# The Developing Person

## Through Childhood and Adolescence

**LaunchPad**
macmillan learning

 **LearningCurve**

# for *The Developing Person Through Childhood and Adolescence,* Twelfth Edition

## Available at launchpadworks.com

Each chapter in LaunchPad for *The Developing Person Through Childhood and Adolescence,* Twelfth Edition, features a collection of activities carefully chosen to help master the major concepts. The site serves students as a comprehensive online study guide, available any time, with opportunities for self-quizzing with instant feedback, exam preparation, and further explorations of topics from the textbook. For instructors, all units and activities can be instantly assigned and students' results and analytics are collected in the Gradebook.

### For Students

- Full interactive and accessible e-book of *The Developing Person Through Childhood and Adolescence,* Twelfth Edition
- *Developing Lives* interactive simulation
- Data Connections activities
- LearningCurve Quizzing
- Student Video Activities
- Practice quizzes

### For Instructors

- Gradebook
- Worth Video Collection for Human Development
- Lecture and Image Slides
- Instructor's Resource Guide
- Test Bank
- i-Clicker questions
- Macmillan Learning Psychology Community Newsfeed
- Correlation of *The Developing Person Through Childhood and Adolescence,* Twelfth Edition, to NCLEX-RN Test and NAEYC Standards

## LearningCurve

*What Is LearningCurve?* LearningCurve is a cutting-edge study tool designed to increase your understanding and memory of the core concepts in every chapter. Based on insights from the latest learning and memory research, the LearningCurve system pairs multiple-choice and fill-in-the-blank questions with instantaneous feedback and a rich array of study tools including videos, animations, and lab simulations. The LearningCurve system is adaptive, so the quiz you take is customized to your level of understanding. The more questions you answer correctly, the more challenging the questions become. Best of all, the e-book of *The Developing Person Through Childhood and Adolescence,* Twelfth Edition, is fully integrated, so you can easily review the text as you study and answer questions. LearningCurve is a smart and fun way to study each chapter.

**LearningCurve** is available as part of **LaunchPad** for *The Developing Person Through Childhood and Adolescence,* **Twelfth Edition.** To find out more or purchase access, go to **launchpadworks.com.**

**TWELFTH EDITION**

# The Developing Person

## Through Childhood and Adolescence

Kathleen Stassen Berger

Bronx Community College
City University of New York

**worth publishers**
Macmillan Learning

New York

*Senior Vice President, Content Strategy:* Charles Linsmeier
*Program Director, Social Sciences:* Shani Fisher
*Senior Executive Program Manager:* Christine Cardone
*Developmental Editor:* Andrea Musick Page
*Assistant Editor:* Dorothy Tomasini
*Executive Marketing Manager:* Katherine Nurre
*Marketing Assistant:* Steven Huang
*Executive Media Editor:* Laura Burden
*Director of Media Editorial, Social Sciences:* Noel Hohnstine
*Assistant Media Editor:* Conner White
*Director, Content Management Enhancement:* Tracey Kuehn
*Senior Managing Editor:* Lisa Kinne
*Senior Content Project Manager:* Peter Jacoby
*Senior Project Manager:* Arindam Bose, Lumina Datamatics, Inc.
*Media Project Manager:* Brian Nobile
*Senior Workflow Supervisors:* Susan Wein & Paul Rohloff
*Senior Photo Editor:* Sheena Goldstein
*Photo Researcher:* Krystyna Borgen, Lumina Datamatics, Inc.
*Design Services Manager:* Natasha Wolfe
*Cover Designer:* John Callahan
*Interior Design:* Studio Montage and Lumina Datamatics, Inc.
*Art Manager:* Matthew McAdams
*Illustrations:* Lumina Datamatics, Inc., Charles Yuen, Matthew McAdams
*Composition:* Lumina Datamatics, Inc.
*Printing and Binding:* LSC Communications
*Cover Photograph:* Jim Cummins/Getty Images

*Library of Congress Control Number:* 2020945062
ISBN-13: 978-1-319-19174-0
ISBN-10: 1-319-19174-6

Printed in the United States of America
1   2   3   4   5   6        25   24   23   22   21   20

Worth Publishers
One New York Plaza
Suite 4600
New York, NY 10004-1562
www.macmillanlearning.com

**Kathleen Stassen Berger** received her undergraduate degree at Stanford University and Radcliffe College. Then she earned an M.A.T. from Harvard University and an M.S. and Ph.D. from Yeshiva University. Her broad experience as an educator includes directing a preschool, serving as chair of philosophy at the United Nations International School, and teaching child and adolescent development to graduate students at Fordham University in New York and undergraduates at Montclair State University in New Jersey and Quinnipiac University in Connecticut. She also taught social psychology to inmates at Sing Sing Prison who were earning paralegal degrees.

Currently, Berger is a professor at Bronx Community College of the City University of New York, as she has been for most of her professional career. She began there as an adjunct in English and for the past decades has been a full professor in the Social Sciences Department, which includes psychology, sociology, economics, anthropology, political science, and human services. She has taught Introduction to Psychology, Child and Adolescent Development, Adulthood and Aging, Social Psychology, Abnormal Psychology, and Human Motivation. Her students—from diverse ethnic, economic, and educational backgrounds, of many ages, ambitions, and interests—honor her with the highest teaching evaluations.

Berger is also the author of *Invitation to the Life Span*, *The Developing Person Through the Life Span*, and *A Topical Approach to the Developing Person Through the Life Span*. Her developmental texts are currently being used at more than 700 colleges and universities worldwide and are published in Spanish, French, Italian, and Portuguese as well as English. Her research interests include adolescent identity, immigration, bullying, and grandparents, and she has published articles on developmental topics in the *Wiley Encyclopedia of Psychology*, *Developmental Review*, and in publications of the American Association for Higher Education and the National Education Association for Higher Education. She continues teaching and learning from her students, her four daughters, and three grandsons. She is also the author of *Grandmothering: Building Strong Ties with Every Generation* (2019).

© 2016 Macmillan

# CONTENTS

Leren Lu/DigitalVision/Getty Images

## PART I
## The Beginnings

GlobalStock/E+/Getty Images

David A Land/Blend Images/Media Bakery

# PART II
# The First Two Years

JBryson/iStock/Getty Images

# PART III
# Early Childhood

# PART IV
# Middle Childhood

# PART V

# Adolescence

"Fresh brains."

That is what a child told me when I asked why she might understand something that I did not.

"Children have fresh brains," she said. She implied that my brain had been around for a long time, so it might no longer be able to think very well.

I disagree, of course. I believe that my years of teaching, thinking, studying, and writing have led to some important knowledge that is far beyond what any child knows. But that child reminded me of one of the discoveries of child development: Children raise adults while adults raise them. As a professor, author, and mother, I recognize that each new generation changes society, culture, and every adult who listens to them.

Older generations have accumulated important knowledge about child development, which I hope to convey in this textbook. Some of what we know is lifesaving: The child death rate has plummeted over the past century, in part because more is known about infection, education, attachment, and more. As you will learn, in every nation, child health, intelligence, and probably happiness have increased over the past decades.

But at the same time, careful listening and attention to fresh brains is needed. This edition of this textbook, I hope, will help you with both.

When I first began to teach child development to college students, I realized not only that this topic is fascinating but also that what scholars have discovered is important information for everyone. I searched for a textbook that would respect my students and the science. I could not find such a book, so I wrote the first edition of this one. I continue to believe that a text can convey critical insights about child development without ignoring the joy of actual children. Accordingly, this edition recognizes problems and possibilities not imagined in earlier editions.

Our old brains must protect, admire, and appreciate the fresh brains of the two billion or so children alive today. This is my contribution to that goal.

sarahwolfephotography/Moment/Getty Images

## New Topics and Research

Every year, scientists discover and explain new concepts and research. The best of these are integrated into the text, including hundreds of new references on many topics, such as epigenetics, prenatal nutrition, the microbiome, early-childhood education, autism spectrum disorder, vaping, high-stakes testing, gender identity, the COVID-19 pandemic's impact on emerging adults, and diversity of all kinds—ethnic, economic, gender, and cultural.

Cognizant that the science of human development is interdisciplinary, I include recent research in biology, sociology, neuroscience, education, anthropology, political science, and more—as well as my home discipline, psychology. A list highlighting this material is available at macmillanlearning.com.

## NEW and Updated Coverage of Neuroscience

Of course, neuroscience continues in the text as well. In addition to Inside the Brain features, cutting-edge research on the brain appears in virtually every chapter, often with charts, figures, and photos. A list highlighting this material is available at macmillanlearning.com.

## NEW! Career Alerts

In several chapters, students will read about career options for various applied settings related to development through childhood and adolescence. These Career Alerts are informed by the U.S. Bureau of Labor Statistics' Occupational Outlook Handbook, which describes duties, education and training, pay, and outlook for hundreds of occupations.

## NEW! Chapter Apps

Free Chapter Apps that students can download to their smartphones have been added, offering a real-life application of the science of life-span development. Callouts to the Chapter Apps (one per chapter) appear in the margins, along with brief descriptions and links to their iTunes and/or Google Play downloads.

## Renewed Emphasis on Critical Thinking in the Pedagogical Program

Critical thinking is essential for all of us lifelong, as we try to distinguish opinion from science, fake news from facts. Virtually every page of this book presents not only facts but also questions with divergent interpretations, sometimes with references to my own need to reconsider my assumptions. Marginal Think Critically questions encourage students to examine the implications of what they read.

Every chapter is organized around learning objectives. Much of what I hope students will always remember from this course is a matter of attitude, approach, and perspective—all hard to quantify.

The What Will You Know? questions at the beginning of each chapter indicate important ideas or provocative concepts—one for each major section of the chapter. In addition, after every major section, What Have You Learned? questions help students review what they have just read. Some of these questions are straightforward, requiring only close attention to the chapter. Others are more complex, seeking comparisons, implications, or evaluations.

Cognitive psychology and research on pedagogy show that vocabulary, specific knowledge, and critical thinking are all part of learning. These features are designed to foster all three.

## Updated Features: Opposing Perspectives, A View from Science, A Case to Study, and Inside the Brain

In this edition of *The Developing Person Through Childhood and Adolescence*, I've included four unique features. Opposing Perspectives focuses on controversial topics—from prenatal sex selection to e-cigarettes. I have tried to present information and opinions on both sides of each topic so that students will weigh evidence, assess arguments, and recognize their biases while reaching their own conclusions.

A View from Science, which explains research, and A Case to Study, which illustrates development via specific individuals, have been updated. Since new discoveries in neuroscience abound, Inside the Brain features explore topics such as the intricacies of prenatal and infant brain development, brain specialization and speech development, and brain maturation and emotional development.

## NEW and Updated Visualizing Development Infographics

Data are often best understood visually and graphically. Every chapter of this edition includes a full-page illustration of a key topic that combines statistics, maps, charts, and photographs. These infographics focus on key issues such as immunization trends, media use among children, and college and later income. My editors and I worked closely with noted designer and 2018 Guggenheim Fellow Charles Yuen to develop these Visualizing Development infographics.

## Updated Online Data Connections Activities

Evidence is crucial for scientists, and I hope students will understand this experientially via the interactive activities that require interpretation of the latest data on important topics, from economic inequality to child care to risk-taking. These activities engage students in active learning, promoting a deeper understanding of the science of development. Instructors can assign the Data Connections in the online LaunchPad that accompanies this book.

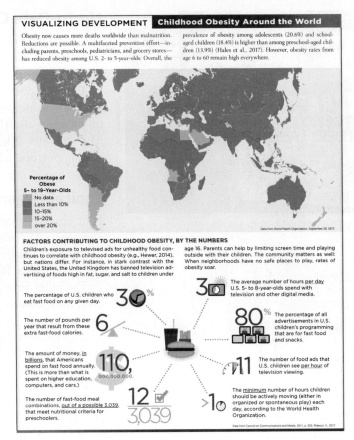

# Ongoing Features

Many characteristics of this book have been acclaimed since the first edition.

## Writing That Communicates the Excitement and Challenge of the Field

An overview of the science of human development should be lively, just as people are. To that end, each sentence conveys tone as well as content. Chapter-opening vignettes describe real (not hypothetical) situations to illustrate the immediacy of development. Examples and explanations abound, helping students make the connections between theory, research, and their own experiences.

## Coverage of Diversity

Cross-cultural, international, intersectional, multiethnic, sexual orientation, socioeconomic status, age, gender identity—all of these words and ideas are vital to appreciating how people develop. Research uncovers surprising similarities and notable differences: We have much in common, yet each human is unique. From the emphasis on contexts in Chapter 1 to the coverage of emerging adulthood in the Epilogue, each chapter highlights variations.

New research on family structures, immigrants, bilingualism, and ethnic differences are among the many topics that illustrate human diversity. Respect for human diversity is evident throughout. Examples and research findings from many parts of the world are included, not as add-ons but as integral parts of each age. A list highlighting multicultural material is available at macmillanlearning.com.

Biz Jones/AGE Fotostock

Dinendra Haria/SOPA Images/AP Images

## Up-to-Date Coverage

My mentors welcomed curiosity, creativity, and skepticism; as a result, I read and analyze thousands of articles and books on everything from how biology predisposes infants to autism spectrum disorder to the many ways the COVID-19 pandemic has affected people of all ages. The recent explosion of research in neuroscience and genetics has challenged me once again, first to understand and then to explain many complex findings and speculative leaps. My students ask nuanced questions and share current experiences, always adding perspective.

## Topical Organization Within a Chronological Framework

Four chapters begin the book with discussions of definitions, theories, genetics, and prenatal development. These chapters provide a foundation for a life-span perspective on plasticity, nature and nurture, multicultural awareness, risk analysis, gains and losses, family bonding, and many other basic concepts.

The other four parts correspond to the major periods of development and proceed from biology to cognition to emotions to social interaction because human growth usually follows that path. Puberty begins adolescence, for instance. The ages of such events vary among people, but 0–2, 2–6, 6–11, and 11–18 are the approximate and traditional ages of the various parts. Ages 18–25 (emerging adulthood) are discussed in the Epilogue.

I know, as you do, that life is not chunked—each passing day makes us older, each aspect of development affects every other aspect, and each social context affects us in a multitude of ways. However, we learn in sequence, with each thought building on the previous one. Thus, a topical organization within a chronological framework scaffolds comprehension of the interplay between age and domain.

## Photographs, Tables, and Graphs That Are Integral to the Text

Students learn a great deal from this book's illustrations because Worth Publishers encourages their authors to choose the photographs, tables, and graphs and to write captions that extend the content. Observation Quizzes accompany some of them, directing readers to look more closely at what they see. The online Data Connections further this process by presenting numerous charts and tables that contain detailed data for further study.

## Integration with LaunchPad

Callouts to accompanying online materials are in the margins throughout the book. These point to special videos of contemporary and classic research (e.g., an interview with Susan Beal, M.D., who discovered a link between infant sleep position and sudden infant death syndrome).

## Child Development and Nursing Career Correlation Guides

Many students taking this course hope to become nurses or early-childhood educators. This book and accompanying test bank are correlated to the NAEYC (National Association for the Education of Young Children) career preparation goals and the NCLEX (nursing) licensure exam. These two supplements are available in LaunchPad.

## Teaching and Learning Aids

Supplements can make or break a class, as I and every other experienced instructor know. Instructors use many electronic tools that did not exist a few decades ago. The publisher's representatives are trained every year to guide students and professors in using the most effective media for their classes. I have adopted texts from many publishers; the Worth representatives are a cut above the rest. Ask them for help with media, with testing, and with content.

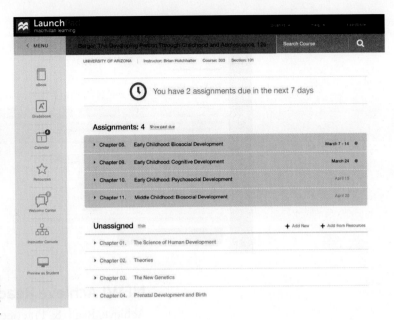

## LaunchPad with Developing Lives, LearningCurve Quizzing, and Data Connections Activities

Built to solve key challenges in the course, LaunchPad provides everything students need to prepare for class and exams, and it gives instructors everything they need to set up a course, shape the content, craft lectures, assign homework, and monitor the learning of each student and the class as a whole.

LaunchPad (preview at launchpadworks.com) includes:

- An **interactive e-book**, which integrates videos and short self-assessments, and includes an interface that simplifies highlighting and notetaking.
- **Developing Lives**, the robust interactive experience in which students "raise" their own virtual child. This simulation integrates more than 200 videos and animations, with quizzes and questions to assign and assess.
- **Data Connections**, interactive activities that allow students to interpret data.
- **LearningCurve adaptive quizzing**, based on current research on learning and memory. It combines individualized question selection, immediate and valuable feedback, and a gamelike interface to engage students. Each LearningCurve quiz is fully integrated with other resources in LaunchPad through the Personalized Study Plan, so students can review using Worth's extensive library of videos and activities. Question analysis reports allow instructors to track the progress of individuals and the entire class.
- Worth's **Video Collection for Human Development** is an extensive archive of video clips and activities that covers the full range of the course, from classic experiments (like Ainsworth's Strange Situation and Piaget's conservation task) to illustrations of many topics. Instructors can assign these videos to students through LaunchPad or choose from 50 activities that combine videos with short-answer and multiple-choice questions. (For presentations, our videos are also available on flash drive.) The Video Assignment Tool makes it easy to assign and assess video-based activities and projects, and provides a convenient way for students to submit video coursework.
- **iClicker** offers active learning simplified, and now includes the REEF mobile app (iClicker.com). iClicker's simple, flexible tools in LaunchPad help you give students a voice and facilitate active learning in the classroom. Students can use iClicker remotes, or the REEF mobile app on their phone, tablet, or laptop to participate more meaningfully. LaunchPad includes a robust collection of iClicker questions for each chapter—readily available for use in your class.

## NEW! Achieve Read & Practice

Achieve Read & Practice combines LearningCurve adaptive quizzing and our mobile, accessible e-book in one easy-to-use and affordable product. Among the advantages of Achieve Read & Practice are the following:

- It is easy to get started;
- Students are better prepared: They can read and study in advance;
- Instructors can use analytics to help their students; and
- Students learn more.

## Instructor's Resources

Now fully integrated with LaunchPad, and available with Achieve Read & Practice, this collection has been hailed as the richest collection of instructor's resources in developmental psychology. Included are learning objectives, topics for discussion and debate, handouts for student projects, course-planning suggestions, ideas for term projects, and a guide to videos and other online materials.

## Test Bank

The test bank includes at least 100 multiple-choice and 70 fill-in-the-blank, true–false, and essay questions for every chapter. Good test questions are crucial; each has been carefully crafted. More challenging questions are included, and all questions are keyed to the textbook by topic, page number, and level of difficulty. Questions are also organized by NCLEX, NAEYC, and APA goals and Bloom's taxonomy. Rubrics for grading short-answer and essay questions are also suggested.

The **Macmillan Learning Test Bank** is an online assessment system that allows you to create and deliver tests through a secure online test center. You can:

- Create paper or online tests that you can export to your LMS using your web browser;
- Drag and drop questions to create tests; and
- Create and edit your own questions and edit publisher-created question sets.

The gradebook in LaunchPad enables instructors to: (1) record students' grades; (2) sort student records; (3) view detailed analyses of test items; (4) curve tests; (5) generate reports; and (6) weight some items more than others.

## Thanks

I would like to recognize the academic reviewers who have read this book in every edition and who have provided suggestions, criticisms, references, and encouragement. They have all made this a better book. I want to thank those of you who have reviewed this edition and the prior editions, including:

Chris Alas, *Houston Community College*
Adrienne Armstrong, *Long Star College*
William Robert Aronson, *Florida International University*
T.M. Barratt, *Arizona State University*
Gina Brelsford, *Pennsylvania State University — Harrisburg*
Melissa Bright, *University of Florida*
Carol Carielli, *CUNY Kingsborough Community College*
Alda Cekrezi, *Lone Star College*
Margaret Cooley, *Eastern Michigan University*
Kristi Cordell-McNulty, *Angelo State University*
Shannon Coulter, *Moorpark College*
Barbara Crosby, *Baylor University*
Faith T. Edwards, *University of Wisconsin — Oshkosh*
Naomi Ekas, *Texas Christian University*
Michael Erickson, *Hawaii Pacific University*
Diane Kleiger Feibel, *University of Cincinnati — Blue Ash College*
Lori Neal Fernald, *The Citadel Military College*
Valerie C. Flores, *Loyola University Chicago*
Stacie Foster, *Arizona State University*
Christopher Gade, *Berkeley City College*
Erica Gelven, *Quinnipiac University*
Dan Grangaard, *Austin Community College*
Jerry Green, *Tarrant County College*
Jiansheng Guo, *California State University — East Bay*
Pinar Gurkas, *Clayton State University*
E. Allison Hagood, *Arapahoe Community College*
Tony Stepter Harris, *Virginia State University*
Raquel Henry, *Lone Star College*
Danelle Hodge, *California State University — San Bernadino*
Regina Kijewski, *Naugatuck Valley Community College*
Vernell Larkin, *Hopkinsville Community College*
Richard Marmer, *American River College*
Jerry Marshall, *Green River College*
T. Darin Matthews, *The Citadel Military College*
Elizabeth McCarroll, *Texas Women's University*
Alejandra Albarran Moses, *California State Univeristy — Los Angeles*
Cindy Sledge, *Lone Star College — CyFair*
Bernadette Stunder, *Holy Family University*
Donna Vaught, *University of North Carolina — Wilmington*
Christie Verarde, *Chabot College*
Kelly A. Warmuth, *Providence College*
Debbie Whitmer, *Shasta College*
Angela Williamson, *Tarrant County College*

New York
August 2020

# APPLICATION TO DEVELOPING LIVES PARENTING
## SIMULATION INTRODUCTION AND PRENATAL DEVELOPMENT

In the Introduction module of Developing Lives, you will begin to customize the developmental journey of your child with information about your personality, cognitive abilities, and demographic characteristics. Next, as you progress through the Prenatal simulation module, how you decide the following will impact the biosocial, cognitive, and psychosocial development of your baby.

| Biosocial | Cognitive | Psychosocial |
|---|---|---|
| • Will you modify your behaviors and diet during pregnancy?<br>• Will you find out the gender of your baby prior to delivery?<br>• What kind of delivery will you and your partner plan for (in the hospital with medication, at home with a doula, etc.)? | • Are you going to talk to your baby while he or she is in the womb?<br>• How much does your baby understand during prenatal development? | • How will your relationship with your partner change as a result of the pregnancy?<br>• Will you begin bonding with your baby prior to birth? |

# The Beginnings

# PART I

**T**he science of human development includes many beginnings. Each of the first four chapters of this text forms one corner of a solid foundation for our study.

**Chapter 1** introduces definitions and dimensions, explaining research strategies and methods that help us understand how people develop. The need for science, the power of culture, and insights from the life-span perspective are explained.

Without theories, our study would be only a jumble of haphazard observations. **Chapter 2** provides organizing guideposts: Five clusters of theories, each leading to hypotheses and controversies, are described.

Heredity is explained in **Chapter 3**. Genes never act alone, yet no development — anywhere in the body or brain of anyone at any time — is unaffected by epigenetics.

**Chapter 4** details the growth of each developing person from a single-celled zygote to a breathing, grasping newborn. Many circumstances — from the mother's diet to the father's care, from the place of birth to the customs of the culture — affect every moment of embryonic and fetal growth.

As you see, the science and the wonder of human life begin long before the first breath. Understanding the beginnings prepares us to understand all the rest. ●◐

# The Science of Development

## What Will You Know?

1. Why is science crucial for understanding how people develop?
2. Are all children the same, or does time and place make each unique?
3. Can we experiment on people to learn how they develop?
4. What questions about child development are hard to ask?

When I was 4 years old, journalists came to our house to photograph my mother and me, wearing matching dresses. I was bathed and dressed, toys were put away, my mother wore lipstick and perfume. While she was getting ready, I found a scissors and cut my hair. My mother stopped me before I could finish, but some tufts were short. She laughed, tying bows to make my hair presentable. I remember none of this, but Mom told this anecdote many times. There are photographs to prove it.

Several aspects of this event suggest another era or place, including photographers coming to homes, mother–daughter dresses, lipstick, ribbons, sharp scissors that a child can reach.

Are you puzzled? Troubled? Do you think it normal for children to misbehave and for mothers to laugh, or do you see defiance or neglect? Would you have punished me if I were your child? Why did Mom laugh?

Everyone was once a child and likely experienced dozens of incidents like this one. How powerful are genes, culture, or child rearing? Is each person's life and experience unique, or is every child like every other child? This chapter shows how to find answers.

## Understanding How and Why

The **science of human development** seeks to understand how and why people—all kinds of people, everywhere, of every age—change or remain the same over time. Development is *multidirectional, multicontextual, multicultural, multidisciplinary*, and *plastic*, five terms that will be explained soon. The goal is for the 7.8 billion people on Earth, especially the 2.6 billion under age 20, to fulfill their potential (population estimates are from United Nations, Department of Economic and Social Affairs, Population Division, 2019).

First, however, we need to emphasize that developmental study is a *science*. It depends on theories, data, analysis, critical thinking, and sound methodology, just like every other science. All scientists ask questions and seek answers in order to ascertain "how and why."

This is especially useful when scientists study people: Lives depend on it.

- Should mothers give birth at home or in hospitals?
- Should babies sometimes cry themselves to sleep?

- How, when, and for what should children be punished?
- Should schools encourage independence or obedience, be optional or required, begin at age 2 or 6?
- Should education continue through high school or college, be free or expensive?

People disagree about almost everything related to child development. That is why we need science.

## The Scientific Method

Science begins with curiosity. Biologists seek to understand how cells function, chemists to investigate the interactions of the elements, physicists to fathom the force of black holes, astronomers to learn what is beyond our galaxy, developmentalists to wonder about everything people do and think.

## Step by Step

As you surely realize, facts may be twisted, opinions may lead people astray, and false assumptions may overwhelm data. To counter prejudices and narrow observations, scientists follow the five steps of the **scientific method** (see **Figure 1.1**):

1. *Begin with curiosity.* Ask questions: Consider theory, study research, and gather observations, all of which suggest issues to be studied.
2. *Develop a hypothesis.* Form a **hypothesis**, a prediction that can be verified. Theories are comprehensive ideas; hypotheses are specific predictions.
3. *Test the hypothesis.* Design a study and conduct research to gather **empirical evidence** (data) to test the hypothesis. When human development is the focus, pay special attention to the selection of participants, the measurement of variables, and the assumptions of the researchers. (More on this later in the chapter.)
4. *Draw conclusions.* Use evidence (Step 3) to support or refute the hypothesis (Step 2). Consider alternative interpretations, unexpected results, and possible biases.
5. *Report the results.* Share data, conclusions, and limitations. Suggest further research to explore new questions and to corroborate conclusions (back to Step 1).

Thus, developmental scientists begin with curiosity and then collect data, drawing conclusions after analyzing the evidence. The process arises not only from observations and personal experience but also from careful study of the reports (Step 5) of other scientists. Each researcher builds on the past, considers the present, and predicts the future—always using critical thinking.

**science of human development** The science that seeks to understand how and why people of all ages and circumstances change or remain the same over time.

**scientific method** A way to answer questions using empirical research and data-based conclusions.

**hypothesis** A specific prediction that can be tested.

**empirical evidence** Evidence that is based on observation, experience, or experiment; not theoretical.

**FIGURE 1.1**
**Process, Not Proof** Built into the scientific method—in questions, hypotheses, tests, and replication—is a passion for possibilities, especially unexpected ones.

1. Curiosity

2. Hypothesis

3. Test

4. Analyze data and draw conclusions

5. Report the results

## Replication

**replication** Repeating a study, usually using different participants, perhaps of another age, SES, or culture.

Repeating a study's procedures and methods with different participants is called **replication**. Scientists study the reports of other scientists (Step 5) and build on what has gone before (back to Step 1). Sometimes they try to duplicate a study exactly, with different participants, to find out if the results apply to everyone. Often they follow up with closely related research (Stroebe & Strack, 2014). Conclusions are revised, refined, rejected, or confirmed after replication.

Obviously, the scientific method is not foolproof. Scientists may draw conclusions too hastily, misinterpret data, or ignore alternative perspectives. Very rarely (about 1 in 5,000 reports), data are falsified (Brainard, 2018). Conclusions are not generally accepted (called *robust*) until several studies confirm them. Ideally, results are replicated not only by other researchers repeating the design of the study (Step 3) but also by other studies with somewhat different designs to verify, refine, and extend the hypothesis (Larzelere et al., 2015).

Of course, no study will exactly mirror another because humans and cultures differ (De Boeck & Jeon, 2018). Perfect replication is impossible; that is why new research is inspired by what has gone before. A View from Science shows this process in more detail.

---

**A VIEW FROM SCIENCE**

## Music and the Brain

An illustration of the scientific method at work comes from research on music and the mind. Does music make people smarter? That question arose from the results of one study 30 years ago, in which 36 college students who listened to Mozart for 10 minutes had higher scores on tests of spatial intelligence than other students who did not hear the music (Rauscher & Shaw, 1993).

That study did not replicate or generalize, but the popular press did not wait. Nor did some politicians. The governor of Georgia in the mid-1990s proposed a budget item of $105,000 to give every Georgia newborn a free CD of classical music. (The legislature voted it down.) Some popular manuals for parents advocated playing classical music for children to help their minds.

Although the original study was flawed in many ways, the topic intrigued scientists, who asked new questions (Step 1). Dozens of studies have since investigated the relationship between music and cognition (Perlovsky et al., 2013).

Sometimes the researchers investigate tiny details. For example, one study compared what happens in the brain when someone listens to Mozart versus listening to Bach (Verrusio et al., 2015).

Another group of researchers examined how rats react to hearing Mozart (Sampaio et al., 2017). Studying rats may seem odd; however, the reactions of rodents, dogs, and other primates might suggest hypotheses regarding people. The impact of music on learning has become a thriving area of research within psychology.

The evidence shows that the noises of hospital nurseries affect the newborn brain, and preterm infants benefit from hearing music, not machines (Lordier et al., 2019). Further, children with special needs may benefit from learning via music (Sharda et al., 2018).

Does music benefit typical children? Decades of research have found that merely listening to music does not aid cognition, but that learning to play a musical instrument may advance intelligence and academic achievement (Herholz & Zatorre, 2012; Rose et al., 2019). The hypothesis (Step 2) is that learning to play an instrument also teaches emotional control, creativity, and memory, which are all crucial cognitive skills. But tests of that hypothesis find more nuanced results.

In one study, three groups of 6-year-olds, all from similar low-income families, were compared. Each week, one group spent six to seven hours learning to play an instrument (usually the violin), one group spent three to four hours in a special sports program (soccer or swimming), and a third group had no after-school programing. After two years, the researchers found (Step 4) that children in the music group improved on several measures of brain development and cognition (Habibi et al., 2018). Surprisingly, the sports group also improved more than the children with no special lessons. The researchers suggested that:

> participation in activities other than music may in fact be associated with . . . [cognitive skills] . . . provided that the activities are socially interactive and comparably motivating and engaging.
>
> [Habibi et al., 2018, p. 79]

This research demonstrates a basic lesson of science: Do not leap to conclusions. Any one study—even one that fails to replicate—can raise new questions. Questions, data, replication, surprises, and alternative explanations are the basics of science.

## The Nature–Nurture Controversy

An easy example of the need for science concerns a great puzzle of life, the *nature–nurture debate*. **Nature** refers to the influence of the genes that people inherit. **Nurture** refers to environmental influences, beginning with the health, diet, and stress of the future person's mother at conception, and continuing life-long, including experiences in the family, school, community, and nation.

The nature–nurture debate has many manifestations, among them *heredity–environment*, *maturation–learning*, and *sex–gender*. Under whatever name, the basic question is, "How much of any characteristic, behavior, or emotion is the result of genes, and how much is the result of experience?"

## Born That Way?

Some people believe that most traits are inborn, that children are innately good ("an innocent child") or bad ("beat the devil out of them"). Others stress nurture, crediting or blaming parents, or neighborhoods, or drugs, or even additives in the food, when someone is good or bad, a hero or a villain.

Neither belief is accurate. As one group of scholars explain, human characteristics are neither born nor made (Hambrick et al., 2018). Genes and the environment *both* affect every characteristic: Nature always affects nurture, and then nurture affects nature. Any attempt to decide exactly how much of a trait is genetic and how much is environmental is bound to fail, because genetic and environmental influences continuously interact, sometimes increasing the influence of the other and sometimes decreasing it.

A further complication is that the impact of any good or bad experience might be magnified or inconsequential, depending on particular genes or past events. For example, a beating, or a beer, or a blessing might be a turning point, or it might not matter.

Every adult can remember a remark, or an incident, in their childhood that is seared in memory because it caused pain, or shame, or joy. That very remark might have been forgotten by the person who said it, or it might have been said to another child with no effect. Each aspect of nature and nurture depends on other aspects of nature and nurture in ways that, themselves, vary because of the nature and nurture of each individual.

## Differential Susceptibility

This illustrates **differential susceptibility** (Ellis et al., 2011a). People vary in how sensitive they are to particular words, or drugs, or experiences, either because of the particular genes they have inherited or because of events years earlier.

Asthma is an obvious example. Because of genes, some people begin wheezing when they are near a cat, but others never do. Yet because of past experience (primarily the reactions of adults), some children are terrified at the first signs of an attack; others are nonchalant.

A more dramatic example involves dogs as well as cats (Krzych-Fałta et al., 2018). If a person lives in a rural area, fur-bearing pets reduce the rate of asthma, but in urban areas, such animals increase the incidence. That is differential susceptibility.

Developmentalists use a floral metaphor to express this idea. Some people are like *dandelions*—hardy, growing and thriving in good soil or bad, with or without ample sun and rain. Other people are like *orchids*—quite wonderful, but only under ideal growing conditions (Ellis & Boyce, 2008; Laurent, 2014). The child who takes asthma or any other illness in stride is a dandelion; the one who experiences terror may be an orchid.

**Chopin's First Concert** Frederick Chopin, at age 8, played his first public concert in 1818, before photographs. But this photo shows Piotr Pawlak, a contemporary prodigy playing Chopin's music in the same Polish Palace where that famous composer played as a boy. How much of talent is genetic, and how much is cultural? This is a nature–nurture question that applies to both boys, 200 years apart.

**nature** In development, nature refers to the traits, capacities, and limitations that each individual inherits genetically from their parents.

**nurture** In development, nurture includes all of the environmental influences that affect the individual after conception. This includes everything from the mother's nutrition while pregnant to the cultural influences in the nation.

**differential susceptibility** The idea that people vary in how sensitive they are to particular experiences. Often such differences are genetic, which makes some people affected "for better or for worse" by life events. (Also called *differential sensitivity*.)

> **THINK CRITICALLY:** Why not assign a percent to nature and a percent to nurture so that they add up to 100 percent?

## Childhood and Adulthood

In the first half of the twentieth century, the focus of developmental psychology was on children. It was thought that once a person was fully grown, development stopped. But as the study of development expanded to include cognitive and emotional development, it became clear that development occurs lifelong.

Each life reflects what has happened in earlier years. This text focuses on children, but you will see many reminders that what happens before age 18 affects what happens after that. Accordingly, when we study children, we note how childhood influences adulthood. The five perspectives that arose from the study of the lifespan—multidirectional, multicontextual, multicultural, multidisciplinary, and plasticity—apply to every age of human development.

## Development Is Multidirectional

The study of development highlights "how and why people change over time." At every stage, gains and losses occur. A simplistic understanding of the direction of development from birth to death—up, steady, and down—is imprecise and sometimes flat-out wrong.

### Continuity and Discontinuity

Instead, multiple changes, in every direction, characterize life. Traits appear and disappear, with increases, decreases, and zigzags (see **Figure 1.2**). An earlier idea—that growth advances until about age 18, steadies, and then declines—has been soundly rejected. Do not let anyone tell you that a child was "born bad" or that someone will never change.

Sometimes *discontinuity* is evident. Change can occur rapidly and dramatically: Caterpillars become butterflies, shy children become social teenagers, and loners fall in love.

Sometimes *continuity* is found. Growth can be gradual: Redwoods add rings over hundreds of years; toddlers stand, take steps, walk, and run. Humans experience simple growth, radical transformation, improvement, and decline as well as stability, stages, and continuity—day to day, year to year, and generation to generation.

### Critical and Sensitive Periods

The timing of losses and gains, impairments or improvements, is affected by age and maturation. Some changes are sudden and profound because

**FIGURE 1.2**

**Patterns of Developmental Growth** Many patterns of developmental growth have been discovered. Although linear progress seems most common, scientists now find that almost no aspect of human change follows the linear pattern exactly.

of a **critical period**, which is either when something *must* occur to ensure normal development or the *only* time when an abnormality might occur.

For instance, the human embryo grows arms and legs, hands and feet, fingers and toes, each over a critical period between 28 and 54 days after conception. After that, it is too late: Unlike some insects, humans never grow replacement limbs.

We know this because of a tragedy. Between 1957 and 1961, thousands of newly pregnant women in 30 nations took *thalidomide*, an antinausea drug. This change in nurture (via the mother's bloodstream) disrupted nature (the embryo's genetic program). If an expectant woman ingested thalidomide during the critical period for limb formation, her newborn's arms or legs were malformed or absent (Moore et al., 2015). Whether all four limbs or just arms, hands, or fingers were missing depended on exactly when the drug was taken. If thalidomide was ingested only after day 54, no harm occurred.

Life has few critical periods. Often, however, a particular development occurs more easily—but not exclusively—at a certain time. That is called a **sensitive period**.

An example is learning language (Werker & Hensch, 2015). If children do not communicate in their first language between ages 1 and 3, they might do so later (these years are not critical), but their grammar is impaired (these years are sensitive). Childhood is a particularly sensitive period for learning to pronounce a second or third language with a native accent: Some brilliant immigrants master the nuances of the English language, sometimes publishing profound and riveting novels, and yet their speech still reflects their native tongue.

One review of the brain structures for second-language learning strongly recommends hearing both languages during the first year of life. The evidence suggests that adults who learn a new language never master a native accent "even after years of practice, and despite high proficiency in all other aspects of language function" (Berken et al., 2017, p. 222). The critical period for hearing and repeating nuances of accent was over.

## Development Is Multicontextual

The second insight is that "human development is fundamentally contextual" (Pluess, 2015, p. 138). Among the many contexts are three obvious clusters: physical surroundings (including climate, noise, streets, trees), family structures (legal status, family size, ages of relatives), and community characteristics (urban, suburban, or rural; diverse or not).

## The Social Context

Humans are intensely social creatures, so a fourth category, the social context, is especially crucial. The social context includes everyone who influences each individual, both immediately and over time, both directly and indirectly.

For example, a 20-year-old college student might be persuaded to stop by a party instead of heading to the library. The host furnishes the setting, with drinks, food, and music. The people—friends, acquaintances, strangers—provide the immediate social context, and that affects whether the student will stay till 3 A.M. or leave soon after arriving. The next morning, that social context will affect the student in class—another social context.

In the same way, we each experience several contexts each day, some by choice and some involuntarily, and they affect our later thoughts and actions. A hard day

**Domov Is Home?** This is Milan Kundera, world-famous author of *The Unbearable Lightness of Being*. He left his Czech *domov* (home) at age 46, becoming a French citizen but writing in Czech until age 64. He now writes in French, with a literate French native to check his work. For example, native speakers know that la maison, le domicile, and chez moi all mean home; they use the appropriate one with no problem. Now Kundera writes fluent French, and speaks it too—with an accent.

**critical period** A time when something *must* happen for normal development to occur.

**sensitive period** A time when something (such as a toxin, or nutrient, or experience) has the greatest impact on development, but recovery is possible if it occurs later.

**ecological-systems approach** A perspective on human development that considers all of the influences from the various contexts of development. (Later renamed *bioecological theory*.)

**microsystem** In Bronfenbrenner's ecological approach, the immediate social contexts that directly affect each person, such as family, peer group, work team.

**exosystem** In Bronfenbrenner's ecological approach, the community institutions that affect the immediate contexts, such as churches and temples, schools and colleges, hospitals and courts.

**macrosystem** In Bronfenbrenner's ecological approach, the overarching national or cultural policies and customs that affect the more immediate systems, such as the effect of the national economy on local hospitals (an exosystem) or on families (a microsystem).

**chronosystem** In Bronfenbrenner's ecological approach, the impact of historical conditions (wars, inventions, policies) on the development of people who live in that era.

**mesosystem** In Bronfenbrenner's ecological approach, a connection between one system and another, such as parent–teacher conferences (connecting home and school) or workplace schedules (connecting family and job).

at work might make a parent impatient with the children—and then the children might pick a fight with a friend.

In these examples, the effect is almost immediate, but much of development is affected by contexts over the long term. Childhood social play may affect adult work habits, for instance. A child's family and neighborhood contexts predispose adult psychological disorders—with differential susceptibility (Keers & Pluess, 2017).

## Ecological Systems

A leading developmentalist, Urie Bronfenbrenner (1917–2005), emphasized contexts. Just as a naturalist studying an organism examines the ecology (the relationship between the organism and its environment) of a tiger, or tree, or trout, Bronfenbrenner told developmentalists to take an **ecological-systems approach** (Bronfenbrenner & Morris, 2006).

This approach recognizes three nested levels (see **Figure 1.3**).

- Most obvious is the **microsystem**—each person's immediate social contexts, such as family and peer group.
- Also important is the **exosystem** (local institutions such as school and church).
- Beyond that is the **macrosystem** (the larger setting, including cultural values, economic policies, and political processes).

Two more systems affect these three.

- One is the **chronosystem** (literally, "time system"), which is the historical context.
- The other is the **mesosystem**, consisting of the connections among the other systems.

**FIGURE 1.3**

**The Ecological Model** According to developmental researcher Urie Bronfenbrenner, each person is significantly affected by interactions among a number of overlapping systems, which provide the context of development. Microsystems—family, peer group, classroom, neighborhood, house of worship—intimately and immediately shape human development. Surrounding and supporting the microsystems are the exosystems, which include all the external networks (such as community structures and local educational, medical, employment, and communications systems) that affect the microsystems. Influencing both of these systems is the macrosystem, which includes cultural patterns, political philosophies, economic policies, and social conditions. Mesosystem refers to interactions among systems, as when parents and teachers coordinate to educate a child. Bronfenbrenner eventually added a fifth system, the chronosystem, to emphasize the importance of historical time.

Before he died, Bronfenbrenner renamed his theory *bioecological* to emphasize the impact of the person, including their genes and body systems. Increasingly, he and all developmentalists recognized biological systems, because signals from the stomach, lungs, heart, hormones, and neurotransmitters affect all the other systems. Recently, the *microbiome*, which is all the microbes within each person, is also recognized as a crucial part of each person (more on this in Chapter 3).

In the student-at-party example above, the student's immediate social circle is the microsystem, the college culture (is it a "party school?") is the exosystem, and the national emphasis on higher education is part of the macrosystem. The party itself is a mesosystem, in that it connects the microsystem and the exosystem.

Every gathering reflects the chronosystem. Party food and drink vary with each decade, and even the fact of a college party reflects history: Many 20-year-olds a century ago were already parents, and if they were in college, they spent evenings studying, not partying. Further, the food, drink, and air at the party affect the biosystem, with some substances changing how people feel and interact.

Bronfenbrenner's perspective remains useful, especially when considering children within families (Ferguson & Evans, 2019). For example, children who have been sexually abused are likely to be abused again, in childhood and adulthood. Why? Is there something amiss in the person, or is the fault in the culture?

Psychologists have used Bronfenbrenner's systems approach to answer this question, finding causes in all systems simultaneously (Pittenger et al., 2016). For example, an abused adult is likely to have been abused in their family as a child (macrosystem), to belong to a church that is silent about sexuality (exosystem), and to live within a culture that does not prosecute abuse (macrosystem and chronosystem). Past abuse affects brain networks (biosystem).

**cohort** People born within the same historical period who therefore move through life together, experiencing the same events, new technologies, and cultural shifts at the same ages. For example, the effect of the Internet varies depending on what cohort a person belongs to.

## The Historical Context

Bronfenbrenner's chronosystem is useful in understanding social movements, including current ones such as Black Lives Matter or Extinction Rebellion or Me Too. In each case, a historical shift occurred. For example, people are now separating plastic and paper, composting scraps, and recycling bags. That illustrates historical change.

All persons born within a few years of one another are called a **cohort**, a group defined by its members' shared age. Cohorts travel through life together, at each age experiencing particular values, events, and technologies. Imagine being a child before contraception, or cell phones, or social media. A person's entire life would be affected. Although many of the elderly now have electronic devices and modern medical care, their assumptions and values reflect an earlier era, which gives rise to the dismissive saying "OK, boomer."

Even something that seems private and personal reflects history. Consider a person's name (see **Table 1.1**). If you know someone named Emma, she is probably young: Emma is the most common name for girls born between 2014 and 2018 but was not in the top 1,000 in 1990. If you know someone named Mary, she is probably old: Mary was the first or second most popular name from 1900 to 1965; now only 1 baby in 800 is named Mary.

These rankings are from the United States (U.S. Social Security Administration, 2019). Variation is evident by nation, by culture, and by region—within the United States and elsewhere. For example, Wyatt is the third most common boy's name in Alaska, but it's not in the first 100 in California.

| TABLE 1.1 |
| --- |
| **Most Popular First Names by Cohort** |
| **Girls** |
| 2018: Emma, Olivia, Ava, Isabella, Sophia |
| 1998: Emily, Hannah, Sarah, Samantha, Ashley |
| 1978: Jennifer, Melissa, Jessica, Amy, Heather |
| 1958: Mary, Susan, Linda, Karen, Patricia |
| 1938: Mary, Barbara, Patricia, Betty, Shirley |
| **Boys** |
| 2018: Liam, Noah, William, James, Oliver |
| 1998: Michael, Jacob, Matthew, Joshua, Christopher |
| 1978: Michael, Jason, Christopher, David, James |
| 1958: Michael, David, James, Robert, John |
| 1938: Robert, James, John, William, Richard |
| Information from U.S. Social Security Administration, 2019. |

**socioeconomic status (SES)** A person's position in society as determined by income, occupation, education, and place of residence. (Sometimes called *social class*.)

## The Socioeconomic Context

Some scholars believe that the economic context is even more important than the historical one. Each person's **socioeconomic status**, abbreviated **SES** (SES is basic to understanding human development, so the abbreviation is used often in this text), affects every stage of development. SES is not solely about income. Socioeconomic status also reflects education, occupation, and neighborhood. The combination affects development much more than money alone.

Imagine two U.S. families comprised of an infant, an unemployed mother, and a father who earns less than $20,000 a year. That family's income is markedly below the 2019 federal poverty line for a family of three ($21,330).

Suppose one family depends on the father's minimum wage job, which provides $16,965 annual income ($7.25 per hour × 45 hours a week × 52 weeks), with neither parent a high school graduate, living in a run-down neighborhood. Their SES would be low. Suppose the other family is headed by a father who is a postdoctoral student living on campus with his college graduate wife. Even though his income might be a grant of $20,000 a year, that family is middle class.

Particularly significant for our study of human development are SES differences by age and cohort (see **Figure 1.4**). In the United States, 50 years ago, the poor were most often elderly, but Medicare changed that. Now young children with young parents suffer most: Poverty in early childhood reduces academic achievement even more than poverty during adolescence (Wagmiller et al., 2015).

There are many reasons. Before age 5, children are almost totally dependent on their families and communities. Since excellent early education is pivotal for later success, and since low-SES parents have little money, limited education, and inadequate housing and thus cannot afford good preschools or provide excellent learning at home, their young children suffer.

This varies by microsystem (nation and community). Some jurisdictions provide excellent early education for all children. It also varies by family. If young children have no cousins or siblings who might need attention from

**FIGURE 1.4**

**Top and Bottom 1 Percent** The gap between rich and poor (measured by the Gini coefficient) is greatest in developing nations, because the poor are below subsistence. Worldwide, inequality is reduced recently, in that there are fewer of the most destitute families. The United States, as you see, is trending toward greater inequality. If both the United States and Mexico continue in their respective trends, Mexico will be closer to income equality than the United States by 2030.

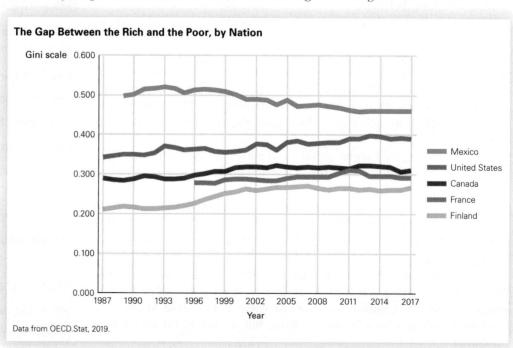

**The Gap Between the Rich and the Poor, by Nation**

Data from OECD.Stat, 2019.

nearby grandparents and great-grandparents, they might benefit from family love and money, even though their parents struggle to pay the rent.

In this example, it is apparent that deprivation begins with income, the *capital* referred to in capitalism. However, *family capital* (the support that families provide for each other) and *social capital* (the support that comes from neighbors, religious institutions, and the larger society) create the context for development (Lin, 2017).

 **DATA CONNECTIONS: Economic Equality and Human Development** explores various nations' Gini indices, which measure economic equality in a particular society.

## Development Is Multicultural

In order to learn about "all kinds of people, everywhere, at every age," it is necessary to study people of many cultures. For social scientists, **culture** is "the system of shared beliefs, conventions, norms, behaviors, expectations and symbolic representations that persist over time and prescribe social rules of conduct" (Bornstein et al., 2011, p. 30).

## Social Constructions

Thus, culture is far more than food or clothes; it is a set of ideas, beliefs, and patterns. Culture is a powerful **social construction**, that is, a concept created, or *constructed*, by a society. Social constructions affect how people think and act—what they value, ignore, and punish.

Each group of people creates a culture, which means there are ethnic cultures, national cultures, family cultures, college cultures, and so on. Thus, everyone is multicultural, sometimes finding that one culture clashes with another. One of my students wrote:

> My mom was outside on the porch talking to my aunt. I decided to go outside; I guess I was being nosey. While they were talking I jumped into their conversation which was very rude. When I realized what I did it was too late. My mother slapped me in my face so hard that it took a couple of seconds to feel my face again.

*[C., personal communication]*

Notice that my student reflects her family culture; she labels her own behavior "nosey" and "very rude." She later wrote that she expects children to be seen but not heard and that her own son makes her "very angry" when he interrupts.

However, her "rude" behavior may have been encouraged by the culture of her school, because she attended a public school far from her mother's native land. In the United States, many teachers want children to speak up; children's talk is welcomed. Do you think my student was nosey or, on the contrary, that her mother should not have slapped her? Your answer reflects your culture.

## Deficit or Just Difference?

As with my student's mother, everyone is inclined to believe that their culture is better than others. This tendency has benefits: Generally, people who appreciate their own culture are happier, prouder, and more willing to help strangers. However, that belief becomes destructive if it reduces respect for people from other groups. Too quickly and without thought, differences are assumed to be problems (Akhtar & Jaswal, 2013).

**culture** A system of shared beliefs, norms, behaviors, and expectations that persist over time and prescribe social behavior and assumptions.

**social construction** An idea that is built on shared perceptions, not on objective reality. Many age-related terms (such as *childhood, adolescence, yuppie,* and *senior citizen*) are social constructions, connected to biological traits but strongly influenced by social assumptions.

**CHAPTER APP 1**

## 📱 SDGs in Action

**IOS:**
https://tinyurl.com/u6hpjwl

**ANDROID:**
https://tinyurl.com/uo4vaqp

**RELEVANT TOPIC:**
Income inequality and social justice

Organized around the United Nations' Sustainable Development Goals (a global to-do list for tackling poverty, inequality, and climate change), this app educates users about challenges in the world today and motivates them to take action.

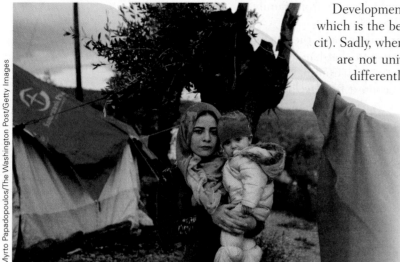

Myrto Papadopoulos/The Washington Post/Getty Images

**Difference, But Not Deficit** This Syrian refugee living in a refugee camp in Greece is quite different from the aid workers who assist there. But the infant, with a pacifier in her mouth and a mother who tries to protect her, illustrates why developmentalists focus on similarities rather than on differences.

● **Observation Quiz** Two religions that sometimes clash are evident here. What are they? (see answer, page 31) ↑

---

**difference-equals-deficit error** The mistaken belief that a deviation from some norm is necessarily inferior to behavior or characteristics that meet the standard.

**ethnic group** People whose ancestors were born in the same region and who often share a language, culture, and religion.

**race** A group of people who are regarded by themselves or by others as distinct from other groups on the basis of physical appearance, typically skin color. Social scientists think race is a misleading concept, as biological differences are not signified by outward appearance.

---

Developmentalists recognize the **difference-equals-deficit error**, which is the belief that people unlike us (different) are inferior (deficit). Sadly, when humans realize that their ways of thinking and acting are not universal, they may believe that people who think or act differently are to be pitied, feared, and encouraged to change.

The difference-equals-deficit error is one reason that a careful multicultural approach is necessary. Never assume that another culture is wrong and inferior—or the opposite, right and superior. Assumptions can be harmful.

For example, one immigrant child, on her first day in a U.S. school, was teased about the food she brought for lunch. The next day, she dumped the contents of her lunchbox in the garbage soon after she arrived at school, choosing hunger over being different.

This example illustrates the problem of difference and deficit. A child's lunch of another culture might, or might not, be more nutritious than conventional peanut butter and jelly sandwiches. In this example, the children noticed only difference; the mothers thought the lunch they packed was best; the student wanted to be accepted. The difference was misjudged as a deficit, and then it harmed that girl (hungry children learn less).

## Ethnic and Racial Groups

Cultural clashes fuel wars and violence when differences are seen as deficits. To prevent that, we need to understand the terms *ethnicity* and *race*. Members of an **ethnic group** almost always share ancestral heritage and often have the same national origin, religion, and language. Ethnicity is a social construction, a product of the social context, not biology.

Ethnic groups often share a culture, but not necessarily. There are "multiple intersecting and interacting dimensions" to ethnic identity (Sanchez & Vargas, 2016, p. 161). People may share ethnicity but differ culturally (e.g., people of Irish descent in Ireland, Australia, and North America), and people of one culture may come from several ethnic groups (consider British culture). [**Developmental Link**: The major discussion of ethnic identity is in Chapter 16.]

Historically, most North Americans thought that ethnicity was cultural but that race was an inborn biological characteristic that differentiated one group from another. A person could not be multiracial. Races were categorized by skin color: white, black, red, and yellow (Coon, 1962). It was not obvious that color words are a gross exaggeration of relatively minor physical differences. No one has skin that is white (like this page) or black (like these letters) or red or yellow.

Biologists now recognize **race** as a social construction. Genetic diversity is evident within groups, and genes are shared by people with quite different appearance. One team writes:

> We believe the use of biological concepts of race in human genetic research—so disputed and so mired in confusion—is problematic at best and harmful at worst. It is time for biologists to find a better way.

> [*Yudell et al., 2016, p. 564*]

The fact that race is a social construction does not make it meaningless, given history. Adolescents who are proud of their racial ancestry are likely to achieve academically, resist drug addiction, and feel better about themselves (Zimmerman, 2013).

The relationship between racial pride and racial prejudice is complex. Ethnic pride, but not personal experiences with discrimination, predicts more positive attitudes about oneself and about other groups. In the United States, this was found in a study of 15- to 25-year-old Black and Hispanic youth but was not apparent among White youth—who usually did not consider themselves as belonging to a racial group (Sullivan & Ghara, 2015).

There is an interesting historical twist on that. A hundred years ago, Americans of Irish, Italian, and Greek ethnicity were *not* considered part of the White race (Gordon, 2017). This confirms, of course, that race is social construction.

## Intersectionality

**Intersectionality** begins with the idea that we each are pushed and pulled—sometimes strongly, sometimes weakly, sometimes by ourselves, sometimes by authorities—by our gender, religion, generation, nation, age, culture, and ethnicity. Our many identities interact with and influence each other (see **Figure 1.5**). Intersectionality then recognizes that those identities can be used to divide—White women versus Black women, Asian men versus Latino men, immigrant children versus immigrant elders, and so on—instead of uniting us, as all women, or all immigrants, or, even better, as all people.

Intersectionality focuses attention on power differences between groups, bringing special attention to the needs of people who are simultaneously in several marginalized groups. They are most harmed when their intersectional identities are ignored. For example, when Crenshaw (1989) first introduced the term "intersectionality," she recognized that the courts allowed discrimination against African American women because the laws did not acknowledge that racism and sexism combined to harm them.

Intersectionality highlights discrimination in many institutions. For example, do judges give African Americans harsher prison sentences than European Americans for the same crimes? The data say yes. That is unfair, but unfairness may be deeper than that.

A careful study of all sentences meted out to convicted criminals in Pennsylvania found more age and gender disparities than ethnic ones. For the same crime, young adults were sentenced more harshly than older ones, and men more harshly than women (Steffensmeier et al., 2017). Thus, young Black men may be particularly misjudged; older White women particularly protected. Note that this was in Pennsylvania. Would this be better or worse in Minnesota or Montana, Bermuda or Brazil? We need more data to know.

More generally, like interlocking gears, systems of social categorization and group power intersect to influence everyone, every day. How would your life be different if you were of another gender, ethnicity, family background, sexual orientation, health, ability, and so on? Cultures matter for everyone.

## Development Is Multidisciplinary

In order to examine each aspect of human growth, development is often considered in three domains—*biosocial*, *cognitive*, and *psychosocial*. Each domain is the focus of several academic disciplines:

- Biosocial includes biology, neuroscience, and medicine.
- Cognitive includes psychology, linguistics, and education.
- Psychosocial includes economics, sociology, and history.

Typically, each scholar follows a particular thread within one discipline and one domain, using clues and conclusions from other scientists

Mike Coppola/Getty Images Entertainment/Getty Images

**Fitting In** The best comedians are simultaneously outsider and insider, giving them a perspective that helps people laugh at the absurdities in their lives. Trevor Noah—son of a Xhosa South African mother and a German Swiss father—grew up within, yet outside, his native culture. For instance, he was seen as "Coloured" in his homeland but as "White" on a video, which once let him escape arrest!

**intersectionality** The idea that the various identities need to be combined. This is especially important in determining if discrimination occurs.

**FIGURE 1.5**
**Identities Interacting** We all are in the middle, with many identities. Our total selves are affected by them all, with variation by culture and context as to which are more salient.

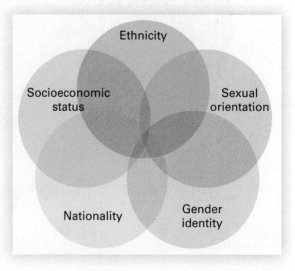

Ethnicity · Socioeconomic status · Sexual orientation · Nationality · Gender identity

# Diverse Complexities

It is often repeated that "the United States is becoming more diverse," a phrase that usually refers only to ethnic diversity and not to economic and religious diversity (which are also increasing and merit attention). From a developmental perspective, two other diversities are also important—age and region, as shown below. What are the implications for schools, colleges, employment, health care, and nursing homes in the notable differences in the ages of people of various groups? And are attitudes about immigration, or segregation, or multiracial identity affected by the ethnicity of one's neighbors?

## THE CHANGING ETHNIC AND RACIAL MAKEUP OF THE UNITED STATES

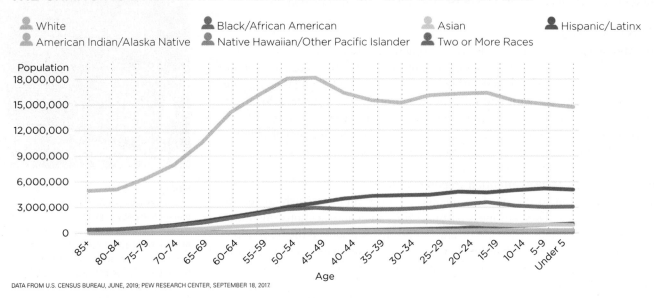

DATA FROM U.S. CENSUS BUREAU, JUNE, 2019; PEW RESEARCH CENTER, SEPTEMBER 18, 2017.

## Regional Differences in Ethnicity Across the United States

In the United States, there are both regional and age differences in ethnicity. This map shows which counties have an ethnic population greater than the national average. Counties where more than one ethnicity or race is greater than the national average are shown as multiethnic. Areas for which data are unavailable are left unshaded.

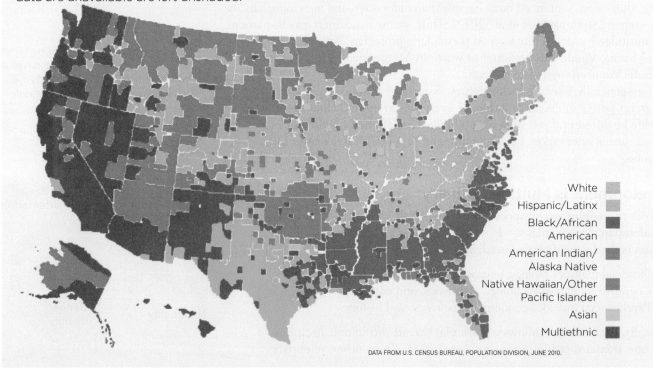

DATA FROM U.S. CENSUS BUREAU, POPULATION DIVISION, JUNE 2010.

who have concentrated on that same thread. They try to avoid the *silo effect*, named after the silos on farms that store grain until it is needed. Those silos typically are tall, round towers, standing alone. In academia, public health, and business, the silo effect is the tendency of each discipline and organization to communicate only with others in the same silo. That reduces their scope, insight, and effectiveness (Tett, 2015).

By contrast, a comprehensive understanding of development requires insights and information from many scientists, past and present, in many disciplines. This is evident when trying to understand any one person. A child who has trouble learning in school might need family counseling, glasses, treatment for chronic illness, recognition of religious prohibitions, tutoring to overcome dyslexia, and more. No single element will solve the child's problem. As in this example, our understanding of every person, and every topic, benefits from a multidisciplinary understanding.

**Criminology and Medicine** Punishment of criminals and the health of newborns are central concerns of the disciplines of criminology and medicine, not psychology or political science. However, here you see 100 psychologists about to inform the U.S. Congress about the hazards of using restraints (e.g., handcuffs) on women giving birth, which is the practice in many prisons. As in this example, many human problems require a multidisciplinary approach.

Lloyd Wolf

## Genetics

Avoiding silos is ideal but not always achieved. Consider genetics. When the human genome was first mapped nearly two decades ago, some people assumed that humans became whatever their genes destined them to be—heroes, killers, or ordinary people. However, multidisciplinary research quickly showed otherwise.

Yes, genes affect every aspect of behavior. But even monozygotic twins, with identical genes, differ biologically, cognitively, and socially. [**Developmental Link**: Twins are discussed in Chapter 3.] Among the many reasons each is unique are position in the womb, non-DNA influences in utero, birthweight, birth order, and then dozens of influences throughout life (Carey, 2012). Thus, to understand any person, one must consider findings from many disciplines: genes, nutrition, psychology, sociology, education, and more. Breaking out of silos can illuminate topics that mystified scientists who were stuck in their own discipline.

A dramatic example comes from autism spectrum disorder (ASD). Autism was not recognized as distinct from schizophrenia until about 1940, and then it remained in the silo of psychiatry for decades. For most of the twentieth century, psychiatrists traced psychological disorders to early mother–child relationships.

Accordingly, since many children with ASD do not look at people, or let their mothers hug them, some blamed cold, unaffectionate "refrigerator mothers," reflecting a perspective of many psychiatrists (Bettelheim, 1972). Thousands of mothers suffered from that judgment (Jack, 2014). Then a reversal came from biology, specifically genetics.

Geneticists collected data proving that autism is inborn. A discipline once thought to be irrelevant to mental disorders was now considered pivotal for autism spectrum disorder, schizophrenia, mood disorders, and so on (Kandel, 2018). However, although the genetic evidence released mothers from guilt, it convinced people that nothing could be done to help such children. Then another silo weighed in: Educators found that children "on the spectrum" can be taught language and social skills.

Soon neuroscientists found signs of autism in the brain; nutritionists suggested dietary changes; medical doctors prescribed drugs; public health workers were appalled when parents blamed vaccinations; demographers traced the increase in cases (now estimated among U.S. 8-year-old boys at about 1 in 23 [Baio et al., 2018]); and so on.

We still do not know all the causes and treatments of ASD. [**Developmental Link**: Autism spectrum disorder is discussed in Chapter 11.] But, we do know that insights from many disciplines are needed. If anyone suggests *the* cause or *the* cure for autism spectrum disorder, that is a mistaken silo approach.

Overall, multidisciplinary research broadens and deepens our knowledge of human development. People are complex, and to properly grasp all the systems—from the workings of the microbiome in the gut to the effects of climate change throughout the entire world—requires a multidisciplinary approach. Adding to this complexity: People change. That leads to the final theme of the life-span perspective, plasticity.

## Development Is Plastic

**plasticity** The idea that abilities, personality, and other human characteristics can change over time. Plasticity is particularly evident during childhood, but even older adults are not always "set in their ways."

The term **plasticity** denotes two complementary aspects of development: Human traits can be molded (as plastic can be), yet people maintain a certain durability of identity (as plastic does). The concept of plasticity in development provides both hope and realism—hope because change is possible, and realism because development builds on what has come before.

## Dynamic Systems

**dynamic-systems approach** A view of human development as an ongoing, ever-changing interaction between the physical, cognitive, and psychosocial influences. The crucial understanding is that development is never static but is always affected by, and affects, many systems of development.

Plasticity is basic to our contemporary understanding of human development. This is evident in the **dynamic-systems approach**. The idea is that human development is an ongoing, ever-changing interaction between the body and mind and between each person and every aspect of the environment. This includes all the systems of the ecological-systems approach.

Note the word *dynamic*: Physical contexts, emotional influences, the passage of time, each person, and every aspect of the ecosystem are always active, always in flux, always in motion.

Thus, a dynamic-systems approach to understanding the role of fathers takes into account the sex and age of the child, the role of the mother, and the cultural norms of fatherhood. The result is a complex mix of complementary effects—and this dynamic mix affects each child in diverse ways (Cabrera, 2015).

Plasticity is also apparent in social norms. Inside the Brain highlights plasticity in culture as well as in the brain.

**INSIDE THE BRAIN**

## Thinking About Marijuana

Brains are affected by drugs, for better or worse. This is evident both in structure (parts of the brain change size because of drug exposure) and activity (connections between neurons are strengthened or weakened).

Consider marijuana. First, the brain. Fear arising from the amygdala and pleasure from the basal ganglia precede drug use, and the size and activity of both are powerfully affected by childhood. Then those parts of the brain continue to be molded, evident in how various generations of adults think about marijuana as well as whether they use the drug.

The plasticity of attitudes is dramatic. In the United States in the 1930s, marijuana was declared illegal. The

1936 movie *Reefer Madness* was shown until about 1960, with vivid images connecting marijuana with a warped brain, suicide, and insanity. Before 1960, most Americans feared and shunned "weed."

Then, that 1960s cohort of adolescents (the baby boomers) had many rebels. They listened to music from the Beatles, Bob Dylan, James Brown, and Bob Marley (all of whom sang about smoking marijuana) and rejected adult fears, values, and rules about drugs, sex, and everything else. This is charted in the annual *Monitoring the Future* report (Johnston et al., 1978–2014; Miech et al., 2015 to present).

By 1978, only 12 percent of high school students thought experimental use of marijuana was harmful, and more than half had tried the drug. That frightened the adults, whose emotional reactions to marijuana had been formed decades earlier. President Nixon declared drug abuse (especially marijuana, but not cigarettes or alcohol) "Public Enemy Number One" and Nancy Reagan (First Lady from 1981 to 1989) exhorted, "Just Say No" to drugs.

Marijuana was declared a "gateway drug," because it was thought that if someone walked through that gate they would be led to heroin use and addiction (Kandel, 2002). People were arrested and jailed for possession of even a few grams. By 1991, 80 percent of high school seniors thought there was "great risk" in regular use of marijuana, and only 21 percent of high school seniors had ever smoked it.

Obviously, attitudes continue to shift, in part because the anti-marijuana generation are now quite old (see **Figure 1.6**). Few teenagers think regular use of marijuana is "a great risk." By 2018, marijuana had become legal in Canada, Uruguay, Argentina, Ecuador, and in 30 U.S. states (often only for

medical use). According to a Gallup poll, two-thirds of Americans believe smoking marijuana should be legal for adults. About half of all high school seniors have smoked marijuana.

Since we know that the brain is plastic, affected by many drugs, scientists ask "How does marijuana change the brain?" Some find that marijuana relieves pain by decreasing pain neurotransmitters, with less addiction or neurological risk than opioids and improved thinking (Gruber et al., 2018). By contrast, some find a correlation between marijuana use and "structural abnormalities in the brains of young people" (DuPont & Lieberman, 2014, p. 557).

Evidently, not only are attitudes about marijuana plastic, so are its effects on the brain, influenced by the age of the smoker, their genes, and perhaps the specifics of the marijuana (where grown, additives) (Dow-Edwards & Silva, 2017; Mandelbaum & de la Monte, 2017). Marijuana may impair brain structures that support memory and motivation—but not for everyone. Plasticity!

In all these ebbs and flows of public attitudes, scientists have no consensus about the long-term effects of marijuana because the federal government made it illegal for scientists to undertake objective research. Currently, many researchers are concerned that the political push to accept marijuana did not consider the neurological effects.

We know that the effects of the drug on the brain vary and that simply thinking about marijuana triggers neurotransmitters, causing phobias, ecstasy, and emotions between those extremes. We know that adults who smoked marijuana decades ago are a select group, so we cannot be sure their current situation is caused by their past drug use. Are current attitudes (mostly positive) more rational than those (mostly negative) of our great-grandparents? More science is needed.

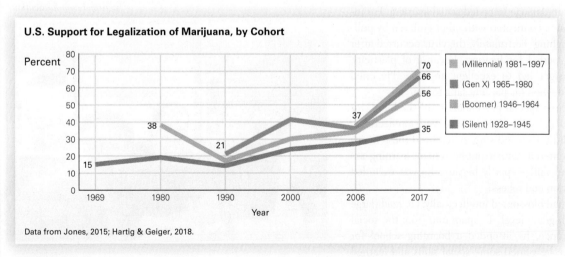

**U.S. Support for Legalization of Marijuana, by Cohort**

Legend:
- (Millennial) 1981–1997
- (Gen X) 1965–1980
- (Boomer) 1946–1964
- (Silent) 1928–1945

Data from Jones, 2015; Hartig & Geiger, 2018.

**FIGURE 1.6**

**Double Trends** Both cohort and generational trends are evident. Note that people of every age are becoming more accepting of marijuana, but the effect is most obvious for adults who never heard about "reefer madness."

**Observation Quiz** Why is the line for the 1981–1997 cohort much shorter than the line for the older cohorts? (see answer, page 31) ↑

Plasticity underlies all the other four aspects of the life-span perspective: multi-directional, multicontextual, multicultural, and multidisciplinary. With any topic, stage, or problem, the dynamic-systems approach urges consideration of all the interrelated aspects, every social and cultural factor, over days and years.

Individuals, families, and societies are moldable. In the United States 20 years ago, no one predicted that teen births, cigarette smoking, and midlife cardiovascular death would be down by half, or that rates of same-sex marriage and single parenthood would double. Each of those changes has altered development for children and adults.

Plasticity is apparent when developmentalists consider any individual. Every brain and body would have been different if that same person had been born in another culture, grown up in another era, eaten other food, witnessed particular events, with different parents, friends, teachers, and so on. My nephew David is one example.

**A CASE TO STUDY**

## My Brother's Son David

My sister-in-law, Dot, contracted *rubella* (also called *German measles*) early in her third pregnancy. The disease was not diagnosed until David was born, blind and dying. Immediate heart surgery saved his life. Then surgery to remove a cataract destroyed one eye.

The doctor was horrified that operating had disturbed the virus and killed the eye, so he did not remove the other cataract until David was 6. One dead eye and one thick cataract meant that young David's visual system was severely impaired. It soon became apparent that other parts of his body—thumbs, ankles, teeth, toes, spine, and brain—were also affected.

Blindness and brain damage impeded social learning. For instance, 3-year-old David connected with other children by pulling their hair and laughing. Fortunately, the virus occurred after the critical prenatal period for hearing. Because of plasticity, David's diminished sight led to excellent audition. He cried often but was quieted when his parents sang to him.

David attended three special preschools—for the blind, for children with cerebral palsy, for children who were intellectually disabled. At age 6, after a second surgery removed the remaining cataract, David entered regular public school, learning academic but not social skills—partly because he was excluded from physical education and recess.

By age 10, David had blossomed intellectually. He read (large print) at the eleventh-grade level. To spare him from the social demands of adolescence, he attended a boarding school for blind children, where he gained some social skills and learned to swim. Before age 20, he spoke a second and a third language. In young adulthood, he enrolled in college.

The interplay of developmental systems was evident. David's family and community contexts (a rural Appalachian region, where the culture is more collectivistic) helped him to become a productive and happy adult. He told me, "I try to stay in a positive mood."

David's listening skills continue to be impressive. He once told me:

I am generally quite happy, but secretly a little happier lately, especially since November, because I have been consistently getting a pretty good vibrato when I am singing, not only by myself but also in congregational hymns in church. [*I asked, what is vibrato? David answered*] When a note bounces up and down within a quartertone either way of concert pitch, optimally between 5.5 and 8.2 times per second.

[*personal communication*]

**My Brother's Children**   Michael, Bill, and David (*left to right*) are adults now, with quite different personalities, abilities, numbers of offspring (4, 2, and none), and contexts (in Massachusetts, Pennsylvania, and California). Yet despite genes, prenatal life, and contexts, I see the shared influence of Glen and Dot, my brother and sister-in-law—evident here in their similar, friendly smiles.

David works as a translator of German texts, which he enjoys because, as he says, "I like providing a service to scholars, giving them access to something they would otherwise not have."

Plasticity does not undo a person's genes, childhood, or permanent damage. The prenatal brain destruction remains, and David, age 52, still lives with his mother. When his father died in 2014, David was better than the rest of us in accepting the death (he said, "Dad is in a better place"). He comforted his mother. She applied to enter a senior citizen residence, but they would not allow David; he is too young. Instead of getting angry, Dot found another apartment for both of them near one of her other children. She laughingly said that David gives her a reason for living, because in another decade, they will be able to stay in senior housing together.

As his aunt, I have seen him repeatedly overcome handicaps. Plasticity is dramatically evident; my intellectually disabled nephew became a very intelligent adult. His case illustrates all five aspects of the life-span perspective (see **Table 1.2**).

### TABLE 1.2

#### Five Characteristics of Development

| Characteristic | Application in David's Story |
|---|---|
| *Multidirectional.* Change occurs in every direction, not always in a straight line. Gains and losses, predictable growth, and unexpected transformations are evident. | David's development seemed static (or even regressive, as when early surgery destroyed one eye), but then it accelerated each time he entered a new school or college. |
| *Multidisciplinary.* Numerous academic fields—especially psychology, biology, education, and sociology, but also neuroscience, economics, religion, anthropology, history, medicine, genetics, and many more—contribute insights. | Two disciplines were particularly critical: medicine (David would have died without advances in surgery on newborns) and education (special educators guided him and his parents many times). |
| *Multicontextual.* Human lives are embedded in many contexts, including historical conditions, economic constraints, and family patterns. | The high SES of David's family made it possible for him to receive daily medical and educational care. His two older brothers protected him. |
| *Multicultural.* Many cultures—not just between nations but also within them—affect how people develop. | In Appalachian regions, like the one in which David lived, the culture is more collectivistic and therefore supportive of all members of the community. |
| *Plasticity.* Every individual, and every trait within each individual, can be altered at any point in the life span. Change is ongoing, although it is neither random nor easy. | David's measured IQ changed from about 40 (severely intellectually disabled) to about 130 (far above average), and his physical disabilities became less crippling as he matured. |

### WHAT HAVE YOU LEARNED?

1. What aspects of development show continuity?
2. What is the difference between a critical period and a sensitive period?
3. Why is it useful to know when sensitive periods occur?
4. What did Bronfenbrenner emphasize in his ecological-systems approach?
5. How does cohort differ from age group?
6. What factors comprise a person's SES?
7. How are culture, race, and ethnicity distinct from each other?
8. What is the problem with each discipline having its own silo?
9. What does it mean to say that human development is plastic?

## Using the Scientific Method

To verify or refute a hypothesis (Step 2), researchers seek the best of hundreds of research designs, choosing exactly who and what to study, how and when (Step 3), in order to gather results that will lead to valid conclusions (Step 4) that are worth publishing (Step 5). Often they use statistics to discover relationships between various aspects of the data.

To understand the science of development, it helps to understand three research designs, and three strategies to learn how people change or remain the same over time.

## Observation

**scientific observation** A method of testing a hypothesis by unobtrusively watching and recording participants' behavior in a systematic and objective manner—in a natural setting, in a laboratory, or in searches of archival data.

**Scientific observation** requires researchers to record behavior systematically and objectively. Observations can occur in a naturalistic setting such as a home, or in a laboratory, where scientists observe what people do. It is also possible to analyze data collected for some other reason but observable to researchers, such as records of Twitter words, or cell phone data, or birth statistics.

Observations suggest hypotheses for further study. Especially when children are observed, a major benefit of this method is that the scientist watches what naturally occurs, without artificial conditions.

For example, in one study (Colditz et al., 2019), mothers and their 2-year-olds were video-taped in a playroom set up to encourage interaction. Only the mother–child dyad was in the room, but the tapes were viewed later by observers who recorded negative (child complains, disobeys, and so on) or positive (child is affectionate, engaged, happy) behaviors every 10 seconds.

Behaviors were carefully defined. For example, disobedience was counted if it was direct, such as responding "no" to a specific request. (If the child simply ignored a suggestion, that did not count as disobedience.)

Beyond clear definitions, note two other ways these scientists sought to make observations objective and scientific. First, raters were not in the room, so mothers or toddlers were not affected by having an observer nearby. Second, ratings were made every 10 seconds, so the observers were not influenced by their overall perceptions or by what had happened a minute before. Scientists use many such methods to make observations accurate.

The rating scale used in this study has been replicated, and is now part of a standard observation measure (Carter & Briggs-Gowan, 2006). As in previous research, toddlers displayed about three times as many positive as negative behaviors. This illustrates the benefits of observation: It is good to know that overall, positive behaviors predominate. Perhaps the "terrible twos" is a stereotype.

This particular study used observation partly because these toddlers were a special group: They all had been born two months before they were due. The observation data found that their mix of positive and negative behaviors were similar to the mix for typical 2-year-olds.

The same study examined language and motor skills, again via observation. For that, the researchers used a scale developed by Nancy Bayley, who published a set of norms for the development of infants and young children (Bayley, 1966). Researchers observed how well the toddlers could talk, walk, run, stack blocks and so on. They corrected for gestational age, which means that they subtracted the number of weeks of prematurity from chronological age in order to accurately assess developmental abilities.

Some cognitive differences between preterm and typical children were dramatic: 3 percent of the preterm 2-year-olds could not walk normally, and most were slower in language development compared to babies born on time. Was this nature or nurture? Observation does not tell us, which is why experiments are sometimes needed.

## The Experiment

An **experiment** establishes causality. In the social sciences, experimenters typically impose a particular treatment or condition on a group of participants and note how they react. If they respond unlike similar people who have no special treatment, then the treatment made a difference.

## Standard Terminology

In technical terms, the experimenters manipulate an **independent variable**, which is the extra treatment or special condition (also called the *experimental variable*; a *variable* is anything that can vary). They note whether this independent variable affects whatever they are studying, called the **dependent variable** (which *depends* on the independent variable).

Thus, the independent variable is the new, special treatment; any change in the dependent variable is the result. The goal is to find out what causes what, that is, whether an independent variable affects the dependent variable.

A typical experiment (as diagrammed in **Figure 1.7**) has two groups of participants. One group, the *experimental group*, experiences the particular treatment or condition (the independent variable); the other group, the *comparison group* (also called the *control group*), does not.

**experiment** A research method in which the scientist tries to determine the cause-and-effect relationship between two variables by manipulating one (called the *independent variable*) and then observing and recording the ensuing changes in the other (called the *dependent variable*).

**independent variable** In an experiment, the variable that is introduced to see what effect it has on the dependent variable. (Also called *experimental variable*.)

**dependent variable** In an experiment, the variable that may change as a result of whatever new condition or treatment the experimenter adds. Thus, the dependent variable *depends* on the independent variable.

**The Experiment**

Many participants, measured on many characteristics, including the dependent variable (the behavior being studied)

(two equal groups)

→ Experimental group → Special treatment (independent variable) → Significant change in the dependent variable

(predicted outcome)

→ Comparison (or control) group → No special treatment → No change in the dependent variable

Procedure:

1. Divide participants into two groups that are matched on important characteristics, especially the behavior that is the dependent variable on which this study is focused.

2. Give special treatment, or intervention (the independent variable), to one group (the experimental group).

3. Compare the groups on the dependent variable. If they now differ, the cause of the difference was probably the independent variable.

4. Publish the results.

**FIGURE 1.7**

**How to Conduct an Experiment** The basic sequence diagrammed here applies to all experiments. Many additional features, especially statistical measures and various ways of reducing experimenter bias, affect whether publication occurs. (Scientific journals reject reports of experiments that were not rigorous.)

**What Can You Learn?** Scientists first establish what is, and then they try to change it. In one recent experiment, Deb Kelemen (shown here) established that few children under age 12 understand a central concept of evolution (natural selection). Then she showed an experimental group a picture book illustrating the idea. Success! The independent variable (the book) affected the dependent variable (the children's ideas), which confirmed Kelemen's hypothesis: Children can understand natural selection if instruction is tailored to their ability.

🌓 **Especially for Nurses** In the field of medicine, why are experiments conducted to test new drugs and treatments? (see response, page 31)

**survey** A research method in which information is collected from a large number of people by interviews, written questionnaires, or some other means.

## Experimental Design

The observation study on the previous page, of the positive and negative behaviors of the preterm 2-year-olds, also had an experimental and control group. All had received the usual specialized care for underweight infants, but the parents of the experimental group attended hospital classes regarding expectations and appropriate care, and then had lengthy phone consultations with experts after they brought their babies home.

The result: The two groups of babies did not differ in behavior (the positive and negative actions at age 2, as just described), but they did differ in cognition and motor skills (the Bayley scales). More of the intervention group were able to stack three blocks on top of each other, for instance.

You can see why a control group was needed. The crucial question was not whether the experimental group were behind the norms. [They were.] The question was whether they were as behind as another group who were also premature. [They were not.] This experiment confirmed that parents of fragile newborns need extra support, so they can support their infants.

Details of the experimental intervention, such as content and timing, may be crucial (Milgrom et al., 2019). Experiments have revealed that many well-intentioned interventions are not really helpful. That is why we need experiments, to know exactly what interventions cause positive results.

## The Survey

A third research method is the **survey**, in which information is collected from a large number of people by interview, questionnaire, or some other means. This is a quick, direct way to obtain data. Surveys keep people from assuming that everyone is like people we know. The wording of a survey may be crucial.

For example, a survey described the epidemic of opioid deaths and then explained life-saving sites, where people can take drugs purchased elsewhere. At such places, medical professionals are nearby to save people who otherwise might die of an overdose, and counselors are available for people who want to quit. Such sites are common in Europe but illegal in most of the United States, because local authorities believe that the public is adamantly opposed. Public health doctors hope those authorities were wrong; they used a survey to find out.

In the survey, adults were asked if such sites should be legal. Descriptions of the sites were identical in every survey, but the titles differed. When the survey title was "Overdose Prevention" 45 percent approved; when the title was "Safe Consumption" only 29 percent approved (Davis et al., 2018).

This illustrates a problem with every survey: As is well known to political pollsters, *how* a question is asked influences the response. In my classes, more of my students approve of "terminating a pregnancy that could not produce a viable infant" than approve of "killing a fetus who could live only a few days after birth."

In late 2019, the U.S. public was surveyed regarding impeachment of President Trump. Surveys worded by Trump supporters found that the public did not support impeachment; surveys worded by Democrats found that the public to be increasingly in favor of impeachment.

Another problem is that survey respondents may lie to researchers, or to themselves. For instance, every two years since 1991, high school students in the United States have been surveyed confidentially in the Youth Risk Behavior Survey. Always a wide and diverse sample is sought: 14,956 students from public, private, and parochial schools answered the 2017 survey (MMWR, June 15, 2018).

One question asked of those 15,000 students was whether they had sexual intercourse *before* age 13. Every year, more ninth-grade boys than eleventh-grade boys say yes, yet those eleventh-graders were ninth-graders two years before (see **Figure 1.8**). Why? Do some teenage boys lie, with ninth-graders bragging? Or have eleventh-graders forgotten? Surveys do not tell us.

## Meta-Analysis

As you see, every research design has strengths as well as weaknesses. No single study is conclusive. Some studies might have too few participants, or some unknown bias in the design, or some oddity in the results. Accordingly, some scholars use **meta-analysis**, which combines the results of many studies. When dozens of studies are gathered, a meta-analysis reveals significant trends.

In the best meta-analyses, the researchers begin by stating exactly how they chose studies that are the grist for their analysis. Care is taken to find all relevant studies, published and unpublished, on a particular topic. Only those that are rigorous are included. A meta-analysis "has become widely accepted as a standardized, less biased way to weigh the evidence" (de Vrieze, 2018, p. 1186).

However, even meta-analyses do not always reach clear conclusions. For instance, does media violence encourage actual violence? Some politicians blamed video games for the massing shooting at Marjory Stoneman Douglas High School in Florida. Were they right? Does shooting in video games provoke real killing? One meta-analysis says yes (Anderson et al., 2010), another no (Ferguson & Kilburn, 2010), and a third says yes but not very much (Hilgard et al., 2017).

The main reason for these differences is that, in order to avoid publication bias (journals tend to publish only dramatic results, called the *file-drawer problem*), the authors included unpublished studies. However, they disagreed about which unpublished studies to use.

For scientists, disagreements are healthy: All the foregoing descriptions of methods and analysis confirm that alternate explanations are part of science. Researchers scrutinize the details and data of published studies (Step 5) in order to interpret the results (Step 4).

## Studying Development over the Life Span

In addition to conducting observations, experiments, and surveys, developmentalists must measure how people *change or remain the same over time*, as the definition stresses. Remember that systems are dynamic, ever-changing. To capture that dynamism, developmental researchers use one of three basic research designs: *cross-sectional*, *longitudinal*, and *cross-sequential*.

## Cross-Sectional Research

The quickest and least expensive way to study development over time is with **cross-sectional research**, in which groups of people of one age are compared with people of another age. You saw that with attitudes about marijuana. Younger people are more likely to approve of legalization than older people.

Cross-sectional design seems simple. However, the people being compared may differ in several ways, not just age. Attitudes about many political and social issues originate in childhood and are solidified in early adulthood. Since many contemporary older adults were taught that marijuana was a dangerous gateway drug, their opinions are still influenced by what Nancy Reagan said when they were teenagers. Their attitudes about same-sex marriage, about war, about religion, and so on are influenced by what their cohort believed decades ago.

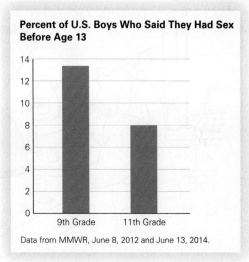

**Percent of U.S. Boys Who Said They Had Sex Before Age 13**

Data from MMWR, June 8, 2012 and June 13, 2014.

**FIGURE 1.8**
**I Forgot?** If these were the only data available, you might conclude that ninth-graders have suddenly become more sexually active than eleventh-graders. But we have 20 years of data—those who are ninth-graders now will answer differently by eleventh grade.

**meta-analysis** A technique of combining results of many studies to come to an overall conclusion. Meta-analysis is powerful, in that small samples can be added together to lead to significant conclusions, although variations from study to study sometimes make combining them impossible.

**cross-sectional research** A research design that compares groups of people who differ in age but are similar in other important characteristics.

"It's a one-year timer. It gives an added sense of urgency to my research grant."

**Not Long Enough** For understanding the human life span, scientists wish for grants that are renewed for decades.

**longitudinal research** A research design in which the same individuals are followed over time, as their development is repeatedly assessed.

**cross-sequential research** A hybrid research design in which researchers first study several groups of people of different ages (a cross-sectional approach) and then follow those groups over the years (a longitudinal approach). (Also called *cohort-sequential research* or *time-sequential research*.)

## Longitudinal Research

To help discover whether age itself rather than cohort causes a developmental change, scientists undertake **longitudinal research**. They collect data repeatedly on the same individuals over time. Longitudinal research can span a few years, or the same individuals may be studied for decades. Long-term research requires patience and dedication from many scientists, but it can pay off.

For example, a longitudinal study of 790 infants born in Baltimore to low-income parents found that only 4 percent of them had graduated from college by age 28 (Alexander et al., 2014). Why don't more low-SES young adults complete college? Many people blame high school guidance counselors, or college admission practices, or university faculty, for this result.

However, this longitudinal study began with infants. Researchers traced when children were pushed away from college or toward it. It began very early in life. Early education and friendly neighbors were more influential than high school!

Longitudinal data are cherished by developmentalists; they show when in the life span to focus on better health practices, education, family interactions. For instance, we now know that the best way to reduce lung cancer deaths is not better diagnosis, or advanced chemotherapy, but prevention of adolescent smoking. Longitudinal data show that if people do not start smoking before age 20, they are unlikely to develop lung cancer in later adulthood, because the sensitive period is over. Almost no one begins smoking in adulthood, but many who became addicted as teenagers are still damaging their lungs as adults.

Another study considered when teaching parents better ways to discipline their children is most likely to improve child behavior. It is widely assumed that earlier is better, but a meta-analysis of many studies using longitudinal research found that interventions during middle childhood were as effective as interventions earlier on (Gardner et al., 2019).

Unfortunately, technology, culture, and politics alter life experiences, so data collected on children years ago might not be relevant for today's children. For example, many recent substances and practices might be harmful or beneficial, among them *phthalates* and *bisphenol A (BPA)* (chemicals used in manufacturing plastic containers), *hydrofracking* (a process used to extract natural gas or oil from rocks), *e-waste* (from old computers and cell phones), *chlorpyrifos* (an insecticide), and *electronic cigarettes* (vaping). Some nations and states ban or regulate each of these; others do not. Data showing the long-term effects of these substances and practices are not yet possible.

A current conundrum is climate change. Some predict global civil wars, agriculture failure, disaster deaths — and that life on our planet may be snuffed out because of atmospheric warming that is happening now. Others call that alarmist, suggesting that mitigation can protect humanity (C. Murphy et al., 2018). Waiting for longitudinal data means we will not know until it is too late.

## Cross-Sequential Research

Developmentalists use a third strategy, combining cross-sectional and longitudinal methods. This is **cross-sequential research** (also referred to as *cohort-sequential* or *time-sequential*). With this design, scientists begin with people of different ages (a cross-sectional approach), follow them for years (a longitudinal approach), and combine the results.

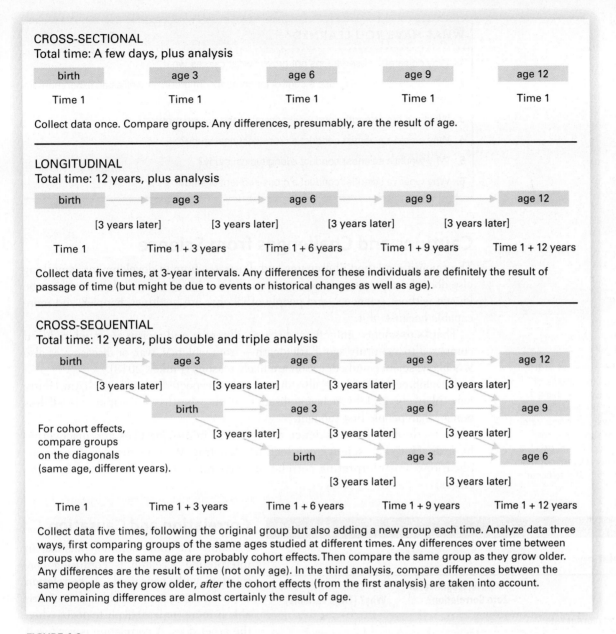

**CROSS-SECTIONAL**
Total time: A few days, plus analysis

| birth | age 3 | age 6 | age 9 | age 12 |
|---|---|---|---|---|
| Time 1 | Time 1 | Time 1 | Time 1 | Time 1 |

Collect data once. Compare groups. Any differences, presumably, are the result of age.

**LONGITUDINAL**
Total time: 12 years, plus analysis

birth ⟶ age 3 ⟶ age 6 ⟶ age 9 ⟶ age 12

[3 years later]   [3 years later]   [3 years later]   [3 years later]

Time 1     Time 1 + 3 years     Time 1 + 6 years     Time 1 + 9 years     Time 1 + 12 years

Collect data five times, at 3-year intervals. Any differences for these individuals are definitely the result of passage of time (but might be due to events or historical changes as well as age).

**CROSS-SEQUENTIAL**
Total time: 12 years, plus double and triple analysis

birth ⟶ age 3 ⟶ age 6 ⟶ age 9 ⟶ age 12

[3 years later]   [3 years later]   [3 years later]   [3 years later]

birth ⟶ age 3 ⟶ age 6 ⟶ age 9

For cohort effects, compare groups on the diagonals (same age, different years).

[3 years later]   [3 years later]   [3 years later]

birth ⟶ age 3 ⟶ age 6

[3 years later]   [3 years later]

Time 1     Time 1 + 3 years     Time 1 + 6 years     Time 1 + 9 years     Time 1 + 12 years

Collect data five times, following the original group but also adding a new group each time. Analyze data three ways, first comparing groups of the same ages studied at different times. Any differences over time between groups who are the same age are probably cohort effects. Then compare the same group as they grow older. Any differences are the result of time (not only age). In the third analysis, compare differences between the same people as they grow older, *after* the cohort effects (from the first analysis) are taken into account. Any remaining differences are almost certainly the result of age.

**FIGURE 1.9**
**Which Approach Is Best?** Cross-sequential research is the most time-consuming and complex, but it yields the best information. One reason that hundreds of scientists conduct research on the same topics, replicating one another's work, is to gain some advantages of cohort-sequential research without waiting for decades.

A cross-sequential design lets researchers compare findings for, say, 3-year-olds with findings for the same individuals as newborns, as well as with data for people who were 3 long ago, who are now ages 6, 9, and 12 (see **Figure 1.9**). Cross-sequential research is complicated, in recruitment and analysis, but it enables scientists to disentangle age from history.

Cross-sequential research is useful for young adults as well. For example, drug addiction (called *substance use disorder*, or *SUD*) is most common in the early 20s and decreases by the late 20s. But one cross-sequential study found that the origins of SUD are in adolescent behaviors and in genetic predispositions (McGue et al., 2014). Other research finds that heroin deaths are more common after age 30, but the best time to prevent such deaths is before age 20 (Carlson et al., 2016).

● **Especially for Future Researchers**
What is the best method for collecting data?
(see response, page 31)

## WHAT HAVE YOU LEARNED?

1. Why do careful observations not prove "what causes what"?

2. Why do experimenters use a control (or comparison) group as well as an experimental group?

3. What are the strengths and weaknesses of the survey method?

4. Why would a scientist conduct a cross-sectional study?

5. Why would a scientist conduct a longitudinal study?

6. Why would a scientist conduct a cross-sequential study?

## Cautions and Challenges from Science

The scientific method illuminates and illustrates human development as nothing else does. Facts, consequences, and possibilities have emerged that would not be known without science—and people of all ages are healthier, happier, and more capable because of it.

Thanks to science, infectious diseases, illiteracy, and racism are much reduced compared to a century ago. Early death—from violence, war, or disease—is also less likely; science and education are likely reasons (Pinker, 2018).

Developmentalists have also discovered unexpected sources of harm. Furry baby blankets, childhood hospitalization, lead, asbestos, and vaping are all less benign than people first thought.

Thus, the benefits of science are many, in improving lives and discovering hazards. However, science can lead us all astray. We now discuss three complications: misinterpreting correlation, depending on numbers, and ignoring ethics.

**correlation** A number between +1.0 and –1.0 that indicates the degree of relationship between two variables, expressed in terms of the likelihood that one variable will (or will not) occur when the other variable does (or does not). A correlation indicates only that two variables are somehow related, not that one variable causes the other to occur.

### TABLE 1.3

#### Quiz on Correlation

| Two Variables | Positive, Negative, or Zero Correlation? | Why? (Third variable) |
|---|---|---|
| 1. Ice cream sales and murder rate | _____ | _____ |
| 2. Reading ability and number of baby teeth | _____ | _____ |
| 3. Adult's sex assigned at birth and average number of offspring | _____ | _____ |

For each of these three pairs of variables, indicate whether the correlation between them is positive, negative, or nonexistent. Then try to think of a third variable that might determine the direction of the correlation. The correct answers appear below.

**Answers:**
1. Positive; third variable: heat
2. Negative; third variable: age
3. Zero. Each child must begin with a sperm from a male and an ovum from a female. No third variable.

## Correlation and Causation

Probably the most common mistake in interpreting research is confusing correlation with causation. A **correlation** exists between two variables if one variable is more (or less) likely to occur when the other does. A correlation is *positive* if both variables tend to increase together or decrease together, *negative* if one variable tends to increase while the other decreases, and *zero* if no connection is evident. (Try the quiz in **Table 1.3**.)

Expressed in numerical terms, correlations vary from +1.0 (the most positive) to –1.0 (the most negative). Correlations are almost never that extreme; a correlation of +.3 or –.3 is noteworthy; a correlation of +.8 or –.8 is astonishing.

Many correlations are unexpected. For instance: First-born children are more likely to develop asthma than are later-born children; teenage girls have higher rates of mental health problems than do teenage boys; and counties in the United States with more dentists have fewer obese residents. That last study controlled for the number of medical doctors and the poverty of the community. The authors suggest that dentists provide information about nutrition that improves health (Holzer et al., 2014).

That explanation may be wrong. Every scientist knows the mantra: *Correlation is not causation.* Just because two variables are correlated does not mean that one causes the other—even if it seems logical that it does. It proves only that the variables are connected somehow.

In the dentist correlation, the cause could be from either direction. Seeing the dentist might encourage people to eat better, or dentists may choose to practice where people are healthier. Or a third variable might cause both if, for instance, a particular community values both exercise and preventive medicine. Unless people remember that correlation is not causation, they may draw mistaken conclusions.

## Quantity and Quality

A second caution concerns whether scientists should rely on data produced by **quantitative research** (from the word *quantity*). Quantitative research data are ranked or numbered, allowing easy translation across cultures. One example of quantitative research is using children's achievement scores to assess education within a school or a nation.

Since quantities can be easily summarized, compared, charted, and replicated, many scientists prefer quantitative research. Statistics require numbers. Quantitative data are easier to replicate and less open to bias.

However, when data are presented in categories and numbers, some nuances and individual distinctions are lost. Moreover, exactly how the raw data are turned into statistics may itself reflect bias. Many developmental researchers thus turn to **qualitative research** (from the word *quality*)—asking open-ended questions, reporting answers in narrative (not numerical) form.

Qualitative research reflects cultural and contextual diversity, and it may reflect the biases of the scientist. Qualitative research is harder to replicate. Both types of research are needed (Morgan, 2018).

Some studies now use both methods, which provides richer, but also more verifiable, details. For example, when a child has a psychological disorder that would benefit from professional help, less than half of all parents access such care. A review that included both quantitative studies (22 of them) and qualitative ones (24 of them) found many factors that reduced care-seeking, including cost (quantitative) and trust in providers (qualitative) (Reardon et al., 2017).

## Ethics

The most important challenge for all scientists is to follow ethical standards. Each professional society involved in research of human development has a *code of ethics* (a set of moral principles). Most colleges and hospitals have an *Institutional Review Board* (IRB) that requires research to follow ethical guidelines set by the federal government.

Some research conducted before IRBs were established was clearly unethical, especially when the participants were children, members of minority groups, prisoners, or animals. Even with IRBs, serious ethical dilemmas remain, particularly when research occurs in developing nations (Leiter & Herman, 2015).

**quantitative research** Research that provides data that can be expressed with numbers, such as ranks or scales.

**qualitative research** Research that considers qualities instead of quantities. Descriptions of particular conditions and participants' expressed ideas are often part of qualitative studies.

◗ **Especially for Future Researchers and Science Writers** Do any ethical guidelines apply when an author writes about the experiences of family members, friends, or research participants? (see response, page 31)

## Ebola and Coronavirus

Many ethical dilemmas arose in the 2014–2015 West African Ebola epidemic (Gillon, 2015; Rothstein, 2015; Sabeti & Sabeti, 2018). Those problems have reemerged in the recent Ebola crisis (Gostin et al., 2019) and the coronavirus pandemic (Wang et al., 2020). Among them:

- Should vaccines be given before their safety is demonstrated with large control and experimental groups?
- What kind of informed consent is needed to avoid both false hope and false fears?
- Should children with Ebola or coronavirus be isolated from family, even though social isolation is harmful?
- Is it fair for public health care systems to be inadequate in some countries and high-tech in others?
- When should each nation be responsible for the health of their own people, and when and how should other nations or the United Nations intervene?
- Should quarantine restrict the travel of healthy people?

Medicine tends to focus on individuals, ignoring the customs and systems that make some people in some nations more vulnerable. One observer noted:

> When people from the United States and Europe working in West Africa have developed Ebola, time and again the first thing they wanted to take was not an experimental drug. It was an airplane that would cart them home.

*[Cohen, 2014, p. 911]*

These issues have led to some international efforts, including funding secure biocontainment laboratories in many nations, in order to quickly recognize deadly diseases (Le Duc & Yuan, 2018). Nonetheless, no developmentalist believes that the political and economic cooperation necessary for world health is adequate. This is evident not only for diseases such as Ebola, Zika, coronavirus, and polio, but also for many developmental concerns, such as early-childhood care, drug control, and public education. Multidirectional, multicontextual, multicultural, multidisciplinary, and plastic perspectives are needed.

An underlying problem is that people everywhere have strong opinions about children that they expect research to confirm. Scientists might try (sometimes without noticing it) to achieve results that confirm their national and cultural values.

Obviously, collaboration, replication, and transparency are essential ethical safeguards. Hundreds of questions regarding human development need answers, and researchers have yet to find them. That is the most important ethical mandate of all. For instance:

- Do we know enough about prenatal drugs to protect every fetus?
- Do we know enough about education to ensure that every child is ready for the future?
- Do we know enough about poverty to enable everyone to be healthy?
- Do we know enough about transgender children, or contraception, or romance to ensure that every child is loved?
- Do we know enough about single parenthood, or divorce, or same-sex marriage to ensure optimal family life?

**Risky Shot?** Most vaccines undergo years of testing before they are used on people, but vaccines protecting against Ebola were not ready until the 2014 West African epidemic finally waned after 11,000 deaths. Thus, the effectiveness of Ebola vaccines is unknown. However, when deadly Ebola surfaced again in the Democratic Republic of Congo in 2018, public health doctors did not wait for longitudinal data. Here Dr. Mwamba, a representative of Congo's Expanded Program on Immunization, receives the vaccine. He hopes that it will protect him and thousands of other Congolese. We will know by 2021 if the vaccine halted a new epidemic.

AP Images/John Bompengo

The answer to these questions is *NO, NO, NO, NO, and NO.*

Scientists and funders tend to avoid questions that might produce unwanted answers. People have strong opinions about drugs, schools, economics, sexuality, and families (the five questions above) that may conflict with scientific findings and conclusions. Religion, politics, and customs shape scientific research, sometimes stopping investigation before it begins.

Consider research on guns, a leading cause of child death from age 2 to 20. In 1996, the U.S. Congress, in allocating funds for the Centers for Disease Control and Prevention, passed a law stating that "None of the funds made available for injury prevention and control at the Centers for Disease Control and Prevention may be used to advocate or promote gun control." The National Rifle Association (NRA) interpreted this as a reason to stop research on guns, even though guns are the most common means of suicide in the United States and the most used weapon of homicide.

Ten highly respected scientists summarize research on gun deaths:

> There is only very sparse scientific evidence [regarding] . . . which policies will be effective. . . . Even the seemingly popular view that violent crime would be reduced by laws prohibiting the purchase or possession of guns by people with mental illness was deemed to have only moderate supporting evidence.

*[Leshner & Dzau, 2018, p. 1195]*

It is unfair to blame Congress, or to focus on guns. Indeed, there are unanswered questions about almost every aspect of human development. Culture, context, and politics distort research on many topics. That is why everyone, left, right, and center, needs science.

Awareness of bias is only the first step for the next cohort of developmental scientists. They will build on what is known, mindful of what needs to be explored, raising questions that earlier cohorts have not asked. The goal of our study remains the same, to help everyone fulfill their potential. The next 15 chapters are a beginning.

> **THINK CRITICALLY:** Can you think of an additional question that researchers should answer?

---

### WHAT HAVE YOU LEARNED?

1. Why does correlation not prove causation?

2. What are the advantages and disadvantages of quantitative research?

3. What are the advantages and disadvantages of qualitative research?

4. What is the role of the IRB?

5. Why might a political leader avoid funding developmental research?

6. What questions about human development remain to be answered?

---

## SUMMARY

### Understanding How and Why

**1.** The study of human development is a science that seeks to understand how people change or remain the same over time. As a science, it begins with questions and hypotheses and then gathers empirical data. The data are analyzed, and conclusions are drawn.

**2.** Research is published with sufficient detail to allow other scientists to confirm or refute the conclusions. Replication is needed before a particular result is considered solid.

**3.** The universality of human development and the uniqueness of each individual's development are evident in both nature (the genes) and nurture (the environment); no person is quite like another. Nature and nurture always interact, and each human characteristic is affected by that interaction.

**4.** Differential susceptibility is evident when we study nature and nurture. Genes and experiences affect our vulnerability to developmental change, for better or worse. Some people are impervious to conditions that affect others, as the metaphor of dandelions and orchids illustrates.

## Childhood and Adulthood

**5.** The assumption that growth is linear has been replaced by the realization that both continuity and discontinuity are part of every life. Developmental gains and losses are apparent lifelong, because development is multidirectional.

**6.** Time is a crucial variable. Everyone changes with age. Critical periods are times when something *must* occur for normal development; sensitive periods are times when a particular kind of development occurs most easily.

**7.** Development is multicontextual and multicultural; it occurs within many contexts and cultures. Those ideas were emphasized by Urie Bronfenbrenner's ecological-systems approach. Each person is situated within larger systems of family, school, community, and culture.

**8.** Each cohort is influenced by the innovations and events of their historical period, and each person is affected by his or her socioeconomic status (SES), with effects of both cohort and SES varying depending on the age and circumstances of the person.

**9.** Culture includes beliefs and patterns; ethnicity refers to ancestral heritage. Race is a social construction, sometimes mistakenly thought to be biological. Developmentalists guard against the assumption that if something is unusual, it is not as good as the usual, called the difference-is-deficit error.

**10.** A multidisciplinary, dynamic-systems approach is needed because each person develops in many ways—biosocially, cognitively, and psychosocially—simultaneously, yet scientists tend to focus on a small part of a larger issue. A multidisciplinary approach has corrected many narrow ideas of the past.

**11.** Throughout life, human development is plastic. Brains and behaviors are molded by experiences. Cultures as well as individuals adjust to social needs.

## Using the Scientific Method

**12.** Commonly used research methods are observation, experiments, and surveys. Each of these methods use techniques, such as having experimental and control groups, that reduce bias. Each study can provide insight, yet each is limited. Meta-analyses summarize conclusions of many studies.

**13.** Developmentalists study change over time, often with cross-sectional and longitudinal research. Cross-sequential research, which combines the other two methods, attempts to avoid the pitfalls of cross-sectional and longitudinal studies.

## Cautions and Challenges from Science

**14.** A correlation is a statistic that indicates that two variables are connected, both increasing or both decreasing together, or, with a negative correlation, one increasing as the other decreases. Correlation does not prove which of two variables causes the other. Sometimes neither is the cause, because two variables correlate because of a third variable.

**15.** Quantitative research provides numerical data, which is best for comparing contexts and cultures via verified statistics. By contrast, more nuanced data come from qualitative research, which reports on individual lives. Both are useful.

**16.** Ethical behavior is crucial in all of the sciences. Results must be fairly gathered, reported, and interpreted. Participants must be informed and protected.

**17.** The most important ethical question is whether scientists are designing, conducting, analyzing, publishing, and applying the research that is most critically needed. The next cohort of developmental scholars will add to our scientific knowledge.

## KEY TERMS

science of human development (p. 3)
scientific method (p. 3)
hypothesis (p. 3)
empirical evidence (p. 3)
replication (p. 4)
nature (p. 5)
nurture (p. 5)
differential susceptibility (p. 5)
critical period (p. 7)
sensitive period (p. 7)

ecological-systems approach (p. 8)
microsystem (p. 8)
exosystem (p. 8)
macrosystem (p. 8)
chronosystem (p. 8)
mesosystem (p. 8)
cohort (p. 9)
socioeconomic status (SES) (p. 10)
culture (p. 11)
social construction (p. 11)

difference-equals-deficit error (p. 12)
ethnic group (p. 12)
race (p. 12)
intersectionality (p. 13)
plasticity (p. 16)
dynamic-systems approach (p. 16)
scientific observation (p. 20)
experiment (p. 21)
independent variable (p. 21)
dependent variable (p. 21)

survey (p. 22)
meta-analysis (p. 23)
cross-sectional research (p. 23)
longitudinal research (p. 24)
cross-sequential research (p. 24)
correlation (p. 26)
quantitative research (p. 27)
qualitative research (p. 27)

## APPLICATIONS

1. It is said that culture is pervasive but that people are unaware of it. List 30 things you did *today* that you might have done differently in another culture. Begin with how and where you woke up.

2. How would your life be different if your parents were much higher or lower in SES than they are? Consider all three domains.

3. A longitudinal case study can be insightful but is also limited in generality. Interview one of your older relatives and explain what aspects of his or her childhood are unique and what might be relevant for everyone.

## Especially For ANSWERS

**Response for Nurses** (from p. 22) Experiments are the only way to determine cause-and-effect relationships. If we want to be sure that a new drug or treatment is safe and effective, an experiment must be conducted to establish that the drug or treatment improves health.

**Response for Future Researchers** (from p. 25) There is no best method for collecting data. The method used depends on many factors, such as the age of participants (infants can't complete questionnaires), the question being researched, and the time frame.

**Response for Future Researchers and Science Writers** (from p. 27) Yes. Anyone you write about must give consent and be fully informed about your intentions. They can be identified by name only if they give permission. For example, family members gave permission before anecdotes about them were included in this text. My nephew David read the first draft of his story (see pages 18–19) and is proud to have his experiences used to teach others.

## Observation Quiz ANSWERS

**Answer to Observation Quiz** (from p. 12) Islam (notice the hijab) and Christianity (notice the cross).

**Answer to Observation Quiz** (from p. 17) Surveys rarely ask children their opinions, and the youngest cohort on this graph did not reach adulthood until about 2005.

## What Will You Know?

1. What is practical about a theory?
2. Do childhood experiences affect adults?
3. Would you be a different person if you grew up in another place or century?
4. Why do we need so many theories?

I have become the head of a family of nine, the other eight of whom are my descendants. Technically one of them is not a descendant, my son-in-law Oscar, but I include him in the count, not only because he is the father of two of my grandchildren, but also because he is an integral part of the family. For instance, his humor lightens our family gatherings.

One family gathering is the springboard of this chapter, because it illustrates why theories are needed. It began when we were all together on a hot summer day. Our thoughts turned to winter. "Maybe we should all go to Iowa for Christmas," someone said.

Iowa for the holidays may be surprising for a professor who teaches in the Bronx, but Rachel recently moved to Iowa, and neither her mother (me) nor her three sisters have seen her new home. That "maybe we should" started dozens of conversations and emails, beginning with questioning the premise (why should we?) and with Oscar laughing at "another Berger trip." He knows by now that we propose a dozen versions of every gathering, with different ideas of who, when, how, and where. Even "why" is debated: Why should all nine of us gather for Christmas? Travel is more expensive then. One previous year, we opened presents together on Skype.

Months of discussion ensued. What about holiday traffic, snow, ice, money, time off work? Does the Iowa daughter want us there in December, an intense work month for her? Flying uses lots of fossil fuel, but the train takes a day and a night and goes only to Chicago; driving is more direct but less safe; planes will fly with or without us; we should reduce our carbon emissions; we should not do that if it harms our family; the money could go to better causes; family bonding is a good cause. . . . It went on for months, Oscar smiling and everyone else considering options but no one deciding. How did we choose? Theories helped; so did facts.

Finally we agreed that we should go to Iowa; then "when" became an issue. Who has days off from work, when is best to avoid crowds, how many days together is long enough but not too long?

As in this example, every human decides what to do with each minute, each day, each month of their lives, selecting among many possibilities, and thus, everyone must set priorities and clarify perspectives. With nine of us, this quickly gets complex. Without theories we would be confused and scattered, unable to agree and each stuck in their own place. The eight of us are used to the complexity of alternate views; Oscar is not. (Is that because he is an only child? That question prompts another set of theories. But not now.)

This chapter explains five comprehensive theories that guide human behavior. Each theory helped us with our Iowa dilemma, as we assessed (in order of the theories, not in order of our months-long, far-ranging discussions) family memories, past experiences, personal beliefs, cultural pressures, innate emotions. At the end of this chapter, you will learn what we did.

## What Theories Do

Theories organize scattered facts and confusing observations into patterns, weaving the details into a meaningful whole. A **developmental theory** is a comprehensive statement of general principles that provides a framework for understanding how and why people change as they grow older. This is much more than a hunch or speculation: Developmental theories emerge from data, survive analysis, lead to experiments, and raise new questions.

### Theory and Practice

Sometimes people think of theories as impractical. Not at all. As a leading social scientist once quipped, "Nothing is as practical as a good theory" (Lewin, 1945). He used humor to counter the idea that theory and practice are opposites. Like many other scientists, he knew not only that theories organize thoughts and experiences to help scientists grasp generalities and reach solid conclusions, but also that they aid everyone in daily life.

For example, if a child yells "I hate you," a mother might be shocked, stunned, sad, and angry. Each of the five theories in this chapter might suggest different responses, but all agree that a thoughtless, reactive "I hate you, too" is not ideal. Without theories, we would be lost with a jumble of observations and reactions, confused as to how they fit together to make a life.

Of course, theories differ; some are more comprehensive than others, and some reflect one culture more than another. In some cultures, children would never say "I hate you" to a parent: In every culture a developmental scientist would ask how old the child was, because "I hate you" means something different at age 2 than at 20.

Overall, children's needs change with age: Theories help adults respond. What should adults do when infants cry, or 3-year-olds refuse to eat their dinner, or 6-year-olds crawl into bed with their parents, or 10-year-olds multiply $7 \times 8$ correctly . . . or incorrectly? Answers reflect theories, ideally theories that have stood the tests of time and science.

It may be easier to understand the role of theory with a metaphor. Imagine trying to build a house without a design. You might have willing workers and all the raw materials: the bricks, the wood, the nails. But without tools and a plan you could not proceed. Science provides the tools; theories provide the plan; scientists are the workers who follow the plan.

Sometimes, over the years, the house needs more work—another bedroom, a new roof, an additional door. Likewise, theories are revised over time. Theories are meant to be tested and refined. Sometimes a theory leads to a hypothesis that turns out to be false, an outcome that is considered a benefit, not a liability, of theory.

**developmental theory** A group of ideas, assumptions, and generalizations that interpret and illuminate thousands of observations about human growth. A developmental theory provides a framework for explaining the patterns and problems of development.

Aaron Bacall/Cartoon Collections/Cartoon Stock

"I'm going to refer to an educational theory which was first published in February and is still applicable today."

**The Test of Time** Grand theories have endured for decades and still guide contemporary scientists.

Theories can be very useful. To be more specific:

- Theories produce *hypotheses*.
- Theories generate *discoveries*.
- Theories offer *practical guidance*.

Remember from Chapter 1 that testing a hypothesis is the third step of science, the middle of the five steps. To get to that pivot, scientists need a question and a hypothesis. That is one reason that theories are needed, to stimulate questions.

Once the question is framed as a hypothesis, the actual research begins, which then leads to analysis and conclusions to be shared with other scientists, to confirm, extend, revise, or refute the theory. For scientists, that is a practical result.

## Facts and Possibilities

Sometimes people say dismissively, "that's just a theory," as if theories were disconnected from facts. In truth, facts are essential: A good theory begins with facts and discovers more of them. As one scientist explained, imagine a world without facts, "a world of ignorance where many possibilities seem equally likely . . . [with] unreliable conclusions . . . [and] shoddy evidence" (Berg, 2018, p. 379). Theories and facts work together. Facts lead to theories, and then theories lead to discovery of previously unrecognized possibilities, which need testing to discover new facts.

It is a fact, not a theory, that everywhere and for all time, part of being a person is to be "perpetually driven to look for deeper explanations of our experience, and broader and more reliable predictions about it" (Gopnik, 2001, p. 66). The perpetual need to understand is evident in history. All five of the theories in this chapter echo ideas written by ancient sages in Greece, China, India, and elsewhere.

Dozens of other theories have been formulated to explain some aspect of development. The five theories here are comprehensive, relevant at every age. None is the final word. As explained in Chapter 1, human growth is dynamic, always affected by cohort and culture.

Science begins with questions, which often spring from theory. Among the thousands of important questions are the following, each central to one of the five theories in this chapter:

1. Do early experiences — of breast-feeding or attachment or abuse — shape adult personality?
2. Does learning depend on encouragement, punishment, and/or role models?
3. Do children learn best if they figure out ideas for themselves?
4. Does culture determine parents' behavior, such as how to respond to an infant's cry?
5. Is survival an inborn instinct, underlying all personal and social decisions?

The answer to each of these questions is "yes" when examined in order by the following theories: psychoanalytic, behaviorism, cognitive, sociocultural, and evolutionary. Each question is answered "no" or "not necessarily" by several others. For every answer, more questions arise: Why or why not? When and how? SO WHAT? This last question is crucial; implications and applications affect everyone's daily life.

---

**WHAT HAVE YOU LEARNED?**

1. How are facts and theories connected?
2. What three things do theories do?
3. Why do people need theories to move forward with their lives?
4. Who develops theories — everyone or just scientists?
5. What is the relationship between theories and facts?

# Grand Theories

In the first half of the twentieth century, two opposing theories—psychoanalytic and behaviorism—dominated psychology, each with extensive applications to child development. In about 1960, a third theory—cognitive—arose, and it, too, was widely applied.

These three are called "grand theories." They are explained here because they are comprehensive, enduring, and far-reaching. In developmental research, they continue to be useful. But be forewarned: None is now considered as grand as once believed.

## Psychoanalytic Theory: Freud and Erikson

Inner drives, deep motives, and unconscious needs rooted in childhood—especially the first six years—are the focus of **psychoanalytic theory.** These unconscious forces are thought to influence every aspect of thinking and behavior, from the smallest details of daily life to the crucial choices of a lifetime.

### Freud's Ideas

Psychoanalytic theory originated with Sigmund Freud (1856–1939), an Austrian physician who treated patients suffering from mental illness. He listened to their remembered dreams and uncensored thoughts. From that, he constructed an elaborate, multifaceted theory.

According to Freud, development in the first six years of life occurs in three *psychosexual* stages, each characterized by sexual interest and pleasure arising from a particular part of the body.

In infancy, the erotic body part is the mouth (the *oral stage*); in early childhood, the anus (the *anal stage*); in the preschool years, the penis (the *phallic stage*), a source of pride and fear among boys and a reason for sorrow and envy among girls. Then, after a quiet period (*latency*), the *genital stage* arrives at puberty, lasting throughout adulthood. (**Table 2.1** on page 36 describes stages in Freud's theory.)

Freud maintained that sensual satisfaction (from stimulation of the mouth, anus, or penis) is linked to major developmental stages, needs, and challenges. During the oral stage, for example, sucking provides not only nourishment for the infant but also erotic joy and attachment to the mother. Kissing between lovers is a vestige of the oral stage. Next, during the anal stage, pleasures arise from self-control, initially with toileting but later with wanting everything to be clean, neat, and regular (an "anal personality").

One of Freud's most influential ideas was that each stage includes its own struggles. Conflict occurs, for instance, when parents wean their babies (oral stage), toilet-train their toddlers (anal stage), deflect the sexual curiosity and fantasies of their 5-year-olds (phallic stage), and limit the sexual interests of adolescents (genital stage). Freud thought that the experiences surrounding these conflicts determine later personality.

Freud did not believe that any new stage occurred after puberty; rather, he believed that adult personalities and habits reflected childhood. As Freud explained it, unconscious conflicts rooted in early life were evident in adult behavior—for instance, cigarette smoking (oral) or meticulous housekeeping (anal) or driving big cars (phallic).

AKG/Science Source

**Freud at Work** In addition to being the world's first psychoanalyst, Sigmund Freud was a prolific writer. His many papers and case histories, primarily descriptions of his patients' symptoms and sexual urges, helped make the psychoanalytic perspective a dominant force for much of the twentieth century.

**psychoanalytic theory** Freud's theory of the stages of development, each of which emphasizes the sexual nature of the child. As its first grand theorist, Freud believed that irrational, unconscious drives and motives, often originating in childhood erotic impulses, underlie human behavior.

**TABLE 2.1**

Comparison of Freud's Psychosexual and Erikson's Psychosocial Stages

| Approximate Age | Freud (psychosexual) | Erikson (psychosocial) |
|---|---|---|
| Birth to 1 year | *Oral Stage*<br><br>The lips, tongue, and gums are the focus of pleasurable sensations in the baby's body, and sucking and feeding are the most stimulating activities. | *Trust vs. Mistrust*<br><br>Babies either trust that others will satisfy their basic needs, including nourishment, warmth, cleanliness, and physical contact, **or** develop mistrust about the care of others. |
| 1–3 years | *Anal Stage*<br><br>The anus is the focus of pleasurable sensations in the baby's body, and toilet training is the most important activity. | *Autonomy vs. Shame and Doubt*<br><br>Children either become self-sufficient in many activities, including toileting, feeding, walking, exploring, and talking, **or** feel shame, **or** doubt their own abilities. |
| 3–6 years | *Phallic Stage*<br><br>The phallus, or penis, is the most important body part, and pleasure is derived from genital stimulation. Boys are proud of their penises; girls wonder why they don't have them. | *Initiative vs. Guilt*<br><br>Children either try to undertake many adultlike activities **or** internalize the limits and prohibitions set by parents. They feel either adventurous **or** guilty. |
| 6–11 years | *Latency*<br><br>Not really a stage, latency is an interlude. Sexual needs are quiet; psychic energy flows into sports, schoolwork, and friendship. | *Industry vs. Inferiority*<br><br>Children busily practice and then master new skills **or** feel inferior, unable to do anything well. |
| Adolescence | *Genital Stage*<br><br>The genitals are the focus of pleasurable sensations, and the young person seeks sexual stimulation and satisfaction in heterosexual relationships. | *Identity vs. Role Confusion*<br><br>Adolescents ask themselves "Who am I?" They establish sexual, political, religious, and vocational identities **or** are confused about their roles. |
| Adulthood | Freud believed that the genital stage lasts throughout adulthood. He also said that the goal of a healthy life is "to love and to work." | *Intimacy vs. Isolation*<br><br>Young adults seek companionship and love **or** become isolated from others, fearing rejection.<br><br>*Generativity vs. Stagnation*<br><br>Middle-aged adults contribute to future generations through work, creative activities, and parenthood **or** they stagnate.<br><br>*Integrity vs. Despair*<br><br>Older adults try to make sense of their lives, either seeing life as a meaningful whole **or** despairing at goals never reached. |

## Erikson's Ideas

Many of Freud's followers became famous theorists themselves—Carl Jung, Alfred Adler, and Karen Horney among them. They agreed with Freud that early-childhood experiences affect everyone, often unconsciously, but they also expanded and modified his ideas. Many prefer to call their approach *psychodynamic*, to emphasize that they do not adhere strictly to Freud's approach.

For scholars in human development, one psychodynamic theorist, Erik Erikson (1902–1994), is particularly insightful. He was born in Denmark, spent his childhood in Germany, and traveled in Italy as a young man. His interest in psychoanalytic theory was fostered by his work as a teacher in Austria in a school for children of patients who were analyzed by Freud. When Hitler's rise forced all the Freudians to flee, Erikson and his American wife, Joan, came to the United States.

Those multicultural experiences led him to develop his **psychosocial theory** of the entire life span.

Erikson described eight developmental stages, each characterized by a particular challenge, or *developmental crisis*. Although Erikson named two polarities at each crisis, he recognized a wide range of outcomes between those opposites. Typically, development at each stage leads to neither extreme but to something in between.

In the stage of *initiative versus guilt*, for example, 3- to 6-year-olds undertake activities that exceed the limits set by their parents and their culture. They leap into swimming pools, pull their pants on backward, make cakes according to their own recipes, and wander off alone.

Erikson thought that those preschool initiatives produce feelings of pride or failure, depending on adult reactions. Should adults pretend to like the cake that a preschooler made or, instead, punish that child for wasting food and messing up the kitchen? According to Erikson's theory, a child will feel guilty lifelong if adults are too critical or if social norms are too strict regarding the young child's initiatives.

As you can see from Table 2.1, Erikson's first five stages are closely related to Freud's stages. Like Freud, Erikson believed that unresolved childhood conflicts echo throughout life, causing problems in adulthood.

Erikson considered the first stage, *trust versus mistrust*, particularly crucial. For example, an adult who has difficulty establishing a secure, mutual relationship with a life partner may never have resolved that first crisis of life. If you know people who are "too trusting" or "too suspicious," Erikson might suggest that you ask about their early care.

In his emphasis on childhood, Erikson agreed with Freud. However, in two crucial aspects, Erikson was unlike his mentor.

1. Erikson's stages emphasized family and culture, not sexual urges.
2. Erikson recognized the entire life span, with three stages after adolescence.

## Behaviorism: Conditioning and Learning

The comprehensive theory that dominated psychology in the United States for most of the twentieth century was **behaviorism.** This theory began in Russia, with Pavlov, who first described conditioning.

### Classical Conditioning

Early in the twentieth century, Ivan Pavlov (1849–1936) did hundreds of experiments to examine the link between something that affected a living creature (such as a sight, a sound, a touch) and how that creature reacted. Technically, he was interested in how a *stimulus* effects a *response*.

While studying salivation in his laboratory, Pavlov began by studying dogs. He noticed that his research dogs drooled (response) not only at the smell of food (stimulus) but also, eventually, at signals that food was coming, even before any sight or smell of the food. This observation led to a series of famous experiments: Pavlov conditioned dogs to salivate (response) when hearing a particular noise (stimulus).

Pavlov began by sounding a tone just before presenting food. After a number of repetitions of the tone-then-food sequence, dogs began salivating at the sound

**psychosocial theory** Erikson's theory of the stages of development, emphasizing the interaction between the psychic needs of the individual and the surrounding social network of family and community.

**A Legendary Couple** In his first 30 years, Erikson never fit into a particular local community, since he frequently changed nations, schools, and professions. Then he met Joan. In their first five decades of marriage, they raised a family and wrote several books. If Erikson had published his theory at age 73 (when this photograph was taken) instead of in his 40s, would he still have described life as a series of crises?

**Especially for Teachers** Your kindergartners are talkative and always moving. They almost never sit quietly and listen to you. What would Erik Erikson recommend? (see response, page 61)

**behaviorism** A grand theory of human development that studies observable behavior. Behaviorism is also called *learning theory* because it describes the laws and processes by which behavior is learned.

**classical conditioning** The learning process in which a meaningful stimulus (such as the smell of food to a hungry animal) is connected with a neutral stimulus (such as the sound of a tone) that had no special meaning before conditioning. (Also called *respondent conditioning*.)

**A Contemporary of Freud** Ivan Pavlov was a physiologist who received the Nobel Prize in 1904 for his research on digestive processes. It was this line of study that led to his discovery of classical conditioning, when his research on dog saliva led to insight about learning.

● **Observation Quiz** How is Pavlov similar to Freud in appearance, and how do both look different from the other theorists pictured? (see answer, page 61) ↑

even when there was no food. This simple experiment demonstrated **classical conditioning** (also called *respondent conditioning*).

In classical conditioning, a person or animal learns to associate a neutral stimulus with a meaningful one, gradually responding to the neutral stimulus in the same way as to the meaningful one. In Pavlov's original experiment, the dog associated the tone (the neutral stimulus) with food (the meaningful stimulus) and eventually responded to the tone as if it were the food itself. The conditioned response to the tone, no longer neutral but now a conditioned stimulus, was evidence that learning had occurred.

Behaviorists see dozens of examples of classical conditioning. Infants learn to smile at their parents because they associate them with food and play; toddlers learn to fear busy streets if the noise of traffic repeatedly frightens them; students learn to enjoy—or hate—school, depending on their kindergarten experience.

This theory alerts us to many reactions linked to stimuli that once were neutral. Think of how some people react to a wasp, or a final exam, or a police car in the rearview mirror.

In my early years teaching seventh-graders, I once strode up to the desk of one boy to tell him directly to get out his notebook and start writing, because he was not responding to my general request to the entire class. He put up his arm in self-defense. That startled me. I would never hit any student, but he had been conditioned to expect a blow.

All our reactions are learned; the mere announcement about a future exam triggers sweat or chills in some students—as would not happen to a child with no exam experience. Many students find that the stress hormones triggered by seeing the exam paper makes them forget what they know—an unwelcome conditioned response.

## Behaviorism in the United States

Pavlov's ideas seemed to bypass most Western European developmentalists but were welcomed in the United States, because many North Americans disputed the psychoanalytic emphasis on the unconscious. The first of three famous Americans who championed behaviorism was John B. Watson (1878–1958). He argued that if psychology was to be a true science, psychologists should examine only what they could measure, not invisible, unconscious impulses. In his words:

> Why don't we make what we can *observe* the real field of psychology? Let us limit ourselves to things that can be observed, and formulate laws concerning only those things. . . . We can observe *behavior—what the organism does or says.*
>
> *[Watson, 1924/1998, p. 6]*

According to Watson, if the focus is on behavior, it is apparent that everything is learned. He wrote:

> Give me a dozen healthy infants, well-formed, and my own specified world to bring them up in and I'll guarantee to take any one at random and train him to become any type of specialist I might select—doctor, lawyer, artist, merchant-chief, and yes, even beggar-man and thief, regardless of his talents, penchants, tendencies, abilities, vocations, and race of his ancestors.
>
> *[Watson, 1924/1998, p. 82]*

Other American psychologists agreed. They chose to study observable behavior, objectively and scientifically. For every creature at every age, behaviorists believe there are natural laws of behavior, and they seek to discover those laws to understand how simple, repeated actions become complex competencies, because stimuli in the environment affect each response.

Learning in behaviorism is far more comprehensive than the narrow definition of learning, which focuses on academics, such as learning to read or multiply. Instead, for behaviorists, everything that people think, do, and feel is learned, step by step, via conditioning.

For example, newborns *learn* to suck on a nipple; infants *learn* to smile at a caregiver; preschoolers *learn* to hold hands when crossing the street. Such learning is conditioned and can endure when no longer useful. That explains why children suck lollipops, adults smile at strangers, and I still grab my children's hands in traffic.

## Operant Conditioning

The most influential North American proponent of behaviorism was B. F. Skinner (1904–1990). Skinner agreed with Watson that psychology should focus on observable behavior. He did not dispute Pavlov's classical conditioning, but, as a good scientist, he built on Pavlov's conclusions. His most famous contribution was to recognize another type of conditioning—**operant conditioning** (also called *instrumental conditioning*)—in which animals (including people) act and then something follows that action.

In other words, Skinner went beyond learning by association, in which one stimulus is paired with another stimulus (in Pavlov's experiment, the tone with the food). He focused instead on what happens *after* the response. If the consequence that follows is enjoyable, the creature (any living thing—a bird, a mouse, a child) tends to repeat the behavior; if the consequence is unpleasant, the creature does not do it again.

Consequences that increase the frequency or strength of a particular action are called *reinforcers*; the process is called **reinforcement** (Skinner, 1953). Pleasant consequences are sometimes called *rewards*, but behaviorists do not call them that because they want to avoid confusion. What some people consider a "reward" may actually be a *punishment*, an unpleasant consequence. For instance, a teacher might reward good behavior by giving the class extra recess time, but if a child hates recess, that is punishment not reinforcement.

The opposite is true as well: Something thought to be a punishment may be reinforcing. For example, parents "punish" their children by withholding dessert. But a particular child might dislike the dessert, so being deprived of it is no punishment.

Culture matters, too. Japanese parents threaten to punish their children by refusing to let them come home; American parents threaten to make the children stay home. Whether these opposite strategies are really punishments depends on the child as well as the culture (Bornstein, 2017).

The crucial question is, "What works as a reinforcement or punishment for that individual?" The answer varies by personal history as well as by age. For instance, adolescents find risk and excitement particularly reinforcing, and they consider punishments much less painful than adults do. That was one conclusion of a study of teenagers who were violent: For them, the thrill of breaking the law was reinforcing, outweighing the pain of getting caught (Shulman et al., 2017).

Consider a common practice in schools: Teachers send misbehaving children out of the classroom. Then, principals suspend the worst violators from school.

However, if a child hates the teacher, leaving class is rewarding; and if a child hates school, suspension is a reinforcement. Indeed, research on school discipline finds that some measures, including school suspension, *increase* later disobedience (Osher et al., 2010). Educators have learned that, to stop misbehavior, it is often more effective to encourage good behavior, to "catch them being good" (Polirstok, 2015, p. 932).

AP Photo

**Rats, Pigeons, and People** B. F. Skinner is best known for his experiments with rats and pigeons, but he also applied his knowledge to human behavior. For his daughter, he designed a glass-enclosed crib in which temperature, humidity, and perceptual stimulation could be controlled to make her time in the crib enjoyable and educational. He encouraged her first attempts to talk by smiling and responding with words, affection, or other positive reinforcement.

**operant conditioning** The learning process by which a particular action is followed by something desired (which makes the person or animal more likely to repeat the action) or by something unwanted (which makes the action less likely to be repeated). (Also called *instrumental conditioning*.)

**reinforcement** When a behavior is followed by something desired, such as food for a hungry animal or a welcoming smile for a lonely person.

**LaunchPad**
macmillan learning

**VIDEO ACTIVITY: Modeling: Learning by Observation** features the original footage of Albert Bandura's famous experiment.

**social learning theory** An extension of behaviorism that emphasizes the influence that other people have over a person's behavior. Even without specific reinforcement, every individual learns many things through observation and imitation of other people. (Also called *observational learning*.)

**modeling** The central process of social learning, by which a person observes the actions of others and then copies them.

**cognitive theory** A grand theory of human development that focuses on changes in how people think over time. According to this theory, our thoughts shape our attitudes, beliefs, and behaviors.

In the United States, the chance of an African American child being suspended from school is three times higher than for a European American child. The rate is also high for children designated as needing special education (Tajalli & Garba, 2014; Shah, 2011). Those statistics raise a question: Is suspension a child's punishment or a teacher's reinforcer?

The data show that children who are suspended from school are more likely than other children to be incarcerated years later. That is a correlation. It does not prove that suspension *causes* later imprisonment; it may be that children who do not obey teachers become adults who do not obey laws. But, behaviorist theory suggests that suspension does not improve child behavior, and it might make it worse (Mallett, 2016). [**Developmental Link:** Correlation and causation are discussed in Chapter 1.]

Remember, behaviorists focus on the *effect* that a consequence has on future behavior, not whether it is intended to be a reward or not. They contend that children who repeatedly misbehave have been reinforced, not punished, for misbehavior—perhaps by their parents or teachers, perhaps by their friends or themselves.

## Social Learning

At first, behaviorists thought that all behavior arose from a chain of learned responses, the result of (1) the association between one stimulus and another (classical conditioning) or (2) past reinforcement (operant conditioning). Thousands of experiments inspired by learning theory have demonstrated both classical conditioning and operant conditioning in everyday life.

However, behaviorists realized people do more than respond to their personal associations, reinforcements, and punishments. They "act on the environment. They create it, preserve it, transform it, and even destroy it. . . . [in] a socially embedded interplay" (Bandura, 2006, p. 167).

That social interplay is the foundation of **social learning theory** (see **Table 2.2**), which holds that humans sometimes learn from what they see, even if they themselves have not been conditioned. As Albert Bandura, the primary proponent of this theory, explained, this learning often occurs through **modeling,** when people copy what they see others do (also called *observational learning*) (Bandura, 1986, 1997).

Modeling is not simple imitation: Some people are more likely to follow, or to be, role models than others. Indeed, humans copy only some actions, of some individuals, in some contexts. If people do the opposite of what they have seen, that could be social learning as well: Humans learn from other humans' mistakes.

Modeling is especially likely when the observer is uncertain or inexperienced and the model is admired, powerful, nurturing, or similar to the observer. That's why role models are crucial in childhood.

Social learning occurs not only for behavior and preferences (haircuts, clothing styles, slang) but also for morals. Deciding what is right is less a personal decision than one profoundly affected by other people (Bandura, 2016).

## Cognitive Theory: Piaget and Information Processing

According to **cognitive theory,** each person's thoughts and expectations profoundly affect their attitudes, values,

---

### TABLE 2.2

#### Three Types of Learning

Behaviorism is also called *learning theory* because it emphasizes the learning process, as shown here.

| Type of Learning | Learning Process | Result |
|---|---|---|
| Classical conditioning | Learning occurs through association. | Neutral stimulus becomes conditioned stimulus leading to conditioned response. |
| Operant conditioning | Learning occurs through reinforcement and punishment. | Weak or rare responses become strong and frequent—or, with punishment, unwanted responses become extinct. |
| Social learning | Learning occurs through modeling what others do. | Observed behaviors become copied behaviors. |

emotions, and actions. The core idea is that *how* and *what* people think is a crucial influence on human behavior.

Cognitive theory diverged from psychoanalytic theory (which emphasized hidden impulses) and behaviorism (which emphasized observed actions) to stress that thoughts are the crucial link between those impulses and actions.

## Piaget's Stages of Development

Jean Piaget (1896–1980) transformed our understanding of cognition. He may have been "the greatest developmental psychologist of all time" (Haidt, 2013, p. 6). His academic training was in biology, with a focus on shellfish, which taught him to look closely at small details.

Before Piaget, most scientists believed that babies could not yet think. But Piaget used scientific observation with his own three infants. He took meticulous notes, finding infants curious and thoughtful; babies develop new concepts month by month.

Later Piaget studied hundreds of schoolchildren. From this work emerged the central thesis of cognitive theory: *How* children think changes with time and experience. According to cognitive theory, to understand the behavior of humans of any age, we need to understand their thinking.

Piaget maintained that cognitive development occurs in four age-related periods, or stages: *sensorimotor*, *preoperational*, *concrete operational*, and *formal operational* (see **Table 2.3**). Each period is characterized by particular mental processes: Infants think via their senses; preschoolers have language but not logic; school-age children have simple logic; adolescents and adults can use formal, abstract logic (Inhelder & Piaget, 1958/2013b; Piaget, 1952/2011).

At every age, Piaget found that intellectual advancement occurs because humans seek **cognitive equilibrium**—a state of mental balance. The easiest way to achieve this balance is to interpret new experiences through the lens of preexisting ideas.

Cognition is easier when the mind simplifies ideas. For instance, once children grasp the concept of "dog," they can see unfamiliar animals on the street, from

**Would You Talk to This Man?** Children loved talking to Jean Piaget, and he learned by listening carefully—especially to their incorrect explanations, which no one had paid much attention to before. All his life, Piaget was absorbed with studying the way children think. He called himself a "genetic epistemologist"—one who studies how children gain knowledge about the world as they grow.

**cognitive equilibrium** In cognitive theory, a state of mental balance in which people are not confused because they can use their existing thought processes to understand current experiences and ideas.

### TABLE 2.3

**Piaget's Periods of Cognitive Development**

| | Name of Period | Characteristics of Period | Major Gains During Period |
|---|---|---|---|
| Birth to 2 years | Sensorimotor | Infants use senses and motor abilities to understand the world. Learning is active, without reflection. | Infants learn that objects still exist when out of sight (*object permanence*) and begin to think through mental actions. (The sensorimotor period is discussed further in Chapter 6.) |
| 2–6 years | Preoperational | Children think symbolically, with language, yet children are *egocentric*, perceiving from their own perspective. | The imagination flourishes, and language becomes a significant means of self-expression and social influence. (The preoperational period is discussed further in Chapter 9.) |
| 6–11 years | Concrete operational | Children understand and apply logic. Thinking is limited by direct experience. | By applying logic, children grasp concepts of conservation, number, classification, and many other scientific ideas. (The concrete-operational period is discussed further in Chapter 12.) |
| 12 years through adulthood | Formal operational | Adolescents and adults use abstract and hypothetical concepts. They can use analysis, not only emotion. | Ethics, politics, and social and moral issues become fascinating as adolescents and adults use abstract, theoretical reasoning. (The formal-operational period is discussed further in Chapter 15.) |

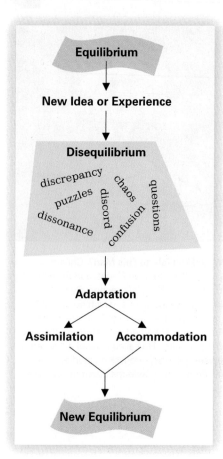

**FIGURE 2.1**

**Challenge Me** Most of us, most of the time, prefer the comfort of our conventional conclusions. According to Piaget, however, when new ideas disturb our thinking, we have an opportunity to expand our cognition with a broader and deeper understanding.

**assimilation** The reinterpretation of new experiences to fit into old ideas.

**accommodation** The restructuring of old ideas to include new experiences.

**information-processing theory** A perspective that compares human thinking processes, by analogy, to computer analysis of data, including sensory input, connections, stored memories, and output.

Great Danes to Chihuahuas, and say "doggie." They also expect dogs to sniff, bark, wag tails, and so on. Some children want to pet every dog they see; some fear them all—but in either case, generalities of "dogness" are evident.

Achieving cognitive equilibrium is not always easy, however. Sometimes a new experience or question is jarring or incomprehensible—such as learning that some dogs (Basenjis) do not bark. Then the individual experiences *cognitive disequilibrium*, an imbalance that creates confusion.

As **Figure 2.1** illustrates, disequilibrium advances cognition if it leads to adaptive thinking. Piaget describes two types of adaptation:

- **Assimilation:** New experiences are reinterpreted to fit, or *assimilate*, into old ideas. [A Basenji could bark if it wanted to, or Basenjis are not really dogs.]
- **Accommodation:** Old ideas are restructured to include, or *accommodate*, new experiences. [Some dogs do not bark.]

Ideally, when two people disagree, adaptation is mutual. Think of a lovers' quarrel. If both parties listen sympathetically to the other, they both accommodate. Then the quarrel strengthens their relationship, and they reach a new, better equilibrium.

As you see, accommodation requires more effort than assimilation, but it advances thought. Children—and everyone else—actively develop new concepts when the old ones fail.

In Piagetian terms, they *construct* ideas based on their experiences. He thought that knowledge is constructed (built) in the mind, an inner construction as ideas link together, not unlike the external process of construction by linking wood, metal, or whatever. For example, infants first assimilate everything using their senses—they taste and touch everything. But experience requires accommodation: They learn what should *not* be put in their mouths.

## Information Processing

A newer version of cognitive theory is called **information-processing theory,** inspired by the input, programming, memory, and output of the computer. When conceptualized in that way, thinking is affected by the neurons, synapses, and neurotransmitters of the brain.

Information processing is "a framework characterizing a large number of research programs" (Miller, 2011, p. 266). Instead of interpreting *responses* by infants and children, as Piaget did, this cognitive theory focuses on the *processes* of thought—that is, when, why, and how neurons fire to activate a thought.

Information-processing theorists contend that cognition begins when *input* is picked up by one of the senses. It proceeds to brain reactions, connections, and stored memories, and it concludes with some form of *output*. For infants, output consists of moving a hand, making a sound, or staring a split second longer at one stimulus than at another. As children mature, output studied by information-processing scientists include words, hesitations, neuronal activity, and bodily reactions (heartbeat, blood pressure, hormones, and the like) (see Inside the Brain).

Information-processing theory is particularly helpful in understanding social reactions. For example, one study began by studying how parents interpreted social information before their babies were born. Later, when their 6-month-olds cried, parents reverted to their earlier assumptions: Some interpreted crying as an attempt to communicate, and others as selfish and angry. Abuse sometimes followed that interpretation (Rodriguez et al., 2019). This research advises parents to change their cognition—breathe deeply, sleep, take a walk, whatever works—when their thoughts go negative.

# Measuring Mental Activity

A hundred years ago, people thought that emotions came from the heart. That's why we still send hearts on Valentine's Day and why we speak of "broken hearts" or people who are "soft-hearted" or who have "hardened their hearts."

But now we know that everything begins inside the brain. It is foolish to dismiss a sensation with "It's all in your head." Of course it is your head; everything is.

Until quite recently, the only way scientists assessed brains was to measure heads. Of course, measuring produced some obvious discoveries—babies with shrunken brains (microcephaly) suffered severe intellectual disability, and brains grew bigger as children matured.

Measuring also led to some obvious errors. In the nineteenth and early twentieth centuries, many scientists believed the theory that bumps on the surface of the head reflected intelligence and character, a theory known as *phrenology*.

Psychiatrists would run their hands over a person's skull to measure 27 traits, including spirituality, loyalty, and aggression. Another discredited example was suggesting that women could never be professors because their brains were too small (Swaab & Hofman, 1984).

Within the past half-century, neuroscientists developed ways to use electrodes, magnets, light, and computers to measure brain activity, not just brain size (see **Table 2.4**).

Raised areas on the head and head size (within limits) were proven irrelevant to intellectual processes. Researchers now study cognitive processes between input and output. Some results are cited later. In this feature we describe methods.

## TABLE 2.4

### Some Techniques Used by Neuroscientists to Understand Brain Function

#### EEG (electroencephalogram)

Robert J. Herko/Getty Images

The EEG measures electrical activity in the cortex. This can differentiate active brains (beta brain waves—very rapid, 12 to 30 per second) from sleeping brains (delta waves—1 to 3 per second) and brain states that are half-awake, or dreaming. Complete lack of brain waves, called flat-line, indicates brain death.

#### ERP (event-related potential)

Langlios Social Development Lab

The amplitude and frequency of brain electrical activity changes when a particular stimulus (called an event) occurs. First, the ERP establishes the usual patterns, and then researchers present a stimulus (such as a sound, an image, a word) that causes a blip in electrical activity. ERP indicates how quickly and extensively people react—although this method requires many repetitions to distinguish the response from the usual brain activity.

#### MRI (magnetic resonance imaging)

Pasieka/Science Source

The water molecules in various parts of the brain each have a magnetic current, and measuring that current allows measurement of myelin, neurons, and fluid in the brain.

#### fMRI (functional magnetic resonance imaging)

Kul Bhatia/Science Source

In advanced MRI, function is measured as more oxygen is added to the blood flow when specific neurons are activated. The presumption is that increased blood flow means that the person is using that part of the brain. fMRI has revealed that several parts of the brain are active at once—seeing something activates parts of the visual cortex, and may also activate parts of the brain far from the visual areas.

### PET (positron emission tomography)

Tim Beddow/Science Source

When a specific part of the brain is active, the blood flows more rapidly in that part. If radioactive dye is injected into the bloodstream and a person lies very still within a scanner while seeing pictures or other stimuli, changes in blood flow indicate thought. PET can reveal the volume of neurotransmitters; the rise or fall of brain oxygen, glucose, amino acids; and more. PET is almost impossible to use with children (who cannot stay still).

### fNIRS (functional near-infrared spectroscopy)

Pat Greenhouse/The Boston Globe via Getty Images

This method also measures changes in blood flow. But it depends on light rather than magnetic charge and can be done with children, who merely wear a special cap connected to sensors and do not need to lie still in a noisy machine (as they do for PET or fMRI). By measuring how each area of the brain absorbs light, neuroscientists infer activity of the brain (Ferrari & Quaresima, 2012).

### DTI (diffusion tensor imaging)

Living Art Enterprises/Science Source

DTI is another technique that builds on the MRI. It measures the flow (diffusion) of water molecules within the brain, which shows connections between one area and another. This is particularly interesting to developmentalists because life experiences affect which brain areas connect with which other ones. Thus, DTI is increasingly being used by clinicians who want to individualize treatment and monitor progress (Van Hecke et al., 2016).

For both practical and ethical reasons, it is difficult to use these techniques on large, representative samples. One of the challenges of neuroscience is to develop methods that are harmless, quick, acceptable to parents and babies, and comprehensive. A more immediate challenge is to depict the data in ways that are easy to interpret and understand.

As you see from the table, measurement and interpretation of brain activity is still difficult, but newer techniques are developing. Neuroscientists and developmentalists often disagree about the specific meaning of various results.

Nonetheless, brain imaging has revealed many surprises. For example, fNIRS finds that the brains of newborns are more active when they hear the language that their mother spoke when they were in the womb than when they hear another language (May et al., 2011). Brain scans of new mothers reveal that babies change their mothers' brains (P. Kim et al., 2016).

With adolescents, fMRI has found that a fully grown brain does not mean a fully functioning brain: The prefrontal cortex is not completely connected to the rest of the brain until about age 25, with substantial variation from one teenager to another (Foulkes & Blakemore, 2018).

Interpreting brain scans is not straightforward. Even with advanced techniques, all that scientists know for certain is which parts of the brain are functioning and active. Changes in light absorption, or magnetism, or oxygenated blood flow in the brain are miniscule from one moment to the next.

For example, the conventional lie detector is unreliable. Could brain imaging replace it? In theory, yes; in practice, no. Current technology is not ready (Rose, 2016).

Variations within and between people make it difficult to know what someone is thinking via brain scans. Once again, this confirms the need for theory: Without an idea of what to look for, or what it might mean, the millions of data points from all brain images might lead to the same trap as earlier measurements of the skull—human bias.

The latest techniques to study the brain have produced insights from neuroscience on the sequence and strength of neuronal communication. With the aid of sensitive technology, information-processing research has overturned some of Piaget's findings, as you will later read. However, the basic tenet of cognitive theory is equally true for Piaget, neuroscience, and information processing: *Ideas matter*.

Countless studies find that how children interpret a hypothetical social situation, such as whether they anticipate acceptance or rejection, affects their actual friendships; how teenagers conceptualize heaven and hell influences their sexual activity; how stressed adults feel (about their work, or income, or health) affects how they relate to children. For everyone, cognition frames situations and affects actions (see A View from Science).

## A VIEW FROM SCIENCE

### Walk a Mile

The folk saying "Walk a mile in my shoes," memorialized in a song that asks if "I could be you and you could be me for just an hour," reflects social perspective-taking, a cognitive accomplishment that is absent in babies and evident by adulthood. When humans understand the circumstances of each other's lives, that might lead to more caring behavior because, according to cognitive theory, thoughts guide actions.

Piaget wondered at what age are children able to understand the perspective of someone else. In one famous study, children sat in front of a sculpture of three mountains and were asked how that display would appear to someone else. Preoperational children assumed that a person sitting on the opposite side of the table would view the display exactly as they themselves did. With cognitive maturation that egocentrism disappeared: Concrete operational children could imagine the viewpoint of another (Piaget & Inhelder, 1956/2013).

Many other researchers have studied perspective-taking, building on Piaget. For example, thousands of studies focus on how to diminish bias, from Gordon Allport's work on Black–White prejudice (Allport, 1954) and continuing to "cognitive liberalization" (Hodson et al., 2018). Researchers in the past few decades have focused on *theory of mind*, which is how children understand the thoughts and emotions of other people. (e.g., Ebert, 2020; Bowman et al., 2019).

As you have read, the information-processing perspective encourages scientists to connect thinking, behavior, and brain structures not in stages but bit by bit. An international team of seven scientists did just that, with 293 participants, aged 7 to 26 (Tamnes et al., 2018).

In that study, the main test of perspective-taking was a modification of the dictator task (Keysar et al., 2000). In that task, the participants view objects in a display case that has 16 cubicles, 5 of which have backs so that the contents are not seen by someone on the other side while the other 11 are open front and back. A man on the other side (the dictator) supposedly tells the participant to move one of the objects. (See **Figure 2.2**.)

If participants are adept at theory of mind, they realize that the dictator cannot see the objects in some of the boxes. For example, three of the cubicles hold balls—large, medium, and small—but the dictator can see only the first two.

Thus, when the dictator commands "Move the small ball," the participant must decide whether to move the medium ball or the smallest ball. The correct answer would be the medium ball, because from the dictator's restricted view that ball is smallest.

Perspective-taking increases as children mature. In this study, children (up to age 11) were wrong about one-third of the time; adolescents (ages 12 to 18) were wrong about one-seventh of the time; and emerging adults were wrong about one-twentieth of the time (Tamnes et al., 2018).

This replicates many other studies: Maturation brings gradual increases in perspective-taking, although even in adulthood, sometimes people do not understand another's viewpoint. Contrary to Piaget, theory of mind increases gradually; there is no sudden transformative stage when perspective-taking appears.

The researchers in the dictator study asked the participants to answer the Strength and Difficulties questionnaire, a questionnaire often vetted and used (Goodman et al., 1998). The focus was on six questions that measured social awareness, including whether the person never, sometimes, or always was "helpful if someone is hurt, upset, or feeling ill."

Accuracy on perspective-taking in the dictator task correlated with prosocial behavior on Strength and Difficulties. Participants who were better at figuring out what the dictator could see were also better at caring for other people.

Finally—and this is the feature that makes this study an example of information processing—the scientists measured the brain, specifically the distance was between gray and white matter in various regions of the cortex.

Each of the three components above had been studied in isolation, but here the scientists combined them. They found that cognition, behavior, and brain were correlated: Those with the

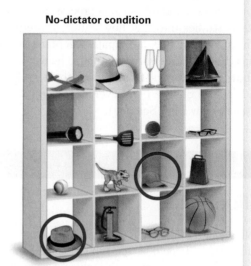

**Dictator condition**

**No-dictator condition**

**FIGURE 2.2**

**Do You See What I See?** If a man behind a set of shelves, some open and some closed, told you to move the small hat or the big ball, what would you do? Probably you would move the mid-sized objects (red) because you would realize that he could not see what you see. Young children, however, might move the wrong objects (blue).

thinner cortexes—especially in regions of the brain known for social cognition (the medial prefrontal, lateral prefrontal, and anterior cingulate)—were most likely to help other people and to understand the views of others.

This raises the possibility that, by developing perspective-taking (perhaps by having people read biographies, or engage in conversations with people unlike them), prosocial behavior might increase. Longitudinal research on the brain might verify that development.

---

**WHAT HAVE YOU LEARNED?**

1. What is the basic emphasis of psychoanalytic theory?
2. What are the similarities and differences between psychosexual and psychosocial theory?
3. How does the central focus of behaviorism differ from psychoanalytic theory?
4. When is a reward actually a punishment?
5. At what time in human development is social learning most powerful?
6. What did Piaget discover that earlier psychologists did not realize?
7. What is the emphasis of information processing?

---

## Newer Theories

The three theories just explained are comprehensive and enduring, which is why they are called *grand*. But they all share a major limitation: They began with men in Europe a century ago. Of course, background factors limit women and non-Europeans as well, but at least newer theories reflect broader perspectives.

Developmental scientists today are as often women as men, benefiting from extensive global, historical, and multidisciplinary research.

This is evident in the two newer theories we now describe. Sociocultural theorists reflect insight from anthropologists who report on cultures in every part of the globe; evolutionary psychologists use data from archeologists who examine the bones of humans who died 200,000 years ago.

Neither has been refined by decades of later application and clarification. Nonetheless, each provides what theories do best: a practical way to organize the many thoughts, observations, and sensations that appear in our everyday life.

## Sociocultural Theory: Vygotsky and Beyond

The central thesis of **sociocultural theory** is that human development results from the dynamic interaction between developing persons and their surrounding society. Culture is not something external that impinges on developing persons; it is internalized, integral to everyday attitudes and actions. This idea is so central to understanding the life span that it was first explained in the multicultural perspective discussion in Chapter 1. Now we explain it in more detail.

**sociocultural theory** A newer theory that holds that development results from the dynamic interaction of each person with the surrounding social and cultural forces.

### Teaching and Guidance

The pioneer of the sociocultural perspective was Lev Vygotsky (1896–1934). Like the three original grand theorists, he was born at the end of the nineteenth century, but unlike them, he studied Asian and European groups of many faiths, languages, and social contexts. That was possible when Russia spanned two continents in one nation, not the 14 nations it now is.

Vygotsky noted that people everywhere were taught whatever beliefs and habits were valued within their community. He studied those variations. For example, his research included how Asian farmers used tools, how illiterate people thought of abstract ideas, and how deaf children in Moscow learned in school.

He was both celebrated and marginalized during his lifetime, as the turbulent politics of Russia lurched from one government to another. After his death from tuberculosis at age 38, his work was admired and then banned. Partly because of international politics, his writing was not translated and widely read in the United States until the end of the twentieth century (e.g., Vygotsky, 2012).

Vygotsky stressed that people do not develop in isolation but rather in relationship to the culture of their community, as transmitted by the words and actions of other people. In Vygotsky's view, everyone, schooled or not, is guided by mentors in an **apprenticeship in thinking** (Vygotsky, 2012).

The word *apprentice* once had a specific meaning, often spelled out in a legal contract that detailed what a novice would learn from a master, and what that learner must do. For example, in earlier centuries, a boy wanting to repair shoes would be apprenticed to a cobbler, learning the trade while assisting his teacher.

Vygotsky believed that children become apprentices as they learn, guided by knowledgeable parents, teachers, and other people. Mentors teach children how to think within their culture by explaining ideas, asking questions, demonstrating actions.

To describe this process, Vygotsky developed the concept of **guided participation,** the method used by parents, teachers, and entire societies to teach novices expected skills, values, and habits. Tutors engage learners (*apprentices*) in joint activities, offering "mutual involvement in several widespread cultural practices with great importance for learning: narratives, routines, and play" (Rogoff, 2003, p. 285).

Guided participation is particularly useful in the medical profession. Guidance, not merely instruction, teaches new parents how to feed their fragile newborns,

Dr. James Wertsch

**Affection for Children** Vygotsky lived in Russia from 1896 to 1934, when war, starvation, and revolution led to the deaths of millions. Throughout this turmoil, Vygotsky focused on learning. His love of children is suggested by this portrait: He and his daughter have their arms around each other.

**apprenticeship in thinking** Vygotsky's term for how cognition is stimulated and developed in people by more skilled members of society.

**guided participation** The process by which people learn from others who guide their experiences and explorations.

helps children develop habits that keep them healthy, and allows adolescents with special needs to monitor their own care (Pridham et al., 2018).

Active apprenticeship and sensitive guidance are central to sociocultural theory. Sociocultural theorists contend that most human beliefs are social constructions, not natural laws, and thus societies need to develop and incorporate them, ideally via mutual interaction.

For example, Vygotsky thought that children with disabilities should be educated (Vygotsky, 1994b), a belief that was not part of U.S. culture until about 1970. Then parents insisted that their children with special needs could, and should, learn. That propelled a sociocultural revolution, and now children with special needs are educated rather than excluded from school. Many other social constructions—about women's work, about same-sex relationships, about divorce—have been revised in the past half century.

Sociocultural theory stresses that customs are shaped by people, as well as vice versa. The culture provides tools, or *artifacts*, that aid a particular kind of learning. In contemporary North America, smartphones are such an artifact, teaching children patterns of thought, behavior, and skills. In past generations, televisions, paper diapers, and even rubber balls were tools that changed how children develop.

## The Zone of Proximal Development

**zone of proximal development (ZPD)**
In sociocultural theory, a metaphorical area, or "zone," surrounding a learner that includes all of the skills, knowledge, and concepts that the person is close ("proximal") to acquiring but cannot yet master without help.

According to sociocultural theory, all learning is social, whether people are learning a manual skill, a social custom, or a language. As part of the apprenticeship of thinking, a mentor (parent, peer, or professional) finds the learner's **zone of proximal development (ZPD),** an imaginary area surrounding the learner that contains the skills, knowledge, and concepts that are close (proximal) to being grasped but not yet reached.

Vygotsky wrote that ZPD is "the distance between the actual developmental level as determined by independent problem solving and the level of potential development as determined through problem solving under adult guidance or in collaboration with more capable peers" (Vygotsky, 1980, p. 86). The ZPD pulls together all the other concepts of sociocultural theory (Eun, 2019).

Through sensitive assessment of each learner, mentors engage mentees within their zone. Together, in a "process of joint construction," new knowledge is attained. The mentor must avoid two opposite dangers: boredom and failure. Some frustration is permitted, but the learner must be actively engaged, never passive or overwhelmed (see **Figure 2.3**).

A mentor must sense whether support or freedom is needed and how peers can help (they may be the best mentors). Skilled teachers know when a person's zone of proximal development expands and shifts. The shared language of both mentor and mentee is an integral part of the sociocultural process of education. Words are the tools of thought.

Excursions into and through the zone of proximal development are everywhere. At the thousand or so science museums in the United States, exhibits are designed to guide children's scientific learning (Haden, 2010). Fifty years ago, there were no science museums: Now almost every city has one—a sociocultural shift as the culture recognizes the significance of STEM (science, technology, engineering, math).

Consider another example. North American children are expected to know how to ride a bicycle. How do they learn that? Many possibilities, but to illustrate the sociocultural understanding of apprenticeship, consider how a father might teach a daughter.

The dad begins by rolling his child along on a small bike, supporting her weight while telling her to keep her hands on the handlebars, to push the right and left pedals in rhythm, and to look straight ahead. As she becomes more comfortable

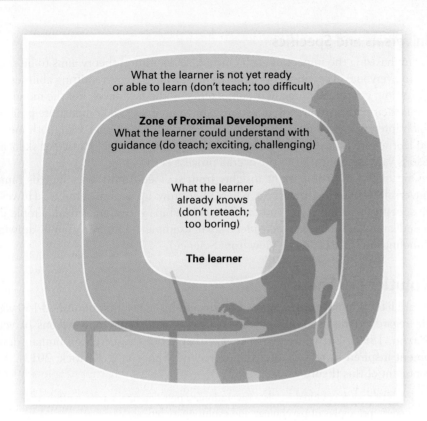

**FIGURE 2.3**
**The Magic Middle** Somewhere between the boring and the impossible is the zone of proximal development, where interaction between teacher and learner results in knowledge never before grasped or skills not already mastered. The intellectual excitement of that zone is the origin of the joy that both instruction and study can bring.

and confident, he jogs beside the bike, still holding it upright himself, praising her for steadily pedaling.

In later days or weeks, he runs beside her, lightly holding only the handlebars. When he senses that she can maintain her balance, he urges her to pedal faster while he loosens his grip. Perhaps without realizing it, she rides on her own, ideally in a wide place without cars or hard pavement. If she falls, he picks her up, reassuring her that she is not seriously hurt and that she is getting better. Someday soon she waves goodbye and bikes around the block.

Note that this is not instruction by preset rules. Sociocultural learning is interactive: No one learns bike-riding by reading and memorizing written instructions, and no good teacher merely repeats a memorized script. Guided practice in the zone of proximal development is essential: The mentor must know exactly what, when, and how support is needed.

Role models and cultural tools also teach, according to sociocultural theory. The bicycle-riding child wants to learn because she has seen other children biking, and stores sell tricycles, training wheels, and small bikes without pedals. Thus, cultural artifacts guide learning.

In another culture, everything might be different. In some nations, no females ride bikes, and no fathers teach their daughters, or even allow them outside the house without a female companion. Recognizing such cultural differences is crucial for understanding development, according to this theory. Children in every culture are taught to walk, dress, and behave in ways that their culture believes are proper.

Every day I witness the power of sociocultural learning. On crowded subways, usually someone sees my white hair and offers a seat. This is the result of apprenticeship: People respond to cultural norms rather than biology (I may be more able to stand than the person who gets up for me). Some sociocultural norms come from childhood (one young man said, in response to my thank you, "My mother would kill me if I didn't give you a seat"), and some are broadcast by loudspeaker announcements: "Offer your seat to someone who is pregnant or elderly."

## Universals and Specifics

By emphasizing the impact of each culture, sociocultural theory aims to be sensitive to everyone, everywhere. Thus, mentors, attuned to ever-shifting abilities and motivation, continually urge new competence—the next level, not the moon.

For their part, learners ask questions, show interest, and demonstrate progress, which informs and inspires the mentors. When education goes well, both mentor and learner are fully engaged and productive within the zone. Particular skills and lessons vary enormously, but the overall process is the same.

One of the most important insights from sociocultural theory regards family. Universally, children thrive best when they grow up within families. However, the specifics of family type and family relationships vary a great deal, a topic discussed later. Now, however, consider a small example—children's family drawings (Rübeling et al., 2011; see A View from Science).

## Evolutionary Theory

You are likely familiar with Charles Darwin and his ideas, first published 150 years ago, regarding the evolution of plants, insects, and birds over billions of years (Darwin, 1859). But you may not realize that serious research on human development inspired by this theory is quite recent (Simpson & Kenrick, 2013). As a proponent of this theory wrote:

> Evolutionary psychology . . . is a revolutionary new science, a true synthesis of modern principles of psychology and evolutionary biology.
>
> *[Buss, 2015, p. xv]*

The basic idea of evolutionary psychology is that in order to understand the emotions, impulses, and habits of humans over the life span, we must appreciate how those same emotions, impulses, and habits developed within *Homo sapiens* over the past 200,000 years.

---

**A VIEW FROM SCIENCE**

## Children's Drawings

Children's drawings may reflect their emotions. In the United States and Western Europe, well-adjusted children draw their families with smiling people, holding on to each other or with their arms raised. By contrast, if a child draws a family with small people, neutral facial expressions, and arms downward and not touching, that suggests a troubled child (Fury et al., 1997).

This interpretation is increasingly challenged by drawings produced by children in Africa (Gernhardt et al., 2013), as explored in detail in a study that compared the family drawing of 32 middle-class 6-year-olds from Berlin, Germany, with the family drawings of 31 children from rural areas of Cameroon. This study allowed a triple sociocultural contrast: by nation, by livelihood, and by income (Gernhardt et al., 2016). The Cameroonian children were no less happy or less cherished, but they drew small people (see **Figure 2.4**).

The drawings of the children were rated on 20 features used to describe the attachment of children to their caregivers (Kaplan & Main, 1986). (Attachment is considered a universal indicator of the caregiver–child relationship, and thus, measuring it is part of many studies).

The drawings of children from the two cultures were quite different. Yet other research finds that children in Cameroon are as securely attached to their families as children elsewhere. From this and many other sociocultural studies comes a clear message: Before anyone intervenes to improve the families, consider the culture (Morelli et al., 2018).

This research illustrates why we need sociocultural theory: The cultural context needs to be considered in order to understand people of any age, from newborns to centenarians. The authors "substantiated children's family drawings as an important cultural document for learning more about children's representation of their social world. However, the interpretation of drawing signs has to be derived from local cultural models of relationships" (Gernhardt et al., 2016, p. 1076).

**FIGURE 2.4**
**Standing Firm** When children draw their families, many child therapists look for signs of trouble—such as small, frowning people with hands down floating in space. But cross-cultural research shows that such depictions reflect local norms: The Cameroonian 6-year-olds were as well adjusted in their local community as the German children.

## Why We Fear Snakes More Than Cars

**Evolutionary theory** has intriguing explanations for many issues in human development, including 1-year-olds' attachment to their parents, pregnant women's nausea, and adult attraction to major sports contests. These may have evolved to help human survival.

**evolutionary theory** When used in human development, the idea that many current human emotions and impulses are a legacy from thousands of years ago.

Another example comes from phobias, which are hard to understand without considering human life in prehistoric times. You know that terror of snakes makes some people scream and sweat upon seeing one. People with that phobia may be frightened by photos of snakes, by plastic ones, or by snakes behind glass at a zoo. However, snakes currently cause less than one death in a million. That compares to a death rate a thousand times higher from motor vehicles (OECD, 2014). Why is no one terrified of automobiles?

The answer from evolutionary theory is that human fears began when snakes were common killers. Thus,

> ancient dangers such as snakes, spiders, heights, and strangers appear on lists of common phobias far more often than do evolutionarily modern dangers such as cars and guns, even though cars and guns are more dangerous to survival in the modern environment.

*[Confer et al., 2010, p. 111]*

Since our fears have not caught up to automobiles, evolutionary theory explains that our instincts will not automatically protect us. Instead, we need laws: infant seats, child-safety restraints, seat belts, red lights, speed limits, air bags, guard rails. Such measures are succeeding: The 2018 U.S. motor-vehicle death rate was 11 per 100,000, half the rate of 40 years earlier.

Other modern killers—climate change, drug addiction, obesity, pollution—also require social management, because instincts are contrary to what we know. Evolutionary theory lets us recognize the origins of destructive urges—such as the desire to eat calorie-dense cake—in order to control them (King, 2013). For instance, many adolescents find fast cars irrationally attractive rather than instinctively frightening. That is why we restrict teen drivers, set speed limits, mandate seat belts, and so on.

## Why We Protect Babies

According to evolutionary theory, every species has two long-standing, biologically based drives: (1) survival and (2) reproduction. Understanding these provides insight into protective parenting, newborn deaths, infant dependency, child immaturity, puberty onset, family formation, and much more (Konner, 2010).

Here is one example. Adults see babies as cute, even though babies have little hair, no chins, stubby legs, and round stomachs—none of which is attractive in adults. The reason, evolutionary theory contends, is that adults instinctually protect and cherish infants. That was essential when survival of the species was in doubt, 200,000 years ago.

But humans do not protect every baby. Indeed, another evolutionary instinct is that all creatures seek to perpetuate their own descendants more than those who are unrelated. They might kill newborns who are not their own.

Some primates do exactly that: Chimpanzee males who take over a troop murder babies of the deposed male. This occurred among ancient humans as well. The Christian Bible chronicles several examples, including two in the story of Moses and one in the birth of Jesus. Modern humans, of course, have created laws against infanticide—a necessity to control evolutionary instincts (Hrdy, 2009).

Critics point out that people do not always act as evolutionary theory predicts: Parents sometimes abandon newborns, adults sometimes handle snakes, political leaders sometimes separate parents and children, and so on. However, evolutionary theorists counter that ancient impulses within our species need to be understood in order to protect the children of today.

Sanjay Kanoja/AFP/Getty Images

**A Sacred River?** This is the Ganges river at Allahabad in 2013, which the Indian government is working to clean—a monumental task. No nation is working to rid the Pacific Ocean of a much bigger garbage site. What would evolutionary theory recommend?

**Observation Quiz** Beyond the pollution of the Ganges by humans' garbage, what characteristics of the river, visible here, contribute to the pollution? (see answer, page 61) ↑

**THINK CRITICALLY:** What would happen if lust were the only reason one person would mate with another?

## Genetic Links

This inborn urge to protect is explained by another concept from evolutionary theory: **selective adaptation.** Biology as well as culture favors traits that promote survival of the next generation. This explains some ancient practices that we now condemn, such as letting a newborn die because it was a girl, or a twin, or a burden on the family in some other way. Biology also worked to help the healthiest children survive and grow to become parents themselves.

Some of the best qualities of people—cooperation, spirituality, and self-sacrifice— may have originated thousands of years ago when tribes and then nations became prosperous because they took care of one another (Rand & Nowak, 2016).

Selective adaptation works as follows: If one person happens to inherit a trait that makes survival more likely, the gene (or combination of genes) responsible for that trait is passed on to the next generation, because that person will live long enough to reproduce (see **Figure 2.5**). Anyone with such a fortunate genetic inheritance has a better chance than those without that gene to survive, mate, and bear many children—half of whom would inherit the genes for that desirable trait.

For example, originally almost all human babies lost the ability to digest lactose at about age 2. All older children and adults were *lactose intolerant*, unable to digest milk from cows or goats (Suchy et al., 2010). This was no problem, as non-dairy foods are nourishing, and our hunter-gatherer ancestors had no farm animals. Indeed, they had no farms until the agricultural revolution, about 12,000 years ago. At that point, cattle were domesticated and raised for their meat. In those places, "killing the fatted calf" provided a rare feast for the entire community.

As you will see in Chapter 3, genes are not always copied exactly from one generation to the next; *spontaneous mutations* occur. In those cattle-raising regions, occasionally a girl would have an aberrant but beneficial gene for the enzyme that allows digestion of cow's milk. If she drank milk intended for a calf, she could digest it and be better nourished than other girls. Her body fat would allow earlier puberty, successful pregnancy, and then ample breast milk.

For all of those reasons, her mutant gene allowing lactose tolerance would spread to half of her many descendants. Here malnourished sisters would have fewer children. Thus, the next generation would include more people who inherited that odd gene, becoming lactose tolerant like their mother. Because of the reproductive advantages, with each generation their numbers would increase. Eventually, that gene would become the new norm.

Interestingly, there are several distinct genetic versions of lactose tolerance: Apparently in each cattle-raising region, when a mutant gene allowed digestion

**selective adaptation** The process by which living creatures (including people) adjust to their environment. Genes that enhance survival and reproductive ability are selected, over the generations, to become more prevalent.

| | Women With (Sex-Linked) Advantageous Gene | Women Without (Sex-Linked) Advantageous Gene |
|---|---|---|
| Mothers (1st generation) | 👤 | 👤👤👤👤👤👤👤👤 |
| Daughters (2nd generation) | 👤　👤 | 👤👤👤👤👤👤👤👤 |
| Granddaughters (3rd generation) | 👤👤👤👤 | 👤👤👤👤👤👤👤👤 |
| Great-granddaughters (4th generation) | 👤👤👤👤👤👤👤👤 | 👤👤👤👤👤👤👤 |
| Great-great-granddaughters (5th generation) | 👤👤👤👤👤👤👤👤👤👤👤👤👤👤👤👤 | 👤👤👤👤👤👤👤 |

**FIGURE 2.5**

**Selective Adaptation Illustrated** Suppose only one of nine mothers happened to have a gene that improved survival. The average woman had only one surviving daughter, but this gene mutation might mean more births and more surviving children such that each woman who had the gene bore two girls who survived to womanhood instead of one. As you see, in 100 years, the "odd" gene becomes more common, making it a new normal.

of milk, selective adaptation increased the prevalence of that spontaneous mutation (Ranciaro et al., 2014).

For humans (unlike fast-breeding creatures, such as insects) selective adaptation takes centuries, but lactose tolerance has gradually become widespread. That is why few Scandinavians are lactose intolerant but many Africans are — but not those Africans in regions of Kenya and Tanzania where cattle are raised (Ranciaro et al., 2014).

Once it was understood that milk might make some African and Asian children sick, better ways to relieve hunger were found. Fewer children are malnourished today than decades ago, partly because nutritionists know which foods are digestible, nourishing, and tasty for whom. Evolutionary psychology has helped with that.

For groups as well as individuals, evolutionary theory notices how the interaction of genes and environment affects survival and reproduction. Genetic variations are particularly beneficial when the environment changes, which is one reason genetic diversity benefits humanity as a whole.

Evolutionary adaptation is in the human genes that allow people to adapt to many climates (Tattersall, 2017). That explains why the Inuit, an ethnic group who have survived in the Arctic for thousands of years, have genes that make them relatively short and plump. That body shape is protective against frigid temperatures. Ordinarily that would make them at high risk for heart disease, except selective adaptation has also bestowed genes that reduce heart damage (Rudkowska et al., 2013).

If a species' gene pool does not include variants that allow survival in difficult circumstances (such as exposure to a new disease or to an environmental toxin), the entire species becomes extinct, true for many nonhuman species. That has not occurred for *Homo sapiens*, because every human has some gene variants that are rare, making us all distinct from our neighbors. Evolutionary theory recognizes and praises such diversity which might mean survival.

**Especially for Teachers and Counselors of Teenagers** Teen pregnancy is destructive of adolescent education, family life, and sometimes even health. According to evolutionary theory, what can be done about this? (see response, page 61)

---

**WHAT HAVE YOU LEARNED?**

1. Why is the sociocultural perspective particularly relevant within the United States?
2. How do mentors and mentees interact within the zone of proximal development?
3. How do the customs and manufactured items in a society affect human development?
4. Why are behaviors and emotions that benefited ancient humans still apparent today?
5. How does understanding ancient peoples protect modern humans?

---

## What Theories Contribute

Each major theory discussed in this chapter has contributed to our understanding of human development (see **Table 2.5**):

- *Psychoanalytic theories* make us aware of the impact of early-childhood experiences, remembered or not, on subsequent development.
- *Behaviorism* shows the effect that immediate responses, associations, and examples have on learning, moment by moment and over time.
- *Cognitive theories* bring an understanding of intellectual processes, since thoughts and beliefs affect every aspect of our development.
- *Sociocultural theories* remind us that development is embedded in a rich and multifaceted cultural context, evident in every social interaction.
- *Evolutionary theories* suggest that human impulses need to be recognized before they can be guided.

## TABLE 2.5

**Five Perspectives on Human Development**

| Theory | Area of Focus | Fundamental Depiction of What People Do | Relative Emphasis on Nature or Nurture? |
|---|---|---|---|
| Psychoanalytic | Psychosexual (Freud) or psychosocial (Erikson) stages | Battle unconscious impulses and overcome major crises. | More nature (biological, sexual impulses, and parent–child bonds) |
| Behaviorism | Conditioning through stimulus and response | Respond to stimuli, reinforcement, and models. | More nurture (direct environment produces various behaviors) |
| Cognitive | Thinking, remembering, analyzing | Seek to understand experiences while forming concepts. | More nature (mental activity and motivation are key) |
| Sociocultural | Social control, expressed through people, language, customs | Learn the tools, skills, and values of society through apprenticeships. | More nurture (interaction of mentor and learner, within cultures) |
| Evolutionary | Needs and impulses that originated thousands of years ago | Develop impulses, interests, and patterns to survive and reproduce. | More nature (needs and impulses apply to all humans) |

Remember that each theory is designed to be practical. This is evident with a very practical issue for many parents: how to toilet-train their children (see Opposing Perspectives).

No comprehensive view of development can ignore any of these theories, yet each has encountered severe criticism: *psychoanalytic theory* for being too subjective; *behaviorism* for being too mechanistic; *cognitive theory* for undervaluing emotions; *sociocultural theory* for neglecting individual choice; *evolutionary theory* for ignoring the power of current morals, laws, and norms.

Most developmentalists prefer an **eclectic perspective,** choosing what they consider to be the best aspects of each theory. Rather than adopt any one of these theories exclusively, they make selective use of all of them.

All theories reflect the personal background of the theorist, as do all criticisms of theories. If you find yourself drawn to one theory, or dismissive of another, ask yourself what in your own background led to your reaction.

Ideally, you can see the reasons each of these five is relevant to the study of child development. Being eclectic, not tied to any one theory, is beneficial, because everyone, scientist as well as layperson, is biased. However, even being eclectic may be limiting: Choosing the best from each theory may be too picky or the opposite, too tolerant.

For developmentalists, all of these theories merit study and respect. It is easy to dismiss any one of them, but using several perspectives opens our eyes and minds to aspects of development that we might otherwise ignore. As one overview of seven developmental theories (including those explained here) concludes,

> Because no one theory satisfactorily explains development, it is critical that developmentalists be able to draw on the content, methods, and theoretical concepts of many theories.

[*Miller, 2016, p. 434*]

**eclectic perspective** The approach taken by most developmentalists, in which they apply aspects of each of the various theories of development rather than adhering exclusively to one theory.

---

**CHAPTER APP 2**

 My Token Board

**IOS:**
https://tinyurl.com/yy6hmbuq

**RELEVANT TOPIC:**
Behaviorism and positive reinforcement for children

My Token Board is a visual reward system for children of all ages and abilities that helps motivate them to learn and complete tasks. The app's use of reinforcers is based on the principles of operant conditioning and effective with children who are on the autism spectrum.

# Toilet Training—How and When?

Parents hear opposite advice about almost everything regarding infant care, including feeding, responding to cries, bathing, and exercise. Often a particular parental response springs from one of the theories explained in this chapter—no wonder advice is sometimes contradictory.

One practical example is toilet training. In the nineteenth century, many parents believed that bodily functions should be controlled as soon as possible in order to distinguish humans from lower animals. Pushed by that theory (as opposed to the theory of evolution) many parents began toilet training in the first months of life (Accardo, 2006). Then, Freud pegged the first year as the oral stage, not anal (when toilet training was supposed to occur), and Erikson stressed that infants need to develop trust.

Accordingly, many psychologists and pediatricians recommended postponing training to avoid serious personality problems later on. This was soon part of many manuals on child rearing. For example, a leading pediatrician, Barry Brazelton, wrote a popular book for parents. He advised delaying toilet training until the child was cognitively, emotionally, and biologically ready—around age 2 for daytime training and age 3 for nighttime dryness.

> As a society, we are far too concerned about pushing children to be toilet trained early. I don't even like the phrase "toilet training." It really should be toilet learning.
>
> [Brazelton & Sparrow, 2006, p. 193]

When the second grand theory took hold in the United States, behaviorists explained that learning results from conditioning. That led to the belief that toilet training could occur whenever the parent wished, not at a particular age.

Parents often wished for early training before disposable diapers (about 1970) because parents experienced unpleasant consequences from changing diapers for years. But now stores carry diapers designed for 4-year-olds, so parents no longer are inconvenienced by late toilet training (that is, by having to contend with dirty diapers). That is a sociocultural shift: A practical impact on parents, not a deep psychoanalytic need of babies, affected the age of toilet training.

In one application of behaviorism, children drank quantities of their favorite juice, sat on the potty with a parent nearby to keep them entertained, and then, when the inevitable occurred, the parent praised and rewarded them—a powerful reinforcement for the child and soon for the adult as well. Children were conditioned (in one day, according to some behaviorists) to head for the potty whenever the need arose (Azrin & Foxx, 1974).

Cognitive theory would consider such a concerted effort unnecessary, suggesting that parents wait until the child can understand why to urinate and defecate in the toilet. Thinking leads to behavior—which explains why older adults are mortified by urinary incontinence.

This raises the importance of modeling, as well as the sociocultural theory. In some African communities, children toilet-train themselves by following slightly older children to the surrounding trees and bushes. This is easier, of course, if toddlers wear no diapers—a practice that makes sense in some climates and ecosystems.

Finally, evolutionary theory notes that control of urination and defecation is part of every human culture, because it promotes survival by reducing the spread of pathogens. That is why dogs and cats readily learn where to eliminate waste (and instinctively scratch to bury their feces) and why humans worldwide learn bathroom hygiene. The contemporary emphasis on handwashing (a cognitive innovation) is the latest manifestation of ancient impulses.

Each of these theories would be critical of one U.S. mother who began training her baby just 33 days after birth. She noticed when her son was about to defecate, held him above the toilet, and had trained him by 6 months (Sun & Rugolotto, 2004).

- Psychoanalytic theorists would wonder what made her such an anal person, valuing cleanliness and order without considering the child's needs.
- Behaviorists would say that the mother was trained, not the son. She taught herself to be sensitive to his body; she was reinforced when she read his clues correctly.
- Cognitive theory would question the mother's thinking. For instance, did she have an irrational fear of normal body functions?
- Sociocultural theory would be aghast that the U.S. drive for personal control took such a bizarre turn.
- Evolutionary theory would expect that such early training would be a rare event unless it was adaptive to the species—and would note that every mother reading about this woman would probably consider her more whacky than wise.

What is best? Some parents are reluctant to train, and the result, according to one book, is that many children are still in diapers at age 5 (Barone, 2015). Dueling theories and diverse parental practices have led the authors of an article for pediatricians to conclude that "despite families and physicians having addressed this issue for generations, there still is no consensus regarding the best method or even a standard definition of toilet training" (Howell et al., 2010, p. 262).

One comparison study of toilet-training methods found that the behaviorist approach was best for older children with serious disabilities but that almost every method succeeded with the average young child. Many sources explain that human diversity means that there is no "right" way: "the best strategy for implementing training is still unknown" (Colaco et al., 2013, p. 49).

That may return us to the multicontextual, multicultural perspectives of Chapter 1 that explain the vast differences from one community to another. A study of parents' opinions in Belgium found that single mothers who were of low socioeconomic status waited until age 3 or so to train their children, which was too long according to those researchers (van Nunen et al., 2015). Of course, both "too soon" and "too late" are matters of opinion.

Many parents firmly believe in one approach or another. Everyone has theories, sometimes strongly held, whether they know it or not. That is one goal of this chapter, to help us recognize the theories that affect our everyday lives.

As you will see in many later chapters, theories provide a fresh look at behavior. Imagine a mother, father, teacher, coach, and grandparent discussing the problems of a particular child. Each might suggest a possible explanation that makes the others say, "I never thought of that." If they listen to each other with an open mind, together they might understand the child better and agree on a beneficial strategy.

Using five theories is like having five perceptive observers. All five are not always on target, but it is better to use theory to consider alternate possibilities than to stay in one narrow groove. A hand functions best with five fingers, although each finger is different and some fingers are more useful than others.

What finally happened with my family, Iowa, and travel?

- The children enjoyed the overnight train ride (*psychoanalytic*).
- The culture provides days off school and work, and people ask "what are you doing for the holidays?" (*sociocultural*).
- We need to protect the planet (four took the train to Chicago; four flew to Minneapolis; all eight drove many hours to avoid a multi-stop flight) (*cognitive*).
- We ignored the possibility of ice and blizzards (we have never driven in the Midwest in December, so no past conditioning) (*behaviorist*).
- Family togetherness is a priority (*evolutionary*).

What happened with all that thinking and theorizing? One happy grandmother, who was told by the other eight that our Iowa trip was a good one. But a lesson from this chapter is that perspectives differ, sometimes radically: My perception may be biased. We all need to consider alternate perspectives on whatever we think about child development!

## WHAT HAVE YOU LEARNED?

1. What are the criticisms of each of the five theories?

2. Why are most developmentalists eclectic in regard to theories?

3. Why is it useful to know more than one theory to explain human behavior?

# Historical Highlights of Developmental Science

As evident throughout this textbook, much more research and appreciation of the brain, social context, and the non-Western world has expanded our understanding of human development in the 21st century. This timeline lists a few highlights of the past.

**200,000–50,000 BCE**  With their large brains, long period of child development, and extensive social and family support, early humans were able to sustain life and raise children more effectively than other primates.

**c. 400 BCE** In ancient Greece, ideas about children from philosophers like Plato (c. 428–348 BCE) and Aristotle (384–322 BCE) influenced further thoughts about children. Plato believed children were born with knowledge. Aristotle believed children learn from experience.

**1650–1800** European philosophers like John Locke (1632–1704) and Jean Jacques Rousseau (1712–1778) debate whether children are born as "blank slates" and how much control parents should take in raising them.

**1797** First European vaccination: Edward Jenner (1749–1823) publicizes smallpox inoculation, building on vaccination against smallpox in Asia, the Middle East, and Africa.

**1750–1850** Beginning of Western laws regulating child labor and protecting the rights of children.

**1879** First experimental psychology laboratory established in Leipzig, Germany.

**1885** Sigmund Freud (1856–1939) publishes *Studies on Hysteria*, one of the first works establishing the importance of the subconscious and marking the beginning of the theories of psychoanalytic theory.

**1895** Ivan Pavlov (1849–1936) begins research on dogs' salivation response.

**1905** Max Weber (1864–1920), the founder of sociology, writes *The Protestant Work Ethic*, about human values and adult work.

**1905** Alfred Binet's (1857–1911) intelligence test published.

**1907** Maria Montessori (1870–1952) opens her first school in Rome.

**1913** John B. Watson (1878–1958) publishes *Psychology As the Behaviorist Views It*.

**140 BCE** In China, imperial examinations are one of the first times cognitive testing is used on young people.

**500–1500** During the Middle Ages in Europe, many adults believed that children were miniature adults.

**1100–1200** First universities founded in Europe. Young people pay to be educated together.

**1837** First kindergarten opens in Germany, part of a movement to teach young children before they entered the primary school system.

**1859** Charles Darwin (1809–1882) publishes *On the Origin of Species*, sparking debates about what is genetic and what is environmental.

**1900** Compulsory schooling for children is established for most children in the United States and Europe.

**1903** The term "gerontology," the branch of developmental science devoted to studying aging, first coined.

**1920** Lev Vygotsky (1896–1934) develops sociocultural theory in the former Soviet Union.

**1923** Jean Piaget (1896–1980) publishes *The Language and Thought of the Child*.

**1933** Society for Research on Child Development, the preeminent organization for research on child development, founded.

**1939** Mamie (1917–1983) and Kenneth Clark (1914–2005) receive their research grants to study race in early childhood.

**Timeline axis:** 50,000 BCE — 400 BCE — 0 — 500 — 1000 — 1500 — 1650 — 1700 — 1750

**1943** Abraham Maslow (1908–1970) publishes *A Theory of Motivation*, establishing the hierarchy of needs.

**1950** Erik Erikson (1902–1994) expands on Freud's theory to include social aspects of personality development with the publication of *Childhood and Society*.

**1951** John Bowlby (1907–1990) publishes *Maternal Care and Mental Health*, one of his first works on the importance of parent–child attachment.

**1953** Publication of the first papers describing DNA, our genetic blueprint.

**1957** Harry Harlow (1905–1981) publishes *Love in Infant Monkeys*, describing his research on attachment in rhesus monkeys.

**1961** The morning sickness drug thalidomide is banned after children are born with serious birth defects, calling attention to the problem of teratogens during pregnancy.

**1961** Alfred Bandura (b. 1925) conducts the Bobo Doll experiments, leading to the development of social learning theory.

**1979** Urie Bronfenbrenner (1917–2005) publishes his work on ecological systems theory

**1986** John Gottman (b. 1942) founded the "Love Lab" at the University of Washington to study what makes relationships work.

**1987** Carolyn Rovee-Collier (1942–2014) shows that even young infants can remember in her classic mobile experiments.

**1990–Present** New brain imaging technology allows pinpointing of brain areas involved in everything from executive function to Alzheimer's disease.

**1994** Steven Pinker (b. 1954) publishes *The Language Instinct*, focusing attention on the interaction between neuroscience and behavior.

**1996** Giacomo Rizzolatti publishes his discovery of mirror neurons.

**2000** Jeffrey Arnett conceptualizes emerging adulthood.

**2003** Mapping of the human genome is completed.

**2013** DSM-5, which emphasizes the role of context in understanding mental health problems, is published.

| 1800 | 1850 | 1900 | 1950 | 2000 |

**1953** B.F. Skinner (1904–1990) conducts experiments on rats and establishes operant conditioning.

**1955** Emmy Werner (b. 1929) begins her Kauai study, which focuses on the power of resilience.

**1956** K. Warner Schaie's (b. 1928) Seattle Longitudinal Study of Adult Intelligence begins.

**1965** Head Start, an early childhood education program, launched in the United States.

**1965** Mary Ainsworth (1913–1999) starts using the "Strange Situation" to measure attachment.

**1966** Diana Baumrind (1928–2018) publishes her first work on parenting styles.

**1972** Beginning of the Dunedin, New Zealand, study—one of the first longitudinal studies to include genetic markers.

**1990** Barbara Rogoff (b. 1950) publishes *Apprenticeship in Thinking*, making developmentalists more aware of the significance of culture and context. Rogoff provided new insights and appreciation of child-rearing in Latin America.

**1993** Howard Gardner (b. 1943) publishes *Multiple Intelligences*, a major new understanding of the diversity of human intellectual abilities. Gardner has since revised and expanded his ideas in many ways.

**2013** U.S. President Barack Obama announces his administration's Brain Research through Advancing Innovative Neurotechnologies (BRAIN) Initiative.

**2017** Several U.S. cities expand public funding for early-childhood education (universal pre-K).

**2020 and beyond** Onward. Many more discoveries are chronicled in this book, as researchers continue to test and explore.

# SUMMARY

### What Theories Do

1. A theory provides general principles to guide research and explain observations. Each of the five major developmental theories—psychoanalytic, behaviorist, cognitive, sociocultural, and evolutionary—interprets human development from a distinct perspective, providing a framework for understanding human emotions, experiences, and actions.

2. Theories are neither true nor false. They begin with facts and lead to facts, but they are not themselves facts. Instead, they generate hypotheses to be tested and interpretations of the myriad human behaviors. Good theories are practical: They aid inquiry, interpretation, and daily life.

### Grand Theories

3. Psychoanalytic theory emphasizes that adult actions and thoughts originate from unconscious impulses and childhood conflicts. Freud's theory is called psychosexual, because he recognized sexual urges that arise during three stages of childhood—oral, anal, and phallic—and continue, after latency, in the genital stage.

4. Erikson's psychosocial theory described eight successive stages of development, each involving a crisis to be resolved. The early stages are crucial, with lifelong effects, but unlike Freud, Erikson emphasized social more than sexual needs.

5. Behaviorists, or learning theorists, believe that scientists should study observable and measurable behavior. Behaviorism emphasizes conditioning—a lifelong learning process in which an association between one stimulus and another (classical conditioning) or the consequences of reinforcement and punishment (operant conditioning) guide behavior.

6. Social learning theory recognizes that people learn by observing others, even if they themselves have not been reinforced or punished. Children are particularly susceptible to social learning, but all humans are affected by what they notice in other people.

7. Cognitive theorists believe that thoughts and beliefs powerfully affect attitudes, actions, and perceptions, which in turn affect behavior. Piaget proposed four age-related periods of cognition, each propelled by an active search for cognitive equilibrium. Like Freud, his last stage occurred at adolescence.

8. Information processing focuses on each aspect of cognition—input, processing, and output. This perspective has benefited from technology, first from understanding computer functioning and more recently by the many ways scientists monitor the brain.

### Newer Theories

9. Sociocultural theory explains human development in terms of the guidance, support, and structure provided by each social group through culture and mentoring. Vygotsky described how learning occurs through social interactions in which mentors guide learners through their zone of proximal development.

10. Sociocultural learning is also encouraged by the examples and tools that each society provides. These are social constructions, which guide everyone but also which can change.

11. Evolutionary theory contends that contemporary humans inherit genetic tendencies that have fostered survival and reproduction of the human species for tens of thousands of years. Through selective adaptation, the fears, impulses, and reactions that were useful 100,000 years ago for *Homo sapiens* continue to this day.

12. Evolutionary theory provides explanations for many human traits, from lactose intolerance to affection toward babies. Selective adaptation is the process by which genes enhance human development over thousands of years. Societies use laws and customs to protect people from some genetic impulses.

### What Theories Contribute

13. Psychoanalytic, behavioral, cognitive, sociocultural, and evolutionary theories have aided our understanding of human development. However, no single theory describes the full complexity and diversity of human experience. Most developmentalists are eclectic, drawing on many theories, aware that any one perspective might be too narrow.

# KEY TERMS

developmental theory (p. 33)
psychoanalytic theory (p. 35)
psychosocial theory (p. 37)
behaviorism (p. 37)
classical conditioning (p. 38)
operant conditioning (p. 39)

reinforcement (p. 39)
social learning theory (p. 40)
modeling (p. 40)
cognitive theory (p. 40)
cognitive equilibrium (p. 41)
assimilation (p. 42)

accommodation (p. 42)
information-processing theory
  (p. 42)
sociocultural theory (p. 47)
apprenticeship in thinking
  (p. 47)

guided participation (p. 47)
zone of proximal development
  (ZPD) (p. 48)
evolutionary theory (p. 51)
selective adaptation (p. 53)
eclectic perspective (p. 55)

## APPLICATIONS

**1.** Developmentalists sometimes talk about "folk theories," which are developed by ordinary people. Choose three sayings in your culture, such as (from the dominant U.S. culture) "A penny saved is a penny earned" or "As the twig is bent, so grows the tree." Explain the underlying assumptions, or theory, that each saying reflects. Why might the theory be wrong?

**2.** Cognitive theory suggests the power of thoughts, and socio-cultural theory emphasizes the power of context. Find someone who disagrees with you about some basic issue (e.g., abortion, immigration, socialism) and listen carefully to their ideas and reasons (encourage them to explain; don't contradict). Then analyze how cognition and experience shaped their ideas *and* your own.

**3.** Ask three people to tell you their theories about male–female differences in mating and sexual behaviors. Which of the theories described in this chapter is closest to each explanation, and which theory is not mentioned?

## Especially for ANSWERS

**Response for Teachers** (from p. 37) Erikson would note that the behavior of 5-year-olds is affected by their developmental stage and by their culture. Therefore, you might design your curriculum to accommodate active, noisy children.

**Response for Teachers and Counselors of Teenagers** (from p. 54) Evolutionary theory stresses the basic human drive for reproduction, which gives teenagers a powerful sex drive. Thus, merely informing teenagers of the difficulty of caring for a newborn (some high school sex-education programs simply give teenagers a chicken egg to nurture) is not likely to work. A better method would be to structure teenagers' lives so that pregnancy is impossible—for instance, with careful supervision or readily available contraception.

## Observation Quiz ANSWERS

**Answer to Observation Quiz** (from p. 38) Both are balding, with white beards. Note also that none of the other theorists in this chapter have beards—a cohort difference, not an ideological one.

**Answer to Observation Quiz** (from p. 52) The river is slow-moving (see the boat) and shallow (see the man standing). A fast-moving, deep river is able to flush out contaminants more quickly.

# The New Genetics

## What Will You Know?

1. Genetically, how is each zygote unique?
2. How do twins differ from other siblings?
3. Who is likely to carry genes that they do not know they have?
4. When should people see a genetic counselor?

For 30 years I have spent Thanksgiving with my four daughters. Now adults, they fly or drive many miles to gather together; they have their own jobs and homes. One tradition is that each of us says what we are thankful for in the past year, and that typically includes each other. The family connections are strong.

It is apparent that we are closely related. Strangers say we look alike, people on the phone mistake us for one another, we laugh in the same way at the same jokes. Our similarities go far deeper. We all express strong opinions (disagreeing on specifics but sharing values); we all make our living by teaching and writing (in different places and professions); and we all have similar habits (we pick up litter; yesterday we had a robust discussion about the best strategy to encourage our neighbors to do so).

Our differences are obvious, too, at least to us. When we are together, each prepares her own coffee—caffeinated or decaf, brewed or instant, black or not, canned or bottled milk, sugar or honey or neither. One daughter was upset this year that I didn't have 2-percent milk in a carton. Without telling her, I asked our neighbor, who gave me some. She was grateful that I did that, but another daughter was troubled that I bothered that neighbor. That illustrates the general truth: We each are distinct—in cooking, eating, cleaning, sleeping, socializing . . . and so on.

In all of this, my family reflects the themes of this chapter. Genes and family background shape human lives, yet each person is unique. The rest of this chapter continues those themes—nature and nurture interwoven, from conception onward.

## The Genetic Code

First, we begin with biology. All living things are composed of cells. The work of cells is done by proteins, aided by other cells. Cells manufacture proteins according to a code of instructions stored by molecules of **deoxyribonucleic acid (DNA)** at the heart of the cell. These coding DNA molecules are on a **chromosome**.

### 46 to 21,000 to 3 Billion

Humans have 23 pairs of chromosomes (46 in all, half from each parent), which direct the manufacture of proteins needed for life and growth (see **Figure 3.1**).

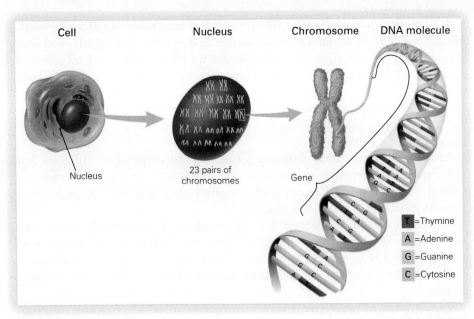

**FIGURE 3.1**

**How Proteins Are Made** The genes on the chromosomes in the nucleus of each cell instruct the cell to manufacture the proteins needed to sustain life and development. The code for a protein is the particular combination of four bases, T-A-G-C (thymine, adenine, guanine, and cytosine).

The instructions on the 46 chromosomes are organized into genes, with every **gene** usually situated at a precise location on a particular chromosome.

When one **gamete** (a reproductive cell, sperm from a man or ovum from a woman) combines with another, those two gametes create a new cell called a **zygote**. Each gamete is formed from a particular variation of chromosomes and genes. Each man or woman produces many possible variations of their 46 chromosomes on each gamete—8 million possible combinations of 23 chromosomes ($23^{23}$ or 8,388,608).

Zygotes have a total of about 21,000 coding genes, each directing the formation of specific proteins made from a string of 20 amino acids. The instructions on those 21,000 genes are on about 3 billion *base pairs*, which are pairs of four chemicals (adenine paired with thymine and guanine paired with cytosine).

The entire packet of instructions to make a living organism is called the **genome**. There is a genome for every species and variety of plant and animal—even for every bacterium and virus. Most human genes are also present in other creatures, yet genes define each species.

Members of the same species are similar genetically—more than 99 percent of any human's base pairs are identical to those of any other person because, although they differ in tiny details, all human chromosomes contain the same basic genes. The definition of a species is that its members can interbreed successfully. Since humans are one species, a man and a woman from opposite ends of the world can mate and produce a new human with all the genes that define a person.

## Same and Different

Decoding the genome of *Homo sapiens* was a major breakthrough in genetic research in 2003. Since then, the genomes of thousands of other species have been decoded and thousands of variations in the human genome have been discovered.

**deoxyribonucleic acid (DNA)** The chemical composition of the molecules that contain the genes, which are the chemical instructions for cells to manufacture various proteins.

**chromosome** One of the 46 molecules of DNA (in 23 pairs) that virtually each cell of the human body contains and that, together, contain all the genes. Other species have more or fewer chromosomes.

**gene** A small section of a chromosome; the basic unit for the transmission of heredity. A gene consists of a string of chemicals that provide instructions for the cell to manufacture certain proteins.

**gamete** A reproductive cell. In humans it is a sperm or an ovum.

**zygote** The single cell formed from the union of two gametes, a sperm and an ovum.

**genome** The full set of genes that are the instructions to make an individual member of a certain species.

It is human nature to notice differences. But remember our shared genetic bonds. Not only do all humans have similar bodies (two eyes, hands, and feet; the same organs, blood, and bones) but also we all use words, we all love and hate, we all hope and fear, for ourselves and for descendants, friends, and strangers.

Yet none of us is exactly like anyone else, and our individuality starts with genes. Any variation in a gene, such as a differences in the precise sequence of the base pairs, is called an **allele**.

**allele** A variation that makes a gene different in some way from other genes for the same characteristics. Many genes never vary; others have several possible alleles.

Most alleles cause small differences (such as the shape of an eyebrow), but some are crucial. Another way to state this is that some genes are *polymorphic* (literally, "many forms"). Because each person's variations differ from every other person's variations, each of us is unique.

You can recognize at a glance that two people are not identical, even if both are the same age, gender, and ethnicity. When you search for a well-known friend among a crowd of thousands, you do not mistakenly greet someone who superficially looks like them. Tiny variations distinguish each face and each body—inside and out.

## Beyond the Genes

*RNA* (*ribonucleic acid*, another molecule) and additional DNA surround each gene. RNA material does not code, which means RNA does not directly determine human traits. This noncoding material used to be called *junk*—but no longer.

In a process called *methylation*, the material surrounding each gene enhances, transcribes, connects, empowers, silences, and alters genetic instructions. Methylation continues throughout life, from conception until death. Obviously, genes are crucial, but even more crucial is whether and how genes are expressed. RNA regulates and transcribes genetic instructions, turning some genes and alleles on or off.

**Not All Genetic** Every child becomes their own person—not what their parents fantasize.

THE WORLD'S FIRST GENETICALLY ENGINEERED HUMAN HITS ADOLESCENCE

We buy you the best genes in the world—FOR THIS?

So, I got my nose pierced. So *what*, man.

I remember checking "genius" on the order form—AND NOW LOOK!

Roz Chast/The New Yorker Collection/The Cartoon Bank

In other words, a person can have the genetic tendency for a particular trait, disease, or behavior, but that tendency might never appear because it was never turned on. Think of a light switch: A lamp might have a new bulb and be plugged into power, but the room stays dark unless the switch is flipped.

Scientists continually discover new functions—for good or ill—of the noncoding genetic material (Iorio & Palmieri, 2019; Larsen, 2018). Applications are many—treating and controlling diseases, genetically modifying crops to resist pathogens, developing vaccines to protect people and animals.

Most scientists are hopeful that research on genes and development will help humankind. Many others are fearful. This divergence is reflected in national and international guidelines.

As one article explains, we have "fast science and sluggish policy," which is "enveloped by UN procedures that promote inclusiveness but are typically slow, lumbering, and inflexible, making it difficult to adapt to fast-moving events in the outside world" (Wynberg & Laird, 2018, p. 1).

## Epigenetics

The science of the interaction between nature and nurture is explored in **epigenetics**, the study of how the environment alters genetic expression, beginning at conception and continuing lifelong. The Greek root *epi-*, meaning "around, above, below," focuses attention on the vital noncoding elements.

Events and circumstances surrounding (around, above, below) the genes determine whether genes are expressed or silenced (Ayyanathan, 2014). Contrary to what some people assume—the assumption that "genetic" means that a trait is unchangeable—we now know that nutrients, toxins, and experiences affect prenatal and postnatal development in the brain as well as in every genetic function. Plasticity is lifelong.

It might be easy to believe that biological forces, such as malnutrition, affect genes. But it is harder to recognize that social experiences, such as chronic loneliness, can change the brain (Cacioppo et al., 2014).

One new area of research is hospital care for preterm infants. Protective factors (being held and comforted by the mother, skin-to-skin) and stressful factors (painful intubations, punctures) affect the genes of the tiny person, with epigenetic changes evident years later (Provenzi et al., 2018). Thanks to research on

> **epigenetics** The study of how environmental factors affect genes and genetic expression—enhancing, halting, shaping, or altering the expression of genes.

---

**A CASE TO STUDY**

## Women Engineers

It was once thought that genes made females inferior in math, specifically that prenatal neurological connections made their brains less adept at spatial understanding. That explained why women scored lower than men on tests of math, and why no woman was allowed to study engineering.

The only way a woman could be an engineer was as a dutiful wife. For example, Elizabeth Roebling was called the "secret engineer" of the Brooklyn Bridge (completed in 1883), because the man designated as chief engineer was her husband, and he became so ill that he could not leave his bed (Dougherty, 2019; Wagner, 2017). She told people that he told her what to do (although he was actually too sick to do so).

A century later another woman, Sheri Sheppard, became a professor of engineering, as her father had done. But at first she thought that she did not belong. She remembers:

> My second year in college [at the University of Michigan], I hit my first engineering class. And at the time I was, in most of my engineering classes, the only woman. And the professor got in front of us and was lecturing and he was using words that I had no idea what he was speaking. And I'm thinking that every guy in the room knows exactly what he's talking about, I mean they were born knowing that. [Still feeling that I did not belong] I went to the next class and one of the other students . . . raised his hand right at the beginning of the class and he said to the professor, "I don't have the foggiest notion of what you're talking about." And it was just like, "they don't know it either!" And after that it became really fun because education is all about asking questions.

> [Retelas, 2017]

Beginning in the 1960s, millions of women insisted that nurture, not nature, kept women from advanced math, and thus from professions that required it. Sheppard was one of the first women to study engineering; now she is a professor of engineering at Stanford, with many female students.

Many college women now major in engineering, physics, math, and chemistry (Brown & Lent, 2016). This does not erase genetic tendencies: Some people excel at math and others struggle with it, but those genes are not exclusive to people of one gender or another, or, for that matter, one family or ethnic background or another.

In the twenty-first century, many women who were hired as engineers quit. A third of them cite hostility from male co-workers as the reason. Some male co-workers were helpful, especially younger ones. However, some female engineers left because of another genetic force—the urge to become a mother.

Fortunately, a recent study of female engineers in large British companies found that social support and role models are changing (Fernando et al., 2018). One young woman engineer said:

> My boss' boss is a woman. She has a daughter. The team leader for one of the other big assets in the North Sea is a woman and she works four days a week. She's very well respected as an engineer. . . . so there is hope for me—in the beginning I didn't think there was any hope especially if I wanted to have children. But now it makes sense to develop a career here.

> [Rosie, quoted in Fernando et al., 2018, p. 491]

Currently, not only are more women employed as engineers, but their brains also reflect their profession: They can envision spatial relations with the best of them—and far better than their mothers and grandmothers. That is an epigenetic result.

epigenetics and preterm infants, newborn care is changing: Lights are dimmed, noises quieted, and parental touch encouraged.

More generally, even when a particular person inherits genes for a serious disease, epigenetic factors matter. As one review explains, "there are, indeed, individuals whose genetics indicate exceptionally high risk of disease, yet they never show any signs of the disorder" (Friend & Schadt, 2014, p. 970). Why? Epigenetics.

## The Microbiome

**microbiome** All the microbes (bacteria, viruses, and so on) with all their genes in a community; here the millions of microbes of the human body.

One aspect of both nature and nurture that profoundly affects each person is the **microbiome**, which refers to all of the microbes (bacteria, viruses, fungi, archaea, yeasts) that live within every part of the body. The microbiome includes "germs," the target of disinfectants and antibiotics. Nonetheless, most microbes are helpful, enhancing life, not harming it.

Microbes have their own DNA, influencing immunity, weight, diseases, moods, and much more (Dominguez-Bello et al., 2019; Dugas et al., 2016). Particularly crucial is how the microbiome affects nutrition, since gut bacteria break down food for nourishment.

In one telling study, researchers in Malawi studied twins when one was malnourished and the other was not, even though both lived together and were fed the same foods. Did a greedy twin grab food from his brother? No! When scientists analyzed each twin's microbiome, they found crucial differences. That is why only one suffered (H. Smith et al., 2014).

## Genetic Diversity

It might seem as if each child is half mother and half father, since each child has 23 chromosomes from each parent. But that is not true, because the genes and alleles of each chromosome interact with those on the other pair (chromosome 1 from the father with chromosome 1 from the mother, 2 with 2, and so on), and that interaction produces a zygote unlike either parent. Thus, each new person is a product of two parents but is not like either one.

That diversity is added to the epigenetic diversity just described. And there is more! Mutations occur before, during, and after conception. Each zygote carries genes that "are themselves transmitted to individual cells with large apparent mistakes—somatically acquired deletions, duplications, and other mutations" (Macosko & McCarroll, 2013, p. 564). Small variations, mutations, or repetitions in the 3 billion base pairs could make a notable difference in the proteins and thus, eventually, in the person.

**Twelve of 3 Billion Pairs** This is a computer illustration of a small segment of one gene. Even a tiny difference in one gene can cause major changes in a person's phenotype.

Attention has focused on **copy number variations**, which are genes with repeats or deletions (from one to hundreds) of base pairs. Copy number variations are at least five times as common as variations in single genes (Saitou & Gokcumen, 2020). Copy number variations correlate with heart disease, intellectual disability, mental illness, and many cancers.

**copy number variations** Genes with various repeats or deletions of base pairs.

Usually, all this genetic diversity helps the species, because creativity, prosperity, and survival are enhanced when one person is unlike another. Two economists suggest that there is an optimal balance between diversity and similarity: Human societies prosper when they are close to that ideal (Ashraf & Galor, 2013). That idea is controversial. Nonetheless, most scholars agree that too much genetic insularity is problematic (Spolaore & Wacziarg, 2018).

## Matching Genes and Chromosomes

**genotype** An organism's entire genetic inheritance, or genetic potential.

The genes on the chromosomes constitute an organism's genetic inheritance, or **genotype**. The code of the original cell is duplicated again and again, in every cell.

## Autosomes

In 22 of the 23 pairs of chromosomes, both members of the pair (one from each parent) are closely matched. Some of the genes have alternate alleles, but each chromosome finds its comparable chromosome, making a pair. Those 44 chromosomes are called *autosomes*, which means that they are independent (*auto-* means "self") of the sex chromosomes (the 23rd pair).

Each autosome, from number 1 to number 22, contains hundreds of genes in the same positions and sequence. If the code of a gene from one parent is exactly like the code on the same gene from the other parent, the gene pair is **homozygous** (literally, "same-zygote").

However, the match is not always letter-perfect because the mother might have a different allele of a particular gene than the father has. If a gene's code differs from that of its counterpart, the two genes still pair up, but the zygote (and, later, the person) is **heterozygous**.

Only half of a man's genes are on each sperm and only half of a woman's genes are on each ovum, so the combination creates siblings who will be, genetically, both similar and different. Thus, which particular homozygous or heterozygous genes my brother and I inherited on our autosomes from our parents is a matter of chance. It is irrelevant, genetically, that I am a sister, not a brother.

**homozygous** Referring to two genes of one pair that are exactly the same in every letter of their code. Most gene pairs are homozygous.

**heterozygous** Referring to two genes of one pair that differ in some way. Typically one allele has only a few base pairs that differ from the other member of the pair.

## Sex Chromosomes

However, for the **23rd pair** of chromosomes, it matters which chromosome I inherited from my father. When his 23rd pair split to make gametes, half carried an X and half a Y.

This is how it happens. In males, the 23rd pair has one X-shaped chromosome and one Y-shaped chromosome. It is called **XY**. In females, the 23rd pair is composed of two X-shaped chromosomes. It is called **XX**.

The X chromosome is bigger, with about 100 more genes, but the Y has a crucial gene, called *SRY*, that directs the embryo to make male hormones and organs. Thus, sex at birth depends on which sperm penetrates the ovum—a Y sperm with the SRY gene, creating a boy (XY), or an X sperm, creating a girl (XX) (see **Figure 3.2**).

It sometimes matters whether a zygote is XY or XX, because genes on all the chromosomes might be affected, a phenomenon called *parental imprinting*. The best-known example occurs with a small deletion or duplication on chromosome 15 (Kalsner & Chamberlain, 2015).

**23rd pair** The chromosome pair that, in humans, determines sex. The other 22 pairs are autosomes, inherited equally by males and females.

**XY** A 23rd chromosome pair that consists of an X-shaped chromosome from the mother and a Y-shaped chromosome from the father. XY zygotes become males.

**XX** A 23rd chromosome pair that consists of two X-shaped chromosomes, one each from the mother and the father. XX zygotes become females.

Biophoto Associates/Science Source.

**Intersex** Every now and then, a baby is born with "ambiguous genitals," meaning that the child's sex is not abundantly clear. When this happens, analysis of the chromosomes may reveal that the zygote was XX or XY. The karyotypes shown here indicate a typical baby boy (*left*) and girl (*right*).

**FIGURE 3.2**
**Determining a Zygote's Sex** Any given couple can produce four possible combinations of sex chromosomes; two lead to female children and two, to male. In terms of the future person's sex, it does not matter which of the mother's Xs the zygote inherited. All that matters is whether the father's Y sperm or X sperm fertilized the ovum. However, for X-linked conditions it matters a great deal because typically one, but not both, of the mother's Xs carries the trait.

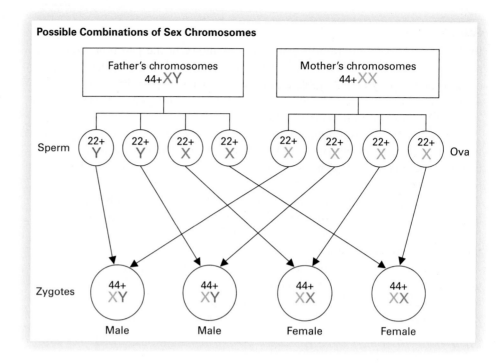

**Possible Combinations of Sex Chromosomes**

**Especially for Medical Doctors** Can you look at a person and then write a prescription that will personalize medicine to their particular genetic susceptibility? (see response, page 89)

If that harmful allele on chromosome 15 came from the father, the child will develop Prader-Willi syndrome and be obese, slow-moving, and stubborn. If that same allele came from the mother's chromosome 15, the child will have Angelman syndrome and be thin, hyperactive, and happy—sometimes too happy, laughing when no one else does. Other diseases and conditions are affected by imprinting, again sometimes in opposite ways (Couzin-Frankel, 2017).

## More Than Sex Organs

Although biology and culture (nature and nurture) constantly interact, the word *sex* generally refers to one's assigned sex at birth, and the word *gender* refers to social and cultural constructs.

The sex chromosomes direct the development of hormones that affect the brain, skeleton, body fat, and muscles, beginning in the first weeks of prenatal development and continuing to old age. Of course, culture (gender) affects every sex difference as well. One review suggests "gender identity is a multifactorial complex trait with a heritable polygenic component" (Polderman et al., 2018, p. 95).

For example, at conception, about 120 XY zygotes are conceived for every 100 XX, probably because the sperm with fewer genes have a slight advantage in the race to the ovum. From that moment on, male life is more fragile. At birth, the male/female ratio is 105:100 in developed nations and 103:100 in the poorest ones. That ratio, no longer 120:100, reveals that male embryos die at higher rates, and that, when pregnant women are sick and malnourished, surviving newborns are more often female.

For most of history people could not learn the sex of the fetus until birth, when someone looked at the genitals and shouted "It's a ------!" Because no one knew that the 23rd pair is present at conception, millions of pregnant women ate special foods, slept on one side, or repeated certain prayers, all to control their baby's sex—which was already determined.

Now prospective parents can learn whether a fetus is male or female. Prenatally, biological sex might be fatal because of gender bias in the culture (see Opposing Perspectives).

# Too Many Boys?

In past centuries, millions of newborns were killed because they were the wrong sex, a practice that would be considered murder today. Now, advances in science are enabling the same goal long before birth in various ways, such as inactivating X or Y sperm before conception.

Recently, millions of couples have used these methods to choose their newborn's sex. Should this be legal? It is against the law, in at least 36 nations. It is legal in the United States (Murray, 2014).

To some prospective parents, those 36 nations are unfair—most allow similar measures to avoid severely disabled newborns. Why is that legal but sex selection is not? There are moral reasons. But, should governments legislate morals? People disagree (Wilkinson, 2015).

One nation that recently tried to forbid prenatal sex selection is China. In about 1979, China began a "one-child" policy, urging, and sometimes forcing, couples to have only one child. That achieved the intended goal: fewer children to feed . . . or starve. Severe poverty was almost eliminated.

But the Chinese tradition is that sons care for aging parents, so couples wanted their only child to be male. Among the unanticipated results:

- Since 1980, an estimated 9 million abortions of female fetuses
- Adoption of thousands of newborn Chinese girls by Western families
- By 2010, far more unmarried young men than women

In 1993, the Chinese government forbade prenatal testing for sex selection. In 2013, China rescinded the one-child policy. Yet in 2020, there are 113 preschool boys for every 100 girls. Apparently, not every Chinese family follows the law.

The argument in favor of sex selection is freedom from government interference. Some fertility doctors and many individuals believe that each couple should be free to decide when, how many, and the sex of their progeny (Murray, 2014).

But one argument against is social harm. In China, many more young Chinese men than women die. The developmental explanation is that unmarried men take risks to attract women. They become depressed if they remain alone, risking early death

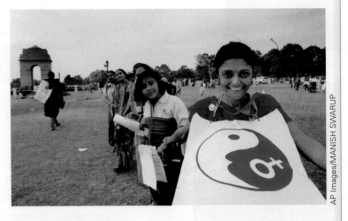

**My Strength, My Daughter** That's the slogan these girls in New Delhi are shouting at a demonstration against abortion of female fetuses in India. The current sex ratio of children in India suggests that this campaign has not convinced every couple.

from accidents, suicide, drug overdoses, and poor health practices (Srinivasan & Li, 2018).

This is a warning to other nations. A society with an excess of males might also have an excess of problems, since males are more likely to abuse drugs, commit crimes, kill each other, die of heart attacks, and start wars. This is true in every nation.

But wait: Chromosomes and genes do not *determine* behavior. Even traits that originate with biology are affected more by environment. Heart attacks, for instance, correlate more with diet and cigarette-smoking. Already, improved diagnosis and declines in smoking (changes in nurture) have reduced male heart attacks. In 1950, four times as many middle-aged men as women died of heart disease; by 2015, the rate was lower for both sexes, but especially for men (2:1, not 4:1) (Centers for Disease Control and Prevention, July 3, 2018).

Historically, some cultures have adjusted to battle deaths of young men (and thus too many young single women) by encouraging polygamy. Societies could change customs to adapt to an excess of males as well. But should they?

**THINK CRITICALLY:** Might laws prohibiting prenatal sex selection be unnecessary if culture shifted?

## WHAT HAVE YOU LEARNED?

1. How many chromosomes and genes do people have?
2. What is an allele?
3. What effect does the microbiome have?
4. Does it matter whether a gene pair is homozygotic or heterozygotic?
5. What determines a baby's sex?

(a)

(b)

(c)

Anatomical Travelogue/Science Source

**First Stages of the Germinal Period** The original zygote as it divides into *(a)* two cells, *(b)* four cells, and *(c)* eight cells. Occasionally at this early stage, the cells separate completely, forming the beginning of monozygotic twins, quadruplets, or octuplets.

**stem cells** Cells from which any other specialized type of cell can form.

# New Cells, New People

Within hours after conception, the zygote begins *duplication* and *division*. First, the 23 pairs of chromosomes (carrying all of the genes) duplicate to form two complete sets of the genome. These two sets move toward opposite sides of the zygote, and the single cell splits neatly down the middle into two cells, each containing the original genetic code.

These first two cells duplicate and divide, becoming four, which duplicate and divide, becoming eight, and so on. The name of the developing mass changes as cells multiply—the zygote (one cell) becomes a *morula*, then a *blastocyst*, then an *embryo*, then a *fetus*—and then, at birth, a *baby*. [**Developmental Link**: Prenatal growth is detailed in Chapter 4.]

## Cells and Identity

Nine months after conception, a newborn has about 26 billion cells, influenced by nutrients, drugs, hormones, viruses, microbes, and so on from the pregnant woman. Adults have about 37 trillion cells, each with the same 46 chromosomes and the same thousands of genes of the original zygote. This explains why DNA testing of any body cell, even from a drop of saliva or a snip of hair, can identify "the real father," "the guilty criminal," "the long-lost brother."

Because the Y chromosome is passed down to every male descendant, and because the Y changes very little from one generation to the next, men today have the Y of their male ancestors who died thousands of years ago.

Female ancestors also live on. Each zygote has *mitochondria*, biological material that provides energy for the cell. The mitochondria come from the mother, and her mother, and her mother, and thus each person carries evidence of maternal lineage.

As with all genetic material, mitochondria sometimes predispose a person to disease, especially problems with the heart (Bonora et al., 2019). Although males are more vulnerable to heart attacks than females are, the problem may originate with their mothers!

## Stem Cells

The cells that result from the early duplication and division are called **stem cells**; they can produce any other cell and thus become a complete person. After about the eight-cell stage, although duplication and division continue, a third process, *differentiation*, begins.

In differentiation, cells specialize, taking different forms and reproducing at various rates depending on where they are located. For instance, some cells become part of an eye, others part of a finger, still others part of the brain. They are no longer stem cells.

Another method, called CRISPR, has been developed to edit genes so that the stem cells have additions or deletions. CRISPR has been used to develop rice that is better adapted to various growing conditions, with the potential to feed billions of people (Endo et al., 2019). Medical researchers are excited about the possibility of using CRISPR to control the mosquitos that spread malaria, Zika, and other diseases (Liu et al., 2019).

In theory, CRISPR could be used to edit human genes as well, but that raises serious ethical questions (Boggio et al., 2020; McConnell & Blasimme, 2019). At the moment, CRISPR is forbidden for human organisms. A scientist's attempt in

China to use CRISPR in human embryos caused a storm of protest and a prison sentence (Cohen, 2018; Mills, 2019).

## In Vitro Fertilization

The ethical implications of CRISPR raise the issue of **in vitro fertilization (IVF)**, which was pronounced "sacrilegious" and "against God" when first attempted in 1960. That did not stop the scientists, who finally succeeded with a live baby, Louise Brown, in 1978.

Over the past half-century, procedures have improved and IVF has become "a relatively routine way to have children" (C. Thompson, 2014, p. 361). The European Society of Human Reproduction and Embryology estimated in 2018 that 8 million IVF babies have been born, some from every nation.

The two daughters of former President Barack Obama were both conceived via IVF. So was the younger sister of Louise Brown. Both Brown daughters have had babies of their own, conceived naturally, but said they would use IVF if need be.

A study of more than 2 million ninth-graders in Sweden reported that specifics of conception made little difference in school achievement (Norrman et al., 2018). Psychologically, IVF children have also fared well. For all children, genes and family life are far more influential than details of conception.

Nonetheless, IVF differs markedly from typical conceptions, almost half of which are unintended (Finer & Zolna, 2016). When a couple opts for IVF, the woman takes hormones to increase the number of ripe ova, and several are surgically removed while the man ejaculates into a sterile container. Then a technician combines ova and sperm in a laboratory dish (*in vitro* means "in glass"), often by inserting one viable sperm into each ovum.

Zygotes that fail to duplicate properly are rejected, but several days after conception, one or more blastocysts are inserted into the uterus. Implantation succeeds about half the time, with the age of the couple an important predictor. Some older women choose IVF with an ovum donated by a younger woman in order to increase the chance of pregnancy.

Since young eggs are more viable, women in their 20s who do not yet want children may freeze their ova for IVF years later. This has prompted a debate. Some suggest that women who don't want motherhood before age 35 or so are selfish, and others contend that such women are making a responsible choice, becoming mothers when they are ready to care for a new life (Carroll & Kr**ø**kke, 2018).

Several European nations limit the numbers of blastocysts inserted into the uterus at one time, partly because national health care pays for both IVF and infant care. The United States has no legal restrictions, although income matters. The cost varies from clinic to clinic within the United States, perhaps $20,000 for drugs, monitoring, and the procedure itself.

IVF offers many possibilities, often raising ethical and legal questions. One woman miscarried seven times and was in her early 40s when her mother, Anastassia Ontou, offered to carry her embryo and fetus. The 67-year-old woman gave birth in the Ukraine (where IVF has no legal restrictions) to her granddaughter.

Medical societies provide some oversight. For example, the California Medical Board removed the license from the physician who inserted 12 blastocysts in Nadya Suleman. She gave birth to eight surviving babies in 2009, a medical miracle but a developmental disaster.

Stuart Atkins/Shutterstock

**From Miracle to Routine** This is Louise Brown, whose birth was an international front-page headline when she became the first IVF baby born decades ago. Here she is holding twins who were also born via IVF, now a routine event at this clinic and thousands of others worldwide. Or, are all births, IVF or not, always a miracle? Perhaps you agree with an Indian mystic who once said that "every newborn is a sign that God has not yet given up on the world."

**in vitro fertilization (IVF)** Fertilization that takes place outside a woman's body (as in a glass laboratory dish). The procedure involves adding sperm to ova that have been surgically removed from the woman's ovary. If a zygote is produced, it is inserted into a woman's uterus, where it may implant and develop into a baby.

**THINK CRITICALLY:** When is it selfish to add another baby to the world?

sarahwolfephotography/Moment/Getty Images

**Not Exactly Alike** These two 4-year-old boys in South Carolina are identical twins, which means they originated from one zygote. But one was born first and heavier, and, as you see here, one appears to be more affectionate to his brother.

**monozygotic (MZ) twins** Twins who originate from one zygote that splits apart very early in development. (Also called *identical twins*.) Other monozygotic multiple births (such as triplets and quadruplets) can occur as well.

Another IVF miracle is that adults can have children who have no genetic connection to them because others have donated the sperm, the ova, and/or the womb. (The word *donate* is misleading, since most donors—often college students—are paid.) Some couples even travel to other nations with less restrictive laws and more women willing to be surrogate mothers (Reddy et al., 2018).

Is that international exploitation? Many aspects of fertility and infertility raise moral questions, within nations and between them.

## Twins and More

Thus far, we have described conception as if one sperm and one ovum resulted in one baby. About once in 350 human conceptions, one zygote becomes two fetuses, or even four (see Visualizing Development on page 74).

### Monozygotic Twins

Remember that each stem cell contains the entire genetic code. In IVF, before implantation, one stem cell can be removed and analyzed. If that cell carries a known destructive gene, or if the chromosomes are not exactly 46, then that blastocyst is not inserted into the uterus.

If genetic testing finds no problems, the remaining cell mass is inserted, where it might implant and grow normally. Removing one stem cell does not harm development, because each of the remaining stem cells has all of the instructions needed to create a person.

Twins *could* be created by separating the cells of the blastocyst before implantation, resulting in two or more identical babies if the separated cells were implanted and then grew. This is illegal with human zygotes in IVF.

However, nature within the woman's body sometimes does what doctors are forbidden to do—it splits those early cells. One separation can create **monozygotic (MZ) twins**, so called because they came from one (*mono-*) zygote (also called *identical twins*). Separations at the four- or eight-cell stage create monozygotic quadruplets or octuplets.

Because monozygotic multiples originate from one zygote, they have identical genetic instructions. Remember, however, that epigenetic influences begin as soon as conception occurs: Monozygotic twins look and act very much alike, but their prenatal environment is not identical.

For example, the particular spot in the uterus where each twin implants may allow one fetus to be better nourished than the other: Malnutrition affects the fetal brain, so it affects a twin lifelong. Experiences after birth can differ markedly, as occurred with monozygotic triplets who were adopted by three different families (as shown in the film *Three Identical Strangers*).

Monozygotic multiples are fortunate in several ways. They can donate a kidney or other organ to each other with no organ rejection. They can also befuddle their parents and teachers, who may need visible ways (such as different earrings or haircuts) to tell them apart.

Usually, monozygotic twins establish their own identities. For instance, both might inherit athletic ability, but one might choose to play basketball and the other, soccer.

As one monozygotic twin writes:

> Twins put into high relief *the* central challenge for all of us: self-definition. How do we each plant our stake in the ground, decide how sensitive, callous, ambitious, conciliatory, or cautious we want to be every day? . . . Twins

come with a built-in constant comparison, but defining oneself against one's twin is just an amped-up version of every person's life-long challenge: to individuate—to create a distinctive persona in the world.

[Pogrebin, 2010, p. 9]

That woman and her twin sister married and had a son and then a daughter within months of each other. Coincidence? Genetic? Sister pressure?

## Dizygotic Twins

About once in 60 natural conceptions, **dizygotic (DZ) twins** are conceived. They begin life when two ova are fertilized by two sperm at about the same time. Usually, women release only one ovum per month, so most human newborns are singletons. However, when multiple ovulation occurs, dizygotic twins are possible.

IVF in the United States produces DZ twins about half the time. All those statistics are for natural conceptions. Rates rise with IVF (see **Figure 3.3**). Indeed, multiple pregnancy increases the risk of preterm birth, but many infertile couples think two babies is a welcome miracle.

Dizygotic twins are sometimes called *fraternal twins*, although because *fraternal* means "brotherly" (as in *fraternity*), fraternal is inaccurate. Of course, MZ twins are always the same sex (their 23rd chromosomes are either XX or XY), but for DZ twins (as with any two siblings) some are brothers, some are sisters, and some are brother and sister.

People say that twinning "skips a generation," but actually it skips fathers, not mothers. Since dizygotic twinning requires multiple ovulation, the likelihood of a woman ovulating two ova and thus conceiving twins depends on her genes from her parents. Her husband's genes are irrelevant.

**VIDEO ACTIVITY: Identical Twins: Growing Up Apart** gives a real-life example of how genes play a significant role in people's physical, social, and cognitive development.

**dizygotic (DZ) twins** Twins who are formed when two separate ova are fertilized by two separate sperm at roughly the same time. (Also called *fraternal twins*.)

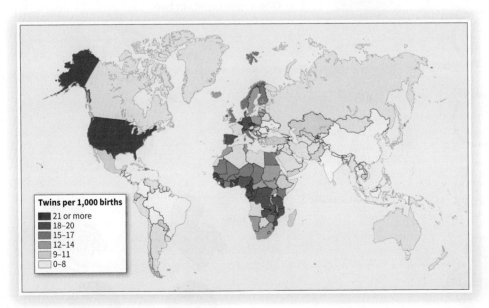

**FIGURE 3.3**

**More Is Not Always Better** Twinning is more common in Africa, and less common in East Asia. That has been true historically and continues to be the case in the twenty-first century, as this map shows. In medically advanced nations such as the United States, fertility drugs and IVF doubled the number of twins in the early twenty-first century, reaching a peak of 33.9 per 1,000 births in 2014. Recently, U.S. rates have fallen slightly as the challenges of low-birthweight newborns become more apparent.

# One Baby or More?

Humans usually have one baby at a time, but sometimes twins are born. Most often they are from two ova fertilized by two sperm (*lower left*), resulting in dizygotic twins.

Sometimes, however, one zygote splits in two (*lower right*), resulting in monozygotic twins; if each of these zygotes splits again, the result is monozygotic quadruplets.

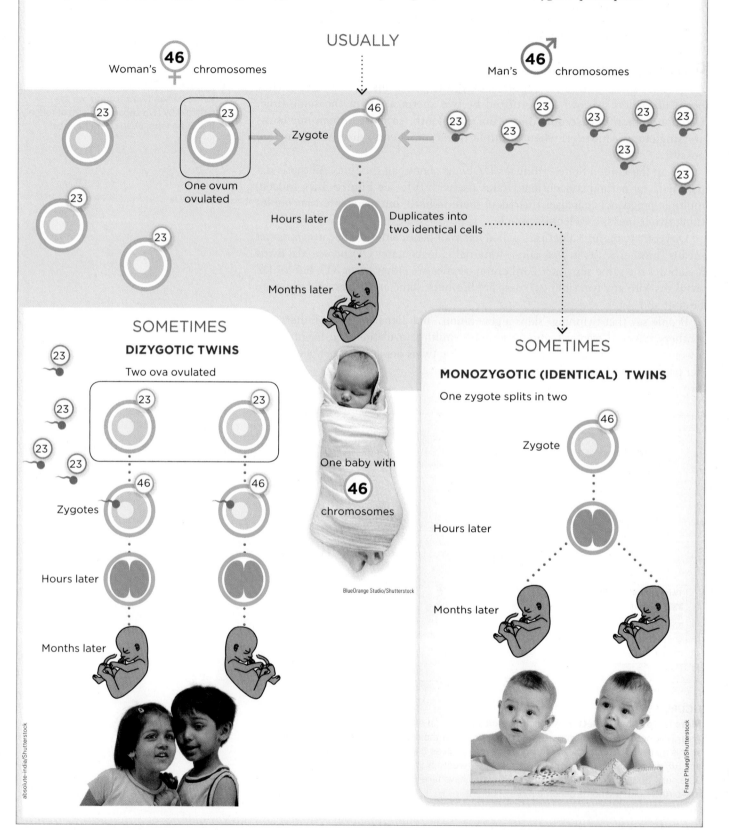

USUALLY

Woman's **46** chromosomes

Man's **46** chromosomes

23

23

One ovum
ovulated

23

23

46
Zygote

23

23

23

23

23

23

Hours later

Duplicates into
two identical cells

Months later

SOMETIMES

**DIZYGOTIC TWINS**

Two ova ovulated

23

23

23

23

23

23

46
46

Zygotes

Hours later

Months later

One baby with

**46**

chromosomes

BlueOrange Studio/Shutterstock

SOMETIMES

**MONOZYGOTIC (IDENTICAL) TWINS**

One zygote splits in two

46
Zygote

Hours later

Months later

absolute-india/Shutterstock

Franz Pfluegl/Shutterstock

However, half of a man's genes are from his mother. If he inherited her gene for multiple ovulation, there is a 50-percent chance that his genes include the multiple ovulating one. Then his daughters may have twins because their paternal grandmother did.

When dizygotic twinning occurs naturally, the incidence varies by ethnicity either because of genes or diet (Smits & Monden, 2011). Age matters, too: Older women more often double-ovulate and thus have more twins.

Like all children from the same parents, dizygotic twins have about half of their genes in common. They can differ markedly in appearance, or they can look so much alike that only genetic tests determine whether they are MZ or DZ. In the rare incidence that a woman releases two ova at once *and* has sex with two men over a short period, twins can have different fathers. Then they share only one-fourth of their genes.

---

### WHAT HAVE YOU LEARNED?

1. How does DNA establish identity?

2. What makes a cell a "stem cell"?

3. Why is CRISPR illegal for humans?

4. What is similar and different in an IVF pregnancy and a traditional pregnancy?

5. What is the difference between monozygotic twins and dizygotic twins?

6. For whom is twinning more likely?

---

## From Genotype to Phenotype

As already explained, when a sperm and an ovum create a zygote, the *genotype* (all the genes of the developing person) is established. This initiates several complex processes that form the **phenotype**—the person's actual appearance, behavior, and brain and body functions.

**phenotype** The observable characteristics of a person, including appearance, personality, intelligence, and all other traits.

### Many Factors

The phenotype depends on the genotype and thousands of factors in the environment. Completely accurate prediction of the phenotype is impossible, even if the genotype is entirely known (Lehner, 2013). One reason is *differential susceptibility*, as explained in Chapter 1. Because of a seemingly minor allele, or a transient environmental influence, a particular person may be profoundly changed—or not affected at all—by experiences.

Diabetes is a notable example. Several distinct alleles put people at risk for diabetes, but weight and exercise awaken that genetic risk. Yet some people are overweight and inactive but never develop diabetes because it is not in their genotype.

The same may be true for other developmental changes over the life span. Substance abuse—cocaine, cigarettes, alcohol, and so on—may produce epigenetic changes. Once addicted, people who have not used the drug for years are still vulnerable and cannot use that drug again as an unaffected person could (Bannon et al., 2014). Their brain has changed; they are "clean" but still have a substance use disorder.

**Human Genome Project** An international effort to map the complete human genetic code. This effort was essentially completed in 2001, though analysis is ongoing.

**Especially for Future Parents**
Suppose you wanted your daughters to be short and your sons to be tall. Could you achieve that? (see response, page 89)

**dominant** Reflected in the phenotype. Dominant genes have more influence on traits than recessive genes.

**recessive** Hidden, not dominant. Recessive genes are carried in the genotype and are not evident in the phenotype, except in special circumstances.

**carrier** A person whose genotype includes a gene that is not expressed in the phenotype. The carried gene occurs in half of the carrier's gametes and thus is passed on to half of the carrier's children. If such a gene is inherited from both parents, the characteristic appears in the phenotype.

## Gene–Gene Interactions

Many discoveries have followed the completion of the **Human Genome Project** in 2003. Once it was apparent that few disorders or talents arose from any single gene, increased attention focused on the complex interactions between one human gene and another.

### Additive Heredity

Interactions among genes and alleles are often called *additive* because their effects *add up* to influence the phenotype. The phenotype then reflects the contributions of every additive gene. Height, hair curliness, and skin color, for instance, are usually the result of additive genes. Indeed, height is probably influenced by 700 genes, each contributing a very small amount (Marouli et al., 2017).

Most Americans have ancestors of varied height, hair curliness, skin color, and so on, with background variations much more nuanced than any simple idea of race. A child's phenotype may not mirror the parents' phenotypes (although the phenotype always reflects the genotype), in part because of the interactions of their unique set of genes.

I see this in my family: Our daughter Rachel is of average height, shorter than her father and me but taller than either of our mothers. She apparently inherited some of her grandmothers' height genes via our gametes. And none of my four daughters has exactly my shape or coloring—apparent when we borrow clothes from each other and notice that a shirt that is flattering to one is ugly on another.

Genetic variations are apparent in every family, particularly among African Americans in the United States. Historically, the continent of Africa was, genetically, the most diverse (Choudhury et al., 2018). Added to that, current North Americans who identify as Black are not only the product of African diversity but also carry genes from many parts of Europe and from many tribes of indigenous Americans.

### Dominant–Recessive Heredity

Not all genes are additive. In one nonadditive form, some alleles are **dominant** and others are **recessive**. In a heterozygotic dominant/recessive pair, the *dominant gene* is more influential. It overpowers the *recessive gene*, hidden on the genotype, not apparent in the phenotype.

A person is called a **carrier** of the recessive gene when it is on the genotype but not the phenotype. In other words, people might carry a gene in their DNA, which they will transmit to half of their gametes. Only if someone inherits a recessive gene from each parent, which means there are two recessive genes but no dominant gene for that trait, does the recessive trait emerge on the phenotype.

Most recessive genes are harmless. One example is eye color. Brown eyes are dominant. Everyone with brown eyes has at least one dominant brown-eye gene.

Blue eyes are recessive. If both parents have blue eyes, then every eye-color gene on every gamete will have one or the other of their pair of blue-eye genes. In that case, all their children will all have blue eyes. If a child has one blue-eyed parent (who always has two recessive blue-eye genes) and one brown-eyed parent, that child will usually have brown eyes.

*Usually*, not always. Brown-eyed parents all have one brown-eye gene (otherwise they would not have brown eyes), but they might carry a blue-eye gene. In

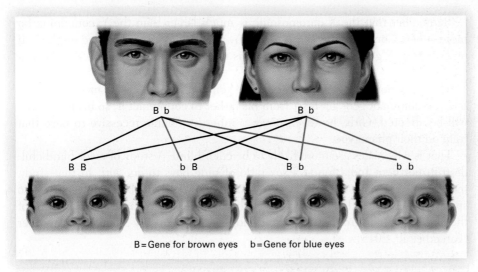

B = Gene for brown eyes     b = Gene for blue eyes

**FIGURE 3.4**
**Changeling?** No. If two brown-eyed parents both carry the blue-eye gene, they have one chance in four of having a blue-eyed child. Other recessive genes include the genes for red hair, Rh negative blood, and many genetic diseases.

⬤⬤ **Observation Quiz** Why do these four offspring look identical except for eye color? (see answer, page 89) ⬆

that case, in a blue-eyed/brown-eyed couple, every child has at least one blue-eye gene (from the blue-eyed parent), and half of the children will have a blue-eye recessive gene (from the carrier parent).

That half will have blue eyes because they have no dominant brown-eye gene. The other half will have a brown-eye dominant gene. Their eyes will be brown, but they will be carriers of the blue-eye gene, just like their brown-eyed parent. Sometimes both parents are carriers. If two brown-eyed parents both have the blue-eye recessive gene, the chances are one in four that their child will have blue eyes (see **Figure 3.4**).

This eye color example presumes that only one pair of genes determines eye color. However, as with almost every trait, eye color is polygenic, so other genes affect eye color, making eyes various shades of blue and brown, greenish or greyish.

## Mother to Son

A special case of the dominant–recessive pattern occurs with genes that are **X-linked** (located on the X chromosome). If an X-linked gene is recessive—as are the genes for red–green color blindness, several allergies, a few diseases, and some learning disorders—the fact that it is on the X chromosome is critical (see **Table 3.1**).

**X-linked** A gene carried on the X chromosome. If a male inherits an X-linked recessive trait from his mother, he expresses that trait because the Y from his father has no counteracting gene. Females are more likely to be carriers of X-linked traits but are less likely to express them.

### TABLE 3.1

**The 23rd Pair and X-Linked Color Blindness**

| 23rd Pair | Phenotype | Genotype | Next Generation |
|---|---|---|---|
| **1.** XX | Typical woman | Not a carrier | No color blindness |
| **2.** XY | Typical man | Typical X from mother | No color blindness |
| **3.** ⊗X | Typical woman | Carrier from father | Half her children will inherit her ⊗. The girls with her ⊗ will be carriers; the boys with her ⊗ will have color blindness. |
| **4.** X⊗ | Typical woman | Carrier from mother | Half her children will inherit her ⊗. The girls with her ⊗ will be carriers; the boys with her ⊗ will have color blindness. |
| **5.** ⊗Y | Color-blind man | Inherited from mother | All his daughters will have his ⊗. None of his sons will have his ⊗. All his children will have typical vision, unless their mother also had an ⊗ for color blindness. |
| **6.** ⊗⊗ | Color-blind woman (rare) | Inherited from both parents | Every child will have one ⊗ from her. Therefore, every son will have color blindness. Daughters will be only carriers, unless they also inherit an ⊗ from the father, as their mother did. |

⊗ = X that carries recessive gene for color blindness

Remember that the X chromosome is much larger than the Y, containing far more genes. Consequently, the X has many genes that are unmatched on the Y. If one of those X genes is recessive, there is no dominant gene on the Y to keep it hidden.

Thus, if a boy (XY) inherits a recessive gene on his X from his mother, he will have no dominant gene on his Y from his father to counteract it, so his phenotype will be affected. Girls, however, need to inherit a double recessive to have that train on their phenotype.

That is why males are more likely to be color blind. A study of color-blind children in northern India found a sex ratio of nine boys to one girl. In that study, marriages were almost always within a small group of neighbors and relatives, so specific genes tended to stay within each group. That explains why 7 percent of the children in one group were color blind, compared to only 3 percent in another (Fareed et al., 2015).

---

**WHAT HAVE YOU LEARNED?**

1. Why do humans vary so much in skin color and height?

2. What is the difference between additive and dominant–recessive inheritance?

3. How can a blue-eyed child have brown-eyed parents?

4. Why are sons more likely to inherit recessive conditions from their mothers than their fathers?

---

## Nature and Nurture

One goal of this chapter is for readers to grasp the complex interaction between genotype and phenotype. This is not easy. For decades, millions of scientists have struggled to understand this complexity. Each year brings advances in statistics and molecular analysis with new data to uncover various patterns, all resulting in hypotheses to be explored.

Now we examine three specific disorders: alcohol addiction, nearsightedness, and schizophrenia. As you will see, understanding the progression from genotype to phenotype has many practical implications.

### Alcohol Use Disorder

At various times throughout history, people have considered the abuse of drugs to be a moral weakness, a social scourge, or a personality defect. Historically and internationally, the main focus has been on alcohol, since people everywhere discovered fermentation thousands of years ago—to the joy of many. About 12 percent of the drinkers, however, become addicted, unable to stop drinking even when it interferes with the rest of their life.

Alcohol has been declared illegal (as in the United States from 1919 to 1933) or considered sacred (as in many religious rituals). Those who cannot control their drinking have been jailed, jeered, or burned at the stake.

We now know that inherited biochemistry affects alcohol metabolism (Preedy, 2019). Punishing those with the genes does not stop addiction. There is no single "alcoholism gene," but dozens of genes and alleles make alcohol use disorder more or less likely (Edenberg et al., 2019). Alleles create an addictive pull that can be overpowering, extremely weak, or somewhere in between, or can render alcohol repulsive. Each person's biochemistry reacts to alcohol, causing sleep, nausea, aggression, joy, relaxation, forgetfulness, or tears.

**Especially for Drug Counselors** Is the wish for excitement likely to lead to addiction? (see response, page 89)

If metabolism allows people to "hold their liquor," they might drink too much; others (including many East Asians) sweat and become red-faced after just a few sips. This inherited "flushing" tendency not only reduces the risk of alcohol use disorder but also improves metabolism (Kuwahara et al., 2014).

Although scientists first sought the genes that affected the *biology* of addiction, they soon learned that genetic personality traits (including a quick temper, sensation seeking, and high anxiety) are as crucial as biology (Macgregor et al., 2009). Age matters, too. Teenagers feel the pressure to drink if their best friends are drinking, while adults find it easier to say "no thank you."

Social contexts matter. Fraternity parties encourage drinking; church socials in a "dry" county make it difficult to swallow anything stronger than lemonade.

Finally, both sex and gender are relevant. For biological reasons (body size, fat composition, metabolism), women become drunk on less alcohol than men. Heavy-drinking females double their risk of mortality compared to heavy-drinking males (C. Wang et al., 2014). That may be why many cultures encourage men to drink but not women (Chartier et al., 2014). Or, sexism and chauvinism may be the reason.

As you see by all this, explaining a particular habit—drinking alcohol—quickly becomes very complex. A review of many current studies from every continent emphasizes that "genetic risk is only a piece of the complex architecture of risk and protective factors" for alcohol abuse (Edenberg et al., 2019). Again, phenotype is affected by both genotype and environment.

## Nearsightedness

Age, genes, and culture affect vision as well. Consider *myopia* (nearsightedness), the most common visual problem.

The effects of age are universal. Newborns focus only on things within 1 to 3 feet of their eyes; vision improves steadily until about age 10. The eyeball changes shape at puberty (increasing myopia) and again in middle age (decreasing myopia). Vision of all kinds becomes less acute in late adulthood, and serious problems increase.

Added to those developmental patterns, nearsightedness is strongly influenced by genes. Heritability is about 75 percent—which is quite high (Williams & Hammond, 2016). If one monozygotic twin is nearsighted, the other twin is virtually always nearsighted, too.

However, **heritability** indicates only how much of the variation in a particular trait, *within a particular population, in a particular context and era*, can be traced to genes. For example, the heritability of height is very high (about 95 percent) when children receive good medical care and nutrition, but it is low (about 20 percent) when children are severely malnourished. Children who are chronically underfed are short, no matter what their genes.

Thus, although nearsightedness is highly heritable, nurture may be crucial. Indeed, it is. In some African and Asian communities, heritability of nearsightedness is close to zero because of diet. Severe vitamin A deficiency blinds more than 250,000 children every year (Ehrenberg, 2016). For them, the genetic tendency to be nearsighted is irrelevant.

To prevent blindness, scientists have developed strains of local staples such as "golden rice" that are high in vitamin A, although use is limited by fears of genetically modified food (Ehrenberg, 2016). Some nations (Zambia and Cameroon) avoid genetic food modification by adding vitamin A directly to cooking oil and sugar. This must be carefully done—excessive, nonfood vitamin A causes health problems, but the risks are far less serious than blindness (Tanumihardjo et al., 2016).

What about children who consume adequate vitamin A in their food? Is their vision entirely inherited? No. Changes in the environment led one ophthalmologist

**Welcome Home** For many women in the United States, white wine is part of the celebration and joy of a house party, as shown here. Most people can drink alcohol harmlessly; there is no sign that these women are problem drinkers. However, danger lurks. Women get drunk on less alcohol than men, and females with alcoholism tend to drink privately and secretly, often at home, feeling more shame than bravado. All of that makes their addiction difficult to recognize.

**heritability** A statistic that indicates what percentage of the variation in a particular trait within a particular population, in a particular context and era, can be traced to genes.

Lai xinlin/AP Images

**Applauding Success** These eager young men are freshmen at the opening convocation of Shanghai Jiao Tong University. They have studied hard in high school, scoring high on the national college entrance exam. Now their education is heavily subsidized by the government. Although China has more college students than the United States, the proportions are far lower, since the population of China is more than four times that of the United States.

⬤⬤ **Observation Quiz** Name three visible attributes of these young men that differ from a typical group of freshmen in North America. (see answer, page 89) ⬆

to predict "an epidemic of pathological myopia . . . in the next few decades in Asia" (Saw, quoted in Seppa, 2013a, p. 23).

That prediction is based on three decades of research. Nearsightedness increased from 26 percent to 43 percent in one decade (1980 to 1990) in the army-mandated medical exams of all 17-year-old males in Singapore (Tay et al., 1992). Similar increases are evident in China, India, and the United States (Holden, 2010).

An article in the leading British medical journal (*The Lancet*) suggests that although genes are usually to blame for severe myopia, "any genetic differences may be small" for common nearsightedness (I. Morgan et al., 2012, p. 1739). Nurture must somehow be involved. But how?

One possible culprit is homework. Fifty years ago, most Asian children were working outside; now almost all are diligent students. As their developing eyes focus on their books, those with a genetic vulnerability to myopia may lose acuity for objects far away—which is exactly what nearsightedness means.

A related culprit is too much time indoors. Data from the United States on children playing sports have led some ophthalmologists to suggest that the underlying cause is inadequate exposure to daylight (I. Morgan et al., 2012). If North American children spent more time outside, would fewer need glasses?

Between the early 1970s and the early 2000s, nearsightedness in the U.S. population increased from 25 percent to 42 percent (Vitale et al., 2009). Urbanization, screen time, and fear of strangers have kept many U.S. children indoors most of the time, unlike children of earlier generations. The result may be reduced visual flexibility.

## Schizophrenia

In the United States, a 2017 survey of adults found the prevalence of mental illness to be 19 percent, with the highest rates (26 percent) among young adults (see **Figure 3.5**). The rate of depression among college students is said to be 16 percent (American College Health Association, 2017).

**FIGURE 3.5**

**Not Just Genetic** Details here may be questioned, as the diagnosis of mental illness is complex. But general trends have been found in other studies as well: Women have higher rates of major depression than men, and some mental illness (such as schizophrenia) "age out," which means they are less common among older adults.

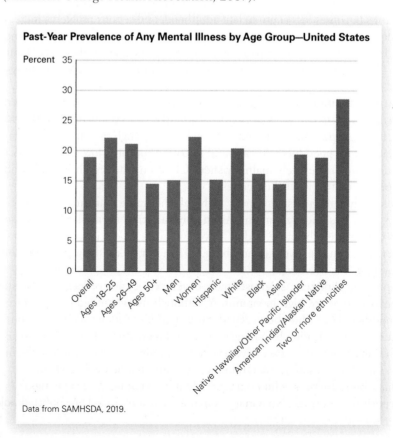

**Past-Year Prevalence of Any Mental Illness by Age Group—United States**

Percent (0–35 scale) by group: Overall, Ages 18–25, Ages 26–49, Ages 50+, Men, Women, Hispanic, White, Black, Asian, Native Hawaiian/Other Pacific Islander, American Indian/Alaskan Native, Two or more ethnicities

Data from SAMHSDA, 2019.

Among the common disorders with genetic origins are depression, anxiety, bipolar disorder, schizophrenia, and autism spectrum disorder (Knopik et al., 2017; Sandstrom et al., 2019). Although both genes and environment are crucial for all of these, we focus here on the relatively rare disorder of schizophrenia, because scientists have seesawed between thinking schizophrenia was caused entirely by destructive parenting, to thinking is was entirely genetic. Because of that seesaw, extensive research has focused on the origins of this particular disorder.

One study reported on the entire population of Denmark, where good medical records and decades of free public health care make research accurate (Gottesman et al., 2010). If *both* Danish parents developed schizophrenia, 27 percent of their children developed it; if one parent had it, 7 percent of their children developed it. Evidence for genes?

These same statistics can be presented in another way: Even if both parents had schizophrenia, almost three-fourths (73 percent) of their children did not. Thus, the data confirm both nature and nurture. Similarly, if one monozygotic twin develops schizophrenia, often—but not always—the other twin also develops a psychological disorder of some sort, not necessarily schizophrenia.

As for nurture, research on MZ twins found specific risk factors (Pepper et al., 2018). One is the stress of adolescence. If one MZ twin is diagnosed with schizophrenia before age 23, almost half the time (54 percent) the other twin will be diagnosed with the disorder. However, if the first diagnosis does not occur until after age 30, the incidence for the other twin is less than a third (30 percent).

Another risk factor is the family context. If one parent has schizophrenia, and one MZ twin develops it as well, chances are 63 percent that the genetic twin will also develop the disease. However, if neither parent had schizophrenia but one MZ twin does, odds are reduced by a third.

Many factors in the environment trigger schizophrenia in vulnerable people, including prenatal viruses, early maltreatment, adolescent drug use, and moving from one culture to another during early adulthood. Indeed, considering all the environmental influences led one team to write that schizophrenia was a *pseudogenetic* disease, with the inherited aspects overestimated (Torrey & Yolken, 2019).

No doubt there is a genetic risk, but also no doubt that childhood experiences matter for schizophrenia as well as for all psychological disorders (Ottesen et al., 2018; Sullivan et al., 2000). It is a mistake to blame any condition *entirely* on genes or *entirely* on childhood or *entirely* on adult experiences. That leads to many questions: How much, for whom, and what are the triggers, the interactions, the treatments, the outcomes?

## Practical Applications

Since genes affect every disorder, no one should be blamed or punished for inherited problems. We all have them: They are not our fault, nor the fault of our parents.

However, knowing that genes never act alone opens the door to prevention. For instance, if alcohol use disorder is in the genes, parents can keep alcohol out of the home and explain the dangers of addiction (neither exaggerating nor ignoring), hoping their children become cognitively and socially mature before imbibing. If nearsightedness runs in the family, parents can play outdoors with their children every day. If mental illness is a problem, children need stability and reassurance.

Of course, avoiding alcohol, playing outdoors, and maintaining stability are recommended for all children, as are dozens of other behaviors, such as flossing twice a day, saying "please," sleeping 10 hours each night, eating five servings of vegetables, and promptly writing thank-you notes. It is unrealistic to expect parents to make their children do all of these; awareness of genetic risks can guide priorities.

The same principles apply lifelong. Recognizing that each of us has a genetic pull toward some unwanted behaviors or conditions is the beginning of self-acceptance as well as a path toward prevention. Adults who know that diabetes is in their genes can avoid overeating—good advice for everyone, but especially needed for some.

---

**WHAT HAVE YOU LEARNED?**

1. Is alcohol dependence a genetic condition or a cultural one?

2. What suggests that nearsightedness is affected by nurture?

3. What does *heritability* mean?

4. If a particular genetic problem is common in a family, what should the parents do with their children?

---

**LaunchPad**
macmillan learning

**VIDEO: Genetic Disorders** offers an overview of various genetic disorders.

**Down syndrome** A condition in which a person has 47 chromosomes instead of the usual 46, with 3 rather than 2 chromosomes at the 21st site. People with Down syndrome typically have distinctive characteristics, including unusual facial features, heart abnormalities, and language difficulties. (Also called trisomy-21.)

**Universal Happiness** All young children delight in painting brightly colored pictures on a big canvas, but this scene is unusual for two reasons: Daniel has trisomy-21, and this photograph was taken at the only school in Chile where typical and special-needs children share classrooms.

# Chromosomal and Genetic Problems

We now focus on conditions caused by an extra chromosome or a single destructive gene. If all notable anomalies and disorders are included, 92 percent of people do <u>not</u> develop a serious genetic condition by early adulthood—but that means 8 percent do (Chong et al., 2015).

## Not Exactly 46

As you know, most humans have 46 chromosomes, created by two gametes, each with 23 chromosomes. However, the 46 chromosomes on the parents' cell do not always split exactly in half to make sperm or ova.

About half of all zygotes have more than or fewer than 46 chromosomes (Milunsky & Milunsky, 2016). Most of them fail to duplicate, divide, differentiate, and implant. They stop growing before anyone knew that conception occurred. Those who survive that initial period usually are spontaneously aborted (miscarried). Ninety-nine percent of newborns have the usual 46 chromosomes (Benn, 2016).

## Trisomies

If an entire chromosome is added, that leads to a recognizable *syndrome*, a cluster of distinct characteristics that tend to occur together. Usually the cause is three chromosomes at a particular location instead of the typical two (a condition called a *trisomy*). One in 10,000 newborns has three chromosomes at the 13th site (called Patau syndrome), and 1 in 5,000 has three at the 18th (called Edwards syndrome). For those trisomies, if a fetus survives prenatal life, death usually occurs soon after birth (Acharya et al., 2017).

A much more common trisomy is at the 21st site, which occurs about once in 700 births (Parker et al., 2010). Trisomy 21 is called **Down syndrome**, named after Dr. and Mrs. Langdon Down. In 1868, they opened the first home for such children (then called "Mongolian Idiots").

No individual with Down syndrome is just like another, but this trisomy usually produces telltale characteristics—a thick tongue, round face, and slanted eyes, as well as distinctive hands, feet, and fingerprints. The hippocampus (important for memory) is usually smaller.

Many people with Down syndrome also have hearing problems, heart abnormalities, muscle weakness, and short stature. They are slow to develop intellectually, especially in language, with a notable deficit in the ability to rhyme (Næss, 2016).

By middle age, many people with Down syndrome develop Alzheimer's disease (AD), because one gene on chromosome 21 increases amyloid plaque—a sign of AD. Since everyone with Down syndrome has an extra chromosome 21, many also have too much amyloid. A blood test may indicate their risk early enough to forestall Alzheimer's disease, and thus research on adults with Down syndrome may help all adults avoid dementia (Hamlett et al., 2018).

A group of researchers asked parents about the positive and negative aspects of having a child with Down syndrome. Happily, positives outweighed negatives. One parent said:

> He not only is a positive force in my life, but in the world. When I push him around the neighborhood in his stroller he loves to wave at people, including those who are homeless. He has a big heart that does not discriminate.

[Farkas et al., 2019, p. 525]

### Problems of the 23rd Pair

Every human has at least 44 autosomes and one X chromosome; an embryo cannot develop without those 45. However, miscounts at the 23rd pair are more common and less deadly than miscounts in the autosomes. About 1 in every 300 infants is born with only one sex chromosome (no Y) or with three or more (not just two) (Benn, 2016). Most of them reach adulthood.

Each particular combination of sex chromosomes results in a specific syndrome (see **Table 3.2**), but all affect cognition, fertility, and sexual maturation (Hong & Reiss, 2014). One problem with the 23rd pair, called Turner syndrome, occurs when only one sex chromosome is present. The result is a girl with a wide neck and low hairline. But many children with an extra sex chromosome (XXY, for instance) seem normal until adolescence or adulthood, when sexual maturation and fertility are impaired.

### Gene Disorders

More common than chromosomal problems are gene disorders. Each person carries about 40 alleles that *could* cause serious diseases. The phenotype is seriously affected only when the inherited gene is dominant or when both parents carry the same allele. Even then, only one child in two (for dominant disorders), or in four (for recessive disorders), inherits the genetic problem.

**Especially for Teachers** Suppose you know that one of your students has a sibling who has Down syndrome. What special actions should you take? (see response, page 89)

### TABLE 3.2

**Common Abnormalities Involving the Sex Chromosomes**

| Chromosomal Pattern | Physical Appearance | Psychological Characteristics | Incidence* |
|---|---|---|---|
| XXY (Klinefelter Syndrome) | Males. Usual male characteristics at puberty do not develop—penis does not grow, voice does not deepen. Usually sterile. Breasts may develop. | Can have some learning disabilities, especially in language skills. | 1 in 700 males |
| XYY (Jacob's syndrome) | Males. Typically tall. | Risk of intellectual impairment, especially in language skills. | 1 in 1,000 males |
| XXX (Triple X syndrome) | Females. Normal appearance. | Impaired in most intellectual skills. | 1 in 1,000 females |
| XO (only one sex chromosome) (Turner syndrome) | Females. Short, often "webbed" neck. Secondary sex characteristics (breasts, menstruation) do not develop. | Some learning disabilities, especially related to math and spatial understanding; difficulty recognizing facial expressions of emotion. | 1 in 6,000 females |

*Incidence is approximate at birth.
Information from Aksglaede et al., 2013; Benn, 2016; Hamerton & Evans, 2005; Powell, 2013; Stochholm et al., 2010.

**Who Has the Fatal Dominant Disease?**
The mother, but not the children. Unless a cure is found, Amanda Kalinsky will grow weak and experience significant cognitive decline, dying before age 60. She and her husband, Bradley, wanted children without Amanda's dominant gene for a rare disorder, Gerstmann-Straussler-Scheinker disease. Accordingly, they used IVF and pre-implantation testing. Only zygotes without the dominant gene were implanted. This photo shows the happy result.

**fragile X syndrome** A genetic disorder in which part of the X chromosome seems to be attached to the rest of it by a very thin string of molecules. The cause is a single gene that has more than 200 repetitions of one triplet.

## Dominant Disorders

Many of the 7,000 *known* single-gene disorders are dominant (Milunsky & Milunsky, 2016). Most are relatively mild. Severe dominant disorders are rare because people who have them usually die before puberty, and thus never pass that gene to another generation.

However, if a dominant disorder does not appear until adulthood it could stay in the gene pool, because adults might have several children before they know of their condition. That is the case for adult-onset Alzheimer's disease, one form of muscular dystrophy, Marfan syndrome, and Huntington's chorea, a fatal central nervous system condition caused by a copy number variation—more than 35 repetitions of a particular set of three base pairs.

Although the dominant gene for all these conditions sometimes affects children or adolescents (Milunsky & Milunsky, 2016), serious symptoms usually do not arise until midlife. The folk singer Woody Guthrie, who wrote "This Land Is Your Land," died of Huntington's, as did two of his daughters. Fortunately, his son, Arlo, inherited his talent but not his disorder.

## Recessive Disorders

Recessive diseases are more numerous than dominant ones because they are passed down by carriers who are unaware of their recessive genes. There are thousands of recessive diseases; advance carrier detection is now possible for several hundred.

A few recessive conditions are X-linked, including hemophilia, Duchenne muscular dystrophy, and **fragile X syndrome**, which is caused by more than 200 repetitions on one stretch of one gene (Plomin et al., 2013). (Some repetitions are normal, but not this many.)

The deficits caused by fragile X syndrome are the most common form of *inherited* intellectual disability. (Many other forms, such as trisomy-21, begin with gametes, not genes.) Boys are more often impaired by fragile X syndrome than are girls, because they have only one X.

## Common Recessive Disorders

About 1 in 10 North American adults carries an allele on their autosomes for cystic fibrosis, thalassemia, or sickle-cell disease. Why so common? Because carriers benefited from the gene, which makes the gene frequent in the population.

Consider the most studied example: sickle-cell disease. Carriers of the sickle-cell gene die less often from malaria, which is prevalent and lethal in parts of Africa. Indeed, four distinct alleles cause sickle-cell disease, each originating in a malaria-prone region.

The gene protected more people (the carriers) than it harmed. If a carrier had children with a noncarrier, half of the children would be carriers and half not, and none of the children would have the disease. If a malaria epidemic swept through that region, and that family had many children, those who were carriers would be more likely to survive to become parents themselves, so the next generation would have more carriers.

What if both parents were carriers? If they had four children, odds were that only one would inherit the double recessive and die young. The other three would not have the disease, and two of the three would be carriers, somewhat protected against an early malaria death. Consequently, each generation included more carriers, and thus the gene became widespread.

This connection between genes and local diseases is common. Almost every lethal disease is more frequent in one place than in another (Weiss & Koepsell, 2014). If a particular allele is protective, it becomes more common in that population.

About 8 percent of Americans with African ancestors have the recessive gene for sickle-cell disease—they are protected against malaria. Cystic fibrosis is more common among people with ancestors from northern Europe, because carriers may have been protected from cholera.

Additive genes can also be beneficial. Dark skin is protective against skin cancer if a person is often exposed to direct sun. Light skin allows more vitamin D to be absorbed from the sun, if a person lives where sunlight is scarce. Being relatively short is beneficial in cold climates, or when food is scarce.

Modern Europeans inherited between 1 and 4 percent of their genes from Neanderthals, who became extinct about 30,000 years ago. Neanderthal genes protect contemporary humans against some skin conditions and other diseases but may also make them vulnerable to allergies and depression—depending on which bits of Neanderthal genes they happen to inherit (Saey, 2016).

Some genetic risks are simultaneously beneficial. Anxiety, for instance, causes people to anticipate problems. Communities benefit if that genetic risk leads to better preparation for hurricanes, earthquakes, wars, and epidemics.

The Greek mythological character Cassandra envisioned wars and other devastation in the future. No one believed her; they thought she was insane. She became depressed, was shunned and eventually murdered. According to the myth, she was later considered a prophet, not a madwoman.

Even schizophrenia may have a benefit. Bruce Springsteen's father was an angry, emotionally abusive man, who probably had schizophrenia (Springsteen, 2017). Did that help his son become a creative musical genius? Indeed, many great artists and writers apparently suffered from serious mental illness, from Vincent Van Gogh to Virginia Woolf, from Anthony Bourdain to Andrew Solomon—you can think of many more. Is there any connection here?

---

 **DATA CONNECTIONS: Common Genetic Diseases and Conditions** describes several different types of gene disorders.

---

## Genetic Counseling and Testing

Until recently, after the birth of a child with a severe disorder, couples blamed witches or fate, not genes or chromosomes. Those children usually died in infancy. Currently, however, most children with genetic disorders survive, which means that everyone has relatives with a disease that is partly genetic.

A simple blood test reveals some recessive diseases, including sickle cell, and the cost of analyzing a person's entire genome has plummeted, from more than a million dollars to less than a hundred. However, there are many problems with genome-wide analysis (Tam et al., 2019).

- Data can reveal risks, but not reality: Almost every condition is better or worse depending on nongenetic factors, as apparent in our discussion of nature and nurture.
- Most reported research has been on people with western European heritage: Much more needs to be learned about the other 80 percent of humankind.
- Genetic research is proceeding faster than practical care: People might learn that they are vulnerable to a particular problem, but not how to prevent or treat it.
- Most genetic oddities are "variants of unknown significance." That means that even experts do not know what to make of them, causing carriers to worry.

Another danger arises from genetic testing that people pay for privately, mailing a saliva sample to learn about their ancestry and genes. The results may be misleading. Worse is that the emotional needs of the person are not addressed.

MICHELLE DEL GUERCIO/Science Source

**Reassurance and Gratitude** Karen is pregnant and just learned that a relative has the gene for a serious condition. Here, a genetic counselor is explaining all the possibilities. Several months after this photo was taken, she gave birth to a healthy baby!

**LaunchPad**
macmillan learning

**VIDEO: Genetic Testing** examines the pros and cons of knowing what diseases may eventually harm us or our offspring.

## Genetic Counseling

A rapidly expanding profession, much needed, is genetic counseling. There are an estimated 7,000 professional genetic counselors in 28 nations (Ormond et al., 2018). Their job is vital but not easy.

The task is to explain that we all have genes that push us in one direction or another, and that part of life is not only accepting but also celebrating this fact in ourselves and our children. At the same time, counseling can help people understand their personal risks of having a child with a serious genetic disorder and to help all of us realize that spontaneous mutations occur, so that prediction is never certain.

Both reassurance and warning may be needed. For example, a genetic counselor may explain that serious problems are unusual. On the other hand, if there is a specific risk, counselors alert prospective parents to organizations for caregivers of children with special needs, to adoption (both nationally and internationally) risks and joy, and to treatment that is experimental but that might soon be proven (a couple might decide to postpone conception), and so on. Counselors are trained to help clients understand and explore many possibilities.

This requires up-to-date information. New genetic disorders—and treatments—are revealed almost weekly. An inherited disorder that once meant lifelong neurological impairment (e.g., phenylketonuria, or PKU) might now mean a normal life.

Accuracy, effect, and interpretation of testing varies: Sometimes a particular gene increases the risk of a problem by only a tiny amount, perhaps 0.1 percent. Counselors need to help clients understand both risks and uncertainty.

## CAREER ALERT The Genetic Counselor

An understanding of life-span development is useful for every career. As students contemplate their future work, they should consult career counselors and check the Occupational Handbook of the Department of Labor, which lists prospects, salary, and qualifications.

Beyond those basics, however, these Career Alerts raise questions and issues that arise from a developmental perspective, issues that might not be found in a standard description of the career. You will see this in this discussion of genetic counseling.

There is far greater demand for genetic counselors than there are people trained in this area, so job prospects are good. Salary is good, too: The median in 2017 was $77,500. Training requires a master's degree and then passing an exam to be certified (though this is not required in every state). That all seems simple, but the reality is much more challenging.

The first challenge is to understand and communicate complex biological and statistical material, so that clients understand the implications of whatever genes they have. This is difficult: Not only are new discoveries made every day, but every disorder is polygenic and multifactorial, and mosaicism, methylation, and the microbiome are all relevant.

One reason this is a rapidly growing career is that many people are curious about their ancestry and pay for commercial tests (such as 23 and Me) to identify where their ancestors lived. In the process, they may discover confusing implications for their health, making genetic counseling essential (Smart et al., 2017). Further, since is it now apparent that almost every disease is partly genetic, many people are concerned about their own health, the health of their family members, or the health of their prospective children, and they want answers.

This is complex regarding the genes of an adult, but it is doubly difficult when discussing a prospective child, who will inherit only half of the genes from each parent.

Facts, medical treatments, and quality of life for a future, not-yet-conceived child are difficult to explain, but genetic counselors must consider much more than that. Each adult has emotions, assumptions, and values that differ between a husband and wife, and those values are not identical to those of the counselor. Not only does each person have a particular attitude about risk, religion, and abortion but also communication is complex. People misunderstand results; counselors must draw charts, rephrase results, and repeat basic facts.

Thus, counselors must not only know facts, recent discoveries, and explain odds and consequences but also must be sensitive to complex social dynamics, respecting everyone—especially when a couple decides to terminate or continue a pregnancy when the counselor would have made the opposite choice.

Theoretical decisions often conflict with reality. If a woman knows that her embryo has trisomy-21, should she terminate the pregnancy? About two-thirds of prospective parents say no, but about two-thirds of pregnant women at high risk (e.g., over age 35) say yes, as do almost all (87 to 96 percent) women who know they are carrying a Down syndrome embryo (Choi et al., 2012).

Similarly, variation was evident when 152 pregnant women in Wisconsin learned that their embryo had trisomy-13 or trisomy-18. Slightly more than half of the women decided to abort; most of the rest decided to give birth but provide only comfort care for the newborn; and three chose full intervention to preserve life (their three babies lived for a few days but died within the first weeks) (Winn et al., 2018).

Many factors—including childhood memories, prior children, religion, opinions of others—make a difference (Choi et al., 2012). Unfortunately, no matter what the decision, outsiders sometimes tell parents they made the wrong choice—something genetic counselors never do.

Before deciding on this profession, ask yourself what you would do in the following situations, each of which has occurred:

- Parents of a child with a disease caused by a recessive gene from both parents ask whether another baby will suffer the same condition. Tests reveal that the husband does not carry that gene. Should the counselor tell the parents that their next child won't have this disease because the husband is not the father of the first child?
- A woman learns that she is at high risk for breast cancer because she carries the BRAC1 gene. She wants to have her breasts removed, but she refuses to inform her four sisters, half of whom probably carry BRAC1.
- A pregnant couple are both "little people," with genes for short stature. They want to know whether their embryo will have typical height. They plan to abort such a fetus.

- A person is tested for a genetic disease that runs in the family. The results are good (not a carrier) and bad (the person carries another serious condition). Should the counselor reveal a risk that the client did not ask about?

This fourth issue is new: Even a few years ago, the cost of testing precluded learning about unrequested results. But now *genome-wide association study* (*GWAS*) is routine, capturing the entire genome, so counselors learn about thousands of unsuspected conditions.

Even with careful counseling, people with identical genetic conditions often make opposite choices. For instance, 108 women who had one child with fragile X syndrome were told that another pregnancy would have a 50/50 chance of fragile X. Most decided to avoid pregnancy, but some (20 percent) deliberately conceived another child (Raspberry & Skinner, 2011).

In another study, pregnant women learned that their fetus had an extra sex chromosome. Half the women aborted; half did not (Suzumori et al., 2015). That highlights why this career is not for everyone. Professionals explain facts and probabilities; people decide. Can you live with that?

## Who Needs Counseling?

Rational and informed understanding is elusive, not only among prospective parents but also among professionals not trained in counseling. Consider the experience of one of my students. A month before she became pregnant, Jeannette's employer required her to have a rubella vaccination. Hearing that Jeannette had had the shot, her obstetrician gave her the following prognosis:

> My baby would be born with many defects, his ears would not be normal, he would be intellectually disabled. . . . I went home and cried for hours and hours. . . . I finally went to see a genetic counselor. Everything was fine, thank the Lord, thank you, my beautiful baby is okay.
>
> *[Jeannette, personal communication]*

Jeannette may have misunderstood, but that is exactly why the doctor should have spoken more carefully. Genetic counselors are trained to make information clear. If sensitive counseling is available, then preconception, prenatal, or even prenuptial (before marriage) testing is especially useful for:

- individuals who have a parent, sibling, or child with a serious genetic condition;
- couples who have had several spontaneous abortions or stillbirths;
- couples who are infertile;
- women over age 35 and men over age 40; and
- couples from the same ethnic group, particularly if they are relatives.

The latter is especially crucial among populations who often intermarry. This is true for Greeks in Cyprus, where about one-third of the population carries the recessive gene for thalassemia. In the 1970s, one Cypriot baby in 158 was born with thalassemia, which led to repeated hospitalization and premature death.

Then Cyprus encouraged testing, before conception or at least prenatally. Some lovers decided not to marry, some married couples decided on adoption or IVF with preconception testing. Now virtually no newborns in Cyprus have thalassemia (Hvistendahl, 2013).

**CHAPTER APP 3**

 **Gene Screen**

**IOS:**
https://tinyurl.com/yxvxbzun

**RELEVANT TOPIC:**
Genetic disorders, counseling, and testing

The Gene Screen app provides information about the inheritance and prevalence of recessive genetic diseases in different cultures and ethnicities.

**THINK CRITICALLY:** Instead of genetic counseling, should we advocate health counseling?

This chapter raised many ethical questions. There is one more, that arises throughout. Does our current emphasis on genes distracts us from public health hazards (poverty, pollution, pesticides, and so on) that harm development more than genes? Developmentalists recognize genes, but they also know that plasticity characterizes development. Context and culture matter.

As you have read many times in this chapter, genes are part of the human story, influencing every page, but they do not determine the plot or the final paragraph. The remaining chapters describe the rest of the story.

---

**WHAT HAVE YOU LEARNED?**

1. What chromosomal miscounts might result in a surviving child?
2. What is the cause and consequence of Down syndrome?
3. How common are recessive conditions?
4. Why is sickle-cell disease very common in some parts of Africa?
5. What is the role of the genetic counselor?
6. What ethical mandates are required of genetic counselors?

---

## SUMMARY

### The Genetic Code

1. Genes are the foundation for all development, first instructing the developing creature to form the body and brain, and then affecting thought, behavior, and health lifelong. Human conception occurs when two gametes (a sperm with 23 chromosomes and an ovum with 23 chromosomes) combine to form a single cell called a zygote.

2. A zygote usually has 46 chromosomes (half from each parent), which carry a total of about 21,000 genes. Genes and chromosomes from each parent match up to make the zygote, but the match is not always letter-perfect because of genetic variations called alleles, or polymorphisms.

3. Genetic variations occur in many ways, from the chromosomes of the parent to the epigenetic material surrounding the zygote and the microbiome of every body part. Spontaneous mutations, copy number variations, and much more make each person unique.

4. The most notable mismatch is in the 23rd pair of chromosomes, which is XX in females and XY in males. The sex of the embryo depends on the sperm, since only men have a Y chromosome and thus can make Y gametes.

### New Cells, New People

5. The first duplications of the one-celled zygote create stem cells, each of which could become a person if it developed.

6. Monozygotic twins occur if those first stem cells split completely. Dizygotic twins occur if two ova are fertilized by two sperm at about the same time. Genetically, they have half of their genes in common, as do all full siblings.

7. In vitro fertilization (IVF) has led to millions of much-wanted babies and also to an increase in multiple births, who often are preterm and of low birthweight. Ethical concerns regarding standard IVF have quieted, but new dilemmas appear. CRISPR is the most recent example.

### From Genotype to Phenotype

8. Genes interact in many ways, sometimes additively with each gene contributing to development and sometimes in a dominant–recessive pattern. If a recessive trait is X-linked, it is passed from mother to son.

### Nature and Nurture

9. Genetic makeup can make a person susceptible to many conditions. Examples include substance use disorder (especially alcohol use disorder) and poor vision (especially nearsightedness). Culture and family affect both of these conditions dramatically.

10. Every adult is a carrier of harmful genes. Their expression depends on the genes of the other parent, as well as on many influences from the environment. Genetic understanding can help caregivers protect people from potentially harmful genes.

### Chromosomal and Genetic Problems

11. Often a gamete has fewer or more than 23 chromosomes, which may create a zygote with 45, 47, or 48 chromosomes. Usually such zygotes do not duplicate, implant, or grow.

12. Infants may survive if they have three chromosomes at the 21st site (Down syndrome). These individuals may have fulfilling lives, although they are vulnerable to heart and lung problems, and, in midlife, to Alzheimer's disease.

13. Another possible problem is a missing or extra sex chromosome. Such people have intellectual disabilities or other problems, but they may also lead a fulfilling life.

14. Everyone is a carrier for genetic abnormalities. Usually these conditions are recessive, not apparent unless the mother and the

father both carry the gene. Serious dominant disorders usually do not appear until midlife.

**15.** Serious recessive diseases can become common if carriers have a health advantage. This is true for sickle-cell disease, which protected carriers against malaria.

**16.** Genetic testing and counseling can help many couples. Testing provides information about possibilities, which are difficult for people to understand when their emotions are overwhelming. The final decision about what to do with the information rests with the client, not the counselor.

## KEY TERMS

deoxyribonucleic acid (DNA) (p. 63)
chromosome (p. 63)
gene (p. 63)
gamete (p. 63)
zygote (p. 63)
genome (p. 63)
allele (p. 64)

epigenetics (p. 65)
microbiome (p. 66)
copy number variations (p. 66)
genotype (p. 66)
homozygous (p. 67)
heterozygous (p. 67)
23rd pair (p. 67)
XY (p. 67)

XX (p. 67)
stem cells (p. 70)
in vitro fertilization (IVF) (p. 71)
monozygotic (MZ) twins (p. 72)
dizygotic (DZ) twins (p. 73)
phenotype (p. 75)

Human Genome Project (p. 76)
dominant (p. 76)
recessive (p. 76)
carrier (p. 76)
X-linked (p. 77)
heritability (p. 79)
Down syndrome (p. 82)
fragile X syndrome (p. 84)

## APPLICATIONS

**1.** Pick one of your traits and explain the influences that both nature *and* nurture have on it. For example, if you have a short temper, explain its origins in your genetics, your culture, and your childhood experiences.

**2.** Many adults have a preference for having a son or a daughter. Interview adults of several ages and backgrounds about their preferences. If they give the socially preferable answer ("It does not matter"), ask how they think the two sexes differ. Listen and take notes—don't debate. Analyze the implications of the responses you get.

**3.** Draw a genetic chart of your biological relatives, going back as many generations as you can, listing all serious illnesses and causes of death. Include ancestors who died in infancy. Do you see any genetic susceptibility? If so, how can you overcome it?

**4.** List a dozen people you know who need glasses (or other corrective lenses) and a dozen who do not. Are there any patterns? Is this correlation or causation?

## Especially For ANSWERS

**Response for Medical Doctors** (from p. 68): No. Personalized medicine is the hope of many physicians, but appearance (the phenotype) does not indicate alleles, recessive genes, copy number variations, and other genetic factors that affect drug reactions. Many medical researchers seek to personalize chemotherapy for cancer, but although this is urgently needed, success is still experimental, even when the genotype is known.

**Response for Future Parents** (from p. 76): Possibly, but you wouldn't want to. You would have to choose one mate for your sons and another for your daughters, and you would have to use sex-selection methods. Even so, it might not work, given all the genes on your genotype. More important, the effort would be unethical, unnatural, and possibly illegal.

**Response for Drug Counselors** (from p. 78): Maybe. Some people who love risk become addicts; others develop a healthy lifestyle that includes adventure, new people, and exotic places. Any trait can lead in various directions. You need to be aware of the connections so that you can steer your clients toward healthy adventures.

**Response for Teachers** (from p. 83): As the text says, "information combats prejudice." Your first step would be to make sure you know about Down syndrome, by reading material about it. You would learn, among other things, that it is not usually inherited (your student need not worry about his or her progeny) and that some children with Down syndrome need extra medical and educational attention. This might mean you need to pay special attention to your student, whose parents might focus on the sibling.

## Observation Quiz ANSWERS

**Answer to Observation Quiz** (from p. 77): This is a figure drawn to illustrate the recessive inheritance of blue eyes, and thus eyes are the only difference shown. If this were a real family, each child would have a distinct appearance.

**Answer to Observation Quiz** (from p. 80): Not nearsightedness! Rates of corrective lenses (estimated at 85 percent) might be as high among university students in the United States, but Americans

would typically have contacts. Two other visible differences: uniforms and gender. Except for in the military, no U.S. university issues uniforms and the majority of North American students are women. A fourth difference may be inferred from their attentiveness: The graduation rate of incoming college students in China is about 90 percent, compared to about 50 percent in the United States.

# Prenatal Development and Birth

## What Will You Know?

1. Why do most zygotes never become babies?
2. How are home births better and worse than hospital births?
3. What can a pregnant woman do to ensure a healthy newborn?
4. Why do new mothers and fathers sometimes become depressed?

I did not tell her, but I was worried about my eldest daughter's pregnancy. She was almost 40, and in the previous few years had a miscarriage as well as surgery to remove a fibroid tumor. If all went well, this would be her first birth. I kept my worries quiet (pregnant women have more than enough worries of their own), but I clung to every reassuring report: The fetus gained weight on schedule, measurements of the fetal neck precluded Down syndrome, blood tests confirmed a typically developing boy. My daughter was eating well, avoiding drugs, counting kicks. I was honored and grateful that she asked me to be her birth partner.

The due date was weeks after final exams, but I recruited one of my colleagues to proctor for me if the birth happened early, as about 12 percent of U.S. births do. I waited for the call telling me that labor had started. Exams were over, grades were calculated, due date had come and gone. No call. Waiting became hard.

So I drove to stay with her, two hours away, to be with her as soon as contractions began. For three days I cooked, read, took the dog to the vet. My daughter heard that walking might start labor; we hiked up a small mountain. One night a thunderstorm woke me; future mother and baby stayed asleep. The next day, another prenatal checkup. The midwife monitored the fetal heartbeat (fine), the maternal blood pressure (fine), the birth position (head down, fine), and the amniotic fluid. Not fine! Too low.

She recommended induction; we checked into the hospital. Another midwife examined her, with surprising news. Labor had started hours earlier. That's why the fluid was low. The nurse said the thunderstorm did it; something about the air.

The actual birth also held surprises, detailed later in this chapter. Spoiler alert: Mother and babe were fine. The grandmother was not.

The scientific study of human development is not only about how individuals change over time; it is about historical change (Bronfenbrenner's chronosystem), family support (microsystem), and social contexts (macro- and exosystems). All are evident in this chapter, as well as in the text above. Elective surgery to remove fibroids? Measuring the fetal neck? Midwives? Sonogram of amniotic fluid? Induction? Never in other times and places, and uncommon in most nations now.

Currently in the United States it is uncommon for the grandmother to be the birth partner, but that was not unusual in past centuries. It is apparent in this chapter, as well as in my daughter's experience, that each birth is affected by every system, reflecting unique experiences (climbing that mountain after the due date) and universal forces (that thunderstorm?). This chapter describes both.

# Prenatal Development

Universally, the months before birth are the time of the most dramatic and extensive transformation of the entire life span. To make it easier to study, prenatal development is often divided into three main periods. The first two weeks are the **germinal period;** the third through the eighth week is the **embryonic period;** from then until birth is the **fetal period.** (Alternative terms are presented in **Table 4.1**.)

## Germinal: The First 14 Days

You learned in Chapter 3 that the one-celled zygote duplicates, divides, multiplies, and differentiates, when those early cells take on distinct characteristics. About a week after conception, the developing mass forms two distinct parts—a shell that will become the *placenta* and a nucleus that will become the *embryo*. The first task of the shell is *implantation*, embedding into the nurturing lining of the uterus. This is far from automatic; most zygotes never implant (Kim & Kim, 2017) (see **Table 4.2**).

## Embryo: From the Third Week Through the Eighth Week

The start of the third week after conception initiates the *embryonic period*, during which the mass of inner cells takes shape—not recognizably human but worthy of the name, **embryo.** (The word *embryo* is often used loosely, but here, embryo refers to day 14 to day 56.)

## Day by Day

About two weeks after conception, a thin line called the *primitive streak* appears down the middle of the embryo; it forms the neural tube, which develops into the central nervous system, that is, the brain and spinal column. Soon the head

**germinal period** The first two weeks of prenatal development after conception, characterized by rapid cell division and the beginning of cell differentiation.

**embryonic period** The stage of prenatal development from approximately the third week through the eighth week after conception, during which the basic forms of all body structures, including internal organs, develop.

**fetal period** The stage of prenatal development from the ninth week after conception until birth, during which the fetus gains about 7 pounds (more than 3,000 grams) and organs become more mature, gradually able to function on their own.

**embryo** The name for a developing human organism from about the third week through the eighth week after conception.

---

**TABLE 4.1**

**Timing and Terminology**

Popular and professional books use various phrases to segment the stages of pregnancy. The following comments may help to clarify the phrases used.

*Beginning of pregnancy:* Sometimes pregnancy is said to begin at conception, which is the start of *gestational age*. However, the organism does not become an *embryo* until about two weeks later, and pregnancy does not affect the woman (and is not confirmed by blood or urine testing) until implantation, so some do not consider the woman pregnant until then. On the other hand, some obstetricians and publications count from the woman's last menstrual period (LMP), usually about 14 days *before* conception.

*Length of pregnancy:* Full-term pregnancies last 266 days, or 38 weeks, or 9 months. If the LMP is used as the starting time, pregnancy lasts 40 weeks, sometimes expressed as 10 lunar months. (A lunar month is 28 days long.)

*Trimesters:* Instead of *germinal period, embryonic period*, and *fetal period*, as used in this text, some writers divide pregnancy into three-month periods called *trimesters*. Months 1, 2, and 3 are the *first trimester;* months 4, 5, and 6, the *second trimester;* and months 7, 8, and 9, the *third trimester*.

*Due date:* Although a specific due date based on the LMP is calculated, only 5 percent of babies are born on that exact day. Babies born between two weeks before and one week after that date are considered *full term*. [This is recent; until 2012, three weeks before and two weeks after were considered full term.] Because of increased risks for postmature babies, labor is often induced if the baby has not arrived a week after the due date.

Omikron/Science Source

(a)

Petit Format/Science Source

(b)

**The Embryonic Period** *(a)* At 4 weeks past conception, the embryo is only about 1/8 inch (3 millimeters) long, but already the head has taken shape. *(b)* By 7 weeks, the organism is somewhat less than an inch (2 centimeters) long. Eyes, nose, the digestive system, and even the first stage of toe formation can be seen.

**cephalocaudal**  Growth and development that occurs from the head down.

**proximodistal**  Growth or development that occurs from the center or core in an outward direction.

**fetus**  The name for a developing human organism from the start of the ninth week after conception until birth.

| TABLE 4.2 |
| --- |
| **Vulnerability During Prenatal Development** |
| **The Germinal Period** |
| An estimated 65 percent of all zygotes do not grow or implant properly and thus do not survive the germinal period. |
| **The Embryonic Period** |
| About 20 percent of all embryos are aborted spontaneously. This is usually called an early *miscarriage,* a term that falsely implies something wrong with the woman. In fact the most common reason for a spontaneous abortion is a chromosomal abnormality. |
| **The Fetal Period** |
| About 5 percent of all fetuses are aborted spontaneously before viability at 22 weeks or are *stillborn,* defined as born dead after 22 weeks. This is much more common in poor nations. |
| **Birth** |
| Because of all these factors, only about 27 percent of all zygotes grow and survive to become living newborn babies. |
| Information from Cunningham et al., 2014; Kim & Kim, 2017. |

appears, as eyes, ears, nose, and mouth start to form and a minuscule blood vessel that will become the heart begins to pulsate.

By the fifth week, buds that will become arms and legs emerge. Upper arms and then forearms, palms, and webbed fingers grow. Legs, knees, feet, and webbed toes, in that order, appear a few days later, each with the beginning of a skeleton. Then, 52 and 54 days after conception, respectively, the fingers and toes separate (Sadler, 2015).

At the end of the eighth week after conception (56 days), the embryo weighs just one-thirtieth of an ounce (1 gram) and is about 1 inch (2½ centimeters) long. It moves frequently, about 150 times per hour, but this is imperceptible to the woman. Random arm and leg movements are more frequent early in pregnancy than later on (Rakic et al., 2016).

By eight weeks post conception, the developing embryo has all of the organs and body parts of a human being, including elbows and knees. Development is **cephalocaudal** (literally, "head-to-tail") and **proximodistal** (literally, "near-to-far"): The head forms first and the extremities last. This directional pattern continues until puberty, when it reverses. (Feet first, brain last!)

The early embryo has both male (via *Wolffian ducts*) and female (via *Müllerian ducts*) potential, in a tiny intersex gonad. At the end of the embryonic period, hormonal and genetic influences typically cause one or the other to shrink, and then ovaries or testes, and a vagina or penis, grow from that omnipotent gonad (Zhao et al., 2017).

## Fetus: From the Ninth Week Until Birth

The organism is called a **fetus** from the beginning of the ninth week after conception until birth. The fetal period encompasses dramatic change, from a tiny creature smaller than the final joint of your thumb to a newborn about 20 inches (51 centimeters) long.

Early growth is rapid. By three months, the fetus weighs about 3 ounces (87 grams) and is about 3 inches (7.5 centimeters) long. Those numbers—3 months, 3 ounces, 3 inches—are approximate. (Metric measures—100 days, 100 grams, 100 millimeters—are similarly imprecise, but useful as a memory guide.)

One of the Tiniest Rumaisa Rahman was born after 26 weeks and 6 days, weighing only 8.6 ounces (244 grams). Nevertheless, now age 16, she is living a full, normal life. Rumaisa gained 5 pounds (2,270 grams) in the hospital and then, six months after her birth, went home. Her twin sister, Hiba, who weighed 1.3 pounds (590 grams) at birth, had gone home two months earlier. At their one-year birthday, the twins seemed typical, with Rumaisa weighing 15 pounds (6,800 grams) and Hiba 17 pounds (7,711 grams) (Nanji, 2005).

## The Middle Three Months

The 4-month-old fetus is very active, with "large body movements—whole body flexion and extension, stretching and writhing, and vigorous leg kicks that somersault the fetus through the amniotic fluid" (Adolph & Franchak, 2017). The heartbeat becomes stronger and faster when the fetus is awake and moving. Digestion and elimination develop. Fingernails, toenails, and buds for teeth form, and hair grows, including eyelashes!

Those developments inspire awe, but the crucial mid-pregnancy development is that the central nervous system becomes active, regulating heart rate, breathing, and sucking. This brain maturation allows the fetus to reach the **age of viability,** when a fetus born far too early might survive.

Every day of prenatal life within the uterus increases viability. If birth occurs before 22 weeks, death is certain because advanced technology cannot maintain life without some brain response. (Reports of survivors born before 22 weeks are unreliable, because the date of conception is unknown.)

After the age of viability, life is still fragile. Currently, if birth occurs in an advanced neonatal unit, some very preterm babies survive, and some of those reach age 2 without major impairments. Rates vary by nation, by sex (girls do better), and by medical advances.

Among the best survival rates are those in Japan and France. In Japan, about half of 22-week-old newborns born alive survive the first week of life, and about half of those survivors escape major cognitive disabilities (Kono et al., 2018). In France, when membranes are ruptured prematurely because continued pregnancy might be fatal to the woman, only 11 percent of 22-week fetuses survive to age 2 (most die at birth or soon thereafter) but 66 percent do so if they were born 25 weeks past conception (Lorthe et al., 2018).

## The Final Three Months

Each day of the final three months benefits the fetal brain and body. Many aspects of prenatal life are awe-inspiring; the fact that any ordinary woman provides a far better home for a fetus than the most advanced medical technology is one of them.

**age of viability** The age (about 22 weeks after conception) at which a fetus might survive outside the mother's uterus if specialized medical care is available.

**CHAPTER APP 4**

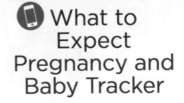 What to Expect Pregnancy and Baby Tracker

**IOS:**
https://tinyurl.com/y6esrn5a

**ANDROID:**
https://tinyurl.com/nufnyqg

**RELEVANT TOPICS:**
Prenatal health and development, birth

Based on the well-known book *What to Expect When You're Expecting*, this app guides users through pregnancy day-by-day. Users receive personalized updates, tips, and articles on their baby's development, and are joined with a virtual community of other parents-to-be.

Loyola Univ. Medical Center/Getty Images News/Getty Images

## Essential Connections

In earlier decades, a newborn's chance of survival was pegged to weight. Today we know better: Some 1-pound babies live and some 3-pound babies die. Brain maturation is more crucial than body fat.

Accordingly, research on prenatal development has become "a frontier of science." However, research on the fetal brain is "exceptionally difficult" (Vasung et al., 2019). Remember the need for interdisciplinary research, explained in Chapter 1? That is essential for learning about early brain development. As one review explains:

> [C]ollaboration between at least three major expert groups is necessary: 1. biological experts (ex. neuroscientists, geneticists and developmental biologists), 2. technical experts (ex. physicists, engineers, computer scientists and mathematicians) and 3. clinical experts (ex. radiologists, neonatologists, neurologists, cardiologists and obstetricians).
>
> *[Vasung et al., 2019, p. 245]*

This collaboration has led to some verified aspects of prenatal growth. The central nervous system is the first body system to begin development. The embryonic stage starts with the primitive streak, which becomes the neural tube even before the facial features are formed and the first pulsating blood vessel appears.

Already by the third week after conception some cells specialize to become *neural progenitor cells,* which duplicate and multiply many times until some of them create neurons (brain cells). Neurons do not duplicate but may endure lifelong. Those early neurons migrate to a particular part of the brain (brainstem, cerebellum, hypothalamus, visual cortex, and so on) and specialize. For example, some neurons are dedicated to seeing faces, others to seeing red and green, others to blue and yellow, and so on.

By mid-pregnancy, in *neurogenesis*, the brain has developed billions of neurons, and folding allows the cortex to be larger and more complex than the brains of other animals (Stiles & Jernigan, 2010). [**Developmental Link:** The cortex and other brain structures are described in Chapter 5.]

Following the proximodistal (near-to-far) sequence, the six layers of the cortex are produced, with the bottom (sixth) layer first and then each new layer above the previous one so that the top, outer layer is the last to form. Similarly, the brainstem above the back of the neck, then the midbrain, and finally the forebrain develop and connect.

Synchronized connections between parts of the brain develop in the second half of pregnancy. That indicates they are working together — as in an adult who sees and smells something delicious, experiences hunger, and reaches for the food, all in a flash.

These four responses arise from different brain regions, a synchrony that begins prenatally (see **Figure 4.1**). In the later months of pregnancy, and not before, the reflexes of heartbeat, breath, and movement coordinate, giving a preterm infant a chance at survival. A relative lack of synchrony after 20 weeks predicts a newborn at risk (Thomason et al., 2017).

(a) 25 days

(b) 50 days

(c) 100 days

(d) 20 weeks

(e) 28 weeks

(f) 38 weeks (full term)

**FIGURE 4.1**

**Prenatal Growth of the Brain** Just 25 days after conception *(a)*, the central nervous system is already evident. The brain looks distinctly human by day 100 *(c)*. By the 28th week of gestation *(e)*, at the very time brain activity begins, the various sections of the brain are recognizable. When the fetus is full term *(f)*, all parts of the brain, including the cortex (the outer layers), are formed, folding over one another and becoming more convoluted, or wrinkled, as the number of brain cells increases.

What makes prenatal brain development a particularly complex area of study is that brain development switches from the first six months to the final three (Vasung et al., 2019). In the first part, basic structures are formed, including the limbic system (for emotions), the prefrontal cortex (for analysis), and the six layers of the cortex (for conscious awareness). Impairments in any of these structures affect the mind and behavior lifelong.

But then the environment becomes more crucial, as the brain of the future person is affected by the prenatal environment, such as maternal stress, nutrition, patterns of sleep, and exercise.

Detailed study of one crucial brain region, the *hippocampus* (the major site for memory formation), reveals an explosion of new cells during the fourth prenatal month, followed by a gradual slowdown, while other parts of the fetal body (legs, arms, etc.) increase (Ge et al., 2015).

In the final months, when somewhat fewer new neurons in the brain are formed, existing neurons begin to be affected by the environment. For example, if the mother is worried, sleeps fitfully, and/or is addicted to drugs, her newborn might have the same problems in the early weeks after birth. The fetal brain is responsive to many signals from maternal actions, and that can affect the future child's social development (Manczak & Gotlib, 2019).

This mid-gestation burst of neurogenesis and then slowdown is characteristic of the entire brain, with each area following its own timetable, prenatally and postnatally (Gilmore et al., 2018).

This is an example of the biosocial development detailed in every later biosocial chapter: Each age has a pattern of growth, and each age has particular challenges. Prenatally, the challenge is for the brain to develop as well as genes allow.

In the final three prenatal months, the neurological, respiratory, and cardiovascular systems all develop. The lungs expand and contract, and breathing muscles strengthen as the fetus swallows and spits out amniotic fluid. The valves of the heart go through a final maturation, as do the arteries and veins throughout the body; the testicles of the male fetus descend.

The various lobes and areas of the brain are also established, and pathways between one area and another are forged. For instance, sound and sight become coordinated: Newborns quickly connect voices heard during pregnancy with faces. That may be why they recognize their mother after seeing her only once or twice.

That phenomenal accomplishment (recognizing Mother) occurs within a day or two after birth. Neurological plasticity allows the fetus to recognize the voices of familiar people by the sixth month after conception (Webb et al., 2015). If a baby is born prematurely, impairments are more common in movement, intelligence, and/or vision than in hearing (Kono et al., 2018).

By full term, human brain growth is so extensive that the cortex has become wrinkled, with *gyri* and *sulci*, as the hills and valleys of the cortex are called (see **Figure 4.2**). Although some huge mammals (whales, for instance) have bigger brains than humans, no other creature needs as many folds because, relative to body size, the human brain is much larger.

**FIGURE 4.2**

**Bigger Brains, Better Connections** From 15 weeks (*far left*) to full term (*far right*), the fetal brain increases not only in size, but also in connections. The top row shows size and complexity—those folds in the cortex are necessary for all aspects of human thought. The bottom row shows the thickness of the subplate compartments, needed mid-gestation to keep one lobe from interfering with another, and then needed to disappear by full-term birth.

Lana Vasung

**LaunchPad**
macmillan learning

**VIDEO: Brain Development
Animation: Prenatal** shows how the
brain develops from just after conception
until birth.

Beyond brain growth, with an estimated 86 billion neurons at birth, another process occurs in the final months of pregnancy—cell death, called *apoptosis*. Research on apoptosis has primarily centered on nonhuman creatures. It is apparent that programmed cell death is widespread in prenatal development, and the effects may be transmitted from one generation to the next (Hamada & Matthews, 2019).

Some apoptosis is easy to understand: Abnormal and immature neurons, such as those with missing or extra chromosomes, are lost. So are neurons if the woman is exposed to toxins, such as drugs or stress. Sometimes, however, seemingly normal neurons die: One estimate finds that almost half of all brain cells are gone before birth (Underwood, 2013). Why?

Perhaps death of any neuron that is not fully functioning creates space in the brain for the remaining neurons to coordinate thinking, remembering, and responding. Surviving preterm babies often have intellectual and emotional deficits, with gestational age the chief predictor (Heitzer et al., 2020). There are many hypotheses for this correlation; less time for prenatal brain development and apoptosis is one of them.

That is speculation. However, it is known that protections of the brain occur in the final months of pregnancy. One critical development is thickening of the membranes and bones covering the brain. This helps prevent "brain bleeds," a hazard of preterm birth if paper-thin blood vessels in the cortex collapse.

Another development pertains to the *fontanels*, which are areas on the top of newborn head where the bones of the skull have not yet fused. Fontanels enable the fetal head to become narrower as it moves through the vagina during birth. During the first weeks of life, the fontanels gradually close. Preterm babies have larger fontanels, making them vulnerable to brain damage (Frémondière et al., 2019).

The average fetus in the United States gains about 4½ pounds (2.1 kilograms) in the third trimester, increasing to about 7½ pounds (about 3.4 kilograms) at birth, with boys a few ounces heavier than girls. Of course, some quite healthy babies born to well-nourished women weigh more, and some weigh less. Variation depends on genes and national diet; northern European newborns tend to be heavier, East Asian to be lighter (Kiserud et al., 2018).

Reflexes (listed at the end of this chapter) are a better indication of health than weight. Unless something is amiss, most newborns are ready by the end of prenatal life to thrive at home on mother's milk—no expert help, oxygenated air, or special feeding required. For thousands of years, that is how humans survived: We would not be alive if any of our ancestors had been born before the last three months of pregnancy.

---

**WHAT HAVE YOU LEARNED?**

1. What are the three stages of prenatal development?
2. Why are the first days of life the most hazardous?
3. What parts of the embryo form first?
4. When do sex organs appear?
5. What distinguishes a fetus from a baby?
6. What is the prognosis of a baby born before 25 weeks of gestation?
7. What occurs in the final three months of pregnancy?

**Choice, Culture, or Cohort?** Why do it that way? Both of these women (in Peru, on the *left*, in England, on the *right*) chose methods of labor that are unusual in the United States, where birth stools (Peru) and birthing pools (England) are uncommon. However, in all three nations, most births occur in hospitals—a rare choice a century ago.

# Birth

About 38 weeks (266 days) after conception, the fetal brain signals massive increases in the hormone *oxytocin* to start labor. Birth occurs after 12 hours of active labor for first births and 7 hours for subsequent ones. These are averages: Birth is still *full term* two weeks before or after the due date, and labor may take twice or half as long. Some women believe they are in active labor for days, and others say 10 minutes.

## Variations in How and Where

When considering birth from a life-span perspective, the multicultural and multicontextual variations are astounding. Birth may be universal, but specifics vary tremendously.

## Birth Positions

Women's birthing positions vary—sitting, squatting, lying down. Some women labor in a tub of warm water, which helps the woman relax (the fetus continues to get oxygen via the umbilical cord). Preferences and opinions on birthing positions (as on almost every other aspect of prenatal development and birth) are partly cultural and partly personal.

In general, physicians find it easier to see the head emerge if the woman lies on her back. However, women find it easier to push the fetus out if they sit up.

## Home or Hospital?

Once, all family members and neighbors were nearby as the mother labored at home, sometimes with an experienced older woman (called a "granny midwife" in the United States) to help. Then, in developed nations in the middle of the twentieth century, almost all babies were born in hospitals, attended only by doctors and nurses. Now most hospitals allow one family member, usually the father, sometimes a friend or grandmother (as in my case).

An innovation in the United States and other nations is to involve a **doula,** a person trained to support the laboring woman. Doulas time contractions, use massage, provide encouragement, and do whatever else is helpful. Often doulas come to the woman's home during early labor and return after birth to encourage breast-feeding. Doulas are chosen by many women, but they have proven to be particularly helpful for immigrant, low-income, or unpartnered women who may be intimidated by doctors (Kang, 2014; Saxbe, 2017).

In many poor nations, births often occur at home. Lack of prenatal care and absence of trained birth attendants correlate with higher death rates, for both

**doula** A woman who helps with the birth process. Traditionally in Latin America, a doula was the only professional who attended childbirth. Now doulas are likely to arrive at the woman's home during early labor and later work alongside a hospital's staff.

**They Called It "Catching" the Baby** Midwife Mahala Couch shows her strong hands that "caught" thousands of newborns in the back woods of Southern Appalachia. Midwife births became illegal in about 1920, but many women still preferred home birth with Mahala over hospital birth with a doctor. Currently, midwives are trained, certified, and legal in most states and nations.

**Apgar scale** A quick assessment of a newborn's health, from 0 to 10. Below 5 is an emergency—a neonatal pediatrician is summoned immediately. Most babies are at 7, 8, or 9—almost never a perfect 10.

babies and mothers (Tekelab et al., 2019). However, uncomplicated home births, facilitated by a trained attendant, may be safer than births in poorly staffed and ill-equipped hospitals (Kunkel et al., 2019; Manasyan et al., 2019).

In developed nations, home births are rarely chosen. In the United States, less than 1 percent of babies are born at home, about half of them unexpected, which is hazardous because no one is nearby to rescue a newborn in distress. Planned home births are better, although sometimes illegal and not covered by insurance. Some contend that home births are risky for newborns (Wendland, 2018).

Even in advanced nations that support home births, few women choose it. In Great Britain, "based on her wishes and cultural preferences and any medical and obstetric needs she and her baby may have" the national health care system pays for home births. Nonetheless, hospital births are chosen by about 90 percent; birthing centers by 8 percent; and home births by only 2 percent (quoted in Hinton et al., 2018).

In the Netherlands, about a third of all low-risk women choose home births. National health care supports that choice, not only financially but with special ambulances called *flying storks,* which speed mother and newborn from home to a hospital if sudden complications arise. In that nation, compared to hospital births, mothers have fewer complications, and infants have better survival rates if born at home (de Jonge et al., 2015).

## The Newborn's First Minutes

Newborns usually breathe and cry on their own. The first breaths of air bring oxygen to the lungs and blood, and the infant's color changes from bluish to reddish. ("Reddish" refers to blood color, visible beneath the skin, and applies to newborns of all skin tones.) Eyes open wide; tiny fingers grab; even tinier toes stretch and retract. Usually full-term babies are instantly, zestfully, ready for life.

Newborn health is often measured by the **Apgar scale,** first developed by Dr. Virginia Apgar (see Visualizing Development). When she earned her M.D. in 1933, Apgar wanted to work in a hospital but was told that only men did surgery. She became an anesthesiologist, present at many births but never the doctor in charge.

Apgar saw that "delivery room doctors focused on mothers and paid little attention to babies. Those who were small and struggling were often left to die" (Beck, 2009, p. D1). To save those young lives, Apgar developed a simple rating scale of five vital signs—color, heart rate, cry, muscle tone, and breathing. Nurses could use the scale and sound the alarm immediately if the score was 6 or lower.

Since 1950, birth attendants worldwide have used the Apgar (often using the name as an acronym: Appearance, Pulse, Grimace, Activity, and Respiration) at one minute and again at five minutes after birth, assigning each vital sign a score.

A study comparing Apgar scores in 23 nations found that the ratings of birth attendants were influenced by their culture: In some nations, 97 percent of newborns scored 9 or 10, whereas in other nations only 73 percent had such scores. Whether attendants tended to rate high or low did not correlate with quality of obstetrics. However, in every nation, an Apgar below 7 always indicated risk (Siddiqui et al., 2017).

## Medical Assistance at Birth

The specifics of birth depend on the fetus, the mother, the birth attendant, the birthplace, and the culture. (See Opposing Perspectives on page 101.)

## Surgery

Fifty years ago, in developed nations, hospitals banned midwives, but now many hospitals allow certified midwives to deliver babies. Midwife births have lower

Eliot Elisofon/The LIFE Picture Collection/Getty Images

# The Apgar

Just moments after birth, babies are administered their very first test. The APGAR score is an assessment tool used by doctors and nurses to determine whether a newborn requires any medical intervention. It tests five specific criteria of health, and the medical professional assigns a score of 0, 1, or 2 for each category. A perfect score of 10 is rare—most babies will show some minor deficits at the 1-minute mark, and many will still lose points at the 5-minute mark.

## GRIMACE RESPONSE/REFLEXES

(2) Healthy babies indicate their displeasure when their airways are suctioned—they will grimace, pull away, cough, or sneeze.

(1) Baby grimaces during suctioning.

(0) Baby shows no response to being suctioned and requires immediate medical attention.

## RESPIRATION

(2) A good, strong cry indicates a normal breathing rate.

(1) Baby has a weak cry or whimper, or slow/irregular breathing.

(0) Baby is not breathing and requires immediate medical intervention.

## PULSE

(2) A pulse of 100 or more beats per minute is healthy for a newborn.

(1) Baby's pulse is less than 100 beats per minute.

(0) Baby has no heartbeat and requires immediate medical attention.

## APPEARANCE/COLOR

(2) Body and extremities show good color, with pink undertones indicating good circulation.

(1) Baby has some blueness in the palms and soles of the feet. Many babies exhibit some blueness at both the 1- and 5-minute marks; most warm up soon after.

(0) Baby's entire body is blue, grey, or very pale and requires immediate medical intervention.

## ACTIVITY AND MUSCLE TONE

(2) Baby exhibits active motion of arms, legs, and body.

(1) Baby shows some movement of arms and legs.

(0) Baby is limp and motionless and requires immediate medical attention.

## REFLEXES IN INFANTS

Never underestimate the power of a reflex. For developmentalists, newborn reflexes are mechanisms for survival, indicators of brain maturation, and vestiges of evolutionary history. For parents, they are mostly delightful and sometimes amazing.

**THE SUCKING REFLEX** A newborn, just a few minutes old, demonstrates that he is ready to nurse by sucking on a doctor's finger.

**THE GRASPING REFLEX** When the doctor places a finger on the palm of a healthy infant, he or she will grasp so tightly that the baby's legs can dangle.

**THE STEP REFLEX** A 1-day-old girl steps eagerly forward on legs too tiny to support her body.

Sekundator/Shutterstock.com; Astier/BSIP/Science Source; Petit Format/Science Source; Jennie Woodcock; Reflections Photolibrary/Corbis Documentary/Getty Images

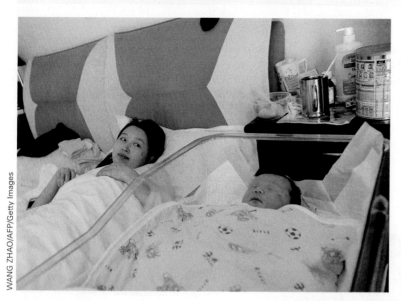

WANG ZHAO/AFP/Getty Images

**Pick Up Your Baby!** Probably she can't. In this maternity ward in Beijing, China, most patients are recovering from cesarean sections, making it difficult to cradle, breast-feed, or carry a newborn until the incision heals.

**cesarean section (c-section)** A surgical birth in which incisions through the mother's abdomen and uterus allow the fetus to be removed quickly instead of being delivered through the vagina. (Also called simply *section*.)

**◑ Especially for Conservatives and Liberals** Do people's attitudes about medical intervention at birth reflect their attitudes about medicine at other points in their life span, in such areas as assisted reproductive technology (ART), immunization, and life support? (see response, page 117)

rates of various complications and interventions than physician births, in part because midwives emphasize breathing, massage, and social support (Bodner-Adler et al., 2017; Raipuria et al., 2018; Renfrew et al., 2014).

Nonetheless, most U.S. births are attended by physicians. They are the only ones allowed to perform certain medical measures, including **cesarean sections (c-sections),** when the fetus is removed though incision in the mother's abdomen instead of being pushed by contractions through the vagina.

C-sections were once rare, a last-ditch effort to save a new life when the mother was dying and vaginal birth was impossible. Now, with much better anesthesia and fetal monitoring, more than one birth in five worldwide (21 percent in 2015, compared to 12 percent in 2000) is a c-section (Boerma et al., 2018).

Cesareans are medically indicated for about 10 percent of births. Multiple births (twins or more), breech births (fetus is not positioned head down), prior c-section, long active labor (more than 24 hours), a narrow pelvis, a large fetus, and advanced maternal age are all conditions that suggest surgery. However, none of these *requires* a c-section.

For instance, a large study of all births (78,880) in the state of Washington focused on the relationship between age and various complications. Sixty percent of new mothers aged 50 or older delivered via c-section; 40 percent delivered vaginally (Richards et al., 2016).

Public health experts are troubled by increases in c-sections in the past decade and by international disparities. Too few (4 percent) cesareans are performed in central Africa, including about 1 percent in South Sudan, where childbirth is still a leading cause of death. Too many occur in the Caribbean and Latin America (44 percent), with the highest of all in the Dominican Republic (58 percent) (Boerma et al., 2018).

Nations with very low cesarean rates also have high numbers of childbirth deaths, but nations with high cesarean rates are not necessarily healthier. In the United States, the cesarean rate was 32 percent in 2018 (Martin et al., 2019).

Cesareans have immediate advantages for hospitals (easier to schedule, quicker, and more expensive than vaginal deliveries) and for women (advance planning, quick birth). Disadvantages appear later.

After a c-section, breast-feeding is harder and medical complications more likely. Babies born via c-section are more likely to develop asthma or become obese as children (Chu et al., 2017; Mueller et al., 2017). One reason: Vaginal deliveries provide newborns with beneficial microbiomes (Wallis, 2014).

---

**WHAT HAVE YOU LEARNED?**

1. What is the typical birth process?

2. Who was Virginia Apgar and what did she do?

3. What are the immediate and long-term results of a cesarean birth?

4. Why do cesarean rates vary internationally?

5. What are the advantages and disadvantages of a hospital birth versus a home birth?

## Interventions in the Birth Process

As you just read, some nations seem to have too few cesareans and others too many. International variations are also evident in drugs to reduce pain, or to start or speed labor.

Particular concern has focused on two aspects of pain relief. First, in developed nations, many hospital births include prescription of opioids, which can become addictive. Second, more than half of all hospital births in the United States include an *epidural*, which is an injection in the spine to stop sensation in the lower body while allowing the birthing woman to be awake. Opioids and epidurals increase the rate of cesarean sections and decrease the rate of breast-feeding (Kjerulff, 2014; Mahomed et al., 2019; Mourad et al., 2019).

Another frequent intervention is the injection of Pitocin, a synthetic version of the hormone *oxytocin*, to start or speed up labor contractions. This hormone is produced naturally to start labor, promote breast-feeding, and encourage infant care. Pitocin correlates with cesarean births and other complications (Grivell et al., 2012; Mikolajczyk et al., 2016).

Someone who has never given birth might conclude that birth should be allowed to proceed without intervention. However, many laboring women and attending professionals want to ease the pain and avoid the risks. Those are reasonable goals, much more possible today than a few decades ago. In 1950, in the world, birth led to death five times more often than it does today. The difference is primarily medical intervention.

I saw this with my daughter. Remember that she was admitted to the hospital because a sonogram revealed that the amniotic fluid was low. That could harm the fetus, a problem that could not have been detected a few decades ago. To avert the problem, the midwife advised that birth should be soon, and she prescribed

Pitocin. After four hours of hard labor, my daughter requested an epidural.

The answer: "You can have an epidural, but the fetal position means that if you can't push, you might need a cesarean."

"No epidural," my daughter responded. She had listened to other women, and her birth plan said no surgery.

Yet, hearing about someone else's experience is not the best way to decide about medical care. Further, correlation is not causation. Does intervention (drugs, surgery, and so on) cause complications, or is it the other way around, with complications causing the intervention? Many doctors believe that concerns about harm to the fetus are considered "premature" when induction is medically indicated (Lønfeldt et al., 2018).

However, the data raised troubling questions. A study of 750,000 births in the United States divided hospitals into three categories—low, average, and high quality. Compared to high-quality hospitals, low-quality hospitals had five times more complications after a cesarean (20 percent versus 4 percent) and twice as many after a vaginal birth (23 versus 11 percent) (Glance et al., 2014). Is hospital quality the issue, not intervention?

Further, intervention rates vary more by doctor, region, and nation than by medical condition. Are some doctors too hasty or are some doctors are too slow to intervene?

In the United States, births are more common during weekdays than on nights and weekends because of more c-sections and Pitocin (Fischetti & Armstrong, 2017). Does that indicate better care or too much intervention? Is birth a natural process that should be left alone or a medical event that requires doctors, technology, and hospitals?

## Problems and Solutions

The early days of life place the future person on the path toward health and success—or not. Problems can begin before conception, if the sperm, the ovum, or the uterus was affected by the parents' health. Indeed, the grandmother's health when the mother and father were born may affect the grandchild, although this epigenetic effect is not proven to the satisfaction of most scientists (Arshad et al., 2017).

Fortunately, healthy newborns are the norm, not the exception. However, if something is amiss, it is often part of a sequence that may become overwhelming (Rossignol et al., 2014).

### Risk Analysis

Life requires risks: We routinely decide which chances to take and how to minimize harm. For example, we know the danger as well as the benefits of

**cerebral palsy** A disorder that results from damage to the brain's motor centers. People with cerebral palsy have difficulty with muscle control, so their speech and/or body movements are impaired.

**anoxia** A lack of oxygen that, if prolonged, can cause brain damage or death.

**teratogen** An agent or condition, including viruses, drugs, and chemicals, that can impair prenatal development and result in birth defects or even death.

**behavioral teratogens** Agents and conditions that can harm the prenatal brain, impairing the future child's intellectual and emotional functioning.

crossing the street, so we hold the hands of young children, teaching them how to safely cross.

That is a small illustration of risk analysis. Risks need to be taken, but they also need to be controlled. Pregnancy and birth entail many risks, but the outcome—a new baby—seems well worth it. The goal is to avoid problems and to mitigate damage of those that occur. Development is lifelong: Single events rarely cause problems, but a cascade often does.

A dramatic example is **cerebral palsy** (a condition marked by difficulties with movement. Cerebral palsy was once thought to be caused solely by birth procedures (excessive medication, slow breech birth, or misused forceps). However, it now seems that cerebral palsy begins with genetic sensitivity, prenatal insults, and maternal infection (Mann et al., 2009) and is exacerbated by insufficient oxygen to the fetal brain at birth.

This lack of oxygen is called **anoxia.** Contractions during labor may affect the fetal heart rate, indicating a moment of anoxia, but recovery occurs when the contraction is over. Similarly, anoxia often occurs for a second or two during birth, indicated by a slower fetal heart rate, with no harm done. Because their births take longer, twins and breech births are more likely to experience anoxia.

To prevent prolonged anoxia, the fetal heart rate is monitored during labor. If anoxia lasts too long, that can harm the fetus. To prevent prolonged anoxia, a cesarean may be indicated. After birth, if the Apgar indicates slow breathing or bluish color, immediate oxygen is given.

How long anoxia can continue without harming the brain depends on genes, birthweight, gestational age, drugs in the bloodstream (either taken by the mother before birth or given by the doctor during birth), and many other factors. Thus, anoxia is part of a cascade that may cause cerebral palsy. Almost every other birth complication is also the result of many factors.

## Harmful Substances

Monthly, even weekly, scientists discover another **teratogen,** which is anything—drugs, viruses, pollutants, malnutrition, stress, and more—that increases the risk of prenatal abnormalities and birth complications.

But don't be like one of my students, who said that now that she knew all the things that can go wrong, she never wants a baby. As I told her, problems can be avoided, and damage can be remedied. Pregnancy is not a dangerous period to be feared; it is a natural process to be protected.

## Visible and Invisible Damage

People once thought that the placenta protected the fetus against every insult. Then, about six decades ago, rubella and thalidomide (both mentioned in Chapter 1) proved otherwise.

Since then, it was apparent that teratogens caused birth defects—such as blindness from rubella or missing limbs from thalidomide—but few realized that teratogens might cause no visible harm but instead make a child hyperactive, antisocial, or intellectually disabled. Those **behavioral teratogens** are common, and, over the life span, more disabling than teratogens that do not affect the brain.

## The Critical Time

Timing is crucial. Some teratogens cause damage only during a *critical period*, which may occur before a woman knows she is pregnant (see **Figure 4.3**). [**Developmental**

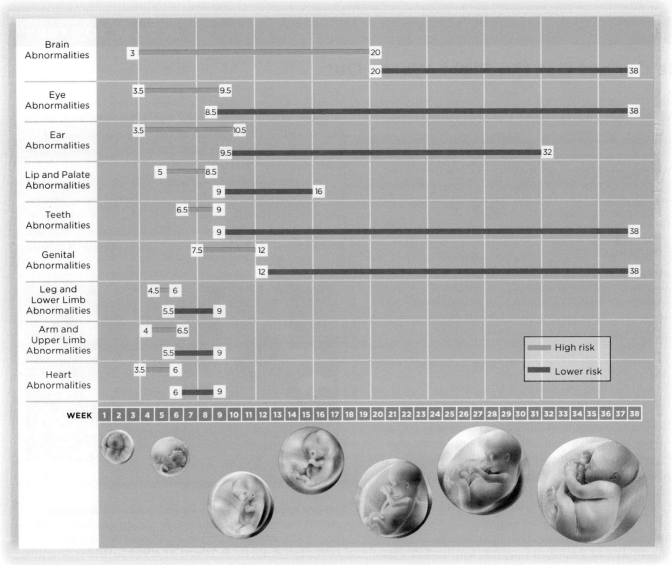

**FIGURE 4.3**

**One More Reason to Plan a Pregnancy** The embryonic period, before a woman knows she is pregnant, is the most sensitive time for causing structural birth defects. However, at no time during pregnancy is the fetus completely safe from harm. Individual differences in susceptibility to teratogens may be caused by a fetus's genetic makeup or peculiarities of the mother, including the effectiveness of her placenta or her overall health. The dose and timing of the exposure are also important.

**Observation Quiz** What part of the embryo and fetus has the longest period of vulnerability? What has the shortest? (see answer, page 117) ↑

**Link:** Critical and sensitive periods are described in Chapter 1.] Consequently, women need to avoid drugs, supplement a balanced diet with folic acid and iron, update their immunizations, and gain or lose weight if needed *before* pregnancy occurs.

The first days and weeks after conception (the germinal and embryonic periods) are critical for body formation, but behavioral teratogens affect the fetus at any time. Cigarettes, for instance, are harmful when the mother smokes before or during pregnancy, but quitting by mid-pregnancy may allow the fetus to grow normally (Kvalvik et al., 2017). Similarly, a longitudinal study of 7-year-olds who were exposed to alcohol prenatally found surprising results: Although alcohol

# He Cannot Get the Right Words Out

Many children have difficulties in thinking and behavior that *could* be connected to teratogens. One of my students wrote:

> I was nine years old when my mother announced she was pregnant. I was the one who was most excited. . . . My mother was a heavy smoker, Colt 45 beer drinker and a strong caffeine coffee drinker.
>
> One day my mother was sitting at the dining room table smoking cigarettes one after the other. I asked "Isn't smoking bad for the baby?"
>
> She made a face and said "Yes, so what?"
>
> I said "So why are you doing it?"
>
> She said, "I don't know.". . .
>
> During this time I was in the fifth grade and we saw a film about birth defects. My biggest fear was that my mother was going to give birth to a fetal alcohol syndrome (FAS) infant. . . . My baby brother was born right on schedule. The doctors claimed a healthy newborn. . . . Once I heard healthy, I thought everything was going to be fine. I was wrong, then again I was just a child. . . .
>
> My baby brother never showed any interest in toys . . . he just cannot get the right words out of his mouth . . . he has no common sense . . .
>
> Why hurt those who cannot defend themselves?
>
> *[J., personal communication]*

As you remember from Chapter 1, one case is not proof. J. blames her mother, but genetic risks, inadequate prenatal care, and troubling postnatal experiences may be part of her brother's sorry cascade. Moreover, her mother was of low SES (itself a correlate of harm) and was poorly nourished. Boys and later-born children are more vulnerable, which may explain why J. was a good student, unlike her brother.

It is not unusual for a newborn to seem to have escaped a teratogen, yet have a damaged brain. The long reach of a seemingly harmless teratogen is evident in the *Zika virus* (ZIKV), caused by the bite of an infected mosquito.

ZIKV was not recognized until 2015, when an epidemic led to dozens of Brazilian newborns with abnormally small brains (*microcephaly*). That epidemic spread to several nations and led to research suggesting that ZIKV has infected humans for hundreds of years, undetected.

Only the most severely affected ZIKV infants have small heads. Many appear typical but have impaired vision, hearing, and emotions (Rosen, 2016; van den Pol, 2017). When pregnant monkeys were infected with Zika, brain patterns suggested schizophrenia, depression, and Alzheimer's disease (Christian et al., 2018; Waldorf et al., 2018).

Schneyder Mendoza/European Pressphoto Agency/Cúcuta/Norte de Santander/Colombia/Newscom

**No One Knows** Dozens of newborns in northern Brazil alerted doctors that the Zika virus could cause microcephaly. More is now known: Zika brain damage is sometimes invisible, and newborns in North, Central, and South America are affected. However, long-term damage is still unknown. No wonder these pregnant women in a clinic in Colombia are worried, especially Sandra Ovallos (*middle*), who recently had a fever and rash.

affects body structures early in pregnancy, it is the second half of pregnancy when binge drinking is an especially potent behavioral teratogen (Niclasen et al., 2014).

Timing may be important in another way. When pregnancy occurs soon after a previous pregnancy, risk increases. For example, one study found that second-born children are twice as likely to have autism spectrum disorder if they are born within a year of the first-born child (Cheslack-Postava et al., 2011).

## How Much Is Too Much?

A second factor that affects the harm from teratogens is the dose and/or frequency of exposure. Many teratogens have a **threshold effect;** they are virtually harmless until exposure reaches a certain level, and then they "cross the threshold" to damage the fetus.

**threshold effect** In prenatal development, when a teratogen is relatively harmless in small doses but becomes harmful once exposure reaches a certain level (the threshold).

Is there a safe dose or timing for psychoactive drugs? Research has focused on alcohol, a drug ingested by most young women in many nations. Early in pregnancy, a woman's heavy drinking can cause **fetal alcohol syndrome (FAS)**, which distorts the facial features of a child (especially the eyes, ears, and upper lip). Later in pregnancy, behavior can be affected; *fetal alcohol effects (FAE)* occur, not FAS (Hoyme et al., 2016).

Currently, pregnant women are advised to avoid all alcohol, but many women in France (between 12 and 63 percent, depending on specifics of the research) do not heed that message (Dumas et al., 2014). Most of their babies seem fine. Should all women who *might* become pregnant refuse a legal substance that most men use routinely? Wise? Probably. Necessary? Maybe not.

## Innate Vulnerability

Genes are a third factor that influences the effects of teratogens. When a woman carrying dizygotic twins drinks alcohol, for example, the twins' blood alcohol levels are equal, yet one twin may be more severely affected because of different alleles for the enzyme that metabolizes alcohol (Hemingway et al., 2019). Similar differential susceptibility occurs for many teratogens (McCarthy & Eberhart, 2014).

Although the links from genes to teratogens to damage are sometimes difficult to verify, two examples of genetic susceptibility are proven. First, male fetuses are more often spontaneously aborted, stillborn, or harmed by teratogens than are female fetuses. The male–female hazard rate differs from one teratogen to another (Lewis & Kestler, 2012).

Second, one maternal allele reduces folic acid, and that deficit can produce *neural-tube defects*—either *spina bifida*, in which the tail of the spine is not enclosed properly (enclosure normally occurs at about week 7), or *anencephaly*, when part of the brain is missing. Neural-tube defects are more common in certain ethnic groups (e.g., Irish, English, and Egyptian), but even those with the gene usually have healthy babies.

In one study (R. Smith et al., 2011), about half of a group of 550 mothers of a child with a neural-tube disorder (and hence genetically at risk) took folic acid supplements. The other half ate normally. The rate of newborns with neural-tube defects was 1 in 250 among the supplemented mothers and 13 in 300 in the non-supplemented ones, proof that folic acid helps. But, note that almost 96 percent of the women who were at genetic risk and did *not* take supplements had healthy babies. Also, one supplemented woman bore a second child with a neural-tube defect. Why? Was the dose too low, or did she skip taking the pills, or was some other genetic risk the problem?

---

📊 **DATA CONNECTIONS: Teratogens** examines the effects of various teratogens and the preventive measures that reduce their risk to a developing fetus. 📚 **LaunchPad.**

---

## Prenatal Diagnosis

Early prenatal care has many benefits: Women learn what to eat, what to do, and what to avoid. Some serious conditions, syphilis and HIV among them, can be diagnosed and treated in the first prenatal months before they harm the fetus.

Tests of blood, urine, fetal heart rate, and ultrasound reassure parents, facilitating the crucial parent–child bond. It is now possible to know the sex of the fetus within the first few months. This allows parents to name the fetus, bonding with that small individual long before birth.

**fetal alcohol syndrome (FAS)** A cluster of birth defects, including abnormal facial characteristics, slow physical growth, and reduced intellectual ability, that may occur in the fetus of a woman who drinks alcohol while pregnant.

**Smoke-Free Babies** Posters such as this one have had an impact. Smoking among adults is only half of what it was 30 years ago. One-third of women smokers quit when they know they are pregnant, while the other two-thirds cut their smoking in half. Unfortunately, the heaviest smokers are least likely to quit—they need more than posters to motivate them to break the habit.

🔵 **Especially For Future Doctors and Nurses** How can medical professionals explain tests without causing anxiety? (see answer, page 117).

In general, early care protects fetal growth, connects women to their future child, makes birth easier, and renders parents better able to cope. When complications (such as twins, gestational diabetes, and infections) arise, early recognition increases the chance of a healthy birth.

Unfortunately, however, about 20 percent of early pregnancy tests *increase* anxiety instead of reducing it. For instance, the level of alpha-fetoprotein (AFP) may be too high or too low, or ultrasound may indicate multiple fetuses, abnormal growth, Down syndrome, or a mother's narrow pelvis. Many such warnings are **false positives;** that is, they falsely suggest a problem that does not exist. On the other hand, advice about fetal growth can alert women to avoid underweight newborns, a serious problem.

**false positive** The result of a laboratory test that reports something as true when in fact it is not true. This can occur for pregnancy tests, when a woman might not be pregnant even though the test says she is, or during pregnancy, when a problem is reported that actually does not exist.

## Safe During Pregnancy?

As explained in Chapter 1, the scientific method is designed to be cautious. It takes years—for replication, for alternate designs, and for exploration of conflicting hypotheses—to reach sound conclusions. Scientists, governments, and the internet disagree about what is safe for pregnant women, as you will now see.

### Which Drugs Are Harmless?

Many women assume that herbal medicines or over-the-counter drugs are safe. Not so. As pediatrics professor Allen Mitchell explains, "Many over-the-counter drugs were grandfathered in with no studies of their possible effects during pregnancy" (quoted in Brody, 2013, p. D5). ("Grandfathered" means that if they were legal in days past, they remain legal—no testing needed.) And, many herbal products are not classed as drugs and hence are not studied and regulated.

To learn which medications are safe, women consult the internet. However, 235 medications were listed as safe on at least one of 25 Web sites but TERSIS (a group of expert teratologists who analyze drug safety) had declared only 60 (25 percent) of them safe, and the others had insufficient evidence to confirm safety (Peters et al., 2013). On those 25 sites, some drugs declared safe on one site were on the danger list of another.

### Pesticides

No biologist doubts that pesticides harm frogs, fish, and bees, but the pesticide industry insists that careful use (e.g., spraying plants, not workers) benefits people, in the form of fresh, low-cost food. That certain benefit may outweigh any possible risk.

Developmentalists, however, fear that pregnant women who breathe or ingest these toxins will bear brain-damaged babies (Heyer & Meredith, 2017). One scientist said, "Pesticides were designed to be neurotoxic. Why should we be surprised if they cause neurotoxicity?" (Lanphear, quoted in Mascarelli, 2013, p. 741).

Since 2000, the United States removed one pesticide, *chlorpyrifos*, from household use (it had been used to kill roaches and ants). It was banned from U.S. agriculture in the last month of the Obama administration but reinstated in the first year of the Trump administration—to the distress of many scientists and doctors (Lipton, 2017; Rauh, 2018).

Is that a developmental issue, an economic issue, or a political issue? Chlorpyrifos is widely used in other nations, in homes as well as farms, and is very profitable.

Analysis of umbilical cord blood finds that fetuses exposed to chlorpyrifos become children with lower IQs and more behavior problems than other children (Horton et al., 2012). However, the companies that sell chlorpyrifos argue that confounding factors need to be considered (Mascarelli, 2013).

What might those confounding factors be? For one thing, pregnant women who use roach spray are more likely to live in stressful, inner-city neighborhoods, a context that reduces children's intelligence whether pesticides are used or not. Likewise, parents who harvest sprayed crops are often migrants who move from place to place and fear deportation. Moving, and fear, disrupts children's schooling.

Could factors such as these be a third variable that explains the correlation between pregnant women exposed to pesticides and their children's education? Further, even if chlorpyrifos is a teratogen, does that outweigh the economic benefits for farmers, chemical companies, and parents who need to buy fruits and vegetables? Risk analysis is needed.

## Food

Pregnant women hear conflicting advice about what to eat and how much to eat. For example, the U.S. government advises them to eat less fish, but the United Kingdom advises them to eat more fish. The reason for these opposite messages is that fish contains mercury (a teratogen) but also DHA (an omega-3 fatty acid that promotes brain development) (Lando & Lo, 2014).

Should governments protect the unborn, or should each woman do her own risk analysis to judge fish, fruits, and vegetables? Some will choose organic produce, while others will choose the cheapest products. Should pregnant women be allowed to take that risk? Should chemical companies decide what to sell, to whom?

To make all of this more difficult, stress and anxiety affect the fetus, yet pregnancy itself increases fear (Rubertsson et al., 2014). Prospective parents want clear, immediate answers about diet, habits, and circumstances. Scientists take years to find them; laws take even longer. We do know, at least, that women should not eat too little, as now explained.

**No More Pesticides** Carlos Candelario, shown here at age 9 months, was born without limbs, a birth defect that occurred when his mother (Francisca, show here) and father (Abraham) worked in the Florida fields. Since his birth in 2004, laws prohibit spraying pesticides while people pick fruit and vegetables, but developmentalists worry about the effect of the residue on developing brains.

## Low Birthweight: Causes and Consequences

The World Health Organization defines **low birthweight (LBW)** as under 2,500 grams (5 ½ pounds). LBW babies are further grouped into **very low birthweight (VLBW)**, under 1,500 grams (3 pounds, 5 ounces), and **extremely low birthweight (ELBW)**, under 1,000 grams (2 pounds, 3 ounces).

About 8 percent of babies born in the United States are low birthweight, a rate similar to Brazil, Greece, and Lebanon. About 50 nations have fewer low-birthweight newborns than the United States, with the lowest rate of all in Sweden (less than 4 percent). About 100 nations are worse than the United States, with several (including Bangladesh, Nepal, and Mozambique) having rates of 20 percent or more (Blencowe et al., 2019).

It would be better for everyone—mother, father, baby, and society—if all newborns were in the womb for at least 36 weeks and weighed more than 2,500 grams (5½ pounds). (Usually, this text gives pounds before grams. But hospitals worldwide report birthweight using the metric system, so grams precede pounds and ounces here.) Being underweight at birth has lifelong consequences, including heart disease, less education, and more obesity, and since such marked variability occurs, we need to understand this better.

## Too Soon or Too Small

Babies born **preterm** (two or more weeks early; no longer called *premature*) are often LBW, because fetal weight normally doubles in the last trimester of pregnancy, with 900 grams (about 2 pounds) of that gain occurring in the final three

**low birthweight (LBW)** A body weight at birth of less than 2,500 grams (5½ pounds).

**very low birthweight (VLBW)** A body weight at birth of less than 1,500 grams (3 pounds, 5 ounces).

**extremely low birthweight (ELBW)** A body weight at birth of less than 1,000 grams (2 pounds, 3 ounces).

**preterm** A birth that occurs two or more weeks before the full 38 weeks of the typical pregnancy—that is, at 36 or fewer weeks after conception.

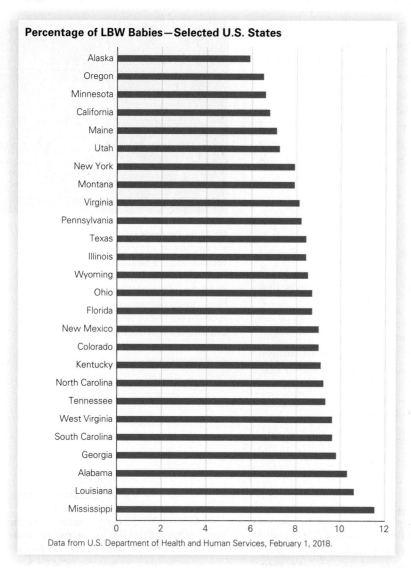

**Percentage of LBW Babies—Selected U.S. States**

Data from U.S. Department of Health and Human Services, February 1, 2018.

**FIGURE 4.4**

**Where Were You Born?** Rates of low birthweight vary by nation, from about 4 to 20 percent, and, as you see here, within nations. Why? Poverty is a correlate—is it also a cause?

**small for gestational age (SGA)** A term for a baby whose birthweight is significantly lower than expected, given the time since conception. For example, a 5-pound (2,265-gram) newborn is considered SGA if born on time but not SGA if born two months early. (Also called *small-for-dates*.)

**immigrant paradox** The surprising, paradoxical fact that low-SES immigrant women tend to have fewer birth complications than native-born peers with higher incomes.

weeks. As already mentioned, every week past week 22 adds weight and maturation.

Other LBW babies have gained weight slowly throughout pregnancy and are *small-for-dates*, or **small for gestational age (SGA).** A full-term baby weighing only 2,600 grams and a 30-week-old fetus weighing only 1,000 grams are both SGA, even though the first is not technically low birthweight. Low birthweight varies dramatically from nation to nation, and, within the United States, from county to county as both a cause and a predictor of lifelong poverty (Robertson & O'Brien, 2018) (see **Figure 4.4**).

In most nations, malnutrition is the most common reason for slow fetal growth. Women who begin pregnancy underweight, who eat poorly during pregnancy, or who gain less than 3 pounds (1.3 kilograms) per month in the last six months often have underweight infants. This problem is particularly common in Africa and South Asia, but it can occur in developed nations as well.

The second common reason, particularly in developed nations, is drug use. Almost every psychoactive drug—including legal ones such as cigarettes and alcohol—reduces nutrition and birthweight.

A third reason is multiple births. Twins gain weight more slowly in pregnancy and are born, on average, three weeks early. As you remember from Chapter 3, multiple births are more common in IVF, with some hopeful parents choosing to implant several blastocysts—against medical advice.

Unfortunately, many risk factors tend to occur together. For example, undernourished mothers often live in urban neighborhoods where pollution is high—another risk factor (Erickson et al., 2016). Women in rural areas have yet another cascade of risks—distance from prenatal care, unwanted pregnancies, and exposure to pesticides (American College of Obstetricians and Gynecologists, 2011).

## What About the Father?

The causes of low birthweight rightly focus on the pregnant woman. However, "Fathers' attitudes regarding the pregnancy, fathers' behaviors during the prenatal period, and the relationship between fathers and mothers . . . influence risk for adverse birth outcomes" (Misra et al., 2010, p. 99).

Indeed, everyone who affects a pregnant woman also affects a fetus. Her mother, her boss, her mother-in-law, her doctor, and especially her partner can add to her stress, or reduce it. Thus, it is not surprising that unintended pregnancies increase the incidence of low birthweight and birth defects, a link strongest in women of low income (Finer & Zolna, 2016). Obviously, intentions are in the mind, not in the body, and are affected by the father and the community, influencing a woman's nutrition and drug use.

Evidence for this is in the **immigrant paradox.** As already mentioned, low SES correlates with low birthweight, especially in the United States (Martinson & Reichman, 2016). Many immigrants have difficulty with high school, college, and employment; hence their socioeconomic status is low. Thus, one might imagine that their babies are underweight. However, the opposite is true.

Babies born to immigrants tend to be heavier and healthier than newborns of native-born women of the same SES and ethnicity (Marks et al., 2014). This is true not only when women from Latin America are compared to Hispanic women whose families have lived in the United States for generations, but also when women born in the Caribbean, Africa, eastern Europe, and Asia are compared to U.S.-born women with similar genes.

Why? One hypothesis is that immigrant fathers and communities cherish pregnant women, keeping them drug-free and well-fed, appreciated and healthy, buffering the stress of poverty (Luecken et al., 2013). Ironically, in families of the same groups who lived in the United States for longer periods, community protection decreases and prenatal as well as postnatal development suffers (Fox et al., 2018).

## Consequences of Low Birthweight

Every developmental milestone—smiling, holding a bottle, walking, talking—is delayed in low-birthweight infants, and rates of cognitive, visual, and hearing impairments increase. As toddlers, LBW children cry often, pay attention less, and disobey more (Aarnoudse-Moens et al., 2009; Stolt et al., 2014).

Problems continue, especially if birthweight was very low. Children who were extremely SGA or preterm tend to have neurological problems in middle childhood, including smaller brain volume, lower IQ, and behavioral difficulties (Clark et al., 2013; Howe et al., 2016; Hutchinson et al., 2013). Even in adulthood, risks persist, with higher rates of diabetes, obesity, heart disease, and depression (Lyall et al., 2016).

However, remember plasticity. By age 4, some ELBW infants exhibit typical brain development, especially if they had no medical complications and their mother was well educated. For some adults, early birth may no longer matter. This was true for those with good experiences, including happy marriages, even when the adult weighed less than 3 pounds at birth (R. Xu et al., 2019).

## International Comparisons

As you remember from Chapter 1, scientists collect empirical data and then draw conclusions based on facts. Regarding low birthweight, the facts are clear; the conclusions are not. No less than six hypotheses might explain a puzzling fact: Low birthweight is less common in most nations than it was, with a worldwide average of 14.6 percent in 2015 compared to 17.5 percent in 2000. However, it is increasing in some nations—the United States among them. We begin with what is known.

In some northern European nations, only 4 percent of newborns weigh under 2,500 grams; in several South Asian and African nations, more than 20 percent do. Two conclusions are proven: First, fewer pregnant women are severely malnourished, so their fetuses weight more. Because babies have more body fat, they are more likely to survive the first month of life, when 36 per thousand babies died in 1990, and only 19 per thousand in 2017 (World Bank, 2018).

Second, national goals matter. In China, Cuba, and Chile low birthweight has plummeted since 2000 because prenatal care has become a national priority. That is one conclusion of a study provocatively titled *Low birth weight outcomes: Why better in Cuba than Alabama?* (Neggers & Crowe, 2013).

In other nations, the LBW rate is rising. Many of those nations are in sub-Saharan Africa, and their rise is troubling but not puzzling: Global warming, HIV/AIDS, food shortages, and civil wars are all worse problems in that part of the world than elsewhere.

**Not the Fetus, the Mother!** Alicia Beltran, age 28, shown here pregnant with her first child, confided at her initial prenatal visit that she had been addicted to a painkiller but was now clean (later confirmed by a lab test). She refused a prescription to keep her away from illegal drugs. But that led to the police taking her to court in handcuffs and shackles when she was 14 weeks pregnant. She was not represented nor allowed to defend herself, but a state-appointed lawyer for the fetus argued that she should be detained. After more than two months in involuntary confinement, a nonprofit lawyer got her released. More than a year later, a judge finally considered her petition that her constitutional rights had been violated but dismissed the case because the state had dropped the charges.

DARREN HAUCK/The New York Times/Redux

Watch **VIDEO: Low Birthweight in India,** which discusses the causes of LBW among babies in India.

**THINK CRITICALLY:** Food scarcity, drug use, and unmarried parenthood have all been suggested as reasons for the LBW rate in the United States. Which is it—or are there other factors?

**Especially for Judges and Juries**
How much protection, if any, should the legal system provide for fetuses? Should women with alcohol use disorder who are pregnant be jailed to prevent them from drinking? What about people who enable them to drink, such as their partners, their parents, bar owners, and bartenders? (see response, page 117)

However, in other nations, an increasing rate of LBW is unexpected. The LBW rate in the United States fell throughout most of the twentieth century, reaching a low of 7.0 percent in 1990. But then it rose, dipping slightly around 2010 but increasing every year since 2012 and reaching 8.28 percent in 2018 (Martin et al., 2019). That is higher than almost every other developed nation.

Added to the puzzle is the belief that several changes in maternal ethnicity, age, and health since 1990 should have *decreased* LBW. For instance, although the rate of LBW among African Americans is higher than the national average (14 percent compared with 8 percent), and although teenagers have smaller babies than do women in their 20s, the birth rate among both groups was much lower in 2018 than in 1990.

Similarly, unintended pregnancies are less common (Finer & Zolna, 2016), and two conditions that produce heavier babies (maternal obesity and diabetes) have increased since 1990. Yet, more underweight babies are born in the United States currently than decades ago. What could the explanation be?

Is prenatal care the crucial variable? Perhaps in some nations, but not in the United States. The rates of women giving birth without prenatal care have decreased, but prenatal care as currently offered does not seem to reduce the occurrence of low birthweight (Krans & Davis, 2012).

Another hypothesis is that multiple births have increased because of fertility measures. However, LBW rates are rising for naturally conceived singletons as well as for IVF twins, and the rate of multiple births has decreased over the past five years, while the LBW rate continues to increase (Martin et al., 2019).

Perhaps the problem is nutrition. The U.S. Department of Agriculture (Coleman-Jensen et al., 2017) reported an increase in the rate of *food insecurity* (measured by skipped meals, use of food stamps, and outright hunger) between the first seven years of the twenty-first century and the next seven, from about 11 percent to about 15 percent (see **Figure 4.5**).

The group most likely to be food insecure are young mothers. Some undereat so that their children have food—unaware that they are harming a future child. Their undernourishment adds stress to their children, who become stressed in return, affecting everyone—including weight gain of a future baby (King, 2018).

**FIGURE 4.5**

**And Recovery?** As you can see, all family types were affected by the Great Recession that began in 2007—especially single fathers, who were most likely to lose their jobs and not know how to get food stamps. But why are children of single mothers hungry more often than children of single fathers and three times as often as children of married parents? The data show correlation; researchers do not agree about causes.

 **Observation Quiz** Is the gap between single mothers and single fathers increasing or decreasing? (see answer, page 117) ↑

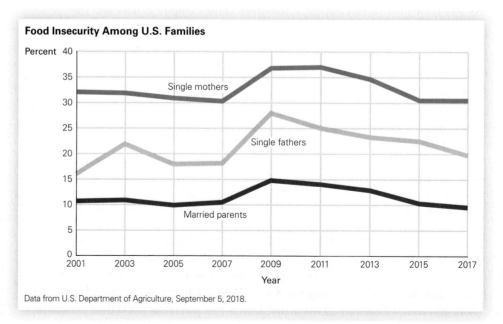

Data from U.S. Department of Agriculture, September 5, 2018.

A related possibility is lack of health care among the poorest Americans, especially young adults. Since untreated infections and chronic illness correlate with LBW, health care may be an explanation.

A fifth possible culprit is drug use, more common among young women in the United States than in most other nations (Natarajan, 2017). In the United States, the birth rate is highest among 20- to 24-year-olds, and so is drug use—in that age group, 11 percent smoke during pregnancy (Drake et al., 2018).

Looking beyond the United States, some trends are ominous. In recent years, low birthweight has decreased markedly in Asia, but smoking and drinking among young women are now increasing in those nations.

In Japan, low birthweight was slightly more than 6 percent in 2000 but almost 10 percent in 2015. Smoking and drinking are among the possible culprits, but so are low weight gain during pregnancy, increasing mercury in food, and more births after age 35 (Tamura et al., 2018).

In every hypothesis, we must distinguish correlation from causation. Since low birthweight varies from nation to nation and year to year, obviously forces beyond normal, natural variation are at work. Since LBW correlates with problems throughout life, we need to know more about causes so that we can prevent the consequences. For developing nations, the first steps are obvious—less hunger and better prenatal care. But for developed nations, more science is needed: Many hypotheses need to be explored.

---

**WHAT HAVE YOU LEARNED?**

**1.** How do we know that the placenta does not screen out all harmful substances?

**2.** What factors increase the harm from a teratogen?

**3.** Why is it difficult to be certain that a behavioral teratogen affected a child?

**4.** What is the difference between low, very low, and extremely low birthweight?

**5.** What are the causes and consequences of low birthweight?

**6.** What is puzzling about national and ethnic differences in low birthweight?

---

# The New Family

Humans are social creatures, seeking interaction with their families and their societies. That begins before birth, and it may have a crucial impact on parents and baby after birth.

## The Newborn

Before birth, the fetus already affects their mother by moving, and by hormones that affect hunger, sleep, emotions. The newborn's appearance (big hairless head, tiny feet, and so on) stirs the human heart. Both parents may be enraptured by their scraggly newborns; mothers and their partners may appreciate each other more than ever, for hormonal and practical reasons.

Newborns respond to people, even in the first hours of life (Zeifman, 2013). They listen, stare, cry, stop crying, and cuddle. In the first day or two, a professional might administer the **Brazelton Neonatal Behavioral Assessment Scale (NBAS),** which records 46 behaviors, including 20 reflexes. Watching the NBAS may help parents appreciate and understand their infant (Barlow et al., 2018).

**Brazelton Neonatal Behavioral Assessment Scale (NBAS)** A test that is often administered to newborns; it measures responsiveness and records 46 behaviors, including 20 reflexes.

**reflex** An unlearned, involuntary action or movement in response to a stimulus. A reflex occurs without conscious thought.

Technically, a **reflex** is an involuntary response to a particular stimulus. The strength of reflexes varies, depending on genes, drugs, and health. Three sets of reflexes aid survival:

- *Reflexes that maintain oxygen supply*. The *breathing reflex* begins even before the umbilical cord, with its supply of oxygen, is cut. Additional reflexes that maintain oxygen are reflexive *hiccups* and *sneezes*, as well as *thrashing* (moving the arms and legs about) to escape something that covers the face.
- *Reflexes that maintain constant body temperature*. When infants are cold, they *cry*, *shiver*, and *tuck their legs* close to their bodies. When they are hot, they try to *push away* blankets and then stay still.
- *Reflexes that manage feeding*. The *sucking reflex* causes newborns to suck whatever touches their lips—fingers, toes, blankets, and rattles, as well as nipples of various textures and shapes. In the *rooting reflex*, babies turn their mouths toward anything brushing against their cheeks—a reflexive search for a nipple—and start to suck. *Swallowing* also aids feeding, as does *crying* when the stomach is empty and *spitting up* when too much is swallowed quickly.

**LaunchPad**
macmillan learning

**VIDEO: Newborn Reflexes** shows several infants displaying the reflexes discussed in this section.

Other reflexes promoted survival of the species in ancient times but now they signify healthy brain development. Among them:

- *Babinski reflex*. When a newborn's feet are stroked, the toes fan upward.
- *Stepping reflex*. When newborns are held upright, feet touching a flat surface, they move their legs as if to walk.
- *Swimming reflex*. When held horizontally on their stomachs, newborns stretch out their arms and legs.
- *Palmar grasping reflex*. When something touches newborns' palms, they grip it tightly.
- *Moro reflex*. When someone bangs on the table they are lying on, they fling their arms out and then bring them together on their chests, crying with wide-open eyes.

**postpartum depression** A new mother's feelings of inadequacy and sadness in the days and weeks after giving birth.

These 18 reflexes (in italics), and all the senses, are present at birth. If the baby tested on the Brazelton NBAS were your own, you would be proud and amazed.

## New Mothers

When birth hormones decrease, between 8 and 15 percent of women experience **postpartum depression,** a sense of inadequacy and sadness (called *baby blues* in the mild version and *postpartum psychosis* in the most severe form). That 8 to 15 percent may be an underestimate: Some sources say that for low-SES and adolescent mothers the rate is 25 percent (Kozhimannil & Kim, 2014).

With postpartum depression, baby care (feeding, diapering, bathing) feels very burdensome. The newborn's cry may not compel the mother to carry and nurse her infant. Instead, the mother may have thoughts of neglect or abuse, thoughts so terrifying that she is afraid of herself. She may be overprotective, insisting that no one else care for the baby. This signifies a fearful mother, not a healthy one.

A mother who experiences postpartum depression feels terrible ("the worst time of my life," one said). She usually recovers by the time the baby is 6 months old. Unfortunately, if she does not have help in the early months, her limited interaction with the baby can affect that developing human lifelong, because those early months are crucial for brain development.

Marty Bucella/CartoonStock

"Of course I know what he wants when he cries. He wants you."

The first sign that something is amiss may be euphoria after birth. A new mother may be unable to sleep, stop talking, or eat normally. After that initial high, severe depression may set in, with long-term impact on the child. Postpartum depression may not be evident right away; anxiety and depression symptoms are stronger two or three months after birth (Kozhimannil & Kim, 2014).

Postpartum depression is not due to hormonal changes alone. From a developmental perspective, some causes (such as financial stress) predate pregnancy. Others (such as marital problems) occur during pregnancy; still others correlate with birth itself (especially if the mother is alone and expected a different birth than what actually occurred).

Finally, the baby may be disappointing. One single mother who experienced postpartum depression thought:

> My only problem in life was that I didn't have a baby. On the day I had a baby, I discovered that no, I had other problems. I hadn't any money, I was in debt, the family was fighting about the debt, it was partly my fault . . . and I started to see I wasn't such a good mother as I had thought I would be. I used to think what could be difficult? It's enough for you to love the baby and everything will be fine. This didn't happen because the baby didn't respond. I'm affectionate, I'd come and take her, hug her and the baby didn't like this. She didn't like to be hugged, she didn't like affection.

> [O'Dougherty, 2013, p. 190]

Successful breast-feeding mitigates maternal depression, but while most new mothers try to nurse their newborn, many quit—which increases depression. A supportive family member, friend, midwife, or lactation consultant may hasten recovery.

Fortunately, postpartum depression can be prevented, diagnosed, and treated (O'Hara & McCabe, 2013). To help with diagnosis, consider the questions of the Edinburgh Postnatal Depression scale (see **Table 4.3**).

## New Fathers

Not every depressed mother reduces her baby's development. The research finds that if she manages to respond sensitively to her baby's needs, within a well-functioning, supportive family (with good emotional management, communication, and clear roles and routines) the baby may develop well (Parade et al., 2018). Fathers may be crucial in keeping the family supportive and caring for the baby.

Fathers may experience pregnancy and birth biologically, not just psychologically. Many fathers have symptoms of pregnancy and birth, including weight gain and indigestion during pregnancy and pain during labor (Leavitt, 2009).

Paternal experiences of pregnancy and birth are called **couvade,** expected in some cultures, a normal variation in many, and considered pathological in others (M. Sloan, 2009). A study in India found that couvade was common (Ganapathy, 2014). In the United States, many fathers are intensely involved during prenatal development, birth, and infancy (Brennan et al., 2007; Raeburn, 2014).

Fathers are usually the first responders when the mother experiences postpartum depression; they may be the support that the mother and baby need. But fathers are vulnerable to depression, too, with the same stresses that mothers feel (Gutierrez-Galve et al., 2015). Indeed, sometimes the father experiences more emotional problems than the mother (Bradley & Slade, 2011). Friends and relatives need to help both parents in the first weeks after birth.

Many new fathers not only feel stressed but also do not talk about their mixed emotions. In reality, both partners are affected by pregnancy and birth. Some fathers do not sleep well during pregnancy, and many fear serious problems, or even deaths,

**Mutual Joy** For thousands of years hormones and instincts have propelled fathers and babies to reach out to each other, developing lifelong connections.

**couvade** Symptoms of pregnancy and birth experienced by fathers.

**Especially for Nurses in Obstetrics** Can the father be of any practical help in the birth process? (see response, page 117)

## TABLE 4.3

### The Edinburgh Postnatal Depression Scale

The Edinburgh Postnatal Depression Scale asks women how they felt *in the past week*.

1. *I have been able to laugh and see the funny side of things*
   - 0-As much as I always could
   - 2-Definitely not so much now
   - 1-Not quite so much now
   - 3-Not at all

2. *I have looked forward with enjoyment to things*
   - 0- As much as I ever did
   - 2-Definitely less than I used to
   - 1-Rather less than I used to
   - 3-Hardly at all

3. *I have blamed myself unnecessarily when things went wrong*
   - 3-Yes, most of the time
   - 1-Not very often
   - 2-Yes, some of the time
   - 0-No, never

4. *I have been anxious or worried for no good reason*
   - 0-No, not at all
   - 2-Yes, sometimes
   - 1-Hardly ever
   - 3-Yes, very often

5. *I have felt scared or panicky for no very good reason.*
   - 3-Yes, quite a lot
   - 1-No, not much
   - 2-Yes, sometimes
   - 0-No, not at all

6. *Things have been getting on top of me*
   - 3-Yes, most of the time I haven't been able to cope at all
   - 2-Yes, sometimes I haven't been coping as well as usual
   - 1-No, most of the time I have coped quite well
   - 0-No, I have been coping as well as ever

7. *I have been so unhappy that I have had difficulty sleeping*
   - 3-Yes, most of the time
   - 1-Not very often
   - 2-Yes, sometimes
   - 0-No, not at all

8. *I have felt sad or miserable*
   - 3-Yes, most of the time
   - 1-Not very often
   - 2-Yes, quite often
   - 0-No, not at all

9. *I have been so unhappy that I have been crying*
   - 3-Yes, most of the time
   - 1-Only occasionally
   - 2-Yes, quite often
   - 0-No, never

10. *The thought of harming myself has occurred to me*
    - 3-Yes, quite often
    - 1-Hardly ever
    - 2- Sometimes
    - 0-Never

The total score ranges from zero to thirty. Below 9 indicates no problem; 9–12 suggests normal "baby blues"; above 12 indicates depression. High scores indicate that more intense screening is needed by a trained clinician, to discern if the new mother is truly depressed, anxious, or suicidal. (A 2 or 3 on question 10 is alarming, even if the rest are 0 or 1.)

of mothers and their babies at birth. Yet, many feel they have no right to complain. One said, "I'm always conscious that [partner]'s has it a lot worse." Another said at the birth, "I felt a bit more like a spare part . . . I just felt in the way" (quoted in Darwin et al., 2017).

Some men find relief at work, where they put the stress of fatherhood behind them or talk about their feelings with other men. An engineer said, "We probably spend half the day talking about babies and kids and that sort of thing. . . . I know that there's guys there that have had similar experiences or they know what it's like. They know how I'm feeling if I say, oh, we've had a rough night. . . . Some people have had worse experiences, so you think, what we're going through is normal" (quoted in Darwin et al., 2017).

In this discussion, we have assumed that each newborn has a mother and a father, a woman and a man who conceive a child. Biologically, that is always true: An ovum and a sperm are required to create a zygote. However, not every father is a biological father, just as not every mother is a biological mother. As one review of fathering states:

> Defining who is a father must account for the diversity of fathering that occurs. Most children have a father, whether he is currently residing with them or living separately. Some children have a single father or 2 parents who are both fathers. Children in a blended family may have both a biological nonresident father and a stepfather. Some gay men and lesbians have created families in which children have 3 or 4 adults in a parenting role, with 1 or 2 of them being fathers.

*[Yogman et al., 2016, p. e2]*

Whether couvade or postpartum depression occurs in nonbiological fathers is not known, but there is no doubt that children benefit from someone in a fathering role, who is involved with and committed to that child at every stage of development, from before birth through adulthood.

The crucial question regarding fathering begins with whether or not a man is responsive to the needs of family members, not with his biological connection (Brown, 2019). As you read regarding women and postpartum depression, parental emotions are not always simple and happy, evident with parents no matter what their gender or biological connection to a child.

## Family Bonding

Are the first hours after birth crucial for the **parent–infant bond,** the strong, loving connection that forms when parents hold their newborn? It has been claimed that this bond develops with touch, just as sheep and goats nurture their newborns if, and only if, they immediately smell and nuzzle them (Klaus & Kennell, 1976).

However, the hypothesis that early skin-to-skin contact is *essential* for human nurturance is false (Eyer, 1992; Lamb, 1982). Substantial research on monkeys begins with *cross-fostering,* when newborns are removed from their biological mothers in the first days of life and raised by another monkey, female or male. A strong and beneficial relationship between the infant and the foster parent may develop (Suomi, 2002).

For people, bonding can begin before birth, or it may not be established until days later. It is good, but not essential, for both parents to be actively involved in pregnancy, birth, and newborn care. Encouraging parents to nurture their newborns benefits all three family members lifelong, as proven with mice, monkeys, and humans (Champagne & Curley, 2010).

The benefits of early contact are evident with **kangaroo care,** in which the newborn lies between the mother's breasts, skin-to-skin, listening to her heartbeat and feeling her body heat. A review of 124 studies confirms that kangaroo-care newborns sleep more deeply, gain weight more quickly, and spend more time alert than do infants with standard care, and they are healthier overall (Boundy et al., 2016). Father involvement, including father–infant kangaroo care, also fosters newborn's health (Feeley et al., 2013).

ROLEX DELA PENA/European Pressphoto Agency/ MANILA/Philippines/Newscom

**Better Care** Kangaroo care benefits mothers, babies, and hospitals, saving space and medical costs in this ward in Manila. Kangaroo care is one reason Filipino infant mortality in 2010 was only one-fifth of what it was in 1950.

**parent–infant bond** The strong, loving connection that forms as parents hold, examine, and feed their newborn.

**kangaroo care** A form of newborn care in which mothers (and sometimes fathers) rest their babies on their naked chests, like kangaroo mothers that carry their immature newborns in a pouch on their abdomen.

## Other Relatives

The birth experience may affect other family members: A birth not only changes names (a baby can make someone suddenly a brother or sister, aunt or uncle, grandmother or grandfather) but also can have a powerful effect on emotions. Time to tell more about the birth first mentioned in the beginning of this chapter.

I held a bent right leg in place with all my strength, fighting against strong muscles to move it. A nurse strained as she held the left. The midwife commanded "push . . . push . . . push." Bethany's arm muscles bulged as she pulled a sheet tied to a mental stanchion above her. A circle of fetal skull visible, then larger, then crowning. Tissues tore, Bethany pushed once more.

"Yes! Yes! Yes!" the midwife shouted. A head emerged, quickly followed by all 4,139 grams of Caleb. Apgar was a stellar 9, every other number was good.

Bethany, smiling, began to nurse. Four professionals looked on, relaxed now. This is grandmother bliss. Decades of praying, studying, teaching, and mothering led me to a miracle, 6:11 A.M., my firstborn with her firstborn. Celestial music rang in my ears.

The ringing grew louder, a buzzing, roaring crescendo. Bethany shimmered, overhead lights became stars, flashing bright and then dark. I was flat on the floor, looking up at four faces staring down. I had fainted.

I know about birth, personally and professionally. I interpret numbers and jargon; I analyze monitors and body language; I judge doctors and nurses; I evaluate hospitals, notice stray paper on floors, hear sharp voices in corridors, see faded pictures on walls. Nothing here amiss; this hospital was excellent.

I also know Bethany: strong, healthy, drug-free. All through the night, indeed all through the nine months, I followed this pregnancy. I expected Caleb to be well-formed and Bethany to be okay. I was relieved and happy—not surprised—when my almost perfect daughter began nursing my quite perfect grandson.

Then why did I faint when all the drama was over? Indeed, why faint at all?

*[Berger, 2019]*

When I analyzed it, I realized that the hormones and evolutionary forces that foster bonding between parents and newborns, as well as depression in parents, affect grandmothers as well. All that aids development of everyone.

As we will see in later chapters, the relationships among family members develop over decades, not merely hours. Birth is one step of a lifelong journey.

---

### WHAT HAVE YOU LEARNED?

1. How are newborns socially interactive?
2. What causes postpartum depression?
3. How are fathers affected by birth?
4. Why is kangaroo care beneficial?
5. When does the parent–infant bond form?

---

## SUMMARY

### Prenatal Development

**1.** In the first two weeks of prenatal growth (the germinal period), the single-celled zygote multiplies into more than 100 cells that will eventually form both the placenta and the embryo. About half the time, the growing organism fails to implant in the uterus, ending pregnancy.

**2.** The embryonic period (the third week through the eighth week after conception) begins with the primitive streak, the start of the central nervous system. The future heart begins to pulsate, and eyes, ears, nose, mouth, and brain form. By the eighth week, the first traces of all of the basic organs and features are present.

**3.** Early in the fetal period (ninth week until birth), male and female organs form, and hormones start to shape the brain. At 22 weeks, the brain can regulate basic body functions, and viability is possible but unlikely. Babies born before the 24th week are at high risk of death or disability.

**4.** In the final three months, the average fetus gains approximately 4½ pounds (2,040 grams), weighing 7½ pounds (3,400 grams) at birth. Maturation of brain, lungs, and heart ensures survival of more than 99 percent of all full-term babies.

### Birth

**5.** Ideally, hormones (oxytocin) start labor and birth approximately 38 weeks after conception. The Apgar scale provides a quick evaluation of the newborn's health.

**6.** Medical assistance speeds contractions, dulls pain, and saves lives. However, many interventions, including about half of cesarean sections, have been criticized.

### Problems and Solutions

**7.** Every birth complication, such as an unusually long and stressful labor that includes anoxia, has a cascade of causes. Long-term handicaps are not inevitable.

**8.** Some teratogens cause physical impairment. Others, called behavioral teratogens, harm the brain and therefore impair cognitive abilities and affect personality.

**9.** Whether a teratogen harms an embryo or fetus depends on timing, dose, and genes. Family members affect the pregnant woman's health.

**10.** Low birthweight (under 5½ pounds, or 2,500 grams) may arise from early or multiple births, placental problems, maternal illness, malnutrition, smoking, drinking, illicit drug use, and age.

**11.** Underweight babies experience medical difficulties and psychological problems for many years. Babies that are small for gestational age (SGA) are especially vulnerable.

### The New Family

**12.** Newborns are primed for social interaction. The Brazelton Neonatal Behavioral Assessment Scale measures 46 newborn behaviors, 20 of which are reflexes. Some reflexes help survival; others measure brain maturation.

**13.** Fathers can be supportive during pregnancy as well as helpful in birth. Paternal support correlates with shorter labor and fewer complications. Some fathers become very involved with the pregnancy and birth, experiencing couvade.

**14.** Many women feel unhappy, incompetent, or unwell after giving birth. Postpartum depression gradually disappears with appropriate help; fathers can be crucial in baby care, or they can experience depression themselves.

**15.** Kangaroo care benefits all babies, but especially those who are vulnerable. The parent–infant bond depends on many factors in addition to birth practices.

## KEY TERMS

germinal period (p. 91)
embryonic period (p. 91)
fetal period (p. 91)
embryo (p. 91)
cephalocaudal (p. 92)
proximodistal (p. 92)
fetus (p. 92)
age of viability (p. 93)
doula (p. 97)
Apgar scale (p. 98)

cesarean section (c-section) (p. 100)
cerebral palsy (p. 102)
anoxia (p. 102)
teratogen (p. 102)
behavioral teratogens (p. 102)
threshold effect (p. 104)
fetal alcohol syndrome (FAS) (p. 105)
false positive (p. 106)

low birthweight (LBW) (p. 107)
very low birthweight (VLBW) (p. 107)
extremely low birthweight (ELBW) (p. 107)
preterm (p. 107)
small for gestational age (SGA) (p. 108)
immigrant paradox (p. 108)

Brazelton Neonatal Behavioral Assessment Scale (NBAS) (p. 111)
reflex (p. 112)
postpartum depression (p. 112)
couvade (p. 113)
parent–infant bond (p. 115)
kangaroo care (p. 115)

## APPLICATIONS

**1.** Go to a nearby greeting-card store and analyze the cards about pregnancy and birth. Do you see any cultural attitudes (e.g., variations depending on the sex of the newborn or of the parent)? If possible, compare those cards with cards from a store that caters to another economic or ethnic group.

**2.** Interview three mothers of varied backgrounds about their birth experiences. Make your interviews open-ended—let the mothers choose what to tell you, as long as they give at least a 10-minute description. Then compare and contrast the three accounts, noting especially any influences of culture, personality, circumstances, and cohort.

**3.** People sometimes wonder how any pregnant woman could jeopardize the health of her fetus. Consider your own health-related behavior in the past month—exercise, sleep, nutrition, drug use, medical and dental care, disease avoidance, and so on. Would you change your behavior if you were pregnant? Would it make a difference if you, your family, and your partner did not want a baby?

## Especially For ANSWERS

**Response for Conservatives and Liberals** (from p. 100): Yes, some people are much more likely to want nature to take its course. However, personal experience often trumps political attitudes about birth and death; several of those who advocate hospital births are also in favor of spending one's final days at home.

**Response for Future Doctors and Nurses** (from p. 105) This is not easy, as people tend to consider the worst case more readily than the best case. Useful might be a graph that depicts the odds, or comparisons with something nonmedical. For example, chance that

your birthday is tomorrow, 1:365. Chance that your fetus has Down syndrome, 1:1000.

**Response for Judges and Juries** (from p. 110): Some laws punish women who jeopardize the health of their fetuses, but a developmental view would consider the micro-, exo-, and macrosystems.

**Response for Nurses in Obstetrics** (from p. 113): Usually not, unless they are experienced, well taught, or have expert guidance. But their presence provides emotional support for the woman, which makes the birth process easier and healthier for mother and baby.

## Observation Quiz ANSWERS

**Answer to Observation Quiz** (from p. 103): Brain. Legs.

**Answer to Observation Quiz** (from p. 110): Decreasing. The reason may be related to greater gender equity. Note, however, that the

recession impacted fathers dramatically, as many wage-earners lost their jobs and did not immediately know how to get public or private help in feeding their families.

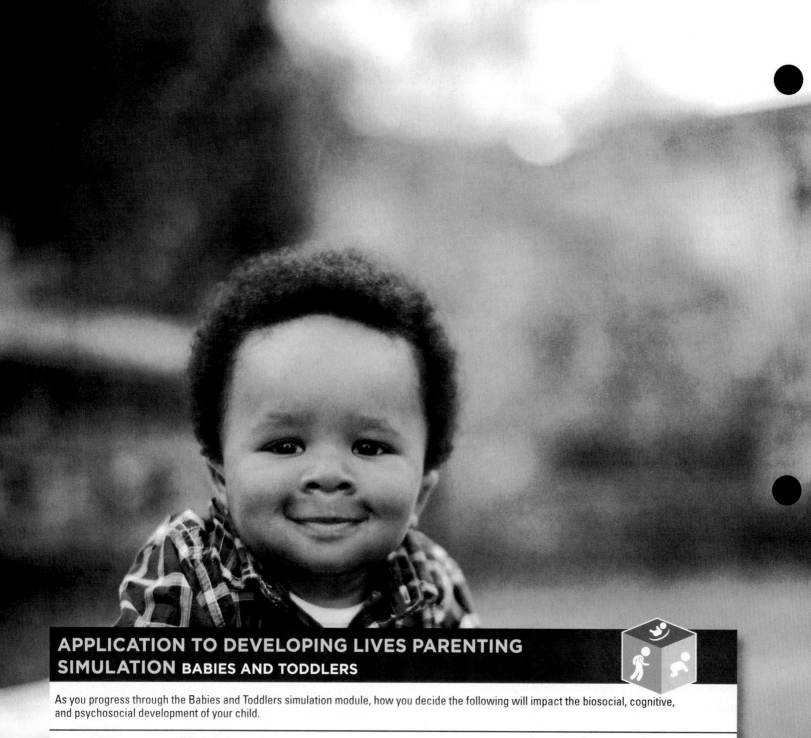

## APPLICATION TO DEVELOPING LIVES PARENTING
## SIMULATION BABIES AND TODDLERS

As you progress through the Babies and Toddlers simulation module, how you decide the following will impact the biosocial, cognitive, and psychosocial development of your child.

|  | Biosocial | Cognitive | Psychosocial |
|---|---|---|---|
| | • Will you vaccinate your baby?<br>• Will you breast-feed your baby? If so, for how long?<br>• What kind of foods will you feed your baby during the first year?<br>• How will you encourage motor skill development?<br>• How do your baby's height and weight compare to national norms? | • What activities will you expose your baby to (music class, reading, educational videos)?<br>• What activities will you do to promote language development?<br>• Which of Piaget's stages of cognitive development is your child in? | • How will you soothe your baby when he or she is crying?<br>• Can you identify your baby's temperament style?<br>• Can you identify your baby's attachment style?<br>• What kind of discipline will you use with your child? |

**PART II**

# The First Two Years

**A**dults don't change much in a year or two. They might have longer, grayer, or thinner hair; they might gain or lose weight; they might learn something new. But if you saw friends you hadn't seen for two years, you'd recognize them immediately.

Imagine caring for your sister's newborn every day for two months. You would learn everything about that baby—how to dress, when to play, what to feed, where to sleep. Toward the end of the two months, the baby would recognize you, smiling broadly, nestling comfortably in your arms, responding with happy noises when you spoke. Then imagine you had to live in another country for two years.

When you returned, your sister might ask you to pick up the toddler at the day-care center. You would need to ask the teacher which child to take, because several of them could be your sister's child. In those two years, weight quadruples, height increases by a foot, hair grows. Emotions change, too—less crying, new fear—including fear of you, now a stranger.

Two years are less than 3 percent of the average human life. However, in those 24 months, people reach half their adult height, learn to run, climb and talk in sentences, and express every emotion—not just joy and fear but perhaps jealousy and shame. Invisible growth of the brain is even more awesome; plasticity is extraordinary during infancy, enabling all these changes and more. The next three chapters describe this transformation. ●●

Left: David A Land/Blend Images/Media Bakery
Right: JBryson/iStock/Getty Images

# The First Two Years: Biosocial Development

## What Will You Know?

1. What part of an infant grows most in the first two years?
2. Are babies essentially blind and deaf at birth?
3. What happens if infants do not get their vaccinations?

Our first child, Bethany, was born when I was in graduate school. At 14 months, the pediatrician said she was growing well. But my husband was worried; she had not yet taken her first step. I told him that genes determine age of walking: I had read that babies in Paris are late to walk, and my grandmother was French.

To our relief, Bethany soon began to walk. A few years later, she was the fastest runner in kindergarten. Our next two children, Rachel and Elissa, were also slow to walk, and my students with Guatemalan and Ghanaian ancestors bragged about their infants who walked before a year; those from China and France were quiet. Genetic, I thought.

Fourteen years after Bethany, Sarah was born. I could finally afford a full time caregiver, Mrs. Todd. She thought Sarah was the most advanced baby she had ever known, except for her own daughter, Gillian.

"She'll be walking by a year," Mrs. Todd told me. "Gillian walked at 10 months."

"We'll see," I graciously replied.

I underestimated Mrs. Todd. She bounced my delighted baby on her lap, day after day, and spent hours giving her "walking practice." Sarah took her first step at 12 months — late for a Todd, early for a Berger, and a humbling lesson for me.

As a scientist, I know that a single case proves nothing. My genetic explanation might be not valid, especially since Sarah shares only half her genes with Bethany and since my daughters are only one-eighth French, a fraction I had conveniently ignored.

Nonetheless, decades of research since Bethany was born confirm that caretakers influence every aspect of biosocial growth. You will soon read many examples of caregiving that enables babies to grow, move, see, and learn. Nurture is at least as important as nature.

Genes provide the scaffold, but daily circumstances shape and guide infant development. Bethany completed a marathon; her grandmother could not walk independently in her final years. Both outcomes were the result of their early experiences: Bethany admired her older cousins who won trophies in races, and Grandma had polio as a child, which weakened her legs in late adulthood.

## Body Changes

In infancy, growth is so rapid and the consequences of neglect so severe that gains are closely monitored. Medical checkups, including measurement of height, weight, and head circumference, reveal whether an infant is progressing as expected—or not.

## Body Size

Newborns lose several ounces in the first three days and then gain an ounce a day for months. Birthweight doubles by 4 months and triples by a year, so the average 7-pound newborn might be 21 pounds at 12 months (9,525 grams, up from 3,175 grams at birth).

Variation is substantial, depending not only on genes and nutrition but also on birthweight—small babies may double their weight in two months and quadruple by age 1, a phenomenon called *catch-up growth*. Height also increases rapidly, with variation: A typical newborn grows 10 inches (25 centimeters) by age 1, measuring about 30 inches (76 centimeters).

Physical growth then slows, but not by much. Most 24-month-olds weigh about 28 pounds (13 kilograms) and have added another 4 inches (10 centimeters) in the previous year. Typically, 2-year-olds are half their adult height and about one-fifth their adult weight (see **Figure 5.1**).

## Compared to Themselves

Growth is often expressed in a **percentile,** indicating how one person compares to another. Thus, a 12-month-old's weight at the 30th percentile means that 29 percent of 12-month-old babies weigh less and 69 percent weigh more. Healthy children vary in size, so any percentile between 10 and 90 is okay, as long as the percentile is close to the previous one for that individual.

When an infant's percentile moves markedly up or down, that could signify trouble. A notable drop, say from the 50th to the 20th percentile, suggests poor nutrition. A sudden increase, perhaps from 30th to 60th signifies overfeeding, especially if their height remains at the 30th percentile.

Parents were once blamed if their infant was not gaining weight. It was thought that parents made feeding stressful, leading to *failure to thrive*. Currently, however,

**LaunchPad**
macmillan learning

**VIDEO: Physical Development in Infancy and Toddlerhood** offers a quick review of the physical changes that occur during a child's first two years.

**percentile** A point on a ranking scale of 0 to 100. The 50th percentile is the midpoint; half the people in the population being studied rank higher and half rank lower.

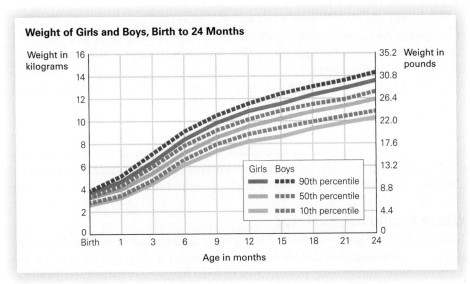

**FIGURE 5.1**

**Averages and Individuals** Norms and percentiles are useful—most 1-month-old girls who weigh 10 pounds should be at least 25 pounds by age 2. But although females weigh less than males on average lifelong, it is obvious that individuals do not always follow the norms. Do you know a 200-pound woman married to a 150-pound man?

**REM (rapid eye movement) sleep**
A stage of sleep characterized by flickering eyes behind closed lids, dreaming, and rapid brain waves.

we know that many organic conditions, such as allergies, the microbiome, and liver problems, combine with nonorganic factors, in the caregiver or in infant feeding practices (Lazzara et al., 2019).

Similarly, obesity is now thought to be cultural and organic, as well as familial. Both conditions may begin during infancy; both conditions require diagnosis and intervention. Blaming the caregivers is neither accurate nor helpful.

## Sleep

Throughout childhood, regular and ample sleep correlates with normal brain maturation, learning, emotional regulation, academic success, and psychological adjustment (Maski & Kothare, 2013). Sleep deprivation can cause poor health, and vice versa. As with many health habits, sleep patterns begin in the first year.

### Patterns of Infant Sleep

Newborns spend most of their time sleeping, about 15 to 17 hours a day. With maturity, hours of sleep decrease rapidly and the patterns change, with longer night sleep and less daytime napping. For example, one study that included infants of many ethnic and economic backgrounds found that the average 1-month-old slept six hours during the day, and nine hours at night, waking up two to three times. By 6 months, the average was three hours of daytime sleep and ten hours at night, waking up once or twice (Ash et al., 2019).

Remember that norms are simply averages: Some infants sleep substantially more, and others less. Babies born preterm seem to be dozing most of the time, but that may be partly caused by the constant bright lights and frequent feeding of the traditional neonatal intensive care unit (NICU). When they come home, preterm babies usually adjust to a day/night schedule (Bueno & Menna-Barreto, 2016).

Newborns dream a lot: About half their sleep is **REM (rapid eye movement) sleep.** REM sleep declines over the early weeks, as does "transitional sleep," the dozing, half-awake stage. At 3 or 4 months, quiet sleep (also called *slow-wave sleep*) increases markedly.

Sleep varies not only because of biology (maturation and genes), but also because of caregiving. Sleep environment matters, since at every age, noise and light disrupt sleep. Some infants sleep where they hear others arguing, traffic noises, or television. When they are very tired, they sleep despite such disruptions, but they sleep fewer hours overall when the environment is stimulating. Pain also keeps them awake: Colicky babies sleep less, and their parents sleep less also.

Insufficient sleep becomes a problem for parents as well as for infants, because "[p]arents are rarely well-prepared for the degree of sleep disruption a newborn infant engenders, and many have unrealistic expectations about the first few postnatal months." As a result, many parents become "desperate" and institute patterns they may later regret (C. Russell et al., 2013, p. 68).

Adey Bryant/Cartoonstock

**Danger Here** Not with the infant (although those pillows should be removed), but for the family. It is hard to maintain a happy marriage if the parents are exhausted.

**co-sleeping** A custom in which parents and their children (usually infants) sleep together in the same room.

**bed-sharing** When two or more people sleep in the same bed.

### Where Should Babies Sleep?

Traditionally, most middle-class North American infants slept in cribs in their own rooms; it was feared that they would be traumatized if their parents had sex in the same room. By contrast, most infants in Asia, Africa, and Latin America slept near their parents, a practice called **co-sleeping,** and sometimes in their parents' bed, called **bed-sharing.** In those cultures, nighttime parent–child separation was considered cruel.

Asian and African mothers still worry more about separation, whereas European and North American mothers worry more about privacy. A 19-nation survey found that parents act on these fears: The extremes were 82 percent of Vietnamese babies co-sleeping compared with 6 percent in New Zealand (Mindell et al., 2010) (see **Figure 5.2**). Although co-sleeping is more common in nations with high poverty rates, culture matters, too: In Japan—one of the wealthiest nations of the world—mothers often sleep with their babies.

In the United States, bed-sharing doubled from 1993 to 2010 (6.5 percent to 13.5 percent) (Colson et al., 2013). In Canada, younger women are more likely to bed-share: A large, nationwide study found that more than 40 percent of new mothers under age 25 sleep with their infants (Gilmour et al., 2019).

The infant's feeding patterns have an effect: Bed-sharing is more common among breast-feeding mothers. A study in Sweden of preterm infants (who need to be fed every two or three hours) found that most slept with their mothers—especially if the mother had trouble getting back to sleep if she got up to feed her infant (Blomqvist et al., 2017).

The argument for co-sleeping is that the parents can quickly respond to a hungry or frightened baby. Moreover, a close physical connection at night fosters bonding. A popular book on infant care advocates "attachment parenting," advising keeping the infant nearby day and night (Sears & Sears, 2001).

Responsive attachment correlates with co-sleeping (Kim et al., 2017). However, bed-sharing doubles the risk of *sudden infant death syndrome (SIDS)*, when a baby dies unexpectedly while asleep (Vennemann et al., 2012).

For that reason, some pediatricians advise against co-sleeping. That advice may be ignored by tired mothers, especially in cultures where bed-sharing is the norm. Canadian mothers are told not to share a bed with their infant, but two-thirds of those with Asian or Caribbean heritage do so (Gilmour et al., 2019).

Consequently, many experts seek ways to safeguard the practice (Ball & Volpe, 2013). Their advice includes *never* sleeping beside a baby if the parent has been drinking, and *never* using a soft comforter, pillow, or mattress near a sleeping infant.

Developmentalists remind parents that babies learn from experience. If they become accustomed to bed-sharing, they may climb into their parents' bed long past infancy. Parents might lose sleep for years because they wanted more sleep when their babies were small. Sleeping alone may encourage independence—a trait appreciated in some cultures, abhorred in others. The entire social context matters, which explains why some studies find benefits from co-sleeping, and other studies find danger (Baddock et al., 2019).

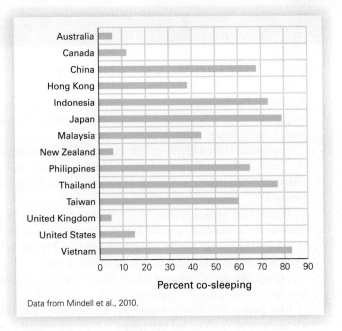

Data from Mindell et al., 2010.

**FIGURE 5.2**

**Awake at Night** Why the disparity between Asian and non-Asian rates of co-sleeping? It may be that Western parents use a variety of gadgets and objects—monitors, night-lights, pacifiers, cuddle cloths, sound machines—to accomplish some of what Asian parents do by having their infant next to them.

**Especially for New Parents** You are aware of cultural differences in sleeping practices, which raises a very practical issue: Should your newborn sleep in bed with you? (see response, page 145)

## Brain Development

From two weeks after conception to two years after birth, the brain grows more rapidly than any other organ. Brain size about 25 percent of adult weight at birth and 75 percent at age 2. Prenatal and postnatal brain growth affects later cognition (Gilles & Nelson, 2012). If teething or a stuffed-up nose temporarily slows eating, body weight is affected before brain weight, a phenomenon called **head-sparing.** That term expresses well what nature does—protect the brain.

Many other terms in neuroscience are not as self-explanatory, but they are useful to understand the brain. Accordingly, they are explained in the following.

**head-sparing** A biological mechanism that protects the brain when malnutrition disrupts body growth. The brain is the last part of the body to be damaged by malnutrition.

# Neuroscience Vocabulary

To understand the impressive brain growth that occurs throughout childhood, it is helpful to know some basic terms of neurological development.

Communication within the *central nervous system (CNS)*—the brain and spinal cord—begins with nerve cells, called **neurons.** At birth, the human brain has about 86 billion neurons.

Within and between areas of the central nervous system, neurons are connected to other neurons by intricate networks of nerve fibers called **axons** and **dendrites** (see **Figure 5.3**). Each neuron has a single axon and numerous dendrites, which spread out like the branches of a tree. Most of the brain growth in infancy is increases in dendrites.

The axon of one neuron meets the dendrites of other neurons at intersections called **synapses,** which are critical communication links within the brain. Infancy is "characterized by overproduction of synapses followed by a period of gradual pruning" (Bernier et al., 2016, p. 1159). Synapse formation and demise is remarkably plastic, heavily dependent on experience.

Neurons communicate by *firing,* or sending electrochemical impulses through their axons to synapses to be picked up by the dendrites of other neurons. The dendrites bring the message to the cell bodies of their neurons, which, in turn, may fire, conveying messages via their axons to the dendrites of other neurons. Some firing is involuntary—such as the reflexes cited in Chapter 4. Most infant brain development requires new connections between one neuron and another, as dendrites grow (Gao et al., 2017).

Axons and dendrites do not touch at synapses. Instead, the electrical impulses in axons typically cause the release of **neurotransmitters,** which stimulate other neurons. There are about a hundred neurotransmitters.

Neurotransmitters carry information from the axon of the sending neuron, across a pathway called the *synaptic gap,* to the dendrites of the receiving neuron, a process speeded up by **myelin,** a coating on the outside of the axon. Myelin increases over childhood—lack of it is one reason infants are slow to react to something pleasurable or painful. [**Developmental link**: Myelination is discussed in Chapter 8.]

Some neurons are deep inside the brain in a region called the *hindbrain,* which controls automatic responses such as heartbeat, breathing, temperature, and arousal. Others are in the *midbrain,* in areas that affect emotions and memory. And in humans most neurons (about 70 percent) are in the *forebrain,* especially the **cortex,** the brain's six outer layers (sometimes called the *neocortex*). Most thinking, feeling, and sensing occur in the cortex (Johnson & de Haan, 2015; Kolb & Whishaw, 2015).

The forebrain has two halves and four lobes, which are general regions, each containing many parts. No important human activity is exclusively left- or right-brain, or in one lobe or another. Although each lobe and hemisphere has specialized functions, thousands of connections transmit information among the parts. The specialization of various parts is the result of various constraints and experiences, not foreordained by genes (Johnson & de Haan, 2015).

The back of the forebrain is the *occipital lobe,* where vision is located; the sides of the brain are the *temporal lobes,* for hearing; the top is the *parietal lobe,* which includes smell, touch, and spatial understanding; and the front is the *frontal lobe,* which enables people to plan, imagine, coordinate, decide, and create. Humans have a much larger frontal cortex relative to body size than any other animal.

The very front of the frontal lobe is called the **prefrontal cortex.** It is not, as once thought, "functionally silent during most of infancy" (Grossmann, 2013, p. 303), although the prefrontal cortex is very immature at birth. [**Developmental Link**: Major discussion of adolescent growth of the prefrontal cortex is in Chapter 14.]

Pleasure and pain may arise from the **limbic system,** a cluster of brain areas deep in the forebrain that is heavily involved in emotions and motivation. Two crucial parts of the limbic system are the amygdala and the hippocampus.

**neuron** One of billions of nerve cells in the central nervous system, especially in the brain.

**axon** A fiber that extends from a neuron and transmits electrochemical impulses from that neuron to the dendrites of other neurons.

**dendrite** A fiber that extends from a neuron and receives electrochemical impulses transmitted from other neurons via their axons.

**synapse** The intersection between the axon of one neuron and the dendrites of other neurons.

**neurotransmitter** A brain chemical that carries information from the axon of a sending neuron to the dendrites of a receiving neuron.

**myelin** The coating on axons that speeds transmission of signals from one neuron to another.

**cortex** The outer layers of the brain in humans and other mammals. Most thinking, feeling, and sensing involves the cortex.

**prefrontal cortex** The area of the cortex at the very front of the brain that specializes in anticipation, planning, and impulse control.

**limbic system** The parts of the brain that interact to produce emotions, including the amygdala, the hypothalamus, and the hippocampus. Many other parts of the brain also are involved with emotions.

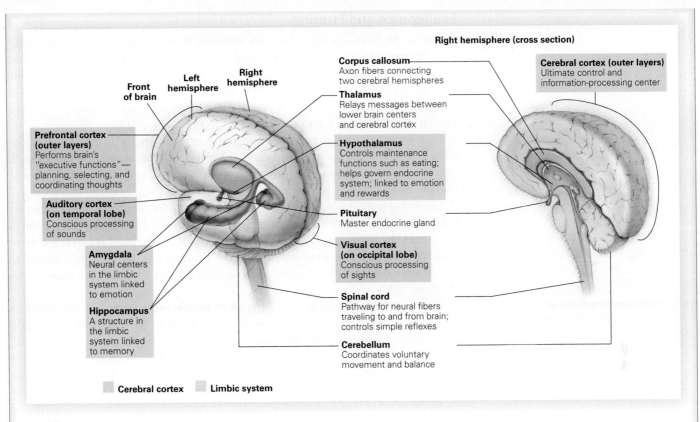

**FIGURE 5.3**

**Connections** A few of the hundreds of named parts of the brain are shown here. Although each area has particular functions, the entire brain is interconnected. The processing of emotions, for example, occurs primarily in the limbic system, where many brain areas are involved, including the amygdala, hippocampus, and hypothalamus.

The **amygdala** is a tiny structure, about the same shape and size as an almond. It registers strong emotions, both positive and negative, especially fear. The amygdala is present in infancy, but growth depends partly on early experience. Increased amygdala activity may cause terrifying nightmares or sudden terrors.

Another structure in the emotional network is the **hippocampus,** located next to the amygdala. A central processor of memory, especially memory for locations, the hippocampus responds to the amygdala by summoning memory. Some places feel comforting (perhaps a childhood room) and others evoke fear (perhaps a doctor's office), even when the experiences that originated those emotions are long gone.

Sometimes considered part of the limbic system is the **hypothalamus,** which responds to signals from the amygdala and to memories from the hippocampus by producing hormones, especially **cortisol,** a hormone that increases with stress. Another nearby brain structure, the **pituitary,** responds to the hypothalamus by sending out hormones to various body parts.

Brain research is one area of international collaboration. For example, a 5-billion-dollar, 12-year project in the United States called BRAIN (Brain Research Through Advancing Innovative Neurotechnologies) began in 2014 and is developing new tools (Huang & Luo, 2015). Given new methods and thousands of neuroscientists worldwide, the names and functions of various parts of the brain may be described differently from one source to another.

The descriptions here are only a beginning. From a developmental perspective, what is crucial to know is that all human thoughts and actions originate in the complexity of the brain, and that understanding the brain adds insight to our effort to understand how humans live their lives. Extensive neurological plasticity is evident as all these parts of the infant brain adapt to experience (Gao et al., 2017).

**amygdala** A tiny brain structure that registers emotions, particularly fear and anxiety.

**hippocampus** A brain structure that is a central processor of memory, especially memory for locations.

**hypothalamus** A brain area that responds to the amygdala and the hippocampus to produce hormones that activate other parts of the brain and body.

**cortisol** The primary stress hormone; fluctuations in the body's cortisol level affect human emotions.

**pituitary** A gland in the brain that responds to a signal from the hypothalamus by producing many hormones, including those that regulate growth and that control other glands, among them the adrenal and sex glands.

## Exuberance and Pruning

At birth, the brain contains far more neurons than a person needs. Some neurons disappear in programmed cell death, and some new ones develop. That loss is counterbalanced by massive gains: Dendrites, axons, synapses, and myelin increase rapidly. Because of all that, the brain is twice as large at age 1 as it was at birth (Gao et al., 2017). The first year of life is a time of massive brain growth, at a rate far more than any later year (Vannucci & Vannucci, 2019).

Between birth and age 2, an estimated fivefold increase in dendrites in the cortex occurs, with about 100 trillion synapses present at age 2. According to one expert, "40,000 new synapses are formed every second in the infant's brain" (Schore & McIntosh, 2011, p. 502).

Extensive *postnatal* brain growth is highly unusual for other mammals. It occurs in humans because birth would be impossible if the fetal head were large enough to contain the brain networks humans need. (As it is, the head is by far the most difficult part of the human birth process). Because the human brain grows so much after birth, humans must nurture and protect children for many years (Konner, 2010).

Early dendrite growth is called **transient exuberance:** *exuberant* because it is so rapid and *transient* because some of it is temporary. Just as a gardener might prune a rose bush by cutting away some growth to enable more, or more beautiful, roses to bloom, unused brain connections atrophy and die. Thinking and learning require connections among many parts of the brain. This process is made more efficient because some potential connections are pruned (Gao et al., 2017).

As one expert explains it, there is an "exuberant overproduction of cells and connections followed by a several year long sculpting of pathways by massive elimination" (Insel, 2014, p. 1727). Notice the word *sculpting*, as if a gifted artist created an intricate sculpture from raw marble or wood. Human infants are gifted artists, developing their brains to adjust to whatever family, culture, or society they are born into.

For example, to understand any sentence in this text, you need to know the letters, the words, the surrounding text, the ideas they convey, and how they relate to your other thoughts and experiences. Those connections are essential for your comprehension, which differs from other people whose infant brains developed in homes unlike yours. Thus, your brain automatically interprets these roman letters, and, for most of you, is befuddled when viewing Arabic, Cyrillic, or Chinese.

Further evidence of the benefit of cell death comes from a sad symptom of fragile X syndrome (described in Chapter 3), "a persistent failure of normal synapse pruning" (Irwin et al., 2002, p. 194). Without **pruning,** the dendrites of children with fragile X are too dense and long, making thinking difficult. Similar problems occur for children with autism spectrum disorder: Their brains are unusually large and full, making communication between neurons less efficient and some sounds and sights overwhelming (Lewis et al., 2013).

Thus, pruning is essential. As brains mature, the process of extending and eliminating dendrites is exquisitely attuned to experience, as the appropriate links in the brain are established, protected, and strengthened (Gao et al., 2017). As with the rose bush, pruning needs to be done carefully, allowing further growth.

## Necessary and Possible Experiences

A scientist named William Greenough identified two experience-related aspects of brain development (Greenough et al., 1987). Understanding

**transient exuberance** The great but temporary increase in the number of dendrites that develop in an infant's brain during the first two years of life.

**pruning** When applied to brain development, the process by which unused connections in the brain atrophy and die.

**Connecting** The color staining on this photo makes it obvious that the two neurons (stained chartreuse) grow dendrites to connect with each other. This tangle is repeated thousands of times in every human brain. Throughout life, those fragile dendrites will grow or disappear as the person continues thinking.

Francois Paquet-Durand/SPL/Science Source

these helps adults avoid the difference/deficit problem explained in Chapter 1, yet still provide the experiences every baby needs.

- **Experience-expectant growth.** Certain functions require basic experiences in order to develop, just as a tree requires water. Those experiences are part of almost every infant's life, and thus, almost all human brains grow as their genes direct. Brains *expect* such experiences; development suffers without them.
- **Experience-dependent growth.** Human brains are quite plastic, again as explained in Chapter 1. Particular brain connections grow as specific experiences occur. These experiences are not essential: They happen in some families and cultures but not in others.

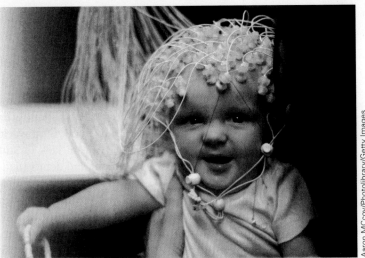

**Face Lit Up, Brain Too** Thanks to scientists at the University of Washington, this young boy enjoys the electroencephalogram (EEG) of his brain activity. Such research has found that babies respond to language long before they speak. Experiences of all sorts connect neurons and grow dendrites.

The basic, expected experiences *must* happen for normal brain maturation to occur, and they almost always do. For example, in deserts and in the Arctic, on isolated farms and in crowded cities, almost all babies have things to see, objects to manipulate, and people to love them. Babies everywhere welcome such experiences: They look around, they grab for objects, they smile at people. As a result, babies' brains develop. Without such expected experiences, brains wither.

In contrast, dependent experiences *might* happen; because of them, one brain differs from another, even though both brains are developing normally. Experiences vary, such as the language they hear, the faces they see, the emotions their caregivers express, and, as you just read, where they sleep. *Depending* on those particulars, infant brains are structured and connected one way or another; some dendrites grow and some neurons thrive while others die (Stiles & Jernigan, 2010).

Consequently, experience-expectant events make all people similar, yet everyone is unique because each undergoes particular experience-dependent events.

The distinction between essential and variable input to the brain's networks can be made for all creatures. Some of the most persuasive research has been done with birds. All male songbirds have a brain region dedicated to listening and reproducing sounds (experience-expectant), but birds of the same species produce slightly different songs (experience-dependent) depending on where they live (Konner, 2010).

Birds inherit genes that produce the neurons they need, perhaps dedicated to learning new songs (canaries) or to finding hidden seeds (chickadees). That is experience-expectant: Songs and seeds are essential for those species. Then, depending on their ecological niche, birds *depend* on specific experiences with learning songs or finding seeds.

Indeed, human babies learn language in much the same way as birds sing (Prather et al., 2017). Unless something is seriously wrong, adults talk to babies whose brains *expect* language. But the particular language *depends* on the specific culture.

**experience-expectant** Brain functions that require certain basic common experiences (which an infant can be expected to have) in order to develop normally.

**experience-dependent** Brain functions that depend on particular, variable experiences and therefore may or may not develop in a particular infant.

**Especially for Parents of Grown Children** Suppose you realize that you seldom talked to your children until they talked to you and that you often put them in cribs and playpens. Did you limit their brain growth and their sensory capacity? (see response, page 145)

## Harming the Infant Body and Brain

Thus far, we have focused on the many variations that families offer babies. Most infants develop well. Feeding and health care vary, but every family tries to ensure that their children survive in good health, and thrive within their culture.

For brain development, it does not matter whether a person learns French or Farsi, or expresses emotions dramatically or subtly (e.g., throwing themselves to

**shaken baby syndrome** A life-threatening injury that occurs when an infant is forcefully shaken back and forth, a motion that ruptures blood vessels in the brain and breaks neural connections.

the floor or merely pursing their lips, a cultural difference). However, infant brains do not grow normally if they lack basic, expected experiences.

## Necessary Stimulation

To begin with, infants need stimulation. Some adults imagine that babies need quiet, perhaps in a room painted one neutral color. That is a mistake. Babies need sights and sounds, emotional expression, and social interaction that encourages movement (arm waving, then crawling, grabbing, and walking).

Severe lack of stimulation stunts the brain. As one review explains, "enrichment and deprivation studies provide powerful evidence of . . . widespread effects of experience on the complexity and function of the developing system" of the brain (Stiles & Jernigan, 2010, p. 345).

Proof came first from rodents! Some "deprived" rats (raised alone in small, barren cages) were compared with "enriched" rats (raised in large cages with toys and other rats). At autopsy, brains of the enriched rats were larger, with more dendrites (Diamond, 1988; Greenough & Volkmar, 1973).

Subsequent research with other mammals confirms that isolation and sensory deprivation stunt development. That is now sadly evident in longitudinal studies of human orphans from Romania, described in Chapter 7.

## Stress and the Brain

Some infants experience the opposite problem, too much of the wrong kind of stimulation (Bick & Nelson, 2016). If the brain produces an overabundance of *cortisol* (the stress hormone) early in life, that derails the connections from parts of the brain, causing odd responses to stress lifelong. Years later, that child or adult may be hypervigilant (always on the alert) or emotionally flat (never happy or sad).

Note that the brain is responding to fear, not directly to physical pain. Of course infants should never be hit, and occasional pain or stress—routine inoculations, temporary hunger, an unwanted bath or diaper change—is part of normal infant life. If a reassuring caregiver communicates comfort, the infant can handle the stress. However, intense and frequent stress can flood the brain with cortisol, causing damage to later cognition. For example, if infants witness a violent fight between their parents, they may suffer lasting harm, evident in brain and behavior (Mueller & Tronick, 2019).

This distinction is important for caregivers to know. All babies cry. Because the prefrontal cortex has not yet developed, telling infants to stop crying is pointless because they cannot *decide* to stop crying. Some adults yell at babies (which may terrify the baby) or even worse, shake the infant. That makes blood vessels in the brain rupture and neural connections break, causing **shaken baby syndrome,** an example of *abusive head trauma* (Christian & Block, 2009). Death is the worst consequence; lifelong intellectual impairment is the more likely one.

Not every infant who has neurological symptoms of head trauma is the victim of abuse: Legal experts worry about false accusations (Byard, 2014). Nonetheless, infants are vulnerable, so the response to a screaming, frustrating baby should be to comfort or walk away, never to shake, yell, or hit.

Lest you cannot imagine the frustration that some parents feel when their baby cries, consider what one mother in Sweden said about her colicky baby, now age 4 and much beloved.

> There were moments when, both me and my husband . . . when she was apoplectic and howling so much that I almost got this thought, 'now I'll take a pillow and put over her face just until she quietens down, until the screaming stops.'

*[quoted in Landgren et al., 2012, p. 55]*

Discoveries about early development have many other implications. First, since early growth is so rapid, well-baby checkups are needed often, in order to spot, and treat, any problems. Sight and hearing are springboards for growth, so sensory impairments should be remedied.

Fortunately, one characteristic of infants is called **self-righting,** an inborn drive to compensate and overcome problems. Infants with few toys develop their brains by using sticks, or empty boxes, or whatever is available. Malnourished newborns have catch-up growth, so a 5-pound newborn may gain weight faster than an 8-pound one. Plasticity is apparent from the beginning of life (Tomalski & Johnson, 2010).

**self-righting** The inborn drive to remedy a developmental deficit; literally, to return to sitting or standing upright after being tipped over. People of all ages have self-righting impulses, for emotional as well as physical imbalance.

---

### WHAT HAVE YOU LEARNED?

1. What facts indicate that infants grow rapidly in the first year?

2. Why are pediatricians not troubled when an infant is consistently small, say at the 20th percentile in height and weight?

3. How do sleep patterns change from birth to 18 months?

4. What are the arguments for and against bed-sharing?

5. How can pruning increase brain potential?

6. How do experience-expectant and experience-dependent growth differ?

7. What are the effects of stress and social deprivation on early development?

8. What should caregivers remember about brain development when an infant cries?

---

## Perceiving and Moving

Young human infants combine immature motor abilities and acute sensory awareness (Konner, 2010). That is the opposite combination for most mammals, such as kittens who are born deaf, with eyes sealed shut, yet can walk immediately. Human senses are crucial from birth on; movement skills take months and years.

### The Senses

All the senses function at birth. Newborns have open eyes, sensitive ears, and responsive noses, tongues, and skin. Indeed, very young babies use all their senses to attend to everything. For instance, in the first days of life, they stare at everyone and suck almost anything in their mouths.

**Sensation** occurs when a sensory system detects a stimulus, as when the inner ear reverberates with sound, or the eye's retina and pupil intercept light. Thus, sensations begin when an outer organ (eye, ear, nose, tongue, or skin) meets anything that can be seen, heard, smelled, tasted, or touched.

Genetic selection over more than 200,000 years affects all the senses. Humans cannot hear what mice hear, or see what bats see, or smell what puppies smell; humans do not need to do that. However, survival requires babies to respond to people, and newborns do so with every sense (Konner, 2010; Zeifman, 2013).

### Hearing

The sense of hearing develops during the last trimester of pregnancy. At birth, certain sounds trigger reflexes, even without conscious perception. Sudden noises startle newborns, making them cry.

Familiar, rhythmic sounds, such as a heartbeat, are soothing: That is one reason kangaroo care reduces newborn stress, as the infant's ear rests on the mother's

**sensation** The response of a sensory organ (eyes, ears, skin, tongue, nose) when it detects a stimulus.

NEIL M. BORDEN/Science Source

**Listen, Imagine, Think, and Tap** A person has just heard "banana" and "round, red fruit," and is told to tap if the two do not match. An MRI reveals that 14 areas of the brain are activated. As you see, this simple matching task requires hearing (the large region on the temporal lobe), imagined seeing (the visual cortex in the occipital lobe at the bottom), motor action (the parietal lobe), and analysis (the prefrontal cortex at the top). Imagine how much more brain activation is required for the challenges of daily life.

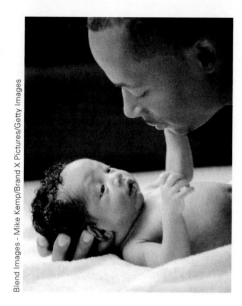

Blend Images - Mike Kemp/Brand X Pictures/Getty Images

**Who's This?** Newborns don't know much, but they look intensely at faces. Repeated sensations become perceptions, so in about six weeks this baby will smile at Dad, Mom, a stranger, the dog, and every other face. If this father in Utah responds like typical fathers everywhere, cognition will be apparent by 6 months: The baby will chortle with joy at seeing him but become wary of unfamiliar faces.

**binocular vision** The ability to focus the two eyes in a coordinated manner in order to see one image.

**THINK CRITICALLY:** Which is most important in the first year of life, accurate hearing or seeing?

chest. [**Developmental Link**: Kangaroo care is explained in Chapter 4.] Soon, infants turn their heads to see the source of a voice—an ability that requires instant calculation of the difference between when the sound reaches the left and right ears.

Newborn hearing is routinely checked at most hospitals in North America and Europe, since deaf infants benefit from early remediation. If they have cochlear implants by age 1, they may not be delayed in speech or comprehension—unlike for those whose deafness is remedied after age 2 (Tobey et al., 2013).

## Seeing

By contrast, vision is immature at birth. Although in mid-pregnancy the eyes open and are sensitive to bright light (if the pregnant woman is sunbathing in a bikini, for instance), the fetus has nothing much to see. Consequently, newborns are legally blind; they focus only on things between 4 and 30 inches (10 and 75 centimeters) away (Bornstein et al., 2005).

Almost immediately, experience combines with maturation of the visual cortex to improve the ability to see shapes and notice details. Movement captures attention, as does contrast. For example, by 6 weeks, when babies see a person, they focus on the eyes—those colorful dots on a plain surface.

Vision improves so rapidly that researchers are hard-pressed to describe the day-by-day improvements (Dobson et al., 2009). By 2 months, infants not only stare at faces but also, with perception and cognition, smile. (Smiling can occur earlier, but not because of perception.) In many ways, the vision of the young infant is attracted to the eyes of other people, and by age 1, they interpret emotions, follow gaze, and use their own eyes to communicate (Grossman, 2017).

Because **binocular vision** (coordinating both eyes to see one image) is impossible in the womb (nothing is far enough away), many newborns seem to use their two eyes independently, momentarily appearing wall-eyed or cross-eyed. Typically, experience leads to rapid focus and binocular vision, and binocular vision emerges at about 13 weeks (Kavšek & Braun, 2016). Early screening for visual ability is as important as early screening for hearing, because good vision is crucial for learning.

Vision allows infants to develop their motor skills. For instance, unlike younger infants, by about 6 months a baby can see something and grab it.

Toddlers who are experienced crawlers and walkers scan the immediate environment to decide whether a slope is safe to cross upright or is best traversed sitting or crawling. This illustrates early coordination of the senses and motor skills (Kretch & Adolph, 2013). (This does *not* mean that toddlers can be trusted not to fall off tables or out of windows.)

## Tasting and Smelling

As with vision and hearing, taste and smell rapidly adapt to the social context. Babies appreciate what their mothers eat, prenatally through amniotic fluid, then through breast milk, and finally through smells and spoonfuls of the family dinner.

The foods of a particular culture may aid survival because some natural substances are medicinal. For example, bitter foods provide some defense against malaria; hot spices help preserve food and thus work against food poisoning (Krebs, 2009). Thus, a taste for the family cuisine may save young lives.

Families pass on cultural taste preferences, despite immigration or changing historical circumstances. A feeding pattern that was protective may no longer be so. Indeed, when starvation was a threat, humans developed a taste for high-fat foods; now their descendants enjoy French fries, whipped cream, and bacon, jeopardizing their health.

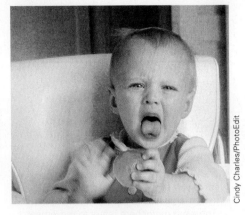

**Learning About a Lime** As with every other typical infant, Jacqueline's curiosity leads to taste and then to a slow reaction, from puzzlement to tongue-out disgust. Jacqueline's responses demonstrate that the sense of taste is acute in infancy and that quick brain perceptions are still to come.

Adaptation also occurs for the sense of smell. When breast-feeding mothers used a chamomile balm to ease cracked nipples during the first days of their babies' lives, those babies preferred that smell almost two years later, compared with babies whose mothers used an odorless ointment (Delaunay-El Allam et al., 2010).

As babies learn to recognize each person's scent, they prefer to sleep next to their caregivers, and they nuzzle into their caregivers' chests—especially when the adults are shirtless. One way to help infants who are frightened of the bath (some love bathing, some hate it) is for the parent to join the baby in the tub. The smells of the adult's body mixed with the smell of soap, and the pleasant touch, sight, and voice of the caregiver make the warm water comforting.

## Touch and Pain

The sense of touch is acute in infants. Wrapping, rubbing, massaging, and cradling are each soothing to many new babies. Even when their eyes are closed, some infants stop crying and visibly relax when held securely by their caregivers.

Gentle touch is effective to sooth an infant only a few weeks old (Tuulari et al., 2019). The infant heartbeat becomes slow and rhythmic, not rapid and erratic (as with stress), when stroked gently and rhythmically on the arm (Fairhurst et al., 2014).

Pain and temperature are not among the traditional five senses, but they are often connected to touch. Some babies cry when being changed, distressed at the sudden coldness on their skin. Some touches are unpleasant—a poke, pinch, or pat—although this varies from one baby to another.

Facial expressions, heart rate, and body movements suggest that pain can be felt, but less so than later on when the axons of the brain are better connected. Digestive difficulty (colic) and teething are said to be painful. However, this is unproven: Crying or lack of crying is an imperfect measure of pain at every stage of life.

Physiological measures, including hormones, heartbeat, and rapid brain waves, are studied to assess infant pain: The conclusions are mixed. Infant brains are immature: They have some similar responses to pain and some dissimilar ones when compared to adults (Moultrie et al., 2016).

However, the past assumption that newborns feel no pain is replaced by the idea that pain in the newborn is not the same intensity, or for the same reasons, as adult pain, but that medical professionals nevertheless need to assess and relieve infant pain (Koress et al., 2019; Maxwell et al., 2019).

For many newborn medical procedures, from a pinprick to minor surgery, a taste of sugar right before the event is an anesthetic. Breast-feeding also relieves pain (Gad et al., 2019). There are two possible reasons for that: (1) Distraction is a way to manage pain (the brain processes one sensation at a time), and (2) breast milk

**The First Blood Test** This baby will cry, but most experts believe the heel prick shown here is well worth it. The drops of blood will reveal the presence of any of several genetic diseases, including sickle-cell disease, cystic fibrosis, and phenylketonuria. Early diagnosis allows early treatment, and the cries subside quickly with a drop of sugar water or a suck of breast milk.

is thought to contain a mild anesthetic. Doctors hesitate to use drugs, because that may slow down breathing.

Many newborn care units in hospitals have adopted practices that make the first days of life better for babies, including allowing parents to touch their fragile infants, eliminating bright lights and noisy monitors, reducing pain and distress through careful swaddling, positioning, and so on. The result is better social and cognitive development later on (Montirosso et al., 2017).

## Motor Skills

**motor skill** The learned abilities to move some part of the body, in actions ranging from a large leap to a flicker of the eyelid. (The word *motor* here refers to movement of muscles.)

A **motor skill** is any skilled movement of the body, from the newborn's head-lifting to the toddler's stair-climbing and, later, from the teenager's legible and sometimes artistic handwriting to the latest dance move. Every skill requires basic maturation and then depends on motivation and practice.

Motor skills begin with reflexes, explained in Chapter 4. Reflexes become skills if they are practiced and encouraged. As you saw in the chapter's beginning, Mrs. Todd set the foundation for my fourth child's walking when Sarah was only a few months old. Similarly, some very young babies can swim—if adults build on the swimming reflex by floating with them in calm, warm water.

### Gross Motor Skills

**gross motor skills** Physical abilities involving large body movements, such as walking and jumping. (The word *gross* here means "big.")

Deliberate actions that coordinate many parts of the body, producing large movements, are called **gross motor skills.** These skills emerge directly from reflexes and proceed in a *cephalocaudal* (head-down) and *proximodistal* (center-out) direction. Infants first control their heads, lifting them up to look around. Then they control their upper bodies, their arms, and finally their legs and feet. (See At About This Time, which shows age norms for gross motor skills.)

Sitting requires muscles to steady the torso, no simple feat. By 3 months, most babies can sit propped up in a lap. By 6 months, they can usually sit unsupported, but "novice sitting and standing infants lose balance just from turning their heads

**Observation Quiz** Which of these skills has the greatest variation in age of acquisition? Why? (see answer, page 145) ➜

### AT ABOUT THIS TIME

**Age Norms (in Months) for Gross Motor Skills**

|  | When 50% of All Babies Master the Skill | When 90% of All Babies Master the Skill |
|---|---|---|
| Sit unsupported | 6 | 7.5 |
| Stand holding on | 7.4 | 9.4 |
| Crawl (creep) | 8 | 10 |
| Stand not holding | 10.8 | 13.4 |
| Walk well | 12.0 | 14.4 |
| Walk backward | 15 | 17 |
| Run | 18 | 20 |
| Jump up | 26 | 29 |

*Note:* As the text explains, age norms are affected by culture and cohort. The first five norms are based on babies from five continents [Brazil, Ghana, Norway, United States, Oman, and India] (World Health Organization, 2006). The next three are from a U.S.-only source [Coovadia & Wittenberg, 2004; based on Denver II (Frankenburg et al., 1992)]. Mastering skills a few weeks earlier or later does not indicate health or intelligence. Being very late, however, is a cause for concern.

or lifting their arms" (Adolph & Franchak, 2017). Babies never propped up (as in some institutions for orphaned children) sit much later, as do babies who cannot use vision to adjust their balance.

Crawling is another example of the head-down and center-out direction of skill mastery. As they gain muscle strength, infants wiggle, attempting to move forward by pushing their arms, shoulders, and upper bodies against whatever surface they are lying on. Motivation is crucial: Babies want to move forward to explore objects just out of reach.

Usually by 5 months, infants add their legs to this effort, inching forward (or backward) on their bellies. Exactly when this occurs depends partly on how much "tummy time" the infant has had to develop the muscles, and that, of course, is affected by the caregiver's culture (Zachry & Kitzmann, 2011).

Between 8 and 10 months after birth, most infants can lift their midsections and move forward—or sometimes backward first. Some babies never crawl, but they all find some way to move before they can walk (inching, bear-walking, scooting, creeping, or crawling). As soon as they are able, babies walk (falling frequently but getting up undaunted and trying again), since walking is quicker than crawling, and has another advantage—free hands (Adolph et al., 2012). That illustrates the drive that underlies every motor skill: Babies are powerfully motivated to do whatever they can as soon as they can.

Beyond motivations, the dynamic-systems perspective highlights the interaction of strength, maturation, and practice. We illustrate these three with walking.

1. *Muscle strength.* Newborns with skinny legs and 3-month-olds buoyed by water make stepping movements, but 6-month-olds on dry land do not; their legs are too chubby for their underdeveloped muscles. As they gain strength, they stand and then walk—easier for thin babies than heavy ones.
2. *Brain maturation.* The first leg movements—kicking (alternating legs at birth and then both legs together or one leg repeatedly at about 3 months)—occur without much thought. As the brain matures, deliberate and coordinated leg action becomes possible.
3. *Practice.* Unbalanced, wide-legged, short strides become a steady, smooth gait.

Once toddlers are able to walk by themselves, they practice obsessively, barefoot or not, at home or in stores, on sidewalks or streets, on lawns or in mud. This depends a great deal on caregivers providing the opportunity—holding them to walk—in the bath, after diapering, around the house, on the sidewalk.

Indeed, "Practice, not merely maturation, underlies improvements. . . . In 1 hour of free play, the average toddler takes about 2400 steps, travels the length of about 8 U.S. football fields, and falls 17 times" (Adolph & Franchak, 2017).

## Fine Motor Skills

Small body movements are called **fine motor skills.** The most valued fine motor skills are finger movements, enabling humans to write, draw, type, tie, and so on. Movements of the tongue, jaw, lips, and toes are fine movements, too.

Regarding hand skills, newborns have a strong reflexive grasp but lack control. During their first 2 months, babies excitedly stare and wave their arms at objects dangling within reach. By 3 months, they can usually touch such objects, but because of limited eye–hand coordination, they cannot yet grab and hold on unless an object is placed in their hands.

By 4 months, infants sometimes grab, but their timing is off: They close their hands too early or too late. Finally, by 6 months, with a concentrated, deliberate

onebluelight/E+/Getty Images

**Advancing and Advanced** At 8 months, she is already an adept crawler, alternating hands and knees, intent on progress. She will probably be walking before a year.

**fine motor skills** Physical abilities involving small body movements, especially of the hands and fingers, such as drawing and picking up a coin. (The word *fine* here means "small.")

**LaunchPad**
macmillan learning

**VIDEO: Fine Motor Skills in Infancy and Toddlerhood** shows the sequence in which babies and toddlers acquire fine motor skills.

## AT ABOUT THIS TIME

### Age Norms (in Months) for Fine Motor Skills

| | When 50% of All Babies Master the Skill | When 90% of All Babies Master the Skill |
|---|---|---|
| Grasp rattle when placed in hand | 3 | 4 |
| Reach to hold an object | 4.5 | 6 |
| Thumb and finger grasp | 8 | 10 |
| Stack two blocks | 15 | 21 |
| Imitate vertical line (drawing) | 30 | 39 |

Data from World Health Organization, 2006.

stare, most babies can reach, grab, and grasp almost any object that is the right size. Some can even transfer an object from one hand to the other.

Toward the end of the first year and throughout the second, finger skills improve as babies master the pincer movement (using thumb and forefinger to pick up tiny objects). They become able to feed themselves, first with hands, then fingers, then utensils (Ho, 2010). (See At About This Time.)

## Cultural Variations

Practice of every motor skill advances development, not only of the skill but over-all (Leonard & Hill, 2014). When U.S. infants are grouped by ethnicity, generally African American babies are ahead of Latinx babies when it comes to walking. In turn, Latino babies are ahead of those of European descent.

Internationally, the earliest walkers are in several nations of Africa. For exam-ple, about a third of the infants in Benin walk at 10 months (Dossou et al., 2019). As evident in the opening anecdote of this chapter, variations that might seem to be genetic may instead be cultural.

Nonetheless, some infants in every culture need early intervention. World Health Organization guidelines now reflect local norms for development, because infants with disabilities need to be recognized and treated before cognitive impair-ment occurs (Lancaster et al., 2018).

In some cultures, babies are massaged and stretched from birth onward and are encouraged to walk as soon as possible. They do so, long before a year (Adolph & Franchak, 2017). The latest walkers (15 months) may be in rural China, where infants are bundled up against the cold (Adolph & Robinson, 2013). Some cul-tures discourage walking because danger lurks (venomous snakes, open fires, speeding cars), making toddlers safer since they cannot wander. By contrast, some cultures encourage running over long distances: Their children can run marathons (Adolph & Franchak, 2017).

Remember that difference is not deficit. However, slow development *relative to local norms* may indicate a problem that needs attention: Lags are much easier to remedy during infancy than later on.

If one sense or motor skill is impaired, the others are affected as well. This is true throughout childhood: Fine motor skills are aided by the ability to sit, lan-guage development depends on hearing, reading depends on vision—so careful monitoring of basic sensory and motor skills in infancy is part of good infant care.

skynesher/E+/Getty Images

**No Stopping Him** Something compels infants to roll over, sit, stand, and walk as soon as their bodies allow it. This boy will fall often, despite his balancing arms, but he will get up and try again. Soon he will run and climb. What will his cautious mother (behind him) do then?

# Sticky Mittens

As with gross motor skills, fine motor skills are shaped by practice. In the first year, when "infants flap their arms, rotate their hands, and wiggle their fingers, and exhibit bouts of rhythmical waving, rubbing, and banging while holding objects" (Adolph & Franchak, 2017), they are practicing fine motor skills that will lead to better thinking later on.

Although infants have an inner compulsion to move their bodies and practice seeing, hearing, and all their motor skills, opportunity is crucial. This has been studied in detail in dozens of studies involving "sticky mittens" (with Velcro) that reward grabbing small toys that also have Velcro on them. With those special mittens, infants master hand skills sooner than usual, and their perceptual skills advance as well (Libertus & Needham, 2010; Libertus et al., 2016; Nascimento et al., 2019; Needham et al., 2017; Soska et al., 2010).

One follow-up of the original research suggests that the special mittens are not necessary, but that play that includes reaching for objects may be. In that study, healthy 2- to 3-month-olds were assigned to one of three groups. Over 16 days, one group had daily reaching practice with sticky mittens, another group had similar reaching practice but their mittens were not sticky, and a third control group had no special practice. The results: The two experimental groups advanced in the motor skill of reaching and the perceptual skill of focusing on objects. The control group also improved a little, but much less so (Leonard & Hill, 2014).

Another follow-up provided not only active exploration with sticky mittens, but it also compared one group who explored in silence and another group who received auditory reinforcement. The details demonstrate how carefully scientists contrast independent variables:

> In the less auditory feedback condition, the table was covered with foam core that was itself covered with thin foam to reduce sounds

the soft toys might make when contacting the table. In the less auditory feedback condition, the toys were silent while moving. In the more auditory feedback condition, no foam was used on the table and the toys made loud impact noises when hitting the table. In addition, in the more auditory feedback condition, bells were sewn onto the sticky mittens and a few small bells were placed inside the toys to produce rattling and jingling sounds during the movement of the toys.

*[Needham et al., 2017, p. 218]*

The infants who could hear as well as see the effects of their activity showed more exploration and perception. That makes sense, because some *sensory redundancy* is characteristic of infant learning. Babies use "multiple sensory modalities: infants look at an object while banging it against a table surface or they explore an object manually, orally, and visually in quick succession" (Needham et al., 2017, p. 221). They not only reach to touch their caregivers, they look, listen, smell, and (if the adult lets them) taste them!

All the research on infant reaching and brain development leads to a solid conclusion: Even early in life, infant senses and motor skills reinforce each other, as steps in an ongoing, experience-expectant, learning process. As authors of one book explain:

> Achievements are not ends or goals but rather they are points in a cascade of developmental change and themselves influence future developmental outcomes. . . . different abilities, functions, or behaviors at another point in time.

*[Oakes & Rakison, 2019, p. xi]*

To advance the cognitive and social development of a person lifelong, early sensory and motor skills are the foundation. Encourage the baby to explore!

---

## WHAT HAVE YOU LEARNED?

1. What particular sounds and patterns do infants pay attention to?

2. How does an infant's vision change over the first year?

3. Why is hearing more acute than vision in the early weeks?

4. Why do some babies prefer certain tastes and smells that others dislike?

5. What is known and unknown about infant pain?

6. What is universal and what is cultural in the development of gross motor skills in infancy?

7. What is the relationship between motor skills and the senses?

8. Why do caregivers vary in which motor skills they encourage?

## Surviving in Good Health

Public health measures have dramatically reduced infant death. United Nations statistics show that in 1950, worldwide, one infant in six died before age 1; in 2020, the rate was about 1 in 40. Marked income differences are evident, from 1 in 200 in the most developed nations to 1 in 10 in the poorest ones (United Nations, June 17, 2019). Progress is most dramatic in large developing nations (China and India).

All told, about 2 million people are alive today who would have died if they had been born 70 years ago. Improvements are everywhere. Infant mortality has been reduced by 900 percent in Poland, Japan, Chile, China, and Finland.

## Better Days Ahead

Most child deaths occur in the first month. In the twenty-first century in developed nations, 99.9 percent of 1-month-olds live to adulthood. Public health measures (clean water, nourishing food, immunization of older children who might catch a disease that could kill a newborn) deserve most of the credit.

Not only survival but life itself is better for children, because parents have fewer births and thus attend more to each one. Maternal education is pivotal. Especially in low-income nations, educated women have far fewer, but much healthier, children than women who never went to school (de la Croix, 2013).

## Considering Culture

Many cultural variations are simply alternate ways to raise a healthy child, a difference, not a deficit. Sometimes, however, one mode of infant care is much better than another. To discover those, international comparisons become useful. Consider the dramatic worldwide reduction in **sudden infant death syndrome (SIDS)**.

Every year until the mid-1990s, tens of thousands of infants died of SIDS, called *crib death* in North America and *cot death* in England. Tiny infants smiled at their caregivers, waved their arms at rattles that their small fingers could not yet grasp, went to sleep, and never woke up. Scientists tested hypotheses (the cat? the quilt? natural honey? homicide? spoiled milk?) to no avail. Grief-ridden parents were sometimes falsely accused. Sudden infant death was a mystery. Finally, one major risk factor—sleeping on the stomach—was discovered, thanks to the work of one scientist, described on the next page, in A Case to Study.

## Immunization

Diseases that could be deadly (including measles, chicken pox, polio, mumps, rotavirus, and whooping cough) are now rare because of **immunization,** which primes the body's immune system to resist a particular disease. Immunization (often via *vaccination*) is said to have had "a greater impact on human mortality reduction and population growth than any other public health intervention besides clean water" (Baker, 2000, p. 199).

In the first half of the twentieth century, almost every child had at least one of these diseases. Usually they recovered, and then they were immune. Indeed, some parents took their toddlers to play with a child who had an active case of chicken pox, for instance, hoping their child would catch the disease and then become immune. That protected that child later in life.

**Well Protected** Disease and early death are common in Ethiopia, where this photo was taken, but neither is likely for 2-year-old Salem. He is protected not only by the nutrition and antibodies in his mother's milk but also by the large blue net that surrounds them. Treated bed nets, like this one provided by the Carter Center and the Ethiopian Health Ministry, are often large enough for families to eat, read, and sleep in together, without fear of malaria-infected mosquitoes.

**sudden infant death syndrome (SIDS)** A situation in which a seemingly healthy infant, usually between 2 and 6 months old, suddenly stops breathing and dies unexpectedly while asleep.

**immunization** A process that stimulates the body's immune system by causing production of antibodies to defend against attack by a particular contagious disease. Creation of antibodies may be accomplished naturally (by having the disease), by injection, by drops that are swallowed, or by a nasal spray.

# Scientist at Work

Susan Beal, a 35-year-old scientist with five young children, began to study SIDS deaths in South Australia. She responded to phone calls, often at 5 or 6 A.M., notifying her that another baby had died. Her husband supported her work, often becoming the sole child-care provider so she could leave home at a moment's notice.

Sometimes she was the first professional to arrive, before the police or the coroner. Initially she was embarrassed to question the grief-stricken parents. But soon she learned that parents were grateful to talk, in part because they tended to blame themselves and they needed to express that emotion to someone who was not likely to accuse them. Beal reassured them that scientists shared their bewilderment.

She was more than a sympathetic listener. She was a scientist, so she took detailed, careful notes on dozens of circumstances at each of more than 500 deaths. She found that some things did not matter (such as birth order), and some increased the risk (maternal smoking and lambskin blankets).

A breakthrough came when Beal noticed an ethnic variation: She saw far more SIDS victims in Australia among people of European descent than of Chinese descent. Genetic? Most experts thought so. But Beal's notes revealed that almost all SIDS babies died while sleeping on their stomachs, contrary to the Chinese custom of placing infants on their backs to sleep. She developed a new hypothesis: Sleeping position mattered.

To test her hypothesis, Beal convinced a large group of non-Chinese parents to put their newborns to sleep on their backs. Almost none of them died suddenly.

After several years of gathering data, she drew a surprising conclusion: Back-sleeping protected against SIDS. Her published report (Beal, 1988) caught the attention of doctors in the Netherlands, where pediatricians had told parents to put their babies to sleep on their stomachs. Two Dutch scientists (Engelberts & de Jonge, 1990) recommended back-sleeping; thousands of parents took heed. SIDS was reduced in Holland by 40 percent in one year—a stunning replication.

In the United States, Benjamin Spock's *Baby and Child Care*, first published in 1946, sold more copies than any book other than the Bible. He advised stomach-sleeping, and millions of parents followed that advice. In 1984, SIDS killed 5,245 babies.

But Beal's 1988 article, and the Dutch 1990 data, spread to America. By 1994, a "Back to Sleep" campaign cut the SIDS rate dramatically in every nation (Kinney & Thach, 2009; Mitchell, 2009). By 1996, the U.S. SIDS rate was half of what it had been. By 2015, the U.S. Centers for Disease Control and Prevention reported 1,600 SIDS deaths, even though the population of infants had increased over the past decades. Consequently, in the United States alone, about 100,000 people are alive who would be dead if they had been born before 1990 (see **Figure 5.4**).

Stomach-sleeping is a proven, replicated risk, but it is not the only one. Other risks include low birthweight, winter, being male, exposure to cigarettes, soft blankets or pillows, bed-sharing, and physical abnormalities (in the brainstem, heart, mitochondria, or microbiome) (Neary & Breckenridge, 2013; Ostfeld et al., 2010). Most SIDS victims experience several risks, a cascade of biological and social circumstances.

That does not surprise Susan Beal. She sifted through all the evidence and found the main risk—stomach-sleeping—but she continues to study other factors. She praises the courage of the hundreds of parents who talked with her hours after their baby died; the entire world praises her.

**LaunchPad**
macmillan learning

**Interview with Susan Beal** https://tinyurl.com/t5xtyjr

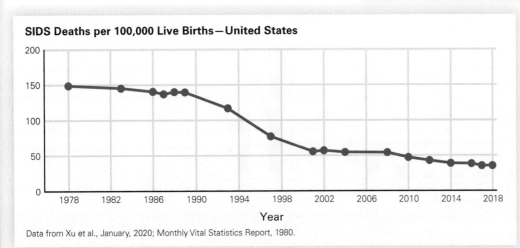

**SIDS Deaths per 100,000 Live Births—United States**

Data from Xu et al., January, 2020; Monthly Vital Statistics Report, 1980.

**FIGURE 5.4**

**Alive Today** As more parents learn that a baby should be on his or her "back to sleep," the SIDS rate continues to decrease. Other factors are also responsible for the decline—fewer parents smoke cigarettes in the baby's room.

Scott Eels/Redux

**True Dedication** This young Buddhist monk lives in a remote region of Nepal, where until recently measles was a common, fatal disease. Fortunately, a UNICEF porter carried the vaccine over mountain trails for two days so that this boy—and his whole community—could be immunized.

**THINK CRITICALLY:** What developmental questions are raised by the recent COVID-19 outbreak?

## Success and Survival

Beginning with smallpox in the nineteenth century, doctors discovered that giving a small dose of a virus to healthy people stimulates antibodies and provides protection. Stunning successes in immunization include the following:

- Smallpox, the most lethal disease for children in the past, was eradicated worldwide as of 1980. Vaccination against smallpox is no longer needed.
- Polio, a crippling and sometimes fatal disease, has been virtually eliminated in the Americas. Only 784 cases were reported anywhere in the world in 2003. However, false rumors halted immunization in northern Nigeria. Polio reappeared, sickening 1,948 people in 2005, almost all of them in West Africa. Public health workers and community leaders rallied and Nigeria's polio rate fell again, to 6 cases in 2014. However, poverty and wars in South Asia prevented immunization there: In 2019, 116 victims were in Pakistan and Afghanistan, four times the rate in 2018. An added complication is that in nations where some children are not immunized, those who are immunized might develop a new strain of polio, as occurred with 196 children in 12 nations of Africa (Roberts, 2020).
- Measles (rubeola, not rubella) is disappearing, thanks to a vaccine developed in 1963. Prior to that time, 3 to 4 million cases occurred each year in the United States alone (Centers for Disease Control and Prevention, May 15, 2015). In 2012 in the United States, only 55 people had measles, although globally about 20 million measles cases occurred that year. (See **Figure 5.5**)

However, if a traveler brings measles back to the United States, and if some parents decide not to immunize their children, outbreaks of measles may occur. That happened in dozens of nations including the United States in 2019, where at least 1,249 people had measles (including a newborn who caught it from the mother)—the highest rate since 1994 (Patel et al., 2019).

Immunization protects not only from temporary sickness but also from complications, including deafness, blindness, sterility, and meningitis. Sometimes such damage from illness is not apparent until decades later. Having mumps in childhood, for instance, can cause sterility and doubles the risk of schizophrenia in adulthood (Dalman et al., 2008).

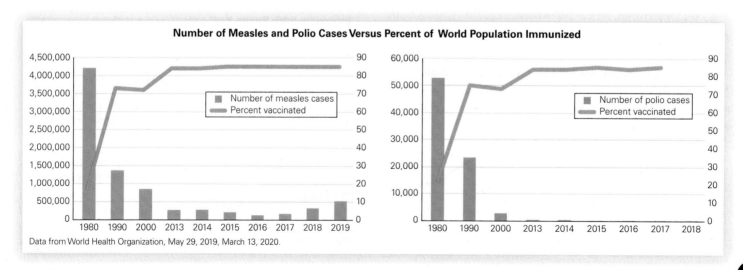

**Number of Measles and Polio Cases Versus Percent of World Population Immunized**

Data from World Health Organization, May 29, 2019, March 13, 2020.

**FIGURE 5.5**

**Ask Grandma** Neither polio nor measles is completely eradicated, because some parents do not realize the danger. They may never have seen the serious complications of these diseases.

## CAREER ALERT    The Pediatrician and the Pediatric Nurse

Many people studying human development hope to enter the medical field as doctors, nurses, physical therapists, or in dozens of related careers. Often their ultimate goal is to become a pediatrician, a medical doctor who helps children grow strong and healthy.

From an educational perspective, that is a lofty goal indeed. To become a pediatrician, one must first become a medical doctor (M.D.) after earning a bachelor's degree. This entails entering medical school, first with two years of advanced classes and then working as an intern for two more years in many aspects of medicine.

At that point, a fledgling doctor might decide to be a pediatrician, which requires a residency in pediatrics for at least three more years. Finally, the doctor can be licensed in pediatrics. The pediatrician can then work in a hospital or other institution that treats children or begin a private practice.

If someone wants to work directly for the health of children, yet remaining a student for more than ten years after college graduation seems impossible, then the person should consider one of many other medical professions that help children, among them nurses, physician assistants, physical therapists, and pediatric psychologists. Nursing itself consists of many levels, from aide, to practical nurse (L.P.N), to registered nurse (R.N.), to nurse practitioner (who can do many of the same things as an M.D.).

For all these, the job outlook is good: The Occupational Outlook Handbook reports that the United States will need 15 percent more pediatricians in the next decade. Nurses fare even better: The projection for registered nurses is 16 percent; for nurse-midwives, 22 percent; and for nurse practitioners, 36 percent. Nurse practitioners must complete two more years of education after earning a bachelor's degree and becoming a registered nurse (RN), but the reward is higher salary, more responsibility, and job security.

How can child health be an expanding field, since the birth rate is falling? There are two reasons: First, the field of medicine is increasingly focused on prevention, and child health is the foundation for adult health. That means that well-child care is increasingly important. Second, as parents have fewer children, they have become more intensely concerned about each child.

The joy of all these professions is working with children and watching them grow into happy and successful adults. However, the children who need the most care are the ones in poor health. Often medicine can cure an illness, or at least pave a path toward a satisfying adulthood. This is now true for many common problems, such as sickle cell anemia or Down's syndrome, that once led to suffering and death. However, some children still suffer and a few die, which is devastating not only to the parents but also to medical professionals.

The other problem is that helping children requires helping caregivers. Often parents are grateful for medical advice, but sometimes they are not. Specializing in child health requires a person to also specialize in providing information and respect to whomever is responsible for the direct care of the child. That may be difficult.

For example, currently, many parents hesitate to vaccinate their children. Medical professionals know the evidence and have treated children with measles, mumps, and other childhood diseases that could have been prevented. That makes them understandably impatient with parents who choose not to protect their children. Yet parents have picketed and sued doctors who advocate vaccination. Thus, becoming a medical professional in child health requires courage as well as knowledge.

Worst of all, some parents mistreat their children, and the doctor or nurse is the first one to notice it. They are "mandated reporters"; they must report their concerns. However, as this text makes clear, reporting is only the first step toward helping a mistreated child. Medical professionals may be the best ones to support caregivers and children, making sure that the child recovers from any harm.

Thus, caring for children is a noble and joyous task, but it requires courage and strong human relations skills. As your study of human development makes clear, children do not grow in isolation: A skilled medical professional is a crucial team member, allowing every child to thrive.

---

Immunization also protects those who cannot be safely vaccinated, such as infants under 3 months and people with impaired immune systems (HIV-positive, aged, or undergoing chemotherapy). Fortunately, each vaccinated child stops transmission of the disease, a phenomenon called **herd immunity.** Usually, if 90 percent of the people in a community (a herd) are immunized, no one dies of that disease.

All 50 of the United States exempt vaccination requirements for children with certain medical conditions (such as undergoing chemotherapy for cancer), but 15 states allow parents to refuse vaccination because of "personal belief," and 45 states allow religious exemptions (see Visualizing Development). This horrifies public health workers, who know that the risks of the diseases—especially to babies—are far greater than the risks from immunization.

Measles, for example, can be deadly, and the "anti-vax" movement has undercut herd immunity in some nations. That makes it especially crucial for any child over 6 months who is travelling to be protected (Wong et al., 2020). The most recent outbreak was in Samoa, from October 2019 to February 2020. Vaccination rates had fallen to 31 percent for young children. After several child deaths, the government mandated vaccination, and now it is 95 percent. That was too late for some: Of the 83 deaths recorded as of January 2020, most (85 percent) were infants and children, aged 1 day to 4 years.

**herd immunity** The level of immunity necessary in a population (the herd) in order to stop transmission of infectious diseases. The rate is usually above 90 percent, and even higher for very infectious diseases. Newborns, and people with certain diseases (e.g., cancer patients taking immunosuppressant drugs), cannot be vaccinated; herd immunity protects them.

# Immunization

Before the measles vaccine was introduced in 1963, 30 million people globally contracted measles each year. About 2 million of them died, usually because they were both malnourished and sick. (World Health Organization, April 28, 2017). Thankfully, worldwide vaccination efforts now mean that no child need die of measles.

Measles is highly infectious, so 95 percent of the population must be immunized in order for herd immunity to protect the entire community. The United States achieved that: A decade ago, measles incidence was close to zero. Experts thought it would soon be eliminated in all developed countries, so public health workers focused on the very poorest nations.

## ESTIMATED MEASLES VACCINE COVERAGE – SELECTED NATIONS

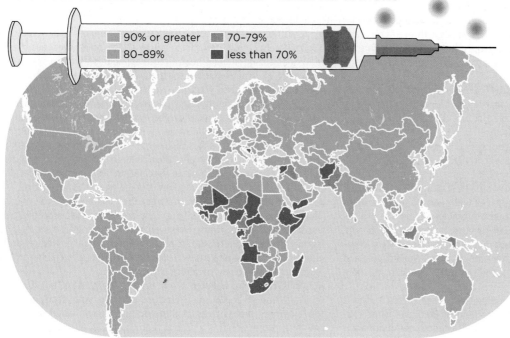

- 90% or greater
- 80–89%
- 70–79%
- less than 70%

By June 2019, more than 1,000 measles cases had been reported in 28 U.S. states, the most since 1992 (measles was declared eliminated in 2000) (Centers for Disease Control and Prevention, June 17, 2019). To understand what went wrong, note that many states allow personal or religious exemptions to immunization requirements. Thus, as the U.S. map below shows, several states are not at that safe 94 percent—leaving many vulnerable, not only to discomfort but also to complications, including pneumonia, encephalitis, and even death.

Data from World Health Organization, May 29, 2019.

## VACCINE EXEMPTION AND HERD IMMUNITY – UNITED STATES

MMR vaccination rate >94%

Nonmedical exemption rate above U.S. median (2%)

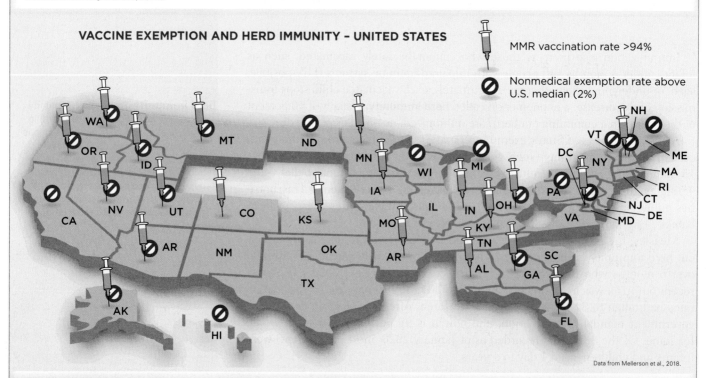

Data from Mellerson et al., 2018.

Ethicists also are concerned, because sometimes allowing individuals to make their own choices clashes with the need to protect the community. If private choices reduce herd immunity, the public is burdened with hospital costs and deaths (Giubilini & Savulescu, 2019).

Children may react to immunization by being irritable or even feverish for a day, to the distress of their parents. However, parents do not notice if their child does *not* get polio, measles, or so on. Before the varicella (chicken pox) vaccine, more than 100 people in the United States died each year from that disease, and 1 million were itchy and feverish for a week. Now, far fewer people get chicken pox, and almost no one dies of varicella.

Many parents are concerned about the potential side effects of vaccines, in part because the rare event of one person sickened by vaccination is broadcast widely. Psychologists find that a common source of irrational thinking is overestimating the frequency of a memorable case (Ariely, 2010). As a result, the rate of missed vaccinations in the United States has been rising over the past decades.

An example of the benefits of immunization comes from Connecticut, where in 2012 flu vaccination was required for all 6- to 59-month-olds in licensed day-care centers. Most children were not in day-care centers, but parents became aware of the law and many immunized their children. That winter, far fewer Connecticut children were hospitalized for flu, although rates rose everywhere else. Meanwhile, Colorado (one of the states that allowed many exemptions, with kindergartners well below herd immunity) had the highest rate of flu hospitalizations (MMWR, March 7, 2014).

**Especially for Nurses and Pediatricians** A mother refuses to have her baby immunized because she wants to prevent side effects. She wants your signature for a religious exemption, which in some jurisdictions allows the mother to refuse vaccination. What should you do? (see response, page 145)

**DATA CONNECTIONS: Saving Lives: Immunization in the United States** describes the vaccines that are recommended for children and the rates at which U.S. children are immunized. 🎬 **LaunchPad.**

## Nutrition

As already explained, infant mortality worldwide has plummeted in recent years for several reasons: fewer sudden infant deaths, advances in prenatal and newborn care, and, as you just read, immunization. One more measure is making a huge difference: better nutrition.

## Breast-Feeding

Ideally, nutrition starts with *colostrum*, a thick, high-calorie fluid secreted by the mother's breasts at birth. This benefit is not understood in some cultures, where the mother is not allowed to breast feed until her milk "comes in" two or three days after birth. (Sometimes other women nurse the newborn; sometimes herbal tea is given). Worldwide research confirmed that colostrum saves infant lives, especially if the infant is preterm (Andreas et al., 2015; Moles et al., 2015).

**Same Situation, Far Apart: Breast-Feeding** Breast-feeding is universal. None of us would exist if our foremothers had not successfully breast-fed their babies for millennia. Currently, breast-feeding is practiced worldwide, but it is no longer the only way to feed infants, and each culture has particular practices.

Compared with formula using cow's milk, human milk is sterile, more digestible, and rich in nutrients (Wambach & Riordan, 2014). Allergies and asthma are less common in children who were breast-fed, and in adulthood, their obesity, diabetes, and heart disease rates are lower.

The composition of breast milk adjusts to the age of the baby, with milk for premature babies distinct from that

**VIDEO: Nutritional Needs of Infants and Children: Breast-Feeding Promotion** shows UNICEF's efforts to educate women on the benefits of breast-feeding.

for older infants. Quantity increases to meet the demand: Twins and even triplets can be exclusively breast-fed for months.

Formula is advised for medical reasons only in unusual cases, such as when the mother uses toxic drugs or is HIV-positive. Even with HIV, however, breast milk without supplementation is advised by the World Health Organization. In some nations, the infants' risk of catching HIV from their mothers is lower than the risk of dying from infections, diarrhea, or malnutrition as a result of bottle-feeding (A. Williams et al., 2016).

Doctors worldwide recommend breast-feeding with no other foods—not even juice—for the first six months of life. (**Table 5.1** lists some of the benefits of breast-feeding.) Some pediatricians suggest adding foods (rice cereal and bananas) at 4 months; others advise waiting until 6 months (Fewtrell et al., 2011).

Breast-feeding was once universal, but by the mid-twentieth century, many mothers thought formula was better. Fortunately, that has changed again. In 2016 in the United States, most (84 percent) newborns were breast-fed, as were more than half (57 percent) of all 6-month-olds and more than a third (36 percent) of all 1-year-olds (Centers for Disease Control and Prevention, 2019).

Encouragement of breast-feeding from family members, especially fathers, is crucial. In addition, ideally nurses visit new mothers weekly at home; such visits (routine in some nations, rare in others) increase the likelihood that breast-feeding will continue.

Although every expert agrees that breast milk is beneficial, given the complexity and variation of human families, mothers should not feel guilty for feeding formula. Indeed, some critics contend that breast-feeding has reached cult status, shaming those who do not do it (Jung, 2015). No single behavior, even those recommended (breast-feeding, co-sleeping, hand-washing, exercising, family planning, immunization) defines good motherhood.

### TABLE 5.1

#### The Benefits of Breast-Feeding

| For the Baby | For the Mother |
|---|---|
| Balance of nutrition (fat, protein, etc.) adjusts to age of baby | Easier bonding with baby |
| Breast milk has micronutrients not found in formula | Reduced risk of breast cancer and osteoporosis |
| Less infant illness, including allergies, ear infections, stomach upsets | Natural contraception (with exclusive breast-feeding, for several months) |
| Less childhood asthma | Pleasure of breast stimulation |
| Better childhood vision | Satisfaction of meeting infant's basic need |
| Less adult illness, including diabetes, cancer, heart disease | No formula to prepare; no sterilization |
| Protection against many childhood diseases, since breast milk contains antibodies from the mother | Easier travel with the baby |
| Stronger jaws, fewer cavities, advanced breathing reflexes (less SIDS) | **For the Family** |
| Higher IQ, less likely to drop out of school, more likely to attend college | Increased survival of other children (because of spacing of births) |
| Later puberty, fewer teenage pregnancies | Increased family income (because formula and medical care are expensive) |
| Less likely to become obese or hypertensive by age 12 | Less stress on father, especially at night |

## Malnutrition

**Protein-calorie malnutrition** occurs when a person does not consume enough food to sustain normal growth. A child may suffer from **stunting,** being short for their age because chronic malnutrition kept them from growing, or **wasting,** being severely underweight for their age and height (2 or more standard deviations below average). Many nations, especially in East Asia, Latin America, and central Europe, have seen improvement in child nutrition in the past decades, with an accompanying decrease in wasting and stunting (see **Figure 5.6**).

In other nations, however, primarily in Africa, wasting has increased (Black et al., 2013). Although only 17 percent of the world's population live in Africa, a third of all the infants worldwide who suffer from malnutrition are in African nations south of the Sahara Desert (Akombi et al., 2017). Explanations include high birth rate, maternal AIDS deaths, climate change, and civil wars.

Chronically malnourished infants and children suffer in three ways:

1. Learning suffers. If malnutrition continues long enough to affect height, it also affects the brain. If hunger reduces energy and curiosity, learning suffers.
2. Diseases are more serious. About half of all childhood deaths occur because malnutrition makes a childhood disease lethal, especially from leading causes of childhood deaths—diarrhea and pneumonia—as well as from milder diseases such as measles (Imdad et al., 2011; Walker et al., 2013).
3. Some diseases result directly from malnutrition—including both *marasmus* during the first year, when body tissues waste away, and *kwashiorkor* after age 1, when growth slows down, hair becomes thin, skin becomes splotchy, and the face, legs, and abdomen swell with fluid (edema).

Prevention, more than treatment, is needed. Sadly, some children hospitalized for marasmus or kwashiorkor die even after being fed because their digestive systems were already failing (M. Smith et al., 2013). Ideally, prenatal nutrition, then breast-feeding, and then supplemental iron and vitamin A stop malnutrition before it starts. Once malnutrition is apparent, highly nutritious formula (usually fortified peanut butter) often restores weight—but not always.

Ironically, one of the factors that correlates with wasting and stunting in children from sub-Saharan African nations is breast-feeding that continues after a year, especially if the mother herself is malnourished. Thus, public health recommendations

**protein-calorie malnutrition** A condition in which a person does not consume sufficient food of any kind. This deprivation can result in several illnesses, severe weight loss, and even death.

**stunting** The failure of children to grow to a normal height for their age due to severe and chronic malnutrition.

**wasting** The tendency for children to be severely underweight for their age as a result of malnutrition.

**VIDEO: Malnutrition and Children in Nepal** shows the plight of Nepalese children who suffer from protein-energy malnutrition.

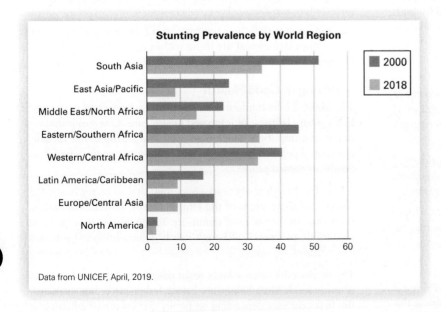

Data from UNICEF, April, 2019.

**FIGURE 5.6**
**Evidence Matters** Genes were thought to explain height differences among Asians and Scandinavians, until data on hunger and malnutrition proved otherwise. The result: starvation down and height up almost everywhere—especially in Asia. Despite increased world population, far fewer young children are stunted (255 million in 1970; 156 million in 2015). Evidence now finds additional problems: Civil war, climate change, and limited access to contraception have increased stunting in East and Central Africa in the past decade.

**Observation Quiz** Which regions have the most and least improvement since 1990? (see answer, page 145) need to consider nutrition in the entire family and community: Infants survive best if breast-fed, but after 6 months, ample, digestible food is also needed (Akombi et al., 2017).

A combination of factors—genetic susceptibility, poor nutrition, infection, and abnormal bacteria in the digestive system (the microbiome)—may be fatal (M. Smith et al., 2013). Giving severely ill children an antibiotic to stop infection saves lives—but always, prevention is best (Gough et al., 2014).

---

**WHAT HAVE YOU LEARNED?**

1. Why is polio still a problem in some nations?

2. Why do doctors worry about immunization rates in the United States?

3. What are the reasons for and against breast-feeding until a child is at least 1 year old?

4. When is it advisable that a woman not breast-feed?

5. What is the relationship between malnutrition and disease?

6. Which is worse, stunting or wasting? Why?

---

## SUMMARY

### Body Changes

1. In the first two years of life, infants grow taller, gain weight, and increase in head circumference—all indicative of development. On average, birthweight doubles by 4 months, triples by 1 year, and quadruples by 2 years.

2. By age 2, the average well-nourished child weighs about 28 pounds (12.7 kilograms) and has gained more than a foot since birth, reaching about half their adult height.

3. Medical checkups in the first months of a child's life focus especially on weight, height, and head circumference because early detection of slow growth can halt later problems. Percentile changes can signify difficulties.

4. The amount of time a child sleeps decreases over the first two years. Variations in sleep patterns are normal, caused by both nature and nurture. Bed-sharing is the norm in many developing nations, although it increases the risk of SIDS. Co-sleeping and bed-sharing are increasingly common in developed nations; many breast-feeding mothers choose it.

5. Brains grow dramatically, from about 25 to about 75 percent of adult brain weight in the first two years. Complexity increases as well, with cell growth, development of dendrites, and formation of synapses.

6. Some stimulation is experience-expectant, needed for normal brain development. Both exuberant growth and pruning aid cognition, as the connections that are experience-dependent are strengthened.

7. Experience is vital for brain development. An infant who is socially isolated, overstressed, or deprived of stimulation may be impaired lifelong.

### Perceiving and Moving

8. At birth, the senses already respond to stimuli. Prenatal experience makes hearing the most mature sense. Vision is the least mature sense at birth, but it improves quickly with experience. Infants use all their senses to strengthen their early social interactions.

9. The senses of smell, taste, and touch are present at birth, and they help infants respond to their social world. Pain is experienced, but infant pain is not identical to adult pain.

10. Infants gradually improve their motor skills as they begin to grow and brain maturation continues. Control of the body proceeds from the head downward (cephalocaudal) and the core to the extremities (proximodistal). Mastery of motor skills aid cognition.

11. Gross motor skills are mastered throughout infancy, depending on practice, motivation, and maturation. Major advances are sitting up (at about 6 months), walking (at about 1 year), and running (before age 2).

12. Fine motor skills also improve, as infants learn to grab, aim, and manipulate almost anything within reach. Development of the senses and motor skills are mutually reinforcing.

### Surviving in Good Health

13. About 2 billion infant deaths have been prevented in the past half-century because of improved health care. One major innovation is immunization, which has eradicated smallpox and virtually eliminated polio and measles. Herd immunity remains crucial, as deaths in Samoa prove.

14. Public health workers are concerned that some regions of the world, and some states of the United States, have immunization rates that are below herd immunity. Young infants may be most vulnerable to viruses, although deaths from childhood diseases can occur at any age.

15. Breast milk helps infants resist disease and promotes growth of every kind. Most babies are breast-fed at birth, but rates over the first year vary depending on family and culture. Pediatricians

now recommend breast milk as the only nourishment for the first 4–6 months.

**16.** Severe malnutrition stunts growth and can cause death, both directly through marasmus or kwashiorkor and indirectly

through vulnerability if a child becomes sick. Stunting and wasting are both signs of malnutrition, which is become less common worldwide except in some nations of sub-Saharan Africa.

## KEY TERMS

percentile (p. 121)
REM (rapid eye movement) sleep (p. 122)
co-sleeping (p. 122)
bed-sharing (p. 122)
head-sparing (p. 123)
neuron (p. 124)
axon (p. 124)
dendrite (p. 124)
synapse (p. 124)

neurotransmitter (p. 124)
myelin (p. 124)
cortex (p. 124)
prefrontal cortex (p. 124)
limbic system (p. 124)
amygdala (p. 125)
hippocampus (p. 125)
hypothalamus (p. 125)
cortisol (p. 125)
pituitary (p. 125)

transient exuberance (p. 126)
pruning (p. 126)
experience-expectant (p. 127)
experience-dependent (p. 127)
shaken baby syndrome (p. 128)
self-righting (p. 129)
sensation (p. 129)
binocular vision (p. 130)
motor skill (p. 132)
gross motor skills (p. 132)

fine motor skills (p. 133)
sudden infant death syndrome (SIDS) (p. 136)
immunization (p. 136)
herd immunity (p. 139)
protein-calorie malnutrition (p. 143)
stunting (p. 143)
wasting (p. 143)

## APPLICATIONS

**1.** Immunization regulations and practices vary, partly for social and political reasons. Ask at least two faculty or administrative staff members what immunizations the students at your college must have and why. If you hear "It's a law," ask why.

**2.** Observe three infants (whom you do not know) in public places such as a store, playground, or bus. Look closely at body size and motor skills, especially how much control each baby has over his or her legs and hands. From that, estimate the

baby's age in months, and then ask the caregiver how old the infant is.

**3.** *This project can be done alone, but it is more informative if several students pool responses.* Ask 3 to 10 adults whether they were bottle-fed or breast-fed and, if breast-fed, for how long. If someone does not know, or expresses embarrassment, that itself is worth noting. Do you see any correlation between adult body size and infant feeding?

## Especially For ANSWERS

**Response for New Parents** (from p. 123): From the psychological and cultural perspectives, babies can sleep anywhere as long as the parents can hear them if they cry. The main consideration is safety: Infants should not sleep on a mattress that is too soft, nor beside an adult who is drunk or on drugs. Otherwise, families should decide for themselves.

**Response for Parents of Grown Children** (from p. 127): Probably not. Brain development is programmed to occur for all infants, requiring only the stimulation that virtually all families provide—warmth, reassuring touch, overheard conversation, facial expressions, movement. Extras such as baby talk, music, exercise, mobiles, and massage may be beneficial but are not essential.

**Response for Nurses and Pediatricians** (from p. 141): It is difficult to convince people that their method of child rearing is wrong, although you should try. In this case, listen respectfully and then describe specific instances of serious illness or death from a childhood disease. Suggest that the mother ask her grandparents whether they knew anyone who had polio, tuberculosis, or tetanus (they probably did). If you cannot convince this mother, do not despair: Vaccination of 95 percent of toddlers helps protect the other 5 percent. If the mother has genuine religious reasons, talk to her clergy adviser.

## Observation Quiz ANSWERS

**Answer to Observation Quiz** (from p. 132): Jumping up, with a three-month age range for acquisition. The reason is that the older an infant is, the more impact both nature and nurture have.

**Answer to Observation Quiz** (from p. 143): Most is East Asia, primarily because China has prioritized public health. Least is western and central Africa, primarily because of civil wars. In some nations, high birth rates have dramatically increased the numbers of stunted children, even though rates in the region are lower.

# The First Two Years: Cognitive Development

## What Will You Know?

1. What do infants remember before they can talk?
2. Why did Piaget compare 1-year-olds to scientists?
3. When does a typical baby say a first word?

A neuroscientist learned about a Korean fortune-telling ritual for 1-year-olds:

The unsuspecting baby is placed in front of an assortment of objects and is encouraged to pick one. . . . If the baby picks up a banana, she will never go hungry; choosing a book means she is destined for academia; a silver coin foretells wealth, or a paintbrush, creativity.

I was intrigued. The very same evening I placed Olivia [her infant daughter] in front of a collection of items.

A stethoscope: would she be a doctor? A stuffed dog: a vet? A plant: a Green Peace activist? A piece of pastry: a chef? And a colorful model of the brain; a neuroscientist?

Olivia inspected the objects closely, took her time, and then went straight for the iPhone I had happened to leave at the corner of the table.

I shouldn't have been surprised. The little girl was obsessed with this piece of machinery. She would skillfully roll herself from one side of the room to the other to grab hold of it. . . . . When she finally grabbed hold of the phone she would quickly insert it into her mouth and attempt to chew. . . . She had other bright, musical toys that she did not desire as much. The iPhone was the item she wanted because from the day she was born she had observed her parents constantly interacting with it with great interest. Although she was only a few months old and could not even say a word she was able to infer that these metal rectangles must be extremely valuable. Little Livia's fondness for iPhones tells us something important about how our brains work.

[Sharot, 2017, pp. 152–153]

This incident introduces the chapter on cognitive development during infancy for three reasons.

First, this topic is intriguing: We all wonder what thoughts, aspirations, and abilities the newest humans will have. We hope they will do well and perpetuate our own values and choices. Did you notice that the mother thought a stethoscope meant doctor (not nurse), that a plant signified Greenpeace (not farmer), and that a model of the brain was among the options (for the daughter of a neuroscientist)?

The second reason is to highlight that infants are curious and social. Of course all those Korean babies reach for something, as Olivia did—every baby would. And of course they are influenced by what they have observed in their parents.

The third is that caregiver behavior is pivotal. Without realizing it, every family and each culture molds the infant mind. This social influence on infants is obvious when babies begin to speak their native language, not any of the 6,000 other languages that infants elsewhere speak; but caregivers also affect curiosity, persistence, and logic, as you will soon learn.

This chapter describes the process of infant cognition, as well as its accomplishments. From the moment when newborns open their eyes, to the insistent grabbing, experimenting, and talking of 2-year-olds, infants are active learners.

## The Eager Mind

Chapter 5 chronicled the intense human drive to use every sensory and motor ability. Newborns look and listen; toddlers run and climb. Brain growth makes sensory and motor development possible; babies obsessively use their abilities as soon as they can.

The same phenomenon occurs with cognitive development. One team suggests that infants are "scientist[s] in the crib" (Gopnik et al., 1999), a suggestion that was "frequently met with incredulity" (Halberda, 2018, p. 1215). However, "the field of developmental neuroscience has burgeoned over the last 20 years with advances in technology and methods that are well suited for measuring the human brain in vivo in infants" (Guyer et al., 2018, p. 687). Incredulity faded as evidence accumulated.

As scientists discover more about the infant brain, they are increasingly impressed by its inborn readiness to learn. One team wrote: "from early on in development, infants display perceptual biases and attentional patterns that strongly suggest a motive to acquire information" (Lucca & Wilbourn, 2018, p. 942).

Brains do much more than increase in size (Chapter 5); infant brains are preset to understand the world, using every step of the scientific method. Curiosity leads to hypothesizing, observing, experimenting, analyzing, and concluding.

### Listening to Learn

Remember that newborns' hearing is acute. Infants can hear all noises—traffic on the street, clanking of dishes in the kitchen, the hum or crackle of the radiator—but they ignore most of what they hear. Thus, sensation does not usually become perception, and perception does not necessarily become cognition. However, babies listen closely to certain sounds, particularly the human voice.

### Distinguishing Speech Sounds

Newborns do not understand words, of course, but they have an inborn affinity for language, probably because, for humans, most learning occurs via words.

Vast differences are audible in adult speech: Russian does not sound like a tonal language such as Chinese; English does not pronounce the *r* as French does; the cadence of German is quite different from that of Spanish. Babies need to learn from whatever language their caregivers speak, which means that every linguistic nuance must be perceived.

That is how it happens. Even in the early weeks, babies distinguish the difference between the sound of *pa* and *ba*, for example, and they hear the nuances of many other speech sounds—some insignificant in one language but crucial in another. They are called *universalists* because they hear the differences in any language (Kuhl, 2004).

By one year after birth, however, that ability to distinguish sounds in never-heard languages deteriorates, a loss that continues throughout childhood. Babies at first

"Is THIS THE WAY YOU PLAN TO SPEND YOUR PEAK LEARNING YEARS?"

**Still Wrong** Parents used to ignore infant cognition. Now some make the opposite mistake, assuming that infants learn via active study.

SIDNEY HARRIS/CARTOONSTOCK

| TABLE 6.1 | |
| --- | --- |
| **Examples of Mispronunciations in the Bergelson and Swingley Study** | |
| Apple | *opel* |
| Banana | *banoona* |
| Milk | *mulk* |
| Hair | *har* |
| Mouth | *mith* |
| Nose | *nazz* |

**LaunchPad**
macmillan learning

**VIDEO: Event-Related Potential (ERP) Research** shows a procedure in which the electrical activity of an infant's brain is recorded to see whether the brain responds differently to familiar versus unfamiliar words.

**Especially for Educators** An infant day-care center has a new child whose parents speak a language other than the one the teachers speak. Should the teachers learn basic words in the new language, or should they expect the baby to learn the teachers' language? (see response, page 170)

attend to all linguistic sounds; by adulthood people literally cannot hear some sound differences that are crucial in languages they have never learned. That is evidence for cognitive maturation.

Babies from English-speaking families were shown pictures of 17 common objects while hearing the names of the objects (Bergelson & Swingley, 2018). Sometimes the name was deliberately mispronounced, as in the examples shown in **Table 6.1.**

Six-month-olds were tested for knowledge of these words. Performance overall was poor, but some babies already knew a few of the 17. Importantly, their understanding was equally good in three conditions: (1) their mother saying the words correctly; (2) their mother mispronouncing the words; and (3) a stranger saying the words correctly.

By 1 year of age, however, not only did they know more but also their brains had already learned correct U.S. English pronunciation. They were significantly better at understanding correct speech from strangers than mispronunciation by their own mothers.

This study shows, first, that very young babies are primed to learn language, and second, that 1-year-olds already know the accepted way to pronounce words. (English-speaking babies in Jamaica, or England, or India learn other nuances.)

## Learning Two Languages

Bilingual proficiency begins in the first year of life—every young human brain can learn several languages. Ideally, parents often speak in two languages, and then their children become doubly fluent as well. The brains of bilingual 1-year-olds respond to both languages (Ramirez et al., 2017), because infant brains are primed to understand whatever speech they hear.

Infants also are attuned to the social context. Have you noticed that most bilingual adults use one language with friends and family and the other one in more formal settings? Very young infants notice that, too: They figure out which language is most important to the adults and respond preferentially to that one.

This was one conclusion from a study of 94 newborns (age 0 to 5 days) in Vancouver, Canada (Byers-Heinlein et al., 2010). For half of them, their mother spoke English and Tagalog (a language native to the Philippines); for one-third, their mothers spoke only English; and for one-sixth, their mothers spoke English and Chinese.

The infants in all three groups sucked on a pacifier connected to a recording of 10 minutes of English and 10 minutes of Tagalog. To make sure there were no subtle biases in the streams of speech, such as one language spoken with more animation, the two languages were matched for pitch, duration, and number of syllables.

As evident in the rate and intensity of their sucking (which activated the recording), babies with English-only mothers preferred English and those with bilingual mothers preferred Tagalog (Byers-Heinlein et al., 2010). They had already connected Tagalog with more animated, emotional talk—and that is what they wanted to learn first.

## Looking to Learn

Developmentalists have long known that very young infants spend more time simply looking around than doing anything else. They scan their surroundings, fixate on faces, follow moving objects with their eyes. Experienced caregivers know that one way to quiet fussy 3-month-olds is to take them to see something—cars moving on the street, dogs coming to be petted, flowers in a garden, toys that move.

## Gaze-Following

Until recently, however, developmentalists did not appreciate how important vision is for cognition. Very young babies choose to look at whatever is likely to advance their understanding. They wisely focus on whatever captures their caregivers' attention, via *gaze-following*, instinctively knowing that what caregivers look at might tell them something important.

For example, following adults' lead, they look at the face of someone entering the room, ignoring the ceiling, the floor, or the person's feet. Have they learned that adults look at faces because expressions are informative, or is gaze-following natural for infants?

Both. It was thought that gaze-following occurred only as a response to adults, who alert the babies to opportunities to learn. Adults say, "Javier, look, here comes Daddy," or "Sophia, here is your teddy bear." Such guides to gaze-following are part of adults' natural tendency to teach babies through *natural pedagogy* (Gergely & Csibra, 2013).

Natural pedagogy is evident whenever caregivers direct the baby's gaze, calling their name, pointing at an object, and so on. Adults try to advance infant cognition; very young babies respond by looking at whatever the adult shows.

But we now know that infants will follow an adult's gaze even without caregiver cues (Gredeback et al., 2018). If a tilt of the head and movement of the pupils indicates that something interests the caregiver, the baby follows the gaze. Thus, gaze-following arises from both nature and nurture.

**No Fear** Like all infants, this 11-month-old girl is eager to explore through sight and touch. Praise to all three—this mother for encouraging learning, this baby for reaching out, and this dog for gently licking her hand. Most dogs recognize babies, tolerating actions they would not accept from adults of any species.

## Early Logic

Nature and nurture may also give babies some understanding of the laws of physics. In one study, a toy dinosaur was removed from a display where it had been next to a flower. A screen then covered the display. A moment later, the screen was lifted to reveal the dinosaur instead of the flower (Cesana-Arlotti et al., 2018).

Cameras and computers measured how long the babies looked at that unexpected event. Infants stared longer when the flower was surreptitiously replaced with the dinosaur than when the flower was still there. This indicated that they knew how things should be and were surprised when their basic understanding was wrong.

Many other events that contradict the basic laws of physics (such as a ball that is suspended in the air rather than falling, or a toy that becomes two toys) elicit the same surprise. From such research, many developmentalists believe that infants have some innate logic. Scientific reasoning may not be a "hard-won accomplishment mastered later in life," but rather an "inherent attribute of the mind" (Halberda, 2018, p. 1214).

## Core Knowledge

To explain infants' cognition, scientists suggest that babies are born with an understanding of how the world works, which they call *core knowledge* (Stahl & Feigenson, 2017). Examples are that moving objects stop when they bump into a solid wall, and that adult gaze signals important information.

Core expectations not only prime learning but also alert the baby when something unexpected happens. Surprise triggers curiosity, which triggers more learning. No one thinks that babies are born with the knowledge and logic they will display in a few months or years. But core knowledge and plasticity make rapid learning possible as the brain grows (remember, it triples in size by age 2) and experiences accumulate.

Consider how this works when infants see pictures (LoBue, 2013). Infants are *not* instinctively afraid of snakes. However, when they look at pictures of flowers and snakes, they focus more on the snakes. Their brains seem to know that snakes may be important; then, during early childhood, they are taught whether or not to be afraid.

## Recognizing Faces

Another example comes from attention to faces. Unless you have *prosopagnosia* (face blindness), the *fusiform face area* of your brain is astonishingly adept. This is innate. Compared to older children and adults, newborns are quicker to recognize a face that they have seen just once (Zeifman, 2013).

Because of experience-expectant brain development, every face is fascinating: Babies stare at pictures of monkey faces and photos of human ones, at drawings and toys with faces, as well as at live faces. At 6 weeks, they smile at almost anyone whose face is about 2 feet away. That fact indicates that faces are part of core knowledge.

Soon, with experience-dependent learning, babies smile more readily at familiar people, differentiate men from women, and distinguish among faces from their own ethnic group (called the *own-race effect*). This fact could be worrisome: Does it suggest that humans are naturally sexist and racist? No, as A View from Science explains. Brains are primed to pay attention to familiar faces, and most babies see faces of a particular kind.

**A VIEW FROM SCIENCE**

## Face Recognition

The own-race effect refers to the fact that infants are better at recognizing individuals from their own ethnic group than at distinguishing individuals from other groups. Researchers test infant recognition by showing babies photos of strangers from various groups and measuring their looking time and attention, to determine if they notice differences between individuals.

This measure of looking time is used in thousands of studies that assess infant cognition. Infants pay less attention to seeing the same thing again and again (that's called *habituation*), so if a baby were to look longer at a particular picture, that suggests that the baby notices the difference between that picture and the previous one (Csibra et al., 2016).

When the experience of a baby or a child under age 12 is multiracial, the own-race effect is less evident; that is, they recognize individuality between photos of people of another race as well as of their own race. Research on children adopted from China and raised in Canada found that if a child of one ethnicity (Chinese) is raised exclusively by people of another ethnicity (European), that child recognizes differences among the people they see, not among people of their biological group (McKone et al., 2019).

The importance of experience is confirmed by two studies. The first study occurred in Malaysia, where many people of two ethnic groups (Malay and Chinese) live and where women, but not men, interact with babies. A group of Chinese infants were shown photos of people who varied by gender and ethnicity. The babies recognized individuality among Chinese women by 3 months and among Malaysian women by 8 months. However, they did not perceive individuality among Europeans or among men of any ethnicity—apparently because they had limited experience with them (Tham et al., 2019).

In another study, parents repeatedly "read" a book to their 6-month-old infants (Scott & Monesson, 2010). The book depicted six monkey faces. One-third of the parents said each monkey's name while showing the pictures; one-third said only "monkey" as they turned each page; the final one-third simply turned the pages with no verbal labeling.

At 9 months, infants in all three groups viewed pictures of six *unfamiliar* monkeys. The infants who had heard names of monkeys were better at distinguishing one new monkey from another than were the infants who saw the same picture book but did not hear each monkey's name (Scott & Monesson, 2010).

Evidently, by hearing the names, the babies realized that monkeys vary in appearance, and they learned to distinguish one monkey from another. This applies to humans' understanding of racial and national groups as well. Interacting with several *named* people of any group helps people understand that members of that group are individuals, not stereotypes (Thorup et al., 2018).

As with almost every type of infant development, experience combines with inborn brain proclivities. An intriguing study found that this innate preference is evident in all primates, not just in humans.

In that study, researchers prevented macaque monkeys from seeing faces (including those of other monkeys and of humans) for the first three months of life. Then they showed pictures, some with faces and some not. Those deprived 3-month-olds looked more attentively at photos of faces than photos of other objects, demonstrating that inborn attraction to faces. Indeed, every face—of chimpanzees, otters, humans, as well as other monkeys—was almost equally interesting.

Then, in the next few months, the monkeys were granted some experiences with other macaques. By 6 months, the researchers found that these monkeys paid more attention to the faces of their own species than of other primates (Simpson et al., 2017). That is just what human babies do: They look intently at every face-like image at first but zero in on the faces that are most important to them.

This research has important practical applications. If parents hope their children become adults who relate well with people of many ages, genders, and ethnicities, they need to expose them early on to friends, caregivers, neighbors, and so on from diverse backgrounds.

Dario    Boris    Anice    Iona    Flora    Louis

Republished with permission of Elsevier, from Experience-dependent neural specialization during infancy 1857-1861, Scott, L., 48, 2010; DOI: 10.1016/J.NEUROPSYCHOLOGIA. 2010.02.008. Permission conveyed through Copyright Clearance Center, Inc.

**Iona Is Not Flora** If you heard that Dario was not Louis or Boris, would you stare at unfamiliar monkey faces more closely in the future? For 6-month-olds, the answer is yes.

## How to Learn

One other aspect of cognition merits mention—babies learn how to learn. As you remember from Chapter 4, infants are born with reflexes. Some of those reflexes fade and others build, depending on experience.

Curiosity is an inborn reflex; newborns look at and listen to everything. Then, some infants are allowed to explore and experiment (fingering their toys, reaching for people, and so on); others are not ("Don't touch!"). It matters whether caregivers encourage curiosity, respond to noises, and build on reflexes (as Mrs. Todd did in Chapter 5) . For example, if a baby utters a sound, some caregivers stop and respond, others ignore the sound, and some others tell the baby to be quiet.

By the second year of life, some toddlers are eager to explore and investigate while others are much more hesitant. One quality, sometimes called *grit* or effort, fosters learning throughout life.

In one experiment, 15-month-olds observed adults trying to get a toy from a container (Leonard et al., 2017). The adult said, "How can I get this toy out of here?" and then worked to do so. Half the infants saw the toy come out quickly, and the other half watched the adult working hard for half a minute to release the toy (see **Figure 6.1**).

Then the babies were handed another toy. The experimenter pushed a button to demonstrate that the toy played music. However, the toy was rigged to play once for the experimenter, but not after that. Not surprisingly, every baby tried to make the toy play music again, since they had just observed this could happen.

But the crucial question is how persistent the babies were. One baby quickly threw the toy to the floor in frustration and another kept trying for more than two minutes. Why the difference? Some is probably temperament, but observation mattered. If babies had seen the adult keep trying for half a minute before getting

**FIGURE 6.1**

**If At First You Don't Succeed . . . Quit?** Two times, with two toys, babies watched an adult try to get toys from a container. One group saw the toys quickly released, and another group saw them released only after some effort. Then the babies were shown another toy. This third toy played music when the adult turned it on, but then (unbeknownst to the babies) the music-playing was deactivated. When babies were handed the quiet toy, how long did they try to turn on the music? (Answer is in the text.) If you don't take time to read the text, what does that suggest about your childhood?

the toy, they pushed the button an average of 22.5 times. However, if they had seen the adult succeed quickly, they pushed, on average, only 12 times (Leonard et al., 2017).

The authors conclude that adults should sometimes let children see them struggle to complete a task. The idea that hard work pays off is a learning strategy that helps throughout a person's education—and it may begin in infancy.

## Theories of the Infant Mind

Two theories are relevant to this new understanding of the infant mind: information-processing theory and evolutionary theory.

As you remember from Chapter 2, *information-processing theory* originated from understanding the processing built into computers, which gather millions of bits of information and then compute a result. The central idea is that the human mind is like a computer, accumulating experiences and then establishing knowledge. Thus, information processing might lead to the hypothesis that the infant mind is programmed for cognitive development, so the myriad sights and sounds produce understanding.

The other theory that provides insight into early cognition is *evolutionary theory* (Bjorklund, 2018). The idea is that the human brain, unique among mammals, has evolved to be extraordinarily plastic so that human babies can learn everything they need within their culture. According to evolutionary theory, this occurs in two steps.

- First, infants innately attend to caregivers as well as to things that, millennia ago, were crucial for survival. That is why they listen to voices, like to be held snugly, and look at snakes more than flowers.
- Second, the diversity of human culture requires that the infant brain be amazingly plastic, allowing inborn predispositions to be shaped so people

can adapt to whatever life may bring. Over the millennia, people with flexible brains were likely to survive and procreate, advancing the genes for plasticity.

Consider one more example: the sucking reflex. For hundreds of thousands of years, the sucking/swallowing/breathing reflexes had to function well in newborns so they could survive, even though no other motor ability needed to work at birth.

You also remember that breast milk is good for the brain; babies who are breast-fed tend to have higher IQs than those who are formula-fed. That was recently proven again, this time carefully controlling for third variables, such as the mother's intelligence and education, that might cause the correlation. Babies who were breast-fed for at least a month had, by age 5, IQ scores that averaged 3 points higher than babies who were not breast-fed at all, or whose mothers gave up breast-feeding in the first few weeks (Strøm et al., 2019).

These two facts are particularly relevant for babies born very early. The sucking reflex does not begin until about 33 weeks after conception, which meant that, in prior centuries, preterm babies died. Now respirators, incubators, and so on allow viable preterm babies to live. They are tube-fed, ideally with breast milk that their mothers have expressed with a breast pump. At about 34 weeks, in the hospital, they begin to suck, either via a special bottle and nipple designed for their tiny mouths or directly from the nipples of their mothers.

NICU professionals prefer the bottle approach, since the mothers do not need to be physically present and nurses can more easily measure nutrition. Doctors thought that babies could easily switch to direct breast-feeding at home. However, that idea ignored what cognitive psychologists now know about infant learning: Sucking for nourishment is core knowledge, evident in newborns.

As evolutionary theory explains, babies refine their evolutionary impulses with experience, because plasticity is part of human nature. Tiny babies who are bottle-fed learn that this is how sucking brings milk. By contrast, those who are directly breast-fed in the hospital (for very preterm infants this means many times a day, often supplemented with tube-feeding) learn that breasts give milk. Babies who are breast-fed in the hospital are released earlier and are more often breast-fed at home (Suberi et al., 2018), which benefits their cognition.

This is an example of the infant's eager mind, because these tiny babies quickly learned to adapt an inborn ability (sucking) with experience (as evolutionary theory suggests). Sucking knowledge is plastic; it adapts.

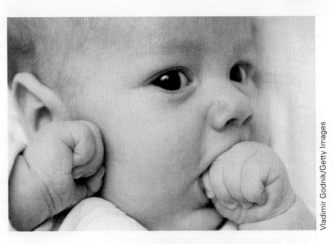

**Time for Adaptation** Sucking is a reflex at first, but adaptation begins as soon as an infant differentiates a pacifier from her mother's breast or realizes that her hand has grown too big to fit into her mouth. This infant's expression of concentration suggests that she is about to make that adaptation and suck just her thumb from now on.

## Infant Memory

Are infant skills and cognition impressive, or are they markedly immature? Both. To further understand this, we need to look in detail at one more ability—memory, which "is crucial for the acquisition of the tremendous amount of knowledge and skills infant[s] and children acquire in the first years of life" (Vöhringer et al., 2018, p. 370).

To see the relationship between early cognition and memory, we need to appreciate that children remember what they need to remember instead of noticing

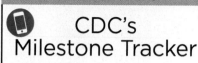

**CHAPTER APP 6**

## CDC's
## Milestone Tracker

**IOS:**
https://tinyurl.com/ycppyalv

**ANDROID:**
https://tinyurl.com/y98yh6lv

**RELEVANT TOPIC:**
Cognitive development during infancy

Featuring the CDC's illustrated checklists, this app enables parents to track important milestones from age 2 months to 5 years. It also offers tips for encouraging their child's development and resources to consult if they have concerns.

their many "faults or shortcomings relative to an adult standard" (Bjorklund & Sellers, 2014, p. 142). Newborns quickly remember who their caregivers are, and they learn how their own behaviors can affect their experiences.

Of course, they remember almost nothing at first. Repeated sensations and brain maturation are required in order to recall whatever happens, as is true life-long (Bauer et al., 2010). Everyone's memory fades with time, especially if that memory was never encoded into language, never compared with similar events, or never discussed with anyone—all of which make infant memory fragile.

## Forget About Infant Amnesia!

That does not mean that babies do not remember. Piaget, Freud, and other early developmentalists described *infant amnesia*, the idea that people forget everything that happened to them before age 3. However, we now know that infant brains are adapted to learn, which means that they can remember.

An insight regarding infant amnesia begins with the distinction between *implicit* and *explicit* memory. Implicit memory is not verbal; it is memory for movement, emotions, or thoughts that are not put into words. Implicit memory is evident by 3 months, begins to stabilize by 9 months, and varies from one infant to another as well as within each infant during the early months.

The reason it appears so early is partly because it comes from Implicit memory comes from the old parts of the brain—including the cerebellum and the amygdala (Vöhringer et al., 2018). Those parts mature rapidly in the first months of life, and then change relatively little, unlike the forebrain, which grows for decades. That's why implicit memory is evident so early in life.

Explicit memory takes longer to emerge, as it depends on language. It arises mainly from the cortex. Explicit memory improves dramatically throughout childhood (Hayne et al., 2015). Verbal memory, especially vocabulary, continues to increase throughout adulthood. When adults tested memory by asking questions, they were testing explicit memory, which seemed absent for the early years. Infant amnesia? Yes for some kinds of memory, especially the kind learned in school and traditionally tested by scientists. But not for many other kinds of memory.

Thus, when people say "I don't remember," they mean "I cannot recall," because something is not in explicit memory. Unconsciously and implicitly, they might remember. A person might have an irrational fear of doctors or hospitals, for instance, because of early terrifying and painful experiences that they do not recall.

## Remind Me!

The most dramatic proof of very early memory comes from a series of innovative experiments in which 3-month-olds learned to move a mobile by kicking their legs (Rovee-Collier, 1987, 1990). The infants lay on their backs connected to a mobile by means of a ribbon tied to one foot.

Virtually all babies realized that kicking made the mobile move. They then kicked more vigorously and frequently, sometimes laughing at their accomplishment. So far, this is no surprise—observing self-activated movement is highly reinforcing to infants.

When infants as young as 3 months had the mobile-and-ribbon apparatus reinstalled and reconnected *one week later*, most started to kick immediately, proof that they remembered their previous experience. But when other 3-month-old infants were retested *two weeks later*, they kicked randomly. Had they forgotten? It seemed so.

But then, *two weeks after* the initial training, the lead researcher, Carolyn Rovee-Collier, allowed some infants to watch the mobile move when they were not connected to it. The next day, when a ribbon again tied their leg to the mobile, they kicked almost immediately.

 **LaunchPad**
macmillan learning

**VIDEO: Contingency Learning in Young Infants** shows Carolyn Rovee-Collier's procedure for studying instrumental learning during infancy.

He Boddy/SPL/Science Source

**He Remembers!** Infants are fascinated by moving objects within a few feet of their eyes—that's why parents buy mobiles for cribs and why Rovee-Collier tied a string to a mobile and a baby's leg to test memory. Babies not in her experiment, like this one, sometimes flail their limbs to make their cribs shake and thus make their mobiles move. Piaget's stage of "making interesting sights last" is evident to every careful observer.

⬤⬤ **Observation Quiz** Do you see anything here that is less than ideal? (see answer, page 171) ↑

Apparently, watching the mobile the previous day reminded them about what they had previously experienced. Other research similarly finds that reminders are powerful. If Daddy routinely plays with a 3-month-old, goes on a long trip, and the mother shows Daddy's picture and says his name on the day before his return, the baby might grin broadly when he reappears. Otherwise, he might seem to be forgotten.

At 12 months, memory improves because brains have added tens of thousands of dendrites and synapses. Babies have learned from parents and strangers, from other babies and older siblings, from picture books and family photographs, and soon from their own walking and talking (Hayne & Simcock, 2009).

Every day of their young lives, infants are processing information and storing memories. Indeed, if you saw a photo of a grandmother who cared for you every day when you were an infant and who died when you were 2, your brain would still react, even though you thought you forgot her. Information-processing research finds evidence of early memories, with visual memories particularly strong (Gao et al., 2017; Leung et al., 2016).

Evolutional theory is confirmed as well. The extraordinary plasticity of the human brain and the core knowledge of how the world might work have together astonished twenty-first-century cognitive psychologists.

Some suggest that a new theory—*evolutionary developmental psychology*—may replace the traditional approach to infant cognition, as expounded by Piaget (Bjorklund, 2018). This theory benefits from twenty-first-century neuroscience and technology that allows researchers to discover the amazing abilities of the infant brain.

---

**WHAT HAVE YOU LEARNED?**

1. What is the developmental pattern of hearing the sound of speech?

2. Why do babies look at whatever they look at?

3. What suggests that infants have an understanding of how objects move?

4. What does face recognition tell us about infant cognition?

5. What suggests that infants develop strategies for learning by watching adults?

6. Why is information-processing theory relevant for infant cognition?

7. Why is evolutionary theory relevant for infant cognition?

**VIDEO: Sensorimotor Intelligence in Infancy and Toddlerhood** shows how senses and motor skills fuel infant cognition.

**sensorimotor intelligence** Piaget's term for the way infants think—by using their senses and motor skills—during the first period of cognitive development.

# Piaget's Sensorimotor Intelligence

Now we turn to Jean Piaget, the groundbreaking theorist who studied infant cognition a century ago. Of course, Piaget lacked the technological advances that undergird our current understanding of infant cognition, but his insights were revolutionary in his day. Consequently, many contemporary developmentalists consider Piaget's six stages of infant cognition a foundation on which to build.

In 1918, when Piaget earned his doctorate in biology, most scientists thought infants only ate, cried, and slept. His Ph.D. research was on shellfish, specifically how they adapt to their environment. That required meticulous observation to understand details such as how a clam interacted with sandy water, or how a snail moved along a particular surface.

When he became a father, Piaget used his scientific observation skills with his own three infants. Contrary to conventional wisdom, he detailed active learning from birth on, recording his children's cognitive development day by day.

Early reflexes, senses, and body movements are the raw materials for infant cognition, Piaget surmised. That is why he called cognition in the first two years **sensorimotor intelligence.** He subdivided this period into six stages (see **Table 6.2**). [**Developmental Link:** Piaget's theory of cognitive development over all the years of childhood is introduced in Chapter 2.]

---

### TABLE 6.2

**The Six Stages of Sensorimotor Intelligence**

For an overview of the stages of sensorimotor thought, it helps to group the six stages into pairs.

**Primary Circular Reactions**

The first two stages involve infants' responses to their own bodies.

| | |
|---|---|
| *Stage One* (birth to 1 month) | *Reflexes:* sucking, grasping, staring, listening |
| | *Example:* sucking anything that touches the lips or cheek |
| *Stage Two* (1–4 months) | *The first acquired adaptations:* accommodation and coordination of reflexes |
| | *Examples:* sucking a pacifier differently from a nipple; attempting to hold a bottle to suck it |

**Secondary Circular Reactions**

The next two stages involve infants' responses to objects and people.

| | |
|---|---|
| *Stage Three* (4–8 months) | *Making interesting sights last:* responding to people and objects |
| | *Example:* clapping hands when mother says "patty-cake" |
| *Stage Four* (8–12 months) | *New adaptation and anticipation:* becoming more deliberate and purposeful in responding to people and objects |
| | *Example:* putting mother's hands together in order to make her start playing patty-cake |

**Tertiary Circular Reactions**

The last two stages are the most creative, first with action and then with ideas.

| | |
|---|---|
| *Stage Five* (12–18 months) | *New means through active experimentation:* experimentation and creativity in the actions of the "little scientist" |
| | *Example:* putting a teddy bear in the toilet and flushing it |
| *Stage Six* (18–24 months) | *New means through mental combinations:* thinking before doing; new ways of achieving a goal without resorting to trial and error |
| | *Example:* before flushing the teddy bear again, hesitating because of the memory of the toilet overflowing and mother's anger |

## Stages One and Two: Primary Circular Reactions

Piaget described the interplay of sensation, perception, action, and cognition as *circular reactions*, emphasizing that, as in a circle, there is no beginning and no end. Each experience leads to the next, which loops back (see **Figure 6.2**).

In **primary circular reactions,** the circle is within the infant's body. Stage one, called the *stage of reflexes,* lasts only a month. Reflexes become deliberate; sensation leads to perception, perception leads to cognition, and then cognition leads back to sensation.

Stage two, called *first acquired adaptations* (also called *stage of first habits*), begins as the mind of the infant allows adjustment to whatever responses they elicit. Adaptation is cognitive; it includes repeating old patterns (assimilation) and developing new ones (accommodation). [**Developmental Link:** Assimilation and accommodation are explained in Chapter 2.]

Here is one example. As you remember, full-term newborns reflexively suck anything that touches their lips (stage one). They must learn to suck, swallow, and suck again without spitting up too much—a major circular reaction that takes a few days to learn.

Then, infants *adapt* their sucking reflex to bottles or breasts, pacifiers or fingers, each requiring specific types of tongue pushing. You already read about this in preterm babies who, at 33 weeks, first are able to suck (Suberi et al., 2018). This adaptation signifies that infants have begun to interpret sensations; as they *accommodate*, they are thinking—ready for stage two.

During stage two, which Piaget pegged from about 1 to 4 months of age, additional adaptation of the sucking reflex begins. Infant cognition leads babies to suck in some ways for hunger, in other ways for comfort—and not to suck fuzzy blankets or hard plastic. Once adaptation occurs, it sticks.

Adaptation is specific. For instance, 4-month-old breast-fed babies may reject milk from the nipple of a bottle if they have never experienced it. Early cognition can endure, as evolutionary theory contends. That explains why children like to suck lollipops and why some adults still like to suck things.

**primary circular reactions** The first of three types of feedback loops in sensorimotor intelligence, this one involving the infant's own body. The infant senses motion, sucking, noise, and other stimuli and tries to understand them.

**(a) Primary circular reaction**
Baby's action
Feels good—keep sucking
Baby's reaction

**(b) Secondary circular reaction**
Baby's action
Interesting object—keep shaking
Repeated reaction from object or person

**(c) Tertiary circular reaction**
Baby's action
Fascinating reaction—what else can I do?
Novel reaction from object or person

**FIGURE 6.2**
**Never Ending** Circular reactions keep going because each action produces pleasure that encourages more action.

● **Especially for Parents** When should parents decide whether to feed their baby only by breast, only by bottle, or by using some combination of the two? When should they decide whether or not to let their baby use a pacifier? (see response, page 170)

**secondary circular reactions** The first of three types of feedback loops in sensorimotor intelligence, involving the infant and an object or another person, as with shaking a rattle or playing peek-a-boo.

**object permanence** The realization that objects (including people) still exist when they can no longer be seen, touched, or heard.

**Family Fun** Peek-a-boo makes all three happy, each for cognitive reasons. The 9-month-old is discovering object permanence, his sister (at the concrete operational stage) enjoys making her brother laugh, and their mother understands more abstract ideas—such as family bonding.

Bambu Productions/The Image Bank/Getty Images

Now, suppose 4-month-olds have discovered how to suck their thumbs and have practiced thumb sucking to their joy and satisfaction. Then, when this stage is over, suppose at 6 months the parents decide that a pacifier is better—perhaps healthier for teeth. Adaptation has already occurred; the baby might spit out the pacifier and insert the thumb.

In the same way at every age, Piaget found that older children and adults tend to stick to their early learning. This is apparent if you ever try to convince someone that something they have done all their life is wrong. Habits of thought and deed are hard to change, from infancy on.

## Stages Three and Four: Secondary Circular Reactions

In stages three and four, development advances from primary to **secondary circular reactions.** These reactions extend beyond the infant's body; this circular reaction is between the baby and something else.

During stage three (4 to 8 months), infants attempt to produce exciting experiences, a stage called *making interesting sights last*. Realizing that rattles make noise, for example, they wave their arms and laugh whenever someone puts a rattle in their hand. The sight of something delightful—a favorite squeaky toy, a smiling parent—can trigger active efforts for interaction.

Next comes stage four (8 months to 1 year), called *new adaptation and anticipation* (also called the *means to the end*). Babies may ask for help (fussing, pointing, gesturing) to accomplish what they want. Thinking is more innovative because adaptation is more complex. For instance, instead of always smiling at Grandpa, an infant might first assess his mood. Stage-three babies continue an experience; stage-four babies initiate and anticipate.

### Pursuing a Goal

An impressive attribute of stage four is that babies work hard to achieve their goals. A 10-month-old girl might crawl over to her mother, bringing a bar of soap to signal she loves baths, and then start to remove her clothes—finally squealing with delight when the bath water is turned on. Similarly, if a 10-month-old boy sees his father putting on a coat to leave, he might drag over his own jacket.

In both cases, infants have learned from repeated experience—Daddy may have often brought the baby along when he went out. With a combination of experience and brain maturation, babies become attuned to the goals of others, an ability that is more evident at 10 months than 8 months (Brandone et al., 2014).

According to Piaget, a major accomplishment of stage four is **object permanence**—the concept that objects or people continue to exist when they are not visible. At about 8 months—not before—infants look for toys that have fallen from the crib, rolled under a couch, or disappeared under a blanket.

As another scholar explains:

> Many parents in our typical American middle-class households have tried out Piaget's experiment in situ: Take an adorable, drooling 7-month-old baby, show her a toy she loves to play with, then cover it with a piece of cloth right in front of her eyes. What do you observe next? The baby does not know what to do to get the toy! She looks around, oblivious to the object's continuing existence under the cloth cover, and turns her attention to something else interesting in her environment. A few months later, the same baby will readily reach out and yank away the cloth cover to retrieve the highly desirable toy. This experiment has been done thousands of times and the phenomenon remains one of the most compelling in all of developmental psychology.
>
> [Xu, 2013, p. 167]

This is one of Piaget's most well-known, as well as most controversial, insights, as Opposing Perspectives explains.

## Object Permanence

Piaget found that:

- Infants younger than 8 months do not search for an attractive object momentarily covered by a cloth. They do not have the concept of object permanence.
- At about 8 months, infants remove the cloth immediately after the object is covered but not if they have to wait a few seconds.
- At 18 months, infants search after a wait. However, if they have seen the object put first in one place (A) and then moved to another (B), they search in A but not B.
- By 2 years, children fully grasp object permanence, progressing through several stages, including A and B displacements (Piaget, 1954/2013a).

This research provides many practical suggestions. If young infants fuss because they see something they cannot have (keys, a cell phone, candy), caregivers can put that coveted object out of sight. Fussing stops if object permanence has not yet appeared.

By contrast, for toddlers, hiding an object is not enough. It must be securely locked up, lest the child later retrieve it, climbing onto the kitchen counter or under the bathroom sink to do so. That much is evident to every developmental scientist. Then why is this an "opposing perspective"?

The opposition comes from researchers who thought Piaget underestimated infant cognition. Piaget believed that failure to search before 8 months meant that infants had no concept of object permanence—that "out of sight" literally means "out of mind." That is where the controversy begins.

Does a baby need to be able to remove a cover from a hidden toy to demonstrate object permanence? No, according to information-processing research. The best-known example is a series of studies by Renee Baillargeon which proved that 3-month-old infants grasp object permanence, long before 8 months, when Piaget said it emerged. How did information-processing measures lead to this conclusion?

Baillargeon devised clever experiments that entailed showing infants an object, then covering it with a screen, and then removing the screen. If the object vanished behind the screen, the babies' brain waves, heart rate, or focused eyes showed surprise. This meant that they expected the object to still be present—that is, they believed an object's existence was permanent (Baillargeon & DeVos, 1991; Spelke, 1993).

Later research on object permanence has continued to question Piaget's conclusions. Many other creatures (cats, monkeys, dogs, birds) develop object permanence faster than human infants. The animal ability seems to be innate, not learned—wolves and dogs develop it, but neither is as adept as human 2-year-olds at A-not-B displacement (Fiset & Plourde, 2013). Nonhuman animal species vary in their object permanence abilities, with other primates better than dogs, for instance (Majecka & Pietraszewski, 2018).

Current research finds that early experiences combine with inherited brain dispositions, making the age of object permanence (especially A-not-B displacements) much more variable than Piaget described (MacNeill et al., 2018). The current context matters as well. When testers look at B (not A), infants are likely to guess correctly. Does that indicate gaze sensitivity, not object permanence? (Dunn & Bremner, 2019).

Most scientists agree with Baillargeon that surprise, and looking time, are evidence for early object permanence. Other scientists are less convinced (Marcovitch et al., 2016; Mareschal & Kaufman, 2012). Some stress that Piaget is essentially correct, in that object permanence is fragile until later infancy (Bremner et al., 2015).

Thus, perspectives differ on exactly how infant cognition should be measured and what gaze reveals (Dunn & Bremner, 2017). But, everyone now agrees that babies are thinking long before Piaget found that they move their hands to uncover a hidden object.

## Stages Five and Six: Tertiary Circular Reactions

In their second year, infants start experimenting in thought and deed—or, rather, in the opposite sequence, deed and thought. They act first (stage five) and think later (stage six).

**Tertiary circular reactions** begin when 1-year-olds take independent actions to discover the properties of other people, animals, and things. Infants no longer respond only to their own bodies (primary reactions) or to other people or objects (secondary reactions). Their cognition is more like a spiral than a closed circle, increasingly creative with each discovery.

Piaget's stage five (12 to 18 months), called *new means through active experimentation*, builds on the accomplishments of stage four. Now, goal-directed and purposeful activities become more expansive.

**tertiary circular reaction** Piaget's description of the cognitive processes of the 1-year-old, who gathers information from experiences with the wider world and then acts on it. The response to those actions leads to further understanding, which makes this circular.

**Imitation Is Lifelong** As this photo illustrates, at every age, people copy what others do—often to their mutual joy. The new ability at stage six is "deferred imitation"—this boy may have seen another child lie on a tire a few days earlier.

BruesWu/Getty Images

**"little scientist"** Piaget's term for toddlers' insatiable curiosity and active experimentation as they engage in various actions to understand their world.

Toddlers delight in squeezing all the toothpaste out of the tube, drawing on the wall, or uncovering an anthill—activities they have never observed. Piaget referred to the stage-five toddler as a **"little scientist"** who "experiments in order to see." As you read, a scientific approach may be evident earlier, but authors who studied 12- to 19-month-olds report that "flexible and productive hypothesis testing does begin in infancy, with a vengeance" (Cesana-Arlotti et al., 2018, p. 1263).

Toddlers' preferred research method is trial and error. Their devotion to discovery is familiar to every adult scientist—and to every parent. Protection is needed. A curious toddler might swallow bleach, flush a doll down the toilet, or throw a cat out the window, all to see what happens next.

Finally, in the sixth stage (18 to 24 months), toddlers use *mental combinations*, intellectual experimentation via imagination that can supersede the active experimentation of stage five. Because they combine ideas, stage-six toddlers can pretend as well as think about the consequences of what they do, hesitating a moment before yanking the cat's tail or dropping a raw egg on the floor.

Stage-six toddlers can remember what they have seen and do it later themselves, an ability Piaget called *deferred imitation*. Newer research finds that some accomplishments that Piaget pegged for stage six—including pretending and deferred imitation—begin much earlier.

However, although he was wrong on the timing of his stages, Piaget was right to describe babies as avid and active learners who "learn so fast and so well" (Xu & Kushnir, 2013, p. 28). His main mistake was underestimating how rapidly their learning can occur.

**Especially for Parents** One parent wants to put all breakable or dangerous objects away because the toddler is able to move around independently. The other parent says that the baby should learn not to touch certain things. Who is right? (see response, page 171)

---

### WHAT HAVE YOU LEARNED?

**1.** Why did Piaget call cognition in the first two years "sensorimotor intelligence"?

**2.** How does stage one of sensorimotor intelligence lead to stage two?

**3.** In sensorimotor intelligence, what is the difference between stages three and four?

**4.** What is the significance of the concept of object permanence for infant cognition?

**5.** What does the active experimentation of the stage-five toddler suggest for parents?

**6.** Why did Piaget underestimate infant cognition?

# Language: What Develops in the First Two Years?

Human linguistic ability by age 2 far surpasses that of full-grown adults from every other species. Very young infants listen intensely, responding as best they can. One scholar explains, "infants are acquiring much of their native language before they utter their first word" (Aslin, 2012, p. 191). How do they do it?

## The Universal Sequence

The sequence of language development is the same worldwide (see At About This Time). Some children learn several languages, some only one; some learn rapidly, others slowly. But all follow the same path.

## Listening and Responding

In every spoken language, adults use higher pitch, simpler words, repetition, varied speed, and exaggerated emotional tone when talking to infants. Babies respond with attention and emotion. By 7 months, they begin to recognize words that are distinctive: *Bottle, doggie,* and *mama,* for instance, might be differentiated, not *baby, Bobbie,* and *Barbie.*

Infants also like alliteration, rhymes, repetition, melody, rhythm, and varied pitch. Think of your favorite lullaby (itself an alliterative word); obviously, babies prefer sounds over content and singing over talking (Tsang et al., 2017). Early listening abilities and preferences are the result of brain function.

## Babbling and Gesturing

Between 6 and 9 months, babies repeat certain syllables (*ma-ma-ma, da-da-da, ba-ba-ba*), a vocalization called **babbling** because of the way it sounds. Babbling is universal; even deaf babies babble.

**babbling** An infant's repetition of certain syllables, such as *ba-ba-ba*, that begins when babies are between 6 and 9 months old.

### AT ABOUT THIS TIME

**The Development of Spoken Language in the First Two Years**

| Age* | Means of Communication |
|------|------------------------|
| Newborn | Reflexive communication—cries, movements, facial expressions. |
| 2 months | A range of meaningful noises—cooing, fussing, crying, laughing. |
| 3–6 months | New sounds, including squeals, growls, croons, trills, vowel sounds. |
| 6–10 months | Babbling, including both consonant and vowel sounds repeated in syllables. |
| 10–12 months | Comprehension of simple words; speechlike intonations; specific vocalizations that have meaning to those who know the infant well. Deaf babies express their first signs; hearing babies also use specific gestures (e.g., pointing) to communicate. |
| 12 months | First spoken words that are recognizably part of the native language. |
| 13–18 months | Slow growth of vocabulary, up to about 50 words. |
| 18 months | Naming explosion—three or more words learned per day. Much variation: Some toddlers do not yet speak.* |
| 21 months | First two-word sentence. |
| 24 months | Multiword sentences. Half of the toddler's utterances are two or more words long. |

*The ages in this table reflect norms. Many healthy, intelligent children attain each linguistic accomplishment earlier or later than indicated here. However, if a baby is late to babble, speak a word, or put words together, that may indicate a speech, hearing, or cognitive problem. A professional should determine whether something is amiss.

**Who Is Babbling?** Probably both the 6-month-old and the 27-year-old. During every day of infancy, mothers and babies communicate with noises, movements, and expressions.

**holophrase** A single word that is used to express a complete, meaningful thought.

**Show Me Where** Pointing is one of the earliest forms of communication, emerging at about 10 months. As you see here, pointing is useful lifelong for humans.

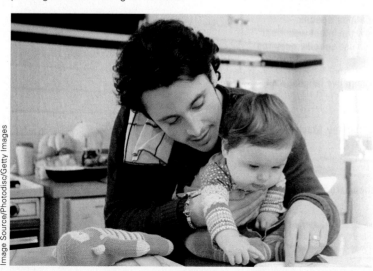

Caregivers usually encourage those noises, and it is wise that they do so. Babbling predicts later vocabulary, even more than the other major influence—the education of the mother (McGillion et al., 2017).

Before uttering their first word, infants notice patterns of speech, such as which sounds are commonly spoken together. A baby who often hears that something is "pretty" expects the sound of *prit* to be followed by *tee* (MacWhinney, 2015) and is startled if someone says "prit-if."

Infants also learn the relationship between mouth movements and sound. In one study, 8-month-olds watched a film of someone speaking, with the audio a fraction of a second ahead of the video. Even when the actor spoke an unknown language, babies noticed the mistiming (Pons & Lewkowicz, 2014).

Some caregivers, recognizing the power of gestures, teach "baby signs" to their 6- to 12-month-olds, who communicate with hand signs months before they move their tongues, lips, and jaws to make words. There is no evidence that baby signing accelerates talking (as had been claimed), but it may make parents more responsive, which itself is an advantage (Kirk et al., 2013). Every gesture and movement aid communication.

For deaf babies, sign language is crucial in the first year: It not only predicts later ability to communicate with signs but also advances cognitive development (Hall et al., 2017). Remember how important gaze-following was for infant learning? Deaf infants are even better at gaze-following than hearing infants, because they rely on visual signs from their caregivers (Brooks et al., 2019).

Even for hearing babies and without adult signing, gestures are a powerful means of communication (Goldin-Meadow, 2015). One early gesture is pointing and responding to pointing from someone else. The latter requires something quite sophisticated—understanding another person's perspective.

Most animals cannot interpret pointing, but before they are a year old most humans look toward wherever someone else points and already point with their tiny index fingers. Pointing is well developed by 12 months, especially when the person who is pointing also speaks (e.g., "look at that") (Daum et al., 2013).

Infants younger than a year old who are adept at pointing tend to be those who will soon begin talking. That is one reason adults need to respond to pointing as if it is intended to communicate—which it is (Bohn & Köymen, 2018).

## First Words

Finally, at about a year, the average baby utters a few words, understood by caregivers if not by strangers. Those words often coincide with the age when walking begins. It may be that a certain amount of brain maturation is needed for both, or it may be that walking allows a new set of questions and makes it more important that people talk to the baby (Walle & Campos, 2014). Following the first words, spoken vocabulary increases gradually (perhaps one new word a week). Meanings are learned rapidly; babies understand about 10 times more than they can say.

Initially, the first words are merely labels for familiar things (*mama* and *dada* are common), but each early word soon becomes a **holophrase,** a single word that expresses an entire thought. That phrase is accompanied by gestures, facial expressions, and nuances of tone, loudness, and cadence. Imagine meaningful communication in "Dada," "Dada?" and "Dada!" Each is a holophrase.

## The Naming Explosion

Spoken vocabulary builds rapidly once the first 50 words are mastered, with 21-month-olds typically saying twice as many words as 18-month-olds (Adamson & Bakeman, 2006). This language spurt is called the **naming explosion** because many early words are nouns, that is, names of persons, places, or things.

Before the explosion, names are already favored. Infants learn the names of each significant caregiver (often *dada, mama, nana, papa, baba, tata*), sibling, and pet. (See Visualizing Development, page 166.) Other frequently uttered words refer to favorite foods (*nana* can mean "banana" as well as "grandma") and to elimination (*pee-pee, wee-wee, poo-poo, ka-ka, doo-doo*).

Notice that all of these words have two identical syllables, a consonant followed by a vowel. Many early words follow that pattern—not just *baba* but also *bobo, bebe, bubu, bibi*. Some of the first words are only slightly more complicated— *ma-me, ama*, and so on. The meanings vary by language, but every baby says such words, and every culture assigns meaning to them. Words that are hard to say are simplified: Rabbits are "bunnies," stomachs are "tummies," and no man waits until his son or daughter can call him Father; he is Daddy or Papa instead.

>  **DATA CONNECTIONS: The Development of Spoken Language in the First Two Years** reviews communication milestones for infants and toddlers. 📱 **LaunchPad.**

## Cultural Differences

Early communication transcends culture. In one study, 102 adults listened to 40 recorded infant sounds and were asked which of five possibilities (pointing, giving, protesting, action request, food request) was the reason for each cry, grunt, or

**naming explosion** A sudden increase in an infant's vocabulary, especially in the number of nouns, that begins at about 18 months of age.

---

**A CASE TO STUDY**

# Early Speech

As you read, sensitive caregiving is crucial for early cognition, as babies innately look at and listen to their caregivers in order to learn. For their part, caregivers are sensitive and responsive to the infant's attempts to understand words. This is evident in early language: Parents may understand what an infant is trying to say long before other people do.

Consider 13-month-old Kyle, who was advanced in language development. He knew standard words such as *mama*, but he also knew *da, ba, tam, opma*, and *daes*, which his parents knew to be, respectively, "downstairs," "bottle," "tummy," "oatmeal," and "starfish." He also had a special sound to call squirrels (Lewis et al., 1999).

When acquaintances came to visit, they were often mystified by Kyle's attempts to speak. Who would know that *daes* meant starfish, or how a person might call squirrels? Only Kyle and his very astute parents.

Even a caring grandmother might not interpret correctly. I know this personally. I was caring for my 16-month-old grandson when he said, "Mama, mama." He looked directly at me, and he didn't seem wistful.

"Mommy's not here," I told him. That didn't stop him; he repeated "mama, mama," more as a command than a complaint. I tried several things. I know that some languages use "ma" for milk. I offered some in his sippy cup. He said, "No, no."

When his father appeared, Isaac repeated "mama." Then his dad lifted him, and Isaac cuddled in his arms. I asked Oscar what "mama" means. His reply: "Pick me up."

I now understand Isaac's logic: When he saw his mother, he said "mama" and she picked him up. His parents understood and responded to his words and gestures.

Now Isaac is a proficient talker, explaining about bird families (pigeons are the parents, because they are bigger), about who should get a seat on the subway (it is Isaac, because, as he says very plaintively to other riders, "I need to sit down"; to my embarrassment, he usually gets a seat, so his words are reinforced), and about what his brother has done wrong (explained in detail to his parents, who listen sympathetically but almost never punish the older boy).

I also listen to Isaac's current chatter, repeating some of his phrases and saying "uh-huh," knowing that early adult responses continue to affect later talking. Isaac is well on his way to becoming a highly verbal adult.

**What Does He See?** All children stare out of windows, but only some are told the names of the various cloud formations and the landscape below. Does this matter for language learning?

**grammar** All of the methods—word order, verb forms, and so on—that languages use to communicate meaning, apart from the words themselves.

whatever. Half of the sounds, and about half of the adults, were from Scotland and the other half from Uganda.

Adults in both cultures scored significantly better than chance (although no group or individual got everything right). The number correct was close to the same whether the sounds came from Scottish or Ugandan infants, or whether the adults were parents or not (Kersken et al., 2017). Human baby sounds are understood by humans no matter what language the community speaks.

However, cultures and families vary in how much child-directed speech children hear. Some parents read to their infants, teach them signs, and respond to every burp or fart as if it were an attempt to talk. Other parents are much less verbal. They use gestures and touch; they say "hush" and "no" instead of expanding vocabulary.

Traditionally, in small agricultural communities, the goal was for everyone to be "strong and silent." If adults talked too much, they might be called blabbermouths or gossips; a good worker did not waste time in conversation.

In some rural areas of the world, that notion remains. One such place is in Senegal, where mothers traditionally feared talking to their babies lest that might encourage evil spirits to take over the child (Zeitlin, 2011).

However, communication is crucial in the twenty-first-century global economy. Government, teachers, and most parents recognize this: A child's first words may be celebrated as much or more than a child's first steps. But some parents are unaware that responding to preverbal vocalizations promotes speech later on.

In one study in Senegal, professionals from the local community (fluent in Woloff, the language spoken by the people) taught mothers in some villages about infant development, including language. A year later those babies were compared to babies in similar villages where the educational intervention had not been offered.

The newly educated mothers talked more to their babies, and the babies, in turn, talked more, with 20 more utterances in five minutes than the control group (A. Weber et al., 2017). The researchers were careful not to challenge the traditional notions directly; instead they taught how early language development advanced infant cognition. The mothers applied what they learned, and the babies responded.

## Putting Words Together

**Grammar** includes all of the methods that languages use to communicate meaning. There are many ways to add letters to words and to put words together—that is grammar.

Word order, prefixes, suffixes, intonation, verb forms, pronouns and negations, prepositions and articles—all of these are aspects of grammar. Grammar can be discerned in holophrases because one word can be spoken differently depending on meaning. However, grammar becomes essential when babies combine words (Bremner & Wachs, 2010). That typically happens between 18 and 24 months.

For example, "Baby cry" and "More juice" follow grammatical word order. Children do not usually say "Juice more," and even toddlers know that "Cry baby" is not the same as "Baby cry." By age 2, children combine three words. English grammar uses subject–verb–object order; the grammar of other languages use other sequences and their toddlers do the same.

For example, English-speaking toddlers say, "Mommy read book" rather than any of the five other possible sequences of those three words. Adults might say the same three-word sentence with a few grammatical changes, "Mom reads e-books," not "e-books reads Mom." As you see, grammar changes meanings markedly.

Children's proficiency in grammar correlates with sentence length, which is why **mean length of utterance (MLU)** is used to measure a child's language progress (e.g., Miyata et al., 2013). The child who says, "The baby is crying" is more advanced than the child who says, "Baby crying" or simply, "Baby cry!"

**mean length of utterance (MLU)** The average number of words in a typical sentence (called utterance because children may not talk in complete sentences). MLU is often used to measure language development.

## Theories of Language Learning

Worldwide, people who are not yet 2 years old express hopes, fears, and memories—sometimes in more than one language. By adolescence, people communicate with nuanced words and gestures, some writing poems and lyrics that move thousands of their co-linguists. How is language learned so easily and so well?

Answers come from at least three schools of thought. The first theory says that infants are directly taught, the second that social impulses propel infants to communicate, and the third that infants understand language because of genetic brain structures that arose more than 100,000 years ago.

### Theory One: Infants Need to Be Taught

One idea arises from behaviorism. The essential idea is that learning is acquired, step by step, through association and reinforcement.

B. F. Skinner (1957) noticed that spontaneous babbling is usually reinforced. Often, when a baby says "ma-ma-ma-ma," a grinning mother appears, repeating the sound and showering the baby with attention, praise, and perhaps food. This is especially likely if the baby is a firstborn, which may explain why later-born children, on average, have smaller vocabularies than the oldest child in a family.

Repetition strengthens associations, so infants learn language faster if parents speak to them often. Few parents know this theory, but many use behaviorist techniques by praising and responding to the toddler's simple, mispronounced speech, thus teaching language.

Behaviorists note that some 3-year-olds converse in elaborate sentences; others just barely put one simple word before another. Such variations correlate with the amount of language each child has heard.

Indeed, to some extent infants are "statistical learners" of language, deciding the meanings and boundaries of words based on how often those sounds are heard (Saffran & Kirkham, 2018). Parents of the most verbal children teach language throughout infancy—singing, explaining, listening, responding, and reading to their babies every day, giving their children a rich trove of verbal data, long before the infant utters a first spoken word (see **Figure 6.3**).

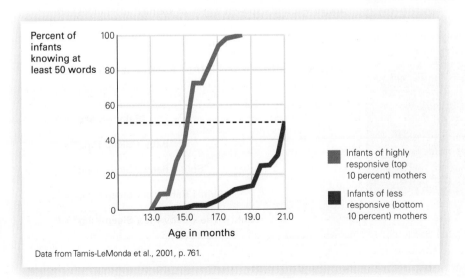

Data from Tamis-LeMonda et al., 2001, p. 761.

**FIGURE 6.3**

**Maternal Responsiveness and Infants' Language Acquisition** Learning the first 50 words is a milestone in early language acquisition, as it predicts the arrival of the naming explosion and the multiword sentence a few weeks later. Researchers found that half of the infants of highly responsive mothers (top 10 percent) reached this milestone at 15 months. The infants of less responsive mothers (bottom 10 percent) lagged significantly behind, with half of them at the 50-word level at 21 months.

# Early Communication and Language

## Communication Milestones: The First Two Years

These are norms. Many intelligent and healthy babies vary in the age at which they reach these milestones.

| Months | Communication Milestone |
|---|---|
| 0 | Reflexive communication—cries, movements, facial expressions |
| 1 | Recognizes some sounds<br>Makes several different cries and sounds<br>Turns toward familiar sounds |
| 3 | A range of meaningful noises—cooing, fussing, crying, laughing<br>Social smile well established<br>Laughter begins<br>Imitates movements<br>Enjoys interaction with others |
| 6 | New sounds, including squeals, growls, croons, trills, vowel sounds<br>Meaningful gestures including showing excitement (waving arms and legs)<br>Expresses negative feelings (with face and arms)<br>Capable of distinguishing emotion by tone of voice<br>Responds to noises by making sounds<br>Uses noise to express joy and unhappiness<br>Babbles, including both consonant and vowel sounds repeated in syllables |
| 10 | Makes simple gestures, like raising arms for "pick me up"<br>Recognizes pointing<br>Makes a sound (not in recognizable language) to indicate a particular thing<br>Responds to simple requests |
| 12 | More gestures, such as shaking head for "no"<br>Babbles with inflection, intonation<br>Names familiar people (like "mama," "dada," "nana")<br>Uses exclamations, such as "uh-oh!"<br>Tries to imitate words<br>Points and responds to pointing<br>First spoken words |
| 18 | Combines two words (like "Daddy bye-bye")<br>Slow growth of vocabulary, up to about 50 words<br>Language use focuses on 10–30 holophrases<br>Uses nouns and verbs<br>Uses movement, including running and throwing, to indicate emotion<br>Naming explosion may begin, three or more words learned per day |
| 24 | Combines three or four words together; half the toddler's utterances are two or more words long<br>Uses adjectives and adverbs ("blue," "big," "gentle")<br>Sings simple songs |

Information from American Academy of Pediatrics

## Universal First Words

Across cultures, babies' first words are remarkably similar. The words for mother and father are recognizable in almost any language. Most children will learn to name their immediate family and caregivers between the ages of 12 and 18 months.

| Language | Mother | Father |
|---|---|---|
| English | mama, mommy | dada. daddy |
| Spanish | mama | papa |
| French | maman, mama | papa |
| Italian | mamma | bebbo, papa |
| Latvian | mama | te-te |
| Syrian Arabic | mama | babe |
| Bantu | be-mama | taata |
| Swahili | mama | baba |
| Sanskrit | nana | tata |
| Hebrew | ema | abba |
| Korean | oma | apa |

ampyang/iStock/Getty Images

## Mastering Language

Children's use of language becomes more complex as they acquire more words and begin to master grammar and usage. A child's spoken words or sounds (utterances) are broken down into the smallest units of language to determine their length and complexity:

MEAN LENGTH OF UTTERANCE (MLU), ILLUSTRATED

"Baby!" = 1

"Baby + Sleep" = 2

"Baby + Sleep + ing" = 3

"Shh! + Baby + Sleep + ing" = 4

"Shh! + Baby + is + Sleep + ing" = 5

"Shh! + The + Baby + is + Sleep + ing" = 6

## Theory Two: Social Impulses Foster Infant Language

The second theory arises from the sociocultural reason for language: communication. According to this perspective, infants communicate because humans are social beings, dependent on one another for survival and joy.

All human infants (and no chimpanzees) seek to master words and grammar in order to join the social world (Tomasello & Herrmann, 2010). According to this perspective, it is the social function of speech, not the words, that undergirds early language.

This theory challenges child-directed videos, CDs, and downloads named to appeal to parents (*Baby Einstein*, *Brainy Baby*, and *Mozart for Mommies and Daddies—Jumpstart your Newborn's I.Q.*). Since early language development is impressive, even explosive, some parents who allow infants to watch such programs believe that the rapid language learning is aided by video. Commercial apps for tablets and smartphones, such as *Shapes Game HD* and *VocabuLarry*, have joined the market.

However, developmental research finds that screen time during infancy may be harmful, because it avoids the social interaction that is essential for learning to communicate. One recent study found that toddlers could learn a word from either a book or a video but that only book-learning, not video-learning, enabled children to use the new word in another context (Strouse & Ganea, 2017). When the parents read the books, they often held their baby, spoke with clear and animated words, and allowed the child to grab pages, make noises, and point to pictures. That was an engaging social experience.

Another study focused on teaching baby signs, 18 hand gestures that refer to particular objects (Dayanim & Namy, 2015). The babies in this study were 15 months old, an age at which all babies use gestures and are poised to learn object names. The 18 signs referred to common early words, such as *baby*, *ball*, *banana*, *bird*, *cat*, and *dog*.

In this study, the toddlers were divided into four groups: (1) video only, (2) video with parent watching and reinforcing, (3) book instruction with parent reading and reinforcing, and (4) no instruction. Not surprisingly, the no-instruction group learned words (as every normal toddler does) but not signs, and the other three groups learned some signs. The two groups with parent instruction learned most, with the book-reading group remembering signs better than either video group. Why?

The crucial factor seemed to be parent interaction. When parents watch a video with their infants, they talk less than when they read a book or play with toys (Anderson & Hanson, 2016). Since adult input is essential for language learning, cognitive development is reduced by video time. Infants are most likely to understand and apply what they have learned when they learn directly from another person (Barr, 2013).

Screen time cannot "substitute for responsive, loving face-to-face relationships" (Lemish & Kolucki, 2013, p. 335). Direct social interaction is pivotal for language, according to theory two.

## Theory Three: Infants Teach Themselves

A third theory holds that language learning is genetically programmed. Adults need not teach it (theory one), nor is it a by-product of social interaction (theory two). Instead, it arises from a particular gene (FOXP2), brain maturation, and the overall human impulse to imitate.

**Caught in the Middle** Parents try to limit screen time, but children are beguiled and bombarded from many sides.

*"Keep in mind, this all counts as screen time."*

Emily Flake/The New Yorker Collection/The Cartoon Bank

For example, English articles (*the*, *an*, *a*) signal that the next word will be the name of an object. Since babies have "an innate base" that primes them to learn, articles facilitate learning nouns (Shi, 2014, p. 9). Articles prove to be a useful clue for infants learning English but are frustrating for anyone who learns English as an adult. Adults from other linguistic communities may be highly intelligent and motivated, but their language-learning genes are past the sensitive learning time.

Our ancestors were genetically programmed to imitate for survival, but until a few millennia ago, no one needed to learn languages other than their own. Thus, human genes allow experience-dependent language learning, pruning the connections that our particular language does not need. If we want to learn another language in adulthood, our brains cannot resurrect the connections we lost in infancy.

The prime spokesman for this perspective was Noam Chomsky (1968, 1980). Although behaviorists focus on variations among children in vocabulary size, Chomsky focused on similarities in language acquisition—the evolutionary universals, not the differences.

Noting that all young children master basic grammar according to a schedule, Chomsky hypothesized that children are born with a brain structure he called a **language acquisition device (LAD),** which allows children, as their brains develop, to derive the rules of grammar quickly and effectively from the speech they hear every day.

For example, everywhere, a raised tone indicates a question, and infants prefer questions to declarative statements (Soderstrom et al., 2011). This suggests that infants are wired to talk, and caregivers universally ask them questions long before they can answer back.

According to theory three, language is experience-expectant, as the developing brain quickly and efficiently connects neurons to support whichever language the infant hears. Because of this experience-expectancy, the various languages of the world are all logical, coherent, and systematic. Then some experience-dependent learning occurs as each brain adjusts to a particular language.

The LAD works for deaf infants as well. All 6-month-olds, hearing or not, prefer to look at sign language over nonlinguistic pantomime. For hearing infants, this preference disappears by 10 months, but deaf infants begin signing at that time, which is their particular expression of the universal LAD.

## All True?

A master linguist explains that "the human mind is a hybrid system," perhaps using different parts of the brain for each kind of learning (Pinker, 1999, p. 279).

The idea that every theory is partially correct may seem idealistic. However, many scientists who are working on extending and interpreting research on language acquisition have arrived at this conclusion. They contend that language learning is neither the direct product of repeated input (behaviorism) nor the result of a specific human neurological capacity (LAD). Rather, from an evolutionary perspective, "different elements of the language apparatus may have evolved in different ways," and thus, a "piecemeal and empirical" approach is needed (Marcus & Rabagliati, 2009, p. 281).

Neuroscience is the most recent method to investigate the development of language. It was once thought that language was located in two specific regions of the brain (Wernicke's area and Broca's area). But now neuroscientists are convinced that language arises from other regions as well. Some genes and regions are crucial, but hundreds of genes and many brain regions contribute to linguistic fluency.

Neuroscientists describing language development write about "connections," "networks," "circuits," and "hubs" to capture the idea that language is interrelated and complex (Dehaene-Lambertz, 2017; Pulvermüller, 2018). Even when the

---

**language acquisition device (LAD)** Chomsky's term for a hypothesized mental structure that enables humans to learn language, including the basic aspects of grammar, vocabulary, and intonation.

**Family Values** Every family encourages the values and abilities that their children need to be successful adults. For this family in Ecuador, that means strong legs and lungs to climb the Andes, respecting their parents, and keeping quiet unless spoken to. A "man of few words" is admired. By contrast, many North American parents babble in response to infant babble, celebrate the first spoken word, and stop their conversation to listen to an interrupting child. If a student never talks in class, or another student blurts out irrelevant questions. Culture talks!

**Observation Quiz** If this is a typical scene, what family values are evident? (see answer, page 171) ↓

Steven J. Kazlowski/Alamy

focus is simply on talking, one neuroscientist notes that "speech is encoded at multiple levels in different parallel pathways" (Dehaene-Lambertz, 2017, p. 52).

That neuroscientist begins her detailed description of the infant brain and language with the same amazement that traditional linguists have expressed for decades:

> For thousands of years and across numerous cultures, human infants are able to perfectly master oral or signed language in only a few years. No other machine, be it silicon or carbon based, is able to reach the same level of expertise.
>
> *[Dehaene-Lambertz, 2017, p. 48]*

Language is closely linked, in the early months, with cognition. As one review of the many pathways between learning to talk and understanding the world concludes:

> A constellation of factors that are unique to human development—infants' prolonged period of dependency, exquisite sensitivity to experience, and powerful learning strategies—collectively spark a cascade of developmental change whose ultimate result is the acquisition of language and its unparalleled interface with cognition.
>
> *[Perszyk & Waxman, 2018, p. 246]*

The words *constellation* and *cascade* signify that many brain structures and social inputs result in both language and learning.

From this we are led to an overall conclusion. Infants are amazing and active learners who advance their cognition in many ways—through understanding of people, objects, memory, and communication. Remember that before Piaget, many experts assumed that babies did not yet learn or think. How wrong they were!

---

**WHAT HAVE YOU LEARNED?**

1. What aspects of language develop in the first year?

2. When does vocabulary develop slowly and when does it develop quickly?

3. What is typical of the first words that infants speak?

4. What indicates that toddlers use some grammar?

5. According to behaviorism, how do adults teach infants to talk?

6. According to sociocultural theory, why do infants try to communicate?

7. Do people really have a language acquisition device?

8. Why do developmentalists accept several theories of language development?

## SUMMARY

### The Eager Mind

**1.** Infants learn so quickly that developmentalists now suggest that some basic understanding is programmed into the brain—no experience necessary.

**2.** Infants distinguish all of the possible sounds that human languages use. This ability decreases as babies become more attuned to whatever languages they hear.

**3.** Infants observe events and people to learn what merits their attention. Face recognition is an inborn ability that is refined by experience. They particularly attend to where adults are looking, an inborn impulse called gaze-following.

**4.** Information-processing theory, which looks at each step of the thinking process, helps researchers understand that every moment of experience aids cognition, enhanced by the innate programming of the infant mind.

**5.** Evolutionary theory is also relevant, as it emphasizes the basic cognitive capacities that humans have needed to survive. The emphasis is not only on inborn cognitive structures but also on plasticity, which allows each infant to adapt to the environment.

**6.** Infant memory is fragile but not completely absent. Reminder sessions help trigger memories, and young brains learn motor sequences and respond to repeated emotions (their own and those of other people) long before explicit memory, using words.

### Piaget's Sensorimotor Intelligence

7. Piaget realized that very young infants are active learners who seek to understand their complex observations and experiences. The six stages of sensorimotor intelligence involve early adaptation to experience.

8. Sensorimotor intelligence begins with reflexes and ends with mental combinations. The six stages occur in pairs, with each pair characterized by a circular reaction.

9. Infants first react to their own bodies (primary), then respond to other people and things (secondary), and finally, in the stage of tertiary circular reactions, infants become more goal-oriented, creative, and experimental as "little scientists."

10. Infants gradually develop an understanding of objects. According to Piaget's classic experiments, infants understand object permanence and begin to search for hidden objects at about 8 months. Newer research finds that Piaget underestimated infant cognition.

### Language: What Develops in the First Two Years?

11. Attempts to communicate are apparent in the first weeks and months, beginning with noises, facial expressions, and avid listening. Infants babble at about 6 months, understand words and gestures by 10 months, and speak their first words at about 1 year.

12. Vocabulary builds slowly until the infant knows approximately 50 words. Then the naming explosion begins. Grammar is evident in the first holophrases, and combining words together in proper sequence is further evidence that babies learn grammar as well as vocabulary.

13. Toward the end of the second year, toddlers express wishes and emotions in short sentences. Variation is evident, in part because of caregiver attention. Some babies are already bilingual.

14. Theories differ in explaining how infants learn language—whether infants must be taught or that social impulses foster language learning or that brains are genetically attuned to language as soon as the requisite maturation occurs.

15. Each theory of language learning is confirmed by research. Developmental scientists find that many parts of the brain, and many strategies for learning, result in early language accomplishments. Current research, with the benefit of advances in neuroscience, confirms that conclusion.

## KEY TERMS

sensorimotor intelligence
  (p. 156)
primary circular reactions
  (p. 157)
secondary circular reactions
  (p. 158)

object permanence (p. 158)
tertiary circular reactions
  (p. 159)
"little scientist" (p. 160)

babbling (p. 161)
holophrase (p. 162)
naming explosion (p. 163)
grammar (p. 164)

mean length of utterance
  (MLU) (p. 165)
language acquisition device
  (LAD) (p. 168)

## APPLICATIONS

1. Elicit vocalizations from an infant—babbling if the baby is under age 1, using words if the baby is older. Write down all of the baby's communication for 10 minutes. Then ask the primary caregiver to elicit vocalizations for 10 minutes, and write these down. What differences are apparent between the baby's two attempts at communication? Compare your findings with the norms described in the chapter.

2. Many educators recommend that parents read to babies every day, even before 1 year of age. What theory of language development does this reflect and why? Ask several parents whether they did so, and why or why not.

3. Test a toddler's ability to pretend and to imitate, as Piaget would expect. Use a doll or a toy car and pretend with it, such as feeding the doll or making the car travel. Then see whether the child will do it. This experiment can be more elaborate if the child succeeds.

## Especially For ANSWERS

**Response for Educators** (from p. 148): Probably both. Infants love to communicate, and they seek every possible way to do so. Therefore, the teachers should try to understand the baby and the baby's parents, but they should also start teaching the baby the majority language of the school.

**Response for Parents** (from p. 158): Both decisions should be made within the first month, during the stage of reflexes. If parents wait until the infant is 4 months or older, they may discover that they are too late. It is difficult to introduce a bottle to a 4-month-old who has never sucked on an artificial nipple or a pacifier to a baby who has already adapted the sucking reflex to a thumb.

**Response for Parents** (from p. 160): It is easier and safer to babyproof the house because toddlers, being "little scientists,"

want to explore. However, it is important for both parents to encourage and guide the baby. If having untouchable items prevents a major conflict between the adults, that might be the best choice.

## Observation Quiz ANSWERS

**Answer to Observation Quiz** (from p. 155): The mobile is a good addition—colorful and too high for the baby to reach. (Let's hope it is securely fastened and those strings are strong and tight!) But there are two things that are not what a cognitive developmentalist would recommend. First, the crib and the wall are both plain white, limiting what the baby can focus on, and second, the crib bumper is a SIDS risk.

**Answer to Observation Quiz** (from p. 168): Not social interaction, not talking. Instead, all quietly stare at sky and terrain; awe of nature may be a family value. Hierarchy and gender seem significant: The father is distant and above all, the mother is busy, the children are below the parents. Do only males wear hats?

# The First Two Years: Psychosocial Development

## What Will You Know?

1. Will a difficult newborn become a difficult child?
2. What do infants do if they are securely attached to their caregivers?
3. Is it ideal for infants to be cared for exclusively by their mothers?

**B**one-tired after a day of teaching, I was grateful to find a seat on the crowded downtown train. At the next stop, more people boarded, including a mother who stood in front of me. She held a well-dressed baby, about 18 months old, in one arm, and she wrapped her other arm around a pole as she held several heavy bags. I thought of offering my seat. Too tired. But at least I could hold her bags on my lap.

"Can I help you?" I asked, offering a hand. Wordlessly she handed me . . . the baby! The toddler sat quietly and listened as I expressed admiration for her socks, pointed out the red and blue stripes, and then sang a lullaby. I could feel her body relax. Her eyes stayed on her mother.

I should not have been surprised. Mothers everywhere need help with infant care, and strangers everywhere are *allomothers*. We all attend to infant cries, bring gifts to newborns, and study, consult doctors, or volunteer to become helpers. I noticed other riders on that train watching me with that little girl. Mother, strangers, and I were doing what our culture expects. And the baby did what healthy babies do. She responded to my off-key singing, reassured by the sight of her mother.

This example opens this chapter because it illustrates infant emotions and caregiver responses. You will read about psychosocial changes over the first two years, from synchrony, to attachment, to social referencing, quite evident in this baby.

At the end of the chapter, we explore a controversy: Who should care for infants? Only mothers, or also fathers, grandmothers, day-care teachers, and strangers? Would you have handed me your baby? Families and cultures answer this question in opposite ways.

Fortunately, as this chapter explains, despite diversity of temperament and caregiving, most infants develop well if their basic emotional needs are met. This baby seemed fine.

## Emotional Development

Psychosocial development during infancy can be seen as two interwoven strands — nature/nurture, or universal/particular, or experience-expectant/experience-dependent. To portray these strands with words in a book, we must pull them apart, so this chapter is a zigzag, turning from universal to particular and back, again and again.

## Early Emotions

We begin with universal: In their first two years, all infants progress from reactive pain and pleasure to complex patterns of socioemotional awareness, a movement from basic instincts to learned responses (see At About This Time).

At first, comfort predominates: Newborns are content and relaxed when fed and drifting off to sleep. Discomfort is also part of daily life: Newborns cry when they are hurt or hungry, tired or frightened (as by a loud noise or a sudden loss of support).

By the second week and increasing to six weeks, some infants have bouts of uncontrollable crying, commonly referred to as *colic*, perhaps the result of immature digestion or the infant version of a migraine headache (Gelfand, 2018). Others have *reflux*, probably the result of immature swallowing. About 10 to 20 percent of babies cry "excessively," defined as more than three hours a day, more than three days a week, for more than three weeks.

Fortunately, early emotions do not necessarily predict later life. A longitudinal study of 291 infants found that, by age 2, infants with colic were no more likely to have behavioral problems than those without (G. Bell et al., 2018). As you will later read, newborn temperament is shaped by caregiver response.

## Smiling and Laughing

Soon, crying decreases and additional emotions become recognizable. Colic usually subsides by 3 months. Happiness is expressed by a fleeting **social smile**, evoked by a human face at about 6 weeks (Wörmann et al., 2012).

Preterm babies smile later, because the social smile is affected by age since conception, not age since birth (White-Traut et al., 2018). The social smile is universal; all babies do it when they are old enough, evidence of the human social impulse.

Laughter builds over the first months, often in tandem with curiosity: A typical 6-month-old chortles upon discovering new things, particularly social experiences that balance familiarity and surprise, such as Daddy making a funny face. That is just what Piaget would expect, "making interesting experiences last." Very young infants prefer seeing happy faces over sad ones, even if the happy faces are not looking at them (Kim & Johnson, 2013).

Soon happiness becomes more discriminating. In one study, infants first enjoyed a video of dancing to music as it normally occurs, on the beat. Then some watched a video in which the sound track was mismatched with dancing. Eight- to twelve-month-old babies, compared to younger ones, were quite curious—but less delighted—about offbeat dancing. The researchers concluded "babies know bad dancing when they see it" (Hannon et al., 2017).

## Anger and Sadness

Crying in pain and smiling in pleasure are soon joined by emotions more responsive to external experiences. Anger is notable at 6 months, usually triggered by frustration.

For example, to study infant emotions, researchers "crouched behind the child and gently restrained his or her arms for 2 min[utes] or until 20 s[econds] of hard crying ensued" (Mills-Koonce et al., 2011, p. 390). "Hard crying" was not rare: Infants hate to be strapped in, caged in, closed in, or just held in place when they want to explore.

In infancy, anger is a healthy response to frustration, unlike sadness, which also may appear in the first months (Thiam et al., 2017). Sadness indicates withdrawal instead of a bid for help, and it is accompanied by a greater increase in the body's

### AT ABOUT THIS TIME

**Developing Emotions**

| Birth | Distress; contentment |
|---|---|
| 6 weeks | Social smile |
| 3 months | Laughter; curiosity |
| 4 months | Full, responsive smiles |
| 4–8 months | Anger |
| 9–14 months | Fear of social events (strangers, separation from caregiver) |
| 12 months | Fear of unexpected sights and sounds |
| 18 months | Self-awareness; pride; shame; embarrassment |

As always, culture and experience influence the norms of development. This is especially true for emotional development after the first 8 months.

**social smile** A smile evoked by a human face, normally first evident in infants about six weeks after birth.

**Developmentally Correct** Both Santa's smile and Olivia's grimace are appropriate reactions for people of their age. Adults playing Santa must smile no matter what, and if Olivia smiled, that would be troubling to anyone who knows about 7-month-olds. Yet every Christmas, thousands of parents wait in line to put their infants on the laps of oddly dressed, bearded strangers.

REUTERS/Suzanne Plunkett

production of cortisol. For that reason, developmentalists are troubled if a very young baby is sad.

## Fear

Fear begins with unexpected events, such as fear of falling or of loud noises, but soon it involves human interaction. Indeed, being frightened of something, from snakes to strangers, may depend on three factors: awareness of discrepancy, inborn temperament, and social context. Two kinds of social fear are typical, increasing from the middle of the first year:

**separation anxiety** An infant's distress when a familiar caregiver leaves; most obvious between 9 and 14 months.

**stranger wariness** An infant's expression of concern—a quiet stare while clinging to a familiar person, or a look of fear—when a stranger appears.

- **Separation anxiety**—clinging and crying when a familiar caregiver is about to leave. Some separation anxiety is normal at age 1, may be more intense by age 2, and then usually subsides.
- **Stranger wariness**—fear of unfamiliar people, especially when they move too close, too quickly. Knowing that, in the subway incident that opened this chapter, I first distracted the baby by talking about her socks, and then sang to her. Babies everywhere respond to song.

If separation anxiety and stranger fear remain intense after age 3, impairing a child's ability to leave home, to go to school, or to play with other children, that is an emotional disorder. According to the DSM-5, separation anxiety becomes a disorder when it lingers into childhood or adolescence (American Psychiatric Association, 2013); clinicians may diagnose it in adults, as well, especially if symptoms persist for at least six months (Bögels et al., 2013).

Likewise, stranger wariness may continue, becoming social phobia or generalized anxiety (Rudaz et al., 2017). Both emotions are expected at age 1, becoming possible problems later. And both are experience-expectant and then experience-dependent, responsive to context (LoBue & Adolph, 2019). Infants at home with their mothers when a stranger comes to visit are likely to smile, not be afraid. But if a stranger yells and approaches quickly to a few inches from the babies face with an angry expression, almost any 1-year-old cries and tries to move away.

Many 1-year-olds are curious but wary of anything unexpected, from the flush of the toilet to the pop of a jack-in-the-box, from closing elevator doors to the tail-wagging approach of a dog. With repeated experience and reassurance, older infants might enjoy flushing the toilet (again and again) or calling the dog (crying if the dog does *not* come). Note the transition from instinct to learning to thought, from the amygdala to the cortex.

**◖◗ Especially for Nurses and Pediatricians** Parents come to you concerned that their 1-year-old hides her face and holds onto them tightly whenever a stranger appears. What do you tell them? (see response, page 201)

## Toddlers' Emotions

Emotions take on new strength during toddlerhood, as both memory and mobility advance. Context is crucial for fear (LoBue & Adolph, 2019). Throughout the second year and beyond, emotions become less frequent but more focused, targeted toward infuriating or terrifying or exhilarating experiences. Both laughing and crying are louder and more discriminating.

### Temper Tantrums

The new strength of emotions is apparent in temper tantrums. Toddlers are famous for fury. When something angers them, they might yell, scream, cry, hit, and throw themselves on the floor. Logic is beyond them: If adults tease or get angry, that makes it worse. Parental insistence on obedience exacerbates the tantrum (Cierpka & Cierpka, 2016).

One child said, "I don't want my feet. Take my feet off. I don't want my feet." Her mother tried logic, which didn't work, and then offered to get scissors and cut off the offending feet. A new wail erupted, with a loud shriek "Nooooo!" (Katrina, quoted in Vedantam, 2011).

With temper tantrums, soon sadness comes to the fore. Then comfort—not punishment—is helpful (Green et al., 2011). Outbursts of anger are typical at ages 1 and 2, but if they persist and become destructive, that signifies trouble, in parent or child (Cierpka & Cierpka, 2016).

As with these examples, a toddler's innate reactions may evolve into moral values and psychic responses, with specifics depending on parents and experiences. For example, many children take off their clothes in public, unaware that nudity is taboo. Children are born curious and uninhibited: Shame and self-consciousness are learned.

## Self and Others

Temper can be seen as an expression of selfhood, as can other common toddler emotions: pride, shame, jealousy, embarrassment, disgust, and guilt. These emotions may begin with inborn sensitivities, but they involve social awareness.

Such awareness typically emerges from family interaction, especially the relationship between caregiver and baby. For instance, in a study of infant jealousy, mothers ignored their own baby and attended to another infant. That made the babies move closer to their mothers, bidding for attention. Their brain activity also registered social emotions (Mize et al., 2014).

Positive emotions also show social awareness and learning. Many toddlers try to help a stranger who has dropped something or who is searching for a hidden object, and some express sympathy for someone who hurt themselves (Aitken et al., 2019).

Over time, children learn when and whom to help by watching adults. Some adults donate to panhandlers, others look away, and still others complain to the police. Attitudes about ethnicity, or immigration, or clothing, begin with the infant's preference for the familiar and interest in novelty, and then upbringing adds appreciation or rejection.

## Recognizing the Self

In addition to social awareness, another foundation for emotional growth is **self-awareness**, the realization that one's body, mind, and activities are distinct from those of other people. Closely following the new mobility that results from walking is an emerging sense of individuality.

In a classic experiment (Lewis & Brooks, 1978), 9- to 24-month-olds looked into a mirror after a dot of rouge had been surreptitiously put on their noses. If they reacted by touching the red dot on their noses, that meant they knew the mirror showed their own faces. None of the babies younger than 12 months did that, although they sometimes smiled and touched the dot on the "other" baby in the mirror.

Between 15 and 24 months, babies become self-aware, touching their own red noses with curiosity and puzzlement. Self-recognition in the mirror/rouge test (and in photographs) usually emerges with two other advances: pretending and using first-person pronouns (*I, me, mine, myself, my*) (Lewis, 2010). Thus, "an explicit and hence reflective conception of the self is apparent at the early stage of language acquisition at around the same age that infants begin to recognize themselves in mirrors" (Rochat, 2013, p. 388).

This illustrates the interplay of infant abilities—walking, talking, social awareness, and emotional self-understanding all combine to make the 18-month-old quite unlike the 8-month-old. To repeat a now-familiar theme, timing and expression of self-awareness are affected by the social context (Ross et al., 2017).

**LaunchPad**
macmillan learning

**VIDEO ACTIVITY: Self-Awareness and the Rouge Test** shows the famous assessment of how and when self-awareness appears in infancy.

**self-awareness** A person's realization that he or she is a distinct individual whose body, mind, and actions are separate from those of other people.

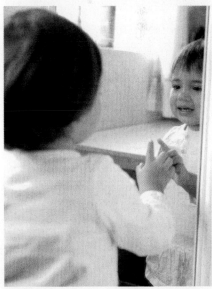

© 2016 Macmillan

**My Finger, My Body, and Me** Mirror self-recognition is particularly important in her case, as this 2-year-old has a twin sister. Parents may enjoy dressing twins alike and giving them rhyming names, but each baby needs to know she is an individual, not just a twin.

Some cultures value independence and others do not, and each individual within each culture may reinforce those cultural values or may resist them. If you asked a toddler to put away some toys and were told "No," would you be angry or amused? Your answer reflects your culture; babies learn to reflect that as well.

> **WHAT HAVE YOU LEARNED?**
>
> **1.** What experiences trigger happiness, anger, and fear?
>
> **2.** How do emotions differ between the first and second year of life?
>
> **3.** What evidence suggests that caregivers affect infant emotions?
>
> **4.** What is the significance of how toddlers react to seeing themselves in a mirror?
>
> **5.** How much of infant emotions is inborn, and how much depends on caregiving?

## Temperament and Personality

The early smiles, curiosity, and wariness are universal, but the intensity of those emotions reflects temperament as well as the situation. The same is true for caregivers, whose personality interacts with temperament (their own as well as that of their infant) and the result is a complex cauldron, mixing nature and nurture. Accordingly, you will see that understanding temperament is an important, but complicated topic.

## The Biology of Temperament

**temperament** Inborn differences between one person and another in emotions, activity, and self-regulation. It is measured by the person's typical responses to the environment.

**Temperament** is defined as the "biologically based core of individual differences in style of approach and response to the environment that is stable across time and situations" (van den Akker et al., 2010, p. 485). "Biologically based" means temperament begins with genes and prenatal determinants, the early manifestation of epigenetics.

Is that accurate? Are babies born with different temperaments? Yes! One team recorded the tone, duration, and intensity of infant cries after the first inoculation, before much experience outside the womb. Cries at this very early stage correlated with later temperament: The loudest and longest screamers become quickest to protest later on (Jong et al., 2010).

By contrast, some young infants are wonderfully sunny, smiling at everyone, fussing more than wailing when hungry or hurt. If their caregivers smile in return, they tend to become happy children (Bridgett et al., 2013). Determining the direction of this correlation, from infant-to-parent or parent-to-infant or both influenced by some third variable (such as poverty or nutrition), is difficult. But various patterns of temperament seem innate, and some stability in temperament is evident over the early months (Planalp & Goldsmith, 2019).

Temperament can make later life easier or more difficult. Even caregiver abuse and neglect seem to be weathered by some babies, with no long-lasting damage to adult personality. Of course, maltreatment is never excusable, but the effects vary, and temperament is one reason (Maltby et al., 2019).

## Dimensions of Temperament

In laboratory studies of temperament, 4-month-old infants might see spinning mobiles or hear unusual sounds, and older babies might confront a clown who approaches quickly. During such experiences, some children laugh, some cry, and others are quiet.

Analyzing many studies of temperament, researchers find three distinct traits:

- Effortful control (regulating attention and emotion, self-soothing)
- Negative mood (fearful, angry, unhappy)
- Exuberance (active, social, not shy)

[*Lengua et al., 2019*]

## Personality

Temperament is *not* the same as personality, although temperament may lead to personality differences. Generally, personality traits (e.g., honesty and humility) are heavily influenced by parents and culture, whereas temperamental traits (e.g., shyness and aggression) arise from genes. Of course, nature and nurture always interact. For both temperament and personality, family influences are powerful: Not only do parents affect their children in temperament and personality, but also children affect their parents (Lengua et al., 2019).

In general, infants with difficult temperaments are more likely than other babies to develop emotional problems, especially if their mothers had a difficult pregnancy and were depressed or anxious caregivers (Garthus-Niegel et al., 2017). In that case, the difficult baby affects the stressed parent, as well as vice versa.

Personality of the adult may be a crucial factor; some adults are more relaxed and others more stressed because of their genes and experiences. Researchers have settled on five clusters of personality in adults, known as the *Big Five*: Openness to experience, Conscientiousness, Extraversion, Agreeableness, and Neuroticism. Agreeable adults find parenthood easy; neurotic (worried, anxious) parents are stressed by difficult babies.

## Temperament Over the Years

One longitudinal study analyzed temperament at least eight times, in infancy, early childhood, middle childhood, adolescence, and adulthood. The scientists designed laboratory experiments to evoke emotions appropriate for the age of the participants, collected detailed reports from mothers and later from participants themselves, and gathered observational data and physiological evidence, including brain scans (Fox et al., 2001, 2005, 2013; Jarcho et al., 2013; Shechner et al., 2018; Williams et al., 2010).

In early childhood, change was most likely for the inhibited, fearful infants and least likely for the exuberant ones (see **Figure 7.1**). Why was that? Do some parents coax frightened infants to be brave, letting exuberant babies stay happy?

When the fearful children grew up, about half were still fearful. The half who overcame their anxiety had more activation in another part of the brain (the *anterior cingulate cortex*), which signals safety (Shechner et al., 2018). Perhaps if fearful infants were quickly reassured by their caregivers, a neurological link formed between fear and comfort, so that, when anxiety rose later in life, the brain automatically counteracted it.

The researchers found unexpected gender differences. As teenagers, formerly inhibited boys had relatively high rates of drug abuse, but the opposite was found for inhibited girls (Williams et al., 2010). A likely explanation is cultural: Shy boys use drugs

**FIGURE 7.1**

**Do Babies' Temperaments Change?**
Sometimes it is possible—especially if they were fearful babies. Adults who are reassuring help children overcome fearfulness. If fearful children do not change, it is not known whether that's because their parents are not sufficiently reassuring (nurture) or because the babies themselves are temperamentally more fearful (nature).

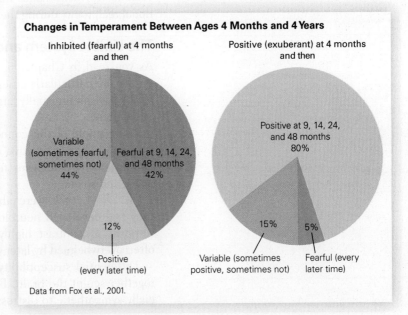

Changes in Temperament Between Ages 4 Months and 4 Years

Data from Fox et al., 2001.

⬤ **Especially for Nurses** Parents come to you with their fussy 3-month-old. They have read that temperament is "fixed" before birth, and they are worried that their child will always be difficult. What do you tell them? (see response, page 201)

to mask their social anxiety, but shy girls may be more accepted as they are. Other research also finds that shyness is more stable in girls than boys (Poole et al., 2017).

## Brain Variations

You read that temperament is "biologically based." That means that brain maturation is crucial for emotional development, particularly for emotions that respond to other people. Experience connects the amygdala and the prefrontal cortex (van Goozen, 2015), teaching infants to align their own feelings with those of their caregivers (Missana et al., 2014). Joy, fear, and excitement become shared, mutual experiences—as anyone who successfully makes a baby laugh knows.

Essentially, connections between innate emotional impulses from the amygdala and experience-based learning shows "dramatic age-dependent improvement," with genes, prenatal influences, and early caregiving all affecting brain growth (Gao et al., 2017). Infant experience leads to adult reactions: If you know someone who cries, laughs, or angers quickly, ask about their first two years of life.

## Hormones and Temperament

All social emotions, particularly sadness and fear, affect the hormones and hence the brain. Caregiving matters. Sad and angry infants whose mothers are depressed usually become fearful toddlers and depressed children (Dix & Yan, 2014).

Abuse and unpredictable responses from caregivers are likely among the "early adverse influences [that] have lasting effects on developing neurobiological systems in the brain" (van Goozen, 2015, p. 208). Even worse is a lack of any social responses: That leads to significant brain shrinkage (Marshall, 2014; Sheridan et al., 2018). In-depth studies of the brain and emotions confirm this.

Remember that oxytocin is high in birthing mothers: It predisposes them to bond with their infants. Now consider the other half of the dyad. Infants vary in their level of oxytocin, in part because of how their parents care for them, and that affects their social responses (Feldman, 2012a).

Over the years of childhood, infants have the highest levels of oxytocin, which strongly correlates with an infant's interest in social stimuli (Nishizato et al., 2017). This suggests that hormones that begin with brain signals affect early extraversion. Oxytocin makes infants watch faces, and then people respond, an emotional reciprocity during the early months.

## The Limbic System and Temperament

As you read in Chapter 5, those regions of the brain that comprise the limbic system are particularly crucial for emotions. Depending on past experience, some adults have an unusually large amygdala and small hippocampus. For this, caregiving matters.

An example of the connection between the brain and caregiving came from a study of "highly reactive" infants (i.e., intensely fearful, angry, active). If they had responsive caregivers (not hostile or neglectful), they became less fearful, less angry, and so on.

By age 4, they were able to regulate their emotions, presumably because they had developed neurological links between brain excitement and emotional response. By contrast, highly reactive toddlers with less responsive caregivers were often overwhelmed by later emotions (Ursache et al., 2013).

Differential susceptibility is apparent: Innate reactions and caregiver actions together sculpt the brain. Both are affected by culture: Some parents are especially sympathetic to distress, while others ignore crying. Caregiver responses are crucial in infancy, even though the emotional manifestations are more apparent later on (Cole & Hollenstein, 2018).

Genes and prenatal influences on the brain are evident. Some fetuses are exposed to toxic drugs; some to inherit genes, making them vulnerable to autism spectrum disorder; some newborns spend many days in the hospital. Especially for them, postnatal experiences are crucial for emotional development (Gao et al., 2017; White-Traut et al., 2018). (See **Figure 7.2**.)

The social smile, for instance, is fleeting when 2-month-olds, especially those who began life in difficult circumstances, see almost any face. As the brain develops and experience builds, those infants smile more at a familiar caregiver than a stranger, and more at responsive, smiling caregivers than at less interactive caregivers.

When neurons repeatedly fire together, the dendrites and synapses become closely connected. Experience, even at 2 months, matters.

**FIGURE 7.2**

**Seven Arrows Pointing Up** This figure is intended to show the ongoing development of the brain. Prenatal, genetic, and experiential influences continue lifelong.

## Mothers of Mice

Many studies of emotions begin with mice, mammals with many genetic similarities to people! In classic research, the brains of infant mice released more serotonin when their mothers licked them. That not only increased the mouselings' pleasure but also started epigenetic responses, reducing cortisol from brain and body, including the adrenal glands. The effects were lifelong; those baby mice became smarter and more social adults, with larger brains.

That research with mice has been replicated and extended to many other mammals, including humans. Neuroscientists are awed by the early "remarkable capacity for plastic changes that influence behavioural outcomes throughout the lifetime" (Kolb et al., 2017, p. 1218).

Too much fear and stress makes the brain grow more slowly. Maltreated infants develop abnormal responses to stress, anger, and other emotions, apparent in the hypothalamus, amygdala, hippocampus, and prefrontal cortex (Bernard et al., 2014; Cicchetti, 2013a).

The immune system is also impaired (Hostinar et al., 2018). Consequently, abused children typically become sickly, slow-thinking adults, with erratic emotions, because of what happened inside their brains decades earlier.

---

**WHAT HAVE YOU LEARNED?**

1. What is the difference between temperament and personality?

2. What are the three dimensions of temperament?

3. How does caregiving affect temperament?

4. What is the relationship between temperament and maltreatment?

---

## The Development of Social Bonds

Now we return to what is universally true. Humans are, by nature, social creatures. The specifics of social interaction during infancy depend on the age of the person.

## Synchrony

Early parent–infant interactions are described as **synchrony**, a mutual exchange with split-second timing. Metaphors for synchrony are often musical—a waltz,

**synchrony** A coordinated, rapid, and smooth exchange of responses between a caregiver and an infant.

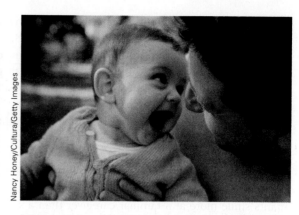

**Open Wide** Synchrony is evident worldwide. Everywhere, babies watch their parents carefully, hoping for exactly what these three parents express, and responding with such delight that adults relish these moments.

 **Observation Quiz** The universality of synchrony is evident here, not only in the babies but also in the parents, each of whom began at birth with a quite different relationship to the baby. Can you guess what those differences are? (see answer, page 201) ↑

a jazz duet—to emphasize that each partner must be attuned to the other, with moment-by-moment responses. Synchrony increases over the first year. Physiological measures, especially hearts that beat in synch, also indicate synchrony (McFarland et al., 2020).

Long before they can control their hands, infants respond excitedly to caregiver attention by waving their arms. Adults with animated expressions move close, letting that waving arm touch a face or, even better, letting a hand grab hair. This synchrony is part of early adaptation and then "making interesting events last," Piaget's stages 2 and 3 of sensorimotor development (described in Chapter 6). Thus, synchrony aids cognition.

Synchronizing adults open their eyes wide, raise their eyebrows, smack their lips, and emit nonsense sounds. Hair-grabbing might make adults bob their heads back and forth, in a playful attempt to shake off the grab, to the infant's joy. Over the early months, an adult and an infant might develop a routine of hair-grabbing in synchrony.

Another adult and infant might develop a different routine, perhaps with hand-clapping, or lip-smacking, or head-turning. Synchrony becomes a mutual dance, with both knowing the steps. Often mothers and infants engage in "social games," which are routines passed down from adult to infant in that culture. Social games soon become synchronized, with the infant anticipating and reacting to each move (Markova, 2018).

## Both Partners Active

Direct observation reveals synchrony; anyone can see it when watching a caregiver play with an infant who is far too young to talk. Adults rarely smile much at newborns until that first social smile, weeks after birth. Smiling is like a switch that lights up the adult and the baby. Soon both partners synchronize smiles, eyes, noises, and movements.

Detailed research, typically with two cameras, one focused on the infant and one on the caregiver, examines the timing of every millisecond of arched eyebrows, widening eyes, pursed lips, and so on. That confirms the tight relationship between adult and infant (Messinger et al., 2010).

Physiological measures, such as heart rate and brain waves, also measure synchrony. That reveals why maternal depression leads to infant depression—the baby picks up on the mother's responses (Atzil et al., 2014).

In every interaction, infants read emotions and develop social skills. Synchrony usually begins with adults imitating infants (not vice versa), responding to barely perceptible facial and bodily motions (Beebe et al., 2016). This helps infants connect their internal state with expressions and behavior.

**CHAPTER APP 7**

📱 **Playground Buddy**

**IOS:**
https://tinyurl.com/waplr56

**ANDROID:**
https://tinyurl.com/r9jykb7

**RELEVANT TOPIC:**
Psychosocial development during infancy

With a worldwide database of over 200,000, this app shows caregivers the location and street views of nearby playgrounds. Users can also send the details to others, even those who do not have the app.

## The Need for Synchrony

Caregiver responsiveness to infant actions aids psychosocial and biological development, evident in heart rate, weight gain, and brain maturation. Experiments involving the **still-face technique** suggest that synchrony is experience-expectant (needed for normal brain growth) (Hari, 2017; Tronick, 1989; Tronick & Weinberg, 1997). [**Developmental Link:** Experience-expectant and experience-dependent brain function are described in Chapter 5.]

In still-face studies, at first an infant is propped in front of an adult who responds normally. Then, on cue, the adult stops all expression, staring quietly with a "still face" for a minute or two. Sometimes by 2 months, and clearly by 6 months, infants are upset when their caregiver is unresponsive. Babies frown, fuss, drool, look away, kick, cry, or suck their fingers. By 5 months, they also vocalize, as if to say, "React to me!"

One study looked in detail at 4-month-olds during and immediately after a still-face episode (Montirosso et al., 2015). The researchers found three clusters: "socially engaged" (33 percent), "disengaged" (60 percent), and "negatively engaged" (7 percent).

When the mothers were still-faced:

- The socially engaged babies remained active, looking around at other things, apparently expecting that the caregivers would soon resume connection. When the still face was over, they quickly reengaged.
- The disengaged infants became passive, looking sad. When the still face was over, they did not quickly return to normal, although they eventually did.
- The negatively engaged infants were visibly upset and angry, crying during the still face and continuing to cry when it was over.

The mothers of each type differed in how they played with their infants before and after the still face. The socially engaged mothers matched the infants' actions (bobbing heads, opening mouth, and so on), but the negatively engaged mothers almost never matched and sometimes expressed anger—not sympathy—when the baby cried (Montirosso et al., 2015). That absent synchrony is a troubling sign for future emotional and brain development.

## Attachment

**Attachment**—the connection between one person and another, measured by how they respond to each other—is a lifelong process, beginning before birth and continuing even when an aged parent has Alzheimer's disease (Arguz Cildir et al., 2019; Lang & Fowers, 2019). Developmentalists are convinced that attachment is basic to the survival of *Homo sapiens*, with the manifestation dependent on culture and the age of the person.

Attachment continues to be studied in many nations, ages, cultures, genders, with caregivers who are not parents, children at many points in time, typical children, those with special needs, families, romances, friendships, and more (e.g., Cassidy & Shaver, 2016; Pinto & Figueiredo, 2019; Voges et al., 2019).

Thus, attachment is a universal; expression is particular. An analogy is language development, as reviewed in Chapter 6. Every human is predisposed to develop attachment, just as every infant is predisposed to develop language. However, the particular manifestations of that need, for example, which of the 6,000 languages a person speaks, or how attachment is manifest, depends on particular childhood experiences. Then that attachment style influences later life, even across generations, just as children learn a particular language and then have difficulty mastering another.

For instance, Ugandan mothers never kiss their infants, but they often massage them, unlike most Westerners. Some U.S. adults phone their mothers every

**still-face technique** An experimental practice in which an adult keeps their face unmoving and expressionless in face-to-face interaction with an infant.

> **THINK CRITICALLY:** What will happen if no one plays with an infant?

**attachment** According to Ainsworth, "an affectional tie" that an infant forms with a caregiver—a tie that binds them together in space and endures over time.

**VIDEO ACTIVITY: Mother Love and the Work of Harry Harlow** features classic footage of Harlow's research on attachment, showing the setup and results of his famous experiment.

**Same or Different?** A theme of this chapter is that babies and mothers are the same worldwide, yet dramatically different in each culture. Do you see more similarities or differences between the Huastec mother in Mexico *(left)*, the mothers waiting in a clinic in Uganda *(middle)*, and supermodel Gisele Bündchen in Boston, Massachusetts *(right)*? (Her husband is Tom Brady, star quarterback of the New England Patriots.)

day—even when the mothers are a thousand miles away—and others connect with their mothers only on holidays. Some attached family members all sit in the same room of a large house, each reading quietly. All of these signify attachment.

The concept began with research in the 1950s and 1960s by John Bowlby in England and Mary Ainsworth in Uganda and the United States on mother–infant relationships when the infants were about age 1. That is our focus in this chapter. Once infants can walk, the moment-by-moment, face-to-face synchrony is less common. Instead, attachment comes to the fore.

Two signs indicate attachment: *contact-maintaining* and *proximity-seeking.* Both take many forms in infancy. Caregivers often keep a watchful eye on their baby, initiating contact with expressions, gestures, and sounds. Before going to sleep at midnight they might tiptoe to the crib to gaze at their sleeping infant, or, in daytime, absentmindedly smooth their toddler's hair.

For their part, 1-year-olds look to their caregivers, ask to be picked up, fall asleep with their legs or arms touching them. When awake and stressed, their attachment is literal: They grab a hand, a leg, a pant leg, achieving contact and proximity.

## Secure and Insecure Attachment

**secure attachment** A relationship in which an infant obtains both comfort and confidence from the presence of his or her caregiver.

Attachment is classified into four types: A, B, C, and D. Infants with **secure attachment** (type B) feel comfortable and confident. The caregiver is a *base for exploration,* providing assurance and enabling discovery.

A securely attached toddler might, for example, scramble down from the caregiver's lap to play with an intriguing toy but periodically look back and vocalize (contact-maintaining), or bring the toy to the caregiver for inspection (proximity-seeking).

The caregiver's presence gives the child courage to explore; departure causes distress; return elicits positive contact (such as smiling or hugging) and then more playing. This balanced reaction—the child concerned but not overwhelmed by comings and goings—indicates security.

**insecure-avoidant attachment** A pattern of attachment in which an infant avoids connection with the caregiver, as when the infant seems not to care about the caregiver's presence, departure, or return.

By contrast, insecure attachment (types A and C) is characterized by fear, anxiety, anger, or indifference. Some insecure children play independently without seeking contact; this is **insecure-avoidant attachment** (type A). The opposite reaction is **insecure-resistant/ambivalent attachment** (type C). Children with type C cling to their caregivers and are angry at being left.

**insecure-resistant/ambivalent attachment** A pattern of attachment in which an infant's anxiety and uncertainty are evident, as when the infant becomes very upset at separation from the caregiver and both resists and seeks contact on reunion.

Infants may be securely or insecurely attached to mothers, fathers, or other caregivers—sometimes just to one person, sometimes to several. Is secure attachment innate? Are difficult children always insecurely attached? No. Every baby seeks attachment: Temperament may affect the expression, but not the need (Groh et al., 2017).

Ainsworth's original schema differentiated only types A, B, and C. Later researchers discovered a fourth category (type D), **disorganized attachment**. Type D infants may suddenly switch from hitting to kissing their mothers, from staring blankly to crying hysterically, from pinching themselves to freezing in place.

Among the general population, almost two-thirds of infants are secure (type B). About one-third are insecure, either indifferent (type A) or unduly anxious (type C), and about 5 to 10 percent are disorganized (type D).

Type D infants are especially worrisome to developmentalists, because they have no consistent strategy for social interaction, even avoidance or resistance. Without intervention to improve early attachment, type D toddlers are at risk for later psychopathology, including severe aggression and major depression (Cicchetti, 2016; Groh et al., 2012). Of course, much more information about family life is needed before type D attachment is considered evidence that a particular child needs to be in foster care (White et al., 2019).

Recently some people have begun advocating *attachment parenting*, which prioritizes the mother–infant relationship during the first three years of life far more than Ainsworth or Bowlby did (Komisar, 2017; Sears & Sears, 2001). Attachment parenting mandates that mothers should always be near their infants (co-sleeping, "wearing" the baby in a wrap or sling, breast-feeding on demand). Some experts suggest that attachment parenting is too distant from the research concept and evidence (Ennis, 2015).

Although attachment parenting may be an exaggeration, the consensus of many researchers is not only that attachment is important for infant development but also that mothers can learn some of the behaviors that increase the bond between mother and child. That is one reason that the federal government has supported more than a thousand programs of home visiting. The emphasis is on early education fostered by the mother, but guidance to increase secure attachment is sometimes included (Berlin et al., 2018).

**disorganized attachment** A type of attachment that is marked by an infant's inconsistent reactions to the caregiver's departure and return.

A VIEW FROM SCIENCE

## Measuring Attachment

Scientists take great care to measure what they purport to measure. This is especially important when they want to measure emotions. They develop an *operational definition*, which is a measurement of an observable behavior that indicates the construct so that other scientists know what is measured and can replicate the study.

For instance, if you wanted to study love between romantic partners, what would your empirical measurement be?

- Ask each partner how much they loved each other, rated on a scale of 1 to 10?
- Ask other questions, such as whether they had, in the past year, thought of breaking up the relationship or sacrificed something for their partner?
- Video their interaction, and count how often they made eye contact, or expressed agreement, or how many inches apart they sat?

- Check details of cohabitation, marriage, physical affection, shared finances?

None of these is exactly what people call "love," and some of these are better than others as operational definitions, but all might be useful, and all could be measured.

Measuring the connection between caregiver and infant is similarly complicated. Fortunately, Mary Ainsworth (1973) developed a now-classic laboratory procedure called the *Strange Situation* to measure attachment, a measurement protocol that has been used in thousands of studies. The Strange Situation measures details on 1-year-olds' reactions to stress, with and without the mother.

The specifics of that measurement are as follows: In a well-equipped playroom, an infant is observed for eight episodes, each lasting no more than three minutes. First, the child and mother are together. Next, according to a set sequence, the mother and then a stranger come and go. Infants' responses to their mother indicate which type of attachment they have formed.

Researchers focus on the following:

*Exploration of the toys.* A secure toddler plays happily.
*Reaction to the caregiver's departure.* A secure toddler notices when the caregiver leaves and shows some sign of missing him or her. A pause in playing, a plaintive sound, a worried expression are all significant signs of attachment.
*Reaction to the caregiver's return.* A secure toddler welcomes the caregiver's reappearance, seeking contact, and then plays again. Typically toddlers run to their mothers for a hug, and then resume investigation of the toys.

Scientists are carefully trained in measuring attachment in 1-year-olds, via watching videos, calibrating ratings, and studying manuals. Researchers are certified only when they reach a high standard of accuracy. They learn which common behaviors signify insecurity, contrary to what untrained observers might think. For instance, clinging to the caregiver may be type C; being too friendly to the stranger suggests type A.

Many scientists who study attachment in older children and adults have developed other measures—again empirical. For instance, detailed questionnaires and interviews, calibrated to signify secure or insecure attachment, with a particular measure based on Ainsworth indicators (the *Adult Attachment Interview*, or *AAI*), are often used.

A sign of a past insecure childhood attachment is not only rejection of one's mother ("I never want to see her again"), but also sanctification of her ("she was a saint"). It is especially troubling if an adult is confused and incoherent, with few details about their awful, or perfect, childhood. This has been found in adults of every gender and cultural background, confirming that attachment is needed at every age (Haltigan et al., 2019).

The measurement of attachment via the Strange Situation has made longitudinal studies possible, assessing the later development of infants who are types A, B, C, or D. We now know that infant–caregiver attachment affects brain development and the immune system (Bernard et al., 2019), and that particular circumstances, such as domestic violence among the parents, can weaken the links between childhood attachment and adult relationships (Fearon & Roisman, 2017).

Thanks to procedures developed by Mary Ainsworth half a century ago, the importance of early caregiver–infant relationships is now recognized. Securely attached infants *are* more likely to become secure toddlers, socially competent preschoolers, high-achieving schoolchildren, partners in loving couples, capable parents, and healthy adults.

> **THINK CRITICALLY:** Is the Strange Situation a valid way to measure attachment in every culture, or is it biased toward the Western idea of the ideal mother–child relationship?

© 2016 Macmillan

**Excited, Troubled, Comforted** This sequence is repeated daily for 1-year-olds, which is why the same sequence is replicated to measure attachment. As you see, toys are no substitute for mother's comfort if the infant or toddler is secure, as this one seems to be. Some, however, cry inconsolably or throw toys angrily when left alone.

## Orphanages in Romania

No scholar doubts that attachments should develop in the first year of life and that the lack of close caregiver–infant relationships predicts lifelong problems. Unfortunately, thousands of children born in Romania verify that conclusion.

When Romanian dictator Nicolae Ceauşescu forbade birth control and abortions in the 1980s, illegal abortions became the leading cause of death for Romanian women aged 15 to 45 (Verona, 2003), and 170,000 children were abandoned and sent to crowded, impersonal, state-run orphanages (Marshall, 2014). The children were severely deprived of social contact, experiencing virtually no synchrony, attachment, or conversation.

In the two years after Ceauşescu was ousted and killed in 1989, thousands of those children were adopted by North American, western European, and Australian families. Infants under 6 months of age fared best; the adoptive parents established synchrony and attachment. Many infants adopted between 6 months and 1 year also fared well.

For those adopted after age 1, early signs were encouraging: Skinny toddlers gained weight, started walking, and grew quickly, developing motor skills they had lacked (H. Park et al., 2011). However, if social deprivation had lasted more than a year, emotions and cognition suffered.

Many of the late adoptees were overly friendly to strangers, a sign of insecure attachment. By age 11, their average IQ was only 85, which is 15 points lower than the statistical norm. The older they had been at adoption, the worse they fared (Nelson et al., 2014). Some became impulsive, angry teenagers. Apparently, the stresses of adolescence and emerging adulthood exacerbated their cognitive and social deficits (Merz & McCall, 2011). (See **Table 7.1**.)

These children are now adults, many with serious emotional or conduct problems (Sonuga-Barke et al., 2017). Some overly friendly 4-year-olds, as adolescents, suffer from *disinhibited social engagement disorder* (Guyon-Harris et al., 2018). That makes them vulnerable throughout adulthood: They follow people who will harm them.

None of this is inevitable. Other research on children adopted nationally and internationally finds that many develop well. However, every stress—such as parental maltreatment, institutional life, cultural loss, and the adoption process—makes it more difficult for children to become happy, well-functioning adolescents and adults (Barroso et al., 2017; Grotevant & McDermott, 2014).

All images copyrighted Thomas B. Szalay

**Hands on Head** These children in Romania, here older than age 2, probably spent most of their infancy in their cribs, never with the varied stimulation that infant brains need. The sad results are evident here—that boy is fingering his own face, because the feel of his own touch is most likely one of the few sensations he knows. The girl sitting up in the back is a teenager. This photo was taken in 1982; Romania no longer destroys children so dramatically.

---

### TABLE 7.1

#### Predictors of Attachment Type

***Secure* attachment (type B) is more likely if:**

- The parent is usually sensitive and responsive to the infant's needs.
- The infant–parent relationship is high in synchrony.
- The infant's temperament is "easy."
- The parents are not stressed about income, other children, or their marriage.
- The parents have a working model of secure attachment to their own parents.

***Insecure* attachment is more likely if:**

- The parent mistreats the child. (Neglect increases type A; abuse increases types C and D.)
- The mother is mentally ill. (Paranoia increases type D; depression increases type C.)
- The parents are highly stressed about income, other children, or their marriage. (Parental stress increases types A and D.)
- The parents are intrusive and controlling. (Parental domination increases type A.)
- The parents have alcohol use disorder. (Father with alcoholism increases type A; mother with alcoholism increases type D.)
- The child's temperament is "difficult." (Difficult children tend to be type C.)
- The child's temperament is "slow-to-warm-up." (This correlates with type A.)

Romania no longer permits international adoption, even though some infants are still institutionalized. Research confirms that early emotional deprivation, not genes or nutrition, is their greatest problem. Infants develop best in their own families, second best in foster families, and worst in institutions (Nelson et al., 2014).

This is true for infants everywhere: Families usually nurture their babies better than strangers who provide good physical care but not emotional attachment. The longer children live in hospitals and orphanages, the more social and intellectual harm occurs (Julian, 2013).

Many institutions have improved or closed, and many adoptive families are securely attached, as A Case to Study illustrates.

**A CASE TO STUDY**

## Can We Bear This Commitment?

Parents and children capture my attention, wherever they are. Recently I spotted one mother ignoring her stroller-bound toddler on a crowded subway (I resisted my impulse to tell her to talk to her child), another mother breast-feeding a 7-month-old in a public park (I smiled approvingly, because that was illegal three decades ago).

A third mother loudly and unfairly berated her 8-year-old (I intervened, only to be criticized by another witness, an older man who said if the mother were hitting her child, he would be the first to intervene, but words were not harmful). The mother glared at me and told her son to come with her, far away from me. He followed her. Should I have ignored the verbal abuse?

I cannot help noticing signs of secure or insecure attachment—the contact-maintaining and proximity-seeking moves that parents do, seemingly unaware that they are responding to primordial depths of human love. I particularly observe families I know. I am struck by the powerful bond between parent and child, as strong (or stronger) in adoptive families as in genetic ones.

One adoptive couple is Macky and Nick. Two examples:

- When Alice was a few days old, I overheard Nick phone another parent, asking which detergent is best for washing baby clothes. That reminded me that I also switched detergents for my newborn.
- Years later, when Macky was engrossed in conversation, Nick interrupted to say they needed to stop talking because the girls needed to get home for their naps. Parents at social occasions everywhere do that, with one parent telling the other it's time to leave.

My appreciation of their attachment was cemented by a third incident. In Macky's words:

I'll never forget the Fourth of July at the spacious home of my mother-in-law's best friend. It was a perfect celebration on a perfect day. Kids frolicked in the pool. Parents socialized nearby, on the sun-drenched lawn or inside the cool house. Many guests had published books on parenting; we imagined they admired our happy, thriving family.

My husband and I have two daughters, Alice who was then 7 and Penelope who was 4. They learned to swim early and are always the first to jump in the pool and the last to leave. Great children, and doesn't that mean great parents?

After hours of swimming, the four of us scrambled up to dry land. I went inside to the library to talk with my father, while most people enjoyed hot dogs, relish, mustard, and juicy watermelon.

Suddenly we heard a heart-chilling wail. Panicked, I raced to the pool's edge to see the motionless body of a small child who had gone unnoticed underwater for too long. His blue-face was still. Someone was giving CPR. His mother kept wailing, panicked, pleading, destroyed. I had a shameful thought—thank God that is not my child.

He lived. He regained his breath and was whisked away by ambulance. The party came to a quick close. We four, skin tingling from the summer sun, hearts beating from the near-death of a child who was my kids' playmate an hour before, drove away.

Turning to Nick, I asked, "Can we bear this commitment we have made? Can we raise our children in the face of all hazards—some we try to prevent, others beyond our control?"

That was five years ago. Our children are flourishing. Our confidence is strong and so are our emotions. But it takes only a moment to recognize just how entwined our well-being is with our children and how fragile life is. We are deeply grateful.

*Victor J. Blue/The New York Times/Redux*

**A Grateful Family** This family photo shows (from *left* to *right*) Nick, Penelope, Macky, and Alice with their dog Cooper. When they adopted Alice as a newborn, the parents said, "This is a miracle we feared would never happen."

## Politics and Children Without Parents

Many nations now restrict international adoptions, in part because some children were literally snatched from their biological parents to be sent abroad. Romania halted international adoptions in 2004, although many adoptable Romanian children are still in institutions (Popescu et al., 2019).

According to government records, the number of international adoptees in the United States was 4,058 in 2018, down from 22,884 in 2004 (see **Figure 7.3**). The decrease may be influenced more by international politics than by infant needs, with Russia particularly refusing to allow any more U.S. adoptions. Ideally, every baby would be wanted, every parent would be supported, and no infant would be institutionalized. But if that ideal is not reached, scientists advocate family care over institutional care, because attachment to a dedicated caregiver is crucial for well-being (McCall, 2013).

Developmentalists of every political stripe are horrified that thousands of children of immigrants are separated from their parents at the border between Mexico and the United States (Roth et al., 2018). Attachment research confirms that children need dedicated caregivers, and that disrupting that relationship causes lifelong harm. Here again, politics, rather than what we know about attachment, interferes with good care.

**International Adoptions by U.S. Citizens, All Nations**

Data from U.S. Department of State, 2019.

**FIGURE 7.3**

**Declining Need?** No. More couples seek to adopt internationally, and millions of children in dozens of nations have no families. This chart does not reflect changing needs of families; it reflects increasing nationalism within and beyond the United States. Sadly, babies have become weapons in national politics.

## Social Referencing

The third social connection that developmentalists look for during infancy, after synchrony and attachment, is **social referencing**. Much as a student might consult a dictionary or other reference work, social referencing means seeking emotional responses or information from other people. A reassuring glance, a string of cautionary words, a facial expression of alarm, pleasure, or dismay—those are social references.

As you read in Chapter 6, gaze-following begins in the first months of life, as part of cognition. After age 1, when infants can walk and are "little scientists," their need to consult others becomes urgent and more accurate—for emotional input, not merely cognition.

Toddlers search for clues in gazes, faces, and body position, paying close attention to emotions and intentions. They focus on their familiar caregivers, but they also use relatives, other children, and even strangers to help them assess objects and events.

From early infancy to late adolescence, children are remarkably selective, noticing that some strangers are reliable references and others are not. For instance, infants as young 14 months old were less likely to accept social referencing from a stranger whose emotions did not fit experiences (e.g., infants distrusted adults who smiled happily at opening an empty box) (Crivello & Poulin-Dubois, 2019). The infant's own emotions and desires spring from social referencing (Wellman, 2014).

Social referencing has many practical applications. Consider mealtime. Caregivers the world over pretend to taste and say "yum-yum," encouraging toddlers to eat beets, liver, or spinach. Toddlers read expressions, insisting on the foods that the adults *really* like.

If a mother enjoys eating it, and then presents some to the toddler, then they eat it—otherwise not. Some tastes (spicy, bitter, sour) are rejected by very young infants, but if they see their caregivers eat it, they learn to like it (Forestel & Mennella, 2017).

**social referencing** Seeking information about how to react to an unfamiliar or ambiguous object or event by observing someone else's expressions and reactions. That other person becomes a social reference.

**Rotini Pasta?** Look again. Every family teaches their children to relish delicacies that other people avoid. Examples are bacon (not in Arab nations), hamburgers (not in India), and, as shown here, a witchetty grub. This Australian aboriginal boy is about to swallow an insect larva.

Bill Bachman/Alamy Stock Photo

# Developing Attachment

Attachment begins at birth and continues lifelong. Much depends not only on the ways in which parents and babies bond, but also on the quality and consistency of caregiving, the safety and security of the home environment, and individual and family experience. While the patterns set in infancy may echo in later life, they are not determinative.

## How Many Children are Securely Attached?

The specific percentages of children who are secure and insecure vary by culture, parent responsiveness, context, and specific temperament and needs of both the child and the caregiver. Generally, about a third of all 1-year-olds seem insecure.

| 50–70% | 10–20% | 10–20% | 5–10% |
|---|---|---|---|
| Secure Attachment (Type B) | Avoidant Attachment (Type A) | Ambivalent Attachment (Type C) | Disorganized Attachment (Type D) |

## Attachment in the Strange Situation May Influence Relationships Through the Life Span

Attachment patterns formed in infancy affect adults lifelong, but later experiences of love and rejection may change early patterns. Researchers measure attachment by examining children's behaviors in the Strange Situation where they are separated from their parent and play in a room with an unfamiliar caregiver. These early patterns can influence later adult relationships. As life goes on, people become more or less secure, avoidant, or disorganized.

**Securely Attached [Type B]**
In the Strange Situation, children are able to separate from caregiver but prefer caregiver to strangers.

Later in life, they tend to have supportive relationships and positive self-concept.

**Insecure-Avoidant [Type A]**
In the Strange Situation, children avoid caregiver.

Later in life, they tend to be aloof in personal relationships, loners who are lonely.

**Insecure-Resistant/Ambivalent [Type C]**
In the Strange Situation, children appear upset and worried when separated from caregiver; they may hit or cling.

Later in life, their relationships may be angry, stormy, unpredictable. They have few long-term friendships.

**Disorganized [Type D]**
In the Strange Situation, children appear angry, confused, erratic, or fearful.

Later in life, they can demonstrate odd behavior—including sudden emotions. They are at risk for serious psychological disorders.

## The Continuum of Attachment

Avoidance and anxiety occur along a continuum. Neither genes nor cultural variations were understood when the Strange Situation was first developed (in 1965). Some contemporary researchers believe the link between childhood attachment and adult personality is less straightforward than this table suggests.

Low Avoidance

Secure · Resistant

Low Anxiety · High Anxiety

Avoidant · Disorganized

High Avoidance

Through this process, some children develop a taste for raw fish or curried goat or smelly cheese—foods that children in other cultures refuse. Similarly, toddlers use social cues to understand the difference between real and pretend eating, as well as to learn which objects, emotions, and activities are forbidden.

## Fathers as Social Partners

Synchrony, attachment, and social referencing are evident with fathers as well as with mothers. Indeed, fathers tend to elicit more smiles and laughter from their infants than mothers do. They tend to play more exciting games, swinging and chasing, while mothers do more caregiving and comforting.

This gender difference should not be exaggerated: Both parents do some soothing and some exciting play. Nonetheless, fathers tend to do much more rough-and-tumble play than mothers do, and infants benefit from that (Cabrera et al., 2018). It is also true that children develop well when the roles are reversed, or when both parents are male or both parents are female. Each couple coordinates; children thrive (Shwalb et al., 2013).

Gender differences in child rearing vary more by nation, by income, by cohort, and by ideology than by natal sex or by ethnic background (Roopnarine & Yildirim, 2019). Variation is dramatic, from fathers who had nothing to do with infants to fathers who are intensely involved. The latter is common in the United States in the twenty-first century, unlike in former times (Abraham & Feldman, 2018).

Contemporary fathers worldwide tend to be more involved with their children than their own fathers were (Sriram, 2019). The effects are evident not only in infants but in fathers themselves. As one man in India said, "my child transformed me" (Kaur, 2019).

For both sexes, stress decreases parent involvement. That brings up another difference between mothers and fathers. When money is scarce and stress is high, some fathers opt out. That choice is less possible for mothers (Qin & Chang, 2013; Roopnarine & Hossain, 2013).

The reactions of both men and women to infants is also affected by their temperament, genes, and early-childhood experiences (Senese et al., 2019). This is another reason why babies of every sex need responsive caregiving: The effects will endure decades later when they have children of their own.

---

### WHAT HAVE YOU LEARNED?

1. Why does synchrony affect early emotional development?
2. How are proximity-seeking and contact-maintaining attachment expressed by infants and caregivers?
3. How does infant behavior differ in each of the four types of attachment?
4. How might each of the four types of attachment be expressed in adulthood?
5. What has been learned from the research on Romanian orphans?
6. How is social referencing important in toddlerhood?

---

## Theories of Infant Psychosocial Development

That infants are emotional and social creatures is one of those universal truths, recognized by everyone who studies babies. However, each of the theories discussed in Chapter 2 has a distinct perspective on this universal reality, as you will now see.

## Psychoanalytic Theory

Psychoanalytic theory connects biosocial and psychosocial development. Sigmund Freud and Erik Erikson each described two distinct stages of early development, one in the first year and one beginning in the second year.

### Freud: Oral and Anal Stages

**Especially for Nursing Mothers** You have heard that if you wean your child too early, he or she will overeat or develop alcohol use disorder. Is it true? (see response, page 201)

According to Freud (1935/1989, 2001), the first year of life is the *oral stage*, so named because the mouth is the young infant's primary source of gratification. In the second year, with the *anal stage*, pleasure comes from the anus—particularly from the sensual satisfaction of bowel movements and, eventually, the psychological pleasure of controlling them.

Freud believed that the oral and anal stages are fraught with potential conflicts. If a mother frustrates her infant's urge to suck—weaning too early or too late, for example, or preventing the baby from sucking a thumb or a pacifier—that may later lead to an *oral fixation*. Adults with an oral fixation are stuck (fixated) at the oral stage, and therefore they eat, drink, chew, bite, or talk excessively, still seeking the mouth-related pleasures of infancy.

Similarly, if toilet training is overly strict or if it begins before maturation allows sufficient control, that causes a clash between the toddler's refusal—or inability—to comply and the wishes of the adult, who denies the infant normal anal pleasures. That may lead to an *anal personality*—an adult who seeks self-control, with a strong need for regularity and cleanliness in all aspects of life.

### Erikson: Trust and Autonomy

**trust versus mistrust** Erikson's first crisis of psychosocial development. Infants learn basic trust if the world is a secure place where their basic needs (for food, comfort, attention, and so on) are met.

According to Erikson, the first crisis of life is **trust versus mistrust**, when infants learn whether or not the world can be trusted to satisfy basic needs. Babies feel secure when food and comfort are provided with "consistency, continuity, and sameness of experience" (Erikson, 1993a, p. 247). If social interaction inspires trust, the child (later the adult) confidently explores the social world.

**autonomy versus shame and doubt** Erikson's second crisis of psychosocial development. Toddlers either succeed or fail in gaining a sense of self-rule over their actions and their bodies.

The second crisis is **autonomy versus shame and doubt**, beginning at about 18 months, when self-awareness emerges. Toddlers want autonomy (self-rule) over their own actions and bodies. Without it, they feel ashamed and doubtful. Like Freud, Erikson believed that problems in early infancy could last a lifetime, creating adults who are suspicious and pessimistic (mistrusting) or easily shamed (lacking autonomy).

## Behaviorism

From the perspective of behaviorism, emotions and personality are molded as adults reinforce or punish children. Behaviorists believe that parents who respond joyously to every glimmer of a grin will have children with a sunny disposition. The opposite is also true:

> Failure to bring up a happy child, a well-adjusted child—assuming bodily health—falls squarely upon the parents' shoulders. [By the time the child is 3] parents have already determined . . . [whether the child] is to grow into a happy person, wholesome and good-natured, whether he is to be a whining, complaining neurotic, an anger-driven, vindictive, over-bearing slave driver, or one whose every move in life is definitely controlled by fear.
>
> [*Watson, 1928/1972, pp. 7, 45*]

Empathy, for instance, is an emotion that appears in direct proportion to the parents' responses (Grady & Hastings, 2018; Heyes, 2018). Shy boys, in particular,

**All Together Now** Toddlers in an employees' day-care program at a flower farm in Colombia learn to use the potty on a schedule. Will this experience lead to later personality problems? Probably not.

JOSE MIGUEL GOMEZ/REUTERS/Newscom

become more outgoing if their fathers' talk with them about emotions (Grady & Hastings, 2018).

## Social Learning

Behaviorists also recognize that infants' behavior reflects social learning, when infants learn from observing other people. You already saw an example, social referencing. Social learning occurs throughout life, not necessarily via direct teaching but often through observation (Shneidman & Woodward, 2016). Toddlers express emotions in various ways—from giggling to cursing—just as their parents or older siblings do.

For example, a boy might develop a hot temper if his father's outbursts seem to win his mother's respect; a girl might be coy, or passive-aggressive, if that is what she has seen at home. These examples are deliberately sexist: Gender roles, in particular, are learned, according to social learning theory.

## Keeping Baby Close

Parents often unwittingly encourage certain traits in their children. Should an infant explore, or learn that danger lurks if they wander off? Should babies have many toys, or will that make them greedy? When babies cry, should their mothers pick them up, feed them, give a pacifier, ignore them? Should an infant breastfeed until age 2, switch to a bottle, or sip from a cup?

These questions highlight the distinction between **proximal parenting** (being physically close to a baby, often holding and touching) and **distal parenting** (keeping some distance—providing toys, encouraging self-feeding, talking face-to-face instead of communicating by touch). Caregivers tend to behave in proximal or distal ways very early, when infants are only 2 months old (Kärtner et al., 2010). Each pattern reinforces some behavior.

For instance, toddlers who, as infants, were often held, patted, and soothed (proximal) became toddlers who were more obedient but less likely to recognize themselves in a mirror. This finding has been replicated in Greece, Cameroon, Italy, Israel, Zambia, Scotland, and Turkey: Distal child rearing correlates with cultures that value individual independence; proximal care correlates with cultures that value collective action and family interdependence (Borke et al., 2007; Carra et al., 2013; Kärtner et al., 2011; Keller et al., 2010; Ross et al., 2017; Scharf, 2014).

Indeed, international variations of parenting practices, including not only proximal and distal parenting but also frequency of synchrony, secure attachment, and social referencing, suggest that children are taught to respond in a particular way because of how their parents treat them (Foo, 2019). That is what behaviorists believe.

## Cognitive Theory

Cognitive theory holds that thoughts determine a person's perspective. Early experiences are important because beliefs, perceptions, and memories make them so, not because they are buried in the unconscious (psychoanalytic theory) or burned into the brain's patterns (behaviorism).

From this perspective, cognitive processes, including language and information, affect attachment, as children and caregivers develop a mutual understanding. Together they build (co-construct) a **working model**, which is a set of assumptions that becomes a frame of reference for later life (Posada & Waters, 2018). It is a "model" because early relationships form a prototype, or blueprint; it is "working" because it is a work in progress, not fixed or final; it is cognitive because the child's understanding and interpretation is crucial.

---

**proximal parenting** Caregiving practices that involve being physically close to the baby, with frequent holding and touching.

**distal parenting** Caregiving practices that involve remaining distant from the baby, providing toys, food, and face-to-face communication with minimal holding and touching.

**Especially for Pediatricians** A mother complains that her toddler refuses to stay in the car seat, spits out disliked foods, and almost never does what she says. How should you respond? (see response, page 201)

**working model** In cognitive theory, a set of assumptions that the individual uses to organize perceptions and experiences. For example, a person might assume that other people are trustworthy and be surprised by an incident in which this working model of human behavior is erroneous.

*"Which one generates the most synapses?"*

**Brainy Baby** Fortunately, infant brains are designed to respond to stimulation of many kinds. As long as the baby has moving objects to see (an animated caregiver is better than any mobile), the synapses proliferate.

Ideally, infants develop "a working model of the self as lovable and competent" because the parents are "emotionally available, loving, and supportive of their mastery efforts" (Harter, 2012, p. 12). However, reality does not always conform to this ideal.

A 1-year-old girl might develop a model, based on her parents' erratic actions, that people are unpredictable. She will continue to apply that model to everyone: Her childhood friendships will be insecure, and her adult relationships will be guarded.

The crucial idea, according to cognitive theory, is that an infant's early experiences themselves are less influential than the interpretation of those experiences is (Olson & Dweck, 2009). Children may misinterpret their experiences, or parents may offer inaccurate explanations, and these form ideas that affect later thinking and behavior.

In this way, working models formed in childhood echo lifelong. A hopeful message from cognitive theory is that people can rethink and reorganize their thoughts, developing new models. That mistrustful girl in the example above might marry someone who is faithful and loving, so she may gradually develop a new working model.

## Evolutionary Theory

Remember that evolutionary theory stresses two needs: survival and reproduction. Human brains are extraordinarily plastic, in order to survive in a vast range of local conditions. This adjustment requires extensive experience: A human child must be nourished, protected, and taught for two decades, which is much longer than the offspring of any other species. Since survival depends on this lengthy protection, it is part of our DNA (Hrdy, 2009).

### Emotions for Survival

Infant emotions are part of this evolutionary mandate. All of the reactions described in the first part of this chapter—from the hunger cry to the temper tantrum—can be seen from this perspective (Konner, 2010).

For example, newborns are extraordinarily dependent, unable to walk or talk or even sit up and feed themselves for months after birth. They must attract adult devotion—and they do. That first smile, the sound of infant laughter, and their role in synchrony are all powerfully attractive to adults—especially to parents.

Adults call their hairless, chinless, round-faced, big-stomached, small-limbed offspring "cute," "handsome," "beautiful," "adorable," yet each of these characteristics is often considered ugly in adults. Parents willingly devote hours to carrying, feeding, changing, and cleaning their infants, who never express gratitude. The love of a parent for a child is part of evolution: For hundreds of thousands of years, humans have needed that love to survive.

Why do people have children, especially now when contraception allows sex without procreation? If humans were motivated solely by money or power, no one would do so. Yet evolution has created adults who find parenting worth every sacrifice.

The same scientific advancements that make it possible to have sex without pregnancy have also compelled many infertile adults to endure pain, embarrassment, and expense to have a baby. Because of that innate desire for progeny, parents are devoted to their children, and that devoted care allows children to develop well (Narvaez et al., 2013).

Evolutionary theory holds that both caregiver and children have powerful emotions—love, jealousy, even clinginess and anger—that keep toddlers near caregivers who remain vigilant. Infants fuss at still faces, fear separation, and laugh when adults play with them—all to sustain caregiving. Emotions are our genetic legacy; we would die without them.

## Allocare

**allocare** Literally, "other-care"; the care of children by people other than the biological parents.

Evolutionary social scientists note that if mothers were the exclusive caregivers of each child until children were adults, a given woman could rear only one or two offspring—not enough for the species to survive. Instead, before the introduction of reliable birth control, the average interval between births for humans was two to four years.

Humans birth children at relatively short intervals because of **allocare**—the care of children by *alloparents*, caregivers who are not the mother. Allocare is essential for *Homo sapiens'* survival. Compared with many other species (mother chimpanzees space births by four or five years and never let another chimp hold their babies), human mothers have evolved to let other people help with child care.

This is not only because mothers need help from, and thus prevail on, fathers and grandmothers, but also because evolution has programmed the human brain so that fathers and grandmothers want to help (Abraham & Feldman, 2018). This explains why that mother on the subway was willing to hand me her baby, and why I was happy that she did.

Allocare is universal for our species—but each community has distinct values and preferences for who should care for children and when (Konner, 2018). Indeed, cultures and theories differ in every aspect of infant care, as you have read regarding breast-feeding, co-sleeping, language, and much else. Now we consider mother care versus other care.

**Same Situation, Far Apart: Safekeeping** Historically, grandmothers were sometimes crucial for child survival. Now, even though medical care has reduced child mortality, grandmothers still do their part to keep children safe, as shown by these two—in the eastern United States *(top)* and Vietnam *(bottom)*.

### WHAT HAVE YOU LEARNED?

1. According to Freud, what might happen if a baby's oral needs are not met?

2. How might Erikson's crisis of "trust versus mistrust" affect later life?

3. How do behaviorists explain the development of emotions and personality?

4. What does the term *working model* mean within cognitive theory?

5. What is the difference between proximal parenting and distal parenting?

6. How does evolution explain the parent–child bond?

7. Why is allocare necessary for survival of the human species?

## Who Should Care for Babies?

Summarizing the research on infant care is difficult, because people tend to believe that the practices of their own family or culture are best. They may be right: Each community tries to provide good care for their babies. However, that belief risks the difference-equals-deficit error.

Variations in perspectives, in norms, and in priorities lead to diverse practices. All humans seek confirmation of their opinions, and research provides it. Contradictory research may be ignored. Your opinions may be right, but that does not make others wrong.

Some cultures assume that mothers should care for young children until age 5 or so; other communities believe that early group care is better. Some cultures expect fathers to avoid infant care, with mothers as "gatekeepers" who criticize how men hold, feed, or play with babies. Mothers may discourage grandparents

Marcus McKinney/U.S. Army

**Together At Last** When Kristian Myrick was deployed to Afghanistan nine months ago, he was not sure he would be a father. His daughter weighed about an ounce, not yet viable. But here, Amelia and her mother (at left) welcome him back to Colorado. Father and infant will smile, laugh, and bond in the next few weeks. Only one year before this photo (in 2019), the U.S. military recognized the benefits of father–infant synchrony and attachment. Now soldiers on active duty have three weeks of paid paternal leave, a more generous policy than any other U.S. agency offers.

and others as well. By contrast, some mothers expect other relatives to help, and some nations pay professionals to provide infant and child care, just as they pay firefighters or the police.

Beyond national differences, opinions are affected by personal experience (adults who experienced nonparental care are likely to approve of it), by gender (males are more often critical of day-care centers), and by education (higher education increases support for nonparental care) (Galasso et al., 2017; Rose et al., 2018; Shpancer & Schweitzer, 2018).

## In the United States

In the United States, norms do not mandate exclusive mother care. Only 20 percent of infants are cared for *exclusively* by their mothers (i.e., no other relatives or babysitters) throughout their first year (Babchishin et al., 2013). In 2018, 58 percent of the mothers of infants under age 1 were in the labor force (U.S. Bureau of Labor Statistics, April 18, 2019).

One reason why most mothers of young children work is that they need the money. The United States is the only developed nation that does not require paid parental leave. Consequently, mothers enlist family members (especially fathers and grandmothers) to care for babies. Professional infant day care, either in a center or at home, is privately paid, and thus too expensive for many families.

In the United States, after a long fight among the men and women in the U.S. Congress, laws require companies with 50 employees or more to offer *unpaid* maternity leave for 12 weeks. Some employers are better, offering more time or some pay. Paternal leave is almost never paid with one exception: As of 2018, the U.S. military allows 21 days of paid leave for new fathers who are secondary caregivers, and up to 6 weeks for mothers or fathers in the military who are primary caregivers.

## Problems with Nonmaternal Care

Is there anything wrong with allocare? It depends: Some relatives provide good care, some not. Some day-care centers are excellent; some not. As you might imagine, since child care is not seen as a public right in the United States, cost is a major concern, and quality may suffer.

Beyond price, two worries are often expressed regarding babies with extensive allocare: (1) insecure attachment, and (2) emotional problems later on.

The first worry has been disproven. Secure mother–infant attachment (as measured by the Strange Situation) is as common for infants with regular father care, with professional day care, and with care from other caregivers, as with exclusive maternal care.

In retrospect, this makes sense. Even when fathers or day-care centers care for a baby 40 hours a week, mothers still spend more hours (especially nights and weekends) with their babies. Further, father–infant attachment is more likely when fathers provide major care, and infants benefit when they are securely attached to both parents (Cabrera et al., 2018).

Regarding behavioral problems, the evidence is not as clear. A mega-analysis of research on infant caregiving (Dearing & Zachrisson, 2017) reported that half of the studies of group care found that the children had more externalizing problems (such as aggression, particularly in boys) later on. However, that was not found in the other half of the studies, including one that reported better emotional adjustment when children had extensive day care.

As an earlier review explained: "This evidence now indicates that early nonparental care environments sometimes pose risks to young children and sometimes confer benefits" (Phillips et al., 2011, p. 44).

The most often cited longitudinal research comes from the Early Child Care Research Network of the National Institute of Child Health and Human Development (NICHD), which followed, from birth through adolescence, over 1,300 children born in 1991. Early day care correlated with many cognitive advances, especially in language. Children who were enrolled in high-quality preschools had higher achievement throughout elementary school and high school.

Most analyses of that group found that secure attachment was as common among infants in center care as among infants cared for at home. Like other, smaller studies, the NICHD research confirmed that the mother–child relationship was pivotal. A summary of that research found:

> higher quality of child care was linked to higher academic-cognitive skills in primary school and again at age 15. Higher hours of child care were associated with teacher reports of behavior problems in early primary school and youth reports of greater impulsivity and risk taking at age 15.

> [Burchinal et al., 2014, p. 542]

Why is the research not definitive about behavior problems? Perhaps the adults, not the infants, are the deciding factor. Many studies confirm that infants with neglectful mothers benefit from day care, but if the mother is responsive and the allocare is inferior, children fare better if their mother provides care. Inferior day care usually means not enough teachers. Even if they spend most of their time engaging with children, they cannot have enough time to spend with each child to provide the quality interactions needed.

## Historical Changes

Most currently reported longitudinal studies began with children who were in day care 30 years ago. Many educators and researchers believe that infant day care is of higher quality, as well as more common, than it was (Huston et al., 2015; Singer & Wong, 2019).

For example, the National Association for the Education of Young Children (NAEYC, the profession organization for educators who teach children under age 6), updated its standards for care of babies from birth to 15 months (NAEYC, 2014). Group size should be small (no more than eight infants), and the ratio of adults to babies is 1:4 or fewer (see **Table 7.2**).

| TABLE 7.2 |
| --- |
| **High-Quality Day Care** |
| **High-quality day care during infancy has five essential characteristics:** |
| 1. *Adequate attention to each infant*<br>A small group of infants (no more than eight) needs two reliable, familiar, loving caregivers. Continuity of care is crucial. |
| 2. *Encouragement of language and sensorimotor development*<br>Infants need language—songs, conversations, and positive talk—and easily manipulated toys. |
| 3. *Attention to health and safety*<br>Cleanliness routines (e.g., handwashing), accident prevention (e.g., no small objects), and safe areas to explore are essential. |
| 4. *Professional caregivers*<br>Caregivers should have experience and degrees/certificates in early-childhood education. Turnover should be low, morale high, and enthusiasm evident. |
| 5. *Warm and responsive caregivers*<br>Providers should engage the children in active play and guide them in problem solving. Quiet, obedient children may indicate unresponsive care. |

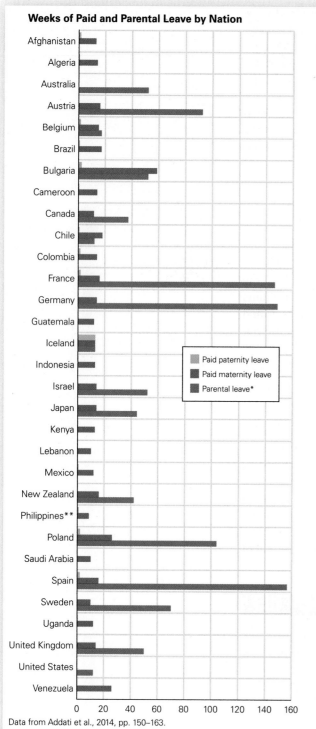

**Weeks of Paid and Parental Leave by Nation**

Legend:
- Paid paternity leave
- Paid maternity leave
- Parental leave*

Data from Addati et al., 2014, pp. 150–163.

*Notes:* *In some cases, leave can be shared between parents or other family members. Many nations have increased leave since these data were gathered.
**In the Philippines, parents must be married in order to receive paid leave.

**FIGURE 7.4**

**A Changing World** No one took maternity leave a century ago because the only jobs mothers had were unregulated ones. Now, virtually every nation has a maternity leave policy, revised every decade or so. As of 2019, only Belgium, Denmark, France, Latvia, Luxembourg, and Sweden had laws ensuring gender equality. That may be the next innovation in many nations.

Each infant is given personal attention, and the curriculum focuses on emotional and intellectual growth. For instance, teachers "engage infants in frequent face-to-face social interactions"—including talking, singing, smiling, and touching (NAEYC, 2014, p. 4). Every staff member must respect cultural differences and try to follow the mother's wishes. Maternal involvement is encouraged, including breast-feeding (bottles of pumped milk are stored for each baby).

Does that mean high-quality infant care is as good or better than mother care? People in the United States do not agree. Let us look at other nations, to see what we can learn.

## Other Nations

For cultural, ideological, and economic reasons, nations differ. Publicly paid infant care is rare in most nations of South Asia, sub-Saharan Africa, and South America, where many adults believe it is harmful. Those nations also have laws that require paid maternal leave, and sometimes paid paternal leave, evidence of the belief that mothers should stay home to care for infants.

By contrast, people in some nations believe that subsidized infant care is a public right, just like fire and police protection, and thus taxes pay for child care. Government-sponsored and regulated child care is prevalent in France, Israel, China, Chile, Norway, Sweden, Denmark, Finland, Iceland, and the Netherlands, and has recently been instituted in Australia and Germany. (See **Figure 7.4**.)

In the Scandinavian nations, legislators believe that the first years are crucial for later life, so quality is high (Garvis et al., 2019), and teachers are relatively well trained and paid.

That is less true in Germany and Australia, because those nations instituted low-cost day care primarily to increase the birth rate. In both nations, many young adults were not having children, as the sacrifice seemed too great. The legislators hope that by paying for early child care, more women will give birth (Harrison et al., 2014).

## France Compared to Norway

In France, subsidized care can begin at 12 weeks, but only about 10 percent of all infants receive it. The waiting list is long, parents pay part of the cost, and the adult–infant ratio is 1:5 under age 1 and 1:8 from age 1 until 3, when it increases again. That ratio reduces cost, but quality suffers. In France, "ensuring high-quality provision seems at odds with affordability and availability of places for under threes" (Fagnani, 2013, p. 92). The government emphasizes expansion so more mothers can work, rather than quality.

Norway takes the opposite course. Norwegians believe that the youngest babies are best cared for by their mothers, so they pay employed women full salary to stay home with their babies for 47 weeks after birth, and provide some paid leave for fathers as well. Beginning at age 1, high-quality, center day care is available for everyone, including in the sparsely populated rural counties. In 2016, many Norwegian 1-year-olds

(72 percent) were in center care, as were most 2-year-olds (92 percent) and almost all 3-year-olds (96 percent) (Statistics Norway, 2018).

## Aggressive or Assertive?

Longitudinal results in Norway find no detrimental results of early center care. What U.S. researchers consider aggression is not aggression in Norway. Instead, Norwegians praise early experiences with other children: That makes shy children bolder (Solheim et al., 2013).

This raises the need for operational definitions, as already explained regarding *attachment*. How should "behavioral problems" be assessed? The usual measure is teacher judgment. Do teachers judge differently in Norway than in the United States? Similar questions can be raised about risk-taking. Adults consider risk-taking a negative trait, but many teenagers disagree.

A study in the Netherlands found that, if anything, children who attended day care were less likely to have emotional problems than other children (Broekhuizen et al., 2018). In that nation, day care may begin before age 1, but most children attend center care part time, two or three days a week (see **Figure 7.5**). Do children benefit from part-time preschool more than full-time preschool?

## Fathers, Grandmothers, and Sisters

As you have already read, humans have evolved to allow allocare, which is help with infant care from many people in addition to the mother. Recent research in neuroscience finds that the human brain is plastic, not only in general, but also in the specifics of infant care. If a particular community encourages father–infant care, the brains of men adjust to make this a priority (Rogers & Bales, 2019).

In the nineteenth and twentieth centuries in the United States, fathers were usually designated as wage-earners, not baby minders. Families were large, and the older children cared for the younger ones. My own mother was the middle born of

Jeff Chiu/AP Images

**Double Winner** These parents brought their babies to the San Francisco legislature to advocate for paid parental leave. They won! The San Francisco Board of Supervisors voted yes, making this the first jurisdiction in the United States to mandate fully paid leave. The law went into effect in 2017—too late for both the mother and father shown here. Perhaps their next babies?

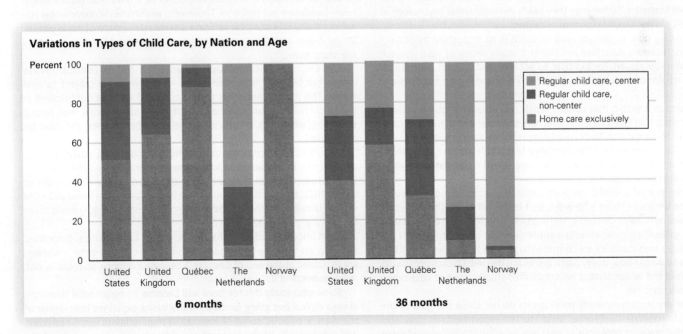

**Variations in Types of Child Care, by Nation and Age**

Legend:
- Regular child care, center
- Regular child care, non-center
- Home care exclusively

6 months: United States, United Kingdom, Québec, The Netherlands, Norway

36 months: United States, United Kingdom, Québec, The Netherlands, Norway

**FIGURE 7.5**

**Who Cares for the Baby?** Infants are the same everywhere, but cultures and governments differ dramatically. Does a 6-month-old need their mother more than a 3-year-old? Norway and Quebec say yes; the United States, United Kingdom, and the Netherlands say no.

**Observation Quiz** Which nation has the most extreme shift at age 1? (see answer, page 201) ↑

12 children. Two of her older sisters did not marry, in part because they cared for the younger ones. When I was an infant, those two maiden aunts moved in with my family, in part to help with child care as they had done when they were teenagers.

However, in the twenty-first century, families are smaller, and in 2018, 76.4 percent of the mothers whose oldest children were aged 6 to 17 were in the labor force (U.S. Bureau of Labor Statistics, April 18, 2019). Currently, fathers and grandmothers provide substantial allocare. It is unusual, but no longer rare, for a father to be the primary caregiver of an infant while the mother is employed.

Research in Europe finds that grandmothers are *more* likely to babysit in nations with extensive public care for infants (Price et al., 2018). The reason may be that, in those nations, exclusive mother care is not idealized. In nations where mothers are expected to be solely responsible for infants, if a particular woman wants or needs to have a job, her own mother is the most common caregiver (not the father or a day-care provider). Thus, in Italy for instance, fewer grandmothers babysit, but those who do put in more hours. Obviously, all of these differences are affected by culture, economics, and politics more than by universal needs of babies.

## CAREER ALERT    The Developmental Scientist

The need for developmental scientists is apparent: Much more must be learned about "how and why people—all kinds of people—change over time." Would-be researchers must become scholars who know what has already been studied—earning at least a master's degree. Leaders in developmental science almost always need a Ph.D. as well.

Often scholars need further study as they work as "post-docs," researching and writing after their doctoral degree under the direction of a leading scientist at a major university. Sometimes they work in government offices such as the Centers for Disease Control or the Bureau of Labor Statistics. Sometimes they teach developmental psychology at colleges, universities, or community centers.

Learning how to design valid research is an important beginning. Beyond the basics described in Chapter 1, many details of valid research have been developed. For example, to achieve multicultural understanding, a scholar often lives in another culture, absorbing its practices and values.

In research within that culture, words and phrases of questionnaires are typically translated by a bilingual native speaker and then back-translated by someone else. Back translation requires someone who is fluent in both languages to read the translated text and restore it to English (or whatever the first language was) to make sure the translation conveys the original meaning.

Then, in a pilot study, the questionnaire is administered to people who are similar to those who will take it in the full study. They interpret the questions, raise concerns, and suggest whether a particular question is misleading or whether the entire direction of the study is off the mark. Experts in statistics are consulted to suggest the proper analysis, as well as to advise how many participants are needed. The scientists who undertake the research must read published studies, consult colleagues, and work together.

In many instances, study participants do not know the goal of the research: They are said to be "blind" to the experimenter's goal. This deception prevents conscious or unconscious efforts to either validate or undermine the study. An ethical mandate is that any deception must be explained to the participants after their involvement.

Scientists may need to be "blind," as well: They do not directly interact with the participants of the study so that they cannot inadvertently clue responses. The entire endeavor requires many people to design, implement, and interpret the research. This is where novice scientists are crucial. Depending on the particulars, novices may do most of the hard work of implementing the design.

All of this is expensive: Some of the work of the scientist is to convince other people (foundations, government, private philanthropists) to support a particular study.

Another necessity is knowledge of statistics. There are many ways to analyze numbers and verbal responses to ensure that results which seem conclusive are really so. Those who wish to be developmental scientists study statistics for at least a semester—more often a year or longer. Some statistical measures are shown in the Appendix, but there are many more.

Once a study is completed and analyzed and its conclusions are drawn, but before it is published, the written report is subject to peer review. This means that other scientists (peers) who are not involved in the study read the unpublished report, make suggestions, and, finally, determine whether it is sufficiently well designed, honest, and clear for publication.

If students are preparing to become developmental scientists, they are likely to take courses in which they summarize and critique published studies so that they are ready to be peer reviewers. In order to earn a Ph.D., a student must undertake innovative research and write the results, usually in a thesis that is at least 100 pages long—more often double or triple that.

Most important of all is that the scientists follow ethical guidelines, always protecting the participants. This is so crucial that some mandates are explained at the end of Chapter 1 because everyone, scientist or not, must understand it.

Some who study this textbook will become developmental scientists, always ethical but going far beyond the basics explained here. Some of the work is tedious, some of the course requirements seem irrelevant, and some results of the research are discouraging. However, for those who choose this career, the joy of new discovery seems well worth the effort, and the potential reward—a better life for thousands of people who benefit from the research—makes all of the work worthwhile. Go for it!

## Conclusions from the Science

A strength of the scientific method is when various measures and populations lead to divergent conclusions; cumulative research rather than any one study or any personal experience makes good science. As you see, in much of the research on infant care, conclusions from one study may differ from another. However, among researchers, there is consensus on four principles:

1.  Mutual attachment to one or several familiar caregivers is beneficial.
2.  Quality of care, whether at home or in a day-care program, matters.
3.  Babies need loving and responsive caregivers.
4.  Frequent changes and instability in care are problematic.

On the last item on this list, it is now apparent that every disruption undercuts the infant's effort to understand their world. If a neighbor, a grandmother, a day-care center, and then another grandmother, each provide care on a different day of the week, or if a baby lives with the biological mother, then a foster mother, then with the biological father, then back with the biological mother, that is harmful. By age 3, children with unstable care histories are more aggressive than those with stable care (Pilarz & Hill, 2014).

As is true of many topics in child development, questions remain. But one fact is without question: Each infant needs personal responsiveness. Someone should serve as a partner in the synchrony duet, a base for secure attachment, and a social reference who encourages exploration. Then, infant emotions and experiences—cries and laughter, fears and joys—will ensure that development goes well.

---

 **DATA CONNECTIONS: A Look at Early Child Care in the United States** explores how various maternal demographics affect child-care arrangements. 🎓 **LaunchPad**.

---

### WHAT HAVE YOU LEARNED?

1.  Why do people disagree about who should provide care for infants?
2.  What are the advantages of maternal care for babies?
3.  What are the advantages of nonmaternal care for babies?
4.  What is the difference between infant care in France and Norway?
5.  What is the role of fathers and grandmothers in providing infant care?
6.  What distinguishes high-quality from low-quality infant day care?
7.  What aspects of infant care are agreed on by everyone?

## SUMMARY

### Emotional Development

**1.** Two emotions, contentment and distress, appear in newborns. Smiles and laughter are soon evident. Between 4 and 8 months of age, anger emerges in reaction to restriction and frustration, and it becomes stronger by age 1.

**2.** Reflexive fear is apparent in very young infants. Fear of something specific depends on the context. Typically, some fear of strangers and of separation is strong by age 1 and continues until age 2. After that, these fears may become disorders.

**3.** Self-recognition (measured by the mirror/rouge test) emerges at about 18 months. Social awareness and self-awareness produce more selective and intense emotions, as well as pride, shame, affection, and explosive temper.

### Temperament and Personality

**4.** Temperament is inborn, but the expression of temperament is influenced by the context, with evident plasticity.

### The Development of Social Bonds

**5.** Often by 2 months, and clearly by 6 months, infants become more responsive and social, and synchrony is evident. Caregivers and infants engage in reciprocal interactions, with split-second timing.

**6.** Attachment is the relationship between two people who try to be close to each other (proximity-seeking and contact-maintaining). It is measured in infancy by a baby's reaction to the caregiver's presence, departure, and return in the Strange Situation.

**7.** Secure attachment provides encouragement for infant exploration, and its influence is lifelong. Adults are attached as well, evident not only as parents but also as romantic partners.

**8.** As they become more mobile and engage with their environment, infants use social referencing (looking to other people's facial expressions and body language) to detect what is safe, frightening, or fun.

**9.** Infants frequently use fathers as partners in synchrony, as attachment figures, and as social references, developing emotions and exploring their world. Contemporary fathers often play with their infants.

## Theories of Infant Psychosocial Development

**10.** According to all major theories, caregivers are especially influential in the first two years. Freud stressed the mother's impact on oral and anal pleasure; Erikson emphasized trust and autonomy. Both believed that the impact of these is lifelong.

**11.** Behaviorists focus on learning. They note that parents teach their babies many things, including when to be fearful or joyful, and how much physical and social distance (proximal or distal parenting) is best.

**12.** Cognitive theory holds that infants develop working models based on their experiences. Interpretation is crucial, and that can change with maturation.

**13.** Evolutionary theorists recognize that both infants and caregivers have impulses and emotions that have developed over millennia to foster the survival of each new member of the human species. Attachment is one example.

## Who Should Care for Babies?

**14.** Research confirms that every infant needs responsive caregiving, secure attachment, and cognitive stimulation. These three can occur at home or in a good day-care center. Quality matters, as does consistency of care.

**15.** Some people believe that infant day care benefits babies and that governments should subsidize high-quality infant care, just as governments pay professional firefighters to put out any fire. Other cultures believe the opposite—that infant care is best done by the mothers, who are solely responsible for providing it.

**16.** National and international research finds much variation in policies and opinions regarding infant day care. Some nations provide extensive day care for young children, and virtually all nations (except the United States) mandate paid maternal leave for employed women who have a baby.

## KEY TERMS

social smile (p. 173)
separation anxiety (p. 174)
stranger wariness (p. 174)
self-awareness (p. 175)
temperament (p. 176)
synchrony (p. 179)

still-face technique (p. 181)
attachment (p. 181)
secure attachment (p. 182)
insecure-avoidant attachment (p. 182)

insecure-resistant/ambivalent attachment (p. 182)
disorganized attachment (p. 183)
social referencing (p. 187)
trust versus mistrust (p. 190)

autonomy versus shame and doubt (p. 190)
proximal parenting (p. 191)
distal parenting (p. 191)
working model (p. 191)
allocare (p. 193)

## APPLICATIONS

**1.** One cultural factor that influences infant development is how infants are carried from place to place. Ask four mothers whose infants were born in each of the past four decades how they transported them—front or back carriers, facing out or in, strollers or carriages, in car seats or on mother's laps, and so on. Why did they choose the mode(s) they chose? What are their opinions and yours on how such cultural practices might affect infants' development?

**2.** Record video of synchrony for three minutes. Ideally, ask the parent of an infant under 8 months of age to play with the infant.

If no infant is available, observe a pair of lovers as they converse. Note the sequence and timing of every facial expression, sound, and gesture of both partners.

**3.** Contact several day-care centers to try to assess the quality of care they provide. Ask about factors such as adult/child ratio, group size, and training for caregivers of children of various ages. Is there a minimum age? Why or why not? Analyze the answers, using Table 7.2 as a guide.

## Especially For ANSWERS

**Response for Nurses and Pediatricians** (from p. 174): Stranger wariness is normal up to about 14 months. This baby's behavior actually might indicate secure attachment.

**Response for Nurses** (from p. 178): It's too soon to tell. Temperament is not truly "fixed" but variable, especially in the first few months. Many "difficult" infants become happy, successful adolescents and adults, if their parents are responsive.

**Response for Nursing Mothers** (from p. 190): Freud thought so, but there is no experimental evidence that weaning, even when ill-timed, has such dire long-term effects.

**Response for Pediatricians** (from p. 191): Consider the origins of the misbehavior—probably a combination of the child's inborn temperament and the mother's distal parenting. Acceptance and consistent responses (e.g., avoiding disliked foods but always using the car seat) is more warranted than anger. Perhaps this mother is expressing hostility toward the child—a sign that intervention may be needed. Find out.

## Observation Quiz ANSWERS

**Answer to Observation Quiz** (from p. 180) The first baby is adopted, the second was born at home, and the third parent is the father, not the mother. Synchrony is universal! Although not evident here, it is also true that each is in a different nation: United States, Ethiopia, and England.

**Answer to Observation Quiz** (from p. 197) Norway. Almost every mother stays home with her infant for the first year (she is paid her salary to do so), and almost every mother enrolls her 1-year-old in public day care.

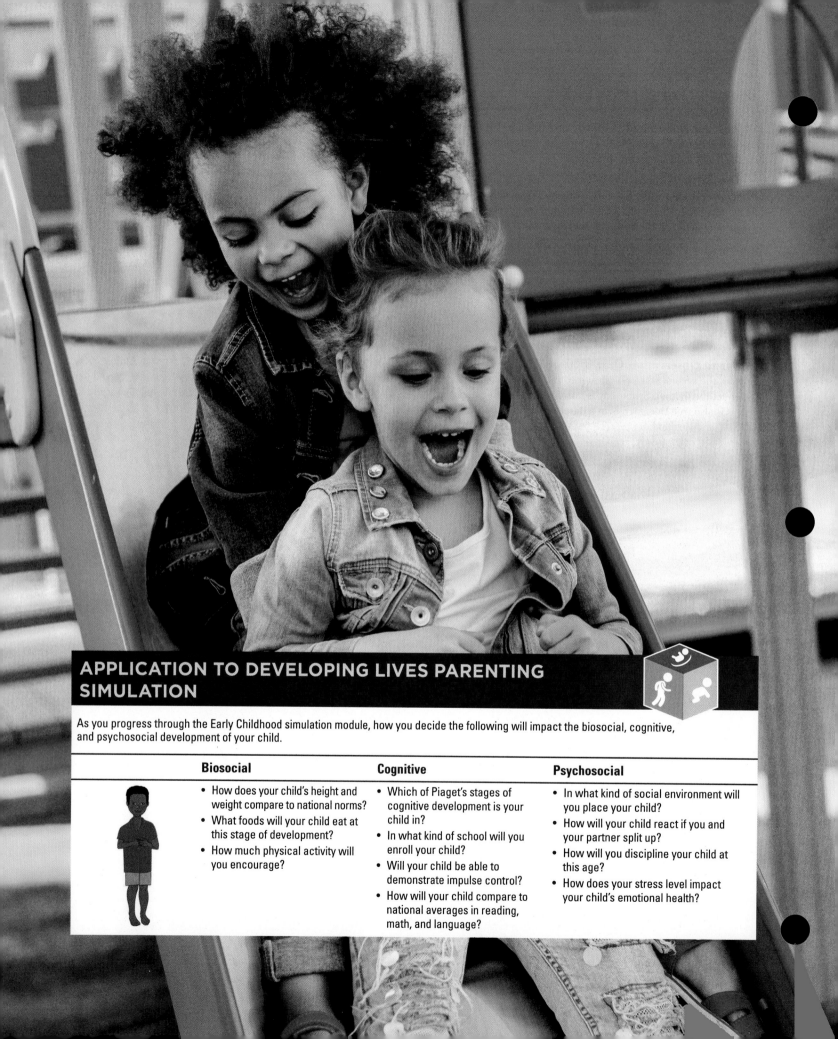

# APPLICATION TO DEVELOPING LIVES PARENTING SIMULATION

As you progress through the Early Childhood simulation module, how you decide the following will impact the biosocial, cognitive, and psychosocial development of your child.

| | Biosocial | Cognitive | Psychosocial |
|---|---|---|---|
| | • How does your child's height and weight compare to national norms?<br>• What foods will your child eat at this stage of development?<br>• How much physical activity will you encourage? | • Which of Piaget's stages of cognitive development is your child in?<br>• In what kind of school will you enroll your child?<br>• Will your child be able to demonstrate impulse control?<br>• How will your child compare to national averages in reading, math, and language? | • In what kind of social environment will you place your child?<br>• How will your child react if you and your partner split up?<br>• How will you discipline your child at this age?<br>• How does your stress level impact your child's emotional health? |

# PART III

# Early Childhood

**F**rom ages 2 to 6, children spend most of their waking hours discovering, creating, laughing, and imagining—all the while acquiring the skills they need. They chase each other and attempt new challenges (developing their bodies); they play with sounds, words, and ideas (developing their minds); they invent games and dramatize fantasies (learning social skills and morals).

These were once called the *preschool years* because school started in first grade. But first grade is no longer first; most children begin school long before age 6. Instead, these years are called *early childhood*; those who were once called *preschoolers* are now *young children*. By whatever name, these years are a time for extraordinary growth, impressive learning, and spontaneous play, joyful not only for young children but also for anyone who knows them. ●●

Left: LightField Studios/Shutterstock.Com
Right: baona/iStock/Getty Images

# Early Childhood: Biosocial Development

## What Will You Know?

1. Do young children eat too much, too little, or the right amount?
2. If children never climb trees or splash in water, do they suffer?
3. Why is injury control needed more than accident prevention?
4. Which is worse, neglect or abuse?

**M**any children, including my grandsons, play in the yard after school. The 4- and 5-year-olds are always in motion, running and chasing; they are not ready for the play of the older children, which includes team sports and sitting and talking.

I am struck not only by their compulsion to move and explore but also by their readiness to touch each other. They greet each other with hugs; they go down the slide together so they all bunch up at the end; they get each other's attention by grabbing an arm. Danger does not stop them: The children scramble to sit on a high ledge, not protected by a fence or safety surface.

Once my grandson came to me, crying.

"I bumped my head," he told me.

I said, "Tell me what pole you bumped it on, and I will tell that pole never to bump my grandson again."

"I bumped it on another head," he said as he ran back to play, no longer crying.

I am not surprised that two young heads bumped each other. Nature makes young children active and social. This chapter describes active growth during early childhood—in body, brain, and motor skills—and what adults do to protect it.

I hold my grandson's wrist when we cross the street, make sure he has his coat, and am ready with a Band-Aid to cover any scrape. His immaturity is evident: A bandage stops the crying. I wish every young child was as easy to comfort. As you will read in this chapter, all young children are active, but some encounter far more serious problems than another child's head.

## Body Changes

In early childhood, as in infancy, the body and brain grow according to powerful epigenetic forces—biologically driven and socially guided, experience-expectant and experience-dependent.

## Growth Patterns

Compare an unsteady 24-month-old with a cartwheeling 6-year-old. Physical differences are obvious. Height and weight increase in those four years by about a foot and 16 pounds, or almost 30 centimeters and 8 kilograms.

Shape changes, too: Children slim down, the lower body lengthens, fat is replaced by muscle. The average *body mass index* (or *BMI*, a ratio of weight to height) is lower at ages 5 and 6 than at any other time of life. [**Developmental Link:** Body mass index is defined in Chapter 11.]

Gone are the infant's protruding belly, round face, short limbs, and large head. The center of gravity moves from the breast to the belly, enabling cartwheels, somersaults, and many other accomplishments. The joys of dancing, gymnastics, and pumping legs on a swing become possible; changing proportions enable new achievements.

During each year of early childhood, well-nourished children grow about 3 inches (about 7½ centimeters) and gain almost 4½ pounds (2 kilograms). By age 6, the average child in a developed nation:

- is at least 3½ feet tall (more than 110 centimeters).
- weighs between 40 and 50 pounds (between 18 and 23 kilograms).
- looks lean, not chubby.
- has adultlike body proportions (legs constitute about half the total height).

## Nutrition

Although they rarely starve, young children sometimes are malnourished, even in nations with abundant food. Small appetites are often satiated by unhealthy snacks, crowding out needed vitamins.

## Obesity Among Young Children

Older adults often encourage overeating, protecting children against famine that no longer occurs in most places. Now, the world's most serious food problem is obesity, which eventually reduces immunity and causes disease (Rook et al., 2014).

Obesity correlates with poverty for many reasons. Families with little money or education are more likely to get less exercise, watch more TV, eat fewer vegetables, drink more sugary drinks, and buy more fast food (Cespedes et al., 2013). This is partly related to where they live, often in communities that are less safe for walking or bike-riding, with fewer stores selling fresh vegetables.

Problems endure lifelong. Children who grow up in food-insecure households learn to eat whenever food is available, becoming less attuned to hunger and satiety signals in their bodies. Consequently, as adults, they overeat when they are not hungry (S. Hill et al., 2016).

Appetite naturally decreases between ages 2 and 6, as growth slows down. Parents need to know this, neither enticing children to eat nor giving them junk food to fill them up. However, parents often underestimate their children's weight. A review of 69 studies found that half of the parents of overweight children believe their children are thinner than they actually are (Lundahl et al., 2014).

Early childhood is the best time for prevention, because overweight increases with age. In 2016, 14 percent of 2- to 5-year-olds, 18 percent of 6- to 11-year-olds, and 21 percent of 12- to 19-year-olds in the United States were obese (Fryar et al., 2018).

Surprisingly, parental recognition that a child is overweight may lead to an *increase* in that child's weight, according to research on 2,823 Australian 4- and 5-year-olds followed until mid-adolescence (Robinson & Sutin, 2017). Similar results were found in Ireland and the United States.

The reason may be, according to the authors of that Australian study, that parents add stress without changing family eating patterns. If parents criticize the child, the child may react by cycling between dieting and overeating. Childhood

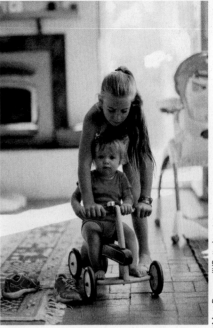

Marc Romanelli/Getty Images

**Short and Chubby Limbs No Longer** Siblings in New Mexico, ages 7 and almost 1, illustrate the transformation of body shape and skills during early childhood. Head size is almost the same, but the older child's arms are twice as long, evidence of proximodistal growth.

**Observation Quiz** Can this toddler pedal the tricycle? (see answer, page 227) ↑

obesity is linked to childhood depression (Sutaria et al., 2019) as well as to lack of exercise and excess screen time, both of which make the problems worse.

Immigration may also increase childhood weight. Few adults realize that traditional diets in low-income nations are healthier than foods advertised in developed nations (de Hoog et al., 2014). Instead, they may urge destructive patterns. One study of immigrants from many nations reported that "universally, caregivers described a concern for whether or not their children were eating enough and a perceived need to force feed them" (Dawson-Hahn et al., 2019, p. 279).

The problem is a major export, as people in many nations are adopting Western diets, buying cars and labor-saving devices, and moving to cities where long walks outside are unusual. As a result, "childhood obesity is one of the most serious public health challenges of the 21st century. The problem is global and is steadily affecting many low- and middle-income countries, particularly in urban settings" (Sahoo et al., 2015, pp. 187–188).

There has been some good news, however. In the United States, school lunches include more fruit and less fat, and the rate of obesity in 2- to 5-year-olds has not shown a steady increase. Pediatric awareness, corporate policies, and parental action are all credited with this improvement, as is former First Lady Michelle Obama, who made child nutrition and exercise her major goal. The real credit may go to her pediatrician, who said that her daughters were gaining weight more quickly than ideal. She resolved to do something about it, first for her daughters and later, as First Lady, for all children (Obama, 2018).

Many day-care centers now promote exercise and provide healthy snacks— carrot sticks and apple slices, not cookies and chocolate milk (Sisson et al., 2016). Obesity among 2- to 6-year-olds fell slightly in about 2015. Similar trends are apparent in Germany, with rates of childhood obesity steady among older children but dropping among young children (Schienkiewitz et al., 2018).

However, after leveling off for a few years, rates of preschool obesity in the United States have risen again to 13.9 percent (Fryar et al., 2018). That bad news has a hopeful twist: Since weight gain in early childhood is fluid, parents and communities can make a difference.

---

 **DATA CONNECTIONS: Food Insecurity Around the World and in the United States** explores how rates vary by nation and by U.S. household. 🔲 **LaunchPad**

---

## Nutritional Deficiencies

Although many young children consume more than enough calories, they do not always obtain adequate iron, zinc, and calcium. For example, North American children now drink less milk than formerly. Less calcium means weaker bones later on.

Compared with the average child, young children who eat more dark-green and orange vegetables and less fried food benefit in many ways. They gain bone mass but not fat, according to a study that controlled for other factors that correlate with body fat, such as gender (girls have more), ethnicity (people of some ethnic groups are genetically thinner), and income (poor children have worse diets) (Wosje et al., 2010).

Sugar is a major problem. Many cultural customs entice children to eat sweets— in birthday cake, holiday candy, desserts, sweetened juice, soda, and so on. Children prefer tastes that are more sweet and less bitter than what adults prefer, which means that adults should not let children eat what they wish. Some mothers add sugar to increase appetite: Those children develop a lifelong sweet tooth that can harm them (Mennella & Bobowski, 2015).

In early childhood, the American Heart Association recommends no more than six teaspoons of natural or added sugars, including high-fructose corn

Dave Carpenter/Cartoonstock

" IT SAYS RIGHT HERE IN THE INGREDIENTS, 'THIS PRODUCT CONTAINS NO YUCKY STUFF'. "

**Who Is Fooling Whom?** He doesn't believe her, but maybe she shouldn't believe what the label says, either. For example, "low fat" might also mean high salt.

syrup. The average child consumes three times that. Too much sugar causes poor circulation—with heart attacks likely 50 years later (Vos et al., 2016).

Advertisements may mislead. For example, vitamin C is usually found in abundance in the normal diet of young children and is a cheap vitamin to add to food, so sweetened juice with 100 percent of the daily requirement of vitamin C is no bargain. Many nutrients in food have not yet been identified, much less listed on food labels.

## Oral Health

The most immediate harm from sugar is cavities and decaying teeth before age 6. Thus, children should see a dentist and brush their teeth regularly during early childhood—practices that were unnecessary before widespread sugar consumption (Gibbons, 2012).

"Baby" teeth are replaced naturally from ages 6 to 10. The schedule is genetic, with girls averaging a few months ahead of boys. However, tooth brushing and dentist visits should become habitual in early childhood because poor oral health harms those permanent teeth (forming below the first teeth) and can cause jaw malformation, chewing difficulties, and speech problems.

Teeth are affected by diet and illness. Thus, a young child's teeth alert the dentist to other health problems. The process works in reverse as well: Infected teeth can affect the rest of the child's body. In adulthood, tooth infections can cause preterm births, another reason good oral health habits need to be established early (Puertas et al., 2018).

## Allergies and Food

An estimated 6 to 8 percent of children are allergic to a specific food, almost always a common, healthy one: Milk, eggs, peanuts, tree nuts (such as almonds and walnuts), soy, wheat, fish, and shellfish are the usual culprits. Diagnostic standards for allergies vary (which explains the range of estimates), and treatment varies even more.

Some experts advocate total avoidance of the offending food—there are peanut-free schools, where no one is allowed to bring a peanut-butter sandwich for lunch. However, some allergists give children who are allergic to peanuts a tiny bit of peanut powder (under medical supervision), which may decrease a child's allergic reaction (Couzin-Frankel, 2018).

Indeed, exposure to peanuts can begin before birth: A study of pregnant women who ingested peanuts found that their children were less likely to be allergic (Frazier et al., 2014). Many childhood food allergies are outgrown, but ongoing allergies make a balanced diet even harder to maintain.

Other allergies increase as children grow older, depending on preventive measures, such as avoiding air pollution or having a pet (Nowak & Schaub, 2018). Diet matters. Children who eat many fast foods (which have more saturated fatty acids, trans fatty acids, sodium, carbohydrates, and sugar than home-cooked food) have higher rates of asthma, nasal congestion, watery eyes, and itchy skin.

© Burger/Phanie/The Image Works

**Not Allergic Anymore?** Many food allergies are outgrown, so young children are more likely to have them than older ones. This skin prick will insert a tiny amount of a suspected allergen. If a red welt develops in the next half hour, the girl is still allergic. Hopefully, no reaction will occur; but if her breathing is affected, an EpiPen is within reach.

---

### WHAT HAVE YOU LEARNED?

1. About how much does a well-nourished child grow in height and weight from age 2 to age 6?

2. Why do some adults overfeed children?

3. Why are today's children more at risk of obesity than children 50 years ago?

4. How do childhood allergies affect nutrition?

## Brain Growth

By age 2, most neurons have connected to other neurons and substantial pruning has occurred. The 2-year-old's brain already weighs 75 percent of what it will weigh in adulthood; the 6-year-old's brain is 90 percent of adult weight.

Since most of the brain is already present and functioning by age 2, what remains to develop? The most important parts! Most important for people, that is.

## Myelination

**myelination** The process by which axons become coated with myelin, a fatty substance that speeds the transmission of nerve impulses from neuron to neuron.

After infancy, the increase in brain weight is primarily in **myelination**. Sometimes called the *white matter* of the brain, *myelin* is a fatty coating on the axons that protects and speeds signals between neurons. (The *gray matter* is the neurons themselves.)

Myelin is far more than mere insulation around the axons. It smooths the connections between neurons that are far from each other. "Myelin organizes the very structure of network connectivity . . . and regulates the timing of information flow through individual circuits" (Fields, 2014, p. 266).

### Connecting Left and Right

**corpus callosum** A long, thick band of nerve fibers that connects the left and right hemispheres of the brain and allows communication between them.

Myelination is especially evident in the major link between the left and the right halves of the brain, the **corpus callosum** (see Inside the Brain).

Left-handed people tend to have thicker, better myelinated corpus callosa than right-handed people do, perhaps because they often switch between the two sides of their bodies. When they can choose which hand to use, they prefer their left (e.g., brushing their teeth), but the culture often requires using the right hand (e.g., shaking hands). Therefore, the corpus callosum must be well-developed.

Acceptance of left-handedness is more widespread now than a century ago. More adults in Great Britain and the United States claim to be left-handed today (about 10 percent) than in 1900 (about 3 percent) (McManus et al., 2010). Developmentalists advise against forcing a left-handed child to become right-handed, since the brain is the origin of handedness.

**lateralization** Literally, sidedness, referring to the specialization in certain functions by each side of the brain, with one side dominant for each activity. The left side of the brain controls the right side of the body, and vice versa.

Indeed, the brain is the source of all types of **lateralization** (literally, *sidedness*). The entire human body is lateralized, apparent not only in right- or left-handedness but also in the feet, the eyes, the ears, and the brain itself.

Genes, prenatal hormones, and early experiences all affect which side does what, and then the corpus callosum puts it all together. Left-handedness (which means a stronger right brain) is an advantage in some professions, especially those involving creativity and split-second, emotional responses.

A disproportionate number of artists, musicians, and sports stars were/are left-handed, including Pele, Babe Ruth, Monica Seles, Bill Gates, Oprah Winfrey, Jimi Hendrix, Lady Gaga, and Justin Bieber. Five of the past seven presidents of the United States were/are lefties: Gerald Ford, Ronald Reagan, George H.W. Bush, Bill Clinton, and Barack Obama. Each was able to coordinate with many nations and opinions in Congress: Perhaps flexibility is a trait that correlates with a strong corpus callosum.

Zephyr/SPL/Science Source

**Mental Coordination?** This brain scan of a 38-year-old depicts areas of myelination (the various colors) within the brain. As you see, the two hemispheres are quite similar, but not identical. For most important skills and concepts, both halves of the brain are activated.

## Humans and Other Animals

Although the brains and bodies of other primates are better than those of humans in some ways (they climb trees earlier and faster, for instance), and although many animals have abilities that humans lack (smell in dogs, hearing in bats), humans have intellectual capacities far beyond any other animal. Much of this is the ability to use many parts of the brain at once, an ability aided by extensive white matter.

# Connected Hemispheres

The brain is divided into two halves called *hemispheres*. Those two are connected by the corpus callosum, a long, thick band of nerve fibers that myelinates and grows particularly rapidly in early childhood (Ansado et al., 2015). For that reason, compared to toddlers, young children become much better at coordinating the two sides of their brains and, hence, both sides of their bodies. They can hop, skip, and gallop at age 5; they cannot at age 2.

Both sides of the brain are usually involved in every skill, not only gross motor skills such as hopping, skipping, and galloping but also fine motor skills such as eating with utensils or buttoning one's coat. Intellectual skills also use many parts of the brain, as do social responses to other people.

As you see, the corpus callosum is crucial. With myelination, signals between the two hemispheres become quicker and clearer, enabling children to become better thinkers, to be less clumsy, and eventually to read, write, and add—all skills that require the whole brain.

The development of the corpus callosum is easy to see when comparing infants and older children. For example, no 2-year-old can hop on one foot, but most 6-year-olds can—an example of brain balancing. Many songs, dances, and games that young children love involve moving the body in some coordinated way—challenging, but fun because of that. Logic (left brain) without emotion (right brain) is a severe impairment, as is the opposite (Damasio, 2012).

Emotions also need to be balanced. In adulthood, depression is more common in people with impaired balance between the two sides of the brain (Bruder et al., 2017).

Serious disorders are caused when the corpus callosum fails to develop. That almost always results in intellectual disability. Abnormal growth of the corpus callosum is one symptom of autism spectrum disorder, as well as of dozens of other disorders (Al-Hashim et al., 2016; Travers et al., 2015; J. Wolff et al., 2015).

This imbalance is partly genetic, but it also is prenatal, as evidenced by smaller corpus callosa when the mother drank heavily during pregnancy (Biffen et al., 2018).

Astonishing studies of humans whose corpus callosa were severed to relieve severe epilepsy, as well as research on humans and other vertebrates with intact corpus callosa, reveal how the brain's hemispheres specialize.

- The left half controls the body's right side, as well as areas dedicated to logical reasoning, detailed analysis, and the basics of language.
- The brain's right half controls the body's left side and areas dedicated to emotional and creative impulses, including appreciation of music, art, and poetry.

Thus, the left half notices details, and the right half grasps the big picture. This left–right distinction has been exaggerated, especially when applied to people. No one is exclusively left-brained or right-brained, except individuals with severe brain injury in childhood, who may use half of their brain to do all of the necessary thinking. Nonetheless, we should all be grateful that many parts of our brains coordinate with other parts.

---

With other creatures, evolution is sometimes called "survival of the fittest." But humans have developed "a mode of living built on social cohesion, cooperation and efficient planning. It was a question of survival of the smartest" (Corballis, 2011, p. 194). Myelination from ages 3 to 6 is crucial for that, because it enables the parts of the brain to communicate with each other (Forbes & Gallo, 2017).

## Maturation of the Prefrontal Cortex

The entire frontal lobe continues to develop for many years after early childhood; dendrite density and myelination continue increasing after age 20. Nonetheless, neurological control advances significantly between ages 2 and 6, evident in several ways:

- Sleep becomes more regular.
- Emotions become more nuanced and responsive.
- Temper tantrums subside.
- Uncontrollable laughter and tears are less common.

One example of the maturing brain is evident in the game Simon Says. Players are supposed to follow the leader *only* when orders are preceded by the words

**Especially for Early-Childhood Teachers** You know you should be patient, but frustration rises when your young charges dawdle on the walk to the playground a block away. What should you do? (see response, page 227)

**Open Your Arms!** But four children keep their arms closed because Simon didn't say to do so. You can almost see their prefrontal cortices (above the eyes) hard at work.

"Simon says." Thus, if leaders touch their noses and say, "Simon says touch your nose," players touch their noses; but when leaders touch their noses and say, "Touch your nose," no one is supposed to follow that example. The youngest children lose at this game because they impulsively do what they see and hear; their prefrontal cortex is too slow.

Another example is overwhelming fear. Because the amygdala is not well connected to more reflective and rational parts of the brain, many young children become suddenly terrified—even of something that exists only in imagination. Common phobias in young children are of the dark, of the ocean, of strangers. Since the emotional parts of the brain are immature, comfort and reassurance are needed, not logic. Then the fear will diminish.

## Inhibition and Flexibility

Neurons have only two kinds of impulses: on–off or, in neuroscience terms, *activate–inhibit*. Each is signaled by biochemical messages from dendrites to axons to neurons. (The consequences are evident in *executive function* and *emotional regulation*, both crucial aspects of cognition that are discussed in the next two chapters.)

### Impulsiveness

A balance of activation and inhibition (on/off) is necessary for thoughtful adults, who neither leap too quickly nor hesitate too long, neither lash out angrily nor freeze in fear. This is needed lifelong: One sign of cognitive loss in adulthood is a person who is too cautious or too impulsive.

The immaturity of the young brain is evident in this on/off function because many young children are notably unbalanced neurologically. They are impulsive, flitting from one activity to another. That explains why many 3-year-olds cannot stay quietly on one task, even in "circle time" in preschool, where each child is supposed to sit in place.

**impulse control** The ability to postpone or deny the immediate response to an idea or behavior.

Some preschool teachers tell the children to sit on their hands, or assign each child to a designated spot on the carpet, because children have difficulty not touching their neighbor. Poor **impulse control** signifies a personality disorder in adulthood but not in early childhood. Few 3-year-olds are capable of sustained attention to tasks that adults want them to attend to.

### Perseveration

**perseverate** To stay stuck, or persevere, in one thought or action for a long time. The ability to be flexible, switching from one task to another, is beyond most young children.

The opposite reaction is also apparent. Some young children **perseverate**, which is to stick to (persevere) one thought or action. A child might play with one toy or hold one fantasy for hours. This is characteristic of children on the autism spectrum but also occurs in some typical 3-year-olds.

Young children may repeat a phrase or question again and again, or they may not be able to stop giggling once they start. That is perseveration. Crying may become uncontrollable because the child is stuck in whatever triggered the outburst.

These behaviors are linked to brain maturation. No young child is perfect at regulating attention, because immaturity of the prefrontal cortex makes controlling the limbic system almost impossible. Consequently, impulsiveness and perseveration occur.

A study of children from ages 3 to 6 found that the ability to attend to adult requests gradually increased. That correlated with academic learning and behavioral control (fewer outbursts or tears) (L. Metcalfe et al., 2013). Development continues as brain maturation (innate) and emotional regulation (learned) allow most children to pay attention and switch activities as needed, with neurological maturation related to cultural demands (Posner & Rothbart, 2017).

In childhood as well as adulthood, perseveration leads to procrastination ("Not now, I am busy"). Impulsivity and procrastination seem to be opposites, but they are closely correlated, because the same brain regions (particularly the left dorso-lateral prefrontal cortex) govern both (Liu & Feng, 2017).

Caregivers need to be patient as well as provide guidance. The comforting truth is that brains mature. Most North American teenagers are able to change tasks at the sound of the school bell, although at every age, people resist demands to stop mid-thought and attend to some other task.

## Stress and the Brain

The relationship between stress and brain activity depends partly on the age of the person and partly on the degree of stress. Both too much stress and too little stress impair learning.

In an experiment, brain scans and hormone measurements were taken of 4- to 6-year-olds immediately after a fire alarm (Teoh & Lamb, 2013). As measured by their cortisol levels, some children were upset and some were not. Two weeks later, they were questioned about the event. Those with higher cortisol reactions to the alarm remembered more details. That is found in other research as well—some stress, but not too much, aids cognition (Keller et al., 2012).

However, especially with children, if an adult creates stress by asking questions sternly, demanding immediate yes-or-no answers, memories are less accurate. There are evolutionary reasons for that: People need to remember experiences that arouse emotions so that they can avoid, or adjust to, similar experiences in the future. At the same time, brains need to shut down to protect from excess stress.

Generally, a balance between arousal and reassurance is needed, again requiring coordination among many parts of the brain. For instance, if children are witnesses to a crime (a stressful experience) or experience abuse, memory is more accurate when an interviewer is warm and attentive, listening carefully but not suggesting answers (Johnson et al., 2016).

Direct maltreatment is worse, causing not only shrinkage of various regions of the brain but also decreases in white matter—and thus reduced connections between parts of the brain (Puetz et al., 2017; Rock et al., 2018). Shutdown might be best. Otherwise, child abuse might make an adult get stuck—on fear, or fantasy, or on an irrational thought, unable to feel the mixed emotions of most experiences.

Sadly, this topic leads again to the Romanian children mentioned in Chapter 7. When some adopted Romanian children saw pictures of happy, sad, frightened, or angry faces, their limbic systems were less reactive than were those of Romanian children who were never institutionalized. Their brains were also less lateralized, suggesting less efficient thinking (C. Nelson et al., 2014). Thus, institutional life, without stress reduction provided by loving caretakers, impaired their brains.

**LaunchPad**
macmillan learning

**VIDEO ACTIVITY: The Childhood Stress–Cortisol Connection** examines how high cortisol levels can negatively impact a child's overall health.

## Advancing Motor Skills

Maturation and myelination allow children to move with greater speed, agility, and grace as they age. Brain growth, motivation, and guided practice undergird all motor skills. In addition, the size of the child and skeletal maturation (measured by assessing the growth of the wrist bones) affect the development of motor skills, maturing faster in girls than in boys.

## Gross Motor Skills

Gross motor skills improve dramatically during early childhood. When playing, many of the youngest children fall down and bump into each other. By contrast, some 5-year-olds perform coordinated dance steps, tumbling tricks, or sports moves.

**CHAPTER APP 8**

 Wuf Shanti
Yoga Fun
Machine

**IOS:**
https://tinyurl.com/y5hzbsmc

**ANDROID:**
https://tinyurl.com/yxyo7nfn

**RELEVANT TOPIC:**
Motor skills and general well-being in early childhood

Featuring the motto "Think well to be well," this app for young children includes brief videos of yoga poses, songs, meditations, and positive thoughts. There are also games and coloring pages on the app, all of which encourage health, wellness, happiness, and positivity in children.

There remains much to learn, especially in adjusting to other people and situations. Thus, some 5-year-olds can kick a ball with precision but cannot be good team players on a soccer team. (Learning about people and controlling emotions are discussed in Chapters 9 and 10.)

Many North American 5-year-olds can ride a tricycle, climb a ladder, and pump a swing, as well as throw, catch, and kick a ball. A few can do these things by age 3, and some 5-year-olds can already skate, ski, dive, and ride a bike—activities that demand balanced coordination and both brain hemispheres. Elsewhere, some 5-year-olds swim in oceans or climb cliffs. All this depends on practice—some 5-year-olds can do none of these, because they have never had a chance.

Adults need to make sure that children have a safe space to play, with time, appropriate equipment, and playmates. Children learn best from peers who do whatever the child is ready to try, from catching a ball to climbing a tree. Culture and locale matter: Some children learn skateboarding, others sailing.

Urbanization worries many scientists (Acuto & Parnell, 2016; Wigginton et al., 2016). A century ago, children with varied skills played together in empty lots or fields without supervision, but now most of the world's children live in cities, with few places to throw balls, to play tag, to hide-and-seek.

Busy or violent streets not only impede development of gross motor skills but also add to the natural fears of the immature amygdala, compounded by the fears of adults. Gone are the days when parents told their children to go out and play, only to return when hunger, rain, or nightfall brought them home.

Parents may fear strangers and traffic, keeping their 3- to 5-year-olds from playing freely with peers. That distresses developmentalists. As one team, expressing the official opinion of the American Academy of Pediatrics, wrote, "Play is not frivolous; it is brain building" (Yogman et al., 2018).

## Learning from Nature

Many childhood educators believe that children need space and freedom in order to develop well (Moore & Sabo-Risley, 2017). Indeed, some view nature as "another teacher having the power to enhance children's sense of wonder and capacity for learning" (Stremmel, 2012, p. 136). Balancing on branches and jumping over fences, squeezing mud and throwing pebbles, chasing birds and catching bugs—each forbidden now by some adults—educated millions of children in former cohorts.

Play is considered crucial for every aspect of child development, cognitive and social as well as physical. Accordingly, it is discussed in detail in Chapter 10. Here we need to acknowledge that motor skills—running, climbing, leaping, jumping—develop when children play freely with other children.

Some researchers analyze which environments are best for active play. A large (over 4,000 children) study of 4- to 15-year-olds in 130 U.S. communities found that children were most likely to play actively outside on dead-end streets, cul-du-sacs, or side streets where there was some visible litter (Kaczynski et al., 2018). The "counterintuitive" discovery that streets with litter were also streets with more play was explained by the researchers as a sign of fewer adults and more children.

## Fine Motor Skills

Fine motor skills improve dramatically in early childhood, again with practice. This is particularly apparent for today's children in eating. Most 1-year-olds grab food in their hands, and they prefer finger foods—sandwiches, chips, carrots, cookies. Indeed, many very young children eat spaghetti, or ice cream, or mashed potatoes with their hands, despite the obvious difficulties.

# Developing Motor Skills

Every child can do more with each passing year. These examples detail what one child might be expected to accomplish from ages 2 to 6. But each child is unique, and much depends on culture, practice, and maturity.

**SKILLS**

**AVERAGE HEIGHT IN INCHES**
**BOYS 45.5    GIRLS 45.0**

Draw and paint recognizable images
Write simple words
Read a page of print
Tie shoes
Catch a small ball

**6 years**

Jose Luis Pelaez Inc/Getty Images

**BOYS 43.0    GIRLS 42.5**

Skip and gallop in rhythm
Clap, bang, sing in rhythm
Copy difficult shapes and letters
Climb trees, jump over things
Use a knife to cut
Wash face, comb hair

**5 years**

Ramona Heim/Shutterstock.com

**BOYS 40.5    GIRLS 40.0**

Catch a beach ball
Use scissors
Hop on either foot
Feed self with fork
Dress self
Copy most letters
Pour juice without spilling
Brush teeth

**4 years**

naluwan/Shutterstock.com

**BOYS 37.5    GIRLS 37.0**

Kick and throw a ball
Jump with both feet
Pedal a tricycle
Copy simple shapes
Walk down stairs
Climb ladders

**3 years**

Nejron Photo/Shutterstock.com

**BOYS 34.1    GIRLS 33.5**

Run without falling
Climb out of crib
Walk up stairs
Feed self with spoon
Draw spirals

**2 years**

Artem Efimov/Shutterstock.com

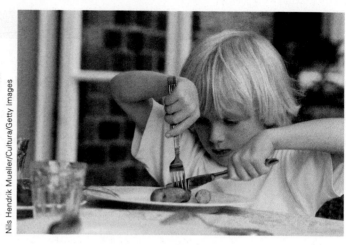

**Same Situation, Far Apart: Finger Skills**
Children learn whatever motor skills their culture teaches. Some master chopsticks, with fingers to spare; others cut sausage with a knife and fork. Unlike these children in Japan *(above left)* and Germany *(above right)*, some never master either, because about one-third of adults worldwide eat directly with their hands.

Gradually, however, they learn to use spoons, and then forks, and eventually knives. This is culture-specific. Asian 4-year-olds master chopsticks, unlike many 40-year-olds in North America.

Other fine motor skills are gradually developed. Young children try to mash a puzzle piece into a space, not only because their spatial visualization is immature but also because their fingers are not yet adept at rotation. That's why many puzzles for young children have wooden pieces with knobs for easier manipulation.

Sewing, knitting, drawing, buttoning, and much more take years to master. Ideally, equipment for children takes skill immaturity into account. That's why shoes are Velcro or slip-on.

Gender differences are evident; girls master fine motor skills earlier than boys. One reason is maturation: Girls are ahead of boys, evident in baby teeth eruption and word pronunciation. But another reason is practice: Girls are more often given sewing cards or dolls with clothes that require fine motor skills.

---

### WHAT HAVE YOU LEARNED?

1. Why is myelination important for thinking and motor skills?

2. How does brain maturation affect impulsivity and perseveration?

3. When is being left-handed an asset, and when is it a liability?

4. How do stress hormones affect brain development?

5. What factors help children develop their gross motor skills?

6. What factors help children develop their fine motor skills?

---

## Harm to Children

The goal of our study is for everyone to develop their full potential lifelong. All cultures cherish the young. Communities provide education, health care, and playgrounds; parents, grandparents, and strangers of every income, ethnicity, and nation seek to protect children while fostering their growth.

Nevertheless, more children are harmed by deliberate or accidental violence, by acts of commission or omission (action or neglect), than from disease. In the United States, almost four times as many 1- to 4-year-olds die of accidents than of cancer, which is the leading cause of disease death during these years (the numbers in one recent year were 1,267 and 325, respectively) (Kochanek et al., 2019).

**Same Situation, Far Apart: Keeping Everyone Safe** Preventing child accidents requires action by both adults and children. In the United States *(above left)*, adults passed laws and taught children to use seat belts—including this boy who buckles his stuffed companion. In France *(above right)*, teachers stop cars while children hold hands to cross the street—each child keeping his or her partner moving ahead.

## Avoidable Injury

Worldwide, injuries that could have been prevented cause millions of premature deaths. Not until age 40 does any specific disease overtake accidents as a cause of mortality.

In some nations, malnutrition, malaria, and other infectious diseases *combined* cause more infant and child deaths than injuries do, but those nations also have high rates of child accidents. For example, southern Asia and sub-Saharan Africa have the highest rates of child motor-vehicle deaths, even though they have fewer cars per person (World Health Organization, 2015). Most children who die are pedestrians, or passengers—with no helmets—on motorcycles.

## Age-Related Dangers

When accidents occur, 2- to 6-year-olds are more often seriously hurt than 6- to 10-year-olds. Why are they so vulnerable?

Immaturity of the prefrontal cortex makes young children impulsive; they plunge into danger. Unlike infants, their motor skills allow them to run, leap, scramble, and grab in a flash, before a caregiver can stop them. Their curiosity is boundless; their impulses uninhibited; their analysis limited.

Meanwhile, adults overestimate what children understand (Morrongiello, 2018). Parents teach not to run with scissors, for example, and their children can repeat that rule. They obey when the parents are nearby. Those same parents think that their children know the reason for that rule—but most do not. A child who suddenly feels angry may deliberately break a rule—unaware of the danger. Children are infamous for playing with fire, and then trying to put a fire out themselves if it gets out of hand.

Parents think they can predict what hazards will be attractive to their children, yet "young children routinely do unpredictable things that lead to injuries" (Morrongiello, 2018, p. 218). A child who has never seemed interested in, for instance, the kitchen knife rack might one day carve, cut, or stab, never having learned that knives can be dangerous. I did exactly that when I was learning to write: One of my parents' cherished coffee tables had "KATL" carved in it.

Almost all young children do something that they know is forbidden and hide it from their parents. This could be quite harmless, such as hiding broccoli in their napkin or sweeping up shards of the glass that should have stayed on the shelf. But, it could also be dangerous: Children run away and get lost or swallow pills but never tell their parents that they feel sick.

Age-related trends are apparent. Falls are more often fatal for the youngest (under 24 months) and oldest (over 80 years) people; 1- to 4-year-olds have high rates of poisoning and drowning; motor-vehicle deaths peak from age 15 to 25.

Generally, as income falls, accident rates rise, but not for every cause. In the United States, wealthier young children drown in swimming pools six times more often than children and adults who are low SES. Usually the deadly pool is in their own backyard, a luxury few low-income children enjoy. Fire, however, is more likely to kill the youngest, poorest children, as their homes have fewer smoke alarms and sprinkler systems.

## Injury Control

Instead of using the term *accident prevention*, public health experts prefer **injury control** (or **harm reduction**). Consider the implications. *Accident* implies that an injury is random, unpredictable; if anyone is at fault, it's a careless parent or an accident-prone child. Instead, *injury control* suggests that the impact of an injury can be limited, and *harm reduction*, that harm can be minimal.

If young children are allowed to play to develop their skills, minor mishaps (scratches and bruises) are bound to occur. As already explained, children benefit from play. A child with no scrapes may be overprotected.

However, playing children need protection. Serious injury is unlikely if a child falls on a safety surface instead of on concrete, if a car seat and airbags protect the body in a crash, if a bicycle helmet cracks instead of a skull, or if swallowed pills come from a tiny bottle. Reducing harm requires effort from professionals and parents, as I know from my own experience (see A Case to Study).

Less than half as many 1- to 4-year-olds in the United States were fatally injured in 2020 as in 1980, thanks to laws that limit poisons, prevent fires, and regulate cars. Control has not yet caught up with newer hazards, however.

For instance, many new homes in California, Florida, Texas, and Arizona have swimming pools: In those states, drowning is a leading cause of child death. As for poisons, children under age 5 are now less often poisoned from prescribed medicines and more often poisoned by cosmetics, recreational drugs, or personal care products (deodorant, hair colorant, etc.) (Mowry et al., 2015).

## Prevention

Prevention begins long before any particular child, parent, or legislator does something foolish. Unfortunately, few people notice injuries and deaths that did *not* happen. Scientists analyze data, however, and have learned what prevention succeeds. That has reduced accidental deaths dramatically.

### Levels of Prevention

Three levels of prevention apply to every health and safety issue.

- **Primary prevention** considers the overall conditions that affect the likelihood of harm. Laws and customs are crucial to reduce injury for people of every age.

**Especially for Urban Planners** Describe a neighborhood park that would benefit 2- to 5-year-olds. (see response, page 227)

**injury control/harm reduction** Practices that are aimed at anticipating, controlling, and preventing dangerous activities; these practices reflect the beliefs that accidents are not random and that injuries can be made less harmful if proper controls are in place.

**primary prevention** Actions that change overall background conditions to prevent some unwanted event or circumstance, such as injury, disease, or abuse.

## "My Baby Swallowed Poison"

Many people think that the way to prevent injury to young children is to educate parents. However, public health research finds that laws are more effective than education, especially if parents are overwhelmed by the daily demands of child care and money management. Injury rates rise when parents have more than one small child, and not enough money.

For example, thousands of lives have been saved by infant car seats. However, before the law required it, few parents voluntarily installed car seats. Research has found that parents are more likely to use car seats if they are given them to take their newborn home from the hospital, and if an expert installs the seat and shows the parents how to use it—not simply tells them or makes them watch a video (Tessier, 2010). New laws mandating car seats and new programs at hospitals have had an effect. In 2017, in the entire United States, only 81 infant passengers died in car accidents, about one-sixth the number 15 years earlier (Insurance Institute for Highway Safety, 2019).

The research concludes that motivation and education help, but laws mandating primary prevention are more effective. I know this firsthand. Our daughter Bethany, at age 2, climbed onto the kitchen counter to find, open, and swallow most of a bottle of baby aspirin. Where was I? In the next room, nursing our second child and watching television. I did not notice what Bethany was doing until a commercial.

Bethany is alive and well today, protected by all three levels of prevention. Primary prevention included laws limiting the number of baby aspirin per container; secondary prevention included my pediatrician's written directions when Bethany was a week old to buy syrup of ipecac; tertiary prevention was my phone call to Poison Control.

I told the helpful stranger who answered the phone, "My baby swallowed poison." He calmly asked me a few questions and then advised me to give Bethany ipecac to make her throw up. I did, and she did.

That ipecac had been purchased two years before, when I was a brand-new mother and ready to follow every bit of my pediatrician's advice. If the doctor had waited until Bethany was able to climb before recommending it, I might not have followed his advice, because by then I had more confidence in my ability to prevent harm.

I still blame myself, but I am grateful for all three levels of prevention that protected my child. In some ways, my own education helped avert a tragedy. I had chosen a wise pediatrician; I knew the number for Poison Control (FYI: 1-800-222-1222). (Ipecac is no longer recommended for inducing vomiting after swallowing poison; call Poison Control for current recommendations.)

As I remember all the mistakes I made in parenting, I am grateful for every level of prevention.

---

- **Secondary prevention** is more targeted, averting harm in high-risk situations or for vulnerable individuals.
- **Tertiary prevention** begins after an injury has already occurred, limiting damage.

Tertiary prevention is the most visible, but primary prevention is the most effective. Much of the research has focused on sports injuries among older children and adults (Emery, 2018), but the same principles apply at every age.

An example comes from data on motor-vehicle deaths. As compared with 50 years ago, far more cars are on the road, but the rate of children killed by cars is only one-fourth of what it was (Centers for Disease Control and Prevention, 2018) (see **Figure 8.1**). How does each level of prevention contribute?

*Primary prevention* includes sidewalks, pedestrian overpasses, streetlights, and traffic circles. Cars have been redesigned (e.g., better headlights, windows, and brakes), and drivers' competence has improved (e.g., stronger penalties for drunk driving). Reduction of traffic via improved mass transit provides additional primary prevention.

*Secondary prevention* reduces danger in high-risk situations. Crossing guards and flashing lights on stopped school buses are secondary prevention, as are salt on icy roads, warning signs before blind curves, speed bumps, and walk/don't walk signals at busy intersections. Laws require safety seats and belt for child passengers, and design improvements are evident every year.

**secondary prevention** Actions that avert harm in a high-risk situation, such as stopping a car before it hits a pedestrian.

**tertiary prevention** Actions, such as immediate and effective medical treatment, that are taken after an adverse event (such as illness or injury) and that are aimed at reducing harm or preventing disability.

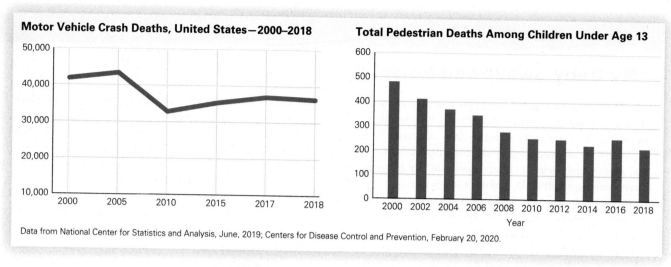

**Motor Vehicle Crash Deaths, United States—2000–2018**

**Total Pedestrian Deaths Among Children Under Age 13**

Data from National Center for Statistics and Analysis, June, 2019; Centers for Disease Control and Prevention, February 20, 2020.

**FIGURE 8.1**

**No Matter What Statistic** Motor-vehicle fatalities of pedestrians, passengers, and drivers, from cars, trucks, and motorcycles, for people of all ages, were all lower in 2018 than in 2000, a dramatic difference since the population had increased by a third and the number of cars increased as well. Proof could be shown in a dozen charts, but here is one of the most telling: deaths of child pedestrians. All three levels of prevention—in roads, cars, drivers, police, care-givers, and the children themselves—contributed to this shift.

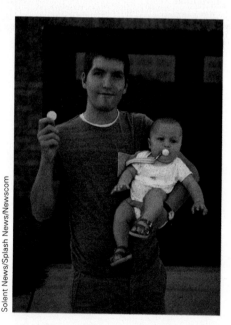

Solent News/Splash News/Newscom

**Forget Baby Henry?** Infants left in parked cars on hot days can die from the heat. Henry's father invented a disc to be placed under the baby that buzzes his cell phone if he is more than 20 feet away from the disc. He hopes all absent-minded parents will buy one.

Finally, *tertiary prevention* reduces damage after an accident. Examples include speedy ambulances, efficient emergency room procedures, effective follow-up care, and laws against hit-and-run drivers, all of which are better than decades ago. Medical personnel speak of the *golden hour*, the hour following an accident in which a victim should be treated. Of course, there is nothing magical about 60 minutes in contrast to 61 minutes, but the faster an injury victim reaches a trauma center, the better the chance of recovery (Schroeder et al., 2019).

The child death rate is lower for other reasons, as well. Air pollution has been reduced, so fewer children die of asthma. Poison control is more readily available, so fewer children die of swallowing chemicals. And many pesticides are banned from home use, so fewer children swallow them.

A most dramatic advance in harm prevention has been in accidental firearm death. In 1970, that rate was 10 per million children ages 1 to 14; in 2015, the rate was half that (National Center for Health Statistics, 2017), even though more guns had been sold.

Evidence matters. It has led to community awareness and prevention. Children are no less curious than they were, and guns are no less common. Indeed, "the civilian gun stock has roughly doubled since 1968, from one gun per every two persons to one gun per person" according to a 2012 report to the U.S. Congress (Krouse, 2012, p. 9). However, gun safety has improved: Pediatricians advise parents to hide and lock their guns, so only half as many children die of gun deaths.

The focus of this chapter is on the body, so we consider physical injury, not intellectual growth. However, pollutants in air and water, and chemicals in household products and food, may impair the brain while having no impact on the body. This is particularly true in infancy and childhood, but it continues lifelong (Babadjouni et al., 2017).

No one can prevent all harm, and government regulations are notoriously slow. The entire community needs to understand harm prevention, to protect every child. Prevention may be costly, and some efforts are not effective, which makes this topic important for every developmentalist. Unless the research is understood by everyone, thousands of children suffer. Lead is a sobering example. See A View from Science.

# Lead in the Environment

The need for scientists to understand the impact of various pollutants in the air, water, and food for children is particularly apparent in one sad example. Lead was recognized as a poison a century ago (Hamilton, 1914). The symptoms of *plumbism*, as lead poisoning is called, were obvious—intellectual disability, hyperactivity, and even death if the level reached 70 micrograms per deciliter of blood.

The lead industry defended the heavy metal. Correlation is not causation, they argued. Low-income children (who often had high lead levels) had lower IQs because of third variables, such as malnutrition, inadequate schools, and parents who let their children eat flaking chips of lead paint (which tastes sweet). This made sense to some developmental psychologists (Scarr, 1985) and, I confess, to me in the first edition of my textbook (Berger, 1980).

Lead remained a major ingredient in paint (it speeds drying) and in gasoline (it raises octane) for most of the twentieth century. Finally, chemical analyses of blood and teeth, with careful longitudinal and replicated research, proved that lead in dust and air (not just in eating paint chips) was indeed poisoning children (Needleman et al., 1990; Needleman & Gatsonis, 1990).

The United States banned lead in paint (in 1978) and automobile fuel (in 1996). The blood level that caused plumbism was set at 40 micrograms per deciliter, then 20, and then 10. Danger is now thought to begin at 5 micrograms, but no level has been proven to be risk-free (MMWR, April 5, 2013). Lead is especially destructive of fetal, infant, and young child brains (Hanna-Attisha et al., 2016).

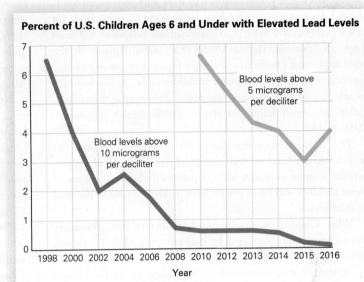

Percent of U.S. Children Ages 6 and Under with Elevated Lead Levels

Blood levels above 5 micrograms per deciliter

Blood levels above 10 micrograms per deciliter

Year

Data from Child Trends Data Bank, 2015; Centers for Disease Control and Prevention, 2018.

**FIGURE 8.2**

**Dramatic Improvement in a Decade** When legislators finally accepted the research establishing the damage from lead in paint, gasoline, and water, they passed laws that helped to make it exceedingly rare for any child to die or suffer intellectual disability because of plumbism. Before 2012, 10 micrograms per deciliter of blood was thought to be completely safe; now less than 1 child in 200 tests at that level, and even 5 micrograms per deciliter alerts pediatricians and parents to find the source. These national data make the tragedy in Flint, Michigan, especially shocking.

Cecil KM, Brubaker CJ, Adler CM, Dietrich KN, Altaye M, et al. (2008) Decreased Brain Volume in Adults with Childhood Lead Exposure. PLoS Med 5(5): e112. doi:10.1371/journal.pmed.0050112

**Toxic Shrinkage** This composite of 157 brains of adults who, as children, had high lead levels in their blood shows reduced volume. The red and yellow hot spots are all areas that are smaller than areas in a normal brain. No wonder lead-exposed children have multiple intellectual and behavioral problems.

Regulation has made a difference: The percentage of U.S. 1- to 5-year-olds with more than 5 micrograms of lead per deciliter of blood was 8.6 percent in 1999–2001, 4.1 percent in 2003–2006, 2.6 percent in 2007–2010, and less than 1 percent in 2010–2014 (Raymond & Brown, 2017) (see **Figure 8.2**).

Prevention matters. Many parents now know to wipe window ledges clean, avoid child exposure to construction dust, test drinking water, discard lead-based medicines and crockery (available in some other nations), and prevent children from eating chips of lead-based paint. A new measure is to make sure that children drink milk, since dairy products eliminate lead from the body (Kordas et al., 2018).

However, private actions alone are not sufficient to protect health. Developmentalists note many examples when blaming parents (for obesity, injury, abuse, low achievement, high blood pressure, neglect, and so on) distracts from blaming industries, laws, or the wider community.

A stark example occurred in Flint, Michigan, where in April 2014 cost-saving officials (appointed by the state to take over the city when the tax base shrunk as the auto industry left) changed the municipal drinking water from Lake Huron to the Flint River. That river contained chemicals from industrial waste that increased lead leaching from old pipes, contaminating tap water for drinking and for mixing infant formula.

The percent of young children in Flint with blood lead levels above 5 micrograms per deciliter doubled in two years, from 2.4 to 4.9 percent, and more than tripled in one neighborhood from 4.6 to 15.7 percent (Hanna-Attisha et al., 2016). Apparently, the state-appointed emergency manager focused on saving money, ignoring possible brain damage to children who, unlike him, are mostly low-income African Americans. This oversight has been called an "abject failure to protect public health" (Bellinger, 2016, p. 1101).

The consequences may harm these children lifelong, not only in their education but also in their activity level (hyperactivity is more common in lead-poisoned children). Some of those children will be in prison later in life because of the lead in their brains.

Why? Children in prison, not bureaucrats? Yes. Teenagers whose brains were damaged by lead are more likely to commit violent crimes than other teenagers.

At least that is what epidemiology suggests. In the United States, about 15 years after the sharp decline in blood lead levels in young children, the rates of violent crimes committed by teenagers and young adults fell sharply (Nevin, 2007).

Research in Canada, Germany, Italy, Australia, New Zealand, France, and Finland finds the same trends. Those nations that were earlier to legislate against lead had earlier crime reductions, about 20 years after the new laws. Research in many nations finds that blood lead levels predict attention deficits, school suspensions, and aggression (Amato et al., 2013; Goodlad et al., 2013; Nkomo et al., 2018).

Not surprisingly, some people think that connecting crime reduction to legislation to reduce lead is unfair, since other factors—fewer unwanted births, improved law enforcement, better education among them—have also reduced crime. But scientists in Sweden, where meticulous longitudinal research is possible, recently concluded that reduced lead levels in children directly produced a reduction of all crimes by 7 to 14 percent (Grönqvist et al., 2014).

There is now no doubt that lead, even at low levels, harms a child's brain. That makes the Flint tragedy more troubling. Developmentalists have known about the dangers of lead for decades. Why didn't the Michigan administrator know better?

---

**child maltreatment** Intentional harm to, or avoidable endangerment of, anyone under 18 years of age.

**child abuse** Deliberate action that is harmful to a child's physical, emotional, or sexual well-being.

# Child Maltreatment

Accidental deaths are common worldwide, but the data reveal a related problem. Many children are harmed, not accidentally but deliberately. Indeed, in recent years, almost as many 1- to 4-year-old U.S. children have been murdered as have died of cancer. (In 2017, the numbers were 303 and 325; see **Figure 8.3**.)

## In the Past 50 Years

Childhood disease deaths have plummeted because of immunization and nutrition, but childhood maltreatment death rates have not decreased. We need to understand maltreatment in order to prevent it.

Until about 1960, people thought child abuse was rare and consisted of a sudden attack by a disturbed stranger, usually a man. Today we know better, thanks to careful observation in one Boston hospital (Kempe & Kempe, 1978). A doctor saw injured children whose X-rays showed prior injuries and began to write about "battered child syndrome."

Maltreatment is neither rare nor sudden, and 90 percent of perpetrators are one or both of the child's parents—more often the mother than the father (U.S. Department of Health and Human Services, January 28, 2019). That makes it worse: Ongoing maltreatment at home, with no protector, is much more damaging than a single outside incident.

**Deaths Among U.S. 1- to 4-year-olds—1980 and 2017**

Data from National Center for Health Statistics, 2012 and 2019.

**FIGURE 8.3**

**Scientists at Work** Medical researchers have reduced child cancer deaths in half, primarily because new drugs have been discovered to destroy cancer cells. Why haven't scientists learned how to stop homicides?

## Definitions and Statistics

**Child maltreatment** now refers to all intentional harm to, or avoidable endangerment of, anyone under 18 years of age. Thus, child maltreatment includes both **child abuse**, which is deliberate action that harms a child's physical, emotional, or sexual well-being, and **child neglect**, which is failure to meet essential needs, such as for food, medical care, or education.

Neglect may be worse than abuse. It is "the most common and most frequently fatal form of child maltreatment" (Proctor & Dubowitz, 2014, p. 27). About three times as many neglect cases occur in the United States as abuse cases (U.S. Department of Health and Human Services, February 1, 2018).

Data on *substantiated* maltreatment in the United States in 2018 indicate that 62 percent of cases were neglect, 11 percent physical abuse, 2 percent psychological abuse, and 7 percent sexual abuse, and 16 percent multiple forms of abuse. Ironically, neglect is often ignored by the public, who are "stuck in an overwhelming and debilitating" concept that maltreatment always causes immediate bodily harm (Kendall-Taylor et al., 2014, p. 810).

**Substantiated maltreatment** means that a case has been reported, investigated, and verified (see **Figure 8.4**). In 2018, 677,529 U.S. children suffered substantiated maltreatment. Every year in the United States substantiated maltreatment harms more than 1 in every 100 children, aged 2 to 5 years old.

**Reported maltreatment** (technically a referral) means simply that the authorities have been informed. Since 1993, the number of children referred to authorities in the United States has ranged from about 2.7 million to 4.1 million per year, with 3.6 million in 2018 (U.S. Department of Health and Human Services, January 28, 2019).

The 5-to-1 ratio of reported versus substantiated cases occurs because:

1. Each child is counted only once, so five verified reports about a single child result in one substantiated case.
2. Substantiation requires proof. Most investigations do not find unmistakable harm or a witness.
3. Many professionals are *mandated reporters*, required to report any signs of *possible* maltreatment. About two-thirds of all reports came from professionals. An investigation usually finds no harm.
4. Some reports are "screened out" as belonging to another jurisdiction, such as the military or a Native American tribe, who have their own systems, or the report is not actually about a child victim. About one-third of all reports are screened out.
5. A report may be false or deliberately misleading (though few are) (Sedlak & Ellis, 2014).

**child neglect** Failure to meet a child's basic physical, educational, or emotional needs.

**substantiated maltreatment** Harm or endangerment that has been reported, investigated, and verified.

**reported maltreatment** Harm or endangerment about which someone has notified the authorities.

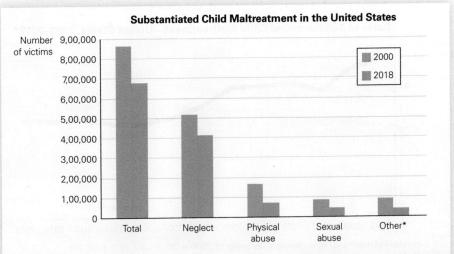

**FIGURE 8.4**
**Not Good News** It might seem to be good news that physical and sexual abuse are increasingly unusual. But the continued high rate of neglect is ominous. Adults can overcome memories of abuse, but neglect is likely to leave enduring traces on the brain.

## Frequency of Maltreatment

How often does maltreatment occur? No one knows. Not all instances are noticed, not all that are noticed are reported, and not all reports are substantiated. Part of the problem is in distinguishing harsh discipline from abuse, and a momentary lapse from ongoing neglect. If the standard were perfect parenting all day and all night from birth to age 18, as judged by neighbors and professionals, then every child is mistreated at least once. Only severe or chronic cases are tallied.

If we rely on official U.S. statistics, positive trends are apparent. Substantiated child maltreatment increased from about 1960 to 1990 but decreased from 1990 to 2010. Other sources also report declines, particularly in sexual abuse.

Perhaps national awareness has led to more effective prevention. However, trends since 2010 suggest that rates may be increasing again (see **Figure 8.5**). There are many possible explanations. The growing gap between rich and poor families is the most plausible, since poverty correlates with neglect. However, no matter what the reason, and even if rates are declining, far too many children are mistreated.

State-by-state reports raise doubt about the data. For example, the National Administration for Children and Families reports that, between 2012 and 2016, investigations increased by 70 percent in Pennsylvania but fell by 6 percent in the neighboring state of Delaware (U.S. Department of Health and Human Services, February 1, 2018). The 2016 rate of child victims was seven times higher in Massachusetts than in Virginia, 23.3 versus 3.2 per thousand children. But no one thinks children are safer in Virginia. Maybe people in Massachusetts are quicker to report harm?

How maltreatment is defined is powerfully influenced by culture (one of my students shocked me when she asked, "When is a child too old to be beaten?"). Willingness to report also varies. The United States has become more culturally diverse, and people have become more suspicious of government but also of each other. Does that reduce reporting or increase it?

From a developmental perspective, another problem is that most maltreatment occurs early in life, before children attend school, where a teacher would be required to report it. One infant in 45 is substantiated as maltreated, as is 1 preschooler in 100 (U.S. Department of Health and Human Services, January 25, 2016). Those are substantiated cases; some of the youngest victims never reach outsiders' attention.

**FIGURE 8.5**

**Still Far Too Many**  The number of substantiated cases of maltreatment of children under age 18 in the United States is too high, but there is some good news: The rate has declined significantly from its peak (15.3 per 1,000) in 1993.

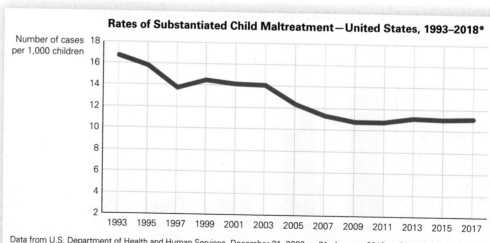

**Rates of Substantiated Child Maltreatment—United States, 1993–2018***

Number of cases per 1,000 children

Data from U.S. Department of Health and Human Services, December 31, 2000, p. 31, January, 2010, p. 34, and January 15, 2020, p. 30.

*As the text explains, none of these is proof of maltreatment, but any of them requires further investigation.

An additional problem is that some children are abused often, by people who should be caregivers not abusers. A single episode of child abuse followed by parental protection and love—never blaming the child—allows children to recover. By contrast, if one family member is abusive and another family member neglects to intervene, that is likely to cause lifelong harm.

## Warning Signs

Instead of relying on official statistics and mandated reporters, every reader of this book can recognize risk and prevent harm. Often the first sign is delayed development, such as slow growth, immature communication, lack of curiosity, or odd social interaction. These characteristics can be noticed in very young children. One factor that predicts maltreatment is insecure attachment: Efforts to improve parent–child relationships can also prevent serious abuse (Toth & Manly, 2019).

**Table 8.1** lists signs of child maltreatment, both neglect and abuse. None of these signs *proves* maltreatment, but investigation is needed whenever they occur. The opposite is also true: Some things that many young children do (not eating much dinner, crying when they must stop playing, imagining things that are not true, throwing things in anger) are common, and usually do not signify maltreatment.

Further, community standards matter. Certain customs (such as circumcision, pierced ears, and spanking) are considered abusive among some groups but not in others; their effects vary accordingly. However, if a child is fearful, easily startled by noise, defensive and quick to attack, and confused between fantasy and reality, that suggests **posttraumatic stress disorder (PTSD)**, first identified in combat veterans, then in adults who had experienced a serious accident, natural disaster, or violent crime. Recently PTSD has been recognized in maltreated children, who suffer neurologically, emotionally, and behaviorally (E. Dunn et al., 2017).

## Consequences of Maltreatment

Children suffer if they think their parents care about them less than most parents they know. If children are punished more severely, or not at all, they might feel unloved. Or if every neighbor girl has earrings, or if every boy is circumcised, a particular child might feel neglected if their parents did not follow that norm. Of course, serious abuse and gross neglect are never acceptable, but community standards matter.

**Especially for Nurses** While weighing a 4-year-old, you notice several bruises on the child's legs. When you ask about them, the child says nothing and the parent says that the child bumps into things. What should you do? (see response, page 227)

**posttraumatic stress disorder (PTSD)** An anxiety disorder that develops as a delayed reaction to having experienced or witnessed a profoundly shocking or frightening event, such as rape, severe beating, war, or natural disaster. Its symptoms may include flashbacks to the event, hyperactivity and hypervigilance, displaced anger, sleeplessness, nightmares, sudden terror or anxiety, and confusion between fantasy and reality.

### TABLE 8.1

**Signs of Maltreatment in Children Aged 2 to 10**

Injuries that are unlikely to be accidents, such as bruises on both sides of the face or body; burns with a clear line between burned and unburned skin

Repeated injuries, especially broken bones not properly tended (visible on X-ray)

Fantasy play with dominant themes of violence or sex

Slow physical growth

Unusual appetite or lack of appetite

Ongoing physical complaints, such as stomachaches, headaches, genital pain, sleepiness

Reluctance to talk, to play, or to move, especially if development is slow

No close friendships; hostility toward others; bullying of smaller children

Hypervigilance, with quick, impulsive reactions, such as cringing, startling, or hitting

Frequent absence from school

Frequent change of address

Frequent change in caregivers

Child seems fearful, not joyful, on seeing caregiver

**Line Up, Single File** These children were separated from their parents at the border between Mexico and the United States. Here, on June 22, 2018, they are in McAllen, Texas, hoping to see their parents again soon. We do not know what happened next.

⬤ **Observation Quiz** Are the older children comforting the younger ones? (see answer, page 227) ↑

The long-term effects of maltreatment depend partly on the current relationship between the adult and the punishing parent. If the grown child has a good relationship with the formerly abusive parent (more common if abuse was not chronic), who expresses regret for past behavior, then recovery is likely (Schafer et al., 2014). Abused children do not necessarily become abusive parents (Widom et al., 2015a). They may avoid the mistakes of their parents, especially if friends or partners show them a better way.

In the chilling memoir *Educated*, Tara Westover (2018) describes the mistreatment she and her five siblings endured as children. With the help of many outsiders and Brigham Young University, she recovered, but three of her siblings did not.

Even for those who recover, however, the consequences of maltreatment may last for decades (Toth & Manly, 2019). Immediate impairment is obvious, when a child is bruised, broken, afraid to talk, or failing in school. More crippling effects endure lifelong, in social skills and self-esteem.

Maltreated children tend to hate themselves and distrust everyone else. Early childhood is a particularly vulnerable time (Toth & Manly, 2019). Even if maltreatment stops at age 5, emotional problems (externalizing for the boys and internalizing for the girls) linger (Godinet et al., 2014). Adult drug abuse, social isolation, and poor health results from maltreatment decades earlier.

Hate is corrosive; love is healing. A warm and enduring friendship can repair some damage, but mistreated children typically regard other people as hostile. They become less friendly, more aggressive, and more isolated than other children.

The earlier that abuse starts and the longer it continues, the worse the children's relationships are. Physically and sexually abused children are likely to be irrationally angry, and neglected children are often withdrawn. Consequently, healthy romances and close friendships are difficult in adulthood.

Finding and keeping a job is a critical aspect of adult well-being, yet adults who were maltreated suffer in this way as well. One study carefully matched 807 children who had experienced substantiated abuse with other children of the same sex, ethnicity, and family SES. About 35 years later, when maltreatment was a distant memory, those who had been mistreated were 14 percent less likely to be employed. The researchers concluded: "Abused and neglected children experience large and enduring economic consequences" (Currie & Widom, 2010, p. 111).

In that study, women had more difficulty finding and keeping a job than men. It may be that self-esteem, emotional stability, and social skills are even more important for female employees than for male ones. That study is just one of hundreds of longitudinal studies, all of which find that maltreatment affects people decades after broken bones, or skinny bodies, or medical neglect.

## Preventing Harm

For accidents, child abuse, and child neglect, the ultimate goal is *primary prevention*, a social network of customs and supports for parents, neighbors, and professionals, so every child is safe. Neighborhood stability, parental education, income support, and fewer unwanted children reduce injury.

However, governments and private foundations are more likely to fund *secondary prevention* for high-risk families (Nelson & Caplan, 2014). The news media also focus on shocking examples of parental abuse or social worker neglect, which ignores the many ways in which families, communities, and professionals stop harm before it begins.

Secondary prevention includes spotting warning signs and intervening early, so a risky situation does not worsen. Many developmentalists believe that it is crucial to foster secure attachment. Relationship problems should be repaired before they become harmful (Toth & Manly, 2019).

Tertiary prevention limits harm after injury has occurred. This begins with reporting and then includes investigating. If abuse is substantiated, the most important step (tertiary prevention) is helping the caregiver provide better care. That may include treating addiction, assigning a housekeeper, locating family helpers, securing better living quarters, and helping the child recover, with special medical, psychological, or education assistance. In the process, the child must be protected, either in the same family or in a better one.

In every case, **permanency planning** is needed: This is planning that addresses how to nurture the child until adulthood (Scott et al., 2013). Uncertainty, moving, a string of temporary placements, and frequent changes in schools are all destructive, even when each one is well-intentioned.

When children are taken from their parents and entrusted to another adult, that is **foster care**. The other adult might be a relative, in which case it is called **kinship care**. Foster care sometimes is informal, as when a grandmother provides custodial care because the parents do not, or may result from Child Protective Services provided by the government.

Every year for the past decade in the United States, almost half a million children have been officially in foster care. At least another million are unofficially in kinship care, because relatives realize that the parents are unable or unwilling to provide good care.

Most foster children are from low-income, ethnic-minority families—a statistic that reveals problems in the macrosystem as well as the microsystem. In the United States, most foster children have physical, intellectual, and emotional problems that arose in their original families. Obviously, foster parents need much more than financial subsidies to provide good care for such children.

Sometimes, a child's best permanency plan is adoption by another family, who will provide care lifelong. However, adoption is difficult, for many reasons:

- Judges and biological parents are reluctant to release children for adoption.
- Most adoptive parents prefer infants, but few infants are available because some adults do not know how hard child care can be until they have tried, and failed, to provide for their children.
- Some agencies screen out families not headed by married, heterosexual couples.
- Some professionals insist that adoptive parents be of the same ethnicity and/or religion as the child.

As you have seen in this chapter, caring for the nutrition, brain development, and safety of a 2- to 6-year-old is not easy for any parent—biological, foster, or adoptive. Yet these years are vital, with consequences lasting for decades. This is as true for cognitive and psychosocial development as for biosocial, as the next two chapters explain.

**She Recovered and Sings** Maya Angelou was abused and neglected as a child, but she also was loved and protected by her brother and other family members. The result was extraordinary insight into the human condition, as she learned "why the caged bird sings."

**permanency planning** An effort by child-welfare authorities to find a long-term living situation that will provide stability and support for a maltreated child. A goal is to avoid repeated changes of caregiver or school, which is particularly harmful.

**foster care** A legal, publicly supported system in which a maltreated child is removed from the parents' custody and entrusted to another adult or family, who is reimbursed for expenses incurred in meeting the child's needs.

**kinship care** A form of foster care in which a relative of a maltreated child, usually a grandparent, becomes the approved caregiver.

## WHAT HAVE YOU LEARNED?

1. What can be concluded from the data on rates of childhood injury?
2. How do injury deaths compare in developed and developing nations?
3. What is the difference between primary, secondary, and tertiary prevention?
4. Why have the rates of child accidental death declined?
5. Why is reported abuse five times higher than substantiated abuse?
6. Why is neglect considered worse than abuse?
7. What are the long-term consequences of childhood maltreatment?
8. When is adoption part of permanency planning?
9. Why does permanency planning rarely result in adoption?

## SUMMARY

### Body Changes

1. Well-nourished children gain weight and height during early childhood at a lower rate than infants do. Proportions change, allowing better body control.

2. Worldwide, an increasing number of children are obese, which puts them at risk for many health problems. Further, many children have an unbalanced diet. Sugar, particularly, is harmful, reducing appetite and harming teeth.

### Brain Growth

3. The brain continues to grow in early childhood, reaching about 75 percent of its adult weight at age 2 and 90 percent by age 6. Much of the increase is in myelination, which speeds transmission of messages from one part of the brain to another.

4. Maturation of the prefrontal cortex allows more reflective, coordinated thought and memory, but this takes decades. Many young children gradually become less impulsive and less likely to perseverate.

5. Childhood trauma may create a flood of stress hormones (especially cortisol) that damage the brain and interfere with learning.

6. Gross motor skills continue to develop; clumsy 2-year-olds become 6-year-olds who move their bodies well, guided by their peers, practice, motivation, and opportunity—all varying by culture. Playing with other children develops skills that benefit children's physical, intellectual, and social development.

7. Fine motor skills are difficult to master during early childhood. Young children enjoy expressing themselves artistically, which helps them develop their body and finger control. Fortunately, self-criticism is not yet strong.

### Harm to Children

8. Accidents cause more child deaths than diseases, with young children more likely to suffer a serious injury or premature death than older children. Close supervision and public safeguards can protect young children from their own eager, impulsive curiosity.

9. In the United States, various preventive measures have reduced the rate of serious injury, and medical measures have reduced disease deaths even faster. Four times as many young children die of injuries than of cancer, the leading cause of disease death in childhood.

10. Injury control occurs on many levels, including long before and immediately after each harmful incident. Primary prevention protects everyone, secondary prevention focuses on high-risk conditions and people, and tertiary prevention occurs after an injury. All three are needed.

11. Child maltreatment includes ongoing abuse and neglect, usually by a child's own parents. In 2018, about 3.6 million cases of child maltreatment were reported in the United States; about a fifth of them were substantiated, with the annual rate of maltreatment about 1 child in 100.

12. Physical abuse is the most obvious form of maltreatment, but neglect is more common and more harmful. Health, learning, and social skills are all impeded by abuse and neglect, not only during childhood but also decades later.

13. Primary prevention is needed to stop child maltreatment before it starts. Secondary prevention should begin when someone first notices a possible problem.

14. Tertiary prevention may include placement of a child in foster care, including kinship care, or in an adoptive family. Permanency planning is required because frequent changes are harmful to children.

## KEY TERMS

myelination (p. 208)
corpus callosum (p. 208)
lateralization (p. 208)
impulse control (p. 210)
perseverate (p. 210)

injury control/harm reduction (p. 216)
primary prevention (p. 216)
secondary prevention (p. 217)
tertiary prevention (p. 217)
child maltreatment (p. 220)

child abuse (p. 220)
child neglect (p. 221)
substantiated maltreatment (p. 221)
reported maltreatment (p. 221)

posttraumatic stress disorder (PTSD) (p. 223)
permanency planning (p. 225)
foster care (p. 225)
kinship care (p. 225)

## APPLICATIONS

1. Keep a food diary for 24 hours, writing down what you eat, how much, when, how, and why. Did you eat at least five servings of fruits and vegetables, and very little sugar or fat? Did you get too hungry, or eat when you were not hungry? Then analyze when and why your food habits began.

2. Go to a playground or another place where young children play. Note the motor skills that the children demonstrate, including abilities and inabilities, and keep track of age and sex. What differences do you see among the children?

3. Ask several parents to describe each accidental injury of each of their children, particularly how it happened and what the consequences were. What primary, secondary, or tertiary prevention measures were in place, and what measures were missing?

4. Think back to your childhood and the friends you had at that time. Was there any maltreatment? Considering what you have learned in this chapter, why or why not?

## Especially For ANSWERS

**Response for Early-Childhood Teachers** (from p. 209): One solution is to remind yourself that the children's brains are not yet myelinated enough to enable them to quickly walk, talk, or even button their jackets. Maturation has a major effect, as you will observe if you can schedule excursions in September and again in November. Progress, while still slow, will be a few seconds faster.

**Response for Urban Planners** (from p. 216): The adult idea of a park—a large, grassy, open space—is not best for young children. For them, you would design an enclosed area, small enough and

with adequate seating to allow caregivers to socialize while watching their children. The playground surface would have to be protective (since young children are clumsy), with equipment that encourages motor skills. Teenagers and dogs should have their own designated areas, far from the youngest children.

**Response for Nurses** (from p. 223): Any suspicion of child maltreatment must be reported, and these bruises are suspicious. Someone in authority must find out what is happening so that the parent as well as the child can be helped.

## Observation Quiz ANSWERS

**Answer to Observation Quiz** (from p. 205): No. There are no pedals! Technically this is not a tricycle; it has four wheels. The ability to coordinate both legs follows corpus callosum development in the next few years, as explained on page 208.

**Answer to Observation Quiz** (from p. 224) Probably not. In many detention centers, children are forbidden to touch each other

except when older children must keep younger ones in line. Notice that the older boy holds the child's wrist (they are not holding hands), and the older girl is pulling the younger girl's arm back, not providing a comforting touch.

# Early Childhood: Cognitive Development

## What Will You Know?

1. Are young children selfish or just self-centered?
2. Do children get confused if they hear two languages?
3. Is it a mistake to let children play all day at preschool?

**M**y grandson, when he was 3 years old, held a large rubber ball. He told me to play basketball with him.
"We can't play basketball; we don't have a hoop," I told him.
"We can imagine a hoop," he answered, throwing the ball up.
"I got it in," he said happily. "You try."
I did.
"You got it in, too," he announced, and did a little dance.
Soon I was tired, and sat down.
"I want to sit and think my thoughts," I told him.
"Get up," he urged. "You can play basketball and think your thoughts."
He was typical. Imagination came easily to him, and he aspired to the skills of older, taller people in his culture. He thought by doing, and his language was impressive, including a sentence eight words long. But he did not yet understand that my feelings differ from his, that I would rather sit than throw a ball at an imaginary basket. He did know, however, that I usually respond to his requests.

This chapter describes these characteristics of young children—imagination, active learning, language, but also their difficulty in understanding another person's perspective. I hope it also conveys the joy of understanding how young children think. When that happens, you might do what I did—get up and play.

## Thinking During Early Childhood

You learned in Chapter 8 about the rapid advances in motor skills, brain development, and impulse control during ages 2 through 6, enabling the young child to do somersaults by kindergarten. Part of the reason this is possible is maturation of the body. Its changing proportions enable head-over-heels moves, because the legs are now much longer than the torso. And part of it is social influence. Few children do somersaults unless they have seen another child do one.

The same two forces allow the mental somersaults of early childhood. Soon you will read about the two major developmental theorists, Piaget and Vygotsky, who focused on young children. Piaget describes cognitive maturation, as children advance from preoperational thought to concrete operational thought. Vygotsky stressed the impact of social forces, as young children learn to talk, think, and explain.

But before describing the contributions of each of these theorists to childhood thinking, we note another aspect of thought that comes to the fore in early childhood.

## Executive Function

At every age, a person's ability to think depends on what has been called *executive function*, a cognitive ability that is nascent at age 2 and that continues to improve throughout life (Diamond, 2012). It is evident, and can be measured, in early childhood (Eisenberg & Zhou, 2016; Espy et al., 2016).

Executive function has been measured at every stage of life. It protects adolescents from destructive emotional outbursts (Poon, 2018), promotes coping skills in adulthood (Nieto et al., 2019), and forestalls death in old age (Reimann et al., 2018).

## Definitions

**Executive function** combines three essential abilities: (1) memory, (2) inhibition, and (3) flexibility. Each requires some further explanation.

The aspect of memory emphasized in executive function is *short-term*, or *working, memory*, which is memory for what was seen a minute ago or yesterday, or what can easily be brought to mind, not for what happened years ago. Young children who are proficient in this aspect of cognition are able to remember what they had for lunch, where they put their mittens, what they saw at the science museum.

*Inhibition* is the ability to control responses, to stop and think for a moment before acting or talking. Young children with this ability are able to restrain themselves from hitting or crying when someone else accidentally bumps them, and to raise their hands without blurting out an answer to a teacher's question.

*Flexibility* (also called *shifting*) is the ability to see things from another perspective rather than staying stuck in one idea. One example from early childhood occurs when a child wants to play with a toy that another child has. Executive function enables the child with the toy to share, and it allows the onlookers to switch to another activity or wait for a turn.

The result, as a leading expert explains, is that young children gain "core skills critical for cognitive, social, and psychological development" that allow "playing with ideas, giving a considered response rather than an impulsive one, and being able to change course or perspectives as needed, resist temptations, and stay focused" (Diamond, 2016). All this is very difficult in early childhood—and it is not easy at any point in the life span.

Developmentalists have many creative ways to measure executive function in young children. To measure memory, for instance, 3- to 5-year-olds are shown a series of barnyard animals and asked to remember them in order. For inhibition, they are asked to push a button when they see a fish but not a shark. For flexibility, they are asked to alternate stamping on a picture of a dog and one of a bone (both are presented together, again and again). Scores on all of these improve with age during early childhood (Espy, 2016).

## A Sensitive Time

It is thought that early childhood is a particularly important time to develop executive function skills. Compared to older children, 2- to 6-year-olds are more open to learning, have much to learn (remember the impulsive and perseverative responses explained in Chapter 8), and are open to suggestion (Walk et al., 2018).

Many educators and parents focus on intelligence and vocabulary, since children's minds need to be engaged, and their language must be encouraged. However, for success in kindergarten and beyond, executive function is crucial.

**executive function** The cognitive ability to organize and prioritize the many thoughts that arise from the various parts of the brain, allowing the person to anticipate, strategize, and plan behavior.

**The Joy of Rivalry** Look closely at this sister and brother in Johannesburg, South Africa. Just as 1-year-olds run as soon as they are able, siblings everywhere quarrel, fight, and compromise, ideally testing their physical and intellectual skills, which, as seems to be the case here, is fun.

Grant Difford/Greatstock/Alamy

It correlates more with brain development than scores on intelligence tests (Friedman & Miyake, 2017).

When experts study executive function in preschool children (Griffin et al., 2016), they emphasize two conclusions:

1. Executive function skills are foundational. They undergird later cognitive abilities and achievements, including in reading and math.
2. Executive function skills are not inborn; they can be taught.

How might that teaching occur? Family life and early schooling are crucial. Instead of explicit, time-limited lessons, executive-function skills should permeate the entire curriculum of a preschool. Young children need to verbalize their emotions, plan their actions, sustain activity, and work with another child or two.

One suggested activity, for example, is for two children to develop a pretend scenario together. They decide on their roles and actions (advance planning) and then carry it out, responding to their playmate's actions (flexibility). They are guided and encouraged, rarely criticized or punished.

Executive function is the product of practice, at home and school. Targeted educational programs inspired by Vygotsky (e.g., Tools of the Mind) are used in preschools (Bodrava & Leong, 2018). One aspect of those programs is that children learn to think about their thinking, and that improves their ability to learn (Marulis et al., 2020).

## Traditional Perspectives

Many cognitive psychologists now focus on executive function, particularly on efforts to advance it. The concept that a combination of memory, inhibition, and flexibility forms a foundation for learning is a useful one.

But this does not reduce the importance of the two traditional theorists, Piaget and Vygotsky, nor of the crucial roles of language development and early education. Indeed, they are basic to our understanding of the mind of the young child, as you will see. We begin with Jean Piaget, the "towering figure in the science of cognitive development throughout much of the 20th century" (Carey et al., 2015, p. 36).

## Piaget: Preoperational Thought

**preoperational intelligence** Piaget's term for cognitive development between the ages of about 2 and 6; it includes language and imagination (which involve symbolic thought), but logical, operational thinking is not yet possible at this stage.

Early childhood is the time of **preoperational intelligence**, the second of Piaget's four periods of cognitive development (described in Table 2.3 on page 41). Piaget referred to early-childhood thinking as *pre*operational because children do not yet use logical operations (reasoning processes) (Inhelder & Piaget, 1964/2013a).

## Symbolic Thought

**symbolic thought** A major accomplishment of preoperational intelligence that allows a child to think symbolically, including understanding that words can refer to things not seen and that an item, such as a flag, can symbolize something else (in this case, a country).

Preoperational children think in symbols, not just via senses and motor skills. In **symbolic thought**, an object or a word can stand for something else, including something out of sight or imagined. The rapid acquisition of vocabulary is a dramatic example of symbolic thought.

However, although vocabulary and imagination soar in early childhood, logical connections between ideas are not yet *operational*. Piaget found that young children cannot yet apply their impressive new linguistic ability to comprehend reality.

Consider how understanding the word *dog* changes over the first three levels of intelligence. During the sensorimotor level, "dog" might mean only the family dog sniffing at the child, not yet a symbol (Callaghan, 2013). By age 3, in contrast, the preoperational child can use the word *dog* as a symbol: It can refer to a remembered dog, or a plastic dog, or an imagined dog, or any new "doggie" the child sees on the street.

Nonetheless, because the child does not yet have the logic of concrete operational thought, if asked what distinguishes dogs from cats, young children mention size and coat. They cannot articulate the difference between dogs and cats, even though they do not mistake one for the other. The essence of "dogness" and "catness" is too abstract.

## Animism

Symbolic thought helps explain **animism**, the belief of many young children that natural objects (such the sun and clouds) are alive and that nonhuman animals have the same characteristics as the child. Many children's stories include animals or objects that talk and listen (Aesop's fables, *Winnie-the-Pooh, Goodnight Gorilla, The Day the Crayons Quit*). Preoperational thought is symbolic and magical, not logical and realistic.

Among contemporary children, animism gradually disappears as the mind becomes more mature, by age 10 if not earlier (Kesselring & Müller, 2011).

Disney/Pixar/Photo 12/Alamy

**All Alive** Animism and egocentrism might make a 4-year-old frightened by this scene in the movie *Toy Story 3*. Very young children have no problem believing that toys (even with three eyes) are alive and have the same emotions that they themselves do.

## Obstacles to Logic

Piaget described symbolic thought as characteristic of preoperational thought. He also noted four limitations that make logic difficult: *centration, focus on appearance, static reasoning*, and *irreversibility*.

**Centration** is the tendency to focus on one aspect of a situation to the exclusion of all others. For example, young children may insist that Daddy is a father, not a brother, because they center on the role that he fills for them. This illustrates a particular type of centration that Piaget called **egocentrism**—literally, "self-centeredness." Egocentric children contemplate the world exclusively from their personal perspective.

Egocentrism is *not* selfishness. One 3-year-old chose to buy a model car as a birthday present for his mother: His "behavior was not selfish or greedy; he carefully wrapped the present and gave it to his mother with an expression that clearly showed that he expected her to love it" (Crain, 2011, p. 133).

A second characteristic of preoperational thought is a **focus on appearance**, to the exclusion of other attributes. For instance, a girl given a short haircut might worry that she has turned into a boy. In preoperational thought, a thing is whatever it appears to be—evident in the joy young children have in wearing the hats or shoes of a grown-up, clomping noisily and unsteadily around the house.

Third, preoperational children use **static reasoning**. They believe that the world is stable, unchanging, always in the state in which they currently encounter it. Many children cannot imagine that their own parents were once children. If they are told that Grandma is their mother's mother, they still do not understand how people change with maturation. One child asked his grandmother to tell his mother not to spank him because "she has to do what her mother says."

The fourth characteristic of preoperational thought is **irreversibility**. Preoperational thinkers fail to recognize that reversing a process might restore whatever existed before. A young girl might cry because her mother put lettuce on her sandwich. She might still reject the food when the lettuce is removed because she thinks what is done cannot be undone.

**animism** The belief that natural objects and phenomena are alive, moving around, and having sensations and abilities that are human-like.

**centration** A characteristic of preoperational thought in which a young child focuses (centers) on one idea, excluding all others.

**egocentrism** Piaget's term for children's tendency to think about the world entirely from their own personal perspective.

**focus on appearance** A characteristic of preoperational thought in which a young child ignores all attributes that are not apparent.

**static reasoning** A characteristic of preoperational thought in which a young child thinks that nothing changes. Whatever is now has always been and always will be.

**irreversibility** A characteristic of preoperational thought in which a young child thinks that nothing can be undone. A thing cannot be restored to the way it was before a change occurred.

**conservation** The principle that the amount of a substance remains the same (i.e., is conserved) even when its appearance changes.

**Especially for Nutritionists** How can Piaget's theory help you encourage children to eat healthy foods? (see response, page 255)

## Conservation and Logic

Piaget reported many examples of the ways in which preoperational intelligence disregards logic. A famous series of experiments involved **conservation**, the notion that the amount of something remains the same (is conserved) despite changes in its appearance.

Suppose two identical glasses contain the same amount of milk, and the milk from one glass is poured into a taller, narrower glass. When children younger than 6 are asked whether one glass contains more or, alternatively, if both glasses contain the same amount, they say that the narrower glass (with the higher level) has more. (See **Figure 9.1** for other examples.)

All four characteristics of preoperational thought are evident in this failure to understand conservation. Young children focus (*center*) on what they see (*appearance*), noticing only the immediate (*static*) condition. They do not realize that pouring the milk back into the wider glass would re-create the level of a moment earlier (*irreversibility*).

Note that this reveals one of the key aspects of cognition that is central to executive function. Unless they are taught, children younger than 6 do not have the memory or flexibility to grasp conservation.

Piaget's original tests of conservation required children to respond verbally to an adult's questions. When scientists make tests of logic simple and playful, young children sometimes succeed, especially when they talk to each other.

This is an important lesson for teachers of young children. To teach about quantity, they must recognize the limitations of preschoolers' thinking (McCray et al., 2018). A teacher might team up two children, ask them to pour milk from one glass to another again and again, and add a stuffed animal who asks about conservation.

**Tests of Various Types of Conservation**

| Type of Conservation | Initial Presentation | Transformation | Question | Preoperational Child's Answer |
|---|---|---|---|---|
| Volume | Two equal glasses of pink lemonade. | Pour one into a taller, narrower glass. | Which glass contains more? | The taller one. |
| Number | Two equal lines of candy. | Increase spacing of candy in one line. | Which line has more candy? | The longer one. |
| Matter | Two equal balls of cookie dough. | Squeeze one ball into a long, thin shape. | Which piece has more dough? | The long one. |
| Length | Two pencils of equal length. | Move one pencil. | Which pencil is longer? | The one that is farther to the right. |

**FIGURE 9.1**

**Conservation, Please** According to Piaget, until children grasp the concept of conservation at about age 6 or 7, they cannot understand that the transformations shown here do not change the total amount of liquid, candies, cookie dough, and pencils.

## A CASE TO STUDY

### Stones in the Belly

As we were reading a book about dinosaurs, my 3-year-old grandson, Caleb, told me that some dinosaurs (*sauropods*) have stones in their bellies. It helps them digest their food and then poop and pee.

"I didn't know that dinosaurs ate stones," I said.

"They don't eat them."

"Then how do they get the stones in their bellies? They must swallow them."

"They don't eat them."

"Then how do they get in their bellies?"

"They are just there."

"How did they get there?"

"They don't eat them," said Caleb. "Stones are dirty. We don't eat them."

I changed the subject, as I knew that his mother had told him not to eat pebbles, or sand, or anything else he found on the ground.

However, at dinner he asked my daughter, "Do dinosaurs eat stones?"

"Yes, they eat stones so they can grind their food," she answered.

At that, Caleb was quiet.

In all of this, preoperational cognition is evident. Caleb is bright; he can name several kinds of dinosaurs, as can many young children.

But logic eludes Caleb. He is preoperational, not operational.

It seemed obvious to me that the dinosaurs must have swallowed the stones. However, in his static thinking, Caleb said the stones "are just there." He rejected the thought that dinosaurs ate stones because he has been told that stones are too dirty to eat.

Caleb is egocentric, reasoning from his own experience, and animistic, in that he thinks other creatures think and act as he himself does. He trusts his mother, who told him never to eat stones. Static thinking prevented him for considering my authority as his mother's mother. He was skeptical that a dinosaur would do something he had been told not to do.

Nonetheless, Caleb is curious, a hallmark of preoperational thought. My question lingered rather than being completely rejected.

Should I have expected him to tell me that I was right when his mother agreed with me? No. That would have required far more understanding of reversibility and far less egocentrism than most young children can muster.

Before age 6, children indicate via eye movements or gestures that they understand conservation, although they cannot yet put their understanding into words (Goldin-Meadow & Alibali, 2013). Conservation and many other logical ideas can be grasped bit by bit, with active, guided experience. Glimmers of understanding may be apparent in children as young as age 4.

As with infants, Piaget underestimated what young children could understand. He was right about his basic idea, however: Young children are not very logical (Lane & Harris, 2014). Their cognitive limits make smart 3-year-olds sometimes foolish, as Caleb was.

**VIDEO ACTIVITY: Achieving Conservation** focuses on the cognitive changes that enable older children to pass Piaget's conservation-of-liquid task.

## Vygotsky: Social Learning

For decades, the magical, illogical, and self-centered aspects of cognition dominated research on early-childhood thought. Scientists were awed by Piaget, who demonstrated many aspects of egocentric thought in children.

Vygotsky emphasized another side of early cognition—that each person's thinking is shaped by other people. His focus on the sociocultural context contrasts with Piaget's emphasis on the individual.

### Mentors

Vygotsky believed that cognitive development is embedded in the social context at every age (Vygotsky, 1987). He stressed that children are curious and observant of everything in their world, and are influenced by their social surroundings.

Young children are famous for their exasperating penchant to ask "why," "how," "where," and "why" again. They want to know how machines work, why weather

**Learning to Button** Most shirts for 4-year-olds are wide-necked without buttons, so preschoolers can put them on themselves. But the skill of buttoning is best learned from a mentor, who knows how to increase motivation.

⬤⬤ **Observation Quiz** Beyond the buttoning, can you see any other signs of scaffolding? (see answer, page 255) ➡

Hero Images/Getty Images

changes, where the sky ends. They seek answers from mentors, who might be parents, teachers, older siblings, or just a stranger, who reply with their own perceptions and assumptions, which they themselves were taught in childhood. Thus, according to Vygotsky, culture shapes thought.

As you remember from Chapter 2, children learn through *guided participation.* Parents are the first guides and mentors, soon joined by many others, especially in an interactive preschool (Broström, 2017).

According to Vygotsky, mentors do the following:

- Present challenges.
- Offer assistance (without taking over).
- Add crucial information.
- Encourage motivation.

Learning from mentors indicates intelligence, according to Vygotsky: "What children can do with the assistance of others might be in some sense even more indicative of their mental development than what they can do alone" (1980, p. 85).

## Scaffolding

**zone of proximal development (ZPD)** Vygotsky's term for the skills—cognitive as well as physical—that a person can exercise only with assistance, not yet independently.

**scaffolding** Temporary support that is tailored to a learner's needs and abilities and aimed at helping the learner master the next task in a given learning process.

Vygotsky believed that all individuals learn within their **zone of proximal development (ZPD)**, an intellectual arena in which new ideas and skills can be mastered. *Proximal* means "near," so the ZPD includes the ideas and skills that children are close to mastering but cannot yet demonstrate independently. Learning requires wise and willing mentors to provide **scaffolding**, or temporary support, to help children within their developmental zone (Mermelshtine, 2017).

Good mentors scaffold in many ways. They encourage children to look both ways before crossing the street (pointing out speeding trucks, cars, and buses while holding the child's hand) or let them stir the cake batter (perhaps covering the child's hand on the spoon handle, in guided participation). Scaffolding might foster emotional control as well. One study encouraged children to take deep breaths, relax, and be less egocentric (Grabell et al., 2019).

Sensitive joint engagement is crucial, because "When providing scaffolding, a teacher or a peer tutor does not make the task easier but instead makes the learner's job easier by giving the child maximum support in the beginning stages and then gradually withdrawing this support as the child's mastery of a new skill increases" (Bodrava & Leong, 2018, p. 226).

Culture matters. Educators agree that book-reading is a crucial scaffold, which adults use to transmit their understanding of what children need to learn (Hoyne & Egan, 2019). Book-reading may be time to encourage questions, or, the opposite, to teach a child to listen quietly.

A study of 27 Head Start classrooms found that children's vocabulary increased when book-reading fostered teacher–student interaction, but some teachers never asked questions and others asked one every 10 seconds. The types of question also varied: Most questions had a single answer ("did the train move?"), but some encouraged dialogue ("what might happen next?") (Hindman et al., 2019).

When reading to their children, some parents emphasize how misbehavior causes problems for the book's characters; others highlight the emotions that the characters experience (Luo et al., 2014). Although every culture teaches specific behaviors, everywhere guided participation involves conversation between children and adults, not yes/no questions.

## Overimitation

Sometimes scaffolding is inadvertent, when children copy something that adults would rather the child not do. Young children curse or kick because someone showed them how.

More benignly, they imitate meaningless habits and customs, a trait called **overimitation**. Children follow mentors: They learn rituals, tool use, grammar, emotional expression. Overimitation is a "flexible and . . . highly functional phenomenon" (Hoehl et al., 2019, p. 104).

Overimitation was demonstrated in a series of experiments with 3- to 6-year-olds, 64 of them from San communities (pejoratively called "Bushmen") in South Africa and Botswana, and, for comparison, 64 from cities in Australia and 19 from aboriginal communities within Australia. Australian middle-class adults often scaffold with words and actions, but San adults rarely do. The researchers expected the urban Australian children but not the San children to follow adult demonstrations (Nielsen et al., 2014). The researchers were wrong.

In part of the study, some children watched an adult open a box, which could easily and efficiently be opened by pulling down a knob by hand. Instead, the adult waved a red stick above the box three times and used that stick to push down the knob to open the box. Then each child (one by one, so they couldn't influence each other) was given the stick and asked to open the box. No matter what their culture, they did what the adult did, waving the stick three times, not touching the knob with their hands.

Other San and Australian children did not see the demonstration. When they were given the stick and asked to open the box, they simply pulled the knob. Then they observed an adult do the stick-waving opening—and they copied those inefficient actions, even though they already knew the easy way. Children everywhere learn from others not only through explicit guidance, but also through observation.

Overimitation is universal: Young children follow what others do. They are naturally "socially motivated," which allows them to learn when adults guide them. Adults everywhere use eyes, facial expressions, and gestures to facilitate learning (Heyes, 2016).

Imitation is innate in our species. Adults enjoy transmitting knowledge, and children like imitating, as long as copying is not too difficult: They imitate adults who seem to know something, even when the adults are unaware that they are modeling (Hoehl et al., 2019; Tomasello, 2016b).

That is exactly what Vygotsky expected and explained: Children learn culture.

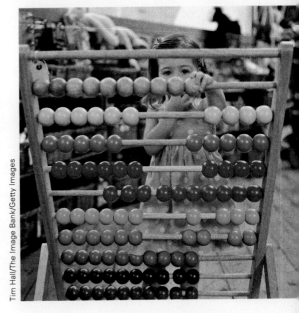

**Count by Tens** A large, attractive abacus could be a scaffold. However, in this toy store the position of the balls suggests that no mentor is nearby. Children are unlikely to grasp the number system without a motivating guide.

● **Observation Quiz** Is the girl above right-handed or left-handed? (see answer, page 255) ↑

**overimitation** When a person imitates an action that is not a relevant part of the behavior to be learned. Overimitation is common among 2- to 6-year-olds when they imitate adult actions that are irrelevant and inefficient.

**private speech** The internal dialogue that occurs when people talk to themselves (either silently or out loud).

**social mediation** Human interaction that expands and advances understanding, often through words that one person uses to explain something to another.

## Language as a Tool

Although all of the elements of a culture guide children, Vygotsky thought language was pivotal, in two ways: private speech and social mediation.

First, talking to oneself, called **private speech**, is evident when young children talk aloud to review, decide, and explain events to themselves (and, incidentally, to anyone else within earshot) (Al-Namlah et al., 2012). Almost all young children sometimes talk to themselves; about a third sing to themselves as well (Thibodeaux et al., 2019).

With time, children become more circumspect, sometimes whispering. Many adults use private speech as they talk to themselves when alone or write down ideas.

Second, language advances thinking by facilitating social interaction (Vygotsky, 2012). This **social mediation** function of speech occurs as mentors guide mentees in their zone of proximal development, learning numbers, recalling memories, and following routines. Adults sometimes are explicit ("do it this way") but often merely encourage ("good job").

## STEM Learning

A practical use of Vygotsky's theory concerns STEM (science, technology, engineering, math) education. Many adults are concerned that too few college students choose a STEM career. This is particularly true for young women and African Americans (Harris, 2019).

Developmentalists find that a person's interest in such vocations begins with learning about numbers and science (counting, shapes, fractions, molecular structure, the laws of motion) in early childhood. Spatial understanding—how one object fits with another—enhances later math skills (Verdine et al., 2017). During the preschool years, knowledge of math and physics develops month by month. Before first grade, children learn to:

- Count objects, with one number per item (called *one-to-one correspondence*).
- Remember times and ages (bedtime at 8 P.M.; a child is 4 years old).
- Understand sequence (first child wins, last child loses; play after dinner.)
- Know which numbers are greater than others (four bites are more than two).
- Understand how to make things move (toy cars, balls, game pieces).
- Appreciate temperature effects, from ice to steam.

By age 3 or 4, children are able to comprehend numbers, store memories, and recognize routines. Whether or not children actually demonstrate this comprehension depends on their families, schools, and cultures (Verdine et al., 2017).

Some 2-year-olds hear sentences such as "One, two, three, takeoff," "Here are two cookies," or "Dinner in five minutes" several times a day. They are encouraged to touch an interesting bit of moss, or are alerted to the phases of the moon outside their window, or are given large puzzle pieces that fit shapes, or hear about the relationship between pace and steepness of a hill they are climbing.

Other children never have such experiences—and they have a harder time with math in first grade, with science in the third grade, and with physics in high school. If, as Vygotsky believed, words mediate between brain potential and comprehension, STEM education begins long before formal education.

Educational software can be "a conduit for collaborative learning" (Cicconi, 2014, p. 58), as Web 2.0 programs respond to each child's abilities and needs. Several children can work together, each mentoring the others, talking aloud as the computer prompts them.

For executive function, however, interactive software needs to be carefully chosen. Video games, for instance, usually encourage rapid responses—the opposite of the planning, inhibition, and memory that are the bedrock of executive function.

Michelle Del Guercio/Science Source/Getty Images

**Future Engineers in the Bronx** Playing with Legos helps children learn about connecting shapes, which makes math and geometry easier to learn in school and makes STEM careers more likely. Once Legos were only marketed to boys, but no longer—there now are kits designed to appeal to girls.

Educators disapprove if a screen replaces human interaction (that is opposite to what Vygotsky advocates), but they also recognize that computers, carefully used (no more than an hour a day), might be learning tools, just as books might be (Alper, 2013; American Academy of Pediatrics, 2016).

A study that compared 226 children and their parents who used the "Bedtime Math" app on computers with 167 matched children found that the former had significantly higher math scores after a year (Berkowitz et al., 2015). The authors cited four reasons:

1. The app required parents and children to discuss math together.
2. The app had few distracting noises or animations.
3. The app helped math-phobic parents talk about numbers and shapes.
4. The app followed each story with questions that encouraged memory and reflection (that aids executive function).

Another reason might be when this interaction occurred. Children, and everyone else, learn best when they have a chance to "sleep on it."

## Children's Theories

Every scholar who studies learning during early childhood notices that children are eager to understand everything. Young children do more than gain words and concepts; they develop theories to help them understand and remember—theories that arise from both brain maturation and personal experience.

## Theory-Theory

In **theory-theory**, the *theory* about how children think is that they construct a *theory*. Humans always want theories (even false ones) to explain their experiences. Children ask questions, and, if they are not satisfied with the answers, they develop their own theories. For example, one child thought Grandpa died because God was lonely; another thought thunder meant God was rearranging the furniture; a third thought mountains were created to stop the world from floating away.

Children follow the same processes that scientists do: asking questions, developing hypotheses, gathering data, and drawing conclusions. As a result, "preschoolers have intuitive theories of the physical, biological, psychological, and social world" (Gopnik, 2012, p. 1623).

Of course, their cognitive methods lack the rigor of scientific experiments, but "infants and young children not only detect statistical patterns, they use those patterns to test hypotheses about people and things" (Gopnik, 2012, p. 1625). Their conclusions are not always correct: Like all good scientists, they allow new data to promote revision, although, also like all humans, they sometimes stick to their old theories instead of newer versions.

A leading developmentalist advocates answering children's questions with valid, research-based explanations, rather than simply smiling at their charming mistakes (Kelemen, 2019). Otherwise mistaken theories continue to prevail, even if later in high school and college, counter evidence is presented. That is how cultural assumptions, fake news, and prejudices, continue. Children theorize that what adults say and do is correct.

**theory-theory** The idea that children attempt to explain everything they see and hear by constructing theories.

> **THINK CRITICALLY:** Are you aware of any misconceptions you learned in childhood that still linger in your adult thinking?

## Theory of Mind

Mental processes—thoughts, emotions, beliefs, motives, and intentions—are among the most complicated and puzzling phenomena that humans encounter every day. Adults wonder why people fall in love with the particular persons they do, why they vote for the political leaders they choose, or why they make foolish decisions, from signing for a huge mortgage to buying an overripe cucumber.

**theory of mind** A person's theory of what other people might be thinking. In order to have a theory of mind, children must realize that other people are not necessarily thinking the same thoughts that they themselves are. That realization seldom occurs before age 4.

**LaunchPad**
macmillan learning

**VIDEO: Theory of Mind: False-Belief Tasks** demonstrates how children's theory of mind develops with age.

**FIGURE 9.2**

**Better with Age?** Could an obedient and honest 3-year-old become a disobedient and lying 5-year-old? Apparently yes, as the proportion of peekers and liars in this study more than doubled over those two years. Does maturation make children more able to think for themselves or less trustworthy?

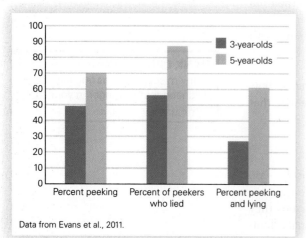

Data from Evans et al., 2011.

Children are likewise puzzled about a playmate's anger, a sibling's generosity, or an aunt's too-wet kiss.

To know what goes on in another's mind, people develop a *folk psychology*, which includes ideas about other people's thinking, called **theory of mind**. Theory of mind is an emergent ability, slow to develop but evident in most children by age 4 (Carlson et al., 2013).

Some aspects of theory of mind develop sooner than others. Longitudinal research finds that typical 2-year-olds do not know that other people think differently than they do, but 6-year-olds have a well-developed theory of mind (Wellman et al., 2011).

Part of theory of mind is understanding that someone else might have a mistaken belief. For example, a child watches a puppet named Max put a toy dog into a red box. Then Max leaves and the child sees the dog taken out of the red box and put in a blue box.

When Max returns the child is asked, "Where will Max look for the dog?" Without a theory of mind, most 3-year-olds confidently say, "In the blue box"; most 6-year-olds correctly say, "In the red box."

Theory of mind actually develops gradually, progressing from knowing that someone else might have different desires (at about age 3) to knowing that someone might hide their true feelings (about age 6). Culture, age, and experience all matter. The most notable variations, however, are neurological, not cultural: Children who are deaf or have autism spectrum disorder are remarkably slow to develop theory of mind (Peterson & Wellman, 2019).

The development of theory of mind can be seen when young children try to escape punishment by lying. Their faces often betray them: worried or shifting eyes, pursed lips, and so on. Parents sometimes say, "I know when you are lying," and, to the consternation of most 3-year-olds, parents are usually right.

In one experiment, 247 children, aged 3 to 5, were left alone at a table that had an upside-down cup covering dozens of candies (Evans et al., 2011). The children were told *not* to peek, and the experimenter left the room.

For 142 children (57 percent), curiosity overcame obedience. They peeked, spilling so many candies onto the table that they could not put them back under the cup. The examiner returned, asking how the candies got on the table. Only one-fourth of the participants (more often the younger ones) told the truth (see **Figure 9.2**).

The rest lied, and their skill at lying increased with their age. The 3-year-olds typically told hopeless lies (e.g., "The candies got out by themselves"); the 4-year-olds told unlikely lies (e.g., "Other children came in and knocked over the cup"). Some of the 5-year-olds, however, told plausible lies (e.g., "My elbow knocked over the cup accidentally").

Another study, this one of prosocial lies (saying that a disappointing gift was appreciated) found that children who were advanced in theory of mind and in executive function were also better liars, able to stick to the lie that they liked the gift (S. Williams et al., 2016). The ability to deceive advances year by year and correlates with theory of mind and executive function (Heyman et al., 2019).

## Brain and Context

Evidence for crucial brain maturation comes from other research on the same 3- to 5-year-olds whose lying was studied. The children who were asked to say "day" when they saw a picture of the moon and "night" when they saw a picture of the sun needed to inhibit their automatic reaction. Their success indicated executive function, which correlated with maturation of the prefrontal cortex. That maturation depends not only on time but also on context, as Inside the Brain explains.

## INSIDE THE BRAIN

# The Role of Experience

Why do executive control, concrete operational thought, social interaction, and even lying improve with age? There are many factors, of course, but developmentalists increasingly recognize the crucial maturation of the prefrontal cortex. With modern neuroscience, this can be traced quite precisely: A notable advance in all of these abilities occurs between ages 4 and 5, probably because the prefrontal cortex matures markedly at this point (Devine & Hughes, 2014).

Children who are slow in language development are also slow in theory of mind, a finding that makes developmentalists suggest that underlying deficits—genetic or neurological—may be crucial for both. Remember the plasticity of the brain: The early years may be particularly important for neurological control.

In studies of adults as well, many brain regions are involved in theory of mind and much depends on past history and context (Preckel et al., 2018). Developmentalists suggest that when a young child is slow in language learning, in addition to targeted work on vocabulary, articulation, and so on, therapists and teachers need to work on executive function (Nilsson & de López, 2016).

Social interactions with other children promote brain development, advancing both theory of mind and executive function. This is especially evident when those other children are siblings of about the same age (McAlister & Peterson, 2013). As one expert in theory of mind quipped, "Two older siblings are worth about a year of chronological age" (Perner, 2000, p. 383).

Indeed, many studies have found that a child's ability to develop theories correlates with neurological maturation, which also correlates with advances in executive processing—the reflective, anticipatory capacity of the mind (Baron-Cohen et al., 2013; Mar, 2011). Detailed studies find that theory of mind activates several brain regions (Koster-Hale & Saxe, 2013).

This makes sense, as theory of mind is a complex ability that humans develop in social contexts, so it is not likely to reside in just one neurological region. Brain research finds that, although each cognitive ability arises from a distinct part of the brain, experience during childhood advances neurological coordination.

Remember that experience strengthens neuronal connections. This is true not only within each neuron and the dendrites reaching another neuron but also in regions of the brain. Thus, while theory of mind promotes empathy in one brain region, and executive function promotes flexibility and memory in another, the prefrontal cortex is able to coordinate the two (Wade et al., 2018).

That is why a correlation is found between theory of mind and executive function. As a child advances in one, that child also advances in the other. Repeated coordination in the brain allows the child, for instance, to comfort a sad friend in exactly the way that sad friend is best comforted.

Even when compared to other children who were the same age, those who failed the day–night tests typically told impossible lies. Their age-mates who were higher in executive function told more plausible lies (Evans et al., 2011).

Does the crucial role of neurological maturation make culture and context irrelevant? Not at all: Nurture is always important. The reason that formal education traditionally began at about age 6 is that by the end of early childhood, maturation of the prefrontal cortex allows sustained attention. Some children are slower in this aspect of brain development (note that ADHD refers to an *attention deficit*), but for everyone experiences before age 6 advance brain development and prepare children for formal education (Blair & Raver, 2015).

Some helpful experiences before age 6 occur naturally: Children develop theory of mind in talking with adults and in playing with other children. Games that require turn-taking encourage memory and inhibitory control, two crucial components of executive control. In daily life, as brothers and sisters argue, agree, compete, and cooperate, and as older siblings fool younger ones, it dawns on 3-year-olds that not everyone thinks as they do, a thought that advances theory of mind.

By age 5, children have learned how to persuade their younger brothers and sisters to give them a toy. Meanwhile, younger siblings figure out how to gain sympathy by complaining that their older siblings have victimized them. "Who started it?" is the wrong question.

## Language Learning

Learning language is often considered the premier cognitive accomplishment of early childhood. Two-year-olds use short, telegraphic sentences ("Want cookie," "Where Daddy go?"), omitting adjectives, adverbs, and articles. By contrast, 5-year-olds seem to be able to say almost anything (see At About This Time), using every part of speech. Some preschoolers understand and speak two or three languages, an accomplishment that many adults struggle for years to achieve.

### The Time for Language Learning

Brain maturation, myelination, scaffolding, and overimitation make early childhood ideal for learning language. As you remember from Chapter 1, scientists

**AT ABOUT THIS TIME**

**Language in Early Childhood**

| Approximate Age | Characteristic or Achievement in First Language |
|---|---|
| 2 years | *Vocabulary:* 100–2,000 words |
| | *Average sentence length:* 2–6 words |
| | *Grammar:* Plurals; pronouns; many nouns, verbs, adjectives |
| | *Questions:* Many "What's that?" questions |
| 3 years | *Vocabulary:* 1,000–5,000 words |
| | *Average sentence length:* 3–8 words |
| | *Grammar:* Conjunctions, adverbs, articles |
| | *Questions:* Many "Why?" questions |
| 4 years | *Vocabulary:* 3,000–10,000 words |
| | *Average sentence length:* 5–20 words |
| | *Grammar:* Dependent clauses, tags at sentence end ("... didn't I?" "... won't you?") |
| | *Questions:* Peak of "Why?" questions; many "How?" and "When?" questions |
| 6 years and up | *Vocabulary:* 5,000–30,000 words |
| | *Average sentence length:* Some seem unending ("... and ... who ... and ... that ... and ...") |
| | *Grammar:* Complex, depending on what the child has heard, with some children correctly using the passive voice ("Man bitten by dog") and subjunctive ("If I were ...") |
| | *Questions:* Some about social differences (male–female, old–young, rich–poor) and many other issues |

once thought that early childhood was a *critical period* for language learning—the *only* time when a first language could be mastered and the best time to learn a second or third one.

It is easy to understand why they thought so. Young children have powerful motivation and ability to sort words and sounds into meaning (theory-theory). That makes them impressive language learners. However, the critical-period hypothesis is false: A new language can be learned after age 6. A first language (even a sign language) is a scaffold for a new language, making learning possible (Mayberry & Kluender, 2018).

Even a first language can be learned after early childhood, although the only reason a child would not learn some language is extreme social isolation. Those few children who were so severely neglected, such as Genie who was rescued in 1970 at age 13 (Curtiss, 2014), never become proficient, although they can learn some language.

Although new language learning in adulthood is possible, it is not easy. Early childhood is a *sensitive period* for language learning—for rapidly mastering vocabulary, grammar, and pronunciation. Young children are language sponges; they soak up every verbal drop they encounter, some learning several languages.

One of the valuable (and sometimes frustrating) traits of young children is that they talk about many things to adults, to each other, to themselves, to their toys—unfazed by misuse, mispronunciation, ignorance, stuttering, and so on (Marazita & Merriman, 2010). Language comes easily, partly because preoperational children are not self-critical. Egocentrism has advantages; this is one of them.

## The Vocabulary Explosion

The average child knows about 500 words at age 2 and more than 10,000 at age 6 (Herschensohn, 2007). That's more than six new words a day.

As with many averages in development, the range is vast: The number of root words (e.g., *run* is a root word, not *running* or *runner*) that 5-year-olds know ranges from 2,000 to 6,000, with several thousand more non-root words (Biemiller, 2009). Counting a child's words is difficult, although building vocabulary is crucial (Treffers-Daller & Milton, 2013).

To understand why vocabulary is difficult to measure, consider the following: Children listened to a story about a raccoon that saw its reflection in the water. The children were asked what *reflection* means. Five of the answers:

1. "It means that your reflection is yourself. It means that there is another person that looks just like you."
2. "Means if you see yourself in stuff and you see your reflection."
3. "Is like when you look in something, like water, you can see yourself."
4. "It mean your face go in the water."
5. "That means if you the same skin as him, you blend in."

*[Hoffman et al., 2014, pp. 471–472]*

Which of the five responses indicated that the child knew what *reflection* means? None? All? Two, three, or four?

In another example, a story included "a chill ran down his spine." Children were asked what *chill* meant. One answer: "When you want to lay down and watch TV—and eat nachos" (Hoffman et al., 2014, p. 473). The child got no credit for "chill"; is that fair?

## Fast-Mapping

Children develop interconnected categories for words, a kind of grid or mental map that aids speedy vocabulary acquisition. Learning a word after one exposure

**LaunchPad**
macmillan learning

**VIDEO ACTIVITY: Language Acquisition in Young Children** features video clips of a new sign language created by deaf Nicaraguan children and provides insights into how language evolves.

Jason Lindsey/Alamy

**What Is It?** These two children at the Mississippi River Museum in Iowa might call this a crocodile, but really it is an alligator. Fast-mapping allows that mistake, and egocentrism might make them angry if someone tells them they chose the wrong name.

**fast-mapping** The speedy and sometimes imprecise way in which children learn new words by tentatively placing them in mental categories according to their perceived meaning.

is called **fast-mapping** (Woodward & Markman, 1998), because, rather than figuring out the exact definition after hearing a word used in several contexts, children hear a word once and quickly stick it into a category in their mental language grid.

Picture books offer many opportunities to advance vocabulary through scaffolding and fast-mapping. A mentor might encourage the next steps in the child's zone of proximal development, such as that tigers have stripes and leopards have spots, or, for an older child, that calico cats are almost always female and that lions with manes are always male.

This process explains children's learning of colors. Generally, 2-year-olds fast-map color names (K. Wagner et al., 2013). For instance, "blue" is used for some greens or grays. It is not that children cannot see the hues. Instead, they apply words they know to broad categories and have not yet learned the boundaries that adults use, or specifics such as chartreuse, turquoise, olive, navy. As one team of scientists explains, adults' color words are the result of slow-mapping (K. Wagner et al., 2013), which is not what young children do.

## Words and the Limits of Logic

Closely related to fast-mapping is a phenomenon called *logical extension:* After learning a word, children use it to describe other objects in the same category. One child told her father that she had seen some "Dalmatian cows" on a school trip to a farm. Instead of telling her there are no such cows, he remembered the Dalmatian dog she had petted the weekend before. He realized that she saw Holstein cows, not Jersey ones.

Bilingual children who don't know a word in the language they are speaking often insert a word from the other language, code-switching in the middle of a sentence. That midsentence switch may be considered wrong, but it is actually evidence of the child's drive to communicate. By age 5, children realize who understands which language, and they avoid substitutions when speaking to a monolingual person. That illustrates theory of mind.

Some words are particularly difficult for every child, such as, in English, *who/whom, have been/had been, here/there, yesterday/tomorrow.* More than one child has awakened on Christmas morning and asked, "Is it tomorrow yet?" A child told to "stay there" or "come here" may not follow instructions because the terms are confusing. It might be better to say, "Stay there on that bench," or "Come here to hold my hand."

All languages have difficult concepts that are expressed in words; children everywhere learn them. Abstractions are particularly difficult for preoperational children; actions are easier to understand. A hole is to dig; love is hugging; hearts beat.

## Acquiring Grammar

Remember from Chapter 6 that *grammar* includes structures, techniques, and rules that communicate meaning. Grammar is essential in speech, reading, and writing. A large vocabulary is useless unless a person knows how to put words together. Each language has its own grammar rules; that's one reason children speak in one-word sentences first.

Children apply rules of grammar as soon as they figure them out, using their own theories about how language works and their experience regarding when and how often various rules apply (Meltzoff & Gopnik, 2013). For example,

English-speaking children quickly learn to add an *s* to form the plural: Toddlers follow that rule, asking for two cookies or more blocks.

Soon children add an *s* to make the plural of words they have never heard before, even nonsense words. If preschoolers are shown a drawing of an abstract shape, told it is called a *wug*, and then shown two of these shapes, they say there are two *wugs* (Berko, 1958). Children comprehend grammar even before they use it.

Sometimes children apply the rules of grammar when they should not. This error is called **overregularization**. By age 4, many children overregularize that final *s*, talking about *foots, tooths,* and *mouses.*

This signifies knowledge, not lack of it: Many children first say words correctly (*feet, teeth, mice*), repeating what they have heard. When they are able to detect the rules of grammar, they overregularize, assuming that all constructions follow the rules (Ramscar & Dye, 2011). The child who says "I goed to the store" needs to hear "Oh, you went to the store?," not criticism.

More difficult to learn is an aspect of language called **pragmatics**—knowing which words, tones, and grammatical forms to use with whom (Siegal & Surian, 2012). In some languages, words differ when talking to someone older, or not a close friend, or when referring to maternal or paternal grandparents.

English does not make those distinctions, but pragmatics is important for early-childhood learning nonetheless. Children learn variations in vocabulary and tone depending on the context and, once theory of mind is established, on the audience.

Knowledge of pragmatics is evident when a 4-year-old pretends to be a doctor, a teacher, or a parent. Each role requires different speech. On the other hand, children often blurt out questions that embarrass their parents ("Why is that lady so fat?" or "I don't want to kiss Grandpa because his breath smells"). The pragmatics of polite speech require more social understanding than many young children possess.

## Learning Two Languages

Language-minority people (those who speak a language that is not their nation's dominant one) suffer if they are not fluent in the majority language. In the United States, non-English speakers are impaired in school achievement, self-esteem, and employment.

Some of the problem is prejudice from English speakers, who think difference means deficit, but some is directly connected to language. Fluency in English erases some liabilities; fluency in another language then becomes an asset.

Early childhood is the best time to learn languages. Neuroscience finds that if adults mastered two languages before age 6, both languages are located in the same areas of the brain with no detriment to the cortex structure (Klein et al., 2014). Being bilingual then benefits the brain lifelong, because executive function is required to inhibit one language in order to speak the other (Cargnelutti et al., 2019). Indeed, the bilingual brain may provide some resistance to Alzheimer's disease in old age (Costa & Sebastián-Gallés, 2014).

By contrast, if a new language is learned in adulthood, proper use of idioms and flawless pronunciation lag behind correct grammar and vocabulary. Thus, many immigrants speak the majority language with an accent but are proficient in comprehension and reading (difference is not deficit).

From infancy on, hearing is more acute than vocalization. Almost all young children mispronounce whatever language they speak, blithely unaware of their mistakes. They comprehend more than they say, they hear better than they speak, and they learn rapidly as long as people speak to them.

**CHAPTER APP 9**

**FaceTalker**

**IOS:**
https://tinyurl.com/y5xycx6p

**RELEVANT TOPIC:**
Language learning in early childhood

FaceTalker is a fun way for teachers to demonstrate the sounds animals make, introduce literature or poetry, and enliven lessons on basic arithmetic, ancient Egypt, music, art, and more.

**overregularization** The application of rules of grammar even when exceptions occur, making the language seem more "regular" than it actually is.

**pragmatics** The practical use of language that includes the ability to adjust language communication according to audience and context.

● **Especially for Immigrant Parents**
You want your children to be fluent in the language of your family's new country, even though you do not speak that language well. Should you speak to your children in your native tongue or in the new language? (see response, page 255)

## Language Loss and Gains

Language-minority parents want their children to master the majority language, but they have a legitimate fear called the *language shift*, when a child becomes fluent in the school language but loses their home language. Language shift occurs whenever theory-theory leads children to conclude that their first language is inferior (Bhatia & Ritchie, 2013).

Some language-minority children in Mexico shift to Spanish; some children of Canada's First Nations shift to French; some children in the United States shift to English. In China, some children shift from Cantonese or another Chinese dialect to Mandarin. Crucial is that adults speak and value both languages, and then children will do the same.

Remember that young children are preoperational: They center on the immediate status of their language (not on future usefulness or past glory), on appearance more than substance. No wonder many children shift toward the language of the dominant culture.

Since language is integral to culture, if a child is to become fluently bilingual, everyone who speaks with the child should respect both cultures, in song, books, and daily conversation. Children learn from listening and talking, so they need to hear twice as much talk to become fluent in two languages.

The same practices make a child fluently trilingual, as some 5-year-olds are. Young children who are immersed in three languages may speak all three with no accent—except the accent of their mother, father, and friends. This was evident in one 6-year-old in the United States who spoke Korean and Farsi with his two parents and English at school, each language with whomever understood it, translating and code-switching as needed (Choi, 2019). [**Developmental Link:** Bilingual education is also discussed in Chapter 12.]

## Listening, Talking, and Reading

Because understanding the printed word is crucial in the twenty-first century, a meta-analysis of about 300 studies analyzed which activities in early childhood aided reading later on. Both vocabulary and phonics (precise awareness of spoken sounds) predicted literacy (Shanahan & Lonigan, 2010). Five specific strategies and experiences were particularly effective for children of all income levels, languages, and ethnicities.

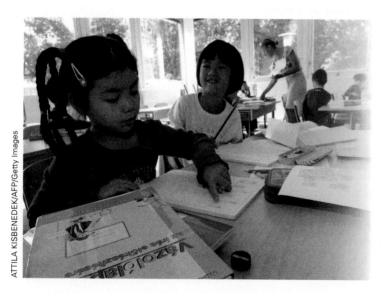

**Bilingual Learners** These are Chinese children learning a second language. Could this be in the United States? No, this is a class in the first Chinese Hungarian school in Budapest. There are three clues: the spacious classroom, the letters on the book, and the trees outside.

ATTILA KISBENEDEK/AFP/Getty Images

1. *Code-focused teaching.* In order for children to read, they must "break the code" from spoken to written words. One step is to connect letters and sounds (e.g., "A, alligators all around" or "B is for baby").
2. *Book-reading.* Vocabulary and print-awareness develop when adults read to children.
3. *Parent education.* When parents know how to encourage cognition (listening and talking), children become better readers. Adult vocabulary expands children's vocabulary.
4. *Language enhancement.* Within each child's zone of proximal development, mentors help children expand vocabulary. That requires teachers who know each child's zone and individualize conversation.
5. *Early-education programs.* Children learn from teachers, songs, excursions, and other children. (We discuss variations of early education next, but every study finds that preschools advance language acquisition.)

**WHAT HAVE YOU LEARNED?**

1. What is the evidence that early childhood is a sensitive time for learning language?
2. How does fast-mapping aid the vocabulary explosion?
3. How is overregularization a cognitive advance?
4. What in language learning shows the limitations of logic in early childhood?
5. What are the advantages of teaching a child two languages?
6. How can the language shift be avoided in children?

## Early-Childhood Schooling

Today, virtually every nation provides some public or private early-childhood education, sometimes for a privileged few, and sometimes for every child. In some nations, as much public money is invested in early education as in primary or secondary school. In other nations, no money at all is allocated for education before age 6 (Barnett et al., 2017; Blossfeld et al., 2017).

Among developed nations, the United States invests relatively little money, and it educates comparatively few children. In 2018, 44 percent of U.S. 4-year-olds and 16 percent of 3-year-old were in publicly funded preschools (Friedman-Krauss et al., 2019). By contrast, in Northern Europe, more than 95 percent of all 3- to 5-year-olds were enrolled in government-funded schools.

The reasons for the international variations are historical, economic, and political, not developmental. The evidence regarding early cognition is no longer disputed: Young children are amazingly capable and eager to learn.

### Homes and Schools

Developmental research does not translate directly into specific practices in early education, so no program can legitimately claim to follow Piaget or Vygotsky exactly (Hatch, 2012). Family practices and parent influences matter even if a young child is in a day-care center from 8 A.M. to 6 P.M., five days a week. Ideally, the teachers and parents collaborate to teach the child, but always, attachment to parents is evident.

Beyond the amazing potential of young children to learn, another robust conclusion from research on children's learning seems not yet universally understood: Quality matters.

Quality cannot be judged by the name of a program or by its sponsorship. Educational institutions for 3- to 5-year-olds are called preschools, nursery schools, day-care centers, pre-primary programs, pre-K classes, and kindergartens. Sponsors can be public (federal, state, or city), private, religious, or corporate.

Indeed, quality is notoriously difficult to judge (Votruba-Drzal & Dearing, 2017); "[B]ecause quality is hard for parents to observe, competition seems to be dominated by price" (Gambaro et al., 2014, p. 22). That is a problem, because to make a profit, programs hire fewer teachers, which means less individualized instruction. Thus, low cost indicates low quality, unless a program is subsidized by a religious, corporate, or government institution.

The converse is not true: High cost does not necessarily mean high quality. Professional assessment of quality seems inadequate (Elicker & Ruprecht, 2019; Sabol et al., 2013). However, one aspect—child–teacher interaction—correlates with learning. Effective teachers do not sit quietly. They talk, laugh, guide, and play with happy, talkative children.

**Tibet, China, India, and . . . Italy?** Over the past half-century, as China increased its control of Tibet, thousands of refugees fled to northern India. Tibet traditionally had no preschools, but young children adapt quickly, as in this preschool program in Ladakh, India. This Tibetan boy is working a classic Montessori board.

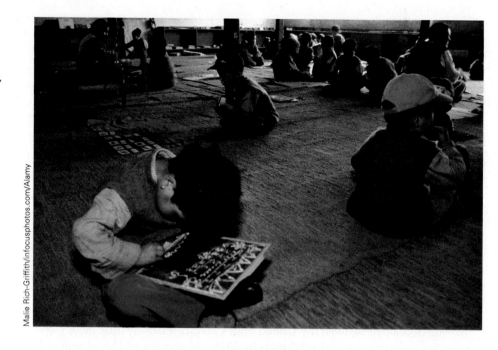

In order to sort through this variety, we consider the goals of preschools. Some aim to encourage each child's creative individuality (*child-centered*), some to prepare the child for formal education (*teacher-directed*).

## Child-Centered Programs

Many programs are called *child-centered*, or *developmental*, because they stress each child's development and growth. The emphasize "teaching the whole child," which means individualized social and emotional growth, not academics (Hyson & Douglass, 2019). Teachers in such programs believe children need to follow their own interests rather than adult directions.

For example, they agree that "children should be allowed to select many of their own activities from a variety of learning areas that the teacher has prepared" (Lara-Cinisomo et al., 2011, p. 101). The physical space and the materials (such as dress-up clothes, art supplies, puzzles, blocks, and other toys) are arranged to allow exploration.

Most child-centered programs encourage artistic expression, including music and drama (Bassok et al., 2016). Some educators believe that young children see the world more imaginatively than older people do. According to advocates of child-centered programs, this peak of creative vision should be encouraged; children need to tell stories, draw pictures, dance, and make music.

Child-centered programs are often influenced by Piaget, who emphasized that each child discovers new ideas if given a chance, or by Vygotsky, who thought that children learn from playing, especially with other children. Neither wanted children to be rushed to adulthood.

## Montessori Schools

One type of child-centered school began in the slums of Rome, Italy, in 1907, when Maria Montessori opened a nursery school (Standing, 1998). She believed that children needed structured, individualized projects to give them a sense of accomplishment. Her students completed puzzles, used sponges and water to clean tables, traced shapes, and so on.

Contemporary **Montessori schools** still emphasize individual pride and achievement, presenting many literacy-related tasks (e.g., outlining letters and looking at books) to young children. Specific materials have changed from those developed by Montessori, but the underlying philosophy is the same. Children are active learners: They do not sit quietly in groups while a teacher instructs them. That makes Montessori programs child-centered (Lillard, 2013).

Montessori schools encourage children to help other children (Lillard & Taggart, 2019). That is something Vygotsky valued as well. Children from Montessori schools seem to enjoy learning together throughout childhood, just as Vygotsky would expect.

## Reggio Emilia

Another form of early-childhood education is **Reggio Emilia**, named after the town in Italy where it began. In Reggio Emilia, children are encouraged to master skills that are not usually taught in North American schools until age 7 or so, such as writing and using tools. Although many educators admire the Reggio philosophy and practice, it is expensive to duplicate in other nations—there are few dedicated Reggio Emilia schools in the United States.

Reggio schools do not provide large-group instruction, with lessons in, say, forming letters or cutting paper. Instead, hands-on activities are chosen by each child. Drawing, cooking, and gardening are stressed. This program begins with the idea that democracy and freedom of personal expression belong in the classroom as well as in the community (McNally & Slutsky, 2017).

Learning is documented via scrapbooks, photos, and daily notes, not to measure progress but to make each child and parent proud of accomplishments. This also enhances memory, a crucial part of executive function.

Appreciation of the arts is evident. Every Reggio Emilia school originally had a studio, an artist, and space to encourage creativity (Forbes, 2012). A spacious, plant-filled playground is part of the curriculum, because "the environment is the third teacher." Big mirrors are part of the schools' décor—again, with the idea of fostering individuality and self-expression.

## Waldorf Schools

A third type of child-centered program is called a **Waldorf school**, first developed by Rudolf Steiner in Germany in 1919. The emphasis again is on creativity and individuality—with no homework, no tests, no worksheets.

As much as possible, children play outdoors; appreciation of nature is basic to Waldorf education. Children of various ages learn together, because older children serve as mentors for younger ones, and the curriculum follows the interests of the child, not the age of the child.

There is a set schedule—usually circle time in the beginning and certain activities on certain days (always baking on Tuesdays, for instance)—but children are not expected to master specific knowledge at certain ages. All child-centered schools emphasize creativity; in Waldorf schools, imagination is particularly prized (Kirkham & Kidd, 2017).

**Child-Centered Pride** How could Rachel Koepke, a 3-year-old from a Wisconsin town called Pleasant Prairie, seem so pleased that her hands (and cuffs) are blue? The answer arises from northern Italy—Rachel attended a Reggio Emilia preschool that encourages creative expression.

**Montessori schools** Schools that offer early-childhood education based on the philosophy of Maria Montessori, which emphasizes careful work and tasks that each young child can do.

**Reggio Emilia** A program of early-childhood education that originated in the town of Reggio Emilia, Italy, and that encourages each child's creativity in a carefully designed setting.

**Waldorf schools** An early-childhood education program that emphasizes creativity, social understanding, and emotional growth. It originated in Germany with Rudolf Steiner and now is used in thousands of schools throughout the world.

**CAREER ALERT**    **The Preschool Teacher**

Preschool teachers are increasingly in demand, as more and more families and communities understand how much young children can learn, and more and more mothers enter the job market. Added to that is the growing realization by public leaders that social skills and self-confidence developed in early childhood continue lifelong: A child who has good early education is likely to become an adult who is a competent and compassionate member of the community.

For developmentalists, important new insights come from neurological research, which helps preschool teachers understand what, how, and when young children learn. For example, since the auditory, visual, and motor cortexes are undergoing rapid myelination, children need to coordinate both hemispheres of brain and body by running, climbing, and balancing. But the immature motor cortex is not yet ready for writing, or tying shoelaces, or sitting quietly in one place.

Research on the developing brain finds that early childhood is the best time for learning language, so the curriculum should be language-rich—talking, listening, singing, hearing stories, making rhymes, engaging in verbal play. Young children can learn to recognize and name letters just as they learn to distinguish a baseball from a soccer ball.

Fostering control of gross motor skills may be particularly important for children who are at risk for *attention-deficit/hyperactivity disorder (ADHD)*, the label given to active children who find it especially hard

to concentrate, quietly, on one activity. Such children need to exercise their bodies, which helps their brains mature (Halperin & Healey, 2011; Hillman, 2014).

That is another reason for preschool education—children are most likely to develop their brains by playing with other children. Screen time, a common activity for children who are not in preschool, does not foster the brain regulation that children need.

Moreover, preschool teachers help children learn how to cooperate with other children, a valuable life lesson that is best learned in childhood. Thus, preschool teachers can be proud that they are nurturing compassionate, prosocial adults.

The joy and satisfaction of working with young children is crucial, because at the moment, salary and working conditions are not yet what they should be. The U.S. Bureau of Labor Statistics reports that, compared to teachers overall, preschool teachers are most in demand and least well paid—the average annual salary is below $30,000 a year. There is marked variation in state-by-state certification requirements and in neighborhood-by-neighborhood salary levels.

This is changing, but students should enter this field for emotional reasons, not financial ones. If you are interested in early-childhood education, you can find more details from a professional group called the National Association for the Education of Young Children (NAEYC).

## Teacher-Directed Programs

Teacher-directed preschools stress academics, often taught by one adult to the entire group. The curriculum includes learning the names of letters, numbers, shapes, and colors according to a set timetable; every child naps, snacks, and goes to the bathroom on schedule as well. Children learn to sit quietly and listen to the teacher. Praise and other reinforcements are given for good behavior, and time-outs (brief separation from activities) are imposed to punish misbehavior.

The goal of teacher-directed programs is to make all children "ready to learn" when they enter elementary school. For that reason, basic skills are stressed, including precursors to reading, writing, and arithmetic, perhaps through teachers asking questions that children answer together in unison. Behavior is also taught, as children learn to respect adults, to follow schedules, to hold hands when they go on outings, and so on.

Children practice forming letters, sounding out words, counting objects, and writing their names. If a 4-year-old learns to read, that is success. (In a child-centered program, this might arouse suspicion that there was too little time for play or socializing.)

Many teacher-directed programs were inspired by behaviorism, which emphasizes step-by-step learning and repetition, with reinforcement (praise, gold stars, prizes) for accomplishment. Another inspiration for these programs comes from information-processing research indicating that children who have not learned basic vocabulary and listening skills by kindergarten often fall behind in primary school. Many state legislatures mandate that preschoolers master specific concepts, an outcome best achieved by teacher-directed learning (Bracken & Crawford, 2010).

## Intervention Programs

Several programs designed for children from low-SES families were established in the United States decades ago. Typically, they combine some elements that are child-centered and some that are teacher-directed.

# Comparing Child-Centered and Teacher-Directed Preschools

Most developmentalists advocate child-centered programs (Christakis, 2016; Golinkoff & Hirsh-Pasek, 2016). They believe that from ages 3 to 6 young children learn best when they can interact in their own way with materials and ideas (Sim & Xu, 2017). On the other hand, many parents and legislators want proof that early education will improve later school achievement.

The developmental critics of teacher-directed education fear "trad[ing] emotional grounding and strong language skills known to support learning for assembly-line schooling that teaches children isolated factoids" (Hirsh-Pasek & Golinkoff, 2016, p. 1158).

As Penelope Leach wrote, "Goals come from the outside. . . . It is important that people see early learning as coming from inside children because that's what makes clear its interconnectedness with play, and therefore the inappropriateness of many 'learning goals'" (Leach, 2011, p. 17). Another developmentalist asks, "Why should we settle for unimaginative goals . . . like being able to identify triangles and squares, or recalling the names of colors and seasons" (Christakis, 2016).

Critics of child-centered programs point to data finding that children who enter kindergarten without knowing names and sounds of letters may become first-graders who cannot read (Ozernov-Palchik et al., 2017). Children are unlikely to learn literacy skills in creative play (Gellert & Elbro, 2017).

Early familiarity with numbers and shapes predicts school achievement later on. As you will soon read, Head Start programs have shifted over the past decades to be more teacher-directed, largely because national policy directives from the government have advocated that change—to the distress of many developmentalists (Walter & Lippard, 2017).

Many developmentalists resist legislative standards and academic tests for young children, arguing that social skills, emotional development, and creative play are essential but difficult to measure (Hyson & Douglass, 2019). A truly brilliant child is characterized by all the complex skills of executive function, not the easy-to-measure skills of letter recognition (Golinkoff & Hirsh-Pasek, 2016). [Children's play is discussed in Chapter 10.]

However, the divide between child-centered and teacher-directed programs goes deeper than that. It is possible that the emphasis on individual exploration is contrary to the wishes and needs of families who want their children to do as they are told, listen to adults, and master the learning tools of their culture. Indeed, child-centered education may arise from the values of middle-class, Western, European American teachers (Trawick-Smith, 2019).

Finding the right balance between formal and informal assessment, and between child-centered and teacher-directed learning, is the goal; achieving it is the challenge (see **Figure 9.3**).

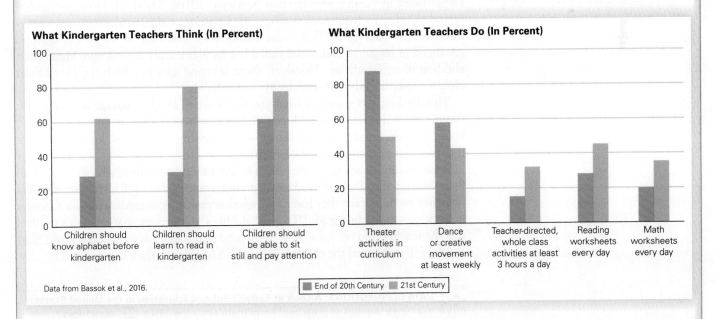

**What Kindergarten Teachers Think (In Percent)**

**What Kindergarten Teachers Do (In Percent)**

Data from Bassok et al., 2016.

■ End of 20th Century   ■ 21st Century

**FIGURE 9.3**

**Less Play, More Work** These data come from a large survey of more than 5,000 public school teachers throughout the United States. In 1998 and 2010, kindergarten teachers were asked identical questions but gave different answers. Smaller, more recent surveys suggest that these trends continue, and they now involve preschool teachers. Some even use worksheets for 3-year-olds.

**Head Start** A federally funded early-childhood intervention program for low-income children of preschool age.

## Head Start

In the early 1960s, millions of young children in the United States were thought to need a "head start" on their formal education to foster better health and cognition before first grade. Consequently, since 1965, the federal government has funded a massive program for 4-year-olds called **Head Start**.

The goals for Head Start have changed over the decades, from lifting families out of poverty to promoting literacy, from providing dental care and immunizations to teaching Standard English, from focusing on 4-year-olds to including 2- and 3-year-olds. In 2018, more than 9 billion dollars in federal funds were allocated to Head Start, which enrolled almost 1 million children.

Head Start is a massive program, but there are about 8 million 3- and 4-year-olds in the United States, which means that only about 12 percent of U.S. children that age attend Head Start. Many other children are in state or municipal programs, or, if they can afford it, private preschools. About twice as many 3- to 5-year-olds from high-SES families are in preschools compared to children from low-SES families.

Many U.S. states provide early education. Some do so for all 4-year-olds (Oklahoma, Florida, and Vermont), but some do so for none (Idaho, Indiana, Utah, South Dakota, and Wyoming). Curriculum, teacher training, and quality vary, with only three (Alabama, Michigan, and Rhode Island) reaching 10 quality goals (Friedman-Krauss et al., 2019).

As you read in Opposing Perspectives, although many Head Start programs were child-centered initially, they have become increasingly teacher-directed as waves of legislators have shaped them. In 2016, new requirements were put in place for Head Start, mandating that programs be open at least six hours a day (initially, most programs were half-day) and 180 days a year (that allows for 81 holidays and 104 weekend days).

Special support is required in Head Start for children who are homeless, have special needs, or are learning English. Research finds that Head Start is most beneficial for them as well as for children in poverty, or who live in rural areas (U.S. Department of Health and Human Services, 2010). Those children are underserved by other early-education programs (Crosnoe et al., 2016).

Historical data show that most Head Start children of every background advanced in language and social skills, but by elementary school non–Head Start children often caught up. However, there was one area in which the Head Start children maintained their superiority—vocabulary.

That finding also supports what you just learned about language development. Almost every preschool introduces children to words they would not learn at home. Children will fast-map those words, gaining a linguistic knowledge base that facilitates expanded vocabulary throughout life.

A longitudinal study of children born in 2001 found that those who went to Head Start were advanced in math and language, but, compared to similar children who had only their mother's care, they had more behavior problems, according to their teachers in kindergarten and first grade (R. Lee et al., 2014). One interpretation of this result is that the teachers did not know how to respond to the self-assertion of the Head Start children: They blamed the children rather than welcoming their independence.

---

**DATA CONNECTIONS: A Look at Early-Childhood Education in the United States** examines changes in preschool enrollment since the 1960s. 🔎 **LaunchPad**

---

## Long-Term Gains from Intensive Programs

This discussion of philosophies, practices, and programs may give the impression that the research on early-childhood cognition is contradictory. That is not true.

Octavio Jones/Tampa Bay Times/ZUMAPRESS/Alamy

**If You're Happy and You Know It** Gabby Osborne (pink shirt) has her own way of showing happiness, not the hand-clapping that Lizalia Garcia tries to teach. The curriculum of this Head Start class in Florida includes learning about emotions, contrary to the wishes of some legislators, who want proof of academics.

Specifics are debatable, but empirical evidence and longitudinal evaluation find that preschool education advances learning.

The best longitudinal evidence comes from three intensive programs that enrolled children for years—sometimes beginning with home visits in infancy, sometimes continuing in after-school programs through first grade. One program, called *Perry* (or *High/Scope*), was spearheaded in Michigan (Schweinhart & Weikart, 1997); another, called *Abecedarian*, got its start in North Carolina (Campbell et al., 2001); a third, called *Child–Parent Centers*, began in Chicago (Reynolds, 2000). They all focused on children from low-SES families.

All three programs compared experimental groups of children with matched control groups, and all reached the same conclusion: Early education has substantial long-term benefits that become most apparent when children are in the third grade or later. By age 10, children who had been enrolled in any one of these three programs scored higher on math and reading achievement tests than did other children from the same backgrounds, schools, and neighborhoods. They were less likely to be placed in classes for children with special needs, or to repeat a year of school, or to drop out of high school before graduation.

An advantage of decades of longitudinal research is that teenagers and adults who received early education can be compared with those who did not. For all three programs, early investment paid off:

- In adolescence, the children who had undergone intensive preschool education had higher aspirations, possessed a greater sense of achievement, and were less likely to have been abused.
- As young adults, they were more likely to attend college and less likely to go to jail.
- As middle-aged adults, they were more often employed, paying taxes, healthy, and not in need of government subsidies (Reynolds & Temple, 2019).

All three research projects found that providing direct cognitive training, with specific instruction in various school-readiness skills, was useful. Each child's needs and talents were considered—a circumstance made possible because the child/adult ratio was low. This combined child-centered and teacher-directed programs, with all of the teachers working together on the same goals so that children

◑ **Especially for Teachers** In trying to find a preschool program, what should parents look for? (see response, page 255)

Frank Porter Graham Child Development Institute.

**Lifetime Achievement** The baby in the framed photograph escaped the grip of poverty. The woman holding the photograph proved that early education can transform children. She is Frances Campbell, who spearheaded the Abecedarian Project. The baby's accomplishments may be the more impressive of the two.

were not confused. The parents reinforced what the children learned. In all three, teachers deliberately involved parents, and each program included strategies to enhance the home–school connection.

These programs were expensive (ranging from $7,500 to $23,000 annually per young child in 2020 dollars). From a developmental perspective, the decreased need for special education and other social services later on made early education a "wise investment" (Duncan & Magnuson, 2013, p. 128). Additional benefits to society over the child's lifetime, including increased employment and tax revenues, as well as reduced crime, save an estimated $329,000 in later expenses per child (Schweinhart, 2019).

Ironically, the children *least* likely to be in such programs are Spanish-speaking, or from families with income slightly above poverty-level, or whose mothers are not employed. These are precisely the children for whom early education may be especially helpful, a conclusion found not only in Head Start but in other research as well. That makes early education an issue of educational justice (Morgan, 2019; Nxumalo & Adair, 2019).

Many professionals try to steer away from political issues, but this one transcends partisanship. Any cuts to preschool education not only mean less child-centered learning (which is more expensive) but also less high-quality, teacher-directed learning. In most U.S. states, full-day kindergarten programs (always locally funded) are optional and sometimes unavailable.

Scientists who know the research on early-childhood education are dismayed when the wishes of the adults (lower taxes) supersede the needs of the children. Professionals disagree about details, but they do not debate whether every young child should be offered high-quality preschool education (they should). Instead, the debate is whether the government should pay for every child, thus making education a public right like the police or fire protection, or whether the government should save money by paying only for those who cannot afford private programs.

Compared to a decade ago, much more is known about early cognition: 2- to 5-year-olds are capable of learning languages, concepts, math, theory of mind, and more. What a child learns before age 6 is pivotal for later schooling and adult life. The amazing potential of young children is also a theme of the next chapter, where we discuss other kinds of learning, such as in emotional regulation and social skills.

---

**WHAT HAVE YOU LEARNED?**

1. What do most preschools provide that most homes do not?

2. In child-centered programs, what do the teachers do?

3. What makes the Reggio Emilia program different from most other preschool programs?

4. Why are Montessori schools still functioning 100 years after the first such schools opened?

5. What are the advantages and disadvantages of teacher-directed preschools?

6. What are the goals of Head Start?

7. What are the long-term gains from intervention preschools?

# Early-Childhood Schooling

Preschool can be an academic and social benefit to children. Around the world, increasing numbers of children are enrolled in early-childhood education.

Programs are described as "teacher-directed" or "child-centered," but in reality, most teachers' styles reflect a combination of both approaches. Some students benefit more from the order and structure of a teacher-directed classroom, while others work better in a more collaborative and creative environment.

### TEACHER-DIRECTED APPROACH
**Focused on Getting Preschoolers Ready to Learn**

Direct instruction
Teacher as formal authority
Students learn by listening
Classroom is orderly and quiet
Teacher fully manages lessons
Rewards individual achievement
Encourages academics
Students learn from teacher

### CHILD-CENTERED APPROACH
**Focused on Individual Development and Growth**

Teacher as facilitator
Teacher as delegator
Students learn actively
Classroom is designed for collaborative work
Students influence content
Rewards collaboration among students
Encourages artistic expression
Students learn from each other

Worth Publishers

## DIFFERENT STUDENTS, DIFFERENT TEACHERS

There is clearly no "one right way" to teach children. Each approach has potential benefits and pitfalls. A classroom full of creative, self-motivated students can thrive when a gifted teacher acts as a competent facilitator. But students who are distracted or annoyed by noise, or who are shy or intimidated by other children, can blossom under an engaging and encouraging teacher in a more traditional environment.

**Done Well**

| Teacher-Directed | Child-Centered |
|---|---|
| • engaging teacher<br>• clear, consistent assessment<br>• reading and math skills emphasized<br>• quiet, orderly classroom<br>• all students treated equally | • emphasizes social skills and emotion regulation<br>• encourages critical thinking<br>• builds communication skills<br>• fosters individual achievement<br>• encourages creativity and curiosity |
| • bored students<br>• passive learning<br>• less independent, critical thinking<br>• teacher may dominate | • chaotic/noisy classrooms<br>• students may miss important knowledge and skills<br>• inconclusive assessment of student progress<br>• some students may dominate others |

**Done Poorly**

# SUMMARY

## Thinking During Early Childhood

**1.** An important part of developing cognition during early childhood is the emergence of executive function, or cognitive control, as children learn to regulate and control their sensory impulses in order to use their minds more effectively.

**2.** Three components are usually included in executive function: memory, inhibition, and flexibility. Executive function can be improved during early childhood, and that advances later learning more than a high score on an IQ test or extensive vocabulary.

**3.** Piaget stressed the egocentric and illogical aspects of thought during early childhood. He called this stage of thinking preoperational intelligence because young children do not yet use logical operations to think about their observations and experiences.

**4.** Young children, according to Piaget, sometimes focus on only one thing (centration) and see things only from their own viewpoint (egocentrism), remaining stuck on appearances and current reality. They may believe that living spirits reside in inanimate objects and that nonhuman animals have the same characteristics they themselves have, a belief called animism.

**5.** Vygotsky stressed the social aspects of childhood cognition, noting that children learn by participating in various experiences, guided by more knowledgeable adults or peers. Such guidance assists learning within the zone of proximal development, which encompasses the knowledge that children are close to understanding and the skills they can almost master.

**6.** According to Vygotsky, the best teachers use various hints, guidelines, and other tools to provide a child with a scaffold for new learning. Language is a bridge that provides social mediation between the knowledge that the child already has and the learning that society hopes to impart. For Vygotsky, words are tools for learning.

**7.** Children develop theories, especially to explain the purpose of life and their role in it. One theory about children's thinking is called "theory-theory"—the hypothesis that children develop theories because all humans innately seek explanations for everything they observe.

**8.** An example of the developing cognition of young children is theory of mind—an understanding of what others may be thinking. Theory of mind begins at around age 4, partly as a result of maturation of the brain. Culture and experiences also influence its development.

## Language Learning

**9.** Language develops rapidly during early childhood, a sensitive period but not a critical one for language learning. Vocabulary increases dramatically, with thousands of words added between ages 2 and 6. In addition, basic grammar is mastered.

**10.** The child's ability to learn language is evident in fast-mapping (the quick use of new vocabulary words) and in overregularization (applying the rules of grammar even when they are not valid).

**11.** Many children learn to speak more than one language, gaining cognitive as well as social advantages. Early childhood is the best time to learn two languages. The benefits of bilingualism are lifelong. Pronunciation lags behind production, which lags behind comprehension.

## Early-Childhood Schooling

**12.** Organized educational programs during early childhood advance cognitive and social skills, although specifics vary a great deal. The quality of a program cannot be judged by the name or by appearance.

**13.** Montessori and Reggio Emilia are two child-centered programs that began in Italy and are now offered in many nations. Waldorf, which began in Germany, is another child-centered program.

**14.** Behaviorist principles led to many specific practices of teacher-directed programs. Children learn to listen to teachers and become ready for kindergarten. Teacher-directed programs are preferred by many parents and legislators, and these programs are increasingly popular—to the consternation of many child developmentalists.

**15.** Head Start is a U.S. federal government program primarily for low-income children. Longitudinal research finds that early-childhood education reduces the risk of later problems, such as needing special education. High-quality programs increase the likelihood that a child will become a law-abiding, gainfully employed adult.

**16.** Many types of preschool programs are successful. It is the quality of early education that matters. The training, warmth, and continuity of early-childhood teachers benefit children in many ways.

**17.** Some nations provide early education for all 3- and 4-year-olds. The United States is behind on this metric, with only about half of all 4-year-olds in preschool, and far fewer 3-year-olds.

# KEY TERMS

executive function (p. 229)
preoperational intelligence (p. 230)
symbolic thought (p. 230)
animism (p. 231)
centration (p. 231)
egocentrism (p. 231)

focus on appearance (p. 231)
static reasoning (p. 231)
irreversibility (p. 231)
conservation (p. 232)
zone of proximal development (ZPD) (p. 234)

scaffolding (p. 234)
overimitation (p. 235)
private speech (p. 236)
social mediation (p. 236)
theory-theory (p. 237)
theory of mind (p. 238)
fast-mapping (p. 242)

overregularization (p. 243)
pragmatics (p. 243)
Montessori schools (p. 247)
Reggio Emilia (p. 247)
Waldorf schools (p. 247)
Head Start (p. 250)

## APPLICATIONS

The best way to understand thinking in early childhood is to listen to a child, as Applications 1 and 2 require. If you have no access to children, consider Application 3 or 4.

**1.** Replicate one of Piaget's conservation experiments. The easiest one is conservation of liquids (see Figure 9.1). Work with a child under age 5 who tells you that two identically shaped glasses contain the same amount of liquid. Then carefully pour one glass of liquid into a narrower, taller glass. Ask the child whether one glass now contains more or the glasses contain the same amount.

**2.** To demonstrate how rapidly language is learned, show a preschool child several objects and label one with a nonsense word that the child has never heard. (*Toma* is often used; so is *wug*.) Or choose a word that the child does not know, such as *wrench*, *spatula*, or the name of a coin from another nation. Test the child's fast-mapping.

**3.** Theory of mind emerges at about age 4, but many adults still have trouble understanding other people's thoughts and motives. Ask several people why someone in the news did whatever he or she did (e.g., a scandal, a crime, a heroic act). Then ask your informants how sure they are of their explanation. Compare and analyze the reasons as well as the degrees of certainty. (One person may be sure of an explanation that someone else thinks is impossible.)

**4.** Think about an experience in which you learned something that was initially difficult. To what extent do Vygotsky's concepts (guided participation, zone of proximal development) explain the experience? Write a detailed, step-by-step account of your learning process as Vygotsky would have described it.

## Especially For ANSWERS

**Response for Nutritionists** (from p. 232): Take each of the four characteristics of preoperational thought into account. Because of egocentrism, having a special place and plate might assure the child that this food is exclusively theirs. Since appearance is important, the food should look tasty. Since static thinking dominates, if something healthy is added (e.g., grate carrots into the cake, add milk to the soup), do it before the food is given to the child. In the reversibility example in the text, the lettuce should be removed out of the child's sight and the "new" hamburger presented.

**Response for Immigrant Parents** (from p. 244): Children learn by listening, so it is important to speak with them often. Depending on how comfortable you are with the new language, you might prefer to read to your children, sing to them, and converse with them primarily in your native language and find a good preschool where they will learn the new language. The worst thing you could do is to restrict speech in either tongue.

**Response for Teachers** (from p. 251): Tell parents to look at the people more than the program. Parents should see the children in action and note whether the teachers show warmth and respect for each child.

## Observation Quiz ANSWERS

**Answer to Observation Quiz** (from p. 234): The name "Jack" above the bed is an obvious scaffold. Egocentric children pay special attention to their names, and those who are as fortunate as Jack can read and spell their names before kindergarten. Jack is also learning what his culture expects of a boy, evident in his haircut, room decor, and furniture.

**Answer to Observation Quiz** (from p. 235): Right-handed. Her dominant hand is engaged in something more comforting than exploring the abacus.

# Early Childhood: Psychosocial Development

## What Will You Know?

1. Why do 2-year-olds have more sudden tempers, tears, and terrors than 6-year-olds?
2. What happens if parents let their children do whatever they want?
3. How does spanking affect children?

At age 4, my youngest grandson considers himself a "big kid." When we wait for the bus, he begs his brother to play "the monster game." The older boy usually says no. Then the 4-year-old cries, and the big brother usually stops the wailing by pretending to be a blind monster, clomping around with arms outstretched to catch the smaller boy, who laughs as he runs ahead, never caught. Should I intervene, telling one not to cry, telling the other not to reward the tears?

In running, the 4-year-old sometimes bumps into strangers who are also waiting for the bus. Some smile, some seem annoyed, but no one expresses anger. I would not mind if they did; I wish my grandson were wiser about other people.

One stranger asked the boy his name, which he readily gave, as well as his address.

"Don't tell strangers where you live," the man said.

He repeated his address.

With strangers as well as older siblings, it is apparent that young children have much to learn. Adults—parents and, in this case, grandmothers—need to figure out when and how to guide, encourage, and discipline.

## Emotional Development

As with the body growth and cognitive development, which the previous two chapters described as changing dramatically from age 2 to 6, emotions change as well.

### Emotional Regulation

Controlling the expression of feelings, called **emotional regulation**, is the preeminent psychosocial task between ages 2 and 6. Emotional regulation is a lifelong endeavor, with particularly rapid development during early childhood, influenced by both peers and parents (Hu et al., 2017).

Think of what happens when you give someone a gift. If the receiver is a young child, you can probably tell whether the child liked the present, because emotions are visible (Galak et al., 2016). If the receiver is an adult, you may not be sure, because adults have learned to disguise their disappointment. People learn to regulate their emotions.

By age 6, most children can feel angry, frightened, sad, anxious, or proud without the explosive outbursts of temper, or terror, or tears of 2-year-olds. Depending on a child's training and temperament, some emotions are easier to control than others, but even temperamentally angry or fearful children learn to regulate their emotions (Moran et al., 2013; Suurland et al., 2016; Tan et al., 2013).

Among the middle class in in the United States, postponement of gratification is valued as a sign of maturity: Dieters must resist some foods today so they will be thinner next summer; students are told to study now for an exam next week, not cram at the last minute; adults are supposed to save for the future, not spend immediately. This aspect of emotional regulation is very difficult for young children (see A View from Science on page 258).

**emotional regulation** The ability to control when and how emotions are expressed.

## Initiative Versus Guilt

Erikson's third developmental stage is **initiative versus guilt**. *Initiative* includes saying something new, beginning a project, expressing an emotion. Depending on what happens next, children feel proud or guilty. Gradually, they learn to rein in boundless pride and avoid crushing guilt.

Pride is common in early childhood. As one team expressed it:

> Compared to older children and adults, young children are the optimists of the world, believing they have greater physical abilities, better memories, are more skilled at imitating models, are smarter, know more about how things work, and rate themselves as stronger, tougher, and of higher social standing than is actually the case.

*[Bjorklund & Ellis, 2014, p. 244]*

**initiative versus guilt** Erikson's third psychosocial crisis, in which young children undertake new skills and activities and feel guilty when they do not succeed at them.

**self-concept** A person's understanding of who they are, in morality, intelligence, appearance, personality, talents, and skills.

That *protective optimism* helps young children try new things, and thus, initiative advances learning. As Erikson predicted, their optimistic **self-concept** protects young children from guilt and shame and encourages them to learn.

Young children often brag about what they have accomplished. As long as the boast is not a lie, other young children like them for it. At about age 7, a developmental shift occurs, and children as well as adults begin to appreciate modesty more than boasting (Lockhart et al., 2018). By then, children have usually learned some emotional regulation; they can finally keep quiet about how wonderful they are.

Many young children believe that whatever they are is good. They may feel superior to children of another nationality or religion. This arises because of maturation: Cognition enables them to understand group categories, not only of ethnicity, gender, and nationality but even categories that are irrelevant.

For instance, children remember more about cartoon characters whose names begin with the same letter as theirs (Ross et al., 2011). If their parents or other adults express prejudice against another group, they may mirror those prejudices (Tagar et al., 2017).

## Brain Maturation

The new initiative that Erikson described results from myelination in the limbic system, growth of the prefrontal cortex, and a longer attention span—all indicative of neurological maturation. Emotional regulation and cognitive maturation develop together, each enabling the other to advance (Bridgett et al., 2015; Frydenberg, 2017).

Already before age 2, primary emotions, such as sadness and joy, have developed, becoming more nuanced with every passing year. Now brain maturation and social awareness allow development of secondary emotions, such as pride, envy, and guilt (Frydenberg, 2017). Usually, emotional control of both primary and secondary emotions becomes more evident by age 4 or 5.

**Learning Emotional Regulation** Like this girl in Hong Kong, all 2-year-olds burst into tears when something upsets them—a toy breaks, a pet refuses to play, or it's time to go home. Mothers who comfort young children and help them calm down are teaching them to regulate their emotions.

## Waiting for the Marshmallow

You probably have heard of the famous marshmallow test (Mischel et al., 1972; Mischel, 2014). Young children were seated in front of a marshmallow and told they could eat it immediately or wait—sometimes as long as 15 minutes—while the researcher left the room. They were promised another marshmallow if they didn't eat the first one before the adult returned.

Those who waited used various tactics—they looked away, closed their eyes, or sang to themselves. Decades later, the researchers contacted the children to see how their lives turned out. Those who delayed gobbling up one marshmallow in order to get two became more successful as teenagers, young adults, and even middle-aged adults—doing well in college, for instance, and having happy marriages.

This experiment is often replicated. The average child waits about 6 minutes; relatively few 4-year-olds sit in front of a marshmallow for 15 minutes without eating it; those who wait are likely to become more successful years later (Shoda et al., 1990).

Some cultures encourage instant gratification; others teach children to wait patiently. In a replication of the marshmallow test, children of the Nso people in Cameroon waited longer than the California children in Mischel's original experiment (Lamm et al., 2018).

In another replication, this one in the United States, children twice experienced a reliable or unreliable examiner. Specifically, the children were told they should wait for better crayons, and better stickers, but after two minutes, for half of them the examiner returned to say that no better crayons or stickers was available, and the other half got the much better crayons or stickers.

Then children were given the marshmallow test, which they could eat immediately or wait for two marshmallows, which the examiner brought after 15 minutes of waiting. Those with the reliable examiner waited, on average, 12 minutes, with 64 percent waiting the full 15 minutes. Those with the unreliable experimenter waited an average of only three minutes, with only 7 percent waiting 15 minutes (Kidd et al., 2013).

The conclusion of these experimenters is that children make rational decisions about delaying gratification. If their parents and cultures teach patience and keep their promises, children learn to control their impulses. Emotional regulation is the product of experience, not just maturation.

Jose Luis Pelaez Inc/DigitalVision/Getty Images

**Both Accomplished** Note the joy and pride in this father and daughter in West New York, New Jersey. Who has achieved more?

Children strengthen and develop their neuronal connections in response to the emotions of other people. The process is reciprocal and dynamic: Anger begets anger, which leads to more anger; joy begets joy, and so on.

This reciprocity is not just a matter of words and facial expression, it also directly involves the brain. For instance, researchers scanned the brains of mothers and children as they did a difficult puzzle together. When the mothers became frustrated, the children did, too—and vice versa. As the scientists explain, "mothers and children regulate or deregulate each other" (Atzaba-Poria et al., 2017, p. 551).

The practical application of shared emotionality benefits adults as well as children. If a happy young boy runs to you, you might laugh, pick him up, and swing him around; if a grinning young girl drums on the table, catch the rhythm and pound in return, smiling broadly. In both adults and children, laughter and happiness increase endorphins and lower cortisol. Emotions are infectious: Catch the good ones, and drop the bad ones.

## Motivation

Motivation is the impulse that propels someone to act. It comes either from a person's own desires or from the social context.

### From Within

**intrinsic motivation** A drive, or reason to pursue a goal, that comes from inside a person, such as the joy of reading a good book.

**Intrinsic motivation** arises from within, when people do something for the joy of doing it: A musician might enjoy making music even if no one else hears it; the sound is intrinsically rewarding. Intrinsic motivation is thought to advance creativity, innovation, and emotional well-being (Weinstein & DeHaan, 2014).

All of Erikson's psychosocial needs—including the young child's initiatives—are intrinsic: A child feels inwardly compelled to act. The power of that internal impulse is sometimes frustratingly evident, especially if an adult in a hurry is walking with a child. The adult's "hurry, we are late" clashes with the child's intrinsic motivation. The child may jump up to walk along a ledge, may stop to throw a snowball, or may pick up a piece of trash to explore.

When playing a game, few young children keep score; intrinsic joy is the goal, more than winning. In fact, young children often claim to have won when objective scoring would say they lost; in this case, the children may really be winners.

## From the Culture

**Extrinsic motivation** comes from outside the person, when external praise or some other reinforcement is the goal, such as when a musician plays for applause or money. Four-year-olds might brush their teeth because they are praised and rewarded with musical toothbrushes and tasty toothpaste.

If an extrinsic reward is removed, the behavior may stop unless it has become a habit. Young children might not brush their teeth if parents don't notice and praise them. For most of us, tooth-brushing was extrinsically rewarded at first, and that continued long enough for it to become habitual. Then motivation becomes intrinsic: Tooth-brushing has become a comforting, internally motivated routine for many adults.

## Spontaneous Joy

Intrinsic motivation is evident in childhood. Young children play, question, exercise, create, destroy, and explore for the sheer joy of it. That serves them well. For example, a longitudinal study found that 3-year-olds who were strong in intrinsic motivation were, two years later, advanced in early math and literacy (Mokrova et al., 2013). The probable reason: They enjoyed counting things and singing songs—when alone.

In contrast, exaggerated external praise ("Your drawing is amazingly wonderful!") undercuts motivation (Brummelman et al., 2017). If young children believe the praise, they might be afraid to try again, thinking they will not be able to do as well. If they suspect that the praise was inaccurate, they may discount the entire activity.

## Imaginary Friends

Intrinsic motivation is apparent when children invent dialogues for their toys, concentrate on creating a work of art or architecture, or talk to imaginary friends. Invisible companions are rarely encouraged by adults (thus, no extrinsic motivation), but many children have them.

An international study of 3- to 8-year-olds found that about 1 child in 5 said that they had an invisible companion, with notable variation by culture: 38 percent of children in the Dominican Republic, but only 5 percent in Nepal, said they had such a friend (Wigger, 2018).

Another study, this one in the United States, found that about half the children had imaginary friends, either completely invisible ones or objects, such as stuffed animals, upon which they bestowed independent opinions, speech, and action. Many of those children also imagined entire worlds! (Taylor et al., 2020).

---

### CHAPTER APP 10

📱 **Peek-a-Zoo**

**IOS:**
https://tinyurl.com/wdhttw6

**RELEVANT TOPIC:**
Emotional development in early childhood

This simple app prompts preschoolers to identify behaviors or emotions exhibited by different animals ("Who is surprised?"), helping them to learn social cues.

---

**extrinsic motivation** A drive, or reason to pursue a goal, that arises from the wish to have external rewards, perhaps by earning money or praise.

---

**● Especially for College Students** Is extrinsic or intrinsic motivation more influential in your study efforts? (see response, page 281)

---

### WHAT HAVE YOU LEARNED?

1. Why is emotional regulation an important skill that children need to develop?
2. How might protective optimism lead to new skills and competencies?
3. How are emotional regulation, emotional control, and executive function related?
4. What did Erikson think was the dominant psychic need of young children?
5. What is an example (not in the text) of intrinsic motivation?
6. What is an example (not in the text) of extrinsic motivation?

## Play

Play is timeless and universal—apparent in every part of the world over thousands of years. Many developmentalists believe that play is children's most productive, enjoyable activity. As you will see, not everyone agrees.

### The Historical Context

As Chapter 9 explained, one dispute in early education is whether child-centered creative play or teacher-directed learning is more important. To further understand that debate, we need to consider how attitudes have changed over the past 100 years.

### Parten's Stages of Play

In 1932, American sociologist Mildred Parten described five stages of play, each more advanced than the previous one:

1. *Solitary*: A child plays alone, unaware of other children playing nearby.
2. *Onlooker*: A child watches other children play.
3. *Parallel*: Children play in similar ways but not together.
4. *Associative*: Children interact, sharing materials or activities, but not taking turns.
5. *Cooperative*: Children play together, creating dramas or taking turns.

Parten described play as intrinsic, with children from age 1 to 6 gradually advancing from solitary to cooperative play. This was apparent as toddlers watched older children play, and as the older children gradually learned how to play together.

Research on contemporary children finds much more age variation than Parten did, in part because children's experiences with other children vary. Those who stay home until kindergarten might be onlookers (stage 2) in kindergarten, whereas those who have been in interactive, child-centered preschools might reach cooperative play (stage 5) by age 4.

THINK CRITICALLY: Is "play" an entirely different experience for adults than for children?

### The Current Controversy

Whether play is essential or merely fun is "a controversial topic of study" (Pellegrini, 2011, p. 3; Johnson & Wu, 2019). Some educators want children to play less in order to learn reading and math; others predict emotional and academic problems if children rarely play (Golinkoff & Hirsh-Pasek, 2016).

Developmental psychologists are particularly impressed with the young child's ability to use play to express their own emotions. One source notes that play varies, with "twists and turns . . . abrupt changes in play patterns—between seriousness and frolic, earnestness and whimsy, reality and pretense, often leading to higher levels of play" (Johnson & Wu, 2019, p. 81).

### Screen Time

The largest historical change is that active play time has been reduced because of *screen time*, which is when children watch television, tablets, smartphones, or computer screens. That troubles developmentalists for many reasons. Pediatricians, psychologists, and teachers all report extensive research that screen time reduces conversation, imagination, and outdoor activity (Downing et al., 2017).

A recent study in Canada of 2,441 children, followed longitudinally from before birth until age 5, found that the average 3-year-old watched more than two hours a day (Madigan et al., 2019). One result was to "disrupt interactions with caregivers"; another was to reduce cognitive and emotional development. Because this was

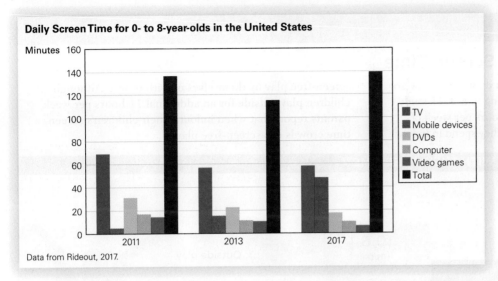

**Daily Screen Time for 0- to 8-year-olds in the United States**

Minutes

Legend:
- TV
- Mobile devices
- DVDs
- Computer
- Video games
- Total

Data from Rideout, 2017.

**FIGURE 10.1**

**Learning by Playing** Fifty years ago, the average child spent three hours a day in outdoor play. Screens have largely replaced that, with specifics changing over the years. In this chart "video games" referred to separate game consoles; now "mobile devices" are often used for games. Children seem safer if parents can keep an eye on them at home, but what are they learning? The long-term effects on brain and body may be dangerous.

a careful longitudinal study, the finding that screen time reduced emotional maturation was not merely correlational but also causal.

Similar results are found in many nations, with many young children using screens three hours a day, and with far-reaching consequences, in obesity, emotional immaturity, and intellectual growth (see **Figure 10.1**). Overall, the American Academy of Pediatrics (2016) recommends no more than an hour a day of any screen time for 2- to 6-year-olds. They also urge parents never to let their children watch programs or play games that include violent or sexual media, or racist and sexist stereotypes. Parent should always watch with the child, interpreting and reinforcing.

However, most young children watch more than is recommended, unsupervised, not only in the North America but also in other developed nations. If you have no children, you might wonder why any parent would allow children to look at screens more than occasionally, or, worse, give their child an iPad for their birthday. If you are a parent, you know why.

## Social Play

Young children play best with *peers,* that is, people of about the same age and social status. Although infants are intrigued by other children, babies do not play together because peer play requires some social maturation (Bateson & Martin, 2013). Gradually, from age 2 to 6, most children learn how to join a peer group, manage conflict, take turns, find friends, and keep the action going (Göncü & Gaskins, 2011; Şendil & Erden, 2014).

## Playmates

Children need peers. Even the most playful parent is outmatched by a child at negotiating the rules of tag, at play-fighting, at pretending to be sick, at killing dragons, and so on.

As they interact with peers, children learn emotional regulation, empathy, and cultural understanding. Specifics vary, but "play with peers is one of the most important areas in which children develop positive social skills" (Xu, 2010, p. 496).

Peers provide an audience, role models, and sometimes competition. For instance, running skills develop best when

**Good Over Evil or Evil Over Good?** Boys everywhere enjoy "strong man" fantasy play, as the continued popularity of Spider-Man and Superman attests. These boys follow that script. Both are Afghan refugees now in Pakistan.

REUTERS/Akhtar Soomro

# More Play Time, Less Screen Time

Play is universal—all young children do it when they are with each other, if they can. According to a 2017 study, U.S. 2- to 10-year-olds average 19 hours per week of screen time, exceeding the 15 hours they spend in indoor screen-free play by themselves or with others. Although children play outside for an additional 11 hours per week, parents report that when indoors, their children's screen time crowds out screen-free play.

## WHAT 2- TO 10-YEAR-OLDS DO WITH THEIR FREE TIME

Screen time

**18.6** hours per week — Screen-based Play

**10.6** hours per week — Outside play

**14.6** hours per week — Indoor play

Screen-free Play

Hours per Week (0, 10, 20, 30)

Data from Gallup, 2017.

## WAY TOO MUCH SCREEN TIME

Very few children have the recommended less than an hour of screen time per day. Some have much more. This is particularly evident on weekends, when they should be playing outside or interacting with their families. What did children do before 1950, without TV or computers? Talking, reading, cooking, cleaning, board games, ball games, playing music, drawing pictures, writing letters ... the list of things that some children never do could go on and on!

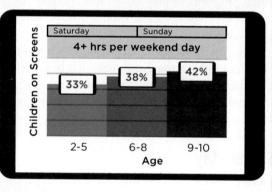

Children on Screens

| Saturday | Sunday |
| --- | --- |

**4+ hrs per weekend day**

33% (2-5)   38% (6-8)   42% (9-10)

Age

Data from Gallup, 2017.

## WHAT CAREGIVERS CAN DO TO ENCOURAGE PLAY

### at Ages 1–3

Choose childcare and preschools that emphasize unstructured playtime.

Offer simple, inexpensive objects (blocks, empty containers, puzzles, etc.), not screens or fancy gadgets.

Organize caregiver-supervised playdates with peers.

Encourage make-believe play.

Sing songs and play rhythms that invite participation.

### at Ages 4–6

Provide opportunities for singing and dancing.

Encourage a variety of movements in a safe environment—e.g., hopping, swinging, climbing, and somersaulting.

Blend make-believe games and reality—e.g., "playing house" and helping with chores.

Encourage school officials to offer recess and play-centered learning approaches, not just reading, memorization, and worksheets.

Information from American Academy of Pediatrics, 2018.

children chase or race each other, not when a child runs alone. Active social play—not solitary play—correlates with physical, emotional, and intellectual growth.

The importance of peer interaction has become increasingly clear, now that many children attend preschools, early-childhood centers, or other institutions of group care and learning. As you learned in Chapter 9, preschools advance language and other aspects of cognition. It is also clear that play with peers also advances social understanding.

## Technology Play

Adults once feared that technology would cause children to become socially isolated. A more nuanced view considers the social setting. When a child watches a video alone, interpersonal emotional understanding is reduced. However, if children are with other children, digital play can advance development.

One detailed study of 3- to 5-year-olds in a Scotland preschool focused on digital technology such as computers, SMART boards, digital cameras, and so on. All of that was available during free play time, in the same way that puzzles, dress-up clothes, and dolls were available (Arnott, 2016).

Children used various digital tools as part of social interaction. Sometimes the digital object encouraged cooperation, as with this boy and girl, both aged 4:

> Grace begins to use the SMART board and Chris begins to use his finger to point at the screen to illustrate which selection she should choose as he verbally directs. Chris continues this process for each step of the way and Grace obeys. Then, when the game reaches a section where Grace does not need to make a selection and she needs to wait, he holds up his hand and says, "now wait."

Sometimes one child was the leader, with onlookers encouraging. For example:

> Three boys have formed a cluster around the computer. Chris is controlling the computer by using the mouse. Harvey is sitting next to him in front of the computer and Steven is hovering close by. Harvey offers encouragement to Chris, "You got 10!" he shouts with an excited tone. Steven becomes more and more excited with this activity and begins to show it by bouncing up and down while he stands next to the computer. He begins to cheer. Suddenly, Harvey turns to Steven and sharply says "Shhh—Don't do that!" Steven is immediately silent and observes quietly.

> [Arnott, 2016, p. 280]

In this study, children's technology use was almost always a social activity. Sometimes they shared, sometimes they mentored each other, sometimes they merely watched, providing encouragement, and later tried it themselves. The social context, including the physical space and the overall routines and rules, framed the interactions. It was unusual for the children to be hostile or to fight for control. (Rarely, the teachers intervened.)

## Rough-and-Tumble Play

One form of social play, often unrecognized for the emotional growth it fosters, is called **rough-and-tumble**, because it looks rough and children seem to tumble over one another. The term was coined by British scientists who studied animals in East Africa (Blurton-Jones, 1976). They noticed that young monkeys often chased, attacked, rolled over in the dirt, and wrestled quite roughly without injuring one another, all while seeming to smile (showing a *play face*).

When the scientists who studied monkeys in Africa returned to London, they saw that puppies, kittens, and even their own children engaged in rough-and-tumble

**VIDEO: The Impact of Media on Early Childhood** explores how screen time can affect young children's cognition.

**rough-and-tumble play** Play that seems to be rough, as in play wrestling or chasing, but in which there is no intent to harm.

2016 Macmillan

**Joy Supreme** Pretend play in early childhood is thrilling and powerful. For this dancing 7-year-old from Park Slope, Brooklyn, pretend play overwhelms mundane realities, such as an odd scarf or awkward arm.

**sociodramatic play** Pretend play in which children act out various roles and themes in plots or roles that they create.

play. Children chase, wrestle, and grab each other, with established rules, facial expressions, and gestures to signify "just pretend."

Developmentalists now recognize that rough-and-tumble play happens everywhere, with every mammal species, and it has for thousands of years (Fry, 2014). It is more common among males than females, and it flourishes best in ample space with minimal supervision (Pellegrini, 2013).

Neurological benefits from such play are evident. The easiest example comes from watching rodents. Young rats try to bite the nape of another's neck. If a bite occurs, the two rats switch roles and the bitten tries to bite the other's nape. This is all playful. If rats want to hurt each other, they try to bite organs, not napes. Rat rough-and-tumble play increases rat brain development (Pellis et al., 2018). Watching puppies, kittens, and human children also shows that the participants are careful not to hurt each other.

Controlled experiments on humans, with some children allowed to play and a matched control group never playing, would be unethical, but correlations suggest that the limbic system connects more strongly with the prefrontal cortex because children engage in rough-and-tumble play. Indeed, longitudinal research on boys who played carefully but roughly with peers and parents (usually with fathers) finds that they become caring, compassionate men (Fry, 2014; Raeburn, 2014).

## Sociodramatic Play

Another major type of social play is called **sociodramatic**, in which children act out various roles and plots. Through such acting, children:

- explore and rehearse social roles;
- learn to explain their ideas and persuade playmates;
- practice emotional regulation by pretending to be afraid, angry, brave, etc.; and
- develop self-concept in a nonthreatening context.

As children combine their imagination with that of their friends, they advance in theory of mind, gaining emotional regulation as they do so (Goldstein & Lerner, 2018; Kavanaugh, 2011).

---

**WHAT HAVE YOU LEARNED?**

1. What are children thought to gain from play?
2. Why do pediatricians want to limit children's screen time?
3. How can technology enhance children's learning instead of inhibiting it?
4. Why does playing with peers increase physical development and emotional regulation?
5. What do children learn from rough-and-tumble play?
6. What do children learn from sociodramatic play?

---

## Challenges for Caregivers

Every developmentalist, and every parent, realizes that caring for a young child is difficult. Young children are energetic and curious but not wise. Some children, by temperament, are especially challenging. They, even more than compliant children, need patient parents (Ayoub et al., 2018).

## Styles of Caregiving

One challenge for caregivers is choosing how strict or permissive to be. Variations in parenting styles are astonishing: Some are so strict that they seem abusive, and others are so lenient that they seem neglectful. Variations are apparent within nations, within ethnic groups, within neighborhoods, and sometimes within marriages.

## Baumrind's Categories

Although thousands of researchers have traced the effects of parenting on child development, the work of one person, 60 years ago, remains influential. Diana Baumrind (1967, 1971) studied 100 preschool children, all from California, almost all middle-class European Americans.

She found that parents differed on four important dimensions:

1. *Expressions of warmth.* Some parents are warm and affectionate; others are cold and critical.
2. *Strategies for discipline.* Parents vary in how they explain, criticize, persuade, and punish.
3. *Expectations for maturity.* Parents vary in expectations for responsibility and self-control.
4. *Communication.* Some parents listen patiently; others demand silence.

On the basis of these dimensions, Baumrind identified three parenting styles: *authoritarian, permissive,* and *authoritative* (summarized in **Table 10.1**). A fourth style, *neglectful,* not described by Baumrind, was suggested by other researchers.

**Authoritarian parenting**. The authoritarian parent's word is law, not to be questioned. Misconduct brings strict punishment, usually physical. Authoritarian parents set down clear rules and hold high standards. Discussion about emotions and expressions of affection are rare. One adult raised by authoritarian parents said that "How do you feel?" had only two possible answers: "Fine" and "Tired."

**Permissive parenting**. Permissive parents (also called *indulgent*) make few demands. Discipline is lax, partly because expectations are low. Permissive parents are nurturing and accepting, listening to whatever their offspring say, which may include "I hate you"—a remark that authoritarian parents would not tolerate.

**Authoritative parenting**. Authoritative parents set limits, but they are flexible. They consider themselves guides, not authorities (unlike authoritarian parents) and not friends (unlike permissive parents). The goal of punishment is for the child to understand what was wrong and what should have been done differently.

**authoritarian parenting** An approach to child rearing that is characterized by high behavioral standards, strict punishment of misconduct, and little communication from child to parent.

**permissive parenting** An approach to child rearing that is characterized by high nurturance and communication but little discipline, guidance, or control.

**authoritative parenting** An approach to child rearing in which the parents set limits and enforce rules but are flexible and listen to their children.

### TABLE 10.1

**Characteristics of Parenting Styles Identified by Baumrind**

| Style | Warmth | Discipline | Expectations of Maturity | Communication Parent to Child | Communication Child to Parent |
|---|---|---|---|---|---|
| Authoritarian | Low | Strict, often physical | High | High | Low |
| Permissive | High | Rare | Low | Low | High |
| Authoritative | High | Moderate, with much discussion | Moderate | High | High |

**Protect Me from the Water Buffalo** These two are at the Carabao Kneeling Festival. In rural Philippines, hundreds of these large but docile animals kneel on the steps of the church, part of a day of gratitude for the harvest.

**Observation Quiz** Is this father authoritarian, authoritative, or permissive? (see answer, page 281) ➜

REUTERS/Erik de Castro

**neglectful/uninvolved parenting** An approach to child rearing in which the parents seem indifferent toward their children, not knowing or caring about their children's lives.

**Neglectful/uninvolved parenting.** Neglectful parents are oblivious to their children's behavior; they seem not to notice. Their children do whatever they want. The child's behavior may be similar to those of the permissive parent, but the parents' attitude is quite different: Neglectful parents do not care, whereas permissive parents care very much.

Long-term effects of parenting styles have been reported in many nations. Cultural and regional differences are apparent, but everywhere authoritative parenting seems best (Pinquart & Kauser, 2018). The following trends have been found in many studies, although you will soon read that results are not as universal as the early research found.

- *Authoritarian* parents raise children who become conscientious, obedient, and quiet but not especially happy. Such children may feel guilty or depressed, internalizing their frustrations and blaming themselves when things don't go well. As adolescents, they sometimes rebel, striking out on their own. As adults, they are quick to blame and punish.
- *Permissive* parents raise children who lack self-control. Inadequate emotional regulation makes them immature and impedes friendships, so they are unhappy. They tend to continue to live at home, still dependent on their parents in adulthood.
- *Authoritative* parents raise children who are successful, articulate, happy with themselves, and generous with others. These children are usually liked by teachers and peers, especially in cultures that value individual initiative (e.g., the United States).
- *Neglectful/uninvolved* parents raise children who are immature, sad, lonely, and at risk of injury and abuse, not only in early childhood but also lifelong.

## Problems with the Research

Baumrind's classification schema has been criticized, especially because she did not consider cultural norms and child temperament. How much protection, encouragement, and guidance does a particular child need? Differential susceptibility suggests that fearful children require reassurance, and impulsive ones need strong guidelines. Parents of such children may, to outsiders, seem permissive or authoritarian.

A study of parenting at age 2 and children's competence in kindergarten (including emotional regulation and friendships) found "multiple developmental pathways." The best outcomes depended on both the child and the adult (Blandon et al., 2010).

Simplistic advice—from a professional, a neighbor, or a textbook author (me) who does not know the child—may be misguided. Longitudinal, unbiased observation of parent–child interactions is needed before judging a caregiver.

## Discipline

Children misbehave. Sometimes adults demand too much of an immature child, but sometimes children deliberately do exactly what they know they should not do.

Misbehavior is part of growing up, as is testing the limits of what is acceptable. However, children need guidance to keep them safe and strong. Parents must respond when the child does something forbidden, dangerous, or mean. During early childhood, most parents use several methods to discipline their children (Thompson et al., 2017). Every form of discipline has critics as well as defenders (Larzelere et al., 2017).

## Physical Punishment

In the United States, young children are slapped, spanked, or beaten more often than are infants or older children, and more often than children in Canada or western Europe. Spanking is more frequent:

- in the southern United States than in New England;
- by mothers than by fathers;
- among conservative Christians than among nonreligious families;
- among African Americans than among European Americans;
- among European Americans than among Asian Americans;
- among U.S.-born Hispanics than among immigrant Hispanics; and
- in low-SES families than in high-SES families.

[*MacKenzie et al., 2011; S. Lee et al., 2015; Lee & Altschul, 2015*]

These are general trends, but do not stereotype. Contrary to these generalizations, some African American mothers living in the South never spank, and some secular, European American, high-SES fathers in New England routinely do. Local norms matter, but individual parents make their own decisions, despite what their neighbors do.

In some nations, **corporal punishment** is illegal; in other nations, it is the norm. A massive international study of low- and moderate-income nations found that 63 percent of 2- to 5-year-olds had been physically punished (slapped, spanked, hit with an object) in the past month (Deater-Deckard & Lansford, 2016).

Given a multicultural, multicontextual perspective, it is not surprising that many spanked children become fine adults, who believe they were not harmed by spanking. Nonetheless, a correlation between spanking and aggression is found in all ethnic groups, in many nations (Lansford et al., 2014; Wang & Liu, 2018).

"He's just doing that to get attention."

Harry Bliss/The New Yorker Collection/The Cartoon Bank

**Pay Attention** Children develop best with lots of love and attention. They shouldn't have to ask for it!

**corporal punishment** Disciplinary techniques that hurt the body (*corpus*) of someone, from spanking to serious harm, including death.

**Smack** Will the doll learn never to disobey her mother again?

Children who are *not* spanked are *more* likely to develop emotional regulation.

Although some adults believe that physical punishment will "teach a lesson," others argue that the lesson learned is that "might makes right." Children who were physically disciplined tend to become more aggressive, and more likely to use corporal punishment on others—first on their classmates, and later on their partners, and then on their children (Thompson et al., 2017).

## Paddling in Schools

This dispute about corporal punishment echoes in schools. In more than 100 nations, physical punishment is illegal in any educational setting. However, each U.S. state sets its own law, and teachers may legally paddle children in 19 of them. Overall, in the United States, more than 100,000 children were corporally punished at school. A disproportionate number were African American boys (Gershoff et al., 2019; Morones, 2013).

Boys are also more likely to be harshly punished by their parents, until adolescence, when boys have more freedom and less punishment at home. However, beginning at puberty, males are at least twice as likely to be imprisoned than females, with gender differences particularly stark for violent offenses.

A study in one U.S. state that allows corporal punishment in school (Arkansas) reports that whether or not a child is physically punished depends more on the school culture than on the state or district policy (McKenzie & Ritter, 2017). The rate of discipline in Arkansas in the 2015–2016 school year was 59 per 100 students, with 5 per 100 including physical punishment.

Interpret those statistics carefully. A ratio of 59 punishments per 100 students does not mean that more than half of the students were disciplined. Instead, some students experienced more than 10 punishments (some were paddled several times), while most (especially the younger girls) were never punished. Rates were much higher in middle schools than elementary schools.

The most common infractions were "minor, non-violent," when students did not obey their teacher or follow school guidelines. The goal is for children to learn more because they are more obedient. But that may not be the result. One study found that children who were physically punished had lower grades in high school, were less likely to graduate, and were more likely to become depressed (Gershoff et al., 2019).

In Arkansas as well as nationwide, school culture is changing. Once every state allowed corporal punishment; the 19 that still allow it include Alabama, Arkansas, Arizona, Colorado, Florida, Georgia, Idaho, Indiana, Kansas, Kentucky, Louisiana, Missouri, Mississippi, North Carolina, Oklahoma, South Carolina, Tennessee, Texas, and Wyoming.

Even within those states, some school districts forbid it. However, suspensions (the school equivalent of time-out) have increased in Arkansas (McKenzie & Ritter, 2017). Longitudinally, over some of the same years (2011–2019), suspensions for the million children in the New York City public schools were cut in half (from 70,000 per year to 33,000). Data from those two states make it clear that policies regarding school discipline change politically, not based on actual misbehavior.

**THINK CRITICALLY:** The varying rates of physical punishment in schools could be the result of prejudice, or they could be because some children misbehave more than others. Which is it?

**psychological control** A disciplinary technique that involves threatening to withdraw love and support, using a child's feelings of guilt and gratitude to the parents.

## Alternatives to Spanking

If spanking is harmful but discipline is necessary, what is a parent to do? Some employ **psychological control**, using children's shame, guilt, and gratitude to control their behavior (Barber, 2002). But this has its own problems (Alegre, 2011).

## Spare the Rod?

Opinions about spanking are influenced by past experience and cultural norms. That makes it hard for opposing perspectives to be understood by people on the other side (Ferguson, 2013). Try to suspend your own assumptions as you read this.

*What might be right with spanking?* Over the centuries, many parents have done it, so it has stood the test of time and has been a popular choice. Spanking is less common in the twenty-first century than in the twentieth (Taillieu et al., 2014).

However, 85 percent of U.S. adolescents who were children at the end of the twentieth century recall being slapped or spanked by their mothers (Bender et al., 2007). In low- and middle-income nations, over a third of the mothers believe that physical punishment is essential to raise a child well (Deater-Deckard & Lansford, 2016).

Those who are pro-spanking need to explain why spanking correlates with later depression, low achievement, aggression, crime, and so on. They suggest that a third variable, not spanking itself, is the reason for that connection. One possible third variable is misbehavior: Perhaps disobedient children cause spanking, not vice versa. Such children may become delinquent, depressed, and so on not *because* they were spanked but *in spite of* being spanked.

Noting problems with correlational research, one team explains, "Quite simply, parents do not need to use corrective actions when there are no problems to correct" (Larzelere & Cox, 2013, p. 284).

Further, since parents who spank their children often have less education and money than other parents, low SES may be the underlying crucial variable. Perhaps spanking is a symptom of poverty and poor parenting skills. If that is true, to reduce the low achievement, aggression, and depression, we need to increase education and income, not to ban spanking (Ferguson, 2013).

Another pro-spanking response to the troubling research is to argue that researchers need to be careful in how they define corporal punishment. If a study does not distinguish between severe corporal punishment and milder, occasional spanking, then the data will show that spanking is harmful—but that conclusion reflects the harm of severe punishment (Larzelere et al., 2017).

Now the opposing perspective.

*What might be wrong with spanking?* One problem is adults' emotions: Angry spankers may become abusive. Children have been seriously injured and even killed by parents who use corporal punishment.

Another problem is the child's immature cognition. Parents assume that the transgression is obvious, but children may think that the parents' anger, not the child's actions, caused spanking (Harkness et al., 2011). Most parents tell their children why they are being spanked, but when they are hit, children are less likely to listen or understand, much less learn.

Almost all of the research finds that children who are physically punished suffer overall (Grogan-Kaylo et al., 2018). Compared to children punished in other ways, they are more depressed, antisocial, and lonely. Many hate school and have few close friends. Emotional and social problems in adulthood are more common in people who were spanked as children—true for relatively mild spanking as well as for more severe spanking.

One reason for these correlations is that spanked children more often have angry, depressed, unloving parents. However, even among children of warm and loving parents, spanked children tend to be more anxious, worried they will do something to lose their parents' affection (Lansford et al., 2014).

*So who is right?* I know which perspective is mine. Most developmentalists believe that alternatives to spanking are better for children and a safeguard against abuse. I agree with that. The same study that found spanking common in developing nations also reported that 17 percent of the children experienced severe violence that no developmentalist would condone (Bornstein et al., 2016). That alone is reason to stop.

I recognize that there are exceptions—spanked children who become happy and successful adults. For example, one study found that conservative evangelical parents spank their children more often than other parents, but if that spanking occurred *only* in early (not middle) childhood, the children did not develop low self-esteem and increased aggression (Ellison et al., 2011).

The authors of the study suggest that, since spanking was the norm in that group, spanked children did not feel unloved. Moreover, religious leaders told the parents never to spank in anger. As a result, some children may "view mild-to-moderate corporal punishment as legitimate, appropriate, and even an indicator of parental involvement, commitment, and concern" (Ellison et al., 2011, p. 957).

Another study of conservative Christians found that many thought their faith condoned spanking. Only when they learned that the Bible opposed spanking (e.g., that "sparing the rod" refers to the guiding rod that shepherds use, which was never used to punish), and learned research on the long-term harm, did they change their minds (Perrin et al., 2017). Many then concluded that physical punishment is contrary to their belief in love and forgiveness.

A dynamic-systems, multicultural perspective reminds me that everyone is influenced by background and context. I know that I am; so is every scientist; so are you. Probably my opinions are wrong about several developmental controversies that I explain in this text. I do not think this is one of them.

**time-out** A disciplinary technique in which a person is separated from other people and activities for a specified time.

**induction** A disciplinary technique that involves explaining why a particular behavior was wrong. To be successful, explanation must be within the child's ability to understand.

**Especially for Parents** Suppose you agree that spanking is destructive, but you sometimes get so angry at your child's behavior that you hit him or her. Is your reaction appropriate? (see response, page 281)

Consider Finland, where corporal punishment is forbidden, but psychological control is not. The higher parents scored on four measures of psychological control, the lower the children's math scores were—and this connection grew stronger over time. Moreover, the children tended to have negative emotions (depression, anger, and so on) (Aunola et al., 2013).

Another disciplinary technique is the **time-out**, in which a misbehaving child is required to sit quietly, without toys or playmates, for a short time. Time-out is not to be done in anger, or for too long; it is recommended that parents use a calm voice and that the time-out last only one to five minutes (Morawska & Sanders, 2011). Time-out is punishment if the child enjoys "time-in," when the child is engaged with parents or with peers.

Time-out is favored by many experts. They advise that time-out is part of a close parent–child relationship, a way to punish a behavior that the child knows is wrong. The message is that the child needs to stop and think, and thus indicates the parent's connection to the child, not rejection (Dadds & Tully, 2019)

Often combined with the time-out is another alternative to physical punishment and psychological control—**induction**, in which the parents discuss the infraction with their child, hoping the children themselves will realize why their behavior was wrong. Ideally, a strong and affectionate parent–child relationship allows children to express their emotions and parents to listen.

Induction takes time and patience, and, like other discipline measures, it does not always succeed. One problem is that young children confuse causes with consequences and tend to think they behaved properly, given the situation. Simple induction ("Why did he cry?") may be appropriate, but even that is hard before a child develops theory of mind. Nonetheless, induction may pay off over time. Children whose parents used induction when they were 3-year-olds became children with fewer externalizing problems in elementary school (Choe et al., 2013b).

What do parents actually do? A survey of discipline in early childhood found that most parents use more than one method (Thompson et al., 2017). In the United States, time-out is the most common punishment, and about half of the parents sometimes spank. The survey found that other methods—induction, counting, distraction, hand-smacking, removal of a toy or activity—were also used.

Specifics of parenting style and punishment seem less crucial than whether or not children know that they are loved, guided, and appreciated (Grusec et al., 2017). If a parent seems too strict, or too lenient, remember that if the children consider discipline fair, and believe they are loved and valued, they are likely to be high achievers, who are happy and proud (Pinquart & Kauser, 2018).

## Becoming Boys and Girls

Another challenge for caregivers is to promote a healthy understanding of sex and gender, so children can be proud of themselves and accepting of others.

### Sex and Gender

**sex differences** Biological differences between males and females, in organs, hormones, and body shape.

**gender differences** Differences in male and female roles, behaviors, clothes, and so on that arise from society, not biology.

**Sex differences** are innate, the results of the XX or XY chromosomes and the hormones they produce. **Gender differences** are cultural, either obviously so, in clothes and hair styles, or more generally, such as differences in achievement scores on tests or an adult's participation in a group conversation.

In theory this distinction between sex and gender seems simple; in practice it is not. Culture and biology are not separate influences but are "interacting components of nature and nurture" (Eagly & Wood, 2013, p. 349). The interaction between sex and gender is such that some scholars propose that we use only one word, sex/gender, to denote both (Hyde et al., 2019).

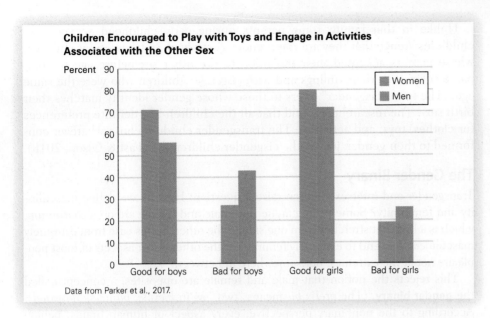

**Children Encouraged to Play with Toys and Engage in Activities Associated with the Other Sex**

Data from Parker et al., 2017.

**FIGURE 10.2**
**Similarities?** What is more remarkable—that most people think girls should be encouraged to play with trucks and boys encouraged to play with dolls, or that some people do not? Your answer probably depends on whether you thought gender equality has been achieved or is still far away.

Be that as it may, during early childhood most children develop distinct gender identities. By age 4, children believe that certain toys (such as dolls or trucks) and roles (Daddy, Mommy, nurse, teacher, police officer, soldier) are reserved for one sex or the other, even when their experience is otherwise. As one expert explains:

> Four year olds say that girls will always be girls and will never become boys. . . . They are often more absolute about gender than adults are. They'll tell their very own pantssuited doctor mother that girls wear dresses and women are nurses.

> [Gopnik, 2016, p. 140]

By age 6, children can become quite rigid. Despite their parents' and teachers' wishes, children say, "girls are stupid; boys stink, no girls [or boys] allowed."

Many parents believe they treat their sons and daughters the same and want to free their children from gender stereotypes. Few adults today would forbid a boy from wanting to push a toy stroller with a doll strapped in it, or a girl from pushing around a truck.

A 2017 survey found that most adults went one step further. They thought parents should *encourage* their children to play with toys associated with the other sex (Parker et al., 2017). Those who disagreed were mostly men who were asked about boys; 43 percent of the men thought boys should *not* be encouraged to do things usually stereotyped for girls, such as care for dolls or wear bracelets (see **Figure 10.2**).

In any case, young children may reject such encouragement. A meta-analysis of 75 studies found that girls have strong preferences for girl toys, especially dolls, and boys for boy toys, especially trucks (Davis & Hines, 2020). A child's absolutism and rejection of the other sex poses a challenge if parents want their children to be less rigid about sex roles.

## Transgender Children

Sex and gender issues are particularly salient when a child is **transgender**, identifying as being a gender other than the one assigned at birth (Rahilly, 2015). It is one thing to allow young girls to play with trucks and young boys to play with dolls, but it may be harder to accept that a child has quite distinct ideas about what gender they are, when that gender is not the one on their birth certificate. One mother said:

**transgender** Identifying oneself with a gender other than the one ascribed at birth. Thus, a transgender girl was thought to be a boy when she was born.

> Since he was two, all he can say is that he wants to be a girl, or that he is a girl. He knows that he is not, but there is no way to change his mind. He is 6 now, and he still asks me everyday "Mom, can I be a girl when I grow up?"

> [quoted in Malpas, 2011, p. 453]

Mike Belleme

**Not Emma** In a North Carolina kindergarten, each child had an "All About Me" day in which the teacher would draw a picture of the child for all of the other children to copy. Emma was born with male sex organs but identifies as a girl. On her day, she proudly wore a light-pink shirt with a heart, pink glittery shoes, and long hair—and she came home bawling because the teacher drew this picture with her "boy name" (barely visible here). Her parents consoled her, had her edit her name and draw longer hair, with some additions. Shouldn't children be allowed to be who they are?

**gender binary** The idea that there are only two (*bi-*) genders, male and female, and that they are opposites. This idea precludes intersex, gender overlap, and gender non-conformity.

Unlike in that family, some parents during early childhood accept their child's insistence that they are transgender. A study of 36 transgender children, whose parents accepted their transition to the other sex before age 6, compared them with their siblings and with *cisgender* children who were the same age. (The term "cisgender" refers to those whose gender identity matches their birth sex.) The researchers found that all the children had definite preferences for clothes, toys, and activities. The transgender children chose whatever conformed to their gender, just as the cisgender children did (Fast & Olson, 2018).

## The Gender Binary

Transgender and intersex children raise a question: How do we define masculinity and femininity? Some people argue that male and female are on a *continuum*, which is a line that stretches from one side to the other, in this case from extremely masculine at one end to extremely feminine at the other. Most aspects of most people are not at the extremes, but somewhere in between.

This rejects the notion that male and female are opposites, a concept called the **gender binary**. (The prefix *bi-* means "two," as in *bicycle, bifurcate, bisexual*). According to the nonbinary perspective, every aspect of human brains, behavior, and bodies is somewhere along that continuum. For example, some men are shorter than the average woman, and some women are more gifted in advanced math than the average man.

That gender traits are not opposites, but instead that there is much overlap between men and women, is now understood by most adults. We expect men to sometimes cry; we cheer the U.S. women's soccer team who won the World Cup. The nonbinary perspective has also become prominent in studies of the human brain. Although male and female brains are alike on most measures, one study found a dozen neurological characteristics that differed notably between the *average* male and female brain (Joel et al., 2015).

However, that study found much overlap, with some men having neurological characteristics typical for women, and vice versa. Fewer than 10 percent of the people in this study had brains that were typical for their sex in all of the dozen traits that distinguish male and female brains (Joel et al., 2015). From studies such as this one, a team of researchers conclude that most human brains and behaviors are a male/female mosaic (Hyde et al., 2019).

The research raises an issue for developmentalists. Why are male and female distinctions recognized by most 2-year-olds, significant to most 4-year-olds, and accepted as natural by 6-year-olds? All of the major theories "devote considerable attention to gender differences. . . . the primary difference among the theories resides in the causal mechanism responsible" (Bornstein et al., 2016, pp. 10, 11). Consider the five comprehensive theories in Chapter 2: psychoanalytic, behaviorism, cognitive, sociocultural, and evolutionary.

## Psychoanalytic Theory

**phallic stage** Freud's third stage of development, when the penis becomes the focus of concern and pleasure.

Freud (1938/1995) called the period from about ages 3 to 6 the **phallic stage**, named after the *phallus,* the Greek word for penis. At age 3 or 4, said Freud, boys become aware of their male sexual organ. They masturbate, fear castration, and develop sexual feelings toward their mother.

**Oedipus complex** The unconscious desire of young boys to replace their fathers and win their mothers' exclusive love.

These feelings make every young boy jealous of his father—so jealous, according to Freud, that he wants to replace his dad. Freud called this the **Oedipus complex**, after Oedipus, son of a king in Greek mythology. Abandoned as an infant and raised in a distant kingdom, Oedipus returned to his birthplace and, without realizing it, killed his father and married his mother. When he discovered the horror, he blinded himself.

Freud believed that this ancient story (immortalized in *Oedipus Rex,* a play written by Sophocles and first presented in Athens in 429 B.C.E.) is still presented every year somewhere in the world because it evokes unconscious wishes in every-one. Every young boy, says Freud, feels guilty about his incestuous and murderous impulses. In self-defense, young boys develop their **superego**, a powerful con-science that is quick to judge and punish.

That marks the beginning of morality, according to psychoanalytic theory. This theory contends that a small boy's fascination with superheroes, guns, kung fu, and the like arises from his unconscious impulse to kill his father. Further, an adult man's homosexuality, homophobia, or obsession with guns, pornography, prostitutes, or hell arises from problems at the phallic stage.

Freud offered several descriptions of the moral development of girls. One, called the *Electra complex,* is again named after an ancient Greek drama. Freud thought that girls also want to eliminate their same-sex parent (mother) and become intimate with the opposite-sex parent (father). For him, that explained why many 5-year-old girls dress in frills and lace and are happy to be "Daddy's girl."

Many psychologists criticize psychoanalytic theory as being unscientific. I know many adults who are gay, lesbian, or asexual, and who have happy, well-adjusted lives. However, scientists seek to reconcile theory and experience. My daughters made me reconsider. (See A Case to Study.)

**superego** In psychoanalytic theory, the judgmental part of the personality that internalizes the moral standards of the parents.

## A CASE TO STUDY

## The Berger Daughters

I dressed my baby girls in blue, trying to create a unisex world for them. I wanted to free them from gender stereotypes. I failed.

My eldest, Bethany, at about 4 years old told me:

**Bethany:** When I grow up, I'm going to marry Daddy.
   **Me:** But Daddy's married to me.
**Bethany:** That's all right. When I grow up, you'll probably be dead.
   **Me:** [*Determined to stick up for myself*] Daddy's older than me, so when I'm dead, he'll probably be dead, too.
**Bethany:** That's OK. I'll marry him when he gets born again.

I was dumbfounded, stunned by how Freudian this sounded. Bethany saw my face fall, and pitied me:

**Bethany:** Don't worry, Mommy. After you get born again, you can be our baby.

A few years later, my second-born daughter Rachel told me:

**Rachel:** When I get married, I'm going to marry Daddy.
   **Me:** Daddy's already married to me.
**Rachel:** [*With joy at her wonderful solution*] Then we can have a double wedding!

My third daughter, Elissa, left a valentine on my husband's pillow on February 14th (see **Figure 10.3**).

Finally, when Sarah turned 5, she also said she would marry her father. I told her she couldn't, because he was married to me. Her response revealed one more hazard of screen time: "Oh, yes, a man can have two wives. I saw it on television."

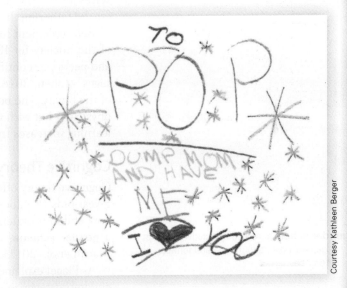

**FIGURE 10.3**
**Pillow Talk** Elissa placed this artwork on my husband's pillow. My pillow, beside it, had a less colorful, less elaborate note—an after-thought. It read, "Dear Mom, I love you too."

As you remember from Chapter 1, a single example (one family with four daughters) does not prove that Freud was cor-rect. I still think Freud was wrong on many counts, and I am proud that all four girls became college-educated, professionally employed women. But in many ways, they are following gender-specific paths. Freud's description of the phallic stage seems less bizarre than I once thought.

## Behaviorism

Gender-typed behavior in play and chores (washing dishes versus fixing cars) is among the most robust findings of decades of research (Eagly & Wood, 2013). Behaviorists believe that those gender distinctions result from reinforcement, punishment, and social learning, evident in early childhood. For example, a 2-year-old boy who asks for both a train and a doll for his birthday is more likely to get the train.

Gender differentiation may be subtle, with adults unaware that they are reinforcing traditional masculine or feminine behavior. For example, parents talking to young children mention numbers and shapes more often with their sons (Pruden & Levine, 2017). Even with infants, fathers interact differently with their children, singing and talking more to their daughters but using words of achievement, such as *proud* and *win*, more with their sons (Mascaro et al., 2017).

According to social learning theory (an extension of behaviorism), people model themselves after people who are nurturing, powerful, and yet similar to themselves. For young children, those people are usually their parents.

Generally, if an employed woman is ever to leave her job to become a housewife, it is when she has a baby. Fathers tend to work longer hours — they are home less often — and mothers work fewer hours when children arrive. Since children learn gender roles from their parents, it is no surprise that they are quite sexist (Hallers-Haalboom et al., 2014).

Thus, adults are the most gender-typed of their entire lives when they are raising young children. According to social learning theory, children model themselves after what they see. They are unaware that their very existence is the reason for the father/mother divide.

Reinforcement for the gender binary extends beyond the family. The president of the Society for Research in Child Development observed, "parents, teachers, and peers . . . continue to encourage, model, and enforce traditional gender messages" (Liben, 2016, p. 24). Peers and social norms are powerful reinforcements of the binary. The boy who brings his Barbie doll to school will be punished — not physically, but with words and social exclusion — by his male classmates. As social learning increases from age 2 to 22, so does gender divergence.

## Cognitive Theory

Cognitive theory offers an alternative explanation for the strong gender identity of 5-year-olds (Kohlberg et al., 1983). Remember that cognitive theorists focus on how children understand various ideas. Regarding boys and girls, they construct a **gender schema**, an understanding of male–female differences (Bem, 1981; Martin et al., 2011).

As Piaget explained, preoperational perceptions are static, not logical. Therefore, children categorize male and female as opposites. Nuances, complexities, exceptions, and gradations about gender (and about everything else) are beyond them.

During the preoperational stage, appearance is stronger than logic. One group of researchers who endorse the cognitive interpretation note that "young children pass through a stage of gender appearance rigidity; girls insist on wearing dresses, often pink and frilly, whereas boys refuse to wear anything with a hint of femininity" (Halim et al., 2014, p. 1091).

Parents who encourage unisex clothes are confronted by daughters who want a bright pink tutu and a sparkly tiara, and sons who want cowboy boots and guns. Children's gender schema overcomes the adult fight against sexism.

During these years, children are especially sensitive to language, which influences the way people think. A study of 45 of the world's languages found that,

**gender schema** A child's cognitive concept or general belief about male and female differences.

if the language assigns gender to asexual objects (as in Spanish, chair is *la* silla, unless it is *el* sillón, the name for a big armchair), children are more likely to see male and female as separate and distinct (DeFranza et al., 2020).

Cognitive theory explains some of the amusing mistakes that children make in their theories of gender. In one preschool, the children decided that one wash-up basin was for boys and the other for girls. That fits the cognitive schema that everything can be divided into male and female. But another cognitive mandate for 3-year-olds is to do whatever it takes to get what you want. A young girl started to use the boys' basin.

> **Boy:** This is for the boys.
> **Girl:** Stop it. I'm not a girl and a boy, so I'm here.
> **Boy:** What?
> **Girl:** I'm a boy and also a girl.
> **Boy:** You, now, are you today a boy?
> **Girl:** Yes.
> **Boy:** And tomorrow what will you be?
> **Girl:** A girl. Tomorrow I'll be a girl. Today I'll be a boy.
> **Boy:** And after tomorrow?
> **Girl:** I'll be a girl.
>
> *[Ehrlich & Blum-Kulka, 2014, p. 31]*

This incident occurred in Israel, where women have been drafted into the army and have served as national leaders for decades. Probably this girl had been told that some gender restrictions are unfair to females, and she appropriated that message when she wanted to wash up. Neither she nor the boy questioned the overall binary, however, perhaps because in Hebrew every object is masculine or feminine.

## Sociocultural Theory

It is evident that gender distinctions are pervasive in every culture (Starr & Zurbriggen, 2016). Some people believe this is no longer true, as women are in professions that

DIPTENDU DUTTA/AFP/GETTY IMAGES

© Ilyas Dean/The Image Works

**Same Situation, Far Apart: Culture Clash?**
He wears the orange robes of a Buddhist monk, and she wears the hijab of a Muslim girl. Although he is at a weeklong spiritual retreat led by the Dalai Lama and she is in an alley in Pakistan, both carry universal toys—a pop gun and a bride doll, identical to those found almost everywhere. Cultures differ; gender roles do not.

were once exclusively male, and many fathers are active caregivers. However, in even the most gender-equal nations, women do much more child care, house cleaning, and meal preparation than do men. This is true when women are the primary wage-earners for their families (as are about 40 percent of mothers in the United States as well as worldwide) (Bornstein & Putnick, 2016).

If you think we have reached gender equality, look closely at the data on professions. Males are more often nurses than they were, but in 2020 only about 10 percent of nurses were male. That this is sociocultural is suggested by data on ethnicity: A higher percent of those male nurses were born in Africa.

In engineering, in 1976 only 2 percent of college women aspired to that profession; now it is slightly above 3 percent for women and 15 percent for college men. This gender divergence is found even when a student's mother is an engineer (Jacobs et al., 2017). Thus, culture seems to overwhelm family influence.

Everywhere, cultures socialize young girls and boys differently. For example, two 4-year-old girls might hug each other and hear "how sweet," but a boy who hugs a boy might be pushed away. Already by age 6, rough-and-tumble play is the only accepted way that boys touch each other, and girls are stopped from rough play more quickly than boys are. No wonder rough-and-tumble is more common among boys than girls.

Cultural differences are expressed by parents who do not realize that they are doing it. For instance, a massive study of 41 low- and middle-income nations found that fathers took their young boys outside more often than their girls. They also were more likely to read to, tell stories to, and count with their sons. The mothers tended to be more unisex in their activities (Bornstein & Putnick, 2016).

By age 6, children are astute "gender detectives," seeking out ways that males and females differ in their culture. They try to conform to their culture, as do all humans of every age. Mia is one example:

> On her first day of school, Mia sits at the lunch table eating a peanut butter and jelly sandwich. She notices that a few boys are eating peanut butter and jelly, but not one girl is. When her father picks her up from school, Mia runs up to him and exclaims, "Peanut butter and jelly is for boys! I want a turkey sandwich tomorrow."

*[Quoted in Miller et al., 2013, p. 307]*

## Evolutionary Theory

Evolutionary theory holds that sexual passion is a basic human drive because all creatures must reproduce. Since conception requires an ovum and a sperm, males and females follow their evolutionary mandate by seeking to attract the other sex—walking, talking, and laughing in traditional feminine or masculine ways. That awakens sexual impulses in the other sex, assuring that the species will continue.

This evolutionary drive may explain why, already in early childhood, boys have a powerful urge to become like the men, and girls like the women. Young boys clomp around in their father's clunky shoes; young girls spray their mother's perfume all over themselves. These impulses prepare them, later on, to mate and conceive a new generation.

Evolutionary theory emphasizes the urge to survive as well as the urge to reproduce. Over millennia of human history, genes, chromosomes, and hormones dictated that young boys were more active (rough-and-tumble play) and girls more domestic (playing house). These also prepared them for adulthood, when fathers needed to defend against predators and mothers needed to care for the home and children.

Many researchers describe the women's liberation movement as a "stalled revolution" with progress evident in the public sphere (signified by employment and education) but not in the domestic one (Scarborough et al., 2019). From an evolutionary perspective, it might be that, in the intimacy of a partnership, wives want the husbands to respond as men traditionally did, even though at the workplace women fight for the same salary and power as the men.

Of course, tigers and bears no longer prowl outside in most places, but evolution takes thousands of years to reverse impulses needed 200,000 years ago. Few adolescents today follow the gendered path of teen marriage and motherhood, but almost all aspire to marry eventually, and almost all live with a sexual partner in adulthood (Sassler & Lichter, 2020). Both partners tend to fall into traditional roles, unless one or the other explicitly says otherwise. Perhaps evolution requires it.

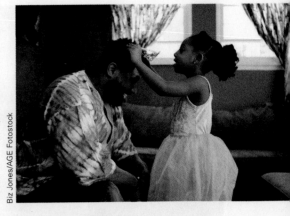

**Gender-Nonconforming** The dad, not the daughter. Like many 6-year-olds, she loves wearing her frilly dress, and like many fathers he allows her to follow traditional roles, here by letting her put a tiara on his head.

## What Is Best?

Each major developmental theory strives to explain the ideas that young children express and the roles they follow. No consensus has been reached. Caregivers know they should not blindly follow the norms of their culture, yet they also know that they need to guide their children regarding male–female differences and everything else.

Some recent research suggests a *gender similarities hypothesis,* the idea that our human emphasis on sex differences blinds us to the reality that the two sexes have far more in common than traditional theories recognize (Hyde, 2016). Perhaps instead of looking for sex differences, we should notice gender similarities. According to some researchers, similarities far outweigh differences in the brain, body, and behavior (Roseberry & Roos, 2016; Hutchison et al., 2019). Each child can be appreciated for themselves.

## Teaching Right and Wrong

A final challenge for parents it to teach moral values. Young children are ready to learn right and wrong, an outgrowth of bonding in infancy, attachment in childhood, and now social understanding. Moral values are essential for our species; we depend on each other for protection, cooperation, and care. That is why our bodies produce hormones (oxytocin, vasopressin) that push people toward trust, love, and morality (Zak, 2012).

**LaunchPad**
macmillan learning

**VIDEO: Interview with Lawrence Walker** discusses what parents can do to encourage their children's moral development.

## Empathy

With the cognitive advances of early childhood, and increased interaction with peers, these innate moral impulses are strengthened. Children develop **empathy**, an understanding of other people's feelings and concerns. Empathy depends on both experiences and brain maturation (Levy et al., 2019; Stern et al., 2019).

Empathy leads to compassion and **prosocial behavior**—"voluntary behavior meant to help another" (Padilla-Walker & Carlo, 2014, p. 6). Expressing concern, offering to share, and including a shy child in a game are examples of children's prosocial behavior. Prosocial behavior seems to result more from emotion than from intellect, more from empathy than from theory.

The link between empathy and prosocial behavior was traced longitudinally in children from 18 months to 6 years. Empathetic 2-year-olds were more likely to share, help, and play with other children in the first grade (Z. Taylor et al., 2013).

Feeling distress when someone else suffers may be a part of nature: Even infants seem distressed at the pain of another. But how and for whom distress leads to action varies by family and culture: Sacrifices are made for family members, or for peers, or not at all (Poelker & Gibbons, 2019).

**empathy** The ability to understand the emotions and concerns of another person, especially when they differ from one's own.

**prosocial behavior** Actions that are helpful and kind but that are of no obvious benefit to the person doing them.

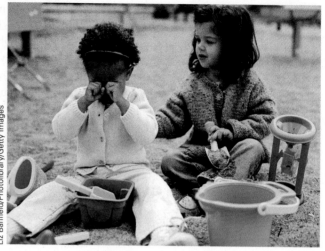

**Pinch, Poke, or Pat** Antisocial and prosocial responses are actually a sign of maturation: Babies do not recognize the impact of their actions. These children have much more to learn, but they already are quite social.

## Antipathy

**antipathy** Feelings of dislike or even hatred for another person.

Empathy appears early in life: Infants mirror the smiles of other people, and young children are happy when other children are happy. **Antipathy** develops a little later, influenced by experience and culture, as children learn to dislike some people.

Just as empathy can lead to prosocial behavior, antipathy can lead to antisocial action, such as avoidance, insults, and physical attacks. A 2-year-old might look at another child, scowl, and then kick hard without provocation.

Generally, parents and teachers teach better behavior, and children become more prosocial and less antisocial with age. A study of children's willingness to belong to a group who did antisocial things found that by age 7, children did not want to be in such a group. That was not true for 5-year-olds: They opted to stay with their group, even when others in the group were antisocial (Wilks et al., 2019).

**antisocial behavior** Actions that are deliberately hurtful or destructive to another person.

At every age, **antisocial behavior** indicates less empathy. That may originate in the brain. An allele or gene may have gone awry. But at least for children, lack of empathy correlates with parents who neither discuss nor respond to emotions (Richards et al., 2014; Z. Taylor et al., 2013). Antisocial parents tend to have antisocial children, a correlation that is probably both genetic and environmental, and may be particularly strong in boys (Li et al., 2017).

## Aggression

Early childhood is prime time for both aggressive behavior and victimization: Almost every young child is both an aggressor and a victim at some point (Saracho, 2016). Not surprisingly, given their moral sensibilities, young children judge whether another child's actions are fair or not.

The focus at first is on effects, not motives: A child who accidentally spilled water on another's painting may be the target of that child's anger. As young children gain in social understanding, particularly theory of mind, they gradually become better at understanding intentions, and that makes them more likely to forgive an accident (Choe et al., 2013a).

The distinction between impulse and intention is critical in deciding when and how adults need to stop a child's aggression. Researchers recognize four general types of aggression, each of which is evident in early childhood (see **Table 10.2**).

### TABLE 10.2

#### The Four Forms of Aggression

| Type of Aggression | Definition | Comments |
|---|---|---|
| Instrumental aggression | Hurtful behavior that is aimed at gaining something (such as a toy, a place in line, or a turn on the swing) that someone else has | Apparent from age 2 to 6; involves objects more than people; quite normal; more egocentric than antisocial. |
| Reactive aggression | An impulsive retaliation for a hurt (intentional or accidental) that can be verbal or physical | Indicates a lack of emotional regulation, characteristic of 2-year-olds. A 5-year-old can usually stop and think before reacting. |
| Relational aggression | Nonphysical acts, such as insults or social rejection, aimed at harming the social connections between the victim and others | Involves a personal attack and thus is directly antisocial; can be very hurtful; more common as children become socially aware. |
| Bullying aggression | Unprovoked, repeated physical or verbal attack, especially on victims who are unlikely to defend themselves | In both bullies and victims, a sign of poor emotional regulation; adults should intervene before the school years. (Bullying is discussed in Chapter 13.) |

**Instrumental aggression** is common among 2-year-olds, who often want something and try to get it. This is called *instrumental* because it is a tool, or instrument, for getting something that is desired. The harm in grabbing a toy, and hitting if someone resists, is not understood.

Because instrumental aggression occurs, **reactive aggression** also is common among young children. Almost every child reacts when hurt, whether or not the hurt was deliberate. The reaction may be aggressive—a child might punch in response to an unwelcome remark. As the prefrontal cortex matures and emotional regulation is possible, the impulse to strike back becomes controlled. Both instrumental aggression and reactive aggression are reduced with maturity (Olson et al., 2011).

**Relational aggression** (usually verbal) destroys self-esteem and disrupts social networks. A child might tell another, "You can't be my friend" or "You are fat," hurting another's feelings. Worse, a child might spread rumors, or tell others not to play with so-and-so.

These are examples of relational aggression, which becomes more hurtful and sometimes more common as social understanding advances. One study found that about one in every five preschool children commonly uses relational aggression (Swit & McMaugh, 2012). Before high school, almost every child has experienced some exclusion from a social group.

The fourth and most ominous type is **bullying aggression**, done to dominate. Bullying aggression occurs among young children but should be stopped before kindergarten, when it becomes more destructive. Not only does it destroy the self-esteem of victims, it also impairs the later development of the bullies, who learn behaviors that harm them lifelong.

A 3-year-old bully needs to learn the effects of their actions; a 10-year-old bully may be feared and admired; a 50-year-old bully may be hated and lonely. (An in-depth discussion of bullying appears in Chapter 13.)

Most types of aggression, including bullying, become less common from ages 2 to 6, as the brain matures, emotional regulation increases, and empathy builds.

**instrumental aggression** Hurtful behavior that is intended to get something that another person has.

**reactive aggression** An impulsive retaliation for another person's intentional or accidental hurtful action.

**relational aggression** Nonphysical acts, such as insults or social rejection, aimed at harming the social connection between the victim and other people.

**bullying aggression** Unprovoked, repeated physical or verbal attack, especially on victims who are unlikely to defend themselves.

Moreover, children understand the social context and thus use aggression selectively, which decreases victimization (Ostrov et al., 2014).

Each type of aggression is influenced by genes as well as by age (Lubke et al., 2018). Thus, some 3-year-olds are innately more aggressive than other children, and they are more likely to be antisocial children and adolescents. That should alert parents and teachers to help such children, particularly, to develop empathy and emotional regulation.

One study found that close teacher–student relationships in preschool decrease aggression and victimization in elementary school. The probable reason—children want to please the teachers, who guide them toward prosocial, not antisocial, behavior (Runions & Shaw, 2013).

---

**WHAT HAVE YOU LEARNED?**

1. What are the four main styles of parenting?

2. What are the consequences of each style of parenting?

3. Why is discipline part of being a parent?

4. What are the arguments for and against corporal punishment?

5. When is a time-out effective and when is it not?

6. What are the differences between the psychoanalytic and behaviorist theories of gender development?

7. What are the differences between the cognitive and evolutionary theories of sex-role development?

8. How might children develop empathy and antipathy as they play with one another?

9. Are prosocial and antisocial behaviors inborn or learned?

10. What are the similarities and differences of the four kinds of aggression?

---

## SUMMARY

### Emotional Development

1. Emotional regulation is crucial during early childhood. It occurs in Erikson's third developmental stage, initiative versus guilt. Children normally feel pride when they demonstrate initiative, but sometimes they feel guilt or even shame at an unsatisfactory outcome.

2. Intrinsic motivation is apparent when a child concentrates on a drawing or a conversation with an imaginary friend. It may endure when extrinsic motivation stops. Extrinsic motivation may discourage intrinsic motivation, or it may result in a habit that continues.

### Play

3. All young children enjoy playing—preferably with other children of the same sex, who teach them lessons in social interaction that their parents do not.

4. Play with other children gradually changes as children mature. Peer experiences, videos, and television affect children's play as they progress from being onlookers to being cooperators.

5. Active play takes many forms, with rough-and-tumble play fostering social skills and sociodramatic play developing emotional regulation. Boys tend to engage in the former, girls in the later, although experts disagree on whether this is nature or nurture.

### Challenges for Caregivers

6. Three classic styles of parenting are authoritarian, permissive, and authoritative. Generally, children are happier and more successful when their parents express warmth and set guidelines.

7. A fourth style of parenting, neglectful/uninvolved, is always harmful. The particulars of parenting reflect the culture as well as the temperament of the child.

8. Parental punishment can have long-term consequences, with both corporal punishment and psychological control teaching lessons that few parents want their children to learn.

9. Even 2-year-olds correctly use sex-specific labels. Young children become aware of gender differences in clothes, toys, playmates, and future careers, and typically become quite strict about male–female distinction. Transgender children show strong gender preferences in early childhood.

10. Every major theory interprets children's awareness of gender differences in a particular way. Freud's emphasized attraction to the

opposite-sex parent; behaviorists stress reinforcement; cognitive theory focuses on gender schemas; sociocultural theory on social norms; and evolutionary theory on the need for species survival.

**11.** Young children's sense of self and social awareness become the foundation for morality, influenced by both nature and nurture. The desire to be part of a group sometimes conflicts with the desire to do the right thing.

**12.** Prosocial emotions lead to caring for others; antisocial behavior includes instrumental, reactive, relational, and bullying aggression.

**13.** Early childhood is an ideal time to teach children how to control their aggression, as well as to learn other aspects of how to navigate the social world in which they find themselves.

## KEY TERMS

emotional regulation (p. 257)
initiative versus guilt (p. 257)
self-concept (p. 257)
intrinsic motivation (p. 258)
extrinsic motivation (p. 259)
rough-and-tumble play (p. 263)
sociodramatic play (p. 264)
authoritarian parenting
 (p. 265)

permissive parenting (p. 265)
authoritative parenting
 (p. 265)
neglectful/uninvolved parenting
 (p. 266)
corporal punishment (p. 267)
psychological control (p. 268)
time-out (p. 270)
induction (p. 270)

sex differences (p. 270)
gender differences
 (p. 270)
transgender (p. 271)
gender binary (p. 272)
phallic stage (p. 272)
Oedipus complex (p. 272)
superego (p. 273)
gender schema (p. 274)

empathy (p. 277)
prosocial behavior (p. 277)
antipathy (p. 278)
antisocial behavior (p. 278)
instrumental aggression
 (p. 279)
reactive aggression (p. 279)
relational aggression (p. 279)
bullying aggression (p. 279)

## APPLICATIONS

**1.** Children's television programming is rife with stereotypes about ethnicity, gender, and morality. Watch an hour of children's TV, especially on a Saturday morning or through a streaming service such as Netflix, and describe the content of both the programs and the commercials. Draw conclusions about stereotyping, citing specific evidence not generalities.

**2.** Gender indicators often go unnoticed. Go to a public place (park, restaurant, busy street) and spend at least 10 minutes recording examples of gender differentiation, such as articles of clothing, mannerisms, interaction patterns, and activities.

Quantify what you see, such as baseball hats on eight males and two females. Or (better, but more difficult) describe four male–female conversations, indicating gender differences in length and frequency of talking, interruptions, vocabulary, and so on.

**3.** Ask three parents about punishment, including their preferred type, at what age, for what misdeeds, and by whom. Ask your three informants how they were punished as children and how that affected them. If your sources all agree, find a parent (or a classmate) who has a different view.

## Especially For ANSWERS

**Response for College Students** (from p. 259): Both are important. Extrinsic motivation includes parental pressure and the need to get a good job after graduation. Intrinsic motivation includes the joy of learning, especially if you can express that learning in ways others recognize. Have you ever taken a course that was not required and was said to be difficult? That was intrinsic motivation.

**Response for Parents** (from p. 270): No. The worst time to spank a child is when you are angry. You might seriously hurt the child, and the child will associate anger with violence. You would do better to learn to control your anger and develop other strategies for discipline and for prevention of misbehavior.

## Observation Quiz ANSWER

**Answer to Observation Quiz** (from p. 266): It is impossible to be certain based on one moment, but the best guess is authoritative. He seems patient and protective, providing comfort and guidance, neither forcing (authoritarian) nor letting the child do whatever he wants (permissive).

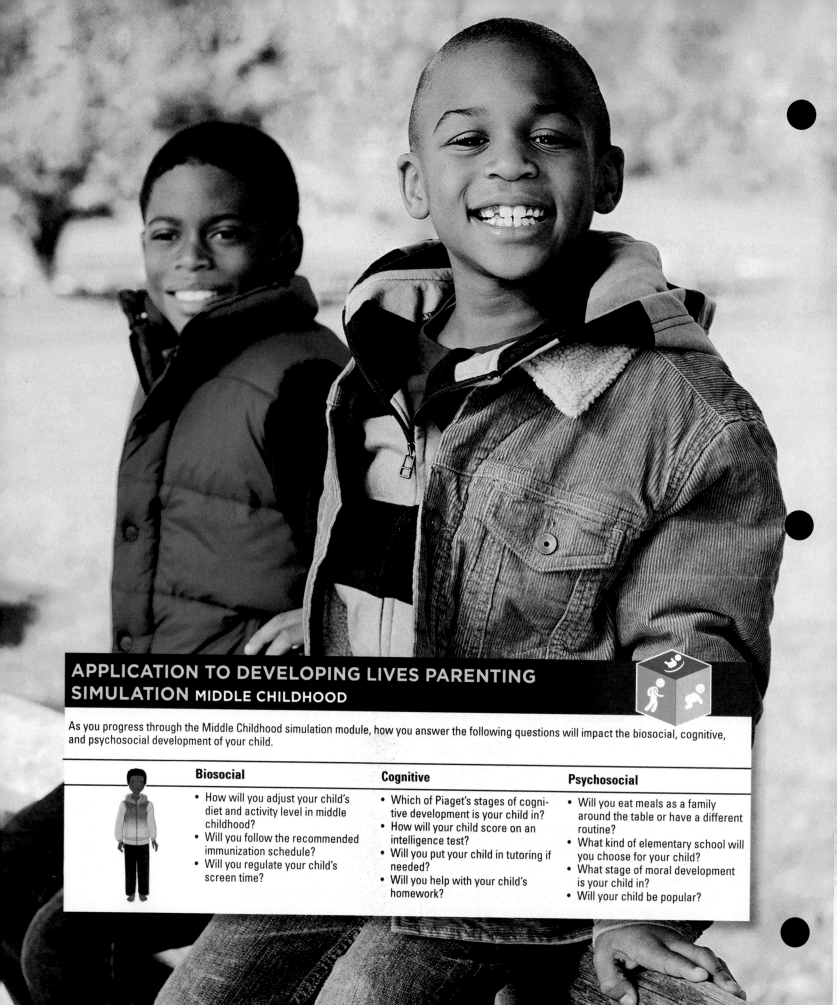

# APPLICATION TO DEVELOPING LIVES PARENTING
## SIMULATION MIDDLE CHILDHOOD

As you progress through the Middle Childhood simulation module, how you answer the following questions will impact the biosocial, cognitive, and psychosocial development of your child.

| | Biosocial | Cognitive | Psychosocial |
|---|---|---|---|
| | • How will you adjust your child's diet and activity level in middle childhood?<br>• Will you follow the recommended immunization schedule?<br>• Will you regulate your child's screen time? | • Which of Piaget's stages of cognitive development is your child in?<br>• How will your child score on an intelligence test?<br>• Will you put your child in tutoring if needed?<br>• Will you help with your child's homework? | • Will you eat meals as a family around the table or have a different routine?<br>• What kind of elementary school will you choose for your child?<br>• What stage of moral development is your child in?<br>• Will your child be popular? |

# Middle Childhood

# PART IV

**E**very year has joys and sorrows, gains and losses. But if you were pushed to choose one best period, you might select middle childhood. The years from 6 to 11 are usually a time of good health and steady growth. Children master new skills, learn thousands of words, and enter a wider social world. They are safe and happy; the dangers of adolescence (drugs, early sex, violence) are distant.

But not always. For some children, these years are the worst, not the best. They hate school or fear home; they suffer with asthma or disability; they are bullied or lonely.

Nor are these years straightforward for every adult who cares for these children. Instead, controversies abound. Should hyperactive children be medicated? Should reading and math crowd out music, or handwriting, or free play? Does single parenthood, divorce, cohabitation, or poverty harm children? The next three chapters explore the joys and complications of middle childhood. ●●

Left: Image Source/DigitalVision/Getty Images
Right: EdZbarzhyvetsky/Deposit Photos

# Middle Childhood: Biosocial Development

## What Will You Know?

1. Who is at fault if a child is obese?
2. How does playing a musical instrument affect brain development?
3. Why are so many children on the autism spectrum?

After school I sit on a bench, watching two of my grandchildren and hundreds of other children play. Many parents, grandparents, and babysitters are there also, sometimes talking to each other, sometimes reading, sometimes interacting with a child who is temporarily hurt or who wants a snack (I always bring fruit; other adults bring cookies, or dried seaweed, or chips).

I admire the few parents who are more active: One father pretends to chase the younger children, including his daughter, to their shrieks of joy. Another father plays soccer with the older children, encouraging both the novices ("Nice kick!") and his own skilled son. One mother walks beside her daughter, who is blind but nonetheless climbs up the ladder to go down the slide. But most adults, like me, sit and watch.

What do we see? Much running, chasing, and climbing. Why do children hang on to metal rings, swinging their legs, grabbing for another metal ring? Why do they run across a bridge designed to be unsteady? Why do they grab each other, falling to the ground (it is rubberized), or, depending on the season, collect leaves, or throw snow, or chase pigeons?

The older children organize games—four square, touch football, kickball—but they do not keep score. Teams are fluid: When a parent tells a player it is time to leave, the remaining children quickly rebalance the team. The game continues until only two or three children remain, or someone takes the ball home.

Even with my warmest coat, I am cold sitting on the bench. Meanwhile, my older grandson wears only a T-shirt. Shivering, I bring his coat to him; he laughs and runs away. ("No. No. I am not cold.") Weather, even drizzle and snow, does not stop the play.

The equipment is designed to be safe (there is a fence around the swings), but children sometimes run into things. Once my younger grandson came to me crying, "I bumped my head." Remembering the animism of young children, I tried to distract him, saying "Tell me what pole hit you, and I will tell that pole not to hurt you again." He said, "I bumped it on another head" and ran off, happy again.

I am awed by their energy and social interaction, a marked contrast to my bench-sitting. This chapter is about that: the actions of children in middle childhood, and the adults who try to keep them safe and healthy, not always doing it well. Examples include allergies, asthma, obesity, and special needs. I hope the mother of the "other head" responded better than I did.

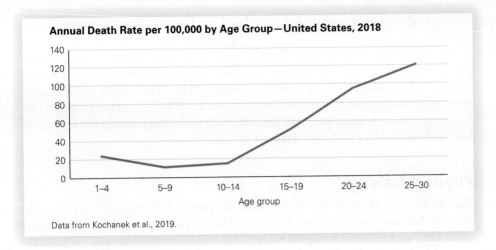

**Annual Death Rate per 100,000 by Age Group—United States, 2018**

Data from Kochanek et al., 2019.

**FIGURE 11.1**
**Death at an Early Age? Almost Never!**
Rates continue to rise with age, up to 13,574 for those aged 85 and older, so this figure cannot portray the entire life span. Details are remarkable as well. Not only are fatal diseases rare, thanks to immunization, but accidents and homicides also dip during middle childhood—and rise rapidly thereafter.

## A Healthy Time

Unlike the first five years or the next ten, middle childhood is a time of slow and steady growth. Children gain about 2 inches and 5 pounds a year (5 centimeters and 2 kilograms). Nature and nurture combine to make these the healthiest years of life (see **Figure 11.1**).

## Statistics on Health

To be specific, the death rate for 5- to 9-year-olds is by far the lowest of any age group, about 1 per 10,000, which is about half the rate of younger or older children, and 1/70th the overall rate (National Center for Health Statistics, 2019). The reasons are both nature and nurture. Genetic diseases are more threatening in infancy or old age; infectious diseases are kept away via immunization; fatal accidents—although the most common cause of child death—are relatively uncommon until late adolescence.

## Health Habits

Children maintain good health if adults teach them good habits, and if regular doctor and dentist visits are part of their lives. Every child needs adequate medical care; without it, health later on is impaired. If a person has good care in adulthood but had poor health and care in childhood, adult health still suffers (Juster et al., 2016; McEwen & McEwen, 2017).

Parents are the major influence on the health habits of 2- to 5-year-olds. By middle childhood, however, peers and teachers become influential, sometimes altering a child's healthy or unhealthy behavior.

This was found in a longitudinal study that tracked children's health habits from early childhood to early adolescence. Children were not necessarily consistent from first through eighth grade, nor were they consistent as individuals: A particular child might be healthy in one way but not another (such as getting adequate exercise but not eating well) (Mollborn & Lawrence, 2018). Schools and friends were part of the reason.

Another study found that, especially in middle childhood, children were influenced not only by learning what they *should* do, but also by learning what other children actually did (Hang et al., 2020). If children see others routinely caring for their own health, social learning pushes them to do the same. Camps for children with asthma, cancer, diabetes, sickle-cell anemia, and other chronic

AP Images/Aijaz Rahi

**Global Progress** Thousands of children in Bangalore, India, gathered to brush their teeth together, part of an oral health campaign. Music, fast food, candy bars, and technology have been exported from the United States, and many developing nations have their own versions (Bollywood replaces Hollywood). That is why western diseases have also reached many nations; preventive health care now follows.

**Observation Quiz** Beyond toothbrushes, what other health tools do most children here have that their parents did not? (see answer, page 309) ↑

illnesses are recommended, because peers and knowledgeable adults teach self-care.

Middle childhood is an ideal time for this, as these children are less likely to question authority recommendations than older children are. Health habits should be established before teenage rebellion erupts: Many adolescents resist special diets, pills, warning signs, and doctors (Dean et al., 2010; Naughton et al., 2014). Some react to authorities by doing the opposite of what they should do, a reaction less likely in middle childhood (Hang et al., 2020).

## Physical Activity

The benefits of physical activity—especially games with rules, which children now can follow—last a lifetime. Exercise advances physical, emotional, and mental health, as well as learning in school. This includes the free play of running around (as I saw in the playground) or organized sports.

Team sports teach cooperation, self-control, and emotional regulation—all essential lessons in middle childhood. Caution is needed here. Games that young children organize themselves are unlikely to cause serious injury, but adults sometimes involve children in adult sports that require child-size protective equipment (helmets, mitts, etc.). Harm is possible.

Organizations have developed guidelines to prevent concussions among 7- and 8-year-olds in football and to halt full-body impact from ice hockey among children under age 12. The fact that regulations are needed to protect children from brain injury is sobering (Toporek, 2012).

## The Influence of Parents

Generally, parental involvement and encouragement of physical activity has increased over recent years, which benefits the children. In some nations, boys and girls are equally influenced by either parent, but in other nations, they follow the adults of their gender. In Portugal, for instance, a child's participation in physical activity follows that of the parents of the same sex (Rodrigues et al., 2018).

Adult emotions may be affected by children's competitive sports. A study found that fathers' testosterone and cortisol rose when they watched their children in a soccer tournament. Effects were stronger for sons than daughters, especially if the men thought the referee was unfair. Hormones were unaffected by winning or losing, as long as the fathers thought their own children and teams played as well as they could (Alvarado et al., 2018).

An important cohort change may be at work here. Both parents are much more engaged in their children's sports activities than they were a few decades ago, according to a detailed study in Norway (Stefansen et al., 2018). Many parents consider this a way to connect with their children, as one father said:

> It's about being acknowledged sort of. To be praised and to be able to talk about [the game] later. [ . . . ] And to share experiences. For instance when [our son] played football [soccer] when he was eight and we could see him score a goal . . . yes. I played football all through my childhood and youth, but my parents did not attend one match. Not one.

*[Quoted in Stefansen et al., 2018, p. 166]*

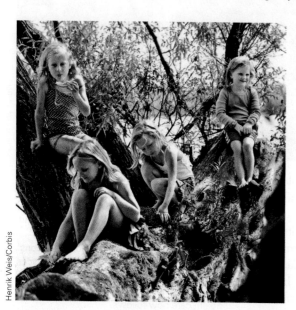

Henrik Weis/Corbis

**Idyllic** Two 8-year-olds, each with a 6-year-old sister, all four daydreaming or exploring in a very old tree beside a lake in Denmark—what could be better? ideally, all of the world's children would be so fortunate, but most are not.

In the United States, parental involvement in children's sports is part of parental investment in each child, which is both a benefit (children know their parents care) and a liability (children feel pressured to perform) (Putnam, 2015).

Parents themselves may be overly concerned about their child's athletic success. One example from that Norwegian study:

> One father . . . had invested a lot in his daughter's talent in handball. He used to be the coach and he had been there for all her practices and games. The daughter had always been "promising" but had never really blossomed. When the development had been good, she had become injured. At the time of the interview the father was feeling lost—not able to stop his intensive support but at the same time questioning if the daughter perhaps should give up handball because of the injuries. The practice of deep involvement thus balances a very thin line between intrusion or pressure and support.
>
> [Stefansen et al., 2018, p. 169]

Most injuries of 6- to 16-year-olds involve sports. Is this because the children take risks or because the adults are not protective? Is it possible that this girl was injured in handball because she sought an acceptable way to escape her father's pressure?

A detailed study in Florida of serious athletic injuries, reported by schools, found that 46 percent of the injuries of 5- to 11-year-olds were concussions (Liller et al., 2019). This does not bode well for later brain health: Concussions before age 25 are unlikely to reveal damage at the time but are one cause of *neurocognitive disorders* (formerly called *dementia*) in late adulthood (Silver et al., 2019).

---

**DATA CONNECTIONS: Death at an Early Age? Almost Never!** shows how middle childhood is typically the healthiest period of the entire life span. 🎮 **LaunchPad.**

---

## The Need for Movement

It is tempting to criticize parents who are too enmeshed in their children's competitive play, or to blame schools that do not protect children's heads from concussions. However, physical activity is crucial for health and learning, and many developmentalists are more troubled when indoor activities crowd out active play. Parents used to tell their children "go out and play"; now they say, "don't leave the house."

To compensate, many parents enroll their children in after-school sports that vary by culture—tennis, karate, cricket, yoga, rugby, football, baseball, or soccer. However, the children who most need to connect their bodies and their minds—those from low-SES families or who have physical disabilities—are least likely to join Little League and the like, even when enrollment is free. The reasons are many, the consequences sad (Dearing et al., 2009).

## Physical Exercise in Japan

The idea that exercise improves the brain is assumed in some cultures, while other cultures assume strong muscles indicate weak minds. Dizzy Dean, a star Major League pitcher in the 1930s, said "The Good Lord was good to me, He gave me a strong right arm, a good body, and a weak mind" (Gregory, 1993).

The opposite sentiment is evident in Japan, where people believe that physical activity promotes learning and character development (Webster & Suzuki, 2014). Many Japanese public schools have swimming pools, indoor gyms, and outdoor yards with structures for climbing, swinging, and so on. Children are allowed over an hour of recess (in several segments) over a long day, in addition to gym classes. Note that Japanese children score high on international tests of achievement.

The Japanese emphasize exercise for everyone lifelong. That may explain why they live longer, on average, than people in any other nation. Of course, longevity could result from many other factors: Correlation is not causation.

Even in Japan, however, teachers are hesitant to teach physical education to students with disabilities (Hodge et al., 2013). From what we know about the

**Same Situation, Far Apart** Given the contrast between the Russian children in front of their rural school *(left)* and the Japanese girls beside their urban school *(right)*, you might see the differences here. But child psychologists notice that children everywhere chase and catch, kick and throw, and as in these photos, jump rope while chanting rhymes.

brain and the body during middle childhood, all children—*especially* those who are not athletically gifted—need daily physical activity.

## Motor Skills and School

Many motor skills are necessary for school achievement: Writing requires finger control; reading print requires eye control; sitting at a desk requires control of gross motor skills.

### Gross Motor Skills

Some schools in the United States have cut sports, recess, and gym in order to focus on reading and math. Yet a study of all elementary schools in Illinois found that schools with low reading scores had the least time for physical activity (Kern et al., 2018).

In this example, understanding correlation provides a novel way to interpret the relationship between reading scores and recess. Remember that correlation does not indicate the direction of the connection, or whether one variable causes the other, or whether a third variable might be involved.

Some educators think that more reading instruction was needed in schools with low scores. But the correlation might occur in the opposite direction: Less physical activity might cause less learning (Kern et al., 2018). Or a third variable—perhaps less support for cluster teachers, such as coaches, counselors, and reading specialists, or the fact that schools with low scores are often low SES schools without grassy fields for recess—might underlie both restricted exercise and low reading achievement.

Unfortunately, even when school policies require exercise, schools may not follow mandates. For instance, although Alabama requires at least 30 minutes daily of physical education in primary schools, the average in one low-SES district was only 22 minutes. No school in that district had recess or after-school sports (Robinson et al., 2014). Other studies also find that as student income decreases, so does school time for physical exercise (Van Dyke et al., 2018). Children's health also declines.

### Fine Motor Skills

Even at age 6, many children are frustrated if their teachers demand that they write neatly, sit still, and cut in a straight line. As you remember from Chapter 9, some adults think preschools should teach readiness for formal education; others suggest that schools should adjust to children, not vice versa.

**THINK CRITICALLY:** How is a person "ready" for school? Are you "ready" for your current education?

Some children seem to need to move their bodies (walking around, jiggling their feet, tapping their pencils) in order to concentrate. As you will see later in this chapter, such children may be diagnosed with *attention deficit/hyperactivity disorder (ADHD)*. There are two opposite dangers: A typical squirmy, active child may be medicated, or an overactive child may be punished instead of treated.

Fine motor skills—like many other biological characteristics, such as bones, brains, and teeth—mature about six months earlier in girls than in boys. By contrast, boys often are ahead of girls in gross motor skills.

These gender differences may be biological, or they may result from practice: Young girls more often dress up and play with dolls (fine motor skills), while boys more often climb and kick (gross motor skills) (Saraiva et al., 2013). Either way, boys may be handicapped in traditional elementary schools. Their female classmates and teachers may criticize their immature handwriting.

**Buddhism in Maine?** Yes. These school-children are performing a play called *Buddha Walks* on St. Patrick's Day (March 17) in 2017. There are many ways to teach children about other cultures: Drama is one of the best, as in this Lebanon, Maine, elementary school.

## Drawing and Drama

Children are imaginative and creative, developing all types of motor skills in the process. They love to express themselves, especially if their parents applaud their performances, display their artwork, and otherwise communicate approval.

The fact that their fine motor skills are immature, and thus a child's artwork lack precision, does not matter. Similarly, the emotional significance of children's theater productions—walking across the stage at the appropriate moment, making the required facial expression, gesturing in the right direction—all these require not only movement but also skill at execution and inhibition, not the impulsive actions of the younger child.

## Making Music

Playing a musical instrument is a fine motor skill, in that the fingers need to move precisely. But as in all motor skills, physical movement is connected to brain function. This seems to be particularly apparent with music.

Some parents enroll their young children in music lessons, hoping they will learn to play. As a result, those children become better at listening to sounds—in speech and music alike. Neurological evidence finds that their brains reflect their new auditory abilities, a remarkable testimony to the connection between motor skills, family influences, and learning (Strait et al., 2013; Zuk et al., 2014).

Music education can also occur as part of school curriculum, with an impact on the brain. In one study, students were divided into groups: (1) music lessons, (2) visual arts, and (3) education as usual. The music and arts curricula were carefully designed for elementary schoolchildren. For example, the music curriculum included singing, clapping in rhythm, and learning to play an instrument of the student's choice.

Before and after the special curriculum, the children in all three groups were tested via several valid tasks. Some were traditional cognitive measures, and three were designed to measure the three aspects (memory, inhibition, flexibility) of executive control. [**Developmental Link:** Executive control is explained in Chapter 9.]

- For memory, children had to reproduce the configuration of dots (on a 4-by-4 matrix) they had just seen.
- For inhibition, a Go/No Go task required pushing a button to indicate whether a plane on the screen went to the left or the right, but not pushing if an X appeared after a few seconds. Those with poor inhibition pushed too soon.

• For flexibility, children were given a modified "Tower of London" task. They had to plan ahead to move colored balls, one at a time according to specific rules, from one stick to another to match a display. Several displays were presented; the children had to change tactics to match them all.

The children in the visual arts curriculum became better at drawing and specific fine motor skills, which was expected. They also became better at seeing shapes and objects and remembering what they had seen, an ability called *visual-spatial memory*. Other cognitive abilities were on par with the control group.

The effects of the music curriculum were more far-reaching. The children became better at various executive control skills, include planning ahead and inhibiting unwanted responses (Jaschke et al., 2018). The authors suggest that an exclusive focus on academic skills that exclude the arts is short-sighted. That echoes what you already read about physical exercise.

## Health Problems in Middle Childhood

Some chronic health conditions, including Tourette syndrome, stuttering, and allergies, may worsen during the school years, drawing unwanted attention to the affected child. Even minor problems—wearing glasses, repeatedly coughing or blowing one's nose, or having a visible birthmark—can affect children's self-esteem. Beyond that, we now focus on two other examples of physical conditions that affect how children feel about themselves.

## Childhood Obesity

**childhood obesity** In a child, having a BMI above the 95th percentile, according to the U.S. Centers for Disease Control's 1980 standards for children of a given age.

**Childhood obesity** is defined as a BMI above the 95th percentile for children of a particular age. That percentile is based on children in the United States, as measured 50 years ago. Now far more than 5 percent of children are in the obese category. For example, in 2016, 18 percent of U.S. 6- to 11-year-olds were obese (Hales et al., 2017). (See **Figure 11.2**.)

What affects children's weight? Once genes were thought to determine weight, then other biological factors (the microbiome) were suspected. Now many environmental factors are recognized as well (Albataineh et al., 2019).

Obesity rates rise if newborns are born too early, if infants are not breast-fed and are fed solid foods before 4 months, if young children have televisions in their bedrooms and drink large quantities of soda, if older children sleep too little but watch screens several hours each day, if people of any age rarely play outside.

During middle childhood, children themselves have *pester power*—the ability to get adults to do what they want (Powell et al., 2011), which often includes pestering their parents to buy calorie-dense snacks that are advertised on television or that other children eat. Parents need to say no, which is easier if they always buy and eat healthy foods, and do not bring pestering children with them as they shop for groceries.

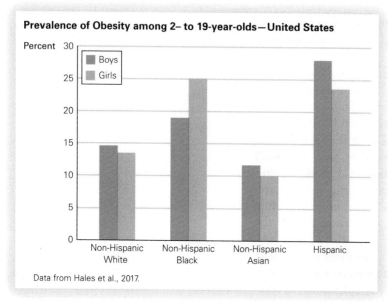

**Prevalence of Obesity among 2- to 19-year-olds—United States**

Data from Hales et al., 2017.

**FIGURE 11.2**

**Ethnic or Economic?** Obesity increases as income decreases. Is that obvious from this figure?

**Observation Quiz** Are boys more likely to be overweight than girls? (see answer, page 309) ↑

The best strategy is to be proactive, before a child is overweight. Rather than targeting parents *or* children, educating parents and their children together may improve weight and health, not just immediately but also over the long term (Yackobovitch-Gavan et al., 2018).

A dynamic-systems approach that considers individual differences, parenting practices, school lunches, fast-food restaurants, television and internet ads, and community norms is needed. Prevention must be tailored to the particular child, family, and culture (Baranowski & Taveras, 2018; Harrison et al., 2011). That makes progress slow—research has found that various interventions, in isolation, have little impact (Bleich et al., 2013).

Solutions in one culture are resisted in another. Every nation is worried about childhood obesity, but diverse practices and policies are evident (Bagchi, 2019).

For example, Mexico taxes sugar-sweetened beverages to reduce obesity, a tax that has met stiff opposition in the United States (Paarlberg et al., 2018). On the other hand, efforts to increase exercise in school have been instituted in many U.S. school districts. Given the long-term effects of childhood obesity, those who care about children must encourage every step—solutions require a concerted effort of parents, communities, and nations.

## Asthma

Another childhood condition that can affect learning is **asthma**, a chronic inflammatory disorder of the airways that makes breathing difficult. Sufferers have periodic attacks, sometimes requiring a rush to the hospital emergency room, a frightening experience for children who know that asthma might kill them (although it almost never does in childhood).

If asthma continues in adulthood, which it does about half the time, it can be fatal (Banks & Andrews, 2015). But a child's most serious problem related to asthma is frequent absence from school. This impedes learning and friendships, which thrive between children who see each other every day.

In the United States, childhood asthma rates more than doubled from 1980 to 2000, increased more gradually from 2000 to 2010, and recently have decreased somewhat (probably because clean-air regulations have meant less smog) (Zahran et al., 2018).

Currently, about 1 in every 10 U.S. 5- to 11-year-olds has been diagnosed with asthma and still suffers from the condition. For more than half of them, asthma has meant missing school and having an attack in the past year, with rates somewhat higher for boys, African Americans, and children of Puerto Rican descent (Zahran et al., 2018).

Rates increase as income falls. For children whose families are under the poverty threshold, 15 percent currently have asthma, as do only 9 percent of those whose annual family income is above $100,000 (Zahran et al., 2018).

Researchers have found many causes. Some genetic alleles have been identified, as have many aspects of modern life—carpets, pollution, house pets, airtight windows, parental smoking, cockroaches, dust mites, less outdoor play. None acts in isolation. A combination of genetic sensitivity to allergies, early respiratory infections, and compromised lung functioning increases wheezing and shortness of breath (Mackenzie et al., 2014).

Some experts suggest a *hygiene hypothesis:* that "the immune system needs to tangle with microbes when we are young. . . . despite what our mothers told us, cleanliness sometimes leads to sickness" (Leslie, 2012, p. 1428).

Children may be overprotected from viruses and bacteria, especially in modern nations. In their concern about hygiene, parents prevent exposure to infections, germs, and family pets

**Especially for Medical Professionals** You notice that a child is overweight, but you are hesitant to say anything to the parents, who are also overweight, because you do not want to offend them. What should you do? (see response, page 309)

**asthma** A chronic disease of the respiratory system in which inflammation narrows the airways from the nose and mouth to the lungs, causing difficulty in breathing. Signs and symptoms include wheezing, shortness of breath, chest tightness, and coughing.

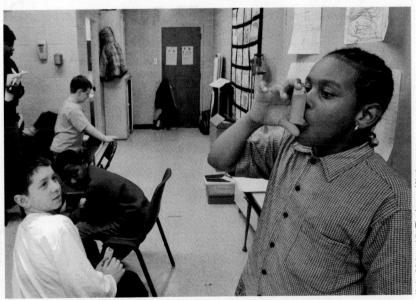

**Pride and Prejudice** In some city schools, asthma is so common that using an inhaler is a sign of pride, as suggested by the facial expressions of these two boys. The "prejudice" is beyond the walls of this school nurse's room, in a society that allows high rates of childhood asthma.

Kathy McLaughlin/The Image Works

**VISUALIZING DEVELOPMENT**

# Childhood Obesity Around the World

Obesity now causes more deaths worldwide than malnutrition. Reductions are possible. A multifaceted prevention effort—including parents, preschools, pediatricians, and grocery stores—has reduced obesity among U.S. 2- to 5-year-olds:

Overall, the prevalence of obesity among adolescents (20.6%) and school-aged children (18.4%) is higher than among pre-school-aged children (13.9%) (Hales et al., 2017). However, obesity rates from age 6 to 60 remain high everywhere.

**Percentage of Obese 5- to 19-Year-Olds**

- No data
- Less than 10%
- 10–15%
- 15–20%
- over 20%

Data from World Health Organization, September 29, 2017.

## FACTORS CONTRIBUTING TO CHILDHOOD OBESITY, BY THE NUMBERS

Children's exposure to ads for unhealthy food continues to correlate with childhood obesity (e.g., Hewer, 2014), but nations differ. For instance, in stark contrast with the United States, the United Kingdom has banned television advertising of foods high in fat, sugar, and salt to children under age 16. The map above shows data from the World Health Organization; other groups' data may differ. However, the overall fact is clear: Childhood obesity is far too common.

The percentage of U.S. children who eat fast food on any given day. **30%**

The number of pounds per year that result from these extra fast-food calories. **6**

The amount of money, <u>in billions</u>, that Americans spend on fast food annually. (This is more than what is spent on higher education, computers, and cars.) **110,000,000,000.**

The number of fast-food meal combinations, <u>out of a possible 3,039</u>, that meet nutritional criteria for preschoolers. **12 / 3,039**

**3** The average number of hours <u>per day</u> U.S. 5- to 8-year-olds spend with television and other digital media.

**80%** The percentage of all advertisements in U.S. children's programming that are for fast food and snacks.

**11** The number of food ads that U.S. children see <u>per hour</u> of television viewing.

**>1** The <u>minimum</u> number of hours children should be actively moving (either in organized or spontaneous play) each day, according to the World Health Organization.

Data from Council on Communications and Media, 2011, p. 202; Rideout, 2017.

that would strengthen their child's immunity. This is suggested as the reason for asthma, as for all other allergies (Liu, 2015).

This hypothesis is supported by data showing that:

- first-born children develop asthma more often than later-born ones;
- asthma and allergies are less common among farm-dwelling children; and
- children born by cesarean delivery (very sterile) have a greater incidence of asthma.

Remember the microbiome—those many bacteria within our bodies. Some microbes in the lungs affect asthma (Singanayagam et al., 2017). Accordingly, changing the microbiome—via diet, drugs, or exposure to animals—may treat asthma. However, asthma has multiple, varied causes and types; no single treatment will help everyone.

---

**WHAT HAVE YOU LEARNED?**

1. How does growth during middle childhood compare with growth earlier or later?

2. Why is middle childhood a healthy time?

3. How do motor skills and physical activity affect a child's education?

4. What are the arguments for and against giving children music lessons?

5. What are the short-term and long-term effects of childhood obesity?

6 What affects the prevalence of asthma?

---

# Brain Development

As already mentioned many times, the most important part of the maturation process for children is in the brain, which enables the entire body to function. As you remember from Chapter 8, the child's brain develops better connections between the various parts every year. This process continues during middle childhood.

One of the distinguishing traits of humans is that the brain is not fully mature until one's mid-20s, an aspect of biological growth that enables all the cognitive and psychosocial aspects of development in middle childhood that are described in the next two chapters. Sadly, children born far too early (under 27 weeks), who escape any obvious brain malfunction (such as cerebral palsy), still have subtle signs of brain abnormalities in middle childhood that impair motor skills (Bolk et al., 2018).

## Brains and Motion

Body movement improves intellectual functioning. How could this be? A review of the research suggests several possible mechanisms, including direct benefits for cerebral blood flow and neurotransmitters as well as indirect results from better moods (Singh et al., 2012). Those better moods themselves loop back to more body movement.

Many studies have found that particular regions of children's brains benefit from physical exercise (Voelcker-Rehage et al., 2018). This can be quite specific: One study found that for boys (not girls), the size of the hippocampus correlated with sports activities (Gorham et al., 2019).

While sports and aerobic exercise may directly affect brain structures, movement of every part of the body, in fine and gross motor skills, can foster learning. Children learn by doing and then express what they know by moving. This is part

**LaunchPad**
macmillan learning

**VIDEO ACTIVITY: Brain Development: Middle Childhood** depicts the changes that occur in a child's brain from age 6 to age 11.

of a concept called *embodied cognition*, the idea that thinking is connected to body movement (Pexman, 2017).

Remember that the study of music and arts education also had a control group. Their abilities improved over the two years, as you would expect, but not as much as the children in the more active learning groups. Moreover, IQ scores, which are thought to reflect brain functioning, also rose in the active groups.

In another example: The physical act of handwriting helps children learn to read (James, 2017). This has implications for students at every level: Taking a screen shot, or printing out a PowerPoint slide, is less likely to result in learning than writing out the assignment.

## Paying Attention

As you remember, one specific aspect of executive control is the ability to inhibit some impulses to focus on others. Neurological advances allow children to pay special heed to the most important elements of their environment. *Selective attention*, concentrating on some stimuli while ignoring others, improves markedly at about age 7.

Selective attention is partly the result of brain maturation, but it is also greatly affected by experience, particularly active play. School-age children not only notice various stimuli (which is one form of attention), but also select appropriate responses when several possibilities conflict (Wendelken et al., 2011). In kickball, soccer, basketball, and baseball, it is crucial to attend to the ball, not to dozens of other stimuli.

For example, in baseball, young batters learn to ignore the other team's attempts to distract them; fielders start moving into position as soon as the bat connects; and pitchers adjust to the height, handedness, and past performance of the person at bat. Another physical activity that seems to foster *executive function* is karate, which requires inhibition of some reactions in order to execute others (Alesi et al., 2014).

## Reaction Time

**reaction time** The time it takes to respond to a stimulus, either physically (with a reflexive movement such as an eyeblink) or cognitively (with a thought).

Physical play combined with brain maturation during middle childhood also improves **reaction time**, which is how long it takes to respond to a stimulus. Preschoolers are sometimes frustratingly slow in putting on their pants, eating their cereal, throwing a ball. Reaction time is reduced every year of childhood, thanks to increasing myelination. As a result, older children can react more quickly.

Skill at games is an obvious example, from scoring in a video game, to swinging at a pitch, to kicking a soccer ball toward a teammate—timing on all of these improves every year from age 6 to 11, depending partly on practice, partly on body growth, and partly on brain connections.

## Measuring the Mind

In ancient times, if adults were strong and hardworking, they were respected members of the community. A child needed to be well fed, protected from injury, and tended to when sick in order to grow into a capable adult. No one was singled out if they could not think quickly, read well, or sit still. Those who had an obvious physical difference, such as being blind or deaf, received special care; no need for diagnosis.

Over the centuries, however, humans have placed more value on brain functioning. Books were printed, making reading important; money was exchanged, so calculating was needed; leaders were chosen by voters instead of kings inheriting kingdoms. This all required learning. It became evident that some people were much better at reading, at math, at analysis.

Schools were built, and some students learned more quickly than others. The slower ones struggled and quit, but adults wondered if poor students were lazy (they could be beaten or forced to stand in a corner wearing a dunce cap), or if their brains rendered learning impossible. It became important to measure intelligence.

Currently, only about 1 percent of all children are diagnosed with obvious physical differences. But in many nations, another 10 to 20 percent are thought to need special education because of something amiss in their intellectual abilities. Their needs are the focus of the last section of this chapter. But before those specifics, we need to understand how brain function is measured.

## Aptitude, Achievement, and IQ

The potential to master a specific skill or to learn a certain body of knowledge is called *aptitude*. A child might have the intellectual aptitude to be a proficient reader, for instance, even though that child has never learned to read or write. Some children have the potential to become a talented athlete, artist, architect, and so on. Most aptitudes are not developed, since motivation and opportunity (or some would say, money and luck) are needed as well.

Aptitude is distinct from *achievement*, which is what is actually mastered. For children, academic achievement is measured by comparing that child with expected accomplishments at each grade. As you remember, children should be able to walk at a year, scribble with a marker at two years, catch a ball at 4 years (depending on the size and speed of the ball). These are achievements of motor skills; the same principle underlies achievement of brain skills.

Thus, a child who is at a second-grade reading level might actually be in the second grade, but it is just as likely for that child to be in the first or the third. If that second-grade reader is 9 years old, and therefore should be reading at the fourth-grade level, then something is amiss—perhaps with aptitude. That reasoning led to intelligence tests, to find out if low achievement was caused by low aptitude or something else.

People assumed that, for intelligence, one general aptitude (often referred to as **"g,"** or **general intelligence**) could be assessed by answers to a series of questions (vocabulary, memory, and so on). The number of correct answers was compared to the average for children of a particular age to compute an *IQ* (*intelligence quotient*), thought to measure brain functioning.

Scores on IQ tests correlated with school achievement: Children with high IQs were able to perform above grade level, because their intellectual potential enabled them to learn quickly. On the other hand, a low IQ score indicated that a child did not have the aptitude to be a quick learner.

People with psychological disorders such as schizophrenia or obsessive-compulsive disorder tend to average lower IQ scores, because their brains do not process ideas as well as other people (Abramovitch et al., 2018). Children whose brains, for one reason or another, make them unable to do expected schoolwork need special treatment, not a dunce cap, a blow with a ruler, or other punishment.

The original IQ tests were developed by Alfred Binet in France at the beginning of the twentieth century. He sought a way to distinguish children who were unable to learn as fast as other children. Thanks to Binet, such children are less often punished or shamed. His IQ test, now called the Stanford-Binet Intelligence Scale, has been revised many times.

In the United States, David Wechsler also developed intelligence tests in the twentieth century. Because he recognized the importance of maturation, he developed different tests for young children, older children, and adults, specifically the WPPSI (Wechsler Preschool and Primary Scale of Intelligence), the WISC (Wechsler Intelligence Test for Children), and the WAIS (Wechsler Adult Intelligence Scale). Each of these tests has five indicators of verbal intelligence

**g (general intelligence)** The idea of *g* assumes that intelligence is one basic trait, underlying all cognitive abilities. According to this concept, people have varying levels of this general ability.

2016 Macmillan

**Typical 7-Year-Old?** In many ways, this boy is typical. He likes video games and school, he usually appreciates his parents, and he gets himself dressed every morning. This photo shows him using blocks to construct a design to match a picture, 1 of the 10 kinds of challenges that comprise the WISC, a widely used IQ test. His attention to the task is not unusual for children his age, but his actual performance is more like that of an older child. Because his mental age is ahead of his chronological age, his IQ is significantly above 100.

(including vocabulary, math problems, and logic) and five indicators of performance intelligence (puzzles, pictures with something missing, and so on).

Added to those standard IQ tests are dozens of other aptitude tests. Some are designed to be culture-free (such as drawing a person), some focus specifically on vocabulary, some on logic, some on spatial relationships, some on motor skills, and so on.

The ones most often used have been developed and revised over the years. Some are explicitly neurological, aimed to measure brain functioning directly, such as another Wechsler test, the WMS (Wechsler Memory Scale).

## Calculating IQ

Originally, IQ tests produced a number that was literally a quotient: *Mental age* (the average age of those who answered a specific number of questions correctly) was divided by the actual age of a person taking the test. The answer from that division (the quotient) was multiplied by 100. An IQ of 100 was exactly average, because when mental age was the same as chronological age, the quotient was 1, and $1 \times 100 = 100$.

Thus, if the average 9-year-old answered, say, exactly 60 questions correctly, then everyone who got 60 questions correct—no matter what their chronological age—would have a mental age of 9. Obviously, for children whose mental age was the same as their chronological age (such as a 9-year-old who got 60 questions right), the IQ would be 100 ($9 \div 9 = 1 \times 100 = 100$), exactly average.

If a 6-year-old answered the questions as well as a typical 9-year-old, the score would be $9 \div 6 \times 100$, or 133. If a 12-year-old answered only 60 questions correctly, the IQ would be 75 ($9 \div 12 \times 100$). The current method of calculating IQ is more complex, but the basic idea is the same: *g* is calculated based on the average mental age of people of a particular chronological age. (See **Figure 11.3**.)

## Plasticity and Intelligence

Probably you have already spotted the underlying problem with assumptions about mental age. Intelligence is much more plastic than people once thought. This is particularly apparent in childhood, but it also may be true in adulthood (Glenn et al., 2018; Patton et al., 2019).

Aptitude is not a fixed characteristic, present at birth, that determines how much a person can learn, or whether an individual can become an artist or architect. Young children with a low IQ sometimes become above-average or even gifted adults, like my nephew David (discussed in Chapter 1).

An added complication is the relationship between intelligence and creativity. If a child scores very high on IQ tests, that qualifies them as gifted, but how that

**FIGURE 11.3**

**In Theory, Most People Are Average**
Almost 70 percent of IQ scores fall within the "average" range. Note, however, that this is a norm-referenced test. In fact, actual IQ scores have risen in many nations; 100 is no longer exactly the midpoint. Furthermore, in practice, scores below 50 are slightly more frequent than indicated by the normal curve (shown here) because severe disability is the result not of normal distribution but of genetic and prenatal factors.

 **Observation Quiz** If a person's IQ is 110, what category are they in? (see answer, page 309) ➔

**Theoretical Distribution of IQ Scores**

Below average — Average
Mild intellectual disability
Above average
Moderate to severe disability — Gifted
Genius
0.14%    2.13%    13.6%    68.26%    13.6%    2.13%    0.14%
40    55    70    85    100    115    130    145    160
IQ Score

## The Flynn Effect

The average IQ scores of more than 30 nations has risen substantially every decade for the past century. This phenomenon is called the **Flynn effect** (Pietschnig & Voracek, 2015; Trahan et al., 2014).

When James Flynn first suggested in the 1980s that the IQ scores had risen throughout the twentieth century, critics said he did not understand the data and was misled by biased samples. Some added that, if Flynn had realized the strong genetic inheritance of IQ, and if he recognized how genes are passed from one generation to the next, he would know that grandchildren could not be much smarter than their grandparents.

Over the past decades, those critics have grown silent, because hundreds of studies found rising scores in nation after nation. Most of those studies have been in industrialized nations of Europe, but the Flynn effect is also evident in poorer nations. For instance, a study in Kenya found that scores on the Raven's matrix (supposed to be culture-free) increased from 12.8 to 17.3 over a 14-year period (Daley et al., 2003).

Scientists no longer question *whether* the Flynn effect exists; they ask *why*. Better education? Better nutrition? Better medical care? More widespread information from newspapers, television, the internet?

The Flynn effect is more apparent for women than for men, and in southern Europe more than northern Europe, as nutrition and education improved (Weber et al., 2017). Rising average IQs are less apparent for upper-class European men. Perhaps even in the early-twentieth century, most of them had good nutrition, education, and opportunity.

Once those benefits are available to everyone, IQ will stabilize. In fact, in the most advanced nations of northern Europe, recent evidence suggests that the Flynn effect may be moving in the other direction, decreasing over time (Pietschnig & Voracek, 2015).

The fact that IQ scores vary by social conditions has changed perceptions. Most psychologists now agree that the brain is like a muscle, affected by mental exercise—which often is encouraged or discouraged by the social setting. This is proven in language and music (brains literally grow with childhood music training), and is probably true in other domains (Moreno et al., 2015; Zatorre, 2013).

Both speed and memory are crucial for *g*, and they are affected by experience, evident in the Flynn effect. Moreover, every test of intelligence is designed to measure what is considered to be intelligence within that culture. Think of someone you believe to be very smart, and then ask yourself if someone in an entirely different context (a rural village in Niger, for instance) would also think that person to be smart. When I feel proud of my intellectual ability, I ask that question. Humility needed.

---

aptitude leads to achievement depends on another trait that differs among people. Some are *divergent thinkers*, who find many solutions and even more questions for every problem, and others are *convergent thinkers*, who quickly find one, and only one, correct answer for every problem.

**Flynn effect** The rise in average IQ scores that has occurred over the decades in many nations.

## Many Intelligences

Since scores change over time (see A View from Science), IQ tests are much less definitive than they were once thought to be, but aptitude remains a useful concept. Every human has a mix of aptitudes and abilities. Some aptitudes are nurtured, and they may become notable achievements; some aptitudes are never developed.

Aptitude is not always crucial. Some people with low aptitude for a particular achievement nonetheless accomplish their goals via extensive effort and practice. In terms of physical abilities, think of those who are relatively weak and uncoordinated who become valued members of sports teams after years of work.

An ongoing debate is whether *g* exists, and thus whether any single test can measure the complexities of the human brain. People may inherit and develop many abilities, some high and some low (e.g., Q. Zhu et al., 2010).

Two leading developmentalists (Robert Sternberg and Howard Gardner) are among those who believe that humans have **multiple intelligences**, not just one. Sternberg originally described three kinds of intelligence: *analytic*, *creative*, and

**multiple intelligences** The idea that human intelligence is composed of a varied set of abilities rather than a single, all-encompassing one.

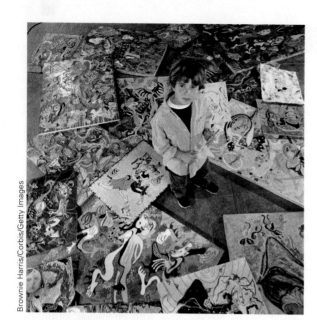

Brownie Harris/Corbis/Getty Images

**A Gifted Child** Gardner believes every person is naturally better at some of his nine intelligences, and then the social context may or may not appreciate the talent. In the twenty-first century, verbal and mathematical intelligence are usually prized far more than artistic intelligence, but Georgie Pocheptsov was drawing before he learned to speak. The reason is tragic: His father suffered and died of brain cancer when Georgie was a toddler, and his mother bought paints and canvases to help her son cope with his loss. By middle childhood (shown here), Pocheptsov was already a world-famous artist. Now a young adult, his works sell for hundreds of thousands of dollars—often donated to brain tumor research.

● ● **Especially for Teachers** What are the advantages and disadvantages of using Gardner's nine intelligences to guide your classroom curriculum? (see response, page 309)

**neurodiversity** The idea that each person has neurological strengths and weaknesses that should be appreciated, in much the same way diverse cultures and ethnicities are welcomed. Neurodiversity seems particularly relevant for children with disorders on the autism spectrum.

*practical* (Sternberg, 2008, 2011). Children who are unusually creative, or very practical, are not be the best students in school, but they may flourish later on.

Gardner originally described seven intelligences: *linguistic, logical-mathematical, musical, spatial, bodily-kinesthetic* (movement), *interpersonal* (social understanding), and *intrapersonal* (self-understanding), each associated with a particular brain region (Gardner, 1983). He subsequently added an eighth (*naturalistic:* understanding nature, as in biology, zoology, or farming) and a ninth (*spiritual/existential:* thinking about life and death) (Gardner, 1999, 2006; Gardner & Moran, 2006).

Although everyone has some of all nine intelligences, Gardner believes each individual excels in particular ones. For example, someone might be gifted spatially but not linguistically (a visual artist who cannot describe her work) or might have interpersonal but not naturalistic intelligence (an astute clinical psychologist whose houseplants die).

Schools, cultures, and families dampen or expand particular intelligences. If two children are born with creative, musical aptitude, the child whose parents are musicians is more likely to develop musical intelligence than the child whose parents are tone-deaf. Gardner (2011) believes that schools often are too narrow, teaching only some aspects of intelligence and thus stunting children's learning.

## Scanning the Brain

Another way to indicate aptitude is to measure the brain directly. In childhood, brain scans do not correlate with IQ scores (except for children with abnormally small brains), but they do later on (Brouwer et al., 2014). Brain scans can measure activity (reaction time, selective attention, emotional excitement) or the size of various brain areas, but they are not accurate in diagnosing cognitive disorders in childhood (Goddings & Giedd, 2014).

Neuroscientists and psychologists agree, however, on four generalities:

- *Brain development depends on experiences.* Thus, a brain scan is accurate only at the moment, not for the future.
- *Dendrites form and myelination changes throughout life.* Middle childhood is crucial, but developments before and after these years are also significant.
- *Children with disorders often have unusual brain patterns, and training may change those patterns.* Normal variation means that diagnosis based on brain patterns is imperfect.
- Each individual brain functions in a particular way, a concept called **neurodiversity**. Diverse neurological patterns are not necessarily better or worse; they are simply different, an example of the *difference is not deficit* idea explained first in Chapter 1 (Kapp et al., 2013).

---

### WHAT HAVE YOU LEARNED?

1. What is the difference between selective attention and quick reaction time?
2. Why were intelligence tests originally developed?
3. What are the arguments for and against *g*?
4. Are aptitude and achievement distinct ideas, or are they part of the same trait?
5. How might the concept of multiple intelligences be useful in schools?

# Children with Special Brains and Bodies

**Developmental psychopathology** links typical with atypical development, especially when the atypical results in special needs. This topic is relevant lifelong, because "[e]ach period of life, from the prenatal period through senescence, ushers in new biological and psychological challenges, strengths, and vulnerabilities" (Cicchetti, 2013b, p. 458).

Most disorders are **comorbid**, which means that more than one problem is evident in the same person. Comorbidity is now considered "the rule, rather than the exception" (Krueger & Eaton, 2015, p. 27). Turning points, opportunities, and past influences are always apparent. Many people of every age have differences that do not meet a diagnostic threshold but that nonetheless impact their lives, making other problems more likely.

At the outset, four general principles should be emphasized.

- *Abnormality is normal*, meaning that everyone has some aspects of behavior that are unusual. The opposite is also true: Everyone with a diagnosed disorder is, in many respects, like everyone else.
- *Disability changes year by year* (Clark et al., 2017). A severe childhood disorder may become insignificant, but a minor problem may become disabling. Some children with significant disabilities (e.g., blindness) become productive adults. Conversely, some conditions (e.g., conduct disorder) become more disabling.
- *Plasticity and compensation are widespread.* Many conditions, especially those that originate in the brain, seem to disappear with age and treatment (Livingston & Happe, 2017).
- *Diagnosis and treatment reflect the social context.* Each individual interacts with the surrounding settings—including family, school, community, and culture—which modify, worsen, cause, or eliminate psychopathology.

DSM-5 (the fifth edition of the *Diagnostic and Statistical Manual of Mental Disorders*, published by the American Psychiatric Association in 2013) is used as a reference here. DSM-5 is only one set of criteria—the World Health Organization has another (ICD-11); some experts use a third (RDoC) for research. Psychiatrists are discussing DSM-6, which again will redefine various disorders (Clark et al., 2017).

Because of the four principles above, it is not always obvious whether a particular child has a disorder or not. No matter what diagnostic method is used, the cutoff between what is, and what is not, a disorder requires some judgment (Clark et al., 2017).

## Many Causes, Many Symptoms

To help children with special needs, it helps to know exactly what caused a problem. Perhaps a child has a chemical imbalance (a drug might correct that), or perhaps a parent or a school has turned a small vulnerability into a huge disorder (then tutoring of parent, teacher, or child is needed), or perhaps an inherited physical weakness is the problem (targeted exercise, or glasses, or a hearing aid might help). Finding the appropriate cause and treatment, however, is more complex than it appears.

One cause can have many final manifestations, a phenomenon called **multifinality** (many final forms). The opposite is also apparent: One symptom can result from several different causes, a phenomenon called **equifinality** (equal in final form). Thus, a direct line from cause to consequence cannot be drawn with certainty.

For example, in multifinality, an infant who has been flooded with stress hormones may become a child who is hypervigilant or irrationally placid, may be easily angered or quick to cry, or may not be affected. Or in equifinality, a child who

**developmental psychopathology** The field that uses insights into typical development to understand and remediate developmental disorders.

**comorbid** Refers to the presence of two or more unrelated disease conditions at the same time in the same person.

**multifinality** A basic principle of developmental psychopathology that holds that one cause can have many (multiple) final manifestations.

**equifinality** A basic principle of developmental psychopathology that holds that one symptom can have many causes.

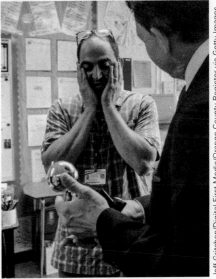

**Expressing Surprise** You would be surprised as Vincent Saporita was when he was named Teacher of the Year in Huntington Beach, California. But you might not express your surprise as he did. His students are hearing impaired, so he has learned to use gestures to express emotions.

does not talk may have autism or hearing impairment, be electively mute or pathologically shy.

To illustrate the complexities in psychopathology, we home in on three conditions: *attention-deficit/hyperactivity disorder (ADHD)*, *specific learning disorders*, and *autism spectrum disorder (ASD)*. The general principles illustrated by these three apply to everyone, since we all have quirks and oddities in behavior, thoughts, and emotions.

## Attention-Deficit/Hyperactivity Disorder

**attention-deficit/hyperactivity disorder (ADHD)** A condition characterized by a persistent pattern of inattention and/or by hyperactive or impulsive behaviors; ADHD interferes with a person's functioning or development.

Someone with **attention-deficit/hyperactivity disorder (ADHD)** is inattentive, active, and impulsive. DSM-5 says that symptoms must start before age 12 (in DSM-IV it was age 7) and must impact daily life. (DSM-IV said *impair*, not merely *impact*.)

Partly because the definition now includes older children, the rate of children diagnosed with ADHD has increased worldwide (Polanczyk et al., 2014). In 1980, about 5 percent of all U.S. 4- to 17-year-olds were diagnosed with ADHD; more recent rates are 8 percent of 4- to 11-year-olds, and 14 percent of 12- to 17-year-olds (Xu et al., 2018).

Every young child is sometimes inattentive, impulsive, and active, gradually settling down with maturation. However, those with ADHD "are so active and impulsive that they cannot sit still, are constantly fidgeting, talk when they should be listening, interrupt people all the time, can't stay on task, . . . accidentally injure themselves." All this makes them "difficult to parent or teach" (Nigg & Barkley, 2014, p. 75).

Because adults are upset by children's moods and actions, and because any physician can write a prescription to quiet a child, thousands of U.S. children may be too readily diagnosed and medicated. *But*, because many parents do not know that their child needs help, and many adults are suspicious of drugs and psychologists (Moldavsky & Sayal, 2013; Rose, 2008), thousands of children suffer needlessly. This dilemma is explored in Opposing Perspectives.

**OPPOSING PERSPECTIVES**

# Drug Treatment for ADHD and Other Disorders

Many child psychologists believe that the public discounts the devastation and lost learning that occur when a child's serious disorder is not recognized or treated. On the other hand, many parents are suspicious of drugs and psychotherapy and avoid recommended treatment (Gordon-Hollingsworth et al., 2015).

In the United States, a non-Hispanic White child is more likely to be diagnosed with ADHD than is a non-Hispanic Black child. As for Hispanic children, their rates of diagnosed ADHD are much lower than for non-Hispanic children of any race (Xu et al., 2018). What do you make of these ethnic differences? Do they reflect genes, or prejudice, or poverty, or culture?

The question of proper diagnosis and treatment is controversial among experts as well. A leading book argues that drug companies and doctors are far too quick to push pills, making ADHD "by far, the most misdiagnosed condition in American medicine" (Schwarz, 2016, p. 2). A critical review of that book notes a failure to mention the millions of people who "have experienced life-changing, positive results" from treatment—including medication (Zametkin & Solanto, 2017, p. 9).

Most children in the United States who are diagnosed with ADHD are medicated; in England and Europe, less than half are (Polanczyk et al., 2014). In China, psychoactive medication is rarely prescribed for children: A child with ADHD symptoms is thought to need correction, not medication (Yang et al., 2013).

In many other nations, an inattentive, overactive child is more likely to be beaten than sent to a psychiatrist. Wise or cruel?

The most common drug for ADHD is Ritalin (methylphenidate), but at least 20 other psychoactive drugs are prescribed for children to treat depression, anxiety, intellectual disability, autism spectrum disorder, disruptive mood dysregulation disorder (sometimes mistaken for bipolar disorder), and many other conditions. Some parents welcome the relief that drugs may provide; others refuse to medicate their children.

Long-term benefits may include less drug abuse later on (Craig et al., 2015). It seems that children with ADHD, with or without medication, are more likely to have psychological and substance abuse problems in adulthood, but that is because of multifinality of the disorder. Those comorbid aspects should be attributed to the underlying cause, not to the medication, which seems to reduce, but not erase, the likelihood of later problems (Uchida et al., 2018).

A meta-analysis finds that medication is likely to help when it is combined with cognitive-behavioral therapy, but also that ADHD is not one simple disorder but a condition that varies from one child, one context, and one nation to another. That illustrates equifinality, and means that no particular drug or therapy, works for every child (López-Pinar et al., 2018).

Research and case study evidence supports both sides of this debate. Some research finds a correlation between medicating children and the rate of mental illness in adulthood (Moran et al., 2015). On the other hand, one expert argues that if children with ADHD are not diagnosed and treated, that increases another outcome—prison.

This outcome may be particularly likely for African American boys who are disruptive. If they are punished, not treated, for ADHD symptoms, they may enter the "school-to-prison pipeline" (Moody, 2016).

All professionals agree that finding the best drug at the right strength is difficult, in part because each child's genes and personality are unique, and in part because children's weight and metabolism change every year. Given that, why are most children who are prescribed psychoactive drugs seen only by a general practitioner who does not follow up on dose and outcome (Patel et al., 2017)? Do pharmaceutical companies mislead parents about the benefits and liabilities of ADHD drugs?

Most professionals believe that contextual interventions (instructing caregivers and schools on child management, changing the diet, increasing outdoor play, eliminating screens) should be tried before drugs. Good advice, but not easy to take if a parent or teacher is trying to manage an overactive, disruptive child every day.

Genes, culture, health care, education, religion, and stereotypes all affect ethnic and economic differences. As two experts explain, "disentangling these will be extremely valuable to improving culturally competent assessment in an increasingly diverse society" (Nigg & Barkley, 2014, p. 98). Given the emotional and practical implications of that tangle, opposing perspectives are not surprising.

In general, three problems are apparent.

- *Misdiagnosis*. If ADHD is diagnosed when another disorder is the problem, treatment might make the problem worse (Miklowitz & Cicchetti, 2010). Many psychoactive drugs alter moods, so a child with disruptive mood dysregulation disorder might be harmed by ADHD medication.
- *Drug abuse*. Although drugs may be therapeutic for true ADHD cases, some adolescents want an ADHD diagnosis in order to obtain legal amphetamines (McCabe et al., 2014). Parents or teachers may also overuse medication to quiet children.
- *Typical behavior considered pathological*. If a child's activity, impulsiveness, and curiosity are diagnosed as ADHD, that child's exuberance and self-confidence may suffer.

"Typical considered pathological" is one interpretation of data on 378,000 children in Taiwan, a Chinese nation whose rates of ADHD are increasing (M-H. Chen et al., 2016). Boys who were born in August, and hence entered kindergarten when they had just turned 5, were diagnosed with ADHD at the rate of 4.5 percent, whereas boys born in September, starting kindergarten when they were almost 6, were diagnosed at the rate of 2.8 percent.

Diagnosis for these Chinese boys typically occurred years after kindergarten, but August birthday boys were at risk throughout their school years. (See **Figure 11.4**.) The data suggest that a year of maturation would have reduced the rate of ADHD by a third.

The example in Taiwan highlights another concern. For ADHD diagnosis, one source reported that "boys outnumber girls 3-to-1 in community samples and 9-to-1 in

**⬤⬤ Observation Quiz** This chart also shows medication rate. Are those August birthdays more likely to be medicated than the September birthdays? (see answer, page 309) ↓

**FIGURE 11.4**

**One Month Is One Year** In the Taiwanese school system, the cutoff for kindergarten is September 1, so some boys enter school a year later because they were born a few days later. Those who are relatively young among their classmates are less able to sit still and listen. They are almost twice as likely to be given drugs to quiet them down.

**Diagnosed with Attention-Deficit/Hyperactivity Disorder (ADHD)**

Data from M.-H. Chen et al., 2016.

clinical samples" (Hasson & Fine, 2012, p. 190). (Clinical samples are those children whose ADHD receives ongoing professional care.) Could typical boy activity be troubling to mothers and teachers? Could that be the reason for this male/female ratio?

Recognizing this possibility, experts recently have been diagnosing more girls with ADHD than was true a decade ago. The most recent report finds the male/female ratio close to 2:1, not 3:1. In a national survey of children's health, parents report that 14 percent of all 4- to 17-year-old boys and 6 percent of all 4- to 17-year-old girls have been diagnosed with ADHD (Xu et al., 2018).

Often a girl's main symptom is inattentiveness, not hyperactivity. Again, the question of the cut-off appears: At what point does a dreamy, distracted child merit a diagnosis? Is there sexism in this diagnosis?

## Specific Learning Disorders

**specific learning disorder** A marked deficit in a particular area of learning that is not caused by an apparent physical disability, by an intellectual disability, or by an unusually stressful home environment.

The DSM-5 diagnosis of **specific learning disorders** now includes problems in both perception and information-processing that cause low achievement in reading, math, or writing (including spelling) (Lewandowski & Lovett, 2014). Differences in these areas undercut academic achievement, destroy self-esteem, and qualify a child for special education (according to U.S. law) or formal diagnosis (according to DSM-5).

**dyslexia** Unusual difficulty with reading; thought to be the result of some neurological underdevelopment.

The most commonly diagnosed learning disorder is **dyslexia**—unusual difficulty with reading. Historically, some children with dyslexia figured out themselves how to cope—as did Hans Christian Andersen and Winston Churchill. Most children with dyslexia, however, endure years of shame and low achievement, as well as punishment for not working hard enough to learn. However, we now know that the origin is in the brain, not the personality (van den Bunt et al., 2018).

Early theories hypothesized visual difficulties—for example, reversals of letters (reading *god* instead of *dog*) and mirror writing (*b* instead of *d*)—as causing dyslexia. That hypothesis was tested and found false. Instead, dyslexia more often originates with speech and hearing difficulties (Elliott & Nicolson, 2016; Swanson, 2013). Language development in the early years correlates with reading development later on.

**dyscalculia** Unusual difficulty with math, probably originating from a distinct part of the brain.

Another common learning disorder is **dyscalculia**, unusual difficulty with math. For example, when asked to estimate the height of a normal room, second-graders with dyscalculia might answer "200 feet," or, when shown both the 5 and 8 of hearts from a deck of playing cards and asked which is higher, schoolchildren might use their fingers to count the hearts on each card (Butterworth et al., 2011).

Although learning disorders can appear in any skill, DSM-5 recognizes only dyslexia, dyscalculia, and one more—*dysgraphia*, difficulty in writing. Few children write neatly at age 5, but practice allows most children to write easily and legibly by age 10.

Because many disorders are comorbid, it is not unusual for a child with one learning disability to also have another, or to be unusually anxious or depressed. This is another example of the interaction of domains, first described in Chapter 1. The biological aspects of brain development affect the cognitive aspects of learning, which influence the emotions.

BSIP/UIG/Getty Images

**Happy Reading** Those large prism glasses keep the letters from jumping around on the page, a boon for this 8-year-old French boy. Unfortunately, each child with dyslexia needs individualized treatment: These glasses help some, but not most, children who find reading difficult.

For every child with a learning disorder, targeted help from teachers and guidance for parents is needed (Crnic et al., 2017). Remember plasticity: Skills improve, not with general practice, such as doing more homework, but with specific practice, such as sounding out letters. The current thinking is that a *multisensory* approach is needed, with hearing, vision, and motor skills all used to overcome the disability.

## Autism Spectrum Disorder

Autism was once a rare disorder affecting fewer than 1 in 1,000 children, who exhibited "an extreme aloneness that, whenever possible, disregards, ignores, shuts out anything . . . from the outside" (Kanner, 1943). Children with autism were usually nonverbal and severely impaired. They were usually institutionalized, and they died young.

That is no longer true. The defining symptom is still impaired social interaction, making children with autism less adept at conversation, at social play, and at understanding emotions. Theory of mind (explained in Chapter 9) develops much later, even if general executive function skills remain (Jones et al., 2018).

However, far more children and adults have signs of autism than once was suspected. Now, in the United States, among all 3- to 17-year-olds, parents say that 1 child in every 36 has been diagnosed as having ASD (Xu et al., 2019). Parents may not be the best course for incidence data, but other sources also suggest high rates. Medical records of 8-year-olds find that 1 in 35 boys and 1 in 143 girls is on the spectrum (Maenner et al., March 27, 2020).

DSM-5 has changed the terminology from autism to **autism spectrum disorder (ASD)**. People "on the spectrum" may have a mild, moderate, or severe form. *Asperger's syndrome* (people who were highly verbal but socially inept) was once considered a separate disorder; now Asperger's is part of that spectrum.

Many scientists are searching for biological ways to detect autism early in life, perhaps with blood tests or brain scans before age 1. At the moment, behavioral signs are the best we have. ASD signs may appear in early infancy (no social smile, for example, or less gazing at faces and eyes). Two scales that measure communication attempts and play patterns are used to diagnose ASD in infants as young as 8 months (Esler et al., 2015; Kiss et al., 2017).

Early diagnosis can produce early treatment, which benefits children and their parents. Currently, some children improve by age 3; others deteriorate (Klinger et al., 2014). Indeed, some children who were diagnosed with autism in early childhood have compensated so well that they are no longer on the spectrum (Livingston & Happe, 2017).

However, diagnosis and treatment are difficult; an intervention that seems to help one child proves worthless for another. It is known, however, that biology (genes, copy number abnormalities, birth complications, prenatal injury, perhaps chemicals during fetal or infant development) is crucial; family nurture is not the cause.

Remember neurodiversity, the concept that each person's brain functions differently? That is apparent with ASD, as those with this disorder seem to have a mixture of perceptions, abilities, and deficiencies that are unlike most children. Because of their diverse abilities, adults should neither be dazzled by their talents nor saddened by their deficits. Some children with ASD have special talents in art or math. Many score above average in IQ (MMWR, March 28, 2014). Others never say a word.

The neurodiversity perspective leads to new criticisms of the many treatments for ASD. When a child is diagnosed with ASD, parental responses vary from irrational hope to deep despair, from blaming doctors and chemical additives to feeling guilty for their genes, for their behavior during pregnancy, or for the circumstances of their child's birth.

A sympathetic observer describes one child who was medicated with

> Abilify, Topamax, Seroquel, Prozac, Ativan, Depakote, trazodone, Risperdal, Anafranil, Lamictal, Benadryl, melatonin, and the homeopathic remedy, Calms Forté. Every time I saw her, the meds were being adjusted again . . . [he also

**VIDEO: Current Research into Autism Spectrum Disorder** explores why the causes of ASD are still largely unknown.

**autism spectrum disorder (ASD)**
A developmental disorder marked by difficulty with social communication and interaction—including difficulty seeing things from another person's point of view—and restricted, repetitive patterns of behavior, interests, or activities.

**Not a Cartoon** At age 3, Owen Suskind was diagnosed with autism. He stopped talking and spent hour after hour watching Disney movies. His father said his little boy "vanished," as chronicled in the Oscar-nominated documentary *Life Animated*. Now, at age 23 (shown here), Owen still loves cartoons, and he still has many symptoms of autism spectrum disorder. However, he also has learned to speak and has written a movie that reveals his understanding of himself, *The Land of the Lost Sidekicks*.

DOGWOOF PICTURES/AF archive/Alamy Stock Photo

**THINK CRITICALLY:** Many adults are socially inept, insensitive to other people's emotions, and poor at communication—might they have been diagnosed as on the spectrum if they had been born more recently?

## CHAPTER APP 11

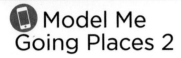

# Model Me Going Places 2

**IOS:**
http://tinyurl.com/y6qj2j27

**RELEVANT TOPIC:**
Autism spectrum disorder and other childhood disorders

This app is designed for children with autism spectrum disorder and other differences, but the tutorials are useful for any child who needs help building social skills. Photos with narration demonstrate appropriate behaviors in public settings, teaching children emotion labels and characteristics, as well as cause and effect.

Kathryn Scott/The Denver Post/Getty Images

**How It Should Be But Rarely Is** In this well-equipped classroom in Centennial, Colorado, two teachers are attentively working with three young children, indicating that each child regularly receives individualized instruction. At this school, students with developmental disabilities learn alongside typical kids, so the earlier a child's education begins the better. Sadly, few nations have classrooms like this, and in the United States, few parents can find or afford special help for their children. Indeed, most children with special needs are not diagnosed until middle childhood.

describes] physical interventions—putting children in hyperbaric oxygen chambers, putting them in tanks with dolphins, giving them blue-green algae, or megadosing them on vitamins . . . usually neither helpful nor harmful, though they can have dangers, are certainly disorienting, and cost a lot.

*[Solomon, 2012, pp. 229, 270]*

### Six Hypotheses

Why is autism so much more common that it once was? Two hypotheses were suggested that now are proven false. One is that unaffectionate or unavailable mothers (the so-called "refrigerator mothers") caused children to withdraw so far from social interaction as to develop autism. Before that idea was proven wrong, thousands of mothers were blamed.

The other disproven hypothesis was that infant vaccinations caused autism. Thousands of studies in many nations refute this idea (only one discredited, fraudulent study backed it), but some parents still refuse to immunize their children. The current quest of millions of health professionals is to figure out how to counter the parents' irrational fears and, thus, to prevent epidemics of measles and mumps that can harm children lifelong. The key professionals in this battle are the nurses: Because they are closest to the parents, they may be able to convince them to immunize their children to stop a "resurgence of childhood diseases" (Kubin, 2019).

Four new groups of hypotheses about increases of autism are suggested.

1. One cluster focuses on the environment, such as new chemicals in food, air, or water.
2. Another cluster considers prenatal influences: mothers who use drugs, eat foods with traces of pesticides or hormones, contract viruses such as some strains of influenza.
3. A third set of hypotheses is that ASD itself has not increased, but diagnosis has. In 2000 in the United States, education for children with ASD became publicly funded, so parents may be more willing to seek a diagnosis and doctors to provide one.
4. Finally, DSM-5 itself may be the reason. Since the definition is expanded, more children fit the category and more doctors recognize the symptoms, so children who once were overlooked are now categorized as having ASD.

## Special Education

The overlap of the biosocial, cognitive, and psychosocial domains is evident to developmentalists, as is the need for parents, teachers, therapists, and researchers to work together to help each child. However, deciding whether a child should be educated differently than other children is not straightforward, nor is it closely related to individual needs. Parents, schools, and therapists often disagree.

In the United States, according to the 1975 Education of All Handicapped Children Act, all children can learn, and all must be educated in the **least restrictive environment (LRE)**. This means that children with special needs are usually educated within a regular class (a practice once called *mainstreaming*), rather than excluded from other children. Sometimes a class is an *inclusion class*, which means that children with special needs are "included" in the general classroom, with "appropriate aids and services" (ideally from a trained teacher who works with the regular teacher).

A more recent strategy is called **response to intervention (RTI)** (Al Otaiba et al., 2015; Morse, 2019; Jimerson et al., 2016). First, all children are taught

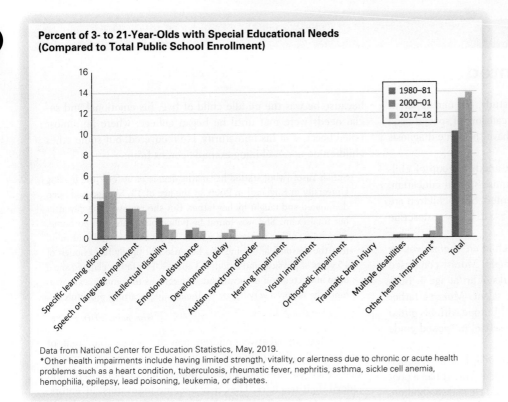

**Percent of 3- to 21-Year-Olds with Special Educational Needs (Compared to Total Public School Enrollment)**

Legend:
- 1980–81
- 2000–01
- 2017–18

Categories (x-axis): Specific learning disorder, Speech or language impairment, Intellectual disability, Emotional disturbance, Developmental delay, Autism spectrum disorder, Hearing impairment, Visual impairment, Orthopedic impairment, Traumatic brain injury, Multiple disabilities, Other health impairment*, Total

Data from National Center for Education Statistics, May, 2019.
*Other health impairments include having limited strength, vitality, or alertness due to chronic or acute health problems such as a heart condition, tuberculosis, rheumatic fever, nephritis, asthma, sickle cell anemia, hemophilia, epilepsy, lead poisoning, leukemia, or diabetes.

**FIGURE 11.5**
**Changing Labels** Note that while fewer children have intellectual disability, more have autism. Many experts think that is a change in name, not substance.

specific skills—for instance, learning the sounds that various letters make. Then the children are tested, and those who did not master the skill receive special "intervention"—practice and individualized teaching, within the regular class.

After the first round of intervention, the children are tested again, and, if need be, intervention occurs again. According to the RTI strategy, only when children do not respond adequately to repeated, focused intervention, are they referred for special education.

At that point, the school proposes an **individual education plan (IEP)**, ideally designed for the particular child. Unfortunately, educators do not always know effective strategies, partly because research on remediation focuses on the less common problems. For example, in the United States "research funding in 2008–2009 for autistic spectrum disorder was 31 times greater than for dyslexia and 540 times greater than for dyscalculia" (Butterworth & Kovas, 2013, p. 304).

As **Figure 11.5** shows, the proportion of children designated with special needs in the United States rose from 10 percent in 1980 to 13 percent in 2016. The greatest rise was in children with learning disorders (National Center for Education Statistics, 2018).

The U.S. school system designates more children as having special needs than does any other nation: Whether or not this is a reason for national pride depends on whether one considers special education a benefit to children, to parents, or to teachers.

How many children really need special education? Some U.S. experts fear that neurodiversity, RTI, and inclusion may boomerang, limiting early and targeted help for children with special needs. If everyone is special, will that prevent help for children who desperately need it (Kauffman et al., 2017)? (See A Case to Study.)

## Early Intervention

One conclusion from all of the research on special education is that diagnosis and intervention often occur too late, or not at all. The numbers of children in public schools who are designated as needing special education increase as children grow

**least restrictive environment (LRE)** A legal requirement that children with special needs be assigned to the most general educational context in which they can be expected to learn.

**response to intervention (RTI)** An educational strategy intended to help children who demonstrate below-average achievement in early grades, using special intervention.

**individual education plan (IEP)** A document that specifies educational goals and plans for a child with special needs.

# The Gifted and Talented

Usually chapters focus on one case to study, but one apparent lesson is that children in any particular category of special need vary among themselves. Children who have the same diagnosis may have quite diverse needs.

To illustrate this point, we highlight another group of children who are sometimes thought to require special education, those who are unusually gifted and talented. Such children are so diverse that it seems best for this A Case to Study to describe several such children.

Historically, parents taught gifted children themselves or hired a special coach or tutor. For example, Mozart composed music at age 3, and Picasso created works of art at age 4. Both boys had fathers who recognized their talent. Mozart's father transcribed his earliest pieces and toured Europe with his gifted son; Picasso's father removed him from school in second grade so that he could create all day.

Although intense early education nourished their talents, neither Mozart nor Picasso had a happy adult life. Mozart had a poor understanding of math, medicine, and money. He had six children, only two of whom survived infancy, and he died in debt at age 35. Picasso regretted not learning to read or write as a child; he married at age 17 and had a total of four children by three women.

When school attendance became universal about a century ago, gifted children were allowed to skip early grades and join other children of the same mental age, not their chronological age. Many accelerated children never learned how to get along with others. As one woman remembers:

> Nine-year-old little girls are so cruel to younger girls. I was much smaller than them, of course, and would have done anything to have a friend. Although I could cope with the academic work very easily, emotionally I wasn't up to it. Maybe it was my fault and I was asking to be picked on. I was a weed at the edge of the playground.
>
> *[Rachel, quoted in Freeman, 2010, p. 27]*

Calling herself "a weed" suggests that she never overcame her conviction that she was less cherished than the other children. Her intellectual needs may have been met by skipping two grades, but her emotional and social needs were severely neglected.

My own father skipped three grades, graduating from high school at age 14. Because he attended a one-room school, and

because he was the middle child of five, his emotional and social needs were met until he began college, where he almost failed because of his immaturity. He recovered, but some other children do not. A chilling example comes from:

> Sufiah Yusof [who] started her maths degree at Oxford [the leading University in England] in 2000, at the age of 13. She too had been dominated and taught by her father. But she ran away the day after her final exam. She was found by police but refused to go home, demanding of her father in an email: "Has it ever crossed your mind that the reason I left home was because I've finally had enough of 15 years of physical and emotional abuse?" Her father claimed she'd been abducted and brainwashed. She refuses to communicate with him. She is now a very happy, high-class, high-earning prostitute.
>
> *[Freeman, 2010, p. 286]*

The fate of creative children may be worse than that of intellectually gifted children. If not given an education that suits them, they joke in class, resist drudgery, ignore homework, and bedevil their teachers. They may become innovators, inventors, and creative forces in the future, but they also may use drugs or drop out of school.

They may find it hard to earn a degree or get a steady job because they are eager to try new things and feel stifled by normal life. Among the well-known creative geniuses who were less-than-stellar students were Bill Gates, Richard Branson, Steve Jobs, and hundreds of thousands of others, probably some of whom you know personally.

One such person was Charles Darwin, whose "school reports complained unendingly that he wasn't interested in studying, only shooting, riding, and beetle-collecting" (Freeman, 2010, p. 283). At the behest of his physician father, Darwin entered college to study medicine, but he dropped out.

Without a degree, he began his famous five-year trip around South America at age 22, collecting specimens and developing the theory of evolution—which disputed conventional religious dogma as only a highly creative person could do.

All these examples suggest that extraordinary children may become extraordinary adults, but that they endure problems because of their abilities. Educators are still not sure what their ideal schooling should be.

older, which is the opposite of what would occur if early intervention were successful. This is apparent in each of the disorders we have discussed.

Sometimes the current approach is called "wait to fail," when ADHD and learning disorders are not diagnosed until a child has been struggling for years without help for sensory, familial, or cultural problems. As one expert says, "We need early identification, and . . . early intervention. If you wait until third grade, kids give up" (Shaywitz, quoted in Stern, 2015, p. 1466).

A similar problem occurs with autism spectrum disorder. You read that autism appears in infancy, but children are not usually diagnosed until age 4, on average (MMWR, March 28, 2014). This is long after many parents have noticed something amiss in their child, and years after the most effective intervention can begin.

In fact, some children diagnosed with ASD before age 4 seem to overcome it later on—an outcome that seems to be related to intense social intervention in the early years (Kroncke et al., 2016). Even with early intervention, most children with ASD have some deficits in adulthood, but the fact that some children overcome social and cognitive symptoms is another argument for early intervention. Plasticity of the brain and behavior is evident.

## Teaching the Gifted and Talented

Children who are unusually gifted are often thought to have special educational needs, although federal laws in the United States do not include them as a special category. Instead, each U.S. state selects and educates gifted-and-talented children in a particular way.

Should children who are unusually intelligent, talented, or creative be home-schooled, skipped, segregated, or enriched? Each of these solutions has been tried and found lacking.

Since both acceleration and intense home schooling have led to later social problems, a third education strategy has become popular, at least in the United States. (See A Case to Study.) Children who are bright, talented, and/or creative—all the same age but each with special abilities—are taught as a group in their own separate class. Ideally, such children are neither bored nor lonely; each is challenged and appreciated by classmates and teachers.

Some research supports the strategy of special education for children with exceptional music, math, or athletic gifts. Their brain structures develop in ways to support their talents (Moreno et al., 2015). Since plasticity means that children learn whatever their context teaches, perhaps some children need gifted-and-talented classes.

Such classes require unusual teachers—bright and creative, and able to individualize instruction. For example, a 7-year-old artist may need freedom, guidance, and inspiration for magnificent art but also need patient, step-by-step instruction in sounding out simple words. Similarly, 7-year-old classmates who already read at the twelfth-grade level might have immature social skills, so the teacher must find another child to befriend them and then must help both share, compromise, and take turns. The teacher must also engage the child who is advanced in reading in conversation about books that most children cannot read until college.

The argument against gifted-and-talented classes is that *every* child needs such teachers, no matter what the child's abilities or disabilities. If each school district (and sometimes each school principal) hires and assigns teachers, as occurs in the United States, then the best teachers may have the most able students, and the school districts with the most money (the most expensive homes) have the highest-paid teachers. Should it be the opposite?

High-achieving students are especially likely to have great teachers if the hidden curriculum includes *tracking*, putting children with special needs together, sorting regular classes by past achievement of the students, and allowing private or charter schools to select only certain students and expel difficult ones.

The problem is worse if the gifted students are in a separate class within the same school as the other students, or if two schools are in the same building, a "regular" school and a "special" school. Then all of the students suffer: Some feel inferior and others superior—with neither group motivated to try

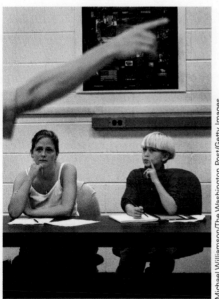

**Mental Age: 18. Chronological Age: 10.** Gregory Smith was a student at Randolph-Macon College in Virginia, shown here in 1999 attending physics class. At age 10, he was quite capable of understanding force and mass, and was one of the best at performing the complicated calculations required in college science. Was he ready to learn all the other things that college teaches?

new challenges and no one learning how to work together (Herrmann et al., 2016; Van Houtte, 2016).

## Every Child Special?

Mainstreaming, IEPs, and so on were developed when parents and educators saw that segregation of children with special needs led to less learning and impaired adult lives. The same may happen if gifted-and-talented children are separated from the rest.

Some nations (China, Finland, Scotland, and many others) educate all children together, assuming that all children could become high achievers if they put in the effort and are guided by effective teachers. Since every child is special, should every child have special education? But since children learn as much from peers as from adults, what does that mean for children who are notably unlike their classmates?

---

**WHAT HAVE YOU LEARNED?**

1. What are the four principles of psychopathology?

2. What is the difference between multifinality and equifinality?

3. What is the difference between ADHD and typical child behavior?

4. What are dyslexia, dyscalculia, and dysgraphia?

5. What are the similarities and differences among the symptoms of autism spectrum disorder?

6. How might the concept of neurodiversity affect treatment for special children?

7. What is the difference between mainstreaming and inclusion?

---

# SUMMARY

### A Healthy Time

**1.** Middle childhood is the healthiest period of the entire life span. Death and disease rates are low, and typically good health habits protect every part of the body.

**2.** Physical activity aids health and joy in many ways. Benefits are apparent in bodies (strength and coordination) and brains (quicker reaction time, more selective attention). However, children who most need physical activity may be least likely to have it.

**3.** Both gross and fine motor skills increase during middle childhood. One particular way to improve fine motor skills is through art and music.

**4.** Worldwide, rates of obesity and asthma are increasing. Children suffer, particularly if they miss time with friends in school and in play.

**5.** International research finds that family habits and national policies interact to increase or decrease the rate of obesity and asthma.

### Brain Development

**6.** Body movement affects brain maturation through blood flow and connections between one part of the brain and another.

**7.** During middle childhood, children gradually become better at paying attention and at reacting quickly. These are valuable skills

in the classroom, which are developed in the team sports that also develop motor skills.

**8.** Intellectual aptitude is usually measured with IQ tests, with scores that can change over time. Achievement is what a person has actually learned, a product of aptitude, motivation, and opportunity.

**9.** Critics of IQ testing contend that intelligence is manifested in multiple ways, which makes *g* (general intelligence) too narrow and limited. Gardner describes nine distinct intelligences.

### Children with Special Brains and Bodies

**10.** Developmental psychopathology uses an understanding of typical development to inform the study of unusual development. Most disorders are comorbid.

**11.** Four general lessons apply to psychopathology at every age: Abnormality is normal; disability changes over time; plasticity and compensation are common; the social context affects manifestation, diagnosis, and treatment. Medication should not be the first response.

**12.** Children with attention-deficit/hyperactivity disorder (ADHD) have potential problems in three areas: inattention, impulsiveness, and activity. DSM-5 recognizes learning disorders, specifically dyslexia (reading), dyscalculia (math), and dysgraphia (penmanship).

**13.** Children on the autism spectrum typically have problems with social interaction and language. ASD originates in the brain, with genetic and prenatal influences, but neurodiversity suggests caution in treatment and analysis.

**14.** Education of children with special needs targets needed treatment. Response to intervention is a first step, before a child is formally adjudicated as a special-needs child.

## KEY TERMS

childhood obesity
  (p. 290)
asthma (p. 291)
reaction time (p. 294)
*g* (general intelligence)
  (p. 295)
Flynn effect (p. 297)

multiple intelligences (p. 297)
neurodiversity (p. 298)
developmental psychopathology
  (p. 299)
comorbid (p. 299)
multifinality (p. 299)
equifinality (p. 299)

attention-deficit/hyperactivity
  disorder (ADHD) (p. 300)
specific learning disorder (p. 302)
dyslexia (p. 302)
dyscalculia (p. 302)
autism spectrum disorder
  (ASD) (p. 303)

least restrictive environment
  (LRE) (p. 305)
response to intervention (RTI)
  (p. 305)
individual education plan (IEP)
  (p. 305)

## APPLICATIONS

**1.** Compare play spaces and school design for children in different neighborhoods—ideally, urban, suburban, and rural areas. Note size, safety, and use. How might this affect children's health and learning?

**2.** Parents of children with special needs often consult internet sources. Pick one disorder and find 10 Web sites that describe causes and educational solutions. How valid, how accurate, and how objective is the information? What disagreements do you find? How might parents react to the information provided?

**3.** Should every teacher be skilled at teaching children with a wide variety of needs, or should some teachers specialize in particular kinds of learning difficulties? Ask professors in your education department. Then ask parents of children with special needs.

**4.** How inclusive are the elementary schools (public, charter, and private) in your community? Get data on ethnic, economic, and ability grouping. Then analyze whether this is best.

## Especially For ANSWERS

**Response for Medical Professionals** (from p. 291): You need to speak to the parents, not accusingly (because you know that genes and culture have a major influence on body weight) but helpfully. Alert them to the potential social and health problems that their child's weight poses. Most parents are very concerned about their child's well-being and will work with you to improve the child's snacks and exercise levels.

**Response for Teachers** (from p. 298): The advantages are that all of the children learn more aspects of human knowledge and that many children can develop their talents. Art, music, and sports should be an integral part of education, not just a break from academics. The disadvantage is that they take time and attention away from reading and math, which might lead to less proficiency in those subjects on standardized tests and thus to criticism from parents and supervisors.

## Observation Quiz ANSWERS

**Answer to Observation Quiz** (from p. 285): Water bottles, sun visors, and ID badges—although the latter might not be considered a healthy innovation.

**Answer to Observation Quiz** (from p. 290): Overall, no. But in some groups, yes. Rates of obesity among Asian American boys are almost three times higher than among Asian American girls.

**Answer to Observation Quiz** (from p. 296): The person is average. Anyone with a score between 85 and 115 has an average IQ.

**Answer to Observation Quiz** (from p. 301): Yes, not only overall but also in response to the diagnosis. When a September birthday boy is diagnosed with ADHD, he is less likely to be medicated than an August birthday boy—the opposite of what would be expected if only boys with real problems were diagnosed.

# Middle Childhood: Cognitive Development

## What Will You Know?

1. Does cognition improve naturally with age, or is teaching crucial to its development?
2. Why do children use slang, curse words, and bad grammar?
3. What type of school is best during middle childhood?

**M**iddle childhood is a time of impressive intellectual capability amid stunning ignorance. Both are explained in this chapter and illustrated by Philip, a delightful 7-year-old with many cognitive skills.

Philip speaks French to his mother and English to everyone else; he can read fluently and calculate Pokémon trades; he does his schoolwork conscientiously. Everyone likes him, in part because he excels at pragmatics: He knows when to use "bathroom words" that make his peers laugh and when to use polite phrases that adults appreciate. Thus, his cognition is impressive. But not always.

Last year, Phillip's mother, Dora, needed open-heart surgery. She and her husband, Craig, told Philip that his mother would be in the hospital for a few days. They explained what this would mean for him, such as that his father would pick him up from school and several others would help with cooking and cleaning. Craig did the explaining; Dora did not want to show her fear.

Philip mirrored his parents' attitude: factual, not emotional. He had a few questions, mostly about exactly what the surgeon would do. A day later he told his parents that when he told his classmates that his mother was having heart surgery, one of them asked, "Is she going to die?" Philip reported this to show his parents how foolish his friend was; he seemed unaware of the insensitivity. His parents, wisely, exchanged wide-eyed glances but simply nodded.

Later, Craig asked Dora, "What is wrong with him? Does he have no heart?"

As you will read, Piaget described concrete operational thought, evident in 6- to 11-year-olds, and Vygotsky explained the power of the social context. Philip's thinking is typical of his age. During these years, if they are told that their parents are divorcing, children might ask, "Where will I live?" instead of expressing sympathy, surprise, or anger. Aspects of cognition that adults take for granted—empathy, emotional sensitivity, hope, and fears for the future—develop gradually.

Dora's operation went well; no repeat surgery is expected. Someday Philip might blame his 7-year-old self for his nonchalance; Craig and Dora can reassure him that he reacted as a child normally does. Later, when they are teenagers, Philip and his classmates will have more than enough "heart."

## Thinking

The human mind from age 6 to 11 is ready to explore and learn from every experience, as children move from the shelter of their family to the wider world of school and community. New intellectual capacities are evident, as described somewhat differently by Piaget, Vygotsky, and information-processing theory.

## Piaget on Middle Childhood

Piaget called this stage of development **concrete operational thought**, characterized by new logical abilities. *Operational* comes from the Latin verb *operare*, meaning "to work; to produce."

By calling this period *operational*, Piaget emphasized productive thinking. By using the word *concrete*, Piaget stressed that the logic of children is focused on specific experiences and observations, not on abstractions. Piaget's theory is a stage theory, expressing the discontinuity first explained in Chapter 1. Preoperational thought ends at about age 6; formal operational thought begins at about age 13; concrete operational thought is the stage between those two, from about age 7 to 12.

Think for a moment about what this means about how children learn. In middle childhood, thinking is *concrete* operational, grounded in actual experience (like the solid concrete of a cement sidewalk). That means it depends on what is visible, tangible, and real, not abstract and theoretical (as at the next stage, formal operational thought). Concrete thinking relies on personal experience. Games, excursions, classroom interactions, family circumstances—all of this is grist for concrete thought.

You read about one concrete example in Chapter 9, conservation. In middle childhood, children know that pouring a liquid into another container does not change the amount of liquid. There are other examples of concrete operational thought that Piaget described.

## A Hierarchy of Categories

One logical operation is **classification**, the organization of things into groups (or *categories* or *classes*) according to some characteristic that they share. For example, *family* includes parents, siblings, and cousins. Other common classes are animals, toys, transportation, and food. Each class includes some elements and excludes others; each is part of a hierarchy.

Food, for instance, is an overarching category, with the next-lower level of the hierarchy being meat, grains, fruits, and so on. Most subclasses can be further divided: Meat includes poultry, beef, and pork, each of which can be divided again.

Adults grasp that items at the bottom of a classification hierarchy belong to every higher level: Bacon is always pork, meat, and food. They also know that each higher category includes many lower ones, but not vice versa (most food, meat, and pork are not bacon). This mental operation of moving up and down the hierarchy is beyond preoperational children.

Gradually, with personal experience (such as eating a variety of foods, meeting many relatives, and using several forms of transportation), concrete operational children can classify. Consider another category, transportation. Children begin to understand, for instance, that planes and motor vehicles are both transportation and that each can be subdivided and further subdivided. Motor vehicles can be buses, trucks, motorcycles, and cars. Then each can be subdivided again: Cars can be sedans, limousines, station wagons, and so on. They know that sedan is a kind of transportation, but not every transportation is a sedan.

Piaget devised many classification experiments. In one, he showed a child a bouquet of nine flowers—seven yellow daisies and two white roses. Then the child is asked, "Are there more daisies or more flowers?" Until about age 7, most children answer, "More daisies."

**concrete operational thought** Piaget's term for the ability to reason logically about direct experiences and perceptions.

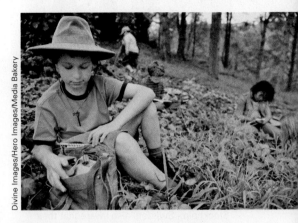

**Notebooks and Weeds** "Write about it," said the teacher to the students on a field trip near San Diego, California. Will this boy describe the air, the plants, the trees—or will his canvas bag distract him? Concrete operational thought is not abstract: He probably won't write about Mother Earth, global warming, or God's kingdom.

**Observation Quiz** Why are these four children sitting far apart from each other? (see answer, page 335) ↑

**classification** The logical principle that things can be organized into groups (or categories or classes) according to some characteristic that they have in common.

Toby Maudsley/The Image Bank/Getty Images

**Numbers and Sequence** Their lockers are numbered, not named, as was true in preschool. Are these children (from Stockholm, Sweden) also aware that their lockers were assigned according to how many inches tall each child is?

**seriation** The concept that things can be arranged in a logical series, such as the number sequence or the alphabet.

The youngest children offer no justification, but some 6-year-olds explain that "there are more yellow ones than white ones" or "because daisies are daisies, they aren't flowers" (Piaget et al., 2015). By age 8, most children can classify: "More flowers than daisies," they say.

## Understanding Sequence

Another example of concrete logic is **seriation**, the knowledge that things can be arranged in a logical *series*. Seriation is crucial for using (not merely memorizing) the alphabet or the number sequence. By age 5, most children can count up to 100, but because they do not yet grasp seriation, most cannot correctly estimate where any particular two-digit number would be placed on a line that starts at 0 and ends at 100.

The ability to remember a sequence of events or actions develops gradually in middle childhood. For example, when children are shown four actions in sequence (for instance, dropping a button into a tube, moving two toys together, putting a stick through a hole, tapping a toy animal with a stick) and are asked to do them in order, most 5-year-olds are unable to do so. By age 8, children are better at this task (Loucks & Price, 2019).

This ability to follow a series may seem inconsequential, but there are dozens of practical applications. Gradually during middle childhood, children learn to get ready for school by performing a series of actions: use the toilet, eat breakfast, brush teeth, put on underwear, then pants and shirt, then socks, then shoes, and so on. This is very hard for 6-year-olds, who need to be reminded what to do next. It is easier with age—and with a list that can be checked off.

## Learning Math

Math begins with familiarity with numbers. As you remember from Chapter 9, some children hear numbers often, such as 10 minutes to play, you are 4 years old, and push the elevator button for the third floor. However, to understand math, children need to grasp the logic behind the numbers, and that develops gradually during concrete operational thought.

Every logical concept helps. Concrete operational thinkers begin to understand that 15 is always 15 (conservation); that numbers from 20 to 29 are all in the 20s (classification); that 134 is less than 143 (seriation); and that because $5 \times 3 = 15$, it follows that $15 \div 5$ must equal 3 (reversibility). By age 11, children use mental categories and subcategories flexibly, inductively, and simultaneously, unlike at age 7.

This learning occurs best when hands-on math (using manipulatives such as blocks, coins, or beans) and verbal descriptions of concepts are both part of instruction (Bachman et al., 2015).

But all children need cognitive maturation before they can, for instance, perform the necessary steps of multidigit multiplication or grasp that four-fifths is greater than seven-tenths.

## Vygotsky and Culture

Like Piaget, Vygotsky felt that educators should consider children's thought processes, not just the outcomes of those processes. He also believed that middle childhood was a time for much learning, with the specifics dependent on the family, school, and culture.

This is evident in the example just given, learning math. Remember that Piaget focused on maturation, with concrete operational thought enabling logic about math. Vygotsky emphasized the social context, noting that children often succeed

**Especially for Teachers** How might Piaget's and Vygotsky's ideas help in teaching geography to a class of third-graders? (see response, page 334)

when they work out math problems together. He predicted what contemporary scholars find, that culture, preschool education, and family attitudes affect math anxiety as well as how quickly children apply math concepts (Scalise et al., 2019).

Vygotsky appreciated children's curiosity and creativity. For that reason, he believed that an educational system based on rote memorization rendered the child "helpless in the face of any sensible attempt to apply any of this acquired knowledge" (Vygotsky, 1994a, pp. 356–357).

Vygotsky would consider a repressive school particularly destructive of cognitive development, because "development depends heavily on the existing diverse social structures" (Lourenço, 2012, p. 284). Thus, the specifics of school organization and curriculum, as well as of family interactions and values, and of cultural mandates and practices, are crucial.

## The Role of Instruction

Unlike Piaget, Vygotsky welcomed direct instruction. With sensitive mentoring, adults and peers provide the scaffold between potential and knowledge, engaging children in their own zone of proximal development. That would explain why children who begin school at age 4 or 5, not 6 or 7, tend to be ahead in academic achievement compared to those who enter later, an effect still apparent at age 15 (Sprietsma, 2010).

Vygotsky would expect children with more social interactions within their zone of proximal development (as would happen in any good kindergarten) to benefit intellectually. The impact of an extra year of early education will vary, because some nations have encouraged more interactive early education than others. Ideally, teachers and other children foster frequent guided participation, and thus cognition advances.

School is one arena for such guided participation, but Vygotsky noted many others. Play with peers, dinner with family, tapping on a screen, greeting neighbors—every experience, from birth on, teaches a child, according to Vygotsky.

On their own, children gradually become more logical during middle childhood, but Vygotsky emphasized the role of mentoring as changing the very structures of the mind. One summary credited Vygotsky (as well as several other twentieth-century developmentalists) with understanding

> "the brain's malleability . . . triggered and organized largely via socially enabled, emotionally driven opportunities for cognitive development. High-quality social interaction therefore presents a critical opportunity and responsibility for education"
>
> [Immordino-Yang et al., 2019, p. 185]

Logic about abstractions is not spontaneously understood until formal operational thought, but when children are taught with high-quality social interaction, they can master logical arguments (even counterfactual ones) by age 11. By the end of middle childhood, some children understand that *if* birds can fly, and *if* elephants are birds, *then* elephants can fly (Christoforides et al., 2016).

Vygotsky emphasized that the lessons a child learns vary by culture and school. Maturation alone is not enough.

He recognized, however, that children are limited by experience and maturation, as in comprehending philosophical issues of life and death. They tend to be quite a matter of fact, absorbing whatever their parents and culture teach rather than seeking the deeper meaning—as was true for Philip (in this chapter's opener on page 310).

ABC/Photofest

**A Boy in Memphis** Moziah Bridges (known as Mo Morris) created colorful bowties, which he first traded for rocks in elementary school. He then created his own company (Mo's Bows) at age 9, selling $300,000 worth of ties to major retailers by age 14. He is shown here with his mother, who encouraged his entrepreneurship.

# Two or Twenty Pills a Day

As you have seen, adults often have opposite points of view on many developmental issues, from racial differences to breast-feeding, from immunization to cesarean births. Here, we present a different kind of opposing perspective, one directly related to the logic and experience of the child.

Researchers presented adults and two groups of children, some at the beginning and some at the end of middle childhood, with the following:

> Marty's ear is red and swollen and hurts a lot. Marty goes to the doctor with his badly infected ear. The doctor takes a look at Marty and gives him some medicine to solve the problem. He tells Marty to take two pills each day, one in the morning when he wakes up and one at night before he goes to bed. He should take those pills for 10 days—so that if Marty takes two pills a day for ten days that would be 20 pills in all.
>
> [Lockhart & Keil, 2018, p. 66]

The participants were asked what would happen if Marty did not take the pills as prescribed but instead:

Took one a day for 20 days.
Took two every morning and none at night for 10 days.
Took two every morning, two at night, for five days.
Took all 20 at once, immediately.

Would Marty get better (rated a 3), stay the same (2), or get worse (rated 1)? The overall results are shown in **Figure 12.1**. As you see, 20 pills at once was quite acceptable to many of the youngest children. Other data showed that only half of them thought this megadose would be harmful, as did 77 percent of the 8- to 11-year-olds and 93 percent of the adults.

This is dramatic evidence that logic by itself is not enough, nor is experience. Virtually all of these children, in their first five years of life, had taken pills prescribed over a period of days, but that experience did not teach them. At the beginning of middle childhood, some understanding began. However, simple logic (more is better) led to a dangerous perspective unless it was tempered by experience. From a developmental perspective, Piaget is inadequate without Vygotsky.

As you also see from these data, children grow wiser in middle childhood, but their concrete, literal thinking is evident. The 8- to 11-year-olds were less willing to deviate from the prescribed dose than the adults were. Most of the adults thought Marty would still get better if he took two pills every morning or only one every day, but many children disagreed. Balanced cognition, using both logic and experience, is not yet available to every 8- to 11-year-old.

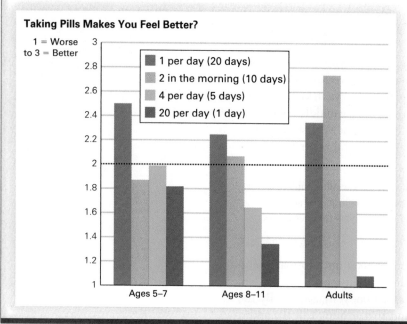

**Taking Pills Makes You Feel Better?**

1 = Worse to 3 = Better

- 1 per day (20 days)
- 2 in the morning (10 days)
- 4 per day (5 days)
- 20 per day (1 day)

Ages 5–7    Ages 8–11    Adults

**FIGURE 12.1**

**Not Doctor's Orders** A doctor diagnosed an infected ear and prescribed 20 pills, with instructions to take one in the morning and one in the evening for ten days. People of various ages were asked how the person would feel if they didn't follow orders. A rating of 3 means "better"; 1 means "worse." The chart shows the average responses, by age. As you see, almost every adult expected improvement if the person took two each morning, and they knew that taking 20 at once was a terrible idea. About half of the youngest children did not know that—most thought the person would still feel okay, and some thought taking 20 pills at once would be fine! Most also thought that one pill a day would be good enough. Given how children think, no wonder their accident rate is so high.

## Information Processing

Contemporary educators and psychologists find both Piaget and Vygotsky insightful. International research confirms the merits of their theories (Mercer & Howe, 2012; Vince, 2018). One scholar wrote:

> [A]sked who are the two main geniuses in the field of developmental psychology, many, if not all, developmentalists would certainly point to Jean Piaget (1896–1980) and Lev Vygotsky (1896–1934).
>
> [Lourenço, 2012, p. 281]

## Coordination and Capacity

Recall that emotional regulation, theory of mind, and left–right coordination emerge in early childhood. The maturing corpus callosum connects the hemispheres of the brain, enabling balance and two-handed coordination, while myelination adds speed. Maturation of the prefrontal cortex—the executive part of the brain—allows the child to plan, monitor, and evaluate.

In middle childhood, increasing maturation results in connections between the brain's various lobes and regions. Connections are crucial for the complex tasks that children must master, which require "smooth coordination of large numbers of neurons" (P. Stern, 2013, p. 577).

Certain areas of the brain, called *hubs*, are locations where massive numbers of axons meet. Hubs tend to be near the corpus callosum, and damage to them correlates with notable brain dysfunction (as in neurocognitive, autism spectrum, and other psychological disorders) (Crossley et al., 2014).

Because of hubs, brain connections forming in middle childhood are crucial. Consider learning to read. Reading is not instinctual: Our ancestors never did it, and until recent centuries, only a few scribes and scholars could interpret letters written on papyrus, carved in wood, or chiseled into stone. Consequently, the brain has no areas dedicated to reading in the way it does for talking or gesturing (Sousa, 2014).

Instead, reading uses many parts of the brain—one for sounds, another for recognizing letters, another for sequencing, another for comprehension, and more. By working together, these parts first foster listening, talking, and thinking, and then they put it all together (Lewandowski & Lovett, 2014).

Children with reading difficulties are variable as well as slow in reaction time. That makes their reading erratic (Tamm et al., 2014). Fluent reading—possible at age 8 or so—requires (1) seeing a long sequence of letters, (2) segmenting them as words, (3) differentiating words spelled alike (such as *read* and *read*, *bark* and *bark*), (4) considering context to grasp unfamiliar words, (5) recognizing oddities and ironies, and (6) understanding meaning related to the previous sentences. For fluency, reactions must be quick and automatic.

More broadly, it is now evident that the prefrontal cortex coordinates many hubs and subcortical regions of the brain "very rapidly (prior to conscious awareness)" as the brain automatically responds to stimulation (Blair, 2016, p. 3). This rapid, unconscious processing is the result of all of the neurotransmitters and neurological hubs of early and middle childhood.

The brain of a typical 6- to 11-year-old is ready to learn rapidly and well. Basic brain functions and connections are in place: Age will bring quantitative changes (increases in size and strength) but not qualitative ones (Engelhardt et al., 2019). Connections are formed that endure lifelong.

What do you remember learning during middle childhood?

Piaget described universal changes; Vygotsky noted cultural impact. However, neither grand theory describes the year-by-year details of cognition in middle childhood. Each domain of achievement may follow a particular path (Siegler, 2016). Developmentalists recognize the need for a third approach to understanding cognition.

As you read in earlier chapters, the *information-processing perspective* benefits from technology that allows much more detailed data and analysis than were possible for Piaget or Vygotsky. Like computers that process information, people accumulate large amounts of facts. They then (1) seek relevant facts (as a search engine does) for each cognitive task, (2) analyze (as software programs do), and (3) express conclusions (as the totals on a spreadsheet might). By tracing the paths and links of each of these functions, scientists better understand the learning process.

The usefulness of the information-processing approach is evident in data on children's school achievement year-by-year and even month-by-month. Absences, vacations, new schools, and even new teachers set back a child's learning because each day builds on the learning of the previous day.

Brain connections and pathways are forged from repeated experiences, allowing advances in processing. Without careful building and repetition, fragile connections between neurons break. Middle childhood is a crucial time for brain connections between one region and another, with the specifics of cultural emphasis aiding those links.

### The Importance of Practice

Neither Vygotsky nor Piaget emphasized the importance of practicing intellectual skills in order to foster cognitive development. However, many more recent studies

**automatization** A process in which repetition of a sequence of thoughts and actions makes the sequence routine so that it no longer requires conscious thought.

of brain development note the importance of practice in reaching **automatization**, the process by which a sequence of thoughts and actions is repeated until no conscious thought is required (e.g., Y. Chen et al., 2019; Rønneberg & Torrance, 2019).

At first, almost all voluntary behaviors require careful thought. But after many repetitions, neurons fire in sequence and less thinking is needed, because the firing of one neuron sets off a chain reaction.

Consider reading again. At age 6, eyes (often aided by a guiding finger) focus intensely, painstakingly making out letters and sounding out each one. Over the years of middle childhood, this leads to the perception of syllables and then words, from emerging literacy at about age 6 to fluent reading by age 10. Eventually, the process becomes so automatic that people driving along a highway read billboards with a glance when they have no interest in doing so.

Automatization aids all academic skills. One longitudinal study of second-graders—from the beginning of the school year to the end—found that each type of academic proficiency aided each other type. Thus, learning became more automatic as automatization fostered more learning (Lai et al., 2014).

Learning a second language, reciting the multiplication tables, and writing one's name are all slow at first, but automatization makes each effortless as the school years go by. Not just academic knowledge but also habits and routines from childhood echo lifelong—and adults find them hard to break. If you have a bad habit that you can't stop, blame your brain. That's automatization.

But, also be proud of your brain's responses, evident toward the end of middle childhood. Quick reaction time and selective attention aid every social and academic skill, without taking any intellectual resources away from the next intellectual task.

For instance, being able to calculate when to utter a witty remark and when to stay quiet is something few 6-year-olds can do. By the end of middle childhood, children can (1) realize that a comment could be made and (2) decide what it could be, (3) think about the other person's possible response and, in the same split second, (4) know when something should NOT be said.

Automatic responses—saying "thank you" for a compliment, "good morning" to an acquaintance, "please" to a stranger—are learned in early childhood (often slowly, with reminders from adults) and become automatic in middle childhood.

**LaunchPad**
macmillan learning

**VIDEO ACTIVITY: Arithmetic Strategies: The Research of Robert Siegler** demonstrates how children acquire math understanding.

**Following Instructions** In middle childhood, children become quite capable of following adults' instructions, as these children in Tallinn, Estonia are. Their teacher told them to put out their right hand, so that Pope Francis could greet each child quickly. The teacher must not have given the most important instruction about greeting a pope: Keep your eyes open.

## Siegler on Math Learning

One of the leaders of the information-processing perspective is Robert Siegler, who studies day-by-day details of children's cognition in math (Siegler & Braithwaite, 2017). Siegler compares the acquisition of knowledge to waves on an ocean beach when the tide is rising. After ebb and flow, eventually a new level is reached.

Like those waves, math understanding accrues gradually, with new and better strategies for calculation tried, ignored, half-used, abandoned, and finally adopted (Siegler, 2016). The specifics are influenced by the culture, which may or may not emphasize math concepts, and the teachers, who may or may not understand the need for patience and practice. Counting itself is the product of culture: Some languages lack words for large numbers, fractions, and so on (Everett, 2017).

Using computer testing and analysis, Siegler and his colleagues have been able to pinpoint lapses in children's understanding of math concepts with precision, which was not possible a century ago for Piaget and Vygotsky. Current scholars find that many children at age 10 are quite capable of adding and subtracting whole numbers, but

Abaca Press/Sipa USA via AP Images

they are woefully inadequate with fractions (Braithwaite et al., 2018). Research such as this uncovers the particular needs that children have.

## Knowledge Leads to Knowledge

The more people already know, the better they can learn. Having an extensive **knowledge base**, or a broad body of knowledge in a particular subject, makes it easier to remember and understand related new information. As children gain knowledge during the school years, they become better able to judge (1) accuracy, (2) what is worth remembering, and (3) what is not important (Woolley & Ghossainy, 2013).

Past experience, current opportunity, and personal motivation all facilitate increases in the knowledge base. Motivation explains why a child may not know what facts parents or teachers prefer.

Some schoolchildren memorize words and rhythms of hit songs, calculate the worth of dozens of game cards, or recite names and statistics of basketball (or soccer, baseball, or cricket) stars. Yet they do not know whether World War I was in the nineteenth or twentieth century, or whether Pakistan is in Asia or Africa.

Concepts are learned best when linked to personal and emotional experiences. For example, children from South Asia, or those with classmates from there, learn the boundaries of Pakistan if teachers appreciate and connect with their students' heritage. On the other hand, children who are new to a nation or a neighborhood may be confused by some kinds of learning that are easy for those who have always lived there.

## Control Processes

The neurological mechanisms that put memory, processing speed, and the knowledge base together are **control processes**; they regulate the analysis and flow of information within the brain. Two terms are often used to refer to cognitive control—*metacognition* (sometimes called "thinking about thinking") and *metamemory* (knowing about memory).

Control processes require the brain to organize, prioritize, and direct mental operations. For that reason, control processes are also called executive processes, and the ability to use them is called executive function (already explained in Chapter 9).

Control processes allow a person to step back from the specifics to consider more general goals and cognitive strategies, with the flexibility, memory, and inhibition that characterize executive processing. The finding, again and again, is that how children use their minds provides the foundation for learning. Maturation and experience matter.

All of these abilities develop spontaneously as the prefrontal cortex matures, but they can also be taught (de Oliveira Cardoso et al., 2018). Examples that may be familiar include spelling rules ("*i* before *e* except after *c*") and ways to remember how to turn a lightbulb ("lefty-loosey, righty-tighty").

Preschoolers ignore such rules or use them only on command; 7-year-olds begin to use them; 9-year-olds can create and master more complicated rules. Efforts to teach executive control succeed if the particular neurological maturation of the child is taken into account, which is exactly what information-processing theorists would predict (Karbach & Unger, 2014).

## Theory of Mind

Closely related to control processes is the ongoing development of theory of mind (Wilson et al., 2018). As you remember, theory of mind begins in early childhood.

Carol Yepes/Getty Images

**What Does She See?** It depends on her knowledge base and personal experiences. Perhaps this trip to an aquarium is no more than a break from the school routine, with the teachers merely shepherding the children to keep them safe. Or, perhaps she has learned about sharks and dorsal fins, about scales and gills, about warm-blooded mammals and cold-blooded fish, so she is fascinated by the swimming creatures she watches. Or, if her personal emotions shape her perceptions, perhaps she feels sad about the fish in their watery cage or finds joy in their serenity and beauty.

**knowledge base** A body of knowledge in a particular area that makes it easier to master new information in that area.

**control processes** Mechanisms (including selective attention, metacognition, and emotional regulation) that combine memory, processing speed, and knowledge to regulate the analysis and flow of information within the information-processing system. (Also called *executive processes*.)

It continues to develop, including more nuanced beliefs and desires, in middle childhood and beyond (Wellman, 2018).

Theory of mind turns out to be pivotal for cognitive development. For example, it aids 6- to 11-year-olds in understanding the scientific process and mathematics. Both of those aspects of cognitive development are far from merely factual; they are facilitated by social awareness (Libertus et al., 2013; Peng et al., 2017; Piekny & Maehler, 2013).

---

**WHAT HAVE YOU LEARNED?**

1. What did Piaget mean when he called cognition in middle childhood *concrete operational thought*?

2. How do Vygotsky and Piaget differ in their explanations of cognitive advances in middle childhood?

3. How does information-processing theory differ from traditional theories of cognitive development?

4. According to Siegler, what is the pattern of learning math concepts?

5. How and why does the knowledge base increase in middle childhood?

6. How might control processes help a student learn?

---

# Language

Language is crucial for cognition in middle childhood. It is the means by which children learn new concepts, and it also indicates how much children have learned. A school-age child who can explain ideas with complex sentences is a child who is thinking well. Every aspect of language—vocabulary, comprehension, communication skills, and code-switching—advances each year from age 6 to 11.

## Vocabulary

Vocabulary builds during middle childhood. Because concrete operational children are logical, they can use prefixes, suffixes, compound words, phrases, and metaphors. That enables them to understand the meaning of a word they have never heard before, a decided advantage over younger children.

For example, 2-year-olds know *egg*, but 10-year-olds also know *egg salad*, *egg-drop soup*, *egghead*, *a good egg*, and *"last one in is a rotten egg"*—a metaphor from my childhood that a recent Google search found still relevant today. By age 10, a child who has never smelled a rotten egg nor heard that phrase can figure out the meaning.

In middle childhood, some words become pivotal for understanding the curriculum, such as *negotiate, evolve, allegation, deficit, molecule*. Consequently, vocabulary is taught in every elementary school classroom.

## Adjusting Language to the Context

A crucial aspect of language that advances markedly in middle childhood is pragmatics, defined in Chapter 9. Pragmatics is evident when a child knows which words to use with teachers (never calling them a rotten egg) and informally with friends (who can be called rotten eggs or worse). For this, the social interaction foundation for cognition is apparent.

**Go with the Flow** This boat classroom in Bangladesh picks up students on shore and then uses solar energy to power computers linked to the internet as part of instruction. The educational context will teach skills and metaphors that peers of these students will not understand.

JONAS GRATZER/LIGHTROCKET/GETTY IMAGES

As children master pragmatics, they become more adept at making friends. Shy 6-year-olds cope far better with the social pressures of school if they use pragmatics well (Coplan & Weeks, 2009). By contrast, children with autism spectrum disorder are usually very poor at pragmatics (Klinger et al., 2014).

Mastery of pragmatics allows children to change styles of speech, or *linguistic codes*, depending on their audience. Each code includes many aspects of language—not just vocabulary but also tone, pronunciation, grammar, sentence length, idioms, and gestures.

Sometimes the switch is between *formal code* (used in academic contexts) and *informal code* (used with friends). Sometimes it is between standard (or proper) speech and dialect or vernacular (used on the street).

All children need instruction because the logic of grammar and spelling (whether *who* or *whom* is correct, or how to spell *you*) is almost impossible to deduce. Yet everyone will be judged by their ability to speak and write the formal code, so children need to learn it.

## Speaking Two Languages

Code changes are obvious when children speak one language at home and another at school. Every nation includes many such children; most of the world's 6,000 languages are not school languages.

In the United States, about one school-age child in four speaks something other than English at home (see **Figure 12.2**). Many other U.S. children speak one or more of the 20 or so English dialects that reflect regional or ethnic word use, pronunciation, and grammar.

A child's comfort using the home language or regional dialect correlates with pride and motivation. At the same time, in the United States, a child's ability to use standard English correlates with school achievement.

Consequently, teachers need to respect the home language while teaching the school language (Terry et al., 2016). However, this is not as simple as it may seem, as adult ideology may conflict with what is best for the child (MacSwan, 2018). It is known, however, that emphasizing language is crucial for school achievement from early childhood on. Children can learn several codes—easily before age 5, with some help in middle childhood, and with effort after puberty.

Educators and political leaders in the United States argue about how to teach English to **English Language Learners (ELLs)**, students whose first language is not

> **THINK CRITICALLY:** Do children from some backgrounds need to become especially adept at code-switching? Does this challenge advance cognitive development?

**English Language Learners (ELLs)** Children in the United States whose proficiency in English is low—usually below a cutoff score on an oral or written test. Many children who speak a non-English language at home are also capable in English; they are *not* ELLs.

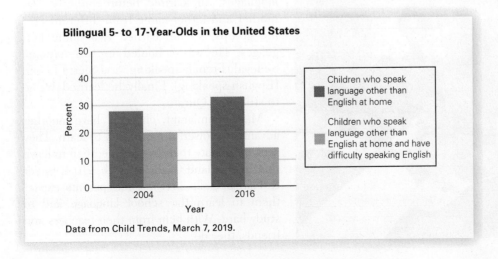

**Bilingual 5- to 17-Year-Olds in the United States**

Legend:
- Children who speak language other than English at home
- Children who speak language other than English at home and have difficulty speaking English

Data from Child Trends, March 7, 2019.

**FIGURE 12.2**
**Home and Country** Do you see good news? A dramatic increase in the number of bilingual children is a benefit for the nation, but the hundreds of thousands of children who still have trouble with English suggests that more education is needed.

Standard English. About 14 percent of the children in middle childhood are designated as ELLs (McFarland et al., 2019). Note that this is significantly lower than the percent who speak another language at home. Many of them are bilingual before they reach primary school.

How should children learn the school language if they have not already done so in early childhood? One strategy is called **immersion**, in which instruction occurs entirely in the new code. The opposite strategy is to teach children in their first language initially and then to add instruction of the second as a "foreign" tongue (a strategy that is rare in the United States but common elsewhere).

Between these extremes lies **bilingual education**, with instruction in two languages, and **ESL (English as a Second Language)**, with all non-English speakers being taught English in one multilingual group, preparing them to join English-only classes. Every method for teaching a second language sometimes succeeds and sometimes fails. A major problem is that language-learning abilities change with age: The youngest children learn a new language fastest, so immersion might succeed for them.

For cognitive advances during middle childhood, the information-processing approach suggests that children should learn two languages. When bilingual individuals are asked to reason about something in their second language, they tend to be more rational and less emotional—which usually (but not always) leads to better thought (Costa et al., 2017).

Bilingual children who are fluent in both languages are able to inhibit one language while using another, advancing in cognitive control. This is obvious in language, but some say it is an asset in other aspects of executive function (Bialystok, 2018). Others dispute that (Nichols et al., 2020). The emphasis here is on proficiency: Children who are not fluent in at least one language are also impaired in cognitive skills.

Parents influence the language fluency of their children, but they are not alone. Children benefit from conversations with relatives, strangers, friends, and teachers, which is one reason going to school every day and playing with children who are proficient in other languages are recommended for language development in middle childhood.

Some bilingual children speak one language at home and learn another language elsewhere, because they spend extensive time with speakers of that second language. That is most likely in childhood; it is difficult in adulthood. One of my African students speaks five languages, all learned before puberty. His mother and father came from different ethnic groups, so he learned two home languages. He was schooled in two nations: Senegal (French-speaking) and Sierra Leone (English-speaking). Finally, he learned Arabic to study the Quran.

Many immigrant children have another advantage, powerful motivation to learn. They seek to validate their parents' decision to leave their native land (Ceballo et al., 2014; Fuller & García Coll, 2010). Their parents expect them to learn the school language and to study hard. With help from their teachers and friends, they do.

**immersion** A strategy in which instruction in all school subjects occurs in the second (usually the majority) language that a child is learning.

**bilingual education** A strategy in which school subjects are taught in both the learner's original language and the second (majority) language.

**English as a Second Language (ESL)** A U.S. approach to teaching English that gathers all of the non-English speakers together and provides intense instruction in English. Students' first languages are never used; the goal is to prepare students for regular classes in English.

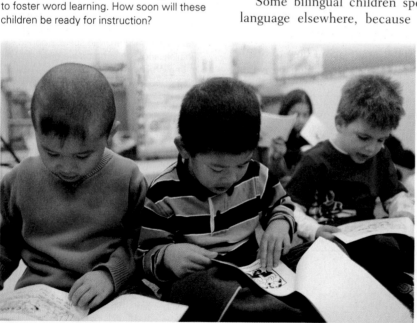

**Months or Years?** ESL classes, like this one in Canada, often use pictures and gestures to foster word learning. How soon will these children be ready for instruction?

Ian Taylor/First Light/Getty Images

## Poverty and Language

Every study finds that SES affects cognitive development, with poor language mastery a prominent sign and perhaps the major cause of low academic achievement in low-income children. Children from low-SES families usually have smaller vocabularies than those from higher-SES families, and they also are impaired in grammar (fewer compound sentences, dependent clauses, and conditional verbs) (Hart & Risley, 1995; Hoff, 2013). That slows down school learning in every subject.

Brain scans confirm that language proficiency is related to brain activity (Romeo et al., 2018). The development of the hippocampus (crucial for memory) is particularly affected by SES, and that may be critical for language learning (Jednoróg et al., 2012).

How can poverty affect the brain? Possibilities include inadequate prenatal care, no breakfast, lead in the bloodstream, crowded and noisy households, few books at home, teenage parents, authoritarian child rearing, inexperienced teachers, air pollution, neighborhood violence, lack of role models . . . the list could go on and on (Cree et al., 2018; Kolb & Gibb, 2015; Rowe et al., 2016). All of these conditions correlate with low SES, slower language development, and less learning. But correlation is not causation: Any one of these might reflect a third variable.

However, one factor definitely is a cause, not just a correlate: language heard early on (Neuman et al., 2018). That explains why maternal education is influential, especially if she continues her quest for learning by reading and asking questions. That also explains why children whose homes have many books accumulate, on average, three more years of education than children who live in homes with no books (Evans et al., 2010).

Of course, the books cannot merely sit on shelves. A study of 16,000 11-year-olds in England found that language proficiency was heavily influenced by how much the parents read to the child—which could begin before the first birthday and continue after the children are able to read on their own (Law et al., 2018).

Remember the plasticity of the brain. In some families, neuronal connections are strengthened, and dendrites grow to support language. This process continues in middle childhood (Perone et al., 2018).

Low income per se is not as influential as maternal talk and listening. Educated parents are more likely to take their children to museums, zoos, and libraries as well as to engage children in conversation about the interesting sights around them. Many sing to their children, not just a few simple songs but dozens of songs with varied vocabulary.

A much-cited study found that vocabulary was directly related to how much language a child heard, and found that, before age 3, children in families low in SES heard 30,000 fewer words than higher SES children (Hart & Risley, 1995). That study led to a nationwide campaign to encourage low-income parents to talk more to their children.

Many later studies also found that low-SES parents talk less to their young children. Consequently, children entered kindergarten already behind other children in their ability to learn in school. That language deficit is thought to be the crucial reason some children score lower on achievement tests, and are much more likely to drop out of high school and find only low-income employment lifelong.

Some research disputes those findings, suggesting that young children from low-SES families overhear much more language than other children. As a result,

**Especially for Parents** You've had an exhausting day but are setting out to buy groceries. Your 7-year-old son wants to go with you. Should you explain that you are so tired that you want to make a quick solo trip to the supermarket this time? (see response, page 334)

there is much more variation within each stratum of socioeconomic status, with some low-SES children hearing more words than some high-SES children (Sperry et al., 2019). Their eventual achievement gaps should not be blamed on their parents, but instead be blamed on the quality of their preschools and primary schools.

Some of the leading scholars in child development argue against that interpretation, contending that overheard speech is not nearly as useful to children as child-directed speech (Golinkoff et al., 2019). They argue that adults need to spend hours every day listening and talking directly to young children. This can occur no matter what the parents' SES. Then the children will develop language and do well in school.

---

**WHAT HAVE YOU LEARNED?**

1. How does language benefit from cognition in middle childhood?
2. What is the relationship between language and cognition?
3. Why would a child's linguistic code be criticized by teachers but admired by peers?
4. How does a person most readily become bilingual?
5. How does family income affect language development?

---

## Teaching and Learning

In middle childhood, anything can be learned. Some children, by age 11, beat their elders at chess, play music that adults pay to hear, publish poems, and solve complex math problems. Others survive on the streets or fight in civil wars, skilled at firing automatic guns that are almost too big to carry.

Children worldwide learn whatever adults in their culture teach, and their brains are ready. (See the At About This Time tables for some of the universally recognized sequences of learning to read and do arithmetic.) Traditionally, children were educated at home, but now almost all of the world's 7-year-olds are in school. It is crucial that adults develop the schools and the curriculum to prepare children for adult life.

Indeed, in many developing nations, the number of students in elementary school exceeds the number of school-age children, because many older children as well as adults now seek basic education. Ghana, El Salvador, and China are among the nations with more students in primary school than the total number of children in middle childhood (UNESCO, 2014).

### The Curriculum

What should children learn? Every nation seeks to teach reading, writing, and arithmetic—the classic "three R's." But beyond literacy and math, nations vary in what they expect.

For example, every nation wants children to become good citizens, but nations disagree about what good citizenship entails or how children can learn it (Cohen & Malin, 2010). Accordingly, many children simply follow their parents' example regarding everything from picking up trash to supporting a candidate for president.

**Math**

| Age | Norms and Expectations |
| --- | --- |
| 4–5 years | • Count to 20.<br>• Understand one-to-one correspondence of objects and numbers.<br>• Understand *more* and *less*.<br>• Recognize and name shapes. |
| 6 years | • Count to 100.<br>• Understand *bigger* and *smaller*.<br>• Add and subtract one-digit numbers. |
| 8 years | • Add and subtract two-digit numbers.<br>• Understand simple multiplication and division.<br>• Understand word problems with two variables. |
| 10 years | • Add, subtract, multiply, and divide multidigit numbers.<br>• Understand simple fractions, percentages, area, and perimeter of shapes.<br>• Understand word problems with three variables. |
| 12 years | • Begin to use abstract concepts, such as formulas and algebra. |

Math learning depends heavily on direct instruction and repeated practice, which means that some children advance more quickly than others. This list is only a rough guide meant to illustrate the importance of sequence.

**Reading**

| Age | Norms and Expectations |
| --- | --- |
| 4–5 years | • Understand basic book concepts. For instance, children learning English and many other languages understand that books are written from front to back, with print from left to right, and that letters make words that describe pictures.<br>• Recognize letters—name the letters on sight.<br>• Recognize and spell own name. |
| 6–7 years | • Know the sounds of the consonants and vowels, including those that have two sounds (e.g., *c, g, o*).<br>• Use sounds to figure out words.<br>• Read simple words, such as *cat, sit, ball, jump*. |
| 8 years | • Read simple sentences out loud, 50 words per minute, including words of two syllables.<br>• Understand basic punctuation, consonant–vowel blends.<br>• Comprehend what is read. |
| 9–10 years | • Read and understand paragraphs and chapters, including advanced punctuation (e.g., the colon).<br>• Answer comprehension questions about concepts as well as facts.<br>• Read polysyllabic words (e.g., *vegetarian, population, multiplication*). |
| 11–12 years | • Demonstrate rapid and fluent oral reading (more than 100 words per minute).<br>• Vocabulary includes words that have specialized meaning in various fields. For example, in civics, *liberties, federal, parliament*, and *environment* all have special meanings.<br>• Comprehend paragraphs about unfamiliar topics.<br>• Sound out new words, figuring out meaning using cognates and context.<br>• Read for pleasure. |
| 13+ years | • Continue to build vocabulary, with greater emphasis on comprehension than on speech. Understand textbooks. |

Reading is a complex mix of skills, dependent on brain maturation, education, and culture. The sequence given here is approximate; it should not be taken as a standard to measure any particular child.

Religious education also varies. The U.S. Constitution forbids overt teaching of religion in public schools (although, of course, children can pray, express beliefs, or wear religious symbols), but other nations believe religious education is part of learning. In the United States, many private schools teach religion, and parents sometimes choose them for precisely that reason.

Another variation is in how much importance is placed on each particular subject. As already mentioned in the previous chapters, the time spent on physical education, on the arts, and on other aspects of the curriculum varies from nation to nation. Most nations have national policies regarding curriculum, but within the United States variation is evident, not only state to state but also school district to school district.

## The Hidden Curriculum

Differences between nations, and between schools in the United States, are stark in the **hidden curriculum**—all of the implicit values and assumptions of schools.

**hidden curriculum** The unofficial, unstated, or implicit patterns within a school that influence what children learn. For instance, teacher background, organization of the play space, and tracking are all part of the hidden curriculum—not formally prescribed, but instructive to the children.

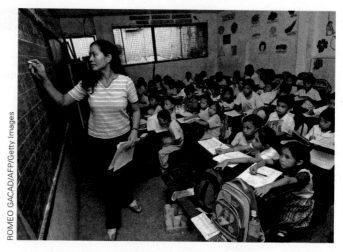

**Room to Learn?** In the elementary school classroom in Florida *(left)*, the teacher is guiding two students who are working to discover concepts in physics—a stark contrast to the Filipino classroom *(right)* in a former storeroom. Sometimes the hidden curriculum determines the overt curriculum, as shown here.

 **Observation Quiz** How many children are in the classroom in the Philippines? (see answer, page 335) ↑

Schedules, tracking, teacher characteristics, discipline, teaching methods, sports competitions, student government, and extracurricular activities are all part of the hidden curriculum. This teaches children far beyond the formal, published curriculum that lists what is taught in each grade.

An obvious example is the physical surroundings. Some schools have spacious classrooms, wide hallways, and large, grassy playgrounds; others have cramped, poorly equipped classrooms and cement play yards. In some nations, school is held outdoors, with no chairs, desks, or books; classes are canceled when it rains. What does that tell the students?

## Teacher Ethnicity

Another aspect of the hidden curriculum is who the teachers are. If their gender, ethnicity, or economic background is unlike that of their students, children may conclude that education is irrelevant to them. School organization is also significant. If the school has gifted classes, those in other classes may conclude that they are not capable of learning.

The United States is experiencing major demographic shifts. Since 2010, half of the babies born are from Hispanic, Asian, African, or Native American families, whereas more than two-thirds of adults are of European background. Because of sexual and racial discrimination, many experienced teachers are older White women.

One result is that most children never have an elementary school teacher who is a man of minority background. Of course, many older White women are excellent teachers, but schools also need more excellent male, minority teachers—not only for the minority boys. The hidden curriculum could teach that caring educators come from many backgrounds. Does it?

## Teacher Expectations

Less visible, yet probably more influential, is the hidden message that comes from teacher attitudes. If a teacher expects a child to be disruptive, or unable to learn, that child is likely to confirm those expectations. Teachers who are themselves African American or Latinx have more favorable attitudes about the learning potential of students from those backgrounds (Glock & Kleen, 2019).

Fortunately, teacher expectations are malleable: Learning increases and absences decrease when teachers believe all of their students are educable and they teach accordingly, encouraging every child (Sparks, 2016).

One cultural value is whether students are expected to talk or be quiet in class. In the United States, adults are encouraged to voice their opinions. Accordingly, many teachers welcome student questions, call on children who do not speak up, ask children to work in pairs so that each child talks, and grant points for participation.

As a result of their schooling, North American students learn to speak, even when they do not know the answers. Teachers say "good question" or "interesting idea" when students say something that the teacher considers wrong. Elsewhere, children are expected to be quiet.

This was dramatically apparent to me when I taught at the United Nations International School. Some of my students shouted out answers, some raised their hands, some never spoke except when I called on them. I found it hard not to favor the talkative students. When I called on one quiet student from South Asia, he immediately stood up to answer—to my surprise and the smiles of his classmates. I hope our reaction did not undercut his learning: I fear it did.

The hidden curriculum affects learning if the teachers' assumptions differ from the students' assumptions. In one study, middle-class children asked questions and requested help from their teachers more often than low-SES students did (Calarco, 2014). The researchers suggested that the low-SES students sought to avoid teacher attention, fearing it would lead to criticism. Might that have given teachers the impression that they were disinterested? Thus, the hidden curriculum might prevent students who most need encouragement from getting it.

## International Testing

Every nation now wants to improve education. Longitudinal data shows that the national economy advances when school achievement rises (Hanushek & Woessmann, 2015). Better-educated children become healthier and more productive adults. That is one reason many developing nations are building more schools and colleges.

Nations seek not only education for everyone, but also more effective education. To measure that, almost 100 nations have participated in at least one massive international test of children's learning.

Achievement in science and math is tested in the **Trends in Math and Science Study (TIMSS)**. The main test of reading is the **Progress in International Reading Literacy Study (PIRLS)**. A third test is the **Programme for International Student Assessment (PISA)**, which is designed to measure the ability to apply learning to everyday issues. East Asian nations always rank high, and scores for more than a dozen nations (some in Europe, most in Asia) surpass those for the United States (see **Tables 12.1** and **12.2**).

One surprising example is that Finland's scores increased dramatically after a wholesale reform of its public education system. Reforms occurred in several waves (Sahlberg, 2011, 2015). In 1985 ability grouping was abolished, and in 1994 the curriculum began to encourage collaboration and active learning rather than competitive passive education.

Currently, in Finland, all children learn together—no tracking—and teachers are mandated to help each child. Over the past two decades, Finland has instituted strict requirements for becoming a teacher. Only the top 3 percent of Finland's high school graduates are admitted to teachers' colleges. They study for five years at the university at no charge, earning a master's degree, studying both the theory and the practice of education.

**Trends in Math and Science Study (TIMSS)** An international assessment of the math and science skills of fourth-graders and eighth-graders. Although the TIMSS is very useful, different countries' scores are not always comparable because sample selection, test administration, and content validity are hard to keep uniform.

**Progress in International Reading Literacy Study (PIRLS)** Inaugurated in 2001, a planned five-year cycle of international trend studies in the reading ability of fourth-graders.

**Programme for International Student Assessment (PISA)** An international test taken by 15-year-olds in 50 nations that is designed to measure problem solving and cognition in daily life.

## TABLE 12.1

**TIMSS Ranking and Average Scores of Math Achievement for Fourth-Graders, 2011 and 2015**

|  | 2011 | 2015 |
|---|---|---|
| Singapore | 606 | 618 |
| Hong Kong | 602 | 615 |
| Korea | 605 | 608 |
| Chinese Taipei | 591 | 597 |
| Japan | 585 | 593 |
| N. Ireland | 562 | 570 |
| Russia | 542 | 564 |
| England | 542 | 546 |
| Belgium | 549 | 546 |
| United States | 541 | 539 |
| Canada (Quebec) | 533 | 533 |
| Finland | 545 | 532 |
| Netherlands | 540 | 530 |
| Germany | 528 | 522 |
| Sweden | 504 | 519 |
| Australia | 516 | 517 |
| Canada (Ontario) | 518 | 512 |
| Italy | 508 | 507 |
| New Zealand | 486 | 491 |
| Iran | 431 | 431 |
| Kuwait | 342 | 353 |

## TABLE 12.2

**PIRLS Distribution of Reading Achievement for Fourth-Graders, 2011 and 2016**

|  | 2011 | 2016 |
|---|---|---|
| Hong Kong | 571 | 569 |
| Russian Federation | 568 | 581 |
| Finland | 568 | 566 |
| Singapore | 567 | 576 |
| N. Ireland | 558 | 565 |
| United States | 556 | 549 |
| Denmark | 554 | 547 |
| Chinese Taipei | 553 | 559 |
| Ireland | 552 | 567 |
| England | 552 | 559 |
| Canada | 548 | 543 |
| Italy | 541 | 548 |
| Germany | 541 | 537 |
| Israel | 541 | 530 |
| New Zealand | 531 | 523 |
| Australia | 527 | 544 |
| Poland | 526 | 565 |
| France | 520 | 511 |
| Spain | 513 | 528 |
| Iran | 457 | 428 |

Information from Mullis et al., 2012b, 2017.

**Bragging or Blaming** Test scores are proof for national education systems when they improve (Hong Kong, Ireland, Singapore) and as reflecting parents and the economy when they fail (Netherlands, United States). Which interpretation is better?

**THINK CRITICALLY:** Finland's success has been attributed to many factors, some mentioned here and some regarding the geography and population of the nation. What do you think is the most influential reason?

Finnish teachers are granted more autonomy within their classrooms than is typical in other nations. Since the 1990s, they have had more time and encouragement to work with colleagues (Sahlberg, 2011, 2015). They are encouraged to respond to each child's temperament as well as the child's skills. This strategy has led to achievement, particularly in math (Viljaranta et al., 2015).

As explained in Chapter 11, every educational system includes children with special educational needs. In Finland, such children are usually educated within the regular classes. Some teachers who have attained all the credentials and credits necessary for a regular teacher then gain additional credits, including classroom experience, to become a specialist for children with special needs (Takala et al., 2019).

Often teachers with such specialized training co-teach with regular teachers. However, about 3 percent of Finnish students are thought to have such pervasive special needs that they are educated in special classes (Sundqvist et al., 2019).

## Problems with International Comparisons

Elaborate and extensive measures are in place to make the PIRLS, TIMSS, and PISA valid. Test items are designed to be fair and culture-free, and participating children represent the diversity (economic, ethnic, etc.) of each nation's child population. Thousands of experts work to ensure validity and reliability. Consequently, most social scientists respect the data gathered from these tests.

The tests are far from perfect, however. Creating questions that are equally valid for everyone is impossible. For example, in math, should fourth-graders be expected to understand fractions, graphs, decimals, and simple geometry? Nations introduce these concepts at different ages, and some schools stress math more than others: Should every fourth-grader be expected to divide fractions?

After such general issues are decided, items are written. The following item tested math:

Three thousand tickets for a basketball game are numbered 1 to 3,000. People with ticket numbers ending with 112 receive a prize. Write down all the prize-winning numbers.

Only 26 percent of fourth-graders worldwide got this one right (112; 1,112; 2,112—with no additional numbers). About half of the children in East Asian nations and 36 percent of the U.S. children were correct. Those national scores are not surprising; children in Singapore, Japan, and China have been close to the top on every international test for 30 years, and the United States has been above average but not by much.

Children from North Africa did especially poorly; only 2 percent of Moroccan fourth-graders were correct. Does that suggest inferior education, or is that item biased in favor of some cultures? Is basketball, or 3,000 tickets for one game, or a random prize, rare in North Africa?

Another math item gives ingredients—4 eggs, 8 cups of flour, ½ cup of milk—and asks:

> The above ingredients are used to make a recipe for 6 people. Sam wants to make this recipe for only 3 people. Complete the table below to show what Sam needs to make the recipe for 3 people. The number of eggs he needs is shown.

The table lists 2 eggs, and the child needs to fill in amounts of flour and milk. Fourth-grade children in Ireland and England scored highest on this item (about half got it right), while those in Korea, China, and Japan scored lower (about 33 percent). The United States scored higher than East Asian nations but lower than England.

This is puzzling, since East Asians usually surpass others in math. Why not on this question? Are English and Irish children experienced with recipes that include eggs, flour, and milk, unlike Japanese children? Or are Asian children distracted by a question that assumes that a boy is cooking?

*"Big deal, an A in math. That would be a D in any other country."*

Mike Twohy/The New Yorker/Conde Nast

| | |
|---|---|
| Eggs | 2 |
| Flour | ?___ |
| Milk | ?___ |

## Who Takes the Test?

Beyond the problem of writing items that are fair for children throughout the world is the problem of student selection. In theory, all children in school at a particular grade level take the test, but in practice the school dropout rate in some nations means that many of the lowest achieving children are not tested.

China has consistently scored far higher than the United States, but some critics say that comparison is unfair because the tested populations are not comparable (Singer & Braun, 2018). For one thing, the Chinese children who take the test are in the major cities, not rural areas. For another, some say that the American children who take the test are not motivated, since the scores are not reflected in school grades. The Chinese children, by contrast, think their personal performance reflects their nation, so they try to do well.

Related to motivation is how much a culture values high scores on achievement tests. A major controversy in the United States is whether children are overtested, with a narrow focus on high achievement. This is discussed in Chapter 15, but the underlying issue is whether or not personality traits that push toward high scores should be encouraged at home.

## Gender Differences in School Performance

In addition to marked national, ethnic, and economic differences, gender differences in achievement scores are reported. The PIRLS finds fourth-grade girls ahead of boys in reading in every nation, by an average of 19 points (Mullis et al., 2017).

The 2016 female verbal advantage on the PIRLS in the United States is only 8 points, which is a difference of less than 2 percent. Several other nations are close to the U.S. norms, including France, Spain, and Hong Kong. Does this mean that those nations are more gender-equitable than the nation with the widest gender gap—Saudi Arabia, with a 65-point gap (464/399)? Maybe, maybe not.

Historically, boys were ahead of girls in math and science. However, TIMSS reported that those gender differences among fourth-graders in math have narrowed, disappeared, or reversed. In many nations, boys are still slightly ahead, with the United States showing a male advantage (7 points—less than 2 percent).

**LaunchPad**
macmillan learning

**VIDEO ACTIVITY: Educating the Girls of the World** examines the situation of girls' education around the world while stressing the importance of education for all children.

# Happiness or High Grades?

Thousands of social scientists—psychologists, educators, sociologists, economists—have realized that for cognitive development from middle childhood through late adulthood, characteristics beyond IQ scores, test grades, and family SES are sometimes pivotal.

One leading proponent of this idea is Paul Tough, who wrote: "We have been focusing on the wrong skills and abilities in our children, and we have been using the wrong strategies to help nurture and teach those skills" (Tough, 2012, p. xv). Instead of focusing on test scores, Tough believes we should focus on characteristics, particularly *grit* (persistence and effort).

Many scientists agree that executive control processes with many names (grit, emotional regulation, conscientiousness, resilience, executive function, effortful control) develop over the years of middle childhood. Over the long term, these aspects of character predict achievement in high school, college, and adulthood.

Developmentalists disagree about exactly which qualities are crucial for achievement, with grit considered crucial by some but not others (Duckworth, 2016; Lam & Zhou, 2019). However, no one denies that success depends on personal traits.

This case study is actually two cases, each reflecting a culture. Does the focus on personal qualities result in blaming children instead of noting that some parents, schools, and cultures create barriers that make learning difficult? Grit could make a child feel personally at fault for low achievement, rather than help that child enjoy life.

Remember that school-age children are ready for intellectual growth (Piaget) and are responsive to mentors (Vygotsky). These universals were evident in one study that occurred in two places, 12,000 miles apart: the northeastern United States and Taiwan.

In that study, more than 200 mothers were asked to recall and then discuss with their 6- to 10-year-olds two learning-related incidents that they knew their child had experienced. In one incident, the child had a "good attitude or behavior in learning"; in the other, "not perfect" (J. Li et al., 2014).

All of the mothers were married and middle-class, and all tried to encourage their children, stressing the value of education and the importance of doing well in school. The researchers noted that the mothers differed in the attitudes they were trying to encourage in their children.

The Taiwanese mothers were far more likely to mention what the researchers called "learning virtues," such as practice, persistence, and concentration—all of which are part of grit. The American mothers were more likely to mention "positive affect," such as happiness and pride.

This distinction is evident in the following two excerpts:

First, Tim and his American mother discussed a "not perfect" incident.

**Mother:** I wanted to talk to you about . . . that time when you had that one math paper that . . . mostly everything was wrong and you never bring home papers like that. . . .

**Tim:** I just had a clumsy day.

**Mother:** You had a clumsy day. You sure did, but there was, when we finally figured out what it was that you were doing wrong, you were pretty happy about it . . . and then you were happy to practice it, right? . . . Why do you think that was?

**Tim:** I don't know, because I was frustrated, and then you sat down and went over it with me, and I figured it out right with no distraction and then I got it right.

**Mother:** So it made you feel good to do well?

**Tim:** Uh-huh.

**Mother:** And it's okay to get some wrong sometimes.

**Tim:** And I, I never got that again, didn't I?

The next excerpt occurred when Ren and his Taiwanese mother discuss a "good attitude or behavior."

**Mother:** Oh, why does your teacher think that you behave well?

**Ren:** It's that I concentrate well in class.

**Mother:** Is your good concentration the concentration to talk to your peer at the next desk?

**Ren:** I listen to teachers.

**Mother:** Oh, is it so only for Mr. Chang's class or is it for all classes?

**Ren:** Almost all classes like that. . . .

**Mother:** So you want to behave well because you want to get an . . . honor award. Is that so?

**Ren:** Yes.

**Mother:** Or is it also that you yourself want to behave better?

**Ren:** Yes. I also want to behave better myself.

*[J. Li et al., 2014, p. 1218]*

Both Tim and Ren are likely to be good students in their respective schools. When parents support and encourage their child's learning, the child almost always masters the basic skills required of elementary school students, and almost never does the child become crushed by life experiences. Instead, the child has sufficient strengths to overcome most challenges (Masten, 2014).

Nonetheless, do parents in Asia emphasize the hard work required for achievement, while parents in North America stress the joy of learning? Could it be, as one group of researchers contend, that U.S. children are happier but less accomplished than Asian ones (F. Ng et al., 2014)? Which is more important: high self-esteem or high grades?

However, in other nations, girls are ahead, sometimes significantly, such as 10 points in Indonesia and 20 points in Jordan. Why? Is there an anti-male bias in the schools or culture?

In middle childhood, girls in every nation have higher report card grades, including in math and science. Is that biological (girls are better able to sit still, to manipulate a pencil)? Or cultural (girls have been taught to do as they are told)? Or does the hidden curriculum favor girls (most of their elementary school teachers were women)?

The popularity of various explanations has shifted. Analysts once attributed girls' higher grades in school to their faster physical maturation. Now explanations are more often sociocultural—that parents and teachers expect girls to be good students and that schools are organized to favor female strengths. The same switch in explanations, from biology to culture, appears for male advantages in science. Is that change itself cultural?

 **DATA CONNECTIONS: Motivation or Achievement?: A Look at Various Nations' PISA Scores** demonstrates how U.S. students compare with students in other nations.

**Future Engineers** After-school clubs now encourage boys to learn cooking and girls to play chess, and both sexes are active in every sport. The most recent push is for STEM (Science, Technology, Engineering, and Math) education—as in this after-school robotics club.

## Schooling in the United States

Some international tests indicate improvements in U.S. children's academic performance over the past decades. However, the United States has the largest disparities between income and ethnic groups. Some blame the disparity on immigration, but other nations (e.g., Canada) have more ethnic groups and immigrants than the United States, yet the achievement gap between groups in other nations is not as large.

## National Standards

For decades, the United States government has sponsored the **National Assessment of Educational Progress (NAEP)**, which is a group of tests designed to measure achievement in reading, mathematics, and other subjects. The NAEP finds fewer children proficient than do state tests. For example, New York's tests reported 62 percent proficient in math, but the NAEP found only 32 percent; 51 percent were proficient in reading on New York's state tests, but only 35 percent according to NAEP (Martin, 2014).

The NAEP also finds that Hispanic American and African American fourth-graders are about 11 percent lower than their European American peers in reading and 9 percent lower in math (McFarland et al., 2019). An even wider achievement gap is evident between high- and low-SES schools.

For some statistics—high school graduation, for instance—Asian American children achieve at higher rates than European Americans. However, this contributes to the "model minority" stereotype, which obscures disadvantages for many children of Asian heritage. For instance, Asian children may suffer from parental pressure and peer jealousy (Cherng & Liu, 2017).

**National Assessment of Educational Progress (NAEP)** An ongoing and nationally representative measure of U.S. children's achievement in reading, mathematics, and other subjects over time; nicknamed "the Nation's Report Card."

**Especially for School Administrators** Children who wear uniforms in school tend to score higher on reading tests. Why? (see response, page 335)

**FIGURE 12.3**

**Where'd You Go to School?** Note that although home schooling is still the least-chosen option, the number of home-schooled children may be increasing. Not shown is the percentage of children attending the nearest public school, which is decreasing slightly because of charter schools and magnet schools. More detailed data indicate that the average home-schooled child is a 7-year-old European American girl living in a rural area of the South with an employed father and a stay-at-home mother.

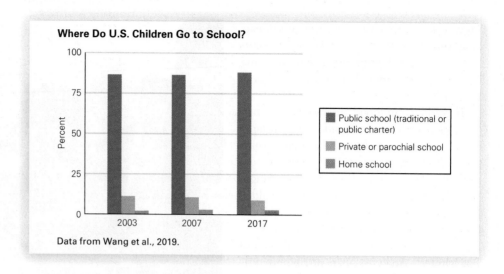

Where Do U.S. Children Go to School?

Data from Wang et al., 2019.

The reason for disparities within the United States seems more economic than ethnic, because African Americans in some of the wealthier states (Massachusetts) score higher than European Americans in the poorer states (Mississippi). Indeed, on international tests, students in Massachusetts are close to the highest-scoring nations, those in East Asia (Singer & Braun, 2018).

Many suggest that the disparity in local funding for schools is at the root of the problem: High-SES children of all groups attend well-funded schools. That raises the first of several issues within U.S. education, 10 of which are mentioned now.

## Ten Questions

1.  Should public schools be well-supported by public funds, or should smaller class sizes, special curricula, and expensive facilities (e.g., a stage, a pool, a garden) be available only in *private schools*, paid via tuition from wealthy parents? All told, about 10 percent of students in the United States attend private schools (see **Figure 12.3**). Other nations have higher or lower rates.

2.  Should parents be given *vouchers* to pay for some tuition at a private school? Each state regulates vouchers differently, but a detailed look at vouchers in Wisconsin found that most parents who used vouchers were inclined to send their children to nonpublic schools in any case, partly for religious and safety reasons (Fleming et al., 2015). Thus, vouchers subsidize schools that differ from public schools, which may allow parents to choose a school that does not follow public school policy or curriculum.

3.  Should more *charter schools* open or close? Charter schools are funded and licensed by states or local districts. Thus, they are public schools but are exempt from some regulations, especially those negotiated by teacher unions (hours, class size, etc.). Most have some control over admissions and expulsions, which makes them more ethnically segregated, with fewer children with special needs (Stern et al., 2015). Quality varies, with African American boys particularly likely to leave or be expelled. However, some charters report that children who stay learn more and are more likely to go to college than their peers in regular public schools (Prothero, 2016). The most devastating criticism is that charter schools undercut the purpose of public education by being exclusive (Ladd, 2019).

4.  Parents can choose to *home-school* their children, never sending them to school. In the United States, home-schooled children must learn certain subjects (reading, math, and so on), but each family decides schedules and discipline. About 2 percent of all U.S. children were home-schooled in 2003 and about

3 percent in 2007. Since then, numbers have leveled off at between 3 and 4 percent (Grady, 2017; Ray, 2013; Snyder & Dillow, 2013). Home schooling requires intense family labor, typically provided by an educated, dedicated, patient mother in a two-parent family.

The major disadvantage for home-schooled children is not academic (some have high test scores) but social: no classmates. To compensate, many parents plan activities with other home-schooling families.

5. Should public education be free of *religion* to avoid bias toward one religion or another? In the United States, thousands of parochial schools were founded when Catholics perceived Protestant bias in public schools. In the past 20 years, many Catholic schools have closed, but schools teaching other religions—Judaism, Islam, evangelical Christianity—have opened.

6. Should *the arts* be part of the curriculum? Music, drama, dance, and visual arts are essential in some places, not in others (Barton & Baguley, 2017). Many North American schools have eliminated requirements for arts education (O'Neill & Schmidt, 2017). By contrast, schools in Finland consider arts education essential (Nevanen et al., 2014).

7. Should children learn a *second language* in primary school? In Canada and in most European nations, almost every child studies two languages by age 10. In the United States, less than 5 percent of children under age 11 study a language other than English in school (Robelen, 2011).

8. Can *computers* advance education? Some enthusiasts hope that connecting schools to the internet or, even better, giving every child a laptop (as some schools do) will advance learning. The results are not dramatic, however. Sometimes computers improve achievement, particularly in math skills (Simms et al., 2019). Widespread, sustainable advances are elusive (Lim et al., 2013). Technology may be only a tool—a twenty-first-century equivalent of chalk—that depends on a creative, trained teacher to use well.

9. Are too many students in each class? Parents typically think that a smaller class size encourages more individualized education. That belief motivates many parents to choose private schools or home schooling. However, mixed evidence comes from nations where children score high on international tests. Sometimes they have large student/teacher ratios (Korea's average is 28-to-1) and sometimes small (Finland's is 14-to-1).

10. Should teachers nurture *soft skills* such as empathy, cooperation, and integrity as part of the school curriculum, even though these skills cannot be tested by multiple-choice questions? Many scholars argue that soft skills are crucial for academic success and later for employment (Reardon, 2013).

## Who Decides?

Overall research in human development guides teachers who want to know exactly which concepts and skills are crucial foundations for mastery of reading, writing, science, math, and human relations. However, the science of child cognition is not necessarily understood by those who determine what children learn.

An underlying issue for almost any national or international school is the proper role of parents. In most nations, matters regarding public education—curriculum, funding, teacher training, and so on—are set by the central government.

Generally, when governments are responsible for education, almost all children attend the local school, whose resources and standards are similar to those of the other schools in that nation. If there are serious religious or cultural differences in the nation, public schools offer alternatives—religious or secular, in one language or another, and so on. The parents' job is to support the teachers and the child's learning.

# Education in Middle Childhood

Only 20 years ago, gender differences in education around the world were stark, with far fewer girls in school than boys. Now girls have almost caught up. However, many of today's children suffer from decades of past educational inequality: Recent data find that the best predictor of childhood health is an educated mother.

## WORLDWIDE PRIMARY SCHOOL ENROLLMENT, 1978–2018

This graph shows net enrollment rate, which is the ratio of enrolled school-age children to the population of children who are the same school age. Progress toward university education and gender equity is evident.

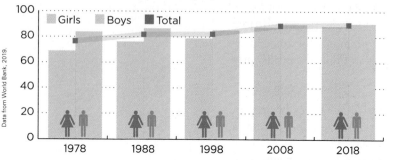

Data from World Bank, 2019.

Worldwide concerns now focus less on the existence of school and more on its quality. International tests usually find the United States is middling. Improvements are evident, but many other nations have improved even more!

### WORLDWIDE, BASIC ELEMENTARY EDUCATION LEADS TO:

**LESS**
- Child and maternal mortality
- Transmission of HIV
- Early marriage and childbirth
- War

**MORE**
- Better paying jobs
- Agricultural productivity
- Use of medical care
- Voting

Information from Hanushek & Woessmann, 2007.

## HOW U.S. FOURTH-GRADERS ARE DOING

Primary school enrollment is high in the United States, but not every student is learning, as these percentages from the National Assessment of Educational Progress (NAEP) show. While numbers are improving, less than half of fourth-graders are proficient in math and reading.

### NAEP PROFICIENCY LEVELS FOR U.S. FOURTH-GRADERS

**MATHEMATICS**

- 40% Proficient or Better
- 40% Basic Understanding
- 20% Below Basic Level

**READING**

- 37% Proficient or Better
- 33% Basic Understanding
- 30% Below Basic Level

Data from National Center for Education Statistics, 2018

### CHANGE IN AVERAGE NAEP SCORES FOR FOURTH-GRADERS

27 pts — 1990 2013 2017

5 pts — 1990 2013 2017

Data from National Center for Education Statistics, 2018

In the United States, however, public schools are open to everyone, which means that no specific religious instruction occurs. Local districts provide most of the funds and guidelines, and parents, as voters and volunteers, are active within the school.

Although most U.S. parents send their children to the nearest public school, almost one-fifth send their children to private schools (10 percent) or charter schools (6 percent), or they educate their children at home (3 percent) (McFarland et al., 2018). Parental choices may vary for each of their children, depending on the child's characteristics, the parents' current economic status, and the political rhetoric at the time. Every option has strengths and weaknesses, both for the child and for society.

It is difficult for parents to determine the best school for their child, partly because neither the test scores of students in any of these schools, nor the moral values a particular school may espouse, correlate with the cognitive skills that developmentalists seek to foster (Finn et al., 2014).

Thus, parents may choose a school that advertises what they value, but this does not mean that the school provides the best educational experience for their child. It is not uncommon for parents to pull children from one school to enroll them in another, a phenomenon that has increased in recent years.

Statistical analysis raises questions about home schooling, vouchers, and charter schools, but continuity benefits children, so the parents' restlessness may not be wise (Finn et al., 2014; Lubienski et al., 2013). However, the data allow many interpretations.

As one review notes, "the modern day, parent-led home-based education movement . . . stirs up many a curious query, negative critique, and firm praise" (Ray, 2013, p. 261). Indeed, for all public and private schools, partisan political controversies swirl around school choice, which makes it hard to make a definitive conclusion about what school is best for a particular child (Quinn & Cheuk, 2018).

Schoolchildren's ability to be logical and teachable—now that they are no longer preoperational and egocentric—makes this a good time for primary school. They will learn whatever adults deem important. Parents, politicians, and developmental experts all agree that school is vital for development, but disagreements about teachers and curriculum—hidden or overt—abound.

**Welcome Home** Laura Stevens returns to her Maine elementary school after a whirlwind trip in Washington, D.C. She received the Presidential Award for Excellence in Math and Science Teaching, and $10,000. Which do you think makes her happier, the award, the hero's welcome from her students and colleagues, or the joy of teaching?

### WHAT HAVE YOU LEARNED?

1. How does the hidden curriculum differ from the stated school curriculum?
2. What are the TIMSS, the PIRLS, and the PISA?
3. Which nations score highest on international tests?
4. How do boys and girls differ in school achievement?
5. How do charter schools, private schools, and home schools differ?
6. How is it decided what curriculum children should receive?

## SUMMARY

### Thinking

1. According to Piaget, middle childhood is the time of concrete operational thought, when egocentrism diminishes and logical thinking begins. Among the most important yet most difficult aspects are the concepts of classification and seriation.

2. By contrast, Vygotsky stressed the social context of learning, including the specific lessons of school and learning from peers, adults, and culture.

3. An information-processing approach examines each step of the thinking process, from input to output, using the computer

as a model. Repeated practice is essential, as cognitive functions become automated.

**4.** One famous researcher who used the information-processing approach is Robert Siegler, who compared learning math to the waves lapping on a beach. Concepts are not learned suddenly.

**5.** Both the knowledge base and intellectual control processes are crucial aspects of the cognitive advances of middle childhood. Information-processing research has helped describe these developments.

### Language

**6.** Language learning advances in many practical ways, including expanded vocabulary and pragmatics.

**7.** Most children use one code, dialect, or language with their friends and another in school. Children who are adept at code-switching, or who are fluently bilingual, have a cognitive advantage.

**8.** Children of low SES are usually lower in linguistic skills, primarily because they hear less language at home. Parent and teacher expectations are crucial.

### Teaching and Learning

**9.** The hidden curriculum may be more influential on children's learning than the formal curriculum. For example, some people believe elementary schools favor girls, although internationally gender similarities seem to outweigh gender differences.

**10.** International assessments are useful as comparisons. Reading is assessed with the PIRLS, math and science with the TIMSS, and practical intelligence with the PISA. Culture affects answers as well as learning: East Asian scores are high, Finland has improved, and the United States is middling.

**11.** In the United States, each state, each district, and sometimes each school retains significant control. This makes education a controversial topic in many communities, with wide variation in curriculum, both hidden and overt. Most children attend their local public school.

**12.** Some parents choose charter schools, others private schools, and still others opt for home schooling. These years are prime time for basic education, but variations among children and cultures make specifics of the overt or hidden curriculum controversial in the United States.

## KEY TERMS

concrete operational thought (p. 311)
classification (p. 311)
seriation (p. 312)
automatization (p. 316)
knowledge base (p. 317)
control processes (p. 317)

English Language Learners (ELLs) (p. 319)
immersion (p. 320)
bilingual education (p. 320)
ESL (English as a Second Language) (p. 320)

hidden curriculum (p. 323)
Trends in Math and Science Study (TIMSS) (p. 325)
Progress in International Reading Literacy Study (PIRLS) (p. 325)

Programme for International Student Assessment (PISA) (p. 325)
National Assessment of Educational Progress (NAEP) (p. 329)

## APPLICATIONS

**1.** Visit a local elementary school and look for the hidden curriculum. For example, do the children line up? Why or why not, when, and how? Does gender, age, ability, or talent affect the grouping of children or the selection of staff? What is on the walls? For everything you observe, speculate about the underlying assumptions.

**2.** Interview a 6- to 11-year-old child to find out what that child knows *and understands* about mathematics. Relate both correct and incorrect responses to the logic of concrete operational thought and to the information-processing perspective.

**3.** What do you remember about how you learned to read? Compare your memories with those of two other people, one at least 10 years older and the other at least 5 years younger than you are. Can you draw any conclusions about effective reading instruction? If so, what are they? If not, why not?

**4.** Talk to two parents of primary school children. What do they think are the best and worst parts of their children's education? Ask specific questions and analyze the results.

## Especially For ANSWERS

**Response for Teachers** (from p. 312): Here are two of the most obvious ways. (1) Use logic. Once children can grasp classification and class inclusion, they can understand cities within states, states within nations, and nations within continents. Organize your instruction to make logical categorization easier. (2) Make use of children's need for concrete and personal involvement. You might have the children learn first about their own location, then about the places where relatives and friends live, and finally about places beyond their personal experience (via books, photographs, videos, and guest speakers).

**Response for Parents** (from p. 321): Your son would understand your explanation, but you should take him along if you can do so without losing patience. You wouldn't ignore his need for food or medicine, so don't ignore his need for learning. While shopping, you can teach vocabulary (does he know pimientos, pepperoni, polenta?), categories (root vegetables, freshwater fish), and math (which size box of cereal is cheaper?). Explain in advance that you need him to help you find items and carry them and that he can choose only one item that you wouldn't normally buy. Seven-year-olds can understand rules, and they enjoy being helpful.

**Response for School Administrators** (from p. 329): The relationship reflects correlation, not causation. Wearing uniforms is more common when the culture of the school emphasizes achievement and study, with strict discipline in class and a policy of expelling disruptive students.

## Observation Quiz ANSWERS

**Answer to Observation Quiz** (from p. 311) As you know from the previous chapter, at this age children like to be near each other. That is your clue: An adult instructed them to sit apart. Their teacher is influenced by Piaget, who thought each person should discover cognitive principles on their own.

**Answer to Observation Quiz** (from p. 324) About 60 (6 rows, 10 in a row). Did trying to count make you realize that the children at the back cannot see or hear the teacher very well? None of them have glasses, so some of them cannot read the board.

# Middle Childhood: Psychosocial Development

## What Will You Know?

1. What helps children thrive in difficult family or neighborhood conditions?
2. Should parents marry, risking divorce, or not marry, risking separation?
3. What can be done to stop a bully?
4. Why would children lie to adults to protect a friend?

**W**ard Sutton is a professional cartoonist who won the prestigious Herblock Prize in 2018. In his acceptance speech, he thanked Kay Brown, a parent of his fifth-grade classmate. Kay noticed that Ward liked to draw, and suggested that he create a cartoon for the community newspaper. As Ward described it, "my first published editorial cartoon pulled no punches on the hard-hitting topic of . . . students leaning back in their chairs in class. Because, if you did that you might, you know, tip over. Hey, I had to start somewhere!"

Ward and Kay start this chapter because their story illustrates the nature of 10-year-olds and the importance of the community that supports them. His focus on the practical problems of fifth-graders—the tipping of chairs—is typical during middle childhood.

Later, bigger issues become salient: Ward praised his small Colorado town for upholding the freedom of speech, including in his cartoons, which were contrary to local opinions because he poked fun at national political leaders. But as a boy, Ward was much more concerned with earning the respect of his peers and teachers.

You will read more about Ward's boyhood later in this chapter. His story provides one example of the thoughts that keep some children up at night or get them out of bed each morning. Among those are friends, bullies, parents, and other adults. Middle childhood is the time when children become aware of the wider community, who might or might not channel their doodles into something meaningful. All children need caring adults like Kay to notice their talents and show them how to use them.

## The Nature of the Child

As explained in the previous chapter, steady growth, brain maturation, and intellectual advances make middle childhood a time for more independence (see At About This Time). One practical result is that between ages 6 and 11, children learn to care for themselves. In contrast to younger children, they not only hold their spoon but also make their lunch, not only zip their pants but also pack their suitcases, not only walk to school but also organize games with friends. They venture outdoors alone.

## AT ABOUT THIS TIME

**Signs of Psychosocial Maturation Over the Years of Middle Childhood\***

Children responsibly perform specific chores.

Children make decisions about a weekly allowance.

Children can tell time and have set times for various activities.

Children have homework, including some assignments over several days.

Children are punished less often than when they were younger.

Children try to conform to peers in clothes, language, and so on.

Children voice preferences about their after-school care, lessons, and activities.

Children are responsible for younger children, pets, and, in some places, work.

Children strive for independence from parents.

\*Of course, culture is crucial. For example, giving a child an allowance is typical for middle-class children in developed nations since about 1960. It was rare, or completely absent, in earlier times and other places.

## Industry and Inferiority

Throughout the centuries and in every culture, school-age children have been industrious. They busily master whatever skills their culture values. Their mental and physical maturation, described in the previous chapter, makes such activity possible.

With regard to his fourth psychosocial crisis, **industry versus inferiority**, Erikson noted that the child "must forget past hopes and wishes, while his exuberant imagination is tamed and harnessed to the laws of impersonal things," becoming "ready to apply himself to given skills and tasks" (Erikson, 1993a, pp. 258, 259). Simply trying new things, as in the previous stage (initiative versus guilt), is no longer sufficient. Sustained activity that leads to accomplishments that make one proud is the goal.

Think of learning to read and learning to add, both of which are painstaking and tedious. For instance, slowly sounding out "Jane has a dog" or writing "3 + 4 = 7" for the hundredth time is not exciting. Yet school-age children busily practice reading and math: They are intrinsically motivated to read a page, finish a worksheet, memorize a spelling word, color a map, and so on. Similarly, they enjoy collecting, categorizing, and counting whatever they gather—perhaps stamps, stickers, stones, or seashells. That is industry.

Overall, children judge themselves as either *industrious* or *inferior*—deciding whether they are competent or incompetent, productive or useless, winners or losers. Self-pride depends not necessarily on actual accomplishments but on how others, especially peers, view one's accomplishments. Social rejection is both a cause and a consequence of feeling inferior (Rubin et al., 2013).

## Parental Reactions

Did you pause a moment ago when you read that 6- to 11-year-olds can "venture outdoors alone"? Cohort and context changes can be dramatic. Recently in the United States, many parents do not allow their children outside without an adult, even to walk to a neighbor's house, much less to go to town with money in their pocket.

Universally, in middle childhood children become capable of doing things themselves that they once could not do, but parents react in diverse ways: Some 10-year-olds

**industry versus inferiority** The fourth of Erikson's eight psychosocial crises, during which children attempt to master many skills, developing a sense of themselves as either industrious or inferior, competent or incompetent.

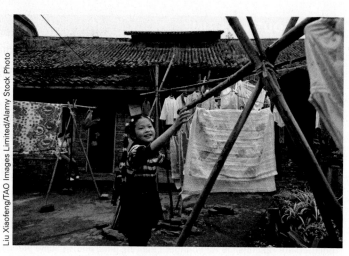

**Same Situation, Far Apart: Helping at Home** Sichuan, in China *(right)*, and Virginia, in the United States *(left)*, provide vastly different contexts for child development. Children everywhere help their families with household chores, as these two do, but gender expectations vary a great deal.

care for younger children, buy groceries, and make dinner while parents are away at work; some use power tools or drive tractors on the family farm; others are closely supervised if they venture outside or even turn on the kitchen stove.

Although variation is apparent, in middle childhood parents shift from providing physical care (bathing, dressing, and so on) to engaging in dialogue, discussion, and shared activities, a trend particularly apparent with boys and their fathers (Keown & Palmer, 2014).

For all children, parents gradually grant more autonomy, which helps children feel happy and capable (Yan et al., 2017). Consequently, time spent with parents decreases while time alone, and with friends, increases. One study of U.S. families found that 8-year-olds, on average, spent 95 minutes a day with their mothers, and 12-year-olds spent 70 minutes, almost half an hour less. This study found substantial variation by context and family structure (Lam et al., 2012).

## Self-Concept

As children mature, they develop their *self-concept*, which is their idea about themselves, including their intelligence, personality, abilities, gender, and ethnic background. As you remember, in toddlerhood children discover that they are individuals, and in early childhood they develop a positive, global self-concept.

That rosy self-concept is modified in middle childhood. The self-concept gradually becomes more specific and logical, the result of increases in cognitive development and social awareness. Fathers, teachers, and peers become more influential, sometimes helping children feel proud of themselves but sometimes not (Verschueren, 2020).

Genes, brain maturation, and family experiences continue to affect 6- to 11-year-olds, advancing or impairing self-concept (Bick et al., 2019). One important insight, called the *adjustment-erosion model*, suggests that a child's emotional problems at the beginning of middle childhood (the aggressive or pathologically shy first-grader) affect later academic difficulties more than vice versa (Deighton et al., 2018). Notice the developmental process: Emotional regulation and social skills developed in early childhood affect school success in middle childhood.

> **THINK CRITICALLY:** When would a realistic, honest self-assessment be harmful?

## Compared to Others

**social comparison** The tendency to assess one's abilities, achievements, social status, and other attributes by measuring them against those of other people, especially one's peers.

Crucial during middle childhood is **social comparison**—comparing oneself to others (Dweck, 2013; Lapan & Boseovski, 2017). Ideally, social comparison helps school-age children value themselves for who they are, abandoning the fantasy self-evaluation of preschoolers.

Social comparison makes the self-concept more realistic, because children incorporate comparison to peers when they judge themselves. The human tendency to think of oneself favorably is present, but it now is grounded in reality (Thomaes et al., 2017).

Some children—especially those from minority ethnic or religious groups—become newly aware of social prejudices that they need to overcome. Children also become aware of gender discrimination, with girls complaining that they are not allowed to play tougher sports and boys complaining that teachers favor the girls (C. Brown et al., 2011).

Over the years of middle childhood, children who affirm pride in their gender and ethnicity are likely to develop healthy self-esteem (Corenblum, 2014). Transgender children particularly experience discrimination. For them, parental support is crucial, but parents themselves experience stress (Hidalgo & Chen, 2019). Overall, parents who feel supported by their community are better able to affirm their own children.

Especially when the outside world seems hostile, parents and schools who teach about successful people from a variety of ethnicities, genders, or nationalities are likely to help children from those groups feel valued (Hernández et al., 2017). Much of the research regarding the impact of role models has focused on African American adolescents, but a recent review suggests that the same influences affect every group. Developing self-acceptance and pride bolsters self-confidence more than alerting children to be wary of possible prejudice (M-T. Wang et al., 2020).

**Learning from Each Other** Middle childhood is prime time for social comparison. Swinging is done standing, or on the belly, or twisted, or head down (as shown here) if someone else does it.

## Culture and Self-Esteem

Both academic and social competence are aided by realistic self-perception. That is beneficial, because unrealistically high self-esteem reduces effortful control, and without some control children are more aggressive and less conscientious than they might be.

The same consequences occur if self-esteem is too low. Obviously, the goal then is to find a middle ground. This is not easy: Children may be too self-critical or not self-critical enough. Their self-control interacts with the reactions of their parents and culture. Cultures differ on what that middle ground is.

High self-esteem is neither universally valued nor universally criticized. Many cultures expect children to be modest, not prideful. For example, Australians say that "tall poppies are cut down"; the Chinese say, "the nail that sticks up is hammered"; and the Japanese discourage social comparison aimed at making oneself feel superior.

This makes self-esteem a moral issue as well as a practical one: *Should* people believe that they are better than other people, as is typical in the United States but not in every nation? Answers vary.

One crucial component of self-concept has received considerable research attention (Dweck, 2013). As children become more self-aware, they benefit from praise for their process, not for their person: for *how* they learn, *how* they relate to others, and so on, not for static qualities such as intelligence and popularity. This encourages growth.

For example, children who fail a test are devastated if failure means they are not smart. However, process-oriented children

**Black Panther** Mythical superheroes, and the perpetual battle between good and evil, are especially attractive to boys in middle childhood but resonate with people of all ages, genders, and ethnic groups. *Black Panther* was first a comic-book hero in 1966 and then became a 2018 movie that broke records for attendance and impact. It features not only African American heroes but also an army of strong women—busting stereotypes and generating self-esteem for many children.

consider failure a "learning opportunity," a time to figure out how to study the next time. They have a "growth mindset."

The self-conscious emotions (pride, shame, guilt) first evident in early child-hood may also develop during middle childhood. They guide social interaction, yet they can overcome a child's self-concept, leading to psychopathology (Muris & Meesters, 2014). Especially during middle childhood (less so in adolescence), school achievement is a crucial factor in developing self-esteem, and that affects later self-concept—as someone who is inferior or not.

In addition, the onset of concrete thinking in middle childhood leads children to notice material possessions. Objects that adults find superficial (name-brand sunglasses, sock patterns) become important.

Insecure 10-year-olds might desperately want the latest jackets, smartphones, and so on. Or they may want something else that makes them seem special, such as les-sons in African dance, or a brilliant light for their bicycle, or—as one of my daughters did—a bread-maker (used often for several weeks, discarded after several years).

From a life-span perspective, a developmental pattern appears. Children in many cultures tend to increase in self-esteem during middle childhood, stabilize in adolescence, and increase again in emerging adulthood. Not until very late adulthood (after age 70 or beyond) does self-esteem decrease (Orth et al., 2018). Thus, parents and grandparents are well-positioned to encourage the child's natu-ral increase in self-esteem.

## Resilience and Stress

In infancy and early childhood, children depend on their immediate families for food, learning, and life itself. In middle childhood, some children continue to ben-efit from supportive families, and others escape destructive families by finding their own niche in the larger world.

Surprisingly, some children seem unscathed by early experiences. They have been called "resilient" or even "invincible." Current thinking about resilience (see **Table 13.1**), with insights from dynamic-systems theory, emphasizes that no one is truly untouched by past history or current context, but some weather early storms and a few not only survive but become stronger because of them (Luthar, 2015; Masten, 2014; Rutter, 2012).

## Defining Resilience

**Resilience** has been defined as "a dynamic process encompassing positive adap-tation within the context of significant adversity" (Luthar et al., 2000, p. 543) and "the capacity of a dynamic system to adapt successfully to disturbances that threaten system function, viability, or development" (Masten, 2014, p. 30). Note that both of these leading researchers emphasize three parts of this definition:

- Resilience is *dynamic*, not a stable trait. That means a given person may be resilient at some periods but not others, and the effects from one period reverberate as time goes on.
- Resilience is a *positive adaptation* to stress. For example, if parental rejec-tion leads a child to a closer relationship with another adult, that is positive resilience, not passive endurance.
- Adversity must be *significant*, a threat to development.

## Cumulative Stress

An important discovery is that stress accumulates over time, including minor dis-turbances (called "daily hassles"). A long string of hassles, day after day, takes a

**LaunchPad**
macmillan learning

Watch **VIDEO ACTIVITY: Interview with Carol Dweck** to learn about how children's mindsets affect their intellectual development.

**resilience** The capacity to adapt well to significant adversity and to overcome serious stress.

## TABLE 13.1

### Dominant Ideas About Resilience, 1965 to Present

| | |
|---|---|
| 1965 | All children have the same needs for healthy development. |
| 1970 | Some conditions or circumstances—such as "absent father," "teenage mother," "working mom," and "day care"—are harmful for every child. |
| 1975 | All children are *not* the same. Some children are resilient, coping easily with stressors that cause harm in other children. |
| 1980 | Nothing inevitably causes harm. Both maternal employment and preschool education, once thought to be risks, are often helpful. |
| 1985 | Factors beyond the family, both in the child (low birthweight, prenatal alcohol exposure, aggressive temperament) and in the community (poverty, violence), can be very risky for children. |
| 1990 | Risk–benefit analysis finds that some children are "invulnerable" to, or even benefit from, circumstances that destroy others. |
| 1995 | No child is invincible. Risks are always harmful—if not in education, then in emotions; if not immediately, then long term. |
| 2000 | Risk–benefit analysis involves the interplay among many biological, cognitive, and social factors, some within the child (genes, disability, temperament), the family (function as well as structure), and the community (including neighborhood, school, church, and culture). |
| 2008 | Focus on strengths, not risks. Assets in child (intelligence, personality), family (secure attachment, warmth), community (schools, after-school programs), and nation (income support, health care) must be nurtured. |
| 2010 | Strengths vary by culture and national values. Both universal ideals and local variations must be recognized and respected. |
| 2012 | Genes as well as cultural practices can be either strengths or weaknesses; differential susceptibility means that identical stressors can benefit one child and harm another. |
| 2015 | Communities are responsible for child resilience. Not every child needs help, but every community needs to encourage healthy child development. |
| 2020 | Resilience is seen more broadly as a characteristic of mothers and communities. |

greater toll than an isolated major stress. Almost every child can withstand one trauma, but "the likelihood of problems increased as the number of risk factors increased" (Masten, 2014, p. 14).

The social context, especially supportive adults who do not blame the child, is crucial. A chilling example comes from the "child soldiers" in the 1991–2002 civil war in Sierra Leone (Betancourt et al., 2013). Children witnessed and often participated in murder, rape, and other traumas. When the war was over, 529 war-affected youth, then aged 10 to 17, were interviewed. Many were severely depressed, with crippling anxiety.

These war-damaged children were interviewed again two and six years later. Surprisingly, many had overcome their trauma and were functioning well. Recovery was more likely if:

- The war occurred when they were in middle childhood, not adolescence;
- at least one caregiver survived and was reunited with the child;
- their communities did not reject them, no matter which side of the civil war they had joined; and
- daily routines (school, family responsibilities) were restored.

**VIDEO ACTIVITY: Child Soldiers and Child Peacemakers** examines the state of child soldiers in the world and then explores how adolescent cognition impacts the decisions of five teenage peace activists.

## Family as a Buffer

In England during World War II, many city children were sent to loving families in rural areas to escape the German bombs dropped every day. To the surprise of researchers, those children who stayed in London with their parents were more resilient, despite nights huddled in air-raid shelters, than those who were physically safe but without their parents (Freud & Burlingham, 1943).

Similar results were found in a longitudinal study of children exposed to a sudden, wide-ranging, terrifying wildfire in Australia. Almost all of the children suffered stress reactions at the time, but 20 years later the crucial factor was not proximity to the fire but whether or not it separated them from their mothers (McFarlane & Van Hooff, 2009).

Whenever war, or economic conditions, or immigration policies separate parents and children, developmentalists predict lifelong problems for the children. Longitudinal studies over the past decades have found significant emotional and social vulnerability in Holocaust survivors from World War II, refugees of African civil wars, and children in Vietnam. Recently, the same consequences have been found in immigrant children in the United States, who suffer from many health problems if their parents are not with them (Perreira & Pedroza, 2019).

For that reason, thousands of developmental scholars and dozens of professional societies have expressed their horror at the 2018 U.S. policy of separating children from their parents at the United States–Mexico border. For example, the Society of Developmental and Behavioral Pediatrics fear that "a generation of children will experience lifelong repercussions" from being forcefully separated from their parents. Their statement reads:

> Children and parents belong together. Children who are separated from their primary caregivers may experience toxic stress and a disruption of attachment that can have severe emotional, behavioral and physical implications.
>
> [Society for Developmental & Behavioral Pediatrics, 2018]

## Cognitive Coping

Obviously, the above examples are extreme, but the general finding is confirmed by many studies. Disasters take a toll, but resilience is possible. Factors in the child (especially problem-solving ability), in the family (consistency and care), and in the community (good schools and welcoming religious institutions) all help children recover (Masten, 2014).

The child's interpretation of events is crucial (Lagattuta, 2014). Cortisol increases in low-income children *if* they interpret events connected to their family's poverty as a personal threat and *if* the family lacks order and routines (thus increasing daily hassles) (Coe et al., 2018). If low-SES children do not feel personally to blame, and if their family is not chaotic, they may be resilient.

In general, children's interpretations of family situations (poverty, divorce, and so on) determine how they are affected. Think of people you know: Some adults from low-SES families did not feel deprived. Only later did they realize that they were poor. For them, childhood poverty is less likely to cast a shadow over adult life.

Some children consider the family they were born into a temporary hardship; they look forward to the day when they can leave childhood behind. If they also have personal strengths, such as the cognitive abilities to imagine a better life, they may shine in adulthood—evident in the United States in thousands of success stories, from Abraham Lincoln to Oprah Winfrey.

The opposite reaction is called **parentification**, when children feel responsible for the entire family, acting as caregivers of everyone, including their actual parents. Here again the child's interpretation is crucial. For instance, suppose a

**THINK CRITICALLY:** Is there any harm in having the oldest child take care of the younger ones? Why or why not?

**parentification** When a child acts more like a parent than a child. Parentification may occur if the actual parents do not act as caregivers, making a child feel responsible for the family.

child witnesses domestic abuse. This is never good, but if the child feels responsible for the abuser and the abused, recovery is less likely (Fortin et al., 2011).

One final example: Many children of immigrants exemplify parentification if they become the translators for their parents, who do not understand the language or the culture. If those children feel burdened by their role as language brokers, that increases their depression. But, if they feel they are making a positive contribution to their family well-being, they themselves benefit (Weisskirch, 2017b).

---

**WHAT HAVE YOU LEARNED?**

**1.** How do Erikson's stages for preschool and school-age children differ?

**2.** Why is social comparison particularly powerful during middle childhood?

**3.** Why do cultures differ in how they value pride or modesty?

**4.** Why and when might minor stresses be more harmful than major stresses?

**5.** How might a child's interpretation of events help that child cope with repeated stress?

---

# Families During Middle Childhood

No one doubts that genes affect personality as well as ability, that peers are vital, and that schools and cultures influence what, and how much, children learn. Some have gone further, suggesting that genes, peers, and communities have so much influence that parents have little impact—unless they are grossly abusive (Harris, 1998, 2002; McLeod et al., 2007). This suggestion arose from studies about the impact of the environment on child development.

## Shared and Nonshared Environments

Many studies have found that children are much less affected by *shared environment* (influences that arise from being in the same environment, such as for two siblings living in one home, raised by their parents) than by *nonshared environment* (e.g., the distinct experiences and surroundings of two people).

Even basic values and traits, or sexual orientation, which once were assumed to be heavily affected by parents, seem much more influenced by genes and nonshared environment than by growing up in a particular household (Twito & Knafo-Noam, 2020; Y. Xu et al., 2020).

Since genes and nonshared environment are more influential than shared, might parents be insignificant? That avoids "misplaced blame on parents for negative outcomes in their children . . . adding guilt to the grief parents are already feeling for their children's suffering" (Sherlock & Zietsch, 2018, p. 155). But then parents should not take credit for the accomplishments of their children.

Could it be that parents are merely caretakers, needed for basic care (food, shelter), harmful when severely neglectful or abusive, but inconsequential in what they do about household routines, prohibitions, and praise? If a child becomes a murderer or a hero, should parents be neither blamed nor credited?

That conclusion is too extreme: Parents are not the only influence, of course, but they are influential. Recent findings reassert parent power. The analysis of shared and nonshared influences was correct, but the conclusion was based on a false assumption. Siblings raised together do *not* share the same environment.

For example, if relocation, divorce, unemployment, or a new job occurs in a family, the impact on each child differs depending on that child's age, genes, resilience, and gender. Moving to another town upsets a school-age child more than an infant; divorce harms boys more than girls; poverty may hurt preschoolers the most; and so on.

**Shared Environment?** All three children live in the same home in Brooklyn, New York, with loving, middle-class parents. But it is not hard to imagine that family life is quite different for the 9-year-old girl than for her sister, born a year later, or their little brother, age 3.

monkeybusinessimages/iStock/Getty Images

**Observation Quiz** Are significant gender differences evident here? (see answer, page 367) ↑

Differential susceptibility adds to the variation: One child might be more affected than another. When siblings are raised together, experiencing the same family conditions, the mix of genes, age, and gender may lead one child to become anti-social, another to be pathologically anxious, and a third to be resilient, capable, and strong. Further, not all characteristics are genetic.

For example, one study of 7-year-old twins found that the child's ability to recognize emotions (whether a particular expression or tone indicated anger or happiness, for instance) was affected by the twins' family experiences but not by genes (Schapira et al., 2019). The authors acknowledged that later on, genes may become more influential, but this was not apparent for these 7-year-olds. Another study also found parental influence on 7-year-olds, as A View from Science makes clear.

---

**A VIEW FROM SCIENCE**

## "I Always Dressed One in Blue Stuff. . ."

To separate the effects of genes and environment, many researchers have studied twins. As you remember from Chapter 3, some twins are dizygotic, with only half of their genes in common, and some are monozygotic, identical in all their genes. Many scientists assumed that children growing up with the same parents would have the same nurture (shared environment).

Therefore, if dizygotic twins are less alike than monozygotic twins are, genes must be the reason. Further, if one monozygotic twin differs from their genetically identical twin, raised by their parents in the same home, those differences must arise from the nonshared environment.

Logically, everyone is influenced by three forces: genes, shared environment (same home), and nonshared environment (different schools, friends, and so on). Many people were surprised when twin research discovered that almost everything could be attributed to genes and nonshared environment, with almost nothing left over for parents.

However, that conclusion is now tempered by another finding: Twins raised in the same home may have quite different family experiences for reasons that are not genetic. A seminal study in this regard occurred with twins in England.

An expert team of scientists compared 1,000 sets of monozygotic twins reared by their biological parents (Caspi et al., 2004). Obviously, the pairs were identical in genes, sex, and age. The researchers asked the mothers to describe each twin. Descriptions ranged from very positive ("my ray of sunshine") to very negative ("I wish I never had her. . . . She's a cow, I hate her") (quoted in Caspi et al., 2004, p. 153). Some mothers noted personality differences between their twins. For example, one mother said:

> Susan can be very sweet. She loves babies . . . she can be insecure . . . she flutters and dances around. . . . There's not much between her ears. . . . She's exceptionally vain, more so than Ann. Ann loves any game involving a ball, very sporty, climbs trees, very much a tomboy. One is a serious tomboy and one's a serious girlie girl. Even when they were babies I always dressed one in blue stuff and one in pink stuff.

> [quoted in Caspi et al., 2004, p. 156]

Some mothers rejected one twin but not the other:

> He was in the hospital and everyone was all "poor Jeff, poor Jeff" and I started thinking, "Well, what about me? I'm the one's just had twins. I'm the one's going through this, he's a seven-week-old baby and doesn't know a thing about it" . . . I sort of detached and plowed my emotions into Mike [Jeff's twin brother].

> [quoted in Caspi et al., 2004, p. 156]

This mother later blamed Jeff for favoring his father: "Jeff would do anything for Don but he wouldn't for me, and no matter what I did for either of them [Don or Jeff], it wouldn't be right" (quoted in Caspi et al., 2004, p. 157). She said Mike was much more lovable.

The researchers measured personality at age 5 (assessing, among other things, antisocial behavior as reported by kindergarten teachers) and then measured each twin's personality two years later. They found that if a mother was more negative toward one of her twins, that twin *became* more antisocial, more likely to fight, steal, and hurt others at age 7 than at age 5, unlike the favored twin.

These researchers recognize that many other nonshared factors—peers, teachers, and so on—are significant. However, most developmental scientists now agree that genes, neighborhood, and parental influences are all important, and that—especially when genes or neighborhood push a child toward unhealthy development—parental intervention can be crucial (Liu & Neiderhiser, 2017).

Genes are still powerful, of course, because "a given DNA sequence operation in different environments can generate different products in different amounts at the cellular and phenotypic levels" (Waldinger & Schulz, 2018, p. 159). That expresses an underlying theme of this book, that human development is multifactorial and complex. It begins with genes (DNA), but a simple calculation of genetic and family influence is impossible.

The fact that parents sometimes treat each of a pair of monozygotic twins differently confirms that parents matter. This will surprise no one who has a brother or a sister. Children from the same family do not always experience their family in the same way.

## Function and Structure

**Family structure** refers to the genetic and legal connections among related people. *Genetic* connections may be from parent to child, between cousins, between siblings, between grandparents and grandchildren, or more distantly, such as from great aunts, second cousins, and so on. *Legal* connections may be through marriage or adoption.

**Family function** is distinct from structure. It refers to how the people in a family actually care for each other. Some families function well; others are dysfunctional.

Function is more important than structure. Ideally, every family provides love and encouragement. For most people, this comes from genetic relatives, so structure and function overlap. For foster children and adopted children who share few distinct genes with their caregivers, family function is crucial (Flannery et al., 2017).

Everyone enters the world with unique genes and a particular prenatal environment, and that differential susceptibility influences how their family affects them. Beyond that, people's needs differ depending on their age: Infants need responsive caregiving, teenagers need guidance, young adults need freedom, the aged need respect. What do school-age children need?

## The Needs of Children in Middle Childhood

Ideally, families that function well for children aged 6 to 11 provide five things:

1. *Physical necessities.* In middle childhood, children can eat, dress, and wash themselves, but they need food, clothing, and shelter. Ideally, their families provide these things.
2. *Learning.* These are prime years for education. Families support, encourage, and guide schooling—connecting with teachers, checking homework, and so on.
3. *Self-respect.* During these years social comparison can deflate self-esteem, so families help each child excel at something—sports, the arts, or academics.
4. *Peer relationships.* Children need friends. Families choose schools and neighborhoods with friendly children and arrange play dates, group activities, overnights, and so on.
5. *Harmony and stability.* Families provide protective, predictable routines in a home that is a safe, peaceful haven. Family conflict and chaos is destructive.

## Harm from Instability

The final item on the list above may be especially significant in middle childhood: Children cherish safety and stability, not change. When children experience many changes in caregivers (e.g., mother, stepmother, aunt, father) and many changes in residence (from one neighborhood to another), they are more likely to develop emotional difficulties.

Several studies find that family instability, such as moving from place to place, and family chaos, such as no routines for sleeping, eating, or homework, increase children's internalizing and externalizing problems. Surprisingly, race might make a difference. At least one study found that harm was less apparent for African American children. The researchers suggested that grandparents and other relatives might buffer the effect of instability (Womack et al., 2019).

Nonetheless, for all children during middle childhood, having a stable network of friends and teachers is an asset, and staying in one neighborhood makes that easier. Children who are homeless suffer physiologically as well as psychologically, evident in cortisol level, blood pressure, weight, and in likelihood of hospitalization (Cutuli et al., 2017).

Also, for all children, a well-functioning family can soften the impact of change. If a child is living in a shelter for homeless families, with a mother who provides

**family structure** The legal and genetic relationships among relatives living in the same home. Possible structures include nuclear family, extended family, stepfamily, single-parent family, and many others.

**family function** The way a family works to meet the needs of its members. Children need families to provide basic material necessities, to encourage learning, to help them develop self-respect, to nurture friendships, and to foster harmony and stability.

**Especially for Scientists** How would you determine whether or not parents treat all of their children the same? (see response, page 367)

**Didn't Want to Marry** This couple was happily cohabiting and strongly committed to each other but didn't wed until they learned that her health insurance would not cover them unless they were legally married. Twenty months after marriage, their son was born.

© 2016 Macmillan

stability, affection, routines, and hope, that child's school achievement may be resilient.

Another example comes from children in military families. Enlisted parents tend to have higher incomes, better health care, and more education than do civilians from the same backgrounds. But they have one major disadvantage: instability.

In general, children whose parents are in military service are no worse off than civilian children. However, for some children, parent deployment (which requires several disruptions in the child's home life) leads to higher rates of depression and aggression (Fairbank et al., 2018; Williamson et al., 2018).

Most military children learn to cope (Russo & Fallon, 2014). To help children whose parents are deployed, the U.S. military offers special programs. Caregivers of such children are encouraged to avoid changes in the child's life during the deployment: no new homes, new rules, or new schools (Lester et al., 2011). Similar transitions occur when deployed parents come home: They are welcomed, of course, but the child's life might change again—and that causes more stress.

On a broader level, children who are displaced because of storms, fire, war, and so on may suffer psychologically. They may try to comfort their parents, not telling them about their distress, but the data on health and achievement show that moving from place to place is highly stressful (Masten, 2014). All children must cope with some disruption: Some children develop good coping skills and other children do not.

## Various Family Structures

A **nuclear family** is a family composed only of children and their parents (married or not). Usually the parents are the biological parents of the children, but other nuclear families are headed by adoptive parents, foster parents, stepparents, or same-sex couples, most of whom provide good care.

Rates of single parenthood vary greatly worldwide (see Visualizing Development, page 350); About a third of 6- to 11-year-olds in the United States live in a **single-parent family**. Many of them are not harmed by that, if their mother is a stable, hopeful caregiver, but obviously good caregiving is more difficult under stress.

An **extended family** includes relatives in addition to parents and children. Usually the additional persons are grandparents or sometimes uncles, aunts, or cousins of the child. The crucial distinction for official tallies is who lives under the same roof. This measures family structure, not family function.

The distinction between one-parent, two-parent, and extended families is not as simple in practice as it is on the census. Many parents of young children live near, but not with, the grandparents, who provide meals, emotional support, money, and child care, functioning as an extended family. The opposite is true as well, especially in developing nations: Some extended families share a household but create separate living quarters for each set of parents and children, making these units somewhat like nuclear families. Similarly some fathers who do not live with their children nonetheless sometimes are involved parents.

In many nations, the **polygamous family** (one husband with two or more wives) is a legal family structure. Generally in polygamous families, income per child is reduced, and education, especially for the girls, is limited—in part because girls are expected to marry young. Polygamy is rare—and illegal—in the United States. Even in nations where it is allowed—most African and many Asian nations—polygamy is less common than it was 30 years ago.

## Cohort Changes

There are more single-parent households, more divorces and remarriages, and fewer children per family than in the past. Specifics vary from decade to decade

**nuclear family** A family that consists of a father, a mother, and their biological children under age 18.

**single-parent family** A family that consists of only one parent and their children.

**extended family** A family of relatives in addition to the nuclear family, usually three or more generations living in one household.

**polygamous family** A family consisting of one man, several wives, and their children.

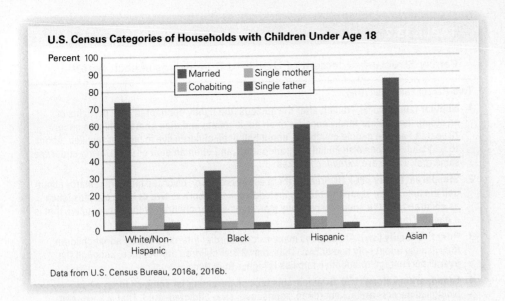

U.S. Census Categories of Households with Children Under Age 18

Data from U.S. Census Bureau, 2016a, 2016b.

**FIGURE 13.1**

**Possible Problems** As the text makes clear, structure does not determine function, but raising children is more difficult as a single parent, in part because income is lower. African American families have at least one asset, however. They are more likely to have grandparents who are actively helping with child care.

and nation to nation. That matters for children. In the United States, divorced, single-parent families were unusual in the 1960s, more common in the 1980s and 1990s, and again are less common in the twenty-first century (see **Figure 13.1**). Children were more likely to suffer from divorce when divorce was rare.

On average, however, children growing up in non-nuclear families have more emotional and academic problems than when both parents live in the same home as the child. Variations in family structures should be acknowledged, but neither exaggerated nor bemoaned. The United States has more single parents than other developed nations, yet almost two-thirds of all U.S. school-age children live with two parents (see **Table 13.2**), most often their biological parents, and some of those children have emotional or academic problems as well.

## Connecting Family Structure and Function

How a family functions is more important for children than their family structure. The two are related; structure influences (but does not determine) function. Some structures increase the possibility that the five family functions mentioned earlier (physical necessities, learning, self-respect, friendship, and harmony/stability) will be fulfilled.

## Two-Parent Families

On average, nuclear families function best; children living with two married parents tend to learn more in school with fewer psychological problems. Why? Does this mean that every mother and father should marry and stay married? No. Some benefits are correlates, not causes.

To understand, remember the longitudinal life-span perspective that considers the family context before the children appear. Education, earning potential, and emotional maturity increase the rate of marriage and parenthood and decrease the rate of divorce. For example, first-time mothers in the United States are usually (78 percent) married when they conceive their first child if they are highly educated, but they are usually unmarried (only 11 percent married at conception) if they are low in SES (Gibson-Davis & Rackin, 2014).

The differences between high- and low-SES individuals in marriage, child-bearing, child rearing, and divorce suggest "close to two different subsystems" of

| **TABLE 13.2** |
| --- |

**Family Structures (percent of U.S. 6- to 11-year-olds in each type)\***

**Two-Parent Families (70%)**

1. **Nuclear family** (57%). Named after the nucleus (the tightly connected core particles of an atom), the nuclear family consists of an adult couple and their shared children under 18 years of age. In middle childhood, about half of all children live in nuclear families. About 10% of such families also include a grandparent, and often an aunt or uncle, living under the same roof. Those are *extended* families.

2. **Stepparent family** (9%). Divorced fathers usually remarry; divorced mothers remarry about half the time. If the stepparent family includes children born to two or more couples (such as children from the spouses' previous marriages and/or children of the new couple), that is a *blended* family.

3. **Adoptive family** (3%). Although as many as one-third of infertile couples adopt children, they usually adopt only one or two. Thus, only 2% of children are adopted, although the overall percentage of adoptive families is higher than that.

4. **Grandparents alone** (1%). Grandparents take on parenting for some children when biological parents are absent (dead, imprisoned, sick, addicted, etc.). That is a *skipped-generation* family.

**Single-Parent Families (30%)**

One-parent families are increasing, with almost half of the newborns now born to unmarried mothers, but such families average fewer children than two-parent families, and many single mothers find partners by the time their children are school age. So, in middle childhood only 31% of children have a lone parent.

1. **Single mother—never married** (14%). In 2018, 40% of all U.S. births were to unmarried mothers; but when children are school age, many such mothers have married or have entrusted their children to their parents' care. Thus, only about 14% of 6- to 11-year-olds, at any given moment, are in single-mother, never-married homes.

2. **Single mother—divorced, separated, or widowed** (12%). Although many marriages end in divorce (almost half in the United States, fewer in other nations), many divorcing couples have no children. Others remarry. Thus, only 12% of school-age children currently live with single, formerly married mothers.

3. **Single father** (3%). About 1 father in 25 has physical custody of his children and raises them without their mother or a new wife. This category increased at the start of the twenty-first century but has decreased since 2005.

4. **Grandparent alone** (1%). Sometimes a grandparent (usually the grandmother) becomes the sole caregiving adult for a child.

**More Than Two Adults (10%)** [Also listed as two-parent or single-parent family]

1. **Extended family** (10%). Some children live with a grandparent or other relatives, as well as with one (5%) or both (10%) of their parents. This pattern is most common with infants (20%) but occurs in middle childhood as well.

2. **Polygamous family** (0%). In some nations (not the United States), men can legally have several wives. This family structure is more favored by adults than children. Everywhere, polyandry (one woman, several husbands) is rare.

\*Less than 1% of children under age 12 live without any caregiving adult; they are not included in this table.

The percentages in this table are estimates (based on data in U.S. Census Bureau, 2019). The category "extended family" in this table is higher than most published statistics, since some families do not tell official authorities about relatives living with them.

family organization in the United States today (Cherlin, 2020, p. 69). Spouses tend to have personal assets *before* they marry and become parents, and their higher income and education benefit the children that marriage might produce. The correlation between child success and married parents occurs partly because of who the spouses are, not because of fact that they marry. These two factors—selection and income—explain some of the correlation between nuclear families and child well-being.

To the surprise of some outsiders, a large study comparing male–female and same-sex couples found that the major predictor of their children's well-being was not the parents' sexual orientation but their income and stability (Cenegy et al., 2018). Similar findings come from adoptive parents, grandparents raising children, and so on. A caregiver's emotional health and the family's economic security benefit the children.

In general, married parents (of whatever gender identity and sexual orientation) are more likely to stay together than unmarried parents, and they are more likely to become wealthier and healthier than either would be alone. Further, living with one's children increases mutual bonding.

By contrast, single parenthood, especially after a bitter divorce, correlates with poor health and low income for everyone. Simply not seeing one parent very often increases internalizing and externalizing problems in children.

Contact tends to increase affection and care. Recent data come from Russia, where economic and social pressures have led many single men to drink and despair, dying years earlier than married men. The reason is thought to be that the husband/father role leads men to take better care of themselves and wives to look out for their husband's health (Ashwin & Isupova, 2014).

Shared parenting also decreases the risk of child maltreatment, because one parent is likely to protect their children if the other is abusive or neglectful. For all children, having two parents around every day makes it more likely that someone will read to them, check their homework, invite their friends over, buy them new clothes, and save for their education. Of course, having two married parents does not guarantee good care. One of my students wrote:

> My mother externalized her feelings with outbursts of rage, lashing out and breaking things, while my father internalized his feelings by withdrawing, being silent and looking the other way. One could say I was being raised by bipolar parents. Growing up, I would describe my mom as the Tasmanian devil and my father as the ostrich, with his head in the sand. . . . My mother disciplined with corporal punishment as well as with psychological control, while my father was permissive. What a pair.

> [C., 2013]

This student is now a single parent, having twice married, given birth, and divorced. She is one example of a general finding: The effects of childhood family function echo in adulthood, financially as well as psychologically.

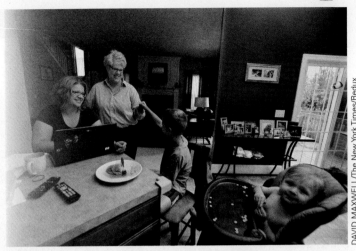

**Middle American Family** This photo shows a typical breakfast in Brunswick, Ohio—Cheerios for 1-year-old Carson, pancakes that 7-year-old Carter does not finish eating, and family photos crowded on the far table.

● **Observation Quiz** What do you notice about this family? (see answer, page 367) ↑

## Single Fathers and Stepfathers

Generally, fathers who do not live with their children become less involved with them every year. When the children reach age 18, fathers are no longer legally responsible, and divorced or unmarried fathers may no longer pay for education or other expenses.

This is a harsh reality in today's world. Emerging adults usually need substantial funds as well as emotional support in order to attend college, find jobs, and become self-sufficient adults. Stepfathers and nonresident biological fathers are less likely to provide that help, in part because each thinks the other should be responsible. There is much variation here, with the biological mother and the father's income often crucial, but generally children of separated parents are less likely to attend college than children living with both biological parents (King et al., 2020; de Leeuw & Kalmijn, 2020).

# Family Structures Around the World

Children fare best when both parents actively care for them every day. This is most likely to occur if the parents are married, although there are many exceptions. Many develop-mentalists focus on the rate of single parenthood, shown on this map. Single parents often raise children well, especially with support from their families, friends, and communities.

## RATES OF SINGLE PARENTHOOD

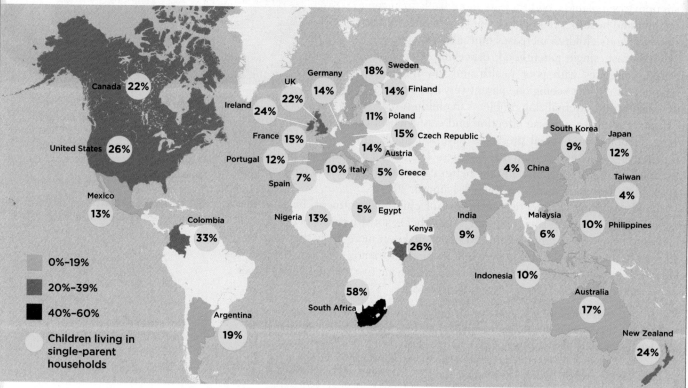

Canada **22%**
United States **26%**
Mexico **13%**
Colombia **33%**
Argentina **19%**
UK **22%**
Ireland **24%**
France **15%**
Portugal **12%**
Spain **7%**
Germany **14%**
Sweden **18%**
Finland **14%**
Poland **11%**
Czech Republic **15%**
Austria **14%**
Italy **10%**
Greece **5%**
Egypt **5%**
Nigeria **13%**
Kenya **26%**
South Africa **58%**
India **9%**
China **4%**
South Korea **9%**
Japan **12%**
Taiwan **4%**
Malaysia **6%**
Philippines **10%**
Indonesia **10%**
Australia **17%**
New Zealand **24%**

Legend:
- 0%–19%
- 20%–39%
- 40%–60%
- Children living in single-parent households

Data from Wilcox, 2011; OECD, 2011.

## LIVING ARRANGEMENTS OF U.S. 0- TO 18-YEAR-OLDS

Note that, while fewer children live with their two married biological parents from birth to age 18, it is not that more children are living in stepfamilies but that more individuals have decided to raise children on their own. Another shift is evident: Single parents once were almost always mothers, but now some are single fathers.

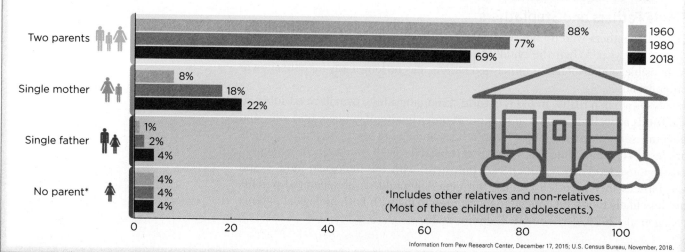

**Two parents**
88% (1960)
77% (1980)
69% (2018)

**Single mother**
8%
18%
22%

**Single father**
1%
2%
4%

**No parent***
4%
4%
4%

Legend:
1960
1980
2018

*Includes other relatives and non-relatives. (Most of these children are adolescents.)

Information from Pew Research Center, December 17, 2015; U.S. Census Bureau, November, 2018.

**Fortunate Boys** This single father *(left)* in Pennsylvania takes his three sons to the playground almost every day, and this nuclear family *(right)* in Mali invests time and money in their only child's education. All four boys have loving fathers. Does family function make family structure irrelevant?

Courts and social workers are increasingly recommending joint physical custody of children after a divorce. In general, when both parents are directly involved in caregiving, children of divorce are healthier, physically and emotionally, than when only one parent has custody (Baude et al., 2016; Braver & Votruba, 2018). A major reason is that the father is a more active parent, and that benefits the children.

When a father is the lone caregiver, he suffers the same problems as single mothers—too much to do and not enough money to do it. Single parents of both sexes often seek a new spouse, in part to help with parenthood. This may not work out as hoped (Booth & Dunn, 2014).

The data suggest that remarriage benefits the adults more than the children. Not only is parental support, emotional as well as financial, diminished for the child, but also the relationship suffers. Children may blame one or both biological parents for the separation, and may reject the stepparent, in part because they are loyal to their absent parent.

Not surprisingly, many stepparents find it hard to bond with a child of their new partner's former lover, especially when the child is hostile. As both a cause and a correlate, adult stepchildren are less likely than biological children to live near their parents.

Practical circumstances matter, too. A major problem for the children when parents remarry is that many parts of their lives change yet again, including such daily routines as where they sleep, what they eat, and where they go to school. Remember that stability and harmony are especially coveted in middle childhood.

One result: Children often are angry or sad, fight with friends, fail in school, rebel against family rules, and harm themselves (e.g., cutting, accidents, eating disorders, and so on). Disputes between half-siblings and stepsiblings are common, because every child is upset.

Their parents often have opposite strategies for discipline and guidance. This occurs with biological parents as well, but a solid parental alliance is particularly elusive when it includes three adults—two of whom disliked each other so much that they divorced, and a third who does not know the history of the child.

Remember that although structure affects function, structure does not determine function. Some stepparent families function well. As a review of research on stepfamilies concludes:

> The case that divorce and family instability reduce children's well-being
> is strong. At the same time, the magnitude of these consequences vary
> considerably across individuals and groups.

*[Raley & Sweeney, 2020, p. 92]*

## Single-Parent Families

On average, the single-parent structure functions less well for children because single parents have less income, time, and stability. Most single parents fill many roles—including wage earner, daughter or son (single parents often depend on their own parents), and lover (many seek a new partner). That reduces time for emotional and academic support for children. If they are depressed (and many are), that makes it worse. Neesha, in A Case to Study, is an example.

However, many parents and communities overcome structural barriers in order to provide love and support to children. Contrary to the averages, thousands of single-parent families are wonderful, children in nuclear families are not guaranteed good care, and extended families, in particular, are sometimes protective.

Culture is always influential. In the slums of Mumbai, India, rates of psychological disorders among school-age children were *higher* in nuclear families than in extended families, presumably because grandparents, aunts, and uncles provided more care and stability in that city than two parents alone (Patil et al., 2013). The opposite is true for many families in the United States: Extended families are

---

**A CASE TO STUDY**

# How Hard Is It to Be a Kid?

Neesha's fourth-grade teacher referred her to the school guidance team because Neesha often fell asleep in class, was late 51 days, and was absent 15 days. Testing found Neesha at the seventh-grade level in reading and writing and at the fifth-grade level in math. Since achievement was not Neesha's problem, something psychosocial must be amiss.

The counselor spoke to Neesha's mother, Tanya, a single parent who was depressed and worried about paying the rent on a tiny apartment where she had moved when Neesha's father left three years earlier. He lived with his girlfriend, now with a new baby as well. Tanya said she had no problems with Neesha, who was "more like a little mother than a kid," unlike her 15-year-old son, Tyrone, who suffered from fetal alcohol effects and whose behavior worsened when his father left.

Tyrone was recently beaten up badly as part of a gang initiation, a group he considered "like a family." He was currently in juvenile detention, after being arrested for stealing bicycle parts. Note the nonshared environment here: Although the siblings grew up together and their father left them both, 12-year-old Tyrone became rebellious whereas 7-year-old Neesha became *parentified*, "a little mother."

The school counselor also spoke with Neesha.

> Neesha volunteered that she worried a lot about things and that sometimes when she worries she has a hard time falling asleep. . . . she got in trouble for being late so many times, but it was hard to wake up. Her mom was sleeping late because she was working more nights cleaning offices. . . . Neesha said she got so far behind that she just gave up. She was also having problems with the other girls in the class, who were starting to tease her about sleeping in class and not doing her work. She said they called her names like "Sleepy"

and "Dummy." She said that at first it made her very sad, and then it made her very mad. That's when she started to hit them to make them stop.

> [Wilmshurst, 2011, pp. 152–153]

Neesha was coping with poverty, a depressed mother, an absent father, a delinquent brother, and classmate bullying. She seemed resilient—her achievement scores were impressive—but shortly after Neesha was interviewed,

> The school principal received a call from Neesha's mother, who asked that her daughter not be sent home from school because she was going to kill herself. She was holding a loaded gun in her hand and she had to do it, because she was not going to make this month's rent. She could not take it any longer, but she did not want Neesha to come home and find her dead. . . . While the guidance counselor continued to keep the mother talking, the school contacted the police, who apprehended [the] mom while she was talking on her cell phone. . . . The loaded gun was on her lap. . . . The mother was taken to the local psychiatric facility.

> [Wilmshurst, 2011, pp. 154–155]

Whether Neesha's resilience would continue depended on her ability to find support beyond her family. Perhaps the school counselor helped:

> When asked if she would like to meet with the school psychologist once in a while, just to talk about her worries, Neesha said she would like that very much. After she left the office, she turned and thanked the psychologist for working with her, and added, "You know, sometimes it's hard being a kid."

> [Wilmshurst, 2011, p. 154]

more chaotic, exactly what children do not need. But not always. One factor is immigration status. In the United States, extended families may function better for immigrant families than for the U.S. born (Areba et al., 2018).

---

**DATA CONNECTIONS: Family Structure in the United States and Around the World** examines the many types of families.

---

## Family Trouble

However, while it is true that structure does not determine function, two factors always correlate with dysfunction: low income and high conflict.

## Wealth and Poverty

Family income affects both function and structure. Marriage rates fall in times of economic recession, and divorce increases with unemployment. Low SES correlates with many other problems, and "risk factors pile up in the lives of some children, particularly among the most disadvantaged" (Masten, 2014, p. 95).

Several scholars have developed the *family-stress model*, which holds that any risk factor (such as poverty, divorce, single parenthood, unemployment) damages a family if, and only if, it increases stress on the parents, making them less patient and responsive to the children (Masarik & Conger, 2017).

Ongoing economic hardship almost always increases family stress (Duran et al., 2019). When parents fear that they cannot provide food and shelter for their children, their worry about the future renders them tense and hostile. The parents' *reaction* to income may exacerbate or minimize stress (Evans & Kim, 2013; Lee et al., 2013; Mazza et al., 2017).

A curious correlation is evident: Children in high-income families are more likely to have developmental problems in adulthood than children of middle-SES parents (Luthar et al., 2018). Stress may be the underlying problem: Some wealthy parents are anxious about maintaining their status, and their stress makes them pressure their children to excel. Their children may have emotional problems in middle childhood and drug abuse, delinquency, and academic failure later on.

But do not conclude that children are better off poor than rich. Poverty always adds stress; high income sometimes does. The crucial question is whether economic pressures affect the parents' ability to provide children the attention and guidance they need (Roubinov & Boyce, 2017). Back to family routines: If parents set clear guidelines for sleep, eating, and homework, children benefit. If parents are too caught up in their own financial concerns, children suffer.

The parents' stress is sometimes mitigated by national policy. In Norway, for instance, family poverty has minimal effect on children because national health care, high-quality early education, and national public schools provide a "buffering effect of the social safety net" (Bøe et al., 2018, p.1). (See **Figure 13.2**.) In the United States, parents must do that buffering themselves.

## Conflict

Every researcher agrees that family conflict harms children, especially when adults fight about child rearing. Such fights are more common in stepfamilies, divorced families, and extended families, but nuclear families are not immune. Children suffer not only if they are abused, physically or

**FIGURE 13.2**

**Families and Schools** This graph shows the score gap in fourth-grade science on the 2015 TIMSS between children in schools where more than 25 percent of the children are from high-SES homes compared to children in schools where more than 25 percent are from low-SES homes. Generally, the nations with the largest gaps are also the nations with the most schools at one or the other end of the spectrum and the fewest in between. For example, 23 percent of the children in the United States attended schools where less than a fourth of the students were from high- or low-SES families, compared with 37 percent of the Japanese children.

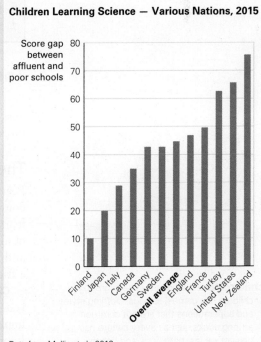

Children Learning Science — Various Nations, 2015

Data from Mullis et al., 2016.

**THINK CRITICALLY:** Can you describe a situation in which having a single parent would be better for a child than having two parents?

emotionally, but also if they merely witness their parents' abuse of each other or of their other children. Fights between siblings can be harmful, too (Buehler, 2020).

This correlation raises a possible hypothesis. Might genes from the parents to the children harm every child, whether or not they witness family fights? If that were so, the correlation between family conflict and child problems is caused by a third variable, specifically genes.

This hypothesis was tested in an amazing longitudinal study of 867 pairs adult twins (388 monozygotic and 479 dizygotic), who had married and had an adolescent child (Schermerhorn et al., 2011). Both parents were asked independently about marital conflict. The teenagers' problems were compared to their cousin, who was the child of their parent's twin.

Thus, this study had data from 5,202 individuals—one-third of them adult twins, one-third of them spouses of twins, and one-third of them adolescents who were genetically linked to another adolescent. If their parent was a monozygotic twin, they had one-fourth of their genes in common with their cousin; if their parent was a dizygotic twin, one-eighth of the same genes.

The researchers found that although genes had some effect, witnessing conflict itself had a powerful impact, increasing externalizing problems in the boys and internalizing problems in the girls. Quiet disagreements did little harm, but open conflict (e.g., yelling heard by the children) and divorce was harmful (Schermerhorn et al., 2011). That leads to an obvious conclusion: Parents should not fight in front of their children.

---

**WHAT HAVE YOU LEARNED?**

1. How might siblings raised together not share the same family environment?

2. What is the difference between family structure and family function?

3. Why is a harmonious, stable home particularly important during middle childhood?

4. What are the advantages for children in a nuclear family structure?

5. Why might the single-parent structure function less well than two-parent structures.

6. How are family structure and family function affected by culture?

7. Using the family-stress model, explain how family income affects family function.

---

# The Peer Group

Peers become increasingly important in middle childhood. With their new awareness of reality (concrete operational thought), children become painfully aware of their classmates' opinions, judgments, and accomplishments.

## The Culture of Children

Peer relationships, unlike adult–child relationships, involve partners who negotiate, compromise, share, and defend themselves as equals. Consequently, children learn social lessons from one another that grown-ups cannot teach (Rubin et al., 2013). Adults may follow a child's lead, but they are always much older and bigger, with their own values and experiences. They cannot substitute for a friend.

**child culture** The idea that each group of children has games, sayings, clothing styles, and superstitions that are not common among adults, just as every culture has distinct values, behaviors, and beliefs.

**Child culture** includes the customs, rules, and rituals that are passed down to younger children from slightly older ones, with no thought about the origins or implications. The child's goal is to join a culture and thus be part of the peer group. Jump-rope rhymes, insults, and superstitions are examples.

For instance, "Ring around the rosy/Pocketful of posies/Ashes, ashes/We all fall down" may have originated as children coped with the Black Death, which killed half the population of Europe in the fourteenth century. (*Rosy* may be short for *rosary*, used by Roman Catholics for prayer.) Children have passed down that rhyme for centuries, laughing together with no thought of sudden death. Rigid distinctions between boys' and girls' culture have eroded, as child culture reflects as well as forecasts changes in the overall culture (Van Rheenen, 2012).

Throughout the world, child culture may clash with adult culture. Many children reject clothes that parents buy as too loose, too tight, too long, too short, or wrong in color, style, brand, decoration, or some other aspect that adults might not notice. If their schools are multiethnic, children may choose friends from other groups, unlike their parents.

Appearance is important for child culture, but more important is independence from adults. Classmates pity those (especially boys) whose parents kiss them ("mama's boy"), tease children who please the teachers ("teacher's pet," "suck-up"), and despise those who betray children to adults ("tattletale," "grasser," "snitch," "rat"). Keeping secrets from parents and teachers is a moral mandate.

The culture of children is not always benign. For example, because communication with peers is vital, children learn whatever language or dialect the other children speak. Immigrant parents proudly note how well their children speak a second language, but all parents are distressed when their children spout their peers' curses, accents, and slang. Because they value independence, children may gravitate toward friends who defy authority, sometimes harmlessly (passing a note in class), sometimes not (shoplifting, smoking).

This is part of the nature of children, who often do what their parents do not want them to do, and it is in the nature of parents to be upset when that happens. This is easier to criticize in other cultures and centuries, as in the following example.

In 1922, the magazine *Good Housekeeping* published an article titled "Aren't you glad you are not your grandmother?" In it, a daughter quotes letters from her dead grandmother that she found in the attic. One describes an incident that occurred when that daughter's father—also long dead—was a boy and snuck out of his house to play with other boys:

**No Toys** Many boys in middle childhood are happiest playing outside with equipment designed for work. This wheelbarrow is perfect, especially because at any moment the pusher might tip it.

> When the door was left unlocked for a moment, out he ran in his little velvet suit. We did not miss him for a while because we thought he was doing his Latin Prose, and then some wealthy ladies . . . saw him literally in the gutter, groping in the mud for a marble. . . . Horace's father was white with emotion when he heard of it. He went out, brought Horace in, gave him another whipping, and, saying that since he acted like a runaway dog he should be treated like one, he went out, bought a dog-collar and a chain, and chained Horace to the post of his little bed. He was there all the afternoon, crying so you could hear nothing else in all the house. . . . I went many times up to the hall before his door and knelt there stretching out my arms to my darling child, the tears flooding down my cheeks. But, of course, I could not open the door and go in to him, to interfere with his punishment.

*[Fisher, 1922, p. 8]*

The author was grateful that mothers now (in 1922!) knew more than did nineteenth-century parents with their "ignorance of child-life" (Fisher, 1922, p. 15). This raises the question: What ignorance of child-life do we have today? If I knew, that would not be ignorance, but this text makes me humble; each new generation develops a child culture that may teach their elders.

## Friendships

Teachers sometimes separate friends, but that may be a mistake. Developmentalists find that children help each other learn both academic and social skills (Bagwell & Schmidt, 2011). The loyalty of children to their friends may work for their benefit or harm (Rubin et al., 2013).

Both aspects of friendship are expressed by these two Mexican American children.

*Yolanda:*

There's one friend . . . she's always been with me, in bad or good . . . She's always telling me, "Keep on going and your dreams are gonna come true."

*Paul:*

I think right now about going Christian, right? Just going Christian, trying to do good, you know? Stay away from drugs, everything. And every time it seems like I think about that, I think about the homeboys. And it's a trip because a lot of the homeboys are my family, too, you know?

[*quoted in Nieto, 2000, pp. 220, 249*]

Yolanda later went to college; Paul went to jail. This is echoed by other children. Many aspects of adult personality are influenced by the personality of childhood friends (Wrzus et al., 2016).

Indeed, quite apart from family, school, and IQ, a study found that the intelligence of a best friend in sixth grade affected intelligence at age 15 (Meldrum et al., 2018). Peers benefit children or not. As one study concludes, if low-achievers "selected similarly low-achieving students as friends, this may dampen their academic achievement over time" (Laninga-Wijnen et al., 2019, p. 347).

Friendships become more intense and intimate over the years of middle childhood, as social cognition and effortful control advance. Six-year-olds may befriend anyone of the same sex and age who will play with them. By age 10, children demand more. They choose carefully, share secrets, expect loyalty, change friends less often, are upset when they lose a friend, and find it harder to make new friends.

Older children tend to choose friends whose interests, values, and backgrounds are similar to their own. By the end of middle childhood, close friendships are almost always between children of the same sex, age, ethnicity, and socioeconomic status (Rubin et al., 2013). Both genders learn how to become good friends, with girls becoming better at sympathetic reassurance and boys becoming better at joint excitement. Everyone finds friendship increasingly satisfying over the years of childhood (Rose & Asher, 2017).

**THINK CRITICALLY:** Do adults also choose friends who agree with them or whose background is similar to their own?

## Popular and Unpopular Children

In the United States, two types of popular children and three types of unpopular children have become apparent in middle childhood (Cillessen & Marks, 2011). First, at every age, children who are friendly and cooperative are well-liked and popular. By the end of middle childhood, as status becomes important, another avenue to popularity begins: Some popular children are also aggressive (Shi & Xie, 2012).

As for the three types of unpopular children, some are *neglected*, not rejected; they are ignored, but not shunned. The other two types are actively rejected, either *aggressive-rejected*, disliked because they are antagonistic and confrontational, or *withdrawn-rejected*, disliked because they are timid and anxious. Children as young as age 6 are aware if they are rejected and decide if they should try to be more accepted or should seek other friends (Nesdale et al., 2014).

Both aggressive-rejected and withdrawn-rejected children often misinterpret social situations, lack emotional regulation, and experience mistreatment at home. Each of these problems not only cause rejection, but the rejection itself makes it worse for the child (Stenseng et al., 2015). If they do not learn when to be assertive and when to be quiet, they may become bullies or victims.

Whether a particular child is popular or not depends on cultural norms, which change over time. As you read in Chapter 7, some parts of temperament are genetic. Some people are temperamentally more aggressive, more outgoing, or more fearful than others. But culture affects whether those inborn traits are accepted, channeled, or curbed.

This is illustrated by research on shyness (X. Chen, 2019). A 1990 survey in Shanghai found that shy children were liked and respected (X. Chen et al., 1992), but 12 years later, when competition with the West became salient, shy children in the same schools were less popular (X. Chen et al., 2005).

Other research found that shyness is more accepted in rural China (Zhang & Eggum-Wilkens, 2018). In general, several aspects of the social context and culture, specifically academic achievement, friendships, and being in middle childhood (not adolescence) all make shy Chinese children more accepted by their peers (X. Chen et al., 2019; X. Chen et al., 2013; Liu et al., 2015).

Within the United States, a similar shift from acceptance to rejection of a personality trait is evident regarding aggression in males. Once that was acceptable ("Boys will be boys!"), but now teachers, both women and men themselves, teach boys to restrain their impulse to lash out. This is most apparent in the new understanding of bullies, as now explained.

## Bullying

**Bullying** is defined as repeated, systematic attacks intended to harm those who are unable or unlikely to defend themselves. It occurs in every nation, in every community, in every kind of school (religious/secular, public/private, progressive/traditional, large/medium/small), and perhaps in every child.

Bullying is of four types:

- *Physical* (hitting, pinching, shoving, or kicking)
- *Verbal* (teasing, taunting, or name-calling)
- *Relational* (destroying peer acceptance)
- *Cyberbullying* (using electronic means to harm another)

The first three types are common in primary school and begin in preschool. Cyberbullying is more common later on and is discussed in Chapter 16.

### Victims

Almost every child experiences an isolated attack or is called a derogatory name during middle childhood. Victims of bullying, however, endure shameful experiences again and again—pushed and kicked, called names, forced to do degrading things, and so on—with no defense. Victims tend to be "cautious, sensitive, quiet . . . lonely and abandoned at school. As a rule, they do not have a single good friend in their class" (Olweus, 1999, p. 15).

Even having a friend who is also a victim helps. Such friends may not be able to provide physical protection, but they can and do provide psychological defense—reassuring victims that their condition is not their fault and that the bully is mean, stupid, racist, or whatever (Schacter & Juvonen, 2018). That is crucial, because the worst harm is loss of self-respect.

**VIDEO ACTIVITY: Bullying: Interview with Nikki Crick** explores the causes and repercussions of the different types of bullying.

**bullying** Repeated, systematic efforts to inflict harm on other people through physical, verbal, or social attack on a weaker person.

**bully-victim** Someone who attacks others and who is attacked as well. (Also called *provocative victims* because they do things that elicit bullying.)

**Especially for Parents of an Accused Bully** Another parent has told you that your child is a bully. Your child denies it and explains that the other child doesn't mind being teased. What should you do? (see response, page 367)

Although it is often thought that victims are particularly unattractive or odd, this is not necessarily the case. Victims are chosen because of their emotional vulnerability and social isolation, not their appearance. Children who are new to a school, whose background and home culture are unlike that of their peers, who are gender nonconforming, who have disabilities, or whose clothes indicate poverty, are especially vulnerable. Bullies can find something (fat or thin, glasses or unruly hair, an odd accent or unusual shoes) in almost any child to belittle.

As one boy said,

> You can get bullied because you are weak or annoying or because you are different. Kids with big ears get bullied. Dorks get bullied. You can also get bullied because you think too much of yourself and try to show off. Teacher's pet gets bullied. If you say the right answer too many times in class you can get bullied. There are lots of popular groups who bully each other and other groups, but you can get bullied within your group too. If you do not want to get bullied, you have to stay under the radar, but then you might feel sad because no one pays attention to you.

[*quoted in Guerra et al., 2011, p. 306*]

Remember the three types of unpopular children? *Neglected* children are not victimized; they are ignored, "under the radar." *Rejected* children fit into the bully network. Withdrawn-rejected children are likely victims; they are isolated, depressed, and friendless. Aggressive-rejected children may be **bully-victims** (or *provocative victims*), with neither friends nor sympathizers (Kochel et al., 2015). They suffer the most, because they strike back ineffectively, which increases the bullying.

## Bullies

Unlike bully-victims, most bullies are *not* rejected. Many are proud, pleased with themselves, with friends who admire them and classmates who fear them. Some are quite popular: Bullying is a form of social dominance and authority (Pellegrini et al., 2011).

The link between bullying and popularity has long been apparent during early adolescence (Pouwels et al., 2016), but bullies are already "quite popular in middle childhood." Adults, however, have become aware that bullying is destructive. As one comprehensive summary of the research explains, bullying "is now recognized as a major and preventable public health problem" (National Academies of Sciences, Engineering, and Medicine, 2016, p. 13).

Bullying begins during the preschool years, and teachers often recognize it and try to stop it. What changes from ages 6 to 12 is that bullies become skilled at avoiding adult awareness, at picking rejected and defenseless victims, and at using nonphysical methods—which avoid adult punishment (Pouwels et al., 2017). As children become better at hiding bullying from adults, the harm to victims increases (Nelson et al., 2019).

Boys are bullies more often than girls, typically attacking smaller, weaker boys. Girl bullies usually use words to demean shyer, more soft-spoken girls. Young boys sometimes bully girls, but by puberty (about age 11), boys who bully girls are not admired, although sexual teasing is. Especially in the final years of middle childhood, boys who are thought to be gay become targets, with suicide attempts as one consequence (National Academies of Sciences, Engineering, and Medicine, 2016).

## Causes and Consequences of Bullying

Bullying may begin early in life. Most toddlers try to dominate other children (and perhaps their parents) at some point. When they hit, kick, and so on, usually their parents, teachers, and peers teach them to find other ways to interact. However, if home life is chaotic, if discipline is ineffectual, if siblings are hostile, or if attachment is insecure, children do not learn how to express their frustration. Instead, vulnerable young children develop externalizing and internalizing problems, becoming bullies or victims (Turner et al., 2012).

By middle childhood, bullying is not the outburst of a frustrated child but an attempt to gain status. That makes it a social action: Bullies rarely attack victims when the two of them are alone. Instead, a bully might engage in a schoolyard fight, with onlookers who are more likely to cheer the victor than stop the fight; or a bully might utter an insult that provokes laughter in all except the target. By the end of middle childhood, bullies choose victims whom other children reject.

Siblings matter. Some brothers and sisters defend each other; children are protected if bullies fear that an older sibling will retaliate. On the other hand, if children are bullied by peers in school *and* siblings at home, they are four times more likely to develop serious psychological disorders by age 18 (Dantchev et al., 2018).

Bullies and victims risk impaired social understanding, lower school achievement, and relationship difficulties, with higher rates of mental illness in adulthood. Many victims become depressed; many bullies become increasingly cruel with higher rates of prison and death (Willoughby et al., 2014). The damage goes even further: In schools with high rates of bullying, all of the children are less likely to focus on academics and more likely to concentrate on the social dynamics of the classroom—hoping to avoid becoming the next victim.

**Power to Peers** Bullying is a way some children gain respect. If, instead, the school gives training and special shirts to bystanders, they can gain status by befriending victims. That seems to work in this school in Bensalem, Pennsylvania.

## Can Bullying Be Stopped?

Many victimized children find ways to halt ongoing bullying—by ignoring, retaliating, defusing, or avoiding. Friendships help.

We know what does *not* work: simply increasing students' awareness of bullying, instituting zero tolerance for fighting, or putting bullies together in a therapy group or a classroom. This last measure tends to make daily life easier for teachers, but it increases aggression.

Since one cause of bullying is poor parent–child interaction, alerting parents may "create even more problems for the child, for the parents, and for their relationship" (Rubin et al., 2013, p. 267). This does not mean that parents should be kept ignorant, but it does mean that parents need help in understanding how to break the bully-victim connection (Nocentini et al., 2019).

This is a theme of an article about parents' attitudes. Many parents were naïve about bullying, some claiming that their child would not experience it because the school was small (Stives et al., 2019). Instead of recognizing that bullies gain status by bullying, some parents thought bullies needed sympathy. One said that, if his son told him he was bullied,

> I would explain to him that bullies usually are very unhappy people and have a tendency to have low self-esteem. Most bullies sometimes don't have a loving/caring home environment. I would tell him to be kind to any bullies. Be a friend whenever possible.

*[quoted in Stives et al., 2019, p. 367]*

That response helps neither victim nor bully.

To decrease bullying, the entire school should be involved, with teachers, aides, children, and parents, all taught to recognize bullying and how to reduce it (Juvonen & Graham, 2014). A Spanish concept, *convivencia*, describes a culture of cooperation and positive relationships within a community. Convivencia has been applied specifically to schools. When teachers are supportive and protective of every child, and the school community encourages friendship, empathy, and cooperation among all students, bullying decreases (Zych et al., 2017).

Programs that seem good might be harmful, especially if they call attention to bullying but do nothing about it (National Academies of Sciences, Engineering, and Medicine, 2016). Longitudinal research on whole-school efforts finds variations depending on the age of the children (younger is easier), on the indicators (peer report, teacher report, absence rate, direct observation), as well as on the tactics (encouraging friendship and decreasing adult hostility is more effective than punishing overt bullying).

Bystanders are crucial: If they do not intervene—or worse, if they watch and laugh—bullying flourishes. Some children who are neither bullies nor victims feel troubled but also feel fearful and powerless. However, if they empathize with victims, feel effective (high in effortful control), and refuse to admire bullies, aggression is reduced. The best way for teachers to help victims is sometimes to encourage bystanders to befriend the victim or stop the bully (Iotti et al., 2020). Bullies ignore, avoid, or even enjoy criticism from authorities; it is harder to do so with peers.

Appreciation of human differences is not innate (remember, children seek friends who are similar to them), so adults need to encourage multicultural sensitivity. Then peers are more effective than teachers at halting bullying (Palmer & Abbott, 2018). As they mature during middle childhood, children become more socially aware, which creates a dilemma: Children become more aware of the emotional harm that bullies do to other children, but also more aware that they themselves might be harmed if they befriend a bullied child.

This explains an odd dynamic: A victimized child is less distressed if their friend is also victimized (Schacter & Juvonen, 2019). This also raises a crucial issue in middle childhood—moral development.

## Children's Morality

Some moral values seem inborn. Babies prefer a puppet who is helpful to other puppets over a mean puppet, and young children believe that desired objects (cookies, stickers, candy) should be shared equally. The ideas of fairness, kindness, and equality are present in the minds of children (Rizzo & Killen, 2016; Van de Vondervoort & Hamlin, 2016).

However, the young child's idea of morality is quite limited. Middle childhood is prime time for moral development. These are

> years of eager, lively searching on the part of children . . . as they try to understand things, to figure them out, but also to weigh the rights and wrongs. . . . This is the time for growth of the moral imagination, fueled constantly by the willingness, the eagerness of children to put themselves in the shoes of others.

> [Coles, 1997, p. 99]

**THINK CRITICALLY:** The text says that both former bullies and former victims suffer in adulthood. Which would you rather be, and why?

Many lines of research have shown that children develop their own morality, guided by peers, parents, and culture (Killen & Smetana, 2014). Children's growing interest in moral issues is guided by three forces: (1) child culture, (2) empathy, and (3) education.

## Moral Rules of Child Culture

First, when child culture conflicts with adult morality, children often align themselves with peers. A child might lie to protect a friend, for instance. Friendship itself has a hostile side: Many close friends (especially girls) resist other children who want to join their play (Rubin et al., 2013). Boys are particularly likely to protect a bully if he is a friend.

## Parents Versus Peers

The fact that children place prime value on being accepted by peers sometimes results in a conflict between the moral values of society and the actions of children. A child may do something that the parents think their child would never do. This is not time to argue, or despair; it is time to teach. This is illustrated by another memory that Ward Sutton (who opened this chapter) told at his Herblock Prize acceptance speech in 2018.

In the summer of 1974, I was seven years old.

There was a kid living in my neighborhood. . . .

For some reason this kid had built up animosity towards a family down the block. He started telling my friend Steve and me that this family had done all sorts of bad things, like hiding razor blades in the apples they gave out to trick-or-treaters at Halloween.

Fake news for seven year olds . . . target people who had done absolutely nothing wrong.

Steve became convinced of the conspiracy theory and fell in line, and then the two of them told me they were starting a club and I couldn't join unless I went along with them. . . .

We snuck behind the family's house in the woods out back. We threw some rocks at the house and when there was no response we realized the family was not home. Then we escalated things, finding bricks, smashing windows, breaking in and vandalizing the home.

I was a shy, introverted kid who never would have ever done anything like this on my own. But once I was swayed to join in,

it was like a switch had been flipped and any sense of right or wrong was thrown by the wayside. Suddenly the unthinkable was okay. . . .

Then the family came home. We ran. Police arrived. Steve was caught. I lied. To my parents. To everyone. Said I didn't know anything about it. Steve confessed, and eventually I did, too. As terrible as it all was, the worst of it was the fact that I had lied. My mother wouldn't speak to me for what felt like an eternity. . . .

My father brought me back to the house to apologize to the family face-to-face. I begged him not to make me do it . . . I expected them to be angry with me, but they weren't. They were gracious, and mostly puzzled at what could have possibly possessed me to do something like this.

I couldn't even explain why I had done it.

As you might imagine, this episode was hugely formative for me. It awakened my moral compass and informed what I would create going forward. . . .

I've . . . never spoken of it publicly until today. For the longest time, I wished I could live that day all over again, and that someone could have talked some sense into me: "Stop and think about what you're doing."

Sutton's cartoons are often ethical comments on world affairs. He says he draws them because he hopes people will smile, and then stop and think.

---

Three moral imperatives of child culture in middle childhood are:

- Defend your friends.
- Don't tell adults about children's misbehavior.
- Conform to peer standards of dress, talk, and behavior.

These three can explain both apparent boredom and overt defiance as well as standards of dress that mystify adults (such as jeans so loose that they fall off or so tight that they impede digestion—both styles worn by my children, who grew up in different cohorts). Given what is known about middle childhood, it is no surprise that children do not echo adult morality.

Part of child culture is that as children become more aware of their peers, they may reject other children who are outsiders as well as stay quiet about their own problems. When teachers ask, "Who threw that spitball?" or parents ask, "How did you get that bruise?" children may be mum.

## Empathy

The second factor, empathy, is key. As middle childhood advances, children become more socially perceptive and more able to learn about other people (Weissberg et al., 2016). This does not always lead to increased morality as adults might define it. One example was just described: Bullies become adept at picking victims, and bystanders become better at noticing victims. However, depending on the culture of their school and home, social awareness may make them either quicker to defend or hesitant to act (Pozzoli & Gini, 2013).

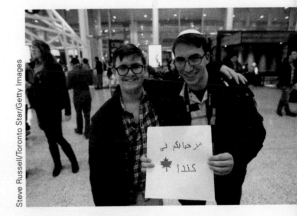

Steve Russell/Toronto Star/Getty Images

**Universal Morality** Remarkable? Not really. By the end of middle childhood, many children are eager to express their moral convictions, especially with a friend. Chaim Ifrah and Shai Reef believe that welcoming refugees is part of being a patriotic Canadian and a devout Jewish person, so they brought a welcoming sign to the Toronto airport where Syrian refugees (mostly Muslim) will soon deplane.

The authors of a study of 7-year-olds "conclude that moral *competence* may be a universal human characteristic, but that it takes a situation with specific demand characteristics to translate this competence into actual prosocial performance" (van Ijzendoorn et al., 2010, p. 1). In other words, school-age children can think and act morally, but they do not always do so because the hidden curriculum, or adult values, or peer pressure may lead them astray.

Here, diversity in schools and neighborhoods can be helpful. Empathy is not an abstract idea as much as a recognition of the basic humanity of other people. In order to achieve that, knowing a child from another group lets children understand. Teachers and parents can help with this, not only through direct contact but, once children can read on their own, by offering books about children in other lands, centuries, and cultures.

## Moral Education

Finally, cognitive development might affect moral development, at least according to Piaget (1932/2013b) and then Kohlberg (1963), who described three levels of moral reasoning and two stages at each level (see **Table 13.3**), with parallels to Piaget's stages of cognition.

**preconventional moral reasoning**
Kohlberg's first level of moral reasoning, emphasizing rewards and punishments.

**conventional moral reasoning**
Kohlberg's second level of moral reasoning, emphasizing social rules.

- **Preconventional moral reasoning** is similar to preoperational thought in that it is egocentric, with children most interested in their personal pleasure or avoiding punishment.
- **Conventional moral reasoning** parallels concrete operational thought in that it relates to current, observable practices: Children watch what their parents, teachers, and friends do and try to follow suit.

### TABLE 13.3

**Kohlberg's Three Levels and Six Stages of Moral Reasoning**

**Level I: Preconventional Moral Reasoning**

The goal is to get rewards and avoid punishments; this is a self-centered level.

- *Stage one: Might makes right* (a punishment-and-obedience orientation). The most important value is to maintain the appearance of obedience to authority, avoiding punishment while still advancing self-interest. Don't get caught!
- *Stage two: Look out for number one* (an instrumental and relativist orientation). Everyone prioritizes their own needs. The reason to be nice to other people is so that they will be nice to you.

**Level II: Conventional Moral Reasoning**

Emphasis is placed on social rules; this is a parent- and community-centered level.

- *Stage three: Good girl and nice boy.* The goal is to please other people. Social approval is more important than any specific reward.
- *Stage four: Law and order.* Everyone must be a dutiful and law-abiding citizen, even when no police are nearby.

**Level III: Postconventional Moral Reasoning**

Emphasis is placed on moral principles; this level is centered on ideals.

- *Stage five: Social contract.* Obey social rules because they benefit everyone and are established by mutual agreement. If the rules become destructive or if one party doesn't live up to the agreement, the contract is no longer binding. Under some circumstances, disobeying the law is moral.
- *Stage six: Universal ethical principles.* Universal principles, not individual situations (level I) or community practices (level II), determine right and wrong. Ethical values (such as "life is sacred") are established by individual reflection and religious ideas, which may contradict egocentric (level I) or social and community (level II) values.

- **Postconventional moral reasoning** is similar to formal operational thought because it uses abstractions, going beyond what is concretely observed, willing to question "what is" in order to decide "what should be."

According to Kohlberg, intellectual maturation advances moral thinking. During middle childhood, children's answers shift from being primarily preconventional to being more conventional: Concrete thought and peer experiences help children move past the first two stages (level I) to the next two (level II). Postconventional reasoning is not usually present until adolescence or adulthood, if then.

Kohlberg posed moral dilemmas to school-age boys (and eventually girls, teenagers, and adults). The most famous example of these dilemmas involves a poor man named Heinz, whose wife was dying. He could not pay for the only drug that could cure his wife, a drug that a local druggist sold for 10 times what it cost to make.

> Heinz went to everyone he knew to borrow the money, but he could only get together about half of what it cost. He told the druggist that his wife was dying and asked him to sell it cheaper or let him pay later. But the druggist said "no." The husband got desperate and broke into the man's store to steal the drug for his wife. Should the husband have done that? Why?

> *[Kohlberg, 1963, p. 19]*

Kohlberg's assessment of morality depends not on what a person answers but why an answer is chosen. For instance, suppose a child says that Heinz should steal the drug. That itself does not indicate the level of morality. The reason could be that Heinz needs his wife to care for him (preconventional), or that people will blame him if he lets his wife die (conventional), or that the value of a human life is greater than the law (postconventional).

Or suppose another child says Heinz should not steal. Again, the reason is crucial. If it is that he will go to jail, that is preconventional; if it is that business owners will blame him, that is conventional; if it is that no one should deprive anyone else of their livelihood, that is postconventional.

Kohlberg has been criticized for not appreciating cultural or gender differences. For example, loyalty to family overrides other values in some cultures, so some people might avoid postconventional actions that hurt their family. Also, Kohlberg's original participants were all boys, which may have led him to discount female values of nurturance and relationships (Gilligan, 1982).

Overall, Kohlberg seemed to value rational principles more than individual needs, unlike other scholars of moral development who consider emotions more influential than logic (Haidt, 2013). Regarding global warming, for instance, the facts about the world's temperature rising by a degree over a decade is less compelling for children in middle childhood than the dilemma of the stranded polar bear cub on a melting ice flow.

In general, over the years of middle childhood, children become more able to understand the difference between intentions and actions (doing harm but intending to be helpful is forgiven) and between lying deliberately and saying something that is untrue by mistake (Rizzo et al., 2019).

## Maturation and Morality

As already discussed, some prosocial values are evident in infancy and early childhood. However, children have much to learn, and middle childhood is the best time for that. Maturation matters. One study measured generosity by counting how many of 10 chosen stickers 5- to 12-year-olds from five nations (United States, Canada, China, Turkey, South Africa) were willing to donate to another unknown child. Generosity increased with age: 5-year-olds gave away two and kept eight, while 12-year-olds gave away five and kept five (Cowell et al., 2017).

Beyond that, culture had an impact. Children from Toronto, Canada, were most generous, and children from Cape Town, South Africa, were least generous, a difference thought to reflect national wealth (Cowell et al., 2017). Those national differences paled when individual behavior was considered: Some children from each of the five nations kept all or almost all stickers to themselves, and some from each nation gave more than half away.

## Teaching Morality

Fortunately, children enjoy thinking about and discussing moral values, and then peers help one another advance in moral behavior. Children may be more ethical than adults (once they understand moral equity, they complain when adults are not fair), and they are better at stopping a bully than adults are, because a bully is more likely to listen to other children than to adults.

Since bullies tend to be low on empathy, they need peers to teach them when their actions are not admired. During middle childhood, morality can be scaffolded just as cognitive skills are, with mentors—peers or adults—using moral dilemmas to advance moral understanding while they also advance the underlying moral skills of empathy and emotional regulation (Hinnant et al., 2013).

Usually, throughout middle childhood, moral judgment becomes more comprehensive, taking into account psychological as well as physical harm, intentions as well as consequences. For example, when 5- to 11-year-olds were presented with anecdotes that differed in whether the harm done was intended to prevent further harm or was simply mean, the younger children judged based on results, but the older children considered intention: They rated justifiable harm as less bad and unjustifiable harm as worse than the younger children did (Jambon & Smetana, 2014).

A detailed examination of the effect of peers on morality began with an update on one of Piaget's moral issues: whether punishment should seek *retribution* (hurting the transgressor) or *restitution* (restoring what was lost). Piaget found that children advance from retribution to restitution between ages 8 and 10 (Piaget, 1932/2013b), which many ethicists consider a moral advance (Claessen, 2017).

To learn how this occurs, researchers asked 133 9-year-olds:

> Late one afternoon there was a boy who was playing with a ball on his own in the garden. His dad saw him playing with it and asked him not to play with it so near the house because it might break a window. The boy didn't really listen to his dad, and carried on playing near the house. Then suddenly, the ball bounced up high and broke the window in the boy's room. His dad heard the noise and came to see what had happened. The father wonders what would be the fairest way to punish the boy. He thinks of two punishments. The first is to say: "Now, you didn't do as I asked. You will have to pay for the window to be mended, and I am going to take the money from your pocket money." The second is to say: "Now, you didn't do as I asked. As a punishment you have to go to your room and stay there for the rest of the evening." Which of these punishments do you think is the fairest?
>
> *[Leman & Björnberg, 2010, p. 962]*

The children were split almost equally in their answers. Then, 24 pairs were formed of children who had opposite views. Each pair was asked to discuss the issue, trying to reach agreement. (The other children did not discuss it.) Six pairs

**THINK CRITICALLY:** If one of your moral values differs from that of your spouse, your parents, or your community, should you still try to teach it to your children? Why or why not?

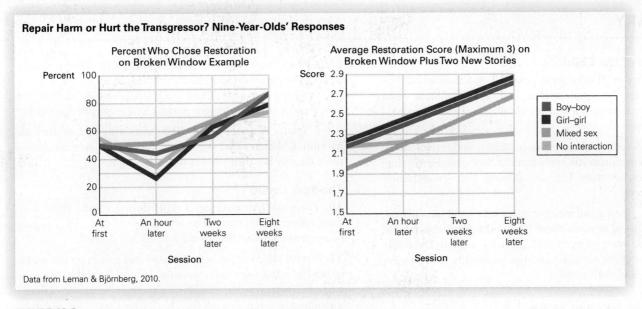

**Repair Harm or Hurt the Transgressor? Nine-Year-Olds' Responses**

Percent Who Chose Restoration on Broken Window Example

Average Restoration Score (Maximum 3) on Broken Window Plus Two New Stories

- Boy–boy
- Girl–girl
- Mixed sex
- No interaction

Data from Leman & Björnberg, 2010.

**FIGURE 13.3**

**Benefits of Time and Talking** The graph on the left shows that most children, immediately after their initial punitive response, became even more likely to seek punishment rather than to repair damage. However, after some time and reflection, they affirmed the response that Piaget would consider more mature. The graph on the right indicates that children who had talked about the broken-window example moved toward restorative justice even in examples that they had not heard before, which was not true for those who had not talked about the first story.

were boy–boy, six were boy–girl with the boy favoring restitution, six were boy–girl with the girl favoring restitution, and six were girl–girl.

The conversations typically took only five minutes, and the retribution side was more often chosen. Piaget would consider a moral backslide, since more restitution than retribution advocates switched.

However, two weeks and eight weeks later all of the children were queried again, and their responses changed toward the more advanced, restitution thinking (see **Figure 13.3**). This advance occurred even for the children who merely thought about the dilemma again, but children who had discussed it with another child were particularly likely to decide that restitution was better.

The main conclusion from this study was that "conversation on a topic may stimulate a process of individual reflection that triggers developmental advances" (Leman & Björnberg, 2010, p. 969). Parents and teachers, take note: Raising moral issues and letting children talk about them may advance morality—not immediately, but soon.

---

### WHAT HAVE YOU LEARNED?

1. How does the culture of children differ from the culture of adults?

2. What are the different kinds of popular and unpopular children?

3. What do victims and bullies have in common?

4. How might bullying be reduced?

5. What three forces affect moral development during middle childhood?

6. What are the main criticisms of Kohlberg's theory of moral development?

7. What role do adults play in the development of morality in children?

## SUMMARY

### The Nature of the Child

**1.** All theories of development acknowledge that school-age children become more independent and capable in many ways. Erikson emphasized industry, when children busily strive to master various tasks.

**2.** Children develop their self-concept during middle childhood, basing it on a more realistic assessment of their competence than they had in earlier years. Cultures differ in their evaluation of high self-esteem.

**3.** Both daily hassles and major stresses take a toll on children, with accumulated stresses more likely to impair development than any single event on its own. Resilience is aided by the child's interpretation of the situation and the availability of supportive adults, peers, and institutions.

### Families During Middle Childhood

**4.** Families influence children in many ways, as do genes and peers. Although most siblings share a childhood home and parents, each sibling experiences different (nonshared) circumstances within the family.

**5.** The five functions of a supportive family are: to satisfy children's physical needs; to encourage learning; to support friendships; to protect self-respect; and to provide a safe, stable, and harmonious home.

**6.** The most common family structure worldwide is the nuclear family, usually with other relatives nearby and supportive. Two-parent families include adoptive, grandparent, and stepfamilies, each of which sometimes functions well for children. However, every family structure also has vulnerabilities.

**7.** Single-parent families have higher rates of change — for example, in where they live and who belongs to the family. Instability is particularly hard during middle childhood, as are changing routines about homework, sleep, food, and so on.

**8.** Income affects family function for two-parent families as well as single-parent households. Poor children are at greater risk for emotional, behavioral, and academic problems because the stresses that often accompany poverty hinder effective parenting.

**9.** No matter what the family SES, instability and conflict are harmful. Children suffer even when the conflict does not involve them directly but their parents or siblings fight.

### The Peer Group

**10.** Peers teach crucial social skills during middle childhood. Each cohort of children has a culture, passed down from slightly older children. Close friends are wanted and needed.

**11.** Popular children may be cooperative and easy to get along with or may be competitive and aggressive. Unpopular children may be neglected, aggressive, or withdrawn, sometimes becoming victims.

**12.** Bullying is common among school-age children. Both bullies and victims have difficulty with social cognition; their interpretation of the normal give-and-take of childhood is impaired.

**13.** Bullies themselves may be admired, which makes their behavior more difficult to stop. Overall, a multifaceted, long-term, whole-school approach — with parents, teachers, and bystanders working together — seems the best way to halt bullying.

**14.** School-age children seek to differentiate right from wrong as moral development increases over middle childhood. Peer values, cultural standards, empathy, and education all affect their personal morality.

**15.** Kohlberg described three levels of moral reasoning, each related to cognitive maturity. His description has been criticized for ignoring cultural and gender differences.

**16.** When values conflict, children often choose loyalty to peers over adult standards of behavior. When children discuss moral issues with other children, they develop more thoughtful answers to moral questions.

## KEY TERMS

industry versus inferiority (p. 337)
social comparison (p. 338)
resilience (p. 340)
parentification (p. 342)
family structure (p. 345)

family function (p. 345)
nuclear family (p. 346)
single-parent family (p. 346)
extended family (p. 346)
polygamous family (p. 346)

child culture (p. 354)
bullying (p. 357)
bully-victim (p. 358)
preconventional moral reasoning (p. 362)

conventional moral reasoning (p. 362)
postconventional moral reasoning (p. 363)

## APPLICATIONS

**1.** Go someplace where many school-age children congregate (such as a schoolyard, a park, or a community center) and use naturalistic observation for at least half an hour. Describe what popular, average, withdrawn, and rejected children do. Note at least one potential conflict. Describe the sequence and the outcome.

**2.** Focusing on verbal bullying, describe at least two times when someone said something hurtful to you and two times when you said something that might have been hurtful to someone else. What are the differences between the two types of situations?

**3.** How would your childhood have been different if your family structure had been different, such as if you had (or had not) lived with your grandparents, if your parents had (or had not) gotten divorced, if you had (or had not) been adopted, if you had lived with one parent (or two), if your parents were both the same sex (or not)? Avoid blanket statements: Appreciate that every structure has advantages and disadvantages.

## Especially For ANSWERS

**Response for Scientists** (from p. 345): Proof is very difficult when human interaction is the subject of investigation, since random assignment is impossible. Ideally, researchers would find identical twins being raised together and would then observe the parents' behavior over the years.

**Response for Parents of an Accused Bully** (from p. 358): The future is ominous if the charges are true. Your child's denial is a sign that there is a problem. (An innocent child would be worried about the misperception instead of categorically denying that any problem exists.) You might ask the teacher what the school is doing about bullying. Family counseling might help. Because bullies often have friends who egg them on, you may need to monitor your child's friendships and perhaps befriend the victim. Talk about the situation with your child. Ignoring the situation might lead to heartache later on.

## Observation Quiz ANSWERS

**Answer to Observation Quiz** (from p. 343): Did you notice that the two males are first, and that the father carries the boy? Everyone should notice gender, ethnic, and age differences, but interpretation of such differences is not straightforward. This scene may or may not reflect male–female roles.

**Answer to Observation Quiz** (from p. 349): Both parents are women. The evidence shows that families with same-sex parents are similar in many ways to families with opposite-sex parents, and children in such families develop well.

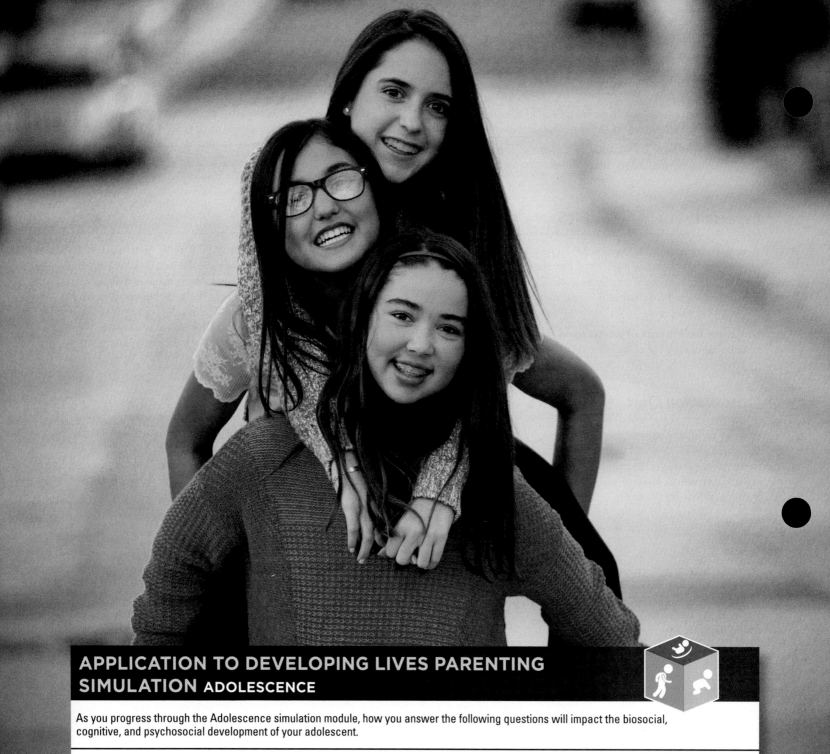

# APPLICATION TO DEVELOPING LIVES PARENTING SIMULATION ADOLESCENCE

As you progress through the Adolescence simulation module, how you answer the following questions will impact the biosocial, cognitive, and psychosocial development of your adolescent.

| | Biosocial | Cognitive | Psychosocial |
|---|---|---|---|
| | • Will your child experiment with smoking, drinking, or drugs during adolescence?<br>• How will you respond if you learn your child is experimenting with drugs?<br>• How will you encourage your child to spend his or her free time after school (sports, part-time job)? | • Which of Piaget's stages of cognitive development is your child in?<br>• What kind of path do you see your teenager pursuing after high school (college, military, work program)? | • How will you respond if your adolescent is struggling to fit in with peers?<br>• How often do you think you and your teenager will have conflicts?<br>• How social will your child be during his or her teen years?<br>• How much privacy will you grant your teenager?<br>• How will you respond when your teenager starts dating? |

# Adolescence

# PART V

A century ago, puberty began at age 15 or so. Soon after that age, most girls married and most boys found work. It is said that *adolescence begins with biology and ends with culture*. If so, then a hundred years ago, adolescence lasted a few months.

Now, adolescence lasts for years. Puberty starts at age 10 or so, and adult responsibilities may be avoided for decades. Indeed, a few observers describe a *Peter Pan syndrome* — men who "won't grow up," too self-absorbed to love and care for anyone else (Kiley, 1983; Snow, 2015). That is unfair to men and to teenagers, but even at age 18, almost no adolescent is ready for all of the responsibilities of adulthood. If high school seniors want marriage, parenthood, and a lifelong career, they should wait at least a few years.

In the next three chapters (covering ages 11 to 18), we begin with biology (Chapter 14), consider cognition (Chapter 15), and then discuss culture (Chapter 16). Adolescence attracts the worst fears of adults, including parents, teachers, police officers, and social workers, yet many children look forward to these years and many adults wish they were young again.

Developmental researchers consider adolescence to be one interval in a long process, as patterns and events can push a teenager toward early death or toward a long, satisfying life. Understanding the possibilities and pitfalls of these years catapults us all toward happy adulthood. ●●

# Adolescence: Biosocial Development

## What Will You Know?

1. How can you predict when puberty will begin for a particular child?
2. Why do many teenagers ignore their nutritional needs?
3. What makes teenage sex often a problem instead of a joy?

**P**uberty was not easy for me. We moved two weeks before my 11th birthday. I left a suburban home with a backyard for an urban row house; I left a single-sex school and enrolled mid-year of the sixth grade, in a school with boys. In retrospect, that move served me well.

- I made friends who accepted me because they had been rejected by the popular clique. One was Mormon, one was Jewish, one was new to the school because she had just moved from Germany. They were my first introduction to the larger world; they are all still my friends, decades later.
- Because I could no longer take long walks in the woods alone, I found a public library a block away. I read dozens of books that my elders would never have chosen.
- I learned to talk to boys; 15 years later that helped me marry one of the best.

But puberty itself was stressful, and only now, as I review the biology of that process, do I realize how hard it was. I reached menarche three weeks after I arrived in the new city; I was afraid of my new male classmates and teachers; I was an awkward, pudgy girl who did not know how to sit at my small desk, to style my changing hair, or to dress my new body.

Once I wore my best taffeta dress to school; it was pale blue with black polka dots. One of the popular girls said, "You must be going somewhere special." "Yes," I lied, suddenly aware that my best dress was not appropriate school attire. Even now no one would call me a fashionable dresser, but I feel sorry for that young girl who hoped that dressing up would bring admiration.

This chapter reviews the physical aspects of puberty, and the problems many adolescents have with appearance, peers, and sexuality. Now that I understand that stress accelerates puberty, I sympathize with my 11-year-old self. Changes are difficult for children at every age, but that is particularly true in the middle of sixth grade, when the growth spurt and sexual changes appear unbidden. I hope you gain some sympathy for your younger self as well.

## Puberty Begins

**Puberty** refers to the years of rapid physical growth and sexual maturation that end childhood, producing a person of adult size, shape, and sexuality. It all begins with a cascade of hormones that produce external growth and internal changes, including heightened emotions and sexual desires.

## Sequence

The visible signs of puberty usually begin sometime between ages 9 and 15. Most biological growth ends about four years after the first signs appear, although some individuals (especially boys) add height, weight, and muscle until age 20 or so. Over the past century, the age of puberty has decreased, probably because of nutrition but perhaps because of increased sexualization of the culture (media, advertisements, clothes).

For girls, the first observable sign is usually nipple growth. Soon a few pubic hairs are visible, followed by a peak growth spurt, widening of the hips, first menstrual period (**menarche**), full pubic-hair pattern, and breast maturation. The average age of menarche in the United States is about 12 years, 4 months (Biro et al., 2013), although nutrition, genes, and stress affect the timing (Brix et al., 2019).

For boys, the usual sequence is growth of the testes, initial pubic-hair growth, growth of the penis, first ejaculation of seminal fluid (**spermarche**), appearance of facial hair, a peak growth spurt, deepening of the voice, and final pubic-hair growth (Dorn & Biro, 2011). The typical age of spermarche is 13 years, almost a year later than menarche.

Age varies markedly. The averages here are for well-nourished adolescents in the United States. Malnutrition delays the start; stress advances it; genes always matter.

## Unseen Beginnings

The changes just listed are visible, but the entire process begins with an invisible event—a marked increase in hormones.

Hormone production is regulated deep within the brain, where biochemical signals from the hypothalamus signal another brain structure, the **pituitary**. The pituitary produces hormones that stimulate the **adrenal glands**, located above the kidneys at either side of the lower back.

These glands produce more hormones. Many hormones that regulate puberty follow this route, the **HPA (hypothalamus–pituitary–adrenal) axis** (see **Figure 14.1**).

## Sex Hormones

Late in childhood, the pituitary activates not only the adrenal glands—the HPA axis—but also the **gonads**, or sex glands (ovaries in females; testes, or testicles,

**puberty** The time between the first onrush of hormones and full adult physical development. Puberty usually lasts three to five years. Many more years are required to achieve psychosocial maturity.

**menarche** A girl's first menstrual period, signaling that she has begun ovulation. Pregnancy is biologically possible, but ovulation and menstruation are often irregular for years after menarche.

**spermarche** A boy's first ejaculation of sperm. Erections can occur as early as infancy, but ejaculation signals sperm production. Spermarche may occur during sleep (in a "wet dream") or via direct stimulation.

**pituitary** A gland in the brain that responds to a signal from the hypothalamus by producing many hormones, including those that regulate growth and sexual maturation.

**adrenal glands** Two glands, located above the kidneys, that respond to the pituitary, producing hormones.

**HPA (hypothalamus–pituitary–adrenal) axis** A sequence of hormone production originating in the hypothalamus and moving to the pituitary and then to the adrenal glands.

**gonads** The paired sex glands (ovaries in females, testicles in males). The gonads produce hormones and mature gametes.

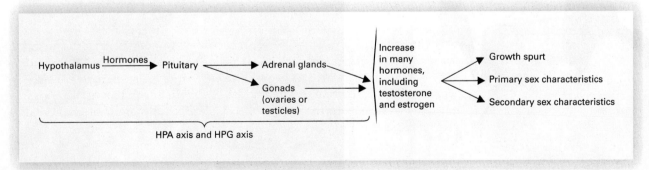

**FIGURE 14.1**
**Biological Sequence of Puberty** Puberty begins with a hormonal signal from the hypothalamus to the pituitary gland, both deep within the brain. The pituitary, in turn, sends a hormonal message through the bloodstream to the adrenal glands and the gonads to produce more hormones.

**HPG (hypothalamus–pituitary–gonad) axis** A sequence of hormone production originating in the hypothalamus and moving to the pituitary and then to the gonads.

**estradiol** A sex hormone, considered the chief estrogen. Females produce much more estradiol than males do.

**testosterone** A sex hormone, the best known of the androgens (male hormones); secreted in far greater amounts by males than by females.

in males), following another sequence called the **HPG (hypothalamus–pituitary–gonad) axis**.

One hormone in particular, *GnRH* (*gonadotropin-releasing hormone*), causes the gonads to enlarge and dramatically increase their production of sex hormones, chiefly **estradiol** in girls and **testosterone** in boys. These hormones affect the body's shape and function, producing more hormones that regulate stress and immunity.

As you recall, hormones are body chemicals that regulate hunger, sleep, moods, stress, sexual desire, immunity, reproduction, and many other bodily functions and processes, including puberty. Throughout adolescence, hormone levels correlate with physiological changes, brain restructuring, and self-reported developments (Goddings et al., 2012; Vijayakumar et al., 2018).

*Estrogens* (including estradiol) are female hormones, and *androgens* (including testosterone) are male hormones, although each sex has some of both. The ovaries produce high levels of estrogens, and the testes produce dramatic increases in androgens. This "surge of hormones" affects bodies, brains, and behavior before any visible signs of puberty appear, "well before the teens" (Peper & Dahl, 2013, p. 134).

The activated gonads soon produce mature ova or sperm. Conception is possible, although peak fertility occurs four to six years later. This is crucial information for teenagers who are sexually active: Some mistakenly believe they cannot become pregnant because they had sex in the past without protection, and no pregnancy occurred. A few years later, that myth may lead to conception.

Hormonal increases may also precipitate psychopathology. Adolescence is the peak time for the emergence of many disorders, with early puberty particularly hazardous (Hamlat et al., 2019). The rush of hormones puts some vulnerable children over the edge.

Stress and genes also matter: Hormones are never the sole cause (Roberts & Lopez-Duran, 2019). Probably because of sex differences in hormones, adolescent males are almost twice as likely as females to develop schizophrenia, and females are more than twice as likely to become severely depressed.

## Hormones and Relationships

If a teenager has emotional problems, no matter what their origin, relationships with other people are crucial. This is evident not only with parents and peers, but also with medical professionals and psychotherapists. When a troubled adolescent develops a good relationship with a therapist, psychopathology is limited.

**Do They See Beauty?** Both young women—the Mexican 15-year-old preparing for her Quinceañara and the Malaysian teen applying a rice facial mask—look wistful, even worried. They are typical of teenage girls everywhere, who do not realize how lovely they are.

Therapists who specialize in treating adolescents understand this and prioritize relationship-building.

This is good news for adults who are aware of the hazards of puberty. For example, one study found that about two-thirds of adolescents receiving psychotherapy report becoming markedly better, as compared to those who sought therapy but were put on a waiting list. Success seems about equally likely for every gender and for adolescents of all ethnic groups, although some conditions (anxiety) have a better improvement rate than others (depression) (Weisz et al., 2017).

For everyone, one psychological effect of estrogen and testosterone is new interest in sexuality. This is evident at the very beginning of puberty, when children become interested in the other gender (who used to be avoided or disparaged) or attracted to members of the same sex (again an unanticipated surprise). This onset of sexual interest can cause joy or depression, depending more on social circumstances than on hormones.

Usually the object of a young adolescent's first attraction is safely unattainable—a film star, a popular singer, a teacher—but by mid-adolescence, fantasies may settle on another young person. Sexual orientation and gender roles and identity are increasingly complex because of the combination of puberty, norms, and variations—a topic discussed in Chapter 16.

Although emotional surges, nurturant impulses, and lustful urges arise with hormones, remember that body, brain, and behavior always interact. Sexual thoughts themselves can *cause* physiological and neurological processes, not just result from them. Cortisol may rise in puberty, and that makes adolescents quick to react with passion, fury, or ecstasy (Goddings et al., 2012; Klein & Romeo, 2013). Then those emotions, in turn, increase various other hormones. Bodies, brains, and behavior all affect one another.

For example, adult reactions to a young person's emerging breasts or beards evoke adolescent thoughts and frustrations, which then raise hormone levels, propel physiological development, and trigger more emotions. Because of hormones, emotions are more likely to be expressed during adolescence (with shouts and tears), which affects everyone's reactions. Thus, the internal and external changes of puberty are reciprocal, each affecting the other.

## Body Rhythms

Because of hormones, the brain of every living creature responds to environmental changes over the hours, days, and seasons. Among the known biorhythms: Children gain weight more rapidly in winter and grow taller more quickly in summer. Another example is *seasonal affective disorder (SAD)*, when people develop symptoms of depression in winter. Those are seasonal changes, but many biorhythms are on a 24-hour cycle, called the **circadian rhythm**. (*Circadian* means "about a day.") Puberty interacts with biorhythms.

For most people, daylight awakens the brain. That's why people experiencing jet lag are urged to take an early-morning walk. But at puberty, night may be more energizing, making some teens wide awake and hungry at midnight but half asleep, with no appetite or energy, all morning. Teenagers become "night owls" more than "early birds" (Gariépy et al., 2018).

In addition to circadian changes at puberty, some individuals (especially males) are naturally more alert in the evening than in the morning, a trait called *eveningness*. To some extent, this is genetic: 351 genes differ in people who are natural "larks" or "owls" (Jones et al., 2019)). Puberty plus eveningness increases risk (drugs, sex, delinquency): Many teenagers are awake when adults are asleep.

Watching late-night TV, working on a computer, or texting friends at 10 P.M. interferes with sleepiness. Any screen time in the evening correlates with later

**LaunchPad**
macmillan learning

**VIDEO: The Timing of Puberty** depicts the usual sequence of physical development for adolescents.

**circadian rhythm** A day–night cycle of biological activity that occurs approximately every 24 hours.

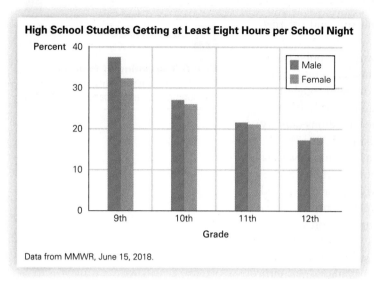

**High School Students Getting at Least Eight Hours per School Night**

Data from MMWR, June 15, 2018.

**FIGURE 14.2**

**Sleepyheads** Three of every four high school seniors are sleep deprived. Even if they go to sleep at midnight, as many do, they must get up before 8 A.M., as almost all do. Then they are tired all day.

 **Observation Quiz** As you see, the problems are worse for the girls. Why is that? (see answer, page 395) ↑

sleep, with social media and Web surfing particularly influential (Hisler et al., 2020). Probably because those activate thoughts as well as biological processes, adolescents have a harder time sleeping when they finally turn out the light.

Schools that provide each student a tablet for homework warn against bedroom use. However, the powerful adolescent urge to stay in touch with friends results in sleeping next to their smartphones—and then they are sleep deprived, nodding off in class. Further, classes are slow and boring compared to video games and human relationship dramas.

Sleep deprivation and irregular sleep schedules increase insomnia, nightmares, mood disorders (depression, conduct disorder, anxiety), and falling asleep while driving. Adolescents are particularly vulnerable to all of these, and tiredness makes it worse (see **Figure 14.2**). In addition, sleepy students do not learn as well as well-rested ones.

Oblivious to adolescent biorhythms, some parents set early curfews or stay awake until their child comes home at night. They might drag their teenager out of bed for school—the same child who, a decade earlier, was commanded to stay in bed until dawn.

Some municipalities fight adolescent biology when they implement community safety measures. In 2014, Baltimore implemented a law that required everyone under age 14 to be home by 9 P.M. and 14- to 16-year-olds to be off the streets by 10 P.M. on school nights and 11 P.M. on weekends. The assumption was that home is a safe place where teenagers will stay out of trouble.

Many high schools remain stuck in schedules set before the hazards of sleep deprivation were known. Although "the science is there; the will to change is not" (Snider, 2012, p. 25). In August 2014, the American Academy of Pediatrics concluded that high schools should not begin until 8:30 or 9 A.M., because adolescent sleep deprivation causes a cascade of intellectual, behavioral, and health problems. The doctors were distressed to report that 43 percent of high schools in the United States start *before* 8 A.M.

Some schools have instituted later start times. One study compared 29 high schools, across seven states, before and after they started school later than 8:30 A.M. Graduation rates increased from 79 to 88 percent, and average daily attendance rose from 90 to 94 percent (McKeever & Clark, 2017). Similar results were found when the city of Seattle began school at 8:45 A.M. instead of 7:50 A.M., with improvement particularly apparent in students from low-SES families (Dunster et al., 2018).

The reality that genes and family affect the circadian rhythm, and that many Western parents grant substantial freedom to their adolescents, raise a question: Is sleep deprivation more problematic for European American teenagers? If parents are lax about bedtime, computer use, and sleeping patterns, might that cause the problems just mentioned?

It seems, however, that adolescent biology is universal, changing circadian rhythms. For example, a study of Mexican American adolescents found that, although parent sleep had some influence, youths were more often awake late at night after their parents were asleep (Bai et al., 2020). Eveningness peaked at about age 16, which is also true for adolescents from other groups. The researchers reported that substance use correlated with late bedtimes, as is also found among teenagers of other groups.

Most developmentalists, pediatricians, and education researchers wonder why adult traditions are preserved while adolescent learning is ignored. There is good news here, however. As the evidence accumulates, schools are postponing their start times, and teenagers are learning more (Lo et al., 2018).

## Brain Growth

A more ominous example of the disconnect between what science tells us and what adolescent brains do concerns cars, guns, sex, and drugs, all of which result in injury and even death. A chilling example comes from teenage driving (legal at age 16 in most U.S. localities). Per mile driven, teenage drivers are three times more likely to die in a motor-vehicle crash than drivers over age 20 (Insurance Institute for Highway Safety, 2018).

### Sequence of Brain Changes

Many aspects of adolescent body growth are uneven. One breast, one foot, or one ear may be bigger than the other—awkward, but harmless. However, the usual sequence of brain maturation, propelled by hormones that activate the limbic system at puberty, is dangerous.

To be specific, the prefrontal cortex matures steadily, advancing gradually as time goes on. Executive function—long-term planning, postponing gratification, thinking flexibly—is better in adults than in young adolescents, because of maturation of the prefrontal cortex. The limbic system, however, is affected more by hormones (the HPG axis) than by time and thus grows dramatically in early adolescence.

Pubertal hormones target the amygdala directly (Romeo, 2013). The instinctual and emotional areas of the adolescent brain develop ahead of the reflective, analytic areas. Puberty means emotional rushes, unchecked by caution. Powerful sensations—loud music, speeding cars, strong drugs—become compelling. Adolescents brag about being wasted, smashed, out of their minds—all conditions that adults try to avoid.

Immediate impulses thwart long-term planning and reflection. My friend said to his neighbor, who had given his son a red convertible as a high school graduation gift, "Why didn't you just give him a loaded gun?" The mother of the 20-year-old who killed 20 first-graders and 7 adults in 2012 in Newtown, Connecticut, did just that. He killed her, too.

Sadly, that is not an isolated example. Guns, including those never used in hunting or target practice, are available to adolescents, who increasingly use them to kill other adolescents or themselves. About three-fourths of all suicides in the United States are by firearms, a rate higher than in other nations (MMWR, March 6, 2020). Especially in adolescence, suicides are often impulsive, which is why suicide by pills is uncommon—that takes time.

It is not that the prefrontal cortex shuts down. Actually, it continues to develop throughout adolescence and beyond (see **Figure 14.3**). Maturation doesn't stop, but the emotional hot spots of the brain zoom ahead. A study compared 886 adolescents (ages 9 to 16) and their parents (average age 44) in Hong Kong and England. All participants were asked questions to assess executive function. The adolescents were less accurate but notably quicker, another indication that the limbic system races ahead while the prefrontal cortex slowly matures (Ellefson et al., 2017).

When stress, arousal, passion, sensory bombardment, drug intoxication, or deprivation is extreme, the adolescent brain is flooded with impulses that overwhelm the cortex. Adults try to keep their thoughts straight, but adolescents may prefer such flooding. Many teenagers choose to spend a night without sleep, to eat nothing all day, to exercise in pain, to play music at deafening loudness, and to drink until they black out.

**THINK CRITICALLY:** If a child seems to be unusually short or unusually slow in reaching puberty, would you give the child hormones? Why or why not?

**FIGURE 14.3**

**Same People, But Not the Same Brain**
These brain scans are part of a longitudinal study that repeatedly compared the proportion of gray matter from childhood through adolescence. (Gray matter refers to the cell bodies of neurons, which are less prominent with age as some neurons are unused.) Gray matter is reduced as white matter increases, in part because pruning during the teen years (the last two pairs of images here) allows intellectual connections to build. As the authors of one study that included this chart explained, teenagers may look "like an adult, but cognitively they are not there yet" (Powell, 2006, p. 865).

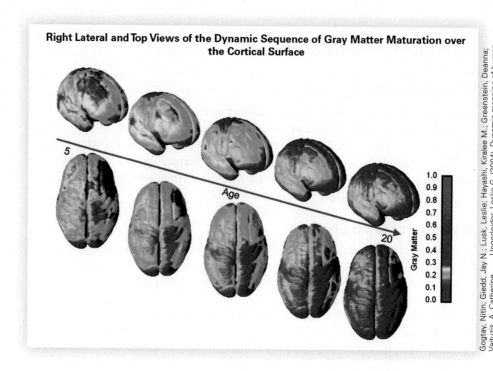

Right Lateral and Top Views of the Dynamic Sequence of Gray Matter Maturation over the Cortical Surface

Gogtay, Nitin; Giedd, Jay N.; Lusk, Leslie; Hayashi, Kiralee M.; Greenstein, Deanna; Vaituzis, A. Catherine, . . . Ungerleider, Leslie G. (2004). Dynamic mapping of human cortical development during childhood through early adulthood. *Proceedings of the National Academy of Sciences of the United States of America, 101*(21), 8174–81. Copyright ©2004 National Academy of Sciences, U.S.A.

A common example comes from reading and sending text messages while driving. Teenagers know that this is illegal almost everywhere, but the "ping" of a text message evokes emotions that compel attention. In one survey of U.S. high school seniors who had driven a car in the past month, 39 percent had texted while driving (MMWR, June 15, 2018). This neurological disconnect is further explained in the following.

## When Will Puberty Begin?

Normally, pubertal hormones begin to accelerate sometime between ages 8 and 14, and visible signs of puberty appear between ages 9 and 15. That six-year range is too great for many parents, teachers, and children, who want to know exactly when a given child will begin puberty. Fortunately, if a child's genes, gender, body fat, and stress level are known, prediction within a year or two is possible.

### Genes and Gender

Genetic sex differences in hormones have a marked effect. In height, the average pubescent girl is about two years ahead of the average boy. Hormones affect sequence as well. The female height spurt occurs *before* menarche; the male increase in height occurs *after* spermarche.

Therefore, unlike height, for hormonal and sexual changes, girls are less than a year ahead of boys. Indeed, a recent study of thousands of Danish teenagers found that the boys took about four years from the beginning to the end of puberty, while the girls took five years. This means that by age 15 the two genders were about equal (Brix et al., 2019).

Thus, a short sixth-grade boy with sexual fantasies about the taller girls in his class is neither perverted nor precocious; his hormones are simply ahead of his height. It also means that, by the last years of high school, most romantic relationships are between students about the same age.

Overall, about two-thirds of age variations in onset of puberty is genetic—not only in the genes associated with the XX or XY chromosomes but also in the genes common in families and ethnic groups. If both of a child's parents were early or late to reach puberty, the child will likely be early or late as well.

# Lopsided Growth

Laurence Steinberg is a noted expert on adolescence (e.g., Steinberg, 2014, 2015). He is also a father.

> When my son, Benjamin, was 14, he and three of his friends decided to sneak out of the house where they were spending the night and visit one of their girlfriends at around two in the morning. When they arrived at the girl's house, they positioned themselves under her bedroom window, threw pebbles against her windowpanes, and tried to scale the side of the house. Modern technology, unfortunately, has made it harder to play Romeo these days. The boys set off the house's burglar alarm, which activated a siren and simultaneously sent a direct notification to the local police station, which dispatched a patrol car. When the siren went off, the boys ran down the street and right smack into the police car, which was heading to the girl's home. Instead of stopping and explaining their activity, Ben and his friends scattered and ran off in different directions through the neighborhood. One of the boys was caught by the police and taken back to his home, where his parents were awakened and the boy questioned.
>
> I found out about this affair the following morning, when the girl's mother called our home to tell us what Ben had done. . . . After his near brush with the local police, Ben had returned to the house out of which he had snuck, where he slept soundly until I awakened him with an angry telephone call, telling him to gather his clothes and wait for me in front of his friend's house. On our drive home, after delivering a long lecture about what he had done and about the dangers of running from armed police in the dark when they believe they may have interrupted a burglary, I paused.
>
> "What were you thinking?" I asked.
>
> "That's the problem, Dad," Ben replied, "I wasn't."
>
> *[Steinberg, 2004, pp. 51, 52]*

Steinberg's son was right: When emotions are intense, especially when friends are nearby, cortisol floods the brain, causing the prefrontal cortex to shut down. This shutdown is not reflected in questionnaires that require teenagers to respond to paper-and-pencil questions regarding hypothetical dilemmas. On those tests, most teenagers think carefully and answer correctly.

In fact, when strong emotions are not activated, teenagers may be more logical than adults (Casey & Caudle, 2013). They remember facts learned in biology or health class about sex and drugs. They know exactly how HIV is transmitted, how pregnancy occurs, and how alcohol affects the brain. However,

the prospect of visiting a hypothetical girl from class cannot possibly carry the excitement about the possibility of surprising someone you have a crush on with a visit in the middle of the night. It is easier to put on a hypothetical condom during an act of hypothetical sex than it is to put on a real one when one is in the throes of passion. It is easier to just say no to a hypothetical beer than it is to a cold frosty one on a summer night.

*[Steinberg, 2004, p. 53]*

Ben reached adulthood safely. Other teenagers, with less cautious police or less diligent parents, do not. Brain immaturity makes teenagers vulnerable to social pressures and stresses, which typically bombard young people today. Emotional control, revealed by fMRI studies, is not fully developed until adulthood, because the prefrontal cortex is less connected to the limbic system (Hartley & Somerville, 2015). Thoughtful reappraisal of emotional impulses is slower in adolescence than later on (Schweizer et al., 2020; Silvers et al., 2015).

Longitudinal research finds that heightened arousal occurs in the brain's reward centers—specifically the *nucleus accumbens*, a region of the ventral striatum that is connected to the limbic system—when adolescent brains are compared to their own brains earlier or later in development (Braams et al., 2015).

When other teens are watching, adolescents thrill to take dramatic risks that produce social acclaim, risks they would not dare take alone. Interestingly, the reward regions that are highly activated when peers are watching decrease in activation when the adolescent's mother is nearby (Telzer et al., 2015).

The research on adolescent brain development confirms two insights regarding adolescent growth in general. First, physiological changes triggered by puberty are dramatic, unlike those of either childhood or adulthood. Second, the social context matters—the body and brain of humans respond not only to hormones and physical maturation but also to friends and family.

Most states in the United States now restrict drivers under age 18, such as mandating no passengers under age 20, or only family members as passengers. That saves lives, because teenagers are less likely to race a train, pass a truck, or zoom around a blind curve when no peers are watching.

On average, African Americans reach puberty about several months before European or Hispanic Americans; Chinese Americans average several months later. These are generalities: Remember that genetic differences *within* each group are greater than differences *between* groups.

The emotional significance of puberty is more gender than sex, more cultural than genetic. Nonetheless, genes exert a strong influence on the biology of puberty (Howard, 2018).

## Body Fat and Chemicals

Another influence on the onset of puberty is body fat, which itself is partly genetic and partly cultural. Body fat is clearly associated with earlier puberty for girls. The effects are more variable for boys: Being overweight seems to accelerate puberty, but being obese slows it down (Reinehr & Roth, 2019). The reasons are probably hormonal: For boys, body fat may interfere with expression of male hormones.

In some nations, inadequate food delays growth of every kind. But, in developed nations, poor eating habits can result in overweight and, thus, early puberty. This is suggested by a study that found that girls who regularly drank several sugar-sweetened beverages each day were likely to experience earlier menarche (Carwile et al., 2015).

Malnutrition explains why youths reach puberty later in some parts of Africa, while their genetic relatives in North America mature much earlier. For example, in Ghana (West Africa) girls in the rural areas reach menarche more than a year later (almost age 14) than African American girls in the United States (just past 12). Even within Ghana, girls in rural areas—where malnutrition is more common—are behind those in urban areas (Ameade & Garti, 2016).

A more dramatic example arises from sixteenth-century Europe. Puberty is thought to have begun several years later than it does today, because those Europeans were often hungry. All of the data suggest that over the past three centuries, puberty has begun at younger and younger ages.

**secular trend** The long-term upward or downward direction of a certain set of statistical measurements, as opposed to a smaller, shorter cyclical variation. As an example, over the past two centuries, because of improved nutrition and medical care, children have tended to reach their adult height earlier and their adult height has increased.

This is an example of what is called the **secular trend**, which is earlier or greater growth as nutrition and medicine improved. Increased food availability has led to more weight gain in childhood, promoting earlier puberty and taller average height. Throughout the nineteenth and twentieth centuries, because of the secular trend, every generation reached puberty before the previous one (Brix et al., 2019; Dorn & Biro, 2011).

One curious bit of evidence of the secular trend is in the height of U.S. presidents. James Madison, the fourth president, was shortest at 5 feet, 4 inches; recent presidents have been much taller. Obama was 6 feet, 1 inch, and Trump says he is 6 feet, 3 inches (although some sources say he is not quite that tall).

The secular trend has stopped in most nations because childhood nutrition allows everyone to attain their genetic potential. Young men no longer look down

**Both the Same?** Yes, they are former U.S. presidents. But what a difference 150 years makes! James Madison *(left)* was the fourth president of the United States, was popular and respected, and at 5 feet, 4 inches tall weighed about 100 pounds. Barack Obama *(right)*, the 44th president, was 6 feet, 1 inch tall, and Donald Trump (#45) is said to be 6 feet, 3 inches tall. Lincoln (#16) was tallest of all—6 feet, 4 inches—which then was a reason to mock his appearance.

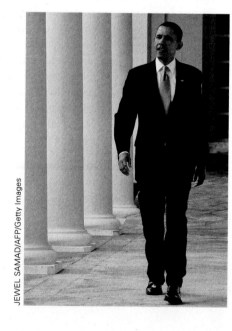

Photo Researchers/Science History Images/Alamy Stock Photo

JEWEL SAMAD/AFP/Getty Images

at their short fathers, or girls at their mothers, unless their parents were born in nations where hunger was common. Future presidents will not be taller than those in the recent past.

Some scientists suspect that precocious (before age 8) or delayed (after age 14) puberty may be caused by hormones in the food supply. Cattle are fed steroids to increase bulk and milk production, and hundreds of chemicals and hormones are used to produce most of the food that children consume. All of these substances *might* affect appetite, body fat, and sex hormones, with effects at puberty (Bourguignon et al., 2016).

**Leptin**, a hormone that is naturally produced by the human body, definitely affects the onset of puberty. Leptin is essential for appetite, energy, and puberty. However, too much leptin correlates with obesity, early puberty, and then early termination of growth. Thus, the heaviest third-grade girl may become the tallest fifth-grader and then the shortest high school graduate.

Most research on leptin has been done with mice; the effects are more complicated for humans (Bohlen et al., 2016). In fact, none of the data on the effects on humans of hormones and other chemicals, whether natural or artificial, are easy to interpret. The female body may be especially sensitive not only to leptin, but also to many other influences. Precise details require much more research, but we do know that many hormones and chemicals, both natural and artificial, affect puberty (Araki & Jensen, 2020; M. Wolff et al., 2015).

**leptin** A hormone that affects appetite and is believed to affect the onset of puberty. Leptin levels increase during childhood and peak at around age 12.

**Especially for Parents Worried About Early Puberty** Suppose your cousin's 9-year-old daughter has just had her first period, and your cousin blames hormones in the food supply for this "precocious" puberty. Should you change your young daughter's diet? (see response, page 395)

## Stress

Stress hastens puberty, especially if a child's parents are sick, drug-addicted, or divorced, or if the neighborhood is violent and impoverished. One study of sexually abused girls found that they began puberty as much as a year earlier than they otherwise would have, a result attributed not only to stress but also to the hormones activated by sexual contact (Noll et al., 2017). Particularly for girls who are genetically sensitive, puberty comes early if their family interaction is stressful but late if their family is supportive.

This may explain the fact that many internationally adopted children experience early puberty, especially if their first few years of life were in an institution or an abusive home. An alternative explanation is that their age at adoption was underestimated: Puberty then seems early but actually is not (Hayes, 2013).

Developmentalists have known for decades that puberty is influenced by genes, hormones, and body fat. The effect of stress is a newer discovery, as A View from Science explains on the next page.

## Too Early, Too Late

For a society's health, early puberty is problematic: It increases the rate of emotional and behavioral problems, including serious psychopathology (Dimler & Natsuaki, 2015; Hamlat et al., 2019). Early puberty is also linked to later health problems, including breast cancer, diabetes, and stroke (Day et al., 2015). Delayed puberty may also be a sign of health problems, including sickle cell anemia (Alexandre-Heymann et al., 2019).

For most adolescents, these links between puberty, stress, and health are irrelevant. Only one aspect of timing matters: their friends' schedules. No one wants to be too early or too late.

## Girls

Think about the early-maturing girl. If she has visible breasts at age 10, the boys her age tease her; they are unnerved by the womanly creature in their midst. She must fit her developing body into a school chair designed for smaller children; she might hide her breasts in large T-shirts and bulky sweaters; she might refuse to undress for gym. Early-maturing girls tend to have lower self-esteem, more depression, and poorer body image than do other girls (Compian et al., 2009; Galvao et al., 2014).

Some early-maturing girls have older boyfriends, who are attracted to their womanly shape and girlish innocence. Having an older boyfriend bestows status among young adolescents, but it also promotes drug and alcohol use (Mrug et al., 2014).

---

**A VIEW FROM SCIENCE**

## Stress and Puberty

Emotional stress, particularly when it has a sexual component, precipitates puberty. This is not always the case, because differential susceptibility means that some young people are more affected by family stress than others, and girls seem more affected than boys. But many lines of research agree that stress is one factor that can lead to early maturation (Ellis & Del Giudice, 2019).

For example, a large longitudinal study in England compared girls whose biological father lived at home with girls whose father was absent. Typically, in that community, when the father was absent, the mother was stressed and often another man lived with her. On average, their daughters were more depressed and reached menarche earlier (Culpin et al., 2015).

The connection between sexual stress and early puberty seems true in developing nations as well as developed ones. For example, in Peru, if a girl was physically and sexually abused, she was much more likely (odds ratio 1.56) to have her first period before age 11 than if she had not been abused (Barrios et al., 2015).

Hypothetically, the connection between stress and early puberty could be indirect. For example, perhaps children in dysfunctional families eat worse and watch TV more. That makes them overweight, which correlates with early menarche. Or, perhaps they inherit genes for early puberty from their distressed mothers, and those genes led the mothers to become pregnant too young, creating a stressful family.

Either obesity or genes *could* cause early puberty, and then stress would be a by-product, not a cause. Plausible hypothesis—but *not* correct.

Instead, longitudinal research links stress directly to early puberty (Ellis & Del Giudice, 2019). Even stress in early childhood matters. For example, one longitudinal study of 756 children found that parents who demanded respect, who often spanked, and who rarely hugged their infants and young children were, a decade later, likely to have daughters who reached puberty earlier than other girls in the same study (Belsky et al., 2007). Perhaps harsh parenting increases cortisol, which precipitates puberty.

A follow-up of the same girls at age 15, controlling for genetic differences, found that harsh treatment in childhood increased sexual problems (more sex, pregnancies, sexually transmitted infections) but *not* other risks (drugs, crime) (Belsky et al., 2010). This suggests that stress triggers earlier increases of sex hormones but not generalized rebellion. The direct impact of stress on puberty seems proven.

Why would higher cortisol accelerate puberty? The opposite effect—delayed puberty—makes more sense. Then stressed teens would still look and act childlike, which might evoke adult protection rather than lust or anger. Protection is especially needed in conflict-ridden or stressed single-parent homes, yet such homes produce earlier puberty and less parental nurturance. Is this a biological mistake? Not according to evolutionary theory:

> Maturing quickly and breeding promiscuously would enhance reproductive fitness more than would delaying development, mating cautiously, and investing heavily in parenting. The latter strategy, in contrast, would make biological sense, for virtually the same reproductive-fitness-enhancing reasons, under conditions of contextual support and nurturance.
>
> [Belsky et al., 2010, p. 121]

In other words, thousands of years ago, when harsh conditions threatened survival of the species, adolescents needed to reproduce early and often, lest the entire community become extinct. By contrast, in peaceful times, with plentiful food and loving care, puberty could occur later, allowing children to postpone maturity and instead enjoy extra years of nurturance from their biological parents and grandparents. Genes evolved to respond differently to war and peace.

Of course, this evolutionary benefit no longer applies. Today, early sexual activity and reproduction are more destructive than protective of communities. However, since the genome has been shaped over millennia, a puberty-starting allele that responds to stress will respond in the twenty-first century as it did thousands of years ago. This idea complements the idea of differential susceptibility (Harkness, 2014). Because of genetic protections, not every distressed girl experiences early puberty, but also for genetic reasons, family stress may speed up age of menarche.

Early-maturing girls enter abusive relationships more often than other girls do. Is that because their social judgment is immature?

## Boys

For girls, early maturation is more harmful than helpful no matter when they were born, but for boys time and place matter. Early-maturing boys who were born around 1930 in the United States often became leaders in high school and earned more money as adults (Jones, 1965; Taga et al., 2006). Since about 1960, however, the risks associated with early male maturation have outweighed the benefits.

In the twenty-first century, early-maturing boys are more aggressive, lawbreaking, and alcohol-abusing than the average boy (Mendle et al., 2012). Although most of the research on the effects of puberty on male delinquency has been on U.S. boys, similar findings come from elsewhere, including a large study in China (Sun et al., 2016).

It is not hard to figure out why. A boy with rapidly increasing testosterone, whose body looks more like a man than a child, whose brain is more affected by emotions than logic, and who seeks approval from peers, is likely to trouble parents, schools, and the police.

Early puberty is particularly stressful if it happens suddenly: The boys most likely to become depressed are those for whom puberty was both early and quick (Mendle et al., 2010). In adolescence, depression is often masked as anger. That fuming, flailing 12-year-old may be more sad than mad.

Late puberty may also be difficult, especially for boys (Benoit et al., 2013). Slow-developing boys tend to be more anxious, depressed, and afraid of sex. Girls are less attracted to them, coaches select them for their teams, peers bully or tease them. If a 14-year-old boy still looks childish, he may react in ways (clowning, fighting, isolating) that are not healthy for him.

**Ancient Rivals or New Friends?** One of the best qualities of adolescents is that they identify more with their generation than their ethnic group, here Turkish and German. Do the expressions of these 13-year-olds convey respect or hostility? Impossible to be sure, but given that they are both about mid-puberty (face shape, height, shoulder size), and both in the same school, they may become friends.

## Ethnic Differences

The specific impact of early puberty varies by both gender and culture. For instance, one study found that, in contrast to European Americans, early-maturing African American girls were not depressed, but early-maturing African American boys were (Hamlat et al., 2014a, 2014b). Another study found that Mexican American boys thought less of themselves as pubertal changes continued, except in one domain—their relationships with girls (Harris et al., 2017).

European research found that early-maturing Swedish girls were likely to encounter problems with boys and early drug abuse, but similar Slovak girls were not, presumably because parents and social norms kept Slovak girls under tight control (Skoog & Stattin, 2014).

Social context also matters in the United States. Early-maturing Mexican American boys experienced trouble (with police and with peers) if their neighborhoods had few Mexican Americans, but not if they lived in ethnic enclaves (R. White et al., 2013). On their home turf, they were leaders, not troublemakers. They responded accordingly.

Puberty that is late by world norms, at age 14 or so, is not troubling if one's friends are late as well. However, if students in the same large high school have diverse ethnic and genetic roots, the fact that some look like tall children and others like grown adults may create tension. Contextual factors interact with biological ones. Peers, parents, and communities make off-time puberty insignificant or a major problem.

**WHAT HAVE YOU LEARNED?**

1. What are the first visible signs of puberty?

2. What body parts of a teenage boy or girl are the last to reach full growth?

3. How do hormones affect the physical and psychological aspects of puberty?

4. Why do adolescents experience sudden, intense emotions?

5. How does the circadian rhythm affect adolescents?

6. What are the consequences of sleep deprivation?

7. What are the ethnic and cultural differences in the timing of puberty?

8. How are girls affected by early puberty?

9. How are boys affected by off-time puberty?

## Growth and Nutrition

Puberty entails transformation of every body part, with each change affecting all of the others. Here, we discuss biological growth and the nutrition that fuels that growth. Then we will focus on sexual maturation.

## Growing Bigger and Stronger

**growth spurt** The relatively sudden and rapid physical growth that occurs during puberty. Each body part increases in size on a schedule: Weight usually precedes height, and growth of the limbs precedes growth of the torso.

The first set of changes is called the **growth spurt**—a sudden, uneven jump in size that turns children into adults. Growth proceeds from the extremities to the core (the opposite of the earlier proximodistal growth). Thus, fingers and toes lengthen before hands and feet, hands and feet before arms and legs, arms and legs before the torso. Because the torso is the last body part to grow, many pubescent children are temporarily big-footed, long-legged, and short-waisted.

If young teenagers complain that their jeans don't fit, they are probably correct—even if those same jeans fit when their parents bought them a month earlier. (Advance warning about rapid body growth occurs when parents first have to buy their children's shoes in the adult section.)

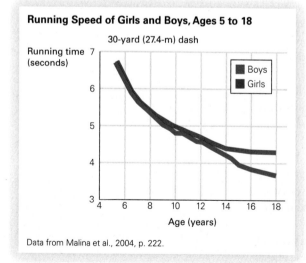

**Running Speed of Girls and Boys, Ages 5 to 18**

30-yard (27.4-m) dash

Running time (seconds) — Boys / Girls

Age (years)

Data from Malina et al., 2004, p. 222.

**FIGURE 14.4**

**Little Difference** Both sexes develop longer and stronger legs during puberty.

## Sequence: Weight, Height, Muscles

As the growth spurt begins, children eat more and gain weight. Exactly when, where, and how much weight they gain depends on heredity, hormones, diet, exercise, and whether they are boys or girls. By age 17, the average girl's body has twice as much body fat as the average boy. Of course, genes and exercise influence body shape; gender and maturation are far from the only influences on body composition.

A height spurt follows the weight spurt. A year or two later, a muscle spurt occurs. Thus, the pudginess and clumsiness of early puberty are usually gone by late adolescence. Keep in mind, however, that puberty may dislodge the usual relationship between height and weight. A child may be eating too much or too little, but that may not be apparent in conventional measures of BMI (Golden et al., 2012).

In the years after puberty, all of the muscles grow. Arm muscles develop particularly in boys, doubling in strength from ages 8 to 18. Other muscles are gender-neutral. For instance, both sexes run faster with each year of adolescence, with boys not much faster than girls (unless the girls choose to slow down) (see **Figure 14.4**).

Muscles are heavier than fat, so merely comparing weight and height, as BMI does, may make it seem as if a strong adolescent is overweight—but that may be inaccurate. Consider athletic activity. If a particular teenage boy is among the 35 percent who are physically active at least an hour every day, he can have a BMI above 25 (technically overweight) and still be in good physical shape. The same applies to girls: 18 percent of them are active every day (MMWR, June 15, 2018).

## Organ Growth

Lungs triple in weight; consequently, adolescents breathe more deeply and slowly. The heart (another muscle) doubles in size as the heartbeat slows, decreasing the pulse rate while increasing blood pressure. Consequently, endurance improves: Some teenagers run for miles or dance for hours. Red blood cells increase, dramatically so in boys, which aids oxygen transport during intense exercise.

Both weight and height increase *before* muscles and internal organs: To protect immature muscles and organs, athletic training and weight lifting should be tailored to an adolescent's size during the previous year. Sports injuries are the most common school accidents, and they increase at puberty. One reason is that the height spurt *precedes* increases in bone mass, making young adolescents particularly vulnerable to fractures.

The other relevant factor is stress—both in competition and in personal life—that accompanies puberty. As stress increases, so does injury, with the average athlete experiencing at least one injury every year. Training should not only be adjusted to the developing body but should also include ways to decrease emotional stress via meditation, mindfulness, deep breathing, and so on (Ivarsson et al., 2017).

One organ system, the lymphoid system (which includes the tonsils and adenoids), *decreases* in size, so teenagers are less susceptible to respiratory ailments. Mild asthma, for example, may switch off at puberty.

In addition, teenagers have fewer colds and allergies than younger children. This reduction in susceptibility is aided by growth of the larynx, which also deepens the voice, dramatically so in boys but also in girls.

Another organ system, the skin, becomes oilier, sweatier, smellier, and more prone to acne—which itself is an early sign of puberty (Brix et al., 2019). Hair also changes, becoming coarser and darker. New hair grows under arms, on faces, and over genitals (pubic hair, from the same Latin root as *puberty*).

## Diet Deficiencies

All of the changes of puberty depend on adequate nourishment, yet many adolescents do not eat well. Teenagers often skip breakfast, binge at midnight, guzzle down unhealthy energy drinks, and munch on salty, processed snacks. In 2017, only 14 percent of U.S. high school seniors ate the recommended three or more servings of vegetables a day (MMWR, June 15, 2018). That is even less than two years earlier (17 percent).

One reason for their eating patterns is that their hormones affect the circadian rhythm of their appetites; another reason is that their drive for independence compels them to avoid family dinners, refusing to eat what their mothers say they should.

Deficiencies of iron, calcium, zinc, and other minerals are especially problematic during adolescence. Because menstruation depletes iron, anemia is more common among adolescent girls than among any other age or sex group. This is true everywhere, especially in South Asia and sub-Saharan Africa, where teenage girls rarely eat iron-rich meat and green vegetables.

**Observation Quiz** Conformity among adolescents may be imposed by adults or chosen by teens. One example of each is evident here—what are they? (see answer, page 395) ↓

**Next Stop: Masterpieces of the Fifteenth Century** These British teens eat chips and soda before they enter the National Gallery in London. Twenty-first century fast food is causing an epidemic of diet deficiencies and disordered eating among youth in every nation.

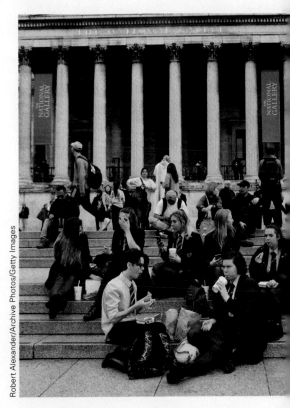

Robert Alexander/Archive Photos/Getty Images

Reliable laboratory analysis of blood iron on a large sample of young girls in developing nations is not available, but all indications suggest that many are anemic. One study of a select group of 168 girls, ages 13 to 16, from one school in India found that two-thirds had anemia, with school grades lower among those who were iron-deficient (Tarun et al., 2016).

Another study on 18- to 23-year-old college women in Saudi Arabia found that a fourth (24 percent) were clinically anemic and another fourth (28 percent) were iron-deficient, although not technically anemic (Al-Sayes et al., 2011). These numbers are especially troubling since almost all college women in Saudi Arabia are in good health, from wealthy families, and have never been pregnant. They are among the better-nourished young women in that nation; rates of anemia are undoubtedly higher among younger, poorer girls.

Boys everywhere may also be iron-deficient, especially if they engage in physical labor or intensive sports: Muscles need iron for growth and strength. Yet, in developed as well as developing nations, adolescents spurn iron-rich foods in favor of chips, sweets, and fries.

Similarly, although the daily recommended intake of calcium for adolescents is 1,300 milligrams, the average U.S. teen consumes less than 500 milligrams a day. About half of adult bone mass is acquired from ages 10 to 20, which means that many contemporary teenagers will develop osteoporosis (fragile bones), a major cause of disability, injury, and death in late adulthood, especially for women.

One reason for calcium deficiency is that milk drinking has declined. In 1961, most North American children drank at least 24 ounces (about three-fourths of a liter) of milk each day, providing almost all (about 900 milligrams) of their daily calcium requirement. Fifty years later, only 8 percent of high school students drank that much milk, and 27 percent (more girls than boys) drank no milk at all in the previous week (MMWR, June 15, 2018).

The decline of milk drinking is one reason for the prevalent deficiency in vitamin D. Skipping breakfast and avoiding dairy products are common for adolescents of every group, particularly African Americans, affecting later health (Van Horn et al., 2011). Some are lactose-intolerant (milk is difficult for them to digest), but they could choose cheese or yogurt. Instead, many choose soda.

## Choices Made

Many economists advocate a "nudge" to encourage people to make better choices, not only in nutrition but also in all other aspects of their lives (Thaler & Sunstein, 2008). Teenagers are often nudged by peers and institutions to make poor choices.

For example, fast-food establishments cluster around high schools, often with extra seating that encourages teenagers to eat and socialize (Walker et al., 2014). This is especially true for high schools with large populations of low-income students, who are most at risk for obesity. This problem seems to be getting worse, not better (Sanchez-Vaznaugh et al., 2019). Price further influences food choices, especially for adolescents: Unhealthy calories are cheaper than healthy ones.

Ethnic and gender factors are also influential. Twenty-two percent of Hispanic girls in U.S. high schools are overweight, as are 21 percent of African American girls. Rates are lower among boys and European Americans (MMWR, June 15, 2018). High schools with many Hispanic or African American students are likely to have fast-food establishments nearby (Sanchez-Vaznaugh et al., 2019).

In rural areas, new high schools are built where land is cheap, and soon a cluster of establishments that cater to students, with salty snacks, e-cigarettes, and sweetened drinks, open nearby.

Rates of obesity are falling in childhood but not in adolescence. In 2003, only three U.S. states (Kentucky, Mississippi, and Tennessee) had high-school obesity rates at

15 percent or more; in 2017, 42 states did (MMWR, June 15, 2018). In Latin America, the nutritional focus is on preventing underweight, not preventing overweight; yet overall, about one teenager in four is overweight or obese (Rivera et al., 2014).

## Body Image

One reason for poor nutrition among teenagers is anxiety about **body image**—that is, the perception of how one's body looks. As one book on body image begins, each person's body "feels, conceives, imagines, represents, evaluates, loves, hates, and manipulates itself" (Cuzzolaro & Fassino, 2018, p. v). This is true lifelong, but since every part of the body changes dramatically in adolescence, the body image must change, too.

Few teenagers welcome every change in their bodies. Instead, they tend to focus on and exaggerate imperfections. They often focus on size and shape. More than half of U.S. high school girls are trying to lose weight, yet only one-sixth are actually overweight or obese (MMWR, June 15, 2018).

One problem is that almost no one has a body like those in magazines, movies, and television programs that are marketed to teenagers. Social media, which features posts of other teens at their most attractive, may lead to depression, body shame, and poor eating habits (Rodgers et al., 2020; Salomon & Brown, 2019).

Unhappiness with appearance—especially with weight for girls—is documented worldwide, including in South Korea, China, Australia, and Greece (Argyrides & Kkeli, 2015; Chen & Jackson, 2009; Kim & Kim, 2009; Murray et al., 2018). Many teenagers try to change their bodies: New diets, drugs, or intensive exercise are tried by almost every adolescent.

## Eating Disorders

Dissatisfaction with body image can be dangerous, even deadly. Many teenagers, mostly girls, eat erratically or ingest drugs (especially diet pills) to lose weight; others, mostly boys, take steroids to increase muscle mass (see **Figure 14.5**). **[Developmental Link:** Teenage drug abuse is discussed in Chapter 16.]

Eating disorders are rare in childhood but increase dramatically at puberty, accompanied by distorted body image, food obsession, and depression. (See Visualizing Development, page 387.) Many adolescents switch from obsessive dieting to overeating to overexercising and back again. Although girls are most vulnerable, boys are at risk, too, especially those who aspire to be pop stars or who train to be wrestlers.

When distorted body image and excessive dieting result in severe weight loss, that indicates **anorexia nervosa**. Fewer than 1 in 100 girls develop anorexia, but those who do dramatically restrict their calorie intake and have a destructive, distorted attitude about their bodies. Their BMI may fall below 17 in cases of mild anorexia or 15 in extreme cases, but clinicians must be alert to any sudden weight loss or weight that is "less than that minimally expected" (American Psychiatric Association, 2013).

About three times as common as anorexia is **bulimia nervosa**. Sufferers overeat compulsively, consuming thousands of calories within an hour or two, and then purge through vomiting or laxatives. Most are close to typical in weight and therefore unlikely to starve. However, they risk serious health problems, including damage to their gastrointestinal system and cardiac arrest from electrolyte imbalance (Mehler, 2018).

**body image** A person's idea of how his or her body looks.

**anorexia nervosa** An eating disorder characterized by self-starvation. Affected individuals voluntarily undereat and often overexercise, depriving their vital organs of nutrition. Anorexia can be fatal.

**bulimia nervosa** An eating disorder characterized by binge eating and subsequent purging, usually by induced vomiting and/or use of laxatives.

**FIGURE 14.5**

**Have You Ever...?** This chart shows lifetime prevalence of eating disorders. Almost all of the adults, and many of the 17- to 18-year-olds, have recovered from an eating disorder. Thus, the .2 percent increase from age 15 to 17 suggests that only 1 adolescent is 500 developed a new eating disorder during the final years of high school. That is reassuring, but two facts from this chart are troubling. One is that almost 1 in 40 young teens (age 13–14) already had an eating disorder, and the other is that the prevalence for the oldest teens is higher than for the adults of all ages. That suggests that the rate of eating disorders is increasing in the twenty-first century.

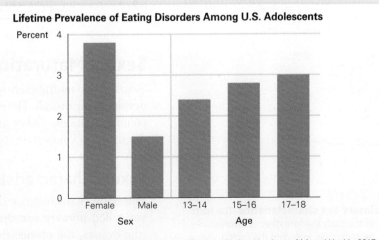

**Lifetime Prevalence of Eating Disorders Among U.S. Adolescents**

Data from U.S. Department of Health and Human Services, National Institute of Mental Health, 2017.

**binge eating disorder** Frequent episodes of uncontrollable overeating to the point that the stomach hurts. Usually the person feels shame and guilt but is unable to stop.

A disorder that is newly recognized in DSM-5 is **binge eating disorder**. Some adolescents periodically and compulsively overeat, quickly consuming large amounts of ice cream, cake, or snack food until their stomachs hurt. When bingeing becomes a disorder, overeating is typically done in private, at least weekly for several months. The sufferer does not purge (hence this is not bulimia) but feels out of control, distressed, and depressed.

## Life-Span Causes and Consequences

From a life-span perspective, teenage eating disorders are not limited to adolescence, even though this is the usual age when first signs typically appear. The origins occur much earlier in family eating patterns if parents do not help their children eat sensibly—when they are hungry, without food being a punishment or a reward. Indeed, the origin could be at conception, since many studies report that anorexia is about half genetic and half environmental.

Of course, as you remember from Chapter 3, disorders that are genetic are also targets for environmental triggers and treatments. For all eating disorders, family function (not structure) is crucial (Tetzlaff & Hilbert, 2014). Peer culture is also crucial during adolescence.

Unfortunately, during the teen years, many parents are oblivious to the first signs of eating disorders. They might have given up trying to get their child to eat breakfast before school or to join the family for dinner. That may be tragic, as the treatment that seems most successful, called family-based treatment, has parents "sit with their children, requiring them to eat" (Couzin-Frankel, 2020, p. 127). The problem is that many parents feel shame and guilt regarding anorexia, and they are told to wait until the patient is ready to be cured.

Some adolescents with eating disorders die before midlife because their body systems are strained by their lack of nutrition. The most common cause of death is heart failure. Most, however, recover (Mehler, 2018).

### WHAT HAVE YOU LEARNED?

1. What is the pattern of growth in adolescent bodies?
2. What complications result from the sequence of growth (weight/height/muscles)?
3. Why are many teenagers deficient in iron and calcium?
4. Why are many adolescents unhappy with their appearance?
5. What are the differences among the three eating disorders explained here?

# Sexual Maturation

Sexuality is multidimensional, complicated, and variable—not unlike human development overall. Here, we consider biological changes at puberty and some cohort variations. Other aspects of adolescent sexuality and gender identity are discussed in Chapter 16.

## Sexual Characteristics

**primary sex characteristics** The parts of the body that are directly involved in reproduction, including the vagina, uterus, ovaries, testicles, and penis.

The body characteristics that are directly involved in conception and pregnancy are called **primary sex characteristics**. During puberty, every primary sex organ (the ovaries, the uterus, the penis, and the testes) increases dramatically in size and matures in function. Reproduction becomes possible.

# Satisfied with Your Body?

Probably not, if you are a teenager. At every age, accepting who you are—not just ethnicity and gender, but also body shape, size, and strength—correlates with emotional health. During the adolescent years, when everyone's body changes dramatically, body dissatisfaction rises. As you see, this is particularly true for girls—but if the measure were satisfaction with muscles, more boys would be noted as unhappy.

## BODY DISSATISFACTION CORRELATES WITH...

| | |
|---|---|
| Unfavorable media comparisons | .26 |
| Weight criticisms from parents | .30 |
| Unfavorable peer comparisons | .55 |
| Low self-esteem | .52 |

Data from Van Vonderen & Kinnally, 2012.

## GENDER DIFFERENCES IN BODY DISSATISFACTION

Females of all ages tend to be dissatisfied with their bodies, but the biggest leap in dissatisfaction occurs when girls transition from early to mid-adolescence (Makinen et al., 2012).

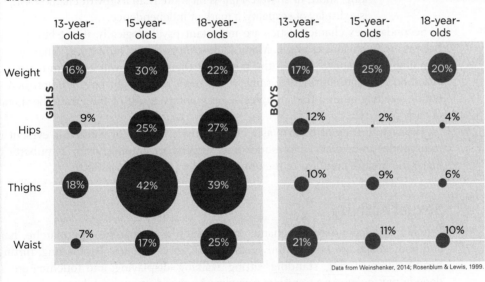

**GIRLS**

| | 13-year-olds | 15-year-olds | 18-year-olds |
|---|---|---|---|
| Weight | 16% | 30% | 22% |
| Hips | 9% | 25% | 27% |
| Thighs | 18% | 42% | 39% |
| Waist | 7% | 17% | 25% |

**BOYS**

| | 13-year-olds | 15-year-olds | 18-year-olds |
|---|---|---|---|
| Weight | 17% | 25% | 20% |
| Hips | 12% | 2% | 4% |
| Thighs | 10% | 9% | 6% |
| Waist | 21% | 11% | 10% |

Data from Weinshenker, 2014; Rosenblum & Lewis, 1999.

### SOCIAL MEDIA AND BODY DISSATISFACTION

- The more time teenage girls spend on social media, the higher their body dissatisfaction.
- 86% of teens say that social network sites hurt their body confidence.

(Information from Proud2Bme, 2012; Tiggemann & Slater, 2014)

## NUTRITION AND EXERCISE

High school students are told, at home and at school, to eat their vegetables and not care about their looks. But they listen more to their peers and follow social norms.

Fortunately, some eventually learn that, no matter what their body type, good nutrition and adequate exercise make a person feel more attractive, energetic, and happy.

**KEY**

Girls 🚺 9th grade  12th grade

Boys 🚹 9th grade  12th grade

| Overweight (by scale) | Trying to lose weight | Active 5 days, an hour or more | Muscle strengthening 3x week | Ate 3+ servings vegetables daily* | Ate/drank 3+ servings fruit daily** | Drank 2+ glasses milk daily |
|---|---|---|---|---|---|---|
| 17% 15% 14% 13% | 57% 62% 35% 33% | 45% 32% 63% 51% | 49% 36% 66% 57% | 12% 13% 15% 16% | 17% 15% 21% 21% | 13% 8% 27% 22% |

*Vegetables includes salad greens, and excludes French fries.
**Fruits include a glass of 100% fruit juice.

Data from MMWR, June 15, 2018.

*"I think I'll be more relaxed once my secondary sex characteristics kick in."*

**Brain Before Body** Hormones affect thoughts, but visible signs reveal maturation.

**secondary sex characteristics** Physical traits that are not directly involved in reproduction but that indicate sexual maturity, such as a man's beard and a woman's breasts.

**LaunchPad**
macmillan learning

**VIDEO: Romantic Relationships in Adolescence** explores teens' attitudes and assumptions about romance and sexuality.

When primary sex characteristics mature, another set of characteristics appear, called **secondary sex characteristics**, which are bodily features that do not directly affect reproduction (hence they are secondary) but that signify masculinity or femininity.

One secondary characteristic is body shape. Young boys and girls have similar shapes, but at puberty males widen at the shoulders and grow about 5 inches taller than females, while girls widen at the hips and develop breasts. Those female curves are often considered signs of womanhood, but neither breasts nor wide hips are required for conception; thus, they are secondary, not primary, sex characteristics.

The pattern of hair growth at the scalp line (widow's peak), the prominence of the larynx (Adam's apple), and several other anatomical features differ for men and women; all are secondary sex characteristics that few people notice. Facial and body hair increases in both sexes, affected by sex hormones as well as genes.

Girls often pluck or wax any facial hair they see and shave their legs, while boys may proudly grow sideburns, soul patches, chinstraps, moustaches, and so on—with specifics dependent on culture and cohort. Hair on the head is cut and styled to be spikey, flat, curled, long, short, or shaved. Hair is far more than a growth characteristic; it is a display of sexuality, a mark of independence.

Secondary sex characteristics are important psychologically, if not biologically. Breasts are an obvious example. Many adolescent girls buy "minimizer," "maximizer," "training," or "shaping" bras in the hope that their breasts will conform to an idealized body image. During the same years, many overweight boys are horrified to notice swelling around their nipples—a temporary result of the erratic hormones of early puberty.

The significance of breasts as a characteristic of men or women is evident in transgender individuals. Hormones and surgery are often chosen at puberty to make the breasts conform to the chosen gender (Patel et al., 2020).

## Sexual Activity

Primary and secondary sex characteristics such as menarche, spermarche, hair, and body shape are not the only evidence of sex hormones. Fantasizing, flirting, hand-holding, staring, standing, sitting, walking, displaying, and touching are all done in particular ways to reflect sexuality. As already explained, hormones trigger sexual thoughts, but the culture shapes thoughts into enjoyable fantasies, shameful obsessions, frightening impulses, or actual contact.

Masturbation is common in both sexes, for instance, but culture determines attitudes, from private sin to mutual pleasure (Driemeyer et al., 2016). Caressing, oral sex, nipple stimulation, and kissing are all taboo in some cultures, expected in others.

The distinction between early and later sexual experience during adolescence may be significant. A detailed longitudinal study in Finland found that depressed and rebellious 13-year-olds were more likely to use drugs and have sex (Kaltiala-Heino et al., 2015). That had flipped by age 19, when those who had experienced intercourse were less likely to be depressed (Savioja et al., 2015).

Emotions regarding sexual experience, like the rest of puberty, are strongly influenced by social norms that indicate what is expected at what age. Recently in the United States, one study found that girls who have sex early in adolescence are likely to be depressed, but those who have sex as older adolescents tend to be quite happy (Golden et al., 2016). Of course, much depends on the specific social context, whether a girl feels shamed or proud of her sexuality.

Indeed, everyone is influenced by hormones and society, biology and culture. All adolescents have sexual interests that they did not previously have (biology), and this propels teenagers in some nations to do things that teenagers in other nations would never do (culture).

Social norms regarding male–female differences are powerful. Traditionally, males were thought to have stronger sexual urges than females, which is why adolescent boys were supposed to "make the first move," from asking for a date to trying for a kiss. Then, girls were supposed to slow down the boys' advances. This was called the *double standard*, in that behaviors of boys and girls were held to different standards.

Many adolescents still expect boys and girls to approach sexual interactions differently, with boys more insistent and girls more hesitant. As one teen girl explained, "that's just how it is" (Tolman et al., 2016).

Nonetheless, many lines of research find that the double standard is less powerful than it once was, not only because of greater freedom for girls but also because many teens question the male–female binary. Interestingly, same-sex couples also find that the double standard is decreasing. A study in Italy found that lesbians experience patterns similar to those of gay males, and both are becoming more similar to straight youth (La Fauci, 2018).

In many nations including the United States, adolescent female rates of sexual activity are now almost even with male rates. For example, among high school seniors, 56 percent of the girls and 59 percent of the boys have had sexual intercourse, with most of them sexually active in the past three months. The one notable difference among high school students is in the number of partners: 8 percent of the girls and 12 percent of the boys have had four or more partners (MMWR, June 15, 2018).

Over the past two decades in the United States, every gender, ethnic, and age group is *less* sexually active than the previous cohort. Between 1993 and 2017, intercourse experience among African American high school students decreased 42 percent (to 46 percent); among European Americans, down 18 percent (to 39 percent); and among Latinos, down 27 percent (to 41 percent) (MMWR, June 15, 2018) (see **Figure 14.6**).

**Everywhere** Glancing, staring, and—when emotions are overwhelming—averting one's eyes are part of the universal language of love. Although the rate of intercourse among teenagers is lower than it was, passion is expressed in simple words, touches, and, as shown here, the eyes on a cold day.

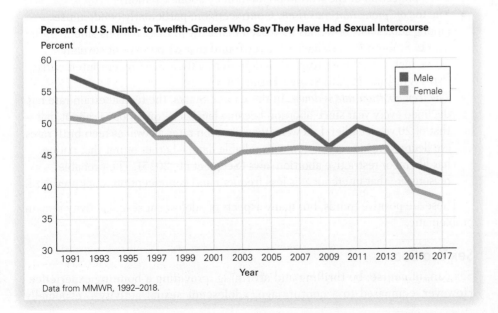

**Percent of U.S. Ninth- to Twelfth-Graders Who Say They Have Had Sexual Intercourse**

Data from MMWR, 1992–2018.

**FIGURE 14.6**

**Boys and Girls Together** Boys tend to be somewhat more sexually experienced than girls during the high school years, but since the Youth Risk Behavior Survey began in 1991, the overall trend has been toward equality in rates of sexual activity.

These were responses to an anonymous questionnaire. As you know from Chapter 1, some inaccuracies may have occurred, but the trends are solid because the same questions were asked over the decades. The data from the 1990s are not as reliable as current numbers, but every study over the past 20 years continues to show that more adolescents are in high school and that fewer are sexually active.

Many reasons for the trends have been suggested: sex education, fear of HIV/AIDS, awareness of the hazards of pregnancy, more female education, less intimacy. To explore these hypotheses, more research is needed.

However, it is apparent, not only in the United States but worldwide, that a universal experience (rising hormones) that produces another universal experience (growth of primary and secondary sex characteristics) is powerfully shaped by cohort, gender, and culture. The most important influence on adolescents' sexual activity is not their bodies but their close friends, who have more influence than either their parents or the norms for their gender and ethnic group (van de Bongardt et al., 2015).

 **DATA CONNECTIONS: Sexual Behaviors of U.S. High School Students** examines how sexually active teens really are.

## Sexual Problems in Adolescence

Sexual interest and interaction are part of adolescence; healthy adult relationships are more likely to develop when adolescent impulses are not haunted by shame and fear (Tolman & McClelland, 2011). Although guidance is needed, teenagers are neither depraved nor degenerate in experiencing sexual urges. Before focusing on the hazards of adolescent sex, we should note that several "problems" are less troubling now than in earlier decades. Here are three specifics:

- *Teen births have decreased.* In the United States, the 2017 rate of births to teenage mothers (aged 15 to 19) was less than half the rate 10 years earlier, with the biggest drop among Hispanic teens (J. Martin et al., 2018). (The 2019 rate was the lowest in 50 years.) Similar declines are evident in other nations. The most dramatic results are from China, where the 2015 teen pregnancy rate was about one-tenth of the rate 50 years ago (reducing the 2015 projection of the world's population by about 1 billion).
- *The use of "protection" has risen.* Contraception, particularly condom use among adolescent boys, has increased markedly in most nations since 1990. The U.S. Youth Risk Behavior Survey found that 61 percent of sexually active high school boys used a condom during their most recent intercourse (MMWR, June 15, 2018) (see **Table 14.1**).
- *The teen abortion rate is down.* In the United States, the teen abortion rate has declined every year since abortion became legal. The rate today is about half that of 20 years earlier. Likewise, teen abortion rates as well as teen birth rates are decreasing in every nation with reliable data, whether or not that nation has liberal or restrictive abortion laws (Sedgh et al., 2015). The probable reasons are that intercourse is less frequent and contraception more prevalent.

These are positive trends, but many aspects of adolescent sexual activity remain problematic.

## Sex Too Soon

Sex can, of course, be thrilling and affirming, providing a bonding experience. However, compared to a century ago, adolescent sexual activity — especially

**TABLE 14.1**

**Condom Use Among High School Students**

| Country | Sexually Active (% of total) | Used Condom at Last Intercourse (% of those sexually active) |
|---|---|---|
| France | 20 | 84 |
| England | 29 | 83 |
| Canada | 23 | 78 |
| Russia | 33 | 75 |
| Israel | 14 | 72 |
| United States | 29 | 54 |

Data from Currie et al., 2009; Centers for Disease Control and Prevention, October 9, 2018.

if it results in birth—is more hazardous because four circumstances have changed:

1. Earlier puberty results in earlier fertility, and sex before age 15 correlates with depression, drug abuse, and lifelong problems (Kastbom et al., 2015).
2. If a teenager has a baby, she usually has no reliable partners to help. A century ago, teenage mothers were often married; now, in the United States, almost all are unwed.
3. Raising a child has become more complex and expensive, and family helpers are scarce. The strategy that most teenage mothers used in former times—having their mother raise the child—is less available, as most young grandmothers are employed.
4. Sexually transmitted infections (STIs) are more common and more dangerous. The rate of all STIs increased markedly over the past decade, with notable increases from 2016 to 2017 (Centers for Disease Control, 2018).

As you read, teen births are declining, as are teen abortions. However, the U.S. rate of adolescent pregnancy is the highest of any developed nation (true among every ethnic group). If a pregnant girl is under 16 (most are not), she is more likely than older pregnant teenagers to experience complications—including spontaneous abortion, high blood pressure, stillbirth, preterm birth, and low birthweight. This is true worldwide, in wealthy as well as low-income nations (Ganchimeg et al., 2014).

There are many reasons for these hazards besides age. Poverty and lack of education correlate with teen pregnancy and with every problem just listed. Sadly, some of the problems begin with family life: Mothers who themselves had teenage births are more likely to have daughters who do the same (N. Liu et al., 2018). One reason for the frequency of complications is that younger pregnant teenagers are frequently undernourished and often postpone prenatal care.

Problems continue from one generation to the next because teenage mothers are less often the responsive mothers that newborns need, so insecure attachment is more common. Although some people imagine that the baby will benefit when an adolescent mother lives with her own mother, the opposite seems more accurate. Troubles begin in infancy, with teenagers living with their mothers less likely to breast-feed their infants than teen mothers living on their own (Pilkauskas, 2014). [**Developmental Link:** Attachment types and the importance of early attachment were discussed in Chapter 7.]

**Especially for Parents Worried About Their Teenager's Risk Taking** You remember the risky things you did at the same age, and you are alarmed by the possibility that your child will follow in your footsteps. What should you do? (see response, page 395)

JEFF KOWALSKY/AFP/Getty Images

**You, Too?** Millions were shocked to learn that Larry Nassar, a physician for gymnasts training for the Olympics and at Michigan State University, sexually abused more than 150 young women. Among the victims was Kaylee Lorenz, shown here addressing Nassar in court. Nassar was convicted of multiple counts of sexual assault and sentenced to 40 to 175 years in prison, but his victims wonder why no one stopped him. The president of Michigan State University resigned in disgrace; many others are still in office.

**child sexual abuse** Any erotic activity that arouses an adult and excites, shames, or confuses a child, whether or not the victim protests and whether or not genital contact is involved.

Even if sexually active adolescents avoid pregnancy, early intercourse increases psychosocial problems. A study of 3,923 adult women in the United States found that those who *voluntarily* had sex before age 16 were more likely to divorce later on, whether or not they became pregnant or later married their first sexual partner. The same study found that adolescents of any age whose first sexual experience was unwanted (either "really didn't want [it]" or "had mixed feelings about [it]") were also more likely to later experience divorce (Paik, 2011, p. 477).

Sexual abuse is much more traumatic, as is now explained.

## Sexual Abuse

Abuse is always devastating: It harms development lifelong. **Child sexual abuse** is defined as any sexual activity (including fondling and photographing) between a juvenile and an adult. Age 18 is the usual demarcation between adult and child (although legal age varies by state). Girls are particularly vulnerable, although boys are also at risk.

Abuse of young children gathers headlines, but young adolescents are, by far, the most frequent victims. The rate of sexual abuse increases at puberty, a particularly sensitive time because many victims are confused about their own sexual urges and identity. Virtually every adolescent problem, including unwanted motherhood, drug abuse, bulimia, and suicide, is more frequent if adolescents are sexually abused.

This is true worldwide. Although solid numbers are unknown for obvious reasons, it is apparent that millions of girls in their early teens are forced into marriage or prostitution each year. Adolescent girls are common victims of sex trafficking, not only because their youth makes them more alluring but also because their immaturity makes them more vulnerable (McClain & Garrity, 2011). Some believe they are helping their families by earning money to support them; others are literally sold by their families (Montgomery, 2015).

It is impossible to know how common child sexual abuse is, but the data suggest that ongoing forced abuse is less common than it was. We do know that fewer girls under age 16 marry older men chosen by their parents, and fewer 16-year-olds have unwanted sex with their 19-year-old boyfriends. Both of the conditions may be considered abuse, and both are less frequent. Estimates of the number of teenage girls being trafficked for sex in the United States range from 1,000 to 336,000 — hardly definitive (Miller-Perrin & Wurtele, 2017).

Trafficking is not the most common form of sexual abuse. Instead, most sexual abuse in the United States occurs at home. Typically, the victims are young adolescents who are not allowed friendships and romances. The abuser may be a biological parent, but more often he is a stepparent, older sibling, or uncle.

Young people who are sexually exploited tend to fear sex, with higher rates of virtually every developmental problem, including repeated abuse (Pittenger et al., 2018). Another developmental consequence is more frequent birth of unwanted babies, who often become mistreated themselves (Noll et al., 2019).

Our discussion of sexual abuse focuses on girls because they are the most common victims. However, teenage boys are also sometimes sexually abused, a direct attack on their fledgling identity as men. Disclosure of past abuse is particularly difficult for men, which makes gathering reliable statistics difficult (Collin-Vézina et al., 2015).

Perpetrators of abuse are often people known to the child. After puberty, although sometimes abusers are parents, coaches, religious leaders, or other authorities, often they are other teenagers. Many high school girls (15 percent) and boys (4 percent) have been kissed, touched, or forced to have sex within a dating relationship when they did not want to (MMWR, June 15, 2018). Chapter 16 discusses sex education; teenagers have much to learn.

## Sexually Transmitted Infections

Unlike teen pregnancy and sexual abuse, the other major problem of teenage sex shows no signs of abating. A **sexually transmitted infection (STI)** (sometimes called a *sexually transmitted disease [STD]*) is any infection transmitted through sexual contact. Worldwide, sexually active teenagers have higher rates of the most common STIs—*gonorrhea*, *genital herpes*, and *chlamydia*—than do sexually active people of any other age group.

In the United States, half of all new STIs occur in people ages 15 to 25, even though this age group has less than one-fourth of the sexually active people (Satterwhite et al., 2013). Rates are particularly high among sexually active adolescents, ages 15 to 19. Biology provides one reason: Pubescent girls are particularly likely to catch an STI compared to fully developed women, probably because adult women have more vaginal secretions that reduce infections. Further, if symptoms appear, teens are less likely to alert their partners or seek treatment unless pain requires it, so STIs spread.

A survey of adolescents in a U.S. pediatric emergency department found that half of the teenagers (average age 15) were sexually active and 20 percent of those had an STI—although that was not why they came for medical help (Miller et al., 2015).

There are hundreds of STIs. Chlamydia is the most frequently reported one; it often begins without symptoms, yet it can cause permanent infertility.

Worse is *human papillomavirus (HPV)*, which has no immediate consequences but increases the risk of cancer in both sexes. Fortunately, in about 1990, an effective vaccine was developed that should be given before sexual activity.

However, less than half of all U.S. adolescents are fully immunized (Hirth, 2019). Among the reasons: Some state health departments do not promote it, the vaccine was originally recommended only for girls (because HPV was most closely associated with cervical cancer), and full immunization requires three doses (many teens do not see a medical professional regularly).

For those who care about infant health, *syphilis* may be the worst STI of all, because mothers transmit the virus to their newborns, who develop lifelong disabilities (and sometimes early death). The U.S. rate of *congenital syphilis* has been increasing since 2009, with the 2017 rate twice as high as the 2014 rate (Umapathi et al., 2019). Fortunately, this STI is still rare, but good, early prenatal care can prevent it, so the increase indicates that national health care does not reach the most vulnerable pregnant women.

Once again, it is apparent that a universal experience (the biology of puberty) varies markedly depending on national and family context. As we stated earlier, adolescence begins with biology and ends with culture. You will see more examples of this in the next chapter, as you learn that schools for adolescents vary a great deal in how and what they teach.

---

 **DATA CONNECTIONS: Major Sexually Transmitted Infections: Some Basics** offers more information about the causes, symptoms, and rates of various STIs.

---

**sexually transmitted infection (STI)**
A disease spread by sexual contact; includes syphilis, gonorrhea, genital herpes, chlamydia, and HIV.

● **Especially for Health Practitioners**
How might you encourage adolescents to seek treatment for STIs? (see response, page 395)

---

**WHAT HAVE YOU LEARNED?**

1. What are examples of the difference between primary and secondary sex characteristics?

2. Why are there fewer problems caused by adolescent sexuality now than a few decades ago?

3. What is problematic regarding adolescent pregnancy?

4. What are the effects of child sexual abuse?

5. Among sexually active people, why do adolescents have more STIs than adults?

# SUMMARY

## Puberty Begins

**1.** Puberty refers to the various changes that transform a child's body into an adult one. Even before the teenage years, biochemical signals from the hypothalamus to the pituitary gland to the adrenal glands (the HPA axis) increase production of testosterone, estrogen, and various other hormones that will soon cause rapid growth and reproductive potential.

**2.** Some emotional reactions, such as quick mood shifts, are directly caused by hormones, as are thoughts about sex. The reactions of others to adolescents and the adolescents' own reactions to the their bodies trigger emotions, which affect hormones.

**3.** Hormones regulate all of the body rhythms of life, by day, by season, and by year. Changes in these rhythms in adolescence often result in sleep deprivation, partly because the natural circadian rhythm makes teenagers wide awake at night. Sleep deprivation causes numerous health and learning problems.

**4.** Various parts of the brain continue to mature until about age 25. The regions dedicated to emotional arousal (including the amygdala) mature before those that regulate and rationalize emotional expression (the prefrontal cortex).

**5.** The outward signs of puberty typically begin between ages 9 and 14. The young person's sex, genetic background, body fat, and level of stress all contribute to this variation in timing.

**6.** Girls generally begin and end puberty before boys do. A two-year gap is evident in height; a one-year gap is evident in sexual development. Girls from stressed families or neighborhoods are likely to reach puberty earlier.

## Growth and Nutrition

**7.** The growth spurt is an acceleration of growth in every part of the body. Peak weight usually precedes peak height, which is then followed by peak muscle growth, a sequence that makes active adolescents particularly vulnerable to injuries. The lungs and the heart also increase in size and capacity.

**8.** All of the changes of puberty depend on adequate nourishment, yet adolescents do not always make healthy food choices. One reason for poor nutrition is the desire to lose (or, less often, gain) weight because of anxiety about body image.

**9.** The precursors of eating disorders are evident during puberty. Many adolescents eat too much of the wrong foods or too little food overall. Deficiencies of iron, vitamin D, and calcium are common, affecting bone growth and overall development.

**10.** Eating disorders vary because of genes, family, and social context. Anorexia involves voluntary starvation, bulimia involves overeating and then purging, and binge eating disorder involves compulsive overeating. All these increase the risk of severe depression and medical complications.

**11.** Because of the sequence of brain development, many adolescents seek intense emotional experiences, unchecked by rational thought. For the same reason, adolescents are quick to react, explore, and learn. As a result, adolescents take risks, bravely or foolishly, with potential for harm as well as for good.

## Sexual Maturation

**12.** Male–female differences in bodies and behavior become apparent at puberty. The maturation of primary sex characteristics means that by age 13 or so, after experiencing menarche or spermarche, teenagers are capable of reproducing, although peak fertility is several years later.

**13.** Secondary sex characteristics are not directly involved in reproduction but signify that the child is becoming a man or a woman. Body shape, breasts, voice, body hair, and numerous other features differentiate males from females. Sexual activity is influenced more by culture than by physiology.

**14.** In the twenty-first century, teenage sexual behavior has changed for the better in several ways. Hormones and nutrition cause sexual thoughts and behaviors at younger ages, but teen pregnancy is far less common, condom use has increased, and the average age of first intercourse has risen.

**15.** Among the problems that adolescents still face is intercourse before their bodies and minds are ready. Giving birth before age 16 takes a physical toll and puts the newborn at risk of physical and psychological problems.

**16.** Sexual abuse is more likely to occur in early adolescence than at other ages. The perpetrators are often family members or close friends. Rates of child sexual abuse are declining in the United States, but globalization has increased international sex trafficking.

**17.** Untreated STIs at any age can lead to infertility and even death. Rates among sexually active teenagers are rising. Immunization to prevent HPV is decreasing rates of cancer in adulthood, but most teenagers are not immunized.

# KEY TERMS

puberty (p. 371)
menarche (p. 371)
spermarche (p. 371)
pituitary (p. 371)
adrenal glands (p. 371)
HPA (hypothalamus–pituitary–adrenal) axis (p. 371)

gonads (p. 371)
HPG (hypothalamus–pituitary–gonad) axis (p. 372)
estradiol (p. 372)
testosterone (p. 372)
circadian rhythm (p. 373)
secular trend (p. 378)

leptin (p. 379)
growth spurt (p. 382)
body image (p. 385)
anorexia nervosa (p. 385)
bulimia nervosa (p. 385)
binge eating disorder (p. 386)

primary sex characteristics (p. 386)
secondary sex characteristics (p. 388)
child sexual abuse (p. 392)
sexually transmitted infection (STI) (p. 393)

## APPLICATIONS

1. Visit a fifth-, sixth-, or seventh-grade class. Note variations in the size and maturity of the students. Do you see any patterns related to gender, ethnicity, body fat, or self-confidence?

2. Interview two to four of your friends who are in their late teens or early 20s about their memories of menarche or spermarche, including their memories of others' reactions. Do their comments indicate that these events are, or are not, emotionally troubling for young people?

3. Talk with someone who became a teenage parent. Were there any problems with the pregnancy, the birth, or the first years of

parenthood? Would the person recommend teen parenthood? What would have been different had the baby been born three years earlier or three years later?

4. Adult reactions to puberty can be reassuring or frightening. Interview two or three people about how adults prepared for, encouraged, or troubled their development. Compare that with your own experience.

## Especially For ANSWERS

**Response for Parents Worried About Early Puberty** (from p. 379): Probably not. If she is overweight, her diet should change, but the hormone hypothesis is speculative. Genes are the main factor; she shares only one-eighth of her genes with her cousin.

**Response for Parents Worried About Their Teenager's Risk Taking** (from p. 391): You are right to be concerned, but you cannot keep your child locked up for the next decade or so. Since you know that some rebellion and irrationality are likely, try to minimize

them by not boasting about your own youthful exploits, by reacting sternly to minor infractions to nip worse behavior in the bud, and by making allies of your child's teachers and the parents of your child's friends.

**Response for Health Practitioners** (from p. 393): Many adolescents are intensely concerned about privacy and fearful of adult interference. This means that your first task is to convince the teenagers that you are nonjudgmental and that everything is confidential.

## Observation Quiz ANSWERS

**Answer to Observation Quiz** (from p. 374): Girls tend to spend more time studying, talking to friends, and getting ready in the morning. Other data show that many girls get less than seven hours of sleep per night.

**Answer to Observation Quiz** (from p. 383): Adults often try to control schoolchildren by making them wear uniforms. Do you see that these students all must wear blue shirts and ties — even the girls? And teens tend to buy and eat the same foods: Notice the large paper cups, all from the same store.

# CHAPTER

## 15

# Adolescence: Cognitive Development

## What Will You Know?

1. Why are young adolescents often egocentric?
2. Why does emotion sometimes overwhelm reason?
3. What kind of school is best for teenagers?

On March 15, 2019, thousands of adolescents in almost 100 nations left their classrooms to gather in the streets. Their inspiration was Greta Thunberg, who began skipping school every Friday when she was 15. She stood in front of the Swedish parliament with a sign to protest adult inaction on climate change.

News media worldwide reported on the 2019 rally, often with students' own words. For example, the BBC interviewed student protesters from a dozen towns in England. In Brighton, a 13-year-old girl said:

> They're messing up our future and we're the ones who are going to have to clean it up, so I think it's important that we come and tell them about it. The school haven't let us go, they say there's consequences but it's more important than school attendance to come here and protest.

Her friend said:

> I really don't care what consequences they give us, it's more important that we fight for our future. This is the world we're going to have to live in.

A 16-year-old boy in Birmingham said:

> We are at the point that in 12 to 20 years the effects of climate change are going to be irreversible. The only way to change it is through the younger generation because the older generation don't really care.

And a 15-year-old in Stockport was torn:

> I tried to come to the last protest but my school said no. My head of year said no this time but I think it is more important to come. I think I'm going to get into trouble though.

That protest stopped public transportation in Manchester, prompting one adult to say

> it's disappointing that they've chosen to disrupt Metrolink—which, ironically, is one of the greenest and most sustainable ways to travel across Greater Manchester.

Five thousand miles away, in Missoula, Montana, students spoke again about the need for adolescents to act because the adults were oblivious. The U.S. reporters tried to put the protest into a political context (O'Brien, 2019). In response, a boy noted "a generation gap between the politicians of today and the politicians of the future."

A 15-year-old in Indiana echoed that when she said:

> This is not a Republican issue; this is not a Democrat issue. This is a human rights issue . . . I don't want to live in a world where the future is unclear. I have big plans for myself . . . People generally perceive it as us kids, we're just whining . . . Unfortunately, adults haven't done enough for us to make this future clear for me and for my peers. So we're taking it into our own hands.

*[Fallahi, quoted in Van Dongen, 2019]*

These quotations begin this chapter on adolescent cognition because they illustrate how adolescents think—sometimes illogically (the public transportation disruption), sometimes considering adults clueless ("they don't really care"), sometimes exaggerating their importance (the young can reverse climate change, "big plans for myself"). Yet, they are still influenced by the schools that adults created ("consequences," "get into trouble") and opinions that adults might have ("whining").

None of this is surprising. Cognition reflects generation and culture. In the United States, reporters see climate change as a political issue; in England, reporters see the young as misguided; in every nation developmental scientists consider the effects on human health. The young reject all that, instead thinking about their own lives.

This chapter attempts to avoid all these narrow judgments. Instead, we describe the facts of adolescent cognition, a mix of egocentrism and abstraction, of emotions and analysis.

We also explore the myriad structures of the schools that educate adolescents. What should the "consequences" be when adolescent thought leads to ditching school? Do the students quoted above illustrate self-centered priorities, or exaggerated self-importance, or admirable analysis?

Six months later, Greta Thunberg took a 15-day boat trip, fueled by solar and hydropower, to address adults at the United Nations. New York students were allowed to leave school to rally with her—no consequences! Reporters lauded her: She was *Time* magazine's person-of-the-year and appeared on its cover. Adults listened: wise or foolish?

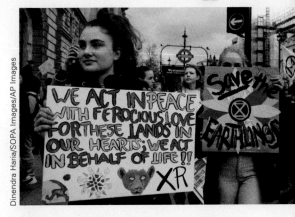

**Ferocious Earthlings** It's hard not to admire the passion of adolescent cognition, not only on climate change, but also on drugs, religion, patriotism, sex, and many other issues. Admiration does not always mean agreement, but that's why adolescents and adults need each other.

● **Observation Quiz** What is the meaning of the four symbols on the bottom of the "ferocious" poster? (see answer, page 422) ↑

## Logic and Self

Brain maturation, additional years of schooling, moral challenges, increased independence, and intense conversations all occur between ages 11 and 18. In some ways, adolescent thought can be understood as two distinct processes, first intense focus on oneself and then moving toward rational thought.

### Egocentrism

During puberty, people center on themselves, in part because body changes heighten self-consciousness. Young adolescents grapple with conflicting feelings about adults and peers, examine details of body changes, and think deeply (not realistically) about the future.

**Adolescent egocentrism**—when adolescents focus on themselves and on what others think of them—was first described by David Elkind (1967). He found that, egocentrically, adolescents regard themselves as much more unique, special, admired, or hated than other people consider them to be. Egocentric adolescents do not understand others' points of view.

**adolescent egocentrism** A characteristic of adolescent thinking that leads young people (ages 10 to 13) to focus on themselves to the exclusion of others.

For example, few girls are attracted to boys with pimples and braces, but one boy's eagerness to be seen as growing up kept him from realizing this. According to his older sister:

> Now in the 8th grade, my brother has this idea that all the girls are looking at him in school. He got his first pimple about three months ago. I told him to wash it with my face soap but he refused, saying, "Not until I go to school to show it off." He called the dentist, begging him to approve his braces now instead of waiting for a year. The perfect gifts for him have changed from action figures to a bottle of cologne, a chain, and a fitted baseball hat like the rappers wear.

> *[adapted from E., personal communication]*

Egocentrism may lead adolescents to interpret what others do as a judgment on them. A stranger's frown or a teacher's critique mean that "No one likes me," and then they deduce that "I am unlovable" or even "I can't leave the house." Positive casual reactions—a smile from a sales clerk or an extra-big hug from a younger brother—could lead to "I am great" or "Everyone loves me."

When a famous singer suddenly died, one of my students complained that everyone cared about her but would not care if he died. "I might be just as wonderful as she was, but nobody knows."

Acute self-consciousness about physical appearance may be more prevalent between ages 10 and 14 than at any other time, in part because adolescents notice changes in their body that do not exactly conform to social norms and ideals (Guzman & Nishina, 2014). Adolescents also instigate changes that they think other teenagers will admire.

For example, piercings, shaved heads, tattoos, and torn jeans—all contrary to the wishes of most parents—signify connection to youth culture. Wearing suits and ties, or dresses and pearls, would attract unwelcome attention from other youth. Notice groups of adolescents waiting in line for a midnight show or clustering near their high school: Their appearance may seem rebellious, but it conforms to teen culture.

Because adolescents are egocentric, their emotions may not be grounded in reality. A study of 1,310 Dutch and Belgian adolescents found that, for many of them, self-esteem and loneliness were closely tied to their *perception* of how others saw them, not to their actual popularity or acceptance among their peers. Gradually, after about age 15, some realized what others actually thought. Then they became less depressed (Vanhalst et al., 2013).

## Rumination

Egocentrism is one reason for *rumination*, which is thinking obsessively about self-focused concerns. Some adolescents go over their problems via phone, text, conversation, social media, and private, quiet self-talk (as when they lie in bed, unable to sleep), thinking about each nuance of everything they have done, are doing, might do, and should have done. Rumination in early adolescence is likely to lead to depression later on (Krause et al., 2018).

Others act impulsively without any rumination at all, blurting out words that they regret and taking risks that they later realize were foolish. Then shame and despair can be overwhelming, again out of proportion to the actual event. Prison administrators know that rates of suicide are higher for jailed adolescent boys than for any other age or gender group (Tartaro, 2019). Impulsive action is one reason.

## The Imaginary Audience

Egocentrism creates an **imaginary audience** in the minds of many adolescents. They believe that they are at center stage, with all eyes on them, and they imagine

**THINK CRITICALLY:** How should you judge the validity of the idea of adolescent egocentrism?

**imaginary audience** The other people who, in adolescents' egocentric belief, are watching and taking note of their appearance, ideas, and behavior. This belief makes many teenagers very self-conscious.

how others might react to their appearance and behavior. One of my students wrote, "If I ran out of hairspray I would refuse to go out because I wouldn't be caught dead outside with flat bangs.... I just knew in my mind that everyone would know I ran out of spray and everyone would laugh." Her mother tried to make her leave the house. She sobbed, "Never" (IP, personal reflection).

One woman who became a noted scholar remembers:

> When I was 14 and in the 8th grade, I received an award at the end-of-year school assembly. Walking across the stage, I lost my footing and stumbled in front of the entire student body. To be clear, this was not falling flat on one's face, spraining an ankle, or knocking over the school principal—it was a small misstep noticeable only to those in the audience who were paying close attention. As I rushed off the stage, my heart pounded with embarrassment and self-consciousness, and weeks of speculation about the consequence of this missed step were set into motion. There were tears and loss of sleep. Did my friends notice? Would they stop wanting to hang out with me? Would a reputation for clumsiness follow me to high school?
>
> [Somerville, 2013, p. 121]

This woman became an expert on the adolescent brain. She wrote that "adolescents are hyperaware of others' evaluations and feel they are under constant scrutiny by an imaginary audience" (Somerville, 2013, p. 124).

## Fables

Egocentrism also leads naturally to a **personal fable**, the belief that one is unique, destined to have a heroic, fabled, legendary life. Some 12-year-olds plan to be star players in the NBA, or to become billionaires, or to cure cancer. The personal fable can extend to their entire generation: Some students quoted in the beginning of this chapter said not only that they understood climate change but also that adults did not care.

One fable is that they are destined to die an early, tragic death. For them, statistics about harm in midlife from STIs, junk food, vaping, or other factors are irrelevant. One of my teenage students said, "That's just a statistic," dismissing its possible application to her.

In one study, teens estimated that their chance of dying before age 20 was 1 in 5. In fact, the odds are less than 1 in 1,000. Even those at highest risk (African American males in urban areas) survive to age 20 more than 99 times in 100. Sadly, if teens think that they will die young, they are likely to risk jail, HIV, drug addiction, and so on (Haynie et al., 2014). If they know someone who did die, their fatalistic response might be "His number was up," unaware that a self-fulfilling prophecy became a nail in the coffin.

The personal fable may coexist with the **invincibility fable**, the idea that death will not occur unless it is destined. Some adolescents believe that fast driving, unprotected sex, or addictive drugs will spare them. Believing that one is invincible removes any attempt at self-control, because personal control is neither needed nor possible (Lin, 2016).

Similarly, teens post comments on Snapchat, Instagram, Facebook, and so on, and they expect others to understand, laugh, admire, or sympathize. Their imaginary audience is other teenagers, not parents, teachers, college admission officers, or future employers, who might have another interpretation (boyd, 2014).

The personal fable is evident worldwide. Boys in teen motorcycle gangs in Indonesia felt "strong and invulnerable against any possible danger while riding [a] motorcycle," which encouraged reckless driving but did not correlate with aggression, as some adults mistakenly assume it does (Saudi et al., 2018, p. 308).

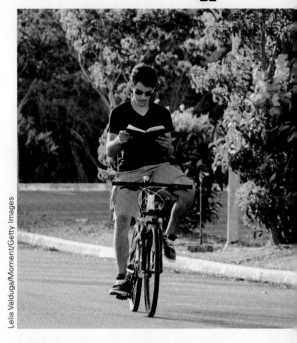

Lelia Valduga/Moment/Getty Images

**Oblivious?** When you see a teenager with purple hair or a nose ring, or riding a bicycle and reading, do you think he or she does not imagine what others think?

**personal fable** An aspect of adolescent egocentrism characterized by an adolescent's belief that his or her thoughts, feelings, and experiences are unique, more wonderful, or more awful than anyone else's.

**invincibility fable** An adolescent's egocentric conviction that he or she cannot be overcome or even harmed by anything that might defeat a normal mortal, such as unprotected sex, drug abuse, or high-speed driving.

Indeed, many researchers assume that adolescent egocentrism is dangerous, but it might have positive effects, giving young people confidence (Hill et al., 2012).

## Formal Operational Thought

**formal operational thought** In Piaget's theory, the fourth and final stage of cognitive development, characterized by more systematic logical thinking and by the ability to understand and systematically manipulate abstract concepts.

Now consider another aspect of adolescent thought. Piaget described a shift to **formal operational thought** as children move past concrete operational thinking and consider abstractions, including "assumptions that have no necessary relation to reality" (Piaget, 1950/2001, p. 163). Is Piaget correct? Many educators think so. They adjust the curriculum between primary and secondary school, reflecting a shift from concrete thought to formal, logical thought. Here are three examples:

- *Math.* Younger children multiply real numbers, such as $4 \times 3 \times 8$; adolescents multiply unreal numbers, such as $(2x)(3y)$ or even $(25xy^2)(-3zy^3)$.
- *Social studies.* Younger children study other cultures by considering concrete expression of daily life—drinking goat's milk or building an igloo, for instance. Adolescents consider how GNP (gross national product) and TFR (total fertility rate) affect global politics.
- *Science.* Younger students grow carrots and feed gerbils; adolescents study invisible particles and distant galaxies.

## Piaget's Experiments

**VIDEO: The Balance Scale Task** shows children of various ages completing the task and gives you an opportunity to try it as well.

Piaget and his colleagues devised many tasks to assess formal operational thought (Inhelder & Piaget, 1958/2013b). They found that "in contrast to concrete operational children, formal operational adolescents imagine all possible determinants . . . [and] systematically vary the factors one by one, observe the results correctly, keep track of the results, and draw the appropriate conclusions" (P. Miller, 2016, p. 52).

One of their experiments (diagrammed in **Figure 15.1**) required balancing a scale by hooking weights onto the scale's arms. To master this task, a person must recognize the reciprocity of distance and weight.

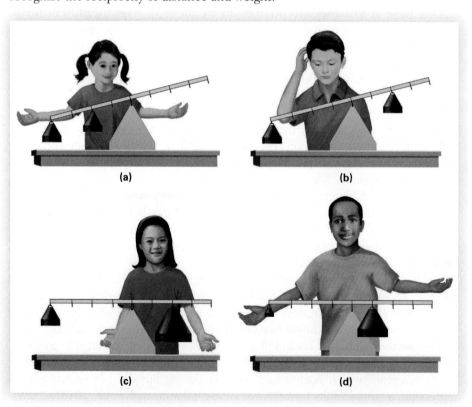

**FIGURE 15.1**

**How to Balance a Scale** Piaget's balance-scale test of formal reasoning, as it is attempted by *(a)* a 4-year-old, *(b)* a 7-year-old, *(c)* a 10-year-old, and *(d)* a 14-year-old. The key to balancing the scale is to make weight times distance from the center equal on both sides of the center; the realization of that principle requires formal operational thought.

(a)   (b)

(c)   (d)

Balancing was not understood by the 3- to 5-year-olds; when tested, they just played with the weights. By age 7, children understood the concept but balanced the scale only by putting identical weights on each arm: They didn't consider distance from the center. By age 10, children experimented, using trial and error, not logic.

By about age 13 or 14, some children hypothesized about reciprocity, realizing that a heavy weight close to the center can be counterbalanced with a light weight far from the center on the other side (Piaget & Inhelder, 1972).

## Hypothetical-Deductive Reasoning

One hallmark of formal operational thought is the capacity to think of possibility, not just reality. "Here and now" is only one of many possibilities, including "there and then," "long, long ago," "not yet," and "never." As Piaget said:

> The adolescent . . . thinks beyond the present and forms theories about everything, delighting especially in considerations of that which is not.
>
> *[Piaget, 1950/2001, p. 163]*

Adolescents are therefore primed for **hypothetical thought**, reasoning about *if–then* propositions. Consider the following question (adapted from De Neys & Van Gelder, 2009):

> If all mammals can walk,
> And whales are mammals,
> Can whales walk?

Children answer "No!" They know that whales swim, not walk; the logic escapes them. Some adolescents answer "Yes." They understand the conditional *if*, and therefore they can use logic to interpret the phrase "if all mammals."

> *Possibility* no longer appears merely as an extension of an empirical situation or of action actually performed. Instead, it is *reality* that is now secondary to *possibility.*
>
> *[Inhelder & Piaget, 1958/2013b, p. 251; emphasis in original]*

Hypothetical thought transforms perceptions, not necessarily for the better. Adolescents might criticize everything from their mother's spaghetti (it's not *al dente*) to the Gregorian calendar (it's not the Chinese or Jewish one). They criticize what *is* because they hypothesize what might be. Added to that is a growing awareness of other families and cultures: history, anthropology, and international studies become intriguing.

In developing the capacity to think hypothetically, by age 14 or so adolescents become more capable of **deductive reasoning**, or *top-down reasoning*, which begins with an idea or premise and then uses logic to draw conclusions. In the example above, "if all mammals can walk" is a premise.

By contrast, **inductive reasoning**, or *bottom-up reasoning*, predominates during concrete operational thought. Children accumulate facts and experiences (the knowledge base) to aid their thinking. Since they know whales cannot walk, knowledge trumps logic.

In essence, a child's reasoning goes like this: "This creature waddles and quacks. Ducks waddle and quack. Therefore, this must be a duck." This is inductive: It progresses from particulars ("waddles" and "quacks") to a general conclusion ("a duck"). By contrast, deduction progresses from the general to the specific: "If it's a duck, it will waddle and quack."

**hypothetical thought** Reasoning that includes propositions and possibilities that may not reflect reality.

**Especially for Natural Scientists** Some ideas that were once universally accepted, such as the belief that the sun moved around Earth, have been disproved. Is it a failure of inductive or deductive reasoning that leads to false conclusions? (see response, page 422)

**deductive reasoning** Reasoning from a general statement, premise, or principle, through logical steps, to figure out (deduce) specifics. (Also called *top-down reasoning.*)

**inductive reasoning** Reasoning from one or more specific experiences or facts to reach (induce) a general conclusion. (Also called *bottom-up reasoning.*)

## Two Modes of Thinking

You just read about the sequence of thought described by Piaget. He considered intellectual development to be sequential, as children move from one cognitive stage to another (sensorimotor to preoperational to concrete to formal). Others disagree, especially when describing adolescent cognition. They suggest that thinking does not develop in sequence but in parallel, with two processes that are not tightly coordinated within the brain (Baker et al., 2015).

Imagine the adolescent as a pianist. One hand plays the high notes and the other the low notes. Sometimes both hands play together, but often the right hand plays a melody that is uncoordinated with the lower chords.

## Dual Processing

Many scholars who describe adolescent cognition note that advanced logic (formal operational thought) is counterbalanced by advancing intuition. Thinking occurs in two ways, called **dual processing**.

The thinking described by the first half of each pair is easier and quicker, preferred in everyday life. Sometimes, however, circumstances necessitate the second mode, when deeper thought is demanded. The discrepancy between the maturation of the limbic system and the prefrontal cortex reflects this duality. So does the movement just explained in this chapter, from egocentrism to abstract logic. [**Developmental Link**: Timing differences in brain maturation are discussed in Chapter 14.]

To some extent, both modes of thinking reflect inborn temperament. Most children who are impulsive by nature learn emotional regulation in childhood, but a dual-processing perspective suggests that this regulation may break down during adolescence (Henderson et al., 2015). Even those who are naturally cautious might act impulsively—joyriding, skinny dipping, table dancing—things their parents never imagined their quiet child would do.

## Intuitive and Analytic Processing

Although many pairs of terms describe dual processing (see **Figure 15.2**), to eliminate confusion we use only one set here, *intuitive* and *analytic*:

- **Intuitive thought** begins with a belief, assumption, or general rule (called a *heuristic*) rather than logic. Intuition is quick and powerful; it feels "right."
- **Analytic thought** is the formal, logical, hypothetical-deductive thinking described by Piaget. It involves rational analysis of many factors whose interactions must be calculated, as in the scale-balancing problem.

To test yourself on intuitive and analytic thinking, answer the following:

1. A bat and a ball cost $1.10 in total. The bat costs $1 more than the ball. How much does the ball cost?

---

**dual processing** The notion that two networks exist within the human brain, one for emotional processing of stimuli and one for analytical reasoning.

**intuitive thought** Thought that arises from an emotion or a hunch, beyond rational explanation, and is influenced by past experiences and cultural assumptions.

**analytic thought** Thought that results from analysis, such as a systematic ranking of pros and cons, risks and consequences, possibilities and facts. Analytic thought depends on logic and rationality.

**Dual Processing**

| System 1 | System 2 |
|----------|----------|
| Intuitive | Analytic |
| Hot | Cold |
| Implicit | Explicit |
| Creative | Factual |
| Gist | Specific |
| Experiential | Rational |
| Qualitative | Quantitative |
| Contextualized | Decontextualized |

**FIGURE 15.2**

**Two Modes** Each pair describes two modes of thought. Although researchers who use each pair differ in what they emphasize, all see two contrasting ways to think.

2. If it takes 5 minutes for 5 machines to make 5 widgets, how long would it take 100 machines to make 100 widgets?

3. In a lake, there is a patch of lily pads. Every day the patch doubles in size. If it takes 48 days for the patch to cover the entire lake, how long would it take for the patch to cover half the lake?

*[From Gervais & Norenzayan, 2012, p. 494]*

Answers are on page 404. As you see, the quick, intuitive responses may be wrong.

Those two processes also reflect experience. Remember *theory of mind*, which began at about age 4? It continues to develop, as children and then adolescents become more aware of what others are thinking and feeling. But distinct aspects of theory of mind are evident, as now explained.

One study assessed 11- to 25-year-olds on two measures: (1) the *Reading the Emotion in the Eyes Test*, which asks participants to looks at faces and say what emotion the person is feeling, and (2) the Social Stories Questionnaire, which asks participants to read a story and note when either of the two characters inadvertently offended the other. On both, theory of mind (ToM) advanced during adolescence, but not in lockstep.

Researchers wrote, "Advanced ToM tasks tap into distinct ToM components that may develop at different rates" (Meinhardt-Injac et al., 2020). With these two ToM tests, it was not the case that one component developed before the other: There is one person playing the piano, one mind developing. But two processes were evident: Each component developed on its own track.

Another demonstration of dual processing occurs when people are asked to report on one half of information and ignore the other half, both presented at the same time. This can be done with an emotionless task, as in the classic *Stroop test*, in which people are told to report the written color of words that spell another color. For example, they must say blue when the word RED is written in blue. This is difficult, but adolescents become better at it as they grow older.

After this "cool" [i.e., analytic] Stroop test, the same adolescents were given what is considered a "hot" task: They were supposed to report the emotion they saw on a face, ignoring the written word presented with the emotion. The word "angry" might accompany a smiling face. This was much harder than the cool task: Adolescents did worse than either children or emerging adults.

In other words, dual processing meant that unemotional processing (cool) gradually improved with age. Emotional processing (hot) created confusion and mistakes, more in adolescence that at younger ages (Aïte et al., 2018).

## Age and Two Processes

When the two modes of thinking conflict, people of all ages sometimes use one and sometimes the other. To use the piano metaphor, a musician (especially a novice) sometimes uses just one hand. The first impulse of most people is to favor the melody without the balance of the chords. We are all "predictably irrational" at times (Ariely, 2010).

Increased myelination reduces reaction time, so adolescent thought and action occurs with lightning speed. They are "fast and furious" intuitive thinkers, unlike their teachers and parents, who wait to add slower, analytic thinking. No wonder "people who interact with adolescents often are frustrated by the mercurial quality of their decisions" (Hartley & Somerville, 2015, p. 112).

**Observation Quiz** Do you see hot or cold thinking here? (see answer, page 422) ↓

**Fire Your Trebuchet!** Denis Mujanovic, Anna Dim, Ahmed Kamaludeen, and Ghader Asal are all high school students participating in the Western Kentucky Physics Olympics. Here they compete with their carefully designed trebuchets, a kind of catapult related to the slingshot.

Bac Totrong/Daily News via AP Images

| ANSWERS | Intuitive | Analytic |
|---------|-----------|----------|
| 1. | 10 cents | 5 cents |
| 2. | 100 minutes | 5 minutes |
| 3. | 24 days | 47 days |

Paul Klaczynski conducted dozens of studies comparing the thinking of children, young adolescents, and older adolescents (usually 9-, 12-, and 15-year-olds, respectively) (Jacobs & Klaczynski, 2005). Klaczynski found that almost every adolescent is analytical and logical on some problems but not on others, with some passing the same questions that others fail. As they grow older, adolescents sometimes gain in logic and sometimes regress, with the social context and training in statistics becoming major influences on cognition (Klaczynski & Felmban, 2014).

Interestingly, as adolescents become more aware of the impact of social structures, they also become more aware of stereotypes and more influenced by them. For some stereotypes, adolescents actually regress, with younger children better able to consider individual variations instead of overgeneralizations.

Among the stereotypes that show regression is one called *gender intensification*, such as believing that certain jobs are best filled by men and others by women. Increased gender stereotyping was temporary, evident in early adolescence until about age 15, and then reduced (Klaczynski et al., 2020).

The finding that neither age nor intelligence alone necessarily makes a person more logical has been confirmed by dozens of other studies (Kail, 2013). Being smarter as measured by an IQ test does not advance cognition as much as having more life experience, statistical knowledge, and linguistic proficiency, each of which can further analytic thought. Even though the adolescent brain is capable of logic, sometimes "social variables are better predictors . . . than cognitive abilities" (Klaczynski & Felmban, 2014, pp. 103–104).

## Preferring Emotions

Why not use formal operational thought? Adolescents learn the scientific method in school, so they know the importance of empirical evidence and deductive reasoning. But they do not always think like scientists. Why?

Dozens of experiments and extensive theorizing have found some answers (Albert & Steinberg, 2011; Blakemore, 2018). Essentially, logic is more difficult than intuition: It requires questioning ideas that are comforting and familiar, and it might lead to conclusions that are rejected by friends and relatives.

Once people of any age reach an emotional conclusion (sometimes called a "gut feeling"), they resist changing their minds. Analysis might lead to an unpopular conclusion. Without deep thought, prejudice is not seen as prejudice; once people have an emotional reaction, they develop reasons to support their intuition (Haidt, 2013). This is evident in "fake news," which people believe when they suspend analysis (Pennycook & Rand, 2020).

As people gain experience in making decisions and thinking things through, they may become better at knowing when the second cognitive process is needed. For example, in contrast to younger students, when judging whether a rule is legitimate, older adolescents are more suspicious of authority and more likely to consider circumstances that might make some regulations more valid than others (Klaczynski, 2011). Ideally that reflection occurs before a quick, egocentric reaction (see A Case to Study).

## What Are Your Priorities?

A developmental approach to cognition seeks to understand how people think at every age. Since adolescents are capable of logical thought, yet they seem to make foolish choices, it is helpful to know what their goals might be.

Perhaps adolescents are not irrational; instead they may rationally seek goals that are not identical to adult goals. Parents want healthy, long-lived children, so they blame faulty reasoning when adolescents risk their lives. Judges want law-abiding citizens, so they punish those who break the law. Adolescents, however, value social warmth and friendship more than old age or social conformity.

> **THINK CRITICALLY:** When might an emotional response be better than an analytic one?

## Biting the Policeman

Remember from the piano metaphor that some experience and practice may be needed before a harmony of chords and melody. Might suspicion of authority lead to impulsive and destructive action unless context is taken into account?

In midday, one of my students, herself only 18 years old, was walking in the Bronx with her younger cousin. A police officer stopped them, asking why the cousin was not in school. He patted down the boy and asked for identification. That cousin was visiting from another state; he did not have ID.

My student had done well in a college class on U.S. government. When the officer began to "stop and frisk" her cousin, she reacted emotionally, telling the cop he had no legal authority to do so. He grabbed her cousin; she bit his hand; he arrested her. After weeks in jail (Rikers Island), she was brought before a judge. Perhaps those weeks, plus a meeting with her public defender, activated her analytic mind. She had prepared a written apology; she read it out loud; the officer did not press charges.

I appeared in court on her behalf; the judge released her to me. She was shivering; the first thing I did was put a warm coat around her.

This was dual processing. In her education, my student had gained a formal understanding of the laws regarding police authority. However, her emotions overwhelmed her logic. She intuitively defended her cousin without analyzing the impact.

It is easy to conclude that more mature thought processes are wiser. The judge thought that my perspective was a needed corrective. Certainly the student should not have bitten the officer. But the entire incident, and the NYPD "stop and frisk" policy in effect at the time, shows that the authorities do not understand the adolescent mind. My student had learned a heuristic in childhood: Protect your family. In the heat of the moment, she reacted emotionally.

She is not alone in that. Do you remember something you did as a teenager that, with the wisdom of time and maturity, you would not do now?

---

Adolescent hormones and brains are more attuned to immediate admiration from peers than to long-term consequences (Blakemore, 2018). Instead of blaming them for foolish choices, their parents should consider that they may be responding to a value system that prioritizes independence.

An evolutionary perspective contends that all primates need to break away from their original family and find mates of their own. Adolescent cognition may push them to do so (Hartley & Somerville, 2015).

Therefore, a young person might be thrilled to ride with many friends in a speeding car, driven by an admired peer. Similarly, a 15-year-old might smoke a cigarette because peer acceptance and possible romance are more valuable than the distant risk of cancer. This is not to condone such actions, but those choices may be less foolish than they appear.

Furthermore, the systematic, analytic thought that Piaget described is slow and costly, not fast and frugal, wasting precious time when a young person seeks action. Adolescents do not want to take time to weigh alternatives and think of how they will feel in middle age. Some risks are taken impulsively, some reactions are intuitive, and that is not always bad.

Indeed, some experts suggest that the adolescent impulse to take risks, respond to peers, and explore new ideas is essential for development and beneficial for the larger society (Ernst, 2016). It may be that adolescent thinking is "adaptive and rational if one considers that a key developmental goal of this period of life is to mature into an independent adult in the context of a social world that is unstable and changing" (Blakemore, 2018, p. 116).

Societies need some people to question assumptions, and that is exactly what adolescents do. As social circumstances change, traditions need reexamination, lest old customs ossify and societies die. The generational tug between rebellion and tradition is part of human life: Neither generation should be too quick to judge the other.

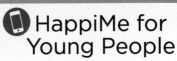

**CHAPTER APP 15**

## HappiMe for Young People

**IOS:**
https://tinyurl.com/y32tsywa

**RELEVANT TOPIC:**
Adolescent cognition

This mindfulness app offers teens strategies for thinking positively. Teens learn to recognize and confront three distinct characters in their thought patterns and can access other tools and techniques for discouraging negative thought patterns.

## Secondary Education

What does our understanding of adolescent cognition imply about school? Educators, developmentalists, political leaders, and parents wonder exactly which curricula and school structures are best. There are dozens of options: academic or vocational, single-sex or coed, competitive or cooperative, large or small, public or private, religious or secular.

To complicate matters, adolescents are far from a homogeneous group. As a result,

> some youth thrive at school—enjoying and benefiting from most of their experiences there; others muddle along and cope as best they can with the stress and demands of the moment; and still others find school an alienating and unpleasant place to be.

> [*Eccles & Roeser, 2011, p. 225*]

A further complication arises from the research on cognition just described. Adolescents are egocentric *and* logical, intuitive *and* analytic, beset by fables *and* capable of advanced reasoning. All forms of thought advance as the brain matures during adolescence, but the connections that allow the entire brain to function as a whole are still developing.

Given all of these variations, no school structure or pedagogy is best for everyone, or even for anyone at every time. Various scientists, nations, schools, and teachers try many strategies, some based on opposite but logical hypotheses. Yet adults want to know what works and that schools are accountable, effectively instructing the teenage mind. To analyze this complexity, we present definitions, facts, and ways to measure what learning occurs.

**Same Situation, Far Apart: How to Learn** Although developmental psychologists find that adolescents learn best when they are actively engaged with ideas, most teenagers are easier to control when they are taking tests (*left*, Winston-Salem, North Carolina, United States) or reciting scripture (*right*, Kabul, Afghanistan).

## Definitions and Facts

**Secondary education**—traditionally grades 7 through 12—denotes the school years after elementary or grade school (known as *primary education*) and before college or university (known as *tertiary education*). Adults are healthier and wealthier if they complete primary education, learning to read and write, and then continue on through secondary and tertiary education. This is true within nations and between them.

Partly because presidents and prime ministers recognize that educated adults advance national wealth and health, every nation is increasing the number of students in secondary schools (see Visualizing Development on the next page). Education is compulsory almost everywhere until at least age 12, and new high schools and colleges open daily in developing nations.

Each year of school advances human potential. As you have read, adolescents are capable of deep and wide-ranging thought, no longer limited by concrete experience; yet they are often egocentric and impulsive.

Quality matters: A year can propel thinking forward or can have little impact. Teachers matter, too (Hanushek et al., 2019). The most effective teachers advance children a year and a half per year, the least effective only a half.

How does anyone know enough about teacher effectiveness to decide that one teacher advances students three times the rate of another? The answer usually involves a test of student learning. As you remember from Chapter 1, scientists try to find ways to measure and evaluate outcomes in order to draw valid conclusions. In this case, many people want to know if students are learning what they should be learning in secondary school.

We want to avoid *social promotion*, promoting students simply because they have spent time in school. A high school diploma is supposed to mean that a student has mastered certain knowledge and skills, and a test might determine that.

On the other hand, as you remember from IQ testing, every test reflects the perspective of the people who write and score the tests. To explore what kind of tests are best for secondary school students, we now look at three types of tests: national "high-stakes" tests, performance assessments, and international tests.

## High Stakes in the United States

Students in the United States take many more tests than they did before 2000, but fewer than they did in 2010. Many of those tests are **high-stakes tests**, so called because of the high cost of failure. In some school districts, *exit exams* determine whether or not a senior can graduate. An 18-year-old might have passed every class for the four years of high school, earning all the required credits (such as two years of a second language, three years of math, four years of English) but still not graduate because of failing a high-stakes test.

Tests also can be high stakes for teachers, who may earn extra pay or lose their jobs based on how their students score. Schools gain resources or are shuttered because of test scores. Entire school systems are rated on test scores. This is said to be one reason that widespread cheating on high-stakes tests occurred in Atlanta, Georgia, beginning in 2009 (Severson & Blinder, 2014).

High-stakes tests sometimes determine whether a child must repeat a grade, beginning at age 8. The 2016 federal education law, the Every Student Succeeds Act (ESSA), required standardized testing from the third grade on.

However, various schools interpret the results differently. For example, Florida was one of several states that mandated that third-graders who failed cannot enter fourth grade. However, in Miami, 15 percent of 28,000 third-graders failed but only half of them were actually left back (Tavassolie & Winsler, 2019).

**secondary education** Literally, the period after primary education (elementary or grade school) and before tertiary education (college). It usually occurs from about ages 12 to 18, although there is some variation by school and by nation.

**high-stakes test** An evaluation that is critical in determining success or failure. If a single test determines whether a student will graduate or be promoted, it is a high-stakes test.

**VISUALIZING DEVELOPMENT**

# How Many Adolescents Are in School?

Attendance in secondary school is a psychosocial topic as much as a cognitive one. Whether or not an adolescent is in school reflects every aspect of the social context, including national policies, family support, peer pressures, employment prospects, and other economic concerns. Rates of violence, delinquency, poverty, and births to girls younger than 17 increase as school attendance decreases.

### PERCENTAGE OF ADOLESCENTS NOT ENROLLED IN SECONDARY SCHOOL

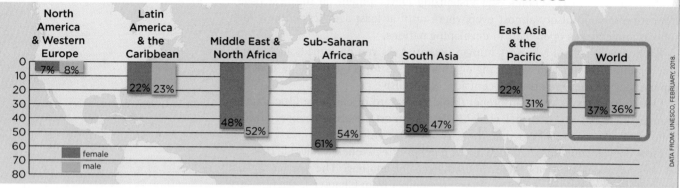

DATA FROM: UNESCO, FEBRUARY, 2018.

### SELECTED SECONDARY SCHOOL GRADUATION RATES - AGE 25 AND UNDER*

| Finland | Japan | Korea | Israel | Greece | Canada | Poland | United States | Germany | United Kingdom | Turkey |
|---------|-------|-------|--------|--------|--------|--------|---------------|---------|----------------|--------|
| 96% | 96% | 94% | 92% | 92% | 87% | 84% | 84% | 79% | 75% | 71% |

DATA FROM: OECD, 2018

*In some nations, some students do not graduate because they go directly into the job market. For example, Germany has an extensive apprenticeship program.

### U.S. HIGH SCHOOL GRADUATION RATE, CLASS OF 2017

Since 2007, the dropout rate among foreign-born youth has declined much faster than for native-born youth, from 27 to 10 percent.

Males are more likely to drop out of high school than their female counterparts, a shift that has occurred since 1980. Before that, more females dropped out, usually because they were pregnant.

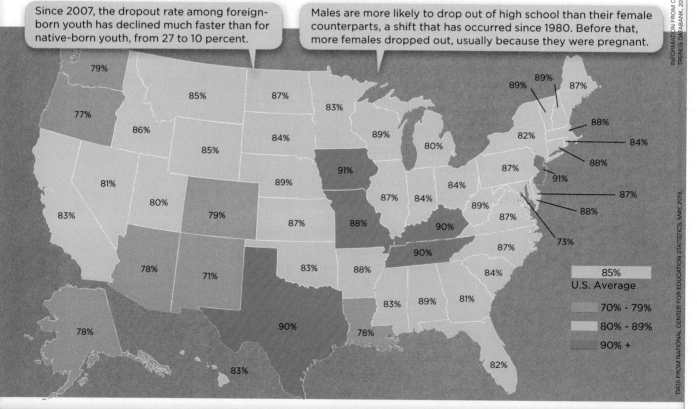

INFORMATION FROM CHILD TRENDS DATABANK, 2018.

DATA FROM: NATIONAL CENTER FOR EDUCATION STATISTICS, MAY, 2019.

For high school students, tests not only determine graduation, but also what college they might enter, and what credits they will earn there. Many colleges use scores on the *SAT (Scholastic Aptitude Test)* or the *ACT (American College Test)* as a crucial factor in deciding admission. Students earn college credits by scoring well on the *AP (Advance Placement)* or *IB (International Baccalaureate)* exams.

The increase in testing is evident in the AP. About 5 million AP tests were taken in 2018, with many students taking several AP tests. That is seven times as many tests as in 2007, when there were only 10 possible AP tests; now there are 38. For example, there was one test in physics and relatively few students took it; now there are three AP physics tests. Each of the 38 AP tests is aligned with a rigorous class in high school (Finn & Scanlan, 2019).

The purpose of mandatory graduation tests was to standardize and improve instruction. Ideally, a diploma earned in one city was equivalent to a diploma in another, and so teachers would try to have all their students reach a high standard.

However, many parents, teachers, and other groups complained that the test narrowed the curriculum, making teachers focus on preparing students to be good test-takers who knew facts, rather than teaching students how to work with other people, analyze problems, and imagine new solutions. In addition, tests were thought to be unfair to African Americans and to English Language Learners (Acosta et al., 2020; Dworkin & Quiroz, 2019; Koretz, 2017).

Those complaints reached lawmakers:

- In 2013, Alabama dropped its high-stakes test for graduation.
- Pennsylvania instituted such a test in that same year, but opponents postponed implementation, and in 2018 the Pennsylvania legislature voted to allow several alternate paths to graduation (including the SAT).
- In 2020, Janet Napolitano, president of the University of California, recommended that the entire California college system scrap the SAT and the ACT as admission requirements and use homegrown tests instead (Hoover, 2020).
- A 2007 law in Texas required 15 tests for graduation; in 2013, Texas law reduced that to four tests (Rich, 2013).

In 2002, more than half of all U.S. states required passing an exit exam before graduation; in 2019, only 13 did (Gewertz, April 9, 2019). However, another trend increased testing: More states (25 by 2019) require all students to take the SAT or ACT, in part to encourage them to plan for college. Overall, high school graduation rates in the United States have increased every year for the past decade (McFarland et al., 2018), reaching 85 percent of fourth-year high school students in 2019 (see **Figure 15.3**). (Graduation rates are higher when they include students who take five or six years to graduate, or who earn an equivalency diploma.) Do these trends reflect increased or decreased testing? If graduation tests are not used, how will employers, parents, or colleges know if a graduate really learned what high school is supposed to teach? Some schools (mostly private ones) use other criteria, such as portfolios or senior papers.

One group of 38 public schools in New York (36 of them in New York City), called the New York Performance Standards Consortium, requires students to

**FIGURE 15.3**
**Mostly Good News** This depicts wonderful improvements in high school graduation rates, especially among Hispanic youth, who drop out only half as often as they did 20 years ago. However, since high school graduation is increasingly necessary for lifetime success, even the rates shown here may not have kept pace with the changing needs of the economy. Future health, income, and happiness for anyone who drops out may be in jeopardy.

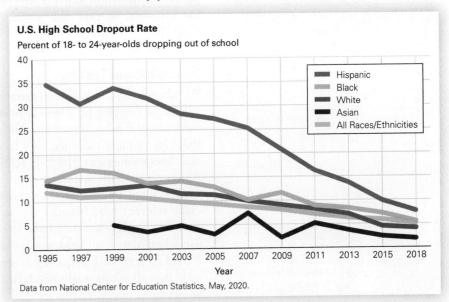

**U.S. High School Dropout Rate**
Percent of 18- to 24-year-olds dropping out of school

Data from National Center for Education Statistics, May, 2020.

**TABLE 15.1**

**Sample of New York Performance Standards Indicators for the Social Science Research Paper**

| | Outstanding | Good | Competent | Needs Revision |
|---|---|---|---|---|
| **Evidence and Sources** | • Supporting arguments include specific, relevant, accurate and verifiable, and highly persuasive evidence, drawn from both primary and secondary sources.<br><br>• Provides specific, relevant, accurate evidence for counterargument, where appropriate.<br><br>• Uses quotations and paraphrasing appropriately to sustain an argument. | • Supporting arguments include relevant, accurate and verifiable, and mostly persuasive evidence, drawn from both primary and secondary sources.<br><br>• Provides relevant, accurate evidence for counterargument, where appropriate.<br><br>• Uses quotations and paraphrasing appropriately to sustain an argument. | • Evidence for supporting arguments is accurate and verifiable, mostly specific and relevant, and generally persuasive drawn from secondary sources.<br><br>• Use of quotations and paraphrasing is mostly evident. | • Supporting arguments may include inaccurate evidence and lack clear, persuasive, or relevant evidence.<br><br>• Quotations and paraphrasing do not effectively support arguments. |

**Only One of Eight!** The entire set of New York Performance Standards for graduation includes several disciplines (including science and literature), each with several measures. Here is just one of eight measures used for the social studies research paper. The other seven include grammar, organization, and analysis. As you see, several evaluators and five levels of success are rated. The high schools in the Consortium consider these rubrics much more demanding than traditional exit exams.

complete four tasks: an essay that analyzes literature, a research paper in the social sciences, a science project that students design and complete, and an applied demonstration of advanced math. Each of these four includes a written and oral test, judged by teachers and outsiders, according to set rubrics (see **Table 15.1**).

Initial results are very positive, with higher graduation rates and college success (Barlowe & Cook, 2016). However, whether or not this can be applied to all of the estimated 43,000 secondary schools in the United States is unknown.

The fact that high-stakes tests have increased and then decreased so dramatically over the past few decades means that change is possible. The fact that virtually every U.S. student takes many standardized achievement tests suggests that eliminating tests completely is unlikely. Even students in the Consortium schools are required, by the New York State Education Department, to take the standardized test to demonstrate proficiency in English.

## International Testing

We already described several international tests, particularly the TIMSS and the PIRLS, in Chapter 12. These tests are given to fourth-, eighth-, and twelfth-grade students in dozens of nations. The results for secondary students are similar to those for younger students, with East Asian nations scoring high, Middle Eastern and South American children scoring low (with some exceptions), and North American students middling.

One more international test, the PISA (mentioned in Chapter 12), is especially relevant here because it was designed to measure high school students' ability to apply what they have learned. The PISA is taken by 15-year-olds, an age when almost all students are still in school but when many will soon stop formal education. The questions are supposed to be practical, measuring knowledge that all adults might need. Recently the emphasis has been on science and analysis.

For example, among the 2012 math questions is this one:

> Chris has just received her car driving license and wants to buy her first car. The table below shows the details of four cars she finds at a local car dealer.
> What car's engine capacity is the smallest?
>
>      A. Alpha      B. Bolte      C. Castel      D. Dezal

| Model | Alpha | Bolte | Castel | Dezal |
|---|---|---|---|---|
| Year | 2003 | 2000 | 2001 | 1999 |
| Advertised price (zeds) | 4,800 | 4,450 | 4,250 | 3,990 |
| Distance traveled (kilometers) | 105,000 | 115,000 | 128,000 | 109,000 |
| Engine capacity (liters) | 1.79 | 1.796 | 1.82 | 1.783 |

For that and the other questions on the PISA, the calculations are quite simple—most 10-year-olds can do them; no calculus, calculators, or complex formulas required. However, almost half of the 15-year-olds worldwide got that question wrong. (The answer is D.) One problem is decimals: Some students do not remember how to interpret them when a practical question, not an academic one, is asked. Even in Singapore and Hong Kong, one out of five 15-year-olds got this question wrong. Another problem is that distance traveled is irrelevant, yet many students are distracted by it.

Overall, U.S. students score lower on the PISA compared to those in many other nations, including Canada, the nation most similar to the United States in ethnicity and location. Compared to peers in other nations, the 2015 results rank U.S. 15-year-olds 25th out of 72 (see **Table 15.2**).

## TABLE 15.2

### Average PISA Scores of 15-Year-Old Students in 2015—Selected Nations

| | Mathematics | Reading | Science |
|---|---|---|---|
| Singapore | 564 | 535 | 556 |
| Japan | 532 | 516 | 538 |
| Canada | 516 | 527 | 528 |
| Netherlands | 512 | 503 | 509 |
| Germany | 506 | 509 | 509 |
| Poland | 504 | 506 | 501 |
| New Zealand | 495 | 509 | 513 |
| Russia | 494 | 495 | 487 |
| Australia | 494 | 503 | 510 |
| United Kingdom | 492 | 498 | 509 |
| Italy | 490 | 485 | 481 |
| United States | 470 | 497 | 496 |
| Chile | 423 | 459 | 447 |
| Mexico | 408 | 423 | 416 |
| Lebanon | 396 | 347 | 386 |
| Indonesia | 386 | 397 | 403 |
| Brazil | 377 | 407 | 401 |
| Dominican Republic | 328 | 358 | 332 |

Some 2015 results were not surprising (China, Japan, Korea, and Singapore were all high), but some were unexpected (high scores for Finland, Vietnam, and Estonia). Among the lowest results were Peru, Indonesia, and the Dominican Republic. The results reflect the educational systems more than geography, since low-scoring Indonesia is close to Singapore.

International analysis finds that the following items correlate with high achievement of high school students on the PISA. The standards were first articulated a decade ago, but they continue to apply (OECD, 2010).

- Leaders, parents, and citizens value education overall, with individualized approaches to learning so that all students learn what they need.
- Standards are high and clear, so every student knows what they must do, with a "focus on the acquisition of complex, higher-order thinking skills."
- Teachers and administrators are valued, and they are given "considerable discretion . . . in determining content" and sufficient salary as well as time for collaboration.
- Learning is prioritized "across the entire system," with high-quality teachers assigned to the most challenging schools.

The PISA and international comparisons of high school students note that students who are immigrants and who are from low-income families do less well. Researchers caution that variations within nations affect results, so comparing one nation to another may be unfair. However, comparing students within nations is illuminating. Generally, girls do less well in science than boys, but this is less true in the United States than in most other nations. However, low-income students in general do especially poorly in the United States.

The scores from Finland have caught international attention, since educators in that nation do not use high-stakes tests. Nor do the students spend much time on homework or after-school education, as is true in some other high-scoring nations, notably South Korea. A Finnish expert proudly states that "schoolteachers teach in order to help their students learn, not to pass tests" (Sahlberg, 2011, p. 26).

International comparisons of 40 nations also show that students in private schools who take the PISA tend to do better than those in public schools, partly because they take the test more seriously and are less likely to guess randomly or skip questions (DeAngelis, 2019). The effort put into learning may be crucial in the United States as well, with different factors relevant depending on whether the student is in middle school or high school, as you will now see.

## Middle School

Often nations provide two levels of secondary education. Traditionally, in the United States, students attended junior high (usually grades 7 and 8) and then senior high (usually grades 9 through 12). As the average age of puberty declined, **middle schools** were created for grades 5 or 6 through 8, as educators recognized that pubescent 12-year-olds are quite different human beings, cognitively and in many other ways, from 17-year-olds.

**middle school** A school for children in the grades between elementary school and high school. Middle school usually begins with grade 6 and ends with grade 8.

Middle school may be the most stressful time in a students' education. Educators find that "teaching is likely to be particularly complex for middle school teachers because it happens amidst a critical period of cognitive, socio-emotional, and biological development of students who confront heightened social pressures from peers and gradual decline of parental oversight" (Ladd & Sorensen, 2017).

Many developmentalists find middle schools to be "developmentally regressive" (Eccles & Roeser, 2010, p. 13), which means that learning goes backward.

**Now Learn This** Educators and parents disagree among themselves about how and what middle school children need to learn. Accordingly, some parents send their children to a school where biology is taught via dissecting a squid *(left)*, others where equality and respect are taught via uniforms and lining up *(right)*.

For students, middle school is a sensitive period, with effects that continue for years (Yeager et al., 2017). Whether or not students go to college is often determined by their middle school experience.

## Engaged Students

Middle school students are dramatically less engaged with school compared to primary school students. The concept of engagement includes how involved students are with school, how active they are in classes, and how much they like their school (Forster et al., 2020; Wang & Eccles, 2013). Every study finds that student engagement drops between primary and secondary education, with the most precipitous drop in middle school.

The most dramatic data come from a 2016 Gallup Student Poll of almost a million students at 3,000 schools in the United States and Canada. They marked whether or not they agreed or disagreed with the following statements:

- At this school, I get to do what I do best every day.
- My teachers make me feel my schoolwork is important.
- I feel safe in this school.
- I have fun at school.
- I have a best friend at school.
- In the last seven days, someone has told me I have done good work at school.
- In the last seven days, I have learned something interesting at school.
- The adults at my school care about me.
- I have at least one teacher who makes me excited about the future.

Every year from the fifth to the ninth grade, fewer students agreed with those statements. By far, the biggest drops were during middle school (see **Figure 15.4**) from three-fourths engaged to less than half (Calderon & Yu, 2017). By high school, engagement was low (about a third), but at least it didn't get much worse each year (active disengagement did, however).

As you remember from Chapter 1, surveys are often inaccurate. Gallup explains that schools and students were self-selected, so specific percentages do not reflect middle school students everywhere. However, the general trends are probably correct, since the same design flaws applied in every grade. Smaller, but more valid studies agree: Many students disengage from school every year of middle school.

**●● Observation Quiz** Although the philosophy and strategy of these two schools are quite different, both share one aspect of the hidden curriculum. What is it? (see answer, page 422) ↑

**FIGURE 15.4**

**Fun, Safe, Exciting . . . School?** A Gallup poll found these results. Do you think that a valid scientific study would also find that three-fourths of primary school students, but less than a third of high school students, are actively engaged in school?

U.S. Student Engagement with School, by Grade

Data from Calderon & Yu, 2017.

## Body and Mind

Puberty itself is part of the problem with education in middle school. Puberty changes the brain, and that affects readiness to learn (Goddings et al., 2019). At least for other mammals, especially when they are under stress, learning is reduced at puberty (McCormick et al., 2010). One problem may be the sexual awakening that occurs with puberty. Sexual conquests are flaunted, girls may be seen as conquests, people of every gender may feel elated, despondent, or obsessed about someone else. Students may have no psychic energy left for homework.

This was the reason that, in 2010, the nation of Trinidad and Tobago changed 20 low-performing schools to single-sex institutions. Achievement rose, in part because the teachers intensified instruction (Jackson, 2019). Would this strategy work elsewhere, or is something unique about that West Indian context?

However, if a student's school achievement suddenly dips, that is both a sign and a cause of psychological as well as academic problems (Rahman et al., 2018). Adults need to understand the reason and change the trajectory; puberty itself should not be blamed. A crucial factor is emotional: whether the students trust and like their teachers (Binning et al., 2019; Riglin et al., 2013).

Signs of a future high school dropout, among them chronic absenteeism, appear in middle school (Ladd & Sorensen, 2017). Those students most at risk are low-SES boys from minority ethnic groups, yet almost no middle school has male guidance counselors or teachers who are African American or Latinx. Given their egocentric and intuitive thinking, many young adolescents need role models of successful, educated men (Morris & Morris, 2013).

Declines in liking school, in trusting teachers, and working hard in class are particularly steep for young adolescents who are African American, Latinx, or Native American, especially when they enter a multiethnic middle school when coming from a neighborhood primary school. As postformal thinking allows them to notice social forces beyond their personal experience, they perceive low expectations and harsh punishment for people of color.

Are they right or biased? One report on 17 middle schools found that for infractions that involved teacher judgment (e.g., disrespect, excessive noise), African Americans were disciplined three times as often as European Americans, but for more objective offenses (cheating, bringing a weapon to school), the rates were more similar (Skiba et al., 2002).

That was decades ago. Has it changed? A more recent report on a large, multi-ethnic school, found that African American sixth-graders (including those not

## CAREER ALERT   The Teacher

Many people who study human development hope to become teachers, for good reason. Teachers can make a huge impact on a child's life. Every adult probably remembers a teacher or two whose interest and insight still affects them.

The need is great, and the demand huge. According to the U.S. Bureau of Labor Statistics' Occupational Outlook Handbook, in 2016 there were 1,500,000 elementary school teachers and 1,008,000 secondary school teachers. But every year, more than 100,000 teachers leave the profession—some retire, some quit, some die. They need to be replaced.

Depending on the local school district, an aspiring teacher can qualify with a bachelor's degree in almost any field. Courses in education can be taken while teaching. Better would be a master's degree in education, which includes on-the-job training with excellent teachers.

Many specialties within the teaching profession are chronically understaffed. In the United States, those trained to teach math, science, a non-English language, or children with special needs will be hired—as long as they are willing to live outside their home community.

Those interested in teaching probably already know that the salary is not that great, but the benefits are adequate, and teaching children can be immensely satisfying as well as challenging. Further, teachers have more vacation days than most professions, and the workday may seem short since most school days end by 3 P.M.

However, good teachers spend as much time preparing and planning as they do in direct teaching. Further, the work is exhausting, physically and emotionally. Teachers become painfully aware that some students have serious problems that teaching cannot solve: abusive or neglectful parents, learning differences, severe poverty, chronic depression.

The greatest openings in the profession are in areas that require special training. Novices may hope to teach high school English or to teach third grade in an affluent suburb. But such jobs are taken by teachers who have seniority; they are unlikely to be filled by new recruits.

Instead, aspiring teachers are most likely to be hired in areas of greatest need: math teachers in cities, teachers who specialize in autism, bilingual teachers, speech teachers who can relate with children and parents of many backgrounds, middle school science teachers.

Some of my students want to be teachers. I encourage them, warning that this profession is more difficult than it may seem. As one leading educator wrote: "Teaching is not rocket science—it is much harder than that" (Sahlberg, 2015, p. 133).

---

personally disciplined) expected biased treatment. Incoming Latinx students did not expect bias, but by the eighth grade, they did. Most White students thought the teachers were fair, but they, too, became less trusting of school authorities over time (Yeager et al., 2017).

Even if there were no discrimination in the larger society, students have reasons to dislike middle school. Parents are less involved than in primary school, partly because students want more independence. It is psychologically healthy for adolescents to push their parents away, but the lack of parental support also increases risk. Bullying increases in the first year of middle school (Baly et al., 2014).

Teacher support also decreases. Unlike teachers in primary school, where each classroom typically has one teacher who knows the families and friends of each student, middle school teachers have hundreds of students. Teachers become impersonal and distant, not the engaging adults that young adolescents need (Meece & Eccles, 2010). Both teachers and students may imagine that the other is hostile toward everyone of their generation, and that imagined hostility harms them both, as now explained.

## Stereotype Threat

It is easy to understand why stereotypes are mistaken, since they do not consider the individuality of each person. Probably every reader of this book knows the sting of being stereotyped and has sometimes too quickly judged someone else, although we are less aware of our own stereotypes than of the stereotypes directed at us.

But more insidious than a direct stereotype may be **stereotype threat**, when someone holds a stereotype that someone else holds a stereotype about them. That mistaken idea can boomerang, harming the person who imagined it.

That boomerang begins with a fact that has troubled social scientists for decades: Secondary school achievement varies by ethnicity. This is evident in tests, grades, and, eventually, graduation. For example, in 2018, 42 percent of public high school

> **Especially for Teachers** You are stumped by a question that one of your students asks. What do you do? (see response, page 422)

> **stereotype threat** The thought a person has that one's appearance or behavior will be misread to confirm another person's oversimplified, prejudiced attitudes.

Hill Street Studios/Blend Images/Newscom

**More Like Him Needed** In 2014 in the United States, half of the public school students were tallied as non-White and non-Hispanic, and half were male. Meanwhile, only 17 percent of teachers are non-White and non-Hispanic, and only 24 percent are male. This Gardena, California, high school teacher is a welcome exception in two other ways—he rarely sits behind his desk, and he uses gestures as well as his voice to explain.

students were Black or Hispanic, but only 38 percent of graduates were. The reasons seem objective: African Americans do not accumulate high school credits at the same rate as other groups.

One sad outcome is ethnic disparity in *status dropouts*, 16- to 24-year-olds who quit school before graduation. Status dropouts have markedly higher rates of unemployment and early death.

Data from 2017 on men aged 16–25, find that 5 percent of non-Hispanic Whites, 7 percent of non-Hispanic Blacks, and 7.5 percent of Hispanics are status dropouts. [Those ethnic categories are the official ones used by the U.S. government]. For women aged 16–24, status dropout rates are 4.3 percent non-Hispanic White, 4.4 percent non-Hispanic Black, and 7.4 percent Hispanic.

There are many explanations for ethnic differences, including poverty, language, genes, and school quality. Each explanation reflects the perceptions of the person offering it.

But look closely at the gender differences among non-Hispanics. Black girls have the same genes, families, and schools as Black boys, yet their status dropout rates are similar to White girls. Why?

Again, many explanations are proposed, each reflecting perceptions. But a novel explanation was suggested by one African American scholar, Claude Steele. He suggested that Black adolescent boys may think that other people have stereotypes about them. The result may be stereotype threat, a "threat in the air," not in reality (Steele, 1997). The mere *possibility* of being negatively stereotyped increases stress, disrupts cognition, and reduces emotional regulation.

Steele suspected that African American males, aware of the stereotypes that they are not smart, become anxious in educational settings. Their anxiety increases stress. Then heightened cortisol undercuts their achievement test scores, so young men protect their pride by denigrating academics. They avoid the anxiety of writing papers, taking exams, and reading textbooks because they anticipate that teachers will not appreciate their work.

In self-defense, they conclude that school doesn't matter, that people who are "book smart" are not "street smart," that Black classmates who study hard are "acting White." They disengage from school, which results in lower achievement.

Stereotype threat occurs within many other groups and skills. It causes college women to underperform in math, bilingual students to stumble with English, older people to be forgetful, and every member of a stigmatized minority in every nation to handicap themselves because of what they imagine others might think (Baysu & Phalet, 2019; Bouazzaoui et al., 2020; Spencer et al., 2016).

Athletic prowess, health habits, and vocational aspiration may be impaired (Aronson et al., 2013). For example, stereotype threat may cause blind people to be underemployed: They hesitate to learn new skills or apply for jobs because they think other people will judge them (Silverman & Cohen, 2014). When star athletes unexpectedly underperform (called *choking*), stereotype threat may be the cause (Smith & Martiny, 2018).

The worst part of stereotype threat is that it is self-imposed. People who are alert to the possibility of prejudice are not only hypersensitive when it occurs, but their minds are hijacked, undercutting potential.

How might this work in secondary school? If students think that teachers expect them to misbehave, anticipating racially biased treatment, that thought will cause them to perceive neutral teacher behavior as disrespectful. That interpretation increases the hormones that, in fact, trigger misbehavior.

Stereotype threat can hobble teachers as well. If they think that students dislike them, in self-defense they might be less personable and more distant, which makes things worse. This becomes a downward spiral, a self-fulfilling prophecy, a sad and hostile teacher.

No one, including Steele, believes that stereotype threat is the only reason for disparities in success and achievement. Further, some adolescents strive to prove the stereotypes wrong. Nonetheless, adolescence may be a crucial time to reduce stereotype threat and increase school engagement (Binning et al., 2019).

Because adolescents are intensely self-conscious, with heightened intuition and irrational personal fables, a teacher's praise for work well done, and explicit expression of respect and anticipation for better work, can transform a threat into a promise. The future can be imagined as worth waiting for—if the adolescent brain can allow anticipation (see Inside the Brain).

## INSIDE THE BRAIN

### Save for a Rainy Day?

You already know that brain growth is uneven in adolescence, with the limbic system advancing ahead of the prefrontal cortex. This explains dual processing, since intuitions arise from the limbic system while analysis is rooted in the prefrontal cortex. It also explains the impulse in middle school to stop studying, and the impulse in high school to quit before graduation.

One topic in cognitive research is called *delay discounting*, the tendency to discount future rewards and instead seek immediate pleasure. Delay discounting is evident when young children eat one marshmallow rather than waiting for two (as described in Chapter 10), when an addicted person takes the drug in front of them instead of thinking about the next day, when middle-aged adults buy a new car instead of saving for retirement.

Delay discounting is particularly strong in adolescence because of uneven growth in the adolescent brain. One part, the *ventral striatum*, is the area that is particularly sensitive to rewards. The striatum grows stronger at puberty, making rewards powerfully attractive (Shulman et al., 2016). As one team expressed it, the "subcortical regions that respond to emotional novelty and reward are more responsive in middle adolescence than in either children or adults" (Harden & Tucker-Drob, 2011, p. 743).

Because the striatum increases the allure of immediate rewards ("don't think about tomorrow"), adolescents are vulnerable to serious problems. Delay discounting is one explanation for impulsive suicide, drug addiction, and eating disorders (Felton et al., 2020).

When delay discounting is added to other aspects of adolescent brain development, with stronger sensations and quicker reactions (sensation-seeking and impulsivity), harm is lifelong. To make it worse, for some adolescents, influences from childhood, such as family chaos and abuse, reduce the brain's ability to wait for future rewards (see **Figure 15.5**) (Acheson et al., 2019).

Fortunately, sensation-seeking and impulsivity are not tightly linked in the brain (Harden & Tucker-Drob, 2011). Both increase, but an adolescent might be drawn to sensory stimulus, but be able to control impulsive reactions. Past family stability and nurturance allows better planning, so destructive impulses are far from inevitable (Acheson et al., 2019). Sensation-seeking might not lead to trouble but might allow a young person to appreciate the moment, such as an exquisite sunset, a sumptuous meal, or a flowering tree more than an adult might.

In many ways, the adolescent brain functions differently from the adult brain. But heightened appreciation of rewards does not always means increased danger. Teachers can find ways to make the immediate classwork more enjoyable, such as encouraging teamwork, laughter, imagination. High school students can visit a college, can plan for a senior prom, can secure a summer job with successful adults.

Everyone of every age is sometimes discouraged by the daily grind. We can learn from the teenagers, even as we try to teach them to plan ahead. Stop to smell the roses?

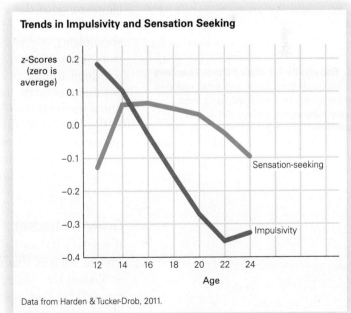

**Trends in Impulsivity and Sensation Seeking**

Data from Harden & Tucker-Drob, 2011.

**FIGURE 15.5**

**Look Before You Leap** As you can see, adolescents become less impulsive as they mature, but they still enjoy the thrill of a new sensation.

## Finding Acclaim

Middle school is a time when children can learn how to cope with challenges, both academic and social. A habit of solving problems rather than blaming oneself—is crucial (Monti et al., 2017). But a habit that worked in primary school may not match the conditions of middle school.

To pinpoint the developmental mismatch between students' needs and the middle school context, note that just when egocentrism leads young people to feelings of shame or fantasies of stardom (the imaginary audience), schools typically require them to change rooms, teachers, and classmates every 40 minutes or so. That context limits friendship and acclaim.

Recognition for academic effort is rare because middle school teachers grade more harshly than their primary school counterparts. Effort without accomplishment is not recognized, and achievement that was previously "outstanding" is now only average. Acclaim for after-school activities is also elusive, because many art, drama, dance, and other programs put adolescents of all ages together, and 11- to 13-year-olds are not as skilled as older adolescents.

Athletic teams become competitive, so those with fragile egos protect themselves by not trying out. If sports require public showers, that is another reason for students in early puberty to avoid them: They do not feel at ease with their changing bodies, and they fear comments from their peers, a fear that is no less powerful if it is a stereotype threat rather than a fact.

As noted in the discussion of the brain, peer acceptance is more cherished at puberty than at any other time. Physical appearance—from eyebrows to foot size—suddenly becomes significant. Status symbols (e.g., trendy sunglasses, a brand-name jacket, the latest smartphone) take on new meaning. Expensive clothes and shoes are coveted.

## High School

Many of the patterns and problems just explained continue in high school. However, once the erratic growth and sudden sexual impulses of puberty are less novel, adolescents are better able to cope. Moreover, peers become more encouraging, and teachers and parents allow more autonomy, which encourages more self-motivation.

Added to that is cognitive maturation. When adolescents are better able to think abstractly, analytically, hypothetically, and logically (all formal operational thought), they can respond to the usual pedagogy of high school.

If a teacher lectures, they can take notes; if someone asks a hypothetical question, they can explore the answer; if a book describes another place and time, they can imagine it. One factor is particularly crucial: whether or not the teacher, and the students themselves, believe that they can master difficult material.

**Especially for High School Teachers** You are much more interested in the nuances and controversies than in the basic facts of your subject, but you know that your students will take high-stakes tests on the basics and that their scores will have a major impact on their futures. What should you do? (see response, page 422)

## Growth Mindset

If teachers do not believe that a student is able to grasp abstract ideas, or if a student believes that they are not able to master calculus, or another language, or Shakespeare, then that perception reduces learning. If a student imagines that they will fail, they avoid the disappointment of failure by not trying. Then they can blame a low grade on their choice ("I didn't study") rather than on their ability. Pivotal is how they think of their potential.

In some schools, children help each other, laugh together, and cooperate on class projects. In other schools, children compete for grades and teacher attention.

This may reflect an attitude toward learning, either a *growth mindset* or *fixed mindset*, also called *incremental* (growth) or *entity* (fixed) (Dweck, 2017).

- The **growth mindset** is that learning grows if people work at it, with one person's growth likely to advance another's. Mistakes are "learning opportunities"; sharing ideas and strategies does not diminish one's own learning, quite the opposite.
- The **fixed mindset** is the belief that ability is determined early on, perhaps at conception. Some people naturally have more talent or ability than others. If students fail, that is evidence of their inadequacy.

To find out inborn ability, students with a fixed mindset use social comparison, ranking themselves among their peers. If they realize that they are not good at math, or that writing is hard, they stop trying, because they are convinced that they will never be good at math, or writing, or whatever. They may deflect attention from their failure ("the dog ate my homework"; "school sucks") and leave school when they can. Teachers with the fixed mindset attribute low performance to the student's personality, neighborhood, family, or intelligence.

On the other hand, students with a growth mindset seek challenges. They work hard at learning, enjoy discussion with their classmates, change their opinions based on what they learn, and choose difficult courses in high school. Teachers with growth mindset believe that every child can succeed, and that their job is to encourage effort, curiosity, collaboration.

This is not hypothetical. In the first year of secondary school, students with a fixed mindset do not achieve much, whereas those with a growth mindset improve academically, and this is true in many nations (e.g., Burnette et al., 2013; Diseth et al., 2014; Zhao & Wang, 2014). By the end of high school, those with a fixed mindset are likely to drop out, and those with a growth mindset are eager for challenging work in college. If they consider a difficult test a challenge, they do better than if they consider the same test a threat (Putwain et al., 2019).

## The College-Bound

From a developmental perspective, the fact that high schools emphasize formal thinking makes sense, since many older adolescents are capable of abstract logic. In several nations, attempts are under way to raise standards so that all high school graduates will be ready for college, where analysis is required.

A mantra in the United States is "college for all"; it is intended to encourage low achievers to aspire for tertiary education, although some authors believe the effect may be the opposite (Carlson, 2016). As already mentioned, many students take difficult classes that are assessed by externally scored exams, either the IB or the AP (Finn & Scanlan, 2019).

Other indicators of increasing standards are greater requirements for academic diplomas and restrictions on vocational or general diplomas. Most U.S. schools require two years of math beyond algebra, two years of laboratory science, three years of history, four years of English, and two years of a language other than English.

## Alternatives to College

In 2018, about 31 percent of U.S. high school graduates did not enter college, and many who enrolled will not graduate. To be specific, only 44 percent at four-year colleges and 33 percent at two-year colleges earn a degree. (These data do not include those who transfer to another institution and graduate there, but transferring itself reduces the chance of graduation [Digest of Education Statistics, May, 2020].) Rates are higher in some nations, lower in others.

**growth mindset** An approach to understanding intelligence that holds that intelligence grows incrementally, and thus can be increased by effort. Those who subscribe to this view believe they can master whatever they seek to learn if they pay attention, participate in class, study, complete their homework, and so on.

**fixed mindset** An approach to understanding intelligence that sees ability as an innate entity, a fixed quantity present at birth. Those who hold this view do not believe that effort enhances achievement.

**What Do They Need to Learn?** Jesse Olascoaga and José Perez assemble a desk as part of a class in Trade Tech High School in Vista, California. Are they mastering skills that will lead to a good job? Much depends on what else they are learning. It may be collaboration and pride in work well done, in which case this is useful education.

San Diego Union-Tribune/ZUMA Press/Newscom

Some high schools encourage college enrollment. For example, high-achieving students in two major cities in neighboring states (Albuquerque, New Mexico, and Fort Worth, Texas) had markedly different college enrollment rates (83 percent compared to 58 percent) (Center for Education Policy, 2012). It is easy to judge Fort Worth harshly, but that itself may be too quick a conclusion.

Instead of encouraging every student to enroll in college, should schools prepare some students for employment after graduation, providing training, social skills, and practical experience? Some nations do that. In Switzerland, students in vocational education have a higher employment rate than students in the academic track, but over a lifetime, their earnings are less (Korber & Oesch, 2019). Which would you rather have at age 40—a steady and secure job or a high salary?

Overall, the data present a dilemma for educators. Suggesting that a student should *not* go to college may be classist, racist, sexist, or worse. On the other hand, since less than half of the students who begin college stay until they graduate, such students may lose time and gain debt when they could have advanced in a vocation. Everyone agrees that adolescents need to be educated for life as well as for employment, but it is difficult to decide what that means.

<table>
<tr><td>

**THINK CRITICALLY:** Is it more important to prepare high school students for jobs or for college?

</td></tr>
</table>

Students who drop out of high school or fail high-stakes tests may have succeeded if they had been offered courses that lead to employment. On the other hand, students who believe that colleges will never accept them, or that employers will never hire them, may handicap themselves, another example of stereotype threat.

## Variability

Adolescents themselves vary: Some are so egocentric that they ruminate obsessively about themselves, some so hypothetical that they think of possibilities no one else imagined. Some are intuitive, some analytic; some foolish, some rational; some ready to quit school in seventh grade, some eager for college; some will thrive in secondary schools, others will disengage.

In fact, these differences appear not only between adolescents but within them; the same person can be intuitive in the morning and analytic in the afternoon. Every adolescent, however, needs respect, personal encouragement, and intellectual challenge.

That brings us to general conclusions for this chapter. The cognitive skills that boost national economic development and personal happiness are creativity, flexibility, relationship building, and analytic ability. Whether or not an adolescent is college-bound, those skills can develop in adolescence, making a wiser adult.

Every cognitive theorist and researcher believes that adolescents' logical, social, and creative potential is not always realized, but that it can be. The two hands on the piano might play beautiful music together. Does that image end this chapter on a hopeful note?

---

**WHAT HAVE YOU LEARNED?**

1. What are the differences between primary, secondary, and tertiary education?
2. What are the advantages and disadvantages of high-stakes testing?
3. How does the PISA differ from other international tests?
4. What characteristics of middle schools make them more difficult for students than elementary schools?
5. Why does puberty affect a person's ability to learn?
6. How does stereotype threat affect learning in secondary school?
7. How do growth mindset and fixed mindset affect motivation and learning?
8. Should high schools prepare everyone for college? Why or why not?

# SUMMARY

### Logic and Self

**1.** Cognition in early adolescence may be egocentric, a kind of self-centered thinking. Adolescent egocentrism gives rise to the personal fable, the invincibility fable, and the imaginary audience.

**2.** Formal operational thought is Piaget's term for the last of his four periods of cognitive development. He tested and demonstrated formal operational thought with various problems that students in a high school science or math class might encounter.

**3.** Piaget realized that adolescents are no longer earthbound and concrete in their thinking; they imagine the possible, the probable, and even the impossible, instead of focusing only on what is real. They develop hypotheses and explore, using deductive reasoning.

### Two Modes of Thinking

**4.** Many cognitive theories describe two types of thinking during adolescence. One set of names for these two types is intuitive and analytic. Both become more forceful during adolescence, but brain development means that intuitive, emotional thinking matures before analytic, logical thought.

**5.** Few teenagers always use logic, although they are capable of doing so. Emotional, intuitive thinking is quicker and more satisfying (and sometimes better) than analytic thought.

**6.** Neurological as well as survey research finds that adolescent thinking is characterized by more rapid development of the limbic system and slower development of the prefrontal cortex. Peers further increase emotional impulses, so adolescents may make choices that their parents believe to be foolish.

### Secondary Education

**7.** Achievement in secondary education—after primary education (grade school) and before tertiary education (college)—correlates with the health and wealth of individuals and nations.

**8.** Educators and political leaders in the United States struggle with how to measure what adolescents learn in secondary school. High-stakes tests have become more popular, and then less popular.

**9.** The PISA test, taken by many 15-year-olds in 50 nations, measures how well students can apply the knowledge they have been taught. Students in the United States have particular difficulty with such tests.

**10.** In middle school, many students struggle both socially and academically. One reason may be that middle schools are not structured to accommodate egocentrism or intuitive thinking. Another reason may be that students become aware of the prejudices of the larger society.

**11.** Education in high school emphasizes formal operational thinking. Students' beliefs about the nature of intelligence—either a growth mindset or a fixed mindset—may also affect their learning.

**12.** About a third of high school students do not graduate or go on to college, and many more leave college without a degree. Current high school education in the United States may not meet their needs. In some other nations, educators pay substantial attention to vocational education in high school so that students are job-ready when they graduate.

# KEY TERMS

adolescent egocentrism (p. 397)
imaginary audience (p. 398)
personal fable (p. 399)
invincibility fable (p. 399)

formal operational thought (p. 400)
hypothetical thought (p. 401)
deductive reasoning (p. 401)
inductive reasoning (p. 401)

dual processing (p. 402)
intuitive thought (p. 402)
analytic thought (p. 402)
secondary education (p. 407)

high-stakes test (p. 407)
middle school (p. 412)
stereotype threat (p. 415)
growth mindset (p. 419)
fixed mindset (p. 419)

# APPLICATIONS

**1.** Describe a time when you overestimated how much other people were thinking about you. How was your mistake similar to and different from adolescent egocentrism?

**2.** Talk to a teenager about politics, families, school, religion, or any other topic that might reveal the way they think. Do you hear any adolescent egocentrism? Intuitive thinking? Systematic thought? Flexibility? Cite examples.

**3.** Think of a life-changing decision you have made. How did logic and emotion interact? What would have changed if you had given the matter more thought—or less?

**4.** Describe what happened and what you thought in the first year you attended a middle school or a high school. What made it better or worse than later years in that school?

## Especially For ANSWERS

**Response for Natural Scientists** (from p. 401): Probably both. Our false assumptions are not logically tested because we do not realize that they might need testing.

**Response for Teachers** (from p. 415): Praise the student by saying, "What a great question!" Egos are fragile, so it's best always to validate the question. Seek student engagement, perhaps asking whether any classmates know the answer or telling the student to discover the answer online or saying you will find out. Whatever you do, don't fake it; if students lose faith in your credibility, you may lose them completely.

**Response for High School Teachers** (from p. 418): It would be nice to follow your instincts, but the appropriate response depends partly on pressures within the school and on the expectations of parents and the administration. A comforting fact is that adolescents can think about and learn almost anything if they feel a personal connection to it. Look for ways to teach the facts your students need for the tests as the foundation for the exciting and innovative topics you want to teach. Everyone will learn more, and the tests will be less intimidating to your students.

## Observation Quiz ANSWERS

**Answer to Observation Quiz** (from p. 397) The first three you can probably guess: Climate change advocates speak of saving the planet, of scientific evidence, and of animals losing their habitats. Extra credit if you know the fourth: "XR" stands for Extinction Rebellion, a group that started with young people in England and has since spread to other nations.

**Answer to Observation Quiz** (from p. 403) Primarily hot! Building the trebuchet requires analysis, but look at their eyes and body positions in this photo.

**Answer to Observation Quiz** (from p. 413) Both are single-sex. What does that teach these students?

# Adolescence: Psychosocial Development

## What Will You Know?

1. Why might a teenager be into sports one year and into books the next?
2. Should parents back off when their teenager disputes every rule, wish, or suggestion they make?
3. Which is more troubling, teen suicide or teen crime?
4. Why are adolescents forbidden to drink and smoke while adults are free to do so?

"**Y**ou're a terrible mother of a teenager!" yelled an angry adolescent.

"I'm learning on the job," the mother shot back. "I've never been a mother of a teenager before."

I sympathize. Often I needed to listen to my daughters to learn how to care for them. One night, Rachel was late coming home. I reassured myself: We had raised her to be cautious and careful; we knew her friends, who would call us if there was serious trouble; we lived in the city, so no one was driving.

Rachel walked in the door before worry overcame my reassurance. I was relieved to see her; I did not think to punish her until she asked, "How long am I grounded?"

That alerted me.

"Two days. Is that fair?"

She agreed.

Parents are not the only ones new to adolescence. Teenagers themselves have never experienced the body transformations described in Chapter 14, nor the cognitive advances described in Chapter 15. The greatest challenges, however, are in this chapter, on psychosocial development.

The social context of adolescent life has never existed before. Sex, drugs, romance, technology, and delinquency are all different for today's youth than for earlier generations. Their parents might remember being an adolescent, but that was before sexting, vaping, and much else. Some things have not changed: Adolescents are more adventurous than their parents. But even the most understanding parent has never viewed adolescence from an adult perspective before.

This developmental perspective is protective but also limiting. When our children were babies, my husband and I discussed the need to be firm, united, and consistent regarding illicit drugs, unsafe sex, and serious law breaking.

We were ready. Yet none of those issues appeared. Instead, their clothes, neatness, and homework made us impatient, bewildered, inconsistent. My husband said, "I knew they would become teenagers. I didn't know we would become parents of teenagers."

This chapter on adolescent psychosocial development includes relationships with friends, parents, partners, authorities. It begins with identity and ends with drugs, both of which may seem to be a personal choice but are strongly affected by social pressures that change from cohort to cohort. Personal traits matter, too, and everyone is unique. Each of my four daughters presented her own challenges, not only because the times had changed, but also because each is an individual, not a younger version of me or of her older sisters.

You will soon read that adults must be alert and supportive, but that they may not know how. Every generation is learning on the job. What did I need to learn? Once Rachel said to her younger sister, "If ever you think of trying cocaine, talk with me first." I was taken aback: I am still learning.

# Identity

Psychosocial development during adolescence is often understood as a search for a consistent understanding of oneself. Self-expression and self-concept become increasingly important at puberty. Each young person wants to know, "Who am I?"

According to Erik Erikson, life's fifth psychosocial crisis is **identity versus role confusion**: Working through the complexities of finding one's own identity is the primary task of adolescence (Erikson, 1968/1994).

Erikson believed that this crisis is resolved with **identity achievement**, when adolescents have reconsidered the goals and values of their parents and culture, accepting some and discarding others, to forge their own identity. They must combine emotional separation from childhood with ongoing reliance on their family and society, a difficult task (Sugimura et al., 2019).

Identity achievement entails neither wholesale rejection nor unquestioning acceptance of national norms. Teenagers maintain continuity with the past so that they can move toward the future, establishing their own identity.

## Not Yet Achieved

Over the past half-century, major psychosocial shifts have lengthened the duration of adolescence, complicating identity achievement (Côté & Levine, 2015). How adolescents experience their identity crisis varies depending on genes, the social context, and family (Markovitch et al., 2017). Moments of rage, anxiety, idealism, and fantasy that seem pathological by adult standards may be part of this search (Côté, 2018).

One developmental scholar provided a useful expansion of Erikson's description of adolescence. James Marcia outlined four ways of coping with the identity crisis: (1) role confusion, (2) foreclosure, (3) moratorium, and finally (4) achievement (Kroger & Marcia, 2011; Marcia, 1966).

**Role confusion** is the opposite of achievement. It is characterized by lack of commitment to any goals or values. It arises early in adolescence, when the hormones of puberty awaken sexual impulses and the cognitive advances of hypothetical thought trigger reexamination of values that were once accepted. The young person's first reaction is confusion: Old assumptions no longer seem valid.

**Foreclosure** occurs when, in order to avoid the confusion of sorting through all the nuances of identity and beliefs, young people lump traditional roles and values together, to be swallowed whole or rejected totally. They might follow every custom from their parents or culture, never exploring alternatives, taking on traditional values, roles, identities.

Or they might do the opposite, foreclosing on an oppositional, *negative identity*— rejecting all their elders' values and routines, again without thoughtful questioning. Foreclosure is comfortable but limiting. It is only a temporary shelter (Meeus, 2011).

A more mature shelter is **moratorium**, a time-out that includes exploration, either in breadth (trying many things) or in depth (following one path but with only tentative commitment). Society offers many ways to postpone identity achievement and choose moratoria instead. Older adolescents may:

- take a gap year before college;
- attend college without a specific career path;

**identity versus role confusion** Erikson's fifth stage of development, when people wonder, "Who am I?" but are confused about which of many possible roles to adopt.

**identity achievement** Erikson's term for the attainment of identity, when people know who they are as unique individuals, combining past experiences and future plans.

**role confusion** When adolescents have no clear identity but fluctuate from one persona to another. (Sometimes called *identity diffusion* or *role diffusion*.)

**foreclosure** Erikson's term for premature identity formation, when adolescents adopt their parents' or society's roles and values without questioning or analysis.

**moratorium** A socially acceptable way to postpone achieving identity. Going to college and joining the military are examples.

- have an intimate sexual relationship with no plans for marriage;
- sign up for two years in the military;
- take a job known to be temporary;
- volunteer for a year of mission work or social justice advocacy;
- intern in a nonprofit for little pay; or
- travel around the world.

All these are moratoria, accepted by our society.

The final outcome, *identity achievement*, is now thought to be a lifelong quest (Topolewska-Siedzik & Cieciuch, 2019). The need to establish identity is most urgent in adolescence, but the self-concept shifts, strengthens, and reverses at many points. This was captured by Anna Quindlen, novelist and grandmother, who wrote:

> It's odd when I think of the arc of my life from child to young woman to aging adult. First I was who I was, then I didn't know who I was, then I invented someone and became her, then I began to like what I'd invented, and finally I was what I was again.

[Quindlen, 2012, p. ix]

## Arenas of Identity Formation

Erikson (1968/1994) highlighted four aspects of identity: religious, political, vocational, and sexual. Terminology and timing have changed, and a fifth identity (ethnic) has been added, yet adolescents still seek identity in every domain.

## Religious Identity

Most adolescents question some aspects of their faith, but their *religious identity* is similar to that of their parents. Few reject their religion totally if they have been raised in it, especially if they have a good relationship with their parents (Kim-Spoon et al., 2012).

The search for religious identity may be universal, as a study of youth in eight nations suggests (Benson et al., 2012). Most of the research has been on Christian youth in Western nations. However, a recent study in Japan reported that Buddhist adolescents also seek to establish their own religious beliefs and practices (Sugimura et al., 2019).

Some become more devout. A Muslim girl might start to wear a headscarf; a Catholic boy might study for the priesthood; a Baptist teenager might join a Pentecostal youth group. In each of these, parents might be surprised, but none of these changes is a reversal. Adults sometimes adopt a completely different faith; adolescents almost never do.

Although becoming more devout than their parents is possible, the more common pattern is rebellion. Attendance at churches, temples, and mosques decreases when parents no longer enforce it. A young person might express the foreclosure of negative identity, criticizing everything about religious customs rather than seeing the benefits as well as the problems.

More common than either extreme is a moratorium that allows later achievement of religious identity. Adolescents question "organized religion" because it seems to be a bundle of beliefs and rituals. They reexamine each part of the package, seeking their own way to be spiritual yet open (Saroglou, 2012). Even those adults who were raised with a strong religious

**VIDEO ACTIVITY: Adolescence Around the World: Rites of Passage** presents a comparison of adolescent initiation customs in industrialized and developing societies.

**Same Situation, Far Apart: Religious Identity** Awesome devotion is characteristic of adolescents, whether devotion is to a sport, a person, a music group, or—as shown here—a religion. This boy *(left)* praying on a Kosovo street is part of a dangerous protest against the town's refusal to allow building another mosque. This girl *(right)* is at a stadium rally for young Christians in Michigan, declaring her faith for all to see. While adults see differences between the two religions, both teens share not only piety but also twenty-first-century clothing. Her T-shirt is a recent innovation, and on his jersey is Messi 10, for a soccer star born in Argentina.

ARMEND NIMANI/AFP/Getty Images

Jim West/The Image Works

background, but who later claim no identifiable religion, nonetheless behave and believe in ways more similar to religious people than to those raised without religion (Van Tongeren et al., 2020). That is achievement, not wholesale rejection.

## Political Identity

Parents also influence their children's *political identity*. In the twenty-first century, more U.S. adults identify as nonpartisan (38 percent) than Republican (26 percent), or Democrat (26 percent), or any other party (5 percent) (Pew Research Center, March 14, 2019). Their teenage children reflect their views, some boasting that they vote for the person, not the party, or that they do not care about politics, echoing their parents without realizing it.

Some proudly vote at age 18—an event that is more likely if they are living at home with voting parents than if they have already left home. Just like other aspects of political involvement, voting is a social activity, influenced by family (Hart & van Goethem, 2017).

In general, adolescents' interest in politics is predicted by their parents' involvement and by current events (Stattin et al., 2017). Adolescents tend to be more liberal than their elders, especially on social issues (same-sex marriage, reproduction, the environment), but major political shifts do not usually occur until later (P. Taylor, 2014).

## Ethnic Identity

Related to political identity is *ethnic identity*, a topic not discussed by Erikson. However, Erikson knew that identity achievement requires interaction between the individual and the historical context. Ethnic identity is now essential.

Parents seek to prepare their adolescents by teaching pride in ethnicity and methods of coping with bias. Such parental socialization becomes a crucial buffer against depression and low achievement (Umaña-Taylor & Hill, 2020).

> **THINK CRITICALLY:** Since identity is formed lifelong, is your current identity different from what it was five years ago?

But because of the chronosystem, the macrosystem, and the microsystem, no parent knows exactly what teenagers will encounter. Teenagers themselves realize that ethnic identity is "not a matter of one's idiosyncratic self-perception, rather, [is] profoundly shaped by one's social context, including one's social role and place in society" (Seaton et al., 2017, p. 683). They must combine parental socialization with current conditions.

In the United States and Canada, about half of all adolescents are of African, Asian, Hispanic, or Native American (First Nations in Canada) heritage. Many also have ancestors of other ethnic groups. The census categories are too broad; teenagers must forge a personal ethnic identity that is more specific.

For instance, youth categorized in school data as Hispanic must figure out how their grandparents' birthplaces (for many U.S. children that might be Mexico, Puerto Rico, or Cuba, and California, Texas, or New York) affect who they are. Many Latinx individuals (some identifying as *Chicano*) also have ancestors from other nations of Central or South America, of Europe and Africa, or of indigenous groups such as the Maya. Non-Hispanics may be surprised to learn that some Mexican Americans do not identify as Hispanic: Mexico recognizes more than 70 national languages, in addition to Spanish.

Identity challenges also confront African American youth as they learn national, global, and family history. Formal operational thought moves them from personal experience into a wider, troubling narrative. For them, parental teachings are often crucial, especially when parents teach racial pride (noting highly successful African American leaders and important cultural values) as well as how to cope with racism (M.-T. Wang et al., 2020).

Similar factors apply for Latinx and American Indian youth who learn a positive narrative regarding their role in the United States. The research suggests that Asian American youth may experience different pressures: For them, racial socialization may reduce self-esteem (M.-T. Wang et al., 2020). Research on adolescents in Hawaii also finds that Native Hawaiian and other Pacific Islander youth have additional complexities establishing their own ethnic identity, a source of conflict with their parents (Wills et al., 2019).

European American adolescents are less likely to hear parents praise their ethnic roots (Loyd & Gaither, 2018) and more likely to hear messages such as "All lives matter," which they realize is a trivialization of the Black Lives Matter movement. Thus, when White children move past concrete operational thought, they also need to figure out how their heritage and ethnicity affect their identity. Some search back to their roots, talking to grandparents, for instance, or sending a saliva sample to be analyzed for DNA origins.

For every adolescent, of every background, peers help sort through stereotypes, resistance, and finally achievement (Santos et al., 2017). Adolescents who are multiracial or adopted by parents of another background encounter additional complications. Their parents usually want to help them but may be less able to do so (Umaña-Taylor & Hill, 2020).

Typically, biracial and adopted youth tend to identify with the ethnic group less powerful in American society. If they are not accepted by that group, they may be depressed (Nishina et al., 2018). Problems may be particularly acute for adoptees from Asia, because parents may be unaware of the racism their children experience (Langrehr et al., 2019). Every adolescent seeks ethnic identity, yet recent cultural shifts make it difficult for adults to understand the particular identity crises of their children.

In general, pride in ethnic identity correlates with academic achievement and overall well-being, but the relationship is "complex and nuanced" (Miller-Cotto & Byrnes, 2016, p. 67). Ethnic pride encourages achievement; ethnic fear fosters depression (Huguley et al., 2019). A positive ethnic identity in early adolescence correlates with intergroup contact later on (Meeus, 2017). Perhaps adolescents who are secure in their own identity are more able to befriend people of other groups.

## Ancestors and Identity

Almost every young person seeks their ancestral roots. Outsiders may not realize how complex this is. Those who have indigenous ancestors (about 1 percent of the population) may want to resurrect customs and lineage that outsiders tried to eliminate, and thus refer to a particular group (Diné, Dakota, Lakota).

Those whose ancestors fought in the American Revolution, or Civil War, or who were enslaved and brought from Africa want to trace their lineage back more than a century. Almost every adolescent encounters identity issues that are acute during the teen years and that may evolve lifelong.

For example, in San Diego, a longitudinal (age 14 to 37) study asked first- and second-generation immigrants, "What do you call yourself?" (Feliciano & Rumbaut, 2019). Few chose pan-ethnic terms (Asian, Latino, etc.). Especially in adolescence, many used specific heritage terms (Cambodian, Mexican, and so on), with a trend toward American (hyphenated or not) as time went on.

One adolescent boy said he was Vietnamese. As an adult, he said he was American, a change facilitated not only by time but also by his surroundings. He said:

> I wouldn't identify myself as Vietnamese. . . . Physically from a phenotype
> perspective, I don't look typical American . . . most people when they think

of Americans they think of just White. But living in San Diego, you see a multicultural group of people.

[*Kim quoted in Feliciano & Rumbaut, 2019, p. 90*]

On the other hand, those who physically appeared White often sought to emphasize their differences from European Americans. Many Latinx individuals claimed to be a "person of color." In this study, none of them said they were simply American. That was a matter of pride. As one said:

For me it's very important to label me Mexican-American because I wanna show people . . . two sides. I wanna show my parents that, hey, I made it. And I'm proud of being Mexican. . . . I'm an immigrant that came to this country and I succeeded and I don't take advantage of the system.

[*Leo quoted in Feliciano & Rumbaut, 2019, p. 93*]

Many reflected the perceptions of other people. One woman with a Filipina mother and a Black father said she was Black-Filipina. She added:

. . . if it was up to me, actually, I'd just say, I'm American [but] I know what they're asking . . . I don't want to be rude about it.

[*Pat quoted in Feliciano & Rumbaut, 2019, p. 93*]

Every individual statement reveals that ethnic identity it is not a private, personal choice but a community one, with differences depending on education (more education led to more specific ethnic identity), family, and national politics. The impact of those influences is not the same on every individual, even those with the same origin. That makes ethnic identity "complex and varied" (Feliciano & Rumbaut, 2018, p. 42).

This is evident in my own family. My brother increasingly identified with his immigrant roots as he grew older, changing how he pronounced his name. My four daughters were required to specify their ethnic heritage as they filled out the 2020 U.S. Census. They sent in their forms and then compared answers; each, with the same eight great-grandparents, wrote a different response.

I have similar impulses myself, which makes me sympathetic when my students resist the identities that strangers assign to them. They are surprised that I bristle if they call me "Caucasian" or "Anglo": Those terms originate from regions where my ancestors did not live. Each of us forges our own ethnic identity, with details that other people may not understand.

## Vocational Identity

Establishing a vocational identity is considered part of growing up, not only by developmental psychologists but also by some adolescents themselves. However, a solid vocational identity is almost impossible in the current U.S. labor market.

Often adolescents imagine what a job might be based on television, not reality, and connect job and personal identity. For that reason, many adolescents aspire to unrealistic careers. Few achieve a vocational identity that they will sustain lifelong, a marked contrast to what Erikson saw, when a young man took a job and stayed with that employer until retirement, or a young woman aspired to work lifelong as a wife and mother. They chose a vocational identity that would shape the rest of their life.

Now, instead, many older adolescents enter the *gig economy*, with temporary, episodic, or independent jobs. They drive cars for hire, tutor children, sell items online, act as social media "influencers," and much more. Those who begin more traditional jobs often quit. Unlike the joke my oldest uncle once told me (that I was going to college to get my "MRS"), few young women now consider marriage *instead* of careers. Between ages 18 and 25, the average U.S. worker has held seven jobs, with the college-educated changing jobs more than the high school graduate (U.S. Bureau of Labor Statistics, August, 2018).

## Gender Identity

Now we come to the most difficult identity for many current adolescents, **gender identity**. As you remember, *sex* refers to certain physical and genetic traits assigned at birth, whereas *gender* refers to the cultural and social factors. A half-century ago, psychoanalytic theorists did not make this distinction. They assumed that adolescents needed to adopt male or female roles (Erikson, 1968/1994; A. Freud, 1958/2000).

Thus, adolescence was once time for "gender intensification," when hormones caused children to identify as one or the other of two *opposite* sexes. That reflected the *gender binary* (the prefix *bi-* means "two," as in *bi*cycle, *bi*nominal, *bi*polar). Many adolescents see sex and gender as *nonbinary*, that they are much more fluid than a male/female dichotomy.

The analytic, hypothetical thinking of adolescents leads to questioning traditional gender norms. This may trouble their elders. One mother thought she was guiding her daughter into a proper female role when she suggested that her daughter's skirt was too tight. Her daughter replied angrily, "Don't slut-shame me."

Similarly, parental comments about appropriate male or female dress, hair, and aspirations may be rejected. Attitudes are powerfully affected by culture, age, and cohort: Gender identity is an example of that. Current adolescents are growing up in a gender world never experienced by their elders.

A new term, *cisgender*, refers to people whose gender identity is the same as their birth sex. The fact that such a term is needed is evidence of the complexity of sex and gender. To be cisgender is not simple, in that exactly how a person is supposed to relate to the other cisgender sex is complicated by conflicting and changing norms of self-presentation, dress, and physical interaction.

Interestingly, more adolescent boys than girls see gender as binary, probably because boys are more strongly pressured to conform to male identity (Horn, 2019). That male identity, however, has changed from what it was, which makes it hard for boys who seek role models in their fathers and grandfathers.

Gender diversity is increasing, and is most evident with transgender identity. In 2016, researchers estimated that 1.4 million people in the United States identified as transgender. That is about .6 percent, twice the rate a decade earlier (Flores et al., 2018).

The reason for the increase is not without controversy. Between 2014 and 2016, three times as many U.S. adolescents who had been designated female at birth identified as male (Littman, 2018; Marchiano, 2017). Some blamed that increase on an encouraging, but mistaken, peer culture. Transgender advocates object to that interpretation, claiming that celebration (not blame) is in order, because more young people can express their identity (Short, 2019; Wadman, 2018).

Among Western psychiatrists in former decades, people who had "a strong and persistent cross-gender identification" were said to have *gender identity disorder*, a serious diagnosis according to *DSM-IV* (1994). However, *DSM-5* (2013) instead describes *gender dysphoria*, when people are distressed at the gender that was assigned to them at birth. *DSM-6* is now in progress: Expect gender updates.

The change from IV to 5 is more than new terminology. A "disorder" means something is amiss with the individual, no matter how they feel about it, whereas "dysphoria" means the problem is in the distress, which can be mitigated by social conditions, by cognitive framing, or by becoming the other gender.

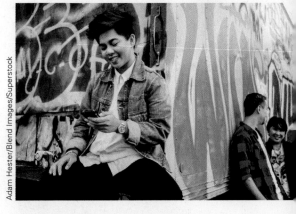

*Adam Hester/Blend Images/Superstock*

**The Opposite Sex?** Every cohort of adolescents rebels against the conventions of the older generations. Earlier generations of boys grew their hair long. A decade later, some girls shaved their heads. Now many teenagers do not see male and female as opposites, choosing instead a nonbinary approach to gender expression.

**gender identity** A person's acceptance of the roles and behaviors that society associates with a particular gender.

## Intersectionality

An added complexity in the identity crisis is that each identity overlaps with every other, not just in individuals, but in society. Each adolescent seeks all five identities just explained, but the various identities combine and conflict, as evident in the concept of *intersectionality* (explained in Chapter 1).

A person aspiring to a particular vocational identity may discover that no one of their ethnic background holds that job, and that itself may discourage them or may cause employers to be unlikely to hire them. Or someone may feel that someone else was chosen for reasons of ethnicity, gender, religion or politics, and that may cause resentment.

Other identities may also conflict: Someone who identifies as a religious conservative may be troubled if they also identify as gender nonbinary, or someone who identifies as African American may be troubled by assumptions about their politics. By adulthood, reconciliation among identities is possible: We all combine aspects of ourselves that others might find contradictory. But, as captured by the term "identity confusion," in adolescence every aspect of identity is in flux.

One psychologist highlighted this with vocational identity:

> career choices faced by individuals inevitably raise the question of the meaning that they intend to give their lives. To choose their work or sector in which they want to evolve is also to consider the purpose of their existence, the priorities (physical, spiritual, social, aesthetic, etc.) that they want to give, the choices that they wish to operate, the overall style of life that they wish to give themselves.
>
> *[Bernaud, 2014, p. 36]*

Given that each identity seems connected to "the purpose of existence" and "the overall style of life," no wonder adolescents experience an identity crisis. Self-definition and then acceptance, not only of oneself but also by other people, is an urgent psychosocial need. Those "other people" are discussed next.

---

**WHAT HAVE YOU LEARNED?**

1. What is Erikson's fifth psychosocial crisis, and how is it resolved?
2. How does foreclosure differ from moratorium?
3. What role do parents play in adolescent religious and political identity?
4. How does ethnic identity affect self-esteem and achievement?
5. What assumptions about gender identity did most adults hold 50 years ago?
6. What is the difference between gender identity disorder and gender dysphoria?

---

## Close Relationships

The focus on adolescent self-definition may imply that teenagers are intensely individualistic, seeking their own identity, apart from their family and society. However, the opposite is more accurate. Parents, peers, grandparents, siblings, teachers, and cultures shape adolescent lives (Seaton et al., 2017).

It is a myth that adolescents choose peers over parents; usually both are supportive. A longitudinal study of all middle school students in one community (almost 800 of them) found that three-fourths had healthy relationships with their parents *and* their peers. That protected them from serious problems during adolescence and early adulthood (Dishion et al., 2019). If parents are not supportive, trouble with friends is also common.

## Family

Family relationships affect identity, expectations, and daily life. Parents shift from providing direct guidance to giving advice when asked, but close parent–child relationships continue (E. Chen et al., 2017).

Older siblings also become influential, as role models and confidants, as bullies or protectors (Aizpitarte et al., 2019; Gallagher et al., 2018). This is especially important if the environment and genes push teens toward negative behavior: An older sibling can be crucial.

### Family Conflict

The fact that families are influential does not mean that family life is peaceful. Disputes are common when biology, cognition, and culture all push for adolescent independence, while parents seek protective control. Consequently, each generation might misjudge the other. Adolescents think parents are overprotective; parents think peers are too loose.

*"So I blame you for everything—whose fault is that?"*

**Not My Fault** Humans always find it easier to blame someone else, but this is particularly true when teenage girls talk to their mothers.

Both may forget that all close relationships include disagreements. Reducing conflict by reducing connection may buy peace at a steep price. Some developmentalists think that conflict increases mutual understanding and emotional growth (Branje, 2018).

Granting too much freedom, too early, is a path toward serious trouble (law breaking, addiction) (Fosco & LoBraico, 2019). On the other hand, too much control, for too long, fractures connection. One of my college students wrote:

> My parents . . . see me as too independent. I see them as too old-fashioned. . . .
> My home life is a lie. I pretend to be their good daughter. . . . I used to argue
> with them all the time when I was in high school but it soon got to the point that
> screaming and yelling got tiring. Now I just want to get by the couple of hours
> I'm at home without any problems.
>
> I never confide in my parents. . . . Whenever I need advice I go to my friends.
> My parents act as if they own my life and that whatever they say goes. It's one of
> the reasons I wanted to run away at thirteen.

*[E., personal communication]*

Authors of research on mothers and their adolescents suggest that "although too much anger may be harmful . . . some expression of anger may be adaptive" (Hofer et al., 2013, p. 276). In this study, as well as generally, the parent–child relationship usually improved with time as both parties adjust to the adolescent's increasing independence. Clearly, as my student shows, sometimes neither generation adjusts.

Crucial is that caregivers avoid either extreme, strictness or leniency, but instead maintain support while increasing autonomy (Yeager et al., 2018). As a review of dozens of studies expressed it: "parent–adolescent conflict might signal the need for families to adapt and change . . . to accommodate adolescents' increasing needs for independence and egalitarianism" (Weymouth et al., 2016, p. 107).

> **THINK CRITICALLY:** When do parents forbid an activity they should approve of, or ignore a behavior that should alarm them?

### Closeness Within the Family

Several specific aspects of parent–child relationships have been studied. Specifically:

1. Communication (Do family members talk openly and honestly?)
2. Support (Do family members rely on each other?)
3. Connectedness (How emotionally close are family members?)
4. Control (Do parents allow independence?)

No social scientist doubts that the first two, communication and support, are crucial. Patterns from childhood continue, ideally buffering the turbulence of adolescence. Regarding the next two, connectedness and control, consequences vary, and observers differ in what they see. How do you react to this example, written by another one of my students?

> I got pregnant when I was sixteen years old, and if it weren't for the support of my parents, I would probably not have my son. And if they hadn't taken care of him, I wouldn't have been able to finish high school or attend college. My parents also helped me overcome the shame that I felt when . . . my aunts, uncles, and especially my grandparents found out that I was pregnant.
>
> *[I., personal communication]*

My student's boyfriend is no longer part of her life. She is grateful that she still lives with her parents, who care for her son. However, did motherhood make her dependent on her parents, preventing her from establishing her own identity? Why didn't her parents monitor her romantic relationship, or at least explain contraception? Is this an example of the best or the worst of parent–adolescent relationships?

One issue here is **parental monitoring** — that is, parental knowledge about each child's whereabouts, activities, and companions. Many studies have shown that when parental knowledge arises from a warm, supportive relationship, adolescents usually become confident, well-educated adults, avoiding drugs and risky sex.

However, if parents are cold and punitive, monitoring may lead to deception and rebellion. If mothers are too controlling, depression increases; if fathers are too controlling, drug addiction is more likely (Eun et al., 2018).

There is a "dynamic interplay between parent and child behaviors," which affects the results of monitoring (Abar et al., 2014, p. 2177). Teenagers choose what to reveal. They share details if their parents are supportive; they lie if their parents are critical (Lushin et al., 2017).

## Cultural Expectations for Parents of Teenagers

Several researchers have compared parent–child relationships in various cultures: Everywhere, parent–child communication and support (numbers 1 and 2 above) reduce teenage depression, suicide, and low self-esteem, and increase motivation and achievement. However, details of connection and control (numbers 3 and 4) vary by culture (Brown & Bakken, 2011).

Parent–child conflict is less evident in cultures that stress **familism**, the belief that family members should sacrifice personal freedom and success to care for one another. For example, most refugee youth (Palestinian, Syrian, Iraqi) in Jordan agree that parents have the right to decide their children's hairstyles, clothes, and music — contrary to what most U.S. teenagers believe (Smetana et al., 2016).

Familism is a strong value in Mexican culture, but a recent study found that Mexican American adolescents do not necessarily value familism as their parents do (Padilla et al., 2020). Fathers, particularly, are likely to endorse familism (e.g., "It is always important to be united as a family"), but older siblings often disagree. A developmental shift may occur when adolescents take "active roles in their identity formation . . . [with] increased autonomy in choosing how and with whom to spend their time" (Padilla et al., 2020, pp. 997, 1001).

In many traditional cultures, teens do not tell their parents anything that might earn disapproval. By contrast, some U.S. adolescents deliberately provoke an argument by advocating marijuana legalization, same-sex romance, immigrant citizenship, or abortion access, especially if they personally are not affected by those policies.

**LaunchPad**
macmillan learning

**VIDEO: Parenting in Adolescence** examines how family structure can help or hinder parent–teen relationships.

**parental monitoring** Parents' ongoing knowledge of what their children are doing, where, and with whom.

**familism** The belief that family members should support one another, sacrificing individual freedom and success, if necessary, in order to preserve family unity and protect the family.

A CASE TO STUDY

## The Naiveté of Your Author

Parents are sometimes unaware of adolescents' desire for respect from their classmates. I did not recognize this with my own children:

- Our oldest daughter wore the same pair of jeans in tenth grade, day after day. She washed them each night by hand, and I put them in the dryer early each morning. [Circadian rhythm—I was asleep hours before she was, and awake hours earlier.] My husband was bewildered. "Is this some weird female ritual?" he asked. Years later, our daughter explained that she was afraid that if she wore different pants each day, her classmates would think she cared about her clothes, which would prompt them to criticize her choices. To avoid that imaginary audience, she wore only one pair of jeans.

- Our second daughter, at 16, pierced her ears for the third time. I asked if this meant she would do drugs; she laughed at my foolishness. Only later did I notice that many of her friends also had multiple holes in their earlobes.

- At age 15, our third daughter was diagnosed with Hodgkin's disease, a kind of cancer. My husband and I consulted four physicians in four hospitals. Their recommendations differed: We selected the one we thought would minimize the risk of death. Our daughter had other priorities: "I don't care what you choose, as long as I keep my hair." (Now her health is good; her hair grew back.)

- Our youngest, in sixth grade, refused to wear her jacket (it was new; she had chosen it), even in midwinter. Years later she told me why—she wanted her classmates to think she was tough.

In retrospect, I am amazed that I was unaware of the power of peers, a stronger and more immediate influence than self-acceptance, personal choice, long life, or even a warm body.

---

Cultural variations in parent–child interaction are evident not only between nations, but also within U.S. ethnic groups. This is illustrated by another study of Mexican American adolescents (Wheeler et al., 2017). This one was longitudinal: Those who were less Americanized were more likely to endorse familism, to obey their parents, to stay in school, and to avoid gangs.

Personality also matters, with differential susceptibility. Impulsive, fearful, or adventurous adolescents are more likely to break the law *unless* their family is supportive, in which case they are more law-abiding than the average adolescent (Rioux et al., 2016).

This contrast is evident in school achievement as well. When parents encourage academics, students do better. However, a longitudinal study of intellectually gifted students found that when parents were harsh at puberty, fewer of the adolescents enrolled in college.

Gender mattered in what they did instead: Boys were likely to become delinquents; girls to become pregnant (Hentges et al., 2018). All these examples suggest that parental support and encouragement is needed, but that parental power over adolescents is limited (see A Case to Study).

### Peer Power

Peers can be crucial. They help each other navigate the physical changes of puberty, the social challenges of leaving childhood, and the intellectual challenges of high school. They also share emotions, and by so doing become closer friends (von Salisch, 2018).

### Choosing Friends

To fully understand the impact of peers, two concepts are helpful: *selection* and *facilitation*. Teenagers *select* friends with similar values and interests, abandoning

**Especially for Parents of a Teenager** Your 13-year-old comes home after a sleepover at a friend's house with a new, weird hairstyle—perhaps cut or colored in a bizarre manner. What do you say and do? (see response, page 453)

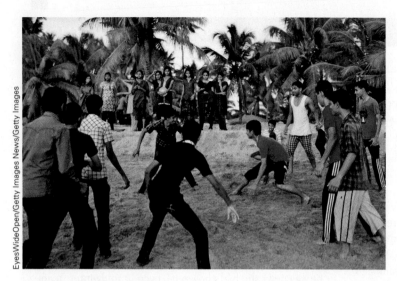

**More Familiar than Foreign?** Even in cultures with strong and traditional family influence, teenagers choose to be with peers whenever they can. These boys play at Cherai Beach in India.

● **Observation Quiz** What evidence do you see that traditional norms remain in this culture? (see answer, page 453) ↑

**peer pressure** Encouragement to conform to friends or contemporaries in behavior, dress, and attitude. Adolescents do many things with peers that they would not do alone.

---

**THINK CRITICALLY:** Why is peer pressure thought to be much more sinister than it actually is?

---

**coercive joining** When others strongly encourage someone to join in their activity, usually when the pressure is that, unless the teenager joins, they will be excluded.

former friends with other interests. Then, friends *facilitate* destructive or constructive behaviors.

It is easier to do wrong ("Let's all skip school on Friday") or right ("Let's study together for the chem exam") with friends. Peer facilitation helps adolescents do things they are unlikely to do alone. This provides an important clue for adults who want to halt destructive patterns in adolescents. Grouping troubled adolescents together (as in special programs in school or residences for young lawbreakers) might make all of them worse, not better (Lochman et al., 2015).

Thus, adolescents select and facilitate, choose and are chosen. Happy, energetic, and successful teens have close friends who themselves are high achievers, with no major emotional problems. A student's grade point average and IQ increase if their friends are highly intelligent (Meldrum et al., 2019).

This works the other way as well. Those who are drug users, sexually active, and alienated from school choose compatible friends. In general, peers provide opportunity, companionship, and encouragement for what adolescents might do.

However, innocent teens are not corrupted by deviants. Adolescents choose their friends and role models—not always wisely, but never randomly. Selection and facilitation are evident lifelong, but the balance between the two shifts. Early adolescence is a time of selection; facilitation is more evident in later adolescence. After age 18 or so, selection becomes important again, as young adults abandon some high school friends and establish new ones (Samek et al., 2016).

## Peer Pressure

**Peer pressure** refers to someone being pushed by their friends to do something that they would not do alone. Peer pressure is especially strong in early adolescence, when adults seem clueless about biological and social stresses. Some teenagers are more susceptible to peer pressure than others, with gender one factor. Boys influence other boys more than girls influence other girls (McCoy et al., 2019).

Adults warn children against peer pressure. However, sometimes having friends is beneficial: Peers pressure each other to study, to apply to college, to plan for their future.

This positive take on peer pressure is tempered by another fact: Peers *can* lead one another into trouble. A study of substance misuse and delinquency among twins found that—even controlling for genes and environment—when one twin became a delinquent, the other was more likely to do so (Laursen et al., 2017). Adolescents who are rejected by other peers tend to choose antisocial friends, who then involve them in drugs, aggression, and so on (Kornienko et al., 2020).

Thus, friends choose, teach, and encourage each other. This is shown in **coercive joining**, when two people join together in making derogatory comments about a third person. A pair of teenagers may compete in who can make the most pointed criticisms. Coercive joining at age 12 predicts antisocial violence at age 21 (Dishion et al., 2019).

## Romantic Partners

Selection is obvious in romance. Adolescents choose and are chosen by romantic partners, and then they influence each other on almost everything—sex, music, work, play, education, food, and so on. Even small things matter: If one gets a new jacket, or tattoo, or sunglasses, the other might, too.

## The Immediacy of Peers

Given the areas of the brain that are quickest to myelinate and mature in adolescence, it is not surprising that the most influential peers are those nearby at the moment. This was found in a study in which all eleventh-graders in several public schools in Los Angeles were offered a free online SAT prep course (worth $200) that they could take if they signed up on a paper distributed by the organizers (Bursztyn & Jensen, 2015).

In this study, most students had several honors classes and several nonhonors classes, depending on their interests as well as what tests (e.g., AP) they planned to take before college. Students were *not* allowed to talk to each other before deciding whether or not to accept the SAT offer.

Consequently, they did not know that, although all of the papers had identical, detailed descriptions of the SAT program, one word differed in who would learn of their decision—either no other students or only the students in that particular class.

The two versions were:

*Your decision to sign up for the course will be kept completely private from everyone, except the other students in the room.*

*Your decision to sign up for the course will be kept completely private from everyone, including the other students in the room.*

It mattered whether students thought their classmates would learn of their decision: The students in an honors class were *more* likely to sign up, and the students in a nonhonors class were *less* likely to sign up, when they thought their classmates would know what they did.

To make sure this was a peer effect, not just divergent motivation and ability between honors and nonhonors individuals, the researchers compared students who took exactly two honors classes and several nonhonors classes. There were 107 such students, some who happened to be in their honors class when they decided whether or not to sign up for SAT prep and some who happened to be in their nonhonors class.

When the decisions of those two-honors-class students were kept totally private, acceptance rates were similar (72 and 79 percent) no matter where students were at the moment. But if students thought their classmates might know their decision, imagined peer pressure affected them. When in an honors class, 97 percent signed up for the SAT program. Of those in a nonhonors class, only 54 percent signed up (Bursztyn & Jensen, 2015).

Evidence from many other studies finds that peers are especially influential in mid-adolescence. That is reflected in brain activity as well as in behavior (Kim-Spoon et al., 2019). Note that peer influence is not necessarily direct, as when one person tells another what to do. Instead, peer influence is contagious (Reiter et al., 2019). Just like catching a cold because someone nearby sneezes, adolescents tend to do what they think nearby peers will admire.

---

Teens' first romances typically occur in high school, with girls having a steady partner more often than boys. Commitment is the ideal, but the fluidity and rapidity of selection disrupt exclusive relationships. Cheating, flirting, switching, and disloyalty are rife; breakups and unreciprocated crushes are common. Emotions range from exhilaration to despair, leading to impulsive sex, cruel revenge, and deep depression.

Peer support is vital: Friends help adolescents cope with ups and downs. They also influence sexual activity, more by what they say than by what they do (which some keep secret). The friend who brags is more influential than the one who stays quiet.

Most peer relationships are nonsexual: Adolescents have platonic friends of all genders (Kreager et al., 2016a). Norms vary from group to group, school to school, city to city, nation to nation. For instance, twice as many high school students in Cleveland as in San Francisco say they have had intercourse (46 percent versus 22 percent) (MMWR, June 15, 2018).

The influence of the social context is undeniable, but sexual impulses are also affected by biology. This is evident in whether or not a romance includes physical activity, and what that physical activity is. Some young people seem driven to risk parental punishment and their own health; others seem content to postpone any sexual activity. Adolescents vary in both the strength of the sexual desire and in their sexual orientation.

**Observation Quiz** What does the body position of these four suggest? (see answer, page 453) ↓

**Hang Loose?** Are these two dating couples or a group of friends at the basketball court? Notice who has the ball and who does not want to show her face.

Hero Images/Getty Images

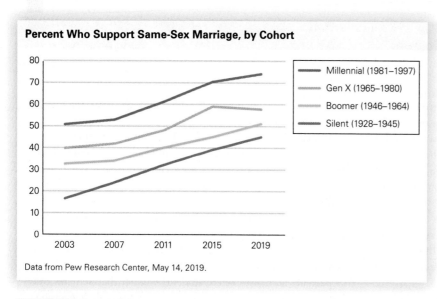

**Percent Who Support Same-Sex Marriage, by Cohort**

Legend:
— Millennial (1981–1997)
— Gen X (1965–1980)
— Boomer (1946–1964)
— Silent (1928–1945)

Data from Pew Research Center, May 14, 2019.

**FIGURE 16.1**

**Young and Old** Everyone knows that attitudes about same-sex relationships are changing. Less well known is that cohort differences may be greater than the shift over the first decade of the twenty-first century.

**sexual orientation** A person's romantic or sexual attraction, which can be to others of the same gender, the other gender, or every gender.

**LaunchPad**
macmillan learning

**VIDEO: Romantic Relationships in Adolescence** explores teens' attitudes and assumptions about romance and sexuality.

**Sexual orientation** refers to the direction of a person's erotic desires. One meaning of *orient* is "to turn toward"; thus, sexual orientation refers to whether a person is attracted to (turned on by) people of the other sex, the same sex, or both sexes. Sexual orientation can be strong, weak, overt, secret, or unconscious. The most apparent—and controversial—evidence for the role of biology and culture occurs with young people who are lesbian, gay, bisexual, transgender, or queer/questioning (LGBTQ).

## Same-Sex Attraction

Sexual orientation is surprisingly fluid during adolescence. In one study, 10 percent of sexually active teenagers had had same-sex romances, but many of those 10 percent nonetheless identified as heterosexual (Pathela & Schillinger, 2010). In that study, those most at risk of abusive relationships and sexually transmitted infections had partners of both sexes, a correlation also found in other studies (e.g., Russell et al., 2014).

In previous decades, LGBTQ adolescents were often "in the closet," unable to tell others (and sometimes themselves) about their sexual orientation. This changed in about 2000, when television aimed at teen audiences began introducing major characters who were gay, and plots portrayed "being out in high school as greatly preferable to being closeted" (Peters, 2016, p. 488). But the depiction was nonetheless homophobic. LGBTQ youth still experience overt prejudice, as well as stereotype threat.

Worldwide, some LGBTQ teens date the other sex to hide their orientation. Deception puts them at risk for binge drinking, suicidal thoughts, and drug use. Those hazards are less common in cultures where same-sex partnerships are accepted (see **Figure 16.1**), especially when parents affirm their offspring's sexuality.

At least in the United States, adolescents have similar difficulties and strengths regardless of their gender identity and sexual orientation. Nonsexual friendships with peers of whatever orientation decrease loneliness and increase resilience (Van Harmelen et al., 2017). However, LGBTQ youth have a higher risk of depression and anxiety, for reasons from every level of Bronfenbrenner's ecological-systems approach (Mustanski et al., 2014).

 **DATA CONNECTIONS: Sexual Behaviors of U.S. High School Students** examines how sexually active teens really are.

## Learning About Sex

Some adolescents have strong sexual urges but minimal logic about pregnancy, disease, lust, and love. Millions of teenagers worry that they are oversexed, undersexed, or deviant, unaware that thousands, maybe millions, of others have the same sexual needs.

The most obvious example is with LGBTQ youth. When suicide data for these young people became public in about 2010, 50,000 gay and lesbian adults posted "It gets better" videos. They wanted young people to learn that same-sex orientation becomes less burdensome in adulthood (Garrett, 2018).

Indeed, every young person has much to learn. As one observer wrote, adolescents "seem to waffle their way through sexually relevant encounters driven both by the allure of reward and the fear of negative consequences" (Wagner, 2011, p. 193). Where can they learn about sex?

## From the Media

Adolescents with intense exposure to sex in music, print, social media, film, and television are more often sexually active, but the direction of this correlation is controversial. The media may reinforce, but not cause, a focus on external appearance, body objectification, and thus sexual activity (Coyne & Ward et al., 2019; Dillman Carpentier & Stevens, 2018).

However, not much practical information comes from the media. Television programs that attract teen audiences include sexual content almost seven times per hour (Steinberg & Monahan, 2011). But almost never does a character develop an STI, deal with an unwanted pregnancy, or mention (much less use) a condom.

For questions regarding sexual health, the internet is a common source (Simon & Daneback, 2013). Unfortunately, Web sites may be frightening (pictures of diseased organs), mesmerizing (pornography), or misleading (false information). A survey of adolescents in England found that they all used the internet for sexual questions, but they had many criticisms—too much material, too technical, too pornographic, or too simplistic (S. Patterson et al., 2019). As one boy said:

> We're talking about adult issues, you know, with our bodies. We're not here to watch like a Thomas the Tank Engine explain it or anything like that.

## From Parents

It may be that "the most important influences on adolescents' sexual behavior may be closer to home than to Hollywood" (Steinberg & Monahan, 2011, p. 575). As that quote implies, sex education begins within the family.

Every study finds that parental communication influences adolescents' behavior. Effective programs of sex education explicitly require parental participation (Silk & Romero, 2014). However, embarrassment and ignorance are common among both generations.

Many parents underestimate their own child's sexual activity while fearing the sexuality of peers and the media (Elliott, 2012). However, those fears do not lead to open and honest discussions about sex, love, and life. According to a survey of young women aged 15 to 24 chosen to represent the U.S. population, only 25 percent of adolescents remember receiving any sex education from either parent (Vanderberg et al., 2016).

Mothers and daughters more often have detailed conversations than do fathers and sons, but the emphasis is on avoiding pregnancy and diseases, not on pleasure and love. That may be less problematic than it seems: The strongest influence from parents on sexual relationships was not via communication about explicit thrills and dangers, but via a strong and supportive parent–child relationship (Cheshire et al., 2019).

Religious values also have some influence, but again the impact comes from general messages about respect and love rather than from specifics. Almost never does either generation share personal details (Coffelt, 2017).

**Laugh and Learn** Emotions are as crucial as facts in sex education.

⬤◗ **Especially for Sex Educators**
Suppose adults in your community never talk to their children about sex or puberty. Is that a mistake? (see response, page 453)

THINK CRITICALLY: Why has sex education become a political issue?

## From Peers

Especially when parents are silent, forbidding, or vague, adolescent sexual behavior is strongly influenced by peers. Boys learn about sex from other boys, girls from other girls. Selection and facilitation are evident again, as adolescents choose friends whose sexual inclinations are similar to their own, and then talk about it (Trinh et al., 2019).

Partners teach each other. However, their lessons are more about pleasure than consequences: Few U.S. adolescent couples decide together *before* they have sex how they will prevent pregnancy and disease, and what they will do if their efforts fail.

In one study, adolescents were asked with whom they discussed sexual issues. Friends were the most common confidants, then parents, and last of all dating partners. Indeed, only half of the them had *ever* discussed specifics of sexual expression with a partner (Widman et al., 2014).

## From Educators

Sex education from teachers varies dramatically by school and by nation. The curriculum for middle schools in most European nations includes information about masturbation, same-sex romance, oral and anal sex, and uses and failure rates of methods of contraception. Those subjects are rarely covered in U.S. classes, even in high school. Rates of teenage pregnancy in European nations are less than half the rates in the United States. Sex education in schools is far from the only reason, but it is one part of it.

Within the United States, the timing and content of sex education vary by state, by community, and by school. Some high schools provide comprehensive education, free condoms, and medical treatment; others provide nothing. Some school systems begin sex education in primary school; others wait until senior year of high school.

A review of official guidelines for sex education in all 50 states found that eight states explicitly condemn same-sex relationships. By contrast, seven states explicitly teach gender diversity of all kinds (Hall et al., 2019). Details about contraception are rarely taught. However, some instructors talk privately with individual students who want more information.

Should such private talks be forbidden? One controversy has been whether schools should teach that abstinence is the only acceptable action. Of course, abstaining from sex (including oral and anal sex) prevents STIs and avoids pregnancy, so some adults and most state curricula favor it (Hall et al., 2019).

But longitudinal data comparing students who were taught to avoid all sexual contact until marriage with those who had comprehensive sex education, showed similar ages for onset of sexual activity. Indeed, abstinence-only programs increased the rate of teen pregnancy and sexually transmitted infections, since students in those programs never learned about prevention (Fox et al., 2019; Santelli et al., 2017).

Legislative support for abstinence-only education is an example of the problem described in Chapter 1: Opinions may ignore evidence (Hall et al., 2019). It also misses evidence from medical, psychological, and neurological research. Teen behavior is driven by peer actions and the limbic system, not by textbook facts and the prefrontal cortex. Consequently, effective sex education must engage emotions and students' opinions (Suleiman & Brindis, 2014).

## Technology and Human Relationships

Technology has changed the adolescent experience, but many adults are not sure whether it is for the better or the worse. Adults over age 50 grew up without the internet, instant messaging, social media, blogs, cell phones, smartphones, MP3 players, tablets, 3-D printers, or digital cameras. Until 2006, only students at a few highly selective colleges could join Facebook.

In contrast, today's teenagers are called *digital natives* because they have been networking, texting, and clicking for definitions, directions, and data all their lives. Their smartphones are always within reach; some teens text hundreds of times a day.

Some observers suggest that this is merely the latest expression of something adults have always feared, and teenagers have always sought: connection with peers. In earlier generations, adults thought that the automobile, or the shopping mall, or rock-and-roll music, would lead their children astray.

The benefits and harms of technology have been brought into focus by the school closings caused by the COVID-19 pandemic, which led to many teenagers spending more time online—75 percent of their waking hours, an average of seven hours a day. However, relatively few are worried about that. Most consider social media more helpful than hurtful, a way to feel connected, entertained, and distracted (Harris Insights and Analytics, June, 2020).

This was the result of an online poll in May 2020 of 1,516 teenagers from every part of the United States. The sample selection was not random or controlled (a teenager had to have access and be willing to answer). However, other data, such as from the American Psychological Association and the Pew Research Center, point in the same direction.

Watch **VIDEO: The Impact of Media on Adolescent Development** to learn more about how digital technology affects cognition during adolescence.

## Cyber Abuse?

Many parents fear that the internet exposes their children to sexual abuse. The facts are reassuring: Although predators lurk online, most teens never encounter them. Sexual abuse is a serious problem, but if sexual abuse is defined as a perverted older stranger taking technological advantage of an innocent teen, it is "extremely rare" (Mitchell et al., 2013, p. 1226).

Almost all teen romances begin with a face-to-face attraction to another peer. Only 6 percent of 13- to 17-year-olds have *ever* had a romance that began online. They know how to block an uncomfortable relationship (Lenhart et al., 2015).

**cyberbullying** When people try to harm others via electronic means, such as social media and cell phone photos or texts.

## Cyberbullies

The facts are less reassuring regarding **cyberbullying**. Rumors, lies, embarrassing truths, or threats can all be sent from the safe distance of the private computer or smartphone, reaching a large audience just when social acceptance is crucial and the imaginary audience makes it worse (Giumetti & Kowalski, 2015). Further, insults, lies, and prejudice can be broadcast, as in "Zoom bombing," bots, and fake news.

Earlier in childhood, the least popular children may be bullied, but the social dynamic changes in high school. Popular students are frequent users of social media, using it to secure their status with prosocial and antisocial comments, which makes them likely to be victims as well as bullies (Ranney & Troop-Gordon, 2020). As with more conventional bullying at earlier ages, parental practices and school climate can mitigate the harm and reduce the prevalence of cyberbullying (Zurcher et al., 2018).

Sadly, ten years out of high school, bullies and victims—online or offline, sexual or otherwise—are less likely to have graduated from college and less likely to have good jobs or any job at all (Sigurdson et al., 2014). Adults need to be more concerned about teens who victimize each other, and less worried about strangers who lurk online.

**Consequences Unknown** Few adolescents think about the consequences of their impulsive rage, responses, or retorts on social media or in text messages. This educator at a community center tries to explain that victims can be devastated—rarely suicidal but often depressed.

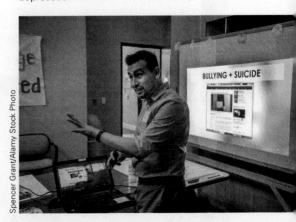

Spencer Grant/Alamy Stock Photo

## VISUALIZING DEVELOPMENT

# Adolescent Bullying

Bullying is defined as repeated attempts to hurt someone else, physically or socially. It can take many forms. For younger children, it is often physical—hitting, shoving, fighting. That is less common among adolescents, who can hurt each other with words or exclusion. Among teenagers, not being invited to a party can be hurtful and is common—as teenagers develop dominance hierarchies and need peer support. The best protection is to have one or more close friends, and adults who encourage whatever talents the child has.

### THE NATURE OF SCHOOL BULLYING

When bullying takes place at school, about two-thirds of it occurs in hallways, schoolyards, bathrooms, cafeterias, or buses. A full one-third occurs in classrooms, while teachers are present. An estimated 30% of school bullying goes unreported.

### FEATURES OF SCHOOL ANTI-BULLYING PROGRAMS

- Increased supervision of students
- A school climate that encourages friendship
- Teachers who promote empathy
- School-wide implementation of anti-bullying policies
- Cooperation among school staff, parents, and professionals across disciplines
- Identification of risk factors for bullying

Success varies, with some programs having no effect. But overall, a good program can reduce bullying by 25% or more.

Data from McCallion & Feder, 2013

Slandered by lies and rumors 44%
Ridiculed or called names 44%
Pushed and shoved 36%
Left out or ignored 32%
Threatened or injured by a weapon 29%
Threatened by peers and classmates 27%
Received sexual comments or gestures 7%
24%

Data from Lessne & Yanez, 2016

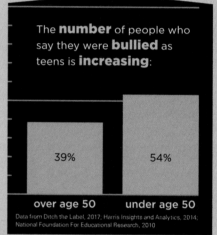

The **number** of people who say they were **bullied** as teens is **increasing**:

over age 50: 39%
under age 50: 54%

Data from Ditch the Label, 2017; Harris Insights and Analytics, 2014; National Foundation For Educational Research, 2010

# CYBERBULLYING

Cyberbullying takes place via e-mail, text messages, Web sites and apps, instant messaging, chat rooms, or posted videos or photos. About 60% of boys and girls have been cyberbullied, but girls are more often the targets of online rumor-spreading or nonconsensual explicit messages (Anderson, 2018).

### WHY DO TEENS CYBERBULLY?

| | |
|---|---|
| to get back at victim | 58% |
| for entertainment | 28% |
| to embarrass victim | 21% |
| to be mean | 14% |
| to show off for friends | 11% |

0  10  20  30  40  50  6

### SOCIAL MEDIA AND CYBERBULLYING

| | |
|---|---|
| 37% | victims who report incidents to their social network |
| 40% | victims who tell their parent or another adult |
| 90% | users who witness cyberbullying on their social media site |
| 35% | witnesses who usually ignore cyberbullying on their social media site |

80  60  40  20  0

Data from Ditch the Label, 2017; Enough Is Enough, 2017; Duggan, 2017

## Benefits and Dangers

The potential for harm from technology should not prevent us from understanding the benefits. Many teachers and students have found that the vast material available online expands education, allowing students to learn far more than any teacher could be expected to know.

Further, remember the need for peer support during adolescence. Teens who were lonely and isolated a few decades ago, such as those with Down syndrome, or who are deaf, or the only one in their neighborhood with their ethnic, religious, or gender identity, can find peers.

The need for peer connection and the benefits of technology are especially obvious with the COVID-19 pandemic. To stave off depression, rage, and despair, many adolescents engaged with their friends online, morning, noon, and night. They also searched for accurate information on death and recovery rates, on effective treatments, on testing locations.

The virus offered some unexpected benefits, not only cleaner air but also family harmony: The generations could work together to separate facts from scams, partisan politics, and wishful thinking.

The danger is that adolescents can connect with people whose views are destructive. The hazards of adolescent egocentrism, and of intuitive rather than analytic cognition, are obvious. Messages are sent in an instant, with no second thoughts. Troubled adolescents can find others who share their prejudices and self-destructive compulsions, such as anorexia, gun use, racism, or cutting.

Benefits and harms are also available for sex. The internet can provide information that the school might not give and allow romantic interaction with no sexual contact. Texting—hundreds of times a day—is common among adolescent lovers. This can include **sexting**, as sending sexual photographs and videos is called.

However, when a romance ends, it may turn ugly. Of those who have quit a romance, 15 percent report being threatened online (Lenhart et al., 2015). If bullying takes a sexual tone, it can be particularly harmful.

At a weekend sleepover, Audrie Pott and her friends found alcohol. She got so drunk that she blacked out. On Monday, three boys in her school bragged that they had had sex with her, showing pictures on their cell phones to classmates. Soon Audrie thought the entire school knew. The next weekend, she hanged herself. Only then did her parents and teachers learn what had happened (Sulek, 2013).

The danger of technology lies not in the equipment but in the mind. As with many adolescent concerns (puberty, sexuality, body image, motivation), cognition and many other factors "shape, mediate, and/or modify effects" of technology (Oakes, 2009, p. 1142).

One careful observer claims that, instead of being *native* users of technology, many teenagers are *naive* users—believing they have privacy settings that they do not have, trusting sites that are markedly biased, believing news that is fake, misunderstanding how to search for and verify information (boyd, 2014).

Adults can help with all of this—but only if they themselves understand technology and adolescence. Teens are intuitive, impulsive, and egocentric, often unaware of the impact of what they send and overestimating the validity of what they see online. Adults should know better.

> **THINK CRITICALLY:** The older people are, the more likely they are to be critical of social media. Why?

**sexting** Sending sexual messages or photographs (usually of one's naked body) via phone or computer.

## Sadness and Anger

Adolescence can be a wonderful time. Nonetheless, troubles plague about 20 percent of youths. In a national survey, 16 percent of 12- to 17-year-olds said that, within the past year, they had received mental health counseling for emotional or behavioral problems. This number did not include those who did not seek help, nor did it include those who were treated for substance abuse (Substance Abuse and Mental Health Services Administration, 2019).

Sadness and anger may dissipate or may become intense, chronic, even deadly. Parents and peers can help a sad or angry child regulate emotions, or they can react with extreme emotions of their own, pushing a teenager toward suicide or prison. Most disorders are *comorbid*, with more than one problem in the same person. Everyone needs to know when normal moodiness becomes pathological, in order to pull someone back from the cliff. That is the goal of the following pages.

## Depression

The general emotional trend from early childhood to early adolescence is toward less confidence. Then, gradually, self-esteem increases. A dip in self-esteem at puberty may occur with children of every ethnicity and gender (Fredricks & Eccles, 2002; Greene & Way, 2005; Kutob et al., 2010; Zeiders et al., 2013a), with notable individual differences, not always the ones expected.

For instance, girls have far higher rates of depression than boys. Children who believe that their nation is without fault are more likely to experience lower self-esteem in adolescence (Godfrey et al., 2019). Generally, self-esteem tends to be higher in African Americans than in European Americans, who themselves have higher self-esteem than Asian Americans. Among Latinos, self-esteem is relatively low, but some Latinas feel quite good about themselves (Zeiders et al., 2013a). One possible reason: Latinas with high familism become increasingly helpful at home, which makes their parents appreciative and them proud, unlike other U.S. teenage girls.

The risk of serious self-harm, such as cutting, is greatest in the years right after puberty (Plener et al., 2015). Gradually toward the end of adolescence and beginning of early adulthood, self-esteem rises (Orth & Robins, 2019). Always, however, specific social experiences and circumstances can outweigh age-related trends. Positive experiences include a fulfilling romance or academic success; negative ones include peer rejection and prison. For every adolescent of every ethnicity, the immediate social context—in the school, the family, and the community—is crucial.

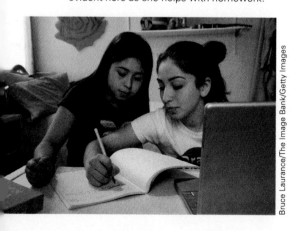

**Sibling Rivalry?** No! This Latina 15-year-old is a role model for her 11-year-old sister, evident here as she helps with homework.

Bruce Laurance/The Image Bank/Getty Images

For instance, you just read that Latinas may have higher self-esteem, but if they have relatives who fear deportation, or they themselves are Dreamers, they may experience sleep disturbances, lower school achievement, and other symptoms of depression (Gulbas et al., 2016; Suárez-Orozco, 2017). You also read that teens during the COVID-19 pandemic have spent more time online, but the online increase did not seem to increase their depression.

What did increase depression and anxiety was social isolation. Most teens cope with stress by talking with friends, but that was more difficult when school was closed. Sadly, two-thirds of the teens who responded in the Harris poll said they felt sad or anxious more often than once a week, and the same proportion said they tried to keep their feelings to themselves, pretending to be happier in order not to worry anyone (Harris Insights and Analytics, June, 2020).

## Major Depressive Disorder

Some adolescents sink into **major depression**, a deep sadness and hopelessness that disrupts all normal, regular activities. The causes predate adolescence, but puberty—with physical and emotional turbulence—pushes some vulnerable children, especially girls, into despair. The rate of serious depression more than doubles during this time to an estimated 15 percent, affecting about 1 in 5 girls and 1 in 10 boys.

Serious, distressing thoughts about killing oneself (called **suicidal ideation**) are most common at about age 15. More than one-third (41 percent) of U.S. high school girls felt so hopeless that they stopped doing some usual activities for two weeks or more in the previous year (an indication of depression), and nearly one-fourth (22 percent) thought seriously about suicide. For boys the rates were 21 and 12 percent (MMWR, June 15, 2018).

Suicidal ideation can lead to **parasuicide**, also called *attempted suicide* or *failed suicide*. Parasuicide includes any deliberate self-harm that could have been lethal. Parasuicide is the preferred term because "failed" suicide implies that to die is to succeed (!). "Attempt" is likewise misleading because, especially in adolescence, the difference between attempt and completion may be luck and treatment, not intent.

As you see in **Figure 16.2**, parasuicide can be divided according to whether or not medical treatment (surgery, pumped stomach, etc.) was needed, but every parasuicide is a warning. Among U.S. high school students in 2017, 9 percent of the girls and 5 percent of the boys attempted suicide in the previous year (MMWR, June 15, 2018).

### CHAPTER APP 16

## My3-Support Network

**IOS:**
https://tinyurl.com/yyzlpmqo

**ANDROID:**
https://tinyurl.com/qgsd6qb

**RELEVANT TOPIC:**
Suicidal ideation among adolescents

My3-Support Network is a crisis-support app for people who experience suicidal thoughts. Users choose three trusted people from their contacts list to place on the app (911 and the National Suicide Hotline are automatically listed). Users create their own safety plan, listing warning signs, coping strategies, distractions, and their "reasons to live." The app also links users to organizations that address the needs of specific groups, such as suicide attempt survivors, LGBTQ youth, and more.

**major depression** Feelings of hopelessness, lethargy, and worthlessness that last two weeks or more.

**suicidal ideation** Serious thinking about suicide, often including extreme emotions and thoughts.

**parasuicide** Any potentially deadly self-harm that does not result in death. (Also called *attempted suicide* or *failed suicide*.)

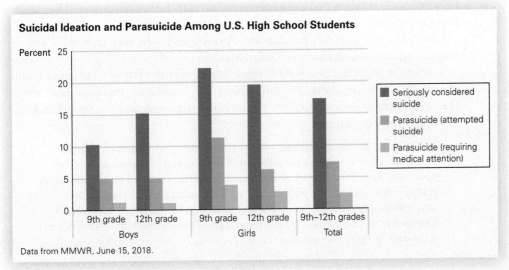

**Suicidal Ideation and Parasuicide Among U.S. High School Students**

Percent

Seriously considered suicide

Parasuicide (attempted suicide)

Parasuicide (requiring medical attention)

9th grade   12th grade   9th grade   12th grade   9th–12th grades
Boys                      Girls               Total

Data from MMWR, June 15, 2018.

**FIGURE 16.2**

**Sad Thoughts** Completed suicide is rare in adolescence, but serious thoughts about killing oneself are frequent. More girls than boys say they have thought about, or attempted, suicide. The rate for boys may be under-estimated for three reasons: (1) boys are less forthcoming about their emotions; (2) boys consider it unmanly to try suicide and fail; and (3) more males than females die by suicide.

**Observation Quiz** Does thinking seriously about suicide increase or decrease during high school? (see answer, page 453) ←

## Completed Suicides

Although suicidal ideation during adolescence is common, completed suicides are not. In the United States in 2016, the rate of completed suicide for White teenagers, aged 15 to 19 (in school or not), was about 5 per 100,000, or 0.005 percent. The rate for non-White teenagers is about half that. Suicides are three times as common among adults, with the highest rate of all among White men in their 80s.

Curiously, although girls have higher rates of parasuicide, boys have higher rates of completed suicide, especially boys who are troubled about their gender identity or sexual orientation. Suicide rates are seven times higher for LGBTQ youth than others (Romanelli et al., 2020).

Of course, even one teen suicide is a tragedy, and it is particularly poignant when the media shares the story along with a photo of the fresh-faced young person. Those stories can cause teen depression and copycat suicides. Adolescent self-harm (parasuicide, cutting, extreme dieting), and clinical depression seem to be increasing; extensive media use (TV, social media, the internet) is a correlate (Twenge et al., 2018).

For example, teen suicide rates increased by almost a third after the release of a Netflix program *Thirteen Reasons Why*, which depicted a girl slitting her wrists (Bridge et al., 2019). Netflix's chief executive, Reed Hastings, said "no one has to watch it." Whether he is naive, cynical, or unfeeling is a matter of opinion.

Because they are more emotional and egocentric than logical and analytical, adolescents are particularly affected when they hear about someone else's suicide. That explains **cluster suicides** (several suicides within a group in the same time period). Although the overall rate is lower in adolescence, a higher proportion are cluster suicides, romantic couple suicides, or suicides by the same means as a recent celebrity suicide (M. Kral, 2019).

**cluster suicides** Several suicides committed by members of a group within a brief period.

## Delinquency and Defiance

Like low self-esteem and suicidal ideation, bouts of anger are common in adolescence. In fact, a moody adolescent could be both depressed and angry: Externalizing and internalizing behavior are closely connected during these years. This may explain suicide in jail: Teenagers incarcerated for assault (externalizing) are at greater risk of suicide (internalizing) than adult prisoners (Ruch et al., 2019).

Externalizing actions are hard to ignore. Many adolescents slam doors, curse parents, and tell friends exactly how badly other teenagers (or siblings or teachers) have behaved. Some—particularly boys—"act out" by breaking laws. They steal, damage property, or injure others.

Internalized behavior is less blatant. A teenager might stay in bed all day, or stop eating, or drink alcohol until oblivious.

Is teenage anger necessary for normal development? That is what Anna Freud (Sigmund's daughter, herself a prominent psychoanalyst) thought. She wrote that adolescent resistance to parental authority was "welcome . . . beneficial . . . inevitable." She explained:

> We all know individual children who, as late as the ages of fourteen, fifteen or sixteen, show no such outer evidence of inner unrest. They remain, as they have been during the latency period, "good" children, wrapped up in their family relationships, considerate sons of their mothers, submissive to their fathers, in accord with the atmosphere, idea and ideal of their childhood background. Convenient as this may be, it signifies a delay of their normal development and is, as such, a sign to be taken seriously.

[*A. Freud, 1958/2000, p. 37*]

However, most contemporary psychologists, teachers, and parents want well-behaved, considerate teenagers, who often become happy adults. A 30-year longitudinal study found that adults who had never been arrested usually earned colleges degrees, "held high-status jobs, and expressed optimism about their own futures" (Moffitt, 2003, p. 61). Thus, teenage acting out, while not unusual, is not essential for healthy development.

## Breaking the Law

Both the *prevalence* (how widespread) and the *incidence* (how frequent) of criminal actions are higher during adolescence than earlier or later. Arrest statistics in every nation reflect this fact, with 30 percent of African American males and 22 percent of European American males being arrested at least once before age 18 (Brame et al., 2014).

Many more broke the law but were not caught, or were caught but not arrested. Self-reports suggest that most adolescents, of every gender, are lawbreakers before age 20. One reason is that many behaviors that are legal for adults—buying cigarettes, having intercourse, skipping school—are illegal for adolescents.

Arrest rates are higher for youth of minority ethnic groups, and boys are three times as likely as girls to be caught, arrested, and convicted. Does this reflect prejudice (Marotta & Voisin, 2017)? Some studies find that female aggression typically targets family and friends. Parents hesitate to call the police to arrest their daughters.

## False Confessions

Determining accurate gender, ethnic, and income differences in actual law-breaking, not just in arrests, is difficult. Self-reports may be false, with boasting or denial. For instance, researchers in the Netherlands contacted teenagers who were interrogated by the police. [The teens did not know that the researchers knew about the interrogations.] They were asked if they had ever had any police contact. One-third said no (van Batenburg-Eddes et al., 2012).

The opposite is also likely. In the United States, about 20 percent of confessions are false, with higher rates among teenagers. Why? Brain immaturity (delay discounting) makes young people ignore long-term consequences. Instead, they may prioritize protecting family members, defending friends, and pleasing adults—including the police (Feld, 2013; Steinberg, 2009).

One dramatic case involved 13-year-old Tyler Edmonds, who confessed to killing his brother-in-law. He was sentenced to life in prison. He then said that he confessed falsely to protect his 26-year-old sister, whom he admired. (She told him to confess, because she said his youth would mean his sentence would be short). His conviction was overturned—after he spent four years behind bars (Malloy et al., 2014).

The researchers who cited Tyler's case interviewed 194 boys, aged 14 to 17, all convicted of serious crimes. More than one-third (35 percent) said they had confessed falsely to a crime (not necessarily the one for which they were serving time). False confessions were more likely after two hours of intense interrogation—the adolescents wanted it to stop; acting on impulse, they said they were guilty (Malloy et al., 2014). And the police believed them.

## A Criminal Career?

Many researchers distinguish between two kinds of teenage lawbreakers (Levey et al., 2019; Monahan et al., 2013), as first proposed by Terri Moffitt (2001, 2003). Both types are usually arrested for the first time in adolescence and for similar crimes, but their future diverges.

**In Every Nation** Everywhere, older adolescents are most likely to protest against government authority. Here, younger adolescents in Alabama celebrate the 50-year anniversary of the historic Selma-to-Montgomery march across the Pettus Bridge. In that historic movement, most of those beaten and killed were under age 25.

**adolescence-limited offender** A person who breaks the law as a teenage but whose criminal activity stops by age 20.

**life-course-persistent offender** A person whose criminal activity begins in adolescence and continues throughout life; a "career" criminal.

- Most juvenile delinquents are **adolescence-limited offenders**, whose criminal activity stops by age 21. They break the law with their friends, facilitated by their chosen antisocial peers.
- Some delinquents are **life-course-persistent offenders**, who become career criminals. Their lawbreaking is more often done alone than as part of a gang, and a contributing factor is neurological impairment (either inborn or caused by early experiences), evident in learning disabilities.

During adolescence, the criminal records of both types may be similar. However, if adolescence-limited delinquents can be protected from various snares (quitting school, incarceration, drug addiction), they outgrow their criminal behavior.

## Causes of Delinquency

The best way to reduce adolescent crime is to notice early behavior that predicts lawbreaking and to change patterns before puberty. Strong and protective social relationships, emotional regulation, and moral values from childhood keep many teenagers from jail. Since learning disabilities and school failure are precursors to crime, effective remediation at age 6 may reduce delinquency at age 16.

Adolescent crime in the United States and many other nations has decreased in the past 30 years. Only a third as many arrests of people under age 18 occurred in 2018 compared to 2000. There are many possible explanations:

- fewer high school dropouts (more education means less crime);
- wiser judges (more community service than prison);
- better policing (arrests for misdemeanors are up, which may warn parents);
- smaller families (parents attend more to each of 2 children than each of 12);
- better contraception (unwanted children often become delinquents);
- less drug use (binge drinking and crack cocaine use increase crime);
- more immigrants (who are more law-abiding); and
- less lead in the blood (lead poisoning reduces brain functioning).

Nonetheless, adolescents remain more likely to break the law than adults, perhaps because of their brains as well as because of the social context. (See Inside the Brain.)

---

**INSIDE THE BRAIN**

## Impulses, Rewards, and Reflection

For almost every crime, in almost every nation, the arrest rate for 15- to 17-year-olds is twice that for those over 18 (exceptions are fraud, forgery, and embezzlement).

What is wrong with those teenagers? Irresponsible parents? Poverty? Drug addiction? Maybe none of these. Perhaps the problem is in the brain, not in outside forces.

The limbic system is activated by puberty while the prefrontal cortex is "developmentally constrained," maturing more gradually (Hartley & Somerville, 2015, p. 109). Thus, adolescents are swayed by their intuition instead of by analysis.

Many studies confirm that adolescents show "heightened activity in the striatum, both when anticipating rewards and when receiving rewards" (Crone et al., 2016, p. 360). In choosing between a small but guaranteed reward and a large possible reward, adolescent brains show more activity for the larger reward than the brains of children or adults.

What does this mean? When teenagers weigh the possible results of a particular action, their brains make them more inclined to imagine success than to fear failure.

Whether this makes them brave and bold or foolish and careless is a matter of opinion, but there is no doubt that neurological circuits tip the balance toward action. Nor is there any doubt that the reward circuits in the brain are powerfully activated in adolescence (Cao et al., 2019).

The thrill of suddenly possessing a coveted jacket, or of joining a group of peers who are beating up a disrespectful stranger, is immediate. Later, if reflection occurs as the teen sits in jail, then another problem appears: According to one review, "incarcerated juveniles are at a four times higher risk of suicide than adolescents in general population" (Joshi & Billick, 2017, p. 141).

A related aspect of adolescent brains is that peer acclaim or rejection is deeply felt, with activation throughout the limbic system as well as other subcortical areas. This may help explain another aspect of adolescent crime: It often occurs in groups, whereas most adult criminals act alone.

Thus, neurological sensitivity may explain why teens readily follow impulses that promise social approval from friends and shun experiences that might bring social rejection. In experiments in which adults and adolescents, alone or with peers, play video games in which taking risks might lead to crashes or gaining points, adolescents are much more likely than adults are to risk crashing, especially when they are with peers.

When they are with their mothers, not their peers, teenagers are much more cautious in such simulations. However, as the connection between two brain regions (the *anterior insula* and the *ventral striatum*) increases in adolescence, risk-taking when the mother is absent increases, especially if the family relationship is not supportive (Guassi Moreira & Telzer, 2018).

There are other notable differences in brain activity (specifically in the ventral striatum) between adolescents and adults. When with other adults, the adult brain signals caution (inhibition)—opposite to the adolescent brain with peers (Albert et al., 2013) (see **Figure 16.3**).

This peer influence is apparent in both sexes but is stronger in boys—particularly when they are with other boys (de Boer et al., 2017). This may explain why adolescent boys use drugs, get arrested, and take dangerous risks, with far higher rates of accidental death than girls.

Teenage drivers like to fill (or overfill) cars with teen passengers who will admire them for speeding, for passing trucks on blind curves, for racing through railroad crossings when the warning lights are flashing, and so on. Fatal accidents are much more likely if the driver and the passengers are adolescents.

The accident rate in adolescence is aided by a third brain change in adolescence. Compared to children, there is a substantial increase in myelination between the emotional and action parts of the brain. This increase in white matter means rapid responses. As a result, adolescents act before slower-thinking adults can stop them (Hartley & Somerville, 2015).

Thus, don't blame teen crashes, juvenile delinquency, or drug use on inexperience; blame it on the brain. Some states now prohibit teen drivers from transporting other teenagers, reducing deaths and banning one source of adolescent excitement. States that allow marijuana always prohibit it before age 18. Some judges hesitate to give life sentences to adolescents.

Teens advocate for some laws, such as those that protect the environment; they do not advocate for laws that restrict drug use, driver's licenses, or gun purchases based on age. After a mass shooting at a high school in Parkland, Florida, students advocated a ban on some kinds of guns; the legislature instead banned gun sales to teenagers. Does this mean they understood the teen brain or that they understood their voters?

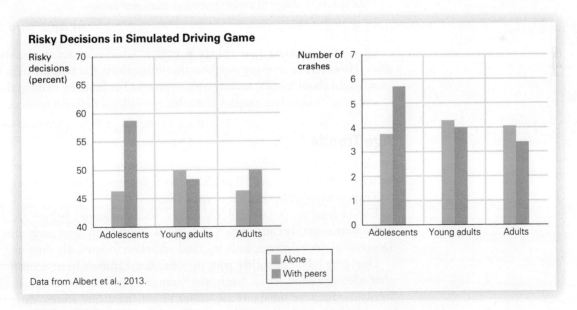

**FIGURE 16.3**
**Losing Is Winning** In this game, risk-taking led to more crashes and fewer points. As you see, adolescents were strongly influenced by the presence of peers, so much so that they lost points that they would have kept if they had played alone. In fact, sometimes they laughed when they crashed instead of bemoaning their loss. Note the contrast with emerging adults, who were more likely to take risks when alone.

# Drug Use and Abuse

Most teenagers try *psychoactive drugs*, that is, drugs that activate the brain. Brain changes in the reward system lead directly to increases in drug abuse, such as binge drinking (Morales et al., 2018). Hormonal surges, the brain's reward centers, and cognitive immaturity make adolescents particularly attracted to the sensations produced by psychoactive drugs. But their immature bodies and brains make drug use especially toxic.

Every psychoactive drug excites the limbic system and interferes with the prefrontal cortex. Because of these neurological reactions, drug users are more emotional (varying from euphoria to terror, from paranoia to rage) and less reflective. By contrast, adult brains have automatic brakes. The rate of every hazard—including car crashes, unsafe sex, and suicide—is higher when teens use psychoactive drugs.

The critical question is what is automatic at what age:

> Our habitual and automatic responses save us valuable effort, energy, and time. The willpower required to make decisions with the prefrontal cortex, deciding how we're going to tie our shoe, or open the door anew each time, would paralyze us from ever living life. . . . stuck giving full attention to routine tasks, and drain our ability to concentrate and learn new things.
>
> [Hendlin, 2019, p. 137]

Of course, learning new things is exactly what adolescent cognition should allow. However, since every psychoactive drug affects the brain, which is not fully grown until about age 25, society tries to protect the brain by making the purchase of any drug—including alcohol and tobacco—illegal before adulthood.

## Age Trends

Adolescence is a sensitive time for experimentation with psychoactive drugs. Use increases from about ages 10 to 25 and then decreases when adult responsibilities and experiences make drugs less attractive.

Use of legal drugs (alcohol, cigarettes, and marijuana) before age 15 is especially worrisome, because brain damage is more likely and early use escalates. Depression, sexual abuse, bullying, and addiction follow early drug use.

One drug follows another pattern—*inhalants* (fumes from aerosol containers, glue, cleaning fluid, etc.). Sadly, the youngest adolescents are most likely to try inhalants, because inhalants are easier to get (hardware stores, drug stores, and supermarkets stock them). Cognitive immaturity means that few pubescent children understand the risks—brain damage and even death (Nguyen et al., 2016).

Cohort differences are evident for every drug, even from one year to the next. Legalization of marijuana, e-cigarettes in many flavors, hundreds of deaths from opioids, dozens of deaths from vaping—these are examples of changes in the adolescent drug scene over the past few years.

Adolescent drug use in the United States has declined since 1976 (see **Figure 16.4**) with one major exception, vaping. Perception of risk, not availability, reduces use, since most high school students have always said that they could easily get alcohol, cigarettes, and marijuana (Miech et al., 2016).

Availability is notable for e-cigarettes. Although the United States prohibits adolescent purchase, 13- to 17-year-olds still manage to buy them, in stores and on the internet. Even when laws are strictly enforced, most young users get their e-cigarettes from other adolescents (Braak et al., 2020; McKeganey et al., 2019). Is that a problem? (See Opposing Perspectives on page 450.)

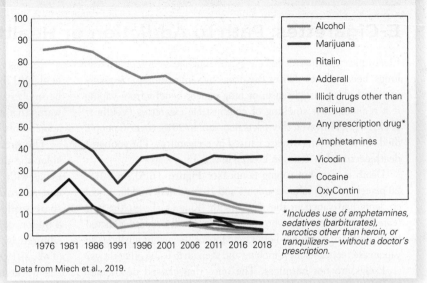

**Percent of U.S. High School Seniors Reporting Drug Use in the Past Year**

Legend:
- Alcohol
- Marijuana
- Ritalin
- Adderall
- Illicit drugs other than marijuana
- Any prescription drug*
- Amphetamines
- Vicodin
- Cocaine
- OxyContin

*Includes use of amphetamines, sedatives (barbiturates), narcotics other than heroin, or tranquilizers—without a doctor's prescription.

Data from Miech et al., 2019.

## Harm from Drugs

Drug use before maturity is particularly likely to harm growth and predict later addiction. However, few adolescents are aware of when they or their friends move past use (experimenting) to abuse (experiencing harm).

Each drug is harmful in a particular way. *Tobacco* impairs digestion and nutrition, slowing down growth. Since internal organs mature after the height spurt, smoking teenagers who appear to be fully grown may damage their developing hearts, lungs, brains, and reproductive systems.

*Alcohol* is the most frequently abused drug in North America. Heavy drinking impairs memory and self-control by damaging the hippocampus and the prefrontal cortex, perhaps distorting the reward circuits of the brain lifelong (Guerri & Pascual, 2010).

Ironically, many antidrug parents condone adolescent drinking. For instance, a careful longitudinal study in Australia found that parents who provided alcohol to their teenagers thought they were teaching responsible drinking, but instead they were increasing binge drinking and substance use disorder six years later (Mattick et al., 2018).

*Marijuana* seems harmless to many people (especially teenagers), partly because users are more relaxed than verbose. Yet adolescents who regularly smoke marijuana are more likely to drop out of school, become teenage parents, be depressed, and later be unemployed—although the evidence comes from years when marijuana was illegal in every U.S. state.

In the next few years, we will learn more. Canada legalized marijuana for adults in the summer of 2018. Canadian health researchers hope that, once the brain is mature, benefits outweigh risks (Lake & Kerr, 2017). Marijuana is illegal in Canada for those under 18, although some doctors wish 21 were the cutoff (Rankin, 2017).

Any age restriction encourages younger adolescents to covet drugs used by older youth, which creates a major problem. This was evident when New Zealand lowered the age for legal purchase of alcohol from 20 to 18. Hospital admissions for intoxication, car crashes, and injuries from assault, increased, not only for 18- to 19-year-olds but also for 16- to 17-year-olds (Kypri et al., 2006, 2014).

## Preventing Drug Abuse: What Works?

Remember that most adolescents think they are exceptions, sometimes feeling invincible, sometimes fearing social disapproval, but almost never being realistic

**FIGURE 16.4**
**Rise and Fall** By asking the same questions year after year, the Monitoring the Future study shows notable historical effects. It is encouraging that something in society, not in the adolescent, makes drug use increase and decrease and that the most recent data show a continued decline in the drug most commonly abused—alcohol.

**Especially for Parents Who Drink Socially** You have heard that parents should allow their children to drink at home, to teach them to drink responsibly and not get drunk elsewhere. Is that wise? (see response, page 453)

# E-Cigarettes: Path to Addiction or Health?

Electronic cigarettes (called e-cigs) are much less damaging to the lungs, because they deliver the drugs by vapor (vaping). Smokers with asthma, heart disease, or lung cancer benefit from vaping if it reduces their smoking of combustible cigarettes (Veldheer et al., 2019). However, the risk is not zero. In 2018, over 50 people died of a severe lung disease caused by e-cigarettes. The youngest death occurred in Texas in 2020. He was 15.

Death is rare, but vaping is not (see **Figure 16.5**). In 2019, 28 percent of high school students and 10 percent of middle school students had vaped in the past month (King et al., 2020). It is feared that adolescents who try e-cigarettes will become addicted to nicotine. Vaping smells better than tobacco, so might inhaling the vapor ease teenagers into smoking and then on to using other drugs?

E-cigs are not harmless. The ones that caused death may have had a particular ingredient (vitamin E) that most of them do not have, but all of them produce *benzene*, a known carcinogen (Pankow et al., 2017). Many contain nicotine, sometimes said to be more addictive than heroin. Some contain THC, a compound in marijuana. If the choice is between smoking and vaping, vaping is better; but if the choice is between not smoking and using e-cigs, vaping is worse.

Developmentalists fear that e-cigarettes will open the door to other drugs. This notion led to a new U.S. law in late 2019 that banned the sale of tobacco products, including e-cigs, to people under age 21. In early 2020, the Food and Drug Administration announced they would crack down on vendors who sold cartridge-based vaping products in kid-friendly flavors.

Teenagers who try e-cigs often smoke tobacco later (Miech et al., 2017b). Do e-cigs open a door, or would those adolescents be smokers no matter what? The American Pediatric Association warns that e-cigs will harm the next generation of children and adolescents (Jenssen & Walley, 2019).

The preceding paragraphs all mentioned harm. Now consider the other perspective. One company (JUUL) designed e-cigs with a sleek delivery gadget that looks like a USB drive, and advertised on Twitter, Instagram, and YouTube. Market share exploded among adolescents, with sales approaching a billion dollars. Inspired design and clever advertising, both admired by many adults, has made them successful (Huang et al., 2019).

The arguments from distributors of e-cigarettes are that their products are healthier than cigarettes, that people should make their own choices, and that the fear of adolescent vaping is exaggerated—part of the irrational fear that everything teenagers do is trouble.

Yet most public health doctors advise against e-cigs, and pediatricians worry that fetal and infant lungs suffer if the mother uses them (Carlsen et al., 2018). With rats, vaping decreases birthweight, which increases risks for early death and brain damage (Orzabal et al., 2019).

The evidence says caution, but caution is scarce at adolescence. The media presents mixed messages: Are strict age restrictions protective or puritanical (Morphett et al., 2020)? Opposing perspectives are apparent: Which perspective is yours?

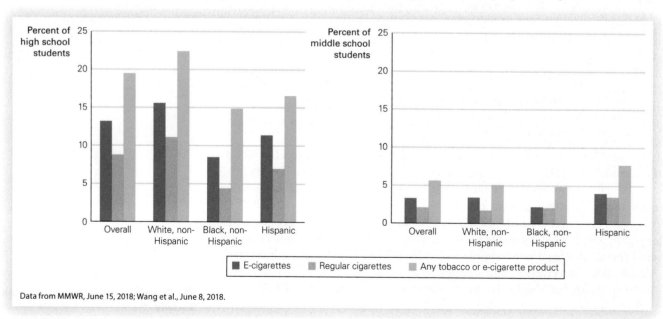

Data from MMWR, June 15, 2018; Wang et al., June 8, 2018.

**FIGURE 16.5**

**Getting Better**  The fact that more than one in five high school students (that's 3 million people) used tobacco—even though purchase of any kind is illegal—in the past month is troubling. This means that more that 3 million students are at risk for addiction and poor health. The surprise (not shown) is that all of these rates are lower than a year earlier. Is that because laws are stricter or teenagers are getting wiser?

about potential addiction or about the reaction if they reject an offer or a toke, a sip, a line. For some, breaking the law is thrilling, defying authority is exciting, and drugs help them feel smarter, more awake, more fun. They do not see that, over time, stress and depression increase, and achievement decreases (Bagot, 2017; McCabe et al., 2017).

With harmful drugs, as with many other aspects of life, people of each generation prefer to learn things for themselves. A common phenomenon is **generational forgetting**, that each new cohort forgets what the previous cohort learned.

Mistrust of the older generation along with a loyalty to one's peers leads not only to generational forgetting but also to a backlash. When adults forbid something, that is a reason to try it, especially if adults exaggerate the dangers. If a friend passes out from drug use, adolescents may be slow to get medical help—a dangerous hesitancy.

Some antidrug curricula and advertisements make drugs seem exciting. Anti-smoking announcements produced by cigarette companies (such as a clean-cut young person advising viewers to think before they smoke) actually increase use (Strasburger et al., 2009).

By contrast, massive ad campaigns by public health advocates in Florida and California cut adolescent smoking almost in half, in part because the publicity appealed to the young. Teenagers respond to graphic images. In one example:

> A young man walks up to a convenience store counter and asks for a pack of cigarettes. He throws some money on the counter, but the cashier says "that's not enough." So the young man pulls out a pair of pliers, wrenches out one of his teeth, and hands it over. . . . A voiceover asks: "What's a pack of smokes cost? Your teeth."
>
> *[Krisberg, 2014]*

Parental example and social changes also make a difference. Throughout the United States, higher prices, targeted warnings, and better law enforcement have led to a marked decline in smoking among younger adolescents. Looking internationally, laws have an effect.

In Canada, cigarette advertising is outlawed, and cigarette packs have lurid pictures of diseased lungs, rotting teeth, and so on; fewer Canadian 15- to 19-year-olds smoke. What effect Canada's legalization of marijuana will have on teenagers is not yet known.

In the past three chapters, we have seen that the universal biological processes do not lead to universal psychosocial problems. Biology does not change, but context does. Rates of teenage births and abortions are declining sharply (Chapter 14), more students are graduating from high school (Chapter 15), and fewer teens drink or smoke (this chapter). Yet each of these chapters shows that much more needs to be done.

As explained at the beginning of these three chapters, adolescence starts with puberty; that much is universal. But what happens next depends on parents, peers, schools, communities, and cultures. In other words, the future of adolescents depends, in part, on you.

**Telling Their Story** Erika Pohl and her mother, Brenda, reflect on a documentary in which Erika had a leading role—as a teenager addicted to opioids who managed to recover. Both hope "never again." That is true for about half of teenagers with addiction; the film was created to improve those odds.

Pat Vasquez-Cunningham/Albuquerque Journal/ZUMAPRESS.com/Alamy Images

**generational forgetting** The idea that each new generation forgets what the previous generation learned. As used here, the term refers to knowledge about the harm drugs can do.

**THINK CRITICALLY:** Might the fear of adolescent drug use be foolish, if most adolescents use drugs whether or not they are forbidden?

---

## WHAT HAVE YOU LEARNED?

1. Why are psychoactive drugs particularly attractive in adolescence?

2. Why are psychoactive drugs particularly destructive in adolescence?

3. What specific harm occurs with tobacco products?

4. How has adolescent drug use changed in the past decade?

5. What methods to reduce adolescent drug use are successful?

# SUMMARY

## Identity

**1.** Adolescence is a time for self-discovery. According to Erikson, adolescents seek their own identity, sorting through the traditions and values of their families and cultures.

**2.** Many young adolescents foreclose on their options without exploring possibilities, and many experience role confusion. Identity achievement takes longer for contemporary adolescents than it did a half-century ago when Erikson first described it.

**3.** Identity achievement occurs in many domains, including religion, politics, ethnicity, vocation, and gender. Each of these domains remains important over the life span, but timing, contexts, and often terminology have changed since Erikson and Marcia first described them. Achieving vocational and gender identity is particularly difficult as many more options seem possible.

## Close Relationships

**4.** Parents continue to influence their growing children, despite bickering over minor issues. Ideally, communication and warmth remain high, while parental control decreases and adolescents develop autonomy. Cultures differ in the timing of conflicts and in the benefits of parental monitoring. Too much parental control is harmful, as is neglect.

**5.** Peers and peer pressure can be beneficial or harmful, depending on who the peers are. Adolescents select their friends, who then facilitate constructive and/or destructive behavior. Peer approval is particularly potent during adolescence.

**6.** Adolescents experience diverse sexual needs and may be involved in short-term or long-term romances, depending in part on their peer group. Contemporary teenagers are less likely to have intercourse than was true a decade ago.

**7.** Some youths are sexually attracted to people of the same sex. Social acceptance of same-sex relationships is increasing, but in some communities and nations, gay, lesbian, bisexual, and transgender youth are bullied, rejected, or worse.

**8.** Many adolescents learn about sex from peers and the media—sources that are not comprehensive. Ideally, parents are the best teachers on topics about sex, but many are silent or naive.

**9.** Some nations provide comprehensive sex education beginning in the early grades, and most U.S. parents want schools to teach adolescents about sex. Abstinence-only education is not effective at slowing down the age of sexual activity, and it may increase STIs.

**10.** Most adolescents in the United States use technology to connect with their peers. Sexting is also common, and adults see dangers in it that peers do not.

## Sadness and Anger

**11.** Almost all young adolescents become more self-conscious and self-critical than they were as children. A few become chronically sad and depressed. Many adolescents (especially girls) think about suicide, and some attempt it. Few adolescents actually kill themselves; most who do so are boys.

**12.** At least in Western societies, almost all adolescents become more independent and angry as part of growing up, although most still respect their parents. Breaking the law and bursts of anger are common; boys are more likely to be arrested for violent offenses than are girls.

**13.** Adolescence-limited delinquents should be prevented from hurting themselves or others; life-course-persistent offenders may become career criminals. Early intervention—years before the first arrest—is crucial to prevent serious delinquency.

## Drug Use and Abuse

**14.** Most adolescents experiment with drugs, which may temporarily reduce stress and increase peer connections but soon add to stress and social problems. Almost every adolescent tries alcohol, and many use e-cigarettes and marijuana. All are technically illegal for those under 18 but are readily available to teenagers.

**15.** All psychoactive drugs are particularly harmful in adolescence, as they affect the developing brain and threaten the already shaky impulse control. Prevention and moderation of adolescent drug use and abuse are possible. Price, perception, and parents have an effect.

# KEY TERMS

identity versus role confusion (p. 424)

identity achievement (p. 424)

role confusion (p. 424)

foreclosure (p. 424)

moratorium (p. 424)

gender identity (p. 429)

parental monitoring (p. 432)

familism (p. 432)

peer pressure (p. 434)

coercive joining (p. 434)

sexual orientation (p. 436)

cyberbullying (p. 439)

sexting (p. 441)

major depression (p. 443)

suicidal ideation (p. 443)

parasuicide (p. 443)

cluster suicides (p. 444)

adolescence-limited offender (p. 446)

life-course-persistent offender (p. 446)

generational forgetting (p. 451)

## APPLICATIONS

1. Locate a news article about a teenager who committed suicide. Were there warning signs that were ignored? Does the report inadvertently encourage cluster suicides?

2. Research suggests that most adolescents have broken the law but that few have been arrested or incarcerated. Ask 10 of your fellow students whether they broke the law when they were under 18 and, if so, how often, in what ways, and with what consequences. (Assure them of confidentiality; remind them that

drug use, breaking curfew, and skipping school were illegal.) Do you see any evidence of gender or ethnic differences? What additional research needs to be done?

3. Cultures vary in expectations for drug use. Interview three people from different backgrounds (not necessarily from different nations; each SES, generation, or religion has different standards) about their culture's drug use, including reasons for what is allowed and when. (Legal drugs should be included in your study.)

## Especially For ANSWERS

**Response for Parents of a Teenager** (from p. 433): Remember: Communicate, do not control. Let your child talk about the meaning of the hairstyle. Remind yourself that a hairstyle in itself is harmless. Don't say, "What will people think?" or "Are you on drugs?" or anything that might give your child reason to stop communicating.

**Response for Sex Educators** (from p. 438): Yes, but forgive them. Ideally, parents should talk to their children about sex, presenting honest information and listening to the child's concerns. However, many parents find it very difficult to do so because they feel

embarrassed and ignorant. You might schedule separate sessions for adults over 30, for emerging adults, and for adolescents.

**Response for Parents Who Drink Socially** (from p. 449): No. Alcohol is particularly harmful for young brains. It is best to drink only when your children are not around. Children who are encouraged to drink with their parents are more likely to drink when no adults are present. It is true that adolescents are rebellious, and they may drink even if you forbid it. But if you allow alcohol, they might rebel with other drugs.

## Observation Quiz ANSWERS

**Answer to Observation Quiz** (from p. 434): The girls are only observers, keeping a respectful distance.

**Answer to Observation Quiz** (from p. 435): Impossible to be sure, but body position suggests dating. The couple on the left seem

happy with each other (she leans toward him, his hand is pulling her close), but the couple may be less so.

**Answer to Observation Quiz** (from p. 443): Both. It increases for boys but decreases for girls.

# Epilogue:
# Emerging Adulthood

## What Will You Know?

1. Is risk-taking an asset or a liability?
2. Does college make you think?
3. Is cohabitation a good prelude to marriage?

Infancy, childhood, and adolescence—the previous 16 chapters—are the foundation of life, but they comprise less than a fourth of the human life span. This epilogue offers a glimpse at what is next, **emerging adulthood**, ages 18–25, when people continue to learn and explore.

Consider this epilogue a brief review and a preview. We follow the same sequence as earlier chapters at each stage—body, mind, and social world—always noting the impact of genetic, prenatal, and early experiences. You will see many familiar themes—family, friends, culture, context, and cohort. The tension between what is universal (true for every human) and what is particular (powerfully influenced by culture and cohort) is apparent at this stage, as it has been throughout.

In considering this period, we include references to the COVID-19 pandemic, which has affected everyone, of every age, emotionally, economically, and educationally. Before going further, remember that the study of human development relies on the scientific method.

Regarding the pandemic, there are many questions (Step 1) and hypotheses (Step 2). What effect will it have on human development? Is this pandemic a temporary detour, or will emerging adults forge an entirely new path for their future? Longitudinal data (Step 3) are needed before we can accept conclusions (Step 4), and then peer review, publication (Step 5), and replication are needed.

The research on COVID-19 reported here is fascinating but speculative. As with many issues raised in the previous 16 chapters, some of you will be the scientists who answer those questions.

## Biological Universals

Certain biosocial characteristics have always characterized 18- to 25-year-olds. Biologically, these years are prime time for high energy, hard physical work, and safe reproduction. As has been true for thousands of years, every body system—digestive, respiratory, circulatory, musculoskeletal, and sexual-reproductive—functions optimally in emerging adulthood. The rapid and sometimes unsettling changes of adolescence are over: Emerging adults are at their peak of fertility and strength.

Consequently, this has been the time for marriage and parenthood, for fighting neighboring groups and growing crops, for undertaking the hard work of raising small children, building a home, starting a job. By age 25, all that was established, and adults continued with the rest of their lives with the same partner, their growing children, and the same work.

No longer.

Remember that one of the goals of our study is to understand what is universal and what is contemporary, to recognize the impact of culture and cohort, and to acknowledge simultaneously that the human species has always experienced similar developmental changes from conception until death. That tension between the universal and the contemporary is an underlying theme of this epilogue.

## Health Habits

As always, human development connects universal, biological maturation with the specific conditions of a particular place and time. The health habits of young adults affect them lifelong. On that score, if emerging adults continue the habits they have now, they will enjoy a long, healthy life.

Exercise is the most obvious good habit. Most young adults are quite active, walking or biking to work, playing on sports teams, going to the gym at higher rates than older adults. Their motivation to exercise includes social reasons (because their friends do it), appearance, as well as health reasons, and that increases their activity (Box et al., 2019). Other health habits are also better than at older ages: Their rates of obesity, excessive drinking, and smoking are lower than older adults (see **Figure EP.1**).

Emerging adults may be protected somewhat from COVID-19, as well as from other diseases. It is not yet known if many have caught the virus with few serious symptoms, or what the long-term effects on their hearts, lungs, and brains might be. But their hospitalization and death rates are low. By contrast, one of every three people over age 70 who were hospitalized in April 2020 had died before June (Petrilli et al., 2020).

The challenge, of course, is for young adults to continue their good habits. If they do, that slows down aging, allowing an extra decade or so of disease-free life in late adulthood (Li et al., 2020). Those habits make a difference lifelong, although the natural reserves and strength of the young means that few emerging adults notice any health problems (see **Table EP.1**).

Nonetheless, research on adults now in midlife finds that some people age three times faster than others, with about half of the difference between fast and slow aging evident by age 26 (Belsky et al., 2015). By the mid-30s, some people have bodies like those in their 20s and some like those in their 40s. Will the current cohort of young adults slow down the aging process?

Later life is directly affected by health habits, but other circumstances matter. College football players, for instance, are exceptionally fit and strong, but also sustain hundreds of hits to their heads. Few have notable concussions, but those hits increase their risk of severe brain disease later on (Sancar, 2019). One COVID-19 question that awaits longitudinal research is whether those who contract the virus after a year or two will be affected later on. Some research finds that heart damage, for instance, endures after recovery (Li et al., 2020), but whether complete recovery is likely in young adulthood remains an open question.

Data from National Center for Health Statistics, 2019.

**FIGURE EP.1**

**Good News Ahead?** Habits established in emerging adulthood tend to persist. Many older adults have suffered through the hard work of quitting smoking, but about 15 percent have tried and failed. We do not yet know what this chart will look like in 2027, but optimism seems realistic!

**emerging adulthood** The period of life between the ages of 18 and 25. Emerging adulthood is now widely thought of as a distinct developmental stage.

| TABLE EP.1 | |
| --- | --- |
| **U.S. Deaths from the Top Two Causes (Heart Disease and Cancer)** | |
| **Age Group** | **Annual Rate per 100,000** |
| 15–24 | 6 |
| 25–34 | 16 |
| 35–44 | 60 |
| 45–54 | 176 |
| 55–64 | 470 |
| 65–74 | 961 |
| 75–84 | 2,119 |
| 85+ | 5,494 |

Data from National Center for Health Statistics, 2018.

**Ashamed to Use a Condom?** This public health effort attempts to remove the stigma, in order to reduce sexually transmitted diseases and unwanted babies.

⬤⬤ **Observation Quiz** Where is this? (see answer, page 467) ↑

## Sex and Pregnancy

Fertility peaks in late adolescence and early adulthood, pregnancy and birth are easier at age 20 than after age 30, which may be why hormones make sexual relationships particularly compelling in early adulthood. Compared to earlier centuries, however, fewer emerging adults seek parenthood.

In 2018, the average U.S. woman gave birth for the first time at age 27 (Martin et al., November 27, 2019), with men choosing fatherhood later than that. Adults of both sexes in some European nations are in their 30s, on average, when they have their first baby.

Thus, biological drives and social preferences diverge in the twenty-first century, unlike in earlier centuries. Medical research has found a solution to this clash: effective contraception. That solution is far from perfect: An estimated 40 percent of all pregnancies in the United States are unintended. However, that rate is decreasing, as is the rate of abortions and unwanted births, especially among emerging adults (Finer & Zolna, 2016; Jatlaoui et al., 2019).

The major sexual problem among emerging adults is now sexually transmitted diseases, which do not seem to be declining. Ironically, the more sexual partners an emerging adult has, the less likely they are to be conscientious with protection (Ashenhurst et al., 2017).

## Risks and Benefits

That is an example of an underlying problem: Early adulthood is a time for taking risks. Remember that each age group has its own gains and losses: Risk-taking in emerging adulthood is an example. Enrolling in college, moving to a new state or nation, independence from parents, committing to a romantic partner, starting a business, filming a documentary, entering a sports competition, enlisting in the military, traveling abroad—all risky and all beneficial.

However, unprotected sex with a new partner, fast driving with no seat belt, carrying a gun, avoiding vaccines, and experimenting with drugs, are more common in early adulthood than later on. The overall death rate of young adults is lower than for older adults, but a higher proportion of those deaths are the result of risks.

In 2018 in the United States, only 10 percent of the deaths of emerging adults were of unavoidable diseases. Most of the rest were related to a risk, such as a drowning, motor vehicle crashes, drug overdose, homicide, or unprotected sex.

Similar trends are apparent even in nations where disease is more common: Young adults rarely die of the scourges of poor nations, such as malaria or malnutrition. Even in underdeveloped nations, motor accidents cause more young-adult deaths than any disease.

---

**WHAT HAVE YOU LEARNED?**
· · · · · · · · · · · · · · · · · · · · · · · · · · · · · · · · · · · · · · · · · · · · · · · · · · · · · · · · · · ·

**1.** What is universal about physical development in emerging adulthood?

**2.** What are the problems and advantages of risk-taking?

**3.** What is similar about disease deaths in developed and developing nations?

# Cognitive Development

In many ways, emerging adulthood is prime time for thinking clearly and well. The prefrontal cortex finally is fully connected to the other three lobes; intuitive and analytic thought can come together; these often are the years of intellectual challenges in college or learning new skills on the job.

**LaunchPad**
*macmillan learning*

**VIDEO ACTIVITY: Brain Development: Emerging Adulthood** shows the changes that occur in a person's brain between ages 18 and 25.

## Postformal Thought

Although *formal operational thought* was the final stage of Piaget's theory, many cognitive psychologists find that postadolescent thinking is a cut above that. Some developmentalists propose a fifth stage, called **postformal thought**, a "type of logical, adaptive problem-solving that is a step more complex than scientific formal-level Piagetian tasks" (Sinnott, 2014, p. 3). In postformal cognition, "thinking needs to be integrated with emotional and pragmatic aspects, rather than only dealing with the purely abstract" (Labouvie-Vief, 2015, p. 89).

As they integrate emotion and pragmatics, postformal thinkers are flexible, with a "more complex, nuanced, and paradoxical" mode of thinking (Gidley, 2016). They consider all aspects of a situation, anticipating problems and dealing with them rather than denying, avoiding, or procrastinating. As a result, postformal thought is practical and creative (Gidley, 2016; Sinnott et al., 2020).

**postformal thought** A proposed adult stage of cognitive development, following Piaget's four stages, that goes beyond adolescent thinking by being more practical, more flexible, and more dialectical (i.e., more capable of combining contradictory elements into a comprehensive whole).

## Combining the Facts and Emotions

This synthesis may entail combining objective and subjective thought. **Objective thought** uses abstract, impersonal logic; **subjective thought** arises from personal experiences and perceptions. As you remember, formal operational thinking values impersonal logic and devalues subjective emotions, the opposite of egocentric preoperational thought. Both may not only come together; they may also produce a more advanced cognition in emerging adulthood.

Some scholars describe this process as *dialectical*, in which one idea (a thesis) leads to a contrary idea (an antithesis), and together they result in a new and better combination (a synthesis). One Canadian study used a dialectical approach to analyze vocational exploration of older adolescents over five years as they entered emerging adulthood, finding that each new career idea could lead to a deeper understanding of the next step (Gagnon et al., 2019).

If people do not reach a synthesis of objective and subjective thought, behavioral extremes (such as binge eating, anorexia, addiction, and violence) and cognitive extremes (such as believing that one is the best, or the worst, person on Earth) are common. Those are typical of the egocentrism of adolescence—and of some adults. By contrast, dialectical thinkers balance opposites, moving forward.

**objective thought** Thinking that is based on facts. It is impartial, and can be verified by anyone who seeks to know.

**subjective thought** Thinking that is based on personal experience and perception. Because it is connected to emotions, it is deeply held and can be quite opposite another's subjective thinking.

**Ideal Versus Real** One indication of adult cognition is the ability to accept some imperfections in oneself, one's family, and one's nation.

## Moral Foundations

The importance of combining emotional and logical perspectives is stressed by Jonathan Haidt, who has studied moral development in many religions and cultures. He wrote many scenarios to uncover which moral principles were important to adults.

- A family dog is killed by a passing car and the family cooks the meat and eats it for dinner.
- A sister and a brother on vacation from college in distant land where no one knows them, using excellent contraception, have intercourse.

"I CAN'T WAIT TILL I'M OLD ENOUGH TO HOLD MY NOSE AND VOTE."

Leo Cullum/Cartoon Collections

- Someone drinks water from a glass that had a dead, sterilized cockroach in it.

Each of these was highly offensive to most adults, who tried to explain their reactions based on logic. In fact, their reactions revealed their deep moral values, which Haidt says we all have in emerging adulthood but fail to recognize. He contends that humans have five moral foundations:

1. care for others, harm no one;
2. promote freedom, avoid oppression;
3. be fair, do not cheat;
4. seek purity, avoid contamination; and
5. respect authority, do not break laws.

The importance of these five varies from nation to nation, with #4, for instance, much stronger in India, and #2 much stronger in the United States. The emphasis on each of the five is influenced by the doctrines of each religion, by the values of each political party, and by the age of the person making the judgment.

## A Weird Perspective

If one culture prioritizes the first two and another the last two, then people will interpret the middle one—fairness—differently. This may explain why people of different religious, political, or cultural backgrounds consider each other immoral; they prioritize differently (Haidt, 2013).

This raises an important question regarding research on cognition. Most published research uses college students from **WEIRD** nations (Western, Educated, Industrialized, and Rich Democracies) as participants. Is that biased?

As one leading researcher expressed it, "the WEIRD group represents maximally 5% of the world's population, but probably more than 90% of the researchers and scientists producing the knowledge that is represented in our textbooks work with participants from that particular context" (Keller, quoted in Armstrong, 2018). Some scholars find that the cognitive abilities of emerging adults are similar worldwide; others disagree. This is another example of the tension between universal and particular.

Consider responses to COVID-19. Emerging adults tend to be most likely to resist government mandates to stay at home. They use logic to buttress their emotional resistance to authority. Research on emerging adults in Italy reports that some of this is cognitive: Those young adults who had a more collectivist perspective (believing more strongly in family and community) were more anxious about spreading the virus, more compliant with quarantine, and, perhaps paradoxically, less maladjusted (Germani et al., 2020). Is that true in the United States as well?

Striking national differences are apparent in limiting the spread of the virus, with New Zealand, South Korea, and Germany having done much better than the United States and England. Emerging adults in the United States are particularly likely to reject quarantine. Is this cognitive? Does national culture combine with developmental age to affect how emerging adults think about their health, or their government, or their family?

## College and Cognition

There is no doubt that college education benefits future health and wealth throughout adulthood (see Visualizing Development, page 460). In the United States, each added level of education correlates with everything from happy marriages to strong teeth, from spacious homes to long lives, from healthy children to working digestive systems (U.S. Department of Health and Human Services, January 28, 2019). Surprisingly, those from low-SES homes who, against the odds, earn a college degree, benefit even more from that degree than those from wealthier backgrounds (Brand & Xie, 2010; Karlson, 2019).

Note, however, that the benefits of college are most evident for those who earn a degree, yet about half the students who enroll in college leave before graduating. That is especially true for low-SES students who are African American, Latinx, and Native American, who often leave within the first year. Some colleges have much higher dropout rates than others, with community college students least likely to persevere until graduation.

Efforts to increase retention are twofold: financial and social. The financial problems include much more than the cost of tuition. Child care, lost income, and transportation may be crucial (Troester-Trate, 2019).

In addition, mentors and fellow students who encourage academic work may be as influential as grants that cover college costs, perhaps especially for students who are interested in science careers (Ceyhan et al., 2019). Note that although the ostensible goal of college is cognitive (to increase knowledge), the attainment of that goal seems more affected by money than the mind.

Intellectual growth, as Vygotsky would note, occurs everywhere in college: The direct academic knowledge that courses provide is only one part. This is evident with COVID-19, as all colleges in the United States temporarily canceled in-person classes, attempting to provide instruction remotely. Many students gained knowledge online, but all students missed the social interaction.

Exposure to new perspectives is a crucial benefit of college. That occurs with books and professors, but a major source is other students who have grown up in diverse communities, or who have had particular experiences, such as parenthood, or military service, or living abroad.

Of course, a diverse student body does not guarantee intellectual growth. Instead, intellectual expansion comes from conversations among people of varied backgrounds and perspectives (Pascarella et al., 2014). Colleges that make use of their diversity—via curriculum, assignments, discussions, cooperative education, learning communities, residence halls, and so on—stretch student understanding, not only of other people but also of themselves (Harper & Yeung, 2013; Shim & Perez 2018).

**Hi Mom and Dad** Like many college graduates, this young man in Idaho is grateful for the support of this family, who helped make this proud moment possible.

### WHAT HAVE YOU LEARNED?

1. What is the difference between formal and postformal thought?
2. Why is most research on emerging adulthood based on WEIRD people?
3. Why do many students quit college before graduating?
4. How does diversity affect college education?

## Psychosocial Development

Emerging adulthood is a time of transition. Young adults emerge from the close nurturance of family and immediate community and enter a broader, more complicated, and independent world. They have new freedom, as well as new restraints. They can now listen to their parents, neither rebelling nor agreeing; they can analyze their national and ethnic legacies. This is a time of extraordinary possibility.

### Personality in Emerging Adulthood

Possibility is evident in personality. Young adults do not shed their genetic and childhood influences. If self-doubt, anxiety, depression, or antisocial behavior characterizes the earlier years, it does not disappear.

# Why Study?

From a life-span perspective, college graduation is a good investment, for individuals (they become healthier and wealthier) and for nations (national income rises). However, when the effort and cost of higher education depend on immediate choices made by students and families, as in the United States, many decide it is not worth it, as illustrated by the number of people who earn Bachelor's degrees.

## CURRENT COLLEGE ENROLLMENT AMONG U.S. 18- TO 24-YEAR-OLDS

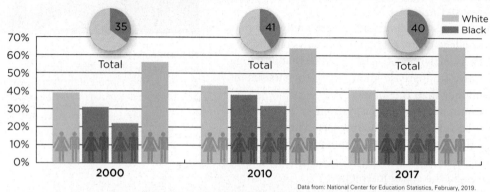

Legend: White, Black, Hispanic, Asian

Pie charts: 2000 Total 35, 2010 Total 41, 2017 Total 40

If this graph showed how many in each group *ever* attended college, the numbers for Black and Hispanic people would be closer to the numbers for Asian people, many of whom earn both Bachelor's and advanced degrees during this six-year period.

Data from: National Center for Education Statistics, February, 2019.

## HIGHEST LEVEL OF EDUCATION ATTAINED BY U.S. ADULTS

The percentage of U.S. residents with high school and college diplomas is increasing as more of the oldest cohort (often without degrees) dies and the youngest cohorts aim for college. The data below are for people ages 25 and older. In 1968, half of them reached high school age when education past eighth grade was a luxury, expected for those who were rich, native-born, and white, not for the general population.

Legend: Male, Female

8 years or less of primary school

4 years of high school

4 years or more of college

Data from U.S. Census Bureau, February 19, 2018.

## INCOME IMPACT

Over an average of 40 years of employment, someone who completes at least a Master's degree earns 1.5 million dollars more than someone who leaves school in eleventh grade. That translates into more than $200,000 for each year of education from twelfth grade to a Master's. The earnings gap is even wider than those numbers indicate because this chart includes only adults who have jobs, yet finding work is more difficult for those with less education.

Legend: 45- to 54-year-olds, 25- to 34-year-olds

Y-axis: Annual income — $160,000, $140,000, $120,000, $100,000, $80,000, $60,000, $40,000, $20,000, 0

X-axis: Education — Not a high school graduate, High school graduate only, Some college, no degree, Associate's degree, Bachelor's degree, Master's degree, Professional degree

Data from National Center for Education Statistics, September, 2018.
Photo: Jupiterimages/Thinkstock/Photos.com/Getty Images Plus.

Yet personality is not static, and each emerging adult combines genes, parental influences, and political contexts in a specific way to form their adult personality. Emerging adulthood has been called the "crucible for personality development" (Roberts & Davis, 2016). Remember the Big Five personality traits? Generally, continuity in those five is evident throughout adulthood. Thus, a young adult who is relatively outgoing becomes an outgoing older adult.

However, especially in emerging adulthood, notable changes are possible (Deventer et al., 2019), and the result is usually positive, with negative personality traits no longer dominant and positive ones strengthened. A study of almost a million adolescents and adults from 62 nations found that "during early adulthood, individuals from different cultures across the world tend to become more agreeable, more conscientious, and less neurotic" (Bleidorn et al., 2013, p. 2530).

This positive push occurs because emerging adults gradually feel more in control of their own lives (Vargas Lascano et al., 2015) and are able to set their own goals (Hill et al., 2011). One longitudinal study found that self-criticism gradually declines from age 23 to 29, and that improves mental health later on (Michaeli et al., 2019).

We need to note that, just as personality may change but rarely transforms, relationship to parents and national culture may change but rarely transforms. Remember the stage Erikson pegged at adolescence, the identity crisis, and remember that *identity achievement* occurs when aspects of earlier life are not rejected wholesale but are reexamined and revised (see **Table EP.2**). That is what emerging adults do.

One example is financial. Emerging adults strive to attain financial independence from their parents, and yet they accept some financial help, either directly with money or indirectly with food, laundry, and so on.

A longitudinal study of 1,719 individuals found that most young adults relied on parental financial help for years, even after college was over. Financial help meant less stress and eventually more independence, from age 18 to 27. Those (about one-fourth) who were totally independent, financially, tended to fare worse at age 27 than those with substantial assistance. The conclusion of this study is that family support is not a barrier to independence but more often the opposite—a helpful launching pad toward adulthood (Bea & Yi, 2019).

---

**CHAPTER APP**

**IOS:**
https://tinyurl.com/jeh8m6y

**ANDROID:**
https://tinyurl.com/y8rb3q5b

**RELEVANT TOPIC:**
Emerging adults and national culture

This app informs users of pending U.S. federal legislation (and soon, state and local legislation) with succinct, nonpartisan, sourced write-ups that include pro and con arguments. Countable also enables users to give instant feedback on pending bills and see how their representatives voted.

---

### TABLE EP. 2

#### Erikson's Eight Stages of Development

| Stage | Virtue / Pathology | Possible in Emerging Adulthood if Not Successfully Resolved |
|---|---|---|
| Trust vs. mistrust | Hope / withdrawal | Suspicious of others, making close relationships difficult |
| Autonomy vs. shame and doubt | Will / compulsion | Obsessively driven, single-minded, not socially responsive |
| Initiative vs. guilt | Purpose / inhibition | Fearful, regretful (e.g., very homesick in college) |
| Industry vs. inferiority | Competence / inertia | Self-critical of any endeavor, procrastinating, perfectionistic |
| Identity vs. role diffusion | Fidelity / repudiation | Uncertain and negative about values, lifestyle, friendships |
| Intimacy vs. isolation | Love / exclusivity | Anxious about close relationships, jealous, lonely |
| Generativity vs. stagnation | Care / rejection | [In the future] Fear of failure |
| Integrity vs. despair | Wisdom / disdain | [In the future] No "mindfulness," no life plan |

Information from Erikson, 1982.

## CAREER ALERT    The Career Counselor

We need more career counselors. Job growth in this occupation is above average, and so is annual income: 13 percent above and $56,000 a year, according to the Occupational Outlook Handbook (U.S. Bureau of Labor Statistics, 2020).

This occupation is both challenging and satisfying: Helping people find the right work for them benefits individuals, families, and communities. Studying human development is a good first step, so you are already on your way! After earning a Bachelor's degree, a Master's in counseling is recommended.

As you know from Erikson, vocational identity is crucial, and work is central to development. Emerging adults often change jobs (every year, on average), sometimes because they expected the job to be temporary (e.g., summer work as a waitress, lifeguard, or office assistant). But many employment shifts occur because young adults are unaware of job availability or of their own skills and values. Education improves job fit and satisfaction (Ilies et al., 2019), but which education for which job?

Many adults have not found the best employment for them. They take jobs that are available; they consult friends and family. They may discover that they hate their work, or an economic shift may put them out of work. Even if they are doing work they enjoy, people may be happier with another employer, or self-employment, or somewhere else. Career counseling might help.

This vocation is especially vital today for at least six reasons:

1. Most current vocations did not exist a generation ago, making past sources of job information (parents and teachers) less reliable.
2. Adult lives change over time, obviously for veterans, for parents with new babies or growing children, and for immigrants, but also for everyone else.
3. The economy is shifting, with start-ups, closed factories, relocated corporations, and emerging markets.
4. Long-term unemployment is one of the worst problems of adulthood, destroying personal happiness, as well as families and communities.
5. Major groups—women, minorities, people with disabilities—who were once shut out of productive work now can be vital workers in today's economy.
6. Adults who enjoy their work, with coworkers, challenges, and hours that make each day a good one, achieve a fulfilling, productive life.

This Career Alert appears in this epilogue chapter on emerging adulthood because floundering is more common than flourishing during these years. Most high school graduates know that they need more education in order to be hired for the work they want, but few know what college courses, requirements, and vocational training satisfy the demands of the job market. Most employees find their work by chance, or through word of mouth, or by stumbling across something on the Internet. Fantasy conflicts with reality; rejection and discouragement are common. Everyone needs guidance by a wise and informed advisor.

A few decades ago, vocational counselors had a simple task. There were valid tests of skills and personality, and the counselor used those to match a person with a career. Currently, however, a skilled counselor must do more than match. Vocational advisors still need to know the current and future job market, but they also must help each person recognize their particular skills and personality, values and aspirations (Rothausen & Henderson, 2019).

Career counselors motivate and guide, helping with searches and applications, role-playing for interviews, crafting résumés, suggesting additional education, gathering recommendations, encouraging applicants after rejection, analyzing offers after acceptance, negotiating benefits, and more.

Can you do this?

## Intimacy Versus Isolation

**intimacy versus isolation** The sixth of Erikson's eight stages of development. Adults seek someone with whom to share their lives in an enduring and self-sacrificing commitment. Without such commitment, they risk profound aloneness and isolation.

In Erikson's theory, after achieving identity, people experience the crisis of **intimacy versus isolation**. He explains:

> The young adult, emerging from the search for and the insistence on identity, is eager and willing to fuse his identity with others. He is ready for intimacy, that is, the capacity to commit himself to concrete affiliations and partnerships and to develop the ethical strength to abide by such commitments, even though they call for significant sacrifices and compromises.
>
> [Erikson, 1993a, p. 263]

Other theorists have different words for the same human need: *affiliation, affection, interdependence, communion, belonging, love*. But all developmentalists agree that social connections are pivotal lifelong (Padilla-Walker et al., 2017). In adulthood, intimacy progresses from attraction to connection to commitment. Each relationship demands vulnerability and compromise, shattering the isolation caused by too much self-protection.

The social context may be particularly influential in emerging adulthood, a period called the "frontier" of efforts to prevent problems and foster positive growth (Schwartz & Petrova, 2019). Individual differences matter, but the trend is toward more social connections, with family relationships maintained and friendships established. That benefits emerging adults (Jorgensen & Nelson, 2018).

## Friendship

Friends are crucial. Throughout life, friends increase each person's understanding via *self-expansion* (Aron et al., 2013); they enlarge perspective as people incorporate each other's experiences and ideas. Since fewer emerging adults today are married and have children, their social world can, and usually does, include friends who provide needed companionship and critical support. Unlike relatives, friends are selected for their ability to be loyal, trustworthy, supportive, and enjoyable—a mutual choice, not an obligatory one.

Thus, friends understand and comfort each other when romance turns sour, and they provide useful information about everything, from which college to attend to which socks to wear. For example, many adolescents are depressed about how their bodies appear. Interviews with 26-year-olds found that negative body image lifted in late adolescence and early adulthood, primarily because of friends who were reassuring (Gattario & Frisén, 2019).

People tend to make more friends during emerging adulthood than at any later period. They often use social media to extend and deepen friendships that begin face-to-face, becoming more aware of the day-to-day tribulations and celebrations of their friends.

Some older adults originally feared that increasing Internet use would diminish the number or quality of friendships. That fear has been proven false. Internet users in early adulthood tend to have more face-to-face friends, to know more about political and social events, and to advance in learning, all examples of self-expansion. Internet use is neither a boon nor a burden to emerging adults; the benefit or harm depends on the person (Blank & Lutz, 2018; Castellacci & Tveito, 2018; Hood et al., 2017).

Friendship patterns change with maturation. Young adults want many friends, and they work to gather them: befriending classmates, attending parties, speaking to strangers at concerts, on elevators, in parks, and so on. At about age 30, a switch begins, when quality becomes more important than quantity (Carmichael et al., 2015). Consequently, some friendships from early adulthood fade away, but others deepen. Social media helps with both processes.

There is a paradox here. Not only do young adults, on average, have more friends and acquaintances that adults of other ages, they also are more likely to be lonely. The only adult age group that seems to have higher rates of loneliness are adults over age 80 (Luhmann & Hawkley, 2016). Some say that social media is part of the reason, since emerging adults know how many "likes" they have, and since others post photos that showcase their most social moments, which makes some viewers feel inferior.

This leads us back to Erikson, who notes that each ongoing relationship demands some personal sacrifice, including vulnerability that brings deeper self-understanding and shatters the isolation of too much self-protection. To establish intimacy, the young adult must

> face the fear of ego loss in situations which call for self-abandon: in the solidarity of close affiliations [and] sexual unions, in close friendship and in physical combat, in experiences of inspiration by teachers and of intuition from the recesses of the self. The avoidance of such experiences . . . may lead to a deep sense of isolation and consequent self-absorption.

*[Erikson, 1963, pp. 163–164]*

**THINK CRITICALLY:** Can a person with many friends also be lonely?

**Especially for Young Men** Why would you want at least one close friend who is a woman? (see answer, page 467)

**Being Intimate** The word "intimacy" was traditionally a euphemism for sexual intercourse, but to developmentalists it is much more than that. Look closely at these two couples, one in Spain *(left)* and one in Malaysia *(right)*. Whether or not they are having sex does not matter: They are intimate in their touching, emotions, and even clothing.

## Romantic Partners

In Europe in the Middle Ages, love, passion, and marriage were each considered to be distinct phenomena: Marriages were not usually for love. This was explained by Sternberg, who said that the current ideal of love includes three dimensions—passion, intimacy, and commitment (see **Table EP.3**).

For developmental reasons, this ideal is difficult to achieve. Passion seems to be sparked by unfamiliarity, uncertainty, and risk, all of which are diminished by the familiarity and security that contribute to intimacy and by the time needed for commitment.

Part of the problem is time. Over the years, passion may fade. Ideally, intimacy grows and commitment deepens as a couple together faces financial ups and downs, child-rearing challenges, and health crises. This pattern can occur for all types of couples—married, cohabiting, and remarried; same-gender and other-gender; young and old; in arranged or self-initiated relationships.

Emerging adults currently hope to find a lifelong partner, but they postpone that commitment until age 30 or so. More than in previous decades, some never find that person—the number of people who never marry is increasing. In former decades, divorce was a young person's experience: It almost always happened in the first years after the wedding. Lately, however, there has been a rise in "gray divorce" after age 50 (Crowley, 2019), and that rising divorce rate is one reason many emerging adults avoid marriage.

A report on the demography of marriage in the United States (Smock & Schwartz, 2020) notes that "despite high levels of aspiration for marriage" among young adults, an increasing number never marry.

That is one reason the birth rate is down, but it also is true that some people—especially those with relatively little education—choose to have a child but not to marry. The average age at first birth is after age 25 (the age when emerging adulthood is said to end) but is younger than the average age of first marriage.

## Connecting with Others

When we consider the psychosocial needs of emerging adults, it seems that Erikson is right: Humans seek an intimate relationship with someone else. However, as you just read, cohort is crucial in how and when this need is met. Marriage is not the

### TABLE EP.3

#### Sternberg's Seven Forms of Love

**Present in the Relationship?**

| Form of Love | Passion | Intimacy | Commitment |
|---|---|---|---|
| Liking | No | Yes | No |
| Infatuation | Yes | No | No |
| Empty love | No | No | Yes |
| Romantic love | Yes | Yes | No |
| Fatuous love | Yes | No | Yes |
| Companionate love | No | Yes | Yes |
| Consummate love | Yes | Yes | Yes |

Information from Sternberg, 1988.

usual solution. One review cites a dramatic statistic: "In 1978, 59% of the population aged 18 to 34 was currently married. By 2018, this percentage was only 29%" (Sassler & Lichter, 2020).

Instead of traditional courtship and marriage, current young adults often use the internet to find possible partners. Virtually all emerging adults have smartphones and social media accounts, and some of them use this technology many times each day to connect with friends and possible partners. Use increased rapidly from 2010 on, but this rise has now stopped—in part because use is near universal (Hitlin, 2018).

Many young adults seeking romance join matchmaking sites that provide dozens of potential partners to meet and evaluate. Often physical attraction is the gateway to a relationship and passion rises, but intimacy and then commitment require much more.

In some ways, **cohabitation**, living with an unmarried partner, has replaced marriage. Cohabitation was relatively unusual 50 years ago: Only one in nine marriages in 1970 began with cohabitation. Now cohabitation is the norm (see **Figure EP.2**). About three of every four U.S. couples cohabit before marriage (Rosenfeld & Roesler, 2019).

Cohabitation rates vary by culture as well as cohort. Almost everyone in Canada and Europe cohabits at some point. Many people in Sweden, France, Jamaica, and Puerto Rico live with a partner for decades, sometimes all their lives, never marrying. In some other nations—including Japan, Ireland, and Italy—cohabitation is not yet the norm, although it is becoming increasingly common.

Although marriage rates are down and cohabitation is up in every demographic group, education increases the chance of marriage and marital childbearing. Cohabiting couples without college degrees have children about five times as often as cohabiting couples the same age who have graduated from college (Lundberg et al., 2016). The probable reason is *not* that college graduates know something that others do not. Instead, college graduates are more likely to marry before becoming parents, because they are more likely to have a steady, well-paying job.

One issue is whether cohabitation is an acceptable substitute for marriage, or a path toward a lifelong commitment, or neither. The research finds many similarities between cohabitation and marriage, but also some crucial differences. Cohabiting couples are more likely to end their relationship, are less likely to have children, and, if they do marry, are more likely to divorce (Sassler & Lichter, 2020).

As you have seen, historical circumstances have an impact on partnership formation. How will COVID-19 affect this? A study of 3,593 adults (age 18 and older) in 57 nations answered questions online about their relationship

**Just Friends?** This photo was taken in a public park in Isfala, Iran. Given that context, these two are probably more than friends.

**Observation Quiz** What indicates that this is romance, not mere friendship? (see answer, page 467) ↑

**cohabitation** An arrangement in which a couple lives together in a committed romantic relationship but is not formally married.

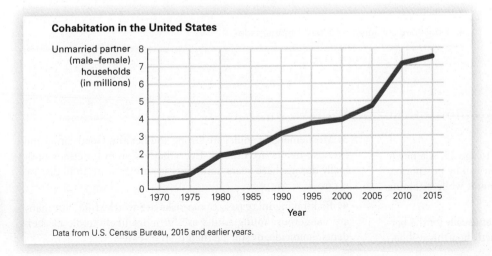

Data from U.S. Census Bureau, 2015 and earlier years.

**FIGURE EP.2**
**More Together, Fewer Married** As you see, the number of cohabiting male–female households in the United States has increased dramatically over the past decades. These numbers are an underestimate: Couples do not always tell the U.S. Census that they are living together, nor are cohabiters counted within their parents' households. Same-sex couples (not tallied until 2000) are also not included here.

(Balzarini et al., 2020). Most were living together; about a third were married. The sample was self-selected: people who responded to online requests.

When governments required lockdowns, conflict stress rose and satisfaction decreased. The most stressed were those who were relatively young, with children and financial insecurity. It seems that socializing with friends, having outside work, and spending time each day away from one's partner, strengthens romantic relationships. Thus, COVID-19 may increase divorce for married couples, separation for cohabiting ones, and domestic abuse for everyone. Of course, longitudinal studies are needed before science can confirm or refute this speculation.

Overall, it seems that contemporary life in general, and the COVID-19 pandemic in particular, are not favorable conditions for romantic relationships.

There is one bright side, however. It also seems that young adults are more connected in current times to their parents and other relatives than they were (Fingerman et al., 2020). That is the conclusion of extensive pre-COVID research, which finds that more young adults are living with a parent than with a romantic partner (most live with housemates or alone). Some suggest that the pandemic has increased young adults' connections to parents and grandparents, although again, more longitudinal research is needed.

---

 **DATA CONNECTIONS: Technology and Romance: Trends for U.S. Adults** examines how emerging adults find romantic partners.

---

## Concluding Hopes

Fortunately, most emerging adults, like humans of all ages, have strengths as well as liabilities. Many survive risks, overcome substance abuse, think more deeply, combat loneliness, and deal with other problems through further education, maturation, friends, and family. If they postpone marriage, prevent parenthood, and avoid a set career until their identity is firmly established and their education is complete, they are ready for all the commitments and responsibilities ahead. I hope this is true.

> **WHAT HAVE YOU LEARNED?**
>
> 1. What personality changes are likely and unlikely in emerging adulthood?
> 2. How do emerging adults meet their need for intimacy?
> 3. What is the difference between support from friends and parents during emerging adulthood?
> 4. How does cohabitation differ from marriage?

# SUMMARY

### Biological Universals

**1.** Emerging adulthood, from about age 18 to age 25, is a newly recognized period of development characterized by postponing parenthood, marriage, and career commitment, while attaining additional education.

**2.** COVID-19 affects adults in many ways, not usually for the better. Research needs confirmation to know exactly how this will be.

**3.** Most emerging adults are strong and healthy. Good eating and exercise habits are crucial. Every body system functions optimally during these years; immunity is strong; death from disease is rare.

**4.** Risk-taking increases. Some risks are worthwhile, but many are dangerous. Young adults are far more likely to die of accidents, homicide, or suicide than from diseases.

## Cognitive Development

**5.** Many researchers believe that the complex and conflicting demands of adult life produce a new cognitive perspective. Postformal thinking is characterized by thinking that is flexible and practical, combing emotion and logic, intuition and analysis.

**6.** How much college education advances cognition in current times is debatable, although research over the past several decades indicates not only that college graduates are wealthier and healthier than other adults but also that they think at a more advanced level.

**7.** Contemporary college students are far more diverse than college students were a few decades ago. Learning from people of different perspectives can advance cognition.

## Psychosocial Development

**8.** Personality tends to be quite stable lifelong, but emerging adulthood is the time when change is most likely to occur. The usual pattern is improvement, according to goals set by the individual.

**9.** Friends are particularly crucial in emerging adulthood. Many emerging adults use social networking and matchmaking sites on the Internet to expand and deepen their friendship circles and mating options.

**10.** Commitment to a partner is increasingly unusual during early adulthood, as both parenthood and marriage are often postponed. Cohabitation, and relationships with parents, are both more common now than a few decades ago.

## KEY TERMS

emerging adulthood (p. 455)      objective thought (p. 457)      WEIRD (p. 458)      cohabitation (p. 465)
postformal thought (p. 457)      subjective thought (p. 457)     intimacy versus isolation (p. 462)

## APPLICATIONS

**1.** Describe an incident during your emerging adulthood when taking a risk could have led to disaster. What were your feelings at the time? What would you do if you knew that a child of yours was about to do the same thing?

**2.** Read a biography or autobiography that includes information about the person's thinking from adolescence through adulthood. How did personal experiences, education, and maturation affect the person's thinking?

**3.** Statistics on cohort and culture in students and in colleges are fascinating, but only a few are reported here. Compare your nation, state, or province with another. Analyze the data and discuss causes and implications of differences.

**4.** Talk to three people you would expect to have contrasting views on love and marriage (differences in age, gender, upbringing, experience, and religion might affect attitudes). Ask each the same questions and then compare their answers.

## Especially For ANSWERS

**Response for Someone Who Has to Make an Important Decision** (from p. 458): Both are necessary. Mature thinking requires a combination of emotions and logic. To make sure you use both, take your time (don't just act on your first impulse) and talk with people you trust. Ultimately, you will have to live with your decision, so do not ignore either intuitive or logical thought.

**Response for Young Men** (from p. 463): Not for sex! Women friends are particularly responsive to deep conversations about family relationships, personal weaknesses, and emotional confusion. But women friends might be offended by sexual advances, bragging, or advice giving. Save these for a future romance.

## Observation Quiz ANSWERS

**Answer to Observation Quiz** (from p. 456) Kyiv, in Ukraine. As evident in the globalization of emerging adulthood, the same challenges are everywhere.

**Answer to Observation Quiz** (from p. 465): Note body position, hands, and her facial expression.

# Appendix
## More About
## Research Methods

This appendix explains how to learn about any topic. One of the most important lessons from the 2020 COVID-19 pandemic is that we need accurate information, reported honestly and analyzed carefully, to protect our mental and physical health. Science is essential to keep speculation and wishful thinking from destroying us.

Remember that almost no conclusion is entirely certain, now and forever. That is why the scientific method requires testing every hypothesis, basing conclusion on evidence, and reporting methods and statistics so the others can confirm, dispute, and replicate.

One of the most important aspects is in the selection of the participants in a study. Ideally, they are diverse in gender, ethnicity, and economic backgrounds, but if not, the biases and limitations of a restricted sample must be acknowledged.

Beyond that, when doing research connected with your own study in learning about human development, here are several suggestions.

## Make It Personal

Think about your life, observe your behavior, and watch the people around you. Pay careful attention to details of expression, emotion, and behavior. The more you see, the more fascinated, curious, and reflective you will become. Ask questions and listen carefully and respectfully to what other people say regarding development.

Whenever you ask specific questions as part of an assignment, remember that observing ethical standards (see Chapter 1) comes first. *Before* you interview anyone, inform the person of your purpose and assure them of confidentiality. Promise not to identify the person in your report (use a pseudonym) and do not repeat any personal details that emerge in the interview to anyone (friends or strangers). Your instructor will provide further ethical guidance. If you might publish what you've learned, get in touch with your college's Institutional Review Board (IRB).

## Read the Research

No matter how deeply you think about your own experiences, and no matter how intently you listen to others whose background is unlike yours, you also need to read scholarly published work in order to fully understand any topic that interests you. Be skeptical about magazine or newspaper reports; some are bound to be simplified, exaggerated, or biased.

## Professional Journals and Books

Part of the process of science is that conclusions are not considered solid until they are corroborated in many studies, which means that you should consult several sources on any topic. Five journals in human development are:

- *Developmental Psychology* (published by the American Psychological Association)
- *Child Development* (Society for Research in Child Development)
- *Developmental Review* (Elsevier)
- *Human Development* (Karger)
- *Developmental Science* (Wiley)

These journals differ in the types of articles and studies they publish, but all are well respected and peer-reviewed, which means that other scholars review each article submitted and recommend that it be accepted, rejected, or revised. Every article includes references to other recent work.

Also look at journals that specialize in longer reviews from the perspective of a researcher.

- *Child Development Perspectives* (from Society for Research in Child Development)
- *Perspectives on Psychological Science* (This is published by the Association for Psychological Science. APS publishes several excellent journals, none specifically on development but every issue has at least one article that is directly relevant.)

Beyond these seven are literally thousands of other professional journals, each with a particular perspective or topic, including many in sociology, family studies, economics, medicine, demography, education, and more. To judge them, look for journals that are peer-reviewed. Also consider the following details: the background of the author (research funded by corporations tends to favor their products); the nature of the publisher (professional organizations, as in the first two journals above, protect their reputations); and how long the journal has been published (the volume number tells you that). Some interesting work does not meet these criteria, so be careful before believing what you read.

Many *books* cover some aspect of development. Single-author books are likely to present only one viewpoint. That view may be insightful, but it is limited. You might consult a *handbook*, which is a book that includes many authors and many topics. One good handbook in development, now in its seventh edition (a sign that past scholars have found it useful) is:

- *Handbook of Child Psychology and Developmental Science* (7th ed.), edited by Richard M. Lerner, 2015, Hoboken, NJ: Wiley.

This handbook is updated about every five years, so a new edition might be out soon. Check on it, and use the newest one. Dozens of other good handbooks are available, many of which focus on a particular age, perspective, or topic.

## The Internet

The *internet* is a mixed blessing, useful to every novice and experienced researcher but dangerous as well. Every library worldwide and most homes in North America, Western Europe, and East Asia have computers that provide access to journals and other information. If you're doing research in a library, ask for help from the librarians; many of them can guide you in the most effective ways to conduct online searches. In addition, other students, friends, and even strangers can be helpful.

Virtually everything is on the internet, not only massive national and international statistics but also accounts of very personal experiences. Photos, charts, quizzes, ongoing experiments, newspapers from around the world, videos, and much more are available at a click. Every journal has a Web site, with tables of contents, abstracts, and sometimes full texts. (An abstract gives the key findings; for the full text, most colleges and universities have access. Again, ask librarians for help.)

Unfortunately, you can spend many frustrating hours sifting through information that is useless, trash, or tangential. *Directories* (which list general topics or areas and then move you step by step in the direction you choose) and *search engines* (which give you all the sites that use a particular word or words) can help you select appropriate information. Each directory or search engine provides somewhat different lists; none provides only the most comprehensive and accurate sites. Sometimes organizations pay, or find other ways, to make their links appear first, even though they are biased. With experience and help, you will find quality on the internet, but you will also encounter some junk no matter how experienced you are.

Anybody can put anything online, regardless of its truth or fairness, so you need a very critical eye. Make sure you have several divergent sources for every "fact" you find; consider who provided the information and why. Every controversial issue has sites that forcefully advocate opposite viewpoints, sometimes with biased statistics and narrow perspectives.

Here are four internet sites that are quite reliable:

- *childtrends.org* A leading U.S. research organization focusing on improving children's lives. Their site contains a wealth of data and evidence-based research.
- *childdevelopmentinfo.com* Child Development Institute. A useful site, with links and articles on child development and information on common childhood psychological disorders.
- *eric.ed.gov* Education Resources Information Center (ERIC). Provides links to many education-related sites and includes brief descriptions of each.
- *www.cdc.gov/nchs/hus.htm* The National Center for Health Statistics issues an annual report on health trends, called *Health, United States*.

Every source—you, your interviewees, journals, books, and the internet—is helpful. Do not depend on any particular one. Avoid plagiarism and prejudice by citing every source and noting objectivity, validity, and credibility. Your own analysis, opinions, words, and conclusions are crucial, backed up by science.

## Additional Terms and Concepts

As emphasized throughout the text, the study of development is a science. Social scientists spend years in graduate school, studying methods and statistics. Chapter 1 touches on some of these matters (observation and experiments; correlation and causation; independent and dependent variables; experimental and control groups; cross-sectional, longitudinal, and cross-sequential research), but there is much more. A few additional aspects of research are presented here to help you evaluate research wherever you find it.

## Who Participates?

The entire group of people about whom a scientist wants to learn is called a **population**. Generally, a research population is quite large—not usually the world's entire population of more than 7 billion, but for statistics on birthweight or unwed mothers of all of the 3,788,235 babies born in the United States in 2019.

The particular individuals who are studied in a specific research project are called the **participants**. They are usually a **sample** of the population. Ideally, the participants are a **representative sample**, that is, a sample that reflects the population. Every peer-reviewed, published study reports details on the sample.

Selection of the sample is crucial. People who volunteer, or people who have telephones, or people who have some particular condition are not a *random sample*; in a random sample, everyone in a particular population is equally likely to be selected. To avoid *selection bias*, some studies are *prospective*, beginning with an entire cluster of people (for instance, every baby born on a particular day) and then tracing the development of some particular characteristic. Ideally, the sample is diverse in gender, ethnicity, and other ways: If it is not, the bias must be explained.

For example, prospective studies find the antecedents of heart disease, or child abuse, or high school dropout rates—all of which are much harder to find if the study is *retrospective*, beginning with those who had heart attacks, experienced abuse, or left school. Thus, although retrospective research finds that most high school dropouts say they disliked school, prospective research finds that some who like school still decide to drop out and then later say they hated school, while others dislike school but stay to graduate. Prospective research discovers how many students are in these last two categories; retrospective research on people who have already dropped out does not.

## Research Design

Every researcher begins not only by formulating a hypothesis but also by learning what other scientists have discovered about the topic in question and what methods might be useful and ethical in designing research. Often they include measures to prevent inadvertently finding only the results they expect. For example, the people who actually gather the data may not know the purpose of the research. Scientists say that these data gatherers are **blind** to the hypothesized outcome. Participants are sometimes "blind" as well, because otherwise they might, for instance, respond the way they think they should.

Another crucial aspect of research design is to define exactly what is to be studied. Researchers establish an **operational definition** of whatever phenomenon they will be examining, defining each variable by describing specific, observable behavior. This is essential in quantitative research, but it is also useful in qualitative research.

For example, if a researcher wants to know when babies begin to walk, does walking include steps taken while holding on? Is one unsteady step enough? Some parents say yes, but the usual operational definition of *walking* is "takes at least three steps without holding on." This operational definition allows comparisons worldwide, making it possible to discover, for example, that well-fed African babies tend to walk earlier than well-fed European babies.

When emotions or personality traits are studied, operational definitions are difficult to formulate but crucial for interpretation of results. How should *aggression* or *sharing* or *shyness* be defined? Lack of an operational definition leads to contradictory results. For instance, critics report that infant day care makes children more aggressive, but advocates report that it makes them more assertive and outgoing. In this case, both may be seeing the same behavior but defining it differently.

---

**population** The entire group of individuals who are of particular concern in a scientific study, such as all the children of the world or all newborns who weigh less than 3 pounds.

**participants** The people who are studied in a research project. Participants is the term now used in psychology; other disciplines still call these people "subjects."

**sample** A group of individuals drawn from a specified population. A sample might be the low-birthweight babies born in four particular hospitals that are representative of all hospitals.

**representative sample** A group of research participants who reflect the relevant characteristics of the larger population whose attributes are under study.

**blind** The condition of data gatherers (and sometimes participants, as well) who are deliberately kept ignorant of the purpose of the research so that they cannot unintentionally bias the results.

**operational definition** A description of the specific, observable behavior that will constitute the variable that is to be studied, so that any reader will know whether that behavior occurred or not. Operational definitions may be arbitrary (e.g., an IQ score at or above 130 is operationally defined as "gifted"), but they must be precise.

For any scientist, operational definitions are crucial, and studies usually include descriptions of how they measured attitudes or behavior.

## Reporting Results

You already know that results should be reported in sufficient detail so that another scientist can analyze the conclusions and replicate the research. Various methods, populations, and research designs may produce divergent conclusions. For that reason, handbooks, some journals, and some articles are called *reviews*: They summarize past research. Often, when studies are similar in operational definitions and methods, the review is a **meta-analysis**, which combines the findings of many studies to present an overall conclusion.

**Table App.1** describes some other statistical measures. One of them is *statistical significance*, which indicates whether or not a particular result could have occurred by chance.

A crucial statistic is **effect size**, a way of measuring how much impact one variable has on another. Effect size ranges from 0 (no effect) to 1 (total transformation, never found in actual studies). Effect size may be particularly important when the sample size is large, because a large sample often leads to highly "significant" results (results that are unlikely to have occurred by chance) that have only a tiny effect on the variable of interest.

Hundreds of statistical measures are used by developmentalists. Often the same data can be presented in many ways: Some scientists examine statistical analysis intently before they accept conclusions as valid. A specific example

**meta-analysis** A technique of combining results of many studies to come to an overall conclusion. Meta-analysis is powerful, in that small samples can be added together to lead to significant conclusions, although variations from study to study sometimes make combining them impossible.

**effect size** A way of indicating statistically how much of an impact the independent variable in an experiment had on the dependent variable.

### TABLE App.1

#### Statistical Measures Often Used to Analyze Search Results

| Measure | Use |
|---|---|
| Effect size | There are many kinds, but the most useful in reporting studies of development is called *Cohen's d*, which can indicate the power of an intervention. An effect size of 0.2 is called small, 0.5 moderate, and 0.8 large. |
| Significance | Indicates whether the results might have occurred by chance. If chance would produce the results only 5 times in 100, that is significant at the 0.05 level; once in 100 times is 0.01; once in 1,000 is 0.001. |
| Cost-benefit analysis | Calculates how much a particular independent variable costs versus how much it saves. This is useful for analyzing public spending, such as finding that preschool education programs or preventative health measures save money. |
| Odds ratio | Indicates how a particular variable compares to a standard, set at 1. For example, one study found that although less than 1 percent of all child homicides occurred at school, the odds were similar for public and private schools. The odds of it in high schools, however, were 18.47 times that of elementary or middle schools (set at 1.0) (MMWR, January 18, 2008). |
| Factor analysis | Hundreds of variables could affect any given behavior. In addition, many variables (such as family income and parental education) overlap. To take this into account, analysis reveals variables that can be clustered together to form a factor, which is a composite of many variables. For example, SES might become one factor, child personality another. |
| Meta-analysis | A "study of studies." Researchers use statistical tools to synthesize the results of previous, separate studies. Then they analyze the accumulated results, using criteria that weigh each study fairly. This approach improves data analysis by combining studies that were too small, or too narrow, to lead to solid conclusions. |

involved methods to improve students' writing ability between grades 4 and 12. A meta-analysis found that many methods of writing instruction have a significant impact, but effect size is much larger for some methods (teaching strategies and summarizing) than for others (prewriting exercises and studying models). For teachers, this statistic is crucial, for they want to know what has a big effect, not merely what is better than chance (significant).

Numerous articles published in the past decade are meta-analyses that combine similar studies to search for general trends. Often effect sizes are also reported, which is especially helpful for meta-analyses since standard calculations almost always find some significance if the number of participants is in the thousands.

An added problem is the *file drawer problem* — that studies without significant results tend to be filed away rather than published. Thus, an accurate effect size may be much smaller than the published meta-analysis finds, or may be nonexistent. For this reason, replication is an important step.

Overall, then, designing and conducting valid research is complex yet crucial. Remember that with your own opinions: As this appendix advises, it is good to "make it personal," but do not stop there.

## A

**23rd pair** The chromosome pair that, in humans, determines sex. The other 22 pairs are autosomes, inherited equally by males and females.

**accommodation** The restructuring of old ideas to include new experiences.

**adolescence-limited offender** A person who breaks the law as a teenage but whose criminal activity stops by age 20.

**adolescent egocentrism** A characteristic of adolescent thinking that leads young people (ages 10 to 13) to focus on themselves to the exclusion of others.

**adrenal glands** Two glands, located above the kidneys, that respond to the pituitary, producing hormones.

**age of viability** The age (about 22 weeks after conception) at which a fetus might survive outside the mother's uterus if specialized medical care is available.

**allele** A variation that makes a gene different in some way from other genes for the same characteristics. Many genes never vary; others have several possible alleles.

**allocare** Literally, "other-care"; the care of children by people other than the biological parents.

**amygdala** A tiny brain structure that registers emotions, particularly fear and anxiety.

**analytic thought** Thought that results from analysis, such as a systematic ranking of pros and cons, risks and consequences, possibilities and facts. Analytic thought depends on logic and rationality.

**animism** The belief that natural objects and phenomena are alive, moving around, and having sensations and abilities that are human-like.

**anorexia nervosa** An eating disorder characterized by self-starvation. Affected individuals voluntarily undereat and often overexercise, depriving their vital organs of nutrition. Anorexia can be fatal.

**anoxia** A lack of oxygen that, if prolonged, can cause brain damage or death.

**antipathy** Feelings of dislike or even hatred for another person.

**antisocial behavior** Actions that are deliberately hurtful or destructive to another person.

**Apgar scale** A quick assessment of a newborn's health, from 0 to 10. Below 5 is an emergency—a neonatal pediatrician is summoned immediately. Most babies are at 7, 8, or 9—almost never a perfect 10.

**apprenticeship in thinking** Vygotsky's term for how cognition is stimulated and developed in people by more skilled members of society.

**assimilation** The reinterpretation of new experiences to fit into old ideas.

**asthma** A chronic disease of the respiratory system in which inflammation narrows the airways from the nose and mouth to the lungs, causing difficulty in breathing. Signs and symptoms include wheezing, shortness of breath, chest tightness, and coughing.

**attachment** According to Ainsworth, "an affectional tie" that an infant forms with a caregiver—a tie that binds them together in space and endures over time.

**attention-deficit/hyperactivity disorder (ADHD)** A condition characterized by a persistent pattern of inattention and/or by hyperactive or impulsive behaviors; ADHD interferes with a person's functioning or development.

**authoritarian parenting** An approach to child rearing that is characterized by high behavioral standards, strict punishment of misconduct, and little communication from child to parent.

**authoritative parenting** An approach to child rearing in which the parents set limits and enforce rules but are flexible and listen to their children.

**autism spectrum disorder (ASD)** A developmental disorder marked by difficulty with social communication and interaction—including difficulty seeing things from another person's point of view—and restricted, repetitive patterns of behavior, interests, or activities.

**automatization** A process in which repetition of a sequence of thoughts and actions makes the sequence routine so that it no longer requires conscious thought.

**autonomy versus shame and doubt** Erikson's second crisis of psychosocial development. Toddlers either succeed or fail in gaining a sense of self-rule over their actions and their bodies.

**axon** A fiber that extends from a neuron and transmits electrochemical impulses from that neuron to the dendrites of other neurons.

## B

**babbling** An infant's repetition of certain syllables, such as *ba-ba-ba*, that begins when babies are between 6 and 9 months old.

**bed-sharing** When two or more people sleep in the same bed.

**behavioral teratogens** Agents and conditions that can harm the prenatal brain, impairing the future child's intellectual and emotional functioning.

**behaviorism** A grand theory of human development that studies observable behavior. Behaviorism is also called *learning theory* because it describes the laws and processes by which behavior is learned.

**bilingual education** A strategy in which school subjects are taught in both the learner's original language and the second (majority) language.

**binge eating disorder** Frequent episodes of uncontrollable overeating to the point that the stomach hurts. Usually the person feels shame and guilt but is unable to stop.

**binocular vision** The ability to focus the two eyes in a coordinated manner in order to see one image.

**body image** A person's idea of how his or her body looks.

**Brazelton Neonatal Behavioral Assessment Scale (NBAS)** A test that is often administered to newborns; it measures responsiveness and records 46 behaviors, including 20 reflexes.

**bulimia nervosa** An eating disorder characterized by binge eating and subsequent purging, usually by induced vomiting and/or use of laxatives.

**bullying** Repeated, systematic efforts to inflict harm on other people through physical, verbal, or social attack on a weaker person.

**bullying aggression** Unprovoked, repeated physical or verbal attack, especially on victims who are unlikely to defend themselves.

**bully-victim** Someone who attacks others and who is attacked as well. (Also called *provocative victims* because they do things that elicit bullying.)

# C

**carrier** A person whose genotype includes a gene that is not expressed in the phenotype. The carried gene occurs in half of the carrier's gametes and thus is passed on to half of the carrier's children. If such a gene is inherited from both parents, the characteristic appears in the phenotype.

**centration** A characteristic of preoperational thought in which a young child focuses (centers) on one idea, excluding all others.

**cephalocaudal** Growth and development that occurs from the head down.

**cerebral palsy** A disorder that results from damage to the brain's motor centers. People with cerebral palsy have difficulty with muscle control, so their speech and/or body movements are impaired.

**cesarean section (c-section)** A surgical birth in which incisions through the mother's abdomen and uterus allow the fetus to be removed quickly instead of being delivered through the vagina. (Also called simply *section*.)

**child abuse** Deliberate action that is harmful to a child's physical, emotional, or sexual well-being.

**child culture** The idea that each group of children has games, sayings, clothing styles, and superstitions that are not common among adults, just as every culture has distinct values, behaviors, and beliefs.

**child maltreatment** Intentional harm to, or avoidable endangerment of, anyone under 18 years of age.

**child neglect** Failure to meet a child's basic physical, educational, or emotional needs.

**child sexual abuse** Any erotic activity that arouses an adult and excites, shames, or confuses a child, whether or not the victim protests and whether or not genital contact is involved.

**childhood obesity** In a child, having a BMI above the 95th percentile, according to

the U.S. Centers for Disease Control's 1980 standards for children of a given age.

**chromosome** One of the 46 molecules of DNA (in 23 pairs) that virtually each cell of the human body contains and that, together, contain all the genes. Other species have more or fewer chromosomes.

**chronosystem** In Bronfenbrenner's ecological approach, the impact of historical conditions (wars, inventions, policies) on the development of people who live in that era.

**circadian rhythm** A day–night cycle of biological activity that occurs approximately every 24 hours.

**classical conditioning** The learning process in which a meaningful stimulus (such as the smell of food to a hungry animal) is connected with a neutral stimulus (such as the sound of a tone) that had no special meaning before conditioning. (Also called *respondent conditioning*.)

**classification** The logical principle that things can be organized into groups (or categories or classes) according to some characteristic that they have in common.

**cluster suicides** Several suicides committed by members of a group within a brief period.

**coercive joining** When others strongly encourage someone to join in their activity, usually when the pressure is being included or excluded in a group and the activity is not approved by authorities (e.g., drug use, bullying.)

**cognitive equilibrium** In cognitive theory, a state of mental balance in which people are not confused because they can use their existing thought processes to understand current experiences and ideas.

**cognitive theory** A grand theory of human development that focuses on changes in how people think over time. According to this theory, our thoughts shape our attitudes, beliefs, and behaviors.

**cohabitation** An arrangement in which a couple lives together in a committed romantic relationship but is not formally married.

**cohort** People born within the same historical period who therefore move through life together, experiencing the same events, new technologies, and cultural shifts at the same ages. For example, the effect of the Internet varies depending on what cohort a person belongs to.

**comorbid** Refers to the presence of two or more unrelated disease conditions at the same time in the same person.

**concrete operational thought** Piaget's term for the ability to reason logically about direct experiences and perceptions.

**conservation** The principle that the amount of a substance remains the same (i.e., is conserved) even when its appearance changes.

**control processes** Mechanisms (including selective attention, metacognition, and emotional regulation) that combine memory, processing speed, and knowledge to regulate the analysis and flow of information within the information-processing system. (Also called *executive processes*.)

**conventional moral reasoning** Kohlberg's second level of moral reasoning, emphasizing social rules.

**copy number variations** Genes with various repeats or deletions of base pairs.

**corporal punishment** Disciplinary techniques that hurt the body (*corpus*) of someone, from spanking to serious harm, including death.

**corpus callosum** A long, thick band of nerve fibers that connects the left and right hemispheres of the brain and allows communication between them.

**correlation** A number between +1.0 and −1.0 that indicates the degree of relationship between two variables, expressed in terms of the likelihood that one variable will (or will not) occur when the other variable does (or does not). A correlation indicates only that two variables are somehow related, not that one variable causes the other to occur.

**cortex** The outer layers of the brain in humans and other mammals. Most thinking, feeling, and sensing involves the cortex.

**cortisol** The primary stress hormone; fluctuations in the body's cortisol level affect human emotions.

**co-sleeping** A custom in which parents and their children (usually infants) sleep together in the same room.

**couvade** Symptoms of pregnancy and birth experienced by fathers.

**critical period** A time when something *must* happen for normal development to occur.

**cross-sectional research** A research design that compares groups of people who differ in age but are similar in other important characteristics.

**cross-sequential research** A hybrid research design in which researchers first study several groups of people of different ages (a cross-sectional approach) and then follow those groups over the years (a longitudinal approach). (Also called *cohort-sequential research* or *time-sequential research*.)

**culture** A system of shared beliefs, norms, behaviors, and expectations that persist over time and prescribe social behavior and assumptions.

**cyberbullying** When people try to harm others via electronic means, such as social media and cell phone photos or texts.

# D

**deductive reasoning** Reasoning from a general statement, premise, or principle, through logical steps, to figure out (deduce) specifics. (Also called *top-down reasoning*.)

**dendrite** A fiber that extends from a neuron and receives electrochemical impulses transmitted from other neurons via their axons.

**deoxyribonucleic acid (DNA)** The chemical composition of the molecules that contain the genes, which are the chemical instructions for cells to manufacture various proteins.

**dependent variable** In an experiment, the variable that may change as a result of whatever new condition or treatment the experimenter adds. Thus, the dependent variable *depends* on the independent variable.

**developmental psychopathology** The field that uses insights into typical development to understand and remediate developmental disorders.

**developmental theory** A group of ideas, assumptions, and generalizations that interpret and illuminate thousands of observations about human growth. A developmental theory provides a framework for explaining the patterns and problems of development.

**difference-equals-deficit error** The mistaken belief that a deviation from some norm is necessarily inferior to behavior or characteristics that meet the standard.

**differential susceptibility** The idea that people vary in how sensitive they are to particular experiences. Often such differences are genetic, which makes some people affected "for better or for worse" by life events. (Also called *differential sensitivity*.)

**disorganized attachment** A type of attachment that is marked by an infant's inconsistent reactions to the caregiver's departure and return.

**distal parenting** Caregiving practices that involve remaining distant from the baby, providing toys, food, and face-to-face communication with minimal holding and touching.

**dizygotic (DZ) twins** Twins who are formed when two separate ova are fertilized by two separate sperm at roughly the same time. (Also called *fraternal* twins.)

**dominant** Reflected in the phenotype. Dominant genes have more influence on traits than recessive genes.

**doula** A woman who helps with the birth process. Traditionally in Latin America, a doula was the only professional who attended childbirth. Now doulas are likely to arrive at the woman's home during early labor and later work alongside a hospital's staff.

**Down syndrome** A condition in which a person has 47 chromosomes instead of the usual 46, with 3 rather than 2 chromosomes at the 21st site. People with Down syndrome typically have distinctive characteristics, including unusual facial features, heart abnormalities, and language difficulties. (Also called trisomy-21.)

**dual processing** The notion that two networks exist within the human brain, one for emotional processing of stimuli and one for analytical reasoning.

**dynamic-systems approach** A view of human development as an ongoing, ever-changing interaction between the physical, cognitive, and psychosocial influences. The crucial understanding is that development is never static but is always affected by, and affects, many systems of development.

**dyscalculia** Unusual difficulty with math, probably originating from a distinct part of the brain.

**dyslexia** Unusual difficulty with reading; thought to be the result of some neurological underdevelopment.

# E

**eclectic perspective** The approach taken by most developmentalists, in which they apply aspects of each of the various theories of development rather than adhering exclusively to one theory.

**ecological-systems approach** A perspective on human development that considers all of the influences from the various contexts of development. (Later renamed *bioecological theory*.)

**egocentrism** Piaget's term for children's tendency to think about the world entirely from their own personal perspective.

**embryo** The name for a developing human organism from about the third week through the eighth week after conception.

**embryonic period** The stage of prenatal development from approximately the third week through the eighth week after conception, during which the basic forms of all body structures, including internal organs, develop.

**emerging adulthood** The period of life between the ages of 18 and 25. Emerging adulthood is now widely thought of as a distinct developmental stage.

**emotional regulation** The ability to control when and how emotions are expressed.

**empathy** The ability to understand the emotions and concerns of another person, especially when they differ from one's own.

**empirical evidence** Evidence that is based on observation, experience, or experiment; not theoretical.

**English as a Second Language (ESL)** A U.S. approach to teaching English that gathers all of the non-English speakers together and provides intense instruction in English. Students' first languages are never used; the goal is to prepare students for regular classes in English.

**English Language Learners (ELLs)** Children in the United States whose proficiency in English is low—usually below a cutoff score on an oral or written test. Many children who speak a non-English language at home are also capable in English; they are *not* ELLs.

**epigenetics** The study of how environmental factors affect genes and genetic expression—enhancing, halting, shaping, or altering the expression of genes.

**equifinality** A basic principle of developmental psychopathology that holds that one symptom can have many causes.

**estradiol** A sex hormone, considered the chief estrogen. Females produce much more estradiol than males do.

**ethnic group** People whose ancestors were born in the same region and who often share a language, culture, and religion.

**evolutionary theory** When used in human development, the idea that many current human emotions and impulses are a legacy from thousands of years ago.

**executive function** The cognitive ability to organize and prioritize the many thoughts that arise from the various parts of the brain, allowing the person to anticipate, strategize, and plan behavior.

**exosystem** In Bronfenbrenner's ecological approach, the community institutions that affect the immediate contexts, such as churches and temples, schools and colleges, hospitals and courts.

**experience-dependent** Brain functions that depend on particular, variable experiences and therefore may or may not develop in a particular infant.

**experience-expectant** Brain functions that require certain basic common experiences (which an infant can be expected to have) in order to develop normally.

**experiment** A research method in which the scientist tries to determine the cause-and-effect relationship between two variables by manipulating one (called the *independent variable*) and then observing and recording the ensuing changes in the other (called the *dependent variable*).

**extended family** A family of relatives in addition to the nuclear family, usually three or more generations living in one household.

**extremely low birthweight (ELBW)** A body weight at birth of less than 1,000 grams (2 pounds, 3 ounces).

**extrinsic motivation** A drive, or reason to pursue a goal, that arises from the wish to have external rewards, perhaps by earning money or praise.

# F

**false positive** The result of a laboratory test that reports something as true when in fact it is not true. This can occur for pregnancy tests, when a woman might not be pregnant even though the test says she is, or during pregnancy, when a problem is reported that actually does not exist.

**familism** The belief that family members should support one another, sacrificing individual freedom and success, if necessary, in order to preserve family unity and protect the family.

**family function** The way a family works to meet the needs of its members. Children need families to provide basic material necessities, to encourage learning, to help them develop self-respect, to nurture friendships, and to foster harmony and stability.

**family structure** The legal and genetic relationships among relatives living in the same home. Possible structures include nuclear family, extended family, stepfamily, single-parent family, and many others.

**fast-mapping** The speedy and sometimes imprecise way in which children learn new words by tentatively placing them in mental categories according to their perceived meaning.

**fetal alcohol syndrome (FAS)** A cluster of birth defects, including abnormal facial characteristics, slow physical growth, and reduced intellectual ability, that may occur in the fetus of a woman who drinks alcohol while pregnant.

**fetal period** The stage of prenatal development from the ninth week after conception until birth, during which the fetus gains about 7 pounds (more than 3,000 grams) and organs become more mature, gradually able to function on their own.

**fetus** The name for a developing human organism from the start of the ninth week after conception until birth.

**fine motor skills** Physical abilities involving small body movements, especially of the hands and fingers, such as drawing and picking up a coin. (The word *fine* here means "small.")

**fixed mindset** An approach to understanding intelligence that sees ability as an innate entity, a fixed quantity present at birth. Those who hold this view do not believe that effort enhances achievement.

**Flynn effect** The rise in average IQ scores that has occurred over the decades in many nations.

**focus on appearance** A characteristic of preoperational thought in which a young child ignores all attributes that are not apparent.

**foreclosure** Erikson's term for premature identity formation, when adolescents adopt their parents' or society's roles and values without questioning or analysis.

**formal operational thought** In Piaget's theory, the fourth and final stage of cognitive development, characterized by more systematic logical thinking and by the ability to understand and systematically manipulate abstract concepts.

**foster care** A legal, publicly supported system in which a maltreated child is removed from the parents' custody and entrusted to another adult or family, who is reimbursed for expenses incurred in meeting the child's needs.

**fragile X syndrome** A genetic disorder in which part of the X chromosome seems to be attached to the rest of it by a very thin string of molecules. The cause is a single gene that has more than 200 repetitions of one triplet.

# G

**g (general intelligence)** The idea of *g* assumes that intelligence is one basic trait, underlying all cognitive abilities. According

to this concept, people have varying levels of this general ability.

**gamete** A reproductive cell. In humans it is a sperm or an ovum.

**gender binary** The idea that there are only two (*bi-*) genders, male and female, and that they are opposites. This idea precludes intersex, gender overlap, and gender non-conformity.

**gender differences** Differences in male and female roles, behaviors, clothes, and so on that arise from society, not biology.

**gender identity** A person's acceptance of the roles and behaviors that society associates with a particular gender.

**gender schema** A child's cognitive concept or general belief about male and female differences.

**gene** A small section of a chromosome; the basic unit for the transmission of heredity. A gene consists of a string of chemicals that provide instructions for the cell to manufacture certain proteins.

**generational forgetting** The idea that each new generation forgets what the previous generation learned. As used here, the term refers to knowledge about the harm drugs can do.

**genome** The full set of genes that are the instructions to make an individual member of a certain species.

**genotype** An organism's entire genetic inheritance, or genetic potential.

**germinal period** The first two weeks of prenatal development after conception, characterized by rapid cell division and the beginning of cell differentiation.

**gonads** The paired sex glands (ovaries in females, testicles in males). The gonads produce hormones and mature gametes.

**grammar** All of the methods—word order, verb forms, and so on—that languages use to communicate meaning, apart from the words themselves.

**gross motor skills** Physical abilities involving large body movements, such as walking and jumping. (The word *gross* here means "big.")

**growth mindset** An approach to understanding intelligence that holds that intelligence grows incrementally, and thus can be increased by effort. Those who subscribe to this view believe they can master whatever they seek to learn if they pay attention, participate in class, study, complete their homework, and so on.

**growth spurt** The relatively sudden and rapid physical growth that occurs during puberty. Each body part increases in size on a schedule: Weight usually precedes height, and growth of the limbs precedes growth of the torso.

**guided participation** The process by which people learn from others who guide their experiences and explorations.

## H

**Head Start** A federally funded early-childhood intervention program for low-income children of preschool age.

**head-sparing** A biological mechanism that protects the brain when malnutrition disrupts body growth. The brain is the last part of the body to be damaged by malnutrition.

**herd immunity** The level of immunity necessary in a population (the herd) in order to stop transmission of infectious diseases. The rate is usually above 90 percent, and even higher for very infectious diseases. Newborns, and people with certain diseases (e.g., cancer patients taking immunosuppressant drugs), cannot be vaccinated; herd immunity protects them.

**heritability** A statistic that indicates what percentage of the variation in a particular trait within a particular population, in a particular context and era, can be traced to genes.

**heterozygous** Referring to two genes of one pair that differ in some way. Typically one allele has only a few base pairs that differ from the other member of the pair.

**hidden curriculum** The unofficial, unstated, or implicit patterns within a school that influence what children learn. For instance, teacher background, organization of the play space, and tracking are all part of the hidden curriculum—not formally prescribed, but instructive to the children.

**high-stakes test** An evaluation that is critical in determining success or failure. If a single test determines whether a student will graduate or be promoted, it is a high-stakes test.

**hippocampus** A brain structure that is a central processor of memory, especially memory for locations.

**holophrase** A single word that is used to express a complete, meaningful thought.

**homozygous** Referring to two genes of one pair that are exactly the same in every letter of their code. Most gene pairs are homozygous.

**HPA (hypothalamus–pituitary–adrenal) axis** A sequence of hormone production originating in the hypothalamus and moving to the pituitary and then to the adrenal glands.

**HPG (hypothalamus–pituitary–gonad) axis** A sequence of hormone production originating in the hypothalamus and moving to the pituitary and then to the gonads.

**Human Genome Project** An international effort to map the complete human genetic code. This effort was essentially completed in 2001, though analysis is ongoing.

**hypothalamus** A brain area that responds to the amygdala and the hippocampus to produce hormones that activate other parts of the brain and body.

**hypothesis** A specific prediction that can be tested.

**hypothetical thought** Reasoning that includes propositions and possibilities that may not reflect reality.

## I

**identity achievement** Erikson's term for the attainment of identity, when people know who they are as unique individuals, combining past experiences and future plans.

**identity versus role confusion** Erikson's fifth stage of development, when people wonder, "Who am I?" but are confused about which of many possible roles to adopt.

**imaginary audience** The other people who, in an adolescent's egocentric belief, are watching and taking note of his or her appearance, ideas, and behavior. This belief makes many teenagers very self-conscious.

**immersion** A strategy in which instruction in all school subjects occurs in the second (usually the majority) language that a child is learning.

**immigrant paradox** The surprising, paradoxical fact that low-SES immigrant women tend to have fewer birth complications than native-born peers with higher incomes.

**immunization** A process that stimulates the body's immune system by causing production of antibodies to defend against attack by a particular contagious disease. Creation of antibodies may be accomplished naturally (by having the disease), by injection, by drops that are swallowed, or by a nasal spray.

**impulse control** The ability to postpone or deny the immediate response to an idea or behavior.

**in vitro fertilization (IVF)** Fertilization that takes place outside a woman's body (as in a glass laboratory dish). The procedure involves adding sperm to ova that have been surgically removed from the woman's ovary. If a zygote is produced, it is inserted into a woman's uterus, where it may implant and develop into a baby.

**independent variable** In an experiment, the variable that is introduced to see what effect it has on the dependent variable. (Also called *experimental variable*.)

**individual education plan (IEP)** A document that specifies educational goals and plans for a child with special needs.

**induction** A disciplinary technique that involves explaining why a particular behavior was wrong. To be successful, explanation must be within the child's ability to understand.

**inductive reasoning** Reasoning from one or more specific experiences or facts to reach (induce) a general conclusion. (Also called *bottom-up reasoning*.)

**industry versus inferiority** The fourth of Erikson's eight psychosocial crises, during which children attempt to master many skills, developing a sense of themselves as either industrious or inferior, competent or incompetent.

**information-processing theory** A perspective that compares human thinking processes, by analogy, to computer analysis of data, including sensory input, connections, stored memories, and output.

**initiative versus guilt** Erikson's third psychosocial crisis, in which young children undertake new skills and activities and feel guilty when they do not succeed at them.

**injury control/harm reduction** Practices that are aimed at anticipating, controlling, and preventing dangerous activities; these practices reflect the beliefs that accidents are not random and that injuries can be made less harmful if proper controls are in place.

**insecure-avoidant attachment** A pattern of attachment in which an infant avoids connection with the caregiver, as when the infant seems not to care about the caregiver's presence, departure, or return.

**insecure-resistant/ambivalent attachment** A pattern of attachment in which an infant's anxiety and uncertainty are evident, as when the infant becomes very upset at separation from the caregiver and both resists and seeks contact on reunion.

**instrumental aggression** Hurtful behavior that is intended to get something that another person has.

**intersectionality** The idea that the various identities need to be combined. This is especially important in determining if discrimination occurs.

**intimacy versus isolation** The sixth of Erikson's eight stages of development. Adults seek someone with whom to share their lives in an enduring and self-sacrificing commitment. Without such commitment, they risk profound aloneness and isolation.

**intrinsic motivation** A drive, or reason to pursue a goal, that comes from inside a person, such as the joy of reading a good book.

**intuitive thought** Thought that arises from an emotion or a hunch, beyond rational explanation, and is influenced by past experiences and cultural assumptions.

**invincibility fable** An adolescent's egocentric conviction that he or she cannot be overcome or even harmed by anything that might defeat a normal mortal, such as unprotected sex, drug abuse, or high-speed driving.

**irreversibility** A characteristic of preoperational thought in which a young child thinks that nothing can be undone. A thing cannot be restored to the way it was before a change occurred.

## K

**kangaroo care** A form of newborn care in which mothers (and sometimes fathers) rest their babies on their naked chests, like kangaroo mothers that carry their immature newborns in a pouch on their abdomen.

**kinship care** A form of foster care in which a relative of a maltreated child, usually a grandparent, becomes the approved caregiver.

**knowledge base** A body of knowledge in a particular area that makes it easier to master new information in that area.

## L

**language acquisition device (LAD)** Chomsky's term for a hypothesized mental structure that enables humans to learn language, including the basic aspects of grammar, vocabulary, and intonation.

**lateralization** Literally, sidedness, referring to the specialization in certain functions by each side of the brain, with one side dominant for each activity. The left side of the brain controls the right side of the body, and vice versa.

**least restrictive environment (LRE)** A legal requirement that children with special needs be assigned to the most general educational context in which they can be expected to learn.

**leptin** A hormone that affects appetite and is believed to affect the onset of puberty. Leptin levels increase during childhood and peak at around age 12.

**life-course-persistent offender** A person whose criminal activity begins in adolescence and continues throughout life; a "career" criminal.

**limbic system** The parts of the brain that interact to produce emotions, including the amygdala, the hypothalamus, and the hippocampus. Many other parts of the brain also are involved with emotions.

**"little scientist"** Piaget's term for toddlers' insatiable curiosity and active experimentation as they engage in various actions to understand their world.

**longitudinal research** A research design in which the same individuals are followed over time, as their development is repeatedly assessed.

**low birthweight (LBW)** A body weight at birth of less than 2,500 grams (5½ pounds).

## M

**macrosystem** In Bronfenbrenner's ecological approach, the overarching national or cultural policies and customs that affect the more immediate systems, such as the effect of the national economy on local hospitals (an exosystem) or on families (a microsystem).

**major depression** Feelings of hopelessness, lethargy, and worthlessness that last two weeks or more.

**mean length of utterance (MLU)** The average number of words in a typical sentence (called utterance because children may not talk in complete sentences). MLU is often used to measure language development.

**menarche** A girl's first menstrual period, signaling that she has begun ovulation. Pregnancy is biologically possible, but ovulation and menstruation are often irregular for years after menarche.

**mesosystem** In Bronfenbrenner's ecological approach, a connection between one system and another, such as parent–teacher conferences (connecting home and school) or workplace schedules (connecting family and job).

**meta-analysis** A technique of combining results of many studies to come to an overall conclusion. Meta-analysis is powerful, in that small samples can be added together to lead to significant conclusions, although

variations from study to study sometimes make combining them impossible.

**microbiome** All the microbes (bacteria, viruses, and so on) with all their genes in a community; here the millions of microbes of the human body.

**microsystem** In Bronfenbrenner's ecological approach, the immediate social contexts that directly affect each person, such as family, peer group, work team.

**middle school** A school for children in the grades between elementary school and high school. Middle school usually begins with grade 6 and ends with grade 8.

**modeling** The central process of social learning, by which a person observes the actions of others and then copies them.

**monozygotic (MZ) twins** Twins who originate from one zygote that splits apart very early in development. (Also called *identical twins*.) Other monozygotic multiple births (such as triplets and quadruplets) can occur as well.

**Montessori schools** Schools that offer early-childhood education based on the philosophy of Maria Montessori, which emphasizes careful work and tasks that each young child can do.

**moratorium** A socially acceptable way to postpone achieving identity. Going to college and joining the military are examples.

**motor skill** The learned abilities to move some part of the body, in actions ranging from a large leap to a flicker of the eyelid. (The word *motor* here refers to movement of muscles.)

**multifinality** A basic principle of developmental psychopathology that holds that one cause can have many (multiple) final manifestations.

**multiple intelligences** The idea that human intelligence is composed of a varied set of abilities rather than a single, all-encompassing one.

**myelin** The coating on axons that speeds transmission of signals from one neuron to another.

**myelination** The process by which axons become coated with myelin, a fatty substance that speeds the transmission of nerve impulses from neuron to neuron.

## N

**naming explosion** A sudden increase in an infant's vocabulary, especially in the number of nouns, that begins at about 18 months of age.

**National Assessment of Educational Progress (NAEP)** An ongoing and nationally representative measure of U.S. children's achievement in reading, mathematics, and other subjects over time; nicknamed "the Nation's Report Card."

**nature** In development, nature refers to the traits, capacities, and limitations that each individual inherits genetically from their parents.

**neglectful/uninvolved parenting** An approach to child rearing in which the parents seem indifferent toward their children, not knowing or caring about their children's lives.

**neurodiversity** The idea that each person has neurological strengths and weaknesses that should be appreciated, in much the same way diverse cultures and ethnicities are welcomed. Neurodiversity seems particularly relevant for children with disorders on the autism spectrum.

**neuron** One of billions of nerve cells in the central nervous system, especially in the brain.

**neurotransmitter** A brain chemical that carries information from the axon of a sending neuron to the dendrites of a receiving neuron.

**nuclear family** A family that consists of a father, a mother, and their biological children under age 18.

**nurture** In development, nurture includes all of the environmental influences that affect the individual after conception. This includes everything from the mother's nutrition while pregnant to the cultural influences in the nation.

## O

**object permanence** The realization that objects (including people) still exist when they can no longer be seen, touched, or heard.

**objective thought** Thinking that is based on facts. It is impartial, and can be verified by anyone who seeks to know.

**Oedipus complex** The unconscious desire of young boys to replace their fathers and win their mothers' exclusive love.

**operant conditioning** The learning process by which a particular action is followed by something desired (which makes the person or animal more likely to repeat the action) or by something unwanted (which makes the action less likely to be repeated). (Also called *instrumental conditioning*.)

**overimitation** When a person imitates an action that is not a relevant part of the behavior to be learned. Overimitation is common among 2- to 6-year-olds when they imitate adult actions that are irrelevant and inefficient.

**overregularization** The application of rules of grammar even when exceptions occur, making the language seem more "regular" than it actually is.

## P

**parasuicide** Any potentially deadly self-harm that does not result in death. (Also called *attempted suicide* or *failed suicide*.)

**parental monitoring** Parents' ongoing knowledge of what their children are doing, where, and with whom.

**parentification** When a child acts more like a parent than a child. Parentification may occur if the actual parents do not act as caregivers, making a child feel responsible for the family.

**parent–infant bond** The strong, loving connection that forms as parents hold, examine, and feed their newborn.

**peer pressure** Encouragement to conform to friends or contemporaries in behavior, dress, and attitude. Adolescents do many things with peers that they would not do alone.

**percentile** A point on a ranking scale of 0 to 100. The 50th percentile is the midpoint; half the people in the population being studied rank higher and half rank lower.

**permanency planning** An effort by child-welfare authorities to find a long-term living situation that will provide stability and support for a maltreated child. A goal is to avoid repeated changes of caregiver or school, which is particularly harmful.

**permissive parenting** An approach to child rearing that is characterized by high nurturance and communication but little discipline, guidance, or control.

**perseverate** To stay stuck, or persevere, in one thought or action for a longtime. The ability to be flexible, switching from one task to another, is beyond most young children.

**personal fable** An aspect of adolescent egocentrism characterized by an adolescent's belief that his or her thoughts, feelings, and experiences are unique, more wonderful, or more awful than anyone else's.

**phallic stage** Freud's third stage of development, when the penis becomes the focus of concern and pleasure.

**phenotype** The observable characteristics of a person, including appearance, personality, intelligence, and all other traits.

**pituitary** A gland in the brain that responds to a signal from the hypothalamus by producing many hormones, including those that regulate growth and that control other glands, among them the adrenal and sex glands.

**plasticity** The idea that abilities, personality, and other human characteristics can change over time. Plasticity is particularly evident during childhood, but even older adults are not always "set in their ways."

**polygamous family** A family consisting of one man, several wives, and their children.

**postconventional moral reasoning** Kohlberg's third level of moral reasoning, emphasizing moral principles.

**postformal thought** A proposed adult stage of cognitive development, following Piaget's four stages, that goes beyond adolescent thinking by being more practical, more flexible, and more dialectical (i.e., more capable of combining contradictory elements into a comprehensive whole).

**postpartum depression** A new mother's feelings of inadequacy and sadness in the days and weeks after giving birth.

**posttraumatic stress disorder (PTSD)** An anxiety disorder that develops as a delayed reaction to having experienced or witnessed a profoundly shocking or frightening event, such as rape, severe beating, war, or natural disaster. Its symptoms may include flashbacks to the event, hyperactivity and hypervigilance, displaced anger, sleeplessness, nightmares, sudden terror or anxiety, and confusion between fantasy and reality.

**pragmatics** The practical use of language that includes the ability to adjust language communication according to audience and context.

**preconventional moral reasoning** Kohlberg's first level of moral reasoning, emphasizing rewards and punishments.

**prefrontal cortex** The area of the cortex at the very front of the brain that specializes in anticipation, planning, and impulse control.

**preoperational intelligence** Piaget's term for cognitive development between the ages of about 2 and 6; it includes language and imagination (which involve symbolic thought), but logical, operational thinking is not yet possible at this stage.

**preterm** A birth that occurs two or more weeks before the full 38 weeks of the typical pregnancy—that is, at 36 or fewer weeks after conception.

**primary circular reactions** The first of three types of feedback loops in sensorimotor intelligence, this one involving the infant's own body. The infant senses motion, sucking, noise, and other stimuli and tries to understand them.

**primary prevention** Actions that change overall background conditions to prevent some unwanted event or circumstance, such as injury, disease, or abuse.

**primary sex characteristics** The parts of the body that are directly involved in reproduction, including the vagina, uterus, ovaries, testicles, and penis.

**private speech** The internal dialogue that occurs when people talk to themselves (either silently or out loud).

**Programme for International Student Assessment (PISA)** An international test taken by 15-year-olds in 50 nations that is designed to measure problem solving and cognition in daily life.

**Progress in International Reading Literacy Study (PIRLS)** Inaugurated in 2001, a planned five-year cycle of international trend studies in the reading ability of fourth-graders.

**prosocial behavior** Actions that are helpful and kind but that are of no obvious benefit to the person doing them.

**protein-calorie malnutrition** A condition in which a person does not consume sufficient food of any kind. This deprivation can result in several illnesses, severe weight loss, and even death.

**proximal parenting** Caregiving practices that involve being physically close to the baby, with frequent holding and touching.

**proximodistal** Growth or development that occurs from the center or core in an outward direction.

**pruning** When applied to brain development, the process by which unused connections in the brain atrophy and die.

**psychoanalytic theory** Freud's theory of the stages of development, each of which emphasizes the sexual nature of the child. As its first grand theorist, Freud believed that irrational, unconscious drives and motives, often originating in childhood erotic impulses, underlie human behavior.

**psychological control** A disciplinary technique that involves threatening to withdraw love and support, using a child's feelings of guilt and gratitude to the parents.

**psychosocial theory** Erikson's theory of the stages of development, emphasizing the interaction between the psychic needs of the individual and the surrounding social network of family and community.

**puberty** The time between the first onrush of hormones and full adult physical development. Puberty usually lasts three to five years. Many more years are required to achieve psychosocial maturity.

## Q

**qualitative research** Research that considers qualities instead of quantities. Descriptions of particular conditions and participants' expressed ideas are often part of qualitative studies.

**quantitative research** Research that provides data that can be expressed with numbers, such as ranks or scales.

## R

**race** A group of people who are regarded by themselves or by others as distinct from other groups on the basis of physical appearance, typically skin color. Social scientists think race is a misleading concept, as biological differences are not signified by outward appearance.

**reaction time** The time it takes to respond to a stimulus, either physically (with a reflexive movement such as an eyeblink) or cognitively (with a thought).

**reactive aggression** An impulsive retaliation for another person's intentional or accidental hurtful action.

**recessive** Hidden, not dominant. Recessive genes are carried in the genotype and are not evident in the phenotype, except in special circumstances.

**reflex** An unlearned, involuntary action or movement in response to a stimulus. A reflex occurs without conscious thought.

**Reggio Emilia** A program of early-childhood education that originated in the town of Reggio Emilia, Italy, and that encourages each child's creativity in a carefully designed setting.

**reinforcement** When a behavior is followed by something desired, such as food for a hungry animal or a welcoming smile for a lonely person.

**relational aggression** Nonphysical acts, such as insults or social rejection, aimed at harming the social connection between the victim and other people.

**REM (rapid eye movement) sleep** A stage of sleep characterized by flickering eyes behind closed lids, dreaming, and rapid brain waves.

**replication** Repeating a study, usually using different participants, perhaps of another age, SES, or culture.

**reported maltreatment** Harm or endangerment about which someone has notified the authorities.

**resilience** The capacity to adapt well to significant adversity and to overcome serious stress.

**response to intervention (RTI)** An educational strategy intended to help children who demonstrate below-average achievement in early grades, using special intervention.

**role confusion** When adolescents have no clear identity but fluctuate from one persona to another. (Sometimes called *identity diffusion* or *role diffusion*.)

**rough-and-tumble play** Play that seems to be rough, as in play wrestling or chasing, but in which there is no intent to harm.

## S

**scaffolding** Temporary support that is tailored to a learner's needs and abilities and aimed at helping the learner master the next task in a given learning process.

**science of human development** The science that seeks to understand how and why people of all ages and circumstances change or remain the same over time.

**scientific method** A way to answer questions using empirical research and data-based conclusions.

**scientific observation** A method of testing a hypothesis by unobtrusively watching and recording participants' behavior in a systematic and objective manner—in a natural setting, in a laboratory, or in searches of archival data.

**secondary circular reactions** The first of three types of feedback loops in sensorimotor intelligence, involving the infant and an object or another person, as with shaking a rattle or playing peek-a-boo.

**secondary education** Literally, the period after primary education (elementary or grade school) and before tertiary education (college). It usually occurs from about ages 12 to 18, although there is some variation by school and by nation.

**secondary prevention** Actions that avert harm in a high-risk situation, such as stopping a car before it hits a pedestrian.

**secondary sex characteristics** Physical traits that are not directly involved in reproduction but that indicate sexual maturity, such as a man's beard and a woman's breasts.

**secular trend** The long-term upward or downward direction of a certain set of statistical measurements, as opposed to a smaller, shorter cyclical variation. As an example, over the past two centuries, because of improved nutrition and medical care, children have tended to reach their adult height earlier and their adult height has increased.

**secure attachment** A relationship in which an infant obtains both comfort and confidence from the presence of his or her caregiver.

**selective adaptation** The process by which living creatures (including people) adjust to their environment. Genes that enhance survival and reproductive ability are selected, over the generations, to become more prevalent.

**self-awareness** A person's realization that he or she is a distinct individual whose body, mind, and actions are separate from those of other people.

**self-concept** A person's understanding of who they are, in morality, intelligence, appearance, personality, talents, and skills.

**self-righting** The inborn drive to remedy a developmental deficit; literally, to return to sitting or standing upright after being tipped over. People of all ages have self-righting impulses, for emotional as well as physical imbalance.

**sensation** The response of a sensory organ (eyes, ears, skin, tongue, nose) when it detects a stimulus.

**sensitive period** A time when something (such as a toxin, or nutrient, or experience) has the greatest impact on development, but recovery is possible if it occurs later.

**sensorimotor intelligence** Piaget's term for the way infants think—by using their senses and motor skills—during the first period of cognitive development.

**separation anxiety** An infant's distress when a familiar caregiver leaves; most obvious between 9 and 14 months.

**seriation** The concept that things can be arranged in a logical series, such as the number sequence or the alphabet.

**sex differences** Biological differences between males and females, in organs, hormones, and body shape.

**sexting** Sending sexual messages or photographs (usually of one's naked body) via phone or computer.

**sexual orientation** A person's romantic or sexual attraction, which can be to others of the same gender, the other gender, or every gender.

**sexually transmitted infection (STI)** A disease spread by sexual contact; includes syphilis, gonorrhea, genital herpes, chlamydia, and HIV.

**shaken baby syndrome** A life-threatening injury that occurs when an infant is forcefully shaken back and forth, a motion that ruptures blood vessels in the brain and breaks neural connections.

**single-parent family** A family that consists of only one parent and their children.

**small for gestational age (SGA)** A term for a baby whose birthweight is significantly lower than expected, given the time since conception. For example, a 5-pound (2,265-gram) newborn is considered SGA if born on time but not SGA if born two months early. (Also called *small-for-dates.*)

**social comparison** The tendency to assess one's abilities, achievements, social status, and other attributes by measuring them against those of other people, especially one's peers.

**social construction** An idea that is built on shared perceptions, not on objective reality. Many age-related terms (such as *childhood, adolescence, yuppie,* and *senior citizen*) are social constructions, connected to biological traits but strongly influenced by social assumptions.

**social learning theory** An extension of behaviorism that emphasizes the influence that other people have over a person's behavior. Even without specific reinforcement, every individual learns many things through observation and imitation of other people. (Also called *observational learning.*)

**social mediation** Human interaction that expands and advances understanding, often through words that one person uses to explain something to another.

**social referencing** Seeking information about how to react to an unfamiliar or ambiguous object or event by observing someone else's expressions and reactions. That other person becomes a social reference.

**social smile** A smile evoked by a human face, normally first evident in infants about six weeks after birth.

**sociocultural theory** A newer theory that holds that development results from the dynamic interaction of each person with the surrounding social and cultural forces.

**sociodramatic play** Pretend play in which children act out various roles and themes in plots or roles that they create.

**socioeconomic status (SES)** A person's position in society as determined by income, occupation, education, and place of residence. (Sometimes called *social class.*)

**specific learning disorder** A marked deficit in a particular area of learning that is not caused by an apparent physical disability, by an intellectual disability, or by an unusually stressful home environment.

**spermarche** A boy's first ejaculation of sperm. Erections can occur as early as infancy, but ejaculation signals sperm production. Spermarche may occur during sleep (in a "wet dream") or via direct stimulation.

**static reasoning** A characteristic of preoperational thought in which a young child thinks that nothing changes. Whatever is now has always been and always will be.

**stem cells** Cells from which any other specialized type of cell can form.

**stereotype threat** The thought a person has that one's appearance or behavior will be misread to confirm another person's oversimplified, prejudiced attitudes.

**still-face technique** An experimental practice in which an adult keeps their face unmoving and expressionless in face-to-face interaction with an infant.

**stranger wariness** An infant's expression of concern—a quiet stare while clinging to a familiar person, or a look of fear—when a stranger appears.

**stunting** The failure of children to grow to a normal height for their age due to severe and chronic malnutrition.

**subjective thought** Thinking that is based on personal experience and perception. Because it is connected to emotions, it is deeply held and can be quite opposite another's subjective thinking.

**substantiated maltreatment** Harm or endangerment that has been reported, investigated, and verified.

**sudden infant death syndrome (SIDS)** A situation in which a seemingly healthy infant, usually between 2 and 6 months old, suddenly stops breathing and dies unexpectedly while asleep.

**suicidal ideation** Serious thinking about suicide, often including extreme emotions and thoughts.

**superego** In psychoanalytic theory, the judgmental part of the personality that internalizes the moral standards of the parents.

**survey** A research method in which information is collected from a large number of people by interviews, written questionnaires, or some other means.

**symbolic thought** A major accomplishment of preoperational intelligence that allows a child to think symbolically, including understanding that words can refer to things not seen and that an item, such as a flag, can symbolize something else (in this case, a country).

**synapse** The intersection between the axon of one neuron and the dendrites of other neurons.

**synchrony** A coordinated, rapid, and smooth exchange of responses between a caregiver and an infant.

## T

**temperament** Inborn differences between one person and another in emotions, activity, and self-regulation. It is measured by the person's typical responses to the environment.

**teratogen** An agent or condition, including viruses, drugs, and chemicals, that can impair prenatal development and result in birth defects or even death.

**tertiary circular reaction** Piaget's description of the cognitive processes of the 1-year-old, who gathers information from experiences with the wider world and then acts on it. The response to those actions leads to further understanding, which makes this circular.

**tertiary prevention** Actions, such as immediate and effective medical treatment, that are taken after an adverse event (such as illness or injury) and that are aimed at reducing harm or preventing disability.

**testosterone** A sex hormone, the best known of the androgens (male hormones); secreted in far greater amounts by males than by females.

**theory of mind** A person's theory of what other people might be thinking. In order to have a theory of mind, children must realize that other people are not necessarily thinking the same thoughts that they themselves are. That realization seldom occurs before age 4.

**theory-theory** The idea that children attempt to explain everything they see and hear by constructing theories.

**threshold effect** In prenatal development, when a teratogen is relatively harmless in small doses but becomes harmful once exposure reaches a certain level (the threshold).

**time-out** A disciplinary technique in which a person is separated from other people and activities for a specified time.

**transgender** Identifying oneself with a gender other than the one ascribed at birth. Thus, a transgender girl was thought to be a boy when she was born.

**transient exuberance** The great but temporary increase in the number of dendrites that develop in an infant's brain during the first two years of life.

**Trends in Math and Science Study (TIMSS)** An international assessment of the math and science skills of fourth-graders and eighth-graders. Although the TIMSS is very useful, different countries' scores are not always comparable because sample selection, test administration, and content validity are hard to keep uniform.

**trust versus mistrust** Erikson's first crisis of psychosocial development. Infants learn basic trust if the world is a secure place where their basic needs (for food, comfort, attention, and so on) are met.

## V

**very low birthweight (VLBW)** A body weight at birth of less than 1,500 grams (3 pounds, 5 ounces).

## W

**Waldorf schools** An early-childhood education program that emphasizes creativity, social understanding, and emotional growth. It originated in Germany with Rudolf Steiner and now is used in thousands of schools throughout the world.

**wasting** The tendency for children to be severely underweight for their age as a result of malnutrition.

**WEIRD** An acronym that refers to people from Western, Educated, Industrialized, Rich Democracies, in other words, to North American college students, not necessarily the rest of humanity.

**working model** In cognitive theory, a set of assumptions that the individual uses to organize perceptions and experiences. For example, a person might assume that other people are trustworthy and be surprised by an incident in which this working model of human behavior is erroneous.

## X

**X-linked** A gene carried on the X chromosome. If a male inherits an X-linked recessive trait from his mother, he expresses that trait because the Y from his father has no counteracting gene. Females are more likely to be carriers of X-linked traits but are less likely to express them.

**XX** A 23rd chromosome pair that consists of two X-shaped chromosomes, one each from the mother and the father. XX zygotes become females.

**XY** A 23rd chromosome pair that consists of an X-shaped chromosome from the mother and a Y-shaped chromosome from the father. XY zygotes become males.

## Z

**zone of proximal development (ZPD)** In sociocultural theory, a metaphorical area, or "zone," surrounding a learner that includes all of the skills, knowledge, and concepts that the person is close ("proximal") to acquiring but cannot yet master without help.

**zygote** The single cell formed from the union of two gametes, a sperm and an ovum.

# References

**Aarnoudse-Moens, Cornelieke S. H.; Smidts, Diana P.; Oosterlaan, Jaap; Duivenvoorden, Hugo J. & Weisglas-Kuperus, Nynke.** (2009). Executive function in very preterm children at early school age. *Journal of Abnormal Child Psychology*, 37(7), 981–993.

**Abar, Caitlin C.; Jackson, Kristina M. & Wood, Mark.** (2014). Reciprocal relations between perceived parental knowledge and adolescent substance use and delinquency: The moderating role of parent–teen relationship quality. *Developmental Psychology*, 50(9), 2176–2187.

**Abraham, Eyal & Feldman, Ruth.** (2018). The neurobiology of human allomaternal care; implications for fathering, coparenting, and children's social development. *Physiology & Behavior*, 193, 25–34.

**Abramovitch, Amitai; Anholt, Gideon; Raveh-Gottfried, Sagi; Hamo, Naama & Abramowitz, Jonathan.** (2018). Meta-analysis of intelligence quotient (IQ) in obsessive-compulsive disorder. *Neuropsychology Review*, 28(1), 111–120.

**Accardo, Pasquale.** (2006). Who's training whom? *The Journal of Pediatrics*, 149(2), 151–152.

**Acharya, Kartikey; Leuthner, Stephen; Clark, Reese; Nghiem-Rao, Tuyet-Hang; Spitzer, Alan & Lagatta, Joanne.** (2017). Major anomalies and birth-weight influence NICU interventions and mortality in infants with trisomy 13 or 18. *Journal of Perinatology*, 37(4), 420–426.

**Acheson, Ashley; Vincent, Andrea S.; Cohoon, Andrew & Lovallo, William R.** (2019). Early life adversity and increased delay discounting: Findings from the Family Health Patterns project. *Experimental and Clinical Psychopharmacology*, 27(2), 153–159.

**Acosta, Sandra; Garza, Tiberio; Hsu, Hsien-Yuan; Goodson, Patricia; Padrón, Yolanda; Goltz, Heather H. & Johnston, Anna.** (2020). The accountability culture: A systematic review of high-stakes testing and English learners in the United States during no Child Left Behind. *Educational Psychology Review*, 32(2), 327–352.

**Acuto, Michele & Parnell, Susan.** (2016). Leave no city behind. *Science*, 352(6288), 873.

**Adamson, Lauren B. & Bakeman, Roger.** (2006). Development of displaced speech in early mother-child conversations. *Child Development*, 77(1), 186–200.

**Addati, Laura; Cassirer, Naomi & Gilchrist, Katherine.** (2014). *Maternity and paternity at work: Law and practice across the world.* Geneva: International Labour Office.

**Adolph, Karen E.; Cole, Whitney G.; Komati, Meghana; Garciaguirre, Jessie S.; Badaly, Daryaneh; Lingeman, Jesse M.; . . . Sotsky, Rachel B.** (2012). How do you learn to walk? Thousands of steps and dozens of falls per day. *Psychological Science*, 23(11), 1387–1394.

**Adolph, Karen E. & Franchak, John M.** (2017). The development of motor behavior. *WIREs*, 8(1/2), e1430.

**Adolph, Karen E. & Robinson, Scott.** (2013). The road to walking: What learning to walk tells us about development. In Zelazo, Philip D. (Ed.), *The Oxford handbook of developmental psychology* (Vol. 1, pp. 402–447). Oxford University Press.

**Ainsworth, Mary D. Salter.** (1967). *Infancy in Uganda: Infant care and the growth of love.* Johns Hopkins Press.

**Ainsworth, Mary D. Salter.** (1973). The development of infant-mother attachment. In Caldwell, Bettye M. & Ricciuti, Henry N. (Eds.), *Child development and social policy* (pp. 1–94). University of Chicago Press.

**Aïte, Ania; Cassotti, Mathieu; Linzarini, Adriano; Osmont, Anaïs; Houdé, Olivier & Borst, Grégoire.** (2018). Adolescents' inhibitory control: Keep it cool or lose control. *Developmental Science*, 21(1), e12491.

**Aitken, Jess; Ruffman, Ted & Taumoepeau, Mele.** (2019). Toddlers' self-recognition and progression from goal- to emotion-based helping: A longitudinal study. *Child Development*.

**Aizpitarte, Alazne; Atherton, Olivia E.; Zheng, Lucy R.; Alonso-Arbiol, Itziar & Robins, Richard W.** (2019). Developmental precursors of relational aggression from late childhood through adolescence. *Child Development*, 90(1), 117–126.

**Akhtar, Nameera & Jaswal, Vikram K.** (2013). Deficit or difference? Interpreting diverse developmental paths: An introduction to the special section. *Developmental Psychology*, 49(1), 1–3.

**Akombi, Blessing J.; Agho, Kingsley E.; Hall, John J.; Wali, Nidhi; Renzaho, Andre M. N. & Merom, Dafna.** (2017). Stunting, wasting and underweight in sub-Saharan Africa: A systematic review. *International Journal of Environmental Research and Public Health*, 14(8).

**Aksglaede, Lise; Link, Katarina; Giwercman, Aleksander; Jørgensen, Niels; Skakkebæk, Niels E. & Juul, Anders.** (2013). 47,XXY Klinefelter syndrome: Clinical characteristics and age-specific recommendations for medical management. *American Journal of Medical Genetics Part C: Seminars in Medical Genetics*, 163(1), 55–63.

**Al Otaiba, Stephanie; Wanzek, Jeanne & Yovanoff, Paul.** (2015). Response to intervention. *European Scientific Journal*, 1, 260–264.

**Al-Hashim, Aqeela H.; Blaser, Susan; Raybaud, Charles & MacGregor, Daune.** (2016). Corpus callosum abnormalities: Neuroradiological and clinical correlations. *Developmental Medicine & Child Neurology*, 58(5), 475–484.

**Al-Namlah, Abdulrahman S.; Meins, Elizabeth & Fernyhough, Charles.** (2012). Self-regulatory private speech relates to children's recall and organization of autobiographical memories. *Early Childhood Research Quarterly*, 27(3), 441–446.

**Al-Sayes, Fatin; Gari, Mamdooh; Qusti, Safaa; Bagatian, Nadiah & Abuzenadah, Adel.** (2011). Prevalence of iron deficiency and iron deficiency anemia among females at university stage. *Journal of Medical Laboratory and Diagnosis*, 2(1), 5–11.

**Albataineh, Samah R.; Badran, Eman F. & Tayyem, Reema F.** (2019). Overweight and obesity in childhood: Dietary, biochemical, inflammatory and lifestyle risk factors. *Obesity Medicine*, 15(100112).

**Albert, Dustin; Chein, Jason & Steinberg, Laurence.** (2013). The teenage brain: Peer influences on adolescent decision making. *Current Directions in Psychological Science*, 22(2), 114–120.

**Albert, Dustin & Steinberg, Laurence.** (2011). Judgment and decision making in adolescence. *Journal of Research on Adolescence*, 21(1), 211–224.

**Alegre, Alberto.** (2011). Parenting styles and children's emotional intelligence: What do we know? *The Family Journal*, 19(1), 56–62.

**Alesi, Marianha; Bianco, Antonino; Padulo, Johnny; Vella, Francesco Paolo; Petrucci, Marco; Paoli, Antonio; . . . Pepi, Annamaria.** (2014). Motor and cognitive development: The role of karate. *Muscle, Ligaments and Tendons Journal*, 4(2), 114–120.

**Alexander, Karl L.; Entwisle, Doris R. & Olson, Linda Steffel.** (2014). *The long shadow: Family background, disadvantaged urban youth, and the transition to adulthood.* Russell Sage Foundation.

**Alexandre-Heymann, Laure; Dubert, Marie; Diallo, Dapa A.; Diop, Saliou; Tolo, Aissata; Belinga, Suzanne; . . . Ranque, Brigitte.** (2019). Prevalence and correlates of growth failure in young African patients with sickle cell disease. *British Journal of Haematology*, 184(2), 253–262.

**Allport, Gordon.** (1954). *The nature of prejudice.* Addison-Wesley.

**Alper, Meryl.** (2013). Developmentally appropriate New Media Literacies: Supporting cultural competencies and social skills in early childhood education. *Journal of Early Childhood Literacy*, 13(2), 175–196.

**Alvarado, Louis; Muller, Martin; Eaton, Melissa & Thompson, Melissa Emery.** (2018). Steroid hormone reactivity in fathers watching their children compete. *Human Nature*, 29(3), 268–282.

**Amato, Michael S.; Magzamen, Sheryl; Imm, Pamela; Havlena, Jeffrey A.; Anderson, Henry A.; Kanarek, Marty S. & Moore, Colleen F.** (2013). Early lead exposure (<3 years old) prospectively predicts fourth grade school suspension in Milwaukee, Wisconsin (USA). *Environmental Research*, 126, 60–65.

**Ameade, Evans Paul Kwame & Garti, Helene Akpene.** (2016). Age at menarche and factors that influence it: A study among female university students in Tamale, northern Ghana. *PLoS ONE*, *11*(5), e0155310.

**American Academy of Pediatrics.** (2016). Media and young minds. *Pediatrics, 138*(5).

**American Academy of Pediatrics.** (2018, May 1). Children and media tips from the American Academy of Pediatrics [Press release]. American Academy of Pediatrics.

**American College Health Association.** (2017). *American college health association-national college health assessment II: Reference group executive summary fall 2016.* Hanover, MD: American College Health Association.

**American College of Obstetricians and Gynecologists Committee on Obstetric Practice.** (2011). Committee opinion no. 476: Planned home birth. *Obstetrics & Gynecology, 117*(2), 425–428.

**American Psychiatric Association.** (2013). *Diagnostic and statistical manual of mental disorders: DSM-5* (5th ed.). American Psychiatric Association.

**Anderson, Craig A.; Shibuya, Akiko; Ihori, Nobuko; Swing, Edward L.; Bushman, Brad J.; Sakamoto, Akira; . . . Saleem, Muniba.** (2010). Violent video game effects on aggression, empathy, and prosocial behavior in Eastern and Western countries: A meta-analytic review. *Psychological Bulletin, 136*(2), 151–173.

**Anderson, Daniel R. & Hanson, Katherine G.** (2016). Screen media and parent–child interactions. In Barr, Rachel & Linebarger, Deborah Nichols (Eds.), *Media exposure during infancy and early childhood: The effects of content and context on learning and development* (pp. 173–194). Springer.

**Anderson, Monica.** (2018, September 27). *A majority of teens have experienced some form of cyberbullying.* Washington, DC: Pew Research Center.

**Andreas, Nicholas J. ; Kampmann, Beate & Le-Doare, Kirsty Mehring.** (2015). Human breast milk: A review on its composition and bioactivity. *Early Human Development, 91*(11), 629–635.

**Ansado, Jennyfer; Collins, Louis; Fonov, Vladimir; Garon, Mathieu; Alexandrov, Lubomir; Karama, Sherif; . . . Beauchamp, Miriam H.** (2015). A new template to study callosal growth shows specific growth in anterior and posterior regions of the corpus callosum in early childhood. *European Journal of Neuroscience, 42*(1), 1675–1684.

**Araki, Atsuko & Jensen, Tina Kold.** (2020). Endocrine-distributing chemicals and reproductive function. In Kishi, Reiko & Grandjean, Philippe (Eds.), *Health impacts of developmental exposure to environmental chemicals* (pp. 101–129). Springer.

**Areba, Eunice M.; Eisenberg, Marla E. & McMorris, Barbara J.** (2018). Relationships between family structure, adolescent health status and substance use: Does ethnicity matter? *Journal of Community Psychology, 46*(1), 44–57.

**Arguz Cildir, Deniz; Ozbek, Aylin; Topuzoglu, Ahmet; Orcin, Esmahan & Janbakhishov, Ceren Evcen.** (2019). Association of prenatal attachment and early childhood emotional, behavioral, and developmental characteristics: A longitudinal study. *Infant Mental Health Journal.*

**Argyrides, Marios & Kkeli, Natalie.** (2015). Predictive factors of disordered eating and body

image satisfaction in Cyprus. *International Journal of Eating Disorders, 48*(4), 431–435.

**Ariely, Dan.** (2010). *Predictably irrational: The hidden forces that shape our decisions* (Revised and Expanded ed.). Harper Perennial.

**Armstrong, Kim.** (2018). The WEIRD science of culture, values, and behavior. *Observer.* Association for Psychological Science.

**Arnott, Lorna.** (2016). An ecological exploration of young children's digital play: Framing children's social experiences with technologies in early childhood. *Early Years, 36*(3), 271–288.

**Aron, Arthur; Lewandowski, Gary W.; Mashek, Debra & Aron, Elaine N.** (2013). The self-expansion model of motivation and cognition in close relationships. In Simpson, Jeffry A. & Campbell, Lorne (Eds.), *The Oxford handbook of close relationships* (pp. 90–115). Oxford University Press.

**Aronson, Joshua; Burgess, Diana; Phelan, Sean M. & Juarez, Lindsay.** (2013). Unhealthy interactions: The role of stereotype threat in health disparities. *American Journal of Public Health, 103*(1), 50–56.

**Arshad, S. Hasan; Karmaus, Wilfried; Zhang, Hongmei & Holloway, John W.** (2017). Multigenerational cohorts in patients with asthma and allergy. *Journal of Allergy and Clinical Immunology, 139*(2), 415–421.

**Ash, Tayla; Davison, Kirsten K.; Haneuse, Sebastien; Horan, Christine; Kitos, Nicole; Redline, Susan & Taveras, Elsie M.** (2019). Emergence of racial/ethnic differences in infant sleep duration in the first six months of life. *Sleep Medicine: X, 1,* 100003.

**Ashenhurst, James R.; Wilhite, Emily R.; Harden, K Paige & Fromme, Kim.** (2017). Number of sexual partners and relationship status are associated with unprotected sex across emerging adulthood. *Archives of Sexual Behavior, 46*(2), 419–432.

**Ashraf, Quamrul & Galor, Oded.** (2013). The 'Out of Africa' hypothesis, human genetic diversity, and comparative economic development. *American Economic Review, 103*(1), 1–46.

**Ashwin, Sarah & Isupova, Olga.** (2014). "Behind every great man . . . ": The male marriage wage premium examined qualitatively. *Journal of Marriage and Family, 76*(1), 37–55.

**Aslam, Kashif; Shabir, Ghulam; Shahid, Muhammad; Sabar, Muhammad; Naveed, Shahzad Amir; Shah, Shahid Masood; . . . Arif, Muhammad.** (2019). Comparative analysis of genomic variation and population structure of rice (oryza sativa). *International Journal of Agriculture and Biology, 21*(6), 1129–1136.

**Aslin, Richard N.** (2012). Language development: Revisiting Eimas et al.'s /ba/ and /pa/ study. In Slater, Alan M. & Quinn, Paul C. (Eds.), *Developmental psychology: Revisiting the classic studies* (pp. 191–203). Sage.

**Atzaba-Poria, Naama; Deater-Deckard, Kirby & Bell, Martha Ann.** (2017). Mother-child interaction: Links between mother and child frontal electroencephalograph asymmetry and negative behavior. *Child Development, 88*(2), 544–554.

**Atzil, Shir; Hendler, Talma & Feldman, Ruth.** (2014). The brain basis of social synchrony.

*Social Cognitive and Affective Neuroscience, 9*(8), 1193–1202.

**Aunola, Kaisa; Tolvanen, Asko; Viljaranta, Jaana & Nurmi, Jari-Erik.** (2013). Psychological control in daily parent–child interactions increases children's negative emotions. *Journal of Family Psychology, 27*(3), 453–462.

**Ayoub, Mona; Briley, Daniel A.; Grotzinger, Andrew; Patterson, Megan W.; Engelhardt, Laura E.; Tackett, Jennifer L.; . . . Tucker-Drob, Elliot M.** (2018). Genetic and environmental associations between child personality and parenting. *Social Psychological and Personality Science.*

**Ayyanathan, Kasirajan (Ed.)** (2014). *Specific gene expression and epigenetics: The interplay between the genome and its environment.* Apple Academic Press.

**Azrin, Nathan H. & Foxx, Richard M.** (1974). *Toilet training in less than a day.* Simon & Schuster.

**Babadjouni, Robin M.; Hodis, Drew M.; Radwanski, Ryan; Durazo, Ramon; Patel, Arati; Liu, Qinghai & Mack, William J.** (2017). Clinical effects of air pollution on the central nervous system; A review. *Journal of Clinical Neuroscience, 43,* 16–24.

**Babchishin, Lyzon K.; Weegar, Kelly & Romano, Elisa.** (2013). Early child care effects on later behavioral outcomes using a Canadian nation-wide sample. *Journal of Educational and Developmental Psychology, 3*(2), 15–29.

**Bachman, Heather J.; Votruba-Drzal, Elizabeth; El Nokali, Nermeen E. & Castle Heatly, Melissa.** (2015). Opportunities for learning math in elementary school: Implications for SES disparities in procedural and conceptual math skills. *American Educational Research Journal, 52*(5), 894–923.

**Baddock, Sally A.; Purnell, Melissa T.; Blair, Peter S.; Pease, Anna S.; Elder, Dawn E. & Galland, Barbara C.** (2019). The influence of bed-sharing on infant physiology, breastfeeding and behaviour: A systematic review. *Sleep Medicine Reviews, 43,* 106–117.

**Bagchi, Debasis (Ed.)** (2019). *Global perspectives on childhood obesity: Current status, consequences and prevention* (2nd ed.). Academic Press.

**Bagot, Kara.** (2017). Making the grade: Adolescent prescription stimulant use. *Journal of the American Academy of Child & Adolescent Psychiatry, 56*(3), 189–190.

**Bagwell, Catherine L. & Schmidt, Michelle E.** (2011). *Friendships in childhood and adolescence.* Guilford Press.

**Bai, Sunhye; Karan, Maira; Gonzales, Nancy A. & Fuligni, Andrew J.** (2020). A daily diary study of sleep chronotype among Mexican-origin adolescents and parents: Implications for adolescent behavioral health. *Development and Psychopathology.*

**Baillargeon, Renée & DeVos, Julie.** (1991). Object permanence in young infants: Further evidence. *Child Development, 62*(6), 1227–1246.

**Baio, Jon; Wiggins, Lisa; Christensen, Deborah L.; Maenner, Matthew J.; Daniels, Julie; Warren, Zachary; . . . Dowling, Nicole F.** (2018, April 27). *Prevalence of autism spectrum disorder among children aged 8 years—Autism and*

*Developmental Disabilities Monitoring Network, 11 Sites, United States, 2014. Morbidity and Mortality Weekly Report, 67*(SS-6), 1–23.

**Baker, Jeffrey P.** (2000). Immunization and the American way: 4 childhood vaccines. *American Journal of Public Health, 90*(2), 199–207.

**Baker, Simon T. E.; Lubman, Dan I.; Yücel, Murat; Allen, Nicholas B.; Whittle, Sarah; Fulcher, Ben D.; . . . Fornito, Alex.** (2015). Developmental changes in brain network hub connectivity in late adolescence. *Journal of Neuroscience, 35*(24), 9078–9087.

**Ball, Helen L. & Volpe, Lane E.** (2013). Sudden infant death syndrome (SIDS) risk reduction and infant sleep location—Moving the discussion forward. *Social Science & Medicine, 79*(1), 84–91.

**Baltes, Paul B.; Lindenberger, Ulman & Staudinger, Ursula M.** (2006). Life span theory in developmental psychology. In Damon, William & Lerner, Richard M. (Eds.), *Handbook of child psychology* (6th ed., Vol. 1, pp. 569–664). Wiley.

**Baly, Michael W.; Cornell, Dewey G. & Lovegrove, Peter.** (2014). A longitudinal investigation of self- and peer reports of bullying victimization across middle school. *Psychology in the Schools, 51*(3), 217–240.

**Balzarini, Rhonda; Muise, Amy; Zoppolat, Giulia; Di Bartolomeo, Alyssa; Rodrigues, David; Alonso-Ferres, María; . . . Slatcher, Richard B.** (2020). Love in the time of COVID: Perceived partner responsiveness buffers people from lower relationship quality associated with COVID-related stressors. *PsyArXiv.*

**Bandura, Albert.** (1986). *Social foundations of thought and action: A social cognitive theory.* Prentice-Hall.

**Bandura, Albert.** (1997). The anatomy of stages of change. *American Journal of Health Promotion, 12*(1), 8–10.

**Bandura, Albert.** (2006). Toward a psychology of human agency. *Perspectives on Psychological Science, 1*(2), 164–180.

**Bandura, Albert.** (2016). *Moral disengagement: How people do harm and live with themselves.* Worth.

**Banks, James R. & Andrews, Timothy.** (2015). Outcomes of childhood asthma to the age of 50 years. *Pediatrics, 136*(Suppl. 3).

**Bannon, Michael J.; Johnson, Magen M.; Michelhaugh, Sharon K.; Hartley, Zachary J.; Halter, Steven D.; David, James A.; . . . Schmidt, Carl J.** (2014). A molecular profile of cocaine abuse includes the differential expression of genes that regulate transcription, chromatin, and dopamine cell phenotype. *Neuropsychopharmacology, 39*(9), 2191–2199.

**Baranowski, Tom & Taveras, Elsie M.** (2018). Childhood obesity prevention: Changing the focus. *Childhood Obesity, 14*(1), 1–3.

**Barber, Brian K. (Ed.)** (2002). *Intrusive parenting: How psychological control affects children and adolescents.* American Psychological Association.

**Barlow, Jane; Herath, Nadeeja; Torrance, Christine B.; Bennett, Cathy & Wei, Yinghui.** (2018). The Neonatal Behavioral Assessment Scale (NBAS) and Newborn Behavioral Observations (NBO) system for supporting caregivers and improving outcomes in caregivers and their infants. *Cochrane Database of Systematic Reviews.*

**Barlowe, Avram & Cook, Ann.** (2016). Putting the focus on student engagement: The benefits of performance-based assessment. *American Educator, 40*(1).

**Barnett, W. Steven & Frede, Ellen C.** (2017). Long-term effects of a system of high-quality universal preschool education in the United States. In Blossfeld, Hans-Peter; Kulic, Nevena; Skopek, Jan & Triventi, Moris (Eds.), *Childcare, early education and social inequality: An international perspective.* Edward Elgar.

**Baron-Cohen, Simon; Tager-Flusberg, Helen & Lombardo, Michael (Eds.).** (2013). *Understanding other minds: Perspectives from developmental social neuroscience* (3rd ed.). Oxford University Press.

**Barone, Joseph.** (2015). *It's not your fault!: Strategies for solving toilet training and bedwetting problems.* Rutgers University Press.

**Barr, Rachel.** (2013). Memory constraints on infant learning from picture books, television, and touchscreens. *Child Development Perspectives, 7*(4), 205–210.

**Barrios, Yasmin V.; Sanchez, Sixto E.; Nicolaidis, Christina; Garcia, Pedro J.; Gelaye, Bizu; Zhong, Qiuyue & Williams, Michelle A.** (2015). Childhood abuse and early menarche among Peruvian women. *Journal of Adolescent Health, 56*(2), 197–202.

**Barroso, Raquel; Barbosa-Ducharne, Maria; Coelho, Vanessa; Costa, Isabel-Sofia & Silva, Ana.** (2017). Psychological adjustment in intercountry and domestic adopted adolescents: A systematic review. *Child and Adolescent Social Work Journal, 34*(5), 399–418.

**Barton, Georgina & Baguley, Margaret (Eds.).** (2017). *The Palgrave handbook of global arts education.* Palgrave Macmillan.

**Bassok, Daphna; Latham, Scott & Rorem, Anna.** (2016). Is kindergarten the new first grade? *AERA Open, 2*(1).

**Bateson, Patrick & Martin, Paul.** (2013). *Play, playfulness, creativity and innovation.* Cambridge University Press.

**Baude, Amandine; Pearson, Jessica & Drapeau, Sylvie.** (2016). Child adjustment in joint physical custody versus sole custody: A meta-analytic review. *Journal of Divorce & Remarriage, 57*(5), 338–360.

**Bauer, Patricia J.; San Souci, Priscilla & Pathman, Thanujeni.** (2010). Infant memory. *Wiley Interdisciplinary Reviews: Cognitive Science, 1*(2), 267–277.

**Baumrind, Diana.** (1967). Child care practices anteceding three patterns of preschool behavior. *Genetic Psychology Monographs, 75*(1), 43–88.

**Baumrind, Diana.** (1971). Current patterns of parental authority. *Developmental Psychology, 4*(1, Pt. 2), 1–103.

**Bayley, Nancy.** (1966). Learning in adulthood: The role of intelligence. In Klausmeier, Herbert J. & Harris, Chester W. (Eds.), *Analyses of concept learning* (pp. 117–138). Academic Press.

**Baysu, Gülseli & Phalet, Karen.** (2019). The up- and downside of dual identity: Stereotype threat and minority performance. *Journal of Social Issues, 75*(2), 568–591.

**Bea, Megan Doherty & Yi, Youngmin.** (2019). Leaving the financial nest: Connecting young adults' financial independence to financial security. *Journal of Marriage and Family, 81*(2), 397–414.

**Beal, Susan.** (1988). Sleeping position and sudden infant death syndrome. *The Medical Journal of Australia, 149*(10), 562.

**Beck, Melinda.** (2009, May 26). How's your baby? Recalling the Apgar score's namesake. *Wall Street Journal.*

**Beck, Martha N.** (2011). *Expecting Adam: A true story of birth, rebirth, and everyday magic.* Three Rivers Press.

**Beebe, Beatrice; Messinger, Daniel; Bahrick, Lorraine E.; Margolis, Amy; Buck, Karen A. & Chen, Henian.** (2016). A systems view of mother–infant face-to-face communication. *Developmental Psychology, 52*(4), 556–571.

**Beilin, Lawrence & Huang, Rae-Chi.** (2008). Childhood obesity, hypertension, the metabolic syndrome and adult cardiovascular disease. *Clinical and Experimental Pharmacology and Physiology, 35*(4), 409–411.

**Bell, Georgie; Hiscock, Harriet; Tobin, Sherryn; Cook, Fallon & Sung, Valerie.** (2018). Behavioral outcomes of infant colic in toddlerhood: A longitudinal study. *The Journal of Pediatrics, 201*, 154–159.

**Bellinger, David C.** (2016). Lead contamination in Flint—An abject failure to protect public health. *New England Journal of Medicine, 374*(12), 1101–1103.

**Belsky, Daniel W.; Caspi, Avshalom; Houts, Renate; Cohen, Harvey J.; Corcoran, David L.; Danese, Andrea; . . . Moffitt, Terrie E.** (2015). Quantification of biological aging in young adults. *Proceedings of the National Academy of Sciences of the United States of America, 112*(30), e4104–e4110.

**Belsky, Jay; Bakermans-Kranenburg, Marian J. & van IJzendoorn, Marinus H.** (2007). For better and for worse: Differential susceptibility to environmental influences. *Current Directions in Psychological Science, 16*(6), 300–304.

**Belsky, Jay; Steinberg, Laurence; Houts, Renate M. & Halpern-Felsher, Bonnie L.** (2010). The development of reproductive strategy in females: Early maternal harshness → earlier menarche → increased sexual risk taking. *Developmental Psychology, 46*(1), 120–128.

**Bem, Sandra L.** (1981). Gender schema theory: A cognitive account of sex typing. *Psychological Review, 88*(4), 354–364.

**Bender, Heather L.; Allen, Joseph P.; McElhaney, Kathleen Boykin; Antonishak, Jill; Moore, Cynthia M.; Kelly, Heather O'Beirne & Davis, Steven M.** (2007). Use of harsh physical discipline and developmental outcomes in adolescence. *Development and Psychopathology, 19*(1), 227–242.

**Benn, Peter.** (2016). Prenatal diagnosis of chromosomal abnormalities through chorionic villus sampling and amniocentesis. In Milunsky, Aubrey & Milunsky, Jeff M. (Eds.), *Genetic disorders and the fetus: Diagnosis, prevention, and treatment* (7th ed., pp. 178–266). Wiley-Blackwell.

**Benoit, Amelie; Lacourse, Eric & Claes, Michel.** (2013). Pubertal timing and depressive symptoms in late adolescence: The moderating role of individual, peer, and parental factors. *Development and Psychopathology*, 25(2), 455–471.

**Benson, Peter L.; Scales, Peter C.; Syvertsen, Amy K. & Roehlkepartain, Eugene C.** (2012). Is youth spiritual development a universal developmental process? An international exploration. *The Journal of Positive Psychology*, 7(6), 453–470.

**Berg, Jeremy.** (2018). Imagine a world without facts. *Science*, 362(6413), 379.

**Bergelson, Elika & Swingley, Daniel.** (2018). Young infants' word comprehension given an unfamiliar talker or altered pronunciations. *Child Development*, 89(5), 1567–1576.

**Berger, Kathleen S.** (1980). *The developing person* (1st ed.). Worth.

**Berger, Kathleen S.** (2019). *Grandmothering: Building strong ties with every generation.* Rowman & Littlefield.

**Berken, Jonathan A.; Gracco, Vincent L. & Klein, Denise.** (2017). Early bilingualism, language attainment, and brain development. *Neuropsychologia*, 98, 220–227.

**Berko, Jean.** (1958). The child's learning of English morphology. *Word*, 14, 150–177.

**Berkowitz, Talia; Schaeffer, Marjorie W.; Maloney, Erin A.; Peterson, Lori; Gregor, Courtney; Levine, Susan C. & Beilock, Sian L.** (2015). Math at home adds up to achievement in school. *Science*, 350(6257), 196–198.

**Berlin, Lisa J.; Martoccio, Tiffany L. & Jones Harden, Brenda.** (2018). Improving early head start's impacts on parenting through attachment-based intervention: A randomized controlled trial. *Developmental Psychology*, 54(12), 2316–2327.

**Bernard, Kristin; Hostinar, Camelia E. & Dozier, Mary.** (2019). Longitudinal associations between attachment quality in infancy, C-reactive protein in early childhood, and BMI in middle childhood: Preliminary evidence from a CPS-referred sample. *Attachment & Human Development*, 21(1), 5–22.

**Bernard, Kristin; Lind, Teresa & Dozier, Mary.** (2014). Neurobiological consequences of neglect and abuse. In Korbin, Jill E. & Krugman, Richard D. (Eds.), *Handbook of child maltreatment* (pp. 205–223). Springer.

**Bernaud, Jean-Luc.** (2014). Career counseling and life meaning: A new perspective of life designing for research and applications. In Di, Fabio A. & Bernaud, J- L. (Eds.), *The construction of the identity in 21st century: A Festschrift for Jean Guichard* (pp. 29–40). Nova Science.

**Bernier, Annie; Calkins, Susan D. & Bell, Martha Ann.** (2016). Longitudinal associations between the quality of mother–infant interactions and brain development across infancy. *Child Development*, 87(4), 1159–1174.

**Betancourt, Theresa S.; McBain, Ryan; Newnham, Elizabeth A. & Brennan, Robert T.** (2013). Trajectories of internalizing problems in war-affected Sierra Leonean youth: Examining conflict and postconflict factors. *Child Development*, 84(2), 455–470.

**Bettelheim, Bruno.** (1972). *The empty fortress: Infantile autism and the birth of the self.* Free Press.

**Bhatia, Tej K. & Ritchie, William C. (Eds.).** (2013). *The handbook of bilingualism and multilingualism* (2nd ed.). Wiley-Blackwell.

**Bialystok, Ellen.** (2018). Bilingualism and executive function: What's the connection? In Miller, David; Bayram, Fatih; Rothman, Jason & Serratrice, Ludovica (Eds.), *Bilingual cognition and language: The state of the science across its subfields* (pp. 283–306). John Benjamins.

**Bick, Johanna & Nelson, Charles A.** (2016). Early adverse experiences and the developing brain. *Neuropsychopharmacology*, 41, 177–196.

**Bick, Johanna; Palmwood, Erin N.; Zajac, Lindsay; Simons, Robert & Dozier, Mary.** (2019). Early parenting intervention and adverse family environments affect neural function in middle childhood. *Biological Psychiatry*, 85(4), 326–335.

**Biemiller, Andrew.** (2009). Parent/caregiver narrative: Vocabulary development (0–60 Months). In Phillips, Linda M. (Ed.), *Handbook of language and literacy development: A roadmap from 0–60* (Online ed.). Canadian Language and Literacy Research Network.

**Biffen, Stevie C.; Warton, Christopher M. R.; Lindinger, Nadine M.; Randall, Steven R.; Lewis, Catherine E.; Molteno, Christopher D.; . . . Meintjes, Ernesta M.** (2018). Reductions in corpus callosum volume partially mediate effects of prenatal alcohol exposure on IQ. *Frontiers in Neuroanatomy*, 11(132).

**Binning, Kevin R.; Cook, Jonathan E.; Purdie-Greenaway, Valerie; Garcia, Julio; Chen, Susie; Apfel, Nancy; . . . Cohen, Geoffrey L.** (2019). Bolstering trust and reducing discipline incidents at a diverse middle school: How self-affirmation affects behavioral conduct during the transition to adolescence. *Journal of School Psychology*, 75, 74–88.

**Biro, Frank M.; Greenspan, Louise C.; Galvez, Maida P.; Pinney, Susan M.; Teitelbaum, Susan; Windham, Gayle C.; . . . Wolff, Mary S.** (2013). Onset of breast development in a longitudinal cohort. *Pediatrics*, 132(6), 1019–1027.

**Bjorklund, David F.** (2018). A metatheory for cognitive development (or "Piaget is dead" revisited). *Child Development*, 89(6), 2288–2302.

**Bjorklund, David F. & Ellis, Bruce J.** (2014). Children, childhood, and development in evolutionary perspective. *Developmental Review*, 34(3), 225–264.

**Bjorklund, David F. & Sellers, Patrick D.** (2014). Memory development in evolutionary perspective. In Bauer, Patricia & Fivush, Robyn (Eds.), *The Wiley handbook on the development of children's memory* (Vol. 1, pp. 126–150). Wiley.

**Black, Robert E.; Victora, Cesar G.; Walker, Susan P.; Bhutta, Zulfiqar A.; Christian, Parul; Onis, Mercedes de & Ezzati, Majid.** (2013). Maternal and child undernutrition and overweight in low-income and middle-income countries. *The Lancet*, 382(9809), 427–451.

**Blair, Clancy.** (2016). Developmental science and executive function. *Current Directions in Psychological Science*, 25(1), 3–7.

**Blair, Clancy & Raver, C. Cybele.** (2015). School readiness and self-regulation: A developmental psychobiological approach. *Annual Review of Psychology*, 66, 711–731.

**Blakemore, Sarah-Jayne.** (2018). Avoiding social risk in adolescence. *Current Directions in Psychological Science*, 27(2), 116–122.

**Blandon, Alysia Y.; Calkins, Susan D. & Keane, Susan P.** (2010). Predicting emotional and social competence during early childhood from toddler risk and maternal behavior. *Development and Psychopathology*, 22(1), 119–132.

**Blank, Grant & Lutz, Christoph.** (2018). Benefits and harms from internet use: A differentiated analysis of Great Britain. *New Media & Society*, 20(2), 618–640.

**Bleich, Sara N.; Segal, Jodi; Wu, Yang; Wilson, Renee & Wang, Youfa.** (2013). Systematic review of community-based childhood obesity prevention studies. *Pediatrics*, 132(1), e201–e210.

**Bleidorn, Wiebke; Klimstra, Theo A.; Denissen, Jaap J. A.; Rentfrow, Peter J.; Potter, Jeff & Gosling, Samuel D.** (2013). Personality maturation around the world: A cross-cultural examination of social-investment theory. *Psychological Science*, 24(12), 2530–2540.

**Blencowe, Hannah; Krasevec, Julia; de Onis, Mercedes; Black, Robert E.; An, Xiaoyi; Stevens, Gretchen A.; . . . Cousens, Simon.** (2019). National, regional, and worldwide estimates of low birthweight in 2015, with trends from 2000: A systematic analysis. *The Lancet Global Health*, 7(7), e849–e860.

**Blomqvist, Ylva Thernström; Nyqvist, Kerstin Hedberg; Rubertsson, Christine & Funkquist, Eva-Lotta.** (2017). Parents need support to find ways to optimise their own sleep without seeing their preterm infant's sleeping patterns as a problem. *Acta Paediatrica*, 106(2), 223–228.

**Blossfeld, Hans-Peter; Kulic, Nevena; Skopek, Jan & Triventi, Moris (Eds.).** (2017). *Childcare, early education and social inequality: An international perspective.* Edward Elgar.

**Blurton-Jones, Nicholas G.** (1976). Rough-and-tumble play among nursery school children. In Bruner, Jerome S.; Jolly, Alison & Sylva, Kathy (Eds.), *Play: Its role in development and evolution* (pp. 352–363). Basic Books.

**Bodner-Adler, Barbara; Kimberger, Oliver; Griebaum, Julia; Husslein, Peter & Bodner, Klaus.** (2017). A ten-year study of midwife-led care at an Austrian tertiary care center: A retrospective analysis with special consideration of perineal trauma. *BMC Pregnancy and Childbirth*, 17, 357–371.

**Bodrava, Elena & Leong, Deborah J.** (2018). Tools of the mind: The Vygotskian-based early childhood program. *Journal of Cognitive Education and Psychology*, 17(3), 223–237.

**Bøe, Tormod; Serlachius, Anna; Sivertsen, Børge; Petrie, Keith & Hysing, Mari.** (2018).

Cumulative effects of negative life events and family stress on children's mental health: The Bergen Child Study. *Social Psychiatry and Psychiatric Epidemiology*, 53(1), 1–9.

**Boerma, Ties; Ronsmans, Carine; Melesse, Dessalegn Y.; Barros, Aluisio J. D.; Barros, Fernando C.; Juan, Liang; . . . Temmerman, Marleen.** (2018). Global epidemiology of use of and disparities in caesarean sections. *The Lancet*, 392(10155), 1341–1348.

**Bögels, Susan M.; Knappe, Susanne & Clark, Lee Anna.** (2013). Adult separation anxiety disorder in *DSM-5*. *Clinical Psychology Review*, 33(5), 663–674.

**Boggio, Andrea; Romano, Cesare P. R. & Almqvist, Jessica (Eds.).** (2020). *Human germline genome modification and the right to science: A comparative study of national laws and policies.* Cambridge University Press.

**Bohlen, Tabata M.; Silveira, Marina A.; Zampieri, Thais T.; Frazão, Renata & Donato, Jose.** (2016). Fatness rather than leptin sensitivity determines the timing of puberty in female mice. *Molecular and Cellular Endocrinology*, 423, 11–21.

**Bohn, Manuel & Köymen, Bahar.** (2018). Common ground and development. *Child Development Perspectives*, 12(2), 104–108.

**Bolk, Jenny; Padilla, Nelly; Forsman, Lea; Broström, Lina; Hellgren, Kerstin & Åden, Ulrika.** (2018). Visual–motor integration and fine motor skills at 6½ years of age and associations with neonatal brain volumes in children born extremely preterm in Sweden: A population-based cohort study. *BMJ Open*, 8(2), e020478.

**Bonora, Massimo; Wieckowski, Mariusz R.; Sinclair, David A.; Kroemer, Guido; Pinton, Paolo & Galluzzi, Lorenzo.** (2019). Targeting mitochondria for cardiovascular disorders: Therapeutic potential and obstacles. *Nature Reviews Cardiology*, 16, 33–55.

**Booth, Alan & Dunn, Judy (Eds.).** (2014). *Stepfamilies: Who benefits? Who does not?* Routledge.

**Borke, Jörn; Lamm, Bettina; Eickhorst, Andreas & Keller, Heidi.** (2007). Father-infant interaction, paternal ideas about early child care, and their consequences for the development of children's self-recognition. *Journal of Genetic Psychology*, 168(4), 365–379.

**Bornstein, Marc H.** (2017). The specificity principle in acculturation science. *Perspectives on Psychological Science*, 12(1), 3–45.

**Bornstein, Marc H.; Arterberry, Martha E. & Mash, Clay.** (2005). Perceptual development. In Bornstein, Marc H. & Lamb, Michael E. (Eds.), *Developmental science: An advanced textbook* (5th ed., pp. 283–325). Lawrence Erlbaum Associates.

**Bornstein, Marc H.; Mortimer, Jeylan T.; Lutfey, Karen & Bradley, Robert.** (2011). Theories and processes in life-span socialization. In Fingerman, Karen L.; Berg, Cynthia; Smith, Jacqui & Antonucci, Toni (Eds.), *Handbook of life-span development* (pp. 27–56). Springer.

**Bornstein, Marc H.; Putnick, Diane L.; Bradley, Robert H.; Deater-Deckard, Kirby & Lansford, Jennifer E.** (2016). Gender in low- and middle-income countries: Introduction. *Monographs of the Society for Research in Child Development*, 81(1), 7–23.

**Bouazzaoui, B.; Fay, S.; Guerrero-Sastoque, L; Semaine, M.; Isingrini, M. & Taconnat, L.** (2020). Memory age-based stereotype threat: Role of locus of control and anxiety. *Experimental Aging Research*, 46(1), 39–51.

**Boundy, Ellen O.; Dastjerdi, Roya; Spiegelman, Donna; Fawzi, Wafaie W.; Missmer, Stacey A.; Lieberman, Ellice; . . . Chan, Grace J.** (2016). Kangaroo mother care and neonatal outcomes: A meta-analysis. *Pediatrics*, 137(1), e20152238.

**Bourguignon, Jean-Pierre; Juul, Anders; Franssen, Delphine; Fudvoye, Julie; Pinson, Anneline & Parent, Anne-Simone.** (2016). Contribution of the endocrine perspective in the evaluation of endocrine disrupting chemical effects: The case study of pubertal timing. *Hormone Research in Paediatrics*, 86(4), 221–232.

**Bowlby, John.** (1983). *Attachment* (2nd ed.). Basic Books.

**Bowman, Lindsay C.; Dodell-Feder, David; Saxe, Rebecca & Sabbagh, Mark A.** (2019). Continuity in the neural system supporting children's theory of mind development: Longitudinal links between task-independent EEG and task-dependent fMRI. *Developmental Cognitive Neuroscience*, 40(100705).

**Box, Allyson G.; Feito, Yuri; Matson, Ashton; Heinrich, Katie M. & Petruzzello, Steven J.** (2019). Is age just a number? Differences in exercise participatory motives across adult cohorts and the relationships with exercise behaviour. *International Journal of Sport and Exercise Psychology*.

**boyd, danah.** (2014). *It's complicated: The social lives of networked teens.* Yale University Press.

**Braak, David; Michael Cummings, K.; Nahhas, Georges J.; Reid, Jessica L. & Hammond, David.** (2020). How are adolescents getting their vaping products? Findings from the international tobacco control (ITC) youth tobacco and vaping survey. *Addictive Behaviors*, 105, 106345.

**Braams, Barbara R.; van Duijvenvoorde, Anna C. K.; Peper, Jiska S. & Crone, Eveline A.** (2015). Longitudinal changes in adolescent risk-taking: A comprehensive study of neural responses to rewards, pubertal development, and risk-taking behavior. *The Journal of Neuroscience*, 35(18), 7226–7238.

**Bracken, Bruce A. & Crawford, Elizabeth.** (2010). Basic concepts in early childhood educational standards: A 50-state review. *Early Childhood Education Journal*, 37(5), 421–430.

**Bradley, Rachel & Slade, Pauline.** (2011). A review of mental health problems in fathers following the birth of a child. *Journal of Reproductive and Infant Psychology*, 29(1), 19–42.

**Brainard, Jeffrey.** (2018). Rethinking retractions. *Science*, 362(6413), 390–393.

**Braithwaite, David W.; Tian, Jing & Siegler, Robert S.** (2018). Do children understand fraction addition? *Developmental Science*, 21(4), e12601.

**Brame, Robert; Bushway, Shawn D.; Paternoster, Ray & Turner, Michael G.** (2014). Demographic patterns of cumulative arrest prevalence by ages 18 and 23. *Crime & Delinquency*, 60(3), 471–486.

**Brand, Jennie E. & Xie, Yu.** (2010). Who benefits most from college?: Evidence for negative selection in heterogeneous economic returns to higher education. *American Sociological Review*, 75(2), 273–302.

**Brandone, Amanda C.; Horwitz, Suzanne R.; Aslin, Richard N. & Wellman, Henry M.** (2014). Infants' goal anticipation during failed and successful reaching actions. *Developmental Science*, 17(1), 23–34.

**Branje, Susan.** (2018). Development of parent–adolescent relationships: Conflict interactions as a mechanism of change. *Child Development Perspectives*, 12(3), 171–176.

**Braver, Sanford L. & Votruba, Ashley M.** (2018). Does joint physical custody "cause" children's better outcomes? *Journal of Divorce & Remarriage*, 59(5), 452–468.

**Brazelton, T. Berry & Sparrow, Joshua D.** (2006). *Touchpoints, birth to 3: Your child's emotional and behavioral development* (2nd ed.). Da Capo Press.

**Bremner, J. Gavin & Wachs, Theodore D. (Eds.).** (2010). *The Wiley-Blackwell handbook of infant development* (2nd ed.). Wiley-Blackwell.

**Brennan, Arthur; Ayers, Susan; Ahmed, Hafez & Marshall-Lucette, Sylvie.** (2007). A critical review of the Couvade syndrome: The pregnant male. *Journal of Reproductive and Infant Psychology*, 25(3), 173–189.

**Bridge, Jeffrey A.; Greenhouse, Joel B.; Ruch, Donna; Stevens, Jack; Ackerman, John; Sheftall, Arielle H.; . . . Campo, John V.** (2019). Association between the release of Netflix's *13 Reasons Why* and suicide rates in the United States: An interrupted times series analysis. *Journal of the American Academy of Child & Adolescent Psychiatry*.

**Bridgett, David J.; Burt, Nicole M.; Edwards, Erin S. & Deater-Deckard, Kirby.** (2015). Intergenerational transmission of self-regulation: A multidisciplinary review and integrative conceptual framework. *Psychological Bulletin*, 141(3), 602–654.

**Bridgett, David J.; Laake, Lauren M.; Gartstein, Maria A. & Dorn, Danielle.** (2013). Development of infant positive emotionality: The contribution of maternal characteristics and effects on subsequent parenting. *Infant and Child Development*, 22(4), 362–382.

**Brix, Nis; Ernst, Andreas; Lauridsen, Lea Lykke Braskhoj; Parner, Erik; Stovring, Henrik; Olsen, Jorn; . . . Ramlau-Hansen, Cecilia Høst.** (2019). Timing of puberty in boys and girls: A population-based study. *Paediatric and Perinatal Epidemiology*, 33(1), 70–78.

**Brody, Jane E.** (2013, February 26). Too many pills in pregnancy. *New York Times*.

**Broekhuizen, Martine L.; Aken, Marcel A. G.; Dubas, Judith S. & Leseman, Paul P. M.** (2018). Child care quality and Dutch 2- and 3-year-olds' socio-emotional outcomes: Does the amount of care matter? *Infant and Child Development*, 27(1), e2043.

**Bronfenbrenner, Urie & Morris, Pamela A.** (2006). The bioecological model of human development. In Damon, William & Lerner, Richard M.

(Eds.), *Handbook of child psychology* (6th ed., Vol. 1, pp. 793–828). Wiley.

**Brooks, Rechele; Singleton, Jenny L. & Meltzoff, Andrew N.** (2019). Enhanced gaze-following behavior in Deaf infants of Deaf parents. *Developmental Science*, e12900.

**Broström, Stig.** (2017). A dynamic learning concept in early years' education: A possible way to prevent schoolification. *International Journal of Early Years Education*, 25(1), 3–15.

**Brouwer, Rachel M.; van Soelen, Inge L. C.; Swagerman, Suzanne C.; Schnack, Hugo G.; Ehli, Erik A.; Kahn, René S.; . . . Boomsma, Dorret I.** (2014). Genetic associations between intelligence and cortical thickness emerge at the start of puberty. *Human Brain Mapping*, 35(8), 3760–3773.

**Brown, Belinda.** (2019). From hegemonic to responsive masculinity: The transformative power of the provider role. In Barry, John A.; Kingerlee, Roger; Seager, Martin & Sullivan, Luke (Eds.), *The Palgrave handbook of male psychology and mental health* (pp. 183–204). Palgrave Macmillan.

**Brown, B. Bradford & Bakken, Jeremy P.** (2011). Parenting and peer relationships: Reinvigorating research on family–peer linkages in adolescence. *Journal of Research on Adolescence*, 21(1), 153–165.

**Brown, Christia Spears; Alabi, Basirat O.; Huynh, Virginia W. & Masten, Carrie L.** (2011). Ethnicity and gender in late childhood and early adolescence: Group identity and awareness of bias. *Developmental Psychology*, 47(2), 463–471.

**Brown, Steven D. & Lent, Robert W.** (2016). Vocational psychology: Agency, equity, and well-being. *Annual Review of Psychology*, 67, 541–565.

**Bruder, Gerard E.; Stewart, Jonathan W. & McGrath, Patrick J.** (2017). Right brain, left brain in depressive disorders: Clinical and theoretical implications of behavioral, electrophysiological and neuroimaging findings. *Neuroscience and Biobehavioral Reviews*, 78, 178–191.

**Brummelman, Eddie; Nelemans, Stefanie A.; Thomaes, Sander & Orobio De Castro, Bram.** (2017). When parents' praise inflates, children's self-esteem deflates. *Child Development*, 88(6), 1799–1809.

**Buehler, Cheryl.** (2020). Family processes and children's and adolescents' well-being. *Journal of Marriage and Family*, 82(1), 145–174.

**Bueno, Clarissa & Menna-Barreto, Luiz.** (2016). Environmental factors influencing biological rhythms in newborns: From neonatal intensive care units to home. *Sleep Science*, 9(4), 295–300.

**Burchinal, Margaret R.; Lowe Vandell, Deborah & Belsky, Jay.** (2014). Is the prediction of adolescent outcomes from early child care moderated by later maternal sensitivity? Results from the NICHD study of early child care and youth development. *Developmental Psychology*, 50(2), 542–553.

**Burnette, Jeni L.; O'Boyle, Ernest H.; VanEpps, Eric M.; Pollack, Jeffrey M. & Finkel, Eli J.** (2013). Mind-sets matter: A meta-analytic review of implicit theories and self-regulation. *Psychological Bulletin*, 139(3), 655–701.

**Bursztyn, Leonardo & Jensen, Robert.** (2015). How does peer pressure affect educational investments? *Quarterly Journal of Economics*, 130(3), 1329–1367.

**Buss, David M.** (2015). *Evolutionary psychology: The new science of the mind* (5th ed.). Routledge.

**Butterworth, Brian & Kovas, Yulia.** (2013). Understanding neurocognitive developmental disorders can improve education for all. *Science*, 340(6130), 300–305.

**Butterworth, Brian; Varma, Sashank & Laurillard, Diana.** (2011). Dyscalculia: From brain to education. *Science*, 332(6033), 1049–1053.

**Byard, Roger W.** (2014). "Shaken baby syndrome" and forensic pathology: An uneasy interface. *Forensic Science, Medicine, and Pathology*, 10(2), 239–241.

**Byers-Heinlein, Krista; Burns, Tracey C. & Werker, Janet F.** (2010). The roots of bilingualism in newborns. *Psychological Science*, 21(3), 343–348.

**Cabrera, Natasha.** (2015). Why do fathers matter for children's development? In McHale, Susan M.; King, Valarie; Van Hook, Jennifer & Booth, Alan (Eds.), *Gender and Couple Relationships* (pp. 161–168). Springer.

**Cabrera, Natasha J.; Volling, Brenda L. & Barr, Rachel.** (2018). Fathers are parents, too! Widening the lens on parenting for children's development. *Child Development Perspectives*, 12(3), 152–157.

**Cacioppo, Stephanie; Capitanio, John P. & Cacioppo, John T.** (2014). Toward a neurology of loneliness. *Psychological Bulletin*, 140(6), 1464–1504.

**Calarco, Jessica McCrory.** (2014). The inconsistent curriculum: Cultural tool kits and student interpretations of ambiguous expectations. *Social Psychology Quarterly*, 77(2), 185–209.

**Calderon, Valerie J. & Yu, Daniela.** (2017, June 1). *Student enthusiasm falls as high school graduation nears*. Washington, DC: Gallup.

**Callaghan, Tara.** (2013). Symbols and symbolic thought. In Zelazo, Philip D. (Ed.), *The Oxford handbook of developmental psychology* (Vol. 1). Oxford University Press.

**Campbell, Frances; Conti, Gabriella; Heckman, James J.; Moon, Seong H.; Pinto, Rodrigo; Pungello, Elizabeth & Pan, Yi.** (2014). Early childhood investments substantially boost adult health. *Science*, 343(6178), 1478–1485.

**Campbell, Frances A.; Pungello, Elizabeth P.; Miller-Johnson, Shari; Burchinal, Margaret & Ramey, Craig T.** (2001). The development of cognitive and academic abilities: Growth curves from an early childhood educational experiment. *Developmental Psychology*, 37(2), 231–242.

**Cao, Zhipeng; Bennett, Marc; Orr, Catherine; Icke, Ilknur; Banaschewski, Tobias; Barker, Gareth J.; . . . Whelan, Robert.** (2019). Mapping adolescent reward anticipation, receipt, and prediction error during the monetary incentive delay task. *Human Brain Mapping*, 40(1), 262–283.

**Carey, Nessa.** (2012). *The epigenetics revolution: How modern biology is rewriting our understanding of genetics, disease, and inheritance*. Columbia University Press.

**Carey, Susan; Zaitchik, Deborah & Bascandziev, Igor.** (2015). Theories of development: In dialog with Jean Piaget. *Developmental Review*, 38, 36–54.

**Cargnelutti, Elisa; Tomasino, Barbara & Fabbro, Franco.** (2019). Language brain representation in bilinguals with different age of appropriation and proficiency of the second language: A meta-analysis of functional imaging studies. *Frontiers in Human Neuroscience*, 13(154).

**Carlsen, Karin C. Lødrup; Skjerven, Håvard O. & Carlsen, Kai-Håkon.** (2018). The toxicity of e-cigarettes and children's respiratory health. *Paediatric Respiratory Reviews*, 28, 63–67.

**Carlson, Robert G.; Nahhas, Ramzi W.; Martins, Silvia S. & Daniulaityte, Raminta.** (2016). Predictors of transition to heroin use among initially non-opioid dependent illicit pharmaceutical opioid users: A natural history study. *Drug & Alcohol Dependence*, 160, 127–134.

**Carlson, Scott.** (2016, May 1). Should everyone go to college?: For poor kids, 'College for all' isn't the mantra it was meant to be. *Chronicle of Higher Education*.

**Carlson, Stephanie M.; Koenig, Melissa A. & Harms, Madeline B.** (2013). Theory of mind. *Wiley Interdisciplinary Reviews: Cognitive Science*, 4(4), 391–402.

**Carmichael, Cheryl L.; Reis, Harry T. & Duberstein, Paul R.** (2015). In your 20s it's quantity, in your 30s it's quality: The prognostic value of social activity across 30 years of adulthood. *Psychology and Aging*, 30(1), 95–105.

**Carra, Cecilia; Lavelli, Manuela; Keller, Heidi & Kärtner, Joscha.** (2013). Parenting infants: Socialization goals and behaviors of Italian mothers and immigrant mothers from West Africa. *Journal of Cross-Cultural Psychology*, 44(8), 1304–1320.

**Carroll, Katherine & Kroløkke, Charlotte.** (2018). Freezing for love: Enacting 'responsible' reproductive citizenship through egg freezing. *Culture, Health & Sexuality*, 20(9), 992–1005.

**Carter, A. S. & Briggs-Gowan, M. J.** (2006). *Infant-toddler social and emotional assessment*. Harcourt.

**Carwile, Jenny L.; Willett, Walter C.; Spiegelman, Donna; Hertzmark, Ellen; Rich-Edwards, Janet W.; Frazier, A. Lindsay & Michels, Karin B.** (2015). Sugar-sweetened beverage consumption and age at menarche in a prospective study of US girls. *Human Reproduction*, 30(3), 675–683.

**Casey, B. J. & Caudle, Kristina.** (2013). The teenage brain: Self control. *Current Directions in Psychological Science*, 22(2), 82–87.

**Caspi, Avshalom; Moffitt, Terrie E.; Morgan, Julia; Rutter, Michael; Taylor, Alan; Arseneault, Louise; . . . Polo-Tomas, Monica.** (2004). Maternal expressed emotion predicts children's antisocial behavior problems: Using monozygotic-twin differences to identify environmental effects on behavioral development. *Developmental Psychology*, 40(2), 149–161.

**Cassia, Viola Macchi; Kuefner, Dana; Picozzi, Marta & Vescovo, Elena.** (2009). Early experience predicts later plasticity for face processing: Evidence for the reactivation of dormant effects. *Psychological Science*, 20(7), 853–859.

**Cassidy, Jude & Shaver, Phillip R. (Eds.).** (2016). *Handbook of attachment: Theory, research, and clinical applications.* Guilford Press.

**Castellacci, Fulvio & Tveito, Vegard.** (2018). Internet use and well-being: A survey and a theoretical framework. *Research Policy, 47*(1), 308–325.

**Ceballo, Rosario; Maurizi, Laura K.; Suarez, Gloria A. & Aretakis, Maria T.** (2014). Gift and sacrifice: Parental involvement in Latino adolescents' education. *Cultural Diversity and Ethnic Minority Psychology, 20*(1), 116–127.

**Cenegy, Laura Freeman; Denney, Justin T. & Kimbro, Rachel Tolbert.** (2018). Family diversity and child health: Where do same-sex couple families fit. *Journal of Marriage and Family, 80*(1), 198–218.

**Center for Education Policy.** (2012). *SDP strategic performance indicator: The high school effect on college-going. The SDP College-Going Diagnostic Strategic Performance Indicators.* Cambridge, MA: Harvard University, Center for Education Policy Research.

**Centers for Disease Control and Prevention.** (2015, May 15). *Epidemiology and prevention of vaccine-preventable diseases* (Hamborsky, Jennifer; Kroger, Andrew & Wolfe, Charles Eds. 13th ed.). Public Health Foundation.

**Centers for Disease Control and Prevention.** (2018). *Sexually transmitted disease surveillance 2017.* Atlanta, GA: U.S. Department of Health and Human Services.

**Centers for Disease Control and Prevention.** (2018, October 9). *Youth risk behavior survey: Data summary & trends report 2007–2017.* Atlanta, GA: National Center for HIV/AIDS, Viral Hepatitis, STD, and TB Prevention, Division of Adolescent and School Health. 328447.

**Centers for Disease Control and Prevention.** (2019). Breastfeeding rates: Breastfeeding among U.S. children born 2009–2016, CDC National Immunization Survey. U.S. Department of Health & Human Services.

**Centers for Disease Control and Prevention.** (2019, June 17). Measles cases and outbreaks. Centers for Disease Control and Prevention.

**Centers for Disease Control and Prevention.** (2020, February 20). WISQARS: Fatal injury reports, national, regional and state, 1981–2018. U.S. Department of Health & Human Services.

**Centers for Disease Control and Prevention, National Center for Health Statistics.** (2018, July 3). *Underlying cause of death, 1999–2017 on CDC WONDER Online Database* [Data set]. CDC WONDER.

**Cesana-Arlotti, Nicoló; Martín, Ana; Téglás, Ernő; Vorobyova, Liza; Cetnarski, Ryszard & Bonatti, Luca L.** (2018). Precursors of logical reasoning in preverbal human infants. *Science, 359*(6381), 1263–1266.

**Cespedes, Elizabeth M.; McDonald, Julia; Haines, Jess; Bottino, Clement J.; Schmidt, Marie Evans & Taveras, Elsie M.** (2013). Obesity-related behaviors of US- and non-US-born parents and children in low-income households. *Journal of Developmental & Behavioral Pediatrics, 34*(8), 541–548.

**Ceyhan, Gaye D.; Thompson, Alia N.; Sloane, Jeremy D.; Wiles, Jason R. & Tillotson,** John W. (2019). The socialization and retention of low-income college students: The impact of a wrap-around intervention. *International Journal of Higher Education, 8*(6).

**Champagne, Frances A. & Curley, James P.** (2010). Maternal care as a modulating influence on infant development. In Blumberg, Mark S.; Freeman, John H. & Robinson, Scott R. (Eds.), *Oxford handbook of developmental behavioral neuroscience* (pp. 323–341). Oxford University Press.

**Chartier, Karen G.; Scott, Denise M.; Wall, Tamara L.; Covault, Jonathan; Karriker-Jaffe, Katherine J.; Mills, Britain A.; . . . Arroyo, Judith A.** (2014). Framing ethnic variations in alcohol outcomes from biological pathways to neighborhood context. *Alcoholism: Clinical and Experimental Research, 38*(3), 611–618.

**Chen, Edith; Brody, Gene H. & Miller, Gregory E.** (2017). Childhood close family relationships and health. *American Psychologist, 72*(6), 555–566.

**Chen, Hong & Jackson, Todd.** (2009). Predictors of changes in weight esteem among mainland Chinese adolescents: A longitudinal analysis. *Developmental Psychology, 45*(6), 1618–1629.

**Chen, Mu-Hong; Lan, Wen-Hsuan; Bai, Ya-Mei; Huang, Kai-Lin; Su, Tung-Ping; Tsai, Shih-Jen; . . . Hsu, Ju-Wei.** (2016). Influence of relative age on diagnosis and treatment of Attention-deficit hyperactivity disorder in Taiwanese children. *The Journal of Pediatrics, 172*, 162–167.e1.

**Chen, Xinyin.** (2019). Culture and shyness in childhood and adolescence. *New Ideas in Psychology, 53*, 58–66.

**Chen, Xinyin; Cen, Guozhen; Li, Dan & He, Yunfeng.** (2005). Social functioning and adjustment in Chinese children: The imprint of historical time. *Child Development, 76*(1), 182–195.

**Chen, Xinyin; Fu, Rui; Li, Dan & Liu, Junsheng.** (2019). Developmental trajectories of shyness-sensitivity from middle childhood to early adolescence in China: Contributions of peer preference and mutual friendship. *Journal of Abnormal Child Psychology, 47*(7), 1197–1209.

**Chen, Xinyin; Rubin, Kenneth H. & Sun, Yuerong.** (1992). Social reputation and peer relationships in Chinese and Canadian children: A cross-cultural study. *Child Development, 63*(6), 1336–1343.

**Chen, Xinyin; Yang, Fan & Wang, Li.** (2013). Relations between shyness-sensitivity and internalizing problems in Chinese children: Moderating effects of academic achievement. *Journal of Abnormal Child Psychology, 41*(5), 825–836.

**Chen, Yalin; Loehr, Janeen D. & Campbell, Jamie I. D.** (2019). Does the min-counting strategy for simple addition become automatized in educated adults? A behavioural and ERP study of the size congruency effect. *Neuropsychologia, 124*, 311–321.

**Cherlin, Andrew J.** (2020). Degrees of change: An assessment of the deinstitutionalization of marriage thesis. *Journal of Marriage and Family, 82*(1), 62–80.

**Cherng, Hua-Yu Sebastian & Liu, Jia-Lin.** (2017). Academic social support and student expectations: The case of second-generation Asian Americans. *Asian American Journal of Psychology, 8*(1), 16–30.

**Cheshire, Emily; Kaestle, Christine E. & Miyazaki, Yasuo.** (2019). The influence of parent and parent–adolescent relationship characteristics on sexual trajectories into adulthood. *Archives of Sexual Behavior, 48*(3), 893–910.

**Cheslack-Postava, Keely; Liu, Kayuet & Bearman, Peter S.** (2011). Closely spaced pregnancies are associated with increased odds of autism in California sibling births. *Pediatrics, 127*(2), 246–253.

**Child Trends.** (2019, March 7). Dual language learners. Child Trends.

**Child Trends Databank.** (2015, March). *Lead poisoning: Indicators on children and youth.* Bethesda, MD: Child Trends.

**Child Trends Databank.** (2018). High school dropout rates. Child Trends.

**Choe, Daniel E.; Lane, Jonathan D.; Grabell, Adam S. & Olson, Sheryl L.** (2013a). Developmental precursors of young school-age children's hostile attribution bias. *Developmental Psychology, 49*(12), 2245–2256.

**Choe, Daniel E.; Olson, Sheryl L. & Sameroff, Arnold J.** (2013b). The interplay of externalizing problems and physical and inductive discipline during childhood. *Developmental Psychology, 49*(11), 2029–2039.

**Choi, Hyunkyung; Van Riper, Marcia & Thoyre, Suzanne.** (2012). Decision making following a prenatal diagnosis of Down syndrome: An integrative review. *Journal of Midwifery & Women's Health, 57*(2), 156–164.

**Choi, Jayoung.** (2019). A child's trilingual language practices in Korean, Farsi, and English: From a sustainable translanguaging perspective. *International Journal of Multilingualism, 16*(4), 534–548.

**Chomsky, Noam.** (1968). *Language and mind.* Harcourt Brace & World.

**Chomsky, Noam.** (1980). *Rules and representations.* Columbia University Press.

**Chong, Jessica X.; Buckingham, Kati J.; Jhangiani, Shalini N.; Boehm, Corinne; Sobreira, Nara; Smith, Joshua D.; . . . Bamshad, Michael J.** (2015). The genetic basis of Mendelian phenotypes: Discoveries, challenges, and opportunities. *American Journal of Human Genetics, 97*(2), 199–215.

**Choudhury, Ananyo; Aron, Shaun; Sengupta, Dhriti; Hazelhurst, Scott & Ramsay, Michèle.** (2018). African genetic diversity provides novel insights into evolutionary history and local adaptations. *Human Molecular Genetics, 27*(R2), R209–R218.

**Christakis, Erika.** (2016). *The importance of being little: What preschoolers really need from grownups.* Viking.

**Christian, Cindy W. & Block, Robert.** (2009). Abusive head trauma in infants and children. *Pediatrics, 123*(5), 1409–1411.

**Christian, Kimberly M.; Song, Hongjun & Ming, Guo-Li.** (2018). A previously undetected pathology of Zika virus infection. *Nature Medicine, 24*(3), 258–259.

**Christoforides, Michael; Spanoudis, George & Demetriou, Andreas.** (2016). Coping with logical fallacies: A developmental training program for learning to reason. *Child Development, 87*(6), 1856–1876.

**Chu, Shuyuan; Chen, Qian; Chen, Yan; Bao, Yixiao; Wu, Min & Zhang, Jun.** (2017). Cesarean section without medical indication and risk of childhood asthma, and attenuation by breastfeeding. *PLoS ONE, 12*(9), e0184920.

**Cicchetti, Dante.** (2013a). Annual research review: Resilient functioning in maltreated children—past, present, and future perspectives. *Journal of Child Psychology and Psychiatry, 54*(4), 402–422.

**Cicchetti, Dante.** (2013b). An overview of developmental psychopathology. In Zelazo, Philip D. (Ed.), *The Oxford handbook of developmental psychology* (Vol. 2, pp. 455–480). Oxford University Press.

**Cicchetti, Dante.** (2016). Socioemotional, personality, and biological development: Illustrations from a multilevel developmental psychopathology perspective on child maltreatment. *Annual Review of Psychology, 67*, 187–211.

**Cicconi, Megan.** (2014). Vygotsky meets technology: A reinvention of collaboration in the early childhood mathematics classroom. *Early Childhood Education Journal, 42*(1), 57–65.

**Cierpka, Manfred & Cierpka, Astrid.** (2016). Developmentally appropriate vs. persistent defiant and aggressive behavior. In Cierpka, Manfred (Ed.), *Regulatory disorders in infants.* Springer.

**Cillessen, Antonius H. N. & Marks, Peter E. L.** (2011). Conceptualizing and measuring popularity. In Cillessen, Antonius H. N.; Schwartz, David & Mayeux, Lara (Eds.), *Popularity in the peer system* (pp. 25–56). Guilford Press.

**Claessen, Jacques.** (2017). *Forgiveness in criminal law through incorporating restorative mediation.* Wolf Legal Publishers.

**Clark, Caron A. C.; Fang, Hua; Espy, Kimberly A.; Filipek, Pauline A.; Juranek, Jenifer; Bangert, Barbara; . . . Taylor, H. Gerry.** (2013). Relation of neural structure to persistently low academic achievement: A longitudinal study of children with differing birth weights. *Neuropsychology, 27*(3), 364–377.

**Clark, Lee Anna; Cuthbert, Bruce; Lewis-Fernández, Roberto; Narrow, William E. & Reed, Geoffrey M.** (2017). Three approaches to understanding and classifying mental disorder: ICD-11, *DSM-5*, and the National Institute of Mental Health's Research Domain Criteria (RDoC). *Psychological Science in the Public Interest, 18*(2), 72–145.

**Coe, Jesse L.; Davies, Patrick T. & Sturge-Apple, Melissa L.** (2018). Family instability and young children's school adjustment: Callousness and negative internal representations as mediators. *Child Development, 89*(4), 1193–1208.

**Coffelt, Tina A.** (2017). Deciding to reveal sexual information and sexuality education in mother-daughter relationships. *Sex Education, 17*(5), 571–587.

**Cohen, Jon.** (2014). Saving lives without new drugs. *Science, 346*(6212), 911.

**Cohen, Jon.** (2018). What now for human genome editing? *Science, 362*(6419), 1090–1092.

**Cohen, Joel E. & Malin, Martin B. (Eds.).** (2010). *International perspectives on the goals of universal basic and secondary education.* Routledge.

**Colaco, Marc; Johnson, Kelly; Schneider, Dona & Barone, Joseph.** (2013). Toilet training method is not related to dysfunctional voiding. *Clinical Pediatrics, 52*(1), 49–53.

**Colditz, Paul B.; Boyd, Roslyn N.; Winter, Leanne; Pritchard, Margo; Gray, Peter H.; Whittingham, Koa; . . . Sanders, Matthew R.** (2019). A randomized trial of Baby Triple P for preterm infants: Child outcomes at 2 years of corrected age. *Journal of Pediatrics, 210*, 48–54.e2.

**Cole, Pamela M. & Hollenstein, Tom.** (2018). *Emotion regulation: A matter of time.* Routledge.

**Coleman-Jensen, Alisha; Rabbitt, Matthew P.; Gregory, Christian A. & Singh, Anita.** (2017). *Household food security in the United States in 2016.* Washington, DC: U.S. Department of Agriculture, Economic Research Service. ERR–237.

**Coles, Robert.** (1997). *The moral intelligence of children: How to raise a moral child.* Random House.

**Collin-Vézina, Delphine; De La Sablonnière-Griffin, Mireille; Palmer, Andrea M. & Milne, Lise.** (2015). A preliminary mapping of individual, relational, and social factors that impede disclosure of childhood sexual abuse. *Child Abuse & Neglect, 43*, 123–134.

**Colson, Eve R.; Willinger, Marian; Rybin, Denis; Heeren, Timothy; Smith, Lauren A.; Lister, George & Corwin, Michael J.** (2013). Trends and factors associated with infant bed sharing, 1993–2010: The National Infant Sleep Position study. *JAMA Pediatrics, 167*(11), 1032–1037.

**Compian, Laura J.; Gowen, L. Kris & Hayward, Chris.** (2009). The interactive effects of puberty and peer victimization on weight concerns and depression symptoms among early adolescent girls. *Journal of Early Adolescence, 29*(3), 357–375.

**Confer, Jaime C.; Easton, Judith A.; Fleischman, Diana S.; Goetz, Cari D.; Lewis, David M. G.; Perilloux, Carin & Buss, David M.** (2010). Evolutionary psychology: Controversies, questions, prospects, and limitations. *American Psychologist, 65*(2), 110–126.

**Coon, Carleton S.** (1962). *The origin of races.* Knopf.

**Coovadia, Hoosen M. & Wittenberg, Dankwart F. (Eds.).** (2004). *Paediatrics and child health: A manual for health professionals in developing countries* (5th ed.). Oxford University Press.

**Coplan, Robert J. & Weeks, Murray.** (2009). Shy and soft-spoken: Shyness, pragmatic language, and socio-emotional adjustment in early childhood. *Infant and Child Development, 18*(3), 238–254.

**Corballis, Michael C.** (2011). *The recursive mind: The origins of human language, thought, and civilization.* Princeton University Press.

**Corenblum, Barry.** (2014). Relationships between racial–ethnic identity, self-esteem and in-group attitudes among First Nation children. *Journal of Youth and Adolescence, 43*(3), 387–404.

**Costa, Albert & Sebastián-Gallés, Núria.** (2014). How does the bilingual experience sculpt the brain? *Nature Reviews Neuroscience, 15*(5), 336–345.

**Costa, Albert; Vives, Marc–Lluís & Corey, Joanna D.** (2017). On language processing shaping decision making. *Current Directions in Psychological Science, 26*(2), 146–151.

**Côté, James E.** (2018). The enduring usefulness of Erikson's concept of the identity crisis in the 21st century: An analysis of student mental health concerns. *Identity, 18*(4), 251–263.

**Côté, James E. & Levine, Charles.** (2015). *Identity formation, youth, and development: A simplified approach.* Psychology Press.

**Council on Communications and Media.** (2011). Policy statement—Children, adolescents, obesity, and the media. *Pediatrics, 128*(1), 201–208.

**Couzin-Frankel, Jennifer.** (2017). Fateful imprints. *Science, 355*(6321), 122–125.

**Couzin-Frankel, Jennifer.** (2018). Toxin or treatment? *Science, 362*(6412), 278–282.

**Couzin-Frankel, Jennifer.** (2020). Rethinking anorexia. *Science, 368*(6487), 124–127.

**Cowell, Jason M.; Lee, Kang; Malcolm-Smith, Susan; Selcuk, Bilge; Zhou, Xinyue & Decety, Jean.** (2017). The development of generosity and moral cognition across five cultures. *Developmental Science, 20*(4), e12403.

**Coyne, Sarah M.; Ward, L. Monique; Kroff, Savannah L.; Davis, Emilie J.; Holmgren, Hailey G.; Jensen, Alexander C.; . . . Essig, Lee W.** (2019). Contributions of mainstream sexual media exposure to sexual attitudes, perceived peer norms, and sexual behavior: A meta-analysis. *Journal of Adolescent Health, 64*(4), 430–436.

**Craig, Stephanie G.; Davies, Gregory; Schibuk, Larry; Weiss, Margaret D. & Hechtman, Lily.** (2015). Long-term effects of stimulant treatment for ADHD: What can we tell our patients? *Current Developmental Disorders Reports, 2*(1), 1–9.

**Crain, William C.** (2011). *Theories of development: Concepts and applications* (6th ed.). Prentice–Hall.

**Cree, Robyn A.; Bitsko, Rebecca H.; Robinson, Lara R.; Holbrook, Joseph R.; Danielson, Melissa L.; Smith, Camille; . . . Peacock, Georgina.** (2018). Health care, family, and community factors associated with mental, behavioral, and developmental disorders and poverty among children aged 2–8 years—United States, 2016. *67*(50), 1377–1383. Atlanta, GA: Centers for Disease Control and Prevention.

**Crenshaw, Kimberle.** (1989). Demarginalizing the intersection of race and sex: A Black feminist critique of antidiscrimination doctrine, feminist theory and antiracist politics. *University of Chicago Legal Forum*, 139–167.

**Crivello, Cristina & Poulin-Dubois, Diane.** (2019). Infants' ability to detect emotional incongruency: Deep or shallow? *Infancy, 24*(4), 480–500.

**Crnic, Keith A.; Neece, Cameron L.; McIntyre, Laura Lee; Blacher, Jan & Baker, Bruce L.** (2017). Intellectual disability and developmental risk: Promoting intervention to improve child and family well-being. *Child Development, 88*(2), 436–445.

**Crone, Eveline A.; van Duijvenvoorde, Anna C. K. & Peper, Jiska S.** (2016). Annual research review: Neural contributions to risk-taking in adolescence—developmental changes and individual differences. *Journal of Child Psychology and Psychiatry, 57*(3), 353–368.

**Crosnoe, Robert; Purtell, Kelly M.; Davis-Kean, Pamela; Ansari, Arya & Benner, Aprile D.** (2016). The selection of children from low-income families into preschool. *Developmental Psychology, 52*(4), 599–612.

**Crossley, Nicolas A.; Mechelli, Andrea; Scott, Jessica; Carletti, Francesco; Fox, Peter T.; McGuire, Philip & Bullmore, Edward T.** (2014). The hubs of the human connectome are generally implicated in the anatomy of brain disorders. *Brain, 137*(8), 2382–2395.

**Crowley, Jocelyn Elise.** (2019). Gray divorce: Explaining midlife marital splits. *Journal of Women & Aging, 31*(1), 49–72.

**Csibra, Gergely; Hernik, Mikołaj; Mascaro, Olivier; Tatone, Denis & Lengyel, Máté.** (2016). Statistical treatment of looking-time data. *Developmental Psychology, 52*(4), 521–536.

**Culpin, Iryna; Heron, Jon; Araya, Ricardo & Joinson, Carol.** (2015). Early childhood father absence and depressive symptoms in adolescent girls from a UK cohort: The mediating role of early menarche. *Journal of Abnormal Child Psychology, 43*(5), 921–931.

**Cunningham, F. Gary; Leveno, Kenneth; Bloom, Steven; Spong, Catherine Y.; Dashe, Jodi; Hoffman, Barbara; . . . Sheffield, Jeanne S.** (2014). *Williams obstetrics* (24th ed.). McGraw-Hill Education.

**Currie, Candace; Nic Gabhainn, Saoirse; Godeau, Emmanuelle & International HBSC Network Coordinating Committee.** (2009). The health behaviour in school-aged children: WHO Collaborative Cross-National (HBSC) study: Origins, concept, history and development 1982–2008. *International Journal of Public Health, 54,* 131–139.

**Currie, Janet & Widom, Cathy S.** (2010). Long-term consequences of child abuse and neglect on adult economic well-being. *Child Maltreatment, 15*(2), 111–120.

**Curtiss, Susan.** (2014). *Genie: A psycholinguistic study of a modern-day wild child.* Academic Press.

**Cutuli, J. J.; Ahumada, Sandra M.; Herbers, Janette E.; Lafavor, Theresa L.; Masten, Ann S. & Oberg, Charles N.** (2017). Adversity and children experiencing family homelessness: Implications for health. *Journal of Children and Poverty, 23*(1), 41–55.

**Cuzzolaro, Massimo & Fassino, Secondo (Eds.).** (2018). *Body image, eating, and weight: A guide to assessment, treatment, and prevention.* Springer.

**d'Alpoim Guedes, Jade; Bestor, Theodore C.; Carrasco, David; Flad, Rowan; Fosse, Ethan; Herzfeld, Michael; . . . Warinner, Christina.** (2013). Is poverty in our genes?: A critique of Ashraf and Galor, "The 'Out of Africa' hypothesis, human genetic diversity, and comparative economic development". *Forum on Public Anthropology, 54*(1).

**Dadds, Mark R. & Tully, Lucy A.** (2019). What is it to discipline a child: What should it be? A reanalysis of time-out from the perspective of child mental health, attachment, and trauma. *American Psychologist, 74*(7), 794–808.

**Daley, Tamara C.; Whaley, Shannon E.; Sigman, Marian D.; Espinosa, Michael P. & Neumann, Charlotte.** (2003). IQ on the rise: The Flynn Effect in rural Kenyan children. *Psychological Science, 14*(3), 215–219.

**Dalman, Christina; Allebeck, Peter; Gunnell, David; Harrison, Glyn; Kristensson, Krister; Lewis, Glyn; . . . Karlsson, Håkan.** (2008). Infections in the CNS during childhood and the risk of subsequent psychotic illness: A cohort study of more than one million Swedish subjects. *American Journal of Psychiatry, 165*(1), 59–65.

**Dalrymple, Rebecca Amy.** (2019). Earlier introduction of solid food is associated with improved sleep in infants. *Archives of Disease in Childhood—Education and Practice.*

**Damasio, Antonio R.** (2012). *Self comes to mind: Constructing the conscious brain.* Vintage.

**Dantchev, Slava; Zammit, Stanley & Wolke, Dieter.** (2018). Sibling bullying in middle childhood and psychotic disorder at 18 years: A prospective cohort study. *Psychological Medicine, 48*(14), 2321–2328.

**Darwin, Charles.** (1859). *On the origin of species by means of natural selection.* J. Murray.

**Darwin, Zoe; Galdas, Paul; Hinchliff, Sharron; Littlewood, Elizabeth; McMillan, Dean; McGowan, Linda & Gilbody, Simon.** (2017). Fathers' views and experiences of their own mental health during pregnancy and the first postnatal year: A qualitative interview study of men participating in the UK Born and Bred in Yorkshire (BaBY) cohort. *BMC Pregnancy and Childbirth, 17*(45).

**Daum, Moritz M.; Ulber, Julia & Gredebäck, Gustaf.** (2013). The development of pointing perception in infancy: Effects of communicative signals on covert shifts of attention. *Developmental Psychology, 49*(10), 1898–1908.

**Davis, Corey S.; Green, Traci C.; Hernandez-Delgado, Hector & Lieberman, Amy Judd.** (2018). Status of US state laws mandating timely reporting of nonfatal overdose. *American Journal of Public Health, 108*(9), 1159–1161.

**Davis, Jac T. M. & Hines, Melissa.** (2020). How large are gender differences in toy preferences? A systematic review and meta-analysis of toy preference research. *Archives of Sexual Behavior, 49,* 373–394.

**Dawson-Hahn, Elizabeth; Koceja, Lorren; Stein, Elizabeth; Farmer, Beth; Grow, H Mollie; Saelens, Brian E.; . . . Pak-Gorstein, Suzinne.** (2019). Perspectives of caregivers on the effects of migration on the nutrition, health and physical activity of their young children: A qualitative study with immigrant and refugee families. *Journal of Immigrant and Minority Health, 22,* 274–281.

**Day, Felix R.; Elks, Cathy E.; Murray, Anna; Ong, Ken K. & Perry, John R. B.** (2015). Puberty timing associated with diabetes, cardiovascular disease and also diverse health outcomes in men and women: The UK Biobank study. *Scientific Reports, 5*(11208).

**Dayanim, Shoshana & Namy, Laura L.** (2015). Infants learn baby signs from video. *Child Development, 86*(3), 800–811.

**De Boeck, Paul & Jeon, Minjeong.** (2018). Perceived crisis and reforms: Issues, explanations, and remedies. *Psychological Bulletin, 144*(7), 757–777.

**de Boer, Anouk; Peeters, Margot & Koning, Ina.** (2017). An experimental study of risk taking behavior among adolescents: A closer look at peer and sex influences. *Journal of Early Adolescence, 37*(8), 1125–1141.

**de Heering, Adelaide; de Liedekerke, Claire; Deboni, Malorie & Rossion, Bruno.** (2010). The role of experience during childhood in shaping the other-race effect. *Developmental Science, 13*(1), 181–187.

**de Hoog, Marieke L. A.; Kleinman, Ken P.; Gillman, Matthew W.; Vrijkotte, Tanja G. M.; van Eijsden, Manon & Taveras, Elsie M.** (2014). Racial/ethnic and immigrant differences in early childhood diet quality. *Public Health Nutrition, 17*(6), 1308–1317.

**de Jonge, Ank; Geerts, C. C.; van der Goes, Birgit Y.; Mol, Ben W.; Buitendijk, S. E. & Nijhuis, Jan.** (2015). Perinatal mortality and morbidity up to 28 days after birth among 743,070 low-risk planned home and hospital births: A cohort study based on three merged national perinatal databases. *BJOG, 122*(5), 720–728.

**de la Croix, David.** (2013). *Fertility, education, growth, and sustainability.* Cambridge University Press.

**de Leeuw, Suzanne G. & Kalmijn, Matthijs.** (2020). The intergenerational transmission of socioeconomic status in stepfamilies: What happens if two fathers are involved in the transmission process? *Journal of Marriage and Family, 82*(2), 657–674.

**De Neys, Wim & Van Gelder, Elke.** (2009). Logic and belief across the lifespan: The rise and fall of belief inhibition during syllogistic reasoning. *Developmental Science, 12*(1), 123–130.

**de Oliveira Cardoso, Caroline; Dias, Natália; Senger, Joana; Colling, Ana Paula Cervi; Seabra, Alessandra Gotuzo & Fonseca, Rochele Paz.** (2018). Neuropsychological stimulation of executive functions in children with typical development: A systematic review. *Applied Neuropsychology: Child, 7*(1), 61–81.

**de Vrieze, Jop.** (2018). The metawars. *Science, 361*(6408), 1184–1188.

**Dean, Angela J.; Walters, Julie & Hall, Anthony.** (2010). A systematic review of interventions to enhance medication adherence in children and adolescents with chronic illness. *Archives of Disease in Childhood, 95*(9), 717–723.

**DeAngelis, Corey A.** (2019). Does private schooling affect noncognitive skills? International evidence based on test and survey effort on PISA. *Social Science Quarterly, 11*(6), 2256–2276.

**Dearing, Eric; Wimer, Christopher; Simpkins, Sandra D.; Lund, Terese; Bouffard, Suzanne M.; Caronongan, Pia; . . . Weiss, Heather.**

(2009). Do neighborhood and home contexts help explain why low-income children miss opportunities to participate in activities outside of school? *Developmental Psychology, 45*(6), 1545–1562.

**Dearing, Eric & Zachrisson, Henrik D.** (2017). Concern over internal, external, and incidence validity in studies of child-care quantity and externalizing behavior problems. *Child Development Perspectives, 11*(2), 133–138.

**Deater-Deckard, Kirby & Lansford, Jennifer E.** (2016). Daughters' and sons' exposure to childrearing discipline and violence in low- and middle-income countries. *Monographs of the Society for Research in Child Development, 81*(1), 78–103.

**Defranza, David; Mishra, Himanshu & Mishra, Arul.** (2020). How language shapes prejudice against women: An examination across 45 world languages. *Journal of Personality and Social Psychology, 119*(1), 7–22.

**Dehaene-Lambertz, Ghislaine.** (2017). The human infant brain: A neural architecture able to learn language. *Psychonomic Bulletin & Review, 24*(1), 48–55.

**Deighton, Jessica; Humphrey, Neil; Belsky, Jay; Boehnke, Jan; Vostanis, Panos & Patalay, Praveetha.** (2018). Longitudinal pathways between mental health difficulties and academic performance during middle childhood and early adolescence. *British Journal of Developmental Psychology, 36*(1), 110–126.

**Delaunay-El Allam, Maryse; Soussignan, Robert; Patris, Bruno; Marlier, Luc & Schaal, Benoist.** (2010). Long-lasting memory for an odor acquired at the mother's breast. *Developmental Science, 13*(6), 849–863.

**Deventer, Jennifer; Wagner, Jenny; Lüdtke, Oliver & Trautwein, Ulrich.** (2019). Are personality traits and relationship characteristics reciprocally related? Longitudinal analyses of codevelopment in the transition out of high school and beyond. *Journal of Personality and Social Psychology, 116*(2), 331–347.

**Devine, Rory T. & Hughes, Claire.** (2014). Relations between false belief understanding and executive function in early childhood: A meta-analysis. *Child Development, 85*(5), 1777–1794.

**Diamond, Adele.** (2012). Activities and programs that improve children's executive functions. *Current Directions in Psychological Science, 21*(5), 335–341.

**Diamond, Adele.** (2016). Why improving and assessing executive functions early in life is critical. In Griffin, James Alan; McCardle, Peggy D. & Freund, Lisa (Eds.), *Executive function in preschool-age children: Integrating measurement, neurodevelopment, and translational research* (pp. 11–43). American Psychological Association.

**Diamond, Adele & Lee, Kathleen.** (2011). Interventions shown to aid executive function development in children 4 to 12 years old. *Science, 333*(6045), 959–964.

**Diamond, Marian C.** (1988). *Enriching heredity: The impact of the environment on the anatomy of the brain.* Free Press.

**Dillman Carpentier, Francesca & Stevens, Elise.** (2018). Sex in the media, sex on the mind: Linking television use, sexual permissiveness, and

sexual concept accessibility in memory. *Sexuality & Culture, 22*(1), 22–38.

**Dimler, Laura M. & Natsuaki, Misaki N.** (2015). The effects of pubertal timing on externalizing behaviors in adolescence and early adulthood: A meta-analytic review. *Journal of Adolescence, 45*, 160–170.

**Diseth, Åge; Meland, Eivind & Breidablik, Hans J.** (2014). Self-beliefs among students: Grade level and gender differences in self-esteem, self-efficacy and implicit theories of intelligence. *Learning and Individual Differences, 35*.

**Dishion, Thomas J.; Mun, Chung; Ha, Thao & Tein, Jenn-Yun.** (2019). Observed family and friendship dynamics in adolescence: A latent profile approach to identifying "mesosystem" adaptation for intervention tailoring. *Prevention Science, 20*(1), 41–55.

**Dix, Theodore & Yan, Ni.** (2014). Mothers' depressive symptoms and infant negative emotionality in the prediction of child adjustment at age 3: Testing the maternal reactivity and child vulnerability hypotheses. *Development and Psychopathology, 26*(1), 111–124.

**Dobson, Velma; Candy, T. Rowan; Hartmann, E. Eugenie; Mayer, D. Luisa; Miller, Joseph M. & Quinn, Graham E.** (2009). Infant and child vision research: Present status and future directions. *Optometry & Vision Science, 86*(6), 559–560.

**Dominguez-Bello, Maria Gloria; Godoy-Vitorino, Filipa; Knight, Rob & Blaser, Martin J.** (2019). Role of the microbiome in human development. *Gut, 68*(6), 1108–1114.

**Dorn, Lorah D. & Biro, Frank M.** (2011). Puberty and its measurement: A decade in review. *Journal of Research on Adolescence, 21*(1), 180–195.

**Dossou, S. G.; M., Lawani M.; Folly, M.; Tigri, N. & Houeto, G.** (2019). Acquisition of motor skills in 784 Benin infants under one year. *International Journal of Development Research, 9*(15334).

**Dougherty, Rachel.** (2019). *Secret engineer: How Emily Roebling built the Brooklyn Bridge.* Roaring Brook.

**Dow-Edwards, Diana & Silva, Lindsay.** (2017). Endocannabinoids in brain plasticity: Cortical maturation, HPA axis function and behavior. *Brain Research, 1654*(Part B), 157–164.

**Downing, Katherine L.; Hinkley, Trina; Salmon, Jo; Hnatiuk, Jill A. & Hesketh, Kylie D.** (2017). Do the correlates of screen time and sedentary time differ in preschool children? *BMC Public Health, 17*(285).

**Drake, Patrick; Driscoll, Anne K. & Mathews, T. J.** (2018). *Cigarette smoking during pregnancy: United States, 2016.* Hyattsville, MD: National Center for Health Statistics. NCHS Data Brief No. 305.

**Driemeyer, Wiebke; Janssen, Erick; Wiltfang, Jens & Elmerstig, Eva.** (2016). Masturbation experiences of Swedish senior high school students: Gender differences and similarities. *The Journal of Sex Research.*

**Duckworth, Angela L.** (2016). *Grit: The power of passion and perseverance.* Scribner.

**Dugas, Lara R.; Fuller, Miles; Gilbert, Jack & Layden, Brian T.** (2016). The obese gut microbiome across the epidemiologic transition. *Emerging Themes in Epidemiology, 13*(1).

**Duggan, Maeve.** (2017, July 11). *Online harassment 2017. Internet & Technology.* Washington, DC: Pew Research Center.

**Dumas, A.; Simmat-Durand, L. & Lejeune, C.** (2014). Pregnancy and substance use in France: A literature review. *Journal de Gynécologie Obstétrique et Biologie de la Reproduction, 43*(9), 649–656.

**Duncan, Greg J. & Magnuson, Katherine.** (2013). Investing in preschool programs. *Journal of Economic Perspectives, 27*(2), 109–132.

**Dunn, Erin C.; Nishimi, Kristen; Powers, Abigail & Bradley, Bekh.** (2017). Is developmental timing of trauma exposure associated with depressive and post-traumatic stress disorder symptoms in adulthood? *Journal of Psychiatric Research, 84*, 119–127.

**Dunn, Kirsty & Bremner, J. Gavin.** (2017). Investigating looking and social looking measures as an index of infant violation of expectation. *Developmental Science, 20*(6), e12452.

**Dunn, Kirsty & Bremner, James Gavin.** (2019). Investigating the social environment of the A-not-B search task. *Developmental Science,* e12921.

**Dunster, Gideon P.; de la Iglesia, Luciano; Ben-Hamo, Miriam; Nave, Claire; Fleischer, Jason G.; Panda, Satchidananda & de la Iglesia, Horacio O.** (2018). Sleepmore in Seattle: Later school start times are associated with more sleep and better performance in high school students. *Science Advances, 4*(12), eaau6200.

**DuPont, Robert L. & Lieberman, Jeffrey A.** (2014). Young brains on drugs. *Science, 344*(6184), 557.

**Duran, Chelsea A. K.; Cottone, Elizabeth; Ruzek, Erik A.; Mashburn, Andrew J. & Grissmer, David W.** (2019). Family stress processes and children's self-regulation. *Child Development, 91*(2), 577–595.

**Dweck, Carol S.** (2013). Social development. In Zelazo, Philip D. (Ed.), *The Oxford handbook of developmental psychology* (Vol. 2, pp. 167–190). Oxford University Press.

**Dweck, Carol S.** (2017). From needs to goals and representations: Foundations for a unified theory of motivation, personality, and development. *Psychological Review, 124*(6), 689–719.

**Dworkin, A. Gary & Quiroz, Pamela Anne.** (2019). The United States of America: Accountability, high-stakes testing, and the demography of educational inequality. In Stevens, Peter A. J. & Dworkin, A. Gary (Eds.), *The Palgrave handbook of race and ethnic inequalities in education* (2nd ed., pp. 1097–1181). Palgrave Macmillan.

**Eagly, Alice H. & Wood, Wendy.** (2013). The nature–nurture debates: 25 years of challenges in understanding the psychology of gender. *Perspectives on Psychological Science, 8*(3), 340–357.

**Ebert, Susanne.** (2020). Theory of mind, language, and reading: Developmental relations from early childhood to early adolescence. *Journal of Experimental Child Psychology, 191*(104739).

**Eccles, Jacquelynne S. & Roeser, Robert W.** (2010). An ecological view of schools and development. In Meece, Judith L. & Eccles, Jacquelynne S. (Eds.), *Handbook of research on schools, schooling, and human development* (pp. 6–22). Routledge.

**Eccles, Jacquelynne S. & Roeser, Robert W.** (2011). Schools as developmental contexts during adolescence. *Journal of Research on Adolescence, 21*(1), 225–241.

**Edenberg, Howard J.; Gelernter, Joel & Agrawal, Arpana.** (2019). Genetics of alcoholism. *Current Psychiatry Reports, 21*(26).

**Ehrenberg, Rachel.** (2016). GMOs under scrutiny. *Science News, 189*(3), 22–27.

**Ehrlich, Sara Z. & Blum-Kulka, Shoshana.** (2014). 'Now I said that Danny becomes Danny again': A multifaceted view of kindergarten children's peer argumentative discourse. In Cekaite, Asta; Blum-Kulka, Shoshana; Grøver, Vibeke & Teubal, Eva (Eds.), *Children's peer talk: Learning from each other* (pp. 23–41). Cambridge University Press.

**Eisenberg, Nancy & Zhou, Qing.** (2016). Conceptions of executive function and regulation: When and to what degree do they overlap? In Griffin, James A.; McCardle, Peggy & Freund, Lisa S. (Eds.), *Executive function in preschool-age children: Integrating measurement, neurodevelopment, and translational research* (pp. 115–136). American Psychological Association.

**Elicker, James & Ruprecht, Karen M.** (2019). Child care quality rating and improvement systems (QRIS): National experiment for improving early childhood education quality. In Brown, Christopher P.; McMullen, Mary Benson & File, Nancy (Eds.), *The Wiley handbook of early childhood care and education* (pp. 515–536). Wiley.

**Elkind, David.** (1967). Egocentrism in adolescence. *Child Development, 38*(4), 1025–1034.

**Ellefson, Michelle R.; Ng, Florrie Fei-Yin; Wang, Qian & Hughes, Claire.** (2017). Efficiency of executive function: A two-generation cross-cultural comparison of samples from Hong Kong and the United Kingdom. *Psychological Science, 28*(5), 555–566.

**Elliott, Julian & Nicolson, Rod.** (2016). *Dyslexia: Developing the debate.* Bloomsbury.

**Elliott, Sinikka.** (2012). *Not my kid: What parents believe about the sex lives of their teenagers.* New York University Press.

**Ellis, Bruce J. & Boyce, W. Thomas.** (2008). Biological sensitivity to context. *Current Directions in Psychological Science, 17*(3), 183–187.

**Ellis, Bruce J.; Boyce, W. Thomas; Belsky, Jay; Bakermans-kranenburg, Marian J. & Van Ijzendoorn, Marinus H.** (2011a). Differential susceptibility to the environment: An evolutionary–neurodevelopmental theory. *Development and Psychopathology, 23*(1), 7–28.

**Ellis, Bruce J. & Del Giudice, Marco.** (2019). Developmental adaptation to stress: An evolutionary perspective. *Annual Review of Psychology, 70*(1), 111–139.

**Ellis, Bruce J.; Shirtcliff, Elizabeth A.; Boyce, W. Thomas; Deardorff, Julianna & Essex, Marilyn J.** (2011b). Quality of early family relationships and the timing and tempo of puberty: Effects depend on biological sensitivity to context. *Development and Psychopathology, 23*(1), 85–99.

**Ellison, Christopher G.; Musick, Marc A. & Holden, George W.** (2011). Does conservative Protestantism moderate the association between corporal punishment and child outcomes? *Journal of Marriage and Family, 73*(5), 946–961.

**Emery, Carolyn A.** (2018). Injury prevention in kids' adventure and extreme sports: Future directions. *Research in Sports Medicine, 26*(Suppl.1), 199–211.

**Endo, Masaki; Mikami, Masafumi; Endo, Akira; Kaya, Hidetaka; Itoh, Takeshi; Nishimasu, Hiroshi; . . . Toki, Seiichi.** (2019). Genome editing in plants by engineered CRISPR–Cas9 recognizing NG PAM. *Nature Plants, 5*(1), 14–17.

**Engelberts, Adèle C. & de Jonge, Guustaaf Adolf.** (1990). Choice of sleeping position for infants: Possible association with cot death. *Archives of Disease in Childhood, 65*(4), 462–467.

**Engelhardt, Laura E.; Harden, K. Paige; Tucker-Drob, Elliot M. & Church, Jessica A.** (2019). The neural architecture of executive functions is established by middle childhood. *NeuroImage, 185*, 479–489.

**Ennis, Linda Rose.** (2015). *Intensive mothering: The cultural contradictions of modern motherhood.* Demeter Press.

**Erickson, Anders C.; Ostry, Aleck; Chan, Hing Man & Arbour, Laura.** (2016). Air pollution, neighbourhood and maternal-level factors modify the effect of smoking on birth weight: A multilevel analysis in British Columbia, Canada. *BMC Public Health, 16*(1).

**Erikson, Erik H.** (1963). *Childhood and society* (2nd ed.). Norton.

**Erikson, Erik H.** (1968). *Identity: Youth and crisis.* Norton.

**Erikson, Erik H.** (1982). *The life cycle completed: A review.* Norton.

**Erikson, Erik H.** (1993a). *Childhood and society* (2nd ed.). Norton.

**Erikson, Erik H.** (1993b). *Gandhi's truth: On the origins of militant nonviolence.* Norton.

**Erikson, Erik H.** (1994). *Identity: Youth and crisis.* Norton.

**Erikson, Erik H.** (1998). *The life cycle completed.* Norton.

**Ernst, Monique.** (2016). A tribute to the adolescent brain. *Neuroscience & Biobehavioral Reviews, 70*, 334–338.

**Esler, Amy N.; Bal, Vanessa Hus; Guthrie, Whitney; Wetherby, Amy; Weismer, Susan Ellis & Lord, Catherine.** (2015). The autism diagnostic observation schedule, toddler module: Standardized severity scores. *Journal of Autism and Developmental Disorders, 45*, 2704–2720.

**Espy, Kimberly Andrews.** (2016). *Monographs of the society for research in child development: The changing nature of executive control in preschool, 81*(4), 1–179.

**Espy, K. A.; Clark, C. A. C.; Garza, J. P.; Nelson, J. M.; James, T. D. & Choi, H.-J.** (2016). Executive control in preschoolers: New models, new results, new implications. *Monographs of the Society for Research in Child Development, 81*(4), 111–128.

**Eun, Barohny.** (2019). The zone of proximal development as an overarching concept: A framework for synthesizing Vygotsky's theories. *Educational Philosophy and Theory, 51*(1), 18–30.

**Eun, John; Paksarian, Diana; He, Jian-Ping & Merikangas, Kathleen R.** (2018). Parenting style and mental disorders in a nationally representative sample of US adolescents. *Social Psychiatry and Psychiatric Epidemiology, 53*(1), 11–20.

**Evans, Angela D.; Xu, Fen & Lee, Kang.** (2011). When all signs point to you: Lies told in the face of evidence. *Developmental Psychology, 47*(1), 39–49.

**Evans, Gary W. & Kim, Pilyoung.** (2013). Childhood poverty, chronic stress, self-regulation, and coping. *Child Development Perspectives, 7*(1), 43–48.

**Evans, M. D. R.; Kelley, Jonathan; Sikora, Joanna & Treiman, Donald J.** (2010). Family scholarly culture and educational success: Books and schooling in 27 nations. *Research in Social Stratification and Mobility, 28*(2), 171–197.

**Everett, Caleb.** (2017). *Numbers and the making of us: Counting and the course of human cultures.* Harvard University Press.

**Eyer, Diane E.** (1992). *Mother-infant bonding: A scientific fiction.* Yale University Press.

**Fagnani, Jeanne.** (2013). Equal access to quality care: Lessons from France on providing high quality and affordable early childhood education and care. In *Equal access to childcare: Providing quality early childhood education and care to disadvantaged families* (pp. 77–99). Policy Press.

**Fairbank, John; Briggs, Ernestine; Lee, Robert; Corry, Nida; Pflieger, Jacqueline; Gerrity, Ellen; . . . Murphy, Robert.** (2018). Mental health of children of deployed and nondeployed US military service members: The millennium cohort family study. *Journal of Developmental & Behavioral Pediatrics, 39*(9), 683–692.

**Fairhurst, Merle T.; Löken, Line & Grossmann, Tobias.** (2014). Physiological and behavioral responses reveal 9-month-old infants' sensitivity to pleasant touch. *Psychological Science, 25*(5), 1124–1131.

**Fareed, Mohd; Anwar, Malik Azeem & Afzal, Mohammad.** (2015). Prevalence and gene frequency of color vision impairments among children of six populations from North Indian region. *Genes & Diseases, 2*(2), 211–218.

**Farkas, Laura; Cless, Jessica D.; Cless, Adam W.; Nelson Goff, Briana S.; Bodine, Ellen & Edelman, Ashley.** (2019). The ups and downs of Down syndrome: A qualitative study of positive and negative parenting experiences. *Journal of Family Issues, 40*(4), 518–539.

**Fast, Anne A. & Olson, Kristina R.** (2018). Gender development in transgender preschool children. *Child Development, 89*(2), 620–637.

**Fearon, R. M. Pasco & Roisman, Glenn I.** (2017). Attachment theory: Progress and future directions. *Current Opinion in Psychology, 15*, 131–136.

**Feeley, Nancy; Sherrard, Kathyrn; Waitzer, Elana & Boisvert, Linda.** (2013). The father at the bedside: Patterns of involvement in the NICU. *Journal of Perinatal & Neonatal Nursing, 27*(1), 72–80.

**Feld, Barry C.** (2013). *Kids, cops, and confessions: Inside the interrogation room.* New York University Press.

**Feldman, Ruth.** (2012a). Oxytocin and social affiliation in humans. *Hormones and Behavior, 61*(3), 380–391.

**Feldman, Ruth.** (2012b). Parent-infant synchrony: A biobehavioral model of mutual influences in the formation of affiliative bonds. *Monographs of the Society for Research in Child Development, 77*(2), 42–51.

**Feliciano, Cynthia & Rumbaut, Rubén G.** (2018). Varieties of ethnic self-identities: Children of immigrants in middle adulthood. *RSF: The Russell Sage Foundation Journal of the Social Sciences, 4*(5), 26–46.

**Feliciano, Cynthia & Rumbaut, Rubén G.** (2019). The evolution of ethnic identity from adolescence to middle adulthood: The case of the immigrant second generation. *Emerging Adulthood, 7*(2), 85–96.

**Felton, Julia W.; Collado, Anahí; Ingram, Katherine; Lejuez, Carl W. & Yi, Richard.** (2020). Changes in delay discounting, substance use, and weight status across adolescence. *Health Psychology, 39*(5), 413–420.

**Ferguson, Christopher J.** (2013). Spanking, corporal punishment and negative long-term outcomes: A meta-analytic review of longitudinal studies. *Clinical Psychology Review, 33*(1), 196–208.

**Ferguson, Christopher J. & Kilburn, John.** (2010). Much ado about nothing: The misestimation and overinterpretation of violent video game effects in Eastern and Western nations—Comment on Anderson et al. (2010). *Psychological Bulletin, 136*(2), 174–178.

**Ferguson, Kim T. & Evans, Gary W.** (2019). Social ecological theory: Family systems and family psychology in bioecological and bioecocultural perspective. In Fiese, Barbara H. (Ed.), *APA handbook of contemporary family psychology: Foundations, methods, and contemporary issues across the lifespan* (Vol. 1, pp. 143–161). American Psychological Association.

**Fernando, Dulini; Cohen, Laurie & Duberley, Joanne.** (2018). What helps? Women engineers' accounts of staying on. *Human Resource Management Journal, 28*(3), 479–495.

**Ferrari, Marco & Quaresima, Valentina.** (2012). A brief review on the history of human functional near-infrared spectroscopy (fNIRS) development and fields of application. *NeuroImage, 63*(2), 921–935.

**Fewtrell, Mary; Wilson, David C.; Booth, Ian & Lucas, Alan.** (2011). Six months of exclusive breast feeding: How good is the evidence? *BMJ, 342*, c5955.

**Fields, R. Douglas.** (2014). Myelin—More than insulation. *Science, 344*(6181), 264–266.

**Finer, Lawrence B. & Zolna, Mia R.** (2016). Declines in unintended pregnancy in the United States, 2008–2011. *New England Journal of Medicine, 374*, 843–852.

**Fingerman, Karen L.; Berg, Cynthia; Smith, Jacqui & Antonucci, Toni C.** (2011). *Handbook of lifespan development.* Springer.

**Fingerman, Karen L.; Huo, Meng & Birditt, Kira S.** (2020). A decade of research on intergenerational ties: Technological, economic, political, and demographic changes. *Journal of Marriage and Family, 82*(1), 383–403.

**Finn, Amy S.; Kraft, Matthew A.; West, Martin R.; Leonard, Julia A.; Bish, Crystal E.; Martin, Rebecca E.; . . . Gabrieli, John D. E.** (2014). Cognitive skills, student achievement tests, and schools. *Psychological Science, 25*(3), 736–744.

**Finn, Chester E. & Scanlan, Andrew E.** (2019). *Learning in the fast lane: The past, present, and future of advanced placement.* Princeton University Press.

**Fischetti, Mark & Armstrong, Zan.** (2017). The baby spike. *Scientific American, 317*(1), 76.

**Fiset, Sylvain & Plourde, Vickie.** (2013). Object permanence in domestic dogs (*Canis lupus familiaris*) and gray wolves (*Canis lupus*). *Journal of Comparative Psychology, 127*(2), 115–127.

**Fisher, Dorothy Canfield.** (1922). *What grandmother did not know.* Pilgrim Press.

**Flannery, Jessica E.; Beauchamp, Kathryn G. & Fisher, Philip A.** (2017). The role of social buffering on chronic disruptions in quality of care: Evidence from caregiver-based interventions in foster children. *Social Neuroscience, 12*(1), 86–91.

**Fleming, David J.; Cowen, Joshua M.; Witte, John F. & Wolf, Patrick J.** (2015). Similar students, different choices: Who uses a school voucher in an otherwise similar population of students? *Education and Urban Society, 47*(7), 785–812.

**Fletcher, Richard; St. George, Jennifer & Freeman, Emily.** (2013). Rough and tumble play quality: Theoretical foundations for a new measure of father–child interaction. *Early Child Development and Care, 183*(6), 746–759.

**Foo, Koong Hean.** (2019). *Intercultural parenting: How Eastern and Western parenting styles affect child development.* Routledge.

**Forbes, Deborah.** (2012). The global influence of the Reggio Emilia Inspiration. In Kelly, Robert (Ed.), *Educating for creativity: A global conversation* (pp. 161–172). Brush Education.

**Forbes, Thomas A. & Gallo, Vittorio.** (2017). All wrapped up: Environmental effects on myelination. *Trends in Neurosciences, 40*(9), 572–587.

**Forestell, Catherine A. & Mennella, Julie A.** (2017). The relationship between infant facial expressions and food acceptance. *Current Nutrition Reports, 6*(2), 141–147.

**Forster, Myriam; Gower, Amy L.; Gloppen, Kari; Sieving, Renee; Oliphant, Jennifer; Plowman, Shari; . . . McMorris, Barbara J.** (2020). Associations between dimensions of school engagement and bullying victimization and perpetration among middle school students. *School Mental Health, 12*, 296–307.

**Fortin, Andrée; Doucet, Martin & Damant, Dominique.** (2011). Children's appraisals as mediators of the relationship between domestic violence and child adjustment. *Violence and Victims, 26*(3), 377–392.

**Fosco, Gregory M. & LoBraico, Emily J.** (2019). Elaborating on premature adolescent autonomy: Linking variation in daily family processes to developmental risk. *Development and Psychopathology, 31*(5), 1741–1755.

**Foster, Eugene A.; Jobling, Mark A.; Taylor, P. G.; Donnelly, Peter; de Knijff, Peter; Mieremet, Rene; . . . Tyler-Smith, C.** (1998). Jefferson fathered slave's last child. *Nature, 396*(6706), 27–28.

**Foulkes, Lucy & Blakemore, Sarah-Jayne.** (2018). Studying individual differences in human adolescent brain development. *Nature Neuroscience, 21*, 315–323.

**Fox, Ashley; Himmelstein, Georgia; Khalid, Hina & Howell, Elizabeth A.** (2019). Funding for abstinence-only education and adolescent pregnancy prevention: Does state ideology affect outcomes? *American Journal of Public Health,* e1–e8.

**Fox, Molly; Thayer, Zaneta M.; Ramos, Isabel F.; Meskal, Sarah J. & Wadhwa, Pathik D.** (2018). Prenatal and postnatal mother-to-child transmission of acculturation's health effects in Hispanic Americans. *Journal of Women's Health, 27*(8), 154–1063.

**Fox, Nathan A.; Henderson, Heather A.; Marshall, Peter J.; Nichols, Kate E. & Ghera, Melissa M.** (2005). Behavioral inhibition: Linking biology and behavior within a developmental framework. *Annual Review of Psychology, 56*, 235–262.

**Fox, Nathan A.; Henderson, Heather A.; Rubin, Kenneth H.; Calkins, Susan D. & Schmidt, Louis A.** (2001). Continuity and discontinuity of behavioral inhibition and exuberance: Psychophysiological and behavioral influences across the first four years of life. *Child Development, 72*(1), 1–21.

**Fox, Nathan A.; Reeb-Sutherland, Bethany C. & Degnan, Kathryn A.** (2013). Personality and emotional development. In Zelazo, Philip D. (Ed.), *The Oxford handbook of developmental psychology* (Vol. 2, pp. 15–44). Oxford University Press.

**Frankenburg, William K.; Dodds, Josiah; Archer, Philip; Shapiro, Howard & Bresnick, Beverly.** (1992). The Denver II: A major revision and restandardization of the Denver Developmental Screening Test. *Pediatrics, 89*(1), 91–97.

**Frayer, David W.** (2017). Talking hyoids and talking Neanderthals. In Marom, Assaf & Hovers, Erella (Eds.), *Human paleontology and prehistory: Contributions in honor of Yoel Rak* (pp. 233–237). Springer.

**Frazier, A. Lindsay; Camargo, Carlos A.; Malspeis, Susan; Willett, Walter C. & Young, Michael C.** (2014). Prospective study of peripregnancy consumption of peanuts or tree nuts by mothers and the risk of peanut or tree nut allergy in their offspring. *JAMA Pediatrics, 168*(2), 156–162.

**Fredricks, Jennifer A. & Eccles, Jacquelynne S.** (2002). Children's competence and value beliefs from childhood through adolescence: Growth trajectories in two male-sex-typed domains. *Developmental Psychology, 38*(4), 519–533.

**Freeman, Joan.** (2010). *Gifted lives: What happens when gifted children grow up?* Routledge.

**Frémondière, Pierre; Marchal, François; Thollon, Lionel & Saliba-serre, Bérangère.** (2019). Change in head shape of newborn infants in the week following birth: Contributing factors. *Journal of Pediatric Neurology, 17*(5), 168–175.

**Freud, Anna.** (1958). Adolescence. *Psychoanalytic Study of the Child, 13*, 255–278.

**Freud, Anna.** (2000). Adolescence. In McCarthy, James B. (Ed.), *Adolescent development and psychopathology* (pp. 29–52). University Press of America.

**Freud, Anna & Burlingham, Dorothy T.** (1943). *War and children.* Medical War Books.

**Freud, Sigmund.** (1935). *A general introduction to psychoanalysis.* Liveright.

**Freud, Sigmund.** (1938). *The basic writings of Sigmund Freud.* Modern Library.

**Freud, Sigmund.** (1989). *Introductory lectures on psycho-analysis.* Liveright.

**Freud, Sigmund.** (1995). *The basic writings of Sigmund Freud.* Modern Library.

**Freud, Sigmund.** (2001). An outline of psychoanalysis. In *The standard edition of the complete psychological works of Sigmund Freud* (Vol. 23). Vintage.

**Friedman, Naomi P. & Miyake, Akira.** (2017). Unity and diversity of executive functions: Individual differences as a window on cognitive structure. *Cortex, 86*, 186–204.

**Friedman-Krauss, Allison H.; Barnett, W. Steven; Garver, Karin A.; Hodges, Katherine S.; Weisenfeld, G. G. & DiCrecchio, Nicole.** (2019). *The state of preschool 2018: State preschool yearbook.* New Brunswick, NJ: National Institute for Early Education Research.

**Friend, Stephen H. & Schadt, Eric E.** (2014). Clues from the resilient. *Science, 344*(6187), 970–972.

**Fry, Douglas P.** (2014). Environment of evolutionary adaptedness, rough-and-tumble play, and the selection of restraint in human aggression. In Narvaez, Darcia; Valentino, Kristin; Fuentes, Agustin; McKenna, James J. & Gray, Peter (Eds.), *Ancestral landscapes in human evolution: Culture, childrearing and social wellbeing* (pp. 169–188). Oxford University Press.

**Fryar, Cheryl D.; Carroll, Margaret D. & Ogden, Cynthia L.** (2018). *Prevalence of overweight, obesity, and severe obesity among children and adolescents aged 2–19 years: United States, 1963–1965 through 2015–2016. Health E-Stats.* Hyattsville, MD: National Center for Health Statistics.

**Frydenberg, Erica.** (2017). *Coping and the challenge of resilience.* Palgrave.

**Fuller, Bruce & García Coll, Cynthia.** (2010). Learning from Latinos: Contexts, families, and child development in motion. *Developmental Psychology, 46*(3), 559–565.

**Fury, Gail; Carlson, Elizabeth A. & Sroufe, Alan.** (1997). Children's representations of attachment relationships in family drawings. *Child Development, 68*(6), 1154–1164.

**Gad, Rasha F.; Dowling, Donna A.; Abusaad, Fawzia E.; Bassiouny, Mohamed R. & Abd El Aziz, Magda A.** (2019). Oral sucrose versus breastfeeding in managing infants' immunization-related pain: A randomized controlled trial. *MCN, 44*(2), 108–114.

**Gagnon, Émilie; Ratelle, Catherine F.; Guay, Frédéric & Duchesne, Stéphane.** (2019). Developmental trajectories of vocational exploration from adolescence to early adulthood: The role of parental need supporting behaviors. *Journal of Vocational Behavior, 115*, 103338.

**Galak, Jeff; Givi, Julian & Williams, Elanor F.** (2016). Why certain gifts are great to give but not to get: A framework for understanding errors in gift giving. *Current Directions in Psychological Science, 25*(6), 380–385.

**Galasso, Vincenzo; Profeta, Paola; Pronzato, Chiara & Billari, Francesco.** (2017). Information and women's intentions: Experimental evidence about child care. *European Journal of Population, 33*(1), 109–128.

**Gallagher, Annabella; Updegraff, Kimberly; Padilla, Jenny & McHale, Susan M.** (2018). Longitudinal associations between sibling relational aggression and adolescent adjustment. *Journal of Youth and Adolescence, 47*(10), 2100–2113.

**Gallup.** (2017, August). *Time to play: A study on children's free time—how it is spent, prioritized and valued.* Washington, DC: Gallup.

**Galvao, Tais F.; Silva, Marcus T.; Zimmermann, Ivan R.; Souza, Kathiaja M.; Martins, Silvia S. & Pereira, Mauricio G.** (2014). Pubertal timing in girls and depression: A systematic review. *Journal of Affective Disorders, 155*, 13–19.

**Gambaro, Ludovica; Stewart, Kitty & Waldfogel, Jane (Eds.).** (2014). *An equal start?: Providing quality early education and care for disadvantaged children.* Policy Press.

**Ganapathy, Thilagavathy.** (2014). Couvade syndrome among 1st time expectant fathers. *Muller Journal of Medical Science Research, 5*(1), 43–47.

**Ganchimeg, Togoobaatar; Ota, Erika; Morisaki, Naho; Laopaiboon, Malinee; Lumbiganon, P.; Zhang, Jun; . . . Mori, Rintaro.** (2014). Pregnancy and childbirth outcomes among adolescent mothers: A World Health Organization multicountry study. *BJOG, 121*(Suppl. 1), 40–48.

**Gao, Wei; Lin, Weili; Grewen, Karen & Gilmore, John H.** (2017). Functional connectivity of the infant human brain: Plastic and modifiable. *Neuroscientist, 23*(2), 169–184.

**Gardner, Frances; Leijten, Patty; Melendez-Torres, G. J.; Landau, Sabine; Harris, Victoria; Mann, Joanna; . . . Scott, Stephen.** (2019). The earlier the better? Individual participant data and traditional meta-analysis of age effects of parenting interventions. *Child Development, 90*(1), 7–19.

**Gardner, Howard.** (1983). *Frames of mind: The theory of multiple intelligences.* Basic Books.

**Gardner, Howard.** (1999). Are there additional intelligences? The case for naturalist, spiritual, and existential intelligences. In Kane, Jeffrey (Ed.), *Education, information, and transformation: Essays on learning and thinking* (pp. 111–131). Merrill.

**Gardner, Howard.** (2006). *Multiple intelligences: New horizons in theory and practice.* Basic Books.

**Gardner, Howard.** (2011). *Frames of mind: The theory of multiple intelligences.* Basic Books.

**Gardner, Howard & Moran, Seana.** (2006). The science of multiple intelligences theory: A response to Lynn Waterhouse. *Educational Psychologist, 41*(4), 227–232.

**Gariépy, Geneviève; Riehm, Kira E.; Whitehead, Ross D.; Doré, Isabelle & Elgar, Frank J.** (2018). Teenage night owls or early birds? Chronotype and the mental health of adolescents. *Journal of Sleep Research,* e12723.

**Garrett, Mallory.** (2018). "It Gets Better" media campaign and gay youth suicide. In Stewart, Chuck (Ed.), *Lesbian, gay, bisexual, and transgender Americans at risk: Problems and solutions* (pp. 119–128). Praeger.

**Garthus-Niegel, Susan; Ayers, Susan; Martini, Julia; von Soest, Tilmann & Eberhard-Gran, Malin.** (2017). The impact of postpartum post-traumatic stress disorder symptoms on child development: A population-based, 2-year follow-up study. *Psychological Medicine, 47*(1), 161–170.

**Garvis, Susanne; Harju-Luukkainen, Heidi; Sheridan, Sonja & Williams, Pia (Eds.).** (2019). *Nordic families, children and early childhood education.* Palgrave Macmillan.

**Gattario, Kristina Holmqvist & Frisén, Ann.** (2019). From negative to positive body image: Men's and women's journeys from early adolescence to emerging adulthood. *Body Image, 28*, 53–65.

**Ge, Xinting; Shi, Yonggang; Li, Junning; Zhang, Zhonghe; Lin, Xiangtao; Zhan, Jinfeng; . . . Liu, Shuwei.** (2015). Development of the human fetal hippocampal formation during early second trimester. *NeuroImage, 119*, 33–43.

**Gelfand, Amy.** (2018). Episodic syndromes of childhood associated with migraine. *Current Opinion in Neurology, 31*(3), 281–285.

**Gellert, Anna S. & Elbro, Carsten.** (2017). Does a dynamic test of phonological awareness predict early reading difficulties? A longitudinal study from kindergarten through grade 1. *Journal of Learning Disabilities, 50*(3), 227–237.

**Gergely, György & Csibra, Gergely.** (2013). Natural pedagogy. In Banaji, Mahzarin R. & Gelman, Susan A. (Eds.), *Navigating the social world: What infants, children, and other species can teach us.* Oxford University Press.

**Germani, Alessandro; Buratta, Livia; Delvecchio, Elisa & Mazzeschi, Claudia.** (2020). Emerging adults and COVID-19: The role of individualism-collectivism on perceived risks and psychological maladjustment. *International Journal of Environmental Research and Public Health, 17*(10), 3497.

**Gernhardt, Ariane; Keller, Heidi & Rübeling, Hartmut.** (2016). Children's family drawings as expressions of attachment representations across cultures: Possibilities and limitations. *Child Development, 87*(4), 1069–1078.

**Gernhardt, Ariane; Rübeling, Hartmut & Keller, Heidi.** (2013). "This is my family": Differences in children's family drawings across cultures. *Journal of Cross-Cultural Psychology, 44*(7), 1166–1183.

**Gershoff, Elizabeth; Sattler, Kierra M. P & Holden, George W.** (2019). School corporal punishment and its associations with achievement and adjustment. *Journal of Applied Developmental Psychology, 63*, 1–8.

**Gervais, Will M. & Norenzayan, Ara.** (2012). Analytic thinking promotes religious disbelief. *Science, 336*(6080), 493–496.

**Gewertz, Catherine.** (2019, April 9). Which states require an exam to graduate?: An interactive breakdown of states' 2016–17 testing plans. Education Week.

**Gibbons, Ann.** (2012). An evolutionary theory of dentistry. *Science, 336*(6084), 973–975.

**Gibson-Davis, Christina & Rackin, Heather.** (2014). Marriage or carriage? Trends in union context and birth type by education. *Journal of Marriage and Family, 76*(3), 506–519.

**Gidley, Jennifer M.** (2016). *Postformal education: A philosophy for complex futures.* Springer.

**Gilles, Floyd H. & Nelson, Marvin D.** (2012). *The developing human brain: Growth and adversities.* Mac Keith Press.

**Gilligan, Carol.** (1982). *In a different voice: Psychological theory and women's development.* Harvard University Press.

**Gillon, Raanan.** (2015). Defending the four principles approach as a good basis for good medical practice and therefore for good medical ethics. *Journal of Medical Ethics, 41*(1), 111–116.

**Gilmore, John H.; Knickmeyer, Rebecca C. & Gao, Wei.** (2018). Imaging structural and functional brain development in early childhood. *Nature Reviews Neuroscience, 19,* 123–137.

**Gilmour, Heather; Ramage-Morin, Pamela L. & Wong, Suzy L.** (2019). Infant bed sharing in Canada. *Health Reports, 30*(7), 13–19.

**Giubilini, Alberto & Savulescu, Julian.** (2019). Vaccination, risks, and freedom: The seat belt analogy. *Public Health Ethics, 12*(3), 237–249.

**Giumetti, Gary W. & Kowalski, Robin M.** (2015). Cyberbullying matters: Examining the incremental impact of cyberbullying on outcomes over and above traditional bullying in North America. In Navarro, Raúl; Yubero, Santiago & Larrañaga, Elisa (Eds.), *Cyberbullying across the globe: Gender, family, and mental health* (pp. 117–130). Springer.

**Glance, Laurent G.; Dick, Andrew W.; Glantz, Christopher; Wissler, Richard N.; Qian, Feng; Marroquin, Bridget M.; . . . Kellermann, Arthur L.** (2014). Rates of major obstetrical complications vary almost fivefold among US hospitals. *Health Affairs, 33*(8), 1330–1336.

**Glenn, Dana E.; Demir-Lira, Özlem Ece; Gibson, Dominic J.; Congdon, Eliza L. & Levine, Susan C.** (2018). Resilience in mathematics after early brain injury: The roles of parental input and early plasticity. *Developmental Cognitive Neuroscience, 30,* 304–313.

**Glock, Sabine & Kleen, Hannah.** (2019). Attitudes toward students from ethnic minority groups: The roles of preservice teachers' own ethnic backgrounds and teacher efficacy activation. *Studies in Educational Evaluation, 62,* 82–91.

**Goddings, Anne-Lise & Giedd, Jay N.** (2014). Structural brain development during childhood and adolescence. In Gazzaniga, Michael S. & Mangun, George R. (Eds.), *The cognitive neurosciences* (5th ed., pp. 15–22). MIT Press.

**Goddings, Anne-Lise; Heyes, Stephanie Burnett; Bird, Geoffrey; Viner, Russell M. & Blakemore, Sarah-Jayne.** (2012). The relationship between puberty and social emotion processing. *Developmental Science, 15*(6), 801–811.

**Goddings, Anne Lise; Beltz, Adriene; Peper, Jiska S.; Crone, Eveline A. & Braams, Barbara R.** (2019). Understanding the role of puberty in structural and functional development of the adolescent brain. *Journal of Research on Adolescence, 29*(1), 32–53.

**Godfrey, Erin B.; Santos, Carlos E. & Burson, Esther.** (2019). For better or worse? System-justifying beliefs in sixth-grade predict trajectories of self-esteem and behavior across early adolescence. *Child Development, 90*(1), 180–195.

**Godinet, Meripa T.; Li, Fenfang & Berg, Teresa.** (2014). Early childhood maltreatment and trajectories of behavioral problems: Exploring gender and racial differences. *Child Abuse & Neglect, 38*(3), 544–556.

**Golden, Neville H.; Yang, Wei; Jacobson, Marc S.; Robinson, Thomas N. & Shaw, Gary M.** (2012). Expected body weight in adolescents: Comparison between weight-for-stature and BMI methods. *Pediatrics, 130*(6), e1607–e1613.

**Golden, Rachel Lynn; Furman, Wyndol & Collibee, Charlene.** (2016). The risks and rewards of sexual debut. *Developmental Psychology, 52*(11), 1913–1925.

**Goldin-Meadow, Susan.** (2015). From action to abstraction: Gesture as a mechanism of change. *Developmental Review, 38,* 167–184.

**Goldin-Meadow, Susan & Alibali, Martha W.** (2013). Gesture's role in speaking, learning, and creating language. *Annual Review of Psychology, 64,* 257–283.

**Goldstein, Thalia R. & Lerner, Matthew D.** (2018). Dramatic pretend play games uniquely improve emotional control in young children. *Developmental Science, 21*(4), e12603.

**Golinkoff, Roberta M. & Hirsh-Pasek, Kathy.** (2016). *Becoming brilliant: What science tells us about raising successful children.* American Psychological Association.

**Golinkoff, Roberta Michnick; Hoff, Erika; Rowe, Meredith L.; Tamis-Lemonda, Catherine S. & Hirsh-Pasek, Kathy.** (2019). Language matters: Denying the existence of the 30-million-word gap has serious consequences. *Child Development, 90*(3), 985–992.

**Göncü, Artin & Gaskins, Suzanne.** (2011). Comparing and extending Piaget's and Vygotsky's understandings of play: Symbolic play as individual, sociocultural, and educational interpretation. In Pellegrini, Anthony D. (Ed.), *The Oxford handbook of the development of play* (pp. 48–57). Oxford University Press.

**Goodlad, James K.; Marcus, David K. & Fulton, Jessica J.** (2013). Lead and Attention-deficit/hyperactivity disorder (ADHD) symptoms: A meta-analysis. *Clinical Psychology Review, 33*(3), 417–425.

**Goodman, R.; Meltzer, H. & Bailey, V.** (1998). The strengths and difficulties questionnaire: A pilot study on the validity of the self-report version. *European Child & Adolescent Psychiatry, 7*(3), 125–130.

**Gopnik, Alison.** (2001). Theories, language, and culture: Whorf without wincing. In Bowerman, Melissa & Levinson, Stephen C. (Eds.), *Language acquisition and conceptual development* (pp. 45–69). Cambridge University Press.

**Gopnik, Alison.** (2012). Scientific thinking in young children: Theoretical advances, empirical research, and policy implications. *Science, 337*(6102), 1623–1627.

**Gopnik, Alison.** (2016). *The gardener and the carpenter: What the new science of child development tells us about the relationship between parents and children.* Farrar, Strauss and Giroux.

**Gopnik, Alison; Meltzoff, Andrew N. & Kuhl, Patricia K.** (1999). *The scientist in the crib: Minds, brains, and how children learn.* William Morrow.

**Gordon, Linda.** (2017). *The second coming of the KKK: The Ku Klux Klan of the 1920s and the American political tradition.* Liveright.

**Gordon-Hollingsworth, Arlene T.; Becker, Emily M.; Ginsburg, Golda S.; Keeton, Courtney; Compton, Scott N.; Birmaher, Boris B.; . . . March, John S.** (2015). Anxiety disorders in Caucasian and African American children: A comparison of clinical characteristics, treatment process variables, and treatment outcomes. *Child Psychiatry & Human Development, 46*(5), 643–655.

**Gorham, Lisa S.; Jernigan, Terry; Hudziak, Jim & Barch, Deanna M.** (2019). Involvement in sports, hippocampal volume, and depressive symptoms in children. *Biological Psychiatry, 4*(5), 484–492.

**Gostin, Lawrence; Phelan, Alexandra; Coutinho, Alex Godwin; Eccleston-Turner, Mark; Erondu, Ngozi; Filani, Oyebanji; . . . Kavanagh, Matthew.** (2019). Ebola in the Democratic Republic of the Congo: Time to sound a global alert? *The Lancet, 393*(10172), 617–620.

**Gottesman, Irving I.; Laursen, Thomas Munk; Bertelsen, Aksel & Mortensen, Preben Bo.** (2010). Severe mental disorders in offspring with 2 psychiatrically ill parents. *Archives of General Psychiatry, 67*(3), 252–257.

**Gough, Ethan K.; Moodie, Erica E. M.; Prendergast, Andrew J.; Johnson, Sarasa M. A.; Humphrey, Jean H.; Stoltzfus, Rebecca J.; . . . Manges, Amee R.** (2014). The impact of antibiotics on growth in children in low and middle income countries: Systematic review and meta-analysis of randomised controlled trials. *BMJ, 348,* g2267.

**Grabell, Adam S.; Huppert, Theodore J.; Fishburn, Frank A.; Li, Yanwei; Hlutkowsky, Christina O.; Jones, Hannah M.; . . . Perlman, Susan B.** (2019). Neural correlates of early deliberate emotion regulation: Young children's responses to interpersonal scaffolding. *Developmental Cognitive Neuroscience, 40*(100708).

**Grady, Jessica Stoltzfus & Hastings, Paul D.** (2018). Becoming prosocial peers: The roles of temperamental shyness and mothers' and fathers' elaborative emotion language. *Social Development, 27*(4), 858–875.

**Grady, Sarah.** (2017, September 26). A fresh look at homeschooling in the U.S. *NCES Blog.* Institute of Education Sciences.

**Gredebäck, Gustaf; Astor, Kim & Fawcett, Christine.** (2018). Gaze following is not dependent on ostensive cues: A critical test of natural pedagogy. *Child Development, 89*(6), 2091–2098.

**Green, James A.; Whitney, Pamela G. & Potegal, Michael.** (2011). Screaming, yelling, whining, and crying: Categorical and intensity differences in vocal expressions of anger and sadness in children's tantrums. *Emotion, 11*(5), 1124–1133.

**Greene, Melissa L. & Way, Niobe.** (2005). Self-esteem trajectories among ethnic minority adolescents: A growth curve analysis of the patterns and predictors of change. *Journal of Research on Adolescence, 15*(2), 151–178.

**Greenough, William T.; Black, James E. & Wallace, Christopher S.** (1987). Experience and brain development. *Child Development, 58*(3), 539–559.

**Greenough, William T. & Volkmar, Fred R.** (1973). Pattern of dendritic branching in occipital cortex of rats reared in complex environments. *Experimental Neurology, 40*(2), 491–504.

**Gregory, Robert.** (1993). *Diz: The story of Dizzy Dean and baseball during the Great Depression.* Penguin.

**Griffin, James A.; McCardle, Peggy & Freund, Lisa S. (Eds.).** (2016). *Executive function in preschool-age children: Integrating measurement, neurodevelopment, and translational research.* American Psychological Association.

**Grivell, Rosalie M.; Reilly, Aimee J.; Oakey, Helena; Chan, Annabelle & Dodd, Jodie M.** (2012). Maternal and neonatal outcomes following induction of labor: A cohort study. *Acta Obstetricia et Gynecologica Scandinavica, 91*(2), 198–203.

**Grogan-Kaylor, Andrew; Ma, Julie & Graham-Bermann, Sandra A.** (2018). The case against physical punishment. *Current Opinion in Psychology, 19*, 22–27.

**Groh, Ashley M.; Narayan, Angela J.; Bakermans-Kranenburg, Marian J.; Roisman, Glenn I.; Vaughn, Brian E.; Fearon, R. M. Pasco & van IJzendoorn, Marinus H.** (2017). Attachment and temperament in the early life course: A meta-analytic review. *Child Development, 88*(3), 770–795.

**Groh, Ashley M.; Roisman, Glenn I.; van IJzendoorn, Marinus H.; Bakermans-Kranenburg, Marian J. & Fearon, R. Pasco.** (2012). The significance of insecure and disorganized attachment for children's internalizing symptoms: A meta-analytic study. *Child Development, 83*(2), 591–610.

**Grönqvist, Hans; Nilsson, J. Peter & Robling, Per Olof.** (2014). *Childhood lead exposure and criminal behavior: Lessons from the Swedish phase-out of leaded gasoline.* Stockholm: Swedish Institute for Social Research. Working Paper 9/2014.

**Grossman, Matthew; Seashore, Carl & Holmes, Alison V.** (2017). Neonatal abstinence syndrome management: A review of recent evidence. *Reviews on Recent Clinical Trials, 12*(4), 226–232.

**Grossmann, Tobias.** (2013). Mapping prefrontal cortex functions in human infancy. *Infancy, 18*(3), 303–324.

**Grossmann, Tobias.** (2017). The eyes as windows into other minds: An integrative perspective. *Perspectives on Psychological Science, 12*(1), 107–121.

**Grotevant, Harold D. & McDermott, Jennifer M.** (2014). Adoption: Biological and social processes linked to adaptation. *Annual Review of Psychology, 65*, 235–265.

**Gruber, Staci A.; Sagar, Kelly A.; Dahlgren, Mary K.; Gonenc, Atilla; Smith, Rosemary T.; Lambros, Ashley M.; . . . Lukas, Scott E.** (2018). The grass might be greener: Medical marijuana patients exhibit altered brain activity and improved executive function after 3 months of treatment. *Frontiers in Pharmacology, 8*(1), 983.

**Grusec, Joan E.; Danyliuk, Tanya; Kil, Hali & O'Neill, David.** (2017). Perspectives on parent discipline and child outcomes. *International Journal of Behavioral Development, 41*(4), 465–471.

**Guassi Moreira, João F. & Telzer, Eva H.** (2018). Family conflict is associated with longitudinal changes in insular-striatal functional connectivity during adolescent risk taking under maternal influence. *Developmental Science, 21*(5), e12632.

**Guerra, Nancy G.; Williams, Kirk R. & Sadek, Shelly.** (2011). Understanding bullying and victimization during childhood and adolescence: A mixed methods study. *Child Development, 82*(1), 295–310.

**Guerri, Consuelo & Pascual, María.** (2010). Mechanisms involved in the neurotoxic, cognitive, and neurobehavioral effects of alcohol consumption during adolescence. *Alcohol, 44*(1), 15–26.

**Gulbas, L. E.; Zayas, L. H.; Yoon, H.; Szlyk, H.; Aguilar-Gaxiola, S. & Natera, G.** (2016). Deportation experiences and depression among U.S. citizen-children with undocumented Mexican parents. *Child, 42*(2), 220–230.

**Gutierrez-Galve, Leticia; Stein, Alan; Hanington, Lucy; Heron, Jon & Ramchandani, Paul.** (2015). Paternal depression in the postnatal period and child development: Mediators and moderators. *Pediatrics, 135*(2), e339–e347.

**Guyer, Amanda E.; Pérez-Edgar, Koraly & Crone, Eveline A.** (2018). Opportunities for neurodevelopmental plasticity from infancy through early adulthood. *Child Development, 89*(3), 687–697.

**Guyon-Harris, Katherine L.; Humphreys, Kathryn L.; Fox, Nathan A.; Nelson, Charles A. & Zeanah, Charles H.** (2018). Course of disinhibited social engagement disorder from early childhood to early adolescence. *Journal of the American Academy of Child & Adolescent Psychiatry, 57*(5), 329–335.e2.

**Guzman, Natalie S. de & Nishina, Adrienne.** (2014). A longitudinal study of body dissatisfaction and pubertal timing in an ethnically diverse adolescent sample. *Body Image, 11*(1), 68–71.

**Habibi, Assal; Damasio, Antonio; Ilari, Beatriz; Sachs, Matthew Elliott & Damasio, Hanna.** (2018). Music training and child development: A review of recent findings from a longitudinal study. *Annals of the New York Academy of Sciences, 1423*(1), 73–81.

**Haden, Catherine A.** (2010). Talking about science in museums. *Child Development Perspectives, 4*(1), 62–67.

**Haidt, Jonathan.** (2013). *The righteous mind: Why good people are divided by politics and religion.* Vintage Books.

**Halberda, Justin.** (2018). Logic in babies. *Science, 359*(6381), 1214–1215.

**Hales, Craig M.; Carroll, Margaret D.; Fryar, Cheryl D. & Ogden, Cynthia L.** (2017, October). *Prevalence of obesity among adults and youth: United States, 2015–2016.* Atlanta, GA: Centers for Disease Control and Prevention, National Center for Health Statistics.

**Halim, May Ling; Ruble, Diane N.; Tamis-LeMonda, Catherine S.; Zosuls, Kristina M.; Lurye, Leah E. & Greulich, Faith K.** (2014). Pink frilly dresses and the avoidance of all things "girly": Children's appearance rigidity and cognitive theories of gender development. *Developmental Psychology, 50*(4), 1091–1101.

**Hall, Matthew L.; Eigsti, Inge-Marie; Bortfeld, Heather & Lillo-Martin, Diane.** (2017). Auditory deprivation does not impair executive function, but language deprivation might: Evidence from a parent-report measure in deaf native signing children. *Journal of Deaf Studies and Deaf Education, 22*(1), 9–21.

**Hall, William J.; Jones, Benjamin L. H.; Witkemper, Kristen D.; Collins, Tora L. & Rodgers, Grayson K.** (2019). State policy on school-based sex education: A content analysis focused on sexual behaviors, relationships, and identities. *American Journal of Health Behavior, 43*(3), 506–519.

**Hallers-Haalboom, Elizabeth T.; Mesman, Judi; Groeneveld, Marleen G.; Endendijk, Joyce J.; van Berkel, Sheila R.; van der Pol, Lotte D. & Bakermans-Kranenburg, Marian J.** (2014). Mothers, fathers, sons and daughters: Parental sensitivity in families with two children. *Journal of Family Psychology, 28*(2), 138–147.

**Halperin, Jeffrey M. & Healey, Dione M.** (2011). The influences of environmental enrichment, cognitive enhancement, and physical exercise on brain development: Can we alter the developmental trajectory of ADHD? *Neuroscience & Biobehavioral Reviews, 35*(3), 621–634.

**Haltigan, John D.; Roisman, Glenn I.; Groh, Ashley M.; Holland, Ashley S.; Booth-Laforce, Cathryn; Rogosch, Fred A. & Cicchetti, Dante.** (2019). Antecedents of attachment states of mind in normative-risk and high-risk caregiving: Cross-race and cross-sex generalizability in two longitudinal studies. *Journal of Child Psychology and Psychiatry, 60*(12), 1309–1322.

**Hamada, Hirotaka & Matthews, Stephen G.** (2019). Prenatal programming of stress responsiveness and behaviours: Progress and perspectives. *Journal of Neuroendocrinology, 31*(3), e12674.

**Hambrick, David Z.; Burgoyne, Alexander P.; Macnamara, Brooke N. & Ullén, Fredrik.** (2018). Toward a multifactorial model of expertise: Beyond born versus made. *Annals of the New York Academy of Sciences, 1423*1(1), 284–295.

**Hamerton, John L. & Evans, Jane A.** (2005). Sex chromosome anomalies. In Butler, Merlin G. & Meaney, F. John (Eds.), *Genetics of developmental disabilities* (pp. 585–650). Taylor & Francis.

**Hamilton, Alice.** (1914). Lead poisoning in the United States. *American Journal of Public Health, 4*(6), 477–480.

**Hamlat, Elissa J.; Shapero, Benjamin G.; Hamilton, Jessica L.; Stange, Jonathan P.;**

**Abramson, Lyn Y. & Alloy, Lauren B.** (2014a). Pubertal timing, peer victimization, and body esteem differentially predict depressive symptoms in African American and Caucasian girls. *Journal of Early Adolescence, 35*(2), 378–402.

**Hamlat, Elissa J.; Snyder, Hannah R.; Young, Jami F. & Hankin, Benjamin L.** (2019). Pubertal timing as a transdiagnostic risk for psychopathology in youth. *Clinical Psychological Science, 7*(3), 411–429.

**Hamlat, Elissa J.; Stange, Jonathan P.; Abramson, Lyn Y. & Alloy, Lauren B.** (2014b). Early pubertal timing as a vulnerability to depression symptoms: Differential effects of race and sex. *Journal of Abnormal Child Psychology, 42*(4), 527–538.

**Hamlett, Eric D.; Ledreux, Aurélie; Potter, Huntington; Chial, Heidi J.; Patterson, David; Espinosa, Joaquin M.; . . . Granholm, Ann-Charlotte.** (2018). Exosomal biomarkers in Down syndrome and Alzheimer's disease. *Free Radical Biology and Medicine, 114*, 110–121.

**Hang, Haiming; Davies, Iain & Schüring, Jennifer.** (2020). Children's conformity to social norms to eat healthy: A developmental perspective. *Social Science & Medicine, 244*(112666).

**Hanna-Attisha, Mona; LaChance, Jenny; Sadler, Richard Casey & Schnepp, Allison Champney.** (2016). Elevated blood lead levels in children associated with the Flint drinking water crisis: A spatial analysis of risk and public health response. *American Journal of Public Health, 106*(2), 283–290.

**Hannon, Erin E.; Schachner, Adena & Nave-Blodgett, Jessica E.** (2017). Babies know bad dancing when they see it: Older but not younger infants discriminate between synchronous and asynchronous audiovisual musical displays. *Journal of Experimental Child Psychology, 159*, 159–174.

**Hanushek, Eric A.; Piopiunik, Marc & Wiederhold, Simon.** (2019). Do smarter teachers make smarter students? International evidence on teacher cognitive skills and student performance. *Education Next, 19*(2).

**Hanushek, Eric A. & Woessmann, Ludger.** (2007). *The role of education quality in economic growth. World Bank Policy Research Working Paper No. 4122.* Washington, DC: World Bank.

**Hanushek, Eric A. & Woessmann, Ludger.** (2015). *The knowledge capital of nations: Education and the economics of growth.* MIT Press.

**Harden, K. Paige & Tucker-Drob, Elliot M.** (2011). Individual differences in the development of sensation seeking and impulsivity during adolescence: Further evidence for a dual systems model. *Developmental Psychology, 47*(3), 739–746.

**Hari, Riitta.** (2017). From brain–environment connections to temporal dynamics and social interaction: Principles of human brain function. *Neuron, 94*(5), 1033–1039.

**Harkness, Sara.** (2014). Is biology destiny for the whole family? Contributions of evolutionary life history and behavior genetics to family theories. *Journal of Family Theory & Review, 6*(1), 31–34.

**Harkness, Sara; Super, Charles M. & Mavridis, Caroline J.** (2011). Parental ethnotheories about children's socioemotional development. In Chen,

Xinyin & Rubin, Kenneth H. (Eds.), *Socioemotional development in cultural context* (pp. 73–98). Guilford Press.

**Harper, Casandra E. & Yeung, Fanny.** (2013). Perceptions of institutional commitment to diversity as a predictor of college students' openness to diverse perspectives. *The Review of Higher Education, 37*(1), 25–44.

**Harris, Cheryl M.** (2019). Quitting science: Factors that influence exit from the stem workforce. *Journal of Women and Minorities in Science and Engineering, 25*(2), 93–118.

**Harris Insights and Analytics.** (2020, June). *Teen mental health.* New York, NY: Harris Interactive.

**Harris, Judith R.** (1998). *The nurture assumption: Why children turn out the way they do.* Free Press.

**Harris, Judith R.** (2002). Beyond the nurture assumption: Testing hypotheses about the child's environment. In Borkowski, John G.; Ramey, Sharon Landesman & Bristol-Power, Marie (Eds.), *Parenting and the child's world: Influences on academic, intellectual, and social-emotional development* (pp. 3–20). Erlbaum.

**Harris, Michelle A.; Wetzel, Eunike; Robins, Richard W.; Donnellan, M. Brent & Trzesniewski, Kali H.** (2017). The development of global and domain self-esteem from ages 10 to 16 for Mexican-origin youth. *International Journal of Behavioral Development.*

**Harrison, Kristen; Bost, Kelly K.; McBride, Brent A.; Donovan, Sharon M.; Grigsby-Toussaint, Diana S.; Kim, Juhee; . . . Jacobsohn, Gwen Costa.** (2011). Toward a developmental conceptualization of contributors to overweight and obesity in childhood: The Six-Cs model. *Child Development Perspectives, 5*(1), 50–58.

**Harrison, Linda J.; Elwick, Sheena; Vallotton, Claire D. & Kappler, Gregor.** (2014). Spending time with others: A time-use diary for infant-toddler child care. In Harrison, Linda J. & Sumsion, Jennifer (Eds.), *Lived spaces of infant-toddler education and care: Exploring diverse perspectives on theory, research and practice* (pp. 59–74). Springer.

**Hart, Betty & Risley, Todd R.** (1995). *Meaningful differences in the everyday experience of young American children.* P. H. Brookes.

**Hart, Daniel & Van Goethem, Anne.** (2017). The role of civic and political participation in successful early adulthood. In Padilla-Walker, Laura M. & Nelson, Larry J. (Eds.), *Flourishing in emerging adulthood: Positive development during the third decade of life* (pp. 139–166). Oxford University Press.

**Harter, Susan.** (2012). *The construction of the self: Developmental and sociocultural foundations* (2nd ed.). Guilford Press.

**Hartig, Hannah & Geiger, Abigail.** (2018, October 8). *About six-in-ten Americans support marijuana legalization. Fact Tank.* Washington, DC: Pew Research Center.

**Hartley, Catherine A. & Somerville, Leah H.** (2015). The neuroscience of adolescent decision-making. *Current Opinion in Behavioral Sciences, 5*, 108–115.

**Hasson, Ramzi & Fine, Jodene Goldenring.** (2012). Gender differences among children with

ADHD on continuous performance tests: A meta-analytic review. *Journal of Attention Disorders, 16*(3), 190–198.

**Hatch, J. Amos.** (2012). From theory to curriculum: Developmental theory and its relationship to curriculum and instruction in early childhood education. In File, Nancy; Mueller, Jennifer J. & Wisneski, Debora B. (Eds.), *Curriculum in early childhood education: Re-examined, rediscovered, renewed.* Routledge.

**Hayden, Elizabeth P. & Mash, Eric J.** (2014). Child psychopathology: A developmental-systems perspective. In Mash, Eric J. & Barkley, Russell A. (Eds.), *Child psychopathology* (3rd ed., pp. 3–72). Guilford Press.

**Hayes, Peter.** (2013). International adoption, "early" puberty, and underrecorded age. *Pediatrics, 131*(6), 1029–1031.

**Hayne, Harlene; Scarf, Damian & Imuta, Kana.** (2015). Childhood memories. In Wright, James D. (Ed.), *International encyclopedia of the social & behavioral sciences* (2nd ed., pp. 465–470). Elsevier.

**Hayne, Harlene & Simcock, Gabrielle.** (2009). Memory development in toddlers. In Courage, Mary L. & Cowan, Nelson (Eds.), *The development of memory in infancy and childhood* (2nd ed., pp. 43–68). Psychology Press.

**Haynie, Dana L.; Soller, Brian & Williams, Kristi.** (2014). Anticipating early fatality: Friends', schoolmates' and individual perceptions of fatality on adolescent risk behaviors. *Journal of Youth and Adolescence, 43*(2), 175–192.

**Heitzer, Andrew M.; Piercy, Jamie C.; Peters, Brittany N.; Mattes, Allyssa M.; Klarr, Judith M.; Batton, Beau; . . . Raz, Sarah.** (2020). Cumulative antenatal risk and kindergarten readiness in preterm-born preschoolers. *Journal of Abnormal Child Psychology, 48*(1), 1–12.

**Hemingway, Susan J. Astley; M. Bledsoe, Julia; K. Davies, Julian; Brooks, Allison; Jirikowic, Tracy; M. Olson, Erin & C. Thorne, John.** (2019). Twin study confirms virtually identical prenatal alcohol exposures can lead to markedly different fetal alcohol spectrum disorder outcomes-fetal genetics influences fetal vulnerability. *Advances in Pediatric Research, 5*(23).

**Henderson, Heather A.; Pine, Daniel S. & Fox, Nathan A.** (2015). Behavioral inhibition and developmental risk: A dual-processing perspective. *Neuropsychopharmacology Reviews, 40*(1), 207–224.

**Hendlin, Yogi Hale.** (2019). I am a fake loop: The effects of advertising-based artificial selection. *Biosemiotics, 12*(1), 131–156.

**Hentges, Rochelle F. & Wang, Ming-Te.** (2018). Gender differences in the developmental cascade from harsh parenting to educational attainment: An evolutionary perspective. *Child Development, 89*(2), 397–413.

**Herholz, Sibylle C. & Zatorre, Robert J.** (2012). Musical training as a framework for brain plasticity: Behavior, function, and structure. *Neuron, 76*(3), 486–502.

**Hernández, Maciel M.; Robins, Richard W.; Widaman, Keith F. & Conger, Rand D.** (2017). Ethnic pride, self-esteem, and school belonging:

A reciprocal analysis over time. *Developmental Psychology*, 53(12), 2384–2396.

**Herrmann, Julia; Schmidt, Isabelle; Kessels, Ursula & Preckel, Franzis.** (2016). Big fish in big ponds: Contrast and assimilation effects on math and verbal self-concepts of students in within-school gifted tracks. *British Journal of Educational Psychology*, 86(2), 222–240.

**Herschensohn, Julia R.** (2007). *Language development and age.* Cambridge University Press.

**Hewer, Mariko.** (2014). Selling sweet nothings: Science shows food marketing's effects on children's minds—and appetites. *Observer*, 27(10).

**Heyer, Djai B. & Meredith, Rhiannon M.** (2017). Environmental toxicology: Sensitive periods of development and neurodevelopmental disorders. *NeuroToxicology*, 58, 23–41.

**Heyes, Cecilia.** (2016). Who knows? Metacognitive social learning strategies. *Trends in Cognitive Sciences*, 20(3), 204–213.

**Heyes, Cecilia.** (2018). Empathy is not in our genes. *Neuroscience and Biobehavioral Reviews*, 95, 499–507.

**Heyman, Gail D.; Li Zhao, Brian J. & Compton, Kang Lee.** (2019). Dishonesty in young children. In Bucciol, Alessandro & Montinari, Natalia (Eds.), *Dishonesty in behavioral economics* (pp. 7–29). Academic Press.

**Hidalgo, Marco A. & Chen, Diane.** (2019). Experiences of gender minority stress in cisgender parents of transgender/gender-expansive prepubertal children: A qualitative study. *Journal of Family Issues*, 40(7), 865–886.

**Hilgard, Joseph; Engelhardt, Christopher R. & Rouder, Jeffrey N. (2017).** Overstated evidence for short-term effects of violent games on affect and behavior: A reanalysis of Anderson et al. (2010). *Psychological Bulletin*, 143(7), 757–774.

**Hill, Patrick L.; Duggan, Peter M. & Lapsley, Daniel K.** (2012). Subjective invulnerability, risk behavior, and adjustment in early adolescence. *Journal of Early Adolescence*, 32(4), 489–501.

**Hill, Patrick L.; Jackson, Joshua J.; Roberts, Brent W.; Lapsley, Daniel K. & Brandenberger, Jay W.** (2011). Change you can believe in: Changes in goal setting during emerging and young adulthood predict later adult well-being. *Social Psychological and Personality Science*, 2(2), 123–131.

**Hill, Sarah E.; Prokosch, Marjorie L.; DelPriore, Danielle J.; Griskevicius, Vladas & Kramer, Andrew.** (2016). Low childhood socioeconomic status promotes eating in the absence of energy need. *Psychological Science*, 27(3), 354–364.

**Hillman, Charles H.** (2014). An introduction to the relation of physical activity to cognitive and brain health, and scholastic achievement. *Monographs of the Society for Research in Child Development*, 79(4), 1–6.

**Hindman, Annemarie H.; Wasik, Barbara A. & Bradley, Donald E.** (2019). How classroom conversations unfold: Exploring teacher-child exchanges during shared book reading. *Early Education and Development*, 30(4), 478–495.

**Hinnant, J. Benjamin; Nelson, Jackie A.; O'Brien, Marion; Keane, Susan P. & Calkins, Susan D.** (2013). The interactive roles of parenting, emotion regulation and executive functioning in moral reasoning during middle childhood. *Cognition and Emotion*, 27(8), 1460–1468.

**Hinton, Lisa; Dumelow, Carol; Rowe, Rachel & Hollowell, Jennifer.** (2018). Birthplace choices: What are the information needs of women when choosing where to give birth in England? A qualitative study using online and face to face focus groups. *BMC Pregnancy and Childbirth*, 18(1).

**Hirsh-Pasek, Kathy & Golinkoff, Roberta M.** (2016, March 11). The preschool paradox: It's time to rethink our approach to early education [Review of the book *The importance of being little: What preschoolers really need from grownups*, by Erika Christakis]. *Science*, 351(6278), 1158.

**Hirth, Jacqueline.** (2019). Disparities in HPV vaccination rates and HPV prevalence in the United States: A review of the literature. *Human Vaccines & Immunotherapeutics*, 15(1), 146–155.

**Hisler, Garrett; Twenge, Jean M. & Krizan, Zlatan.** (2020). Associations between screen time and short sleep duration among adolescents varies by media type: Evidence from a cohort study. *Sleep Medicine*, 66, 92–102.

**Hitlin, Paul.** (2018, September 28). *Internet, social media use and device ownership in U.S. have plateaued after years of growth.* Washington, DC: Pew Research Center.

**Ho, Emily S.** (2010). Measuring hand function in the young child. *Journal of Hand Therapy*, 23(3), 323–328.

**Hodge, Samuel R.; Sato, Takahiro; Mukoyama, Takahito & Kozub, Francis M.** (2013). Development of the physical educators' judgments about inclusion instrument for Japanese physical education majors and an analysis of their judgments. *International Journal of Disability, Development and Education*, 60(4), 332–346.

**Hodson, Gordon; Crisp, Richard J.; Meleady, Rose & Earle, Megan.** (2018). Intergroup contact as an agent of cognitive liberalization. *Perspectives on Psychological Science*, 13(5), 523–548.

**Hoehl, Stefanie; Keupp, Stefanie; Schleihauf, Hanna; Mcguigan, Nicola; Buttelmann, David & Whiten, Andrew.** (2019). 'Over-imitation': A review and appraisal of a decade of research. *Developmental Review*, 51, 90–108.

**Hofer, Claire; Eisenberg, Nancy; Spinrad, Tracy L.; Morris, Amanda S.; Gershoff, Elizabeth; Valiente, Carlos; . . . Eggum, Natalie D.** (2013). Mother-adolescent conflict: Stability, change, and relations with externalizing and internalizing behavior problems. *Social Development*, 22(2), 259–279.

**Hoff, Erika.** (2013). Interpreting the early language trajectories of children from low-SES and language minority homes: Implications for closing achievement gaps. *Developmental Psychology*, 49(1), 4–14.

**Hoffman, Jessica L.; Teale, William H. & Paciga, Kathleen A.** (2014). Assessing vocabulary learning in early childhood. *Journal of Early Childhood Literacy*, 14(4), 459–481.

**Hogan, Jillian; Cordes, Sara; Holochwost, Steven; Ryu, Ehri; Diamond, Adele & Winner, Ellen.** (2018). Is more time in general music class associated with stronger extra-musical outcomes in kindergarten? *Early Childhood Research Quarterly*, 45, 238–248.

**Holden, Constance.** (2010). Myopia out of control. *Science*, 327(5961), 17.

**Holzer, Jessica; Canavan, Maureen & Bradley, Elizabeth.** (2014). County-level correlation between adult obesity rates and prevalence of dentists. *JADA*, 145(9), 932–939.

**Hong, David S. & Reiss, Allan L.** (2014). Cognitive and neurological aspects of sex chromosome aneuploidies. *The Lancet Neurology*, 13(3), 306–318.

**Hood, Michelle; Creed, Peter A. & Mills, Bianca J.** (2017). Loneliness and online friendships in emerging adults. *Personality and Individual Differences*.

**Hoover, Eric.** (2020, May 21). Golden State blockbuster: U. of California will replace ACT and SAT with new test—or None at all. *Chronicle of Higher Education*.

**Horn, Stacey S.** (2019). Sexual orientation and gender identity-based prejudice. *Child Development Perspectives*, 13(1), 21–27.

**Horton, Megan K.; Kahn, Linda G.; Perera, Frederica; Barr, Dana B. & Rauh, Virginia.** (2012). Does the home environment and the sex of the child modify the adverse effects of prenatal exposure to chlorpyrifos on child working memory? *Neurotoxicology and Teratology*, 34(5), 534–541.

**Hostinar, Camelia E.; Nusslock, Robin & Miller, Gregory E.** (2018). Future directions in the study of early-life stress and physical and emotional health: Implications of the neuroimmune network hypothesis. *Journal of Clinical Child & Adolescent Psychology*, 47(1), 142–156.

**Howard, Sasha R.** (2018). Genes underlying delayed puberty. *Molecular and Cellular Endocrinology*, 476, 119–128.

**Howe, Tsu-Hsin; Sheu, Ching-Fan; Hsu, Yung-Wen; Wang, Tien-Ni & Wang, Lan-Wan.** (2016). Predicting neurodevelopmental outcomes at preschool age for children with very low birth weight. *Research in Developmental Disabilities*, 48, 231–241.

**Howell, Diane M.; Wysocki, Karen & Steiner, Michael J.** (2010). Toilet training. *Pediatrics In Review*, 31(6), 262–263.

**Hoyme, H. Eugene; Kalberg, Wendy O.; Elliott, Amy J.; Blankenship, Jason; Buckley, David; Marais, Anna-Susan; . . . May, Philip A.** (2016). Updated clinical guidelines for diagnosing fetal alcohol spectrum disorders. *Pediatrics*, 138(2), e20154256.

**Hoyne, Clara & Egan, Suzanne M.** (2019). Shared book reading in early childhood: A review of influential factors and developmental benefits. *An Leanbh Og*, 12(1), 77–92.

**Hrdy, Sarah B.** (2009). *Mothers and others: The evolutionary origins of mutual understanding.* Harvard University Press.

**Hu, Yousong; Wang, Yifang & Liu, Aizhen.** (2017). The influence of mothers' emotional expressivity and class grouping on Chinese preschoolers' emotional regulation strategies. *Journal of Child and Family Studies*, 26(3), 824–832.

**Huang, Jidong; Duan, Zongshuan; Kwok, Julian; Binns, Steven; Vera, Lisa E.; Kim,**

Yoonsang; . . . Emery, Sherry L. (2019). Vaping versus JUULing: How the extraordinary growth and marketing of JUUL transformed the US retail e-cigarette market. *Tobacco Control*, 28(2), 146.

Huang, Z. Josh & Luo, Liqun. (2015). It takes the world to understand the brain. *Science*, 350(6256), 42–44.

Huguley, James P.; Wang, Ming-Te; Vasquez, Ariana C. & Guo, Jiesi. (2019). Parental ethnic–racial socialization practices and the construction of children of color's ethnic–racial identity: A research synthesis and meta-analysis. *Psychological Bulletin*, 145(5), 437–458.

Huston, Aletha C.; Bobbitt, Kaeley C. & Bentley, Alison. (2015). Time spent in child care: How and why does it affect social development? *Developmental Psychology*, 51(5), 621–634.

Hutchinson, Esther A.; De Luca, Cinzia R.; Doyle, Lex W.; Roberts, Gehan & Anderson, Peter J. (2013). School-age outcomes of extremely preterm or extremely low birth weight children. *Pediatrics*, 131(4), e1053–e1061.

Hutchison, Jane E.; Lyons, Ian M. & Ansari, Daniel. (2019). More similar than different: Gender differences in children's basic numerical skills are the exception not the rule. *Child Development*, 90(1), e66–e79.

Huynh, Jimmy L. & Casaccia, Patrizia. (2013). Epigenetic mechanisms in multiple sclerosis: Implications for pathogenesis and treatment. *The Lancet Neurology*, 12(2), 195–206.

Hvistendahl, Mara. (2013). China heads off deadly blood disorder. *Science*, 340(6133), 677–678.

Hyde, Janet S. (2016). Sex and cognition: Gender and cognitive functions. *Current Opinion in Neurobiology*, 38, 53–56.

Hyde, Janet Shibley; Bigler, Rebecca S.; Joel, Daphna; Tate, Charlotte Chucky & van Anders, Sari M. (2019). The future of sex and gender in psychology: Five challenges to the gender binary. *American Psychologist*, 74(2), 171–193.

Hyson, Marilou & Douglass, Anne L. (2019). More than academics: Supporting the whole child. In Brown, Christopher P.; McMullen, Mary Benson & File, Nancy (Eds.), *The Wiley handbook of early childhood care and education* (pp. 279–300). Wiley.

Ikeda, Martin J. (2012). Policy and practice considerations for response to intervention: Reflections and commentary. *Journal of Learning Disabilities*, 45(3), 274–277.

Ilies, Remus; Yao, Jingxian; Curseu, Petru L. & Liang, Alyssa X. (2019). Educated and happy: A four-year study explaining the links between education, job fit, and life satisfaction. *Applied Psychology*, 68(1), 150–176.

Imdad, Aamer; Sadiq, Kamran & Bhutta, Zulfiqar A. (2011). Evidence-based prevention of childhood malnutrition. *Current Opinion in Clinical Nutrition & Metabolic Care*, 14(3), 276–285.

Immordino-Yang, Mary Helen; Darling-Hammond, Linda & Krone, Christina R. (2019). Nurturing nature: How brain development is inherently social and emotional, and what this means for education. *Educational Psychologist*, 54(3), 185–204.

Inhelder, Bärbel & Piaget, Jean. (1958). *The growth of logical thinking from childhood to adolescence: An essay on the construction of formal operational structures*. Basic Books.

Inhelder, Bärbel & Piaget, Jean. (1964). *The early growth of logic in the child: Classification and seriation*. Harper & Row.

Inhelder, Bärbel & Piaget, Jean. (2013a). *The early growth of logic in the child: Classification and seriation*. Routledge.

Inhelder, Bärbel & Piaget, Jean. (2013b). *The growth of logical thinking from childhood to adolescence: An essay on the construction of formal operational structures*. Routledge.

Insel, Thomas R. (2014). Mental disorders in childhood: Shifting the focus from behavioral symptoms to neurodevelopmental trajectories. *JAMA*, 311(17), 1727–1728.

Insurance Institute for Highway Safety. (2018, December). Child safety: Motor vehicle crashes are a leading cause of death for children younger than 13. Insurance Institute for Highway Safety.

Insurance Institute for Highway Safety. (2018, December). General statistics: Crashes took 37,133 lives in the U.S. in 2017. Insurance Institute for Highway Safety.

Insurance Institute for Highway Safety, Highway Loss Data Institute. (2019, May). Older drivers. Insurance Institute for Highway Safety.

Iorio, Marilena V. & Palmieri, Dario. (2019). Editorial: From "junk DNA" to clinically relevant tools for cancer diagnosis, staging, and tailored therapies: The incredible case of non-coding RNAs. *Frontiers in Oncology*, 9(389).

Iotti, Nathalie Ophelia; Thornberg, Robert; Longobardi, Claudio & Jungert, Tomas. (2020). Early adolescents' emotional and behavioral difficulties, student-teacher relationships, and motivation to defend in bullying incidents. *Child & Youth Care Forum*, 49(1), 59–75.

Irwin, Scott; Galvez, Roberto; Weiler, Ivan Jeanne; Beckel-Mitchener, Andrea & Greenough, William. (2002). Brain structure and the functions of FMR1 protein. In Hagerman, Randi Jenssen & Hagerman, Paul J. (Eds.), *Fragile X syndrome: Diagnosis, treatment, and research* (3rd ed., pp. 191–205). Johns Hopkins University Press.

Ivarsson, Andreas; Johnson, Urban; Andersen, Mark; Tranaeus, Ulrika; Stenling, Andreas & Lindwall, Magnus. (2017). Psychosocial factors and sport injuries: Meta-analyses for prediction and prevention. *Sports Medicine*, 47(2), 353–365.

Jack, Jordynn. (2014). *Autism and gender: From refrigerator mothers to computer geeks*. University of Illinois Press.

Jackson, C. Kirabo. (2019). Can introducing single-sex education into low-performing schools improve academics, arrests, and teen motherhood? *Journal of Human Resources*.

Jacobs, Jerry A.; Ahmad, Seher & Sax, Linda J. (2017). Planning a career in engineering: Parental effects on sons and daughters. *Social Sciences*, 6(1).

Jacobs, Janis E. & Klaczynski, Paul A. (Eds.). (2005). *The development of judgment and decision making in children and adolescents*. L. Erlbaum.

Jambon, Marc & Smetana, Judith G. (2014). Moral complexity in middle childhood: Children's evaluations of necessary harm. *Developmental Psychology*, 50(1), 22–33.

James, Karin H. (2017). The importance of handwriting experience on the development of the literate brain. *Current Directions in Psychological Science*, 26(6), 502–508.

Jarcho, Johanna M.; Fox, Nathan A.; Pine, Daniel S.; Etkin, Amit; Leibenluft, Ellen; Shechner, Tomer & Ernst, Monique. (2013). The neural correlates of emotion-based cognitive control in adults with early childhood behavioral inhibition. *Biological Psychology*, 92(2), 306–314.

Jaschke, Artur C.; Honing, Henkjan & Scherder, Erik J. A. (2018). Longitudinal analysis of music education on executive functions in primary school children. *Frontiers in Neuroscience*, 12(103).

Jatlaoui, Tara C.; Eckhaus, Lindsay; Mandel, Michele G.; Nguyen, Antoinette; Oduyebo, Titilope; Petersen, Emily & Whiteman, Maura K. (2019, November 29). *Abortion surveillance — United States, 2016. Surveillance Summaries*, 68(11), 1–41. Atlanta, GA: Centers for Disease Control and Prevention.

Jednoróg, Katarzyna; Altarelli, Irene; Monzalvo, Karla; Fluss, Joel; Dubois, Jessica; Billard, Catherine; . . . Ramus, Franck. (2012). The influence of socioeconomic status on children's brain structure. *PLoS ONE*, 7(8), e42486.

Jenssen, Brian P. & Walley, Susan C. (2019). E-cigarettes and similar devices. *Pediatrics*, 143(2).

Jimerson, Shane R.; Burns, Matthew K. & VanDerHeyden, Amanda M. (Eds.). (2016). *Handbook of response to intervention: The science and practice of multi-tiered systems of support*. Springer.

Joel, Daphna; Berman, Zohar; Tavor, Ido; Wexler, Nadav; Gaber, Olga; Stein, Yaniv; . . . Assaf, Yaniv. (2015). Sex beyond the genitalia: The human brain mosaic. *Proceedings of the National Academy of Sciences*, 112(50), 15468–15473.

John, George Kunnackal; Wang, Lin; Nanavati, Julie; Twose, Claire; Singh, Rajdeep & Mullin, Gerard. (2018). Dietary alteration of the gut microbiome and its impact on weight and fat mass: A systematic review and meta-analysis. *Genes*, 9(3), 167.

Johnson, James E. & Wu, Viana Mei-Hsuan. (2019). Perspectives on play in early childhood care and education. In Brown, Christopher P. ; McMullen, Mary Benson & File, Nancy (Eds.), *The Wiley handbook of early childhood care and education* (pp. 79–98). Wiley.

Johnson, Jonni L.; McWilliams, Kelly; Goodman, Gail S.; Shelley, Alexandra E. & Piper, Brianna. (2016). Basic principles of interviewing the child eyewitness. In O'Donohue, William T. & Fanetti, Matthew (Eds.), *Forensic interviews regarding child sexual abuse* (pp. 179–195). Springer.

Johnson, Mark H. & de Haan, Michelle. (2015). *Developmental cognitive neuroscience: An introduction* (4th ed.). Wiley.

Jones, Catherine R. G.; Simonoff, Emily; Baird, Gillian; Pickles, Andrew; Marsden, Anita J. S.; Tregay, Jenifer; . . . Charman, Tony. (2018). The association between theory of mind, executive function, and the symptoms of autism spectrum disorder. *Autism Research*, 11(1), 95–109.

Jones, Jeffrey M. (2015, October 21). *In U.S., 58% back legal marijuana use*. Washington, DC: Gallup.

Jones, Mary C. (1965). Psychological correlates of somatic development. *Child Development*, 36(4), 899–911.

Jong, Jyh-Tsorng; Kao, Tsair; Lee, Liang-Yi; Huang, Hung-Hsuan; Lo, Po-Tsung & Wang,

**Hui-Chung.** (2010). Can temperament be understood at birth? The relationship between neonatal pain cry and their temperament: A preliminary study. *Infant Behavior and Development, 33*(3), 266–272.

**Jorgensen, Nathan & Nelson, Larry.** (2018). Moving toward and away from others: Social orientations in emerging adulthood. *Journal of Applied Developmental Psychology, 58,* 66–76.

**Joshi, Kshamta & Billick, Stephen.** (2017). Biopsychosocial causes of suicide and suicide prevention outcome studies in juvenile detention facilities: A review. *Psychiatric Quarterly, 88*(1), 141–153.

**Julian, Megan M.** (2013). Age at adoption from institutional care as a window into the lasting effects of early experiences. *Clinical Child and Family Psychology Review, 16*(2), 101–145.

**Jung, Courtney.** (2015). *Lactivism: How feminists and fundamentalists, hippies and yuppies, and physicians and politicians made breastfeeding big business and bad policy.* Basic Books.

**Juster, Robert-Paul; Russell, Jennifer J.; Almeida, Daniel & Picard, Martin.** (2016). Allostatic load and comorbidities: A mitochondrial, epigenetic, and evolutionary perspective. *Development and Psychopathology, 28*(4), 1117–1146.

**Juvonen, Jaana & Graham, Sandra.** (2014). Bullying in schools: The power of bullies and the plight of victims. *Annual Review of Psychology, 65,* 159–185.

**Kaczynski, Andrew T.; Besenyi, Gina M.; Child, S.; Hughey, Morgan; Colabianchi, Natalie; McIver, Kevin L.; . . . Pate, Russell R.** (2018). Relationship of objective street quality attributes with youth physical activity: Findings from the Healthy Communities Study. *Pediatric Obesity, 13*(Suppl. 1), 7–13.

**Kail, Robert V.** (2013). Influences of credibility of testimony and strength of statistical evidence on children's and adolescents' reasoning. *Journal of Experimental Child Psychology, 116*(3), 747–754.

**Kalsner, Louisa & Chamberlain, Stormy J.** (2015). Prader-Willi, Angelman, and 15q11-q13 Duplication syndromes. *The Pediatric Clinics of North America, 62*(3), 587–606.

**Kaltiala-Heino, Riittakerttu; Fröjd, Sari & Marttunen, Mauri.** (2015). Depression, conduct disorder, smoking and alcohol use as predictors of sexual activity in middle adolescence: A longitudinal study. *Health Psychology and Behavioral Medicine, 3*(1), 25–39.

**Kandel, Denise B. (Ed.)** (2002). *Stages and pathways of drug involvement: Examining the gateway hypothesis.* Cambridge University Press.

**Kandel, Eric R.** (2018). *The disordered mind: What unusual brains tell us about ourselves.* Farrar, Straus and Giroux.

**Kang, Hye-Kyung.** (2014). Influence of culture and community perceptions on birth and perinatal care of immigrant women: Doulas' perspective. *The Journal of Perinatal Education, 23*(1), 25–32.

**Kanner, Leo.** (1943). Autistic disturbances of affective contact. *Nervous Child, 2,* 217–250.

**Kaplan, N. & Main, M.** (1986). *Instructions for the classification of children's family drawings in terms of representation of attachment* [Unpublished manuscript]. University of California.

**Kapp, Steven K.; Gillespie-Lynch, Kristen; Sherman, Lauren E. & Hutman, Ted.** (2013). Deficit, difference, or both? Autism and neurodiversity. *Developmental Psychology, 49*(1), 59–71.

**Karbach, Julia & Unger, Kerstin.** (2014). Executive control training from middle childhood to adolescence. *Frontiers in Psychology, 5*(390).

**Karlson, Kristian Bernt.** (2019). College as equalizer? Testing the selectivity hypothesis. *Social Science Research, 80,* 216–229.

**Kärtner, Joscha; Borke, Jörn; Maasmeier, Kathrin; Keller, Heidi & Kleis, Astrid.** (2011). Sociocultural influences on the development of self-recognition and self-regulation in Costa Rican and Mexican toddlers. *Journal of Cognitive Education and Psychology, 10*(1), 96–112.

**Kärtner, Joscha; Keller, Heidi & Yovsi, Relindis D.** (2010). Mother–infant interaction during the first 3 months: The emergence of culture-specific contingency patterns. *Child Development, 81*(2), 540–554.

**Kastbom, Åsa A.; Sydsjö, Gunilla; Bladh, Marie; Priebe, Gisela & Svedin, Carl-Göran.** (2015). Sexual debut before the age of 14 leads to poorer psychosocial health and risky behaviour in later life. *Acta Paediatrica, 104*(1), 91–100.

**Kauffman, James M.; Anastasiou, Dimitris & Maag, John W.** (2017). Special education at the crossroad: An identity crisis and the need for a scientific reconstruction. *Exceptionality, 25*(2), 139–155.

**Kaur, Arshdeep.** (2019). My child transformed me: Reflections of involved fathers. In Sriram, Rajalakshmi (Ed.), *Fathering in India* (pp. 141–152). Springer.

**Kavanaugh, Robert D.** (2011). Origins and consequences of social pretend play. In Pellegrini, Anthony D. (Ed.), *The Oxford handbook of the development of play* (pp. 296–307). Oxford University Press.

**Kavšek, Michael & Braun, Stephanie K.** (2016). Binocular vision in infancy: Responsiveness to uncrossed horizontal disparity. *Infant Behavior and Development, 44,* 219–226.

**Keers, Robert & Pluess, Michael.** (2017). Childhood quality influences genetic sensitivity to environmental influences across adulthood: A life-course Gene × Environment interaction study. *Development And Psychopathology, 29*(5), 1921–1933.

**Kelemen, Deborah.** (2019). The magic of mechanism: Explanation-based instruction on counterintuitive concepts in early childhood. *Perspectives on Psychological Science, 14*(4), 510–522.

**Keller, Heidi; Borke, Jörn; Chaudhary, Nandita; Lamm, Bettina & Kleis, Astrid.** (2010). Continuity in parenting strategies: A cross-cultural comparison. *Journal of Cross-Cultural Psychology, 41*(3), 391–409.

**Keller, Peggy S.; El-Sheikh, Mona; Granger, Douglas A. & Buckhalt, Joseph A.** (2012). Interactions between salivary cortisol and alpha-amylase as predictors of children's cognitive functioning and academic performance. *Physiology & Behavior, 105*(4), 987–995.

**Kelly, Clare.** (2015). 'Let's do some jumping together': Intergenerational participation in the use of remote technology to co-construct social relations over distance. *Journal of Early Childhood Research, 13*(1), 29–46.

**Kempe, Ruth S. & Kempe, C. Henry.** (1978). *Child abuse.* Harvard University Press.

**Kendall-Taylor, Nathaniel; Lindland, Eric; O'Neil, Moira & Stanley, Kate.** (2014). Beyond prevalence: An explanatory approach to reframing child maltreatment in the United Kingdom. *Child Abuse & Neglect, 38*(5), 810–821.

**Keown, Louise J. & Palmer, Melanie.** (2014). Comparisons between paternal and maternal involvement with sons: Early to middle childhood. *Early Child Development and Care, 184*(1), 99–117.

**Kern, Ben D.; Graber, Kim C.; Shen, Sa; Hillman, Charles H. & McLoughlin, Gabriella.** (2018). Association of school-based physical activity opportunities, socioeconomic status, and third-grade reading. *Journal of School Health, 88*(1), 34–43.

**Kersken, Verena; Zuberbühler, Klaus & Gomez, Juan-Carlos.** (2017). Listeners can extract meaning from non-linguistic infant vocalisations cross-culturally. *Scientific Reports, 7.*

**Kesselring, Thomas & Müller, Ulrich.** (2011). The concept of egocentrism in the context of Piaget's theory. *New Ideas in Psychology, 29*(3), 327–345.

**Keysar, Boaz; Barr, Dale J.; Balin, Jennifer A. & Brauner, Jason S.** (2000). Taking perspective in conversation: The role of mutual knowledge in comprehension. *Psychological Science, 11*(1), 32–38.

**Kidd, Celeste; Palmeri, Holly & Aslin, Richard N.** (2013). Rational snacking: Young children's decision-making on the marshmallow task is moderated by beliefs about environmental reliability. *Cognition, 126*(1), 109–114.

**Kiley, Dan.** (1983). *The Peter Pan syndrome: Men who have never grown up.* Dodd Mead.

**Killen, Melanie & Smetana, Judith G. (Eds.).** (2014). *Handbook of moral development* (2nd ed.). Psychology Press.

**Kim, Bo-Ram; Chow, Sy-Miin; Bray, Bethany & Teti, Douglas M.** (2017). Trajectories of mothers' emotional availability: Relations with infant temperament in predicting attachment security. *Attachment & Human Development, 19*(1), 38–57.

**Kim, Dong-Sik & Kim, Hyun-Sun.** (2009). Body-image dissatisfaction as a predictor of suicidal ideation among Korean boys and girls in different stages of adolescence: A two-year longitudinal study. *The Journal of Adolescent Health, 45*(1), 47–54.

**Kim, Hojin I. & Johnson, Scott P.** (2013). Do young infants prefer an infant-directed face or a happy face? *International Journal of Behavioral Development, 37*(2), 125–130.

**Kim, Pilyoung; Strathearn, Lane & Swain, James E.** (2016). The maternal brain and its plasticity in humans. *Hormones and Behavior, 77,* 113–123.

**Kim, Su-Mi & Kim, Jong-Soo.** (2017). A review of mechanisms of implantation. *Development & Reproduction, 21*(4), 351–359.

**Kim-Spoon, Jungmeen; Deater-Deckard, Kirby; Brieant, Alexis; Lauharatanahirun, Nina; Lee, Jacob & King-Casas, Brooks.** (2019). Brains of a feather flocking together? Peer and individual neurobehavioral risks for substance use across adolescence. *Development and Psychopathology, 31*(5), 1661–1674.

**Kim-Spoon, Jungmeen; Longo, Gregory S. & McCullough, Michael E.** (2012). Parent-adolescent relationship quality as a moderator for the influences of parents' religiousness on adolescents' religiousness and adjustment. *Journal of Youth and Adolescence, 41*(12), 1576–1587.

**King, Brian A.; Jones, Christopher M.; Baldwin, Grant T. & Briss, Peter A.** (2020). The EVALI and youth vaping epidemics—Implications for public health. *New England Journal of Medicine, 382*(8), 689–691.

**King, Bruce M.** (2013). The modern obesity epidemic, ancestral hunter-gatherers, and the sensory/reward control of food intake. *American Psychologist, 68*(2), 88–96.

**King, Christian.** (2018). Food insecurity and child behavior problems in fragile families. *Economics and Human Biology, 28*, 14–22.

**King, Valarie; Pragg, Brianne & Lindstrom, Rachel.** (2020). Family relationships during adolescence and stepchilden's educational attainment in young adulthood. *Journal of Marriage and Family, 82*(2), 622–638.

**Kinney, Hannah C. & Thach, Bradley T.** (2009). The sudden infant death syndrome. *New England Journal of Medicine, 361*, 795–805.

**Kirk, Elizabeth; Howlett, Neil; Pine, Karen J. & Fletcher, Ben.** (2013). To sign or not to sign? The impact of encouraging infants to gesture on infant language and maternal mind-mindedness. *Child Development, 84*(2), 574–590.

**Kirkham, Julie Ann & Kidd, Evan.** (2017). The effect of Steiner, Montessori, and National Curriculum Education upon children's pretence and creativity. *Journal of Creative Behavior, 51*(1), 20–34.

**Kiserud, Torvid; Benachi, Alexandra; Hecher, Kurt; Perez, Rogelio González; Carvalho, José; Piaggio, Gilda & Platt, Lawrence D.** (2018). The World Health Organization fetal growth charts: Concept, findings, interpretation, and application. *American Journal of Obstetrics and Gynecology, 218*(2), S619–S629.

**Kiss, Ivy Giserman; Feldman, Melanie S.; Sheldrick, R. Christopher & Carter, Alice S.** (2017). Developing autism screening criteria for the Brief Infant Toddler Social Emotional Assessment (BITSEA). *Journal of Autism and Developmental Disorders, 47*, 1269–1277.

**Kjerulff, Kristen.** (2014, November 18). *Epidural analgesia use during labor and adverse maternal and neonatal outcomes: A large-scale observational study* [Paper presentation]. Improving Pregnancy Outcomes: Psychosocial Influences on Birth Outcomes, New Orleans, LA, United States.

**Klaczynski, Paul A.** (2011). Age differences in understanding precedent-setting decisions and authorities' responses to violations of deontic rules. *Journal of Experimental Child Psychology, 109*(1), 1–24.

**Klaczynski, Paul A. & Felmban, Wejdan S.** (2014). Heuristics and biases during adolescence: Developmental reversals and individual differences. In Markovits, Henry (Ed.), *The developmental psychology of reasoning and decision-making* (pp. 84–111). Psychology Press.

**Klaczynski, Paul A.; Felmban, Wejdan S. & Kole, James.** (2020). Gender intensification and gender generalization biases in pre-adolescents, adolescents, and emerging adults. *British Journal of Developmental Psychology.*

**Klaus, Marshall H. & Kennell, John H.** (1976). *Maternal-infant bonding: The impact of early separation or loss on family development.* Mosby.

**Klein, Denise; Mok, Kelvin; Chen, Jen-Kai & Watkins, Kate E.** (2014). Age of language learning shapes brain structure: A cortical thickness study of bilingual and monolingual individuals. *Brain and Language, 131*, 20–24.

**Klein, Zoe A. & Romeo, Russell D.** (2013). Changes in hypothalamic–pituitary–adrenal stress responsiveness before and after puberty in rats. *Hormones and Behavior, 64*(2), 357–363.

**Klinger, Laura G.; Dawson, Geraldine; Burner, Karen & Crisler, Megan.** (2014). Autism spectrum disorder. In Mash, Eric J. & Barkley, Russell A. (Eds.), *Child psychopathology* (3rd ed., pp. 531–572). Guilford Press.

**Knopik, Valerie S.; Neiderhiser, Jenae M.; DeFries, John C. & Plomin, Robert.** (2017). *Behavioral genetics* (7th ed.). Worth.

**Kochanek, Kenneth D.; Murphy, Sherry L.; Xu, Jiaquan & Arias, Elizabeth.** (2019, June 24). *Deaths: Final data for 2017. National Vital Statistics Reports, 68*(9). Hyattsville, MD: National Center for Health Statistics.

**Kochel, Karen P.; Ladd, Gary W.; Bagwell, Catherine L. & Yabko, Brandon A.** (2015). Bully/victim profiles' differential risk for worsening peer acceptance: The role of friendship. *Journal of applied developmental psychology, 41*, 38–45.

**Kohlberg, Lawrence.** (1963). The development of children's orientations toward a moral order: I. Sequence in the development of moral thought. *Vita Humana, 6*(1/2), 11–33.

**Kohlberg, Lawrence; Levine, Charles & Hewer, Alexandra.** (1983). *Moral stages: A current formulation and a response to critics.* Karger.

**Kolb, Bryan & Gibb, Robbin.** (2015). Childhood poverty and brain development. *Human Development, 58*(4/5), 215–217.

**Kolb, Bryan; Harker, Allonna & Gibb, Robbin.** (2017). Principles of plasticity in the developing brain. *Developmental Medicine & Child Neurology, 59*(12), 1218–1223.

**Kolb, Bryan & Whishaw, Ian Q.** (2015). *Fundamentals of human neuropsychology* (7th ed.). Worth.

**Komisar, Erica.** (2017). *Being there: Why prioritizing motherhood in the first three years matters.* TarcherPerigee.

**Konner, Melvin.** (2010). *The evolution of childhood: Relationships, emotion, mind.* Harvard University Press.

**Konner, Melvin.** (2018). Nonmaternal care: A half-century of research. *Physiology & Behavior, 193*(Part A), 179–186.

**Kono, Yumi; Yonemoto, Naohiro; Nakanishi, Hidehiko; Kusuda, Satoshi & Fujimura, Masanori.** (2018). Changes in survival and neurodevelopmental outcomes of infants born at <25 weeks' gestation: A retrospective observational study in tertiary centres in Japan. *BMJ Paediatrics Open, 2*(1), e000211.

**Korber, Maïlys & Oesch, Daniel.** (2019). Vocational versus general education: Employment and earnings over the life course in Switzerland. *Advances in Life Course Research, 40.*

**Kordas, Katarzyna; Burganowski, Rachael; Roy, Aditi; Peregalli, Fabiana; Baccino, Valentina; Barcia, Elizabeth; . . . Queirolo, Elena I.** (2018). Nutritional status and diet as predictors of children's lead concentrations in blood and urine. *Environment International, 111*, 43–51.

**Koress, Cody M.; Jones, Mark R. & Kaye, Alan David.** (2019). Development of pain behavior in the fetus and newborn. In Abd-Elsayed, Alaa (Ed.), *Pain* (pp. 53–55). Springer.

**Koretz, Daniel.** (2017). *The testing charade: Pretending to make schools better.* University of Chicago Press.

**Kornienko, Olga; Ha, Thao & Dishion, Thomas J.** (2020). Dynamic pathways between rejection and antisocial behavior in peer networks: Update and test of confluence model. *Development and Psychopathology, 32*(1), 175–188.

**Koster-Hale, Jorie & Saxe, Rebecca.** (2013). Functional neuroimaging of theory of mind. In Baron-Cohen, Simon; Tager-Flusberg, Helen & Lombardo, Michael (Eds.), *Understanding other minds: Perspectives from developmental social neuroscience* (3rd ed., pp. 132–163). Oxford University Press.

**Kozhimannil, Katy B. & Kim, Helen.** (2014). Maternal mental illness. *Science, 345*(6198), 755.

**Kral, Michael J.** (2019). *The idea of suicide: Contagion, imitation, and cultural diffusion.* Routledge.

**Krans, Elizabeth E. & Davis, Matthew M.** (2012). *Preventing Low Birthweight*: 25 years, prenatal risk, and the failure to reinvent prenatal care. *American Journal of Obstetrics and Gynecology, 206*(5), 398–403.

**Krause, Elizabeth D.; Vélez, Clorinda E.; Woo, Rebecca; Hoffmann, Brittany; Freres, Derek R.; Abenavoli, Rachel M. & Gillham, Jane E.** (2018). Rumination, depression, and gender in early adolescence: A longitudinal study of a bidirectional model. *Journal of Early Adolescence, 38*(7), 923–946.

**Kreager, Derek A.; Molloy, Lauren E.; Moody, James & Feinberg, Mark E.** (2016). Friends first? The peer network origins of adolescent dating. *Journal of Research on Adolescence, 26*(2), 257–269.

**Krebs, John R.** (2009). The gourmet ape: Evolution and human food preferences. *American Journal of Clinical Nutrition, 90*(3), 707S–711S.

**Kretch, Kari S. & Adolph, Karen E.** (2013). No bridge too high: Infants decide whether to cross based on the probability of falling not the severity of the potential fall. *Developmental Science, 16*(3), 336–351.

**Krisberg, Kim.** (2014). Public health messaging: How it is said can influence behaviors: Beyond the facts. *The Nation's Health, 44*(6), 1, 20.

**Kroger, Jane & Marcia, James E.** (2011). The identity statuses: Origins, meanings, and interpretations. In Schwartz, Seth J.; Luyckx, Koen & Vignoles, Vivian L. (Eds.), *Handbook of identity theory and research* (pp. 31–53). Springer.

Kroncke, Anna P.; Willard, Marcy & Huckabee, Helena. (2016). Optimal outcomes and recovery. In *Assessment of autism spectrum disorder: Critical issues in clinical, forensic and school settings* (pp. 23–33). Springer.

Krouse, William J. (2012, November 14). *Gun control legislation. CRS Report for Congress.* Washington, DC: Congressional Research Service. RL32842

Krueger, Robert F. & Eaton, Nicholas R. (2015). Transdiagnostic factors of mental disorders. *World Psychiatry, 14*(1), 27–29.

Krzych-Fałta, Edyta; Furmańczyk, Konrad; Piekarska, Barbara; Raciborski, Filip; Tomaszewska, Aneta; Walkiewicz, Artur; . . . Samoliński, Bolesław Krzysztof. (2018). Extent of protective or allergy-inducing effects in cats and dogs. *Annals of Agricultural and Environmental Medicine, 25*(2), 268–273.

Kubin, Laura. (2019). Is there a resurgence of vaccine preventable diseases in the U.S.? *Journal of Pediatric Nursing, 44,* 115–118.

Kuhl, Patricia K. (2004). Early language acquisition: Cracking the speech code. *Nature Reviews Neuroscience, 5*(11), 831–843.

Kunkel, Melissa; Marete, Irene; Cheng, Erika R.; Bucher, Sherri; Liechty, Edward; Esamai, Fabian; . . . Vreeman, Rachel C. (2019). Place of delivery and perinatal mortality in Kenya. *Seminars in Perinatology, 43*(5), 252–259.

Kutob, Randa M.; Senf, Janet H.; Crago, Marjorie & Shisslak, Catherine M. (2010). Concurrent and longitudinal predictors of self-esteem in elementary and middle school girls. *Journal of School Health, 80*(5), 240–248.

Kuwahara, Keisuke; Kochi, Takeshi; Nanri, Akiko; Tsuruoka, Hiroko; Kurotani, Kayo; Pham, Ngoc Minh; . . . Mizoue, Tetsuya. (2014). Flushing response modifies the association of alcohol consumption with markers of glucose metabolism in Japanese men and women. *Alcoholism: Clinical and Experimental Research, 38*(4), 1042–1048.

Kvalvik, Liv G.; Haug, Kjell; Klungsøyr, Kari; Morken, Nils-Halvdan; Deroo, Lisa A. & Skjærven, Rolv. (2017). Maternal smoking status in successive pregnancies and risk of having a small for gestational age infant. *Paediatric and Perinatal Epidemiology, 31*(1), 21–28.

Kypri, Kypros; Davie, Gabrielle; McElduff, Patrick; Connor, Jennie & Langley, John. (2014). Effects of lowering the minimum alcohol purchasing age on weekend assaults resulting in hospitalization in New Zealand. *American Journal of Public Health, 104*(8), 1396–1401.

Kypri, Kypros; Voas, Robert B.; Langley, John D.; Stephenson, Shaun C. R.; Begg, Dorothy J.; Tippetts, A. Scott & Davie, Gabrielle S. (2006). Minimum purchasing age for alcohol and traffic crash injuries among 15- to 19-year-olds in New Zealand. *American Journal of Public Health, 96*(1), 126–131.

La Fauci, Luigi. (2018). The changing sexual life course of gay men and lesbians in contemporary Italy. *European Societies.*

Labouvie-Vief, Gisela. (2015). *Integrating emotions and cognition throughout the lifespan.* Springer.

Ladd, Helen F. (2019). How charter schools threaten the public interest. *38*(4), 1063–1071.

Ladd, Helen F. & Sorensen, Lucy C. (2017). Returns to teacher experience: Student achievement and motivation in middle school. *Education Finance and Policy, 12*(2), 241–279.

Lagattuta, Kristin H. (2014). Linking past, present, and future: Children's ability to connect mental states and emotions across time. *Child Development Perspectives, 8*(2), 90–95.

Lai, Stephanie A.; Benjamin, Rebekah G.; Schwanenflugel, Paula J. & Kuhn, Melanie R. (2014). The longitudinal relationship between reading fluency and reading comprehension skills in second-grade children. *Reading & Writing Quarterly: Overcoming Learning Difficulties, 30*(2), 116–138.

Lake, Stephanie & Kerr, Thomas. (2017). The challenges of projecting the public health impacts of marijuana legalization in Canada. *International Journal of Health Policy Management, 6*(5), 285–287.

Lam, Chun Bun; McHale, Susan M. & Crouter, Ann C. (2012). Parent–child shared time from middle childhood to late adolescence: Developmental course and adjustment correlates. *Child Development, 83*(2), 2089–2103.

Lam, Kelly Ka Lai & Zhou, Mingming. (2019). Examining the relationship between grit and academic achievement within K-12 and higher education: A systematic review. *Psychology in the Schools, 56*(10), 1654–1686.

Lamb, Michael E. (1982). Maternal employment and child development: A review. In Lamb, Michael E. (Ed.), *Nontraditional families: Parenting and child development* (pp. 45–69). Erlbaum.

Lamm, Bettina; Keller, Heidi; Teiser, Johanna; Gudi, Helene; Yovsi, Relindis D.; Freitag, Claudia; . . . Lohaus, Arnold. (2018). Waiting for the second treat: Developing culture-specific modes of self-regulation. *Child Development, 89*(3), e261–e277.

Lancaster, Gillian A.; Mccray, Gareth; Kariger, Patricia; Dua, Tarun; Titman, Andrew; Chandna, Jaya; . . . Janus, Magdalena. (2018). Creation of the WHO Indicators of Infant and Young Child Development (IYCD): Metadata synthesis across 10 countries. *BMJ Global Health, 3*(5), e000747.

Landgren, Kajsa; Lundqvist, Anita & Hallström, Inger. (2012). Remembering the chaos – But life went on and the wound healed: A four year follow up with parents having had a baby with infantile colic. *The Open Nursing Journal, 6,* 53–61.

Lando, Amy M. & Lo, Serena C. (2014). Consumer understanding of the benefits and risks of fish consumption during pregnancy. *American Journal of Lifestyle Medicine, 8*(2), 88–92.

Lane, Jonathan D. & Harris, Paul L. (2014). Confronting, representing, and believing counterintuitive concepts: Navigating the natural and the supernatural. *Perspectives on Psychological Science, 9*(2), 144–160.

Lang, Samantha F. & Fowers, Blaine J. (2019). An expanded theory of Alzheimer's caregiving. *American Psychologist, 74*(2), 194–206.

Langrehr, Kimberly J.; Morgan, Sydney K.; Ross, Jessica; Oh, Monica & Chong, Wen Wen. (2019). Racist experiences, openness to discussing racism, and attitudes toward ethnic heritage activities: Adoptee–parent discrepancies. *Asian American Journal of Psychology, 10*(2), 91–102.

Laninga-Wijnen, Lydia; Gremmen, Mariola C.; Dijkstra, Jan Kornelis; Veenstra, René; Vollebergh, Wilma A. M. & Harakeh, Zeena. (2019). The role of academic status norms in friendship selection and influence processes related to academic achievement. *Developmental Psychology, 55*(2), 337–350.

Lansford, Jennifer E.; Sharma, Chinmayi; Malone, Patrick S.; Woodlief, Darren; Dodge, Kenneth A.; Oburu, Paul; . . . Di Giunta, Laura. (2014). Corporal punishment, maternal warmth, and child adjustment: A longitudinal study in eight countries. *Journal of Clinical Child & Adolescent Psychology, 43*(4), 670–685.

Lapan, Candace & Boseovski, Janet J. (2017). When peer performance matters: Effects of expertise and traits on children's self-evaluations after social comparison. *Child Development, 88*(6), 1860–1872.

Lara-Cinisomo, Sandraluz; Fuligni, Allison Sidle & Karoly, Lynn A. (2011). Preparing preschoolers for kindergarten. In Laverick, DeAnna M. & Jalongo, Mary Renck (Eds.), *Transitions to early care and education* (Vol. 4, pp. 93–105). Springer.

Larsen, Peter A. (2018). Transposable elements and the multidimensional genome. *Chromosome Research, 26*(1/2), 1–3.

Larzelere, Robert E. & Cox, Ronald B. (2013). Making valid causal inferences about corrective actions by parents from longitudinal data. *Journal of Family Theory & Review, 5*(4), 282–299.

Larzelere, Robert E.; Cox, Ronald B. & Swindle, Taren M. (2015). Many replications do not causal inferences make: The need for critical replications to test competing explanations of nonrandomized studies. *Perspectives on Psychological Science, 10*(3), 380–389.

Larzelere, Robert E.; Gunnoe, Marjorie Lindner; Roberts, Mark W. & Ferguson, Christopher J. (2017). Children and parents deserve better parental discipline research: Critiquing the evidence for exclusively "positive" parenting. *Marriage & Family Review, 53*(1), 24–35.

Laurent, Heidemarie K. (2014). Clarifying the contours of emotion regulation: Insights from parent–child stress research. *Child Development Perspectives, 8*(1), 30–35.

Laursen, Brett; Hartl, Amy C.; Vitaro, Frank; Brendgen, Mara; Dionne, Ginette & Boivin, Michel. (2017). The spread of substance use and delinquency between adolescent twins. *Developmental Psychology, 53*(2), 329–339.

Law, James; Rush, Robert; King, Tom; Westrupp, Elizabeth & Reilly, Sheena. (2018). Early home activities and oral language skills in middle childhood: A quantile analysis. *Child Development, 89*(1), 295–309.

Lazzara, Alexandra; Daymont, Carrie; Ladda, Roger; Lull, Jordan; Ficicioglu, Can; Cohen, Jennifer & Aprile, Justen. (2019). Failure to thrive: An expanded differential diagnosis. *Journal of Pediatric Genetics, 8*(1), 27–32.

Le Duc, James W. & Yuan, Zhiming. (2018). Network for safe and secure labs. *Science, 362*(6412), 267.

Leach, Penelope. (2011). The EYFS and the real foundations of children's early years. In House, Richard (Ed.), *Too much, too soon?: Early learning and the erosion of childhood.* Hawthorn.

Leavitt, Judith W. (2009). *Make room for daddy: The journey from waiting room to birthing room.* University of North Carolina Press.

Lee, Dohoon; Brooks-Gunn, Jeanne; McLanahan, Sara S.; Notterman, Daniel & Garfinkel, Irwin. (2013). The Great Recession, genetic sensitivity, and maternal harsh parenting. *Proceedings of the National Academy of Sciences, 110*(34), 13780–13784.

Lee, RaeHyuck; Zhai, Fuhua; Brooks-Gunn, Jeanne; Han, Wen-Jui & Waldfogel, Jane. (2014). Head Start participation and school readiness: Evidence from the early childhood longitudinal study–birth cohort. *Developmental Psychology, 50*(1), 202–215.

Lee, Shawna J. & Altschul, Inna. (2015). Spanking of young children: Do immigrant and U.S.-born Hispanic parents differ? *Journal of Interpersonal Violence, 30*(3), 475–498.

Lee, Shawna J.; Altschul, Inna & Gershoff, Elizabeth T. (2015). Wait until your father gets home? Mother's and fathers' spanking and development of child aggression. *Children and Youth Services Review, 52*, 158–166.

Lehner, Ben. (2013). Genotype to phenotype: Lessons from model organisms for human genetics. *Nature Reviews Genetics, 14*(3), 168–178.

Leiter, Valerie & Herman, Sarah. (2015). Guinea pig kids: Myths or modern Tuskegees? *Sociological Spectrum, 35*(1), 26–45.

Leman, Patrick J. & Björnberg, Marina. (2010). Conversation, development, and gender: A study of changes in children's concepts of punishment. *Child Development, 81*(3), 958–971.

Lemish, Daphna & Kolucki, Barbara. (2013). Media and early childhood development. In Britto, Pia Rebello; Engle, Patrice L. & Super, Charles M. (Eds.), *Handbook of early childhood development research and its impact on global policy.* Oxford University Press.

Lengua, Liliana J.; Garstein, Maria A. & Prinzie, Peter. (2019). Temperament and personality trait development in the family: Interactions and transactions with parenting from infancy through adolescence. In McAdams, Dan P.; Shiner, Rebecca L. & Tackett, Jennifer L. (Eds.), *Handbook of personality development* (pp. 201–220). Guilford.

Lenhart, Amanda; Anderson, Monica & Smith, Aaron. (2015, October 1). *Teens, technology and romantic relationships. Pew Research Center: Internet, Science & Tech.* Washington, DC: Pew Research Center.

Leonard, Hayley C. & Hill, Elisabeth L. (2014). Review: The impact of motor development on typical and atypical social cognition and language: A systematic review. *Child and Adolescent Mental Health, 19*(3), 163–170.

Leonard, Julia A.; Lee, Yuna & Schulz, Laura E. (2017). Infants make more attempts to achieve a goal when they see adults persist. *Science, 357*(6357), 1290–1294.

Lerner, Richard M.; Overton, F. Willis; Freund, Alexandra M. & Lamb, Michael E. (2010). *The handbook of life-span development.* Wiley.

Leshner, Alan I. & Dzau, Victor J. (2018). Good gun policy needs research. *Science, 359*(6381), 1195.

Leslie, Mitch. (2012). Gut microbes keep rare immune cells in line. *Science, 335*(6075), 1428.

Lessne, Deborah & Yanez, Christina. (2016, December 20). *Student reports of bullying: Results from the 2015 School Crime Supplement to the National Crime Victimization Survey.* Washington, DC: National Center for Education Statistics.

Lester, Patricia; Leskin, Gregory; Woodward, Kirsten; Saltzman, William; Nash, William; Mogil, Catherine; . . . Beardslee, William. (2011). Wartime deployment and military children: Applying prevention science to enhance family resilience. In Wadsworth, Shelley MacDermid & Riggs, David (Eds.), *Risk and resilience in U.S. military families* (pp. 149–173). Springer.

Leung, Sumie; Mareschal, Denis; Rowsell, Renee; Simpson, David; Laria, Leon; Grbic, Amanda & Kaufman, Jordy. (2016). Oscillatory activity in the infant brain and the representation of small numbers. *Frontiers in Systems Neuroscience, 10*(4).

Levey, Emma K. V.; Garandeau, Claire F.; Meeus, Wim & Branje, Susan. (2019). The longitudinal role of self-concept clarity and best friend delinquency in adolescent delinquent behavior. *Journal of Youth and Adolescence, 48*(6), 1068–1081. p. 409 Hoover.

Levy, Jonathan; Goldstein, Abraham & Feldman, Ruth. (2019). The neural development of empathy is sensitive to caregiving and early trauma. *Nature Communications, 10*(1).

Lewandowski, Lawrence J. & Lovett, Benjamin J. (2014). Learning disabilities. In Mash, Eric J. & Barkley, Russell A. (Eds.), *Child psychopathology* (3rd ed., pp. 625–669). Guilford Press.

Lewin, Kurt. (1945). The Research Center for Group Dynamics at Massachusetts Institute of Technology. *Sociometry, 8*(2), 126–136.

Lewis, John D.; Theilmann, Rebecca J.; Townsend, Jeanne & Evans, Alan C. (2013). Network efficiency in autism spectrum disorder and its relation to brain overgrowth. *Frontiers in Human Neuroscience, 7*, 845.

Lewis, Lawrence B.; Antone, Carol & Johnson, Jacqueline S. (1999). Effects of prosodic stress and serial position on syllable omission in first words. *Developmental Psychology, 35*(1), 45–59.

Lewis, Michael. (2010). The emergence of human emotions. In Lewis, Michael; Haviland-Jones, Jeannette M. & Barrett, Lisa Feldman (Eds.), *Handbook of emotions* (3rd ed.). Guilford Press.

Lewis, Michael & Brooks, Jeanne. (1978). Self-knowledge and emotional development. In Lewis, Michael & Rosenblum, L. A. (Eds.), *Genesis of behavior* (Vol. 1, pp. 205–226). Plenum Press.

Lewis, Michael & Kestler, Lisa (Eds.). (2012). *Gender differences in prenatal substance exposure.* American Psychological Association.

Li, Bo; Yang, Jing; Zhao, Faming; Zhi, Lili; Wang, Xiqian; Liu, Lin; . . . Zhao, Yunhe. (2020). Prevalence and impact of cardiovascular metabolic diseases on COVID-19 in China. *Clinical Research in Cardiology, 109*(5), 531–538.

Li, Jin; Fung, Heidi; Bakeman, Roger; Rae, Katharine & Wei, Wanchun. (2014). How European American and Taiwanese mothers talk to their children about learning. *Child Development, 85*(3), 1206–1221.

Li, Pin; Becker, Jill B.; Heitzeg, Mary M.; Mcclellan, Michele L.; Reed, Beth Glover & Zucker, Robert A. (2017). Gender differences in the transmission of risk for antisocial behavior problems across generations. *PLoS ONE, 12*(5), e0177288.

Liben, Lynn S. (2016). We've come a long way, baby (but we're not there yet): Gender past, present, and future. *Child Development, 87*(1), 5–28.

Libertus, Klaus; Joh, Amy S. & Needham, Amy W. (2016). Motor training at 3 months affects object exploration 12 months later. *Developmental Science, 19*(6), 1058–1066.

Libertus, Klaus & Needham, Amy. (2010). Teach to reach: The effects of active vs. passive reaching experiences on action and perception. *Vision Research, 50*(24), 2750–2757.

Libertus, Melissa E.; Feigenson, Lisa & Halberda, Justin. (2013). Is approximate number precision a stable predictor of math ability? *Learning and Individual Differences, 25*, 126–133.

Lillard, Angeline S. (2013). Playful learning and Montessori education. *American Journal of Play, 5*(2), 157–186.

Lillard, Angeline S. & Taggart, Jessica. (2019). Pretend play and fantasy: What if Montessori was right? *Child Development Perspectives, 13*(2), 85–90.

Liller, Karen D.; Morris, Barbara; Yang, Yingwei; Bubu, Omonigho M.; Perich, Brad & Fillion, Jessica. (2019). Injuries and concussions among young children, ages 5-11, playing sports in recreational leagues in Florida. *PLoS ONE, 14*(5), e0216217.

Lim, Cher Ping; Zhao, Yong; Tondeur, Jo; Chai, Ching Sing & Tsai, Chin-Chung. (2013). Bridging the gap: Technology trends and use of technology in schools. *Educational Technology & Society, 16*(2), 59–68.

Lin, Nan. (2017). Building a network theory of social capital: Theory and research. In Lin, Nan; Cook, Karen & Burt, Ronald S. (Eds.), *Social capital: Theory and research.* Taylor & Francis.

Lin, Phoebe. (2016). Risky behaviors: Integrating adolescent egocentrism with the theory of planned behavior. *Review of General Psychology, 20*(4), 392–398.

Lipton, Eric. (2017, March 29). E.P.A. chief, rejecting agency's science, chooses not to ban insecticide. *New York Times.*

Littman, Lisa. (2018). Parent reports of adolescents and young adults perceived to show signs of a rapid onset of gender dysphoria. *PLoS One, 13*(8), e0202330.

Liu, Andrew H. (2015). Revisiting the hygiene hypothesis for allergy and asthma. *The Journal of Allergy and Clinical Immunology, 136*(4), 860–865.

Liu, Chang & Neiderhiser, Jenae M. (2017). Using genetically informed designs to understand the environment: The importance of family-based approaches. In Tolan, Patrick H. & L., Leventhal

Bennett (Eds.), *Gene-environment transactions in developmental psychopathology: The role in intervention research* (pp. 95–110). Springer.

**Liu, Junsheng; Chen, Xinyin; Coplan, Robert J.; Ding, Xuechen; Zarbatany, Lynne & Ellis, Wendy.** (2015). Shyness and unsociability and their relations with adjustment in Chinese and Canadian children. *Journal of Cross-Cultural Psychology, 46*(3), 371–386.

**Liu, Ning; Vigod, Simone N.; Farrugia, M. Michèle; Urquia, Marcelo L. & Ray, Joel G.** (2018). Intergenerational teen pregnancy: A population-based cohort study. *BJOG, 125*(13), 1766–1774.

**Liu, Peiwei & Feng, Tingyong.** (2017). The overlapping brain region accounting for the relationship between procrastination and impulsivity: A voxel-based morphometry study. *Neuroscience, 360*, 9–17.

**Liu, Tong; Yang, Wen-Qiang; Xie, Yu-Gu; Liu, Pei-Wen; Xie, Li-Hua; Lin, Feng; . . . Chen, Xiao-Guang.** (2019). Construction of an efficient genomic editing system with CRISPR/Cas9 in the vector mosquito *Aedes albopictus. Insect Science, 26*(6), 1045–1054.

**Livingston, Lucy Anne & Happé, Francesca.** (2017). Conceptualising compensation in neurodevelopmental disorders: Reflections from autism spectrum disorder. *Neuroscience and Biobehavioral Reviews, 80*, 729–742.

**Lo, June C.; Lee, Su Mei; Lee, Xuan Kai; Sasmita, Karen; Chee, Nicholas I. Y. N.; Tandi, Jesisca; . . . Chee, Michael W. L.** (2018). Sustained benefits of delaying school start time on adolescent sleep and well-being. *Sleep, 41*(6).

**LoBue, Vanessa.** (2013). What are we so afraid of? How early attention shapes our most common fears. *Child Development Perspectives, 7*(1), 38–42.

**LoBue, Vanessa & Adolph, Karen E.** (2019). Fear in infancy: Lessons from snakes, spiders, heights, and strangers. *Developmental Psychology, 55*(9), 1889–1907.

**Lochman, John E.; Dishion, Thomas J.; Powell, Nicole P.; Boxmeyer, Caroline L.; Qu, Lixin & Sallee, Meghann.** (2015). Evidence-based preventive intervention for preadolescent aggressive children: One-year outcomes following randomization to group versus individual delivery. *Journal of Consulting and Clinical Psychology, 83*(4), 728–735.

**Lockhart, Kristi L.; Goddu, Mariel K. & Keil, Frank C.** (2018). When saying "I'm best" is benign: Developmental shifts in perceptions of boasting. *Developmental Psychology, 54*(3), 521–535.

**Lockhart, Kristi L. & Keil, Frank C.** (2018). What heals and why? Children's understanding of medical treatments. *Monographs of the Society for Research in Child Development, 83*(2).

**Lønfeldt, Nicole N.; Verhulst, Frank C.; Strandberg-Larsen, Katrine; Plessen, Kerstin J. & Lebowitz, Eli R.** (2018). Assessing risk of neurodevelopmental disorders after birth with oxytocin: A systematic review and meta-analysis. *Psychological Medicine.*

**López-Pinar, Carlos; Martínez-Sanchís, Sonia; Carbonell-Vayá, Enrique; Fenollar-Cortés, Javier & Sánchez-Meca, Julio.** (2018). Long-term efficacy of psychosocial treatments for adults with Attention-deficit/hyperactivity disorder: A meta-analytic review. *Frontiers in Psychology, 9*(638).

**Lordier, Lara; Meskaldji, Djalel-Eddine; Grouiller, Frédéric; Pittet, Marie P.; Vollenweider, Andreas; Vasung, Lana; . . . Hüppi, Petra S.** (2019). Music in premature infants enhances high-level cognitive brain networks. *PNAS, 116*(24), 12103–12108.

**Lorthe, Elsa; Torchin, Héloïse; Delorme, Pierre; Ancel, Pierre-Yves; Marchand-Martin, Laetitia; Foix-L'Hélias, Laurence; . . . Kayem, Gilles.** (2018). Preterm premature rupture of membranes at 22–25 weeks' gestation: Perinatal and 2-year outcomes within a national population-based study (EPIPAGE-2). *American Journal of Obstetrics and Gynecology, 219*(3), 298.e1–298.e14.

**Loucks, Jeff & Price, Heather L.** (2019). Memory for temporal order in action is slow developing, sensitive to deviant input, and supported by foundational cognitive processes. *Developmental Psychology, 55*(2), 263–273.

**Lourenço, Orlando.** (2012). Piaget and Vygotsky: Many resemblances, and a crucial difference. *New Ideas in Psychology, 30*(3), 281–295.

**Loyd, Aerika Brittian & Gaither, Sarah E.** (2018). Racial/ethnic socialization for white youth: What we know and future directions. *Journal of Applied Developmental Psychology, 59*, 54–64.

**Lubienski, Christopher; Puckett, Tiffany & Brewer, T. Jameson.** (2013). Does homeschooling "work"? A critique of the empirical claims and agenda of advocacy organizations. *Peabody Journal of Education, 88*(3), 378–392.

**Lubke, Gitta H.; Mcartor, Daniel B.; Boomsma, Dorret I. & Bartels, Meike.** (2018). Genetic and environmental contributions to the development of childhood aggression. *Developmental Psychology, 54*(1), 39–50.

**Lucca, Kelsey & Wilbourn, Makeba Parramore.** (2018). Communicating to learn: Infants' pointing gestures result in optimal learning. *Child Development, 89*(3), 941–960.

**Luecken, Linda J.; Lin, Betty; Coburn, Shayna S.; MacKinnon, David P.; Gonzales, Nancy A. & Crnic, Keith A.** (2013). Prenatal stress, partner support, and infant cortisol reactivity in low-income Mexican American families. *Psychoneuroendocrinology, 38*(12), 3092–3101.

**Luhmann, Maike & Hawkley, Louise C.** (2016). Age differences in loneliness from late adolescence to oldest old age. *Developmental Psychology, 52*(6), 943–959.

**Lundahl, Alyssa; Kidwell, Katherine M. & Nelson, Timothy D.** (2014). Parental underestimates of child weight: A meta-analysis. *Pediatrics, 133*(3), e689–e703.

**Lundberg, Shelly; Pollak, Robert A. & Stearns, Jenna.** (2016). Family inequality: Diverging patterns in marriage, cohabitation, and childbearing. *Journal of Economic Perspectives, 30*(2), 79–102.

**Luo, Rufan; Tamis-LeMonda, Catherine S.; Kuchirko, Yana; Ng, Florrie F. & Liang, Eva.** (2014). Mother–child book-sharing and children's storytelling skills in ethnically diverse, low-income families. *Infant and Child Development, 23*(4), 402–425.

**Lushin, Viktor; Jaccard, James & Kaploun, Victor.** (2017). Parental monitoring, adolescent dishonesty and underage drinking: A nationally representative study. *Journal of Adolescence, 57*, 99–107.

**Luthar, Suniya S.** (2015). Resilience in development: A synthesis of research across five decades. In Cicchetti, Dante & Cohen, Donald J. (Eds.), *Developmental psychopathology* (2nd ed., Vol. 3). Wiley.

**Luthar, Suniya S.; Cicchetti, Dante & Becker, Bronwyn.** (2000). The construct of resilience: A critical evaluation and guidelines for future work. *Child Development, 71*(3), 543–562.

**Luthar, Suniya S.; Small, Phillip J. & Ciciolla, Lucia.** (2018). Adolescents from upper middle class communities: Substance misuse and addiction across early adulthood. *Development and Psychopathology, 30*(1), 315–335.

**Lyall, Donald M.; Inskip, Hazel M.; Mackay, Daniel; Deary, Ian J.; McIntosh, Andrew M.; Hotopf, Matthew; . . . Smith, Daniel J.** (2016). Low birth weight and features of neuroticism and mood disorder in 83,545 participants of the UK Biobank cohort. *British Journal of Psychiatry Open, 2*(1), 38–44.

**Macgregor, Stuart; Lind, Penelope A.; Bucholz, Kathleen K.; Hansell, Narelle K.; Madden, Pamela A. F.; Richter, Melinda M.; . . . Whitfield, John B.** (2009). Associations of ADH and ALDH2 gene variation with self report alcohol reactions, consumption and dependence: An integrated analysis. *Human Molecular Genetics, 18*(3), 580–593.

**Mackenzie, Karen J.; Anderton, Stephen M. & Schwarze, Jürgen.** (2014). Viral respiratory tract infections and asthma in early life: Cause and effect? *Clinical & Experimental Allergy, 44*(1), 9–19.

**MacKenzie, Michael J.; Nicklas, Eric; Brooks-Gunn, Jeanne & Waldfogel, Jane.** (2011). Who spanks infants and toddlers? Evidence from the fragile families and child well-being study. *Children and Youth Services Review, 33*(8), 1364–1373.

**MacNeill, Leigha A.; Ram, Nilam; Bell, Martha Ann; Fox, Nathan A. & Pérez-Edgar, Koraly.** (2018). Trajectories of infants' biobehavioral development: Timing and rate of A-not-B performance gains and EEG maturation. *Child Development, 89*(3), 711–724.

**Macosko, Evan Z. & McCarroll, Steven A.** (2013). Our fallen genomes. *Science, 342*(6158), 564–565.

**MacSwan, Jeff.** (2018). Academic English as standard language ideology: A renewed research agenda for asset-based language education. *Language Teaching Research.*

**MacWhinney, Brian.** (2015). Language development. In Lerner, Richard M. (Ed.), *Handbook of child psychology and developmental science* (7th ed., Vol. 2, pp. 296–338). Wiley.

**Madigan, Sheri; Browne, Dillon; Racine, Nicole; Mori, Camille & Tough, Suzanne.** (2019). Association between screen time and children's performance on a developmental screening test. *JAMA Pediatrics, 173*(3), 244–250.

**Maenner, Matthew J.; Shaw, Kelly A.; Baio, Jon; Washington, Anita; Patrick, Mary; DiRienzo, Monica; . . . Dietz, Patricia M.**

(2020, March 27). *Prevalence of autism spectrum disorder among children aged 8 years—autism and developmental disabilities monitoring network, 11 sites, United States, 2016. Morbidity and Mortality Weekly Report: Surveillance Summaries,* 69(4), 1–12. Atlanta, GA: Centers for Disease Control and Prevention.

**Mahomed, Kassam; Wild, Kellie; Brown, Consuela & Green, Ann.** (2019). Does fentanyl epidural analgesia affect breastfeeding: A prospective cohort study. *Australian and New Zealand Journal of Obstetrics and Gynaecology,* 59(6), 819–824.

**Majecka, Katarzyna & Pietraszewski, Dariusz.** (2018). Where's the cookie? The ability of monkeys to track object transpositions. *Animal Cognition,* 21(4), 603–611.

**Makinen, Mauno; Puukko-Viertomies, Leena-Riitta; Lindberg, Nina; Siimes, Martti A. & Aalberg, Veikko.** (2012). Body dissatisfaction and body mass in girls and boys transitioning from early to mid-adolescence: Additional role of self-esteem and eating habits. *BMC Psychiatry,* 12(35).

**Malina, Robert M.; Bouchard, Claude & Bar-Or, Oded.** (2004). *Growth, maturation, and physical activity* (2nd ed.). Human Kinetics.

**Mallett, Christopher A.** (2016). The school-to-prison pipeline: A critical review of the punitive paradigm shift. *Child and Adolescent Social Work Journal,* 33(1), 15–24.

**Malloy, Lindsay C.; Shulman, Elizabeth P. & Cauffman, Elizabeth.** (2014). Interrogations, confessions, and guilty pleas among serious adolescent offenders. *Law and Human Behavior,* 38(2), 181–193.

**Malpas, Jean.** (2011). Between pink and blue: A multi-dimensional family approach to gender nonconforming children and their families. *Family Process,* 50(4), 453–470.

**Maltby, Lauren E.; Callahan, Kelly L.; Friedlander, Scott & Shetgiri, Rashmi.** (2019). Infant temperament and behavioral problems: Analysis of high-risk infants in child welfare. *Journal of Public Child Welfare,* 13(5), 512–528.

**Manasyan, Albert; Chomba, Elwyn; Moore, Janet; Wallace, Dennis; McClure, Elizabeth M.; Koso-Thomas, Marion & Carlo, Waldemar A.** (2019). Association between birth attendant type and delivery site and perinatal outcomes. *International Journal of Gynecology & Obstetrics,* 145(2), 187–192.

**Manczak, Erika M. & Gotlib, Ian H.** (2019). Lipid profiles at birth predict teacher-rated child emotional and social development 5 years later. *Psychological Science,* 30(12), 1780–1789

**Mandelbaum, David E. & de la Monte, Suzanne M.** (2017). Adverse structural and functional effects of marijuana on the brain: Evidence reviewed. *Pediatric Neurology,* 66, 12–20.

**Mann, Joshua R.; McDermott, Suzanne; Bao, Haikun & Bersabe, Adrian.** (2009). Maternal genitourinary infection and risk of cerebral palsy. *Developmental Medicine & Child Neurology,* 51(4), 282–288.

**Mar, Raymond A.** (2011). The neural bases of social cognition and story comprehension. *Annual Review of Psychology,* 62, 103–134.

**Marazita, John M. & Merriman, William E.** (2010). Verifying one's knowledge of a name without retrieving it: A U-shaped relation to vocabulary

size in early childhood. *Language Learning and Development,* 7(1), 40–54.

**Marchiano, Lisa.** (2017). Outbreak: On transgender teens and psychic epidemics. *Psychological Perspectives: Gender Diversity,* 60(3), 345–366.

**Marcia, James E.** (1966). Development and validation of ego-identity status. *Journal of Personality and Social Psychology,* 3(5), 551–558.

**Marcovitch, Stuart; Clearfield, Melissa W.; Swingler, Margaret; Calkins, Susan D. & Bell, Martha Ann.** (2016). Attentional predictors of 5-month-olds' performance on a looking A-not-B task. *Infant and Child Development,* 25(4), 233–246.

**Marcus, Gary F. & Rabagliati, Hugh.** (2009). Language acquisition, domain specificity, and descent with modification. In Colombo, John; McCardle, Peggy & Freund, Lisa (Eds.), *Infant pathways to language: Methods, models, and research disorders* (pp. 267–285). Psychology Press.

**Mareschal, Denis & Kaufman, Jordy.** (2012). Object permanence in infancy: Revisiting Baillargeon's drawbridge study. In Slater, Alan M. & Quinn, Paul C. (Eds.), *Developmental psychology: Revisiting the classic studies.* Sage.

**Markova, Gabriela.** (2018). The games infants play: Social games during early mother–infant interactions and their relationship with oxytocin. *Frontiers in Psychology,* 9(1041).

**Markovitch, Noam; Luyckx, Koen; Klimstra, Theo; Abramson, Lior & Knafo-Noam, Ariel.** (2017). Identity exploration and commitment in early adolescence: Genetic and environmental contributions. *Developmental Psychology,* 53(11), 2092–2102.

**Marks, Amy K.; Ejesi, Kida & García Coll, Cynthia.** (2014). Understanding the U.S. immigrant paradox in childhood and adolescence. *Child Development Perspectives,* 8(2), 59–64.

**Marotta, Phillip L. & Voisin, Dexter R.** (2017). Testing three pathways to substance use and delinquency among low-income African American adolescents. *Children and Youth Services Review,* 75, 7–14.

**Marouli, Eirini; Graff, Mariaelisa; Medina-Gomez, Carolina; Lo, Ken Sin; Wood, Andrew R.; Kjaer, Troels R.; . . . Perola, Markus.** (2017). Rare and low-frequency coding variants alter human adult height. *Nature,* 542, 186–190.

**Marshall, Eliot.** (2014). An experiment in zero parenting. *Science,* 345(6198), 752–754.

**Martin, Carmel.** (2014). *Common Core implementation best practices. New York State Office of the Governor Common Core Implementation Panel.* Washington, DC: Center for American Progress.

**Martin, Carol L.; Fabes, Richard; Hanish, Laura; Leonard, Stacie & Dinella, Lisa.** (2011). Experienced and expected similarity to same-gender peers: Moving toward a comprehensive model of gender segregation. *Sex Roles,* 65(5/6), 421–434.

**Martin, Joyce A.; Hamilton, Brady E.; Osterman, Michelle J. K. & Driscoll, Anne K.** (2019, November 27). *Births: Final data for 2018. National Vital Statistics Reports,* 68(13). Hyattsville, MD: National Center for Health Statistics.

**Martin, Joyce A.; Hamilton, Brady E.; Osterman, Michelle J. K.; Driscoll, Anne K. &**

**Drake, Patrick.** (2018, January 31). *Births: Final data for 2016. National Vital Statistics Reports,* 67(1). Hyattsville, MD: National Center for Health Statistics.

**Martinson, Melissa L. & Reichman, Nancy E.** (2016). Socioeconomic inequalities in low birth weight in the United States, the United Kingdom, Canada, and Australia. *American Journal of Public Health,* 106(4), 748–754.

**Marulis, Loren Marie; Baker, Sara T. & Whitebread, David.** (2020). Integrating metacognition and executive function to enhance young children's perception of and agency in their learning. *Early Childhood Research Quarterly,* 50, 46–54.

**Masarik, April S. & Conger, Rand D.** (2017). Stress and child development: A review of the Family Stress Model. *Current Opinion in Psychology,* 13, 85–90.

**Mascarelli, Amanda.** (2013). Growing up with pesticides. *Science,* 341(6147), 740–741.

**Mascaro, Jennifer S.; Rentscher, Kelly E.; Hackett, Patrick D.; Mehl, Matthias R. & Rilling, James K.** (2017). Child gender influences paternal behavior, language, and brain function. *Behavioral Neuroscience,* 131(3), 262–273.

**Maski, Kiran P. & Kothare, Sanjeev V.** (2013). Sleep deprivation and neurobehavioral functioning in children. *International Journal of Psychophysiology,* 89(2), 259–264.

**Masten, Ann S.** (2014). *Ordinary magic: Resilience in development.* Guilford Press.

**Mattick, Richard P.; Clare, Philip J.; Aiken, Alexandra; Wadolowski, Monika; Hutchinson, Delyse; Najman, Jackob; . . . Degenhardt, Louisa.** (2018). Association of parental supply of alcohol with adolescent drinking, alcohol-related harms, and alcohol use disorder symptoms: A prospective cohort study. *The Lancet Public Health,* 3(2), e64–e71.

**Maxwell, Lynne G.; Fraga, María V. & Malavolta, Carrie P.** (2019). Assessment of pain in the newborn. *Clinics in Perinatology,* 46(4), 693–707.

**May, Lillian; Byers-Heinlein, Krista; Gervain, Judit & Werker, Janet F.** (2011). Language and the newborn brain: Does prenatal language experience shape the neonate neural response to speech? *Frontiers in Psychology,* 2, 222.

**Mayberry, Rachel I. & Kluender, Robert.** (2018). Rethinking the critical period for language: New insights into an old question from American Sign Language. *Bilingualism: Language and Cognition,* 21(5), 938–944.

**Mazza, Julia Rachel; Pingault, Jean-Baptiste; Booij, Linda; Boivin, Michel; Tremblay, Richard; Lambert, Jean; . . . Côté, Sylvana.** (2017). Poverty and behavior problems during early childhood: The mediating role of maternal depression symptoms and parenting. *International Journal of Behavioral Development,* 41(6), 670–680.

**McAlister, Anna R. & Peterson, Candida C.** (2013). Siblings, theory of mind, and executive functioning in children aged 3–6 years: New longitudinal evidence. *Child Development,* 84(4), 1442–1458.

**McCabe, Sean Esteban; Veliz, Philip; Wilens, Timothy E. & Schulenberg, John E.** (2017).

Adolescents' prescription stimulant use and adult functional outcomes: A national prospective study. *Journal of the American Academy of Child and Adolescent Psychiatry, 56*(3), 226–233.e4.

**McCabe, Sean Esteban; West, Brady T.; Teter, Christian J. & Boyd, Carol J.** (2014). Trends in medical use, diversion, and nonmedical use of prescription medications among college students from 2003 to 2013: Connecting the dots. *Addictive Behaviors, 39*(7), 1176–1182.

**McCall, Robert B.** (2013). The consequences of early institutionalization: Can institutions be improved?—Should they? *Child and Adolescent Mental Health, 18*(4), 193–201.

**McCallion, Gail & Feder, Jody.** (2013, October 18). *Student bullying: Overview of research, federal initiatives, and legal issues.* Washington, DC: Congressional Research Service. R43254.

**McCarthy, Neil & Eberhart, Johann K.** (2014). Gene–ethanol interactions underlying fetal alcohol spectrum disorders. *Cellular and Molecular Life Sciences, 71*(14), 2699–2706.

**McClain, Natalie M. & Garrity, Stacy E.** (2011). Sex trafficking and the exploitation of adolescents. *Journal of Obstetric, Gynecologic, & Neonatal Nursing, 40*(2), 243–252.

**McConnell, Sean C. & Blasimme, Alessandro.** (2019). Ethics, values, and responsibility in human genome editing. *AMA Journal of Ethics, 21*(12), E1017–1020.

**McCormick, Cheryl M.; Mathews, Iva Z.; Thomas, Catherine & Waters, Patti.** (2010). Investigations of HPA function and the enduring consequences of stressors in adolescence in animal models. *Brain and Cognition, 72*(1), 73–85.

**McCoy, Shelly; Dimler, Laura; Samuels, Danielle & Natsuaki, Misaki N.** (2019). Adolescent susceptibility to deviant peer pressure: Does gender matter? *Adolescent Research Review, 4*(1), 59–71.

**McCray, Jennifer S.; Chen, Jie-Qi & Sorkin, Janet Eisenband (Eds.).** (2018). *Growing mathematical minds: Conversations between developmental psychologists and early childhood teachers.* Routledge.

**McEwen, Craig A. & McEwen, Bruce S.** (2017). Social structure, adversity, toxic stress, and intergenerational poverty: An early childhood model. *Annual Review of Sociology, 43*, 445–472.

**McFarland, David H.; Fortin, Annie Joëlle & Polka, Linda.** (2020). Physiological measures of mother–infant interactional synchrony. *Developmental Psychobiology, 62*(1), 50–61.

**McFarland, Joel; Hussar, Bill; Wang, Xiaolei; Zhang, Jijun; Wang, Ke; Rathbun, Amy; . . . Mann, Farrah Bullock.** (2018, May). *The condition of education 2018.* Washington, DC: National Center for Education Statistics. NCES 2018-144.

**McFarland, Joel; Hussar, Bill; Zhang, Jijun; Wang, Xiaolei; Wang, Ke; Hein, Sarah; . . . Barmer, Amy.** (2019). *The condition of education 2019.* Washington, DC: National Center for Education Statistics. NCES 2019-144.

**McFarlane, Alexander C. & Van Hooff, Miranda.** (2009). Impact of childhood exposure to a natural disaster on adult mental health: 20-year longitudinal follow-up study. *The British Journal of Psychiatry, 195*(2), 142–148.

**McGillion, Michelle; Herbert, Jane S.; Pine, Julian; Vihman, Marilyn; dePaolis, Rory; Keren-Portnoy, Tamar & Matthews, Danielle.** (2017). What paves the way to conventional language? The predictive value of babble, pointing, and socioeconomic status. *Child Development, 88*(1), 156–166.

**McGue, Matt; Irons, Dan & Iacono, William G.** (2014). The adolescent origins of substance use disorders: A behavioral genetic perspective. In Stoltenberg, Scott F. (Ed.), *Genes and the motivation to use substances* (pp. 31–50). Springer.

**McKeever, Pamela M. & Clark, Linda.** (2017). Delayed high school start times later than 8:30 a.m. and impact on graduation rates and attendance rates. *Sleep Health, 3*(2), 119–125.

**McKeganey, Neil; Russell, Christopher; Katsampouris, Evangelos & Haseen, Farhana.** (2019). Sources of youth access to JUUL vaping products in the United States. *Addictive Behaviors Reports, 10*, 100232.

**McKenzie, Sarah C. & Ritter, Gary W.** (2017). School discipline in Arkansas. *Policy Briefs, 14*(4).

**McKone, Elinor; Wan, Lulu; Pidcock, Madeleine; Crookes, Kate; Reynolds, Katherine; Dawel, Amy; . . . Fiorentini, Chiara.** (2019). A critical period for faces: Other-race face recognition is improved by childhood but not adult social contact. *Scientific Reports, 9*(12820).

**McLeod, Bryce D.; Wood, Jeffrey J. & Weisz, John R.** (2007). Examining the association between parenting and childhood anxiety: A meta-analysis. *Clinical Psychology Review, 27*(2), 155–172.

**McManus, I. Chris; Moore, James; Freegard, Matthew & Rawles, Richard.** (2010). Science in the making: Right hand, left hand. III: Estimating historical rates of left-handedness. *Laterality: Asymmetries of Body, Brain and Cognition, 15*(1/2), 186–208.

**McNally, Shelley A. & Slutsky, Ruslan.** (2017). Key elements of the Reggio Emilia approach and how they are interconnected to create the highly regarded system of early childhood education. *Early Child Development and Care, 187*(12), 1925–1937.

**Meece, Judith L. & Eccles, Jacquelynne S. (Eds.).** (2010). *Handbook of research on schools, schooling, and human development.* Routledge.

**Meeus, Wim.** (2011). The study of adolescent identity formation 2000–2010: A review of longitudinal research. *Journal of Research on Adolescence, 21*(1), 75–94.

**Meeus, Wim.** (2017). Adolescent ethnic identity in social context: A commentary. *Child Development, 88*(3), 761–766.

**Mehler, Philip S.** (2018). Medical complications of anorexia nervosa and bulimia nervosa. In Agras, W. Stewart & Robinson, Athena (Eds.), *The Oxford handbook of eating disorders* (2nd ed.). Oxford University Press.

**Meinhardt-Injac, Bozana; Daum, Moritz M. & Meinhardt, Günter.** (2020). Theory of mind development from adolescence to adulthood: Testing the two-component model. *British Journal of Developmental Psychology, 38*(2), 289–303.

**Meldrum, Ryan; Kavish, Nicholas & Boutwell, Brian.** (2018). On the longitudinal association between peer and adolescent intelligence: Can our friends make us smarter? *PsyArXiv.*

**Meldrum, Ryan Charles; Young, Jacob T. N.; Kavish, Nicholas & Boutwell, Brian B.** (2019). Could peers influence intelligence during adolescence? An exploratory study. *Intelligence, 72*, 28–34.

**Mellerson, Jenelle L.; Maxwell, Choppell B.; Knighton, Cynthia L.; Kriss, Jennifer L.; Seither, Ranee & Black, Carla L.** (2018, October 12). *Vaccination coverage for selected vaccines and exemption rates among children in kindergarten—United States, 2017–18 school year. Morbidity and Mortality Weekly Report, 67*(40), 1115–1122. Atlanta, GA: Centers for Disease Control and Prevention.

**Meltzoff, Andrew N. & Gopnik, Alison.** (2013). Learning about the mind from evidence: Children's development of intuitive theories of perception and personality. In Baron-Cohen, Simon; Tager-Flusberg, Helen & Lombardo, Michael (Eds.), *Understanding other minds: Perspectives from developmental social neuroscience* (3rd ed., pp. 19–34). Oxford University Press.

**Mendle, Jane; Harden, K. Paige; Brooks-Gunn, Jeanne & Graber, Julia A.** (2010). Development's tortoise and hare: Pubertal timing, pubertal tempo, and depressive symptoms in boys and girls. *Developmental Psychology, 46*(5), 1341–1353.

**Mendle, Jane; Harden, K. Paige; Brooks-Gunn, Jeanne & Graber, Julia A.** (2012). Peer relationships and depressive symptomatology in boys at puberty. *Developmental Psychology, 48*(2), 429–435.

**Mennella, Julie A. & Bobowski, Nuala K.** (2015). The sweetness and bitterness of childhood: Insights from basic research on taste preferences. *Physiology & Behavior, 152*, 502–507.

**Mercer, Neil & Howe, Christine.** (2012). Explaining the dialogic processes of teaching and learning: The value and potential of sociocultural theory. *Learning, Culture and Social Interaction, 1*(1), 12–21.

**Mermelshtine, Roni.** (2017). Parent–child learning interactions: A review of the literature on scaffolding. *British Journal of Educational Psychology, 87*(2), 241–254.

**Merz, Emily C. & McCall, Robert B.** (2011). Parent ratings of executive functioning in children adopted from psychosocially depriving institutions. *Journal of Child Psychology and Psychiatry, 52*(5), 537–546.

**Messinger, Daniel M.; Ruvolo, Paul; Ekas, Naomi V. & Fogel, Alan.** (2010). Applying machine learning to infant interaction: The development is in the details. *Neural Networks, 23*(8/9), 1004–1016.

**Metcalfe, Lindsay A.; Harvey, Elizabeth A. & Laws, Holly B.** (2013). The longitudinal relation between academic/cognitive skills and externalizing behavior problems in preschool children. *Journal of Educational Psychology, 105*(3), 881–894.

**Michaeli, Yossi; Kalfon Hakhmigari, Maor; Dickson, Daniel J.; Scharf, Miri & Shulman, Shmuel.** (2018). The role of change in self-criticism across young adulthood in explaining developmental outcomes and psychological wellbeing. *Journal of Personality, 87*(4), 785–798.

**Miech, Richard A.; Johnston, Lloyd D.; O'Malley, Patrick M.; Bachman, Jerald G. &**

**Schulenberg, John E.** (2015). *Monitoring the future, national survey results on drug use, 1975–2014: Volume I, secondary school students.* Ann Arbor, MI: Institute for Social Research, The University of Michigan.

**Miech, Richard A.; Johnston, Lloyd D.; O'Malley, Patrick M.; Bachman, Jerald G. & Schulenberg, John E.** (2016). *Monitoring the future, national survey results on drug use, 1975–2015: Volume I, secondary school students.* Ann Arbor, MI: Institute for Social Research, The University of Michigan.

**Miech, Richard A.; Johnston, Lloyd D.; O'Malley, Patrick M.; Bachman, Jerald G.; Schulenberg, John E. & Patrick, Megan E.** (2017a). *Monitoring the future, national survey results on drug use, 1975–2016: Volume I, secondary school students.* Ann Arbor, MI: Institute for Social Research, The University of Michigan.

**Miech, Richard A.; Johnston, Lloyd D.; O'Malley, Patrick M.; Bachman, Jerald G.; Schulenberg, John E. & Patrick, Megan E.** (2018). *Monitoring the future, national survey results on drug use, 1975–2017: Volume I, secondary school students.* Ann Arbor, MI: Institute for Social Research, The University of Michigan.

**Miech, Richard A.; Johnston, Lloyd D.; O'Malley, Patrick M.; Bachman, Jerald G.; Schulenberg, John E. & Patrick, Megan E.** (2019). *Monitoring the future, national survey results on drug use, 1975–2018: Volume I, secondary school students.* Ann Arbor, MI: Institute for Social Research, The University of Michigan.

**Miech, Richard A.; Patrick, Megan E.; O'Malley, Patrick M. & Johnston, Lloyd D.** (2017b). E-cigarette use as a predictor of cigarette smoking: Results from a 1-year follow-up of a national sample of 12th grade students. *Tobacco Control, 26,* e106–e111.

**Miklowitz, David J. & Cicchetti, Dante (Eds.).** (2010). *Understanding bipolar disorder: A developmental psychopathology perspective.* Guilford Press.

**Mikolajczyk, Rafael T.; Zhang, Jun; Grewal, Jagteshwar; Chan, Linda C.; Petersen, Antje & Gross, Mechthild M.** (2016). Early versus late admission to labor affects labor progression and risk of cesarean section in nulliparous women. *Frontiers in Medicine, 3*(26).

**Milgrom, Jeannette; Martin, Paul R.; Newnham, Carol; Holt, Christopher J.; Anderson, Peter J.; Hunt, Rod W.; . . . Gemmill, Alan W.** (2019). Behavioural and cognitive outcomes following an early stress-reduction intervention for very preterm and extremely preterm infants. *Pediatric Research, 86,* 92–99.

**Miller, Cindy F.; Martin, Carol Lynn; Fabes, Richard A. & Hanish, Laura D.** (2013). Bringing the cognitive and the social together: How gender detectives and gender enforcers shape children's gender development. In Banaji, Mahzarin R. & Gelman, Susan A. (Eds.), *Navigating the social world: What infants, children, and other species can teach us* (pp. 306–313). Oxford University Press.

**Miller, Melissa K.; Dowd, M. Denise; Harrison, Christopher J.; Mollen, Cynthia J.; Selvarangan, Rangaraj & Humiston, Sharon.** (2015). Prevalence of 3 sexually transmitted infections in a pediatric emergency department. *Pediatric Emergency Care, 31*(2), 107–112.

**Miller, Patricia H.** (2011). *Theories of developmental psychology* (5th ed.). Worth.

**Miller, Patricia H.** (2016). *Theories of developmental psychology* (6th ed.). Worth.

**Miller-Cotto, Dana & Byrnes, James P.** (2016). Ethnic/racial identity and academic achievement: A meta-analytic review. *Developmental Review, 41,* 51–70.

**Miller-Perrin, Cindy & Wurtele, Sandy K.** (2017). Sex trafficking and the commercial sexual exploitation of children. *Women & Therapy, 40*(1/2), 123–151.

**Mills, Catherine.** (2019, May 14). CRISPR case highlights the ethical concerns over gene editing. *Lens.* Monash University.

**Mills-Koonce, W. Roger; Garrett-Peters, Patricia; Barnett, Melissa; Granger, Douglas A.; Blair, Clancy & Cox, Martha J.** (2011). Father contributions to cortisol responses in infancy and toddlerhood. *Developmental Psychology, 47*(2), 388–395.

**Milunsky, Aubrey & Milunsky, Jeff M.** (2016). *Genetic disorders and the fetus: Diagnosis, prevention, and treatment* (7th ed.). Wiley-Blackwell.

**Mindell, Jodi A.; Sadeh, Avi; Wiegand, Benjamin; How, Ti Hwei & Goh, Daniel Y. T.** (2010). Cross-cultural differences in infant and toddler sleep. *Sleep Medicine, 11*(3), 274–280.

**Mischel, Walter.** (2014). *The marshmallow test: Mastering self-control.* Little, Brown.

**Mischel, Walter; Ebbesen, Ebbe B. & Raskoff Zeiss, Antonette.** (1972). Cognitive and attentional mechanisms in delay of gratification. *Journal of Personality and Social Psychology, 21*(2), 204–218.

**Misra, Dawn P.; Caldwell, Cleopatra; Young, Alford A. & Abelson, Sara.** (2010). Do fathers matter? Paternal contributions to birth outcomes and racial disparities. *American Journal of Obstetrics and Gynecology, 202*(2), 99–100.

**Missana, Manuela; Rajhans, Purva; Atkinson, Anthony P. & Grossmann, Tobias.** (2014). Discrimination of fearful and happy body postures in 8-month-old infants: An event-related potential study. *Frontiers in Human Neuroscience, 8,* 531.

**Mitchell, Edwin A.** (2009). SIDS: Past, present and future. *Acta Paediatrica, 98*(11), 1712–1719.

**Mitchell, Kimberly J.; Jones, Lisa M.; Finkelhor, David & Wolak, Janis.** (2013). Understanding the decline in unwanted online sexual solicitations for U.S. youth 2000–2010: Findings from three Youth Internet Safety Surveys. *Child Abuse & Neglect, 37*(12), 1225–1236.

**Miyata, Susanne; MacWhinney, Brian; Otomo, Kiyoshi; Sirai, Hidetosi; Oshima-Takane, Yuriko; Hirakawa, Makiko; . . . Itoh, Keiko.** (2013). Developmental sentence scoring for Japanese. *First Language, 33*(2), 200–216.

**Mize, Krystal D.; Pineda, Melannie; Blau, Alexis K.; Marsh, Kathryn & Jones, Nancy A.** (2014). Infant physiological and behavioral responses to a jealousy provoking condition. *Infancy, 19*(3), 338–348.

**MMWR.** (2008, January 18). *School-associated student homicides—United States, 1992–2006.*

*Morbidity and Mortality Weekly Report, 57*(2), 33–36. Atlanta, GA: U.S. Department of Health and Human Services, Centers for Disease Control and Prevention.

**MMWR.** (2010, June 4). *Youth risk behavior surveillance—United States, 2009. Morbidity and Mortality Weekly Report Surveillance Summaries, 59*(SS05). Atlanta, GA: U.S. Department of Health and Human Services, Centers for Disease Control and Prevention.

**MMWR.** (2012, June 8). *Youth risk behavior surveillance—United States, 2011. Morbidity and Mortality Weekly Report, 61*(4). Atlanta, GA: U.S. Department of Health and Human Services, Centers for Disease Control and Prevention.

**MMWR.** (2013, April 5). *Blood lead levels in children aged 1–5 Years—United States, 1999–2010. Morbidity and Mortality Weekly Report, 62*(13), 245–248. Atlanta, GA: U.S. Department of Health and Human Services, Centers for Disease Control and Prevention.

**MMWR.** (2014, June 13). *Youth risk behavior surveillance—United States, 2013. Morbidity and Mortality Weekly Report, 63*(4). Atlanta, GA: U.S. Department of Health and Human Services, Centers for Disease Control and Prevention.

**MMWR.** (2014, March 7). *Impact of requiring influenza vaccination for children in licensed child care or preschool programs—Connecticut, 2012–13 influenza season. Morbidity and Mortality Weekly Report, 63*(9), 181–185. Atlanta, GA: U.S. Department of Health and Human Services, Centers for Disease Control and Prevention.

**MMWR.** (2014, March 28). *Prevalence of autism spectrum disorder among children aged 8 years—Autism and Developmental Disabilities Monitoring Network, 11 sites, United States, 2010. Morbidity and Mortality Weekly Report, 63*(2). Atlanta, GA: U.S. Department of Health and Human Services, Centers for Disease Control and Prevention.

**MMWR.** (2016, June 10). *Youth risk behavior surveillance—United States, 2015. Morbidity and Mortality Weekly Report, 65*(6). Atlanta, GA: U.S. Department of Health and Human Services, Centers for Disease Control and Prevention.

**MMWR.** (2018, June 15). *Youth risk behavior surveillance—United States, 2017. Morbidity and Mortality Weekly Report, 67*(8). Atlanta, GA: U.S. Department of Health and Human Services, Centers for Disease Control and Prevention.

**MMWR.** (2020, March 6). *Quickstats: Age-adjusted suicide rates, by sex and three most common methods—United States, 2000–2018. Morbidity and mortality weekly report, 69*(9), 249. Atlanta, GA: U.S. Department of Health and Human Services, Centers for Disease Control and Prevention.

**Moffitt, Terrie E.** (2003). Life-course-persistent and adolescence-limited antisocial behavior: A 10-year research review and a research agenda. In Lahey, Benjamin B.; Moffitt, Terrie E. & Caspi, Avshalom (Eds.), *Causes of conduct disorder and juvenile delinquency* (pp. 49–75). Guilford Press.

**Moffitt, Terrie E.; Caspi, Avshalom; Rutter, Michael & Silva, Phil A.** (2001). *Sex differences in antisocial behaviour: Conduct disorder, delinquency, and violence in the Dunedin Longitudinal Study.* Cambridge University Press.

Mokrova, Irina L.; O'Brien, Marion; Calkins, Susan D.; Leerkes, Esther M. & Marcovitch, Stuart. (2013). The role of persistence at preschool age in academic skills at kindergarten. *European Journal of Psychology of Education*, 28(4), 1495–1503.

Moldavsky, Maria & Sayal, Kapil. (2013). Knowledge and attitudes about Attention-deficit/hyperactivity disorder (ADHD) and its treatment: The views of children, adolescents, parents, teachers and healthcare professionals. *Current Psychiatry Reports*, 15, 377.

Moles, Laura; Manzano, Susana; Fernández, Leonides; Montilla, Antonia; Corzo, Nieves; Ares, Susana; . . . Espinosa-Martos, Irene. (2015). Bacteriological, biochemical, and immunological properties of colostrum and mature milk from mothers of extremely preterm infants. *Journal of Pediatric Gastroenterology & Nutrition*, 60(1), 120–126.

Mollborn, Stefanie & Lawrence, Elizabeth. (2018). Family, peer, and school influences on children's developing health lifestyles. *Journal of Health and Social Behavior*, 59(1), 133–150.

Monahan, Kathryn C.; Steinberg, Laurence; Cauffman, Elizabeth & Mulvey, Edward P. (2013). Psychosocial (im)maturity from adolescence to early adulthood: Distinguishing between adolescence-limited and persisting antisocial behavior. *Development and Psychopathology*, 25(4), 1093–1105.

Montgomery, Heather. (2015). Understanding child prostitution in Thailand in the 1990s. *Child Development Perspectives*, 9(3), 154–157.

Monthly Vital Statistics Report. (1980). *Final mortality statistics, 1978: Advance report. Monthly Vital Statistics Report*, 29(6, Suppl. 2). Hyattsville, MD: National Center for Health Statistics.

Monti, Jennifer D.; Rudolph, Karen D. & Miernicki, Michelle E. (2017). Rumination about social stress mediates the association between peer victimization and depressive symptoms during middle childhood. *Journal of Applied Developmental Psychology*, 48, 25–32.

Montirosso, Rosario; Casini, Erica; Provenzi, Livio; Putnam, Samuel P.; Morandi, Francesco; Fedeli, Claudia & Borgatti, Renato. (2015). A categorical approach to infants' individual differences during the Still-Face paradigm. *Infant Behavior and Development*, 38, 67–76.

Montirosso, Rosario; Tronick, Ed & Borgatti, Renato. (2017). Promoting neuroprotective care in neonatal intensive care units and preterm infant development: Insights from the neonatal adequate care for quality of life study. *Child Development Perspectives*, 11(1), 9–15.

Moody, Myles. (2016). From under-diagnoses to over-representation: Black children, ADHD, and the school-to-prison pipeline. *Journal of African American Studies*, 20(2), 152–163.

Moore, Keith L.; Persaud, T. V. N. & Torchia, Mark G. (2015). *The developing human: Clinically oriented embryology* (10th ed.). Saunders.

Moore, Mary Ruth & Sabo-Risley, Constance (Eds.). (2017). *Play in America: Essays in honor of Joe L. Frost*. Archway.

Morales, Angelica; Jones, Scott; Ehlers, Alissa; Lavine, Jessye & Nagel, Bonnie. (2018). Ventral striatal response during decision making involving risk and reward is associated with future binge drinking in adolescents. *Neuropsychopharmacology*, 43(9), 1884–1890.

Moran, Lyndsey R.; Lengua, Liliana J. & Zalewski, Maureen. (2013). The interaction between negative emotionality and effortful control in early social-emotional development. *Social Development*, 22(2), 340–362.

Moran, Lauren V.; Masters, Grace A.; Pingali, Samira; Cohen, Bruce M.; Liebson, Elizabeth; Rajarethinam, R. P. & Ongur, Dost. (2015). Prescription stimulant use is associated with earlier onset of psychosis. *Journal of Psychiatric Research*, 71, 41–47.

Morawska, Alina & Sanders, Matthew. (2011). Parental use of time out revisited: A useful or harmful parenting strategy? *Journal of Child and Family Studies*, 20(1), 1–8.

Morelli, Gilda; Quinn, Naomi; Chaudhary, Nandita; Vicedo, Marga; Rosabal-Coto, Mariano; Keller, Heidi; . . . Takada, Akira. (2018). Ethical challenges of parenting interventions in low- to middle-income countries. *Journal of Cross-Cultural Psychology*, 49(1), 5–24.

Moreno, Sylvain; Lee, Yunjo; Janus, Monika & Bialystok, Ellen. (2015). Short-term second language and music training induces lasting functional brain changes in early childhood. *Child Development*, 86(2), 394–406.

Morgan, David L. (2018). Living within blurry boundaries: The value of distinguishing between qualitative and quantitative research. *Journal of Mixed Methods Research*, 12(3), 268–279.

Morgan, Hani. (2019). Does high-quality preschool benefit children? What the research shows. *Education Sciences*, 9(1).

Morgan, Ian G.; Ohno-Matsui, Kyoko & Saw, Seang-Mei. (2012). Myopia. *The Lancet*, 379(9827), 1739–1748.

Morones, Alyssa. (2013). Paddling persists in U.S. schools. *Education Week*, 33(9), 1, 10–11.

Morphett, Kylie; Herron, Lisa & Gartner, Coral. (2020). Protectors or puritans? Responses to media articles about the health effects of e-cigarettes. *Addiction Research & Theory*, 28(2), 95–102.

Morris, Vivian G. & Morris, Curtis L. (2013). A call for African American male teachers: The supermen expected to solve the problems of low-performing schools. In Lewis, Chance W. & Toldson, Ivory A. (Eds.), *Black male teachers: Diversifying the United States' teacher workforce* (pp. 151–165). Emerald Group.

Morrongiello, Barbara A. (2018). Preventing unintentional injuries to young children in the home: Understanding and influencing parents' safety practices. *Child Development Perspectives*, 12(4), 217–222.

Morse, Timothy E. (2019). *Response to intervention: Refining instruction to meet student needs*. Rowman & Littlefield.

Moultrie, Fiona; Goksan, Sezgi; Poorun, Ravi & Slater, Rebeccah. (2016). Pain in neonates and infants. In Battaglia, Anna A. (Ed.), *An introduction to pain and its relation to nervous system disorders* (pp. 283–293). Wiley.

Mourad, Mirella; Landau, Ruth; Wright, Jason; Siddiq, Zainab; Duffy, Cassandra; Kern-Goldberger, Adina; . . . Friedman, Alexander. (2019). Oral opioid use during vaginal delivery hospitalizations. *American Journal of Perinatology*.

Mowry, James B.; Spyker, Daniel A.; Brooks, Daniel E.; Mcmillan, Naya & Schauben, Jay L. (2015). 2014 Annual report of the American Association of Poison Control Centers' National Poison Data System (NPDS): 32nd Annual report. *Clinical Toxicology*, 53(10), 962–1146.

Mrug, Sylvie; Elliott, Marc N.; Davies, Susan; Tortolero, Susan R.; Cuccaro, Paula & Schuster, Mark A. (2014). Early puberty, negative peer influence, and problem behaviors in adolescent girls. *Pediatrics*, 133(1), 7–14.

Mueller, Isabelle & Tronick, Ed. (2019). Early life exposure to violence: Developmental consequences on brain and behavior. *Frontiers in Behavioral Neuroscience*, 13(156).

Mueller, Noel T.; Mao, G.; Bennett, Wendy L.; Hourigan, Suchi K.; Dominguez-Bello, Maria G.; Appel, Lawrence J. & Wang, Xiaobin. (2017). Does vaginal delivery mitigate or strengthen the intergenerational association of overweight and obesity? Findings from the Boston Birth Cohort. *International Journal of Obesity*, 41, 497–501.

Mullis, Ina V. S.; Martin, Michael O.; Foy, Pierre & Arora, A. (2012a). *TIMSS 2011 international results in mathematics*. Chestnut Hill, MA: TIMSS & PIRLS International Study Center, Boston College.

Mullis, Ina V. S.; Martin, Michael O.; Foy, Pierre & Drucker, Kathleen T. (2012b). *PIRLS 2011 international results in reading*. Chestnut Hill, MA: TIMSS & PIRLS International Study Center, Boston College.

Mullis, Ina V. S.; Martin, Michael O.; Foy, Pierre & Hooper, Martin. (2016). *TIMSS 2015 international results in mathematics*. Chestnut Hill, MA: TIMSS & PIRLS International Study Center, Boston College.

Mullis, Ina V. S.; Martin, Michael O.; Foy, Pierre & Hooper, Martin. (2017). *International results in reading PIRLS 2016*. Chestnut Hill, MA: TIMSS & PIRLS International Study Center, Boston College.

Muris, Peter & Meesters, Cor. (2014). Small or big in the eyes of the other: On the developmental psychopathology of self-conscious emotions as shame, guilt, and pride. *Clinical Child and Family Psychology Review*, 17(1), 19–40.

Murphy, Colleen; Gardoni, Paolo & McKim, Robert (Eds.). (2018). *Climate change and its impacts: Risks and inequalities*. Springer.

Murray, Kristen; Rieger, Elizabeth & Byrne, Don. (2018). Body image predictors of depressive symptoms in adolescence. *Journal of Adolescence*, 69, 130–139.

Murray, Thomas H. (2014). Stirring the simmering "designer baby" pot. *Science*, 343(6176), 1208–1210.

Mustanski, Brian; Birkett, Michelle; Greene, George J.; Hatzenbuehler, Mark L. & Newcomb, Michael E. (2014). Envisioning an America without sexual orientation inequities in adolescent health. *American Journal of Public Health, 104*(2), 218–225.

**Næss, Kari-Anne B.** (2016). Development of phonological awareness in Down syndrome: A meta-analysis and empirical study. *Developmental Psychology, 52*(2), 177–190.

**NAEYC.** (2014). *NAEYC Early Childhood Program standards and accreditation criteria & guidance for assessment.* Washington, DC: National Association for the Education of Young Children.

**Nanji, Ayaz.** (2005, February 8). World's smallest baby goes home. *CBS News.* AP.

**Narvaez, Darcia; Gleason, Tracy; Wang, Lijuan; Brooks, Jeff; Lefever, Jennifer Burke & Cheng, Ying.** (2013). The evolved development niche: Longitudinal effects of caregiving practices on early childhood psychosocial development. *Early Childhood Research Quarterly, 28*(4), 759–773.

**Nascimento, Andressa Lagoa; Toledo, Aline Martins; Merey, Leila Foerster; Tudella, Eloisa & Soares-Marangoni, Daniele de Almeida.** (2019). Brief reaching training with "sticky mittens" in preterm infants: Randomized controlled trial. *Human Movement Science, 63*, 138–147.

**Natarajan, Mangai (Ed.)** (2017). *Drugs of abuse.* Routledge.

**National Academies of Sciences, Engineering, and Medicine (Ed.)** (2016). *Preventing bullying through science, policy, and practice.* National Academies Press.

**National Center for Education Statistics.** (2018). *The nation's report card.* Washington, DC: Institute of Education Sciences, U.S. Department of Education.

**National Center for Education Statistics.** (2018, September). *Table 502.30. Median annual earnings of full-time year-round workers 25 to 34 years old and full-time year-round workers as a percentage of the labor force, by sex, race/ethnicity, and educational attainment: Selected years, 1995 through 2017.* Washington, DC: Institute of Education Sciences, U.S. Department of Education.

**National Center for Education Statistics.** (2019, February). *Indicator 24: Degrees awarded. Status and trends in the education of racial and ethnic groups.* Washington, DC: Institute of Education Sciences, U.S. Department of Education.

**National Center for Education Statistics.** (2020). *College enrollment rates.* Institute of Education Sciences.

**National Center for Education Statistics.** (2019, May). *Public high school graduation rates. The Condition of Education.* National Center for Education Statistics.

**National Center for Education Statistics.** (2020, May). *Status dropout rates. The Condition of Education.* National Center for Education Statistics, Institute of Education Sciences.

**National Center for Health Statistics.** (2012). *Health, United States, 2011: With special feature on socioeconomic status and health.* Hyattsville, MD: U.S. Department of Health and Human Services, Centers for Disease Control and Prevention.

**National Center for Health Statistics.** (2017). *Health, United States, 2016: With chartbook on long-term trends in health.* Hyattsville, MD: U.S. Department of Health and Human Services.

**National Center for Health Statistics.** (2018). *Health, United States, 2017: With a special feature on mortality.* Hyattsville, MD: U.S. Department of Health and Human Services.

**National Center for Health Statistics.** (2019). *Health, United States, 2018.* Hyattsville, MD: U.S. Department of Health and Human Services.

**National Center for Statistics and Analysis.** (2019, June). *Early estimate of motor vehicle traffic fatalities for 2018. Crash•Stats Brief Statistical Summary.* Washington, DC: National Highway Traffic Safety Administration.

**Naughton, Michelle J.; Yi-Frazier, Joyce P.; Morgan, Timothy M.; Seid, Michael; Lawrence, Jean M.; Klingensmith, Georgeanna J.; . . . Loots, Beth.** (2014). Longitudinal associations between sex, diabetes self-care, and health-related quality of life among youth with type 1 or type 2 diabetes mellitus. *The Journal of Pediatrics, 164*(6), 1376–1383.e1.

**Neary, Marianne T. & Breckenridge, Ross A.** (2013). Hypoxia at the heart of sudden infant death syndrome? *Pediatric Research, 74*(4), 375–379.

**Needham, Amy W.; Wiesen, Sarah E.; Hejazi, Jennifer N.; Libertus, Klaus & Christopher, Caroline.** (2017). Characteristics of brief sticky mittens training that lead to increases in object exploration. *Journal of Experimental Child Psychology, 164*, 209–224.

**Needleman, Herbert L. & Gatsonis, Constantine A.** (1990). Low-level lead exposure and the IQ of children: A meta-analysis of modern studies. *JAMA, 263*(5), 673–678.

**Needleman, Herbert L.; Schell, Alan; Bellinger, David; Leviton, Alan & Allred, Elizabeth N.** (1990). The long-term effects of exposure to low doses of lead in childhood. *New England Journal of Medicine, 322*(2), 83–88.

**Neggers, Yasmin & Crowe, Kristi.** (2013). Low birth weight outcomes: Why better in Cuba than Alabama? *Journal of the American Board of Family Medicine, 26*(2), 187–195.

**Nelson, Charles A.; Fox, Nathan A. & Zeanah, Charles H.** (2014). *Romania's abandoned children: Deprivation, brain development, and the struggle for recovery.* Harvard University Press.

**Nelson, Geoffrey & Caplan, Rachel.** (2014). The prevention of child physical abuse and neglect: An update. *Journal of Applied Research on Children, 5*(1).

**Nelson, Helen; Kendall, Garth; Burns, Sharyn; Schonert-Reichl, Kimberly & Kane, Robert.** (2019). Development of the student experience of teacher support scale: Measuring the experience of children who report aggression and bullying. *International Journal of Bullying Prevention, 1*(2), 99–110.

**Nesdale, Drew; Zimmer-Gembeck, Melanie J. & Roxburgh, Natalie.** (2014). Peer group rejection in childhood: Effects of rejection ambiguity, rejection sensitivity, and social acumen. *Journal of Social Issues, 70*(1), 12–28.

**Neuman, Susan B.; Kaefer, Tanya & Pinkham, Ashley M.** (2018). A double dose of disadvantage: Language experiences for low-income children in home and school. *Journal of Educational Psychology, 110*(1), 102–118.

**Nevanen, Saila; Juvonen, Antti & Ruismäki, Heikki.** (2014). Does arts education develop school readiness? Teachers' and artists' points of view on an art education project. *Arts Education Policy Review, 115*(3), 72–81.

**Nevin, Rick.** (2007). Understanding international crime trends: The legacy of preschool lead exposure. *Environmental Research, 104*(3), 315–336.

**Ng, Florrie Fei-Yin; Pomerantz, Eva M. & Deng, Ciping.** (2014). Why are Chinese mothers more controlling than American mothers? "My child is my report card". *Child Development, 85*(1), 355–369.

**Nguyen, Jacqueline; O'Brien, Casey & Schapp, Salena.** (2016). Adolescent inhalant use prevention, assessment, and treatment: A literature synthesis. *Drug Policy, 31*, 15–24.

**Nic Gabhainn, Saoirse; Baban, Adriana; Boyce, William & Godeau, Emmanuelle.** (2009). How well protected are sexually active 15-year-olds? Cross-national patterns in condom and contraceptive pill use 2002–2006. *International Journal of Public Health, 54*(Suppl. 2), 209–215.

**Nichols, Emily S.; Wild, Conor J.; Stojanoski, Bobby; Battista, Michael E. & Owen, Adrian M.** (2020). Bilingualism affords no general cognitive advantages: A population study of executive function in 11,000 people. *Psychological Science, 31*(5), 548–567.

**Niclasen, Janni; Andersen, Anne-Marie N.; Strandberg-Larsen, Katrine & Teasdale, Thomas W.** (2014). Is alcohol binge drinking in early and late pregnancy associated with behavioural and emotional development at age 7 years? *European Child & Adolescent Psychiatry, 23*(12), 1175–1180.

**Nielsen, Mark; Tomaselli, Keyan; Mushin, Ilana & Whiten, Andrew.** (2014). Exploring tool innovation: A comparison of Western and Bushman children. *Journal of Experimental Child Psychology, 126*, 384–394.

**Nieto, Marta; Romero, Dulce; Ros, Laura; Zabala, Carmen; Martínez, Manuela; Ricarte, Jorge J.; . . . Latorre, Jose M.** (2019). Differences in coping strategies between young and older adults: The role of executive functions. *The International Journal of Aging and Human Development.*

**Nieto, Sonia.** (2000). *Affirming diversity: The sociopolitical context of multicultural education* (3rd ed.). Longman.

**Nigg, Joel T. & Barkley, Russell A.** (2014). Attention-deficit/hyperactivity disorder. In Mash, Eric J. & Barkley, Russell A. (Eds.), *Child psychopathology* (3rd ed., pp. 75–144). Guilford Press.

**Nilsson, Kristine Kahr & de López, Kristine Jensen.** (2016). Theory of mind in children with specific language impairment: A systematic review and meta-analysis. *Child Development, 87*(1), 143–153.

**Nishina, Adrienne; Bellmore, Amy; Witkow, Melissa R.; Nylund-Gibson, Karen & Graham, Sandra.** (2018). Mismatches in self-reported and meta-perceived ethnic identification across the high school years. *Journal of Youth and Adolescence, 47*(1), 51–63.

**Nishizato, Minaho; Fujisawa, Takashi; Kosaka, Hirotaka & Tomoda, Akemi.** (2017). Developmental changes in social attention and oxytocin levels in infants and children. *Scientific Reports, 7*(1), 2540–2540.

**Nkomo, Palesa; Naicker, Nisha; Mathee, Angela; Galpin, Jacky; Richter, Linda M. & Norris, Shane A.** (2018). The association between environmental lead exposure with aggressive behavior, and dimensionality of direct and indirect aggression during mid-adolescence: Birth to Twenty Plus cohort. *Science of the Total Environment*, 612, 472–479.

Nocentini, Annalaura; Fiorentini, Giada; Di Paola, Ludovica & Menesini, Ersilia. (2019). Parents, family characteristics and bullying behavior: A systematic review. *Aggression and Violent Behavior*, 45, 41–50.

Noll, Jennie G.; Guastaferro, Kate; Beal, Sarah J.; Schreier, Hannah M. C.; Barnes, Jaclyn; Reader, Jonathan M. & Font, Sarah A. (2019). Is sexual abuse a unique predictor of sexual risk behaviors, pregnancy, and motherhood in adolescence? *Journal of Research on Adolescence*, 29(4), 967–983.

Noll, Jennie G.; Trickett, Penelope K.; Long, Jeffrey D.; Negriff, Sonya; Susman, Elizabeth J.; Shalev, Idan; . . . Putnam, Frank W. (2017). Childhood sexual abuse and early timing of puberty. *Journal of Adolescent Health*, 60(1), 65–71.

Norrman, Emma; Petzold, Max; Bergh, Christina & Wennerholm, Ulla-Britt. (2018). School performance in singletons born after assisted reproductive technology. *Human Reproduction*, 33(10), 1948–1959.

Nowak, Elisabeth & Schaub, Bianca. (2018). Prevention of allergies. In Agache, Ioana & Hellings, Peter (Eds.), *Implementing precision medicine in best practices of chronic airway diseases* (pp. 63–71). Elsevier.

Nxumalo, Fikile & Adair, Jennifer Keys. (2019). Social justice and equity in early childhood education. In Brown, Christopher P.; McMullen, Mary Benson & File, Nancy (Eds.), *The Wiley handbook of early childhood care and education* (pp. 661–682). Wiley.

O'Brien, Edward. (2019, March 15). Missoula high-schoolers demand action on climate change. *Montana Public Radio*.

O'Dougherty, Maureen. (2013). Becoming a mother through postpartum depression: Narratives from Brazil. In Faircloth, Charlotte; Hoffman, Diane M. & Layne, Linda L. (Eds.), *Parenting in global perspective: Negotiating ideologies of kinship, self and politics* (pp. 184–199). Routledge.

O'Hara, Michael W. & McCabe, Jennifer E. (2013). Postpartum depression: Current status and future directions. *Annual Review of Clinical Psychology*, 9, 379–407.

O'Neill, Susan A. & Schmidt, Patrick. (2017). Arts education in Canada and the United States. In Barton, Georgina & Baguley, Margaret (Eds.), *The Palgrave handbook of global arts education* (pp. 187–202). Palgrave Macmillan.

Oakes, J. Michael. (2009). The effect of media on children: A methodological assessment from a social epidemiologist. *American Behavioral Scientist*, 52(8), 1136–1151.

Oakes, Lisa M. & Rakison, David H. (2019). *Developmental cascades: Building the infant mind*. Oxford University Press.

Obama, Michelle. (2018). *Becoming*. Crown.

OECD. (2010). *Learning mathematics for life: A perspective from PISA*. OECD.

OECD. (2011). *Education at a glance 2011: OECD indicators*. Paris, France: Organisation for Economic Cooperation and Development.

OECD. (2014). *Education at a glance 2014: OECD Indicators*. Paris, France: Organisation for Economic Cooperation and Development.

OECD. (2018). *Education at a glance 2018: OECD indicators*. Paris, France: Organisation for Economic Cooperation and Development.

OECD.Stat. (2019). *Income distribution and poverty* [Data set]. OECD Income Distribution Database.

Olson, Kristina R. & Dweck, Carol S. (2009). Social cognitive development: A new look. *Child Development Perspectives*, 3(1), 60–65.

Olson, Sheryl L.; Lopez-Duran, Nestor; Lunkenheimer, Erika S.; Chang, Hyein & Sameroff, Arnold J. (2011). Individual differences in the development of early peer aggression: Integrating contributions of self-regulation, theory of mind, and parenting. *Development and Psychopathology*, 23(1), 253–266.

Olweus, Dan. (1999). Sweden. In Smith, Peter K.; Morita, Yohji; Junger-Tas, Josine; Olweus, Dan; Catalano, Richard F. & Slee, Phillip T. (Eds.), *The nature of school bullying: A cross-national perspective* (pp. 7–27). Routledge.

Ormond, Kelly E.; Laurino, Mercy Ygoña; Barlow-Stewart, Kristine; Wessels, Tina-Marié; Macaulay, Shelley; Austin, Jehannine & Middleton, Anna. (2018). Genetic counseling globally: Where are we now? *American Journal of Medical Genetics Part C: Seminars in Medical Genetics*, 178(1), 98–107.

Orth, Ulrich; Erol, Ruth Yasemin & Luciano, Eva C. (2018). Development of self-esteem from age 4 to 94 years: A meta-analysis of longitudinal studies. *Psychological Bulletin*, 144(10), 1045–1080.

Orth, Ulrich & Robins, Richard W. (2019). Development of self-esteem across the lifespan. In Shiner, Rebecca L.; Tackett, Jennifer L. & McAdams, Dan P. (Eds.), *Handbook of personality development* (pp. 328–344). Guilford.

Orzabal, Marcus R.; Lunde-Young, Emilie R.; Ramirez, Josue I.; Howe, Selene Y. F.; Naik, Vishal D.; Lee, Jehoon; . . . Ramadoss, Jayanth. (2019). Chronic exposure to e-cig aerosols during early development causes vascular dysfunction and offspring growth deficits. *Translational Research*, 207, 70–82.

Osher, David; Bear, George G.; Sprague, Jeffrey R. & Doyle, Walter. (2010). How can we improve school discipline? *Educational Researcher*, 39(1), 48–58.

Ostfeld, Barbara M.; Esposito, Linda; Perl, Harold & Hegyi, Thomas. (2010). Concurrent risks in sudden infant death syndrome. *Pediatrics*, 125(3), 447–453.

Ostrov, Jamie M.; Kamper, Kimberly E.; Hart, Emily J.; Godleski, Stephanie A. & Blakely-McClure, Sarah J. (2014). A gender-balanced approach to the study of peer victimization and aggression subtypes in early childhood. *Development and Psychopathology*, 26(3), 575–587.

Ottesen, Ninja M.; Meluken, Iselin; Scheike, Thomas; Kessing, Lars V.; Miskowiak, Kamilla W. & Vinberg, Maj. (2018). Clinical characteristics, life adversities and personality traits in monozygotic twins with, at risk of and without affective disorders. *Frontiers in Psychiatry*, 9(401).

Ozernov-Palchik, Ola; Norton, Elizabeth S.; Sideridis, Georgios; Beach, Sara D.; Wolf, Maryanne; Gabrieli, John D. E. & Gaab, Nadine. (2017). Longitudinal stability of pre-reading skill profiles of kindergarten children: Implications for early screening and theories of reading. *Developmental Science*, 20(5), e12471.

Paarlberg, Robert; Mozaffarian, Dariush; Micha, Renata & Chelius, Carolyn. (2018). Keeping soda in SNAP: Understanding the other iron triangle. *Society*, 55(4), 308–317.

Padilla, Jenny; Jager, Justin; Updegraff, Kimberly A.; McHale, Susan M. & Umaña-Taylor, Adriana J. (2020). Mexican-origin family members' unique and shared family perspectives of familism values and their links with parent-youth relationship quality. *Developmental Psychology*, 56(5), 993–1008.

Padilla-Walker, Laura; Memmott-Elison, Madison & Nelson, Larry. (2017). Positive relationships as an indicator of flourishing during emerging adulthood. In Padilla-Walker, Laura M. & Nelson, Larry J. (Eds.), *Flourishing in emerging adulthood: Positive development during the third decade of life* (pp. 212–235). Oxford University Press.

Padilla-Walker, Laura M. & Carlo, Gustavo. (2014). The study of prosocial behavior. In Padilla-Walker, Laura M. & Carlo, Gustavo (Eds.), *Prosocial development: A multidimensional approach*. Oxford University Press.

Paik, Anthony. (2011). Adolescent sexuality and the risk of marital dissolution. *Journal of Marriage and Family*, 73(2), 472–485.

Palmer, Sally B. & Abbott, Nicola. (2018). Bystander responses to bias-based bullying in schools: A developmental intergroup approach. *Child Development Perspectives*, 12(1), 39–44.

Pankow, James F.; Kim, Kilsun; McWhirter, Kevin J.; Luo, Wentai; Escobedo, Jorge O.; Strongin, Robert M.; . . . Peyton, David H. (2017). Benzene formation in electronic cigarettes. *PLoS ONE*, 12(3), e0173055.

Papapetrou, Eirini P. (2016). Induced pluripotent stem cells, past and future. *Science*, 353(6303), 991–992.

Parade, Stephanie H.; Armstrong, Laura M.; Dickstein, Susan & Seifer, Ronald. (2018). Family context moderates the association of maternal postpartum depression and stability of infant temperament. *Child Development*, 89(6), 2118–2135.

Park, Hyun; Bothe, Denise; Holsinger, Eva; Kirchner, H. Lester; Olness, Karen & Mandalakas, Anna. (2011). The impact of nutritional status and longitudinal recovery of motor and cognitive milestones in internationally adopted children. *International Journal of Environmental Research and Public Health*, 8(1), 105–116.

Parke, Ross D. (2013). Gender differences and similarities in parental behavior. In Wilcox, Bradford & Kline, Kathleen K. (Eds.), *Gender and parenthood: Biological and social scientific perspectives* (pp. 120–163). Columbia University Press.

Parker, Kim; Horowitz, Juliana Menasce & Stepler, Renee. (2017, December 5). *On gender differences, no consensus on nature vs. nurture: Americans say society places a higher premium on masculinity than on femininity. Social & Demographic Trends.* Washington, DC: Pew Research Center.

**Parker, Samantha E.; Mai, Cara T.; Canfield, Mark A.; Rickard, Russel; Wang, Ying; Meyer, Robert E.; . . . Correa, Adolfo.** (2010). Updated national birth prevalence estimates for selected birth defects in the United States, 2004–2006. *Birth Defects Research Part A: Clinical and Molecular Teratology*, 88(12), 1008–1016.

**Pascarella, Ernest T.; Martin, Georgianna L.; Hanson, Jana M.; Trolian, Teniell L.; Gillig, Benjamin & Blaich, Charles.** (2014). Effects of diversity experiences on critical thinking skills over 4 years of college. *Journal of College Student Development*, 55(1), 86–92.

**Patel, Ayush; Medhekar, Rohan; Ochoa-Perez, Melissa; Aparasu, Rajender R.; Chan, Wenyaw; Sherer, Jeffrey T.; . . . Chen, Hua.** (2017). Care provision and prescribing practices of physicians treating children and adolescents with ADHD. *Psychiatric Services*, 68(7), 681–688.

**Patel, Harsh; Arruarana, Victor; Yao, Lucille; Cui, Xiaojiang & Ray, Edward.** (2020). Effects of hormones and hormone therapy on breast tissue in transgender patients: A concise review. *Endocrine*, 68(1), 6–15.

**Patel, Manisha; Lee, Adria D.; Clemmons, Nakia S.; Redd, Susan B.; Poser, Sarah; Blog, Debra; . . . Gastañaduy, Paul A.** (2019, October 11). *National update on measles cases and outbreaks—United States, January 1–October 1, 2019. Morbidity and Mortality Weekly Report.* Atlanta, GA: U.S. Department of Health and Human Services.

**Pathela, Preeti & Schillinger, Julia A.** (2010). Sexual behaviors and sexual violence: Adolescents with opposite-, same-, or both-sex partners. *Pediatrics*, 126(5), 879–886.

**Patil, Rakesh N.; Nagaonkar, Shashikant N.; Shah, Nilesh B. & Bhat, Tushar S.** (2013). A cross-sectional study of common psychiatric morbidity in children aged 5 to 14 years in an urban slum. *Journal of Family Medicine and Primary Care*, 2(2), 164–168.

**Patterson, Susan Patricia; Hilton, Shona; Flowers, Paul & McDaid, Lisa M.** (2019). What are the barriers and challenges faced by adolescents when searching for sexual health information on the internet? Implications for policy and practice from a qualitative study. *Sexually Transmitted Infections*, 95(6), 462–467.

**Patton, Mary H.; Blundon, Jay A. & Zakharenko, Stanislav S.** (2019). Rejuvenation of plasticity in the brain: Opening the critical period. *Current Opinion in Neurobiology*, 54, 83–89.

**Pellegrini, Anthony D.** (2011). Introduction. In Pellegrini, Anthony D. (Ed.), *The Oxford handbook of the development of play* (pp. 3–6). Oxford University Press.

**Pellegrini, Anthony D.** (2013). Play. In Zelazo, Philip D. (Ed.), *The Oxford handbook of developmental psychology* (Vol. 2, pp. 276–299). Oxford University Press.

**Pellegrini, Anthony D.; Roseth, Cary J.; Van Ryzin, Mark J. & Solberg, David W.** (2011). Popularity as a form of social dominance: An evolutionary perspective. In Cillessen, Antonius H. N.; Schwartz, David & Mayeux, Lara (Eds.), *Popularity in the peer system* (pp. 123–139). Guilford Press.

**Pellis, Sergio M.; Himmler, Brett T.; Himmler, Stephanie M. & Pellis, Vivien C.** (2018). Rough-and-tumble play and the development of the social brain: What do we know, how do we know it, and what do we need to know? In Gibb, Robbin & Kolb, Bryan (Eds.), *The neurobiology of brain and behavioral development* (pp. 315–337). Academic Press.

**Peng, Peng; Yang, Xiujie & Meng, Xiangzhi.** (2017). The relation between approximate number system and early arithmetic: The mediation role of numerical knowledge. *Journal of Experimental Child Psychology*, 157, 111–124.

**Pennycook, Gordon & Rand, David G.** (2020). Who falls for fake news? The roles of bullshit receptivity, overclaiming, familiarity, and analytic thinking. *Journal of Personality*, 88(2), 185–200.

**Peper, Jiska S. & Dahl, Ronald E.** (2013). The teenage brain: Surging hormones—brain-behavior interactions during puberty. *Current Directions in Psychological Science*, 22(2), 134–139.

**Pepper, Edward J.; Pathmanathan, Sasi; Mcilrae, Shona; Rehman, Faiz-Ur & Cardno, Alastair G.** (2018). Associations between risk factors for schizophrenia and concordance in four monozygotic twin samples. *American Journal of Medical Genetics Part B: Neuropsychiatric Genetics*, 177(5), 503–510.

**Perlovskya, Leonid; Cabanac, Arnaud; Bonniot-Cabanac, \Marie-Claude & Cabanac, Michel.** (2013). Mozart effect, cognitive dissonance, and the pleasure of music. *Behavioural Brain Research*, 244, 9–14.

**Perner, Josef.** (2000). Communication and representation: Why mentalistic reasoning is a life-long endeavour. In Mitchell, Peter & Riggs, Kevin John (Eds.), *Children's reasoning and the mind* (pp. 367–401). Psychology Press.

**Perone, Sammy; Palanisamy, Jeeva & Carlson, Stephanie M.** (2018). Age-related change in brain rhythms from early to middle childhood: Links to executive function. *Developmental Science*, 21(6), e12691.

**Perreira, Krista M. & Pedroza, Juan M.** (2019). Policies of exclusion: Implications for the health of immigrants and their children. *Annual Review of Public Health*, 40, 7.1–7.20.

**Perrin, Robin; Miller-Perrin, Cindy & Song, Jeongbin.** (2017). Changing attitudes about spanking using alternative biblical interpretations. *International Journal of Behavioral Development*, 41(4), 514–522.

**Perszyk, Danielle R. & Waxman, Sandra R.** (2018). Linking language and cognition in infancy. *Annual Review of Psychology*, 69, 231–250.

**Peters, Stacey L.; Lind, Jennifer N.; Humphrey, Jasmine R.; Friedman, Jan M.; Honein, Margaret A.; Tassinari, Melissa S.; . . . Broussard, Cheryl S.** (2013). Safe lists for medications in pregnancy: Inadequate evidence base and inconsistent advice from Web-based information, 2011. *Pharmacoepidemiology and Drug Safety*, 22(3), 324–328.

**Peters, Wendy.** (2016). Bullies and blackmail: Finding homophobia in the closet on teen TV. *Sexuality & Culture*, 20(3), 486–503.

**Peterson, Candida C. & Wellman, Henry M.** (2019). Longitudinal theory of mind (ToM) development from preschool to adolescence with and without ToM delay. *Child Development*, 90(6), 1917–1934.

**Petrilli, Christopher M.; Jones, Simon A.; Yang, Jie; Rajagopalan, Harish; O'Donnell, Luke; Chernyak, Yelena; . . . Horwitz, Leora I.** (2020). Factors associated with hospital admission and critical illness among 5279 people with coronavirus disease 2019 in New York City: Prospective cohort study. *BMJ*, 369, m1966.

**Pew Research Center.** (2015, December 17). *Parenting in America: Outlook, worries, aspirations are strongly linked to financial situation. Social & Demographic Trends.* Washington, DC: Pew Research Center.

**Pew Research Center.** (2019, March 14). *Political independents: Who they are, what they think. U.S. Politics and Policy.* Washington, DC: Pew Research Center.

**Pexman, Penny M.** (2017). The role of embodiment in conceptual development. *Language, Cognition and Neuroscience.*

**Phillips, Deborah A.; Fox, Nathan A. & Gunnar, Megan R.** (2011). Same place, different experiences: Bringing individual differences to research in child care. *Child Development Perspectives*, 5(1), 44–49.

**Piaget, Jean.** (1932). *The moral judgment of the child.* K. Paul, Trench, Trubner & Co.

**Piaget, Jean.** (1950). *The psychology of intelligence.* Routledge & Paul.

**Piaget, Jean.** (1952). *The origins of intelligence in children.* International Universities Press.

**Piaget, Jean.** (1954). *The construction of reality in the child.* Basic Books.

**Piaget, Jean.** (2001). *The psychology of intelligence.* Routledge.

**Piaget, Jean.** (2011). *The origins of intelligence in children.* Routledge.

**Piaget, Jean.** (2013a). *The construction of reality in the child.* Routledge.

**Piaget, Jean.** (2013b). *The moral judgment of the child.* Routledge.

**Piaget, Jean.** (2013c). *Play, dreams and imitation in childhood.* Routledge.

**Piaget, Jean & Inhelder, Bärbel.** (1956). *The child's conception of space.* Routledge.

**Piaget, Jean & Inhelder, Bärbel.** (1972). *The psychology of the child.* Basic Books.

**Piaget, Jean & Inhelder, Bärbel.** (2013). *The child's conception of space.* Routledge.

**Piaget, Jean; Voelin-Liambey, Daphne & Berthoud-Papandropoulou, Ioanna.** (2015). Problems of class inclusion and logical implication. In Campell, Robert L. (Ed.), *Studies in reflecting abstraction* (pp. 105–137). Psychology Press.

**Piekny, Jeanette & Maehler, Claudia.** (2013). Scientific reasoning in early and middle childhood: The development of domain-general evidence evaluation, experimentation, and hypothesis generation skills. *British Journal of Developmental Psychology*, 31(2), 153–179.

**Pietschnig, Jakob & Voracek, Martin.** (2015). One century of global IQ gains: A formal meta-analysis of the Flynn Effect (1909–2013).

*Perspectives on Psychological Science, 10*(3), 282–306.

**Pilarz, Alejandra Ros & Hill, Heather D.** (2014). Unstable and multiple child care arrangements and young children's behavior. *Early Childhood Research Quarterly, 29*(4), 471–483.

**Pilkauskas, Natasha.** (2014). Breastfeeding initiation and duration in coresident grandparent, mother and infant households. *Maternal and Child Health Journal, 18*(8), 1955–1963.

**Pinker, Steven.** (1999). *Words and rules: The ingredients of language.* Basic Books.

**Pinker, Steven.** (2018). *Enlightenment now: The case for reason, science, humanism, and progress.* Viking.

**Pinquart, Martin & Kauser, Rubina.** (2018). Do the associations of parenting styles with behavior problems and academic achievement vary by culture? Results from a meta-analysis. *Cultural Diversity and Ethnic Minority Psychology, 24*(1), 75–100.

**Pinto, Tiago Miguel & Figueiredo, Bárbara.** (2019). Attachment and coparenting representations in men during the transition to parenthood. *Infant Mental Health Journal, 40*(6), 850–861.

**Pittenger, Samantha L.; Huit, Terrence Z. & Hansen, David J.** (2016). Applying ecological systems theory to sexual revictimization of youth: A review with implications for research and practice. *Aggression and Violent Behavior, 26,* 35–45.

**Pittenger, Samantha L.; Pogue, Jessica K. & Hansen, David J.** (2018). Predicting sexual revictimization in childhood and adolescence: A longitudinal examination using ecological systems theory. *Child Maltreatment, 23*(2), 137–146.

**Planalp, Elizabeth M. & Goldsmith, H. Hill.** (2019). Observed profiles of infant temperament: Stability, heritability, and associations with parenting. *Child Development.*

**Plener, Paul L.; Schumacher, Teresa S.; Munz, Lara M. & Groschwitz, Rebecca C.** (2015). The longitudinal course of non-suicidal self-injury and deliberate self-harm: A systematic review of the literature. *Borderline Personality Disorder and Emotion Dysregulation, 2*(1).

**Plomin, Robert; DeFries, John C.; Knopik, Valerie S. & Neiderhiser, Jenae M.** (2013). *Behavioral genetics.* Worth.

**Pluess, Michael.** (2015). Individual differences in environmental sensitivity. *Child Development Perspectives, 9*(3), 138–143.

**Poelker, Katelyn E. & Gibbons, Judith L.** (2019). Sharing and caring: Prosocial behavior in young children around the world. In Tulviste, Tiia; Best, Deborah L. & Gibbons, Judith L. (Eds.), *Children's social worlds in cultural context* (pp. 89–102). Springer.

**Pogrebin, Abigail.** (2010). *One and the same: My life as an identical twin and what I've learned about everyone's struggle to be singular.* Anchor.

**Polanczyk, Guilherme V.; Willcutt, Erik G.; Salum, Giovanni A.; Kieling, Christian & Rohde, Luis A.** (2014). ADHD prevalence estimates across three decades: An updated systematic review and meta-regression analysis. *International Journal of Epidemiology, 43*(2), 434–442.

**Polderman, Tinca J. C.; Kreukels, Baudewijntje P. C.; Irwig, Michael S.; Beach, Lauren; Chan, Yee-Ming; Derks, Eske M.; . . . Davis, Lea K.** (2018). The biological contributions to gender identity and gender diversity: Bringing data to the table. *Behavior Genetics, 48*(2), 95–108.

**Polirstok, Susan.** (2015). Classroom management strategies for inclusive classrooms. *Creative Education, 6,* 927–933.

**Pons, Ferran & Lewkowicz, David J.** (2014). Infant perception of audio-visual speech synchrony in familiar and unfamiliar fluent speech. *Acta Psychologica, 149,* 142–147.

**Poole, Kristie L.; Jetha, Michelle K. & Schmidt, Louis A.** (2017). Linking child temperament, physiology, and adult personality: Relations among retrospective behavioral inhibition, salivary cortisol, and shyness. *Personality and Individual Differences, 113,* 68–73.

**Poon, Kean.** (2018). Hot and cool executive functions in adolescence: Development and contributions to important developmental outcomes. *Frontiers in Psychology, 8*(2311).

**Popescu, Rebeca; Muntean, Ana & Juffer, Femmie.** (2019). Adoption in Romania: Historical perspectives and recent statistics. *Adoption Quarterly, 23*(1), 1–26.

**Posada, Germán E. & Waters, Harriet Salatas.** (2018). The mother-child attachment partnership in early childhood: Secure base behavioral and representational processes. *Monographs of the Society for Research in Child Development, 83*(4).

**Posner, Michael I. & Rothbart, Mary K.** (2017). Integrating brain, cognition and culture. *Journal of Cultural Cognitive Science, 1*(1), 3–15.

**Pouwels, J. Loes; Lansu, Tessa A. M. & Cillessen, Antonius H. N.** (2016). Participant roles of bullying in adolescence: Status characteristics, social behavior, and assignment criteria. *Aggressive Behavior, 42*(3), 239–253.

**Pouwels, J. Loes; Salmivalli, Christina; Saarento, Silja; Van Den Berg, Yvonne H. M.; Lansu, Tessa A. M. & Cillessen, Antonius H. N.** (2017). Predicting adolescents' bullying participation from developmental trajectories of social status and behavior. *Child Development.*

**Powell, Cynthia M.** (2013). Sex chromosomes, sex chromosome disorders, and disorders of sex development. In Gersen, Steven L. & Keagle, Martha B. (Eds.), *The principles of clinical cytogenetics* (pp. 175–211). Springer.

**Powell, Kendall.** (2006). Neurodevelopment: How does the teenage brain work? *Nature, 442*(7105), 865–867.

**Powell, Shaun; Langlands, Stephanie & Dodd, Chris.** (2011). Feeding children's desires? Child and parental perceptions of food promotion to the "under 8s". *Young Consumers: Insight and Ideas for Responsible Marketers, 12*(2), 96–109.

**Pozzoli, Tiziana & Gini, Gianluca.** (2013). Why do bystanders of bullying help or not? A multidimensional model. *Journal of Early Adolescence, 33*(3), 315–340.

**Prather, Jonathan; Okanoya, Kazuo & Bolhuis, Johan J.** (2017). Brains for birds and babies: Neural parallels between birdsong and speech acquisition. *Neuroscience & Biobehavioral Reviews, 81*(Part B), 225–237.

**Preckel, Katrin; Kanske, Philipp & Singer, Tania.** (2018). On the interaction of social affect and cognition: Empathy, compassion and theory of mind. *Current Opinion in Behavioral Sciences, 19,* 1–6.

**Preedy, Victor R.** (2019). *Neuroscience of alcohol: Mechanisms and treatment.* Elsevier.

**Price, Debora; Ribe, Eloi; Di Gessa, Giorgio & Glaser, Karen.** (2018). Grandparental childcare: A reconceptualisation of family policy regimes. In Timonen, Virpi (Ed.), *Grandparenting practices around the world* (pp. 43–64). Policy Press.

**Pridham, Karen; Limbo, Rana & Schroeder, Michele.** (2018). *Guided participation in pediatric nursing practice: Relationship-based teaching and learning with parents, children, and adolescents.* Springer.

**Proctor, Laura J. & Dubowitz, Howard.** (2014). Child neglect: Challenges and controversies. In Korbin, Jill E. & Krugman, Richard D. (Eds.), *Handbook of child maltreatment* (pp. 27–61). Springer.

**Prothero, Arianna.** (2016, April 20). Charters help alums stick with college. *Education Week, 35*(28), 1, 13.

**Proud2Bme.** (2012, March 26). Overall, do social networking sites like Facebook and Twitter help or hurt your body confidence.

**Provenzi, Livio; Guida, Elena & Montirosso, Rosario.** (2018). Preterm behavioral epigenetics: A systematic review. *Neuroscience & Biobehavioral Reviews, 84,* 262–271.

**Pruden, Shannon M. & Levine, Susan C.** (2017). Parents' spatial language mediates a sex difference in preschoolers' spatial-language use. *Psychological Science, 28*(11), 1583–1596.

**Puertas, Alberto; Magan-Fernandez, Antonio; Blanc, Vanessa; Revelles, Laura; O'Valle, Francisco; Pozo, Elena; . . . Mesa, Francisco.** (2018). Association of periodontitis with preterm birth and low birth weight: A comprehensive review. *Journal of Maternal-Fetal and Neonatal Medicine, 31*(5), 597–602.

**Puetz, Vanessa B.; Parker, Drew; Kohn, Nils; Dahmen, Brigitte; Verma, Ragini & Konrad, Kerstin.** (2017). Altered brain network integrity after childhood maltreatment: A structural connectomic DTI-study. *Human Brain Mapping, 38*(2), 855–868.

**Pulvermüller, Friedemann.** (2018). Neural reuse of action perception circuits for language, concepts and communication. *Progress in Neurobiology, 160,* 1–44.

**Putnam, Robert D.** (2015). *Our kids: The American dream in crisis.* Simon & Schuster.

**Putwain, David W.; Symes, Wendy & McCaldin, Tamsin.** (2019). Teacher use of loss-focused, utility value messages, prior to high-stakes examinations, and their appraisal by students. *Journal of Psychoeducational Assessment, 37*(2), 169–180.

**Qin, Desiree B. & Chang, Tzu-Fen.** (2013). Asian fathers. In Cabrera, Natasha J. & Tamis-LeMonda, Catherine S. (Eds.), *Handbook of father involvement: Multidisciplinary perspectives* (2nd ed., pp. 261–281). Routledge.

**Quindlen, Anna.** (2012). *Lots of candles, plenty of cake.* Random House.

**Quinn, Rand & Cheuk, Tina.** (2018). *School vouchers in the Trump era: How political ideology and religion shape public opinion.* Philadelphia, PA: Consortium for Policy Research in Education. CPRE Policy Briefs. PB #2018-1.

**Raeburn, Paul.** (2014). *Do fathers matter?: What science is telling us about the parent we've overlooked.* Farrar, Straus and Giroux.

**Rahilly, Elizabeth P.** (2015). The gender binary meets the gender-variant child: Parents' negotiations with childhood gender variance. *Gender & Society, 29*(3), 338–361.

**Rahman, Muhammad A.; Todd, Charlotte; John, Ann; Tan, Jacinta; Kerr, Michael; Potter, Robert; . . . Brophy, Sinead.** (2018). School achievement as a predictor of depression and self-harm in adolescence: Linked education and health record study. *The British Journal of Psychiatry, 212*(4), 215–221.

**Raipuria, Harinder Dosanjh; Lovett, Briana; Lucas, Laura & Hughes, Victoria.** (2018). A literature review of midwifery-led care in reducing labor and birth interventions. *Nursing for Women's Health, 22*(5), 387–400.

**Rakic, Snezana; Jankovic Raznatovic, Svetlana; Jurisic, Aleksandar; Anicic, Radomir & Zecevic, Nebojsa.** (2016). Fetal neurosonography and fetal behaviour: Genesis of fetal movements and motor reflexes. *Ultrasound in Obstetrics and Gynecology, 48*(Suppl. 1), 196.

**Raley, R. Kelly & Sweeney, Megan M.** (2020). Divorce, repartnering, and stepfamilies: A decade in review. *Journal of Marriage and Family, 82*(1), 81–99.

**Ramírez, Naja Ferjan; Ramírez, Rey R.; Clarke, Maggie; Taulu, Samu & Kuhl, Patricia K.** (2017). Speech discrimination in 11-month-old bilingual and monolingual infants: A magnetoencephalography study. *Developmental Science, 20*(1), e12427.

**Ramscar, Michael & Dye, Melody.** (2011). Learning language from the input: Why innate constraints can't explain noun compounding. *Cognitive Psychology, 62*(1), 1–40.

**Ranciaro, Alessia; Campbell, Michael C.; Hirbo, Jibril B.; Ko, Wen-Ya; Froment, Alain; Anagnostou, Paolo; . . . Tishkoff, Sarah A.** (2014). Genetic origins of lactase persistence and the spread of pastoralism in Africa. *The American Journal of Human Genetics, 94*(4), 496–510.

**Rand, David G. & Nowak, Martin A.** (2016). Cooperation among humans. In Messner, Dirk & Weinlich, Silke (Eds.), *Global cooperation and the human factor in international relations* (pp. 113–138). Routledge.

**Rankin, Jay.** (2017). Physicians disagree on legal age for cannabis. *CMAJ, 189*(4), E174–E175.

**Ranney, John D. & Troop-Gordon, Wendy.** (2020). The role of popularity and digital self-monitoring in adolescents' cyberbehaviors and cyber-victimization. *Computers in Human Behavior, 102*, 293–302.

**Raspberry, Kelly A. & Skinner, Debra.** (2011). Negotiating desires and options: How mothers who carry the fragile X gene experience reproductive decisions. *Social Science & Medicine, 72*(6), 992–998.

**Rauh, Virginia A.** (2018). Polluting developing brains—EPA failure on chlorpyrifos. *New England Journal of Medicine, 378*(13), 1171–1174.

**Rauscher, Frances H.; Shaw, Gordon L. & Ky, Catherine N.** (1993). Music and spatial task performance. *Nature, 365*(6447), 611.

**Ray, Brian D.** (2013). Homeschooling rising into the twenty-first century: Editor's introduction. *Peabody Journal of Education, 88*(3), 261–264.

**Raymond, Jaime & Brown, Mary Jean.** (2017, January 20). *Childhood blood lead levels in children aged <5 Years—United States, 2009–2014. Morbidity and Mortality Weekly Report, 66*(3), 1–10. Atlanta, GA: Centers for Disease Control and Prevention.

**Reardon, Sean F.** (2013). The widening income achievement gap. *Educational Leadership, 70*(8), 10–16.

**Reardon, Tessa; Harvey, Kate; Baranowska, Magdalena; O'Brien, Doireann; Smith, Lydia & Creswell, Cathy.** (2017). What do parents perceive are the barriers and facilitators to accessing psychological treatment for mental health problems in children and adolescents? A systematic review of qualitative and quantitative studies. *European Child & Adolescent Psychiatry, 26*(6), 623–647.

**Reddy, Sunita; Patel, Tulsi; Kristensen, Malene Tanderup & Nielsen, Birgitte Bruun.** (2018). Surrogacy in India: Political and commercial framings. In Mitra, Sayani; Schicktanz, Silke & Patel, Tulsi (Eds.), *Cross-cultural comparisons on surrogacy and egg donation: Interdisciplinary perspectives from India, Germany and Israel.* Palgrave Macmillan.

**Reimann, Zakary; Miller, Jacob R.; Dahle, Kaitana M.; Hooper, Audrey P.; Young, Ashley M.; Goates, Michael C.; . . . Crandall, AliceAnn.** (2018). Executive functions and health behaviors associated with the leading causes of death in the United States: A systematic review. *Journal of Health Psychology.*

**Reinehr, Thomas & Roth, Christian Ludwig.** (2019). Is there a causal relationship between obesity and puberty? *The Lancet Child & Adolescent Health, 3*(1), 44–54.

**Reiter, Andrea M. F.; Suzuki, Shinsuke; O'Doherty, John P.; Li, Shu-Chen & Eppinger, Ben.** (2019). Risk contagion by peers affects learning and decision-making in adolescents. *Journal of Experimental Psychology, 148*(9), 1494–1504.

**Renfrew, Mary J.; McFadden, Alison; Bastos, Maria Helena; Campbell, James; Channon, Andrew Amos; Cheung, Ngai Fen; . . . Declercq, Eugene.** (2014). Midwifery and quality care: Findings from a new evidence-informed framework for maternal and newborn care. *The Lancet, 384*(9948), 1129–1145.

**Retelas, George (Producer).** (2017, December 12). *Interview with Sheri Sheppard, Grace Young, Emily Bohl, Maria Filsinger, Marina Dimitrov, and Ariana Qayumi by undergraduate students at Stanford University.* EngineerGirl @ Stanford University. [Video]. YouTube.

**Reynolds, Arthur J.** (2000). *Success in early intervention: The Chicago Child-Parent Centers.* University of Nebraska Press.

**Reynolds, Arthur J. & Ou, Suh-Ruu.** (2011). Paths of effects from preschool to adult well-being: A confirmatory analysis of the Child-Parent Center Program. *Child Development, 82*(2), 555–582.

**Reynolds, Arthur J. & Temple, Judy A. (Eds.).** (2019). *Sustaining early childhood learning gains: Program, school, and family influences.* Cambridge University Press.

**Reynolds, Jamila E. & Gonzales-Backen, Melinda A.** (2017). Ethnic-racial socialization and the mental health of African Americans: A critical review. *Journal of Family Theory & Review, 9*(12), 182–200.

**Rich, Motoko.** (2013, April 11). Texas considers backtracking on testing. *New York Times.*

**Richards, Jennifer S.; Hartman, Catharina A.; Franke, Barbara; Hoekstra, Pieter J.; Heslenfeld, Dirk J.; Oosterlaan, Jaap; . . . Buitelaar, Jan K.** (2014). Differential susceptibility to maternal expressed emotion in children with ADHD and their siblings? Investigating plasticity genes, prosocial and antisocial behaviour. *European Child & Adolescent Psychiatry, 24*(2), 209–217.

**Richards, Morgan K.; Flanagan, Meghan R.; Littman, Alyson J.; Burke, Alson K. & Callegari, Lisa S.** (2016). Primary cesarean section and adverse delivery outcomes among women of very advanced maternal age. *Journal of Perinatology, 36*, 272–277.

**Rideout, Victoria.** (2017). *The Common Sense Census: Media use by kids age zero to eight.* San Francisco, CA: Common Sense Media.

**Riglin, Lucy; Frederickson, Norah; Shelton, Katherine H. & Rice, Frances.** (2013). A longitudinal study of psychological functioning and academic attainment at the transition to secondary school. *Journal of Adolescence, 36*(3), 507–517.

**Riordan, Jan & Wambach, Karen (Eds.).** (2009). *Breastfeeding and human lactation* (4th ed.). Jones and Bartlett.

**Rioux, Charlie; Castellanos-Ryan, Natalie; Parent, Sophie & Séguin, Jean R.** (2016). The interaction between temperament and the family environment in adolescent substance use and externalizing behaviors: Support for diathesis–stress or differential susceptibility? *Developmental Review, 40*(10), 117–150.

**Rivera, Juan Ángel; de Cossío, Teresita González; Pedraza, Lilia S.; Aburto, Tania C.; Sánchez, Tania G. & Martorell, Reynaldo.** (2014). Childhood and adolescent overweight and obesity in Latin America: A systematic review. *The Lancet Diabetes & Endocrinology, 2*(4), 321–332.

**Rizzo, Michael T. & Killen, Melanie.** (2016). Children's understanding of equity in the context of inequality. *British Journal of Developmental Psychology, 34*(4), 569–581.

**Rizzo, Michael T.; Li, Leon; Burkholder, Amanda R. & Killen, Melanie.** (2019). Lying, negligence, or lack of knowledge? Children's intention-based moral reasoning about resource claims. *Developmental Psychology, 55*(2), 274–285.

**Robelen, Erik W.** (2011). More students enrolling in Mandarin Chinese. *Education Week, 30*(27), 5.

**Roberts, Andrea G. & Lopez-Duran, Nestor L.** (2019). Developmental influences on stress response systems: Implications for psychopathology vulnerability in adolescence. *Comprehensive Psychiatry, 88*, 9–21.

**Roberts, Brent W. & Davis, Jordan P.** (2016). Young adulthood is the crucible of personality development. *Emerging Adulthood, 4*(5), 318–326.

**Roberts, Leslie.** (2020). Global polio eradication falters in the final stretch. *Science, 367*(6473), 14–15.

**Robertson, Cassandra & O'Brien, Rourke.** (2018). Health endowment at birth and variation in intergenerational economic mobility: Evidence from U.S. county birth cohorts. *Demography, 55*(1), 249–269.

**Robinson, Eric & Sutin, Angelina R.** (2017). Parents' perceptions of their children as overweight and children's weight concerns and weight gain. *Psychological Science, 28*(3), 320–329.

**Robinson, Leah E.; Wadsworth, Danielle D.; Webster, E. Kipling & Bassett, David R.** (2014). School reform: The role of physical education policy in physical activity of elementary school children in Alabama's Black Belt region. *American Journal of Health Promotion, 38*(Suppl. 3), S72–S76.

**Rochat, Philippe.** (2013). Self-conceptualizing in development. In Zelazo, Philip D. (Ed.), *The Oxford handbook of developmental psychology* (Vol. 2, pp. 378–397). Oxford University Press.

**Rock, Jacoba; Geier, Charles F.; Noll, Jennie G. & De Bellis, Michael D.** (2018). Developmental traumatology: Brain development in maltreated children with and without PTSD. In Noll, Jennie G. & Shalev, Idan (Eds.), *The biology of early life stress* (pp. 45–56). Springer.

**Rodgers, Rachel F.; Slater, Amy; Gordon, Chloe S.; Mclean, Siân A.; Jarman, Hannah K. & Paxton, Susan J.** (2020). A biopsychosocial model of social media use and body image concerns, disordered eating, and muscle-building behaviors among adolescent girls and boys. *Journal of Youth and Adolescence, 49*(2), 399–409.

**Rodrigues, Daniela; Padez, Cristina & Machado-Rodrigues, Aristides M.** (2018). Active parents, active children: The importance of parental organized physical activity in children's extracurricular sport participation. *Journal of Child Health Care, 22*(1), 159–170.

**Rodriguez, Christina M.; Silvia, Paul J. & Gaskin, Regan E.** (2019). Predicting maternal and paternal parent-child aggression risk: Longitudinal multimethod investigation using social information processing theory. *Psychology of Violence, 9*(3), 370–382.

**Rogers, Forrest Dylan & Bales, Karen Lisa.** (2019). Mothers, fathers, and others: Neural substrates of parental care. *Trends in Neurosciences, 42*(8), 552–562.

**Rogoff, Barbara.** (2003). *The cultural nature of human development.* Oxford University Press.

**Romanelli, Meghan; Xiao, Yunyu & Lindsey, Michael A.** (2020). Sexual identity-behavior profiles and suicide outcomes among heterosexual, lesbian, and gay sexually active adolescents: Sexual identity-behavior profiles and suicide. *Suicide and Life-Threatening Behavior.*

**Romeo, Russell D.** (2013). The teenage brain: The stress response and the adolescent brain. *Current Directions in Psychological Science, 22*(2), 140–145.

**Romeo, Rachel R.; Leonard, Julia A.; Robinson, Sydney T.; West, Martin R.; Mackey, Allyson P.; Rowe, Meredith L. & Gabrieli, John D. E.** (2018). Beyond the 30-million-word gap: Children's conversational exposure is associated with language-related brain function. *Psychological Science, 29*(5), 700–710.

**Rønneberg, Vibeke & Torrance, Mark.** (2019). Cognitive predictors of shallow-orthography spelling speed and accuracy in 6th grade children. *Reading and Writing, 32*(1), 197–216.

**Rook, Graham A. W.; Lowry, Christopher A. & Raison, Charles L.** (2014). Hygiene and other early childhood influences on the subsequent function of the immune system. *Brain Research,* (Corrected Proof).

**Roopnarine, Jaipaul L. & Hossain, Ziarat.** (2013). African American and African Caribbean fathers. In Cabrera, Natasha J. & Tamis-LeMonda, Catherine S. (Eds.), *Handbook of father involvement: Multidisciplinary perspectives* (2nd ed., pp. 223–243). Routledge.

**Roopnarine, Jaipaul L. & Yildirim, Elif Dede.** (2019). *Fathering in cultural contexts: Developmental and clinical issues.* Routledge.

**Rose, Amanda J. & Asher, Steven R.** (2017). The social tasks of friendship: Do boys and girls excel in different tasks? *Child Development Perspectives, 11*(1), 3–8.

**Rose, Dawn; Jones Bartoli, Alice & Heaton, Pamela C.** (2019). Measuring the impact of musical learning on cognitive, behavioural and socio-emotional wellbeing development in children. *Psychology of Music, 47*(2), 284–303.

**Rose, Katherine K.; Johnson, Amy; Muro, Joel & Buckley, Rhonda R.** (2018). Decision making about nonparental child care by fathers: What is important to fathers in a nonparental child care program. *Journal of Family Issues, 39*(2), 299–327.

**Rose, Nikolas.** (2016). Reading the human brain: How the mind became legible. *Body & Society, 22*(2), 140–177.

**Rose, Steven.** (2008). Drugging unruly children is a method of social control. *Nature, 451*(7178), 521.

**Roseberry, Lynn & Roos, Johan.** (2016). *Bridging the gender gap: Seven principles for achieving gender balance.* Oxford University Press.

**Rosen, Meghan.** (2016). Concern grows over Zika birth defects. *Science News, 190*(9), 14–15.

**Rosenblum, Gianine D. & Lewis, Michael.** (1999). The relations among body image, physical attractiveness, and body mass in adolescence. *Child Development, 70*(1), 50–64.

**Rosenfeld, Michael J. & Roesler, Katharina.** (2019). Cohabitation experience and cohabitation's association with marital dissolution: The short-term benefits of cohabitation. *Journal of Marriage and Family, 81*(1), 42–58.

**Ross, Josephine; Anderson, James R. & Campbell, Robin N.** (2011). *I remember me: Mnemonic self-reference effects in preschool children.* Wiley-Blackwell.

**Ross, Josephine; Yilmaz, Mandy; Dale, Rachel; Cassidy, Rose; Yildirim, Iraz & Zeedyk, M. Suzanne.** (2017). Cultural differences in self-recognition: The early development of autonomous and related selves? *Developmental Science, 20*(3), e12387.

**Rossignol, Michel; Chaillet, Nils; Boughrassa, Faiza & Moutquin, Jean-Marie.** (2014). Interrelations between four antepartum obstetric interventions and cesarean delivery in women at low risk: A systematic review and modeling of the cascade of interventions. *Birth, 41*(1), 70–78.

**Roth, Benjamin J.; Crea, Thomas M.; Jani, Jayshree; Underwood, Dawnya; Hasson, Robert G.; Evans, Kerri & Zuch, Michael.** (2018). Detached and afraid: U.S. immigration policy and the practice of forcibly separating parents and young children at the border. *Children Welfare, 96*(5), 29–49.

**Rothausen, Teresa J. & Henderson, Kevin E.** (2019). Meaning-based job-related well-being: Exploring a meaningful work conceptualization of job satisfaction. *Journal of Business and Psychology, 34*(3), 357–376.

**Rothstein, Mark A.** (2015). The moral challenge of Ebola. *American Journal of Public Health, 105*(1), 6–8.

**Roubinov, Danielle S. & Boyce, William Thomas.** (2017). Parenting and SES: Relative values or enduring principles? *Current Opinion in Psychology, 15*, 162–167.

**Rovee-Collier, Carolyn.** (1987). Learning and memory in infancy. In Osofsky, Joy Doniger (Ed.), *Handbook of infant development* (2nd ed., pp. 98–148). Wiley.

**Rovee-Collier, Carolyn.** (1990). The "memory system" of prelinguistic infants. *Annals of the New York Academy of Sciences, 608*, 517–542.

**Rowe, Meredith L.; Denmark, Nicole; Harden, Brenda Jones & Stapleton, Laura M.** (2016). The role of parent education and parenting knowledge in children's language and literacy skills among white, Black, and Latino families. *Infant and Child Development, 25*(2), 198–220.

**Rübeling, Hartmut; Keller, Heidi; Yovsi, Relindis D.; Lenk, Melanie & Schwarzer, Sina.** (2011). Children's drawings of the self as an expression of cultural conceptions of the self. *Journal of Cross-Cultural Psychology, 42*(3), 406–424.

**Rubertsson, C.; Hellström, J.; Cross, M. & Sydsjö, G.** (2014). Anxiety in early pregnancy: Prevalence and contributing factors. *Archives of Women's Mental Health, 17*(3), 221–228.

**Rubin, Kenneth H.; Bowker, Julie C.; McDonald, Kristina L. & Menzer, Melissa.** (2013). Peer relationships in childhood. In Zelazo, Philip D. (Ed.), *The Oxford handbook of developmental psychology* (Vol. 2, pp. 242–275). Oxford University Press.

**Ruch, Donna A.; Sheftall, Arielle H.; Schlagbaum, Paige; Fontanella, Cynthia A.; Campo, John V. & Bridge, Jeffrey A.** (2019). Characteristics and precipitating circumstances of suicide among incarcerated youth. *Journal of the American Academy of Child & Adolescent Psychiatry, 58*(5), 514–524.e1.

**Rudaz, Myriam; Ledermann, Thomas; Margraf, Jürgen; Becker, Eni S. & Craske, Michelle G.** (2017). The moderating role of avoidance behavior on anxiety over time: Is there a difference between social anxiety disorder and specific phobia? *PLoS ONE, 12*(7), e0180298.

**Rudkowska, Iwona; Dewailly, Eric; Hegele, Robert A.; Boiteau, Véronique; Dubé-Linteau, Ariane; Abdous, Belkacem; . . . Vohl, Marie-Claude.** (2013). Gene–diet interactions on plasma lipid levels in the Inuit population. *British Journal of Nutrition, 109*(5), 953–961.

**Runions, Kevin C. & Shaw, Thérèse.** (2013). Teacher–child relationship, child withdrawal and aggression in the development of peer victimization. *Journal of Applied Developmental Psychology, 34*(6), 319–327.

**Russell, Charlotte K.; Robinson, Lyn & Ball, Helen L.** (2013). Infant sleep development: Location, feeding and expectations in the postnatal period. *The Open Sleep Journal, 6*(Suppl. 1: M9), 68–76.

**Russell, Stephen T.; Everett, Bethany G.; Rosario, Margaret & Birkett, Michelle.** (2014). Indicators of victimization and sexual orientation among adolescents: Analyses from youth risk behavior surveys. *American Journal of Public Health, 104*(2), 255–261.

**Russo, Theresa J. & Fallon, Moira A.** (2014). Coping with stress: Supporting the needs of military families and their children. *Early Childhood Education Journal, 43*(5), 407–416.

**Rutter, Michael.** (2012). Resilience as a dynamic concept. *Development and Psychopathology, 24*(2), 335–344.

**Sabeti, Pardis & Salahi, Lara.** (2018). *Outbreak culture: The Ebola crisis and the next epidemic.* Harvard University Press.

**Sabol, T. J.; Soliday Hong, S. L.; Pianta, R. C. & Burchinal, M. R.** (2013). Can rating pre-K programs predict children's learning? *Science, 341*(6148), 845–846.

**Sadler, Thomas W.** (2015). *Langman's medical embryology* (13th ed.). Lippincott Williams & Wilkins.

**Saey, Tina Hesman.** (2016). Neandertal DNA poses health risks. *Science News, 189*(5), 18–19.

**Saffran, Jenny R. & Kirkham, Natasha Z.** (2018). Infant statistical learning. *Annual Review of Psychology, 69*, 181–203.

**Sahlberg, Pasi.** (2011). *Finnish lessons: What can the world learn from educational change in Finland?* Teachers College Press.

**Sahlberg, Pasi.** (2015). *Finnish lessons 2.0: What can the world learn from educational change in Finland?* (2nd. ed.). Teachers College Press.

**Sahoo, Krushnapriya; Sahoo, Bishnupriya; Choudhury, Ashok Kumar; Sofi, Nighat Yasin; Kumar, Raman & Bhadoria, Ajeet Singh.** (2015). Childhood obesity: Causes and consequences. *Journal of Family Medicine and Primary Care, 4*(2), 187–192.

**Saitou, Marie & Gokcumen, Omer.** (2020). An evolutionary perspective on the impact of genomic copy number variation on human health. *Journal of Molecular Evolution, 88*(1), 104–119.

**Salomon, Ilyssa & Brown, Christia Spears.** (2019). The selfie generation: Examining the relationship between social media use and early adolescent body image. *Journal of Early Adolescence, 39*(4), 539–560.

**Samek, Diana R.; Goodman, Rebecca J.; Erath, Stephen A.; McGue, Matt & Iacono,**

**William G.** (2016). Antisocial peer affiliation and externalizing disorders in the transition from adolescence to young adulthood: Selection versus socialization effects. *Developmental Psychology, 52*(5), 813–823.

**SAMHSDA.** (2019). Substance Abuse and Mental Health Services Administration (SAMHSA)'s public online data analysis system: Data from the national survey on drug use and health, 2017. Substance Abuse and Mental Health Services Administration.

**Sampaio, Waneli Cristine Morais; Ribeiro, Mara Cláudia; Costa, Larice Feitosa; Souza, Wânia Cristina de; Castilho, Goiara Mendonça de; Assis, Melissa Sousa de; . . . Ferreira, Vania Moraes.** (2017). Effect of music therapy on the developing central nervous system of rats. *Psychology & Neuroscience, 10*(2), 176–188.

**Sancar, Feyza.** (2019). Subconcussive football hits may leave a telltale signature of brain damage. *JAMA, 322*(16), 1537–1538.

**Sanchez, Gabriel R. & Vargas, Edward D.** (2016). Taking a closer look at group identity: The link between theory and measurement of group consciousness and linked fate. *Political Research Quarterly, 69*(1), 160–174.

**Sanchez-Vaznaugh, Emma V.; Weverka, Aiko; Matsuzaki, Mika & Sánchez, Brisa N.** (2019). Changes in fast food outlet availability near schools: Unequal patterns by income, race/ethnicity, and urbanicity. *American Journal of Preventive Medicine, 57*(3), 338–345.

**Sandstrom, Andrea; Sahiti, Qendresa; Pavlova, Barbara & Uher, Rudolf.** (2019). Offspring of parents with schizophrenia, bipolar disorder, and depression: A review of familial high-risk and molecular genetics studies. *Psychiatric Genetics, 29*(5), 160–169.

**Santelli, John S.; Kantor, Leslie M.; Grilo, Stephanie A.; Speizer, Ilene S.; Lindberg, Laura D.; Heitel, Jennifer; . . . Ott, Mary A.** (2017). Abstinence-only-until-marriage: An updated review of U.S. policies and programs and their impact. *Journal of Adolescent Health, 61*(3), 273–280.

**Santos, Carlos E.; Kornienko, Olga & Rivas-Drake, Deborah.** (2017). Peer influence on ethnic-racial identity development: A multi-site investigation. *Child Development, 88*(3), 725–742.

**Saracho, Olivia N.** (2016). *Contemporary perspectives on research on bullying and victimization in early childhood education.* Information Age.

**Saraiva, Linda; Rodrigues, Luís P.; Cordovil, Rita & Barreiros, João.** (2013). Influence of age, sex and somatic variables on the motor performance of pre-school children. *Annals of Human Biology, 40*(5), 444–450.

**Saroglou, Vassilis.** (2012). Adolescents' social development and the role of religion. In Trommsdorff, Gisela & Chen, Xinyin (Eds.), *Values, religion, and culture in adolescent development* (pp. 391–423). Cambridge University Press.

**Sassler, Sharon & Lichter, Daniel T.** (2020). Cohabitation and marriage: Complexity and diversity in union-formation patterns. *Journal of Marriage and Family, 82*(1), 35–61.

**Satterwhite, Catherine Lindsey; Torrone, Elizabeth; Meites, Elissa; Dunne, Eileen F.;**

**Mahajan, Reena; Ocfemia, M. Cheryl Bañez; . . . Weinstock, Hillard.** (2013). Sexually transmitted infections among US women and men: Prevalence and incidence estimates, 2008. *Sexually Transmitted Diseases, 40*(3), 187–193.

**Saudi, A Nur Aulia; Hartini, Nurul & Bahar, Bahar.** (2018). Teenagers' motorcycle gang community aggression from the Personal Fable and risk-taking behavior perspective. *Psychology Research and Behavior Management, 11*, 305–309.

**Savioja, Hanna; Helminen, Mika; Fröjd, Sari; Marttunen, Mauri & Kaltiala-Heino, Riittakerttu.** (2015). Sexual experience and self-reported depression across the adolescent years. *Health Psychology and Behavioral Medicine, 3*(1), 337–347.

**Saxbe, Darby E.** (2017). Birth of a new perspective? A call for biopsychosocial research on childbirth. *Current Directions in Psychological Science, 26*(1), 81–86.

**Scalise, Nicole R.; Gladstone, Jessica R. & Ramani, Geetha B.** (2019). Motivation and mathematics in early childhood. In Saracho, Olivia N. (Ed.), *Contemporary perspectives on research in motivation in early childhood education* (pp. 101–132). Information Age.

**Scarborough, William J.; Sin, Ray & Risman, Barbara.** (2019). Attitudes and the stalled gender revolution: Egalitarianism, traditionalism, and ambivalence from 1977 through 2016. *Gender & Society, 33*(2), 173–200.

**Scarr, Sandra.** (1985). Constructing psychology: Making facts and fables for our times. *American Psychologist, 40*(5), 499–512.

**Schacter, Hannah L. & Juvonen, Jaana.** (2018). Dynamic changes in peer victimization and adjustment across middle school: Does friends' victimization alleviate distress? *Child development.*

**Schafer, Markus H.; Morton, Patricia M. & Ferraro, Kenneth F.** (2014). Child maltreatment and adult health in a national sample: Heterogeneous relational contexts, divergent effects? *Child Abuse & Neglect, 38*(3), 395–406.

**Schanler, Richard. J.** (2011). Outcomes of human milk-fed premature infants. *Seminars in Perinatology, 35*(1), 29–33.

**Schapira, Rotem; Anger Elfenbein, Hillary; Amichay-Setter, Meirav; Zahn-Waxler, Carolyn & Knafo-Noam, Ariel.** (2019). Shared environment effects on children's emotion recognition. *Frontiers in Psychiatry, 10*(215).

**Scharf, Miri.** (2014). Parenting in Israel: Together hand in hand, you are mine and I am yours. In Selin, Helaine (Ed.), *Parenting across cultures: Childrearing, motherhood and fatherhood in non-Western cultures* (pp. 193–206). Springer.

**Schermerhorn, Alice C.; D'Onofrio, Brian M.; Turkheimer, Eric; Ganiban, Jody M.; Spotts, Erica L.; Lichtenstein, Paul; . . . Neiderhiser, Jenae M.** (2011). A genetically informed study of associations between family functioning and child psychosocial adjustment. *Developmental Psychology, 47*(3), 707–725.

**Schienkiewitz, Anja; Brettschneider, Anna-Kristin; Damerow, Stefan & Rosario, Angelika Schaffrath.** (2018). Overweight and obesity among children and adolescents in Germany: Results of the cross-sectional KiGGS Wave 2 study and trends. *Journal of Health Monitoring, 3*(1), 15–22.

**Schore, Allan & McIntosh, Jennifer.** (2011). Family law and the neuroscience of attachment: Part I. *Family Court Review, 49*(3), 501–512.

**Schroeder, Philip H.; Napoli, Nicholas J.; Barnhardt, William F.; Barnes, Laura E. & Young, Jeffrey S.** (2019). Relative mortality analysis of the "golden hour": A comprehensive acuity stratification approach to address disagreement in current literature. *Prehospital Emergency Care, 23*(2), 254–262.

**Schwartz, Seth & Petrova, Mariya.** (2019). Prevention science in emerging adulthood: A field coming of age. *Prevention Science, 20*(3), 305–309.

**Schwarz, Alan.** (2016). *ADHD nation: Children, doctors, big pharma, and the making of an American epidemic.* Scribner.

**Schweinhart, Lawrence J.** (2019). Lessons on sustaining gains from the life-course study of Perry Preschool. In Reynolds, Arthur J. & Temple, Judy A. (Eds.), *Sustaining early childhood learning gains: Program, school, and family influences* (pp. 254–266). Cambridge University Press.

**Schweinhart, Lawrence J.; Montie, Jeanne; Xiang, Zongping; Barnett, W. Steven; Belfield, Clive R. & Nores, Milagros.** (2005). *Lifetime effects: The High/Scope Perry Preschool Study through age 40.* High/Scope Press.

**Schweinhart, Lawrence J. & Weikart, David P.** (1997). *Lasting differences: The High/Scope Preschool curriculum comparison study through age 23.* High/Scope Educational Research Foundation.

**Schweizer, Susanne; Gotlib, Ian H. & Blakemore, Sarah-Jayne.** (2020). The role of affective control in emotion regulation during adolescence. *Emotion, 20*(1), 80–86.

**Scott, Diane L.; Lee, Chang-Bae; Harrell, Susan W. & Smith-West, Mary B.** (2013). Permanency for children in foster care: Issues and barriers for adoption. *Child & Youth Services, 34*(3), 290–307.

**Scott, Lisa S. & Monesson, Alexandra.** (2010). Experience-dependent neural specialization during infancy. *Neuropsychologia, 48*(6), 1857–1861.

**Sears, William & Sears, Martha.** (2001). *The attachment parenting book: A commonsense guide to understanding and nurturing your baby.* Little Brown.

**Seaton, Eleanor K.; Quintana, Stephen; Verkuyten, Maykel & Gee, Gilbert C.** (2017). Peers, policies, and place: The relation between context and ethnic/racial identity. *Child Development, 88*(3), 683–692.

**Sedgh, Gilda; Finer, Lawrence B.; Bankole, Akinrinola; Eilers, Michelle A. & Singh, Susheela.** (2015). Adolescent pregnancy, birth, and abortion rates across countries: Levels and recent trends. *Journal of Adolescent Health, 56*(2), 223–230.

**Sedlak, Andrea J. & Ellis, Raquel T.** (2014). Trends in child abuse reporting. In Korbin, Jill E. & Krugman, Richard D. (Eds.), *Handbook of child maltreatment* (pp. 3–26). Springer.

**Şendil, Çağla Öneren & Erden, Feyza Tantekin.** (2014). Peer preference: A way of evaluating social competence and behavioural well-being in early childhood. *Early Child Development and Care, 184*(2), 230–246.

**Senese, Vincenzo Paolo; Azhari, Atiqah; Shinohara, Kazuyuki; Doi, Hirokazu; Venuti, Paola; Bornstein, Marc H. & Esposito, Gianluca.** (2019). Implicit associations to infant cry: Genetics and early care experiences influence caregiving propensities. *Hormones and Behavior, 108,* 1–9.

**Seppa, Nathan.** (2013a). Urban eyes: Too much time spent indoors may be behind a surge in nearsightedness. *Science News, 183*(3), 22–25.

**Seppa, Nathan.** (2013b). Home births more risky than hospital deliveries: Records suggest babies born at home are more prone to unresponsiveness after five minutes. *Science News, 184*(8), 14.

**Severson, Kim & Blinder, Alan.** (2014, January 7). Test scandal in Atlanta brings more guilty pleas. *New York Times.*

**Shah, Nirvi.** (2011). Policy fight brews over discipline. *Education Week, 31*(7), 1, 12.

**Shanahan, Timothy & Lonigan, Christopher J.** (2010). The National Early Literacy Panel: A summary of the process and the report. *Educational Researcher, 39*(4), 279–285.

**Sharda, Megha; Tuerk, Carola; Chowdhury, Rakhee; Jamey, Kevin; Foster, Nicholas; Custo-Blanch, Melanie; . . . Hyde, Krista.** (2018). Music improves social communication and auditory–motor connectivity in children with autism. *Translational Psychiatry, 8*(231).

**Sharot, Tali.** (2017). *The influential mind: What the brain reveals about our power to change others.* Henry Holt.

**Shawar, Yusra Ribhi & Shiffman, Jeremy.** (2017). Generation of global political priority for early childhood development: The challenges of framing and governance. *The Lancet, 389*(10064), 119–124.

**Shechner, Tomer; Fox, Nathan A.; Mash, Jamie A.; Jarcho, Johanna M.; Chen, Gang; Leibenluft, Ellen; . . . Britton, Jennifer C.** (2018). Differences in neural response to extinction recall in young adults with or without history of behavioral inhibition. *Development and Psychopathology, 30*(1), 179–189.

**Sheridan, Margaret A.; Mclaughlin, Katie A.; Winter, Warren; Fox, Nathan; Zeanah, Charles & Nelson, Charles A.** (2018). Early deprivation disruption of associative learning is a developmental pathway to depression and social problems. *Nature Communications, 9*(1), 2216.

**Sherlock, James M. & Zietsch, Brendan P.** (2018). Longitudinal relationships between parents' and children's behavior need not implicate the influence of parental behavior and may reflect genetics: Comment on Waldinger and Schul. (2016). *Psychological Science, 29*(1), 154–157.

**Shi, Bing & Xie, Hongling.** (2012). Popular and nonpopular subtypes of physically aggressive preadolescents: Continuity of aggression and peer mechanisms during the transition to middle school. *Merrill-Palmer Quarterly, 58*(4), 530–553.

**Shi, Rushen.** (2014). Functional morphemes and early language acquisition. *Child Development Perspectives, 8*(1), 6–11.

**Shim, Woo-Jeong & Perez, Rosemary Jane.** (2018). A multi-level examination of first-year students' openness to diversity and challenge. *Journal of Higher Education, 89*(4), 453–477.

**Shneidman, Laura & Woodward, Amanda L.** (2016). Are child-directed interactions the cradle of social learning? *Psychological Bulletin, 142*(1), 1–17.

**Shoda, Yuichi; Mischel, Walter & Peake, Philip K.** (1990). Predicting adolescent cognitive and self-regulatory competencies from preschool delay of gratification: Identifying diagnostic conditions. *Developmental Psychology, 26*(6), 978–986.

**Short, Clara Schaertl.** (2019). Comment on "Outbreak: On transgender teens and psychic epidemics". *Psychological Perspectives, 62*(2/3), 285–289.

**Shpancer, Noam & Schweitzer, Stefanie N.** (2018). A history of non-parental care in childhood predicts more positive adult attitudes towards non-parental care and maternal employment. *Early Child Development and Care, 188*(3), 375–386.

**Shulman, Cory.** (2016). *Research and practice in infant and early childhood mental health.* Springer.

**Shulman, Elizabeth P.; Monahan, Kathryn C. & Steinberg, Laurence.** (2017). Severe violence during adolescence and early adulthood and its relation to anticipated rewards and costs. *Child Development, 88*(1), 16–26.

**Shwalb, David W.; Shwalb, Barbara J. & Lamb, Michael E. (Eds.).** (2013). *Fathers in cultural context.* Psychology Press.

**Siddiqui, Ayesha; Cuttini, Marina; Wood, Rachel; Velebil, Petr; Delnord, Marie; Zile, Irisa; . . . Macfarlane, Alison.** (2017). Can the Apgar score be used for international comparisons of newborn health? *Paediatric and Perinatal Epidemiology, 31*(4), 338–345.

**Siegal, Michael & Surian, Luca (Eds.).** (2012). *Access to language and cognitive development.* Oxford University Press.

**Siegler, Robert S.** (2016). Continuity and change in the field of cognitive development and in the perspectives of one cognitive developmentalist. *Child Development Perspectives, 10*(2), 128–133.

**Siegler, Robert S. & Braithwaite, David W.** (2017). Numerical development. *Annual Review of Psychology, 68,* 187–213.

**Sigurdson, J. F.; Wallander, J. & Sund, A. M.** (2014). Is involvement in school bullying associated with general health and psychosocial adjustment outcomes in adulthood? *Child Abuse & Neglect, 38*(10), 1607–1617.

**Silbey, Susan S.** (2016, August 23). Why do so many women who study engineering leave the field? *Harvard Business Review.*

**Silk, Jessica & Romero, Diana.** (2014). The role of parents and families in teen pregnancy prevention: An analysis of programs and policies. *Journal of Family Issues, 35*(10), 1339–1362.

**Silver, Jonathan M.; McAllister, Thomas W. & Arciniegas, David B. (Eds.).** (2019). *Textbook of traumatic brain injury* (3rd ed.). American Psychiatric Association.

**Silverman, Arielle M. & Cohen, Geoffrey L.** (2014). Stereotypes as stumbling-blocks: How coping with stereotype threat affects life outcomes for people with physical disabilities. *Personality and Social Psychology Bulletin, 40*(10), 1330–1340.

**Silvers, Jennifer A.; Shu, Jocelyn; Hubbard, Alexa D.; Weber, Jochen & Ochsner, Kevin N.** (2015). Concurrent and lasting effects of emotion regulation on amygdala response in adolescence and young adulthood. *Developmental Science, 18*(5), 771–784.

**Sim, Zi L. & Xu, Fei.** (2017). Learning higher-order generalizations through free play: Evidence from 2- and 3-year-old children. *Developmental Psychology, 53*(4), 642–651.

**Simms, Victoria; Gilmore, Camilla; Sloan, Seaneen & McKeaveney, Clare.** (2019). *Interventions to improve mathematical achievement in primary school-aged children.* London, UK: Nuffield Foundation.

**Simon, Laura & Daneback, Kristian.** (2013). Adolescents' use of the internet for sex education: A thematic and critical review of the literature. *International Journal of Sexual Health, 25*(4), 305–319.

**Simpson, Elizabeth A.; Jakobsen, Krisztina V.; Damon, Fabrice; Suomi, Stephen J.; Ferrari, Pier F. & Paukner, Annika.** (2017). Face detection and the development of own-species bias in infant macaques. *Child Development, 88*(1), 103–113.

**Simpson, Jeffry A. & Kenrick, Douglas.** (2013). *Evolutionary social psychology.* Taylor & Francis.

**Simpson, Kate; Adams, Dawn; Bruck, Susan & Keen, Deb.** (2019). Investigating the participation of children on the autism spectrum across home, school, and community: A longitudinal study. *Child, 45*(5), 681–687.

**Singanayagam, Aran; Ritchie, Andrew I. & Johnston, Sebastian L.** (2017). Role of microbiome in the pathophysiology and disease course of asthma. *Current Opinion in Pulmonary Medicine, 23*(1), 41–47.

**Singer, Elly & Wong, Sandie.** (2019). Emotional security and daycare for babies and toddlers in social-political contexts: Reflections of early years pioneers since the 1970s. *Early Child Development and Care.*

**Singer, Judith D. & Braun, Henry I.** (2018). Testing international education assessments. *Science, 360*(6384), 38–40.

**Singh, Amika; Uijtdewilligen, Léonie; Twisk, Jos W. R.; van Mechelen, Willem & Chinapaw, Mai J. M.** (2012). Physical activity and performance at school: A systematic review of the literature including a methodological quality assessment. *Archives of Pediatrics & Adolescent Medicine, 166*(1), 49–55.

**Sinnott, Jan; Hilton, Shelby; Wood, Michael & Douglas, Derek.** (2020). Relating flow, mindfulness, cognitive flexibility, and postformal thought: Two studies. *Journal of Adult Development, 27*(1), 1–11.

**Sinnott, Jan D.** (2014). *Adult development: Cognitive aspects of thriving close relationships.* Oxford University Press.

**Sisson, Susan B.; Krampe, Megan; Anundson, Katherine & Castle, Sherri.** (2016). Obesity prevention and obesogenic behavior interventions in child care: A systematic review. *Preventive Medicine, 87*, 57–69.

**Skiba, Russell J.; Michael, Robert S.; Nardo, Abra Carroll & Peterson, Reece L.** (2002). The color of discipline: Sources of racial and gender disproportionality in school punishment. *The Urban Review, 34*(4), 317–342.

**Skinner, B. F.** (1953). *Science and human behavior.* Macmillan.

**Skinner, B. F.** (1957). *Verbal behavior.* Appleton-Century-Crofts.

**Skoog, Therése & Stattin, Håkan.** (2014). Why and under what contextual conditions do early-maturing girls develop problem behaviors? *Child Development Perspectives, 8*(3), 158–162.

**Sloan, Mark.** (2009). *Birth day: A pediatrician explores the science, the history, and the wonder of childbirth.* Ballantine Books.

**Smart, Andrew; Bolnick, Deborah A. & Tutton, Richard.** (2017). Health and genetic ancestry testing: Time to bridge the gap. *BMC Medical Genomics, 10*(1).

**Smetana, Judith G.; Ahmad, Ikhlas & Wray-Lake, Laura.** (2016). Beliefs about parental authority legitimacy among refugee youth in Jordan: Between- and within-person variations. *Developmental Psychology, 52*(3), 484–495.

**Smith, Daniel M. & Martiny, Sarah E.** (2018). Stereotype threat in sport: Recommendations for applied practice and research. *The Sport Psychologist, 32*(4), 311–320.

**Smith, Hannah E.; Ryan, Kelsey N.; Stephenson, Kevin B.; Westcott, Claire; Thakwalakwa, Chrissie; Maleta, Ken; . . . Manary, Mark J.** (2014). Multiple micronutrient supplementation transiently ameliorates environmental enteropathy in Malawian children aged 12–35 months in a randomized controlled clinical trial. *Journal of Nutrition, 144*(12), 2059–2065.

**Smith, Michelle I.; Yatsunenko, Tanya; Manary, Mark J.; Trehan, Indi; Mkakosya, Rajhab; Cheng, Jiye; . . . Gordon, Jeffrey I.** (2013). Gut microbiomes of Malawian twin pairs discordant for kwashiorkor. *Science, 339*(6119), 548–554.

**Smithells, R. W.; Sheppard, S.; Schorah, C. J.; Seller, M. J.; Nevin, N. C.; Harris, R.; . . . Fielding, D. W.** (2011). Apparent prevention of neural tube defects by periconceptional vitamin supplementation. *International Journal of Epidemiology, 40*(5), 1146–1154.

**Smits, Jeroen & Monden, Christiaan.** (2011). Twinning across the developing world. *PLoS ONE, 6*(9), e25239.

**Smock, Pamela J. & Schwartz, Christine R.** (2020). The demography of families: A review of patterns and change. *Journal of Marriage and Family, 82*(1), 9–34.

**Snider, Terra Ziporyn.** (2012). Later school start times are a public-health issue. *Education Week, 31*(31), 25, 27.

**Snow, J. B.** (2015). *Narcissist and the Peter Pan syndrome: Emotionally unavailable and emotionally immature men.* J. B. Snow Publishing, Amazon Digital Services.

**Snyder, Thomas D. & Dillow, Sally A.** (2013). *Digest of education statistics, 2012.* Washington, DC: National Center for Education Statistics, Institute of Education Sciences, U.S. Department of Education.

**Society for Developmental & Behavioral Pediatrics.** (2018, July 18). *SDBP statement related to the separation of children from families at the border.* McLean, VA: Society for Developmental & Behavioral Pediatrics.

**Soderstrom, Melanie; Ko, Eon-Suk & Nevzorova, Uliana.** (2011). It's a question? Infants attend differently to yes/no questions and declaratives. *Infant Behavior and Development, 34*(1), 107–110.

**Solheim, Elisabet; Wichstrøm, Lars; Belsky, Jay & Berg-Nielsen, Turid Suzanne.** (2013). Do time in child care and peer group exposure predict poor socioemotional adjustment in Norway? *Child Development, 84*(5), 1701–1715.

**Solomon, Andrew.** (2012). *Far from the tree: Parents, children, and the search for identity.* Scribner.

**Somerville, Leah H.** (2013). The teenage brain: Sensitivity to social evaluation. *Current Directions in Psychological Science, 22*(2), 121–127.

**Sonuga-Barke, Edmund J. S.; Kennedy, Mark; Kumsta, Robert; Knights, Nicky; Golm, Dennis; Rutter, Michael; . . . Kreppner, Jana.** (2017). Child-to-adult neurodevelopmental and mental health trajectories after early life deprivation: The young adult follow-up of the longitudinal English and Romanian Adoptees study. *The Lancet, 389*(10078), 1539–1548.

**Soska, Kasey C.; Adolph, Karen E. & Johnson, Scott P.** (2010). Systems in development: Motor skill acquisition facilitates three-dimensional object completion. *Developmental Psychology, 46*(1), 129–138.

**Sousa, David A.** (2014). *How the brain learns to read* (2nd ed.). SAGE.

**Sparks, Sarah D.** (2016, July 20). Dose of empathy found to cut suspension rates. *Education Week, 35*(36), 1, 20.

**Spelke, Elizabeth S.** (1993). Object perception. In Goldman, Alvin I. (Ed.), *Readings in philosophy and cognitive science* (pp. 447–460). MIT Press.

**Spencer, Steven J.; Logel, Christine & Davies, Paul G.** (2016). Stereotype threat. *Annual Review of Psychology, 67*, 415–437.

**Sperry, Douglas E.; Sperry, Linda L. & Miller, Peggy J.** (2019). Reexamining the verbal environments of children from different socioeconomic backgrounds. *Child Development, 90*(4), 1303–1318.

**Spolaore, Enrico & Wacziarg, Romain.** (2018). Ancestry and development: New evidence. *Journal of Applied Econometrics, 33*(5), 748–762.

**Sprietsma, Maresa.** (2010). Effect of relative age in the first grade of primary school on long-term scholastic results: International comparative evidence using PISA 2003. *Education Economics, 18*(1), 1–32.

**Springsteen, Bruce.** (2017). *Born to run.* Simon & Schuster.

**Srinivasan, Sharada & Li, Shuzhuo.** (2018). Unifying perspectives on scarce women and surplus men in China and India. In Srinivasan, Sharada & Li, Shuzhuo (Eds.), *Scarce women and surplus men in China and India* (pp. 1–23). Springer.

**Sriram, Rajalakshmi.** (2019). A global perspective on fathering. In Sriram, Rajalakshmi (Ed.), *Fathering in India* (pp. 19–34). Springer.

**Stahl, Aimee E. & Feigenson, Lisa.** (2017). Expectancy violations promote learning in young children. *Cognition, 163*, 1–14.

**Standing, E. M.** (1998). *Maria Montessori: Her life and work.* Plume.

**Starr, Christine R. & Zurbriggen, Eileen L.** (2016). Sandra Bem's gender schema theory after 34 years: A review of its reach and impact. *Sex Roles*.

**Statistics Norway.** (2018). Facts about education in Norway 2018. Statistics Norway's Information Centre.

**Stattin, Håkan; Hussein, Oula; Özdemir, Metin & Russo, Silvia.** (2017). Why do some adolescents encounter everyday events that increase their civic interest whereas others do not? *Developmental Psychology*, 53(2), 306–318.

**Steele, Claude M.** (1997). A threat in the air: How stereotypes shape intellectual identity and performance. *American Psychologist*, 52(6), 613–629.

**Stefansen, Kari; Smette, Ingrid & Strandbu, Åse.** (2018). Understanding the increase in parents' involvement in organized youth sports. *Sport, Education and Society*, 23(2), 162–172.

**Steffensmeier, Darrell; Painter-Davis, Noah & Ulmer, Jeffery.** (2017). Intersectionality of race, ethnicity, gender, and age on criminal punishment. *Sociological Perspectives*, 60(4), 810–833.

**Steinberg, Laurence.** (2004). Risk taking in adolescence: What changes, and why? *Annals of the New York Academy of Sciences*, 1021, 51–58.

**Steinberg, Laurence.** (2009). Should the science of adolescent brain development inform public policy? *American Psychologist*, 64(8), 739–750.

**Steinberg, Laurence.** (2014). *Age of opportunity: Lessons from the new science of adolescence*. Houghton Mifflin Harcourt.

**Steinberg, Laurence.** (2015). The neural underpinnings of adolescent risk-taking: The roles of reward-seeking, impulse control, and peers. In Oettingen, Gabriele & Gollwitzer, Peter M. (Eds.), *Self-regulation in adolescence* (pp. 173–192). Cambridge University Press.

**Steinberg, Laurence & Monahan, Kathryn C.** (2011). Adolescents' exposure to sexy media does not hasten the initiation of sexual intercourse. *Developmental Psychology*, 47(2), 562–576.

**Stenseng, Frode; Belsky, Jay; Skalicka, Vera & Wichstrøm, Lars.** (2015). Social exclusion predicts impaired self-regulation: A 2-year longitudinal panel study including the transition from preschool to school. *Journal of Personality*, 83(2), 212–220.

**Stern, Gavin.** (2015). For kids with special learning needs, roadblocks remain. *Science*, 349(6255), 1465–1466.

**Stern, Jessica A.; Botdorf, Morgan; Cassidy, Jude & Riggins, Tracy.** (2019). Empathic responding and hippocampal volume in young children. *Developmental Psychology*, 55(9), 1908–1920.

**Stern, Mark; Clonan, Sheila; Jaffee, Laura & Lee, Anna.** (2015). The normative limits of choice: Charter schools, disability studies, and questions of inclusion. *Educational Policy*, 29(3), 448–477.

**Stern, Peter.** (2013). Connection, connection, connection . . . *Science*, 342(6158), 577.

**Sternberg, Robert J.** (1988). Triangulating love. In Sternberg, Robert J. & Barnes, Michael L. (Eds.), *The psychology of love* (pp. 119–138). Yale University Press.

**Sternberg, Robert J.** (2008). Schools should nurture wisdom. In Presseisen, Barbara Z. (Ed.), *Teaching for intelligence* (2nd ed., pp. 61–88). Corwin Press.

**Sternberg, Robert J.** (2011). The theory of successful intelligence. In Sternberg, Robert J. & Kaufman, Scott Barry (Eds.), *The Cambridge handbook of intelligence* (pp. 504–526). Cambridge University Press.

**Stiles, Joan & Jernigan, Terry.** (2010). The basics of brain development. *Neuropsychology Review*, 20(4), 327–348.

**Stives, Kristen L.; May, David C.; Pilkinton, Melinda; Bethel, Cindy L. & Eakin, Deborah K.** (2019). Strategies to combat bullying: Parental responses to bullies, bystanders, and victims. *Youth & Society*, 51(3), 358–376.

**Stochholm, Kirstine; Juul, Svend & Gravholt, Claus H.** (2010). Diagnosis and mortality in 47,XYY persons: A registry study. *Orphanet Journal of Rare Diseases*, 5(15).

**Stolt, Suvi; Matomäki, Jaakko; Lind, Annika; Lapinleimu, Helena; Haataja, Leena & Lehtonen, Liisa.** (2014). The prevalence and predictive value of weak language skills in children with very low birth weight—A longitudinal study. *Acta Paediatrica*, 103(6), 651–658.

**Strait, Dana L.; Parbery-Clark, Alexandra; O'Connell, Samantha & Kraus, Nina.** (2013). Biological impact of preschool music classes on processing speech in noise. *Developmental Cognitive Neuroscience*, 6, 51–60.

**Strasburger, Victor C.; Wilson, Barbara J. & Jordan, Amy B.** (2009). *Children, adolescents, and the media* (2nd ed.). Sage.

**Stremmel, Andrew J.** (2012). A situated framework: The Reggio experience. In File, Nancy; Mueller, Jennifer J. & Wisneski, Debora B. (Eds.), *Curriculum in early childhood education: Reexamined, rediscovered, renewed* (pp. 133–145). Routledge.

**Stroebe, Wolfgang & Strack, Fritz.** (2014). The alleged crisis and the illusion of exact replication. *Perspectives on Psychological Science*, 9(1), 59–71.

**Strøm, Marin; Mortensen, Erik Lykke; Kesmodel, Ulrik Schiøler; Halldorsson, Thorhallur; Olsen, Jørn & Olsen, Sjurdur F.** (2019). Is breast feeding associated with offspring IQ at age 5? Findings from prospective cohort: Lifestyle during pregnancy study. *BMJ Open*, 9(5), e023134.

**Strouse, Gabrielle A. & Ganea, Patricia A.** (2017). Toddlers' word learning and transfer from electronic and print books. *Journal of Experimental Child Psychology*, 156, 129–142.

**Suárez-Orozco, Carola.** (2017). Conferring disadvantage: Behavioral and developmental implications for children growing up in the shadow of undocumented immigration status. *Journal of Developmental & Behavioral Pediatrics*, 38(6), 424–428.

**Suberi, Moriya; Morag, Iris; Strauss, Tzipora & Geva, Ronny.** (2018). Feeding imprinting: The extreme test case of premature infants born with very low birth weight. *Child Development*, 89(5), 1553–1566.

**Substance Abuse and Mental Health Services Administration.** (2019). *Key substance use and mental health indicators in the United States: Results from the 2018 National Survey on Drug Use and Health*. Rockville, MD: Center for Behavioral Health Statistics and Quality, Substance Abuse and Mental Health Services Administration. HHS Publication No. PEP19-5068, NSDUH Series H-54.

**Suchy, Frederick J.; Brannon, Patsy M.; Carpenter, Thomas O.; Fernandez, Jose R.; Gilsanz, Vicente; Gould, Jeffrey B.; . . . Wolf, Marshall A.** (2010). National Institutes of Health Consensus Development Conference: Lactose intolerance and health. *Annals of Internal Medicine*, 152(12), 792–796.

**Sugimura, Kazumi; Matsushima, Kobo; Hihara, Shogo; Takahashi, Masami & Crocetti, Elisabetta.** (2019). A culturally sensitive approach to the relationships between identity formation and religious beliefs in youth. *Journal of Youth and Adolescence*, 48(4), 668–679.

**Suleiman, Ahna B. & Brindis, Claire D.** (2014). Adolescent school-based sex education: Using developmental neuroscience to guide new directions for policy and practice. *Sexuality Research and Social Policy*, 11(2), 137–152.

**Sulek, Julia P.** (2013, April 30). Audrie Pott suicide: Parents share grief, quest for justice in exclusive interview. *San Jose Mercury News*.

**Sullivan, Jas M. & Ghara, Alexandra.** (2015). Racial identity and intergroup attitudes: A multiracial youth analysis. *Social Science Quarterly*, 96(1), 261–272.

**Sullivan, Patrick F.; Neale, Michael C. & Kendler, Kenneth S.** (2000). Genetic epidemiology of major depression: Review and meta-analysis. *American Journal of Psychiatry*, 157(10), 1552–1562.

**Sun, Li; Guo, Xin; Zhang, Jing; Liu, Henghui; Xu, Shaojun; Xu, Yuanyuan & Tao, Fangbiao.** (2016). Gender specific associations between early puberty and behavioral and emotional characteristics in children. *Zhonghua Liu Xing Bing Xue Za Zhi*, 37(1), 35–39.

**Sun, Min & Rugolotto, Simone.** (2004). Assisted infant toilet training in a Western family setting. *Journal of Developmental & Behavioral Pediatrics*, 25(2), 99–101.

**Sundqvist, Christel; Björk-Åman, Camilla & Ström, Kristina.** (2019). The three-tiered support system and the special education teachers' role in Swedish-speaking schools in Finland. *European Journal of Special Needs Education*, 34(5), 601–616.

**Suomi, Steven J.** (2002). Parents, peers, and the process of socialization in primates. In Borkowski, John G.; Ramey, Sharon L. & Bristol-Power, Marie (Eds.), *Parenting and the child's world: Influences on academic, intellectual, and social-emotional development* (pp. 265–279). Erlbaum.

**Sutaria, Shailen; Devakumar, Delan; Yasuda, Sílvia Shikanai; Das, Shikta & Saxena, Sonia.** (2019). Is obesity associated with depression in children? Systematic review and meta-analysis. *Archives of Disease in Childhood*, 104(1), 64–74.

**Suurland, Jill; van der Heijden, Kristiaan B.; Huijbregts, Stephan C. J.; Smaling, Hanneke J. A.; de Sonneville, Leo M. J.; Van Goozen, Stephanie H. M. & Swaab, Hanna.** (2016). Parental perceptions of aggressive behavior in preschoolers: Inhibitory control moderates the association with negative emotionality. *Child Development*, 87(1), 256–269.

**Suzumori, Nobuhiro; Kumagai, Kyoko; Goto, Shinobu; Nakamura, Akira & Sugiura-Ogasawara, Mayumi.** (2015). Parental decisions following prenatal diagnosis of chromosomal abnormalities: Implications for genetic counseling practice in Japan. *Journal of Genetic Counseling*, 24(1), 117–121.

**Swaab, D. F. & Hofman, M. A.** (1984). Sexual differentiation of the human brain: A historical perspective. *Progress in Brain Research*, 61, 361–374.

**Swanson, H. Lee.** (2013). Meta-analysis of research on children with learning disabilities. In Swanson, H. Lee; Harris, Karen R. & Graham, Steve (Eds.), *Handbook of learning disabilities* (2nd ed., pp. 627–642). Guilford Press.

**Swit, Cara & McMaugh, Anne.** (2012). Relational aggression and prosocial behaviours in Australian preschool children. *Australasian Journal of Early Childhood*, 37(3), 30–34.

**Taga, Keiko A.; Markey, Charlotte N. & Friedman, Howard S.** (2006). A longitudinal investigation of associations between boys' pubertal timing and adult behavioral health and well-being. *Journal of Youth and Adolescence*, 35(3), 380–390.

**Tagar, Michal Reifen; Hetherington, Chelsea; Shulman, Deborah & Koenig, Melissa.** (2017). On the path to social dominance? Individual differences in sensitivity to intergroup fairness violations in early childhood. *Personality and Individual Differences*, 113, 246–250.

**Taillieu, Tamara L.; Afifi, Tracie O.; Mota, Natalie; Keyes, Katherine M. & Sareen, Jitender.** (2014). Age, sex, and racial differences in harsh physical punishment: Results from a nationally representative United States sample. *Child Abuse & Neglect*, 38(12), 1885–1894.

**Tajalli, Hassan & Garba, Houmma A.** (2014). Discipline or prejudice? Overrepresentation of minority students in disciplinary alternative education programs. *Urban Review*, 46(4), 620–631.

**Takala, Marjatta; Nordmark, Marie & Allard, Karin.** (2019). University curriculum in special teacher education in Finland and Sweden. *Nordic Journal of Comparative and International Education*, 3(2), 20–36.

**Tam, Vivian; Patel, Nikunj; Turcotte, Michelle; Bossé, Yohan; Paré, Guillaume & Meyre, David.** (2019). Benefits and limitations of genome-wide association studies. *Nature Reviews Genetics*, 20(8), 467–484.

**Tamis-LeMonda, Catherine S.; Bornstein, Marc H. & Baumwell, Lisa.** (2001). Maternal responsiveness and children's achievement of language milestones. *Child Development*, 72(3), 748–767.

**Tamm, Leanne; Epstein, Jeffery N.; Denton, Carolyn A.; Vaughn, Aaron J.; Peugh, James & Willcutt, Erik G.** (2014). Reaction time variability associated with reading skills in poor readers with ADHD. *Journal of the International Neuropsychological Society*, 20(3), 292–301.

**Tamnes, Christian K.; Overbye, Knut; Ferschmann, Lia; Fjell, Anders M.; Walhovd, Kristine B.; Blakemore, Sarah-Jayne & Dumontheil, Iroise.** (2018). Social perspective taking is associated with self-reported prosocial behavior and regional cortical thickness across adolescence. *Developmental Psychology*, 54(9), 1745–1757.

**Tamura, Naomi; Hanaoka, Tomoyuki; Ito, Kumiko; Araki, Atsuko; Miyashita, Chihiro; Ito, Sachiko; . . . Kishi, Reiko.** (2018). Different risk factors for very low birth weight, term-small-for-gestational-age, or preterm birth in Japan. *International Journal of Environmental Research and Public Health*, 15(2), 369.

**Tan, Patricia Z.; Armstrong, Laura M. & Cole, Pamela M.** (2013). Relations between temperament and anger regulation over early childhood. *Social Development*, 22(4), 755–772.

**Tanumihardjo, Sherry A.; Gannon, Bryan & Kaliwile, Chisela.** (2016). Controversy regarding widespread vitamin A fortification in Africa and Asia. *Advances in Nutrition*, 7, 5A.

**Tartaro, Christine.** (2019). *Suicide and self-harm in prisons and jails* (2nd ed.). Lexington.

**Tarun, Kumar; Kumar, Singh Sanjeet; Manish, Kumar; Sunita & Ashok, Sharan.** (2016). Study on relationship between anemia and academic performance of adolescent girls. *International Journal of Physiology*, 4(1), 81–86.

**Tattersall, Ian.** (2017). Why was human evolution so rapid? In Marom, Assaf & Hovers, Erella (Eds.), *Human paleontology and prehistory: Contributions in Honor of Yoel Rak* (pp. 1–9). Springer.

**Tavassolie, Tanya & Winsler, Adam.** (2019). Predictors of mandatory 3rd grade retention from high-stakes test performance for low-income, ethnically diverse children. *Early Childhood Research Quarterly*, 48, 62–74.

**Tay, Marc Tze-Hsin; Au Eong, Kah Guan; Ng, C. Y. & Lim, M. K.** (1992). Myopia and educational attainment in 421,116 young Singaporean males. *Annals Academy of Medicine Singapore*, 21(6), 785–791.

**Taylor, Marjorie; Mottweiler, Candice M.; Aguiar, Naomi R.; Naylor, Emilee R. & Levernier, Jacob G.** (2020). Paracosms: The imaginary worlds of middle childhood. *Child Development*, 91(1), e164–e178.

**Taylor, Paul.** (2014). *The next America: Boomers, millennials, and the looming generational showdown*. PublicAffairs.

**Taylor, Zoe E.; Eisenberg, Nancy; Spinrad, Tracy L.; Eggum, Natalie D. & Sulik, Michael J.** (2013). The relations of ego-resiliency and emotion socialization to the development of empathy and prosocial behavior across early childhood. *Emotion*, 13(5), 822–831.

**Tekelab, Tesfalidet; Chojenta, Catherine; Smith, Roger & Loxton, Deborah.** (2019). The impact of antenatal care on neonatal mortality in sub-Saharan Africa: A systematic review and meta-analysis. *PLoS ONE*, 14(9), e0222566.

**Telzer, Eva H.; Ichien, Nicholas T. & Qu, Yang.** (2015). Mothers know best: Redirecting adolescent reward sensitivity toward safe behavior during risk taking. *Social Cognitive and Affective Neuroscience*, 10(10), 1383–1391.

**Teoh, Yee San & Lamb, Michael E.** (2013). Interviewer demeanor in forensic interviews of children. *Psychology, Crime & Law*, 19(2), 145–159.

**Terry, Nicole Patton; Connor, Carol McDonald; Johnson, Lakeisha; Stuckey, Adrienne & Tani, Novell.** (2016). Dialect variation, dialect-shifting, and reading comprehension in second grade. *Reading and Writing*, 29(2), 267–295.

**Tessier, Karen.** (2010). Effectiveness of hands-on education for correct child restraint use by parents. *Accident Analysis & Prevention*, 42(4), 1041–1047.

**Tett, Gillian.** (2015). *The silo effect: The peril of expertise and the promise of breaking down barriers*. Simon & Schuster.

**Tetzlaff, Anne & Hilbert, Anja.** (2014). The role of the family in childhood and adolescent binge eating. A systematic review. *Appetite*, 76(1), 208.

**Thaler, Richard H. & Sunstein, Cass R.** (2008). *Nudge: Improving decisions about health, wealth, and happiness*. Yale University Press.

**Tham, Diana Su Yun; Woo, Pei Jun & Bremner, J. Gavin.** (2019). Development of the other-race effect in Malaysian-Chinese infants. *Developmental Psychobiology*, 61(1), 107–115.

**Thiam, Melinda A.; Flake, Eric M. & Dickman, Michael M.** (2017). Infant and child mental health and perinatal illness. In Thiam, Melinda A. (Ed.), *Perinatal mental health and the military family: Identifying and treating mood and anxiety disorders*. Routledge.

**Thibodeaux, Jordan; Bock, Allison; Hutchison, Lindsey A. & Winsler, Adam.** (2019). Singing to the self: Children's private speech, private song, and executive functioning. *Cognitive Development*, 50, 130–141.

**Thomaes, Sander; Brummelman, Eddie & Sedikides, Constantine.** (2017). Why most children think well of themselves. *Child Development*, 88(6), 1873–1884.

**Thomason, Moriah E.; Scheinost, Dustin; Manning, Janessa H.; Grove, Lauren E.; Hect, Jasmine; Marshall, Narcis; . . . Romero, Roberto.** (2017). Weak functional connectivity in the human fetal brain prior to preterm birth. *Scientific Reports*, 7(39286).

**Thompson, Charis.** (2014). Reproductions through technology. *Science*, 344(6182), 361–362.

**Thompson, Richard; Kaczor, Kim; Lorenz, Douglas J.; Bennett, Berkeley L.; Meyers, Gabriel & Pierce, Mary Clyde.** (2017). Is the use of physical discipline associated with aggressive behaviors in young children? *Academic Pediatrics*, 17(1), 34–44.

**Thorup, Bianca; Crookes, Kate; Chang, Paul P. W.; Burton, Nichola; Pond, Stephen; Li, Tze Kwan; . . . Rhodes, Gillian.** (2018). Perceptual experience shapes our ability to categorize faces by national origin: A new other-race effect. *British Journal of Psychology*, 109(3), 583–603.

**Tiggemann, Marika & Slater, Amy.** (2014). NetTweens: The internet and body image concerns in preteenage girls. *Journal of Early Adolescence*, 34(5), 606–620.

**Tobey, Emily A.; Thal, Donna; Niparko, John K.; Eisenberg, Laurie S.; Quittner, Alexandra

L. & Wang, Nae-Yuh. (2013). Influence of implantation age on school-age language performance in pediatric cochlear implant users. *International Journal of Audiology*, 52(4), 219–229.

Tolman, Deborah L.; Davis, Brian R. & Bowman, Christin P. (2016). "That's just how it is": A gendered analysis of masculinity and femininity ideologies in adolescent girls' and boys' heterosexual relationships. *Journal of Adolescent Research*, 31(1), 3–31.

Tolman, Deborah L. & McClelland, Sara I. (2011). Normative sexuality development in adolescence: A decade in review, 2000–2009. *Journal of Research on Adolescence*, 21(1), 242–255.

Tomalski, Przemyslaw & Johnson, Mark H. (2010). The effects of early adversity on the adult and developing brain. *Current Opinion in Psychiatry*, 23(3), 233–238.

Tomasello, Michael. (2016a). The ontogeny of cultural learning. *Current Opinion in Psychology*, 8, 1–4.

Tomasello, Michael. (2016b). Cultural learning redux. *Child Development*, 87(3), 643–653.

Tomasello, Michael & Herrmann, Esther. (2010). Ape and human cognition. *Current Directions in Psychological Science*, 19(1), 3–8.

Topolewska-Siedzik, Ewa & Cieciuch, Jan. (2019). Modes of personal identity formation: A preliminary picture from the lifespan perspective. *Personality and Individual Differences*, 138, 237–242.

Toporek, Bryan. (2012). Sports rules revised as research mounts on head injuries. *Education Week*, 31(22), 8.

Torrey, E. Fuller & Yolken, Robert H. (2019). Schizophrenia as a pseudogenetic disease: A call for more gene-environmental studies. *Psychiatry Research*, 278, 146–150.

Toth, Sheree L. & Manly, Jody T. (2019). Developmental consequences of child abuse and neglect: Implications for intervention. *Child Development Perspectives*, 13(1), 59–65.

Tough, Paul. (2012). *How children succeed: Grit, curiosity, and the hidden power of character*. Houghton Mifflin Harcourt.

Trahan, Lisa H.; Stuebing, Karla K.; Fletcher, Jack M. & Hiscock, Merrill. (2014). The Flynn Effect: A meta-analysis. *Psychological Bulletin*, 140(5), 1332–1360.

Travers, Brittany G.; Tromp, Do P. M.; Adluru, Nagesh; Lange, Nicholas; Destiche, Dan; Ennis, Chad; . . . Alexander, Andrew L. (2015). Atypical development of white matter microstructure of the corpus callosum in males with autism: A longitudinal investigation. *Molecular Autism*, 6.

Trawick-Smith, Jeffrey. (2019). Not all children grow up the same: Child development, diversity, and early care and education. In Brown, Christopher P.; McMullen, Mary Benson & File, Nancy (Eds.), *The Wiley handbook of early childhood care and education* (pp. 29–58). Wiley.

Treffers-Daller, Jeanine & Milton, J. (2013). Vocabulary size revisited: The link between vocabulary size and academic achievement. *Applied Linguistics Review*, 4(1), 151–172.

Trinh, Sarah L.; Lee, Jaemin; Halpern, Carolyn T. & Moody, James. (2019). Our buddies, ourselves: The role of sexual homophily in adolescent friendship networks. *Child Development*, 90(1), e132–e147.

Troester-Trate, Katy Elizabeth. (2019). Food insecurity, inadequate childcare, & transportation disadvantage: Student retention and persistence of community college students. *Community College Journal of Research and Practice*.

Tronick, Edward. (1989). Emotions and emotional communication in infants. *American Psychologist*, 44(2), 112–119.

Tronick, Edward & Weinberg, M. Katherine. (1997). Depressed mothers and infants: Failure to form dyadic states of consciousness. In Murray, Lynne & Cooper, Peter J. (Eds.), *Postpartum depression and child development* (pp. 54–81). Guilford Press.

Tsang, Christine; Falk, Simone & Hessel, Alexandria. (2017). Infants prefer infant-directed song over speech. *Child Development*, 88(4), 1207–1215.

Turner, Heather A.; Finkelhor, David; Ormrod, Richard; Hamby, Sherry; Leeb, Rebecca T.; Mercy, James A. & Holt, Melissa. (2012). Family context, victimization, and child trauma symptoms: Variations in safe, stable, and nurturing relationships during early and middle childhood. *American Journal of Orthopsychiatry*, 82(2), 209–219.

Tuulari, Jetro J.; Scheinin, Noora M.; Lehtola, Satu; Merisaari, Harri; Saunavaara, Jani; Parkkola, Riitta; . . . Björnsdotter, Malin. (2019). Neural correlates of gentle skin stroking in early infancy. *Developmental Cognitive Neuroscience*, 35, 36–41.

Twenge, Jean M.; Joiner, Thomas E.; Rogers, Megan L. & Martin, Gabrielle N. (2018). Increases in depressive symptoms, suicide-related outcomes, and suicide rates among U.S. adolescents after 2010 and links to increased new media screen time. *Clinical Psychological Science*, 6(1), 3–17.

Twito, Louise & Knafo-Noam, Ariel. (2020). Beyond culture and the family: Evidence from twin studies on the genetic and environmental contribution to values. *Neuroscience & Biobehavioral Reviews*, 112, 135–143.

U.S. Bureau of Labor Statistics. (2018, August). *Labor force characteristics by race and ethnicity, 2017*. BLS Reports. Washington, DC: U.S. Bureau of Labor Statistics.

U.S. Bureau of Labor Statistics. (2019, April 18). Table 6. Employment status of mothers with own children under 3 years old by single year of age of youngest child and marital status, 2017–2018 annual averages. Division of Labor Force Statistics.

U.S. Bureau of Labor Statistics. (2020). Occupational outlook handbook. Division of Labor Force Statistics.

U.S. Census Bureau. (2015). *America's families and living arrangements: 2015: Households (H table series). Table H3: Households by race and Hispanic origin of household reference person and detailed type*. Washington, DC: U.S. Department of Commerce, Economics and Statistics Administration, U.S. Census Bureau.

U.S. Census Bureau. (2016a). *Selected population profile in the United States: 2014 American community survey 1-year estimates. American FactFinder*. Washington, DC: U.S. Department of Commerce.

U.S. Census Bureau. (2016b). *Selected population profile in the United States: 2009 American community survey 1-year estimates. American FactFinder*. Washington, DC: U.S. Department of Commerce.

U.S. Census Bureau. (2018, November). *Historical living arrangements of children: Living arrangements of children under 18 years old: 1960 to present*. U.S. Census Bureau.

U.S. Census Bureau. (2018, February 19). CPS historical time series tables: Table A-1. Years of school completed by people 25 years and over, by age and sex: Selected years 1940 to 2018. U.S. Census Bureau.

U.S. Census Bureau. (2019, June). *Annual estimates of the resident population by sex, age, race, and Hispanic origin for the United States and States: April 1, 2010 to July 1, 2018. American FactFinder*. Washington, DC: U.S. Department of Commerce. PEPASR6H.

U.S. Department of Agriculture. (2018, September 5). *Key statistics & graphics: Food insecurity in the U.S.* Washington, DC: U.S. Department of Agriculture.

U.S. Department of Health and Human Services. (2000, December 31). *Child maltreatment 2000*. Washington, DC: Administration on Children, Youth and Families, Children's Bureau.

U.S. Department of Health and Human Services. (2010). *Head Start impact study: Final report*. Washington, DC: Administration for Children and Families.

U.S. Department of Health and Human Services. (2010, January). *Child maltreatment 2009*. Washington, DC: Administration for Children and Families, Administration on Children, Youth and Families, Children's Bureau.

U.S. Department of Health and Human Services. (2011). *The Surgeon General's call to action to support breastfeeding*. Washington, DC: U.S. Department of Health and Human Services, Office of the Surgeon General.

U.S. Department of Health and Human Services. (2016, January 25). *Child maltreatment 2014*. Washington, DC: Administration for Children and Families, Administration on Children, Youth and Families, Children's Bureau.

U.S. Department of Health and Human Services. (2017, January 19). *Child maltreatment 2015*. Washington, DC: Administration for Children and Families, Administration on Children, Youth and Families, Children's Bureau.

U.S. Department of Health and Human Services. (2018, February 1). *Child maltreatment 2016*. Washington, DC: Administration for Children and Families, Administration on Children, Youth and Families, Children's Bureau.

U.S. Department of Health and Human Services. (2019, January 28). *Child maltreatment 2017*. Washington, DC: Administration for Children and Families, Administration on Children, Youth and Families, Children's Bureau.

**U.S. Department of Health and Human Services.** (2020, January 15). *Child maltreatment 2018*. Washington, DC: Administration for Children and Families, Administration on Children, Youth and Families, Children's Bureau.

**U.S. Department of State.** (2019). Adoption statistics—Adoptions by year. Travel.State.gov.

**U.S. Social Security Administration.** (2019). Popular names by birth year. U.S. Social Security Administration.

**Uchida, Mai; Spencer, Thomas J.; Faraone, Stephen V. & Biederman, Joseph.** (2018). Adult outcome of ADHD: An overview of results from the MGH longitudinal family studies of pediatrically and psychiatrically referred youth with and without ADHD of both sexes. *Journal of Attention Disorders*, 22(6), 523–534.

**Umaña-Taylor, Adriana J. & Hill, Nancy E.** (2020). Ethnic–racial socialization in the family: A decade's advance on precursors and outcomes. *Journal of Marriage and Family*, 82(1), 244–271.

**Umapathi, Kishore Krishna; Thavamani, Aravind & Chotikanatis, Kobkul.** (2019). Incidence trends, risk factors, mortality and healthcare utilization in congenital syphilis-related hospitalizations in the United States: A nationwide population analysis. *The Pediatric Infectious Disease Journal*, 38(11), 1126–1130.

**Underwood, Emily.** (2013). Why do so many neurons commit suicide during brain development? *Science*, 340(6137), 1157–1158.

**UNESCO.** (2014). *Country profiles*. UNESCO Institute for Statistics Data Centre. Montreal, Canada: UNESCO, Université de Montréal at the Montreal's École des hautes études.

**UNESCO.** (2018, February). *One in five children, adolescents and youth is out of school*. Fact Sheet No. 48. Montreal, Canada: UNESCO. UIS/FS/2018/ED/48.

**UNICEF.** (2017, January 13). *Global overview child malnutrition 1990–2015*. UNICEF Data and Analytics: Joint Malnutrition Estimates 2016 Edition. New York: NY: United Nations.

**UNICEF.** (2019, April). *Malnutrition* [Data set]. UNICEF Data.

**United Nations.** (2019, June 17). *UN Data: Life expectancy at birth for both sexes combined (years)* [Data set].

**United Nations, Department of Economic and Social Affairs, Population Division.** (2019). *World population prospects 2019*. New York, NY: (Volumes 1 & 2: ST/ESA/SER.A/426 & ST/ESA/SER.A/427).

**Ursache, Alexandra; Blair, Clancy; Stifter, Cynthia & Voegtline, Kristin.** (2013). Emotional reactivity and regulation in infancy interact to predict executive functioning in early childhood. *Developmental Psychology*, 49(1), 127–137.

**van Batenburg-Eddes, Tamara; Butte, Dick & van de Looij-Jansen, Petra.** (2012). Measuring juvenile delinquency: How do self-reports compare with official police statistics? *European Journal of Criminology*, 9(1), 23–37.

**van de Bongardt, Daphne; Reitz, Ellen; Sandfort, Theo & Deković, Maja.** (2015). A meta-analysis of the relations between three types of peer norms and adolescent sexual behavior. *Personality and Social Psychology Review*, 19(3), 203–234.

**Van de Vondervoort, Julia W. & Hamlin, J. Kiley.** (2016). Evidence for intuitive morality: Preverbal infants make sociomoral evaluations. *Child Development Perspectives*, 10(3), 143–148.

**van den Akker, Alithe; Deković, Maja; Prinzie, Peter & Asscher, Jessica.** (2010). Toddlers' temperament profiles: Stability and relations to negative and positive parenting. *Journal of Abnormal Child Psychology*, 38(4), 485–495.

**van Den Bunt, M. R.; Groen, M. A.; van Der Kleij, S. W.; Noordenbos, M. W.; Segers, E.; Pugh, K. R. & Verhoeven, L.** (2018). Deficient response to altered auditory feedback in dyslexia. *Developmental Neuropsychology*, 43(7), 622–641.

**van den Pol, Anthony N.; Mao, Guochao; Yang, Yang; Ornaghi, Sara & Davis, John N.** (2017). Zika virus targeting in the developing brain. *Journal of Neuroscience*, 37(8), 2161–2175.

**Van Dongen, Rachel.** (2019, March 15). The Energy 202: Kids are skipping school today—to protest climate change. *Washington Post*.

**Van Dyke, Miriam E.; Cheung, Patricia C.; Franks, Padra & Gazmararian, Julie A.** (2018). Socioeconomic and racial/ethnic disparities in physical activity environments in Georgia elementary schools. *American Journal of Health Promotion*, 32(2), 453–463.

**van Goozen, Stephanie H. M.** (2015). The role of early emotion impairments in the development of persistent antisocial behavior. *Child Development Perspectives*, 9(4), 206–210.

**Van Harmelen, A.-L.; Kievit, R. A.; Ioannidis, K.; Neufeld, S.; Jones, P. B.; Bullmore, E.; . . . Goodyer, I.** (2017). Adolescent friendships predict later resilient functioning across psychosocial domains in a healthy community cohort. *Psychological Medicine*, 47(13), 2312–2322.

**Van Hecke, Wim; Emsell, Louise & Sunaert, Stefan (Eds.).** (2016). *Diffusion tensor imaging: A practical handbook*. Springer.

**Van Horn, Linda V.; Bausermann, Robert; Affenito, Sandra; Thompson, Douglas; Striegel-Moore, Ruth; Franko, Debra & Albertson, Ann.** (2011). Ethnic differences in food sources of vitamin D in adolescent American girls: The National Heart, Lung, and Blood Institute Growth and Health Study. *Nutrition Research*, 31(8), 579–585.

**Van Houtte, Mieke.** (2016). Lower-track students' sense of academic futility: Selection or effect? *Journal of Sociology*, 52(4), 874–889.

**van IJzendoorn, Marinus H.; Bakermans-Kranenburg, Marian J.; Pannebakker, Fieke & Out, Dorothée.** (2010). In defence of situational morality: Genetic, dispositional and situational determinants of children's donating to charity. *Journal of Moral Education*, 39(1), 1–20.

**van Nunen, Karolien; Kaerts, Nore; Wyndaele, Jean-Jacques; Vermandel, Alexandra & Van Hal, Guido.** (2015). Parents' views on toilet training (TT): A quantitative study to identify the beliefs and attitudes of parents concerning TT. *Journal of Child Health Care*, 19(2), 265–274.

**Van Rheenen, Derek.** (2012). A century of historical change in the game preferences of American children. *Journal of American Folklore*, 125(498), 411–443.

**Van Tongeren, Daryl R.; DeWall, C. Nathan; Chen, Zhansheng; Sibley, Chris G. & Bulbulia, Joseph.** (2020). Religious residue: Cross-cultural evidence that religious psychology and behavior persist following deidentification. *Journal of Personality and Social Psychology*.

**Van Vonderen, Kristen E. & Kinnally, William.** (2012). Media effects on body image: Examining media exposure in the broader context of internal and other social factors. *American Communication Journal*, 14(2), 41–57.

**Vanderberg, Rachel H.; Farkas, Amy H.; Miller, Elizabeth; Sucato, Gina S.; Akers, Aletha Y. & Borrero, Sonya B.** (2016). Racial and/or ethnic differences in formal sex education and sex education by parents among young women in the United States. *Journal of Pediatric and Adolescent Gynecology*, 29(1), 69–73.

**Vanhalst, Janne; Luyckx, Koen; Scholte, Ron H. J.; Engels, Rutger C. M. E. & Goossens, Luc.** (2013). Low self-esteem as a risk factor for loneliness in adolescence: Perceived – but not actual – social acceptance as an underlying mechanism. *Journal of Abnormal Child Psychology*, 41(7), 1067–1081.

**Vannucci, Robert C. & Vannucci, Susan J.** (2019). Brain growth in modern humans using multiple developmental databases. *American Journal of Physical Anthropology*, 168(2), 247–261.

**Vargas Lascano, Dayuma I.; Galambos, Nancy L.; Krahn, Harvey J. & Lachman, Margie E.** (2015). Growth in perceived control across 25 years from the late teens to midlife: The role of personal and parents' education. *Developmental Psychology*, 51(1), 124–135.

**Vasung, Lana; Abaci Turk, Esra; Ferradal, Silvina L.; Sutin, Jason; Stout, Jeffrey N.; Ahtam, Banu; . . . Grant, P. Ellen.** (2019). Exploring early human brain development with structural and physiological neuroimaging. *NeuroImage*, 187, 226–254.

**Vaughn, Byron P.; Rank, Kevin M. & Khoruts, Alexander.** (2019). Fecal microbiota transplantation: Current status in treatment of GI and liver disease. *Clinical Gastroenterology and Hepatology*, 17(2), 353–361.

**Vedantam, Shankar.** (2011, December 5). *What's behind a temper tantrum? Scientists deconstruct the screams*. Hidden Brain. Washington DC: National Public Radio.

**Veldheer, Susan; Yingst, Jessica; Midya, Vishal; Hummer, Breanna; Lester, Courtney; Krebs, Nicolle; . . . Foulds, Jonathan.** (2019). Pulmonary and other health effects of electronic cigarette use among adult smokers participating in a randomized controlled smoking reduction trial. *Addictive Behaviors*, 91, 95–101.

**Vennemann, Mechtild M.; Hense, Hans-Werner; Bajanowski, Thomas; Blair, Peter S.; Complojer, Christina; Moon, Rachel Y. & Kiechl-Kohlendorfer, Ursula.** (2012). Bed sharing and the risk of sudden infant death syndrome:

Can we resolve the debate? *The Journal of Pediatrics*, *160*(1), 44–48.

**Verdine, Brian N.; Golinkoff, Roberta Michnick; Hirsh-Pasek, Kathy & Newcombe, Nora S.** (2017). Spatial skills, their development, and their links to mathematics. *Monographs of the Society for Research in Child Development: Links between spatial and mathematical skills across the preschool*, *82*(1), 7–30.

**Verona, Sergiu.** (2003). Romanian policy regarding adoptions. In Littel, Victor (Ed.), *Adoption update* (pp. 5–10). Nova Science.

**Verrusio, Walter; Ettorre, Evaristo; Vicenzini, Edoardo; Vanacore, Nicola; Cacciafesta, Mauro & Mecarelli, Oriano.** (2015). The Mozart Effect: A quantitative EEG study. *Consciousness and Cognition*, *35*, 150–155.

**Verschueren, Karine.** (2020). Attachment, self-esteem, and socio-emotional adjustment: There is more than just the mother. *Attachment & Human Development*, *22*(1), 105–109.

**Vijayakumar, Nandita; Op de Macks, Zdena; Shirtcliff, Elizabeth A. & Pfeifer, Jennifer H.** (2018). Puberty and the human brain: Insights into adolescent development. *Neuroscience and Biobehavioral Reviews*, *92*, 417–436.

**Viljaranta, Jaana; Aunola, Kaisa; Mullola, Sari; Virkkala, Johanna; Hirvonen, Riikka; Pakarinen, Eija & Nurmi, Jari-Erik.** (2015). Children's temperament and academic skill development during first grade: Teachers' interaction styles as mediators. *Child Development*, *86*(4), 1191–1209.

**Vitale, Susan; Sperduto, Robert D. & Ferris, Frederick L.** (2009). Increased prevalence of myopia in the United States between 1971–1972 and 1999–2004. *Archives of Ophthalmology*, *127*(12), 1632–1639.

**Voelcker-Rehage, Claudia; Niemann, Claudia & Hübner, Lena.** (2018). Structural and functional brain changes related to acute and chronic exercise effects in children, adolescents and young adults. In Meeusen, Romain; Schaefer, Sabine; Tomporowski, Phillip & Bailey, Richard (Eds.), *Physical activity and educational achievement: Insights from exercise neuroscience* (pp. 143–163). Routledge.

**Voges, Juané; Berg, Astrid & Niehaus, Dana J. H.** (2019). Revisiting the African origins of attachment research—50 years on from Ainsworth: A descriptive review. *Infant Mental Health Journal*, *40*(6), 799–816.

**Vöhringer, Isabel A.; Kolling, Thorsten; Graf, Frauke; Poloczek, Sonja; Fassbender, Iina; Freitag, Claudia; . . . Knopf, Monika.** (2018). The development of implicit memory from infancy to childhood: On average performance levels and interindividual differences. *Child Development*, *89*(2), 370–382.

**von Salisch, Maria.** (2018). Emotional competence and friendship involvement: Spiral effects in adolescence. *European Journal of Developmental Psychology*, *15*(6), 678–693.

**Vos, Amber A.; van Voorst, Sabine F.; Steegers, Eric A. P. & Denktaş, Semiha.** (2016). Analysis of policy towards improvement of perinatal mortality in the Netherlands

(2004–2011). *Social Science & Medicine*, *157*, 156–164.

**Votruba-Drzal, Elizabeth & Dearing, Eric (Eds.).** (2017). *Handbook of early childhood development programs, practices, and policies.* Wiley.

**Vygotsky, Lev S.** (1980). *Mind in society: The development of higher psychological processes.* Harvard University Press.

**Vygotsky, Lev S.** (1987). Thinking and speech. In Rieber, Robert W. & Carton, Aaron S. (Eds.), *The collected works of L. S. Vygotsky* (Vol. 1, pp. 39–285). Springer.

**Vygotsky, Lev S.** (1994a). The development of academic concepts in school aged children. In van der Veer, René & Valsiner, Jaan (Eds.), *The Vygotsky reader* (pp. 355–370). Blackwell.

**Vygotsky, Lev S.** (1994b). Principles of social education for deaf and dumb children in Russia. In van der Veer, Rene & Valsiner, Jaan (Eds.), *The Vygotsky reader* (pp. 19–26). Blackwell.

**Vygotsky, Lev S.** (2012). *Thought and language.* MIT Press.

**Wade, Mark; Prime, Heather; Jenkins, Jennifer; Yeates, Keith; Williams, Tricia & Lee, Kang.** (2018). On the relation between theory of mind and executive functioning: A developmental cognitive neuroscience perspective. *Psychonomic Bulletin & Review*, *25*(6), 2119–2140.

**Wadman, Meredith.** (2018). 'Rapid onset' of transgender identity ignites storm. *Science*, *361*(6406), 958–959.

**Wagmiller, Robert L.** (2015). The temporal dynamics of childhood economic deprivation and children's achievement. *Child Development Perspectives*, *9*(3), 158–163.

**Wagner, Erica.** (2017). *Chief engineer: Washington Roebling, the man who built the Brooklyn Bridge.* Bloomsbury.

**Wagner, Katie; Dobkins, Karen & Barner, David.** (2013). Slow mapping: Color word learning as a gradual inductive process. *Cognition*, *127*(3), 307–317.

**Wagner, Paul A.** (2011). Socio-sexual education: A practical study in formal thinking and teachable moments. *Sex Education: Sexuality, Society and Learning*, *11*(2), 193–211.

**Waldinger, Robert & Schulz, Marc.** (2018). The blind psychological scientists and the elephant: Reply to Sherlock and Zietsch. *Psychological Science*, *29*(1), 158–160.

**Waldorf, Kristina M. Adams; Nelson, Branden R.; Stencel-Baerenwald, Jennifer E.; Studholme, Colin; Kapur, Raj P.; Armistead, Blair; . . . Rajagopal, Lakshmi.** (2018). Congenital Zika virus infection as a silent pathology with loss of neurogenic output in the fetal brain. *Nature Medicine*, *24*, 368–374.

**Walk, Laura M.; Vaidya, Chandan; Evers, Wiebke F.; Quante, Sonja & Hille, Katrin.** (2018). Evaluation of a teacher training program to enhance executive functions in preschool children. *PLoS ONE*, *13*(5), e0197454.

**Walker, Christa L. Fischer; Rudan, Igor; Liu, Li; Nair, Harish; Theodoratou, Evropi; Bhutta, Zulfiqar A.; . . . Black, Robert E.**

(2013). Global burden of childhood pneumonia and diarrhoea. *The Lancet*, *381*(9875), 1405–1416.

**Walker, Renee; Block, Jason & Kawachi, Ichiro.** (2014). The spatial accessibility of fast food restaurants and convenience stores in relation to neighborhood schools. *Applied Spatial Analysis and Policy*, *7*(2), 169–182.

**Walle, Eric A. & Campos, Joseph J.** (2014). Infant language development is related to the acquisition of walking. *Developmental Psychology*, *50*(2), 336–348.

**Wallis, Claudia.** (2014). Gut reactions: Intestinal bacteria may help determine whether we are lean or obese. *Scientific American*, *310*(6), 30–33.

**Walter, Melissa Clucas & Lippard, Christine N.** (2017). Head Start teachers across a decade: Beliefs, characteristics, and time spent on academics. *Early Childhood Education Journal*, *45*(5), 693–702.

**Wambach, Karen & Riordan, Jan.** (2014). *Breastfeeding and human lactation* (5th ed.). Jones & Bartlett.

**Wang, Chen; Horby, Peter W.; Hayden, Frederick G. & Gao, George F.** (2020). A novel coronavirus outbreak of global health concern. *The Lancet*, *395*(10223), 470–473.

**Wang, Chao; Xue, Haifeng; Wang, Qianqian; Hao, Yongchen; Li, Dianjiang; Gu, Dongfeng & Huang, Jianfeng.** (2014). Effect of drinking on all-cause mortality in women compared with men: A meta-analysis. *Journal of Women's Health*, *23*(5), 373–381.

**Wang, Ke; Rathbun, Amy & Musu, Lauren.** (2019). *School choice in the United States: 2019.* Washington, DC: U.S. Department of Education, National Center for Education Statistics. NCES 2019–106.

**Wang, Meifang & Liu, Li.** (2018). Reciprocal relations between harsh discipline and children's externalizing behavior in China: A 5-year longitudinal study. *Child Development*, *89*(1), 174–187.

**Wang, Ming-Te & Eccles, Jacquelynne S.** (2013). School context, achievement motivation, and academic engagement: A longitudinal study of school engagement using a multidimensional perspective. *Learning and Instruction*, *28*, 12–23.

**Wang, Ming-Te; Henry, Daphne A.; Smith, Leann V.; Huguley, James P. & Guo, Jiesi.** (2020). Parental ethnic-racial socialization practices and children of color's psychosocial and behavioral adjustment: A systematic review and meta-analysis. *American Psychologist*, *75*(1), 1–22.

**Watson, John B.** (1924). *Behaviorism.* The People's Institute Pub. Co.

**Watson, John B.** (1928). *Psychological care of infant and child.* Norton.

**Watson, John B.** (1972). *Psychological care of infant and child.* Arno Press.

**Watson, John B.** (1998). *Behaviorism.* Transaction.

**Webb, Alexandra R.; Heller, Howard T.; Benson, Carol B. & Lahav, Amir.** (2015). Mother's voice and heartbeat sounds elicit auditory plasticity in the human brain before full gestation. *Proceedings of the National Academy of Sciences*, *112*(10), 3152–3157.

**Weber, Ann; Fernald, Anne & Diop, Yatma.** (2017). When cultural norms discourage talking to babies: Effectiveness of a parenting program in rural Senegal. *Child Development, 88*(5), 1513–1526.

**Weber, Daniela; Dekhtyar, Serhiy & Herlitz, Agneta.** (2017). The Flynn Effect in Europe—Effects of sex and region. *Intelligence, 60,* 39–45.

**Webster, Collin A. & Suzuki, Naoki.** (2014). Land of the rising pulse: A social ecological perspective of physical activity opportunities for schoolchildren in Japan. *Journal of Teaching in Physical Education, 33*(3), 304–325.

**Weinshenker, Naomi J.** (2014). Teenagers and body image. Education.

**Weinstein, Netta & DeHaan, Cody.** (2014). On the mutuality of human motivation and relationships. In Weinstein, Netta (Ed.), *Human motivation and interpersonal relationships: Theory, research, and applications* (pp. 3–25). Springer.

**Weiss, Noel S. & Koepsell, Thomas D.** (2014). *Epidemiologic methods: Studying the occurrence of illness* (2nd ed.). Oxford University Press.

**Weissberg, Roger P.; Durlak, Joseph A.; Domitrovich, Celene E. & Gullotta, Thomas P.** (2016). Social and emotional learning: Past, present, and future. In Durlak, Joseph A.; Domitrovich, Celene E.; Weissberg, Roger P. & Gullotta, Thomas P. (Eds.), *Handbook of social and emotional learning: Research and practice* (pp. 3–19). Guilford Press.

**Weisskirch, Robert S.** (2017a). A developmental perspective on language brokering. In Weisskirch, Robert S. (Ed.), *Language brokering in immigrant families: Theories and contexts.* Routledge.

**Weisskirch, Robert S.** (2017b). *Language brokering in immigrant families: Theories and contexts.* Routledge.

**Weisz, John R.; Kuppens, Sofie; Ng, Mei Yi; Eckshtain, Dikla; Ugueto, Ana M.; Vaughn-Coaxum, Rachel; . . . Fordwood, Samantha R.** (2017). What five decades of research tells us about the effects of youth psychological therapy: A multilevel meta-analysis and implications for science and practice. *American Psychologist, 72*(2), 79–117.

**Wellman, Henry M.** (2014). *Making minds: How theory of mind develops.* Oxford University Press.

**Wellman, Henry M.** (2018). Theory of mind: The state of the art. *European Journal of Developmental Psychology, 15*(6), 728–755.

**Wellman, Henry M.; Fang, Fuxi & Peterson, Candida C.** (2011). Sequential progressions in a theory-of-mind scale: Longitudinal perspectives. *Child Development, 82*(3), 780–792.

**Wendelken, Carter; Baym, Carol L.; Gazzaley, Adam & Bunge, Silvia A.** (2011). Neural indices of improved attentional modulation over middle childhood. *Developmental Cognitive Neuroscience, 1*(2), 175–186.

**Wendland, Claire.** (2018). Who counts? What counts? Place and the limits of perinatal mortality measures. *AMA Journal of Ethics, 20*(1), 278–287.

**Werker, Janet F. & Hensch, Takao K.** (2015). Critical periods in speech perception: New directions. *Annual Review of Psychology, 66,* 173–196.

**Westover, Tara.** (2018). *Educated: A memoir.* Random House.

**Weymouth, Bridget B.; Buehler, Cheryl; Zhou, Nan & Henson, Robert A.** (2016). A meta-analysis of parent–adolescent conflict: Disagreement, hostility, and youth maladjustment. *Journal of Family Theory & Review, 8*(1), 95–112.

**Wheeler, Lorey A.; Zeiders, Katharine H.; Updegraff, Kimberly A.; Umaña-Taylor, Adriana J.; Rodríguez de Jesús, Sue A. & Perez-Brena, Norma J.** (2017). Mexican-origin youth's risk behavior from adolescence to young adulthood: The role of familism values. *Developmental Psychology, 53*(1), 126–137.

**White, Rebecca M. B.; Deardorff, Julianna; Liu, Yu & Gonzales, Nancy A.** (2013). Contextual amplification or attenuation of the impact of pubertal timing on Mexican-origin boys' mental health symptoms. *Journal of Adolescent Health, 53*(6), 692–698.

**White, Sue; Gibson, Matthew & Wastell, David.** (2019). Child protection and disorganized attachment: A critical commentary. *Children and Youth Services Review, 105*(104415).

**White-Traut, Rosemary C.; Rankin, Kristin M.; Yoder, Joe; Zawacki, Laura; Campbell, Suzann; Kavanaugh, Karen; . . . Norr, Kathleen F.** (2018). Relationship between mother-infant mutual dyadic responsiveness and premature infant development as measured by the Bayley III at 6 weeks corrected age. *Early Human Development, 121,* 21–26.

**Widman, Laura; Choukas-Bradley, Sophia; Helms, Sarah W.; Golin, Carol E. & Prinstein, Mitchell J.** (2014). Sexual communication between early adolescents and their dating partners, parents, and best friends. *The Journal of Sex Research, 51*(7), 731–741.

**Widom, Cathy Spatz; Czaja, Sally J. & DuMont, Kimberly A.** (2015a). Intergenerational transmission of child abuse and neglect: Real or detection bias? *Science, 347*(6229), 1480–1485.

**Widom, Cathy Spatz; Horan, Jacqueline & Brzustowicz, Linda.** (2015b). Childhood maltreatment predicts allostatic load in adulthood. *Child Abuse & Neglect, 47,* 59–69.

**Wigger, J. Bradley.** (2018). Invisible friends across four countries: Kenya, Malawi, Nepal and the Dominican Republic. *International Journal of Psychology, 53*(Suppl. 1), 46–52.

**Wigginton, Nicholas S.; Fahrenkamp-Uppenbrink, Julia; Wible, Brad & Malakoff, David.** (2016). Cities are the future. *Science, 352*(6288), 904–905.

**Wilcox, W. Bradford (Ed.)** (2011). *The sustainable demographic dividend: What do marriage and fertility have to do with the economy?* Social Trends Institute.

**Wilkinson, Stephen.** (2015). Prenatal screening, reproductive choice, and public health. *Bioethics, 29*(1), 26–35.

**Wilks, Matti; Kirby, James & Nielsen, Mark.** (2019). Developmental changes in young children's willingness to copy the antisocial actions of ingroup members in a minimal group context. *Developmental Psychology, 55*(4), 709–721.

**Williams, Anne M.; Chantry, Caroline; Geubbels, Eveline L.; Ramaiya, Astha K.; Shemdoe, Aloisia I.; Tancredi, Daniel J. & Young, Sera L.** (2016). Breastfeeding and complementary feeding practices among HIV-exposed infants in coastal Tanzania. *Journal of Human Lactation, 32*(1), 112–122.

**Williams, Katie M. & Hammond, Christopher J.** (2016). GWAS in myopia: Insights into disease and implications for the clinic. *Expert Review of Ophthalmology, 11*(2), 101–110.

**Williams, Lela Rankin; Fox, Nathan A.; Lejuez, C. W.; Reynolds, Elizabeth K.; Henderson, Heather A.; Perez-Edgar, Koraly E.; . . . Pine, Daniel S.** (2010). Early temperament, propensity for risk-taking and adolescent substance-related problems: A prospective multimethod investigation. *Addictive Behaviors, 35*(2), 1148–1151.

**Williams, Shanna; Moore, Kelsey; Crossman, Angela M. & Talwar, Victoria.** (2016). The role of executive functions and theory of mind in children's prosocial lie-telling. *Journal of Experimental Child Psychology, 141,* 256–266.

**Williamson, Victoria; Stevelink, Sharon A. M.; Da Silva, Eve & Fear, Nicola T.** (2018). A systematic review of wellbeing in children: A comparison of military and civilian families. *Child and Adolescent Psychiatry and Mental Health, 12*(46).

**Willoughby, Michael T.; Mills-Koonce, W. Roger; Gottfredson, Nisha C. & Wagner, Nicholas J.** (2014). Measuring callous unemotional behaviors in early childhood: Factor structure and the prediction of stable aggression in middle childhood. *Journal of Psychopathology and Behavioral Assessment, 36*(1), 30–42.

**Wills, Thomas A.; Okamoto, Scott K.; Knight, Rebecca & Pagano, Ian.** (2019). Parental support, parent-adolescent conflict, and substance use of native Hawaiian and other Pacific Islander youth: Ethnic differences in stress-buffering and vulnerability effects. *Asian American Journal of Psychology, 10*(3), 218–226.

**Wilmshurst, Linda.** (2011). *Child and adolescent psychopathology: A casebook* (2nd ed.). Sage.

**Wilson, Jennifer; Andrews, Glenda; Hogan, Christy; Wang, Si & Shum, David H. K.** (2018). Executive function in middle childhood and the relationship with theory of mind. *Developmental Neuropsychology, 43*(3), 163–182.

**Winn, Phoebe; Acharya, Krishna; Peterson, Erika & Leuthner, Steven R.** (2018). Prenatal counseling and parental decision-making following a fetal diagnosis of trisomy 13 or 18. *Journal of Perinatology, 38*(7), 788–796.

**Wolff, Jason J.; Gerig, Guido; Lewis, John D.; Soda, Takahiro; Styner, Martin A.; Vachet, Clement; . . . Piven, Joseph.** (2015). Altered corpus callosum morphology associated with autism over the first 2 years of life. *Brain, 138*(7), 2046–2058.

**Wolff, Mary S.; Teitelbaum, Susan L.; McGovern, Kathleen; Pinney, Susan M.;**

Windham, Gayle C.; Galvez, Maida; . . . Biro, Frank M. (2015). Environmental phenols and pubertal development in girls. *Environment International*, 84, 174–180.

Womack, Sean R.; Taraban, Lindsay; Shaw, Daniel S.; Wilson, Melvin N. & Dishion, Thomas J. (2019). Family turbulence and child internalizing and externalizing behaviors: Moderation of effects by race. *Child Development*, 90(6), e729–e744.

Wong, Waison; Lam, Ray & Morris, Shaun. (2020). The role of the measles vaccine for travelling infants 6 to 11 months of age in the era of global outbreaks of disease. *Paediatrics & Child Health*, 1–3.

Woodward, Amanda L. & Markman, Ellen M. (1998). Early word learning. In Kuhn, Deanna & Siegler, Robert S. (Eds.), *Handbook of child psychology* (5th ed., Vol. 2, pp. 371–420). Wiley.

Woolley, Jacqueline D. & Ghossainy, Maliki E. (2013). Revisiting the fantasy–reality distinction: Children as naïve skeptics. *Child Development*, 84(5), 1496–1510.

World Bank. (2018). *World development indicators: Mortality rate, infant (per 1,000 live births)* [Data set].

World Bank. (2019). World Bank open data. World Bank.

World Health Organization. (2006). WHO Motor Development Study: Windows of achievement for six gross motor development milestones. *Acta Paediatrica*, 95(Suppl. 450), 86–95.

World Health Organization. (2015). *Global status report on road safety 2015*. Geneva, Switzerland: World Health Organization.

World Health Organization. (2017, April 28). Measles vaccines: WHO position paper – April 2017. *Weekly Epidemiological Record*, 17(92), 205–228.

World Health Organization. (2017, September 29). Global Health Observatory data repository: Prevalence of obesity among children and adolescents, BMI>+2 standard deviation above the median, crude estimates by country, among children aged 5–19 years. World Health Organization.

World Health Organization. (2019, December, 6). Immunization coverage. Fact sheets. World Health Organization.

World Health Organization. (2019, May 29). *WHO vaccine-preventable diseases: Monitoring system—2019 global summary: Global and regional immunization profile* [Data set].

World Health Organization. (2020, March 13). *Immunization, vaccines and biologicals: Measles and rubella surveillance data* [Data set].

Wörmann, Viktoriya; Holodynski, Manfred; Kärtner, Joscha & Keller, Heidi. (2012). A cross-cultural comparison of the development of the social smile: A longitudinal study of maternal and infant imitation in 6- and 12-week-old infants. *Infant Behavior and Development*, 35(2), 335–347.

Wosje, Karen S.; Khoury, Philip R.; Claytor, Randal P.; Copeland, Kristen A.; Hornung, Richard W.; Daniels, Stephen R. & Kalkwarf, Heidi J. (2010). Dietary patterns associated with fat and bone mass in young children. *American Journal of Clinical Nutrition*, 92(2), 294–303.

Wright, Vince. (2018). Vygotsky and a global perspective on scaffolding in learning mathematics. In Zajda, Joseph (Ed.), *Globalisation and education reforms: Globalisation, comparative education and policy research* (pp. 123–135). Springer.

Wrzus, Cornelia & Neyer, Franz J. (2016). Co-development of personality and friendships across the lifespan: An empirical review on selection and socialization. *European Psychologist*, 21(4), 254–273.

Wynberg, Rachel & Laird, Sarah A. (2018). Fast science and sluggish policy: The Herculean task of regulating biodiscovery. *Trends in Biotechnology*, 36(1), 1–3.

Xu, Fei. (2013). The object concept in human infants: Commentary on Fields. *Human Development*, 56(3), 167–170.

Xu, Fei & Kushnir, Tamar. (2013). Infants are rational constructivist learners. *Current Directions in Psychological Science*, 22(1), 28–32.

Xu, Guifeng; Strathearn, Lane; Liu, Buyun; O'Brien, Matthew; Kopelman, Todd G.; Zhu, Jing; . . . Bao, Wei. (2019). Prevalence and treatment patterns of autism spectrum disorder in the United States, 2016. *JAMA Pediatrics*, 173(2), 153–159.

Xu, Guifeng; Strathearn, Lane; Liu, Buyun; Yang, Binrang & Bao, Wei. (2018). Twenty-year trends in diagnosed Attention-deficit/hyperactivity disorder among US children and adolescents, 1997–2016. *JAMA Network Open*, 1(4), e181471.

Xu, Jiaquan; Murphy, Sherry L.; Kochanek, Kenneth D. & Arias, Elizabeth. (2020, January). *Mortality in the United States, 2018. NCHS Data Brief*. U.S. Department of Health and Human Services, Centers for Disease Control and Prevention, National Center for Health Statistics. 355.

Xu, Richard; Poole, Kristie L.; Van Lieshout, Ryan J.; Saigal, Saroj & Schmidt, Louis A. (2019). Shyness and sociability among extremely low birth weight survivors in the third and fourth decades of life: Associations with relationship status. *Journal of Personality*, 87(2), 231–239.

Xu, Yaoying. (2010). Children's social play sequence: Parten's classic theory revisited. *Early Child Development and Care*, 180(4), 489–498.

Xu, Yin; Norton, Sam & Rahman, Qazi. (2020). A longitudinal birth cohort study of early life conditions, psychosocial factors, and emerging adolescent sexual orientation. *Developmental Psychobiology*, 62(1), 5–20.

Yackobovitch-Gavan, Michal; Wolf Linhard, D.; Nagelberg, Nessia; Poraz, Irit; Shalitin, Shlomit; Phillip, Moshe & Meyerovitch, Joseph. (2018). Intervention for childhood obesity based on parents only or parents and child compared with follow-up alone. *Pediatric Obesity*, 13(11), 647–655.

Yan, J.; Han, Z. R.; Tang, Y. & Zhang, X. (2017). Parental support for autonomy and child depressive symptoms in middle childhood: The mediating role of parent–child attachment. *Journal of Child and Family Studies*, 26(7), 1970–1978.

Yang, Rongwang; Zhang, Suhan; Li, Rong & Zhao, Zhengyan. (2013). Parents' attitudes toward stimulants use in China. *Journal of Developmental & Behavioral Pediatrics*, 34(3), 225.

Yeager, David S.; Dahl, Ronald E. & Dweck, Carol S. (2018). Why interventions to influence adolescent behavior often fail but could succeed. *Perspectives on Psychological Science*, 13(1), 101–122.

Yeager, David S.; Purdie-Vaughns, Valerie; Hooper, Sophia Yang & Cohen, Geoffrey L. (2017). Loss of institutional trust among racial and ethnic minority adolescents: A consequence of procedural injustice and a cause of life-span outcomes. *Child Development*, 88(2), 658–676.

Yogman, Michael; Garfield, Craig F. & Committee on Psychosocial Aspects of Child and Family Health. (2016). Fathers' roles in the care and development of their children: The role of pediatricians. *Pediatrics*, 138(1), e20161128.

Yogman, Michael; Garner, Andrew; Hutchinson, Jeffrey; Hirsh-Pasek, Kathy & Golinkoff, Roberta Michnick. (2018). The power of play: A pediatric role in enhancing development in young children. *Pediatrics*, 142(3), e20182058.

Yu, Xinting; Rueschman, Michael; Kaplan, Emily R.; Quante, Mirja; Horan, Christine; Davison, Kirsten; . . . Redline, Susan S. (2019). 0818 actigraphy sleep assessment in early infancy: Associations with socioeconomic factors over ages one to six months. *Sleep*, 42(Suppl. 1), A328.

Yudell, Michael; Roberts, Dorothy; DeSalle, Rob & Tishkoff, Sarah. (2016). Taking race out of human genetics. *Science*, 351(6273), 564–565.

Zachry, Anne H. & Kitzmann, Katherine M. (2011). Caregiver awareness of prone play recommendations. *American Journal of Occupational Therapy*, 65(1), 101–105.

Zahran, Hatice S.; Bailey, Cathy M.; Damon, Scott A.; Garbe, Paul L. & Breysse, Patrick N. (2018). *Vital signs: Asthma in children—United States, 2001–2016. Morbidity and Mortality Weekly Report*, 67(5), 149–155. Atlanta, GA: Centers for Disease Control and Prevention.

Zak, Paul J. (2012). *The moral molecule: The source of love and prosperity*. Dutton.

Zametkin, Alan J. & Solanto, Mary V. (2017). A Review of *ADHD nation* [Review of the book *ADHD nation: Children, doctors, big pharma, and the making of an American epidemic*, by Alan Schwarz]. *The ADHD Report*, 25(2), 6–10.

Zatorre, Robert J. (2013). Predispositions and plasticity in music and speech learning: Neural correlates and implications. *Science*, 342(6158), 585–589.

Zeiders, Katharine H.; Umaña-Taylor, Adriana J. & Derlan, Chelsea L. (2013a). Trajectories of depressive symptoms and self-esteem in Latino youths: Examining the role of gender and perceived discrimination. *Developmental Psychology*, 49(5), 951–963.

Zeiders, Katharine H.; Updegraff, Kimberly A.; Umaña-Taylor, Adriana J.; Wheeler, Lorey A.; Perez-Brena, Norma J. & Rodríguez, Sue A. (2013b). Mexican-origin youths trajectories of depressive symptoms: The role of familism values. *Journal of Adolescent Health, 53*(5), 648–654.

**Zeifman, Debra M.** (2013). Built to bond: Coevolution, coregulation, and plasticity in parent-infant bonds. In Hazan, Cindy & Campa, Mary I. (Eds.), *Human bonding: The science of affectional ties* (pp. 41–73). Guilford Press.

**Zeitlin, Marian.** (2011). *New information on West African traditional education and approaches to its modernization.* Tostan.

**Zhang, Linlin & Eggum-Wilkens, Natalie D.** (2018). Correlates of shyness and unsociability during early adolescence in urban and rural China. *Journal of Early Adolescence, 38*(3), 408–421.

**Zhao, Fei; Franco, Heather L.; Rodriguez, Karina F.; Brown, Paula R.; Tsai, Ming-Jer;**

**Tsai, Sophia Y. & Yao, Humphrey H.-C.** (2017). Elimination of the male reproductive tract in the female embryo is promoted by COUP-TFII in mice. *Science, 357*(6352), 717–720.

**Zhao, Jinxia & Wang, Meifang.** (2014). Mothers' academic involvement and children's achievement: Children's theory of intelligence as a mediator. *Learning and Individual Differences, 35,* 130–136.

**Zhu, Qi; Song, Yiying; Hu, Siyuan; Li, Xiaobai; Tian, Moqian; Zhen, Zonglei; . . . Liu, Jia.** (2010). Heritability of the specific cognitive ability of face perception. *Current Biology, 20*(2), 137–142.

**Zimmerman, Marc A.; Stoddard, Sarah A.; Eisman, Andria B.; Caldwell, Cleopatra H.; Aiyer, Sophie M. & Miller, Alison.** (2013). Adolescent resilience: Promotive factors that inform

prevention. *Child Development Perspectives, 7*(4), 215–220.

**Zuk, Jennifer; Benjamin, Christopher; Kenyon, Arnold & Gaab, Nadine.** (2014). Behavioral and neural correlates of executive functioning in musicians and non-musicians. *PLoS ONE, 9*(6), e99868.

**Zurcher, Jessica D.; Holmgren, Hailey G.; Coyne, Sarah M.; Barlett, Christopher P. & Yang, Chongming.** (2018). Parenting and cyberbullying across adolescence. *Cyberpsychology, Behavior, and Social Networking, 21*(5), 294–303.

**Zych, Izabela; Farrington, David P.; Llorent, Vicente J. & Ttofi, Maria M. (Eds.).** (2017). *Protecting children against bullying and its consequences.* Springer.

# Name Index

# Subject Index

Note: Page numbers followed by f, p, or t indicate figures, photographs, or tables respectively.